ALSO BY STEVEN WOODWORTH

Beneath a Northern Sky

While God Is Marching On

A Scythe of Fire

Six Armies in Tennessee

Davis and Lee and War

Jefferson Davis and His Generals

Nothing but Victory

Nothing but Victory

THE ARMY OF THE TENNESSEE, 1861–1865

STEVEN E. WOODWORTH

ALFRED A. KNOPF, NEW YORK, 2005

THIS IS A BORZOI BOOK
PUBLISHED BY ALFRED A. KNOPF

Copyright © 2005 by Steven E. Woodworth

ISBN 0-375-41218-2

Printed in the United States of America

To Nathan, Jonathan, David, Daniel, Anna, Elizabeth, and Mary.

To God Alone Be the Glory.

CONTENTS

INTRODUCTION

The Army of the Tennessee was the Union field army that fought in the Mississippi Valley during the first three years of the war and then moved east for campaigns in Georgia and the Carolinas during the war's final year. It was present at most of the great battles that became turning points of the war—Fort Donelson, Vicksburg, and Atlanta. Its desperate fight at Shiloh was the nation's first revelation of how bloody the war would be. It made up half of Sherman's army during the March to the Sea and the Carolinas Campaign, operations that more than any others revealed to the nation that the war was ending and the Union had won. Though smaller than the high-profile Army of the Potomac, which fought, as it were, in the shadow of the Capitol dome, the Army of the Tennessee won the decisive battles in the decisive theater of the war. With the Army of the Potomac all but deadlocked with its adversary in Virginia and the Army of the Cumberland advancing slowly through Kentucky and Tennessee, it was the Army of the Tennessee that struck the winning blows and penetrated deeply into the heartland of the South.

Just as George B. McClellan shaped the Army of the Potomac in his own image, so Ulysses S. Grant built the Army of the Tennessee in his. It partook both of his matter-of-fact steadiness and his hard-driving aggressiveness. By the midpoint of the war, it had completely imbibed his quiet, can-do attitude, and this spirit continued to characterize its operations even after Grant had moved on to higher command. As the Army of the Tennessee marched away from its familiar Mississippi Valley in the fall of 1863, slinging its knapsacks for new fields, Capt. Jacob Ritner of the 25th Iowa wrote to his wife back in Mount Pleasant, "Our army never was in better spirits or more enthusiastic in the cause than at present. We all expect a hot fight before long, but we expect nothing but victory."[1] That was typical of the Army of the Tennessee. "Nothing but victory" was what that army expected and was usually what it experienced. Nor is it any coincidence that

Grant's qualities tended to be those of that up-and-coming region of the country, one day to be called the Midwest, from which the army was almost exclusively recruited. The men were quick to adopt Grant's approach to war, because it was the way their own fathers had approached the challenges of carving farms out of the wilderness.

Perhaps a word is in order about nomenclature. Although the army received its official title as the Army of the Tennessee only in October 1862, I decided to cover it from its genesis in the camps around Cairo, Illinois, in the summer of 1861 and, even before that, the recruitment of the soldiers. For simplicity's sake, I will refer to it throughout as the Army of the Tennessee. Another matter of nomenclature has to do with the term "Midwest." It was not in use in the mid-nineteenth century, and therefore some might contend that I should not use it. However, although I am telling this story *about* people who lived in the nineteenth century, I am telling it *to* people who live in the twenty-first. The terms "Midwest" and "Midwestern" communicate well to my intended audience, and therefore I will occasionally use them. The term that mid-nineteenth-century Americans would have used was "Northwest." The "Old Northwest" referred to the states of Ohio, Indiana, Illinois, Michigan, and Wisconsin, but the region had come to include Iowa and Minnesota as well. For the sake of variety and a touch of authenticity, I will sometimes use the term "Northwest" as being synonymous with "Midwest."

In telling the story of the Army of the Tennessee, I have made a number of decisions about what I would cover and what I would regretfully pass over. One fundamental decision was to maintain a focus on that part of the Army of the Tennessee that operated directly under Army of the Tennessee headquarters. Thus, I have not covered the Thirteenth Corps in the trials and tribulations it experienced after its unfortunate transfer to the Department of the Gulf or the triumphs of A. J. Smith's wing of the Sixteenth Corps functioning as Grant's de facto strategic reserve during the last year of the war. I have passed lightly over the activities of the Seventeenth Corps in Mississippi during the autumn of 1863 and of Peter Osterhaus's division when it functioned under the command of Joseph Hooker in that same period. In each of these cases, my decision was based on giving maximum coverage to units functioning with the main Army of the Tennessee.

That said, this is by no means a headquarters history. My goal has been to present a narrative of the army with attention to all levels, from that of commanding general all the way down to the newest recruit. It was the common soldiers that interested me most, and I have endeavored to convey the flavor of their thoughts, attitudes, and actions throughout this account. After years of poring through their diaries and letters, I feel as though I've come to know them on an almost personal basis, and my respect for them continues to grow.

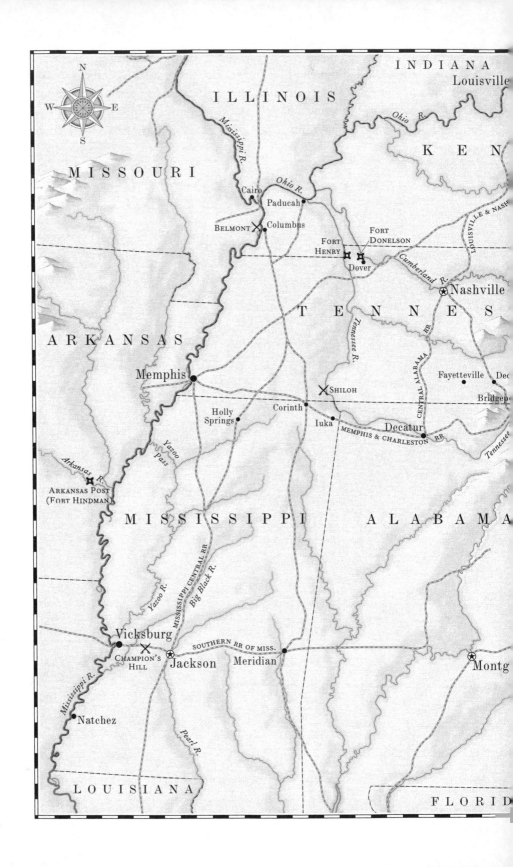

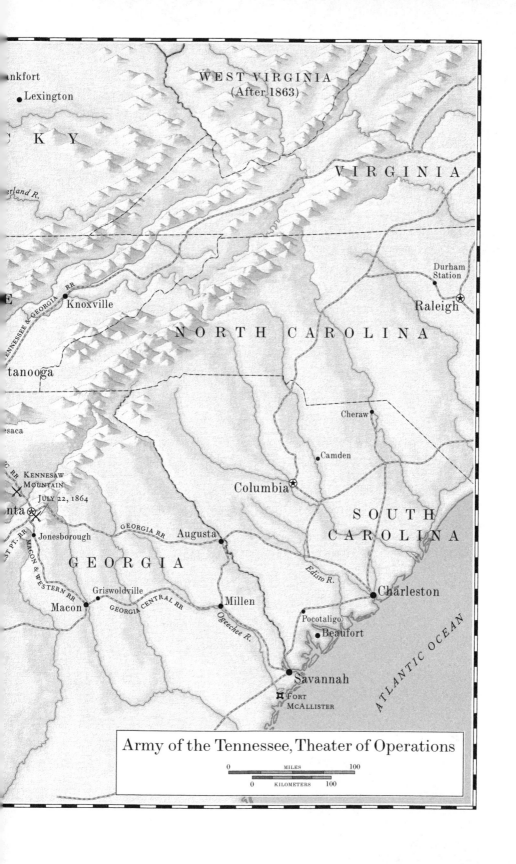

Army of the Tennessee, Theater of Operations

0   MILES   100

0   KILOMETERS   100

PART ONE

Grant's Army

CHAPTER ONE

Raising an Army

"RED SNOW FELL near Iowa City," reported the *Des Moines Sunday Register* on March 5, 1861. Editor George Mills hastened to explain that the color was caused by fine flakes of reddish clay mixed with the precipitation. Wind had swept dust into the atmosphere far to the west, providing the residents of eastern Iowa with a bit of unusual late-winter color. It was a simple scientific explanation, easily understood by modern Americans in this enlightened second half of the nineteenth century. Yet as editor Mills observed, many Iowans could hardly help wondering whether the eerie reddish cast of their normally snow-whitened plains was not some vague but appalling portent of terrible things to come. It may well have occurred to some Hawkeyes that the next winter's snows might be reddened by the bloodshed of civil strife. Americans elsewhere would have asked themselves the same question.[1]

On the same day the red snow fell in Iowa, Abraham Lincoln took the oath of office as president of a country that was tearing itself apart. The issue of slavery had festered between North and South for two generations, and for many people in Iowa, as in the other Midwestern states, the tension in Washington, D.C., was a matter of great concern.

In response to Lincoln's election, on December 20, 1860, South Carolina declared itself no longer a part of the United States. On January 9, Mississippi followed. Florida went on January 10, and the next day it was Alabama. Other Deep South states followed throughout the month. On February 1, Texas became the seventh state to declare itself out of the Union. Later that month, representatives of the rebellious states met in Montgomery, Alabama, organized a government, styled themselves "the Confederate States of America," and elected Jefferson Davis of Mississippi as their president. By March 4, when Lincoln was inaugurated and the red snow fell in Iowa, the dismemberment of the world's only great republic and the establishment of a slaveholders' regime in the Deep South seemed to be faits accomplis.

Throughout the winter, the fire-eaters in the Southern states had spoken of seceding peacefully if possible, violently if necessary, and Southern military preparations had gone on apace. Northerners watched uneasily. The news they read daily in the papers seemed no more credible than the freak of nature that had brought red-tinged snow to Iowa City on the day of Lincoln's inauguration.

Here and there across the North, men began to think of making military preparations of their own. Some towns organized volunteer companies. In January, Henry and George Perkins, brothers and coeditors of the *Cedar Falls Gazette,* began encouraging the formation of such a group in their Iowa town. "We have the material here from which to form a 'crack corps,' which, if properly organized and equipped, would be of great advantage to us on our gala days and public occasions," opined the *Gazette,* "and who knows but in these troublesome times might be the means of preserving the country from ruin and give some of the members an opportunity to cover themselves with immortal glory." By the following month, forty men had formed themselves into the "Pioneer Greys," so named after the common color of militia uniforms at the time. They drilled diligently and were soon gaining additional recruits.[2] Similar companies sprang up elsewhere. Peoria, Illinois, had four: the Peoria Guards, Peoria Rifles, Emmett Guards, and National Blues.[3]

Like the first jarring peal of a prairie thunderstorm came the news in mid-April that Confederate forces ringing the harbor of Charleston, South Carolina, had opened fire on the United States flag and garrison at Fort Sumter in the predawn hours of April 12. Thirty-four hours later, the fort surrendered. On April 15, President Lincoln, following the example of George Washington in the days of the Whiskey Rebellion, called upon the states to provide militia for ninety days of Federal service—75,000 of them—in order to put down the rebellion.

All across the North, thousands of men scarcely waited for Lincoln's call for troops. John L. Maxwell was behind the plow preparing his fields for spring planting when he heard the news of Fort Sumter. He put away the plow and horses, and set out for nearby Canton, Illinois, to join what was to become Company H of the 17th Illinois Regiment.[4] George O. Smith was a student in the city schools of Monmouth, Illinois. Within the week, he had enlisted and, with several other youths, was eagerly working to organize a company. They too would end up in the 17th Illinois.[5] Nearby Peoria, where the 17th would muster, got the news of Fort Sumter on April 13 and went into an uproar. Flags appeared all over town, including at the armories of Peoria's four volunteer companies, now busily preparing to take the field. The enrollment of additional troops began that very evening.[6]

On April 15 in the Illinois capital, the Springfield Grays, who had the advantage of proximity, became the first company to offer its services to the state. The company became part of the state's first regiment for the war, numbered the 7th Illinois out of respect for the six state regiments that had served in the Mexican War. Within nine days, the Springfield Grays had been joined by companies from all over the state in an encampment named Camp Yates in honor of Illinois's governor.[7]

Enthusiasm ran high. Chicago seethed with outrage at the Confederate attack. Thousands of men volunteered to go and fight for the Union. Among them were the Highland Guards, a company of ethnic Scots, making a striking appearance in their Scottish caps. Their captain, John McArthur, a thirty-four-year-old Scottish-born blacksmith and successful proprietor of Chicago's Excelsior Ironworks, won election as colonel of the 12th Illinois Regiment.[8]

Also joining the 12th Illinois was a company from the lead-mining town of Galena, in the far northwest corner of the state. The citizens of Galena held a mass meeting on April 16 to discuss news of the Southern attack. Mayor Robert Brand presided but promptly set the assembly in an uproar when he "gave expression to antiwar sentiments and favored compromise and peace," as an eyewitness recalled. When the tumult subsided, a succession of more patriotic citizens made impassioned speeches pleading for manly resistance to Southern aggression. One of the speakers was a consumptive-looking lawyer named John A. Rawlins. Another was local U.S. congressman Elihu B. Washburne, who concluded by exhorting his fellow citizens to raise two companies of volunteers for the war. "The meeting adjourned with the wildest enthusiasm and cheers for the Union."

Two days later, an even larger meeting convened at the courthouse in Galena, this time explicitly for the purpose of raising troops. Washburne suggested that the appropriate chairman for this meeting would be a quiet-spoken local leather-goods clerk who was a genuine West Point graduate and veteran of the Mexican War. Ulysses S. Grant—"Sam" to his friends— had made captain in the Regular Army but had had to leave the service in the early fifties because of an incident with alcohol. He had certainly seemed sober and reliable enough during the eighteen months he had lived in Galena, clerking at his father's leather-goods store. The assembly elected him to the chair, which Grant took over with some embarrassment and a brief statement of the meeting's purpose. No matter—Washburne and

Rawlins could make the fiery speeches. Wealthy Galena businessman Augustus L. Chetlain chimed in, stating his own intention of going as a volunteer. A number of others stepped forward for military service that night, and in the days that followed, Grant, Chetlain, and the others canvassed the nearby towns of Jo Daviess County for more recruits. They soon had a full company, named it the Jo Daviess Guard, offered it to Gov. Richard Yates, and got orders to head for Springfield. Grant declined to serve as captain of the company. If an officer of his training and experience was of any value at all to the country, it ought to be at a higher rank. Chetlain got the slot instead, but Grant went along to Springfield to assist the company as it became part of a regimental organization.[9]

War meetings like the one in Galena were common all across the Prairie State and its neighbors. In Ottawa, Illinois, a similar meeting resolved "that we will stand by the flag of our country in this her most trying hour, cost what it may of blood or treasure," and likewise determined to raise troops. The first company filled up in a single day. Others followed, including one company composed entirely of men over the age of forty-five and led by a captain who had served with Winfield Scott at Lundy's Lane during the War of 1812. To their dismay, however, they discovered that the government was not accepting enlisted recruits who were over the age of forty-five.[10]

News of Fort Sumter reached Frankfort, Indiana, late on the afternoon of April 13, 1861. In the Clinton County courthouse, lawyer Lewis "Lew" Wallace was addressing a jury. The town's telegraph operator entered and told the judge he had a telegram for Wallace. It was from Wallace's friend, Indiana governor Oliver P. Morton, and read: "Sumter has been fired on. Come immediately." With the judge's permission, Wallace excused himself to the jury and left the case to his law partner. Then he mounted his horse and rode hard the ten miles to Colfax, where he could catch a train to Indianapolis that night. Son of a former governor of the state, Wallace had served as a second lieutenant in the Mexican War and in 1856 organized a militia company called the Montgomery (County) Guards. Now Governor Morton made Wallace Indiana's state adjutant general for the purpose of supervising the raising of troops.

Within days, Lincoln's call for troops arrived, requesting six regiments from Indiana. Wallace asked if he could become colonel of one of the new regiments, and Morton agreed. Before the week was out, Wallace reported to Morton some 130 companies at Camp Morton, near Indianapolis. That was 70 more than the number required by Lincoln's call. As was even then being done in Illinois, Morton and Wallace decided that Indiana's regiments should begin numbering where they left off in the Mexican War, so the first Indiana regiment for the Civil War was the 6th. Wallace carefully selected the ten companies he liked best for his own regiment, the 11th.[11]

Even out in Iowa, beyond the Mississippi River, news arrived and people reacted so quickly as to be ahead of Lincoln's call for troops. In Keosauqua, on the Des Moines River in the southeastern part of the state, citizens suspended their ordinary business and stood around in clusters, discussing the news. They had already scheduled a war meeting by the time word of Lincoln's call arrived, so they used the gathering to discuss the raising of a local company. On that much they agreed, but they disagreed on what kind of company to raise. Some were for raising a "foot company," others a "horse company," and still others preferred service in a "cannon company." Someone called for a word from Van Buren County recorder James M. Tuttle, and that official, who farmed and kept a store in addition to his official duties, referred to the issue in dispute as involving "infantry," "cavalry," and "artillery," and gave his opinion in favor of infantry. The townsmen were so impressed with his military knowledge that they agreed to raise a company of infantry and elected Tuttle to command it. Years later Tuttle admitted that "in giving these definitions I went almost to the limit of my military knowledge."[12]

And so men flocked to the colors all across the Midwest, green as the late-April grass on the prairies and led by lawyers, clerks, and petty officials, but filled with enthusiasm and a deep determination to do their duty. They came in such numbers that the states quickly exceeded their recruiting quotas. The problem for many of the newly raised companies was gaining acceptance into the service. Some companies had to disband, at least for the time being, but most were eventually mustered into service. Some Illinois companies, like the Peoria Zouave Cadets, did so by crossing into Missouri and enlisting there as part of the 8th Missouri Regiment.[13] As a border slave state, Missouri held divided loyalties. Many Missouri men would eventually enlist with the Confederacy, and thus the state would have had some difficulty fulfilling its U.S. recruiting quota if not for the influx of Illinoisans and others eager for a place in the ranks of any Union regiment that would take them. The 13th Missouri included one company from Illinois, six from Ohio, and only three from Missouri. The 9th Missouri Regiment included almost no Missourians at all—just Illinoisans.[14]

The Illinois legislature, foreseeing the nation's need of more troops, authorized the state to raise an additional ten regiments—one from each congressional district—beyond the six of Lincoln's original request. These regiments, the 13th through the 22nd Illinois, were filled almost at once. The

state undertook to pay these 10,000 extra levies until the federal government realized its need for them. In like manner, Indiana's redoubtable Governor Morton authorized additional regiments to be sworn into state service
as "the Indiana Legion," pending another call from the president.[15]

The extra regiments, as well as the other companies clamoring for
acceptance into Federal service in Ohio, Wisconsin, and Iowa, did not have
long to wait. Lincoln and his advisors in Washington soon recognized the
need for more troops than the initial 75,000 and for longer terms than the
original ninety-day enlistments. Early in the summer, the president called
for additional troops to serve for three years. After the Union debacle at the
First Battle of Bull Run in July 1861, Lincoln issued a call for 500,000 three-
year volunteers. With that, there was plenty of opportunity for everyone
who wanted to be a soldier, and the states turned down no more companies,
provided they had the requisite number of enlisted men. Officers, though
usually devoid of training or experience, were never in short supply.

Indeed, the supply of would-be officers sometimes outstripped that of
men prepared to follow them. The result was a bizarre competition for
recruits. The man who successfully recruited a company would get a captain's commission, so the race was on to raise the enlistments of the necessary eighty-four privates. Whereas companies during the first few weeks of
the war had tended to be overstrength, aspiring captains were so numerous
by late summer that many struggled to reach the requisite minimum enrollment for their companies.

Joseph Cormack, a conductor on the southern division of the Illinois
Central Railroad, and Wimer Bedford, a mail agent on the same line, got
permission from Governor Yates to raise a company of infantry. Cormack
was to be captain, Bedford his lieutenant, and when the company was complete, they were to report at Anna, Illinois, and become part of the 18th Illinois Regiment. By the time they started, however, most of the willing
recruits in the district between Centralia and Cairo had already enlisted in
other companies. After several weeks, Cormack and Bedford had only a
handful of recruits to show for their efforts, and most of these had been
brought in by one especially enterprising recruit whom the aspiring officers
promptly made a sergeant. Finally the last day of their recruiting authority
arrived. They must report a full company the next day or give up their hopes
for commissions. That evening their sergeant brought them interesting
news. Camped in the woods not far away was a full-strength company that
another captain had recruited and was taking to Anna to join the 18th. The
rival captain had left his men sitting cold and hungry in the woods while he
went into town and got drunk. Cormack sent his persuasive sergeant to talk

to this leaderless unit and offer them good quarters and rations. The plan worked, and Captain Cormack was soon commanding Company D, 18th Illinois, while the drunken would-be captain, upon sobering up, found the woods empty.[16]

Throughout the summer and fall months, recruitment proceeded. In communities all across the Northwest, individual citizens made the decisions that would eventually place them in the ranks of the Army of the Tennessee. From Pekin, Illinois, Dietrich Smith wrote a friend, "Every young man in our church will go."[17] Hoosier lad Noah Sharp decided to go, but his mother had other ideas. Undeterred, Sharp climbed out his bedroom window one night, slid down the porch column, and walked all the way to Logansport, where the 46th Indiana was forming.[18]

Near Iowa City, Iowa, David Henderson was a twenty-one-year-old student at Upper Iowa University that year. He had been born in Scotland, and his parents brought him to America when he was six. When war came, and the large calls for troops began, he decided to lay aside, for the time being at least, his promising career at the university and, along with two brothers, enlist in the 12th Iowa Regiment. It was not an easy decision. "Three brothers of us met together one night . . . under the old family roof," he recalled, "and agreed that in this great land of our adoption the hour had come for us to lay our lives at the feet of our common country. We slept none that night; all sat up. In the morning, before parting, the old father . . . born in Scotland, too, took down the old family Bible . . . and after reading it, knelt among his little group of Scottish-American children, prayed to the God of nations to guard us and make us brave for the right, finished the prayer and said amen." The three brothers then left to join a company of their fellow students called the University Recruits.[19]

Students at other schools also laid aside their books. The Illinois State Normal University, a teachers' college just north of Bloomington, had a remarkable president. Charles E. Hovey was a well-known educator, described by one contemporary as "an able, earnest and enthusiastic man." Shortly after Fort Sumter, he took the lead in forming a military company composed of teachers and students of the university, and the sight of Hovey and his men drilling became a routine feature on campus during the spring months.

In July, business took Hovey to Washington, and he was there when the eastern Union army set out on its much-heralded "On to Richmond" campaign. Hovey became one of the many civilians who went along to see the show, but when the enemy made a stand behind Bull Run Creek, thirty-five miles from Washington, Hovey proved unlike most of the frock-coated rabble in that, instead of sitting down with a picnic basket, he somehow supplied himself with a rifle and took potshots at the Rebels. Back in the capital after the battle, Hovey paid a call on Lincoln, told him about the Normal Company, and got his blessing to recruit it all the way up to regimental strength.

Hurrying back to Illinois, Hovey raised the additional nine companies in three weeks, and what was soon to become the 33rd Illinois joined other troops just outside Springfield at Camp Butler with Hovey as colonel. The 33rd was nicknamed "the Normal Regiment," "the Teachers' Regiment," or occasionally "the Brain Regiment," and indeed it did include in its ranks an unusual number of college graduates—thirteen in one company, all of whom were privates. A few days after they arrived at Camp Butler, one of the privates received a letter offering him a professorship at a prestigious college back east. He turned it down.[20]

Meanwhile, in the region around Iowa City, some members of the University Recruits helped stage recruiting meetings both to boost their own company's numbers and also to help raise another company known as the Iowa City Temperance Zouaves. The meeting in Clermont was especially effective, as twenty-three men signed up. "Whenever a man was enlisted cheers were given," recalled one of the university men. "The old flag was carried around the room and each man, as he enlisted marched after it while the cheers of the people rent the air."[21]

The Wisconsin River Volunteers tried the same method in their neighborhood around Delton, Wisconsin. With color-bearer, snare drummer, bass drummer, and fifer, the boys would pile into big wagons for the ride to nearby towns, shouting about how being a soldier meant "Fourth of July every day in the year!" The meetings, held in local schoolhouses, were well attended, as a good show was not that common an occurrence in rural Wisconsin in those days. After some stirring music, the captain, sounding much like a camp-meeting preacher, would exhort men to "enlist in the army of the Lord." The young ladies often seemed to become more enthusiastic than the young men at this point, urging their male friends to enlist. One became especially zealous and, turning to her beau, cried, "John, if you do not enlist I'll never let you kiss me again as long as I live! Now you mind, sir, I mean what I say!" The soldiers chimed in: "John, you'd better go with us!" "Come, now, John, if I were in your place I'd enlist!" "Come, John, now's your chance!" It was no use. A member of the company later admitted that they garnered few recruits at these meetings but had a famous time.[22]

Some of the most effective recruiters for the 55th Illinois, a northern Illinois regiment, were several Methodist ministers. Well known from their extensive circuit-riding ministry throughout the region, they traveled widely across the northern counties, eloquently exhorting men to step forward and serve their country and the cause of freedom. Three of the Methodist preachers undertook to raise and lead companies as captains. So effective were they as recruiters that they not only filled their own companies but also helped the other captains of the 55th to fill theirs.[23] Elsewhere across the region, other clergy did the same.[24]

Sometimes recruits preferred to enlist with others of their own ethnic group. In such cases, ethnic identity took the place of the normally strong local connection of individual companies. The 58th Ohio was to be a regiment made up entirely of Germans, the fourth such regiment the state had produced. Though recruits were drawn from all over the state, only enough Germans could be obtained to fill seven companies of regulation size. Much to the Germans' dismay, the state recruiting authorities decided to finish out the regiment with three companies of "ordinary" Ohioans. Many of the men in the three extra companies had good German names, but their forebears had come to America long before, and much to the disgust of the more recent immigrants, they were thoroughly Americanized.[25] Other states had ethnic regiments too, such as the all-German 43rd Illinois.

A company in Eau Claire, Wisconsin, prided itself on having one truly unique recruit. He was a young bald eagle they called Abe. Some Chippewa Indians had caught him near the Flambeau River just after maple sugar season that spring and sold him to Daniel McCann for a bushel of corn. An eaglet was not exactly Manhattan Island, but McCann figured he had made a good bargain. He took the bird to Chippewa Falls and tried selling him to a company recruiting there. To their everlasting obscurity, the Chippewa Falls boys turned him down, so McCann took the eagle downstream to Eau Claire, where Capt. John Perkins was organizing a company known as the Eau Claire Badgers. Perkins and his men knew a first-rate mascot when they saw one. A local businessman bought the bird for $2.50 and presented him to the company. Perkins and his men named the eagle in honor of the new president and then changed the name of their company to the Eau Claire Eagles. There were any number of badger companies in Wisconsin, and some of them actually had badgers for mascots (and very ill-tempered mascots they must have been), but an eagle—that was something special. The Eau Claire Eagles soon became Company C, 8th Wisconsin. Eventually the whole regiment came to call itself "the Eagle Regiment," carrying Abe as a sort of extra ensign, perched on a specially decorated pole whose bearer marched beside the regimental colors.[26]

The companies of new recruits were very much the creatures of their local communities. Raised locally of neighbors and men who had known one another most of their lives, they were bound to their local communities by myriad ties of kinship and friendship and usually by the names they bore before they became simply lettered companies of numbered regiments. The Rockford Zouaves were very much a living element, indeed, a part of the military embodiment, of that northern Illinois town on the banks of the Rock River both before and after they became Company D, 11th Illinois, just as the Wisconsin River Volunteers were of their community of Delton, even after their official name changed to Company E, 12th Wisconsin. Between the part of the community that marched off to war and the part that stayed behind was the age-old unspoken covenant between a soldier and the society for which he fights. The soldier goes forth to face hardship and possible wounds and death, while those who remain at home undertake to back him both by supplying his material needs and by giving him moral support. The latter could come in the form of public ceremonies—parades, rallies, and the like—letters, or the supplying of comfort items beyond the bare needs of warfare. The U.S. Army commissary and quartermaster departments would eventually become the chief conduits of the soldiers' basic material needs, but the local communities remained the source of moral sustenance throughout the war. A soldier in the ranks of the Washington Guards of Dubuque might come to refer to his unit as Company A, 3rd Iowa. He might fight for freedom and the flag, but in his mind the most vivid reality behind that flag was the community on the banks of the Mississippi that was his primary source of moral assurance.

At no time was local support for the troops more starkly visible than in the opening months, when companies were gathering and marching away. Thomas Connelly of the 70th Ohio recalled how the citizens of West Union "would bring in chicken, pies, cakes, honey and jellies" for the men at his regiment's camp of assembly. The members of the regiment "were always bade welcome to any home in West Union," as well as in the local "Sabbath-school" and church, where many of them attended regularly until the regiment transferred out.[27]

In those first months of the war, the soldiers' uniforms, if any, were the product of committees of local seamstresses. Many enthusiastic women strove to make other items of usefulness. Peoria ladies fashioned knapsacks for the National Blues company out of the oilskin capes that had been worn by the Wide-Awakes, the Republican drill teams that had paraded for Lincoln in the 1860 election campaign. Others found more innovative ways to help. A Peoria woman sent the company a large quantity of small feather pillows "because she thought they would be light for the boys to carry on the march."[28] The ladies of Oskaloosa, Iowa, sewed 101 havelocks—cap covers with a large flap in back meant to protect the wearer's neck from sun—for the men of Company B, 5th Iowa, prompting soldier John Campbell to exclaim in his diary, "Who would be a bachelor, while there are single ladies in Oskaloosa?"[29] In fact, however, after the first few days or weeks, Civil War soldiers never wore havelocks.

The women of Cedar Falls, Iowa, not only sewed uniforms for their Pioneer Greys—gray wool trousers and navy blue cotton shirts—but also provided them with shoes, socks, and underclothing.[30] Similarly, the female teachers and students of Miami University in Ohio set themselves to sewing flannel underwear for all the members of the University Rifles. Far too demure to ask about sizes, they simply guessed, and the result, sometimes ill fitting, was "the occasion of not a little merriment" to the recruits.[31]

One of the most useful items made for the departing soldiers was an article called a "housewife," a small, often decoratively stitched, folding pouch designed to carry needles, pins, thread, and buttons. The soldiers kept such articles with them throughout the war, since they were easy to carry and of immense use in repairing damaged uniforms. The ladies of Delton gave one such "housewife" to each of the departing soldiers of the Wisconsin River Volunteers.[32]

The most important and universal local gift to the departing company was its flag. The flag carried enormous significance both as the symbol of the nation and as the company's tangible link with its home community. Wives, mothers, sisters, or sweethearts of the soldiers usually sewed it with their own hands, and a delegation of them presented it to the assembled company in a formal ceremony. A representative of the ladies would make a stylized presentation speech, and then a representative of the company, usually the captain, would reply with a speech of his own. Miss Ellen Fisher's address to the Ottawa Rifles, soon to be Company H, 11th Illinois, was typical of the genre, if a bit shorter than usual. It also expressed clearly the implied covenant between soldier and community. "Beloved soldiers," Miss Fisher began,

we present you this banner. It is the flag of our native land. It represents our dearest hopes for country, home and life. Our hands have made it, yours must defend it, and if needed for the purpose, the choicest blood in your veins, we doubt not will freely pour out. Our best wishes attend you. Our prayers will follow you; and if you fall in your country's cause, we promise that your names shall be often spoken with tender pride so long as we shall

live. See to it that this flag is never insulted with impunity. God bless you, and
God bless our native land. Farewell.

Capt. Theodore C. Gibson responded by thanking the ladies for the flag
and pledging his company's faithful service to it and the cause for which it
stood.[33]

Occasionally the men who were enlisting recorded in diaries or letters
their motivations for going to war. A recruit writing a letter might say what
he thought a man going forth to fight for his country was supposed to say,
but in a diary a man was usually writing for himself. If anything, he seemed
to be setting down his grounds for enlisting, so that he might be reminded
of it if he later forgot. John Campbell of the 5th Iowa wrote in his diary, "I
believe that duty to my country and my *God*, bid me assist in crushing this
wicked rebellion against our government, which rebellious men have insti-
gated . . . to secure the extension of that blighting curse—*slavery*—o'er
our fair land."[34]

For each of the companies, the meetings, speeches, and special services
eventually ended and the day came to march off to the large assembly
camps where they would join other companies to form regiments and larger
units. It was a day anticipated with excitement by the soldiers and with
dread by many they left behind. "Oh that departure!" wrote Dietrich Smith
of his company's exodus from Pekin, Illinois. "As the Volenteers passed
down court street to the levee all was covered with people. The Band playing some cheering others crying."[35]

In Cedar Falls, Iowa, 5,000 were on hand to see the Pioneer Greys off to
the war. Main Street was lined with dense crowds as the parade set off.
Escorting the Greys to the railroad station was the Cedar Falls Brass Band,
followed by about twenty gray-haired veterans of the War of 1812. Then
came the young volunteers, on the way to their own war, proudly wearing
their gray pants and dark blue shirts. The crowd fell in behind and followed
the procession to Cedar Falls's brand-new train station—the tracks had
reached this Iowa town only a few months before. There a special train
waited, decorated with flags, bunting, and cedar boughs. The company
broke ranks for final good-byes, and the jubilation was tempered by at least
one woman who stood sobbing, with two small children clinging to her
skirts. The volunteers then boarded the train, followed by the band and
about fifty civilians who would travel with them as far as Dubuque.[36]

In Delton, Wisconsin, the Wisconsin River Volunteers piled into the
thirteen wagons that were to take them to Madison. Then the village parson
stepped forward and exhorted the new soldiers "to keep up good courage,"

as one of them recalled, "never for a moment to doubt that in our most trying hours—on the battle-field, in sickness, in death—that the prayers of
loving and faithful hearts are ascending for us to the kind Father in heaven."
The preacher led in prayer, and then the wagons rolled forward. The
townspeople walked alongside the slow-moving vehicles until they came to
the bridge over Dell Creek. The wagons crossed, while the citizens stood
on the Delton side, and shouts of "Good-bye" went back and forth across
the narrow stream. Waves from the wagons continued to answer fluttered
handkerchiefs from the bridge until the road passed over a crest and the
departing soldiers disappeared from view.[37]

The journey to the camp of assembly could be an ovation. During the
trip from Oxford to Columbus, Ohio, the University Rifles received such
vociferous cheering that one member recalled, "We began to feel that we
were heroes already."[38] James Dugan had a similar experience as his 14th
Illinois traveled from Shelbyville to Quincy. "At every station . . . the populace had assembled to see those who were going to the war, and our passage all the way, may . . . be called an Ovation." Best of all, "wherever it
was practicable, refreshments were served."[39]

What the recruits encountered when they reached the large camps
where troops were assembling was often their first, slight foretaste of the
hardships of soldiering. Each state hastily established several points of
assembly. Illinois's main installation was Camp Yates, just outside Springfield. In peacetime, Camp Yates had been known as the Fair Grounds. Many
of the new soldiers now quartered in the stalls normally used for animals.
These were three-sided structures open to the out-of-doors on the fourth
side; so the soldiers sometimes rigged makeshift curtains across that side.
They built their campfires just outside on the open side of the stall. That
was a problem since many of the stalls' open sides faced west. "The wind
has been from the west ever since we came in," wrote Cyrus Dickey of the
11th Illinois, "& the smoke from our camp fires (which are in front) fills all
the stalls or quarters with smoke." It was, Dickey concluded, "a pretty
rough life, but not more so than I anticipated."[40] George L. Paddock of the
12th Illinois recalled, "The Fair Ground was not a place of sumptuous
resort; yet those recruits who were transferred to Camp Yates, after a night
or so spent at Camp Taylor, which was another and more military name for
a brickyard near by, deemed it a comparatively spacious and habitable piece
of land."[41] The story was much the same at fairgrounds all over the Midwest. In Chicago, several regiments were housed in the cavernous wooden
Wigwam, the convention hall in which Abraham Lincoln had been nominated the year before.[42]

At Camp Randall, in Madison, Wisconsin, Abe the eagle continued to attract just as much attention as he had in Eau Claire. When the Eau Claire Eagles marched into camp there for the first time, its musicians playing "Yankee Doodle," Abe, who was perched on his platform alongside a small American flag, took one end of the flag in his beak and spread his wings "with a continuously flapping motion," much to the delight of onlookers. The people of Madison flocked to camp to see the bird, and the quartermaster at Camp Randall had a new perch built for him. It featured a shield decorated with the Stars and Stripes and the inscription "8th Reg. W. V." A few inches above the shield was a crosspiece for Abe to roost on. At each end of the crosspiece were three arrows, in imitation of the Great Seal of the United States. A man would carry the whole assembly on the end of a five-foot pole. The base of the pole would fit in a socket attached to a belt that went around the bearer's waist. Abe was kept securely tethered to his perch by a strong cord sixteen to twenty feet long, and when the regiment was on the march, the tether could be shortened to about three feet. The Eau Claire Eagles, now Company C, 8th Wisconsin, bore him proudly right alongside the regimental colors.[43]

Occasions like the Eau Claire Eagles' entrance to Camp Randall were just the sort of scenes many of the young men had pictured themselves being part of when they went off to join the army—"Fourth of July every day in the year." However, at Camp Yates at Springfield, Camp Randall at Madison, Camp Jackson at Columbus, and all the similar facilities across the rest of Illinois, Wisconsin, Iowa, Indiana, and Ohio, the chief reality of military life, aside from boredom and discomfort, was drill. The muzzleloading weapons of the day required that soldiers do most of their fighting while standing in line. Using such linear tactics successfully required hundreds if not thousands of hours of close-order drill. Unfortunately, in many regiments the officers were almost as ignorant of the drill as the men to whom they were supposed to be teaching it. Asa Munn of the 13th Illinois remembered that at the Dixon, Illinois, fairgrounds where his regiment did its first training, the officers seemed to rely very much on a particular lieutenant who had once been to the East. There he had seen some militia "marking time" and gotten the idea that marching in place was a very soldierly thing to do. So the 13th did a great deal of marking time when the lieutenant could not think of any other order to give them. "Yes," Munn wryly observed in later years, "we brought to camp a full stock of military ignorance."[44]

Some of the soldiers practiced a special type of drill known as the Zouave drill. Zouaves were originally French North African colonial troops who had performed well in European wars. They utilized light infantry tactics that emphasized open-order formations, with several feet between soldiers, rather than the customary close order, with its characteristic "touch of elbows." They moved at double time, rather than marching at a stately cadence, and they lay on their backs to load their rifles rather than standing to do so. To fire they rolled prone and sometimes rose on one knee. Later the pressures of war would blur the differences between Zouaves and ordinary troops. The line troops adopted what was useful from the Zouave drill, and the Zouaves abandoned impractical flourishes. At the outset of the war, however, Zouave troops felt much superior.

Zouave units normally adopted special uniforms, more or less inspired by the traditional garb of the French North African regiments. These ranged from the gaudy to the downright bizarre. Among troops destined for the Army of the Tennessee, however, good Midwestern common sense tempered the excesses seen in the more outlandish uniforms of the East Coast Zouaves. Lew Wallace's 11th Indiana Zouaves were an example. Their baggy Zouave breeches were sky blue, with button gaiters connecting to their shoes. Their jackets were of gray twill, in the short, Zouave style. Unlike many Eastern Zouaves, Wallace's men eschewed turbans and fezzes and stuck with the standard kepi, the typical cap of Civil War soldiers. Theirs, however, were gray with red tops.[45]

Lew Wallace believed that the overall effect of the Zouave uniform was "to magnify the men." The Zouave drill, he believed, gave the men confidence, self-reliance, and élan. Many soldiers agreed. The 14th Illinois was no Zouave regiment, but James Dugan recalled how pleased he and his fellow soldiers were when a Regular Army captain came to their camp and "commenced instructing us in the Zoo-Zoo drill."[46]

Whether in Zouave or ordinary tactics, drill was the primary means of making farm boys, clerks, college students, and the like into steady soldiers. At Camp Douglas, near Chicago, the 55th Illinois drilled at least seven hours a day, mostly directed by the regiment's martinet lieutenant colonel, a Swede named Oscar Malmborg, who was supposed to have had some sort of military background in the old country. The men hated him for his unrelenting and unrestrained abuse, but they thought his accent ludicrous—especially when it was belted out with all the force Malmborg's lungs could muster, which was usually the case. "Charge peanuts!" the apoplectic Malmborg would roar, when he obviously meant "Charge bayonets!" "Column py file," the lieutenant colonel would bellow, or "What for you face mit your pack?"

Besides drill, Malmborg was especially ferocious about the need for nighttime sentinels to maintain the highest possible alertness, even though the men as yet had no guns and had to march their beats armed only with stout oaken cudgels. One night Malmborg determined to catch one of the sentinels being inattentive, presumably in order to have the pleasure of ordering him punished. Approaching quietly through the thicket where the soldier was posted, Malmborg received, more or less simultaneously, a startled challenge and a tremendous wallop with the oak club. He survived, though knocked out cold for a few minutes, and for several weeks afterward bossed the regiment through its maneuvers with a very black eye.[47]

The actual colonel of the 55th Illinois was Chicago lawyer David Stuart. Stuart, a man of somewhat scandalous personal life, had only the sketchiest of ideas of the drill manual and therefore made the mistake of having Malmborg direct all the regiment's drills. This was easier in the short run, but it meant that Stuart fell further and further behind his regiment in military knowledge. Naturally his obvious ignorance steadily lost him the respect of the soldiers, which had been none too high to begin with.

Stuart was a prime example of the sort of man who, though prominent and successful in civilian life, simply did not have what it took to become a successful officer. It was not a rare breed. Hugh T. Reid was a highly successful Keokuk lawyer whom the governor of Iowa appointed colonel of the 15th Iowa Regiment. "A man of the purest private character, of the most incorruptible honesty, of undoubted patriotism and loyalty," one of his officers described him, "as brave as ever drew saber, and as ignorant of military tactics as any man that ever gave or attempted to secure the execution of a military command." Reid was, his subordinate concluded, "a most striking illustration of a man not only respectable but eminent in important civic pursuits, who was utterly incapable of acquiring even a respectable knowledge of military drill and maneuvers."[48]

A successful colonel had to have personal integrity as well as knowledge of military drill. One of the best colonels at Camp Yates was William H. L. Wallace. Like Stuart and Reid, Wallace was also a lawyer, and like Reid, at any rate, he was a man of rock-solid integrity, a devout Christian, devoted to his wife, Ann, and their children. Wallace won the respect of his men both by his character and by his skill on the drill field. "Discipline comes hard on volunteers," Wallace admitted, "and I am obliged to be severe sometimes, and expect some dissatisfaction."[49]

Nevertheless, drill was military and made the men feel like soldiers. They were full of youthful enthusiasm and took every opportunity to show it. The boys of one of the Ottawa companies in the 11th Illinois developed their own special cheer for saluting the colors. It featured the name of their town with the three syllables separated and emphasized: "one-two-three Au tau wa." The Ottawa boys were immensely pleased with it and believed it much superior to the popular "tiger" cheer. The Ottawa cheer "commands the admiration of the whole camp," one of them proudly wrote to the folks back home.[50]

One serious problem, both for drilling and for making the men feel like soldiers, was the difficulty of obtaining weapons. Although privately owned rifles were plentiful, the need for at least some semblance of uniformity in ammunition required that the regiments depend on government-issued arms. Whatever drilling was done in hometowns was done with empty hands or with sticks standing in for rifles. The various companies had marched away from their hometowns unarmed, and waited impatiently at the assembly camps to receive their weapons. The fact was that the United States did not have enough military arms on hand to equip the massive flood of recruits, and agents of the U.S. government were vying with those of the Confederacy to buy up surplus arms in the European market.

All regiments hoped for modern Springfield or Enfield rifled muskets, or perhaps, even better, the new breechloading or even repeating rifles. Some regiments got their wish. The men of northwestern Illinois's Lead Mine Regiment, the 45th Illinois, were delighted to receive first-class Enfield muzzleloading rifles and considered their regiment one of the best equipped in the state.[51] Many regiments had to make do with inferior arms. Some got various older model Springfield or Harpers Ferry smoothbore muskets, with less than half the range of the new rifles and atrocious accuracy. Others received grossly inferior imported Belgian or Austrian muskets. Using any of the outmoded weapons could be unpleasant. The 55th Illinois, raised in several of the same northern Illinois counties as the 45th, had been recruited largely with the promise that its men would be equipped with the amazing five-shot Colt revolving rifle. Instead they got the Dresden rifle, a deplorable import from old Europe. "Language fails when attempting to describe the grotesque worthlessness of these so-called arms," recalled a member of the regiment. Others wryly quipped that with the Dresden rifle, it was the shooter who did the revolving, since, if the gun happened to go off when the trigger was pulled (by no means a foregone conclusion), the recoil was terrific.[52]

Excessive recoil was a common complaint about inferior weapons, and it was not limited to guns of foreign make. John Hunt recalled that his 40th Illinois Regiment was originally supplied with "the old Harpers Ferry musket," which, Hunt opined, "was about as dangerous to those behind as to those in front."[53] The 47th Illinois got Belgian muskets, "good hard kickers," wrote one of the soldiers, "and like the human kickers, for the most part, harmless."[54] When the 77th Ohio received Austrian rifled muskets, they were so angry that several companies briefly mutinied, stacking the hated weapons in front of their tents. They soon came around but remained unhappy about those guns. "They were a very heavy, awkward gun," a member recalled, "and had a very unpleasant habit of kicking back when fired."[55]

One of the many activities that took place at the assembly camps was a reminder of this war's odd mixture of the military and the political. All wars are political, but in this one, civilian political methods carried over into the army in unusual ways. When not drilling their companies, the various captains took time out to campaign for higher rank. This began with the assembling of the regiments themselves out of the collections of companies in the camps, and it almost smacked of a political convention with its horse-trading and backroom deal-making. A regiment consisted of ten companies, so many a captain sought to connect his company with just the right list of nine others so as to give himself the best chance of achieving promotion to the resulting regiment's list of field officers—major, lieutenant colonel, or, best of all, colonel. The ten captains would meet and bargain and usually agree on a slate of candidates to put forward when the combined rank and file of the new regiment should vote for field officers.

The regiment that became the 11th Illinois included companies from towns scattered from one end of the state to the other, the result of a great many strategic calculations on the part of their captains. William H. L. Wallace, who had originally come to Springfield as captain of a company from Ottawa, vouchsafed to his wife in a letter he wrote on April 25 that if the right new companies showed up in camp the next day, he thought he might be able to win a colonelcy. If he did not achieve that rank, however, he assured his wife he would come home immediately. As a veteran of the Mexican War, Wallace felt it would be humiliating for him to accept a lower rank. He need not have worried. When the ten captains caucused, they were unanimous for Wallace as their colonel and T. E. G. Ransom, a bright young graduate of Norwich Military Academy who had brought in a company from Vandalia, as major. They could not agree, however, about who should be lieutenant colonel. It came to a vote, and Capt. J. Warren Filler of Effingham beat out George Paddock of Princeton, Illinois. Thereupon, Paddock took his company of disgruntled Princeton men and went in search of a more promising regiment. His place was filled by a company from LaSalle with a more reasonable captain, and on April 26, Wallace was able to report a full-strength regiment to the Regular Army mustering officer on duty at Camp Yates.[56]

CHAPTER TWO

Cairo

ONE BY ONE, the new regiments got their orders to move forward to various posts in the theater of operations. The leave-takings from camps of assembly were often the occasions of ceremonies similar to those that had occurred when the companies left their hometowns. The 14th Illinois had assembled at Jacksonville, Illinois, and when it prepared to depart for its first duty station, the ladies of Jacksonville "sent to Chicago and ordered the most beautiful bunting flag the city could furnish." The formal presentation ceremony took place May 18, with a beautiful young lady giving the oration and handing over the colors. From there, however, the ceremony took a decided turn for the worse. The regiment had obtained a 6-pounder cannon, and the colonel had appointed a squad of amateur artillerists to operate that piece of nonregulation equipment. Now he wanted them to fire a salute for the occasion. The first round went fine, but the gun crew neglected to swab the barrel before attempting to load a second. The resulting premature detonation tore off the loader's arms and gave the regiment its first casualty.[1]

Few send-off ceremonies could have made a more impressive spectacle to the eyes of contemporary beholders than that of Lew Wallace's 11th Indiana Zouaves at the State House Square in Indianapolis. A large crowd was on hand, joining the regiment in cheering and singing patriotic songs. Delegations of ladies from Indianapolis and Terre Haute had prepared state and national flags for the regiment, and a Mrs. Cady presented them to Colonel Wallace.

Wallace expressed his gratitude to the ladies, then turned and made a speech to his men. He alluded to something of which most of those present were probably already aware. At the Mexican War's Battle of Buena Vista, fourteen years earlier, a single Indiana regiment, fighting against long odds, had run away. Many of its scattered members made their way back to the front and fought alongside other U.S. troops, including the 1st Mississippi Regiment, which was commanded by Jefferson Davis, now the Confederate president. Although it was much to the Indiana men's credit that they came back, this apparently drew the attention of the Mississippians, and led to Southerners in general sneering that all Hoosiers were cowards. Wallace rehearsed the story in detail and concluded by pointing out that the reproach of Buena Vista still adhered to the state. "The stain is upon you and me. It attaches no less to these flags just received, because they are now our property, and we of Indiana. So what have we to do, my men? What but recognize that the war we are summoned to is twice holy—for the Union first, then to wipe the blot from our state and infamize our slander?"

The colonel then concluded, "Boys, then, will you ever desert the banners that have been presented to us today?" "Never! Never!" the Zouaves roared back. Wallace had the whole regiment drop to one knee, raise their right hands, and swear, "God helping us, we will remember Buena Vista."[2]

One by one, with fanfare or quietly, the various regiments shipped out. Fortunately for the often ill-equipped and semitrained soldiers of the first levies, operational assignments during the summer of 1861 were not particularly challenging and consisted mostly of garrisoning various key points along the southern and western fringes of Illinois perceived to be threatened by the forces of slavery and secession just across the Ohio and Mississippi rivers. The most important of these posts lay at the confluence of those two streams. Located on a spit of alluvial mud in the acute angle of the rivers, the town of Cairo, Illinois, in the words of one unhappy northern Illinois recruit, was "famous for dirt, filth, mud, mean houses and accommodations, and meaner men."[3] Mary Logan, wife of a Union colonel, wrote of how the waters of the frequent floods "stagnated in every depression and were soon covered by a green scum" that sometimes nearly cut off Cairo from the rest of Illinois.[4] The floodwaters also flushed out the impressive rat population of the wharves until they "literally overran the streets at night." Camp rumor had it that the following January a drunken soldier, passed out in the gutter, was not only killed by the rats but skeletonized by them overnight.[5] Cairo was the sort of place where men could believe stories like that one.

Located not only at the junction of the rivers but also at the southern terminus of the Illinois Central Railroad, Cairo was a strategic location for commerce as well as for war, but it had been hindered throughout its existence by the tendency to flood. The town's population had grown tenfold during the 1850s, but secession, which had stopped the operation of the tri-weekly Cairo–New Orleans steamboats, had paralyzed Cairo's economy.[6] Still, the town was Illinois's gateway to the Deep South. A soldier from the central Illinois corn belt wrote home from Cairo, "We can stand on the levee & see parts of three states at one time," referring to Illinois, Kentucky, and Missouri.[7] In the summer of 1861, some feared that the Rebels just across the Mississippi in Missouri were making plans to occupy the strategic river junction.[8]

Cairo drew the largest portion of the nascent armies of Illinois, initially, and later those of the rest of the Northwest. There, where the southern tip of Illinois, farther south than Richmond, Virginia, pointed like a wedge down the Mississippi Valley, the Army of the Tennessee would first begin to coalesce. Several Illinois regiments got orders for Cairo by the end of April. The 11th Illinois went to Villa Ridge, a dozen or so miles from Cairo; the 7th to nearby Mound City, a half-dozen miles upstream from Cairo on the Ohio River. The 12th encamped at Caseyville, not far from St. Louis, ready in case trouble should develop from the direction of that sharply divided city. Other regiments went to posts in Missouri, where Union authorities were trying to establish and maintain control of the state.[9]

The Rebels across the rivers in Missouri or Kentucky were not the only worry for Union forces that summer. Southern Illinois itself harbored unknown quantities of disloyalty. The southern counties of the Prairie State were known as "Little Egypt" because during the severe winter of 1830 settlers in northern Illinois had imported corn from southern Illinois just as the Old Testament patriarchs had done from the land of Egypt.[10] The area had been settled by Kentuckians and other Southerners, and its population had strong proslavery and possibly pro-Confederate sentiments. John Hunt, a young man living in Benton, Illinois, recalled that during the election campaign of 1860, "it was rather dangerous to express your political sentiments." This was especially true "if you happened to be a Republican and for Abraham Lincoln," in which case it was best to " 'hide out' on election day." Hunt was no Republican. His family had come from the South, and he believed that in the prewar struggle to halt the spread of slavery "the south was being needlessly oppressed by the free-soil element."[11]

Lincoln, Yates, and other Union leaders worried about Little Egypt. It was as easy to imagine the southern Illinoisans shooting one way as the other. First, Governor Yates and, later, Union Western commanding general John C. Frémont, from his headquarters in St. Louis, dispatched troops to guard against possible trouble in Little Egypt. Various detachments of the newly raised regiments took up positions around southern Illinois at likely targets for pro-Confederate saboteurs. For example, two companies of the 8th Illinois spent weeks at the railroad bridge over the Big Muddy River, just north of Carbondale.

In fact, the situation in southern Illinois was not as bad as Lincoln and the others had feared. Hunt later explained: "Like a great many poor misguided individuals living contiguous to the southern border I was almost ready to join the issue with 'our brethren of the south.' " The deciding factor for Hunt, and apparently many others, was Fort Sumter. When the Confederates became "the aggressors, and committed the unpardonable [sin] of firing on the flag, they revolutionized political sentiment in southern Illinois." Most "Egyptians" in 1861 were certainly not ready to fight against slavery, but neither were they prepared to tolerate slaveholders fighting to overthrow the Stars and Stripes and the Constitution of the United States. "The vast majority of our able-bodied male population, myself with the rest," Hunt concluded, "sooner or later enlisted under the banner of 'Old Glory' in defense of our country."[12]

Nevertheless, it would be some time before Lincoln would be able to rest entirely easy about the southern counties of Illinois. Newspapers like the *Jonesboro Gazette* were openly secessionist, and the *Cairo City Gazette* proclaimed "the sympathies of our people are mainly with the South."[13] In May, a band of about thirty-five Egyptians had set off to fight for the Confederacy. Making their way south of the Ohio, the Illinois Rebels joined the 15th Tennessee.[14]

To help ensure the shaky loyalty of Little Egypt, Lincoln called on some of his erstwhile opponents in Illinois politics, prominent Democratic politicians from the southern half of the state who were nevertheless loyal. Chief among these was Congressman John A. McClernand of Shawneetown, near the Ohio River about a hundred miles northeast of Cairo. After the death of his political mentor, Stephen A. Douglas, McClernand was the foremost Democrat in Illinois. Like Douglas, McClernand, though indifferent to slavery, was staunchly for the Union.

In June, McClernand went with fellow southern Illinois Democratic congressman John A. Logan to bolster the patriotic fervor of the troops at Camp Yates. One of the regiments to which they spoke was the 21st Illinois. The 21st had come to the field with an incompetent colonel whom Governor Yates had finally replaced with Ulysses Grant. Prior to that time, Grant had been rather discouraged at his inability to obtain an appropriate command. Now, however, Grant had a problem. His regiment's enlistment was about to expire, and the men, ill trained by his predecessor and not yet accustomed to his strict military regime, were not inclined to reenlist. Thus, Grant invited McClernand to speak, and McClernand brought Logan. Grant had his doubts about the swarthy Logan. A resident of Marion, scarcely more than fifty miles from Cairo, Logan was widely rumored to be a secessionist and had not yet declared his loyalty to the Union. In an 1859 speech to Congress, Logan had boasted of the readiness of Illinois Democrats to enforce the Fugitive Slave Act, returning escaped slaves to bondage, and thus performing the state's constitutional "dirty work." Republican newspapers in Illinois had been calling him "Dirty Work" Logan ever since.[15]

Taking a chance, Grant decided to let both men speak. McClernand gave the expected pro-Union stem-winder. Then Logan rose to speak. It was ridiculous to think of quitting without even getting into the fight, he asserted. "You can't fall out now. If you go home to Mary, she will say, 'Why Tom, are you home from the war so soon?'

" 'Yes.'

" 'How far did you get?'

" 'Mattoon.' "

Logan's reference to the nearby east-central Illinois town brought roars of laughter from the troops, who saw at once the absurdity of marching off under waving flags to battle treason in the Deep South—and then getting no farther than the county seat. Logan concluded with a forceful and successful appeal for the men to reenlist and see the war through. Grant was appreciative.[16]

Despite that speech and another Logan made in June, as well as a letter published in a Springfield paper, his allegiance remained questionable in the eyes of many Illinoisans that summer. Logan was in Washington the following month for a special session of Congress, and he accompanied the army when it marched down to Bull Run and took part—on the Union side—in a skirmish at Blackburn's Ford, three days before the major battle. Returning to southern Illinois, Logan shocked many of his pro-Confederate friends and family by accepting a commission to raise a regiment of troops for the Union, the 31st Illinois, and become its colonel. Naturally the Illinois Republican press was not slow in christening the regiment the "Dirty-first Illinois," but to Lincoln the active support of a southern Illinois Democrat like Logan meant worlds. When Logan first called for volunteers, standing on a wagon in the town square of Marion, Illinois, in the very heart of Little Egypt's pro-Confederate Williamson County, it was for many Egyptians their first definitive news that John Logan was planning to fight for the Union.[17]

Lincoln had won over Logan in the same way he won over many other political opponents and their followers into support for the war: he gave him a commission in the army. In Logan's case, strictly speaking, the appointment came from Governor Yates, but Lincoln no doubt advised his home state's governor in the matter. Politicians coveted military glory in those days, and the people were inclined to look upon their frock-coated leaders as equally fitted to bear shoulder straps and swords—no experience necessary. By making a man a high-ranking officer, preferably a general, Lincoln not only secured his loyalty but the support of his political follow-ing, not necessarily for the Republican Party, but rather for the cause of winning the war and preserving the Union. Lincoln used the same method with McClernand, nominating him in August to be one of several new brigadier generals from the state of Illinois.

McClernand continued to stump for the Union cause in Illinois, to ply Lincoln with unsolicited and unrealistic advice, and to watch carefully for possible angles to improve his own political standing.[18] He had a few weeks' nominal service in the Black Hawk War; Logan had no military experience at all. They were far from the last and certainly not the worst politically motivated appointments Lincoln was to make. Their sort could sometimes be costly on the day of battle. For now, though, Lincoln had no complaints, as Logan and McClernand were both doing their part, in Lincoln's words, to "keep Egypt right side up."[19]

The crisis of loyalty in southern Illinois gradually ebbed away, and recruiting picked up there. Perhaps this came about through the influence of men like Logan and McClernand. Perhaps these wily politicians sensed the early signs of a shift in public opinion and hastened to place themselves in front of it. Or perhaps what happened was a combination of both.

While the politicians maneuvered and additional recruits continued to flock to the colors, the regiments whose organization was complete began shipping out of the assembly camps headed for their first posts of duty in the war. The 11th Illinois Regiment's journey south from Springfield to its new post near Cairo illustrates the challenges of making an efficient army out of a mass of civilians. At Camp Yates on the morning of May 5, the reg-iment got orders to be ready to leave camp at four o'clock that afternoon. Colonel Wallace checked with the commissary officer and received assur-ance that ten days' rations would go with them. Right on time they marched out of camp, made their way to the Great Western Railroad depot in Springfield, and boarded the trains, cheered by thousands of soldier and civilian well-wishers.[20]

The next morning at about six o'clock they rolled into Carbondale under a steady downpour. There, Wallace discovered that no barracks or shelter of any kind awaited his men at Villa Ridge, forty miles away, and his regiment had no tents. While the engine took on wood and water and the colonel worried about his 900 men being turned out on a wooded hillside in a driving rain, some of the rank and file took the opportunity to visit a num-ber of Carbondale's retail establishments. While a crowd of soldiers was in

S. H. Freeland's store, some person or persons unknown boosted sixteen and a half packages of envelopes, sixteen pieces of dried beef, and a tin cup—total value, $5.75, as Freeland informed Wallace the next day in a letter demanding reimbursement.[21]

The train rolled on, with Wallace now making inquiries at each station for any available carpenters and lumber. By the time they got to Villa Ridge, at about ten o'clock that morning, things were looking up. True, the "town" was an uninviting collection of about fifteen houses in a very muddy little valley a dozen miles north of Cairo, but the rain had finally stopped, and Wallace had some twenty carpenters on board ready to go right to work building huts for the troops. In the meantime, Wallace had them retain the railroad cars on a siding as temporary housing, much to the distress of the Illinois Central Railroad, which was receiving more orders to move troops and was hindered in doing so because of the missing rolling stock.[22]

Wallace's second morning in Villa Ridge brought him his next surprise. His men were out of food. Instead of ten days' rations, his regiment had left Camp Yates with only one. Wallace immediately fired off orders for supplies to be sent up from Cairo. He also sent the authorities in Springfield both official notification and a somewhat more strongly worded private note: "By the eternal my men must be fed." Wallace protested, pointing out that if the government did not provide rations regularly, the troops were bound to take to stealing. For several days, the rations were a bit scanty and irregular, but eventually the commissary department made the necessary adjustments.[23]

Behavior continued to be a problem for the new troops, or at least some of them. Three days after the regiment's arrival, the mayor of nearby Mound City wrote Colonel Wallace to complain about "the exceeding bad conduct of a few of your men towards our citizens." The errant soldiers, the mayor reported, "get drunk, insult ladies upon the street and disturb the peace and quiet of our people generally." The city marshal had had to arrest three of them and ship them back to camp at Villa Ridge. Citizens also complained that some of the men had been supplementing their admittedly scanty rations by devouring local livestock. Once again, Wallace took prompt and decisive action. The next day, he issued stringent orders for suppressing such breaches, threatening violators with court-martial and being drummed out of camp in disgrace. That was a very serious punishment to these men. "Drumming out" would take place while the regiment stood in line during evening dress parade; "the culprit was escorted back and forth in front of the line, followed by the band playing the 'Rogue's

March.' " Then the sergeant major cut every last military insignia off of the offender's uniform, including even the buttons on his cap, and at last the condemned was expelled from the camp.[24] A soldier at Cairo at about that time wrote a friend, "I had rather be burned to death than be drumed out of camp." Wallace was determined that "the honor and reputation of the regiment shall not be imperiled by the lawless acts of a few disorderly and dishonest men."[25]

For good measure, the next day Wallace ordered, "On each Sabbath until further orders companies will attend divine service at 10 o'clock a.m. At the first call of the drum which will beat at a ¼ before ten, companies will form upon their parade grounds. At the second call they will march to the place of worship in charge of 1st Sergeants."[26] Wallace meant to have discipline and virtue in his regiment, one way or another.

Other colonels were fighting the same battle. In Cairo, Col. C. C. Marsh of the 20th Illinois took steps to deal with the problem of drunken and "riotous" soldiers, banning both drinking and gambling in the camp. He also "required bathing by companies twice a week," and no soldier was to go into town without a pass.[27] Col. Philip B. Fouke of the 30th Illinois likewise prohibited "card playing and drinking" among his men.[28]

The struggles Wallace faced in moving his regiment from Camp Yates to Villa Ridge and in feeding, housing, and disciplining it illustrated the difficulties of even the simplest operations in an army that was often almost as green at the level of regimental command as it was at that of the private soldier. Wallace, who had been a lieutenant and regimental adjutant in the Mexican War, was among the best of the new volunteer colonels. Smart, dedicated, ambitious, but committed to the well-being of his troops, Wallace still made mistakes, but he was learning fast. His regiment was one of the best drilled of the volunteer outfits. "The men take great interest in drilling," he wrote his wife, "& I am giving them enough of it." The 11th's morale, like that of the other regiments, was high. One evening about a week after the regiment's arrival at Villa Ridge, Company D, the Rockford Zouaves, marched up to headquarters in perfect step and gave the field officers "the Zouave salute." A few minutes later, ten or fifteen of them were back with candles and printed sheet music, from which they sang "The Star-Spangled Banner," and "God Save Our Native Land" while Colonel Wallace beamed with pleasure.[29]

It was well that they began with all the exuberant high spirits of youth, for life in the camps around Cairo was a further step in the education of the new soldiers. Conditions were not bad compared with what came later in the conflict, but the troops were unused to the hardships of war and unlearned in the little tricks that would, later in the conflict, make soldiering more bearable. In after years, some were still describing their first summer of the war in Cairo as the most unpleasant memory of their time in the army.[30]

Usually somewhere in the month of May, the various regiments recorded their first fatalities of the war, not to enemy action or even accident but rather to the foremost killer of every pre-twentieth-century war—and especially of this war and this particular army—sickness. Surviving comrades mentioned typhoid, dysentery, diarrhea, or simply "fever" as the causes of death. For the men of the Army of the Tennessee, the impartial microbe would always be a more persistent and deadly foe than the Confederate armies.[31]

The difficulties and boredom of camp life in southern Illinois and the bordering fringes of the slave states during the long, hot summer of 1861 made it notable that a great many of the men of the original ninety-day regiments reenlisted for another three years. The regiments, the 7th through 12th Illinois, the 7th through 11th Indiana, and so on, simply kept their same designations and organizations as they became long-term U.S. Volunteers rather than short-term federalized state militia. The higher-numbered regiments were already signed up for three-year hitches.[32]

Even with secession territory, and presumably the enemy, just across the river, the business of politicking for promotion went on. Just as regimental officers were elected by their men, so too, among the Illinois troops that summer, was the brigadier general to be chosen by the officers of the regiments in his brigade. The two chief contestants were Capt. John Pope, of the Regular Army, and Col. Benjamin M. Prentiss, a Democratic politician from Quincy who had recently been elected colonel of the 10th Illinois.

Pope was West Point–trained, but Prentiss had received his education in a very different school. "Dear Friend," Prentiss wrote to another Illinois colonel the day before the election. "This will be handed to you by my Friend Captn Tillson of the Quincy Guard who will confer with you as to my chances to be elected Brig Genl." Hinting that it was time to jump on the bandwagon, Prentiss continued, "I will now mention that I have the support of two full Regt and three Companies, in this Camp. I can be elected with your aid." Finally, hoping to sweeten the prospect with a bit of free railroad travel, he added, "I forward some RR Passes for use at your Station." It was the good old formula that rarely failed in peacetime politics. It worked just fine in the army too, and Prentiss became Illinois's first brigadier general.[33] Before the summer was over, however, Lincoln would appoint several more brigadier generals from Illinois, some of whose commissions would be dated prior to Prentiss's.

For the troops stationed in and around Cairo, the monotony of guard, drill, and fatigue duty was broken several times during the summer months by forays across the Mississippi into the swamps of southeastern Missouri in pursuit of Confederate guerrillas led by M. Jeff Thompson. Elements of several regiments took part in the thrusts, and though they usually made no contact with the enemy, it was an exciting outing all the same and involved just enough hardship to feel like real campaigning.[34]

In June, Union troops, including William Wallace's 11th Illinois and Michael Lawler's brawling 18th Illinois, moved across the Mississippi River from Cairo to occupy Bird's Point, Missouri. The camp there was a pleasant one, with a splendid view of the river.[35] In August, a detachment from Bird's Point, including elements of the 11th and the 22nd Illinois, took the railroad to Charleston, Missouri, and defeated a small Confederate force in a skirmish there.[36]

Most tramps or rides into the wilds of Missouri brought no contact with the enemy. Except for those few outings, the summer months were a time of unrelieved boredom. Col. John McArthur and the other officers of the 12th Illinois decided to enliven things a bit by holding a mock battle with blank cartridges. In a large open area covered only with a low growth of stinkweed, they divided the regiment into two wings. McArthur took one wing, Capt. A. C. Ducat the other, and the two sides went at it. Volleys crashed and clouds of sulfurous powder smoke hung over the field as the two embattled lines closed in. Then, forgetting that this was all in good fun, the soldiers waded into one another with musket butts and bare knuckles, despite the officers' frantic efforts to separate them. "Many heads were hurt," recalled regimental surgeon Horace Wardner, "and numerous other casualties were reported." Fortunately there were no fatalities, but the regimental officers were afraid of what their superiors might say about the large number of men reported "unable for duty" the next morning. Some of them begged Wardner to report "an epidemic of measles, diarrhoea, or anything to prevent an investigation." Wardner declined to do so and instead reported the truth. Nevertheless, the affair, known ever afterward in the 12th Illinois as the "Battle of Stinkweed Valley," drew no comment from higher headquarters.[37]

So the troops that were to become the nucleus of the Army of the Tennessee waited at Cairo, Bird's Point, and other nearby posts through the summer months of 1861, even while additional regiments, one day bound to join this army, continued recruiting and organizing all across the Midwest. Yet the waiting at Cairo was not for additional regiments. The components of an army were gradually assembling at the southern tip of Illinois, awaiting only a forceful hand to mold them into a unified force with a clear course of action.

CHAPTER THREE

Paducah

COL. RICHARD J. OGLESBY, 8th Illinois Infantry, and temporary commander of the post of Cairo, was having a busy day, though not an unusual one. On this fourth day of September 1861, his headquarters was, as usual, filled with people clamoring for the post commander's attention. They were mostly Missourians and Kentuckians, and every one seemed to have either a complaint or a plea for some special favor. It had been like this for three weeks, ever since General Prentiss had transferred to Missouri, leaving Oglesby, as senior colonel, in command at Cairo.

One of the people in the office this day was an average-sized, slightly built, somewhat stooped man in a drab suit of civilian clothes. The man looked so ordinary, in fact, that in this crowd he was well-nigh invisible. An aide introduced him to Oglesby, but the colonel did not quite catch his name and was soon distracted by other claimants for his attention. The overlooked man took it in stride and quietly reverted to near-invisibility. The harassed Oglesby did not even notice the newcomer taking a sheet of writing paper from the desk where the colonel was seated, listening to complaints and scribbling orders. The quiet man finished writing his own message and gently but firmly placed it under the colonel's nose. It stated that the bearer was Brig. Gen. Ulysses S. Grant and that he was taking command of the District of Southeast Missouri, with headquarters at Cairo.[1]

Grant had been doing a good deal of traveling lately. Earlier that summer, he and his 21st Illinois had been sent to Missouri to help combat Confederate guerrillas there. A few weeks later he was promoted to brigadier general, in large part, as Grant himself knew very well, because of the unsolicited patronage of Galena congressman Elihu Washburne. Not long after came orders for Cairo.[2]

Giving Grant command of the District of Southeast Missouri, including southern Illinois and western Kentucky, was probably John C. Frémont's greatest contribution to the Union cause, and the importance of the move is not minimized by the fact that all of Frémont's other contributions to the cause were highly questionable. Born in Savannah, Georgia, in 1813, Frémont had served as an officer in the army's Corps of Topographical Engineers. In that capacity he won fame and the nickname "Pathfinder" in the mountains of the West, though some might claim that he could not have found the path to the latrine without the help of experienced guides like mountain man Kit Carson. He took part in the conquest of California during the Mexican War, but then managed to draw a court-martial for insubordination. Out of the army, Frémont achieved wealth when gold was discovered on his California estate. He achieved political prominence when, attracted by his pathfinding celebrity, the brand-new Republican Party chose him as its 1856 presidential candidate. Despite his loss to James Buchanan, many Republicans in 1861 still considered the Pathfinder to be a great leader of men, a fine military mind, and a man of deep moral principle. Any one of those assertions was open to serious question.

Frémont was in fact a tireless self-promoter, and if he had ever grown weary of advancing his prestige and power, his wife, Jessie, daughter of prominent Missouri senator Thomas Hart Benton, would have been more than ready to take up the task. They were an ambitious couple, always alert to possibilities for career enhancement.

Political reality dictated that Lincoln had to make a place for Frémont, and that place was the Department of the West, with headquarters in St. Louis. Frémont's fame extended to Europe and soon brought to his headquarters various European military men, adventurers, and humbugs, whom he gratified with positions on his ornate and oversized staff. The collection of fancy foreign uniforms at department headquarters was like nothing else on the continent and distinctly did not play well to Midwestern tastes. One might have thought that all that prior military experience in Europe should have conferred a fair degree of competence to Frémont's staff. It did not, and the department's affairs were riddled with graft and inefficiency. The Pathfinder may not have realized this, and it certainly would have been hard for anyone to tell him. Obtaining an audience with the Department of the West's commander seemed more difficult than seeing a pope, president, or czar.

The summer of 1861 had seen mixed Union fortunes in Frémont's department. In late August, the Pathfinder became interested in clearing the Rebels out of southeastern Missouri in preparation for a bit of expansion in the Mississippi Valley. For this purpose, he created the District of Southeast Missouri and chose Grant to command it.

In his August 28 order assigning Grant to the position, Frémont explained a set of elaborate movements he had already started in the region.

Various Union forces in southeastern Missouri were marching in an effort to converge and trap a body of Confederate troops under M. Jeff Thompson. Meanwhile, a force from Cairo, McArthur's 12th Illinois under the supervision of Col. Gustav Waagner, chief of artillery at Cairo, was to move down the Mississippi in steamboats, escorted by two navy gunboats, and occupy Belmont, Missouri, a west-bank steamboat landing boasting only a building or two. There Waagner, McArthur, and company were to destroy certain fortifications the Rebels were believed to be erecting and stand by for the sequel, which was to be Union occupation of the commanding bluffs on the east bank of the Mississippi near the town of Columbus, Kentucky.[3]

Columbus beckoned attractively to anyone seeking strategic advantage in the region. The economic lifeblood of the Midwest flowed on the Mississippi, and the towering bluffs around Columbus—the Chalk Bluffs just below town and the Iron Banks, as the bluffs just north of town were called—constituted the most dominating military position in the whole stretch of the Mississippi from Cairo to Memphis. Whichever side first took and fortified the Chalk Bluffs and Iron Banks would have an enormous advantage in the struggle for control of the Mississippi, and whichever side controlled the Mississippi would probably win the war. If Columbus needed additional importance, it also happened to be the northern terminus of the Mobile & Ohio Railroad, the chief north-south line for the midsection of the continent, which ran from Columbus 470 miles southward to Mobile, Alabama.

If taking Columbus made a certain strategic sense, Frémont's program of occupying Columbus during the final week of August showed all the political acumen of a walleyed pike. Kentucky was deeply divided between secession and the Union, and had therefore declared itself neutral. The idea of a state being neutral while the nation went to war was, of course, absurd, but many Kentuckians believed in it, and the state's government strictly warned both Union and Confederate authorities not to violate its neutrality by sending troops into its territory. In the same way that many southern Illinoisans swung to a pro-Union position because the Confederacy became the aggressor at Fort Sumter, so many Kentuckians were prepared to swing into active opposition to whichever side should first appear to be the aggressor in their state. Each president, aware that Kentucky's strategic position could well make it the balance of power, had, up to this point, carefully observed the state's unrealistic status. In short, if Frémont entered Kentucky before the Confederates did, the political damage to the Union cause would far outweigh whatever military advantage he might gain by control of the Chalk Bluffs and Iron Banks.

Into this situation stepped Grant when he took up his new command. After inspecting Union outposts in southeastern Missouri, he hurried to Cairo, the strategic fulcrum of the district. There he surprised Oglesby with his low-key arrival at headquarters on September 4. Grant had gotten rid of his colonel's uniform and ordered a brigadier general's uniform, but the latter had not arrived yet. In any case, Grant always seemed more comfortable with less fuss and feathers.

At the top of his agenda once he got to Cairo was exploration of river routes leading south. Back in the days when Thomas Jefferson had fantasized about the new states that might be carved out of America's Western lands, the sage of Monticello had envisaged Cairo and environs becoming part of a state with the euphonious name of Polypotamia. Among the "many rivers" whose proximity inspired the name were not only the Mississippi and the Ohio but also two tributaries that emptied into the Ohio within about sixty miles upstream of Cairo, the Tennessee and the Cumberland. The Tennessee flowed in from due south, joining the Ohio at Paducah, Kentucky, forty-five miles above Cairo. The Cumberland came from the southeast, and its mouth was at Smithland, Kentucky, fifteen miles upstream from Paducah. Both were navigable far upstream. A trip up the Cumberland would lead to Nashville after about 150 miles. A voyage up the Tennessee would carry the traveler, after some 200 miles, to the northeast corner of the state of Mississippi and to within about twenty miles of the vital southern rail junction at Corinth. The Mississippi River, of course, flowed all the way to the Gulf of Mexico, right through the land of cotton and out the other side. For the 150 or so miles south of Cairo, the Mississippi and Tennessee paralleled each other, the Mississippi flowing south, the Tennessee north, and close enough together—70 to 100 miles—that a force advancing on one river could turn the defenses of the other.

Grant had not had long to contemplate the rivers and their courses from the vantage point of his second-floor office in a bank building in Cairo when events on the river to the south began to demand decisive action. Within hours after he assumed command on September 4, Grant began receiving reports that the Confederates had occupied Columbus and its bluffs.[4]

In fact, Rebel forces under the overall supervision of Maj. Gen. Leonidas Polk and the direct command of Brig. Gen. Gideon J. Pillow had boarded steamboats at New Madrid the night before and taken the short trip to Hickman. Landing there, the Confederates had marched up the east bank to Columbus. With a keen grasp of the tactically obvious and, like Frémont, an obtuse blindness to what should have been politically self-evident, Pillow, a Tennessee lawyer and Mexican War veteran, had for weeks cast longing eyes on the Chalk Bluffs and Iron Banks. With good reason to distrust Pillow's judgment in this and all other matters, Jefferson Davis had in late June appointed his old West Point crony and more recently Episcopal bishop of Louisiana, Polk, to steer Pillow on a safe course. Instead, Polk had adopted one of Pillow's most dangerous ideas and ordered the Tennesseean and his troops to occupy Columbus and fortify the heights, thus shattering Kentucky's neutrality.

Polk got his men to Columbus ahead of Frémont's troops, seizing the dominant heights and saving Frémont from a serious blunder by making it first himself. Yet none of this was as obvious then as it seems in hindsight. Men like Frémont, Polk, and Pillow, all considered intelligent enough for other purposes, all men of repute for their political savvy, had somehow failed to see it in this light. At the time, appearances were simply that Polk and Pillow had stolen a march on Frémont and Grant, slamming, barring, and double-locking the door to the Mississippi Valley in the faces of the would-be invaders. As of the afternoon of September 4, 1861, it required a man of truly unusual strategic acumen to recognize the flaw in Polk's program and exact full payment for it.

The next day, September 5, a member of Frémont's staff, a former Russian army officer named Charles De Arnaud, arrived at Grant's headquarters. De Arnaud was on his way back to St. Louis after doing a bit of espionage south of Cairo. His report not only confirmed that the Confederates had seized Hickman and Columbus but that they intended to take Paducah too, were on their way, in fact, and would have the town at the mouth of the Tennessee River within the next twenty-four hours.

Grant's reaction showed both his strategic sense and his keen political awareness. Up to that time, Grant had been thinking in terms of attacking the Confederates at Columbus before they had time to consolidate their position. Now he quickly reevaluated the situation. There was no time to verify De Arnaud's report. If it was true, there was not a moment to lose. If it was false, taking Paducah was still a good idea. Frémont had previously expressed his desire to capture the place, and clearly the resulting access to the Tennessee River was the ideal strategic countermove to Polk's seizure of the Chalk Bluffs and Iron Banks and thus control of the Mississippi.[5]

Before moving on Paducah, however, Grant took care of necessary political preliminaries. In a letter he wrote that day to the speaker of the Kentucky legislature, Grant stated, "I regret to inform you that Confederate forces in considerable numbers have invaded the territory of Kentucky and are occupying & fortifying strong positions at Hickman & Chalk Bluffs."[6] Grant knew that the legislature was pro-Union, in contrast to the secessionist governor, and that his letter would be sufficient to demonstrate that the Confederates had been the aggressors, the violators of Kentucky's neutrality, and that his move was merely a necessary response. Throughout the day, he sent a series of messages to Frémont, informing him of the situation and of his own intention to occupy Paducah unless Frémont sent orders not to.[7]

Having taken care of the necessary communication, Grant moved quickly into action. Putting the 9th and 12th Illinois regiments in steamboats, along with some artillery, he headed for Paducah, escorted by the gunboats *Tyler* and *Conestoga*. They arrived early on the morning of September 6. When they came in sight of the town, a number of Confederate flags were flying over it, but as the flotilla approached, citizens hauled down the Rebel banners. By the time Grant and his men landed, no flags were to be seen. The people of Paducah were clearly pro-Confederate, and stood here and there on the sidewalks, watching the incoming troops with a mixture of fear and resentment. Not a shot was fired, however, as the Army of the Tennessee occupied its first secessionist town.[8]

Two decades later, Grant would still believe that he had beaten a major Confederate column to Paducah by only a matter of hours, and that the Rebel flags he had seen over the town on his approach had been intended as a welcome to an approaching Confederate force.[9] In fact, it was not so. Polk had intended to take Paducah, but Pillow's men had not yet gotten beyond Columbus. As for De Arnaud's report, everything in it that was news to Grant was also untrue. Yet Grant's course of action was sound nonetheless. Reasoning from what he knew for certain, and taking into account the unconfirmed report of De Arnaud, Grant had arrived at a solution that met all contingencies.[10]

Once in Paducah, Grant deployed his troops around the town so as best to defend it against attack "and least annoy peaceable citizens." The Federal troops proudly raised the Stars and Stripes where Rebel flags had waved only a few minutes before. Grant wrote a proclamation and had it printed and distributed throughout the town. "I have come among you, not as an enemy, but as your friend and fellow-citizen," he wrote, "not to injure or annoy you, but to respect the rights, and to defend and enforce the rights of all loyal citizens." He went on to explain that "an enemy, in rebellion against our common Government," had invaded their state and that he had come to defend them against that enemy. "I have nothing to do with opinions. I shall deal only with armed rebellion and its aiders and abettors."[11]

This was precisely in keeping with Union policy at the time, an approach that emanated all the way from the White House. Lincoln believed that a coterie of influential fire-eaters had stampeded the South into secession, and that much latent Unionism still existed among most white Southerners. Union armies should therefore treat Southern civilians essentially not as enemy but as friendly civilians, thus convincing them both of the power and of the restraint of the Federal government. Once convinced, these conciliated Southerners would return to their allegiance. At least that was the theory.[12]

Grant was serious about applying this policy. Having established the outpost at Paducah, he left the garrison there under the command of Brig. Gen. Eleazer A. Paine, West Point class of 1839 and veteran of the Second Seminole War but a civilian for the past two decades, who until his recent promotion had been colonel of the 9th Illinois. In his parting instructions to Paine, Grant warned, "You are charged to take special care and precaution that no harm is done to inoffensive citizens; that the soldiers shall not enter any private dwelling nor make any searches unless by your orders. . . . Exercise the strictest discipline against any soldier who shall insult citizens or engage in plundering private property."[13] This was definitely going to be a kid-glove occupation.

Then, leaving *Tyler* and *Conestoga* to support Paine if necessary, Grant hurried back down the Ohio to look after affairs in the rest of his department. When he arrived at Cairo, he received a telegram from Frémont, tentatively approving the movement on Paducah if Grant was sure he was strong enough to pull it off. A second telegram from Frémont, however, rebuked Grant for having the temerity to communicate directly with the Kentucky legislature. All communication with state governments, Frémont's aide archly informed Grant, was the exclusive province of "the Major General Commanding the Department."[14]

There was choice unintended irony in this, for Frémont had lately been showcasing his political skills by issuing, on August 30, a proclamation freeing the slaves of disloyal Missourians and prescribing firing squads for Rebels taken in arms. Lincoln was aghast. It was not that such measures did not have a good deal of logic and justice behind them, but they were the worst imaginable violations of Lincoln's policy of conciliation, and the president promptly revoked Frémont's decree.

The contrast with Grant's skillful handling of the Paducah operation could not have been more striking. By taking Paducah, Grant, though he may not yet have fully realized it, had negated the military advantage Polk had hoped to gain by taking Columbus. While the fortifications Polk's men were even now hastily erecting on the Chalk Bluffs and Iron Banks might seal the Mississippi against Union forces, Grant's control of Paducah opened to the Union the Tennessee River, which offered the opportunity of turning Polk's position at Columbus and forcing his withdrawal. Furthermore, the way Grant had handled the affair had the best possible effect on Kentucky. Keeping the picture of Confederate aggression clear in legislators' minds, Grant assured them that his own move was merely a reaction. Within days, the Kentucky legislature had issued a proclamation condemning the Confederate incursion, demanding the withdrawal of Southern forces, and inviting Union cooperation in driving the invaders from Kentucky soil. It was an exceptionally auspicious beginning in major semi-independent command for a man who six months before had been clerking in a leather goods store.

Shrugging off Frémont's niggling, Grant got down to the business of administering his district. The first order of business was to strengthen the all-important outpost at Paducah. During the days that followed, Grant dispatched several regiments from southeastern Missouri to Paducah, including Lew Wallace's 11th Indiana Zouaves. From Paducah, General Paine reported constant rumors that the enemy was about to attack him in heavy force and urged Grant to send him still more troops.[15]

Shortly, however, the command at Paducah was neither Paine's concern nor, in a direct sense, Grant's. No sooner had Grant returned from taking Paducah than he received from Frémont a telegram notifying him that the department commander wanted Grant "to continue personally in command" of Union forces in southern Illinois and southeastern Missouri, and therefore he was sending Brig. Gen. Charles F. Smith to take over command at Paducah, which would then be outside Grant's authority.[16] Of course, there was no reason why Grant could not command the adjoining areas of all three states, as his original instructions had stated, so in one sense this move might have seemed like a slap at Grant, and Frémont may have meant it that way. In Smith, however, he had chosen the officer most respected and admired by Grant, and indeed by a great many others in the "Old Army."

Charles Ferguson Smith was Old Army all the way. A native of Philadelphia, he had entered West Point back in 1821, four years before Robert E. Lee, two years before Leonidas Polk and Polk's newly appointed superior on the Confederate side, Albert Sidney Johnston, whose reputation rivaled Smith's own. That was also one year before Ulysses S. Grant was born. Smith was fourteen at the time. For the next four decades, he had been the ideal soldier. He was commandant of cadets at West Point during Cadet Grant's four years at the academy, and he performed with conspicuous gallantry in the Mexican War, receiving three brevet, or honorary, promotions, the same number as Robert E. Lee. Promotion in the Old Army was notoriously slow, and Smith was a major when the Civil War broke out. Even such an impressive and relatively senior Regular Army officer might be shunted out of the main stream of promotion in the Civil War if he did not have the kind of staunch political backing that Washburne provided for Grant. Thus, Smith had just been promoted to brigadier general of volunteers on August 31, his commission dating more than three months junior to his former cadet, Grant.

Smith arrived at Paducah during the second week of September and immediately made an impression on the troops there. Augustus Chetlain wrote that he was "a splendid-looking soldier, tall, slender, and straight, with close-cut gray hair and a heavy white mustache." Smith was, Chetlain thought, "the embodiment of the ideal soldier."[17] Lew Wallace had much the same impression. The ramrod posture, "long, white mustaches [that] trailed below his chin," bright blue eyes, and ruddy cheeks made Smith "the handsomest, stateliest, most commanding figure I have ever seen, the one who has since remained in memory my idea of a general officer."[18]

Smith was not under Grant's command. To many officers who had been in the Old Army, Grant among them, there would have seemed something profoundly wrong with the idea of "Sam" Grant, as his nickname had been, giving orders to Charles F. Smith, and that may be part of the reason Frémont had made Smith's Paducah command independent of Grant. However, because there was no direct telegraph link between St. Louis and Paducah for the first few weeks, Frémont sent his orders to Grant for forwarding to Smith.[19]

During the weeks that followed, Grant carried on the work of organizing, training, and supplying his nascent army around Cairo and across the river in Missouri, and while the troops learned the rudiments of soldiering, Grant learned more about the finer points of administering a force of well over 10,000 men—twentyfold larger than the regiment for which he had been quartermaster in the Mexican War. Hour after hour, Grant sat in his office on the second floor of the bank building, smoking his meerschaum pipe and filling out the reams of paperwork necessary to keep even a small army running tolerably smoothly. "He did nothing carelessly," an observer noted, "but worked slowly, every now and then stopping and taking his pipe out of his mouth." In this manner, Grant kept his men fed and got them all clothed in army blue and shod with army brogans. He got tent canvas over their heads at night, and he did his best to improve the sanitary and health situation in the regimental camps and post hospitals.[20]

He kept the troops supplied with ammunition, including enough for a bit of ball-cartridge target practice, and that was an especially difficult task given the dozens of different types and calibers of weapons represented in his camps.[21] Grant had to tell the colonel of the 23rd Indiana that he could not supply him with the odd type of ammunition his regiment's weapons required. The colonel wanted Grant to write to the governor of Indiana requesting ammunition and wagons, but Grant declined, noting nevertheless "that if the Gov. of Indiana furnished it he would be doing the Government a service." Word of the matter eventually worked its way back to department headquarters, prompting the Pathfinder to pounce once again. What did Grant mean by communicating with a state governor? Grant assured him he had done nothing of the sort, and Frémont grudgingly subsided.[22]

Handling all of the command's administrative business was laborious work and kept Grant going routinely until two or three o'clock in the morning, then had him up again before dawn.[23] It was thus an especially good thing when in mid-September John A. Rawlins arrived in Cairo to take up the position Grant had offered him as assistant adjutant general. Rawlins was the Galena lawyer who had spoken up so forcefully for the Union back at the war meeting in April. Small of stature, Rawlins had an extremely pale complexion made striking by black hair, beard, and eyes. His hatred for secession was equaled by his hatred for liquor, for the latter had ruined his father. Grant knew him to be a competent and loyal man, and also a useful connection to Grant's indispensable political backer, Elihu Washburne. Grant had offered the job to Rawlins some weeks earlier, but Rawlins's wife was extremely ill with tuberculosis, and he dared not leave her. In late August, she died, and shortly thereafter Rawlins set out to join Grant. His arrival was of great help to Grant both as a competent administrative assistant and as a friend and confidant.[24]

Meanwhile, Grant's thoughts turned frequently to the prospects of doing something about the Confederates in Columbus. That was natural with him. Grant later summed up his philosophy of war: "Get at the enemy as quick as you can, hit him as hard as you can, and keep moving on." He seemed to understand instinctively—or perhaps from his observations of U.S. success in the Mexican War—that speed was a multiplier of force.

Though he knew himself to be somewhat outnumbered by Polk's army at Columbus, Grant was eager to "get at the enemy" as quickly as possible, to strike the Confederates before they could consolidate their position. "If it was discretionary with me," he wrote to Frémont on September 10, "with a little addition to my present force I would take Columbus." Two days later, he wrote Frémont with a plan. If Smith would feint southward from

Paducah, Grant could send a force south along the east bank of the Mississippi while the gunboats and a waterborne force would descend the river to threaten Belmont. That, Grant figured, would suffice to induce the Confederates to leave Columbus. All he needed was a few more regiments and the appropriate orders from Frémont. Meanwhile, Polk worked steadily to build Columbus into the strongest bastion on the continent and soon had some 140 heavy guns in well-dug emplacements, with infantry fortifications for the 16,000 Confederate troops on hand there.[25] In the face of these formidable defenses, Grant continued to be dismayed at his inability to take aggressive action, writing to his wife in late October, "What I want is to advance."[26]

Frémont gave Grant neither the orders nor the means for moving against Columbus, so, like a good subordinate, Grant busied himself about the things for which Frémont did give him orders. These generally involved making his district secure against Confederate attack. At Frémont's behest, he established two fortified outposts on the Kentucky side of the Ohio River just across from Cairo, Forts Holt and Jackson, and manned them with about 3,000 men. He maintained the small garrison at Bird's Point, Missouri—four regiments under the command of the senior colonel, William Wallace. This force provided the bulk of the manpower for the regular forays into the interior of southeastern Missouri in pursuit of the ever-elusive Jeff Thompson.[27]

From Paducah, Smith's soldiers operated in much the same manner. A soldier of the 9th Illinois wrote that the men were "spoiling for a fight" and "felt that now they were ready to fight with and conquer the whole South." Sometimes the probes led to satisfying little skirmishes.[28] More often, however, the forays into no-man's-land brought only a steamboat excursion or some fruitless marching. Such missions helped accustom the troops to moderately difficult marches as well as to the idea of the proximity of the enemy, but the war was not going to be won by foot-sloggers chasing mounted irregular forces through the swamps of southeastern Missouri or western Kentucky.

In the garrison of Cairo itself was John A. McClernand's brigade. Typically, McClernand had been leveraging his political influence for all it was worth, winning a letter from the acting secretary of war that he rather plastically interpreted as entitling his brigade to priority over all other Illinois troops in the scramble for scarce arms and equipment. McClernand even schemed to cut a deal directly with the agent for the Enfield arms factory in Britain to obtain 4,000 state-of-the-art rifles for his brigade and bill the whole transaction to the state of Illinois, maintaining that his letter from the assistant secretary of war meant Uncle Sam would pick up the tab eventually.[29] The deal somehow fell through, but McClernand never tired of pulling every wire in sight that might advance his career.[30]

Throughout September and October, Grant's troops at Cairo, including McClernand's brigade—armed with a miscellaneous collection of smooth-bores and a handful of Springfield rifled muskets—numbered somewhat over 4,200. Even these greenest of troops were chafing under their inactivity. A soldier of the 31st Illinois later recalled, "The volunteers began to tire of camp life, its incidents and monotony, and many began to express their desire to meet the enemy."[31]

In all, Grant had somewhere in the neighborhood of 15,000 men in the various scattered posts of his command.[32] Except for the 2nd and 7th Iowa regiments, they were all Illinoisans. Through these months, Frémont remained concerned with operations in Missouri, not only those involving the pestilent Thompson in the southeastern corner of the state, but also the much larger and more important operations against Confederate general Sterling Price in the middle of the state. Grant, however, kept his eye on Columbus.

On November 1 came new orders from Frémont. Grant was to hold his entire command in readiness to march at an hour's notice, well supplied with ammunition. When the orders came, he was to launch diversionary movements into the interior of southeastern Missouri. Smith too was to feint aggressively toward Columbus and draw Rebel attention.[33] The reason for all this was Frémont's continuing fixation on Missouri and his desire to divert Confederate forces from operations in that state.

Grant had just begun preparations for the ordered movements when the next day brought another dispatch from St. Louis. Thompson, the phantom of the Missouri marshes, was believed to be at Indian Ford on the St. Francis River. Frémont thought he saw at last an opportunity to force the wily Confederate out of Missouri and into Arkansas. The department commander started a force southward from Pilot Knob, eighty miles north of Thompson's alleged position, and ordered Grant to send another force southwestward from Cape Girardeau, sixty miles northeast of Thompson's reported whereabouts, and a third column due west from Bird's Point, seventy-five miles distant. No expenditure of energy or shoe leather seemed too extravagant for Frémont if it would only rid him of that ragtag gadfly Thompson.[34]

Grant promptly dispatched Oglesby with 4,000 men from Bird's Point on one more tramp into the interior, and Col. J. B. Plummer with 3,000 out of Cape Girardeau on a similar expedition. Significantly, Grant's instructions to these officers contained no talk of "driving Thompson into Arkansas," as per Frémont's orders, but rather flatly stated: "The object of the expedition is to destroy [Thompson's] force."[35] Grant probably considered it unlikely they would catch Thompson, but obviously believed that if the operation was worth his soldiers' sore feet, it was worth going for the kill.

Grant seemed to have other purposes as well. He soon ordered Oglesby to turn his column from marching west, toward Indian Ford on the St. Francis River, to marching south, toward the Confederate base at New Madrid, on the Missouri shore of the Mississippi River, twenty-five crow's flight miles below Columbus and about twice that far by the meanderings of the river. This would threaten to turn the left flank of the Confederate position at Columbus. To strengthen Oglesby, Grant dispatched William Wallace, who had just returned from leave, with another 400 men that Oglesby had left behind at Bird's Point. Their combined column would total perhaps 4,400 men. Significantly, Grant's instructions to both Oglesby and Wallace informed them that he would be at Belmont, just across the river from Columbus, and they should communicate with him there by messenger while their column passed some miles to the west.[36]

Grant also sent a message to Smith at Paducah, informing him that he was preparing an expedition to attack Belmont and suggesting, "If you can make a demonstration towards Columbus at the same time with a portion of your command, it would probably keep the enemy from throwing over the river much more force than they now have there, and might enable me to drive those they now have out of Missouri."[37] Such a move by Smith would menace the right flank and rear of the Confederate force at Columbus. Smith was prompt to reply and eager to cooperate. The following afternoon, November 6, he started a brigade of about 3,000 men under Brigadier General Paine, marching southwestward toward the rear of Columbus.[38]

Thus, Smith would threaten the right rear of the Confederates at Columbus. Oglesby would threaten their left rear. All that remained was for someone to threaten them in front, and Grant intended to lead that mission in person. His plan was to take two brigades of infantry, along with a couple of batteries and a couple of companies of cavalry, in all just over 3,100 men, load them on six transports, and, escorted by Flag Officer Andrew H. Foote's gunboats, steam down the river and attack Belmont, where the Confederates were keeping an outpost of one regiment on the Missouri shore opposite Columbus. Taking Belmont would give his men valuable combat experience, and, if all went well, it might accomplish something more. Viewed as a whole, the operation looks remarkably similar to the plan Grant had suggested to Frémont back in September for the purpose of taking Columbus.

However, Grant kept his more optimistic projections to himself and in dispatches continued to refer to the movement as a "reconnaissance in force" to his subordinates, and a "demonstration" in his message to Smith. He no doubt used similar terms in discussing the coming operation with the second-ranking officer in Cairo at that time, McClernand, who would command one of the two brigades headed for Belmont.[39]

On the evening of September 5 and the morning of the 6th, the troops encamped around Cairo and Bird's Point were busy making preparations for an expedition the destination and purpose of which they were still quite ignorant. For William Jones of the 7th Iowa, the order "to be in readiness to march in one hour's notice with 2 days provisions in our haversacks" came as a relief. "Nothing has transpired lately," he had written in his diary that day. "We have had the dullest time that we have had since we left home."[40]

About three o'clock that afternoon, the regiments of McClernand's brigade formed up in their camps and marched down to the levee to board the steamboats. Col. Napoleon Buford, a West Point classmate of Leonidas Polk and Confederate western theater commander Albert Sidney Johnston, brought his 27th Illinois. Col. Philip B. Fouke, who, when not in uniform, served as a Democratic congressman, marched his 30th Illinois to the landing, even as his fellow Illinois Democratic congressman Col. John A. Logan was bringing up the 31st Illinois, proudly sporting new uniforms issued only a few days before but still carrying ancient muskets that kicked wickedly at every discharge. There would be some sore shoulders if they got into a fight. The three regiments filed onto two of the steamers while a small company of cavalry and the expedition's supply wagons embarked on several others.[41]

The loading took several hours, and the sun had just set when the flotilla cast off from the Illinois shore and churned across the Mississippi to Bird's Point. There, Col. Henry Dougherty's 22nd Illinois and Col. Jacob Lauman's 7th Iowa crowded onto the transports, along with Capt. Ezra Taylor's Chicago Light Artillery—officially Battery A, 1st Illinois Light Artillery—and another small company of cavalry. By last light, the vessels once again put out into the stream, escorted by the gunboats *Tyler* and *Lexington,* under the immediate direction of Commander Henry Walke.

As the boats pulled out into the broad waters at the confluence of the Ohio and the Mississippi, many soldiers wondered where this journey would take them. Perhaps they would head up the Ohio to reinforce the garrison at Paducah, perhaps back up the Mississippi to Cape Girardeau, jumping-off point for another wearisome tramp into the wilds of Missouri in pursuit of guerrillas. The clanking engines and slapping paddlewheels at length brought the flotilla to the main channel. Then, by the starlight, the watchers who lined the rails of each steamboat perceived that their bows were swinging to point not up the Ohio or the Mississippi but rather down the Mississippi. They were heading south, toward the enemy's stronghold, and hundreds guessed that the intended target was nothing less than Columbus itself. Cheers drifted across the dark water from boat to boat.[42]

CHAPTER FOUR

Belmont

A T 11:00 P.M. Grant directed the boatmen to halt and tie up for the night on the Kentucky shore eight miles south of Cairo and eleven from Columbus.[1] He would aim to arrive at Belmont, as he had at Paducah, shortly after dawn. A whiff of mystery clings to the events of that night. The troops on the boats were talking, singing, or trying to sleep, as their temperament and the crowded conditions might allow. At 2:00 a.m., Grant later claimed, a courier arrived bearing a message from William Wallace, who was camped at Charleston that night, on his way to join Oglesby. His news, according to Grant's later report, was "that he had learned from a reliable Union man that the enemy had been crossing troops from Columbus to Belmont the day before, for the purpose of following after and cutting off the forces under Colonel Oglesby." That, Grant later explained, was the deciding factor. He would have to attack Belmont in order to protect the columns under Wallace and Oglesby.[2]

In some ways, that sounded plausible enough. Wallace was indeed at Charleston that night, and it would have been feasible for him to send a courier from there to Bird's Point by rail and then down the river by steamboat to overtake Grant. However, Wallace was in the habit of writing long, information-packed letters to his wife back in Ottawa, Illinois. He wrote one about this operation but said nothing of gaining such information or of sending it to Grant. Indeed, in such strictly private letters to his wife, Wallace later criticized Grant as having attacked Belmont for no good reason, discounting Grant's claim that the Rebels were shifting troops into Missouri.[3] It is inconceivable that Wallace would have neglected mentioning the midnight message or failed to understand why Grant would have had to act on it. The fact is that there never was any midnight message or any 2:00 a.m. change of plans entailing a decision to attack Belmont. Grant had made that decision before he left Cairo. The story about a message from Wallace in the early hours of September 7, like that of a message from Frémont two days before, grew out of later exigencies.[4]

Though no messenger arrived at that hour, Grant and his staff were nevertheless busy at 2:00 a.m. on November 7. Over the signature of John A. Rawlins and dated "On Board Steamer Belle Memphis, November 7, 1861–2 o'clock a.m.," they drew up, copied, and distributed Grant's final orders for the coming day. The flotilla would get under way at 6:00 a.m., before daylight in November, and proceed as far down the river as it could without coming under the fire of the Columbus batteries. When Commander Walke judged that they had reached that point, the transports would put in on the Missouri shore and begin unloading troops, McClernand's brigade first, then Dougherty's.[5]

The steamboats moved in against the Missouri shore at a place called Hunter's Farm at about eight o'clock on a clear, crisp autumn morning. They were three miles from Belmont, and though they were in range of the big guns across the river from Belmont on the Iron Banks, they were concealed by the thick woods on the intervening lobe of land inside a broad bend of the river. Unloading took time, especially for the 12-pounders of Taylor's battery. The worst of it was getting the guns up the steep, muddy bank that towered about twenty-five feet above the river, which was unusually low at that time. Taylor's men finally resorted to digging a cut in the rim of the bank and then using a block-and-tackle rig to drag their guns to the top.[6]

Meanwhile, the Confederates on the Iron Banks could see the smoke of the steamboats and lobbed a few inaccurate shots in that direction, several of which sailed right over the boats and embedded themselves in the muddy bank beyond, while others landed in the river. "A very exciting scene it was," wrote one of Grant's soldiers, "to hear the roar of the heavy guns & the whizzing of the balls & shells and see them plunging into the water all about the boats, and throwing up great showers of spray."[7] Commander Walke took his gunboats just around the bend to divert the Confederate gunners while Grant's troops debarked.[8]

Meanwhile, Grant's army formed in line and prepared to advance. Belmont was located at the end of a great bend of the river. Grant's main column, having landed at the base of the bend, would move into the interior of the peninsula and advance toward the Confederates from the west. The Rebels facing Grant would have their backs to their own camp and to the river beyond.[9]

With McClernand's brigade in the lead, the army marched toward Belmont. After about a mile, they encountered Confederate resistance near a long, dry slough. Grant ordered the command to deploy into line of battle, McClernand's three regiments on the right, Dougherty's two on the left.

Grant ordered each of his regiments to advance skirmishers. As the skirmish companies of the 22nd Illinois prepared to advance under the command of Capt. John Seaton, the captain reminded his men, "Today the eyes of Illinois are upon us."[10]

"We could distinctly hear the drums at Columbus beating to arms," recalled Walter Scates of Taylor's battery. He and his comrades could also hear the whistle of steamboats where only Confederate steamboats could be. "It was there," Scates continued, "I experienced the first sensations on a battlefield. But it was not a thrilling fear, only an oppressive, deadly suspense, which seemed to weigh heavier and heavier upon my heart the longer we waited. Our boys were silent and solemn, listening with thrilling intensity for the opening volley, and expecting every moment to be ordered against heavy odds."[11]

In the woods out in front, the skirmishers soon had a hot fight on their hands, and Grant ordered the main body to advance. The regiments shucked knapsacks and overcoats and piled them along the roadside and by the edge of the woods, then formed up and prepared to advance. As the line stepped forward through the woods shortly before 11:00 a.m., the embryonic fighting force that was one day to be called the Army of the Tennessee was about to offer battle for the first time.[12]

The Rebels accepted the challenge. Stretching across the path of Grant's army, partially in woods and partially in open cornfields, was a gray-clad line of battle of slightly greater strength—3,000 to Grant's 2,800 on the field. In response to the Union landing upstream from Belmont, Polk had reinforced the garrison there with another three regiments under the command of Pillow. It was the crossing of these troops that had occasioned the steamboat sounds heard by some of Grant's men as they waited to advance.

The Federals drove in the Confederate skirmishers and the opposing lines of battle became engaged. As the fight started to heat up, two of Grant's subordinates in quick succession ad-libbed maneuvers that proved highly effective. On the far right, McClernand sent Col. Napoleon Buford's 27th Illinois swinging wide around the enemy's left flank. At almost the same time, Col. Jacob Lauman, commanding the 7th Iowa, marching toward the sound of the heaviest firing, acted without orders to shift his regiment across the rear of the Union army from left to right. The 22nd Illinois followed, and the weight of the augmented Federal right wing soon began to tell on the Confederates.[13]

In desperation, Pillow ordered a bayonet charge that tore open the lines of the 7th Iowa. Providentially, however, the skirmish companies of the

22nd Illinois, now following the main body of their regiment, happened to be passing behind the center of the 7th at that moment. Captain Seaton, who had that morning reminded his men that "the eyes of Illinois are upon us," reacted quickly, swinging his force into line and plugging the gap in the 7th Iowa. With their help, the Iowans rallied and beat off the attack. The Rebels fell back and attempted to hold their original line again, but continued pressure from the Union infantry, along with the accurate fire of Taylor's Chicago Light Artillery, finally broke their resistance and sent them back toward their camp on the run.[14]

Fringing the camp on the landward side was an abatis, an entanglement formed by felling trees with their tops toward the enemy. Behind its protection, Confederate officers strove to get their men in line for a concerted defense. Just as Grant's troops began their assault on the front of the camp, Buford's 27th Illinois emerged from a back road squarely athwart the Confederate left flank, which soon began to give way under the pressure of this unexpected attack. Abandoning their tight formations, Grant's troops took cover behind logs and trees "after the old Indian fashion," as one of them described, and fought their way through the abatis and into the Confederate camp. Once again the defenders gave way and ran, scrambling down the twenty-five-foot bank to a narrow shelf of land immediately beside the river. In the confusion, Grant's troops did not pursue but contented themselves with occupying the Rebel cantonment.[15]

So far, Grant's strategy of having Smith and Cook threaten Columbus from the Kentucky side had paid off. Convinced that Grant's assault on Belmont was merely a feint, Polk had sent only four regiments to reinforce the garrison there, holding back others in expectation of a direct attack on Columbus from the Kentucky side.[16]

It was about 2:00 p.m., and the morning's combat, especially the "Indian fashion" assault on the camp, had disorganized Grant's force. A member of the 27th admitted that the men of the regiment "became so badly scattered that they could not be formed again. In fact they were not formed again until they were on the parade ground in Cairo." Then, having taken the encampment, Grant's men—along with many of their officers—decided it was time to celebrate.[17]

Someone went to the flagpole, hauled down the Confederate banner, and raised a big United States flag in its place, while soldiers crowded around, cheering vociferously. The band of the 22nd Illinois showed up, instruments and all, and ran through its repertoire—including "The Star-Spangled Banner," "Yankee Doodle," and "Dixie," which was not yet considered the property of Southerners. The soldiers sang along with all their might, defiantly aiming their performance toward the Rebels watching from the other side of the river. Captain Seaton, who had led the skirmishers of the 22nd Illinois that morning, plugged the gap in the 7th Iowa, and lately captured a cannon in the Confederate camp, now stood perched atop one of the guns, helping to lead the men in one rousing chorus after another.[18]

Cheering, singing, flag-waving—it was all just like a big political rally back in Illinois. McClernand had experience with this sort of thing and knew just what to do. He immediately launched into a stem-winding, "spread-eagle" speech.[19] Soon many of the other officers were doing the same. Grant recalled, "They galloped about from one cluster of men to another and at every halt delivered a short eulogy upon the Union cause and the achievements of the command." Meanwhile, soldiers milled around throughout the camp, browsing through Confederate tents, sampling the Rebels' rations, and examining various booty. It was like a political rally, camp meeting, and Fourth of July picnic all rolled into one.[20]

Grant decided that the only way to regain control of his troops was to set fire to the tents and ordered his staff officers to do the work. Soon the camp was ablaze, and the men began to pour out onto the parade ground. At this point, Bishop Polk, on the other side of the river, lent his unwitting help to Grant's efforts. From the heights of the Iron Banks, the Confederate general had his heavy guns open fire on the camp. That moved Grant's men along even more rapidly, and soon they had sorted themselves out into at least rough approximations of regimental organizations and moved off the parade ground and into the woods. Once again the Confederate fire went high, "the shell passing through the tops of the trees, and making a terrific racket," as one member of Grant's staff noted. Grant himself wrote merely that it helped to bring "officers and men completely under control."[21]

In fact, the danger was greater and more immediate than Grant had yet realized. Even before his troops had driven the Confederates out of the camp at Belmont, Polk had decided that the Union advances on the Kentucky side were in fact feints and that his lines around Columbus would not be attacked. With that he gave orders for two more Confederate regiments to board steamboats and cross to reinforce Pillow. These troops arrived during the big celebration in the captured camp, landing upstream from Belmont, where Pillow's fugitives were sheltering at the base of the bank. While the Federals in the camp had been singing, looting, and listening to speeches, the newly arrived Confederate regiments had pushed inland and taken up a position blocking Grant's route to his steamboats. One of the new Confederate regiments was the 15th Tennessee, and in its ranks was a band of proslavery Illinoisans, who had come south from Williamson County to fight for the Confederacy, including John A. Logan's brother-in-law.

Further exacerbating the Union situation, Gideon Pillow, with the aid of the charismatic Brig. Gen. Frank Cheatham, just arrived from Columbus, had succeeded in rallying about 1,500 men from his original force and moving them inland to take up a position beside the new troops, further blocking Union retreat. Grant now had between him and his only possibility of escape a force larger than his own remaining command and almost exactly equal to that which he had, against the odds, broken through that morning. He would now have to reenact that feat of arms, with his tired and disorganized troops, or else face ignominious surrender.[22]

Some soldiers and officers began to talk of surrender. Instead, Grant informed them that as they had cut their way in, they could cut their way out again. "It seemed a new revelation," Grant wrote. The now thoroughly sobered troops obeyed their officers' orders to get into line of battle once more. Still, Surgeon John H. Brinton observed, there was "considerable confusion; some were tired out, and some did not care much about further fighting." The surgeon put it down to the spirit of volunteer soldiers: "they had done their day's work, and wanted to go home."[23]

The way home, however, now led through Confederate lines. Grant's forces moved forward. The Rebels, advancing from the river, hit Dougherty's brigade hard, especially the 7th Iowa, closest to the river on the army's far right. Lt. Col. Augustus Wentz, now leading the regiment in place of the fallen Lauman, urged his men to hold steady but soon fell, badly wounded. "Let me alone, boys," he protested as his men attempted to carry him off. "I want to die on the battlefield." The combat became hand-to-hand, and several men from each side fell fighting for the 7th's colors. The situation was desperate, but somehow the 7th's major managed to rally the men and lead most of them out of the trap.[24]

Meanwhile, Grant had Taylor's battery blast the center of the Confederate line. Then as the artillerists limbered up, it was time for the infantry to clear the way. At the spearhead of the Union breakout attempt was the 31st Illinois. Logan formed his men and had them fix bayonets. He had a captain take the colors to the head of the column, joined him there, drew his sword, and ordered the men to follow him and the flag. They charged toward the newly landed Confederate regiments, including the 15th Tennessee with its small contingent from Williamson County, Illinois. Neighbors faced one another from both sides of the lines. The regimental column charged headlong toward the Confederate line and burst it asunder, the two halves swinging back like a double gate, and the 31st rushed through the gap.[25]

Behind it the 30th accidentally veered out of column and hit the Rebel line to one side of the hole Logan had made. No matter—that just made the hole bigger. Taylor's battery, minus one of its limbers but still bringing along two of the captured Rebel guns, pulled by captured horses, dashed through the gap. Two of the 31st's company commanders were hit, as was Colonel Logan's horse and his pistol, which at that moment was in the holster on his hip. Three bullets hit Colonel Fouke's saddle, and those or others brought down his horse.[26] H. J. Walter of the 30th Illinois remembered this fight as "much fiercer" than the one they had had that morning on the way in.[27]

The situation in Dougherty's brigade was worse. Essentially the two regiments were overrun, and escaping became a matter of every man for himself. Dougherty got through, along with most of the 22nd Illinois, but then turned back to try to help the 7th Iowa. A Rebel volley put bullets into his shoulder, elbow, and ankle; unable to flee, he was taken prisoner.[28] Lauman had been wounded earlier in the day and carried to the rear atop a caisson. Hearing the sounds of battle and guessing what must be happening, he got someone to help him onto a horse so he could go back and help his men. He did, and escaped without further injury. By the time the survivors were clear, both the 7th Iowa and the 22nd Illinois had suffered approximately 20 percent of their numbers killed or wounded. The 7th lost that many again in missing, mostly captured; the 22nd somewhat fewer.[29] Among those killed was the 7th Iowa's Will Jones, who had lamented in his diary just the day before about the dull times they had been having at Bird's Point.[30]

Once Grant's men had moved past the Confederate lines, what had been a breakthrough degenerated quickly into a rout, with horse and foot fleeing for the landing as fast as they could go. Private Walter recalled becoming separated from his company, unable to see a single member of the familiar group he had marched and fought with. "I never did as fine running and as much of it," he wrote of his journey to the boat landing.[31] Others bore witness to the same confusion and headlong flight. "It was a scene of indescribable confusion," wrote artillerist Scates. "Reg't was mixed with reg't company with company. The unhurt with the wounded and throwing away everything but their guns & cartridge boxes they hurried along only hoping to reach the boats before the enemy came upon them. The poor fellows were exhausted & it was only through terror that they were able to move at all." Some who could not go on tried to hide in the brush alongside the road.[32]

Hoping to make a stand and slow down the enemy pursuit, Grant ordered Taylor's artillerists to unlimber and open fire, and he and Logan tried hard to rally the fleeing infantrymen to support the battery. It was no use. The stampede went on. So Grant ordered Taylor to limber up again and take up a position immediately adjacent to the landing.[33]

As they were leaving, Private Scates took pity on a soldier of the 22nd Illinois, painfully trying to get to the boats despite a wounded thigh. Scates dismounted and gave the man his horse, but though the soldier was so weak he could scarcely hold on to the horse, he insisted that Scates carry his musket, absolutely refusing to leave it behind. "All in fact considered it a dishonor to leave their muskets," Scates observed, "& clung to them as long as they could carry them, but it was a weary two miles to the boats & some had to throw away their guns, which they did with tears in their eyes."[34] There may have been other reasons for the soldiers to drop their muskets. Both Foukes and Logan reported after the battle that large numbers of their regiments' weapons, as many as one-fourth, had burst or otherwise become unserviceable during the fight.[35]

Hurrying after his battery on foot now, Scates was especially impressed by four men carrying a wounded comrade, two men taking him by turns. The men were obviously near exhaustion, and their comrade near death, but they refused to leave him behind, even while others hurried past them on their way to the landing.[36]

Headlong flight brought the first of Grant's fugitives to the landing at Hunter's Farm some thirty minutes before the Confederates moved into the adjoining cornfield. Had the Rebels moved more promptly, the situation would have been desperate. It was bad enough as it was. The men piled into the boats as expeditiously as possible, with little regard for organization— of which little remained in most units anyway. As the Confederates began to move up and took the operation under fire, the Union cavalry and Taylor's amazing battery stood them off, aided eventually by large-caliber fire from Walke's gunboats. Buford's 27th Illinois had somehow failed to reach the landing at all, but that could not be helped. They could not hold the landing five minutes longer, and the expedition had to shove off without the missing regiment. Grant was the last to go aboard the steamboat *Belle Memphis*. Ever the expert horseman, he slid his horse down a muddy bank on its haunches and then trotted it across a narrow gangplank spanning a dozen feet of dark river water to come aboard the transport.[37]

A little ways down the shore, Taylor's men were hurrying to get their guns loaded onto the transport *Chancellor*. They unhitched and ran the teams on board. Then they "fairly tumbled the guns down the bank" and manhandled them onto the boat. "Just as we were getting our last gun down the bank, the cry arose 'They're coming, They're coming.' " Private Scates scrambled to the top of the bank and could hear the vast rustling of a whole line of battle coming at the double-quick through the field of sere cornstalks. Off to the right, he could see other Rebels closing in on *Belle Memphis,* probably at about the moment Grant was going aboard. Scates had no time to notice his commanding general's daring ride over the plank. He and several comrades were trying to get Battery B's big baggage wagon down the bank, but "the bullets came whistling about our ears & we had to leave it." The boatmen swung axes to cut the *Chancellor's* cables as Scates and his comrades tumbled down the bank and leaped aboard.

As the boat slowly began to move, all aboard waited tensely for the Rebel line to appear at the top of the bank. From the deck of the *Chancellor,* Taylor got two of his battery's guns loaded and trained on the bank, along with one of the captured Confederate guns. Those like Scates who were not involved in working the guns grabbed muskets or revolvers and stood on the upper deck, weapons trained on the crest of the bank. "The moment they appeared there was an explosion that shook the heavens." *Tyler* and *Lexington* added the weight of their heavy shells, and the infantrymen on the decks of *Belle Memphis* and other steamboats also took part. "We knocked our wagon all to pieces," Scates wrote. He also believed they had killed large numbers of Rebels. Grant, too, and others thought they had seen numerous gray-clad soldiers falling as casualties before the guns, but later Confederate official reports indicated scarcely any losses in this sector. Light was already failing on this short November day. Powder smoke was dense once fire was opened, and perhaps, too, the Confederates dove for cover very quickly. Certainly their return fire inflicted few if any casualties on the boats.[38]

Even as the flotilla began to gather headway upstream, Grant's men could still see members of the 7th Iowa and 22nd Illinois emerging from the woods far behind in ones and twos to discover that they now had no chance of escaping capture.[39]

Immediately upon boarding, Grant entered a cabin and lay down on a sofa. Hearing the heavy firing between the boats and the shore, he got up and went out to see what was happening. Returning to the cabin, he found that a bullet had come through the bulkhead and drilled a hole in the sofa right where he had been lying.[40] It was an apt metaphor for the entire day's experience for Grant. In his first engagement as a general officer, he had come about as close to ultimate disaster as it was possible to imagine without actually experiencing utter defeat. He had lost control of his army, been surrounded by the enemy, and returned to the transports in inglorious rout. Some of his men, more than he liked to think about, would not be coming back at all. There would be other low points in his career, but never, not even at Shiloh, would he feel the hot breath of complete disaster quite this close on his neck. That catastrophe had not engulfed Grant and his army that day owed much to Providence and much also to his own determination not to fail. He simply would not allow it.[41]

Grant's resolve not to allow failure in the affair at Belmont led him, in coming days, months, and years, to labor somewhat uncharacteristically to put the best possible face on what had happened there. To Will Wallace, he made excuses for even launching the attack. "If he had had regular troops," Grant told the colonel, "he would not have fought" at Belmont, but if he had turned back without a battle, "he never would have been able to convince his volunteer soldiers that he was not afraid to fight." Perhaps, but Wallace was unimpressed.[42]

In the spring of 1864, Grant's staff officers, writing his official report of the operation, recounted the curious story of the messages from Frémont on November 5 and from Wallace received at 2:00 a.m. on the morning of November 7—messages that seem not to have existed. Perhaps Grant signed the report without scrutinizing its contents. Perhaps memories had grown confused. Nearly a quarter century after the Battle of Belmont, Grant would write in his memoirs that after passing out of range of the Confederate guns that evening, he and his troops had gone "peacefully on our way to Cairo, every man feeling that Belmont was a great victory and that he had contributed his share to it."[43] Soon the men would come to interpret their experiences in that light. Grant would see to it. But that evening he did not act like a man who felt he had just contributed his share to a great victory. He sat by himself, Captain Seaton observed, and "said not a word but to the waiter."[44]

For Grant, the butcher's bill for the Battle of Belmont—killed, wounded, and captured—came to about 550 men, or roughly 20 percent of the total force engaged. Confederate losses had been somewhat higher, about 640 men besides the loss of two cannon, which Grant's men had captured and dragged off, and all of their camp equipment at Belmont, which had gone up in flames. About 5,000 Confederates eventually got into the fight, almost twice the number of Grant's force that had actually been engaged.[45]

Grant's losses would have been considerably higher had the 27th Illinois been completely cut off and lost, as it appeared to be at the time of the evacuation. McClernand had his steamboat turn back and put in on the Missouri shore some distance above Hunter's Farm. There he and two of his staff officers landed to look for the missing regiment. They soon made contact with the regimental adjutant, who was hoping to flag down the passing steamers. Thus they succeeded in extracting the 27th Illinois, getting it aboard the boat and back to Cairo.[46]

As soon as Grant arrived in Cairo, he sent orders recalling all of the other expeditions under his command, Cook to Fort Holt, Oglesby and Wallace to Bird's Point. He also notified C. F. Smith that the operation was concluded, so that the latter could recall Paine's column.[47] Smith did so. The advance and return of the column from Paducah illustrated, at the very least, that Grant was not the only senior officer who had underestimated the difficulty of maintaining control of untrained volunteers and, more to the point, their untrained officers.[48]

Hearing the sound of heavy firing from the direction of Belmont, Paine had set his men to marching faster and farther than his orders stipulated, in hopes of getting in on the action.[49] For the men, it was the first time they had heard the sound of battle. Though already tired and footsore, they brightened up and marched along at a lively pace, cheering and singing patriotic songs. They reached Milburn, Kentucky, thirty-one miles from Paducah and only eleven from Columbus, at about nightfall on November 7, and made a weary camp.

Early the next morning came the recall order. The return march started at daybreak and continued at a rapid pace until the lead regiment, the 9th Illinois, reached Paducah in midafternoon. Discipline broke down among the soldiers of the 40th and 41st Illinois, and the regiments virtually disintegrated. Their men straggled into Paducah in ones, twos, and small groups throughout the next two days. Each soldier had left Paducah on November 6, not knowing whether his unit would return or be stationed permanently elsewhere, and therefore the men had brought everything they had in the way of blankets, overcoats, spare clothing, cooking utensils, and personal items. Under the strain of the return march, they littered the roads with their prized possessions. "Many of the boys came into camp on our return destitute of everything but their guns," wrote a member of the 40th.

Things were different in the 9th. Col. August Mersy detailed a guard to march at the rear of the regiment and force the troops to keep going. There was some grumbling, but "the 9th Regiment came into camp in Paducah in splendid order," drawing commendation from the much-admired General Smith. The men of the 9th were so pleased they "almost forgot their heavy marching, and there was no more complaining about rigid discipline."[50] Paine, however, as overall commander of the column, drew a stern rebuke from Smith for allowing two of his regiments to fall apart on the march.[51]

The hasty recall of all those columns made it seem almost as if Belmont had been a defeat, but Grant stoutly maintained nonetheless that he had been successful there, fully accomplishing his purpose. That purpose, he now repeatedly claimed, was to prevent the Rebels from transferring troops into Missouri, but not everyone believed it. An Illinois soldier wrote in his diary, "Why they can't send reinforcements now as well as before, is more than I know."[52] Another soldier was both perceptive and highly critical of Grant. Rejecting Grant's claims about preventing the transfer of troops to Missouri, Charles Wills of the 8th Illinois, part of Oglesby's column, wrote, "I don't believe it. I think the Paducah forces were to take Columbus, Grant was going to swallow Belmont, we were to drive all the guerrillas before us to New Madrid, and then with the Paducah forces and Grant's we were to take Madrid and probably go on to Memphis."[53] That was more or less what Grant had intended. In truth, the expedition accomplished little tangible strategic gain, but it did scare Polk and Pillow, and that should count for something. Besides, if the war was going to be won some day, a start was going to have to be made at fighting. Grant's day at Belmont was the first day's work in a very long task.

On November 8, the day after the battle, Grant sent the steamboat *Belle Memphis*, under flag of truce, down the river with a burial party and a proposal to Polk that they make an informal partial exchange of sick and wounded prisoners. The latter was necessary because as yet no formal arrangement for prisoner exchanges existed between the United States and the rebellious forces. Polk accepted, and thus some of the wounded on both sides got to go home. Meanwhile, the burial detail, under Lt. Col. Harrison E. Hart of the 22nd Illinois, went about its sorrowful task on the battlefield, working alongside Confederate details assigned to the same job. They dug long trenches and laid the dead in them side by side, as many as forty-one in a single trench, then covered them with about two feet of dirt.[54]

Along with the flag-of-truce party had come Rebecka Wentz, wife of Augustus Wentz, lieutenant colonel of the hard-hit 7th Iowa. She came upon his body where his men, at his order, had left him. Mrs. Wentz let out a "low agonizing cry" and dropped down "prostrate upon his body." Capt. McHenry Brooks of the 27th Illinois found his brother dead on the battlefield, buried him in a separate grave, placed a marker, and then sat down and wept. His brother had been a member of the 13th Arkansas. John Logan, also with the flag-of-truce party, had a different experience. He ran into an angry Missouri farmer whose slaves had followed the Union army back north to freedom. The former slaveholder railed and cursed at Logan, who was not accustomed to taking that sort of talk. He had no choice now, but some who witnessed the scene thought Logan meant to have his revenge someday.[55]

"We have met the enemy and they are not ours," telegraphed a correspondent of the *St. Louis Sunday Republican* from Cairo at 3:00 a.m. on November 8. In the immediate aftermath of the battle, many in the North were critical of Grant. Other newspapers in Iowa and Illinois complained of the casualties and pointed to the absence of any tangible result. The tone of the press changed over the next several weeks, however. Perhaps Grant's own insistence that he had won a victory was paying off. That in itself was worth much. By year's end, newspapers across the North were hailing Belmont as a clear-cut triumph.[56]

John A. McClernand certainly intended that it should be a personal victory for him and for his political career. He had performed well in the actual fighting, showing conspicuous courage in the face of the enemy. His role in the recovery of the 27th Illinois was crucial. Grant had high praise for McClernand's performance. "General McClernand . . . acted with great coolness and courage throughout," Grant wrote in a letter to his father the day after the battle, "and proved that he is a soldier as well as a statesman."[57] On the other hand, as Grant was apparently too charitable to mention in his letter, McClernand's performance in the captured Rebel camp had been less creditable, contributing to the loss of control that had been one of the chief causes of the subsequent reverse.

The day after the battle, McClernand sent a dispatch to Union general-in-chief George B. McClellan in Washington. While acknowledging that "Genl. Grant was in chief command," McClernand did not downplay the importance of his own role in the battle. Back at Cairo, McClernand held a victory review, of sorts, for his brigade, issuing a fulsome congratulatory order to his troops. That sort of thing was all very well up to a point, but McClernand showed a tendency to carry it too far.[58] His official report claimed exaggerated credit for himself and his brigade, sounding almost as if his command had been the only one in the fight. That was vintage McClernand.[59] As his behavior in the captured Rebel camp at Belmont had demonstrated, the general from Shawneetown did not know how to stop acting like a politician.

This trait was made all the more dangerous by the fact that McClernand was a personal acquaintance of fellow Illinois lawyer and politician Abraham Lincoln. On November 10, Lincoln wrote McClernand a letter of congratulation. "You and all with you," Lincoln wrote, "have done honor to yourselves and the flag, and service to the country." Though the president noted that the letter was "not official but social," it still seems odd that the commander-in-chief would be congratulating a subordinate general on a battle fought by a superior. For now, though, Grant was safe from McClernand's politicking. In his letter to McClernand, Lincoln mentioned that he had just talked with Congressman Washburne, who had presented to the president Grant's and McClernand's various requests for more and better weapons.[60] As long as Elihu Washburne had Lincoln's ear, Grant's interests would not be neglected.

Grant was prepared to overlook McClernand's failure to attempt to maintain control of his troops in the captured camp because McClernand had fought well and been on hand when needed in the desperate breakout. The same had been true of Logan, Lauman, and Dougherty, all of whom had fought like tigers. Lauman may have acted impetuously, but his battle-field improvisation had worked out well. Dougherty was perhaps the most impressive of the three, but his severe wounds would prevent him from taking the field again.

As for Grant himself, he had by his skill and audacity diverted the Confederates from the true point of the attack, setting up the victorious first stage of the battle. He then had temporarily lost control of his army, preventing him from making his victory over the fleeing Confederates truly complete in such a way as would have prevented the landing of further Rebels on the west bank. When faced with this reverse, however, he had maintained his composure and determination, rallied his semi-demoralized troops, and directed them in cutting their way out of the encirclement.

Some were as yet unable to see the seeds of greatness in Grant's performance. "He had not the courage to refuse to fight," Will Wallace wrote disparagingly after Grant's lame explanation that he had fought at Belmont so that his volunteer soldiers would not think he was afraid to fight.[61] Wallace's criticism sounded lofty, but this war would yield any number of generals who had "the courage to refuse to fight." They were never in short supply. One of the chief things that made Grant rare and valuable as a general, as Lincoln would soon begin to notice, was that he *would* fight and do so with skill and determination.

As for the rank and file of the army Grant had taken to Belmont, their performance had met and exceeded all reasonable expectations. In his congratulatory order to the troops, Grant noted that he had been in most of the great battles of the Mexican War "and never saw one more hotly contested, or where troops behaved with more gallantry." In a letter to his father, Grant wrote, "I feel truly proud to command such men."[62]

Well might Grant praise the men and feel proud of them. Twice they had attacked a superior enemy force and hewed their way straight through it. They had fought aggressively in open order, despite becoming scattered and disorganized, and only the most experienced of troops could have minimized disorganization in those circumstances. They had briefly reverted to acting like civilians during the interval in the captured camp, but their officers had been more to blame for that. Brought to their senses by flames and the exploding shells of the Confederate batteries, they had rallied for another head-on attack on the enemy. "I watched our people rallying in line," wrote Surgeon Brinton, "and I thought that even if they had scattered a little to pillage the enemy's camp, they were still a brave set of men."[63]

Nor were Grant and Brinton the only ones impressed with the courage and fighting prowess of the Illinoisans and Iowans at Belmont. When an Illinoisan asked one of the Confederates captured at Belmont if he still believed the popular Southern boast that one Southerner could lick five Yankees, the Rebel replied, "Oh, we don't mean you Westerners. We thought this morning when you were approaching that we never saw such big men in our lives before. You looked like giants."[64] With a little more drill and a modicum of experience for both officers and men, these "giants," of whatever physical stature, showed promise of becoming truly outstanding fighters. That they were but a sample of scores of other regiments still enlisting or hastening to the front was something in which the North could rightly take great comfort and satisfaction.

One character who did not play a role in the postmortems of Belmont was the old Pathfinder, John C. Frémont. On November 9, Frémont, who was then campaigning, after a fashion, in the interior of Missouri, received orders from Washington relieving him of command. His replacement as western department commander was Maj. Gen. Henry Wager Halleck.[65]

Born in New York in 1814, Halleck had graduated third in the West Point class of 1839 and entered the army's Corps of Engineers. He gained a reputation for scholarship in the Old Army, writing treatises on warfare and translating the work of Swiss military theorist, and historian of Napoleon, Antoine-Henri Jomini. Halleck left the army in 1854 to found the leading law firm in California. Subsequently he turned down offers of a seat on the California Supreme Court as well as a seat in the U.S. Senate. Instead, Halleck turned his attention to business and continued to prosper until the outbreak of the Civil War. Lincoln, at Winfield Scott's behest, appointed him a major general, and his date of rank put him ahead of every other officer save Scott, McClellan, and Frémont.

He did not quite look the part of the dashing commander. Beneath the ponderous dome of his high forehead, the general would gaze goggle-eyed at those who spoke to him, reflecting long before answering and simultaneously rubbing both elbows all the while, leading one observer to quip that the great intelligence he was reputed to possess must be located in his elbows. His Old Army nickname was "Old Brains," so it seemed a safe bet to assume that he knew what he was doing. His first success came very quickly, as he cleaned up Frémont's inefficiency and graft and got the department on a sound administrative basis.[66] Time would tell how he would do as a conceiver and director of active operations.

One of Halleck's first administrative changes was to consolidate Grant's command at Cairo, now renamed the District of Cairo, with Smith's at Paducah. By reason of his earlier date of rank, Grant would command the enlarged district.[67] Halleck had a high regard for Smith and protected him from the machinations of Paine, who was still smarting from Smith's rebuke and consequently using back channels to stir up popular belief that Smith was disloyal.[68] Halleck's Old Army preferences were as strong as anyone's. Indeed, he was far less open to the advancement of volunteer officers than was Grant. Placing Smith under Grant's command can not have been congenial to Old Brains because, though both men were West Pointers, the arrangement was quite the reverse of how things would have been in the Old Army. Nevertheless, the consolidation made good administrative sense, and perhaps something could be done about the command of the district a bit later. For now, Grant was senior and that was that.

The consolidation of Grant's and Smith's commands may have been at least an indirect response to appeals that Grant and McClernand had made—Grant to Washburne and McClernand to Lincoln—both to the effect that a unified command should be created for the purpose of pushing down the Mississippi, and this unified command should have its headquarters in Cairo. McClernand's letter to Lincoln did contain one strange statement. The politician in arms opined that "a combined and simultaneous attack by our forces at Paducah, Cairo and Cape Girardeau upon Columbus, as well as Belmont, would probably have resulted in the reduction of both of the latter places." That was very nearly exactly what Grant had done. It sounded almost as if McClernand was criticizing Grant and coveted the unified command for himself, but then it may simply have been hard for McClernand to sound like a team player even when he was trying to be one.[69]

Another ongoing joint project of Grant's and McClernand's was the equipping of their troops. Both sent various appeals to Washington, and

Grant dispatched McClernand to Springfield to lay the case before Governor Yates.[70] To the adjutant general in St. Louis, Grant wrote, "The condition of this command is bad in every particular, except discipline." Besides a lack of wagons, ambulances, and cavalry equipment, his force suffered from poor-quality uniforms and weapons. "The arms in the hands of the men are mostly the old Flint Lock, altered, the Tower musket and others of still more inferior quality."[71] But better weapons, like other needed items, trickled in slowly and in small quantities.

Another thing Grant urged on Washburne was the promotion of Will Wallace to brigadier general. Wallace, Grant wrote, "is evry inch a soldier. A gentleman by nature and a man of great modesty and great tallent." Ironically, Grant added that Wallace was "not aware that I feel any personal interest in him."[72] Grant was not aware that Wallace was almost simultaneously penning strong criticisms of him in letters to his wife, Ann, back in Ottawa, Illinois. "I . . . feel strongly the necessity of some head—some leading mind upon whom I can rely & feel that in so doing I am directed by a mind that conceives the crisis & comprehends the means of meeting it." However, Wallace tried "to hope for the best," and, above all, kept his criticisms private, strictly between himself and his beloved wife.[73]

At their posts in Cairo, Bird's Point, Fort Holt, and Paducah, the soldiers of what would soon be called the Army of the Tennessee settled in for the winter. Shortly after their return from the Belmont operation, they began building cabins for winter quarters, going into the nearby woods to cut timbers for rafters or traveling to the cypress swamps southwest of Bird's Point to fetch "board timber to cover cabins." The walls of their cabins were logs, the floors and roofs of sawed lumber. On November 28, by order of General Grant, the army observed Thanksgiving Day, though it was not yet a national holiday. At Bird's Point, Will Wallace was so eager to get the cabins done and the men under board roofs that he decided they could "work half the day & go to church in the afternoon." The next day, the first snow fell, two inches deep.[74]

During the winter months, the troops suffered from camp illnesses, as new troops always suffered during their first winter in a Civil War army. From camp near Paducah, Austin Andrews wrote to his sisters back in State Line City, Indiana, that there were sometimes as many as two or three or more funerals in camp in a single day. "One of our Co. was buried yesterday & the capt. says there are two more that he don't think can get well."[75] Measles and pneumonia were among the diseases suffered by the soldiers. Will Wallace wrote, "With the best we can do I fear much suffering & sickness among the men this winter. It will be a trying time for all."[76]

Occasional probes into the interior continued, once again in vain pursuit of the elusive Jeff Thompson. It was a frustrating business. "If I had had two or three hundred more cavalry," Wallace wrote regarding a mid-November foray, "I should have captured Thompson's guns at least."[77] As it was, both Wallace and Grant realized they had very little chance of snaring the Confederate guerrilla. Two months later, regarding "another race after the inevitable Jeff Thompson's forces," Wallace wrote, "I have no faith in finding him."[78] The jaunts were at least good training for the men.

Other training came in the form of the usual exercises on the drill field, carried on whenever the weather permitted.[79] The drill now had a more vivid reality to men who had experience trying to implement these maneuvers in the heat of battle. In the long winter evenings, the veterans of Belmont would tell and retell to one another their individual stories of the fight, sometimes somberly remembering comrades who fell there. For the most part, however, the stories of Belmont that the soldiers told were accounts of courage overcoming adversity. Like their commanding general, they chose to see that which was victorious in their battle at Belmont and draw from it the assurance that when next they met the enemy they would overcome again. When the 31st Illinois went out to drill during the months after the battle, "all that was necessary to rouse the enthusiasm of the regiment was to command 'Belmont charge,' and with a wild cheer the men would move forward in line at the double quick," reveling in the memory of how with fixed bayonets they had carved a path through the encircling Rebel lines. "The volunteers had met the enemy," recalled one of them. "They returned to Cairo, rejoicing in their achievement, self-reliant and confident."[80]

CHAPTER FIVE

Fort Henry

A LL THE TROOPS here are under orders to be ready to move by 12 o'clk tomorrow," Col. William H. L. Wallace wrote to his wife, Ann, on the evening of January 8, 1862. "I don't know what it all means. It may be a new demonstration, or it may be an earnest forward movement."[1] The reasons for the threatened expedition were woven from threads that ran to central Kentucky, East Tennessee, and all the way to Washington, D.C. The citizens of mountainous East Tennessee owned few slaves and consequently felt little stake in the Confederacy's war to make the continent safe for slavery. They remained loyal to the Union when West and Middle Tennessee declared the state part of the Confederacy, and they were now paying a price in terms of oppression from the Rebel authorities, whose high-sounding talk about self-determination did not seem to apply in this case. Lincoln desperately wanted to help the East Tennesseeans, not only because they were suffering for their loyalty but also because he was eager to show all potentially loyal Southerners that they would have the effective support of the national government in opposing the "slave-ocracy" that had stampeded their states into rebellion. In accomplishing this purpose, he had two problems. The first was that East Tennessee was a very difficult place to reach, especially from the north. The second problem was that the general whose sector lay next to East Tennessee, and therefore whose assignment it was to go there, was Don Carlos Buell, who gave no indications of going anywhere at all very soon. A George McClellan protégé, Buell was much like his mentor save that whereas McClellan could look impressive doing nothing, Buell did nothing and simply looked stodgy.

By the beginning of 1862, Lincoln was becoming increasingly impatient at the lack of movement toward East Tennessee—or anywhere else, for that matter. With McClellan temporarily sidelined by illness, Lincoln telegraphed Buell and the commander of the neighboring Union department, Halleck, to find out if they were cooperating with a view to immediate offensive operations. Neither man had any idea of cooperating or of advancing in the near future, concepts that were constitutionally alien to them. Both, however, explained to Lincoln, in terms of military science and to at least their own satisfaction, why the president's desired operations were impossible. "It is exceedingly discouraging," Lincoln wrote at the bottom of a dispatch he had just received from Halleck. "As everywhere else, nothing can be done."[2]

Lincoln did not give up, however, and his prodding finally produced action. Buell got one column of his army in motion toward Cumberland Gap, the northern gateway to East Tennessee, and Halleck agreed to stage demonstrations to prevent the Rebels from shifting troops from his sector to oppose Buell. Halleck's order for the demonstrations went to Grant, whom he directed to advance columns both from Cairo and from Paducah. He enjoined Grant to maintain the strictest secrecy, not even telling his officers the purpose of the expedition, and above all, he forbade Grant under any circumstances to bring on a battle.[3]

This directive was the impetus that sent orders to every regiment in Grant's command on January 8 and had Wallace wondering what was afoot. At Cairo, Bird's Point, Fort Holt, and Paducah, troops began packing their knapsacks, loading wagons, and stuffing as much as they could of five days' rations into their haversacks, while post quartermasters went to work to get as many draft animals as possible ready for what would obviously be a strenuous expedition.[4]

It was going to be strenuous because winter weather was often unfavorable for marching on dirt roads, and current conditions promised to be especially so. Noting the receipt of the order to get ready to move, Wallace wrote in a letter to his wife, "The roads are in an awful condition. It has been raining all last night & today."[5] In the 30th Illinois, David Poak drew the more or less correct conclusion that "there must be something of importance going to happen or they would not take us out in this kind of weather."[6]

Yet even a general as determined as Grant could sometimes be stopped by the weather, at least temporarily. Noon on January 9 passed, and the army remained in its camps while dense fog, brutal cold, and occasional light rain and snow swirled around them. The fog was the element that prevented operations. The riverboats were essential to assembling the column and setting it on the Kentucky shore, and, as Grant explained in a dispatch to Halleck, "The fog is so dense that it is impossible to cross the river. This will defer any movement." Further delays piled up. A steamer ran aground, temporarily blocking the river channel above Cairo. Then Halleck ordered a delay because of movements elsewhere.[7]

Meanwhile, the troops waited for thirty-six hours. Then came the order to unpack and, scarcely twenty-four hours after that, another order to prepare to march again. Finally, on the chilly morning of January 15, amid intermittent snow, sleet, and rain, the troops at Cairo and Bird's Point piled onto steamboats for the ride to the starting point for the march. Shouldering aside the chunks of ice that floated thickly in the river, the transports churned southward through the icy water to deposit the expedition on the Kentucky shore seven miles below Cairo, and the trek began, one division out of Cairo under Grant's direct command and another from Paducah under Smith. In all they numbered about 10,000 men.[8]

The soldiers struggled day after day through roads that were quagmires. The weather remained execrable. Grant and McClernand's column was out for five days, marched a total of about seventy-five miles, including some countermarching to confuse the Rebels, and advanced to within about ten miles of Columbus.[9] Smith's column was out for a cold, wet, and miserable eleven days. About twenty miles from the Confederate stronghold at Fort Henry, Smith's division reached the Tennessee River and rendezvoused with the gunboat *Lexington*. Smith and his chief military engineer, Capt. John Rziha, went aboard *Lexington* and took a ride upstream to see the Rebel fort. *Lexington* exchanged a few rounds with the fort's artillery, and Captain Rziha made some technical observations before heading back downstream to rejoin the division for the return march. By the time Smith's column arrived back in Paducah, it had covered some 125 miles.[10]

Besides attracting the attention of the Rebels and preventing the transfer of troops as intended, the expeditions demonstrated the toughness the men had developed since they had become soldiers. "The weather is pretty rough," Will Wallace wrote his wife during the expedition, "but we all stand it very well. The men are in good health & spirits." He added that they stood up to the fatigue of the march much better than they had done the previous summer. When it was over, he wrote, "The trip we have made has resulted in at least one good thing for us. It has demonstrated that we can move over any kind of roads & that we can stand any kind of weather."[11]

Throughout the January expeditions, Grant was thinking of bigger things. Though his orders from Halleck strictly forbade his making any attack, he continued to desire an opportunity to attempt a major advance, preferably against Columbus, on which his attention had chiefly been focused for the past four months.[12] During the expedition he had quipped, "I wonder if General Halleck would object to another 'skirmish' like Belmont? I suppose, though, that it would hardly do to 'skirmish' hard enough to take Columbus."[13]

Once the columns had returned to base, Smith informed Grant that as a result of information gained in his expedition, he believed it would be possible to take the high ground across the Tennessee River from Fort Henry and capture Fort Henry itself. Grant had been primarily focused on Columbus, but now he came to the realization that the Tennessee and Cumberland rivers represented the best possible avenue of attack for the Union forces in the West. Even before the January expedition, he had sent a request to Halleck for permission to travel to department headquarters at St. Louis to confer on possible future operations, probably against Columbus. Instead, he had received orders for the trek through rain, sleet, and mud. Now, with a new plan for an advance not against Columbus but rather up the Tennessee and Cumberland—confirmed by the highly respected Smith—Grant repeated his request for permission to go to St. Louis.[14]

Halleck grudgingly consented, making it clear that he was not eager to confer with him. When Grant arrived at headquarters, the department commander was so obviously irritated and uninterested that Grant became embarrassed and afterward felt that he had not done a good job of explaining what he wanted to do: launch an offensive up the Tennessee and Cumberland rivers. He had gotten out only a few sentences when Halleck abruptly cut him off and dismissed the whole business, "as if my plan was preposterous," Grant later wrote. "I returned to Cairo very much crestfallen."[15]

Halleck did not consider the plan preposterous. From his point of view, the problem with the plan was that Grant had thought of it. Halleck had plans to advance that way—in due time, as he saw it—and he did not appreciate suggestions from Grant, who might thus get some of the credit. The fact was that the wisdom of advancing via the Tennessee and Cumberland rivers was so transparently obvious that any intelligent person who reflected on a map and a general account of the war situation was bound to see it eventually. Grant, Smith, and Flag Officer Foote, as well as chief engineer of the Department of the Ohio Charles Whittlesey, from his post at Cincinnati, all urged upon Halleck what Whittlesey referred to as "a great movement by land and water up the Cumberland and Tennessee Rivers." Indeed, Whittlesey had sent Halleck his suggestion on November 20, only a couple of days after Old Brains succeeded to the Western command.[16] Various others later asserted that they had come up with the idea first, and loudly claimed credit.[17]

What made Grant special was that he believed the time to act on it was now. He found a ready ally in Foote. The two conferred with each other and both agreed to agitate for action. No sooner had Grant returned to Cairo on

January 28, "very much crestfallen" after his unsuccessful interview, than he telegraphed Halleck suggesting that, "if permitted, I could take and hold Fort Henry on the Tennessee." Foote sent a similar appeal, and the next day Grant followed up his suggestion with another message fully explaining what he proposed to do.[18]

Urging his case strongly, Grant argued, "If this is not done soon there is but little doubt that the defenses on both the Tennessee and Cumberland rivers will be materially strengthened." He was one of very few Union generals at this stage of the war who understood the advantage of seizing the initiative and acting before the enemy was prepared. Another thing he understood was the morale of his troops—their willingness to fight aggressively and their confidence that they would prevail. So he added in his message to Halleck: "It will besides have a moral effect upon our troops to advance them toward the rebel states."[19] Grant's almost instinctive understanding of these two factors was shaping the nascent Army of the Tennessee from the very beginning.

While Grant pled his case in renewed appeals to Halleck, other events conspired to support his position. On January 27, Lincoln had reached a new level of impatience at the inactivity of his generals on all fronts, expressed in General War Order No. 1. That order specified "that the 22d day of February, 1862, be the day for a general movement of the land and naval forces of the United States against the insurgent forces." The president singled out several armies he expected to advance, including "the army and flotilla at Cairo," and concluded, "The heads of Departments . . . with all other commanders and subordinates . . . will severally be held to their strict and full responsibilities for prompt execution of this order."[20] The various generals involved, including Halleck, apparently did not take his order altogether seriously, because they did not obey it. Still, a knowledge that the commander-in-chief strongly desired quick action probably influenced Halleck's thinking. That may have been all Lincoln really intended.

On January 29, Halleck received a further and probably more effective prod. That day a wire arrived from McClellan, in Washington, D.C., informing him that a Confederate prisoner taken in Virginia had revealed that Gen. P. G. T. Beauregard was under orders to go west with fifteen regiments from the Confederate army in Virginia.[21] Faced with the threat that his Rebel foes would soon be heavily reinforced, even Halleck began to see the value of prompt movement. In fact, Beauregard, renowned Confederate victor of Fort Sumter and First Bull Run, was indeed on his way west, but with only a staff officer or two. The rumor, however, had its effect. Halleck was convinced. On January 30, he wired Grant: "Make your preparations to take and hold Fort Henry."[22]

In his telegram, Halleck promised to send full instructions by mail. Those arrived on February 1 and were generally helpful though obvious. Grant should leave only enough troops behind to secure his posts against Rebel attack; otherwise he was to take every last man he could muster. Because roads were few and poor and bound to be in atrocious condition, and because Grant's army was short of wagons by the standards of 1862, Halleck gave the self-evident directive that Grant should rely as much as possible on steamboat transportation. From the very beginning, the Army of the Tennessee was going to be a frequently waterborne force that relied heavily on joint operations. Grant had already used that system at Belmont. Finally, Halleck urged Grant to take the fort before Beauregard could arrive.[23]

One other thing Halleck mentioned: he was sending a "Lieutenant-Colonel McPherson, U.S. Engineers" to serve as Grant's chief engineer for this expedition. By a tradition stretching back to the Mexican War, the chief engineer was expected to be, at least to some degree, the brains of the army, and Halleck believed he had in McPherson an officer who could not only provide plenty of brains but also represent the sort of by-the-book caution that Halleck valued and suspected Grant did not. McPherson might also serve as Halleck's eyes at Grant's headquarters, especially with respect to Grant's unfortunate reputation as a hard drinker.[24]

Born the son of a blacksmith near modern-day Clyde, Ohio, in 1828, James Birdseye McPherson had to go to work in a store at age thirteen to help support the family after his father went insane. The store owner took a shine to the bright young boy and sent him to nearby Norwalk Academy. From there he won a berth at West Point, where he graduated first in the class of 1853. Service in the Corps of Engineers naturally followed. Brilliant, handsome, and charming, with flawless manners and a winning personality, McPherson rose rapidly from first lieutenant to lieutenant colonel during the six months prior to Grant's proposed advance up the Tennessee River. His most recent assignment had been as aide-de-camp to Halleck. Now he would be one of the most important figures on Grant's staff, along with Chief of Staff Joseph D. Webster and Assistant Adjutant General Rawlins.[25]

Grant's soldiers were definitely ready for a movement of some kind—almost any kind. Life in the camps around Cairo and Paducah was sometimes unpleasant and always boring. New regiments continued to arrive as they completed their recruitment and organization in Illinois, Indiana, and

Iowa and went south to discover the pleasures of life in Polypotamia. "Mud! Mud! You never saw so much mud," wrote Capt. Luther H. Cowan to his wife upon his regiment's arrival at Cairo, "enough to plaster all the rest of the Union."[26] The 55th Illinois found snow several inches deep when they arrived at their assigned post of Smithland near the end of January and had no choice but to pitch their tents on top of it. When not struggling to keep tolerably warm and dry, the new arrivals amused themselves by watching the "fantastically dressed and fancifully drilled" 11th Indiana and 8th Missouri, the Zouave regiments.[27]

Yet the weather was variable. So warm and pleasant was the fourth week of January that Allen Geer of the 20th Illinois noted in his diary on the twenty-seventh, "Fine summer weather." The twenty-eighth came in warm, but temperatures dropped during the day. By evening, a cold rain was falling, which quickly gave way to snow. The snow continued to fall, as did the mercury, for the next two days. Then temperatures came back up and the precipitation turned back to rain. The creeks and rivers ran high, brown, and turbid. The Ohio was "perfectly yellow with clay," a soldier of the 12th Iowa observed.[28] Clearly, winter weather in the Ohio Valley could be tricky. Yet there was something about the weather that seemed to say spring was at hand, waiting to burst out in good earnest all over the now gray and sodden woodlands. Will Wallace wrote his wife, "I think that this cold spell will probably be the last of our winter."[29]

Throughout the day of February 1, Grant and his staff hurried to make the necessary arrangements for the expedition, the biggest of the war thus far in the Mississippi Valley. "There was riding in hot haste from camp to camp," wrote the 11th Indiana's Col. Lew Wallace. "Tents went down, and the streets filled with troops in orderly march to the river. The excitement was tremendous, for now no one was so dull as not to know the meaning of the sudden breakup."[30] In the camp of the 45th Illinois, Luther Cowan surmised what the preparations meant but not where the army was headed. "We have put 40 rounds of cartridges into our boxes and start with 3 days rations fixed for a fight," he wrote to his wife, Harriet, back in Warren, Illinois. "Expect the next you hear of us will be that we have knocked the Secesh sky high." Cowan had to admit, "Where we go we don't know," but he was determined to give a good account of himself wherever the fight occurred. "I intend to fight and to kill at least one secesh, God being my helper."[31]

Unlike Cowan, Will Wallace of the 11th Illinois knew exactly where they were going. For security reasons, he would not speak of it to his men yet, but, rather incongruously, he wrote it in a letter to his wife, apparently never suspecting that a mailbag could go astray and fall into the wrong hands. The troops from all over Grant's district, Wallace wrote, were massing to "go up the Tennessee to take Fort Henry." Proudly, Will informed Ann that if the mission was successful, "We will have the honor of being the first Federal troops on Tennessee soil."[32] A man did not need to be one of the army's senior colonels like Wallace to guess as much. "Our destination appears to be Ft. Henry on the Tenn. River," wrote Pvt. Allen Geer of the 20th Illinois. So exciting was the prospect of that destination, or any other that promised a fight with the Rebels, that few of the men even thought to note in their diaries or letters that the weather remained cold and raw, with rain and sleet.[33]

Grant's total force would amount to some 17,000 men, almost six times as many as he had led to Belmont.[34] This larger force would be divided into two divisions: The First, under McClernand, would consist primarily of the forces that had been gathering in the Cairo–Bird's Point–Fort Holt area. The Second, under Smith, would be made up of the regiments that had encamped around Paducah and Smithland. Additional troops continued to arrive from the Midwest, and Halleck hurried them forward, fearful, almost in panic, lest the expedition prove a failure.[35]

"I will leave here tomorrow night," Grant telegraphed Halleck on February 1.[36] That, at least, was his firm intent and fervent hope. No bored and uncomfortable soldier in all the camps around Cairo and Paducah could have been so eager for the expedition to start as was Grant himself. Having at last received the long-sought permission to advance, he worried that perhaps Halleck might change his mind at the last minute and send a recall order. It was frustrating to him, therefore, that the army could not be readied as rapidly as he had planned. The Bird's Point contingent was supposed to board steamboats at 9:00 a.m. on February 2, but did not get off until late afternoon, by which time the Cairo troops were also supposed to be aboard and under way. That too got postponed.[37]

For the troops, it was another chapter in the good old army way of doing things. Lt. Douglas Hapeman of the 11th Illinois noted in his diary that his men had been ready at the appointed time but had been obliged to sit around with their gear waiting until all was in readiness for their departure. Loading of steamboats at the Cairo wharf went on through the night of February 2–3. The 11th Illinois, part of McClernand's First Division, was aboard by 5:00 a.m., but their boat did not start until 9:00. After a slow trip up the surging Ohio, they arrived at Paducah at around 8:00 p.m., stayed only an hour, and then set out steaming southward, up the Tennessee

River.[38] On the other hand, the 7th Illinois, part of Smith's Second Division, fell behind in its embarkation, spent "nearly all day loading the camp and garrison equipage," and did not pass Paducah until midnight.[39] Whether early or late, the other regiments' experience was about the same, packing onto the crowded and uncomfortable steamboats and huddling in the damp cold belowdecks or the pelting sleet above. The men of the 31st Illinois recalled being "packed together like sardines in a box."[40]

Grant did not have enough steamboats available to embark his entire force, so he took McClernand's and some of Smith's troops with him, to land them near Fort Henry, and then sent the boats back down the Tennessee to Paducah to pick up the rest of Smith's troops.[41] Grant traveled in the rear boat of the flotilla that carried McClernand's division. On the evening of February 3, as his boat prepared to leave Paducah, he nervously watched the wharf boat, fearful that even as his steamboat drew away from the shore the smaller boat would pursue with last-minute recall orders from Halleck, whom he correctly guessed to be in a state of near panic at the thought of troops under his command actually making contact with the enemy. When at last Paducah passed out of sight astern around a bend of the river, Grant brightened visibly. Uncharacteristically, he even clapped the nearby Rawlins on the shoulder. "Now we seem to be safe," Grant said, "beyond recall." Safe—with no one but the enemy to contend with, and in Grant's reckoning the enemy would rarely pose as large a threat to the Union war effort as did superiors like Halleck. "We will succeed, Rawlins," Grant added. "We must succeed."[42]

Leading the column of boats steaming up the Tennessee were four craft unlike any previously seen on that or any other river. "Creeping, menacing, ugly objects to look at," Lew Wallace called them. They were ironclad gunboats, specially built riverboats with their boilers below the waterline, their paddlewheels inboard, and much of their deck area covered by a slope-sided casemate partially plated with two and a half inches of iron. Each mounting thirteen heavy guns, they were the most formidable vessels on inland waters and a major component of Grant and Foote's plan to take the forts and open the rivers. The timberclads *Tyler, Lexington,* and *Conestoga*—like every other wooden warship in the world grown suddenly old to the point of obsolescence—came along too, but when the flotilla approached the enemy forts, the ironclads—*Cincinnati, Essex, Carondelet,* and *St. Louis*—were expected to do the heavy lifting.

Right behind the ironclads came the first of the transports, with McClernand on board. At 4:30 on the morning of February 4, they reached Itra

Landing, on the east bank of the river eight miles below Fort Henry. There, McClernand had his division disembark as he and Grant had discussed before leaving Paducah.[43]

While McClernand's troops were eating breakfast, Grant arrived and assessed the situation. After a brief reconnaissance in USS *Essex*, Grant ordered the troops back on board the boats for a five-mile ride up the river to Bailey's Ferry, below the mouth of Panther Creek, and at a range of three or four miles from the fort, just out of reach of its guns. From their new landing place, the troops could see the large Rebel flag floating over the fort. The debarkation brought specially good news to the men of John Logan's 31st Illinois. As they marched off the transport, they traded in their ancient muskets for brand-new Enfield rifles—a definite boost to morale. Once McClernand's division was established ashore, Grant boarded one of the empty transports for the trip downstream to Paducah to bring up the rest of Smith's division.[44]

Meanwhile, McClernand had issued an order to his various subordinate commanders enjoining them to maintain strict discipline among the troops and especially "to punish all depredators upon the persons or property of peaceful citizens."[45] This was an echo of Grant's own orders for the operation, which stated, "Plundering and disturbing private property is positively prohibited."[46] Smith had these or similar orders read out to the troops at Paducah and Smithland before they boarded the steamboats. The commanders might have been unanimous about this, but the rank and file were definitely not in agreement. The men of Company F, 12th Iowa, newly arrived in the war zone, were an example. With mock solemnity they took among themselves a vow that "if any cow, sheep, chicken, goose, lamb, duck, or other ferocious animal should bite a member of the Twelfth Iowa, it should surely die." They later testified to having kept the vow religiously and that no "edible animal was allowed to escape that vow on a technicality, or for want of evidence."[47] For the time being, at least, the men had little opportunity to implement this or similar resolutions about Southerners' property.

The departure of Smith's division from Paducah was a different affair from that of McClernand's division the night before. The rain had paused overnight. Steaming away in broad, if somewhat cloudy, daylight, the Second Division enjoyed the music of the various regimental bands, and the men stood by the rails and cheered. The rear of the army, at least, departed its base in a manner befitting the advance of the Army of the Tennessee moving up its namesake river on the first leg of an odyssey that was to take it through the heart of the Confederacy over the next three years. For many of the boys of the 45th Illinois, and no doubt other regiments as well, the departure offered a less dramatic but more immediate thrill than the sensation of starting off to battle. It was their first steamboat ride.[48]

The weather cleared off that afternoon. The First Division went into camp at about 3:00 p.m. at a bivouac McClernand, eager to curry the favor of the department commander, dubbed "Camp Halleck." The camp was muddy enough, and the soldiers in sardonic mimicry of riverboatmen at their soundings would occasionally shout, "No bottom!"[49] The first elements of Smith's Second Division reached the landing points below Fort Henry late that afternoon, and additional boatloads continued to arrive throughout the night and the next day. For the troops waiting in camp there, a foggy morning gave way to a day that was "heavy and hasey," with threat of further rain. The gunboats lobbed a few long-range shots at the fort, which replied with equal lack of effect. Some of the soldiers climbed nearby hilltops to watch the fireworks as well as the steamboats discharging the troops of Smith's division on the opposite, western, bank of the Tennessee. In the distance, Fort Henry looked formidable.[50]

That evening, Grant issued his orders for the assault the following day. Everyone was to move out at 11:00 a.m. Grant believed he could not order an earlier movement because some units of his army might not be on hand and in position before midmorning. McClernand's division was to swing into position east of the fort. There its mission would be to block the route from Fort Henry to its sister bastion of Fort Donelson, on the Cumberland River eleven miles to the east, preventing either the reinforcement or the escape of the garrison. McClernand was also to hold his command in readiness to "charge and take Fort Henry by storm" when Grant gave the order. Two of the three brigades of Smith's division would move up the west bank to seize a high hill that overlooked the fort. The Confederates had been working on fortifications on the hilltop, and no one knew just how strong they were. When Smith got possession of the hill, he was to put as much artillery as possible on top of it and send as much of his infantry as he could spare back down to the steamboats for transport across the river to join in the assault on the fort. Smith's third brigade would stay on the east bank the whole time, ready to aid McClernand or join the assault when needed. Simultaneously with all of this, Foote would lead his ironclad gunboats into action.[51] On the west bank that evening, Smith read the order from Grant and commented to Lew Wallace. "Everybody is to pull up tomorrow at eleven o'clock," the old Regular explained as he coolly surveyed the threatening skies and the rain-soaked countryside. "It will be a hard road," he added, "but we'll get there."[52]

That night, heavy thunderstorms rolled over the lower Tennessee Valley. Some of the regiments did not have their tents with them, and, as the 11th Illinois's Lt. Douglas Hapeman put it, "We got a little wet."[53] Other regiments, like the 45th Illinois, had tents, but many of them blew over in the storm.[54]

The rain stopped and the skies cleared off a few hours after dawn. Some of Grant's troops were formed up by 9:00 a.m. and waiting to advance, most of the rest of army by 10:00.[55] For many of them, the wait proved to be a long one, as the all-but-inevitable disorganization delayed the start and then the truly inevitable mud slowed the march almost to a standstill. The story was the same for both McClernand's and Smith's columns on opposite sides of the river. "We started in mud half knee deep," wrote Lt. Ira Merchant of the 28th Illinois.[56] Again and again, the artillery mired down all the way to the axles, and even doubled teams could not budge the guns. Then the despairing battery commanders had to appeal to the nearest infantry to help pull them out.[57] The routes selected were meant to take the troops around the worst of the flooded backwaters of the river, but they still had much wading to do, often waist-deep, sometimes neck-deep. Eager to get at the enemy, "the men plunged in cheering and yelling like tigers," recalled an officer. "They had to hold their cartridge boxes up to keep the powder dry."[58]

The troops at the back of the column, or even the middle, had to wait hours for the units ahead of them to make progress enough to allow them a place on the road. The 11th Illinois was in line by 9:00 a.m. but stood waiting until noon before moving out. The 45th had a similar experience. "We stood in line for two hours waiting for the cavalry and artillery to pass," recalled Luther Cowan. When the order to advance finally came, the soldiers stepped off enthusiastically, "shout after shout going up from the whole line for the union, the Stars and strips, the state of Ill. &c. &c."[59]

Yet above the noise of shouting, the marching, wading, struggling soldiers could hear another sound—the deep booming of heavy cannon fire coming from the river and the fort. Flag Officer Andrew Hull Foote was an old navy sea dog in the best tradition of Preble, Decatur, and Perry. He had promised Grant he would launch an attack on the fort at 11:00 a.m., and that is exactly what he did. At first the Rebel gunners scored heavily, hitting the ironclads again and again. The two-and-a-half-inch casemate plates stopped some of the incoming rounds, but some burst through, inflicting casualties. Foote's gunboats pressed the fight, however, and their firepower, along with the discipline of the navy gun crews, began to tell. They were pounding the fort at 200-yard range when at 1:55 p.m. the Confederate colors fluttered down the pole and a white flag waved from the parapet. Rebel officers in a row boat emerged from the fort—so low was the fort and so high the river that they rowed right out the sally port—and approached the flagship, offering the formal surrender of the post. All but about 90 of the 2,900-man garrison had already left.[60]

Still too far away to get into the fight, Grant's soldiers could only listen to the sound of the guns. The noise was "tremendous," Will Wallace wrote to his wife, Ann, the next day.[61] "Almost unintermittent thunder," Lew Wallace described it years later.[62] It sparked both elation and frustration among the blue-clad soldiers. The 11th Indiana, toiling along at the head of Smith's column, cheered when they heard the guns open up, but the 30th Illinois spent most of the battle "standing in line in a meadow," recalled Sgt. David Poak, waiting for some artillery to get up a muddy hill and clear the road for them to advance. The 45th Illinois had not even started its march yet, and listened to the sounds of battle from the encampment, where they too stood in line awaiting the order to advance.[63]

Those who had clear road in front of them strained harder than ever to get into the fight they could hear beyond the surrounding woods. A soldier in the 31st Illinois remembered the officers almost constantly exhorting the men to "Close up! close up," as they slipped and toiled through the mud.[64] On the west side of the river, the leading troops of Smith's column got unwelcome evidence of the raging naval battle, as "overs" from the fort sailed into the woods around them and exploded in treetops, raining leaves, twigs, and limbs on the forest floor. "The effect was to energize everybody in the march," wrote Lew Wallace.[65]

When the firing ceased, the soldiers wondered what it meant. "We could not conjecture for what reason" the guns had fallen silent, an officer noted. The 30th Illinois, part of McClernand's division, double-quicked the last two miles but were still woefully too late to catch the fleeing Rebels.[66] When word of what had happened finally reached the soldiers, their reaction was mixed. "We were tramping along in the mud," recalled Wilbur Crummer of the 45th Illinois, "when a messenger passed along the line announcing the capture of the fort by the gunboats. Some of us cheered, but others were silent and really felt sore at the sailors for their taking of the fort before we had a chance to help them."[67]

The first of Grant's troops to enter the fort and its associated camps found numerous signs of hasty, even panicked, departure. Confederate commanding officer Brig. Gen. Lloyd Tilghman claimed he had sent most of his men marching away before the attack started. If so, the order had come as quite a shock to the Confederate rank and file, as the camps gave unmistakable evidence of precipitate abandonment—"fires burning, food left cooking, and letters unfinished in the tents."[68] As one of Grant's soldiers put it, the Confederates "took leg bail & run."[69]

Across the river, Smith's column found the west-bank Confederate fortifications, known as Fort Heiman, empty, the Rebels having left the post more than forty-eight hours before. From their hilltop position, Smith's men could at last see Fort Henry, "across the swelling flood of the Tennessee within easy cannon range," as Lew Wallace described the scene. "The stars and stripes flew out lazily from the stump of a flagstaff."[70]

CHAPTER SIX

From Henry to Donelson

THE NEXT MORNING many of the soldiers seized the opportunity to look over the captured Confederate camps and fortifications. A favorite activity in the camps was souvenir hunting in the miscellaneous debris the Rebels had left behind. Among the most desirable forms of booty were Bowie knives: large fighting knives, some as much as two feet long and four inches wide.[1] Some soldiers took more practical weapons and reequipped themselves with captured firearms deemed to be of superior quality to those they had had before. Such battlefield rearming, in a least a regiment or two, became a standard postscript to most of the Army of the Tennessee's battles over the next year and a half. The 50th Illinois's Charles Hubert, however, was not impressed with his regiment's haul at Fort Henry. As far as he was concerned, the captured Austrian rifles they picked up were worse than the old, smoothbore muskets they had carried before.[2]

New regiments continued to arrive every day, the 14th Iowa on February 8, as well as the ethnically German 43rd Illinois, both straight down from Benton Barracks, near St. Louis. Peoria's own 17th Illinois came the next day, direct from its most recent posting at Cape Girardeau.[3] The most colorful arrivals, by all odds, were John M. Birge's Western Sharpshooters, who also arrived on February 8. Recruited from all the states of the Northwest, plus Missouri, they were then designated as a Missouri unit, though they would later be redesignated the 66th Illinois. They wore gray coats and gray sugarloaf-style hats with three black squirrel tails attached to each hat. The unit carried a mixture of Dimmick plains rifles and target rifles. Halleck warned Grant of their approach: "Look out for Birge's sharpshooters, they have been committing numerous robberies. I have the Col. locked up in the Military prison."[4]

The men of the 43rd Illinois would have seconded Halleck's warning, at least as to the Sharpshooters' obnoxious behavior. The 43rd had ridden down from St. Louis on the same steamboat with them, and Lt. Col. Adolph Engelmann of the 43rd complained in a letter to his wife that the Sharpshooters had secured all the comfortable berths on the boat. Then when they got to Fort Henry, "the Sharpshooters worked General McClernand for an order moving us into a muddy cornfield so they could get our camp site," and had the 43rd "haul the rest of their stuff up the river bank for them." Much to Engelmann's satisfaction, however, the officers of the 43rd got McClernand to rescind his order about the campsites.[5]

While the soldiers basked in their victory and the new arrivals tried to accommodate themselves as best they could to life in a war zone, the high brass reacted to the capture of Fort Henry in more purposeful ways, though the various generals' purposes were not always the same. McClernand, true to form, began looking for means of turning military success to political advantage. The first step would be renaming the newly captured fort. He had already used the name "Halleck," and naming it "Fort McClernand" would have been a bit too obvious, so he called it Fort Foote, in honor of the naval commander. Foote certainly deserved the honor, and for McClernand the name had the advantage of emphasizing and publicizing that Grant had not been responsible for the capture of the fort. Of course, all of this over-looked the fact that the fort was not McClernand's to rename in the first place. That authority should have inhered in McClernand's superior, Grant, or perhaps even in Halleck. McClernand, however, was not about to let such niceties stand in the way of his own greater glory. Grant chose to ignore it.[6]

McClernand wrote a letter to Lincoln, crowing, "My division was the first into the Fort, and was the only one that pursued the enemy." The "pur-suit" amounted only to rounding up a few stragglers a mile or two east of the fort, and McClernand's letter conveniently neglected to mention that Smith's division had been on the other side of the river and thus had not had opportunity to pursue.[7]

Grant had different objects in view. "Fort Henry is ours," he wrote that night in a dispatch to Halleck. Then after a few sentences of explanation, he added, "I shall take and destroy Fort Donelson on the 8th and return to Fort Henry."[8] Just like that. Grant and his people would take a stroll in the coun-try, capture another vital Confederate bastion, and make a pleasant day's outing of it. And why not? To a reporter, Grant admitted that he had scant knowledge of the size of Fort Donelson's garrison, but he believed he knew what was important: the Rebels seemed to have very little fight left in them.[9] Therefore, almost as a matter of course, Grant and his men would whip them every time. Grant's men were coming to think the same. "Fort Henry was said to be one of the strongest points the rebels had," wrote Philo

Woods of the 12th Iowa, "but they gave it up without much fiting . . . a perfect panic ensued. All ran that could get out, leaving everything just as it was."[10]

Grant was serious about marching on Fort Donelson. The next morning when the surrounding roads continued to be far too muddy to support the movement of supply wagons and artillery, he seriously considered moving against the Confederate fortress with infantry alone and only as much food and ammunition as the foot soldiers could hump. Yet his aggressiveness was tempered by good sense. When a young cavalry officer, after leading a probe to within about a mile of Fort Donelson, reported "that the enemy will make a stand there and that any movement made against the place ought to be accompanied by artillery," Grant saw the wisdom of the young man's advice and decided the advance would have to wait a day or two at least. Another good reason for waiting was that only one of the gunboats was available to support the movement, the rest being either laid up for repairs at Cairo or else detached to make an important probe up the Tennessee River, cutting railroads and telegraph wires.[11]

While Grant and his army waited, the country began to digest the news of Fort Henry. The *New York Times* wrote, "Talk of peace and a restoration of the Union has revived with the taking of Fort Henry," while the *New York Tribune* opined, "A few more events such as the capture of Fort Henry, and the war will be substantially at an end."[12] Rejoicing was most enthusiastic in the Northwest. "Three cheers, and another, and yet another, and one cheer more," exulted the *Cincinnati Gazette*. In Springfield, Illinois, the triumph was the subject of much handshaking and backslapping on the streets of the capital. Excited citizens raised the Stars and Stripes all over town, and artillery fired salutes outside the state arsenal.[13]

The nation's military minds could reflect on just how much had been gained by the capture of a half-finished, poorly sited Confederate fort. The Tennessee River was now open to Union gunboats all the way to Muscle Shoals in northern Alabama. Columbus was effectively turned—rendered a useless position and potential trap for its Confederate garrison, which would now have no time to lose in making its retreat, marching away from the Gibraltar of the West, for which Leonidas Polk had thrown away most of the Confederacy's political hopes in Kentucky. Any other potential defensive position along the Mississippi north of Memphis was now also doomed to fall sooner or later, the only remaining question being how many days or weeks the Confederates could postpone that conclusion. Union troops could now advance up the rivers, carried and supplied by steamboats and supported by gunboats, all the way across the Upper South state of Tennessee and almost into the Deep South beyond. In this manner, they could reach within twenty miles of the strategically important Memphis & Charleston Railroad, the South's only continuous east-west line and, in the words of Confederate secretary of war George W. Randolph, "the vertebrae of the Confederacy."

While Halleck received congratulations from McClellan and exchanged thoughts with him on how the success should be maintained and exploited, Old Brains also gave some thought as to who, besides himself, should get a promotion as a result of this affair. His answer to that question, expressed in a dispatch to the secretary of war, was that the command situation in the West would be greatly facilitated if the War Department would call the sixty-three-year-old Ethan A. Hitchcock out of retirement, promote him to major general, and send him west. That way, Hitchcock would outrank all of the brigadier generals in the department, including Grant. Hitchcock was offered a major general's commission two days after Halleck's recommendation, but he declined it on grounds of ill health.[14] As his next resort, Halleck offered command of the Tennessee and Cumberland river expedition to Brig. Gen. William T. Sherman, then at Paducah, but Sherman expressed support for Grant.[15]

All the while, Grant, who knew nothing of Halleck's efforts to reward him with dismissal, continued to be eager, even fretful, to get his advance moving again. Almost alone among Union commanders in the Civil War, Grant understood the importance of momentum and maintaining the initiative. There might be many things that the enemy could do to him, but Grant seemed to realize that the enemy would not be able to do those things if he acted first, keeping his opponent off balance. One of his most important abilities as a general was that which enabled him to assess a situation, determine a course of action, and execute that course of action while the enemy was still several steps behind in that process, laboriously trying to determine the proper reaction to a situation that, thanks to Grant's quick action, no longer existed. Enforced inactivity in the midst of a campaign therefore chafed him almost beyond endurance.

From day to day, Grant continued to hope that the flooded backwaters would drain, the roads dry out and solidify, and the gunboats return from their various diversions and repairs. On February 8, he wrote Smith, "I may move tomorrow on Fort Donelson," but he could not.[16] The weather that day continued to be atrocious. "Rain, snow, & sleet," Will Wallace wrote on the eighth, "the whole country mud & slush. The roads impassable almost for horses. Movements with artillery impossible."[17] Grant was nothing if not persistent. Two days later, he wrote his sister, "I intend to keep the ball moving as lively as possible."[18]

By then conditions were beginning to look more favorable. The weather began to improve, with warm temperatures and "every indication of an early spring," despite occasional showers and still muddy roads.[19] On February 9, Grant personally reconnoitered within a mile of the outer works of Fort Donelson. He had heard that Gideon Pillow commanded the Confederate troops at Donelson. "I had known General Pillow in Mexico," Grant later wrote, "and judged that with any force, no matter how small, I could march up to within gunshot of any intrenchments he was given to hold."[20] He found that Fort Donelson was strong, built on high ground some eighty feet above the waters of the Cumberland River and situated between two small but now flooded tributaries of the river. Covering the fort on the landward side was an extensive ring of trenches fronted by a dense abatis.[21]

Arriving back at his encampments near Fort Henry, Grant found a lengthy memorandum from McClernand recommending an early advance against Fort Donelson and spelling out—complete with a diagram— exactly what form the campaign should take.[22] Chiefly the plan was one in which McClernand's division took the lead and featured in all of the important movements. If Grant made a direct response to McClernand's missive, we have no record of it. Instead, he sent orders for all of his division and brigade commanders to meet him for a council of war on board the steamboat *New Uncle Sam,* moored at Itra's Landing, the following afternoon, February 10.[23]

When all had arrived, Grant stated quietly: "The question for consideration, gentlemen, is whether we shall march against Fort Donelson or wait for reinforcements. I should like to have your views." Grant turned first to Smith. "There is every reason why we should move without a loss of a day," the doughty old soldier replied. McClernand was next. To the surprise and dismay of Grant and his officers, McClernand produced his written memo and read the entire document with its program for the capture of Fort Donelson by the glorious First Division, with bit parts for various elements of the Second. Lew Wallace, who was also in attendance, thought it would have been better for McClernand to have followed Smith's example and stated a simple recommendation to advance. "The proceeding smacked of a political caucus," Wallace noted, "and I thought both Grant and Smith grew restive before the paper was finished." As soon as McClernand stopped reading, Grant nodded quickly to Wallace, who was next in rank. "Let us go, by all means," chimed the Hoosier general, "the sooner the better." In quick succession all of the others responded with a firm and clipped "Yes."

"Very well, gentlemen," Grant concluded, "we will set out immediately. Orders will be sent you. Get your commands ready."[24]

Thus encouraged by his subordinates, with indications of drying roads and a promise that the gunboat squadron would soon be ready for action again, Grant determined on an immediate advance against Fort Donelson. Best of all for Grant, and perhaps somewhat surprising, was the fact that he had received no message from Halleck forbidding the further advance that Grant had first mentioned in his February 6 dispatch reporting the capture of Fort Henry. It did not seem at all like the nervous, obsessively cautious department commander to let his subordinate thus forge ahead, waging a successful war of momentum, but if Old Brains had suddenly found his nerve—or was providentially distracted—Grant would ask no questions but revel in the freedom he had first felt when Paducah fell out of sight astern.

In fact, Halleck had been neither acquiescent in Grant's plans nor silent at the other end of the telegraph wire. He was in fact characteristically fretful, determined that Grant should cease all forward movement and immediately begin to entrench. Above all he wanted full and constant reports from Grant and could not understand why he did not receive them, despite his own constant stream of telegraphs. The cause of this strange disconnect between Grant at Fort Henry and Halleck in St. Louis was a disloyal telegraph operator in Cairo, who was waylaying the messages between the two Union commanders. Though he was not able to give the messages to the Rebels, he did his best to help the Confederacy by simply failing to transmit them to their intended Union recipients.[25] This actually struck both ways. On the one hand, the artificial silence of Grant nearly provoked Halleck to do what he had a mind to do anyway and remove the most talented field commander of the war. On the other hand, had Halleck's messages gone through, his own pusillanimous counsels would no doubt have prevailed, and Grant would not have advanced against Fort Donelson.

Blissfully ignorant of Halleck's disapprobation, Grant issued his orders. Leaving a detachment at Fort Henry, the command would march for Fort Donelson on the morning of February 12. McClernand's First Division, being closer, would lead the way, followed by Smith's Second Division. They would approach to within two miles of the Confederate entrenchments, form a continuous line of battle, and await Grant's further instructions. New regiments were arriving as fast as the decidedly nervous Halleck could forward them, six of them on the very day of departure for Fort Donelson. Grant had them stay on their transports for the ride around to the Cumberland by way of Paducah and Smithland rather than marching overland with the rest of the army.[26]

As Grant was about to depart, he finally received a somewhat cryptic dispatch from Halleck. Old Brains gave instructions for the elaborate entrenchment of Fort Henry, which he wanted Grant to "hold on to . . . at all hazards." On the other hand, Halleck's dispatch also directed, "If possible, destroy the bridge at Clarksville; it is of vital importance & should be attempted at all hazards." Clarksville was a town on the Cumberland River thirty-eight miles above Fort Donelson. Although it was almost certainly not what Halleck had in mind, Grant might very reasonably have interpreted this directive as encouragement to attack Fort Donelson. In a quick reply, Grant promised to make "every effort" to take Clarksville.[27]

In a brief dispatch the following morning, February 12, Grant dutifully notified Halleck, "We start this morning for Fort Donaldson [*sic*] in heavy force." This dispatch Halleck received.[28] His reaction was another attempt to get rid of Grant. Trying to tempt neighboring department commander Don Carlos Buell, Halleck wrote, "Why not come down and take the immediate command of the Cumberland column yourself? If so, I will transfer Sherman and Grant." Buell made no reply.[29]

As Grant had informed Halleck, the Army of the Tennessee marched at daybreak on February 12, with no tents and minimum baggage.[30] Lew Wallace remembered it as "a day of summer. River, land, and sky fairly shimmered with warmth. Overcoats were encumbrances."[31] From the many hilltops along the way, men craned their necks to look forward and back along the column and were thrilled with the appearance of the biggest army they had yet seen. "In full view there was an army with banners marching to battle," thought Lt. Henry Hicks of the 2nd Illinois Cavalry as he looked back along the Ridge Road from his position in the vanguard. He considered it "a most inspiring scene."[32]

Sgt. F. F. Kiner admitted that he and his comrades "had not been used to marching" and so "got tired very easily."[33] The roads were very hilly and remained just muddy enough to increase the fatigue of the march.[34] "Before noon of that day," Hicks noted, "many an overcoat was thrown away as a useless burden."[35]

McClernand's division had marched four or five miles, almost halfway across the peninsula between the rivers, the evening before. They were soon closing in on Fort Donelson. About noon the tail end of the army's column had scarcely passed out of sight of Fort Henry when the 2nd Illinois Cavalry, leading the march, encountered Confederate pickets a little more than two miles from Donelson. Oglesby's brigade of infantry moved up to help drive back the Rebel outpost. By nightfall, both McClernand's and Smith's divisions were deployed in line of battle facing the entrenchments of Fort Donelson.[36] The troops settled down for a night under the stars, but temperatures remained moderate. Hicks recalled no discomfort sleeping that night, even without a blanket.[37]

Grant established his headquarters in the sector of Smith's division, which he placed on the left of the Union line. McClernand's division would hold the right. Confederate prisoners taken in the afternoon's picket clash revealed that the fort had been reinforced by a brigade under the command of Brig. Gen. John B. Floyd, who by seniority now held top command. They further claimed, fairly accurately, that the garrison numbered between 20,000 and 25,000 men. That meant Grant was outnumbered by at least 5,000, and could definitely use reinforcement.[38]

Grant sent back for Wallace's brigade, left as a garrison for Forts Henry and Heiman, to march at once to join the army at Fort Donelson. This would be a start toward bringing Grant's army up to parity in numbers with the Confederate army he was supposed to be besieging, and it would allow Grant to complete the encirclement of Fort Donelson and the little town of Dover on the land side.[39]

Wallace had been furious that his brigade was selected as the one to be left behind. He blamed the choice on C. F. Smith, whom he believed had a grudge against him. Wallace had been hauling on political wires to try to have Smith brought up on disloyalty charges while the two of them were serving together in Paducah, so his assumption that Smith might resent this was certainly not unreasonable.[40] Grant was apparently unaware of Wallace's machinations against Smith, whom he admired profoundly. Grant liked Wallace as well, thought him a promising young officer, and planned to put together a third division and give Wallace command of it. By the morning of February 14, Wallace's troops were on their way to Donelson.[41]

Throughout February 13, "lively skirmishing" continued all along the lines as Grant's forces spread out to reach from a flooded backwater just downstream of Fort Donelson all the way around the entrenched Confederate lines almost to another flooded backwater just above Dover. Birge's Sharpshooters were in their element during this day's action. Each one "from behind a rock, tree or other cover," wrote an admiring soldier in the 31st Illinois, "picked off the enemy with his rifle."[42] Birge's men were not the only ones sharpshooting. From concealment in the edges of the Confederate abatis, skirmishers all along the Union line took shots "as soon as a head showed above the smooth line of earthworks," while the Confederates "could not safely look over long enough to see us," a member of the 7th Iowa recalled.[43] Both sides were just beginning to discover that for sharp-shooting contests the side behind well-established defensive works was actually at a disadvantage. A Confederate soldier inside the fort recalled the effectiveness of the Union skirmishers. Every head that appeared above the Confederate breastworks was immediately a target, and "it became quite hazardous to pass and repass from the rifle pits to the camp."[44] Nevertheless, the Confederates sometimes scored. Pvt. Edward Buckner took a bullet in the eye that day to become the first combat fatality of the 12th Iowa, and there were sharpshooting casualties in other regiments as well.[45] Artillery fire also continued throughout the day.[46]

Despite Grant's orders not to bring on a general engagement, both of his division commanders this day launched unauthorized assaults. Smith and McClernand had been spoiling for a fight ever since Foote beat them to Fort Henry.[47] Ironically, the first offender was not the pathologically ambitious politician McClernand, but rather the professional soldier Smith. Early that morning, he decided to launch two of his three brigades in an assault on the Confederate fortifications in his front. At 10:00 a.m. the brigades of Col. Jacob Lauman and Col. John Cook formed up, fixed bayonets, and advanced through woods and brush so thick they could not always see the Confederate breastworks ahead of them. Down one slope, up another, then laboriously through the tangled branches of the abatis struggled the soldiers from Iowa, Illinois, Indiana, and Missouri. The complete absence of any remote appearance of a chance of success probably helped keep the casualty lists short. Officers like the 25th Indiana's Col. James Veatch were ready to "halt and direct the men to lie down to save us from very heavy loss" rather than press home a suicidal assault. After two hours spent crouching in unpleasant proximity to the Rebel breastworks, the troops received orders to withdraw. Few of them had even had opportunity to get off an aimed shot. Casualties in the 25th Indiana totaled seventy-five. The other regiments suffered somewhat less, but the overall losses for the operation were well over a hundred.[48]

Around noon, McClernand, deeming that his batteries had gotten much the better of one of the day's artillery exchanges and that the enemy's infantry in his sector had been "thrown into confusion," decided the time was right for an infantry assault to seize one of the Confederate redans opposite him. He selected his small Third Brigade, commanded by Col. William R. Morrison and composed only of the 17th and 49th Illinois regiments, and reinforced it with the 48th Illinois from Will Wallace's brigade. The troops advanced down the ridge they had been occupying and up the one the Rebels held. They struggled over rough ground and through the abatis, pressed up to within fifty yards of the Confederate works, and maintained an unequal contest variously reported to have lasted from fifteen minutes to an hour.[49] In contrast to the battle of the sharpshooters, when it came to frontal infantry assaults, the party defending from behind prepared entrenchments held all the advantages.

McClernand decided to reinforce the failing assault and ordered Wallace to send in the 45th Illinois as well. The Lead Mine Regiment advanced like the others before it, but the attack never had a realistic chance of success. The four regiments had to retreat after suffering 147 casualties—mostly in the 17th and 49th Illinois. Among the wounded was Morrison.[50] "We had smelt powder for the first time and had heard the whiz of the minie-ball," wrote a soldier of the 45th, but that was all the assault had accomplished.[51] Union dead and wounded lay scattered on the ground over which the charge had advanced and retreated. Dead leaves and underbrush had caught fire during the engagement, and now flames spread over much of the area where the wounded lay. A watching Confederate thought this "the most heart-rending scene of the whole battle. . . . The groans and screams of the poor helpless men suffering this double torture were agonizing." Nothing could be done for them, however, "and death finally put an end to their misery."[52]

In his report, McClernand called the attack "one of the most brilliant and striking incidents" of the entire operation and complained that it would have been successful if it had been accompanied by simultaneous attacks by the gunboats and the rest of the Union line. Of course, that was why Grant had ordered McClernand not to attack that day but to wait until the whole army and the river flotilla were ready to advance in concert.[53]

That evening the waterborne troops arrived, along with Foote and the bulk of the gunboat fleet, repaired and once again ready for action. Grant gave his orders. As at Fort Henry, Foote would open the ball with his gunboats. After battering Fort Donelson's guns into silence as they had done to its sister fortification eight days before, the gunboats would steam the two miles upstream to Dover and take up a position just beyond the town, blocking any Confederate escape by the river. With gunfire support from the fleet, McClernand's division on the Union right would then assault the Confederate lines and drive the badly whipped Rebels onto the solidly positioned Union center and right held by Wallace and Smith. Thus trapped, the enemy would have no choice but surrender. The whole operation was to begin the following afternoon at two o'clock.[54]

Fleet, transports, and troops were not the only things moving in from the north that Thursday afternoon. Also arriving that evening was a new weather front. Late in the day "a cold, drizzling rain set in," and the temperature continued to drop. By nightfall the rain had turned to sleet and then to snow, swirling thickly before "a driving north wind."[55] The opposing lines of battle were dangerously close together, and Grant had very reasonably issued an order against campfires, which would have given away positions and drawn the enemy's fire. The order began to seem far less reasonable, however, as the temperatures continued to plunge well below the freezing point. None of the men had tents, and thanks to their improvidence during the warm march on February 12, many were without blankets and overcoats as well.

Sometimes soldiers with blankets shared with their comrades without. Sergeant Kiner found two kindly friends in his 14th Iowa, and the three of them huddled tightly under two blankets. "After our blankets were wet through and we as well as the blankets," Kiner recalled, "it began to freeze and snow. Oh, how we did suffer from cold." Kiner thought that he could not stand it, that he would surely die of the cold. "Our blankets froze stiff around us, and when moved would stand in any position we would put them."[56]

Not all soldiers were as generous as Kiner's two friends. A private in the 11th Illinois later wrote that one rubber poncho had covered his whole company that night, "by being repeatedly stolen from its sleeping owner."[57]

Around midnight, firing flared up along the picket lines in several places, and officers called their men into formation.[58] On rising to answer the summons, Gould Molineaux of the 8th Illinois found his blanket already covered by three inches of snow. Once in line, Molineaux and his comrades could see no targets to shoot at. Out in front, the seemingly pointless firing rattled on. With bullets singing over their heads, the officers ordered their men to the ground, where they crouched miserably in the snow. Once the firing stopped, Molineaux gave up on getting any more sleep and instead spent the rest of the night walking back and forth to try to keep warm.[59] Many others did the same, sometimes whole units. David Reed described the activity of his own 12th Iowa that night as something entirely new to the tactics manual: "By company, in a circle, double quick, march!"[60] In the 7th Illinois, Lt. Col. A. J. Babcock paced up and down a hill with his men as they all tried "to keep from freezing."[61]

Freezing was a very real possibility in temperatures that dropped to 12 degrees Fahrenheit, and there were reports of many severe cases of frostbite as well as some deaths caused by the cold that night.[62] Members of the 12th Iowa found Maj. Samuel D. Brodtbeck of their regiment seated at the foot of a tree, unable to move. "He was roused with some difficulty," a member of the regiment reported, but his health was never the same again.[63]

A couple of hours before dawn, some officers began to look for ways to fulfill the spirit of Grant's orders while bending the letter enough to keep their men from freezing. The colonel of the 12th Iowa allowed half the regiment to go "over into the woods about half a mile away" and build fires to warm them and dry their clothes. After a couple of hours the other half of the regiment took its turn.[64] Throughout Grant's army, many men later described this as "the *hardest* night I yet experienced," and Gould Molineaux added, "I was provoked at the secesh, *provoked to kill.*"[65]

The morning of February 14 dawned "cold and cheerless," though one soldier noted, "Never was morning light more welcome." Sergeant Kiner recalled the men of his 14th Iowa that morning, looking "like chunks of old logs lying beneath the snow." They got up, stood their frozen blankets against trees, and built fires. Some Tennesseeans said it was the coldest day of the year. The snow continued to fall for some time after daybreak, but with the coming of light, the soldiers had more opportunities to build fires safely.[66]

The intermittent artillery firing of the previous day resumed shortly after dawn, as did the sharpshooting. A Rebel soldier recorded that they felt they could deal with the Union artillery, but the Yankee sharpshooters were more deadly and picked off the Confederate gunners one by one.[67] Not every Union soldier was an expert marksman. Company C of the 12th Iowa did its first stint on the skirmish lines that day. "I only shot once at something sticking up over the breastworks," wrote Pvt. Philo Woods, "whether it was a man or not, I do not know. At any rate, I shot away my gun cork"— meant to prevent moisture from entering the barrel of the rifle when it was not in use.[68] Allen Geer of the 20th Illinois was more precise and businesslike about his day's work: "Fired 10 rounds, dropped one man," he noted in his diary.[69]

The main event of the day, however, was to be the attack of the gunboats. At 3:00 p.m., Foote led his squadron up the Cumberland River toward Fort Donelson. Two of the ironclads that had fought at Fort Henry, *Essex* and *Cincinnati*, were not present, having been too badly damaged for repair in the time available. In their place, Foote had the new ironclads *Louisville* and *Pittsburg*—in all, four gunboats, as at Fort Henry.[70] Foote opened fire and pressed in to finish off the enemy at close range. Hearing the sounds of the navy's guns opening up from the river, Grant's soldiers sent up a cheer, remembering the victory eight days before.[71]

But this was not Fort Henry. Much better sited, on an eighty-foot bluff overlooking the river, Fort Donelson was far stronger. In a ninety-minute battle during which Foote closed in to well under 400 yards, the gunboats suffered brutal punishment. Scores of heavy shells hit them, and many burst through the armor and wreaked havoc inside until the decks were slippery with blood. One shell burst in the pilothouse of the flagship *St. Louis*, killing the pilot, carrying away the wheel, and wounding Foote himself. One by one, the gunboats were knocked out and drifted helplessly downstream, away from the fort and out of the fight. This time a great shout rose from the Confederate lines. Rebel losses in the fight totaled one man killed. Over on the Union side, Grant's men had been listening to the fight, heard it end, and the Rebel cheer that followed. "We looked at one another like sick men," wrote a Federal officer.[72]

Grant was disappointed but, being Grant, was not about to give up. He began to consider plans for as long a siege as might be necessary, either bringing up tents for the men or having them build huts.[73] Despite the setback of the gunboats, his position was in some ways the best it had been so far in the campaign. With the arrival of additional troops that Friday, he finally equaled or outnumbered the defenders of the fort. His position during recent days had been, on paper at least, a rather precarious one. Grant had felt justified in taking the risk because he knew the incompetence of his opposing generals, John B. Floyd and Gideon Pillow. Besides, he was much more prone to think of what he was going to do to the enemy than what the enemy might do to him. Now he had all the more reason to think that way.[74]

Lew Wallace and his brigade had arrived overland from Fort Henry around noon. Grant assigned the brigade to assume its accustomed place as part of Smith's Second Division, to which it belonged, but Wallace himself Grant detached to command the new Third Division, composed of new troops that had arrived that day and the day before. Grant assigned Wallace's division to the center of his line, between Smith's Second Division on the left, and McClernand's First Division on the right.[75]

As Wallace's new command marched out to take up its assigned sector, Confederate artillerists detected the movement and opened fire on it at long range. The division had 300 or 400 yards to cross during which it would be exposed to incoming shells. Someone suggested to Wallace having the troops double-quick across that space, but Wallace had a hunch about the effectiveness of long-range artillery fire and wanted to teach his new command "contempt of shells" rather than "fear of them." So he ordered the lead brigade commander to "set all his drums and fifes going" and proceed at the normal step. Their spirits bolstered by the martial music, the troops marched across the open ground jauntily. "The stiffening up was magical," Wallace wrote. They reached their assigned position without a single casualty. Wallace was dismayed, however, to find that his line could not stretch far enough to join hands with both Smith's Second Division and McClernand's First.[76]

Having a large sector of front now covered by Wallace's division was meant to allow McClernand to sidle somewhat to the right and narrow the gap between his right flank and the nearest flooded backwater of the Cumberland River. When McClernand's line still failed to reach the river, Grant had Smith detach John McArthur's brigade and send it marching all the way around to McClernand for use on the far right. The march was an unpleasant one for McArthur's men, as the Confederates shelled them for much of the way. They arrived on the far right just as night was closing in. There, McClernand placed McArthur's three regiments, the 9th, 12th, and 41st Illinois, partially overlapping behind his previous right-flank regiment, the 18th Illinois, and partially extending still farther right. Nonetheless, the new right-flank regiment, the 41st Illinois, was still 400 or 500 yards from the nearest flooded backwater. McClernand tried to cover that ground with a detachment of cavalry.[77] He gave scant instructions to Colonel McArthur, who had had no opportunity to observe the surrounding terrain and would not be able to do so until daylight.[78]

That night the rain, sleet, snow, and penetrating cold came again. Many soldiers still had to spend much of the night in places where they could not build fires, but commanders seemed to do a better job of rotating troops back to sheltered areas to thaw out in the warmth of fires there. "This night . . . was somewhat better than the first one," recalled Sergeant Kiner. "It snowed a little during the night and was middling cold, but then we had the advantage of having good fires, and got along as well as could be expected under the circumstances." It was bad enough for all that. Allen Geer noted in his diary that he "walked a circle all night," as did others, but Geer also added that he "made hot coffee often," indicating frequent access to a fire.[79]

In the 76th Ohio, as in other regiments, the whole outfit, except two companies detailed to the picket line, retired over a hill and built fires. The men of the 76th were also better off than many of the troops around Fort Donelson in that they had both overcoats and blankets. They had just filed off their transport that evening and marched to their position in the line amid the falling snow. Four days ago, they had been in their recruitment camp near their hometown of Newark, Ohio. "We had been playing soldier," wrote the 76th's Lt. R. W. Burt, "but now it was coming right down to real business." Burt crowded around a fire with a dozen other soldiers, brewed and drank a cup of coffee, then rolled himself in his blanket, lay down as close to the fire as seemed prudent, and dropped off to sleep. The next thing he knew, his men were shaking him and shouting, "Lieutenant Burt, your blanket is afire." It was. After extinguishing the flames, the lieutenant found they had left a hole he could put his arm through. "Fortunately," Burt added, "the fire had not reached my coat."[80]

CHAPTER SEVEN

Victory at Fort Donelson

O N THE MORNING of February 15, "before it was yet broad day," a courier from Foote reached Grant at his headquarters. Foote's note informed Grant that the naval commander wanted to talk with him but the previous day's action had left him too badly wounded to travel. Would Grant come to visit him on his flagship?[1] Foote had been exemplary in his cooperation with Grant, straining the bounds of the possible to do all that the general had asked of him, including the previous day's gunboat assault. The Grant-Foote relationship set the tone for the successful joint operations that would be one of the Army of the Tennessee's keys to success in coming years.

Grant immediately made preparations to go to Foote. He had Rawlins notify Smith, Lew Wallace, and McClernand that he would be away for some hours and that during that time they were "to do nothing to bring on an engagement until they received further orders, but to hold their positions." The landing was about five miles away, and the road was not a good one. Wagons, artillery, and thousands of marching soldiers had churned its deep mud into extravagant ruts, ridges, and holes during the wet weather of the past few days. Now, as Grant began his early morning ride, those improbable shapes were frozen rock-hard. "This made travel on horseback even slower than through the mud," Grant recalled, "but I went as fast as the roads would allow."[2]

He did not appoint any officer to command the army during the several hours that he must necessarily be out of contact with it. By seniority the man for that job would have been McClernand. Though not necessarily lacking aptitude for military command, McClernand had the sort of checkered record one would expect from an amateur just learning the job. The most recent example of how much he still had to learn was that appalling four-regiment assault on February 13. Besides his military shortcomings, McClernand was politically dangerous. Grant was not aware of all McClernand's political activities, but he could not have failed to notice that the man had powerful connections and coveted Grant's job. As an additional consideration, Grant could hardly have considered placing McClernand in command of the highly esteemed C. F. Smith. And besides, what could happen in the few hours Grant would be gone?

As Grant's horse stumbled along through the predawn darkness on the rutted road to the landing, at the opposite end of the long Union line around Fort Donelson and Dover, pickets of the 41st Illinois, chilled and shivering in their exposed forward observation posts, wished fervently for the sunrise that was still almost an hour away. They were the extreme right flank of the Union line. To their right a few hundred yards of woods and brush separated them from the nearest flooded backwater of the Cumberland River. In front of them, outlined against the gray sky, was the Confederate parapet. There, at 5:45 a.m., they saw something that made them forget the bitter cold: Confederate troops were streaming over the parapet, forming up into regiments and brigades in front of it, and beginning to advance.[3]

Some of the pickets fired on the advancing Confederates while others scrambled back to the camp of the 41st Illinois to give Col. Isaac C. Pugh the word that the Rebels were "advancing in strong force." Pugh at first did not understand just what he was facing and ordered two companies to go forward and reinforce the picket line. This was no skirmish raid, however, and the companies came under fire almost as soon as they got out of camp. Now Pugh came fully awake and ordered the whole regiment into line, and suddenly they were in a pitched battle, exchanging massed volleys with a powerful formation that bore down on them relentlessly. Pugh ordered a bayonet charge that pushed the enemy back a short distance, but the pressure built again, stronger than ever. Then the colonel realized that the Rebels were streaming around his dangling right flank. He tried to shift to the right to counter the threat, and McArthur, his brigade commander, brought up the 12th Illinois on the right rear of the 41st to try to help, while the 9th Illinois moved up on Pugh's left. For a time the brigade held, but the weight of numbers in front of them was too much. The 41st fell back.[4]

The 12th Illinois, commanded now by Lt. Col. Augustus Chetlain, held on a few minutes longer. Chetlain deployed his companies carefully to take advantage of a conveniently placed fence and some buildings. The gap on the right proved fatal, however. The Rebels were pressing there in overwhelming force, obviously trying to rip the Union right flank away from the Cumberland River and open a way of escape toward Nashville. And it was working. After what Chetlain estimated as twenty to twenty-six minutes of fighting, he ordered the 12th to retire. To cover the retreat of the rest of the regiment, he called on Company F, the Jo Daviess Guard, which Grant had helped recruit and organize back in Galena the year before.[5]

The 9th Illinois's position in line put it on the left of McArthur's brigade, with Oglesby's brigade next on the left. Two companies of the 9th had previously been detached on other duty, and about 600 men were present in the eight remaining companies. The regiment's defensive position was a commanding ridge, and that helped. From its position there it continued to fight long after the 41st and 12th had been driven back on the right.[6]

Conspicuous during the fight was Pvt. James Getty, aged approximately sixty, of Company F and Monmouth, Illinois. Unlike his comrades, Getty refused to lie down to load, but "stood, loaded his gun, and fired as deliberately as if he had been shooting at a target for a wager." "I reckon I know my business," said Getty in reply to the remonstrance of his young lieutenant. A few minutes later, Getty went down, shot in the shoulder, but jumped up again, saying "he guessed he was not much hurt." Taking up his musket, he went back to shooting. Some minutes later a bullet struck his pocketbook, flattening a silver dollar and badly bruising his thigh. The aged private also took two or three buckshot. Yet he continued to stand, coolly loading and firing.[7]

By the estimate of one member of the regiment, the stand of the 9th Illinois on the ridge lasted for some two and a half hours. They exhausted their ammunition, and, as had been the case with the other two regiments of the brigade, the pressure on the right finally became irresistible. With a third of the regiment down, Lieutenant Colonel Phillips gave the order to retreat. As the 9th finally began to withdraw, still maintaining its formation, the Confederate forces continued to flow ominously past its right, clearly bent on getting in the rear of the 9th and the rest of the army as well.[8]

McArthur's entire brigade, the pride of Illinois and the first unit sent to Paducah, was now out of the battle. McArthur himself was wounded. The three regiments had given a good account of themselves, especially the 9th, whose 210 casualties were almost as many as those of the other two regiments combined. Still, the right of the Union line was a gaping hole, and the Rebels were swarming through it to flank and encircle McClernand's division.[9]

By this time, the battle had already spread farther along the Union line, as additional Confederate regiments moved out from their breastworks and struck the right front of Oglesby's brigade, next on McArthur's left. Shortly after the Rebel assault began to hammer at the front of the 9th Illinois, other Confederate troops advanced against the 18th Illinois, the regiment of Oglesby's brigade next on the left of the 9th. The men of the 18th were a combative lot. Their surgeon, between amputations, picked up a rifle and fired forty-five rounds at the enemy.[10] As the fighting grew hot, the 18th's Col. Michael Lawler suffered a severe wound in the arm. Though at first refusing to leave the field, he finally had to give in and allow himself to be carried off. Command of the regiment devolved on a captain. By the time the 9th retreated, the 18th was also almost out of ammunition. To compensate for the absence of the 9th, Oglesby ordered the 18th to shift to the right, so that he could bring up the 30th Illinois on its left. The left wing of the 18th never got the order, however, and the regiment broke apart into two separate bodies. Rebels stormed through the gap and around the right flank, and soon sent the 18th reeling backward in retreat. The 30th filled its place on the right of the 8th.[11]

Next door to the 18th stood the 8th Illinois. The men of the 8th waited in line of battle for about fifteen minutes after the attack hit the 18th. The artillery fire hit them first, and several guns in the nearby battery of Capt. Adolph Schwartz, Battery E, 2nd Illinois, were dismounted by direct hits. Then Rebels emerged from the brush in front, and the 8th was fighting hard. Before the battle reached his regiment, Gould Molineaux's fingers were numb with cold, but once he began loading and firing he noticed that they got warmed up enough to ache. The position was warm enough, to be sure. Besides the heavy musketry and rifle fire of Confederates sheltering in trees and brush only forty yards in front, the 8th caught a great deal of incoming artillery fire, much of it canister. The most deadly of Civil War artillery loads, canister was a bucket of balls that turned a cannon into a giant sawed-off shotgun.[12]

James Jessee remembered the "deafening roar" of gunfire; Molineaux, its effects. A bullet hummed by his head and slammed into the head of the rear-rank man right behind him. The man collapsed in a heap and "never moved afterwards." The two front-rank men to the left of Molineaux fell wounded, one in the face, the other in the neck. When he looked to the right to see how his comrades there were doing, he saw his old friend Edgar Thompson take a bullet in the left eye. Thompson fell flat on his back, "the blood gushing like a fountain from his eye."[13]

The 8th was engaged for perhaps forty-five minutes before the 18th broke. While the two regiments fought desperately to hold what had become, with the retreat of the 9th, the right of the Union line, the fighting spread rapidly along the rest of the front of McClernand's division. Will Wallace, commanding McClernand's center brigade, believed it was about 7:00 a.m. when his two right regiments, the 11th and 20th Illinois, came under attack. Although it is difficult to compare times on Civil War battle-fields because hardly any two watches seemed to agree, this would probably have been sometime before the retreat of the 18th Illinois at the other end of McClernand's line. As Oglesby's brigade, as well as the 9th Illinois, had done, after repulsing the first Rebel onset, Wallace moved his line forward about forty yards to the crest of a ridge where he believed his men would have a better field of fire. Soon his whole line was hotly engaged.[14]

By some eyewitness accounts, Will Wallace's brigade repulsed three Confederate frontal assaults in forty minutes. "We suffered them to advance within 100 yards," recalled a member of the 11th Illinois, "when we opened upon them with terrible effect." The Confederates pressed their attacks home, firing as they came, working their way forward under cover of the forest, sometimes to within twenty-five yards of the Union line. In the 11th Illinois, Lt. James Churchill was standing at his assigned place just behind the firing line when Cpl. John Cronemiller was hit in the forehead immediately in front of him. The stricken corporal fell back into Churchill's arms, his blood spurting into the lieutenant's face. Others fell here and there along the line, but the fire of Wallace's four regiments, combined with canister from Taylor's battery, drove the attackers back. Officers cautioned their men not to waste ammunition but to aim carefully. When the Confederates gave way and retreated, a fierce yell went up along Wallace's lines.[15]

Between Confederate infantry assaults, the artillery carried on the battle with vigor. Will Wallace's men hugged the ground as shells and canister screamed above them. Capt. Ezra Taylor's Battery B, 1st Illinois Light Artillery, which had performed ably at Belmont, was assigned to Wallace's sector of the front and fought back as best it could, contending at times against as many as six batteries. When the Rebel infantry charged, Taylor's gunners switched from shell to canister and helped Wallace's men beat off the attack. Sometimes the incoming fire became so heavy that Taylor and his artillerists were forced to seek shelter behind trees. Then when the firing slowed a bit, they would dash out and work their guns as fast as they could, while the crouching infantrymen "encouraged them with cheer upon cheer." Throughout the bombardment, Wallace, accompanied by a single orderly, rode slowly along the line of his brigade, as one admiring observer in the ranks recorded, "as cool as though he was a thousand miles from an enemy, never dodging or looking around, while the shells were bursting and tearing up the ground close to his horse's feet."[16]

During a midmorning lull, the Confederates broke contact in front of the brigade. Wallace deployed skirmishers forward and sent details to the rear to make coffee and carry it to the cold, tired, hungry troops on the firing line. A few minutes later, the skirmishers came rushing back in time to warn the brigade to brace for an even larger onslaught. Soon they were engaged again, with officers repeating their warnings to conserve ammunition. Now they were also scavenging the cartridge boxes of the dead and wounded.[17]

Getting the wounded back to the field hospitals was a difficult and dangerous task. Medical director John H. Brinton witnessed "one of the most remarkable cases of heroism" of the day's fighting, performed not by a man with a weapon in his hands but rather by one who was retrieving the wounded. The man was a chaplain. Brinton did not know his regiment but knew him as a Methodist. He was probably the 45th Illinois's chaplain William D. Atchison. At any rate, the man Brinton saw would ride his horse to the very forefront of the battle, "absolutely under the enemy's fire." There he would dismount, lift a badly wounded man into the saddle, and then, holding the wounded man with one hand and leading the horse with the other, head for the rear. As soon as he delivered his wounded charge to the field hospital, he would mount up, turn around, and go back for another. Sometimes he took two at a time. Brinton had to admire both his courage and "the sincerity of his religion." Somehow the dedicated chaplain came through the battle unscathed.[18]

Meanwhile, the crisis was continuing to build on the Union right. The situation of Oglesby's brigade was gradually becoming desperate under the relentless front and flank pressure of Confederate attacks. About an hour after the 18th retreated, Lt. Col. Frank L. Rhoads of the 8th reported to Oglesby that his regiment's cartridge boxes were nearly empty. Clearly the brigade was not going to be able to hold much longer.[19]

Reinforcements were on the way. It was about dawn when Lew Wallace, with his division in the center of the Union line, heard the sound of firing on the far right. It got closer and louder "until it bore likeness to a distant train of empty cars rushing over a creaking bridge." The noise had been going on for two hours when a horseman galloped up to Wallace. "I am from General McClernand, sent to ask assistance of you," the man explained. "The general told me to tell you the whole rebel force in the fort massed against him in the night. Our ammunition is giving out. We are losing ground. No one can tell what will be the result if we don't get immediate help."

Wallace explained his orders from Grant—all about holding his position and doing "nothing to bring on an engagement." This was all patent nonsense now, as a major engagement had obviously been in progress for the past two hours at least, but he did not feel right in sending reinforcements without higher approval, so he dispatched a staff officer to army headquarters for permission to help McClernand. The young lieutenant did not spare his horse and soon returned with word that Grant was away visiting Foote and "nobody at headquarters felt authorized to act." The Army of the Tennessee was fighting a major battle without a commander. "The battle," as Wallace later wrote, "roared on," and the troops of the Third Division stayed where they were.[20]

In time a second messenger came from McClernand, the First Division's assistant adjutant general Maj. Mason Brayman.[21] Wallace described him as "a gray-haired man in uniform . . . with tears in his eyes." His message was urgent: "Our right flank is turned. The regiments are being crowded back on the center. We are using ammunition taken from the dead and wounded. The whole army is in danger." Wallace decided he had to take the responsibility of acting. He ordered his First Brigade, under Col. Charles Cruft, to march to the right and report to McClernand. Somehow in the confusion McClernand got the idea that not only Grant but Wallace too was absent, and that Cruft had come on his own responsibility.[22]

Cruft's brigade was a recent transfer from Buell's army and was composed of two Indiana and two Kentucky regiments—the only Kentucky units in Grant's army. Like most of the troops at Fort Donelson, Cruft's men were seeing their first real battle. As the brigade marched into the zone of combat, Pvt. Jesse Connelly of the 31st Indiana saw for the first time a man who had been killed in battle. He was lying beside the road, having been "struck by a cannon ball near the middle of the body, and had almost been cut in two pieces."[23]

Cruft's brigade arrived behind Oglesby's brigade as the latter unit was nearing the breaking point. The 8th Illinois's ammunition was almost completely gone now, and Oglesby was urging Rhoads to keep his regiment in line until the reinforcements could arrive. Cruft, however, was getting very poor directions from a staff officer borrowed from McClernand, and conflicting requests from an officer of one of Oglesby's regiments, probably the 8th, pleading urgently for immediate relief. As the 25th Kentucky began to deploy from column into line of battle, it received an unexpected blast of rifle fire from Confederate troops on the flank of the 8th and working their way through a ravine toward that regiment's rear. The startled Kentuckians responded by triggering off a hasty volley of their own—right into the backs of the 8th Illinois. That was enough for Rhoads's regiment. The 8th departed for the rear in search of more ammunition and someplace where they would not be shot by their own men.[24]

The 25th Kentucky held on briefly on what was then the far right of the army, but soon crumbled and fell back on the 31st Indiana. There the problem was the same. "The Rebels fired into us, front and rear," complained a member of the 31st, while Cruft's men were so confused they could not tell which way to shoot.[25] One by one, the regiments of Cruft's brigade and the remaining regiments of Oglesby's brigade were either driven back or withdrawn as their position became impossible and threatened with encirclement. The Confederates were successfully rolling up the entire right wing of the Army of the Tennessee. By late morning, more than a third of the army had been forced to retreat, usually with heavy casualties. The troops streamed toward the left rear, looking for more ammunition and a place to make another stand.

As noon approached, the only part of Oglesby's brigade still in the fight was its left-flank regiment, John A. Logan's 31st Illinois. It now occupied the right flank of the army, the focus of the Rebel assault. The pressure of attackers in front, on the right-flank, and the right rear had worked like a giant nutcracker to crush one right-flank regiment after another all morning long. Now the 31st was in the nutcracker. Logan refused his regiment's line, that is, pivoted the line back on its left flank so that it faced toward what had been its right rear. In that position, the 31st formed what Capt. Smith Atkins called "an elbow" with the next regiment on its left, Will Wallace's 11th Illinois. Together, the two regiments fought to keep the nutcracker's jaws from closing again.[26]

The fight became intense, with clouds of powder smoke hanging so thickly among the bare forest trees that a colonel could not see his whole regimental front at one time. Logan and the other field officers of the 31st remained on horseback, their visibility inspiring to their own men but also making them targets to the enemy. Logan galloped back and forth along his line, roaring encouragement to his men. "Give it to 'em!" he shouted again and again.[27]

The fact was that Logan's men had precious little left in their cartridge boxes. Riding over to Lt. Col. T. E. G. Ransom of the 11th, commanding the regiment while Wallace led the brigade, Logan notified him that his regiment was out of ammunition and would have to retreat. He recommended that the 11th change front to deal with the threat this would present. About this time Logan was hit in the shoulder. Moments later Lt. Col. John H. White noticed that the enemy had gotten around the 31st's right flank despite all their efforts to prevent it. White had just given the order to change front to face the new danger when a bullet dropped him from the saddle, and he fell dead into the snow. With its ranking officers down and its cartridge boxes empty, the 31st Illinois finally retreated out of the fight.[28]

Now the 11th Illinois felt the full pressure of the Confederate nut-cracker. Bullets flew thickly. Churchill had two of them go through his coat and one through his pant leg, all without touching him. Ransom had had his coat torn by six bullets that morning. Another bullet went through his hat, while yet another felled his horse. Shortly before the 31st Illinois retreated, a bullet struck Ransom in the shoulder. He went to the rear to have the wound bandaged and then five minutes later hurried back to resume command of the regiment. Now he ordered the 11th to swing back to face the threat on the right flank, taking the place of the absent 31st Illinois.[29]

The enemy came on. "It seemed as if the rebels had gathered demoniac courage by their partial success in driving back our line," recalled Capt. Smith Atkins of the 11th, "and followed up every inch of vantage ground, and yelling like devils, they poured in their fire." Casualties mounted rapidly in the 11th, leaving gaps in the line. "We closed up," one of the soldiers in the ranks remembered, "keeping the colors for our center."[30]

Will Wallace knew the situation of the 11th Illinois was becoming critical, but the other regiments of his brigade were hard-pressed too. He had seen Cruft's regiments march by, heading to the right, but the sound and direction of the firing told clearly enough that they had failed to halt the steady unraveling of the army. He asked McClernand for reinforcements, but the general had none to give. That being the case, Wallace felt he had no choice but to order his brigade to retreat rather than wait for its regiments to be savaged one by one in the sort of unequal battles that had wrecked a third of Grant's army that morning. The 48th, 45th, and 20th Illinois regiments got the message all right, but the staff officer sent to inform the 11th was killed before he could deliver the order. The terrain was hilly, wooded, and shrouded in powder smoke, and Ransom and his men did not see the other regiments retiring. In short order the 11th was alone and all but surrounded.[31]

Watching his company's firing line, Churchill was shocked to notice that his men were being hit in the back. The stunned lieutenant grasped for the first time that the regiment was surrounded, with infantry in front and on both flanks and cavalry behind them. Churchill immediately notified Ransom. Realizing at once how desperate the situation was and where the regiment's only chance lay, Ransom gave the order to "face to the rear and charge cavalry." Then, wounded though he was, he led the way himself.[32]

Churchill charged along with the rest, sword in his right hand, revolver in his left. He had gone perhaps a hundred feet when he felt as though he had been "suddenly struck with a leaden whip across the thighs," and fell headlong. His company charged on. Struggling to his feet, the lieutenant discovered that he could still run. A musket ball had struck his left thigh but failed to break the bone. At the time, he could not even tell which leg was hit. Following after his company as best he could, he picked out the place where he would try to break through. As he neared the line of Confederate horsemen, he glanced to his right and saw a cavalryman with a rifle leveled at him scarcely six feet away. Churchill swung his revolver around but was too late. The cavalryman's bullet struck him in the right hip, and he pitched to the ground "among a pile of dead and wounded."[33]

All through the snowy woods, the men of the 11th fought their individual battles to escape. Lt. B. F. Blackstone had already taken two bullets in the back and one in the side but struggled along anyway. A Rebel cavalryman loomed in front of him, raising his revolver, but Blackstone fired his first. The bullet lifted the cavalryman out of the saddle and sent him crashing to the ground. Blackstone was upon him at once, seized the Rebel's saber, and ran him through. Then, still clutching the bloody sword, the lieutenant set out to cover the three-fourths of a mile that still separated him from Union lines.[34]

Pvt. George Carrington never heard the order to charge—or retreat. He simply joined the stampede. As he ran full tilt downhill, his bayonet, fixed to the end of his rifle, jabbed into a log and stuck. He left it and ran on, slipping and sliding in the snow. Already wounded in the back and hand, Pvt. Charles Crane ran frantically from three pursuing horsemen until, realizing he had no chance to outrun the horses, he turned, brought up his rifle, and shot the nearest cavalryman. Then he dived into the branches of a nearby felled tree. The two remaining Rebel riders circled the brushy treetop, unable to ride into it but slashing furiously with their sabers. Crane got out of sight in the brush, then crawled around behind the two Rebels, who were at a disadvantage in the dense thicket. Rushing on them, he slashed at each with his bayonet, thought he got them both but did not pause to see, and made off for safety as fast as he could.[35]

Musician Albert W. Gore had taken up a rifle and fought as an infantryman during the battle. When the order came to leave, Gore, though wounded in the thigh, wanted to stay and fire another round. While taking a parting shot, he was hit in the hand. He dropped the rifle and ran, though with difficulty on his injured leg. He got about twenty yards before collapsing. As he lay behind a log, he saw his comrades dropping one by one around him with grievous wounds. Pvt. Henry C. Ellsbury was dashing past when a bullet struck his head. He toppled dead atop the wounded Gore.[36]

Through the terrible fight and flight, the 11th Illinois somehow held on to its colors. It was the flag that Ellen Fisher had presented to the Ottawa Rifles on behalf of the ladies committee back in April 1861. "Our hands have made it," Miss Fisher had intoned, "yours must defend it, and if needed for the purpose, the choicest blood in your veins, we doubt not will freely pour out." The statement sounds far too melodramatic to twenty-first-century ears, but on February 15, 1862, the Ottawa Rifles, now known as Company H, had, along with the other nine companies of the 11th, made it a simple reality. When the remnant of the regiment rallied after escaping from the trap, Cpl. William S. Armstrong of Company H, though wounded, was still carrying the flag. He was the only member of the color guard still standing.[37]

Of the 509 members of the 11th Illinois who had formed line of battle at the beginning of the fight that morning, 180 were still with the colors, unscathed, at the end of the day. The regiment's casualty rate, 65 percent, was the highest for any regiment in the Army of the Tennessee at Fort Donelson.[38]

Back in Third Division's sector, in the center of the army, Lew Wallace had been listening to the progress of the battle that was out of sight beyond trees and hills. John Rawlins joined him. They watched in dismay as a growing tide of fugitives streamed by from the right, and Wallace had to stop Rawlins from shooting a panicked officer who rode by shrieking, "We're cut to pieces!"

Wallace rode forward to see for himself and met the defeated troops of the First Division, retreating individually and in groups of various sizes. "They were not in the least panicky," Wallace wrote, "not even in a hurry." And they were almost all out of ammunition. The cry of "Cartridges, cartridges!" greeted Wallace as he rode. Finally he saw riding nonchalantly toward him an officer with "one leg thrown over the horn of his saddle and four or five hundred men with a flag behind him." Galloping to meet him, Lew Wallace found that this was his namesake, Will Wallace, "a man above medium height, florid face, wearing a stubby, reddish beard, with eyes of a bluish cast and a countenance grave and attractive." The Illinois Wallace said he needed ammunition, and the Hoosier Wallace directed him to Third Division's wagons. Then Lew Wallace asked how close the enemy were. "Well," replied Will, "you will about have time to form a line of battle here."[39]

That got Lew Wallace moving. He quickly ordered up what he had left of the Third Division—Col. John M. Thayer's brigade, reinforced with three extra regiments that had just arrived that morning, and Lt. Peter Wood's Battery A, Chicago Light Artillery. Thayer's men came double-quicking up the road, and Wallace formed them in a line of battle facing toward the approaching Confederate threat.

Behind Thayer's regiments, Battery A came careening up the road at a gallop, "the horses running low, the riders standing in their stirrups plying their whips, guns and caissons bouncing over root and rut like playthings. The men clinging to their seats like monkeys." "I have lived long," wrote Lew Wallace many years later, "and seen many things thrilling, but never anything to approach that battery." Already gunfire was flaring along the front of Thayer's 1st Nebraska and 58th Illinois. Wood wheeled his guns into battery right in the road, while Wallace shouted for him to hurry and Thayer's men volleyed methodically into the Rebels. Even as the artillerists were unhitching, Wood was yelling for double canister. To Lew Wallace, it seemed the wheels of the guns had hardly stopped rolling before the first blast sent two bundles of iron balls into the faces of the advancing Confederates. The other guns opened in quick succession, and soon the smoke was too dense to see anything distinctly of guns, gunners, or the busy infantrymen, loading and firing as fast as they could.[40]

For forty-five minutes, the Confederates stubbornly assailed Wallace's line. Overextended, however, and disorganized by the morning's battle, they were unable to turn Wallace's flank as they had every previous Union position. Their attacks remained centered on the road held by Battery A, and Wood's gunners had plenty of canister for them. Indeed, Taylor's battery took a position nearby, having retreated intact from the cauldron of battle around Will Wallace's brigade, but with its ammunition—some 1,730 rounds—almost entirely expended. Wood was able to provide Taylor with enough canister to keep his guns in action during this fight.[41]

Thayer's infantry shredded the woodland with its heavy volume of rifle fire. The heavily German 58th Ohio deployed with front rank prone and rear rank on one knee, firing over their comrades' heads, while the artillery fired over them all. The men of the 58th could see no foes in the thick brush in front of them, but the enemy's bullets were constantly passing through the brush over them—at about the height of a standing man's chest or head—so thickly that they were constantly belabored with a hail of severed twigs. The German-Americans kept loading and firing, taking their best guess as to direction.[42]

The green 76th Ohio, less than a week out of the Buckeye State, deployed behind and somewhat uphill from the 1st Nebraska and fired over that regiment into the enemy—in theory at least. "I'll venture to say that neither the Nebraska boys nor the rebels were in much danger from some of our firing," wrote Lt. R. W. Burt, "for I observed that some of them fired much as if they were shooting squirrels in the tops of trees." Burt agreed that it was very hard to see the Rebels, "but their balls whizzing about us convinced us that they were there."[43]

Union casualties were light in this sector, while the attackers suffered severely. The Confederates fell back, and a lull ensued. "How rejoiced we were over our first victory," wrote Lieutenant Burt.[44] When occasional shells sailed out from Confederate lines, the men reacted with jeering and laughter. "Nothing veteranizes soldiers," Lew Wallace observed, "like a successful fight."[45]

The question of what time of day it was when various events took place on the battlefield is a difficult one. Participants' accounts vary by two hours or more for the same events. However, this lull occurred sometime in the early afternoon, perhaps about 1:00 p.m. Though very little firing occurred for about an hour and a half, leaders on both sides made decisions during this time that set the course for the final outcome of the battle.

The purpose of the attack had been to open a route by which all or most of the garrison could withdraw and join the rest of Gen. Albert Sidney Johnston's army somewhere near, or south of, Nashville. To accomplish that end, the Confederates had massed almost their entire force at the south end of their perimeter, where McClernand's division, reinforced by McArthur's brigade, lay across the path of their intended escape. The morning's battle had been eminently successful, except for the bloody repulse by Thayer's brigade, and even that setback did not affect the primary purpose of the operation. Thayer was not in a position to block Confederate escape through the sector that had been held by McClernand. The way to Nashville lay open. All the Confederates had to do was march away.

That they did not was a factor of just the sort of rank incompetence that Grant had expected when he heard that John B. Floyd had the top command in Fort Donelson, seconded by Gideon J. Pillow. During the early afternoon lull, Pillow persuaded Floyd, over the frantic protests of the competent but outranked Simon B. Buckner, to order the whole Confederate force right back into the entrenchments around Dover and Fort Donelson. It may be that Pillow thought Grant's army so soundly defeated that it would go away and allow the Confederates to withdraw at their leisure. Or it may be that the morning's victory had convinced him that the Confederate army need not retreat at all but could stay at Fort Donelson and whip any force the Union might send against it. At any rate, Pillow's counsel prevailed, and the Confederate army returned to its entrenchments. The initiative, which the Confederates had snatched from Grant with devastating effect that morning, now lay on the ground, as it were, for whoever cared to take it.

Grant had had a somewhat discouraging conference with Foote that morning. The flag officer had explained to him that several of his vessels would have to return to Cairo for repairs requiring ten days. Grant saw no alternative but to lay siege to Fort Donelson until the gunboats were ready for action again. At his urging, Foote agreed to leave two of the less damaged boats to support the army while the other vessels were laid up for repairs. It was about noon when Grant emerged from the *St. Louis* and boarded a rowboat that would carry him back to the west bank of the Cumberland. Grant, normally a pipe smoker, now carried a cigar given him by Foote. Just as he was landing, he met Capt. William Hillyer of his staff, looking very pale and very serious. "The enemy," Hillyer informed Grant, "had come out of his lines in full force and attacked and scattered McClernand's division, which was in full retreat."[46]

Grant mounted up at once and rode as fast as the condition of the road would allow. He was a notoriously fast rider, even under inclement conditions. He probably arrived in Smith's sector, the nearest part of the army, before 1:00 p.m., and stopped at headquarters, where staff officers would have told him more about the morning's battle. Finding Smith, Grant immediately ordered him to dispatch a brigade to the right. In strict obedience to his orders, Smith had done nothing so far, but now, with equally precise obedience, he started the brigade at once.[47]

Grant next rode for the hard-hit right wing of his army, galloping along the line with Foote's cigar clenched in his teeth. Chief of Staff Col. Joseph D. Webster rode with him. As they approached the scene of the fighting, they began to encounter soldiers who had been in action that day. Some of these informed Grant that enemy dead had been found wearing knapsacks and haversacks, the latter filled with rations. Grant's soldiers took this to mean that the Rebels were prepared to "stay out and fight just as long as their provisions held out." Grant thought it meant a breakout attempt. To Webster he said, "Some of our men are pretty badly demoralized, but the enemy must be more so, for he has attempted to force his way out, but has fallen back: the one who attacks first now will be victorious and the enemy will have to be in a hurry if he gets ahead of me."[48]

Riding on, Grant and Webster encountered disorganized soldiers and encouraged them to refill their cartridge boxes from the ammunition chests available not far to the rear and then return to their units. "The enemy is trying to escape," Grant told the men, "and he must not be permitted to do so." This seemed a new idea to the men, who probably had been thinking much more of their own escape. They appeared to take new confidence from Grant's orders.[49]

At some point, Grant encountered McClernand and Lew Wallace, discussing the fortunes of the day. When Grant arrived, McClernand ventured to observe snidely, "This army wants a head."

"It seems so," Grant replied. McClernand began to launch into an explanation of his division's retreat, but Grant had no time for that now. "Gentlemen," he announced, "the position on the right must be retaken." Directing Wallace and McClernand to counterattack, Grant informed them that he would ride to Smith's position now and have the Second Division cooperate in their attack.[50]

Grant lost no time getting to Smith. The old soldier was sitting under a tree, serenely awaiting further developments. "All has failed on our right," Grant told his former West Point commandant, "you must take Fort Donelson."

"I will do it," replied Smith, and with that he rose and went off to get to work.[51]

About this time, perhaps 1:45 p.m., Grant scribbled the only written dispatch he took time to send during his scramble to get the army in motion, and from the text of the message it is plain that he did not take very much time on it. Addressed to Foote, who, unbeknownst to him, had already departed, the note asked for a demonstration by the gunboats, even some long-range shelling, to boost the chances of the land attack. Eager to persuade Foote, who he knew would be reluctant, Grant wrote that the advance of the gunboats "may secure us a Victory. Otherwise all may be defeated." Such pessimism was probably intended for persuasive purposes, for Grant did not voice it to anyone else. He knew the decisive moment had come and he intended to throw in every bit of strength he had or could wangle out of the navy. Cdr. Benjamin M. Dove, who received Grant's dispatch in the absence of Foote, dutifully had the two remaining serviceable gunboats cleared for action and steamed back around the bend to engage the fort at long range as Grant had requested.[52]

This fight was going to be decided on land, however, and there Smith had his division ready first. "The general was off in an incredibly short time," wrote Grant.[53] At 2:00 p.m. Smith's troops, who had been waiting under arms, got their orders to prepare to advance. Within fifteen minutes, they moved out. Smith's plan was for Cook's brigade to move up toward the breastworks in line of battle, drawing the Confederates' attention and pinning them down with rifle fire, while Lauman's brigade, on Cook's left, charged forward in column of regiments to punch through the Rebel line. Even the regimental lines would be doubled to form a compact battering ram.[54]

The few minutes during which the regiments formed up and took their places for the assault were tense ones for the soldiers. Many of these troops had never been in combat before Thursday's abortive advance over this same ground, and it had not been a confidence-builder. One thought Sergeant Kiner could not get out of his head as he waited for the order to advance was: some men were going to die in this attack. Who would they be? "The question frequently occurred to me, is it I?" Resolutely he reminded himself that "we had volunteered to fight and we were ready, let the result be as it might."[55]

To lead Lauman's brigade, Smith selected the 2nd Iowa. Riding to the front of that regiment, Smith bellowed, "You must take the fort; take your caps off your guns, fix bayonets, and I will lead you."[56] Placing a percussion cap at the rifle's breech was the last step of loading. Having the men undo that step was meant to keep them from stopping and firing during the advance but still enable them to fire within a matter of seconds once they had taken the enemy's works and needed to repel a possible counterattack. Smith wanted his men to go straight over the breastworks with the cold steel.

At approximately 2:15 p.m., the division strode forward, down into the valley that separated it from the formidable Confederate breastworks. Smith rode in front of the 2nd Iowa, partially to urge the men on and partially to make sure they would not waste time shooting. The formation loosened considerably as they struggled over rough ground and through brush and downed trees. They started up the steep slope toward the Confederate entrenchments and began taking casualties. One of the first to fall was the 2nd Iowa's Maj. N. P. Chipman. He refused to be carried to the rear—that would take bayonets out of the ranks—but instead lay waving his sword and shouting, "Forward, my brave boys! We will gain the fort yet!"[57]

Color Sergeant Harry Doolittle took four bullets in quick succession, and the 2nd Iowa's flag went down. Pvt. John Bell of the 2nd later believed that moment, of all the moments of the battle burned into his memory, made the most powerful impression in his mind. It was a feeling of "personal degradation" to see that flag fall. "It was no longer a combination of stripes and stars in silken texture," Bell explained, "but the vital personification of human liberty battling for its own life, and its downfall, though but temporary, seemed the triumph of wrong, injustice and oppression." Many, like Bell, would have picked up the colors, but Cpl. Solomon Page got there first.[58]

As they pressed on, Bell noticed the "zip" of passing rifle bullets that seemed also to have "a peculiar stinging sound." Around him his comrades were being hit, many with exclamations of "Oh Lord!" or "Oh, my God!" He felt an overpowering rage at the men who were killing his friends. For the moment those enemy soldiers at the top of the ridge were "not human beings, but devils and demons" whom he wished to "slaughter without mercy."[59]

The white-haired general still spurred his horse up the slope, keeping ahead of the 2nd Iowa, waving his hat on the tip of his sword. Somehow he worked his way through the obstructions. Where he went, the soldiers would follow. "I was scared to death," wrote one of the Iowans, "but I saw the old man's white moustache over his shoulder and went on."[60]

"Come on, you volunteers, come on," roared Smith. "This is your chance. You volunteered to be killed for love of country and now you can be!"[61] The men may not quite have agreed with Smith as to the purpose of their enlistment, but they came on just the same. Page was dead by this time, and Cpl. James Churcher carried the colors of the 2nd Iowa. The regiment broke free of the abatis at last and plunged forward to cover the last few yards to the breastworks. A bullet broke Churcher's arm, and the colors fell for the third time in the charge. Cpl. Voltaire. P. Twombley, last man in the color guard, snatched them up. Almost at once a spent bullet slammed into him, knocking him to the ground. Smith was already leaping his horse over the Rebel breastworks. Twombley scrambled to his feet, climbed up the breastworks, and planted the colors atop the Rebel parapet. The 2nd Iowa surged by all around him. Most of the Rebels fled, and the attackers bayoneted those who stayed to fight. Then as the defenders tried to form up for resistance a hundred yards or so in rear of the breastworks, the Iowans quickly capped their rifles and poured a devastating volley into them.[62]

Just to the right of the 2nd Iowa the regiments of Cook's brigade were apparently just in front of the breastworks at this time and fired their volley over the parapet, then leapt over it and joined the fight inside. Members of the 50th Illinois even claimed that their flag reached the Rebel parapet simultaneously with that of the 2nd Iowa, but most eyewitnesses stated that the Iowa banner preceded it by a few seconds.[63] The men of the 12th Iowa never disputed the 2nd's claim to have had the first colors *on* the parapet, but they pointed out that their colors had been the first to go *inside* the parapet, a few seconds later. That banner, sewn by the young ladies of Upper Iowa University the previous April, was carried over the works by Sgt. Henry J. Grannis, to whom the ladies had presented it in formal ceremony all those months before.[64]

Had the Confederate entrenchments been fully manned, all the valor of

Smith and his men would likely have ended in bloody failure. The defensive line here had been weakened, however, as Grant surmised had been the case, when the Confederates had massed at the opposite end of their position for the attack against McClernand. By 3:00 p.m., Smith's division was firmly in control of the outer line of Confederate works. Rebels returning from the fight at the other end of the battlefield were in time to prevent Smith from exploiting his victory during the short winter afternoon, but he now had an extremely advantageous position from which to launch a concerted attack the following morning. No point inside the fort was higher than the ground Smith's men now held. Firing, sometimes heavy, continued throughout the afternoon, but the lines were now stable on this part of the front.[65]

Shortly after Smith launched his attack, action got under way again on the opposite end of the battlefield, scene of the morning's fight. This time Grant's men were the aggressors. Grant had ordered Lew Wallace and McClernand to take the offensive, and since most of McClernand's division needed time to regroup and fill cartridge boxes, the operation was primarily Wallace's. McClernand contributed his small Third Brigade, composed of the 17th and 49th Illinois and now commanded by Col. Leonard Ross of the 17th. These regiments had not seen heavy action since McClernand's ill-conceived foray on February 13. Wallace also planned to use Cruft's brigade of his own division, which had regrouped and was ready for action again. Wallace's main reliance in the attack, however, was on the brigade sent over by Smith at Grant's order. It was, as a member wrote a few days later, "a little brigade, but one calculated to fight."[66] It had been Wallace's own brigade until he had transferred to division command barely twenty-four hours ago, and was composed of Wallace's own 11th Indiana and Morgan L. Smith's 8th Missouri, both Zouave regiments. Morgan Smith, the sometime schoolteacher, soldier, and riverboat man, now commanded the brigade.[67]

The attack would aim to regain key ground that the Rebels had taken that morning, slamming shut the door of escape that they had just battered open. Morgan Smith would take the center, Ross the left, and Cruft the right. Thayer's solid brigade, along with McClernand's regrouping units, would continue to hold the center of the Union line. While Wallace waited for all of the assaulting brigades to get into position, he bantered with his old brigade. Pulling up in front of the 8th Missouri, he asked what hotel they had stayed in the night before.

"At the Lindell, of course," came a voice from the ranks.

"How were the accommodations?" asked Wallace.

"Cold, but cheap," a soldier shouted back, drawing roars of laughter from both Wallace and the ranks.

The general rode on and stopped in front of his own 11th Indiana. "You fellows had been swearing for a long time that I would never get you into a fight," he called. "It's here now. What have you to say?"

"We're ready," a soldier replied. "Let her rip!"

Finally a courier arrived to state that Cruft was in position on the far right and ready to advance. Wallace turned to Smith: "It is time to move."

"Wait until I light a fresh cigar," replied the Missourian. With that important preliminary completed, the attack went forward. It was about 3:30 p.m.[68]

Morgan Smith's brigade advanced toward a Confederate hilltop position using Zouave tactics, which emphasized fighting in open order, advancing on hands and knees and by short rushes, loading while lying on the back, and firing from a prone position. While his men thus sought all the shelter they could in their advance, Smith coolly rode on horseback immediately behind his lead regiment. A bullet shot off his cigar close to his mouth. Pulling out a fresh cigar, he shouted, "Here, one of you fellows bring me a match." A Missourian dashed over and lit the new cigar. Smith thanked him and added, "Take your place now. We are almost up."[69]

Smith deployed the 8th Missouri forward as skirmishers. They engaged the enemy first, while the men of the 11th Indiana, who could hear but not see the fight, "kept cheering to let them know we were there and would be with them," as one of the Hoosiers later explained. Soon the 11th was ordered into action too. Morgan Smith was in the thick of the fight, still riding his horse, and firing his revolver at the enemy. The Rebels resisted stoutly for a time. "They pored the bullets into us thick as hail almost," recalled one of Smith's soldiers, "and the way they whistled around one's ears was enough to make him jerk his head." However, as the Zouave regiments closed in, the Confederates broke and fled. "We could just get a sight of them flying through the brush," wrote Indiana Zouave William Brown. "We poured a volley at them and pitched after them." The pursuit continued for 500 yards and was brought up in front of the original Confederate entrenchments, where Rebel artillery checked the advance.[70]

Immediately on the right of the 8th Missouri charged the left-most regiment of Cruft's brigade, the 44th Indiana. Unlike C. F. Smith and Morgan Smith, Col. Hugh B. Reed dismounted to lead the charge, but he still proved an inspiring example to his men. With a revolver in each hand, he shouted, "Come on," and charged up the hill ahead of his men. The

Hoosiers joined in breaking the Rebel line and pursuing to within sight of the Confederate fortifications. The rest of Wallace's command moved forward to the same line. The new position did not give Wallace the kind of leverage C. F. Smith had gained on the opposite side of the fort, but it closed off the most obvious way of escape for the Confederates, and it was a reasonable jumping-off point for the all-out assault that Lew Wallace and Morgan Smith were planning to deliver in the morning. With sundown, at about 5:30 p.m., most of the firing ceased.[71]

With the darkness came the return of brutal cold. It had not been particularly warm all day. The night was a hard one for the soldiers. Morgan Smith's men had dumped their overcoats and knapsacks, including blankets, before starting their attack that afternoon. Now as they settled down for a night too close to Confederate lines to make fires practical, they wished fervently for the items that were now almost two miles away.[72]

It was worse for the wounded. Lieutenant Churchill still lay where he had fallen around noon of that day as he and the rest of the 11th Illinois were attempting to escape Confederate encirclement. Conscious but unable to move the lower half of his body, Churchill looked around himself and found that within a radius of fifteen feet there lay fifteen dead comrades, plus several wounded. He could hear many around him groaning, some crying "Mother," others "shrieking as though in great agony," and one cursing. One man's head was against his right side. Another head was against his head, requiring him to turn his neck awkwardly, and a third man's head lay against his left side. The first two men were dead, and the last, dying. Churchill in turn was lying with his head across the abdomen of another wounded man.

Throughout the course of the day, he had various visitors, mostly unpleasant. The Confederate battle line was the first to pass him by. Then came the Rebel stragglers, looting and stripping the dead and wounded. Churchill remonstrated with them that the wounded needed all they had to keep from freezing. Seeing some of them stripping the corpse of his friend Sgt. Frank Bellman, he asked them to bring him a memento of the sergeant. They handed him a pocket comb. Later, Confederate surgeons came, taking their wounded and some of the Union. Churchill asked to be taken, but the surgeons explained that it was no use. He was going to die anyway. They could not carry everyone and wanted only those that would live. Dragging the wounded soldier out from under him, they let Churchill's head flop down into the snow. Still later, the 8th Missouri had passed over him in their charge, but they had been able to give no more than encouraging words. Later they fell back to the other side of him, and Churchill found himself between the contending lines of battle, with bullets repeatedly striking the log near which he was lying and showering him with splinters.

The firing stopped and darkness fell. Churchill realized that no one was going to come for him that night, situated as he was in no-man's-land. The man against his left side stopped groaning and grew cold to Churchill's touch. The other bodies around him were "cold as ice." Temperatures were dropping, and "branches and twigs moved with sharp crispy sound." Throughout the long night, he battled alternately with pain, thirst, and cold, but he credited the latter with freezing his wound and saving his life. At one point, he found that his hair had frozen to the ground and only freed it with great difficulty. After that he tried to move his head every few minutes lest it freeze again. It was not until ten o'clock the following morning that members of his company found him and carefully bore him off to the hospital after a twenty-two-hour ordeal on the frozen battlefield. He survived, and after a long convalescence, returned to service.[73]

Soldiers did their best to reach their wounded comrades much more quickly than that, and throughout the night after the battle, stretcher parties and individual soldiers searched the battlefield for their fallen friends, often helping any wounded they found. Near the end of a long night of recovering wounded on the darkened battlefield, Alexander Kinmont, leading a seven-man detail of the 44th Indiana, heard a man crying for help quite near Confederate lines. It took some persuading on Kinmont's part to get his comrades to venture on such dangerous ground with him, but eventually he prevailed on them to go. They found the wounded soldier, like Churchill, with his hair frozen to the ground, freed him by cutting the hair, and successfully brought him to the hospital.[74]

The hospitals themselves—established in every available house and barn—were sobering sights, overcrowded as they were with intensely suffering, often badly disfigured men, and with the surgeons diligently plying their bone saws. In one of the hospitals that night, Capt. Luther Cowan of the 45th Illinois stood over one of his own soldiers who had a stomach wound—a death warrant in those days. He asked Cowan to take a letter he had received recently, and as the doctor gave him a big dose of morphine and left him to die, he said, "I'm not afraid." The letter was from a young lady, and began, "Dear William, I received your letter yesterday and whenever I am alone I read it. I'll be so glad when the terrible war is over and you are safely back home again." The memory of the letter and the dying boy haunted Cowan for months.[75]

No one was more sensitive to the sufferings of the troops than Grant. That evening he came upon a badly wounded Union lieutenant feebly attempting to give a drink from his canteen to a Rebel private lying beside him. Borrowing a flask of brandy from a staff officer, Grant gave each man a swallow. "Thank you, general," murmured the Confederate. The Federal could not speak, but saluted weakly. Grant made sure a stretcher party was brought up at once, and when the detail loaded the Federal first, Grant ordered, "Take this Confederate too. Take them both together; the war is over between them." As Grant and his staff continued through a sector of much-fought-over terrain, their horses shied constantly at the many dead men and horses on the ground. "Let's get away from this dreadful place," Grant said to Webster.[76]

Back at headquarters, before turning in, Grant issued his orders for the next morning—all-out assaults on both sides of the fort.

It had been quite a day for the Army of the Tennessee and its commander. Beginning with near-disaster, it was now ending with victory almost in sight. That Grant would take Fort Donelson was now as certain as human probability could make any future event. That would be a heavy blow to the Confederacy, since it would open the Cumberland River all the way to Nashville. Beyond the seizure of the fort itself, however, with the huge swath of Middle Tennessee it opened up, the sum total of Grant's victory on the Cumberland had not yet been determined when the fighting stopped on the evening of February 15.

Several hours later, the three top Confederate officers at Fort Donelson held a middle-of-the-night conference. Brig. Gen. Simon B. Buckner was irrationally pessimistic, although one can certainly understand his state of mind given the hardship, fatigue, and combat he had experienced, as well as the poor decisions of his superiors. He insisted not only that the fort would fall within thirty minutes of the beginning of the Union attack that was sure to come at dawn, but also that any further attempt to extricate the garrison would result in 75 percent casualties, which, he further claimed, would be immoral. His two superiors, Floyd and Pillow, accepted his judgment as fact.

In reality, the Confederates possessed several possible ways to get most of their troops out of the fort. Their steamboats could still operate on the Cumberland and could have ferried many troops to safety. Floyd killed that option, however, when he sent them all the way to Nashville with the sick and wounded. They could have made many trips back and forth across the Cumberland in that time. Even without the boats, considerable possibility of escape existed for Confederate troops moving upstream along the left bank of the Cumberland. Union lines came no closer to the river on the night of February 15 than they had twenty-four hours before—probably not as close—and the flooded backwater covered the river road to a depth of only three feet. The Confederates would have had to abandon all their baggage and artillery, their infantry would have had to wade waist- or even chest-deep in icy water for several hundred yards, and they might not have been able to get every last man out of the fort before Grant detected the operation and attacked, but they could have extricated a large portion of their force, probably well over half.

Instead, Buckner persuaded Floyd and Pillow that the garrison must surrender. Floyd was already under U.S. indictment for financial corruption while serving as U.S. secretary of war in the James Buchanan administration, and he stood a fair chance of facing charges of treason for having used the office of secretary of war to transfer weapons and munitions, in effect, into the hands of the rebellious Southern states immediately before leaving office. He determined therefore to make his escape from the doomed fort. General Pillow also saw the path of duty leading him out of the fort. He announced that he himself was the man in all the Confederacy that the Yankees most wanted to capture. He too must escape. The two seniors therefore turned command over to Buckner and fled. Pillow and his staff made off in a small boat. Floyd went in style. Two Confederate steamboats arrived after midnight with 400 reinforcements for the garrison. Floyd commandeered the boats and used them to ferry four regiments of his own brigade across the river. He might have continued ferrying troops save that Buckner was in too much of a hurry to surrender and, quite properly, would allow no more evacuations once the white flag went up.

Besides Floyd, Pillow, and Floyd's four regiments, perhaps 3,000 cavalrymen made their escape through the flooded backwater, led by Col. Nathan Bedford Forrest. A few other troops, no one knows how many, simply slipped away through the wooded, hilly terrain and the still fairly porous Union lines. Among the last group was the fort's fourth-ranking officer, Brig. Gen. Bushrod Johnson. The rest remained within Confederate lines when, early on the morning of Sunday, February 16, a bugler sounded the call for parley, and a gray-clad officer emerged from Rebel lines bearing a white flag and a note for Grant.

The flag-of-truce party entered Union lines, appropriately enough, in the sector of the 2nd Iowa, and one of the regiment's officers conducted them to C. F. Smith. "I'll make no terms with rebels with arms in their hands," barked the crusty old general. "My terms are unconditional and immediate surrender." But it was not Smith's place to offer or refuse terms, and he knew it. He conducted the Confederate officer, Maj. Nathaniel F.

Cheairs, to Grant's headquarters and left him waiting outside while going in to see Grant and show him the written message from Buckner.

Grant was sleeping on a mattress on the kitchen floor of the farmhouse he was using as headquarters. Smith, who was half-frozen, went over to the fire to warm himself. Then turning his back to the fire, he said, "There's something for you to read, General Grant." He handed Grant the note from Buckner. Grant read it while Smith borrowed a pull on medical director Brinton's flask and stood before the fire, "twisting his long white moustache and wiping his lips" and looking like all the world's ideal of an old but vigorous soldier.[77]

The letter in Grant's hands read:

> In consideration of all the circumstances governing the present situation of affairs at this station I propose to the Commanding officer of the Federal forces the appointment of commissioners to agree upon terms of capitulation of the forces and post under my command, and in that view suggest an armistice until 12 o'clock today.[78]

It was signed by Simon B. Buckner, an Old Army friend of Grant's.

"What answer shall I send to this, General Smith?" asked Grant. With an oath, Smith said he would not give them any terms at all. Grant chuckled, took out a piece of paper, and began to write. When he finished, he read it aloud:

> Yours of this date proposing Armistice, and appointment of commissioners, to settle terms of capitulation is just received. No terms except an unconditional and immediate surrender can be accepted.
>
> I propose to move immediately upon your works.[79]

There it was: no armistice, no commissioners, no terms. Major Cheairs carried the message back to Buckner, who was shocked at the severity of the reply but knew Grant was not bluffing. Buckner liked to pretend that war was a sort of medieval tournament in which all that mattered was a chivalrous passage of the lists, but Grant had a job to do. The Confederate commander was piqued that Grant would not play along with his game of pretend, but he had no choice but to submit. After the surrender, Grant continued to handle affairs in a businesslike manner, no formal ceremony, lowering of the flag, or delivery of the vanquished commander's sword. Grant had what he wanted; others could have the pomp of war.[80]

Grant's soldiers were in line that morning awaiting orders to assault the Rebel lines. It was a sobering prospect. "We all expected a great slaughter," wrote an officer of the 76th Ohio.[81] In some sectors, news of the fort's surrender came when the soldiers spotted white flags being raised over the Rebel lines. "When we got to the entrenchments," wrote a member of the 12th Iowa, "we saw white flags sticking up all around."[82] Elsewhere, a galloping messenger brought the news, and some units got their first clue that they would not be making a desperate attack this day when they heard thunderous cheering spreading along the battle line toward them.[83] However they learned the news, the men joined at once in the jubilation. "Did we shout?" recalled Wilbur Crummer of the 45th Illinois. "Well, if we didn't use our lungs then we never did."[84]

It was a proud moment for thousands of Midwestern boys when the army marched in to take possession of Fort Donelson and Dover that day, "with every flag flying and band playing"—"Hail Columbia," "Yankee Doodle," "The Star-Spangled Banner," even "Dixie" echoed from the hills and across the Cumberland.[85] "We marched into their stronghold the most exultant men the world ever saw," wrote Jonathan Labrant of the 58th Illinois. "We supposed that would end the war and we would get to go home in a few days."[86] The scene along the riverfront was exciting, with "the gun boats in front, the transports next coming up the river, and the long lines of infantry marching in from every direction," wrote Lt. Victor Stevens of the 20th Illinois. "The bands playing Yankee Doodle and the Star Spangled Banner. The stars and Stripes blowing upon the stronghold of secesherdom. I can't express it."[87]

Some of the Union soldiers sought out the new prisoners of war. "They seemed anxious to converse with us and tried to persuade us that they were our friends," wrote a Confederate prisoner from Tennessee, "but they met with but little success."[88] On the other hand, some of the prisoners told Grant's men that "they were forced into the army and did their fighting unwillingly," reported Wilbur Crummer. "We did not believe a word of it."[89] Mistrust ran deep on both sides.

News of the victory at Fort Donelson brought rejoicing all over the North and especially in the Northwest. The Chicago Board of Trade suspended business, and smiles and backslapping were the order of the day on the streets of towns and cities all over the Midwest. Illinois was especially jubilant, for twenty-one of its regiments made up the bulk of Grant's army. "Every school district in the State had its representative there," boasted the *Chicago Tribune*. Politically, the victory brought a double payoff for the Lincoln administration. Because all three of Grant's division commanders were Democrats, it showed that the war was broader than just an anti-slavery crusade. McClernand, Smith, and Lew Wallace showed that even racist Northerners still had reason to fight to save the Union.[90]

Grant, however, was the hero of the hour and deservedly so. The approximately 15,000 Rebel troops who surrendered at Fort Donelson (after about 6,000 made off that morning) constituted the largest haul of prisoners in the history of warfare on the North American continent, surpassing both Saratoga and Yorktown. Grant's "unconditional surrender" message played splendidly all across the North. Here was a general who meant business. Why, his initials might just as well stand for "Uncondi-tional Surrender." Stories of Grant galloping over the battlefield with the cigar Foote had given him clenched in his teeth made the rounds of newspapers, and the image of the jaunty, determined general lit up imaginations. Many in the North sent congratulatory cigars to Grant, and he received so many that he gave up his previous pipe-smoking habits and became a cigar smoker instead.

Strategically, the victories at Forts Henry and Donelson opened the Tennessee and Cumberland rivers as avenues of irresistible Union advance, completely unraveling Confederate defenses from the Mississippi to Nashville and southward to the southern boundary of Tennessee. Seven days after the fall of Donelson, the Confederates evacuated Nashville. On March 2, the last Rebel troops marched away from the great fortress at Columbus, which Grant had for so long contemplated attacking. Within six weeks, Grant's army would be encamped less than a day's march from the Mississippi state line. His triumph at Donelson also deprived the Confederate army in Tennessee of desperately needed troops that might have made a significant difference in future operations.

The soldiers of the Army of the Tennessee had performed prodigies of valor and endurance during the campaign. The modern observer stands in awe that they could fight as bravely and tenaciously as they did on February 15 after the suffering and fatigue of the previous two days. When forced to retreat after heavy casualties and often for lack of ammunition, they did not panic but proved ready to regroup and face battle again as soon as they could be resupplied with ammunition. Cruft's brigade was the only one that fought in the afternoon action after having been forced back in the morning, but McArthur, Oglesby, and Will Wallace could undoubtedly have done the same. Harder lessons and tougher tests still lay ahead of them, but the young manhood of the Northwest, enlisted in the Army of the Tennessee, had made a good start on soldiering.

Their officers had done well too. Particularly striking is the large num-

ber of outstanding midlevel leaders that were beginning to emerge at this
time. The two Wallaces, Logan, and Morgan Smith were among the most
promising. Oglesby and McArthur had done well too, and Lauman and
Lawler were at least solidly combative. Of course, C. F. Smith, an old Regular, was superb. Scarcely any officer at the regimental level or above failed
to provide at least inspirational leadership in combat. Many did that and
more. Excellent leadership at the division, brigade, and regimental levels,
often provided by men without professional military training, was to be one
of the chief factors in the success of the Army of the Tennessee throughout
its existence. The army's rising leaders still had much to learn. Grant later
pointed out that at the time of the February 15 battle at Fort Donelson "not
all of our commanders of regiments, brigades, or even divisions . . . had
been educated up to the point of seeing that their men were constantly supplied with ammunition during an engagement."[91] He would see to their
education in this mundane but vital matter, as in other areas as well.

Grant had begun to distinguish himself as a great commander. Many
had recognized the opportunity presented by the twin rivers. Grant had
acted. During the course of the war, many generals would suffer severe
reverses as Grant did on the morning of February 15. He was one of a very
few who responded to such circumstances by striking back harder than
ever. Some might say that Grant had been the lucky beneficiary of the three
Confederate generals' moral and psychological breakdown on the night of
February 15–16. It might just as easily be said that under the psychological
stress of intense military confrontation, Grant had remained steadfast until
his opponents broke.

Above all, Grant had given his army its first major lesson that hard fighting would bring success, that the lives of their fallen comrades had not been
wasted, as theirs would not be should they fall in future battles. With Grant
in command, the soldiers of the Army of the Tennessee could enlarge the
native confidence they had grown up with as sons of the pioneer generation, the assurance that by courage, endurance, and patient sacrifice they
could finally accomplish the task on which they had embarked.

CHAPTER EIGHT

Up the Tennessee River

I BELIEVE IT WON'T be over three months now until the rebellion will be squelched and we shall be permitted to go home," wrote an officer of the 45th Illinois to his family a few days after the capture of Fort Donelson.[1] Jubilation was the reaction of both the soldiers and the folks back home to Union success in what William Tebbetts of the 45th described as "the largest battle, in some respects, that ever was fought on the American continent." Despite the casualties suffered in combat, Grant's soldiers felt more determination than ever to see the war through. "We have reasons to praise the Lord that it is as well with us as it is," wrote Tebbetts to his sister, "for I have seen trees a foot and a half through cut entirely off by the cannon balls and I have had balls strike the trees at full force not more than a foot from my head and I have had shells burst within a rod of me and throw the dirt all over me but it appears that the Lord has still more work for me to do. . . . I came here for the purpose of fighting and I expect to fight till the last armed foe expires."[2]

During the days and weeks after the battle, numerous delegations of Midwestern citizens and political leaders traveled to Fort Donelson, partially as tourists and partially to bring comfort and encouragement to the troops. Gov. Samuel J. Kirkwood of Iowa and Gov. Richard Yates of Illinois were among those who came.[3] Citizens of Cincinnati chartered a steamboat and sent it down to Fort Donelson with nineteen surgeons and a full load of medical supplies. "God bless the benevolent people of the Queen City," wrote the 78th Ohio's Lt. William W. McCarty.[4] Elsewhere, citizens sent other tokens of their esteem and gratitude to the soldiers. The ladies of Chicago provided a new flag for the 20th Illinois, and those of Ottawa did the same for the 11th Illinois, thus replacing the battle-torn banners of Fort Donelson with bright new silk.[5]

Yet at the same time the soldiers were basking in the glory of their victory, many of them were also beginning to pay a physical price for the days and nights of extreme exposure to the elements. Sickness was rampant in the

Union camps. "Boys mostly unwell," wrote the 8th Illinois's James Jessee, "suffering from exposure and fatigue on the battlefield."[6] Among those who definitely seemed to suffer adverse health effects from their nights in the snowy woods around Fort Donelson was Gen. C. F. Smith, who was sick in the weeks following the battle.

In part, however, the widespread illness stemmed from larger causes than merely the stresses and fatigues of the campaign just concluded. The Civil War soldier's diet was unhealthy, sometimes consisting of little more than hardtack and salt pork. The water supply could be an even more serious health risk, as knowledge of sanitation was minimal. The longer an army stayed in one place, the more likely were its soldiers to suffer from waterborne diseases. The crowded conditions in camps and on steamboats made for ready transmission of disease. Finally, for a combination of reasons, soldiers were especially prone to illness during their first winter in the army. Since this was everyone's first winter, illness was rampant. "There are not more than ½ the men in the Regt. able for duty," wrote the 45th Illinois's Capt. Luther H. Cowan on March 1. The situation was not always that bad, but the troops continued to suffer from widespread fevers, "bilious attacks," rheumatism, and diarrhea right through the months of March and April.[7]

Despite the sickness, spirits remained high among the troops. They had come victoriously through a great battle, or in the slang expression of the day for experiencing the ultimate thrill, they had "seen the elephant." Now the war was about to end and they would be going home, perhaps without ever again having to see the kind of ghastly scenes they had witnessed of late. "The impression here among the soldiers is that the war is fast coming to a close," wrote the 20th Illinois's Allen Geer.[8] It was common knowledge that Clarksville and Nashville had fallen, and rumor had it that Grant was holding negotiations with Tennessee governor Isham G. Harris for the surrender of the entire state.[9]

What was more, Grant's soldiers believed they had taken the measure of their foes and found the enemy contemptible. "I have always been disposed to give the southerners credit for being equal to northern men," wrote Captain Cowan, "but they are not."[10] In fact, the Union soldiers began to suspect that their enemies were poltroons. "If the secesh had not been such cowards," wrote the 78th Ohio's Francis Bateman to his parents, "we would have lost 50,000 men before we could have taken" Fort Donelson.[11] "Is this a sample of the Southern chivalry?" asked a contemptuous Ira Merchant of the 28th Illinois. "If so I beg to be excused from having any thing more to do with them. Their Officers must certainly have them proficient in the 'double quick' movement. Donnelson has fallen. Bowling Green evacuated. Nashville is in the possession of our troops. Columbus, the Gibralter of the west, reported here evacuated. Where in the name of everything that is warlike can they make a stand?"[12] The clear implication was that the Rebels might not stand and fight at all, and if they did, Grant's men would whip them again.

Like the men in the ranks, the high brass also reacted to the momentous events of February 1862, though they did so in their own ways. McClernand reacted like the politician he was. To the troops of the First Division, he issued a bombastic commendation order. "You have continually led the way in the valley of the Lower Mississippi, the Tennessee and the Cumberland," he told them. "You have carried the flag of the Union further south than any other land forces marching from the interior toward the seaboard." The general went on to praise his men for being the first to enter Fort Henry and to reach and attack Fort Donelson as well as for their hard fighting on February 15.[13]

This was all very well up to a point. It was a wise general who looked to boost the morale of his troops. However, McClernand's victory order was couched in such wording as to imply, subtly or sometimes not so subtly, that his division had won the battle single-handedly. McClernand even spoke as if all of the forty captured cannon, prisoners, and stores were the trophies of the First Division.[14] Heaping praise on his troops was an indirect way of singing his own praises. In fact, his performance had been uneven at best. His February 13 assault had wasted lives; he had panicked during the February 15 fight; and he had not kept his men supplied with ammunition. His self-praise was therefore as unjustified as were his implied slights to his commander and his fellow division leaders.

McClernand cared little if Grant ignored his bombast, but to make sure that Lincoln did not, he sent the president a copy of the order along with a letter claiming, "I was not properly supported."[15] The statement was certainly not intended as a favor to Grant, but at the moment graver dangers were threatening the victor of Fort Donelson.

Halleck also reacted emphatically to news of Grant's success on the Cumberland. "Make Buell, Grant, and Pope major-generals of volunteers, and give me command in the West," he telegraphed to General-in-Chief George B. McClellan. "I ask this in return for Forts Henry and Donelson."[16] It was a remarkable missive in several ways. Realizing that a promotion for Grant was inevitable after the nation's greatest victory since the 1815 Battle of New Orleans, Halleck padded his list with the names of Don Carlos Buell and John Pope, who had done absolutely nothing, in order to diminish the glory for Grant. The shameless demand for an enlarged sphere of authority—oversight of Buell's department as well as his own—was all the more striking when sought as payment for two forts, the latter of which had fallen only because Halleck had been unsuccessful in transmitting his orders not to capture it. If Halleck lacked shame, he certainly had no short-age of persistence, following up his demand three days later with another even more peremptory: "I must have command of the armies in the West. Hesitation and delay are losing us the golden opportunity. Lay this before the President and Secretary of War. May I assume the command? Answer quickly."[17]

Halleck also persisted in his efforts to get C. F. Smith promoted. To McClellan he wrote that Smith, "by his coolness and bravery at Fort Donel-son when the battle was against us, turned the tide and carried the enemy's outworks. Make him a major-general. You can't get a better one. Honor him for this victory and the whole country will applaud."[18] Smith did deserve promotion, but Halleck's urgency in the matter came from his desire to diminish the recognition of Grant.

McClellan answered that he did not see the need of placing Buell under Halleck's command at this time.[19] Lincoln responded by nominating for promotion to major general of volunteers Grant and Grant only. The Sen-ate lost no time in confirming him, and Grant soon had his second star.[20] Smith's promotion would be delayed a decent interval as fitting recognition, by those in Washington at least, that Grant was the man whose vision and drive had won the forts and opened the rivers. Halleck, who at the moment was much distracted with fears of an imaginary Confederate threat to Cairo, could do nothing but acquiesce in Washington's decisions, but he would bide his time. No one was better at intrigue than Henry W. Halleck.

Grant, for his part, had his mind on further advances. "I want to push on as rapidly as possible to save hard fighting," he wrote to his wife. "These terrible battles are very good things to read about for persons who lose no friends but I am decidedly in favor of having as little of it as possible. The way to avoid it is to push forward as vigorously as possible." He realized that the capture of Fort Donelson had brought the added benefit of control of the upriver towns of Clarksville and Nashville, more or less whenever Union forces decided to take them. That was the next step and Grant rightly saw no reason to delay it. Yet he had no orders to proceed. "Clarksville is evacuated," he wrote to Halleck's chief of staff on Febru-ary 19, "and I shall take possession on Friday next with one Division under Gen. Smith. If it is the desire of the Gen. Comdg Dept. I can have Nash-ville on Saturday week."[21]

The next day, Grant decided to pay a visit to Clarksville himself. In company with McClernand, Will Wallace, two companies of the latter's brigade, and the band of the 11th Illinois, he boarded a steamboat at Dover for the forty-mile ride upstream. "It was a pleasant trip and a great relief from the constant & heavy cares incident to our dearly bought victory," wrote Wallace to his wife after they returned to Fort Donelson at about eleven o'clock that night. "Clarksville is a beautiful village or town of 5 or 6000 inhabitants," Wallace continued, but few of the white citizens were on hand to see Grant and the Federal soldiers land. Clarksville was a rabidly secessionist town, and, as was to be the pattern across the South, the more violently a man espoused secession, even though a civilian, the more likely he was to flee the approach of Union troops. "We marched through the streets," wrote Wallace, "but met no welcome except from the negroes."[22]

The next day, February 21, just as he had informed headquarters, Grant ordered Smith to take part of his division up the Tennessee by steamboat and occupy Clarksville. "I have no special directions to give that will not naturally suggest themselves to you," Grant added in his orders, "such as keeping the men from going into private houses and annoying the citizens generally."[23]

That same day, Grant reorganized his troops at Fort Donelson in preparation for further action. By the end of the battle he had 27,000 men on hand. These he now organized into four divisions: the First, Second, and Third under McClernand, Smith, and Wallace as before, and a new Fourth Division, which several days later he placed under the command of Brig. Gen. Stephen A. Hurlbut.[24]

Born in South Carolina to New England parents, Hurlbut had been educated as a lawyer. In 1845, at the age of thirty, Hurlbut had moved to Belvidere, Illinois, where he practiced law and allowed his inordinate political ambitions to engage him in bitter partisan strife with fellow Republican Elihu Washburne, Grant's patron in Galena, whom Hurlbut wished to replace in Congress. He failed in that endeavor but did gain election to the Illinois legislature. With experience in the South Carolina militia during the Second Seminole War, Hurlbut thought he was entitled to something more than a colonelcy in the new conflict and got his political friends and even some of his enemies to belabor Lincoln for a general's commission. His enemies may have thought it the surest way to ruin him. At any rate, Lincoln made him a brigadier general.[25]

The taint of corruption was never far behind Hurlbut. His known vices were a propensity to line his pockets and a fondness for intoxicating drink. He had held various commands in Missouri with very little credit, and it appeared that by the end of the summer of 1861 he had indeed fulfilled his enemies' hopes and thoroughly ruined himself. Hurlbut had a knack of landing on his feet, however, and in his most recent assignment, at Benton Barracks, not far from department headquarters in St. Louis, he had apparently remained sober enough for his administrative skills to attract Halleck's favorable attention. Halleck sent him to Grant, and Grant gave him the Fourth Division. The men of Hurlbut's new command were none too happy to have him. As Hurlbut himself later wrote, "I know full well that no regiment in my old division desired to be under my command when we met at Donelson."[26] But for now they were stuck.

Meanwhile, Grant continued to contemplate the strategic situation. Even two decades later, he still believed that after the fall of Fort Donelson an aggressive policy might well have unraveled the Confederacy before its leadership could gain time to regroup its forces or its population could recover its will to resist.[27] The next step was to take Nashville, and Grant was eager.

Taking the capital of Tennessee posed a greater problem than had Clarksville, though not because of any Confederate resistance. The Rebels had abandoned both cities several days before. What hindered Union forces from occupying Nashville during the last week of February 1862 was their own departmental system and the stubborn pride, timidity, and incapacity of Don Carlos Buell. Nashville was in his department, and since the fall of Fort Donelson and the Confederate abandonment of the city, he had been advancing toward it along the line of the railroad from Bowling Green, Kentucky. From Washington, McClellan had repeatedly urged him to hurry up, and Halleck constantly badgered him to march to Clarksville and go from there by steamboat. Buell, however, was not to be hurried.

On February 24, Brig. Gen. William Nelson reported to Grant at Fort Donelson with his division. During the brief siege of Fort Donelson, Halleck had begged Buell for additional troops, and Buell had complied by dispatching Nelson. Now, typical of any help that might be sent by Buell, Nelson arrived more than a week after the fighting was over at Fort Donelson. Grant saw a way to make use of Nelson anyway, even as he returned him to Buell. He sent Nelson up the Cumberland in steamboats to Nashville, where Buell was slated to arrive shortly. When the latter did arrive on the north bank of the Cumberland opposite Nashville the next day, he was chagrined to find Nelson's division of his own army already in possession of the city.[28]

Despite all the bickering Halleck and Buell had been doing in recent months about who should command the other and whose plans and program should prevail throughout the Western theater, there was one way in which the two were undeniably alike: they both became decidedly nervous when their troops got within three days' march of the enemy. Discovering part of his army already on the south bank of the Cumberland gave Buell the vapors. On February 25, he complained in a dispatch to Smith at Clarksville that Grant's action had now forced him to hold the south bank at Nashville, and he did not have men enough to do it. The Confederates, he opined, were likely to attack him at any time. This was pure moonshine, akin to Halleck's almost simultaneous delusion about vast Rebel hordes about to descend on Cairo, but Buell believed it. So he concluded his dispatch by ordering Smith, who, being on the east bank of the Cumberland was technically in Buell's department, to report to him at once in Nashville with his entire available force.[29]

Meanwhile, Grant had been making plans to visit Nashville himself to check on the situation there. As he did regarding almost every significant action he took, Grant carefully telegraphed Halleck, stating what he intended to do unless he heard otherwise from the department commander. No reply came from Halleck, so Grant assumed all was well and set off for Nashville late on February 26. With him he took McClernand and Will Wallace and their staffs, Col. Jacob Lauman, the redoubtable Capt. Ezra Taylor of Battery A, 1st Illinois Light Artillery, and various others.[30]

On the way, Grant stopped at Clarksville, where he was surprised to see along the shore the same fleet of steamboats in which he had sent Nelson's division to Nashville. Grant had thought Buell would use them to ferry the rest of his troops across the Cumberland and into Tennessee's capital city. Of course, Buell was keeping most of his troops on the north bank of the Cumberland, where he hoped they might be safe from the Rebels, and he had sent the boats to fetch Smith's troops back to help Nelson hold Nashville. Smith showed Buell's order to Grant and commented that it was nonsense. Grant commented that he had better obey it anyway, and Smith replied, "Of course I must obey." The troops, he said, were embarking as quickly as they could.[31]

More eager than ever to get to Nashville, not only to examine conditions but now also to confer with Buell and find out, if he could, whether there was any truth to that general's claims of the enemy's current aggressive plans, Grant continued up the Cumberland. "The weather was beautiful & the trip a very pleasant one," wrote Will Wallace. Grant arrived in Nashville early on the morning of February 27. Once again he was in for a surprise. Buell was not personally present with Nelson's division in the city he imagined to be so seriously threatened but rather was prudently remaining on the north bank of the Cumberland. Grant learned that Buell was expected to cross that day, so he inspected the city and Nelson's position. "We found Nashville a most beautiful city," reported Wallace, "with a magnificent capitol building, & better than all, the old flag waving over it."[32]

After waiting as long as he could, Grant decided he needed to get back to his own command and penned a short note to Buell. "If I could see the necessity of more troops here," he explained, "I would be most happy to supply." As it was, however, he correctly surmised that the Confederates were almost to the southern boundary of Tennessee and heading south. So, although Smith and his men would be along later that day, would Buell please send them back as soon as he could spare them, as Grant might want to use them himself.[33]

As Grant was making his way back to his steamboat, he ran into Buell. The latter, according to a member of Grant's staff, "was an angry man."[34] Grant said that his information "was that the enemy was retreating as fast as possible." Buell said it was not so. Nashville was in imminent danger of enemy attack. Grant demurred. Buell said he "knew."

"Well," Grant replied, "I do not know; but as I came by Clarksville General Smith's troops were embarking to join you." And with that Grant departed to return to his command.[35]

On March 2, Grant received a dispatch from Halleck, dated the previous day, ordering him to prepare to move his army far up the Tennessee River to the southern edge of the state and there launch fast-moving detachments ten or twenty miles into the interior to cut Confederate telegraph lines, first near Eastport, in the northwestern corner of Mississippi, and then wherever else telegraph wires could be reached. Grant immediately began issuing the orders that would, in a matter of days, start the Army of the Tennessee in motion, concentrating at Fort Henry for embarkation in the steamboats that would take it up the river for which it was to be named.[36]

While Grant prepared his campaign against the Rebels, Halleck prepared a campaign of his own—against Grant. Just how many of Grant's dispatches Halleck failed to receive remains unclear. Departmental records show that a number of his messages did get through. At any rate, Halleck learned of Grant's brief visit to Nashville and saw his opportunity. Instead of those tomes on strategy he cribbed from the French to gain his reputation as Old Brains, Halleck really ought to have written a book on bureaucratic infighting.

On March 2, he telegraphed General-in-Chief George McClellan in Washington. "I have had no communication with General Grant for more than a week," Halleck complained. "He left his command without my authority and went to Nashville. His army seems to be as much demoralized by the victory of Fort Donelson as was that of the Potomac by the defeat of Bull Run. It is hard to censure a successful general immediately after a victory, but I think he richly deserves it. I can get no returns, no reports, no information of any kind from him. Satisfied with his victory, he sits down and enjoys it without any regard to the future. I am worn-out and tired with this neglect and inefficiency. C. F. Smith is almost the only officer equal to the emergency."[37]

McClellan responded promptly and with even more vigor than Halleck had hoped: "The future success of our cause demands that proceedings such as Grant's should at once be checked. Generals must observe discipline as well as private soldiers. Do not hesitate to arrest him at once if the good of the service requires it, and place C. F. Smith in command. You are at liberty to regard this as a positive order if it will smooth your way."[38]

That was all Halleck needed. He was not planning to arrest Grant, just sideline him. Then command of the army could go to someone Halleck could respect. As an added benefit, if Grant were set aside and disgraced, more of the credit for the capture of Forts Henry and Donelson would go to Halleck instead of to that upstart general who simply went out and won battles. He fired off a dispatch to Grant: "You will place Maj.-Gen. C. F. Smith in command of the expedition, and remain yourself at Fort Henry. Why do you not obey my orders to report strength and positions of your command?"[39]

Grant received this bombshell just as he and the leading elements of the Army of the Tennessee were about to set out from Fort Donelson to march over to Fort Henry. He was dumbfounded. He had never knowingly disobeyed any order from Halleck and had faithfully reported his actions and intentions. Dutifully, however, he took the army across to Fort Henry and notified Smith that he was in command.[40]

Halleck was not finished, however. Now that Grant was, as it were, facedown in the bureaucratic barnyard, he could not resist stepping on the back of his head. He followed up his dispatch with several more over the next few days, condescendingly lecturing Grant at length about the importance of "order & system in your command," and complaining of how "ashamed" he had felt not to be able to forward reports of Grant's troop strength to Washington. "Don't let such neglect occur again," Halleck scolded.[41] In fact, there is no evidence that Halleck had actually telegraphed to Grant the requests for information to which he complained that Grant had not replied.[42] As for the composition of Grant's force, Halleck knew how many regiments Grant started with and knew, or ought to have known, how many more he had sent to Grant since then—unless he was too flustered to count. With an especially dishonest twist, Halleck salted his messages with such alarming statements as, "The want of order and discipline and the numerous irregularities in your command since the capture of Fort Donelson are matters of general notoriety, and have attracted the serious attention of the authorities at Washington"; and "Your going to Nashville without authority, and when your presence with your troops was of the utmost importance was a matter of very serious complaint at Washington, so much so that I was advised to arrest you on your return."[43] What Halleck did not mention in any of these dispatches was that the only reaction from anyone at the national capital was such as Halleck himself had engineered.

For good measure, Halleck continued his complaining messages to McClellan, in one of which he played his trump: "A rumor has just reached me that since the taking of Fort Donelson General Grant has resumed his former bad habits. If so, it will account for his neglect of my often-repeated orders. I do not deem it advisable to arrest him at present, but have placed General Smith in command of the expedition up the Tennessee. I think Smith will restore order and discipline."[44]

Halleck knew that McClellan, like every other officer in the prewar U.S. Army, would know exactly what he meant by Grant's "former bad habits." The Old Army officer corps was a small community, and news got around—including news about a desperately lonely captain stationed in California, half a continent and a year's journey from his family, who had taken to drink. If Ulysses Grant had never touched another drop of liquor, he would still never have escaped that stigma. Anyone who disliked him had only to whisper a few words like "former bad habits" in order to bring Grant's entire character into question. Now it was Halleck who did the whispering, and Halleck knew the rumor he was passing to McClellan was patently false. Halleck's own staff representative with Grant, Lt. Col. James B. McPherson, had just returned to St. Louis and assured Halleck that Grant was abstaining from alcohol.[45]

Grant knew nothing of Halleck's machinations against him. Just three days before, in writing a letter to his wife, he had referred to Halleck as "one of the greatest men of the age."[46] He had had no inkling of Halleck's displeasure until the fatal stroke fell. Stunned, but still eager to see the war pressed forward and bloodshed minimized, Grant moved ahead with preparations for the expedition he was now forbidden to lead, making sure that the Army of the Tennessee took every available man when it moved up the Tennessee River under its new commander.[47]

On March 4, Grant and his staff rode from Fort Donelson to Fort

Henry, where Grant established his headquarters aboard the steamboat *Tigress*.[48] That same day, the leading elements of the Army of the Tennessee also began their march along the same route. It rained off and on throughout the day. The roads were muddy and progress slow. Lucius Barber of the 15th Illinois noted that when they halted for the night, the regiment's wagons were still stuck in the mud two miles back down the road. Since the wagons carried both their rations and their tents, Barber and his comrades "went to bed supperless and without shelter." They awoke the next morning to find themselves covered with snow. Lt. Col. E. F. W. Ellis, commanding the 15th, insisted that his regiment was not going anywhere until the supply wagons caught up and his men had some food; so they stayed put that day and reached Fort Henry on March 6.[49]

Some regiments finished their tramp through the mud one day earlier; other units got their marching orders up to a week later; but otherwise, the 15th's experience was more or less typical.[50] One factor making the march especially unpleasant was the weight of the loads the soldiers were carrying—"knapsack, overcoat, blanket, in fact, the complete outfit of all personal property, including arms and accoutrements," as a soldier of the 12th Iowa described it.[51] A member of Birge's Sharpshooters recalled that he and his comrades had added to the weight of their loads by taking "all kinds of relics, to take home, as we supposed the war was ended." He admitted to having packed a 6-pound cannonball the whole eighteen miles.[52] Many of the troops found that because of flooding around Fort Henry they had to finish their march by wading about a quarter mile of icy backwater. "I don't mind marchin," wrote the 17th Illinois's Abram Vanauken, "but this wadin don't feel good."[53]

Grant had gathered at Fort Henry every steamboat he could possibly obtain, fifty-eight of them in all, enough to carry 15,000 soldiers and 3,000 horses. As regiment after regiment crowded onto the boats, spirits were high.[54] The troops had grown impatient waiting at Fort Donelson in the cold, wet weather.[55] Once they arrived at the Tennessee River, they realized that they would not be going home right away, but most believed that one more great battle would end the war. "They think they can whip the secesh easily now," noted Capt. Luther Cowan of the 45th Illinois. Rumor had it that they were headed for Florence, Alabama, or perhaps Memphis, Tennessee, via the upriver town of Savannah, Tennessee. At any rate, they would be going southward, up the river, deeper into the territory claimed by the Rebels.[56]

Very few of the troops mentioned Grant's removal in their diaries or letters. He had led them to victory, but they had not had time to grow attached to him. When the news got around, a number of the men gathered on shore in front of *Tigress* to show their support, but the change otherwise passed with little notice. Smith was a highly respected officer, and the men were apparently just as ready to march and fight under him as under Grant.

Some of the officers realized more fully what the army was losing. Several of them—Logan, Oglesby, Cook, and Lawler among others—had gone together to order Grant a magnificent sword in celebration of his victory at Fort Donelson. It arrived shortly after the army shifted back to the Tennessee River, and the officers presented it to Grant aboard *Tigress* while the army was preparing to move up the river. Unofficial word had arrived by this time that several of them were to be promoted to brigadier general at Grant's recommendation. Now with Grant effectively relieved of command and the army about to leave without him, the scene took on added poignancy. Grant was so moved that he had to leave the room to avoid showing emotion. Later, after the delegation of colonels had left, Grant showed the sword to a staff member. "Send it to my wife," said Grant sadly. "I will never wear a sword again."[57]

Smith arrived with his troops, having been released by Buell and returned from Nashville. He and Grant still had a warm relationship. Grant deeply respected him, appreciated his service at Fort Donelson, and believed him the most fit man to command the army.[58] Yet, when Medical Director John H. Brinton observed the two men aboard *Tigress* in the last few days before the expedition set out, he noticed that "there was an unconscious deference on the part of Smith to Grant as a soldier. It was apart from rank; it seemed indescribable; but it was there, it was the recognition of the master." Brinton remembered the two walking up and down the deck of *Tigress* together the evening before the expedition sailed and thought that their relationship seemed "stronger than ever."[59]

The first troops to start up the river belonged to a division new to the Army of the Tennessee. Brig. Gen. William Tecumseh Sherman's division had organized at Paducah during February, mostly from new regiments just arriving from their home states.[60] Sherman's Fifth Division was almost as solidly composed of Ohioans as McClernand's First was of Illinoisans. Nine of Sherman's twelve regiments were from the Buckeye State.

Their division commander was a remarkable man, a nervous, talkative genius whose mind seemed incapable of rest. A journalist described him as "a 'bundle of nerves,' all strung to the highest tension."[61] Two years older than Grant and his senior in rank until Grant's recent promotion to major general, Sherman was the brother of prominent Ohio Republican senator John Sherman. A graduate of West Point and a veteran of the Old Army,

Sherman, like Grant, had left the army but had been unable to achieve success in the civilian world. Thus far in the war, he did not appear to be doing much better in the military world. Appointed colonel of the newly organized 13th U.S. Infantry, Sherman had done well at the otherwise disastrous July 1861 First Battle of Bull Run. Thereafter, he succeeded to command of Union forces in Kentucky east of the Cumberland River, and that assignment had not gone so well. Nervous and excitable, Sherman had come to believe that the Confederates in massive force were about to sweep all the way to the Ohio and had belabored the authorities in Washington with dispatches that sounded downright panicky. In November 1861, Washington sacked him in favor of Buell. Unfriendly newspapers suggested that Sherman had become deranged.[62]

The Kentucky episode might have ended Sherman's career had he not possessed a brother in the Senate. The day after Fort Henry's fall, Halleck had assigned Sherman to command the District of Cairo, including the post of Paducah, in place of Grant, who was formally reassigned to the District of West Tennessee.[63] In that capacity, Sherman had energetically forwarded troops and supplies to Grant and had rebuffed Halleck's overtures toward having him replace Grant. Repeatedly during the siege, he had written him brief notes of encouragement.[64]

At Sherman's request, Halleck ordered him to join the Tennessee River expedition under Smith with most of the troops at Paducah as his division. They were an inexperienced lot. Eight of the Ohio regiments were so new that they had first received their weapons within the past fortnight. The 53rd Ohio received its rifles on the same day it boarded the steamer in preparation to go up the river.[65] Sherman dispatched his troop-laden steamboats on March 6 and 7 and followed them the next day. Arriving at Fort Henry on March 9, he consulted with Smith, who gave him orders for the movement up the Tennessee River. The destination would be Savannah, Tennessee, just thirty-four miles from the strategic rail junction at Corinth, Mississippi. The expedition would start on March 10, with Sherman's green division in the lead.[66]

The first vessels of the main expedition got under way on the morning of March 10, and others followed throughout the next twenty-four hours.[67] The soldiers always found massed movements by steamboat to be some of the most awe-inspiring sights they ever witnessed. Steamboats had been plying the Western waters for scarcely a generation, and many of the soldiers had never ridden one before joining the army. Now here were more steamboats than they had ever seen before moving together up the river, all heavily laden with troops, guns, and horses.

The weather had turned fair at last, balmy and springlike in contrast to recent gray skies and snow. The river and the land were beautiful under blue skies and blazing sunshine. Six hundred yards wide, the Tennessee ran high and strong. The banks were steep, and behind them rose heavily wooded hills lining the horizon on either side. Closer to the river, in the willow thickets and canebrakes and on the overhanging red maples, buds were beginning to appear, adding a touch of spring green to the somber hues of the forest. To almost all the soldiers of the Army of the Tennessee, the river above Fort Henry was an unknown stream, its every bend revealing new vistas.[68]

Through this idyllic scene churned score upon score of vessels that were among the fastest and most powerful products of the technology of the day. "Up and down as far as the eye could see were steamers crowded with blue coats," recalled a soldier, "and still farther, hidden by the bends of the river, we could hear the puffing and snorting and see the smoke curling upward from still other steamers."[69] Few soldiers who later wrote an account of this day failed to mention "the black smoke from more than a hundred tall pipes" that "rolled away in clouds over the forest."[70] To a soldier in the 14th Illinois, "it was a sublime spectacle, far exceeding anything we ever saw. Behind us, down the river, the sky was obscured by dense clouds of smoke, looking like angry storms; while in every other direction it was . . . pure and stainless . . . blue."[71] To the soldiers, those clouds of black coal smoke meant progress and power, the might of a free people and a free market, now harnessed in the cause of liberty and the survival of the world's boldest experiment in self-government.

Most of all, the power of the great republic was represented in the soldiers themselves, who packed every steamboat, lining the rails, observing one another across the sparkling waters of the river, and marveling at the might of the army of which they were a part. "We will live long without seeing such a sight again," wrote an officer of the 3rd Iowa. "A grand army, equipped in splendor and exulting in success, moving far into the enemy's country with the speed of steam. . . . It was a glorious sight, and we could not tire of gazing. From it every soldier seemed to catch a sense of the great moment of the enterprise, and of his own dignity as an agent in it."[72]

Yet conditions on board the steamboats were not ideal. Because there were not enough vessels to carry the entire army at one time, orders were to "place as many on each boat as can be taken, having due regard to the health and comfort of the men."[73] The men's comfort, however, was not much consulted in the matter. "In fact," wrote Sergeant Kiner, "there was not room enough for our men to lay with any kind of comfort."[74]

Crowded as they were, the men of the 48th Ohio had to share their steamer with 200 head of beef cattle, and all the regiments had four-legged company on this cruise. The officers' mounts and regimental draft animals had to be accommodated. A soldier of the 55th Illinois estimated that at this time his regiment had twenty-six six-mule wagons. As Kiner observed, this "necessarily created a great deal of filth, and made the situation of our men more disagreeable." In his boat, which was typical, "there was a large pile of coal, and rows of pork barrels along beside the engines, which only left a very narrow space between them for men to lay." Kiner spent most of the night standing up, listening to the groaning of a friend who was vainly trying to sleep in a very uncomfortable position spanning the heads of three barrels.[75]

Bucking the swift current and stopping occasionally for firewood, some of the overloaded steamboats took more than twenty-four hours to cover the hundred miles to Savannah, where the first transports began arriving on the evening of March 11. Along the way, the men saw many of the local populace who turned out to view the spectacle of the passing fleet. Because the boats often hugged the shorelines in order to avoid the strong current in midstream, encounters with civilians were often close enough for shouted greetings. Most of the population of the Tennessee Valley was Unionist, and their reactions to the expedition were another factor that made the trip exciting for the soldiers. "Men, women, and children, gathered on the high banks, and on the hillsides adjacent to the river," recalled Cpl. Charles Wright, were "waving hats and handkerchiefs, some shouting at the top of their voices, clapping hands." Wright and his comrades could distinctly hear the words "God bless you" coming from the onlookers, some of whom waved United States flags, which the soldiers surmised had been kept hidden in recent months.[76]

Not all of those along the river were friendly, however. Near Fort Henry, the 48th Ohio was passing close to a high bank where, as a member of the regiment described the scene, "a number of women and children were cheering us, by waving their handkerchiefs. When just above them, among the cedars, there was heard the sharp crack of a musket." They heard the sound of the passing musket ball and buckshot too, and one member of the regiment found a buckshot stuck in his coat collar. The Rebel bushwhacker made off through the woods. "This being the first shot the regiment had received from the Rebels," a member recalled, "it created considerable excitement."[77] The 15th Illinois fared worse. From the cover of a thicket, a company of Confederate cavalry fired a surprise volley into the 15th's boat, wounding two men. As the men of the 15th scrambled for their rifles to return fire, one man's weapon went off, fatally shooting one of his comrades in the head.[78] Other sniper incidents resulted in several casualties.[79]

The army remained at Savannah for several days, many of the troops still "jammed and crammed" aboard the steamers, as one of them described their lot.[80] Those who did go ashore received a warm welcome from both whites and blacks, and a number of regiments added Tennessee recruits to their numbers.[81]

Will Wallace's brigade was one of those that disembarked at Savannah. He found it "a quiet sober looking old town, with a single street, a square brick court house, a number of buildings scattered along the street, with some pretty & rather stylish residences in the suburbs." While scouting a camping place for his troops, he met two ladies who greeted him with "Hurrah for the Union!"

"God bless you for saying that," replied Wallace.[82]

Meanwhile, Smith proceeded to the purpose for the expedition. He made plans to break railroads both east and north of the key junction town of Corinth—the Memphis & Charleston east, the Mobile & Ohio north. For the latter target, Smith chose Lew Wallace's division. On the evening of March 12, he took a small boat out to Wallace's headquarters steamer and explained to him the plan for cutting the Mobile & Ohio at Purdy, Tennessee. "I might have sent you an order," Smith explained, "and left you to your own devices, but knowing it is a business new to you, I have come over to try and help you with suggestions." Wallace was grateful. After giving thorough instructions for the operation, Smith headed back to his small boat.

Wallace walked with him to the side of the steamer where it was moored. "He gave me his hand with a friendly good night," Wallace wrote. Perhaps the bitterness that had begun between these two men back at Paducah the winter before was now fading. Smith stooped to get into his boat, lost his balance, and toppled forward, as Wallace recalled, "raking the sharp edge of a seat, and skinning one of his shins from the ankle to the knee—a frightful hurt." The boat crew helped him up, and Wallace urged him to stay aboard that night and let the Third Division staff surgeon look at that leg. "No," replied Smith between clenched teeth, "too much business."[83]

Wallace immediately sent word to his brigade commanders and later claimed that he thought they had their steamers under way before Smith's boat reached the shore. At any rate, the division moved without delay five miles up the river to Crump's Landing, marched inland to Purdy, and successfully destroyed a half-mile-long trestle over a flooded swamp north of

Purdy. Wallace then encamped his division, with one brigade at Crump's Landing, another one two miles inland at Stoney Lonesome, and the third yet another two miles to the west at Adamsville.[84]

As soon as he received word of Wallace's success on the morning of March 14, Smith sent orders for Sherman to break the Memphis & Charleston Railroad somewhere east of Corinth, preferably "in the neighborhood of Burnsville," Mississippi, only twelve miles from the nearest point on the river and the location of valuable railroad repair shops. Sherman received the order at ten o'clock, and his division was in motion by noon. Before leaving, he hurried off a message to Smith, reminding him that his division would have to pass Pittsburg Landing, only ten miles upstream, and suggesting that it might be a good idea to have one of the other divisions take possession of the place lest the Rebels, who had been reported in the area, should reinforce and threaten to cut off Sherman's division above Pittsburg Landing.[85]

Escorted by the gunboat *Tyler,* the division proceeded up the river in its nineteen steamboats. They continued all the way to Eastport, Mississippi, about thirty miles above Savannah. Rebel troops were in evidence there, so the flotilla dropped back down the river about two miles to a place called Tyler's Landing at the mouth of Yellow Creek. They arrived there at 7:00 p.m., and Sherman immediately began disembarking his battalion of cavalry. Rain had fallen all day, though now the weather showed signs of clearing off. Still, the river was high and the ground muddy. Unloading the horses took time, and it was 11:00 before the horsemen rode off into the night on what would now be a nineteen-mile trip. If all went well, they should be near Burnsville by 4:00 a.m., March 15.[86]

Meanwhile, the task of disembarking the infantry and artillery continued. Sherman's plan was to take his infantry about halfway to Burnsville to support the cavalry. Since he had four infantry brigades and they would take considerable time to unload at this half-flooded landing, he would start one at 3:00 a.m., another at 4:00, and the other two at daylight, about 6:00. The rain began again, "as though the windows of heaven had opened," recalled a soldier of the 55th Illinois. As the troops left the boats, they stood in the downpour on the muddy top of the natural levee.[87]

The unloading got behind schedule, and it was daylight before the head of the column left the levee and plunged into the thigh-deep waters of the flooded lower-lying bottomland behind it. After "wallowing and wading" half a mile they reached the bluffs. The going was easier then, but every ravine held a roaring brook, and every stream was a flood. A courier caught up with Sherman at the head of the column to tell him that the water level in the river and the adjoining flooded bottomland was rising at a rate of six inches per hour. Sherman sent back word for the last two brigades not even to leave the landing. Finally the column came to a watercourse, four and a half miles out, that was beyond all fording. Bridging efforts were hampered by the rapidly rising water and took several hours. The cavalry had crossed this stream hours earlier, before it was so high, but the rising waters of other streams at length forced the horsemen to turn back without accomplishing their purpose.[88]

The command almost could not reach the landing again. After struggling across many flooded streams, they came to the top of the bluffs to find the bottomland a lake and the natural levee rapidly disappearing. The soldiers of the two brigades left at the landing had been forced to reembark. Sherman decided to try sending the artillery across the bottomland, but the result was even worse than feared. The artillerymen had to cut the traces to save the horses from drowning. They recovered the abandoned cannon "by the use of long ropes," enabling them to "drag the guns under water through the bayous to reach the bank of the river." Yawls ferried the infantry out to the steamers, and, at about 6:00 p.m., March 15, the cold, wet, tired, and bedraggled expedition steamed away. The river had risen fifteen feet in the past twenty-three hours, and Tyler's Landing, which had been ten feet above water level, was now five feet under.[89]

After casting about for a more propitious landing site and finding all the possibilities in the area inundated, Sherman gave up and took the fleet back down the river. At Pittsburg Landing he encountered not the Rebels but rather Hurlbut's Fourth Division, disembarking from its steamboats and filing up a single road that led to the top of the eighty-foot bluff. Sherman left his own division moored there with Hurlbut's boats and took only his own boat downriver to consult with Smith at Savannah. Smith's orders were to disembark both Sherman's Fifth Division and Hurlbut's Fourth at Pittsburg Landing and move them inland far enough to afford room for the rest of the army to camp between them and the river. Once the whole force was on hand, Smith would lead a forward movement that would accomplish the assigned task of breaking the Memphis & Charleston Railroad.[90]

During the next several days, Sherman's and Hurlbut's divisions, followed by McClernand's and Smith's, came ashore at Pittsburg Landing and moved back into the countryside to camp. The area impressed one Illinois soldier as being "almost a perfect wilderness."[91] The riverbanks in either direction were heavily wooded, with great trees overhanging the water. Beyond the narrow strip of bottomland at the landing rose the bluffs, the edge of a rolling plateau that stretched far inland. The plateau was cut by numerous deep, steep, and rugged ravines, one of which opened onto the river adjacent to the landing, offering an opportunity for the single road to climb its slope in order to reach the plateau.[92]

Pittsburg Landing amounted to very little as a settlement, boasting only a couple of dilapidated log buildings, one of which had pretensions to being a store. Of far more interest to the arriving soldiers was the residue of the March 1 fight between a U.S. Navy gunboat and Confederate troops. Some of the latter had been killed in action and buried in shallow graves that the recent rains had reopened. The only other noticeable feature atop the bluffs, aside from the seemingly endless forest, was a road, which led away from the landing and eventually reached Corinth, twenty-five miles away. A mile or two inland, other roads branched off, one leading to Crump's Landing, five miles down the river (north), and another to the hamlet of Hamburg, about the same distance upstream (south). The Corinth Road branched a little more than a mile from the landing into the main Corinth Road and the Eastern Corinth Road, which rejoined about four miles out. Ambling more or less athwart these various roads, about two miles from the landing, was another connecting Hamburg and Purdy.[93]

In obedience to Smith's orders, Sherman positioned his division to cover a large enough area for the entire army to encamp. He sent one brigade, Col. David Stuart's, about a mile and half out on the road to Hamburg. The other three brigades he placed side by side covering the main Corinth Road a little more than two miles from the landing. While Hurlbut's regiments camped wherever they found a cleared field or a spring of good water, Sherman had his camps laid out so that when each regiment fell in on its color line, the division, or at least the three brigades on the main Corinth Road, would be more or less in line of battle, facing toward Corinth.[94] The division's camps ran along a gentle ridge perpendicular to the road, and where the ridge crossed the road, Sherman made his headquarters in a little log building that on Sundays hitherto had been used by a congregation of local Methodists. They called it Shiloh Church.

CHAPTER NINE

"We Are Attacked!"

WE HAVE A VERY PRETTY place to camp," wrote Lt. John Puter-baugh to his wife back in Salem, Illinois.[1] Pleasant times seemed at hand for the men of the Army of the Tennessee in their camps behind Pitts-burg Landing. Most of the regiments were enjoying the best campsites they had occupied since leaving their hometowns. "All the camps were beauti-ful," recalled an Illinois soldier, "convenient and healthy, with wood, water and parade ground close at hand. The scenery abounded in deep ravines, sparkling waters, rugged bluffs and beautiful foliage."[2] The men, who had been sleeping in the open air or on the crowded steamboats for weeks, now lived in Sibley tents. A conical tent, patterned after the teepees of the Plains Indians and accommodating from twelve to fifteen men, the Sibley was a universal favorite of Civil War soldiers.[3]

The weather remained highly variable through mid-March, with even a couple of unseasonably late snow flurries, but already the peach orchards, of which there were many in this region, were beginning to blossom in pink. The pear trees bloomed too, as did the wild plums and early spring wildflowers. Then the last week of the month the weather turned warm, "extremely warm," wrote Puterbaugh, "so much so that one could hardly be comfortable in the shade."[4] The roads began to be dusty, and those regi-ments that had not camped near good springs found the search for drinking water growing more difficult.[5] All this was "a sort of tropical revelation to these lusty Northern soldiers," recalled a member of the 55th Illinois. "It was a striking contrast to those who had been accustomed to the blustering, cold winds of March, as they rush to and fro over the prairies of Illinois."[6]

The season advanced apace. "Vegetation is starting," wrote Will Wal-lace to his wife, Ann, near the end of the month. "The trees are covered with a green haze."[7] Along with the squirrels, raccoons, and possums, small lizards and snakes began to appear as springtime brought the forest to life.[8] Jonathan Labrant and some of his friends in the 58th Illinois even tried going swimming in the river. "Water very cold," he wrote in his diary that night.[9]

"It is a great sight to pass through the camp and see the men drilling," wrote Capt. Luther Cowan of the 45th Illinois, "for we are all drilling as much as possible, expecting a big fight and wishing to be prepared."[10] Yet life was far from drudgery here in what another Illinois soldier called "this sylvan retreat."[11] Soldiers of the 81st Ohio, having no bricks, made bake ovens out of mud, and the regiment relished the taste of soft biscuits after weeks of hardtack.[12] Company D of the 6th Iowa found a little gristmill powered by the waters of Owl Creek, near their camp, and put it to work grinding corn for the soldiers' use. They also went fishing in the creek.[13]

In the pleasant circumstances, the soldiers' youthful high spirits resurfaced. "There was much fun in camp over the tricks of some of the boys in selling out the rest with all kinds of joshes," wrote the 11th Iowa's William Wade in his diary for April Fool's Day.[14] More organized sorts of fun were popular too. "Playing ball was all the rage today," wrote Lt. Douglas Hapeman of the 11th Illinois in his diary for March 26.[15] The boys of the University Recruits, Company C, 12th Iowa, were a long way now from Upper Iowa University, but they still liked to indulge their taste for both "drive ball," or baseball, as well as "wicket-ball," probably cricket.[16] The men of the 58th Illinois pitched horseshoes, and Jonathan Labrant accidentally hit one of his buddies in the head—no serious damage done.[17]

Pvt. Lucius "Lute" Barber of the 15th Illinois summed up the soldiers' circumstances as March gave way to April. "The weather was delightful," Barber wrote. "Spring had just begun to open and the grand old forest was putting on its leafy covering. Our mail came regularly and we were happy as mortals could be under the circumstances."[18]

At Army of the Tennessee headquarters, ten miles back down the river at Savannah, another change of command took place in mid-March. Grant was back. He had had a very bad two weeks but had maintained his presence of mind under Halleck's bombardment of scolding. In calm tones, Grant had written to his superior, explaining his actions and showing that he was innocent of the accusations, which Grant thought originated not with Halleck but with those above him in Washington. That was exactly what Halleck wanted Grant to think. Then, however, Grant, or someone on his staff, did something that Halleck had not counted on and forwarded copies of the entire correspondence to Elihu Washburne, Grant's congressional patron. Washburne went to Lincoln, who was in any case inclined to support Grant because of his recent victories and because he seemed to be the only army commander the Union had who was not afraid to fight. At the president's behest, Adjutant General Lorenzo Thomas telegraphed Halleck demanding a full report on exactly what it was that Grant had done wrong.[19]

It was a gilt-edged presidential invitation to put up or shut up. Halleck apparently got wind of it a few days before Thomas issued the directive. Old Brains lost no time in slithering out of the way. A few days earlier, Lincoln had removed McClellan as commander of all Union armies nationwide and had promoted Halleck to command all Union armies west of the Appalachians. Having achieved what he long had wanted, Halleck had less desire than ever to have his duplicitous correspondence with Grant scrutinized closely in Washington.[20]

In response to a letter from Grant suggesting "I must have enemies between you and myself," Halleck replied, "You are mistaken. There is no enemy between you and me." He was right about that. Just then Halleck was the worst enemy Grant had. To Grant's request that he be removed from serving under Halleck, the latter replied, "You cannot be relieved from your command. There is no good reason for it. I am certain that all which the authorities in Washington ask, is, that you enforce discipline and punish the disorderly. The power is in your hands; use it, and you will be sustained by all above you. Instead of relieving you, I wish you, as soon as your new army is in the field, to assume the immediate command and lead it on to new victories." To General Thomas's query, Halleck hastily replied that all was now well with Grant.[21]

So Grant boarded a steamboat and rode up the Tennessee to take command once again of the army that already bore the stamp of his personality. He arrived at Savannah on March 17 and made his headquarters in the two-story brick mansion of the leading Union man in the area, W. H. Cherry.[22] Grant found Smith happy to see him but not in good health. The injury to the shin he had received falling into the small boat was becoming inflamed, and the old general could hardly get around. Presently he took to his bed in the Cherry Mansion.

Along with his orders to resume command, Grant also received from Halleck the strictest orders not to do anything that would bring on an engagement. Halleck knew his man well by this time, for Grant was eager to take the offensive against the Confederate force that Gen. Albert Sidney Johnston was reported to be assembling at Corinth, only twenty-five miles from Pittsburg Landing. Yet Halleck had no sooner returned Grant to his command than Old Brains nearly made the mistake of giving his subordinate the opportunity to slip his leash again and proceed toward the winning of the war without a proper regard for bureaucratic detail or Halleck's personal glory. On March 18, he wired Grant to say that he had received a report that the Rebels were abandoning Corinth and moving north so as to take up a position on the Tennessee River below (i.e., in rear of) Grant's army at Savannah. If that was so, Halleck continued, then the Union forces at Pittsburg Landing should strike southwestward and "destroy railroad connection at Corinth."[23]

Grant did not for a moment believe the Rebels were doing any such thing, as indeed they were not, but he saw in this an opportunity to resume the initiative against the Confederates. "Immediate preparations will be made to execute your perfectly feasible order," he wrote back to Halleck. "I will go in person, leaving Genl McClernand in command here," that is, in Savannah.[24] To Smith, Grant issued an order to get the troops ready to go. "Hold all the command at Pittsburg subject to marching orders at any time," Grant directed. "Troops will march with three days rations in Haversack, and seven in wagons," and Grant proceeded with other specifics of how he wanted the expedition organized. He also ordered McClernand to send two of his three brigades from Savannah to Pittsburg Landing at once. No need to leave the politician too large a garrison at Savannah, and Grant wanted to take every possible man to fight the Rebels at Corinth.[25]

Yet Grant was not irresponsible, nor was he seeking an excuse to disobey his orders—just to interpret them in the manner most conducive to Union success. Considering the muddy and difficult state of the roads leading inland from Pittsburg Landing as well as his own intelligence that additional Confederate troops were constantly arriving at Corinth, he suspended the advance until he could get further orders from Halleck. "Corinth cannot be taken without a general engagement," Grant wrote to the department commander, "which from your instructions is to be avoided."[26] Halleck, realizing the mistake he had nearly made, lost no time in setting Grant straight. "By all means keep your forces together until you connect with General Buell," he telegraphed next day. "Don't let the enemy draw you into an engagement now. Wait till you are properly fortified and receive orders."[27]

Johnston's numbers were variously estimated all the way up to 200,000 men, though that figure was patently ridiculous. Grant, who believed Confederate numbers at Corinth were closer to 20,000, felt he could defeat them because the Southern soldiers would be demoralized by recent Union successes. "The temper of the rebel troops is such that there is but little doubt but that Corinth will fall much more easily than Donelson did, when we do move," Grant wrote to Halleck. "All accounts agree in saying that the great mass of the Rank and file are heartily tired."[28]

In fact, Johnston's forces were both less demoralized than Grant thought and less numerous than some sources reported. Had Grant been allowed to advance, he would in all probability have succeeded in taking Corinth within a week or two, though a large battle would probably have resulted. That, however, can never be more than speculation, for Grant was not permitted to make the experiment. Halleck's plan was for Grant to remain planted in the neighborhood of Pittsburg Landing while Buell marched his army overland from Nashville. When those two forces joined at Pittsburg Landing, along with other troops Halleck had ordered up, then Halleck would take personal command and lead the mighty host against Corinth.[29]

Grant's soldiers shared his eagerness to advance and impatience with a delay they instinctively knew could not serve the interests of their cause. Lt. John Puterbaugh of the 15th Illinois wrote, "All seem anxious to be on the move and strike down this rebellion at the earliest moment."[30] Capt. Levi Coman of the 76th Ohio added the reason why: "I long for the order to go forward," Coman wrote. "I cannot bear delay. Every day spent in idle camp life seems like one day farther from home."[31] These pleasant days might be a welcome change from the hard times in February, but sitting in camp was not going to win the war and allow them to go home. For these Midwesterners determined to save the Union, the road home led southward.

Grant's soldiers were convinced, however, that sooner or later their army would advance and give the Rebels battle someplace between Pittsburg Landing and Corinth. "All expect a heavy battle here before long," wrote Abram Vanauken of the 17th Illinois.[32] The soldiers were confident of victory, and many of them hoped that this victory, or perhaps just a few more after it, would win the war. The 6th Iowa's William Richardson wrote, "The roads will be ready to move over in a few days and then God keep the Rebel soldiers for the Lincolnites will not. . . . A few more fights gained by the gallant volunteers, [and] the fuss will be over."[33]

While Grant and his soldiers chafed to advance, McClernand had his own concerns. He had written to Lincoln two days after the surrender of Fort Donelson, sending his laudatory order to his division. He wrote again near the end of the month, complaining that "as a non-regular officer but little can reach you concerning me through official channels." He reiterated to the president how his division had been "first to reach Camp Halleck; Fort Henry, Fort Donelson and Clarksville," and had done most of the fighting along the way. Lincoln, he complained, had not done him justice, presumably by not promoting him to major general at the same time he promoted Grant. At the bottom he wrote a postscript: "I desire this note may come to the President's personal notice."[34]

On March 21, McClernand got the coveted second star, but ten days later he wrote the president again, enclosing a copy of his report of the Battle of Fort Donelson. The report was, as Grant would later tactfully observe, "a little highly colored as to the conduct of the First Division." It also falsely claimed that McClernand had suggested the February 15 counterattack that had led to the surrender of Fort Donelson.[35] But McClernand had more than that to say to Lincoln. Coming to the point, the general wrote, "If you will give me an independent command, in an active and contested field, I will try and reward your confidence with success."[36] For now, Lincoln did not see fit to grant McClernand's request, but the general would keep trying.

Troops continued to arrive at Pittsburg Landing. The remaining brigades of McClernand's and Smith's divisions moved up the river from Savannah during the last week of March, and new troops continued steadily arriving from the North.[37] On March 26, Grant's onetime superior and later fractious subordinate during their service in Missouri, Benjamin Prentiss, reported for duty, and Grant assigned him "to the command of the unattached troops at Pittsburg, Tenn.," with instructions that "as fast as troops arrive they will be brigaded and brigades formed into a division, which will be known as the Sixth Division, and commanded by General Prentiss."[38]

Among the units joining Prentiss's new division was the 16th Wisconsin. The regiment marched out of Camp Randall at Madison 1,000-strong on the Ides of March. Fourteen inches of snow lay on the ground as they boarded the train for Chicago and points south. They crossed the Illinois prairies, sodden but no longer frozen, reached St. Louis, and boarded the steamboat that would take them down the Mississippi and up the Ohio and the Tennessee. South of Paducah, they noticed that "the trees were budding and some had leaves out." On March 20, they disembarked at balmy Pittsburg Landing, just five days out of the snows of Wisconsin. Capt. Henry Culbertson wrote to his family back in Eau Claire, "The woods are alive with men in all directions," bands were playing and bugles blowing, and "you can hear rifles cracking everywhere," as ill-disciplined soldiers shot at small game or "slow deer," or simply wanted to make sure they had dry loads in their weapons after a rainy night. The men of the 16th were definitely not among those firing off their weapons. They had as yet not been issued any ammunition for their Belgian rifles.[39]

Other regiments, equally green, joined the new Sixth Division from

Missouri, Iowa, Michigan, and Illinois. An officer from one of the experienced regiments recalled one of the new men, just a few hours off the boat,
approaching him to ask "if I would kindly show him which end of the bullet should be put into the gun first." The embarrassed soldier was apparently reluctant to reveal his ignorance to his comrades in his own
regiment.[40] Within ten days, Prentiss had one brigade and the beginning of
another encamped on the outer edge of the army, between Sherman's three
brigades near Shiloh Church and his separated brigade on the Hamburg-
Purdy Road.

Grant kept his headquarters in Savannah in order to be able to make
contact with Buell, who was approaching from the northeast, as soon as
possible. He had been content to have Sherman in command of the
encampment at Pittsburg Landing, but once McClernand and Smith arrived
there, that was no longer possible, since both outranked Sherman. Grant
designated Smith to command the encampment, but then the issue arose as
to whether he ranked McClernand. Both men had been promoted to major
general on the same day, March 21. Grant saw no solution for it but to establish his own headquarters at Pittsburg Landing. First, however, he wanted
to wait until he could contact Buell.[41]

Smith was incapacitated by illness and unable to remain with his division; so on April 3, Grant assigned Will Wallace, recently promoted to
brigadier general, to take over the Second Division.[42] It was a heady move
for Wallace, who ten days earlier had written Ann regarding his promotion
to brigadier general, "I shall strive to do my duty relying on our Father for
strength, courage, & wisdom to aid me."[43] For the time being, Sherman
continued to command the encampment at Pittsburg Landing, but that
would have to change once official notice of McClernand's promotion to
major general arrived. Grant hoped by that time to be present at Pittsburg
Landing in person, thus avoiding the specter of having McClernand in
command of five divisions of troops.[44]

The regiments continued to drill diligently. "The officers are putting us
through as if the salvation of the country depended on it," wrote the 11th
Iowa's William Wade.[45] There were big reviews too, a whole brigade or
even division at one time, in the few large open fields available here and
there in the woods. These events were impressive spectacles to the new soldiers. "It is a Splendid Sight to see 12 regts. all armed and equipped, with
Bayonets and Swords gleaming in the bright Sun Shine," wrote Lt. John
Puterbaugh regarding a review of Hurlbut's Fourth Division on the last
day of March. "All drew up in line of Battle, then threw into Divisions

[units of two companies] and marched up in Solid Column."[46] McClernand's First Division had its own "grand review" on April 3.[47]

Meanwhile, beyond the picket lines, patrols were making contact with the enemy with increasing frequency. Rumors vibrated through the camps. When James Oates returned from sick leave on April 3, his friends told him "that there was picket fighting at the front and that a general engagement would soon take place."[48] Sgt. Charles L. Sumbardo's regiment, the 12th Iowa, was encamped not far from a detachment of cavalry that was involved in patrolling beyond the picket lines. On April 3, some of the cavalrymen told him that they had encountered a strong enemy formation at the little hamlet of Monterey, twelve miles from Pittsburg Landing, less than ten from the nearest Union camps.[49]

The frontline brigade and regimental commanders had their men patrolling well out from the camps. That same Thursday, April 3, Col. Ralph Buckland's brigade of Sherman's division pushed out about five miles from Shiloh Church on the road to Corinth, more for exercise than for scouting. The brigade halted to take its noon meal and sent pickets farther down the road. These men ran into a party of Confederate pickets and exchanged shots. Some of Buckland's men thought they heard the long roll sounding in nearby camps that could only be Confederate. Buckland and his officers held a hasty consultation and decided to return to Shiloh Church—Sherman's orders were "not to be drawn into battle."[50] From the camps of Prentiss's division, a battalion probed forward about the same distance that day without contacting the enemy.[51]

Life in the camps continued to be almost festive. That evening, after the grand review of McClernand's division, "the splendid band of the Lead Mine Regiment," the 45th Illinois, serenaded General McClernand at his headquarters. In the custom of the time, McClernand "responded in a stirring speech to his men."[52]

Friday, April 4, brought intermittent thunderstorms and a shower of hail. That morning a captain and two enlisted men of the 77th Ohio, Sherman's division, strolled forward from their camp through the woods to the edge of a nearby farm. Standing by the fence and looking across the fields in front of them, they saw, several hundred yards away, an enormous encampment of Confederates—infantry, cavalry, and artillery—apparently just getting breakfast. The captain sent one of the enlisted men, Sgt. C. J. Eagler, hurrying back to camp to report. Eagler spoke to the major of the 77th, who hurried to pass the word up the chain of command. Some minutes later a message came back from Sherman. Sergeant Eagler was to be placed under arrest "for bringing a false report into camp." His captain ignored the order.[53]

Others noticed the Rebel presence. As Col. Everett Peabody reviewed his brigade of Prentiss's division between thundershowers that day, many soldiers noticed the presence of a squad of Rebel cavalry lurking in the woods on the far side of the field and wondered why nothing was done about them.[54]

That evening, during one of the thunderstorms, Rebel cavalry struck at outposts of Sherman's division. Firing became fairly heavy in the sector and included artillery. The Confederates captured two officers and seven enlisted men along the picket line. One camp rumor had it that the luckless captives had been taken while playing euchre. In the ensuing skirmish, each side lost several killed and wounded. A brigade of Sherman's division pursued the retiring Confederate horsemen and captured several of them.[55]

Throughout the Union camps, colonels had their drummers beat the long roll, the signal for the men to fall in, ready for battle. Down at the landing, Capt. Andrew Hickenlooper's 5th Battery, Ohio Light Artillery, had just finished unloading from the steamboat that had brought it up the river and had set up a temporary camp. Shortly after the sound of "heavy skirmish firing" came orders to hurry forward and join Prentiss's division on the front line. Various infantry formations started forward, but the firing soon stopped as the Rebel cavalry rode off into the night with their prisoners. After standing under arms for several hours, the regiments turned and marched back to their camps.[56]

Ten miles away in Savannah, Grant heard the sound of artillery coming from Pittsburg Landing. He spent most of his days at the army's camps but the nights at the Cherry Mansion in Savannah. He now lost no time heading upriver in his headquarters steamboat, *Tigress*. Arriving at the landing, he disembarked with his horse, mounted, and rode up the steep, muddy road toward the encampments. "The night was one of impenetrable darkness," Grant recalled, "with rain pouring down in torrents; nothing was visible to the eye except as revealed by the frequent flashes of lightning." He had to trust the horse to pick its steps. Not far from the landing, he met Will Wallace together with McPherson. They assured him that all was quiet again at the front, and Grant turned back toward the landing. As he rode through the rain-soaked darkness, his horse slipped and went down hard, right on Grant's leg. "My ankle was very much injured," Grant wrote, "so much so that my boot had to be cut off." For the next several days, he would be able to walk only with crutches.[57]

Hickenlooper never got his battery up to Prentiss's camps that night.

The captain rode ahead of his guns to find the way, and by the time he reached Prentiss, the latter told him the excitement was over and he could bring up his guns in the morning. As Hickenlooper rode back to his battery, he encountered a detachment escorting Confederate prisoners to the rear amid occasional taunts and jeers from Union soldiers. One Federal called out to ask if there were enough "Graybacks" left out in the woods to "make interesting hunting."

"Yes," replied one of the Rebels with spirit, "more than you'ns have ever seen . . . and if you all ain't mighty careful, they'll run you into hell or the river before tomorrow night."[58]

Thunderstorms continued to roll across the Tennessee Valley that night, with torrential rains and high winds, while rumors buzzed through the camps again.[59] Capt. E. C. Dawes of the 53rd Ohio heard that Confederate prisoners were being kept at Shiloh Church and had made statements similar to those Hickenlooper recalled.[60] That rumor was correct. Sgt. Edward Gordon of the 57th Ohio, encamped on the south side of the church, talked to one of them through the chinks in the logs. "You'uns will catch hell tomorrow!" warned the Rebel.[61] Sergeant Sumbardo of the 12th Iowa had his own source of information in the nearby cavalry detachment. They told him that night that the enemy had a powerful force only six miles from the Union outposts.[62]

Lieutenant Colonel Ellis of the 15th Illinois, in Hurlbut's division, may have heard some of the rumors, or he may simply have had a hunch. On Hurlbut's orders, the onetime banker from Rockford, Illinois, had marched his regiment to the front during the fracas on the skirmish lines. Then when nothing came of it, he marched the 15th back to its camp. Before dismissing the men to their tents, however, Ellis had a few words he wanted to say to them. It was a measure of the deep respect the men had for their lieutenant colonel that they did no grumbling at having to stand and listen to him on this stormy night. He spoke of "his connection with the regiment, how pleasant it had been, how he loved it and how proud he was of it." A battle would take place very soon, he told them, and he wanted every man to do his duty no matter what might happen. The 15th was made up of quiet, unemotional men from Illinois's northern tier of counties, but Ellis's speech "brought tears to many eyes."[63]

Sherman was not at all of Ellis's opinion. He believed the Rebels were not going to attack but would stay in Corinth and await the approach of the Union army. The various skirmishes and contact reports reflected merely the presence of some marauding Rebel cavalry, and Sherman became annoyed when people like Eagler insisted on reporting that a major Confederate force was nearby. Late that night, after the skirmish clash, Will Wallace visited Sherman's headquarters along with McPherson of Halleck's staff, once again detached for service with Grant. They found Sherman "in fine spirits." He informed them that he had "driven the enemy back some 3 or 4 miles" before encountering a battery of Confederate artillery. The event strengthened his confidence that no significant Rebel force was present.[64]

Saturday, April 5, dawned clear and pleasant after the heavy rains of the night before. "It was one of those beautiful spring days, when all nature seems to conspire to leave its impress," recalled an officer in Prentiss's division.[65] Temperatures were warmer than they had been of late, and Lt. John Compton told his men of Company E, 11th Iowa, "Now, boys, we drill in earnest for an hour, then return to our quarters, put away our rifles, and then to the branch for bathing." The men drilled diligently in the muggy heat, and then all enjoyed their swim.[66]

Yet at the same time, the army's mood was one of eager anticipation. "Times are getting pretty exciting just now," wrote Pvt. Christian Zook that morning to his friends back in Fairfield County, Ohio, "and maybe we will meet with a big battle in a short time, how soon no one can tell, may be to day, or to night."[67]

Edward Gordon was detailed for picket duty that day. He and his fellow pickets "were pleased with the prospect of some long range target practice"—an occasional potshot at the prowling Confederate cavalry videttes. As he and his comrades took up their post, Gordon asked the men they were relieving if they had seen any rebels. Yes, came the reply, "lots of 'em!" They showed him where to look, and a few minutes later he spotted several riders about a half mile away. Gordon and his squad blazed away at them, and the horsemen retired. The pattern was repeated again and again throughout the day. Gordon kept his superiors informed of the situation, along with the ominous fact that many of the riders did not appear to be cavalrymen but rather officers, observing the Union lines with field glasses. The reports traveled up the chain of command to Gordon's division commander, Sherman.[68]

Sherman was more confident than ever. "I have no doubt that nothing will occur to-day more than some picket firing," he wrote in a note to Grant that day. "The enemy is saucy, but got the worst of it yesterday, and will not press our pickets far. I will not be drawn out far unless with certainty of advantage, and I do not apprehend anything like an attack on our position."[69] Grant fully agreed with his subordinate. In a dispatch to Halleck that day, Grant wrote, "I have scarcely the faintest idea of an attack (general one) being made upon us, but will be prepared should such a thing take place."[70]

That morning the vanguard of Buell's army, the division of Brig. Gen. William Nelson, marched into Savannah.[71] Nelson reported to Grant at the Cherry Mansion just after midday and asked for permission to continue to Pittsburg Landing. "Not immediately," answered Grant. "You will encamp for the present at Savannah." Nelson asked if Grant was not worried about an attack, and said he thought it was a wonder the Confederates had not done so already, but Grant said he was not worried about the Rebels. C. F. Smith chimed in: "They're all back at Corinth, and, when our transportation arrives, we have got to go there and draw them out, as you would draw a badger out of a hole." So Nelson put his division into camp near Savannah.[72] Buell himself was expected on the morrow, and Grant anticipated meeting the Army of the Ohio commander in Savannah before joining his army at Pittsburg Landing.[73]

Will Wallace, in his second full day as commander of the Second Division, reviewed his troops in one of the larger open fields interspersed through the prevailing woodlands. Bands, drums, shouted commands, flags waving in the gentle spring breeze, and long lines of blue-uniformed soldiers still had the power to thrill the men, but Wallace was thinking of the new weight that lay on him now.[74] "It is a great responsibility & does not set easy on me yet," Will wrote to his beloved soul mate, Ann, that evening.[75] Unknown to Will, Ann had already left home to pay him a surprise visit. Her steamboat was even then on its way up the Tennessee. Traveling through the night, it should just reach Pittsburg Landing around dawn Sunday.

Will's primary concern on Saturday was preparing to go to the aid of Lew Wallace at Crump's Landing should the Rebels attack there. On Friday, Grant had sent a note to Will stating, "It is believed that the enemy are re-enforcing at Purdy, and it may be necessary to re-enforce General Wallace to avoid his being attacked by a superior force. Should you find danger of this sort, re-enforce him at once with your entire division."[76] The Second Division was camped closest to Pittsburg Landing and was also the closest to the River Road, which ran to Crump's Landing. The Illinois Wallace and his Hoosier namesake exchanged messages about the best routes between their positions.[77]

Two miles west of Will Wallace's headquarters, and about two and a quarter miles west of Pittsburg Landing, Sherman's division was drilling as usual. A narrow belt of open field fronted the southern half of the division. From just north of Shiloh Church southward for about half a mile ran a long field of varying width, belonging to a farmer named Rea. It was what people called a "deadening," described by one of Sherman's soldiers as "a vast, open, unfenced district, grown up with rank, dry grass." Dead trees dotted the field, "as though some farmer had determined to clear a farm for himself and had abandoned the undertaking in disgust."[78] Sherman's line ended in the north end of this expanse, known as Rea Field, and a gap of several hundred yards separated his southernmost regiment, the 53rd Ohio, from the nearest units of Prentiss's division.

During the drill session that afternoon, members of several regiments spotted horsemen in butternut uniforms watching the drill from the edge of the woods at the south end of Rea Field.[79] Col. Jesse Appler of the 53rd Ohio sent an officer with a platoon of troops to the south end of the field to investigate. The detachment returned some time later reporting that the horsemen had retreated in front of them, and when they had pursued, they had run into a full-scale Rebel skirmish line. Appler ordered the 53rd into line of battle and sent a staff officer to notify Sherman. A few minutes later, the staff officer returned. "Colonel Appler," he said within earshot of many of the soldiers, "General Sherman says: Take your d——d regiment back to Ohio. There is no enemy nearer than Corinth." There was a roar of laughter up and down the 53rd's line, recalled the regimental adjutant, and the men "broke ranks without waiting for an order."[80] They need not respect a colonel for whom their division commander obviously had contempt.

That evening at around 7:00 p.m., a messenger came from brigade headquarters with the latest intelligence Sherman was circulating to his command: the Rebels recently encountered beyond the picket lines consisted of two regiments of cavalry, two of infantry, and a battery of artillery. Tomorrow a detachment of the division would go out and chase them away.

Appler was nervous. His campsite was isolated from the rest of the division, to his right, by the ravine of the east fork of Shiloh Branch. His left was dangling far from the support of the nearest Union troops in that direction. His division commander and his men obviously lacked confidence in him, and worst of all, he lacked confidence in himself. Appler was one of those volunteer colonels who had been a fine community leader but could not quite make the transition to military command. This afternoon's events had been ample demonstration of that. Appler could at least take precautions. He ordered a special picket of sixteen men stationed at the southern end of Rea Field, as Adjutant Ephraim C. Dawes recalled, "with orders to report any movement of troops in their front, and to return to camp at daybreak, but under no circumstances to fire, unless attacked." Mindful of his humiliation that afternoon, Appler refrained from notifying higher head-quarters of his precaution.[81]

Elsewhere around the camps that evening, the 12th Iowa's Sergeant Sumbardo talked to his cavalry friends again. They told him they had encountered solid Rebel forces only three miles outside the Union picket line earlier that day but on reporting their findings at headquarters had been dismissed with a quip that they were "more scared than hurt."[82]

Along the picket line in front of Sherman's division that evening, "as far as the eye could reach," Sergeant Gordon and his comrades could see "through the open woods in our front . . . hundreds of [camp]fires." Gordon tried to count them but gave up. There were too many.[83]

In the camps of Prentiss's division that evening, Methodist chaplain Milton L. Haney preached to the men of the 12th Michigan. Haney actually belonged to the 55th Illinois, part of Sherman's division, but Lt. Col. William H. Graves of the 12th had sent him a "polite note" that day, requesting that he come and speak to the regiment. So that night, Haney earnestly explained to the men how they could be assured of an eternal future in heaven when their lives on earth came to a close.[84]

Sherman took dinner with Prentiss that evening and regaled him with a description of the previous evening's outpost skirmish. Afterward a staff officer thought Prentiss seemed "somewhat worried," complaining that he needed more cavalry to patrol in front of his division.[85] Prentiss had seen the seemingly ubiquitous Confederate horsemen that afternoon while reviewing his division in front of its camps. He had sent out a five-company infantry patrol at 4:00 p.m. They advanced about a mile and a half, saw no enemies, but encountered slaves who said they had seen many Rebel soldiers. They also heard noises that sounded like a large army in motion off beyond the trees.[86]

Around 7:00 p.m., the patrol returned to camp with their report. Prentiss strengthened his picket outposts, in case the Rebels should make another dash at them as they had done to Sherman's pickets the night before. On the division's picket line that night were four companies of the 16th Wisconsin who that evening received their very first cartridges. "It was one of those balmy nights in the Spring, so common in that delightful climate," wrote Pvt. Lloyd Jones of the 16th. He recalled being very nervous that night, his first on picket, but "the stillness was only disturbed by the occasional tinkle of a cow bell, or the movement of some wild animal through the underbrush."[87]

About midnight Maj. James E. Powell of the 25th Missouri took a detachment of the regiment's picket guard on a probe forward, telling the men he had heard that "a squad of rebel cavalry" was camped nearby and "he wanted to take them in 'out of the wet.' " Powell and his men groped forward some distance in the darkness. "We could hear the enemy moving in every direction," recalled Pvt. Daniel B. Baker. Powell decided they had better get back to camp. There he reported to his brigade commander, Col. Everett Peabody, who decided to do something about it. Peabody was thirty-one, a Harvard graduate, successful railroad engineer, and veteran of combat in Missouri the previous year. He suspected that something might be very wrong in the darkened woods in front of his brigade's camp. In order to find whatever it was before it found him, he decided to send out another patrol, without consulting Prentiss. At 3:00 a.m., he ordered Powell to push forward with three companies of his own regiment and two from the 12th Michigan, about 400 men in all.[88]

At his picket post on the Corinth Road about a mile south-southwest of Shiloh Church, Ed Gordon was passing an uneasy night, contemplating the many campfires he had seen in the evening. He guessed it must have been about 3:00 a.m., though it may have been closer to 4:00, when he and his comrades heard a group of men marching toward them from the direction of their own army's camps. "Who goes there?" challenged Gordon.

"Major Powell, in command of three companies of the Twenty-fifth Missouri!" came the reply.

Gordon started. The first thought that crossed his mind was that Missourians were Rebels. How could these enemies have gotten inside the Union picket line? His own division, Sherman's, contained no Missouri regiments. On command, however, Powell advanced and gave the correct countersign. Gordon's fears subsided. Powell and his men were, of course, the patrol Peabody had dispatched. They had come about half a mile southwest of their camps and thus crossed the advanced portion of Sherman's picket line. Powell explained to Gordon that he and his Missourians were "going out to catch some rebels for breakfast." Gordon dutifully reported the previous day's skirmishing and the evening's many distant campfires, "and advised him to be careful, as there were more rebels than he could handle."[89]

Powell and his men marched on and disappeared into the darkness. A few minutes later, the squad of pickets heard three shots in quick succession and saw their flashes. Gordon judged them to be not more than half a mile farther out.[90]

Powell deployed his battalion in skirmish line and kept advancing, crossing a field of cotton stubble belonging to a farmer named Fraley. He soon encountered an opposing skirmish line, and a sharp firefight began.

For more than an hour, the Missourians and Michiganders doggedly kept up a steady tattoo of shots, aiming at the row of muzzle flashes that was all they could see of the enemy.[91] Back at his picket post on the Corinth Road, Gordon began to see wounded soldiers headed back for the camps, either under their own power or with the aid of comrades. Some of them said that Powell needed help.[92]

Back at the camps of Prentiss's division, Peabody heard the distant firing and guessed that his reconnaissance had run into another picket skirmish. He had the long roll sounded in his brigade's camps, and the men of his three regiments left their breakfasts and fell into line. Prentiss heard the firing and the drums and rode over to Peabody's headquarters to ask what was up. On learning of the reconnaissance, he sharply scolded Peabody for starting an unauthorized fight. Prentiss ordered a battalion of the 21st Missouri to support Powell. When the colonel of the 21st met substantial numbers of wounded men coming back the other way, he decided to bring up his whole regiment on the double-quick. The time was about 7:00 a.m., Sunday, April 6, 1862.[93]

Back at Pittsburg Landing, it was a peaceful, pleasant Sunday morning, "one of those beautiful soft spring mornings that seem to come far too seldom in a lifetime," according to Lt. George Mason of the 12th Illinois.[94] Several steamboats had arrived shortly before dawn. Among their passengers were the 15th and 16th Iowa regiments, fresh from their home state and earmarked for Prentiss's new division. The Hawkeyes were terribly afraid that they might miss the great battle. They were much relieved when visiting soldiers from regiments camped near the landing assured them that nothing had happened yet but minor skirmishing. A major battle was expected any day.[95]

Just before the sun rose, Capt. James Day of the 15th Iowa took a leisurely stroll to the top of the bluff. "It was a most invigorating, peaceful, quiet Sabbath morning," recalled Day. "Not a sound fell upon the ear." He walked back down to the river and was startled to notice sudden activity by officers and men at the top of the bluff. Scrambling back up, Day was shocked. "The transformation which a few fleeting minutes had wrought surpasses all powers of description." The roar of battle somewhere to the front was unmistakable. "All Tophet seemed let loose," wrote Day. He rushed back to rejoin his regiment, which was already being hurried off the transport, issued ammunition, and marched forward—"without breakfast," Day added.[96]

Also at the landing that morning was the steamer *Minnehaha*, aboard which Ann Wallace had arrived before daybreak. She had no horse to ride, and so waited on the boat while an officer went ashore to find out where her husband's division was camped. The distant firing broke out, and when the officer returned, he informed her that Will was moving forward with his Second Division. There was nothing for Ann to do but wait on the steamboat.[97]

On the dangling southern flank of Sherman's Shiloh ridge position, Col. Jesse Appler of the 53rd Ohio had been awake hours before dawn. In fact, he had not slept at all. About 4:00 a.m. he roused his adjutant, Lieutenant Dawes. "Get up, quick," said Appler. Dawes rose and accompanied the colonel beyond the regiment's Sibley tents to the southern edge of the camp. There they stood listening to the sound of scattered shots coming from somewhere off to the south. While they stood there, Appler's special picket detail came hurrying back from the far south end of Rea Field. They reported hearing heavy firing.

Appler ordered Dawes to form the regiment, then told him instead to go and report to their brigade commander, Col. Jesse Hildebrand. Again, Appler changed his mind and stopped Dawes. While the colonel continued to dither, a Union soldier ran into camp from the south. The man's arm was bleeding, and he shouted, "Get into line; the rebels are coming!" That was enough for Appler. He ordered the drummer to beat the long roll and dispatched one staff officer to report to Hildebrand and another to Sherman. The officer sent to Sherman got back first. He gave the general's response to Appler in low tones so the men would not hear: "General Sherman says, 'You must be badly scared over there.' "

After that insult, events seemed to hurtle toward Appler in relentless succession with dizzying speed. The officer reporting to Hildebrand returned moments later with orders to reinforce the pickets with two more companies. Appler had just complied when an officer shouted, "Colonel, the rebels are crossing the field!" Everyone looked southward down the long stretch of Rea Field and by the first light of day saw troops moving across the southern end of the field, obviously advancing to attack Prentiss's camps. Appler ordered the regiment to swing to the south side of the tents, facing south.

They were still in motion when the pickets came scampering back from the west, their captain exclaiming, "The rebels out there are thicker than fleas on a dog's back." Another messenger galloped up from Hildebrand ordering the very left wheel they were even then executing, but as Dawes brought the regiment into position, he looked right and saw an amazing sight. A gentle slope led down to the west fork of Shiloh Branch, its banks hidden in dense woods and thickets. Now in those thickets, scarcely a hundred yards away, Dawes saw the slanting rays of the rising sun glinting off a long row of rifle barrels.

Maintaining his composure, Dawes hurried to Appler. "Colonel, look to the right," said the adjutant in a low tone. Appler did and started. "This is no place for us," he gasped. Then he barked out an order for the regiment to wheel back through the camps and take up a line behind them, facing west again, toward the newest threat. Back went the 53rd, line opening and closing as it worked its way through the tents. Cooks, sutlers, and the regiment's sick were still in the camp, and as he passed, Appler shouted repeatedly, "Sick men to the rear." They scrambled to obey. Behind all of them came a spattering of shots from the Confederate skirmishers. Finally the regimental line cleared the tents and halted just inside the edge of the woods and a few steps beyond the crest of the ridge. Appler had them turn and face their camp, and the enemy beyond it, and then lie down in line.[98]

A few hundred yards north, on the other side of the ravine of the east fork of Shiloh Branch, Gordon was in line with his regiment and the rest of Sherman's division. It had been his good fortune to be relieved from the picket line only a few minutes ago, and now the post on the Corinth Road a mile in front of the camps was some other sergeant's worry. The long roll had sounded in all of Sherman's camps thirty minutes before, in response to the sound of firing from Prentiss.[99] Hildebrand's brigade had moved up to a position on the slope of the ridge just to the left, or south, of Shiloh Church, and Buckland was moving up on his right.[100] As Gordon stood in line, he noticed Sherman and his staff galloping along behind the line, heading toward the position of the 53rd on the division's southern flank.[101]

William Tecumseh Sherman was one of the most intelligent men ever to wear the stars of a general, but for the past few days he had played the fool. No narcotic had been necessary to produce the effect. Sherman had formed a theory about the strategic situation and then simply made the data fit that theory. As is normal in humans, observed facts did not form the theory, but rather the theory determined Sherman's interpretation of the facts. Only rarely do external realities so force themselves on a human mind that it is compelled to discard one interpretive theory and adopt an entirely different one. Sherman was about to have such an epiphany.

A few minutes before 7:00 a.m., he rode along the front of the 53rd Ohio, stopped, and raised his field glass to look more closely at the troops crossing the south end of the field, 800 yards away. While he did so, the Confederate battle line along Shiloh Branch emerged from the brush less than 100 yards to Sherman's right, advanced several paces, and began to raise their rifles. "General, look to your right," shouted an officer of the

53rd. Sherman lowered his glass and turned to look. "My God," cried Sherman. "We are attacked!" As he did so, he threw his hand up, as if to ward off a blow. The Confederate volley crashed out, and a bullet clipped Sherman's upraised hand. Sherman's orderly, Pvt. Thomas L. Holliday of the 2nd Illinois Cavalry, fell dead a few feet from him, shot through the head. The general turned his horse and galloped back. "Appler, hold your position," he shouted as he passed the colonel of the 53rd. "I will support you."[102]

Sherman had at last begun to grasp the serious situation that the Army of the Tennessee faced. Confederate Western department commander Albert Sidney Johnston had concentrated his forces at Corinth, along with reinforcements that brought his total numbers to more than 40,000 as compared to the 36,000 Federals camped at Pittsburg Landing. Johnston's object was to destroy Grant's army before Buell could join it. The Confederate general ordered his army to move out on Thursday, April 3, and had hoped to attack Grant the following morning. Muddy roads and an inexperienced army had slowed the march and necessitated the two-day postponement of the attack. The Rebels that Grant's men had spotted on Friday and Saturday had been the first units of Johnston's army slowly moving into position. By Sunday morning, April 6, Johnston's attack was ready. Peabody's reconnaissance had struck the waiting assault lines and triggered the fighting before the Confederate advance could begin. Now, the whole Rebel army bore down on the Union encampments in three broad waves.

About the time Appler was deploying his regiment first on one side of his camp and then on the other, Prentiss was deploying both brigades of his division about a quarter mile in front of his camps. Powell's patrol, along with the 21st Missouri and several companies of the brigade's pickets, had skirmished gamely for almost two hours, but as dawn lit up the sky behind the Union camps, the main Confederate advance began. Powell's force could not hope to stem that tide and fell back toward Prentiss's line. Shortly after 6:00 a.m., Prentiss's entire division prepared to engage the advancing Confederates.[103]

In the ranks of the 61st Illinois, on the left of Prentiss's line, Pvt. Edgar Embley called a warning to his captain as he spotted the enemy advancing through the underbrush. Like Dawes farther north, Embley noticed the glint of sunlight on rifle barrels. Firing started almost immediately. "In a perfect shower the leaves and dust flew around our feet," Embley wrote. "The bark flew off the trees." One of Embley's comrades turned instantly and ran for the rear. The rest of the Illinoisans dropped to one knee and returned the fire as rapidly as they could. Prentiss rode along the line, calling encouragement to the men. They should fire low and make their shots count, the general admonished, "fore every secesh that we killed there would be one less to shoot at us," Embley recalled. "I thought of that several times during the day."[104]

Fighting raged all along Prentiss's line. "We opened fire on them and you should have seen the cusses fall," exulted Henry Culbertson of the 16th Wisconsin, "but at the same time many of our poor fellows fell."[105] Nearby, Hickenlooper's 5th Battery, Ohio Light Artillery, met the advancing Confederates with blasts of double canister that "tore great gaps in their ranks."[106]

On the extreme left of Prentiss's line, the 15th Michigan faced a bizarre dilemma. They had arrived at Pittsburg Landing the night before, marched halfway out to Prentiss's position, and camped. This morning when fighting started, they got orders to join Prentiss and did so, moving up into line with his division. As the Confederates advanced against their position, however, and Michigan men began to fall, the regiment simply stood there, bayonets at the ready, without firing. They had no ammunition but had thought they would be supplied once they reached Prentiss's camps. There was no time for that now, and Col. Madison Miller, commanding Prentiss's left brigade, ordered the 15th to fall back until it could get ammunition from one of the other divisions.[107]

Meanwhile, in Sherman's sector the men of the 53rd Ohio and the other regiments of Hildebrand's and Buckland's brigades prepared to receive the Rebel onslaught a few minutes before 7:00 a.m. The long open space of Rea Field, bordered on the east and north by the ridges where Sherman's men stood, presented a thrilling and appalling spectacle of war to these soldiers, none of whom had ever seen a battle before. The two brigades were in full view of each other and of each other's camps, where the conical Sibley tents were still standing and where the sick, along with teamsters, sutlers, cooks, and various other rear-echelon types, were swarming to the rear, toward the camps of McClernand's division, where even now Sherman's men could hear the long roll sounding. From the direction of Prentiss's camps came the rattle of musketry.[108]

All across the long western edge of Rea Field, a Confederate battle line emerged from the woods and brush along Shiloh Branch. The Rebel line stretched the length of the field's long axis and disappeared from sight into the woods on either side. "The sun was just rising in their front," wrote a Union soldier near Shiloh Church, "and the glittering of their arms and equipments made a gorgeous spectacle."[109]

"In an open space in the Corinth road, a battery was unlimbering," recalled Dawes. "Directly in front of the spot where General Sherman's orderly lay dead, there was a group of mounted officers and a peculiar flag—dark blue, with a white center."[110] That was the flag of William J. Hardee's corps, first wave of the Confederate assault.

"The Confederate battery fired, its first shot cutting off a tree top above our Company A," recalled Dawes. A Union battery barked a reply. Dawes looked at his watch and noted that it was just seven o'clock. Then the Confederate battle line surged through the 53rd's abandoned tents and emerged within fifty yards of the regiment. "Colonel Appler gave the command to fire; there was a tremendous crash of musketry." The assault wave rolled toward the line of all of Hildebrand's and Buckland's regiments, and the roar of massed rifles reverberated from one end of the field to the other. "The battle," noted Dawes, "was fairly on."[111] So little time had elapsed since Sherman had galloped past Shiloh Church on his way to see Appler and make his startling discovery that, years later, Sergeant Gordon did not believe the general could possibly have made it to the 53rd's camp before mass firing broke out all along the line.[112]

The division stood its ground and poured musketry into the advancing Confederates. Dense clouds of heavy white smoke soon shrouded Rea Field. The 53rd Ohio beat off the first Rebel assault on its position, leaving its tents riddled and the ground around them thickly strewn with dead and wounded Confederates. The new soldiers had little time for elation at their first battlefield victory, however, for the Confederates regrouped in the woods along Shiloh Branch and came on again. Again the Buckeyes of the 53rd stood manfully to their work. A Mississippi regiment was all but annihilated in and around the 53rd's camp. Dawes thought the second assault was beginning to recede when he heard Appler, standing behind the left end of the regiment's line, shout, "Retreat and save yourselves." Two-thirds of the regiment streamed to the rear and the rest had to follow.[113]

Appler had never seemed comfortable in command of a regiment. He had been nervous for days, had not slept at all the night before, and had had neither his morale nor his confidence boosted by Sherman's disgraceful actions of the past twenty-four hours. He may also have had other reasons for losing his nerve. Positioned behind the left of his regiment, he was the closest field officer to the north edge of the ominous 800-yard gap between Sherman's and Prentiss's divisions. He may have perceived the Rebels already beginning to work around the 53rd's left flank. That was bound to happen sooner or later, and when it did, the 53rd would have to retreat, if it still could. The gap in the center of the Union line existed off and on for much of the day and, though only sketchily perceived by the Confederates, became one of the keys of the day's fighting.

Prentiss blamed the retreat of the 53rd Ohio for the failure of his own line in front of his division's camps, but he seems to have been looking for a scapegoat.[114] After well over an hour of full-scale, intense combat against a larger attacking force, the green Sixth Division was nearing the end of its endurance. The 53rd's retreat enlarged the gap between Prentiss's and Sherman's divisions, but even while the Ohioans stood their ground, the Rebels were already working around both of Prentiss's flanks.

The Confederates closed in, giving their "Rebel yell." Hickenlooper recalled that the sound made "an involuntary thrill of terror to pass like an electric shock through even the bravest hearts." Prentiss's line began to give way. "Limber to the rear," roared Hickenlooper. The goal now was to get his guns out of there before the Rebel charge engulfed them. Just then a Confederate volley swept the battery, dropping every horse in the left section and dismounting both Hickenlooper and his lieutenant. The officers scrambled to their feet and directed their men in the effort to save the remaining four guns. A glance toward the charging Confederates showed Hickenlooper that he was close enough to see individual faces, "blackened with powder smoke, lighted up by revengeful fury." As the Ohioans got their guns moving, it seemed the Rebel bayonets were only a few feet behind them. Away they went, "over ditches, between trees, through underbrush, over logs, every rider lashing his team."[115]

The Sixth Division fell back, making occasional stands. Hickenlooper had the remaining two sections of his battery alternately unlimber and give the enemy a few rounds, then limber up again and continue the retreat. When the division reached the camps, Prentiss, Peabody, and Miller attempted to rally their troops. The regiments were already losing their organization, however. T. W. Baird recalled that his regiment "was scattered like chaff by the next attack of the rebels."[116] As George Graves of the 16th Wisconsin explained it, "By that time everybody was running, and the rebels were coming down through our camp, so I ran too."[117]

The situation rapidly became hopeless. Peabody fell dead. Confederate pressure increased, and Prentiss ordered what was left of the division to fall back and try to rally on the divisions of Hurlbut and Will Wallace, well to the rear. The remnants of the Sixth streamed back in retreat, all order lost. Most of the fugitives never stopped until they reached the foot of the bluffs at Pittsburg Landing, two miles to the rear. Several hundred pulled up when they reached an old, half-overgrown farm lane that crossed their path about half a mile behind their camps, and there Prentiss and his officers began forming them into line again. Prentiss checked his watch. It was 9:05 a.m.[118]

Back at the north end of the Union front, Sherman's division, less the

53rd Ohio, was still grimly hanging on. The ravine of the east fork of Shiloh Branch, which had made Appler feel isolated, probably helped the remainder of Hildebrand's brigade to hold its ground even after the 53rd stampeded. The Rebels pressed hard along the fronts of both Buckland's and Hildebrand's brigades, advancing to within only a few feet of the 70th Ohio. Each time, however, Sherman's men drove them back with heavy loss. Buckland showed good skill in positioning his regiments, and his men fought stoutly. In the center of Buckland's line, the 48th Ohio's color-bearer fled to the rear only five minutes into the fight. The rest of the regiment wavered but then rallied and held firm. The regimental band put aside its instruments, took up rifles from those who had fallen, and got into the fight. Young drummer Jesse Nelson was in the act of firing a rifle when he was shot through the head and killed.[119]

Sherman himself had recovered well from his shock in front of the 53rd Ohio. In many ways, that moment had been the nadir of his Civil War career. Now that the battle was joined, he seemed to have found himself. Energetically and efficiently, he galloped about the battlefield, positioning his troops and making sure they were fighting well. A young soldier of Buckland's brigade recalled seeing Sherman. "The splendid soldier, erect in his saddle . . . looked a veritable war eagle."[120] Ed Gordon of the 57th Ohio wrote, "I remember how glad we were to see General Sherman, with a rag on his hand, ride along our lines."[121]

Some things, however, neither Sherman's vigor and skill nor the valor of his troops could remedy. The great gap separating him from Prentiss's division offered the Confederates a standing invitation to flank the Fifth Division on its left just as they had flanked the Sixth Division on its right. The 53rd Ohio had been the first victim. As the Rebel attack continued, the rest of Hildebrand's brigade gradually unraveled from left to right, until the whole line south of Shiloh Church was gone. The 57th Ohio went first. Next in line was the 77th, and before it gave way, the men in the left-flank companies had left-faced where they stood and were firing in that direction. "There was no formal movement in falling back," recalled Pvt. Bob Flemming of the 77th, "the men in the left gradually sloughed off and passed to the rear, singly and in squads, as they were flanked."[122] Hildebrand, an old major general of Ohio militia well past his sixtieth birthday, had never excelled as a brigade commander.[123] Now as the brigade began to come apart, he simply abandoned it and spent the rest of the day attaching himself to various generals' staffs.[124]

It was now nearly 10:00 a.m. Buckland's brigade was still holding steady, but obviously could not continue to do so much longer. Sherman ordered it and McDowell's brigade, which had been less heavily engaged on the far right, to fall back to the line of the Hamburg-Purdy Road, about a quarter mile to the rear of their camps.[125] "While this movement was in progress," wrote Thomas Connelly of the 70th Ohio, "the Rebels raised their cornbread yelp, and making a desperate charge, captured our camp; taking full possession of our tents, our blankets, knapsacks and all of our love letters." Behind the retreating Federals came shouted Confederate taunts: "Bull Run, Bull Run," "Get up there, you d—— Yankee S——s of B——s, and fight like men."[126]

The first phase of the Battle of Shiloh was over. Prentiss's and Sherman's divisions had been driven from their positions, their camps overrun. Of Sherman's division, two brigades remained capable of further action; of Prentiss's, only an ad hoc command less than the size of one ordinary brigade. The Union line, two and a half miles from Pittsburg Landing when the opposing lines of battle had first become fully engaged four hours before, lay now from two miles to, in places, as little as a mile and a half from the landing. Eight hours of daylight remained.

CHAPTER TEN

"The Devil's Own Day"

G RANT PLANNED to take an early breakfast on the morning of April 6 and then ride out and meet Buell. The latter had actually arrived in Savannah the evening before, while Grant was visiting his lines at Pittsburg Landing, but Buell, still resentful and jealous of Grant, sent no notice of his arrival. After the planned meeting with Buell, Grant absolutely had to shift his headquarters to Pittsburg Landing this day and had given his staff the necessary preparatory orders for doing so. He had learned just the afternoon before that the official notification of the recent promotions had now arrived. That meant that McClernand was now formally the highest-ranking officer at Pittsburg Landing, and that would not do. Grant would go and take command personally.[1]

As Grant sat at breakfast in the Cherry Mansion, the sound of a cannon shot reverberated down the river—then another and another. He paused, his untasted cup of coffee halfway to his mouth. Then he set it down and stood up. "Gentlemen, the ball is in motion. Let's be off." Grant hastily directed two dispatches, one to Nelson, penned by John Rawlins, ordering the Army of the Ohio general to march his division to the Tennessee River opposite Pittsburg Landing, another to Buell, excusing himself from their meeting. Within a quarter of an hour, Grant, his staff, and their horses were aboard *Tigress,* and the boat was churning its way up the river at the best speed it could make.[2]

About halfway to Pittsburg Landing, *Tigress* approached Crump's Landing. Lew Wallace was there, waiting on board a steamer tied up at the wharf. He had first heard the sound of heavy firing from the south at about daylight. At Crump's it was possible to discern the sounds of both artillery and musketry. Wallace immediately ordered his division under arms. His three brigades were separated; one was at Crump's Landing, one at Stoney Lonesome, two miles inland on the road toward Purdy, and the third at Adamsville, yet another two miles farther out. Tolerable roads led south from Stoney Lonesome, so Wallace ordered his three brigades to concentrate there at once, while he waited at Crump's for some word from Grant. Thus he was on the steamboat *Jesse K. Bell,* gazing eagerly downstream as *Tigress* approached.[3]

Grant's boat came alongside Wallace's, the engines stopped, and deckhands secured the lashings. The two generals talked across the railings of their respective hurricane decks. "Have you heard the firing?" Grant asked, as Wallace recalled the conversation.

"Yes, sir, since daybreak," Wallace replied.

"What do you think of it?" Grant wanted to know.

"It's undoubtedly a general engagement."

"Well," Grant said thoughtfully, "hold yourself in readiness to march upon orders received."

Years later Wallace recalled himself replying, "But, general, I ordered a concentration about six o'clock. The division must be at Stoney Lonesome. I am ready now." That may be what he said, although Grant's volunteer aide, Douglas Putnam, remembered only "My division is in line, waiting for orders." Doubtless, Wallace and his men were eager to get into whatever battle might be on hand. On the other hand, long before Wallace wrote his account of the exchange, hindsight had shown all involved that the Third Division should have marched at once. Grant still did not know what was happening at Pittsburg Landing, and he would not have wanted to send a division marching five miles just because of another skirmish fracas.

"Very well," Wallace recalled Grant replying. "Hold the division ready to march in any direction." Putnam's recollection was similar, with Grant saying "that as soon as he got to Pittsburg Landing and learned where the attack was, he would send him orders." That concluded the interview. *Tigress*'s deckhands cast off, and her captain rang for speed. Soon she had disappeared around the bend of the river in the direction of Pittsburg Landing.[4]

Somewhere above Crump's Landing, *Tigress* met the steamboat *John Warner,* charging downstream. Will Wallace, whose camps were closest to Pittsburg Landing, had dispatched it to notify Grant of the attack. Ironically, Will was still unaware, when he dispatched the steamboat, that his wife, Ann, was aboard one of the other boats moored at the landing. Spotting *Tigress* racing up the river, *John Warner* rounded to and followed Grant's boat back toward Pittsburg Landing.[5]

It was between 8:30 and 9:00 a.m. when *Tigress* hove in sight of Pittsburg Landing. Grant could tell at once that something was wrong. Large numbers of stragglers were beginning to congregate on the riverbank at the foot of the bluffs. The 2,000 or so fugitives of Prentiss's division—all those who were neither killed nor wounded, nor among the determined men even then beginning to rally with Prentiss or with other units to which they had attached themselves—would have had time to reach the landing before Grant arrived. A couple of hundred of the 53rd Ohio may have been on hand, as well as a smattering of representatives from other regiments of Sherman's division that were still fighting along Shiloh Ridge.

Once ashore, Grant had his staff officers help him into the saddle—he was still hobbling from his fall on Friday night—and tie his crutch to the saddle. Then, accompanied by Rawlins, he rode inland. About half a mile from the landing, they met Will Wallace, who filled them in on the situation up to that point. The Rebels were attacking all along the line. Sherman and Prentiss were both engaged, with McClernand and Hurlbut moving up to support them and Wallace's own division in reserve. Grant immediately instructed Rawlins to go back to the river and send Capt. Algernon S. Baxter, the assistant quartermaster on Grant's staff, back up the river aboard *Tigress* to Crump's Landing to tell Wallace to come on. He dispatched another note to Nelson, ordering him to hurry his division to the east side of the river opposite Pittsburg Landing, and he gave orders to get the army's ammunition wagons moving toward the engaged troops at the front. Then he rode on to visit his lines.[6]

Between the landing and the bloody ground for which Prentiss and Sherman had fought during the first hours of daylight were the camps of three other divisions, McClernand's First Division, Will Wallace's Second, and Hurlbut's Fourth. For many of the men of these divisions, the beginning of the morning's battle had been as much of a shock as it had been to the troops on the front line or to Grant back in Savannah. Hurlbut's and Will Wallace's divisions fell into ranks quickly, however, and were waiting and ready to move forward more than half an hour before orders came to advance. Grant rode through the camp of the 41st Illinois, in Hurlbut's division, on his way to the front, then passed through again a few minutes later, telling the men, "You will soon have something to do."[7]

McClernand's division was closer to the scene of the first action. Early that morning, Lt. Abram H. Ryan, adjutant for its Third Brigade, answered a summons from brigade commander Col. James S. Reardon. They met at Reardon's quarters, and the colonel told Ryan that "owing to ill-health he was unable to command the brigade" and would have to depart on sick leave at once. While they were talking, the sound of heavy firing came from Sherman's division. Reardon told Ryan to notify Col. Julius Raith, commander of the 43rd Illinois and the brigade's senior colonel, that he was now in command.[8]

Raith found himself suddenly thrust into brigade command at the very moment the battle was starting, and worse still, his was the first brigade of McClernand's division to receive orders to move up and support Sherman. The day had started as a very ordinary one for Raith. He had sent his lieutenant colonel, Adolph Engelmann, to McClernand's headquarters for permission to discharge the regiment's rifles, which had remained loaded since the scare on Friday evening. Two companies had discharged their rifles when Raith heard the serious firing in front of the army and ordered a halt to the operation.

Shortly came word that he was in command of the brigade, along with orders from McClernand to get it ready to advance into battle. Raith dispatched Engelmann to order the 49th Illinois into line, but when Engelmann reached the regiment's camp with his order, the reply was, "For what purpose?" Engelmann told them that the enemy was attacking, but the officers of the 49th assured him that it was only the men of their own division, getting the old loads out of their rifles. They were so convincing that Engelmann started to doubt his own story and rode off to find out the truth for himself. He had gone scarcely 200 yards from the 49th's camp when he came up behind Sherman's hotly engaged line of battle. Fully convinced now, Engelmann rode back to the 49th and was appalled to find that the regiment had not made the least effort to obey the order he had delivered. This time he could give them eyewitness assurance of the situation, and that sufficed to put the officers of the 49th into rapid motion.[9]

The response was different in the camps of Col. C. Carroll Marsh's brigade, formerly Will Wallace's. The men were astir early that morning, getting ready for routine Sunday inspection. The sound of a cannon shot brought a startled pause. "What's that?" said Sgt. Sam Forbes. The men looked at one another. Then came more cannon shots and heavy volleys of musketry. Soon the drummers were beating the long roll and the men snatched up rifles and threw on accoutrements. The 20th Illinois's brass band grabbed its instruments to provide a bit of music and help nerve the men for battle. Soon they were belting out "Hail Columbia," but before they got through the first verse, the regiment was formed up and double-timing out of camp. Shells were already crashing through the trees overhead.[10]

Quickly and efficiently or in stubborn disbelief, the regiments of the First, Second, and Fourth divisions formed up on the color lines of their camps and then marched off to join the divisions already engaged or to take up supporting positions behind them. Musician John Cockerill of the 70th Ohio was hastening to the rear, rifle in hand, after the collapse of Hildebrand's brigade, when he came upon Brig. Gen. John McArthur's Highland Brigade, whose members wore Scotch caps. "A handsomer body of troops I never saw," recalled Cockerill. The 9th and 12th Illinois, which were the backbone of the brigade, had been counted as crack regiments back in September 1861 when they were the first units Grant took to Paducah. Now they were veterans of Fort Donelson, among the best troops in Grant's army. The Highlanders' band was playing "Hail Columbia," and their flags were unfurled. They stood in ranks awaiting orders to move up into the fight.

As Cockerill was passing the regiment, a "chipper young lieutenant" of the 9th Illinois stopped him.

"Where do you belong?" asked the lieutenant.

"I belong to Ohio," Cockerill replied.

"Well, Ohio is making a bad show of itself here today. I have seen stragglers from a dozen Ohio regiments going past here for half an hour," the officer said, referring to the detritus of Sherman's battle. "Ohio expects better work from her sons than this. Do you want to come and fight with us?"

Cockerill agreed to do so. The lieutenant pulled out a little pocket notebook and carefully recorded Cockerill's name and next of kin. That was important because a Civil War soldier who became separated from his company and then fell in battle was likely to remain an unknown, and his family might never know his fate. A number of other fleeing soldiers responded to the lieutenant's appeals, and he recorded their information as well.[11] In fact, scores of fugitives from frontline collapses subsequently attached themselves to McArthur's and other brigades still waiting to go into battle.[12] Not every soldier whose unit lost its cohesion was destined to join the mob at the base of the bluffs at Pittsburg Landing.

The next division to enter the fight after Prentiss's and Sherman's was McClernand's First Division. That fact was dictated by position as much as anything else. Located as little as 600 yards behind those of Sherman's division, McClernand's camps were directly in the path of the Confederates advancing in pursuit of Sherman and streaming through the gap between Sherman and Prentiss. Raith's brigade had hardly formed in line and advanced a few hundred yards before it made contact with the enemy, "crowding upon us in apparently great numbers," as Engelmann described it.[13] The Confederates drove Raith's brigade back to the line of the Hamburg-Purdy Road at about the time Sherman's division was retreating to that line from Shiloh Ridge. Raith himself received a mortal wound while rallying his troops, and command of the brigade devolved on Engelmann.[14]

The other two brigades of McClernand's division came up and joined Engelmann at about the same time that Sherman's battered division, or the two brigades that were left of it, fell back to join them along the same alignment. The new line ran along the Hamburg-Purdy Road on either side of its intersection with the main Corinth Road. Sherman's division held the right of the line; McClernand's held the left, slanting backward, away from the Hamburg-Purdy Road to follow a line a few dozen yards south of the Corinth Road. The new line was a strong one. Here were two divisions side by side, one of them not only fresh but veteran.

It was probably at about this time that Grant first visited Sherman's front. Sherman had by this point had two horses shot out from under him and had his shoulder bruised by a glancing bullet in addition to the hand wound he had received in the first volley. Douglas Putnam noted that "Sherman's stock had become pulled around until the part that should have been to the front rested under one of his ears, while his whole appearance indicated hard and earnest work."[15] Sherman was performing magnificently, capably directing his division's defense and inspiring his men by his courage. Grant expressed "great satisfaction" at the stand Sherman was making, and well he might. Not only was the hard fighting of Sherman's division winning desperately needed time, it was also drawing Confederate forces toward that side of the battlefield and away from the Union left, where they could potentially do much more damage. Grant explained to Sherman that "things did not look as well over on the left." The good news, however, was that Grant had sent for Lew Wallace, and his division should be appearing on Sherman's right any time now.[16] With that, Grant moved on to visit each of the rest of his division commanders in turn. "I never deemed it important to stay long with Sherman," he later explained.[17]

While Sherman was fighting on Shiloh Ridge and then falling back to the Hamburg-Purdy Road to be joined there by McClernand, Prentiss's troops "over on the left" had been enjoying a lull. This lull was partially the result of Sherman's stiff resistance, which drew Confederate units toward the sound of the heaviest firing. Another cause for the lack of pressure on Prentiss was Confederate soldiers breaking ranks, en masse, to rifle Prentiss's captured camps. It took time for their officers to reform their units and get them advancing again. That was a good thing for Prentiss and his remaining men, for they never would have been able to regroup in the old farm lane had the Confederates been in hot pursuit.

The condition of Prentiss's command was much improved by the arrival of the 23rd Missouri Regiment, another of the new regiments earmarked for his division and just now joining up. As green as any of the division's other regiments, the 23rd was at least fresh, and its undepleted strength of 700 men probably more than doubled Prentiss's numbers.[18]

Prentiss's situation received a more dramatic boost when Hurlbut's and Will Wallace's troops moved up on either side of him. Hurlbut brought his division—less one brigade he had dispatched on urgent request to Sherman—into line on Prentiss's left. Wallace brought his division into line on Prentiss's right, but, like Hurlbut, also detached one of his three brigades. The reason for Wallace's detachment was that Hurlbut's two brigades were not sufficient to cover the gap between Prentiss and David Stuart's detached brigade of Sherman's division on the far Union left. Wallace sent McArthur's brigade to fill the remaining gap on Hurlbut's left, but an interval of several hundred yards, obscured by woods and ravines, lay open between McArthur's left and Stuart's right.[19]

The farm lane along which Prentiss had rallied his division was eroded in some places below the surrounding ground level, the depth ranging from a few inches to a couple of feet, and so it came to be referred to as "the Sunken Road." It offered little protection from enemy fire. In some places, even a man lying prone would be exposed. It did, however, provide a tangible line on which the shaken troops could rally. In front of Prentiss's position lay a section of particularly dense thickets. To Prentiss's right, Wallace's division continued in the Sunken Road, across the Eastern Corinth Road, and all the way to the main Corinth Road. Much of Wallace's line faced an open field of head-high weeds belonging to a farmer named Duncan.[20] For practical purposes, Wallace's right flank joined McClernand's left along the main Corinth Road. Men of the two divisions did not necessarily touch elbows but were close enough to provide direct supporting fire for each other. For the moment, the Confederates could no longer exploit the gap between them.

To Prentiss's left, Hurlbut's line, lengthened by McArthur's brigade, ran through the Sunken Road, behind the same patch of thickets that covered Prentiss's front, then through a peach orchard in full bloom and across the Hamburg-Savannah Road to stop in the woods some yards—and a deep ravine—short of Stuart's position. Much of Hurlbut's line faced another field of cotton stubble, this one belonging to the widow Sarah Bell. Hurlbut's men waited nervously for the Rebel onset. In the ranks of the 44th Indiana, ordered to lie prone in the Sunken Road, George Squier silently prayed, "Ever kind Father, preserve me."[21]

At approximately 10:00 a.m., the first major Confederate assault struck the combined Wallace-Prentiss-Hurlbut position. In the dense thickets in front of Hurlbut's right, the attackers pushed to within ten yards of the lines of the 31st Indiana. Then the Hoosiers, lying prone in the Sunken Road, rose up and poured a volley into their faces. The survivors fell back, only to rally and come on again.[22] Next in line, the 44th Indiana kept up a steady rhythm of fire. "We lay on the ground to load, raised, and fired," wrote George Squier. He found that now he "felt as cool and composed as if sitting down for a chat or shooting squirrells," even though "the bullets whistled over our heads, shells bursting all around us, balls whizing past, tearing trees."[23] Not far away, Sgt. John Boggs fought in the ranks of the 3rd Iowa. "After the first fire we gave them, it put me in mind of a windrow of stumps and chunks piled up," Boggs recalled. "We left a row of their dead and wounded the length of the field."[24]

Captain Hickenlooper had his four remaining guns in action alongside Prentiss's infantry. As the Rebel line closed in, he called instructions to his cannoneers for what ammunition to use. First it was case shot with two-second fuses, then one-second fuses. As the attackers closed to within 200 yards, he shouted the order for canister. Then, as the enemy made preparation for their final dash, "double canister," and his men worked the guns so fast that their separate reports seemed to blend into a continuous roar.[25]

Prentiss's line wavered, and he had to ask Wallace for help. Wallace sent over the 8th Iowa, and Prentiss, riding his line and encouraging his men to hold steady, was able to stabilize the situation.[26] Beside Prentiss's hard-pressed men, the 12th and 14th Iowa, Wallace's left-flank regiments, lay down until the advancing Confederates were thirty paces away. According to Sgt. Frederick F. Kiner of the 14th Iowa, the Rebels were so close "that we could see the whites of their eyes."[27] Rising up, the Iowans triggered a deadly volley into the attackers' faces, then counterattacked and pursued the fleeing Confederates several score yards before returning to their original position on Prentiss's right.[28] At the other end of the position, as the Confederate survivors simultaneously retreated from the front of Hurlbut's division, Col. Hugh B. Reed of the 44th Indiana rode up and down his regiment's line, beaming with pride, and shouted, "Boys, can you give that a cheer?" The Hoosiers responded with "three rousing cheers."[29]

Shortly after the three divisions had succeeded in beating off the Confederate attack, Grant arrived in this sector. He met first with Will Wallace. Firing was still so heavy in this sector that Rawlins, who was with Grant, and Lieutenant Colonel McPherson, who was accompanying Wallace during this phase of the battle, urged Grant not to allow himself to be seen immediately behind the battle line, where he might be shot. Grant responded, as an aide recalled, that he wanted to see and know what was going on."[30] Next he rode on to visit Prentiss. He expressed approval of the defensive position his subordinates had taken up and of the stand they were making, and he ordered Prentiss "to maintain that position at all hazards."[31]

The pause during which Grant visited with Prentiss was brief, only long enough for the Confederates to regroup, bring up fresh troops, and return to the attack. Again the same scenes of slaughter were played out in the thickets and cotton fields in front of the Union position. The brush caught fire in some places, filling the air with even more acrid smoke and threatening the wounded with a hideous death. And no sooner was the second Confederate assault repulsed than the Rebel generals rallied their troops and launched a third. Attack after attack rebounded from the Union position like the blows of a blacksmith's hammer on an anvil.

Brig. Gen. Jacob Lauman, commanding the Kentucky-Indiana brigade now instead of his accustomed Iowans, fought in the Sunken Road and Peach Orchard sector and did an exceptional job of keeping his regiments supplied with ammunition. He alertly used the pauses between attacks to resupply his troops or else held one of his regiments in reserve and rotated it in and out of the line while the relieved regiments resupplied. On average, his troops emptied their cartridge boxes twice and part of a third time during this phase of the fighting, firing about 100 rounds per man.[32] During and after the battle, Confederates came to call the area of dense thickets in front of Prentiss and Lauman "the Hornets' Nest," because at every advance into the area the bullets buzzed past their ears like angry hornets.

The resupply of ammunition was very much a matter to be handled at the brigade level. Right next to Lauman's brigade, Hurlbut's other brigade was not faring quite so well. Its commander, Col. Nelson G. Williams, was wounded almost as soon as the brigade came under fire. His successor, Col. Isaac C. Pugh, decided that the forty rounds in the men's cartridge boxes was enough and no provision for resupply would be necessary.[33]

More or less simultaneous with the beginning of the repeated Confederate assaults against the Sunken Road sector came the renewal of the Rebel offensive on the Union right, against Sherman's and McClernand's line along and near the Hamburg-Purdy Road. In the center of McClernand's division, Marsh's brigade took up its place in line. In front of them, Marsh's men could see "large masses of men filing into line," but from a distance, amid the trees and under the slanting rays of the sun, they were not sure what soldiers those were.[34] They were carrying a flag that appeared to be the Stars and Stripes, recalled Sgt. Wilbur Crummer of the 45th Illinois.[35] Pvt. George Carrington of the 11th Illinois thought the Rebels were wearing blue uniforms and carrying "a blue flag with a single star in the center."[36] The "star" was probably in fact a white disk, and this flag, at least, was once again the banner of Hardee's division that Lieutenant Dawes had noticed in Rea Field three hours before.

Some of the men in the 45th grew impatient as the unidentified forces approached. Here and there along the blue-clad line, several soldiers fired their rifles without permission. An officer ran down the line shouting, "Cease firing, those are our troops."

"The h—— they are!" roared an irreverent soldier. "You will find out pretty d——d soon they are not." But the troops obediently ceased firing.[37]

To find out the truth at last, the 20th Illinois's Maj. Frederick A. Bartleson rode forward to see. Moments later he came galloping back with a badly wounded arm, shouting, "Rebels! Rebels!"[38]

Nobody waited for orders then. Both sides triggered off volleys at almost the same moment. On Marsh's left, the Confederates may have been as close as thirty or forty yards before the 45th and 48th Illinois opened fire. All four of Marsh's regiments were soon fighting for their lives. "Never, never in my life have I seen . . . such a death struggle," recalled Capt. Lloyd Waddell of the 11th Illinois.[39] Next to the 11th fought the 20th Illinois: "We could not see them as they crouched down behind a rise of ground, while we were entirely exposed and within easy range of their guns," wrote Sgt. Ira Blanchard. "We gave them the best we had for half an hour, but their fire was telling fearful on our ranks, so much so, we had to load on our backs and fire on our knees to keep from all being killed, so our fire was not so rapid."[40]

"Everyone was loading and firing as fast as possible," recalled George Carrington regarding his own 11th Illinois, "bullets hissing over our heads and cutting the limbs, twigs and that peculiar chug when a bullet strikes a man." Will Crummer found the memory of those minutes so intense he slid into the present tense when recounting it: "The roar of musketry from either side [is] terrific. The underbrush is mowed down by bullets. Men are shot in several places in the body in a moment. The dead lie where they fall, and the wounded drag themselves to the rear."[41]

A bullet through the calf sent Lt. Nesbitt Baugher of the 45th Illinois sprawling. As he tried to crawl to the rear, another bullet struck him in the buttocks. Thinking that the situation "was getting no better fast," Baugher struggled to his feet and began hobbling to the rear. A bullet hit him in the shoulder. In frustration, he turned and defiantly held up his sword. A bullet struck the edge of the sword, split, and half of it struck Baugher in the cheek. Another round slammed into the hilt of the sword, cutting the lieutenant's fingers. Somehow Baugher managed to get out of range. He probably could not have helped reflecting on the contrast between this woodland slaughter pen and the bucolic tranquillity of the little Pennsylvania town where he had grown up. Surely nothing like this could ever happen in peaceful Gettysburg.[42]

Marsh believed most of his casualties came within the first five minutes. The Rebels may have been aiming for the officers. Lt. Col. T. E. G. Ransom and Maj. Garrett Nevins of the 11th Illinois, as well as the colonel and lieutenant colonel of the 48th Illinois, suffered wounds within the first few minutes. The line broke in the center, with the 48th giving way first. Then the regiments on either side in quick succession broke for the rear with a speed that Marsh found "mortifying."[43] "The enemy rushed forward with a yell," recalled Sergeant Blanchard, "and we had to fly from our position to a safe one in the rear."[44] Marsh and the other brigade commanders tried unsuccessfully to rally the troops. George Smith and eight or ten comrades of the 17th Illinois attempted to wheel a cannon off the field after the horses that should have been pulling it were dead. Smith recalled, "The rebels came on so fast we had to leave the gun and look out for ourselves." Within minutes the entire Hamburg-Purdy Road position had collapsed, and Sherman's and McClernand's divisions were in full retreat. "As private soldiers," Smith added, "we considered that the day was lost."[45]

Marsh attributed the sudden collapse of his brigade, which had fought splendidly at Fort Donelson, to the rapid loss of field officers in the 48th and other regiments.[46] That was no doubt part of the answer. It probably also had something to do with the relatively unfavorable ground of which Sergeant Blanchard spoke, as well as a particularly strong Confederate concentration at that point. The Rebels were having difficulty controlling and coordinating the movements of their units. In this case, they succeeded, almost fortuitously, in bringing sufficient force together to blast a hole through the middle of McClernand's line.

Covering the retreat of Sherman's and McClernand's divisions was the brigade of Col. James C. Veatch, which Hurlbut had detached to reinforce Sherman. McClernand's line was still holding as Veatch's brigade marched up "with drums beating and colors flying." Then, on command, the drummers dropped to the rear, still playing. In the 15th Illinois, Colonel Ellis, who on Friday evening had moved the regiment to tears with his prediction that a battle was coming and his emotional appeal for the men to do their duty, took his stand atop a log to get a better view. As the heavy firing from in front came closer and closer to the brigade's position, officers ordered their men to take cover by lying down.[47]

The fugitives of the broken Hamburg-Purdy Road line fled through Veatch's ranks. Then Veatch's officers ordered their men to rise and commence firing, and the whole onslaught of the Confederate pursuit fell on the brigade, front and flank. The Rebels were highly motivated, riding a tide of victory. A Confederate color-bearer dashed ahead of his regiment to plant his flag on a Union cannon that had been abandoned by its crew. Dozens of Veatch's men fired at him, and he went down, riddled with bullets. Veatch's men were falling too, and the volume of incoming fire seemed incredible. In the ranks of the 15th Illinois, Pvt. Lute Barber almost lost his grip on his rifle as a bullet hit and shattered its stock. Another bullet holed his canteen, and still another passed close enough to cut the straps of his haversack. The heavy volume of firing was rapidly clipping the underbrush to pieces. "The bushes and trees," Barber noted, "would writhe, twist and fall before this blast."[48]

On the brigade's exposed right flank, the 15th Illinois was taking the worst of the Confederate pounding. According to Veatch's official report, Colonel Ellis "heroically held his ground." Early in the fight, a bullet struck his wrist. He got Lt. Frederick A. Smith to bind it up and then continued in command. Capt. Louis D. Kelly could still hear him encouraging the men: "Stand firm"; "Do your duty, boys"; "Stand your ground"; "Take good aim." Then, as Colonel Veatch reported, "while cheering his men and directing their fire [Ellis] fell mortally wounded." The regiment's major was already dead, and eight of its ten captains were down. Lt. John Puterbaugh took a bullet in the shoulder but stayed in the fight.[49]

Death seemed to strike all around Lute Barber. The major went down just a few feet away. Then Barber's captain pointed out a Rebel for Barber to shoot at but was shot himself moments later. Lieutenant Smith was hit next, while standing beside Barber. The private carried his lieutenant a few yards to the rear and then turned back to rejoin his company, now completely without officers. To his shock, he found the whole regiment gone. Outnumbered and outflanked, the 15th Illinois had retreated. Where its line had stood, Barber now saw "the ground swarming with Rebels." "This," he told himself, "is not a safe place for Lute Barber," and took to his heels.[50]

The story was much the same in Veatch's other regiments. The 46th Illinois lost its entire color guard, and Col. John A. Davis was carrying the flag himself when Veatch ordered what was left of the brigade to fall back to avoid encirclement. Veatch's regiments had suffered severely, but they had fulfilled their mission in delaying the Confederate advance enough to allow Sherman's and McClernand's divisions to break contact and regroup.[51]

The two divisions rallied about 500 yards to the rear. Marsh berated the men of his brigade for their precipitate retreat, saying that "this battle would never be won with such fighting."[52] Lieutenant Colonel Ransom, head swathed in a bloody bandage, resumed command of the badly depleted 11th Illinois.[53] Not far away, in the ranks of the 11th Iowa, Thomas Haines showed his comrades what a close call he had had only a few moments before, holding up his hat on the end of his ramrod so the others could see the bullet hole clear through it. Just then a shell burst over the regiment, mortally wounding him.[54]

With their commands once again in hand, Sherman and McClernand, who cooperated closely in the defense of the Union right, decided to launch a counterattack. Their trump card was Sherman's right-flank brigade, that of Col. John McDowell. It had been relatively lightly engaged thus far and was thus in good shape. It also occupied a position that would allow it to slash down onto the left flank of the forces threatening the rest of Sherman's and McClernand's divisions. Around midday they launched their attack and succeeded in driving the Confederates back through McClernand's now badly tattered camps. Marsh's brigade, together with the 11th Iowa of Col. Abraham Hare's brigade, even captured a six-gun Confederate battery.[55] McDowell's brigade had things much its own way for a time.

Then, however, the Confederate advantage in numbers began to tell. New units came up and struck McDowell's right flank, forcing him back. Heavy Rebel attacks again battered McClernand's front as well. In the ranks of the 11th Iowa, Alexander Downing fired his rifle until it became so foul with powder residue that his ramrod stuck fast in the barrel. "I could neither get it up nor down," he wrote. So he proceeded to place a percussion cap on the breech of the rifle and then fired the ramrod off across the battlefield. Without a ramrod, however, his rifle was useless, so he picked up a Belgian rifle and cartridge box from a dead Rebel lying nearby and went on fighting.[56]

Under this pressure, Sherman's and McClernand's divisions once again fell back to the position in which they had rallied before their counterattack, about a mile and a half from the landing. Action on Sherman's and McClernand's fronts now slackened somewhat from the furious frenzy of battle that had raged there almost uninterruptedly since the Confederates had first emerged from the thickets of the Shiloh Branch bottoms and nearly shot Sherman. Smaller numbers of Rebels continued to press on Sherman's and McClernand's battered lines, and some episodes of fighting continued to be intense. Several Union batteries in this sector fought an extensive duel with their Confederate counterparts across the way, but for now, the main weight of the Rebel assault was toward the Union center and left.[57]

It was near noon, and Grant, accompanied by several of his staff, was inspecting his lines on the right when he saw a formation of troops moving up. "Now we are all right, all right," Grant exclaimed, "there's Wallace." But it was not a part of Lew Wallace's Third Division but merely an element from one of the divisions already on the field.[58] Grant could not understand why Wallace was not there yet. He had been counting on the veteran Third Division to help turn the tide in his favor, and he had been expecting to see it much sooner than this. Around 11:00 a.m., "Grant expressed considerable solicitude at the non-appearance of General Wallace," as a staff officer recalled, and sent a lieutenant of cavalry with a message for Wallace to hurry up.[59] Then at 12:30 p.m. he sent his aide-de-camp Capt. W. R. Rowley on a similar mission.[60]

Wallace's "non-appearance" has remained one of the lingering controversies of the Battle of Shiloh. Grant's first message took inexplicably long to reach him. Then Wallace misunderstood what Grant wanted of him and traveled the wrong road. Apprised of his error, he laboriously doubled his column back on itself in order to get to the right one—when he could have simply about-faced. Finally the pace of his movement was reasonably prompt for ordinary circumstances but was far from being the forced march that the present desperate circumstances demanded. As the afternoon wore on, Grant continued to wait in vain for the Third Division.

Meanwhile, Col. David Stuart's detached brigade of Sherman's Fifth Division had been fighting a battle of its own this morning, almost separate from that waged by the rest of the army. It comprised the extreme right flank. Here on the edge of the Shiloh plateau, more and deeper ravines cut through the otherwise rolling terrain. Called to arms when the firing had started that morning, soldiers of the brigade had waited nearly three hours for the Confederates to find them. Stuart's skirmishers fired on Rebels advancing to attack Prentiss's and Hurlbut's troops farther to the left, but for a time no major attack came their way. That was bound to change, however. As resistance stiffened along the Peach Orchard and Sunken Road line, Rebel attackers seeking to flank the position would be heading this way. Even after McArthur took position on Hurlbut's left, a significant gap existed—Stuart thought it was more than a quarter mile—on his right, but Confederate formations would have difficulty getting through that gap until they dealt with Stuart's three regiments, the 54th and 71st Ohio and the 55th Illinois.

The wait was hard on these green soldiers and their equally inexperienced commander. Stuart wondered which way the Confederate attack would come from and where he should place his regiments. He moved them from one position to another, all within a few hundred yards of their camps, making the soldiers more and more nervous and less and less confident in their brigade commander. When the Confederates approached and the skirmishers began exchanging shots, some of the regimental leaders proved even worse than Stuart. With bullets from the skirmish firing buzzing over the heads of his men, Lt. Col. Oscar Malmborg, the Swedish martinet, decided to put his 55th Illinois through a complicated and inappropriate tactical movement. As a result, the men became confused and then panicked and fled 200 yards before rallying, most of them, and forming line again.[61] The 71st Ohio's Col. Rodney Mason apparently led his regiment in a panicked flight, and Stuart saw neither Mason nor the regiment again that day, though small groups of men stayed and attached themselves to the other two regiments.[62]

With about 800 men left in his brigade, mostly members of the 55th Illinois and 54th Ohio, Stuart formed his line on the forward rim of a deep ravine. The time was about noon, and the main line of the brigade had not yet been seriously engaged. In this position, however, Stuart and his men fought for the next two hours. The Confederates should have been able to brush this small force aside, but they were having trouble bringing up men and ammunition. What pressure they did exert during those two hours was just about as much as Stuart's remaining men could hold out against. The drummers cast aside their drums, picked up rifles from the dead and wounded, and joined the fight. Chaplain Haney, who had preached to the 12th Michigan the night before, now supervised the stretcher-bearers and drove one of the 55th Illinois's ambulances through enemy shellfire to reach the field hospital.[63]

Cpl. Robert Oliver of the 55th was lying down, loading his rifle, when Lt. Theodore Hodges approached. Both Oliver and Hodges, like many in Company C, hailed from the little village of Harrison, Illinois, near the confluence of the Sugar and Pecatonica rivers, a few miles from the Wisconsin line. Hodges dropped to one knee beside Oliver and with the point of his sword on the ground, leaned down near Oliver's head in order to make himself heard above the roar of battle. "Oliver," he shouted, "as soon as you get your gun loaded take Ainsbury to the rear; he is . . ." At that moment a bullet slammed into Hodges's head. As the lieutenant sank to the ground, "he hung to the hilt of his sword until his hand came to the ground, bending the sword double," Oliver later recalled, "and when he let go it bounded six feet into the air."[64]

A few hundred yards to the west, the Confederates continued to hammer at the Union line along the Sunken Road and through the Peach Orchard, but Hurlbut's and Will Wallace's divisions and Prentiss's remnant remained solid. Hickenlooper noted how "the ear-piercing and peculiar 'rebel yell' " and the lower-pitched cheers of the Union men "rose and fell" as the tide of battle surged back and forth in front of the Sunken Road. "Again and again . . . this dance of death went on."[65] The underbrush caught fire in front of Lauman's brigade, adding to the thick pall of smoke that hung over the position. Out in front of the Sunken Road, Lauman's men could hear the shrieks of the Rebel wounded caught by the flames. In the vicious cross fire that prevailed, no one from either side dared go to their aid.[66]

Col. James Tuttle, commanding a brigade of Iowans in Wallace's division, rode his horse calmly along the Sunken Road telling his men to "keep cool and remember that we were from Iowa."[67] Like Lauman on the other side of the Hornets' Nest, Tuttle was doing a good job of keeping his men's cartridge boxes filled. Again and again, the Iowans rose up to pour point-blank volleys into the faces of the attackers. Then the defenders charged and pursued the fleeing Rebels some distance before returning to their position in the Sunken Road. In helping to repulse the sixth attack of the day, Pvt. James Guthrie of the 14th Iowa caught a Rebel color-bearer and took his flag. "See here, boys, I've got their flag!" shouted the exultant Guthrie. By the time of the eleventh and twelfth assaults, as counted by the men of the 12th Iowa, Philo Woods of that regiment believed the attacks were landing much more heavily on his own side of the Sunken Road, Wallace's sector. Different observers came up with different tallies for the total number of Confederate charges on the position. Still, the Iowans believed they could go on fighting off as many more onslaughts as the Rebels could launch at them.[68]

Prentiss's and Hurlbut's men might have disagreed about both the chief target of the attacks and how long they could endure them. One event in particular, though unknown to the Union soldiers at the time, was indicative of the high importance the Confederates attached to breaking through Hurlbut's position at the Peach Orchard. Around 2:00 p.m., Confederate commanding general Albert Sidney Johnston personally led an infantry charge across the widow Bell's cotton field toward the Peach Orchard. He turned aside somewhere in the field, allowing his infantry to surge forward against the Union line. As the general turned away, however, a bullet from one of Hurlbut's men struck his leg just behind the knee, tearing his popliteal artery. Most of the copious flow of blood went into his high boot, and Johnston apparently remained unaware of the wound, as did those around him. About thirty minutes later, he lost consciousness, and within an hour of his wounding he was dead. Command of the army passed to Gen. Pierre G. T. Beauregard, a mile and a half to the rear.[69]

Yet along the Sunken Road, in the Hornets' Nest and the Peach Orchard, the battle raged on. In the heart of the Hornets' Nest, a shot from some Confederate battery smashed one of Hickenlooper's four guns, while another incoming round detonated one of his ammunition chests with a mighty roar. In contrast to the Iowans a few yards away, Hickenlooper by late afternoon felt "the line was slowly melting away; our ammunition, several times replenished, was nearly exhausted."[70]

Near the Peach Orchard, in Hurlbut's sector, Battery A, 1st Illinois Light Artillery—the Chicago Light Artillery—ran out of canister, the best type of ammunition for use against attacking infantry. As the assaults continued, the artillerists had to use solid shot and their few remaining shells.[71] Not far away, in the Peach Orchard itself, the men of Pugh's brigade were starting to run out of ammunition, thanks to Pugh's breezy assurance that no resupply would be necessary. The colonel of the 32nd Illinois had his men fix bayonets and prepare to defend themselves with those.[72]

It did not come to that. By now it was about 3:00 p.m., and events elsewhere on the battlefield would dictate the next movements in the Peach Orchard sector. On the far left, Stuart's men, the 54th Ohio and 55th Illinois, were also nearing the end of their supply of ammunition as well as their continued ability to hold off the heavy attacks against their front. With the men rummaging the cartridge boxes of their fallen comrades for the last few rounds, Stuart sent word to Hurlbut that he was going to have to pull back, exposing Hurlbut's left flank. Then he gave the order to retreat. Behind them was a ravine, 100 feet deep and 100 yards wide. The Confederates had already gotten into the ravine on the right, between Stuart's brigade and that of John McArthur, who was operating with Hurlbut.[73]

As Stuart's men plunged down the near slope of the ravine, they immediately came under a deadly cross fire from up the ravine as well as from other Rebels who rushed forward to line the rim of the ravine that Stuart's men had just vacated. "It was like shooting into a flock of sheep," recalled a Rebel officer of the 9th Mississippi. "I never saw such cruel work during the war." As Stuart's men scrambled up the far slope of the ravine, the slaughter only grew worse.[74]

Capt. Lucien Crooker took a bullet in the leg, and Sgt. Parker Bagley came alongside to help him to the rear. Seeing a bloody bandage on Bagley's arm, Crooker realized that he too was wounded and urged him to leave him and go to the rear. "That does not amount to anything," Bagley assured him. "Lean on me just as heavily as you have a mind to; I feel just as well as I ever did." At that instant, Crooker felt a bullet burn across the skin on his back and heard it strike Bagley. The two men toppled to the ground in a heap, the dying Bagley on top.[75]

Those of Stuart's men who survived the gauntlet of the ravine regrouped several hundred yards to the rear, but McArthur's flank was now exposed. From McArthur's left, the officers of the 50th Illinois had some-times caught glimpses of Stuart's fight, farther to the left. In midafternoon they noticed that the firing had ceased from Stuart's sector and assumed that they were about to be attacked. They were right. The Rebels surged up through the ravine on the regiment's left, and the 50th was almost hope-lessly flanked before the fight fairly got started. Lt. Theodore Letton, on the left flank of the 50th, was watching his men engage the Confederate attack-ers in front when he looked to the left and saw a gray-clad line of battle approaching squarely athwart his company's flank. "I saw them plainly when they raised their guns, turned their heads to one side in order to aim, and then fired," Letton recalled. "To say that I was surprised and horrified would fall far short of expressing my feelings at that moment." The 50th broke for the rear.[76]

The rest of McArthur's regiments fought stubbornly but finally had to give way, one by one from left to right, as each in turn was flanked. In the 9th Illinois, young John Cockerill, fugitive from the 70th Ohio, was appalled when the young lieutenant who had noted his name and address fell dead almost at his feet. Now if Cockerill should fall, his family might never learn his fate. With the rest of his adopted regiment, Cockerill kept shooting until his cartridges gave out.[77] The 9th Illinois suffered 62 percent casualties and had only four unwounded officers remaining when it retreated.[78] McArthur himself was wounded, and Hurlbut, realizing that his division was next, shifted Cruft's brigade from the Sunken Road around to his left to try to hold the crumbling flank. The Hoosiers and Kentuckians fought as fiercely as had McArthur's men. The position was exposed to a savage cross fire, and casualties were high. Finally, as George Squier put it, the cross fire became "rather more than even Indiana valor could withstand, and we were ordered to retreat."[79] Hurlbut notified Prentiss that he was falling back. Then he gave his troops the order to withdraw, and the 32nd Illinois did not get to try its bayonets against the Confederate attackers.[80]

For Hurlbut's men, retiring in the face of continued Confederate attacks was no easy matter, however. Sergeant Boggs of the 3rd Iowa thought the order to retreat came "just in time to save our bacon. It was every man for himself." Boggs thought he would find safety in the 3rd Iowa's camp, about half a mile from where he had been fighting. What he did not realize was that by running toward the camp he was actually traveling diagonally across a pocket that was already beginning to form around the entire Sunken Road sector. He was shocked to find the Rebels already pouring into his regiment's camp. "I thought I was a gone goose, but I had good faith in my running qualities, and said to myself, here it goes. With musket in hand, and my neck stretched out like a sandhill [crane], I started through a heavy cross fire from the rebel musketry. At every jump I thought it would be my last. I could see men fall all around me."[81]

The artillerymen did not have the advantage of Boggs's high mobility. When Lt. Peter P. Wood, of the Chicago Light Artillery, shouted, "Limber to the rear. Get your guns out of this," two of his six gun crews had imme-diate problems. The four men left in the crew of gun number five, a heavy 12-pounder howitzer, were too few to pull their piece back and hook it to its limber. Cpl. Adam Hall rode up, jumped off his horse, and put his shoulder to the wheel of the gun. In seconds they had it limbered. Hall jumped back on his horse, but was immediately toppled with a bullet wound in the head. The gun started for the rear with the Rebels only 100 yards behind.

The crew of gun number two had a different problem. Their gun, a light 6-pounder, had only one horse left—enough to pull it for some distance with the crew helping as best they could. The horse balked, however. The Rebels charged closer and closer. Nothing the crew could do would move the beast. Then a Confederate bullet smacked into the horse "squarely in the root of the tail." Artilleryman Charles Kimbell called it "an instanta-neous cure for balking." The horse finally got into motion and the gun got away.[82]

The retreat of Hurlbut's division, though it began on orders, soon became a footrace. "Our men were in full retreat," wrote a staff officer, "running as hard as their legs could carry them for the landing. I never saw such a stampede in my life. Our troops were the most frightened set of men I ever saw." Hurlbut and his staff galloped ahead of them and tried to regain control. Hurlbut had been magnificent this day, riding his horse boldly along his line under heavy enemy fire. His men had noticed and dra-matically revised their estimate of him. Now, however, nothing that he or his staff could do would stop his division's panicked flight. "We fell back in the worst possible confusion," wrote Lt. D. J. Benner of Hurlbut's staff, "men running—cavalry tearing through the woods as if their life depended on it."[83]

With Hurlbut's division gone, Prentiss bent back his left flank to counter the new pressure from that direction. He consulted with Will Wal-lace at this time, and according to Prentiss, they "agreed to hold our position at all hazards."[84] Within minutes, however, something happened to change Wallace's mind. At about 3:00 p.m., McClernand had withdrawn his line to the point that it no longer supported Wallace's right. Partly this was a result of continued Confederate pressure, and partly it was owing to the fact that once again, as at Fort Donelson, some of his regiments were running out of ammunition.[85] At any rate, the infamous central gap that had helped doom Sherman's and Prentiss's early stands was now reopened. Confederate officers, struggling against the disorganization of their army and the rugged, wooded terrain, finally succeeded in massing overwhelming strength against the exposed flank of Wallace's division, the brigade of the one-armed, Irish-born Col. Thomas W. Sweeny. As Sweeny's regiments began to crumble one after another, he sent word to Wallace that he could not last much longer.

For Wallace, this put things in a whole new light. Holding at all hazards was one thing when only one flank was in the air. Now both flanks were open, and the command was in imminent danger of being surrounded. Worse, with Sweeny's brigade collapsing, Tuttle's Iowans could not hope to hold out much longer. Wallace had to get them out of the trap before they suffered a fate similar to what his own 11th Illinois had endured at Fort Donelson. The need for haste was such that Wallace did not take time to consult with Prentiss again but immediately gave the order for Tuttle's regiments to begin withdrawing.

That was going to be difficult, as by now they were taking fire from almost all directions. The path of the withdrawal would be along the main Corinth Road through a gentle hollow behind Tuttle's position. The first regiments to go were the 2nd and 7th Iowa, and Wallace and his staff rode with them, the general riding slowly on the retreat, much as he had been doing at Fort Donelson when Lew Wallace met him. They had come a little more than 100 yards when a staff officer noticed a line of Confederate troops coming toward them over a rise to their left as they retreated. Wallace rose in the stirrups for a better look. As he did so, a bullet struck him behind the left ear and exited through the left eye socket. He fell heavily to the ground. His staff officers carried him about a quarter of a mile, but the Rebels were closing in. Their general's wound was obviously mortal. In fact, they thought he was dead already; so they left him and made off as best they could.[86]

Most of the artillery got away, since both Wallace and Prentiss had started their batteries to the rear some minutes before when things began to look unstable. The 2nd and 7th Iowa also escaped, as did all of Sweeny's regiments except the 58th Illinois. The Confederates trapped that regiment along with the three remaining regiments of Tuttle's brigade just beyond where Wallace was shot. The 12th and 14th Iowa never received the order to retire. The last order Col. Joseph J. Woods of the 12th Iowa received directed him to "hold this position at all hazards." Virtually surrounded, half the Hawkeyes were firing to the front and half to the rear before the two regiments finally attempted a breakout. Running a gauntlet of enemy fire at double-quick time, they made it as far as the hollow behind their position where several of Prentiss's and Sweeny's regiments were milling around in disorder, their escape blocked. All eventually surrendered.[87]

Prentiss also capitulated with the remnant of his command. By this time it was about 5:00 p.m., and the Confederates needed time to pass the prisoners to the rear, and then untangle their many units that had turned toward the Hornets' Nest to help encircle Wallace and Prentiss. Then with perhaps somewhere between thirty minutes and an hour of daylight remaining, the victorious Confederate line advanced once again toward Pittsburg Landing, now less than one mile away.[88]

Throughout the day, Grant continued to ride his lines, sometimes under heavy enemy fire.[89] He designated the cabin at the landing as his official headquarters but checked in there only occasionally to see if anything had been heard yet of the approach of Lew Wallace's division from Crump's Landing or of Nelson's division from Savannah. On one of these visits to the landing, at about 2:00 p.m., Grant met Buell aboard the steamboat on which the Army of the Ohio commander had just come up the river from Savannah.[90] Both the circumstance and their relationship dictated that their greeting be brief. It could not have been warm. That dispatched, Buell got down to business: "What preparations have you made for retreating?"

"I have not yet despaired of whipping them, general," Grant replied.

The exchange was characteristic of both men. Grant went on to explain that he was expecting Lew Wallace any minute. With Wallace's and Nelson's divisions, victory would be certain.[91]

Buell was not necessarily convinced, and, in truth, a look around the landing would have been enough to discourage a stouter heart than his. By this time, the number of stragglers at the base of the bluffs had grown considerably. Grant estimated they numbered "as many as four or five thousand" by this time.[92] Later, Buell and others not particularly well disposed toward Grant would bandy about figures as large as 10,000 or even 20,000. The latter number is patently absurd, but the former is probably exaggerated as well. Eyewitnesses who had extensive opportunity to observe the crowd on the bank estimated it as closer to 5,000. Several pointed out the fact that the area was not very large and would not have held more than that.[93]

As Grant explained in his memoirs, "The distant rear of an army engaged in battle is not the best place from which to judge correctly what is going on in front."[94] Every hotly engaged Civil War army leaked a steady stream of demoralized soldiers to the rear. Some were habitual skulkers; others had simply run out of courage for that day. At Shiloh an added factor was that lack of training and experience contributed to a loss of organization. This loss of small-unit cohesion removed the individual soldier's most effective prop for his courage. Finally, at Shiloh, those who fled the front lines could not go very far to the rear because the river stopped them, creating a pent-up mass of men whose courage had failed them.

Nothing, it seemed, could induce those men to return to the fight. Officers harangued them, appealed to their patriotism, their manhood, or anything else they could think of—all to no avail. Grant tried his hand at the matter, as did Chaplain Haney of the 55th Illinois and numerous others, all without effect. Even threats of immediate shooting, shelling, sabering, or bayoneting failed to move them. The men rightly sensed that neither Grant nor any of their officers—not even Buell—would actually shoot them. And they knew the Rebels would.[95]

The scene at the foot of the bluff was not a sight for the timid, and by all accounts it worked mightily on Buell, who prowled around the landing for some time in a vile temper, apparently with half a mind not to bring his troops across the river at all. Col. Hugh Reed's 44th Indiana, part of Hurlbut's division, had won the nickname "the Iron Forty-fourth" fighting in the Hornets' Nest that day. When the division fell back to the vicinity of the landing, Reed went looking for ammunition. Seeing a general officer he did not know, he approached and asked if the general knew where Reed could get some. The general turned out to be Buell, who contemptuously replied, "No, sir, nor do I believe you want ammunition, sir." Reed asked the general's name. "It makes no difference, sir, but I am General Buell." As Reed turned and rode away, Buell spurred after him and demanded his name. "My answer," Reed later related, "was as fierce and insulting as I could make it."[96]

Throughout that afternoon, Grant had had his chief of staff, Col. Joseph D. Webster, gathering artillery for a final line of defense on the last ridge south of Pittsburg Landing. He started with the Army of the Tennessee's five 24-pounder siege guns, each weighing nearly three tons. Then he added four 20-pounder Parrott rifles, and then every other gun in every battery he could lay hands on. Batteries and parts of batteries, as they retreated from the various stands the army made farther out, would refill their ammunition chests, briefly rest horses and men if they could, and then take up a position in the growing line of guns that finally came to a total of forty-one. The line of artillery faced south, toward the deep ravine of Dill's Branch.[97]

The Chicago Light Artillery was there with all six of its guns—four 6-pounders and two 12-pounder howitzers—including the howitzer that was down to a four-man crew and the 6-pounder that had retired from its last position drawn by one horse and its crew. Before going into battery on the ridge, Lt. Peter Wood took his command down to the lower landing where an ammunition boat was docked. There he had his men refill the ammunition chests on their caissons and limbers with an ample supply of canister for the final struggle.[98]

As Hurlbut's division fell back from its position near the Peach Orchard, the ridge occupied by the line of artillery was the next viable piece of terrain for a defensive stand. It was also the last possible place for a stand short of Pittsburg Landing. If the line overlooking Dill's Branch should collapse, the Confederates would drive the survivors into the Tennessee River or into the swamps of Snake Creek, a tributary just to the north. Either way, the army, as an army, would cease to exist. Only scattered individuals would escape, probably without weapons. "Every one seemed to be imbued with the idea that as this was our last stand," wrote Lt. George Nispel of Battery E, 2nd Illinois Light Artillery, "so should it be the most desperate."[99]

It was the sight of the heavy guns on the ridge above the landing that finally brought Hurlbut's fleeing division to halt its stampede. Lieutenant Benner had about given up on the army's chances of survival. "Our men were panic-stricken—the enemy flushed with victory were in hot pursuit—the river in front of us, and nothing appeared to remain to us at that time but an ignominious surrender." At the sight of the big guns, however, "a new courage was inspired, and our men commenced rallying to support this battery."[100]

The remnants and fragments of Sherman's and McClernand's divisions fell in along the same line, farther out from the landing. From what was once Will Wallace's division, the 2nd and 7th Iowa, and the 9th Illinois—the last with only seventy men still with the colors—took their places in line.[101] Only Hickenlooper's battery and Capt. Emil Munch's 1st Minnesota Battery were left of Prentiss's division. The 15th Iowa was there as well, technically part of Prentiss's division, though it had never joined that command. Around midmorning Grant had sent it to reinforce McClernand instead. After seven hours of combat, it was back within a few hundred yards of where it had filed off the steamboat that morning, its numbers reduced by 28 percent casualties. Grant personally directed it to a place in the final line.[102] Together all of these fragments formed a line that ran from just above the landing westward for about one mile, then curved to the north to cover the Snake Creek bridge, over which Grant and many others had looked in vain all day for Lew Wallace's arrival.

The approximately 18,000 men left in the ranks were enough to man the line fairly heavily, a density of almost seven men per yard of front.[103] The line was continuous, without the gaps and loose joints that had betrayed several of the positions farther out from the landing during the course of the day. Yet only a full-scale Confederate assault would reveal exactly how much fight was left in these soldiers, most of whom had been in intense combat for eight to ten hours by this point. Pvt. Edward Roe felt full of fight and believed his comrades did too. "It was worth several years of common life to feel as we did then," he recalled. "I cannot explain my feelings, only I know that we all felt alike" in sharing a determination to avenge the deaths of fallen comrades.[104]

Shortly after 5:00 p.m., it became apparent that the Confederates were sorting out their units and forming up in preparation for an attack. Out in the river, the gunboats *Tyler* and *Lexington* took up positions opposite the mouth of Dill's Branch, ready to add the fire of their heavy 32- and 64-pounder guns to that of Webster's massed batteries when the inevitable Confederate charge began.[105] The head of Nelson's column had reached the far bank of the river, and his men were already boarding steamboats for ferrying across to join Grant.

On the Hamburg-Savannah Road about three miles north of the landing, Lew Wallace's division was laboring along the muddy road across the Snake Creek swamps. By now Rawlins and McPherson were both with him, dispatched by Grant in a desperate effort to impart some speed to the Third Division's approach. As Wallace had continued his nonchalant progress toward the battlefield, complete with rest stops, Rawlins had been almost ready to place him under arrest. Now some passing civilians informed Wallace that the Snake Creek bridge was in Confederate hands, so Wallace halted the column until his cavalry detachment could scout ahead and find out. In a few minutes, a messenger returned from the cavalry with the reassuring word that the bridge was safe. Still, Wallace remained halted, in Rawlins's words, "waiting for his column to close up and his troops to rest." They were sitting there at about 5:30 p.m. when a new roar of artillery firing, more thunderous than any that had gone before, seemed almost to shake the ground. There was no mistaking, amid the thunderous din, the deeper voices of the big 24-pounders. Rawlins and McPherson had seen Webster placing those heavy guns just above the landing earlier that day and knew what their sound meant. It "filled our minds with terrible apprehension," Rawlins later wrote.[106]

Back at the landing, the Rebel forces surged forward against Grant's final line, and Webster's massed artillery cut loose with a breathtaking roar. The gunboats added their thunder as they blasted shells up the length of Dill's Branch. Those of Grant's own infantry whose field of fire was not obstructed by the artillery added their musketry. "The smoke was so great, however," wrote Charles Hubert of the 50th Illinois, "that I could not see the enemy in our front."[107] This fight was to be primarily an artillery fight. Lieutenant Nispel and his officers urged the infantry near their battery "to stand firm but a short time longer and we would drive [the Rebels] back."[108]

During the attack, Grant sat his horse placidly at the top of the ridge just behind the heavy guns.[109] A few feet away, an incoming cannonball shattered the head of an aide, but Grant remained impassive.[110]

"General," a nearby surgeon remarked, "things are going decidedly against us today."

"Not at all, sir," Grant replied, "we are whipping them there now."[111]

He was right. The massed artillery beat back the Rebel assault across Dill's Branch. In fact, it had been a relatively weak thrust, carried out by only a couple of brigades of the by now badly disorganized Confederate army. While the Rebel generals near the front lines were getting their troops into line for a more concerted assault, they received orders from Beauregard, commanding from several miles to the rear, to halt and pull back for the night. The time was about 6:00 p.m., and the first day's battle at Shiloh was over. As the guns fell silent, somewhere along the Union line a band struck up "The Star-Spangled Banner."[112]

It had been a beautiful spring day, and some men had complained of the heat. That night, however, a cold rain poured down in torrents.[113] The cabin Grant had designated as his headquarters was in use by a surgeon diligently amputating and tossing the severed limbs out a window to join a growing pile outside.[114] The steamboats at the landing were likewise full of wounded men. So the commanding general fared as his soldiers did, without shelter under the pitiless downpour.

Sherman found him that night, standing under the scant shelter of a tree, lantern in one hand, smoking a cigar. "Well, Grant," Sherman quipped, "we've had the devil's own day, haven't we?"

"Yes," Grant replied between puffs on his cigar. "Lick 'em tomorrow, though."[115]

CHAPTER ELEVEN

From Pittsburg Landing to Corinth

AFTER THE GUNS had fallen silent and night was gathering, Lew Wallace's division finally crossed the Snake Creek bridge and approached the rest of the Army of the Tennessee. Wallace and his men did not know who had been victorious in the conflict in which they had been too late to take any part. Uncertain in the darkness and lingering banks of gun smoke as to whether they were approaching friends or newly victorious foes, Wallace had his lead regiment, the 24th Indiana, form line of battle, fix bayonets, and move forward cautiously toward figures dimly seen on the high ground beyond the creek. Out of the murk ahead of them came a challenge: "Who comes there?"

"Hoosiers!" answered the 24th's Col. Alvin P. Hovey, nervously wondering if the response would draw a volley of rifle fire.

"Welcome, Hoosiers!" came the response. Hovey's regiment had encountered Birge's Sharpshooters, assigned to guard the Snake Creek approaches. Wallace's division moved forward until it was completely within Union lines. Then, exhausted after more than sixteen miles of marching on sometimes difficult and muddy roads, they settled down to make the best they could of camp for the night.[1]

"That night, on the shore of the Tennessee River, was one to be remembered," wrote John Cockerill.[2] Few soldiers who were there could ever have forgotten the night of April 6 at Pittsburg Landing and in the woods and fields nearby. The battle had raged intensely for twelve hours, and the men were exhausted, faces blackened with powder residue, minds appalled at what they had witnessed. They had not eaten since the long roll had called most of them away from their breakfasts, and many had no food with them.

Then there was the rain. It began as a drizzle and gradually increased to a downpour. Except for some of the regiments of the Second Division that had been encamped nearest the landing, none of the troops had tents, and many were without blankets or overcoats. "The rain came down in torrents," recalled Pvt. Lloyd Jones of the 16th Wisconsin. "I never saw it rain as it did that night. It literally poured."[3] John Cockerill called it "one of those peculiar, streaming, drenching, semi-tropical downpours."[4] John Hunt of the 40th Illinois sat down with his back to a tree, and as he fell asleep, his head lolled backward against the trunk. "When I awoke," he later recalled, "the water was pouring down through that treetop in great streams into my upturned face." He added, "I never came so near drowning in my life on what may figuratively be termed dry ground."[5] The rain continued with no perceptible pause all through the night. "We were hungry, wet, and miserable," wrote William Wade of the 11th Iowa.[6]

In darkness thickened by sheets of falling rain, it was the sounds of the night that many soldiers remembered. "We heard many gruesome noises that night," recalled John Hunt.[7] The most striking sounds were those of the heavy cannon aboard *Tyler* and *Lexington,* which kept up a harassing fire against the Confederates all night. "The gunboats were firing shells as big as pumpkins up into the heavens every fifteen minutes to drop down into the Confederate line," recalled Oscar Stewart of the 15th Iowa.[8] "I watched these shells all night as it was almost impossible to sleep," wrote an Illinois soldier. "I saw the light and flash at the cannon's mouth and the light of the shell fuse as it rose gracefully up to its extreme altitude, gradually falling until it exploded with a reverberation that shook the earth."[9] Frequently the report of the exploding shell was followed by the sound of splintering wood and the crash of falling limbs and trees.[10]

Soldiers' reactions to the shelling varied. Illinoisan George Mason said it gave "a glad, exultant feeling" to the men of Grant's army.[11] Thomas Connelly of the 70th Ohio agreed, writing that the "terrible shrieking" of the shells "was soul-stirring music to our ears."[12] Others seemed to think the shelling was as harassing to Union troops as to Confederate.[13] For Private Jones, it was a forcible and unwelcome reminder of the deadly business that had brought him into this miserable place. "The thought came to me then, that this was the worst night I ever passed through."[14]

John Cockerill lay on a waterlogged hay bale at the landing about 100 yards from the gunboats and dozed fitfully. "I was aroused every now and then by what appeared to be a tremendous flash of lightning," he wrote, "followed by the most awful thunder ever heard on the face of the earth. These discharges seemed to lift me four or five inches from my water-soaked couch."[15] Many soldiers wrote that the regular booming of the guns made sleep completely impossible.[16] "It was," in the words of Capt. James Day of the 15th Iowa, "a weird, wearisome, wrathful night."[17] In John Cockerill's verdict, "There never was a night so long, so hideous."[18]

Between crashes of natural and man-made thunder, other sounds reached the ears of the thousands of wakeful soldiers. "I will never forget the cries of distress of the wounded who lay on the battlefield that night," wrote George Smith of the 17th Illinois. "They called for mother, sister, wife, sweetheart, but the most piteous plea was for water." Once the rain began in earnest the cries for water ceased. "We hoped that many were refreshed," wrote Smith. "As the wounded lay between the battle lines we could not help them."[19]

From somewhere on the battlefield, not far away, Smith heard a man begin singing the Charles Wesley hymn "Jesus, Lover of My Soul." Others took up the hymn through verse after verse:[20]

> *Jesus, lover of my soul;*
> *Let me to Thy bosom fly.*
> *While the nearer waters roll;*
> *While the tempest still is high.*
> *Hide me, O my Savior, hide!*
> *Till the storm of life is past.*
> *Safe into the haven glide,*
> *O receive my soul at last.*

Elsewhere on the battlefield wounded soldiers took up the hymn "When I Can Read My Title Clear," with its appropriate verse,

> *Let cares like a wild deluge come,*
> *And storms of sorrow fall,*
> *May I but safely reach my home,*
> *My God, my heaven, my all.*[21]

Other wounded suffered aboard the steamboats, where overworked surgeons and others did their best to help them. Ann Wallace served as a volunteer nurse to the hundreds of wounded who were brought aboard *Minnehaha* that day. On another boat, Surgeon Horace Wardner found a soldier "bleeding from a badly shattered arm" and lying exposed to the elements on the hurricane, or upper, deck, as there was no room below. "Amputation was necessary to save his life," Wardner recalled. "With the light of one tallow candle, which a drunken assistant held and protected from the wind as best he could, I amputated and dressed the arm." Somewhat surprisingly, the patient recovered.[22] Others did not even live out the night. Long lines of corpses appeared outside the cabin at the landing and on shore alongside the steamboats where throughout the night attendants laid out one by one those who had succumbed to their wounds.[23]

Soldiers near the landing could also hear the sound of steamboats in motion during the night. "All night long they wheezed and groaned, and came and went" as they hauled load after load of Buell's soldiers across the river. Three divisions totaling some 20,000 men had crossed by morning. Curled up on his soggy hay bale at the landing, Cockerill could also hear the almost constant sound of Buell's troops marching up the road from the landing to the top of the bluff. "By this time the road was churned into mud knee-deep," he recalled. "Regiment after regiment went by with that peculiar slosh, slosh of men marching in mud, and the rattling of canteens against bayonet scabbards, so familiar to the ear of the soldier."[24]

These 20,000 fresh troops, along with the 6,000 veterans of Lew Wallace's division, figured prominently in Grant's plans for April 7. Those plans were uncomplicated but thoroughly settled in his thinking. On the evening of the first day's battle, as Grant and several of his staff officers stood around a smoking fire, McPherson rode up and dismounted. "Well, Mac, how is it?" Grant asked. It was pretty bad. McPherson reported in some detail on the depleted and exhausted condition of the army. Grant listened but said nothing.

"Well, General Grant," McPherson concluded, "under this condition of affairs, what do you propose to do, sir? Shall I make preparations for retreat?" Grant seemed surprised. "Retreat? No! I propose to attack at daylight, and whip them."[25]

Grant reckoned that if his own troops were near the end of their endurance, the enemy's must be too. As he explained to Sherman when visiting his lines shortly after the firing stopped, "At Fort Donelson at the crisis of the battle, both sides seemed defeated, and whoever assumed the offensive was sure to win."[26] With his large reinforcements, Grant had an unusual opportunity for seizing the offensive, and he meant to use it to the fullest. At dawn his forces would come straight at the Rebels in an all-out attack and drive them back until their army crumbled.

It was a simple plan, but as the German philosopher of war Carl von Clausewitz had written, "Everything is simple in war, but the simplest thing is difficult."[27] The first difficulty arose with the absurdly simple task of locating Lew Wallace. In the strict military sense, it was not Grant's responsibility to find Wallace, but Wallace's to find him and report. This would have been much easier, since Pittsburg Landing was a known place to which any officer in the army could have directed the commander of the Third Division or a member of his staff. Wallace neglected this duty, however, leaving to Grant and his staff the problem of tracking down Third Division headquarters, somewhere in the darkened woods south of Snake Creek.

Grant had McPherson out looking for Wallace much of the night. When around midnight the hapless staffer reported that he still had not unearthed Third Division headquarters, Grant remained adamant. "Go again, Colonel," he insisted, "and don't come back until you do find him; and order him to attack at daylight."[28] McPherson had ranked first in the West Point class of 1853, but they never taught this situation at the academy. He dutifully continued searching through the dripping woods and muddy ravines, in constant danger of blundering into enemy lines, but failed to come upon Wallace.

Some of Wallace's officers later claimed that he had searches made for Grant, Sherman, and McClernand, but could find none of them. The night was too dark, the rain too intense. Somehow no one thought to look for the river, or else they could not locate that either. From a passing cavalryman that night, Wallace learned that the valley just west of him contained Tilghman Branch, and that the enemy was on the other side of it. He deployed his three brigades accordingly.[29]

The knowledge of the enemy's presence and of what awaited on the morrow weighed on the minds of many within the Pittsburg Landing perimeter that night. One of them was Col. William L. Sanderson of the 23rd Indiana, in Lew Wallace's division. Like everyone else on the battlefield, he could hear the cries of the wounded and the booming of the guns. What seemed most to interfere with his sleeping, however, was "the Responsibility of my position." He thought of all the things that might go wrong and how if his regiment should "fail to do as much as any other," his family "would be eternally disgraced." After long thought, he reassured himself that the men of his regiment would stand the gaff. "I finally came to the conclusion that the boys were all right." Still, the night seemed unpleasantly long.

With relief Sanderson saw streaks of light spreading across the sky in the east and heard the drums beating reveille. He mounted up and rode along his line, where some of his men were munching hardtack and making coffee. One of them said, "Colonel, I have some coffee for you." Sanderson gratefully accepted the soldier's gift and relished it much, but though he had a haversack full of bread, butter, and ham, he did not feel like eating anything just then. Continuing to ride along the line of his regiment, he "scand every face" and tried to encourage the men. "Boys, mind where you are from," he admonished them, "the glorious state of Indiana. I want you to convince them that you are no home guards. Will you do it?" The men responded with a cheer and shouts of "Yes," "Yes, Colonel," "Take us in!" and "We will follow you any place."[30]

Elsewhere throughout the army, other regiments were rising, eating such breakfast as they possessed, and preparing for battle. Chaplain Haney had spent much of April 6 hauling wounded to the landing and then trying to give them what aid he could. He guessed, however, that the regiment was without food. Going aboard one of the supply boats at the landing, he managed to wangle a sack filled with hams and carried it the short distance to where the regiment was now camped. The men, who had had no food for twenty-four hours, were grateful.[31]

Whatever the day might portend, no one seemed sorry to see it come. "Action of some kind, even if it took us into the very hell of battle," wrote John Hunt, "was preferable to standing in the impenetrable darkness, in the steady downpour of rain, sleepy, hungry and tired."[32]

Grant himself finally found Lew Wallace shortly after daybreak. Wallace had already ordered his batteries to open fire on the Confederates across Tilghman Branch, and the noise of the bombardment may finally have been the beacon that was needed. When he came upon Wallace, Grant's orders were simple: the Third Division was to advance due west, cross the valley of Tilghman Branch, and keep going.[33]

In Grant's overall program that morning, the Army of the Ohio would form his left wing; the Army of the Tennessee, his right. McClernand and Sherman, with the more or less reconstituted First and Fifth divisions, would compose the left and center of the Army of the Tennessee. Hurlbut's Fourth Division would serve as reserve. Prentiss's Sixth Division was no more, and the Second, formerly Will Wallace's, was disorganized. Lew Wallace's Third Division would form the right wing of the Army of the Tennessee and, as a large fresh unit, would provide by far the strongest single element of the army's combat power on this day.

As the advance began, the Federals all across the front initially encountered no serious Confederate opposition. Beauregard's order of the previous evening, calling off the assault, had also directed Confederate units to pull back a considerable distance. The tough fighting did not begin until Union troops had moved forward about a mile to a mile and a half. Then the battle was joined in earnest. Grant's forces continued to press forward against stiff resistance, pausing intermittently in one sector or another to allow other parts of the line to catch up.

During one such interlude, Colonel Sanderson made sure the men of his 23rd Indiana were lying down out of harm's way, but he himself "kept walking up and down the lines, still uneasy, think[ing] something might happen, to cause the boys to run." His men called to him to take cover. "Col., do lay down," they said, but Sanderson laughed and told them "to lay still, that I was all right."[34] During another halt, Sanderson and his adjutant made a lunch of the bread, butter, and ham in Sanderson's haversack. He had been too nervous to eat it for breakfast, but now he was in high feather. His men chafed him good naturedly. "Thought a man did not get hungry in battle!" "Oh, you rascals," replied Sanderson in the same spirit, "you all want some of it." They assured him they did not, showed him their own full haversacks, and offered him some. "Save it," replied the smiling colonel, "you will need it when you whip those fellows that are now firing on you."[35]

That afternoon the Confederates launched several local counterattacks. One such small foray by a detachment of mounted Texas Rangers threatened Wallace's right-flank brigade, commanded by Col. John M. Thayer. Thayer ordered his own right-flank regiment, the 23rd Indiana, to shift right and block the attacking horsemen. Making use of terrain, Sanderson and his men scored a complete success, soundly thrashing the Texans.[36] The colonel had no need to worry about being "eternally disgraced." His boys had done him proud.

On the whole, the battle of the second day did not match the sustained ferocity of the day before. Col. James Veatch, who participated in both days' fighting, wrote of the second day, "There were sudden bursts of battle as furious and intense as any that occurred on the first day, but they were less frequent, and of short duration."[37]

The heaviest fighting of the day came in Sherman's front. Not far from the Hamburg-Purdy Road, where Sherman and McClernand had tried to make their combined stand the previous morning, Confederate forces directed by Gen. Braxton Bragg staged a major attempt to halt the Union advance. A shallow body of water known as Water Oaks Pond became the focal point of intense combat. Sherman's line of advance here converged with that of the right division of the Army of the Ohio, which had been fighting its way along the axis of the main Corinth Road. Sherman's troops, reinforced by Hurlbut's, and joined by Brig. Gen. Alexander McCook's division of the Army of the Ohio, fought for several hours in their efforts to break through the Confederate line near Water Oaks Pond.

Early in the afternoon, the Rebels counterattacked. A brigade of troops from Arkansas, Tennessee, Mississippi, and Alabama charged across Water Oaks Pond—waist-deep in some places—and pushed Sherman's and McClernand's divisions back several hundred yards before they rallied and took up the advance again, aided by Wallace's division on the right.[38]

The battle surged back and forth several times through and around

Water Oaks Pond and the surrounding woods, fields, and thickets as first one side and then the other seemed to gain the upper hand. Sherman described the fighting there as including "the severest musketry fire I ever heard." To break the Confederate resistance there, Sherman sent a staff officer back to find and bring up some additional artillery. "By almost Providential decree," as he put it, the first artillery unit the staff officer came to was a section of Capt. Edward McAllister's Battery D, 1st Illinois Light Artillery, equipped with two 24-pounder howitzers. These were much lighter guns than the heavy siege cannon back at the landing but still unusually large and powerful compared to other field guns. Along with several other batteries nearby, McAllister's men succeeded in neutralizing the opposing Rebel artillery. Then, cooperating with an assault by a brigade of McCook's division, Sherman launched both Buckland's brigade and Stuart's (now commanded by the 54th Ohio's Col. T. Kilby Smith). These troops finally succeeded in securing the area around Water Oaks Pond and pushing the Confederates back from the Hamburg-Purdy Road.[39]

Elements of the Second and Fourth divisions had moved up from reserve and gone into the fight when called for in support of McClernand's and Buell's troops, each undersized regiment or brigade experiencing its own triumphs and setbacks as part of the steady overall advance. The 81st Ohio drove back a Mississippi regiment opposite them and captured several abandoned artillery pieces. "You cannot conceive of the glory of a victory," wrote Maj. W. H. Chamberlin of that moment, "nor can I tell you anything of it." The exultant Ohioans shortly found, however, that they had neither horses with which to remove the guns nor sufficient ammunition left for their own rifles to enable them to hold the cannon against the immediate Confederate counterattack. For the time being, they had to fall back.[40]

During the fight for the guns, Cpl. Charles Wright of the 81st saw a black man come up to the regiment's firing line from the rear. The man was not in uniform but wore a cartridge box and carried a rifle—just now anyone could have his choice of thousands of pieces of such equipment, lying all over the ground. The black man joined the 81st's firing line and blazed away steadily, grinning happily the whole time. Wright was impressed both by his courage and by the good rate of fire he maintained, and it occurred to the corporal from Ohio that he would like to meet and shake hands with that man after the battle.[41] The rifle-wielding black man was probably one of a fairly substantial number of runaway slaves who had sought refuge with the army. Although orders called for returning such persons to their masters, many regiments actively flouted the orders and kept them in camp.

This one apparently decided to strike a blow for his people's freedom almost nine months before Lincoln's final Emancipation Proclamation authorized black soldiers in the Union armies.

About the time Sherman and McCook pushed the Rebels back from the Hamburg-Purdy Road, Beauregard ordered his army to disengage and retreat to Corinth. Grant was near the front at the time, a little east, or to the left, of the area around Water Oaks Pond, and perceived the beginnings of the Confederate withdrawal. He knew his army was too battered and exhausted to make a general pursuit, but he hoped to do the Rebels what damage he could before they got off the field and to start them along at a good brisk pace when they did go. Looking around him he found the 14th and 15th Illinois regiments, belonging to Veatch's brigade, and ordered them to advance. He rode with them to prevent premature and ineffective long-range fire. Then when he reached musket range, he turned aside and ordered them to charge. The movement was successful, as far as it went, but before the Illinoisans could set their bayonets to the fleeing Confederates, Buell, not knowing the advance was Grant's doing, ordered it stopped. By the time things got straightened out, there was no hope of doing further immediate damage to the rapidly retiring enemy.[42]

As the Rebels fled, Grant's men cheered. "Such shouting as went up from our lines—I now felt proud—yesterday's gloom was removed," wrote Lt. D. J. Benner of Hurlbut's staff. "I could have torn my shirt from my back or got drunk, I did not know which. No one can imagine one's feelings under such circumstances."[43]

The Battle of Shiloh was over at last, and Grant ordered his exhausted troops to return to the camps from which most of them had been driven the previous morning. With the fighting over, the men of the 23rd Indiana suddenly discovered powerful appetites and dove hungrily into their haversacks, as their colonel had predicted. Sanderson lay down exhausted that night but could not sleep until he had "fought the battle over again" in his thoughts. Of that evening, he later wrote, "I was never so tired, and yet so happy, and proud, in my life."[44]

In the aftermath of Shiloh, officers' reputations rose and fell. Col. Jesse Appler, of course, was finished. Two weeks after the battle, Sherman filed court-martial charges against him, but he had already resigned and mustered out three days earlier. Here and there, other regimental and company officers faced court-martial and dismissal for displaying cowardice in the face of the enemy.[45] On the other hand, some officers gained new respect for their courage and leadership in battle. "Some of the boys did not like the captain before the battle and thought he would not fight," wrote Sgt. Henry

Culbertson of the 16th Wisconsin, "but they were mistaken, for there was not a braver man on the field. He stood at the head of his company, sword in hand, and the way he would swing that old thing over his head and say, 'Go for them, boys!' "[46]

General officers could gain respect the same way. Hurlbut's stock went sharply up with his troops after Shiloh. His courage on the battlefield changed his image in the Fourth Division from that of a political hack with a drinking problem to that of a brave and capable commander.[47] Sherman's stock rose sharply with everyone. That was odd, in a way, because Sherman had been more at fault for the Sunday morning surprise than any other officer. Yet once the fighting started, he had been magnificent. Halleck, Grant, and the army's rank and file were impressed.[48]

Lew Wallace fell drastically in Grant's estimation. As Augustus Chetlain summed up the belief at Grant's headquarters, "Had Gen. Lew Wallace strictly obeyed orders on the morning of the 6th and taken his place at the right of our line with his division of 6,000 men and two batteries, the battle would, without doubt, have been a decided Union victory by or before 3 o'clock that day."[49] This was not quite correct, but if Grant's facts were wrong, his instincts, in this case, were probably correct. The confusion about which road to take was excusable, but Wallace's unhurried march during the afternoon hours, after he had been informed that the Army of the Tennessee was fighting for its life, was not.

Long before Shiloh produced any visible effect in Wallace's standing, however, it appeared destined to ruin Grant. Politicians, newspaper editors, much of the public, and some officers and soldiers in the army clamored against Grant for the surprise at Shiloh and the appalling casualty list. Included in the newspaper clamor was the inevitable but completely unfounded charge that Grant had been drunk. To make matters worse, the army read the newspapers and believed them. "We waited until the arrival of newspapers from the North to learn what we had ourselves done," wrote soldier Alfred T. Andreas.[50] And *Chicago Tribune* editor Joseph Medill had the nerve to write to Grant's friend Washburne stating that Grant was "played out," because "the soldiers are down on him."[51] Some of Medill's readers certainly were. One Chicagoan later said that "if Gen. Grant had made his appearance in Chicago immediately after the battle of Shiloh, he would have been mobbed, such was the feeling of indignation."[52]

In fact, notwithstanding the efforts of Medill and his ilk, many of the soldiers still had confidence in Grant. "That Pittsburg battle was one awful affair," wrote Charles Wills of the 8th Illinois in a letter home, "but it don't hurt us any. Grant will whip them the next time completely."[53] Jesse Connelly of the 31st Indiana noted in his diary the rumors that the army "was surprised, and that Grant was drunk," but added, "I do not believe either true."[54]

Shiloh had not been a masterpiece of strategy or a specimen of operational genius. The Confederate attack on April 6 was one of the most complete and stunning strategic surprises in the history of warfare. In after years, hot debates would rage in the columns of Union veterans' publications as to whether the army was surprised at Shiloh. The evidence is overwhelming that the army was not surprised, but Grant and Sherman certainly were.

Union scouts and pickets did their jobs in the days and hours leading up to the Confederate attack. Thanks to alert officers like Everett Peabody and even the apparent constitutional coward Jesse Appler, as well as alert sergeants like Edward Gordon, every regiment in the Army of the Tennessee was in line of battle with weapons in hand before coming under attack. In almost every case, they had stood ready in that formation for half an hour or more. No regiment made its initial fight on its color line; except for Appler of the 53rd Ohio, every colonel was able to take his men at least several hundred yards forward and choose a position in which to meet the enemy. Contrary to hysterical newspaper accounts in the weeks that followed, Union soldiers were not bayoneted while they lay sleeping in their tents or chased from their camps unarmed and half dressed.

Grant and Sherman, however, were as completely surprised as it was possible for generals to be. They had had, in Grant's words the day before the battle, "scarcely the faintest idea of an attack (general one) being made upon us." However, there was some particle of truth in the promise Grant had made in the same dispatch to Halleck that he would "be prepared should such a thing take place." It is doubtful that Grant would have done anything very much differently if he had expected a Confederate attack in the first week of April 1862. Sherman's and Prentiss's camps were laid out more or less so that the regiments on their color lines would be in line of battle. Grant probably saw that as sufficient, believing that the yawning gaps between Sherman and Prentiss and between Prentiss and Stuart's detached brigade could be plugged by the First, Second, and Fourth divisions before serious consequences could arise from them. Grant had his army prepare no entrenchments, but such defensive works were the exception rather than the rule at this stage of the war. As Colonel Tuttle of the Iowa brigade later observed, "an officer would have been laughed out of camp had he proposed to build works for the defense of our army at that time."[55]

Though Grant drastically miscalculated his opponent's likely behavior leading up to Shiloh, that was not the mistake that brought his army close to defeat. Rather, the truly dangerous error was in grossly underestimating white Southerners' determination to fight for the Confederacy and therefore underestimating the fighting prowess of their armies. Grant did not expect an attack, but he thought he was adequately prepared for one and could easily cope with it if it came. The biggest surprise for Grant at Shiloh was not that the Confederates attacked but that they attacked as fiercely and effectively as they did.

Writing his memoirs more than two decades later, Grant stated, "Up to the battle of Shiloh I, as well as thousands of other citizens, believed that the rebellion against the Government would collapse suddenly and soon, if a decisive victory could be gained over any of its armies." Shiloh, he said, changed his mind. "I gave up all idea of saving the Union except by complete conquest." Up to this time, it had been Grant's policy, reiterated in dozens of general orders, to spare the property of civilians. "After this, however, I regarded it as humane to both sides to protect the persons of those found at their homes, but to consume everything that could be used to support or supply armies."[56] The passage of two decades had led the 1885 Grant to telescope into a single battle the metamorphosis that had in fact taken place in his thinking over the several months following the Battle of Shiloh. Nor was Grant the only one whose thoughts that summer were migrating away from ideas of a limited police action against a clique of insurgent politicians to an all-out war against a rebellious people. The ferocity of Confederate resistance not only at Shiloh but at battles elsewhere during the spring and early summer of 1862 brought Lincoln to the same conclusion.

Such resolutions, however, and their ramifications both grim and glorious, still lay well in the future as the soldiers of the Army of the Tennessee returned to their camps on the evening of April 7. The camps that had been a "sylvan retreat" thirty-six hours before were now an appalling shambles. The beloved Sibley tents, if still standing at all, were riddled with bullet holes. Dead and wounded men and horses lay all around.[57] "Within a radius of 200 yards of my headquarters some 150 dead bodies were left on the field," General McClernand reported, "and some 30 or 40 horses were killed within the same distance."[58]

The Rebels had ransacked the soldiers' personal belongings. "I lost my shirts, blankets, letters from home, my testament (mother's gift) and a picture of the 'girl I left behind me,'" wrote the 45th Illinois's Will Crummer. "I was more indignant over the loss of my girl's picture than I was over the other articles."[59] Members of the 70th Ohio on returning to their camp found "our old letters torn up and scattered in every direction."[60] In many cases, the Rebels had added insult to larceny by leaving their own filthy, worn-out clothes, shoes, blankets, and other items in place of the corresponding items they took from the tents. "Nearly every thing was gone," wrote William Wade of the 11th Iowa.[61] George Smith of the 17th Illinois may have been the only man in the army who actually gained from the Rebel occupation of his regiment's camp. "I found a Confederate soldier of the 5th Mississippi dead in my bed," he recorded in his diary. "From him I got the big knife that I have."[62]

That night Allen Geer of the 8th Illinois found that "the groans of the dying & wounded were so loud that sleep was almost impossible."[63] Medical personnel, chaplains, and comrades continued to make strenuous efforts to aid the thousands of wounded, but the task was overwhelming.[64] Meanwhile, men found other sorts of sounds disturbing as well. The noises that caused Oscar Stewart "to awaken with a start" in the new camp of the 15th Iowa were those of wagons going over corduroy roads (roads formed of logs laid side by side). "It so much resembled distant musketry firing."[65]

Will Wallace's staff officers were eager to retrieve his body and hastened to the place they had left him as soon as the Union advance reached it. To their astonishment, they found him still living, though cold and wet after the night's rain. Wrapping him in a blanket, they carried him to *Minnehaha*. There Ann met him, a little more than twenty-four hours later than she had originally intended. During the next several days, he was "in a stupor most of the time" but had "occasional intervals of consciousness" and could recognize and talk to his friends and, of course, to Ann. She found quarters for them in Savannah, where Will could rest more comfortably than on the steamboat and have a better chance of recovery. Yet all knew that chance to be very slim. On April 10, he succumbed. His last words to Ann: "We meet in heaven."[66]

Rain, thunder, and lightning came again on the evening of April 7 with the same intensity as the night before. Johann Stuber of the ethnically German 58th Ohio wrote that it rained "as if poured out of buckets," and in the morning "we were lying in a lake."[67] That morning at dawn a false alarm called everyone into ranks under arms, expecting another Rebel attack. "We fell in and stood around without our breakfast for about two hours," wrote William Wade. "Everybody was cross over the affair."[68] Such false alarms were common for the next several days.[69]

The work of burying the dead could not wait. Usually, though not always, the soldiers buried their comrades in individual graves, marked so that the bodies could be exhumed and brought home if desired. Sometimes they laid both Union and Confederate in trenches, though separate trenches.[70] "We buried the rebels in long trenches, laying them in cross wise until the trench was full, putting 150 to 200 in each trench," Wade recorded in his diary. "It is reported that 4000 were buried in this way."[71] That is what the burial parties reported to Army of the Tennessee headquarters, but official Confederate casualty figures listed 1,728 killed. Grant claimed that the Army of the Tennessee "buried, by actual count, more of the enemy's dead in front of the divisions of McClernand and Sherman alone" than were reflected in the Confederate report. Total Union killed and wounded were officially 10,162; Confederate casualties were 9,740. The figures for captured or missing were much less comparable because several Union regiments surrendered late on the afternoon of April 6. Union captured or missing were 2,103; Confederate 957.[72]

The experience of Shiloh, with its unprecedented bloodletting, affected the soldiers' own views of the war. They had left home hoping to "see the elephant," to experience the great adventure of battle. Shiloh was an awakening for these young men. "I came off without a scratch and I am sure I dont know why it was for I stood as good a chance as any of them to get hurt," wrote James Newton of the 14th Wisconsin in a letter home a few days after the battle. "I guess all of the Co[mpany] are perfectly satisfied as to what war is & they would be willing to have the war brought to an end so they could be discharged and sent home."[73] That did not, however, mean that most of them were eager to go home without winning the war. John Hunt of the 40th Illinois summed up the soldiers' desire to go home and their determination to see the job through to completion. "I remember writing to my mother that I had seen the 'Elephant' and had no curiosity to further cultivate his acquaintance," Hunt wrote after the war. "I am sure I reflect the sentiment of the entire army when I say that we would now have been glad if the conflict could have been ended with this great struggle, and peace and unity restored to our suffering country, and were as equally determined to suffer on, struggle and fight on until this much desired end was accomplished."[74]

News of what was then the bloodiest battle ever fought by Americans hit the Midwest hard. "Never since the war broke out had there been such intense anxiety in the Northwest," wrote an Illinoisan years later. "Many hearts were sad over friends who fell at Shiloh," and the public anticipated that another equally bloody battle might follow.[75] Intense sorrow visited many homes across the region. In Salem, Illinois, Mrs. John W. Puterbaugh received a letter from Capt. C. A. Morton beginning with the words "It becomes my painful duty to inform you of the death of your Husband." John had continued to lead his platoon of the 15th Illinois after receiving a wound in the shoulder, but a few minutes later another bullet struck him in the abdomen. He died the following morning.[76] Some families never received any notification at all, their loved ones having suffered the fate that John Cockerill had feared, falling where no friends could see and report their death.

Rapidly changing news brought contrasting reactions in Ottawa, Illinois, hometown of Will Wallace. On Tuesday evening, April 8, word arrived of a Union victory at Pittsburg Landing. "Of course the whole community were thrown into a tumult of enthusiasm & joy," wrote a townsman. "Every flag in the county was at the mast's head and every one shouting the tidings of the victory." At ten o'clock next morning came a report that Wallace was dead. "The news ran like wild fire through Ottawa and in 10 minutes every flag was at half mast," and clusters of teary-eyed townspeople stood in hushed conversation about the streets. Thursday morning brought news that Wallace was not dead but wounded. "As if by magic every flag was hoisted and the streets rang with exclamations of joy." That evening, however, Wallace died, down in Savannah, Tennessee, and news of his death brought public mourning to Ottawa once more.[77]

To Iowa City and Upper Iowa University came the news that their own University Recruits, Company C, 12th Iowa, had been captured, along with the flag that the female students had made and that color-bearer Henry Grannis had carried over the Confederate breastworks at Fort Donelson. "O what a dreadful chill came to our hearts with the news from Pittsburg Landing," wrote one of the young women of the university. Their response, however, was practical. "Our boys are sure to be exchanged," one of them explained, "and we must have a flag ready for them when that time comes around." So the ladies got busy sewing again.[78]

Within ten days of the battle, civilians from the Midwestern states began arriving at Pittsburg Landing either to care for wounded friends and relatives or to retrieve their remains.[79] One such was George Ebey of Winchester, Illinois, "an elderly gentleman, of grave and dignified appearance." His brother-in-law, Lt. Col. Thomas Kilpatrick of the 28th Illinois, had been killed in the battle. His son Fletcher Ebey had died while carrying the colors of the 14th Illinois, and another son, Lt. George Ebey, also of the 14th, was severely wounded. Yet another son had previously succumbed to disease while in the army. The elder Ebey asked Lt. Col. William Cam of the 14th to show him the exact spot where his son Fletcher had fallen, and Cam took him to the place. Standing there, the old man said in a voice choked with emotion: "When this war commenced, I declared I would willingly give up every dollar I had in the world, all my sons, and, if necessary, my own life, for my country. I say so yet, Colonel. I say so yet."[80]

Gov. Richard Yates of Illinois arrived at Pittsburg Landing a few days after the battle with a boatload of "sanitary goods"—medicine, bandages, and the like, as well as healthier and more palatable food than was normally issued in army rations.[81] Gov. Louis Harvey of Wisconsin brought a similar shipment, along with extra surgeons. As soon as word of the battle reached Wisconsin, Harvey inquired of the surgeon general what items would be most helpful to the soldiers and appealed to the people of his state to contribute to the shipment. In Madison on a snowy April 9, schoolteacher Emilie Quiner was one of a large number of citizens who "went up to the Assembly Chamber to assist in preparing and packing articles of necessity and comfort for our wounded." She noted that "there were a great many persons present, and a large amount of work was done."[82]

Harvey left for Pittsburg Landing the next day accompanying the shipment. Milwaukee was the largest donor, sending sixty-one boxes. Madison sent thirteen, with smaller totals from towns like Janesville, Beloit, and Clinton. On the way south, the governor visited with wounded troops at various rear-area hospitals and then with the Wisconsin soldiers at Pittsburg Landing. He was well received and deeply moved by their enthusiasm and dedication. To his wife, he wrote on April 17: "Yesterday was the day of my life. Thank God for the impulse that brought me here. I am well, and have done more good by coming than I can well tell you."[83] He bade farewell to the soldiers on Saturday, April 19, and started back home. That night, however, while changing boats at Savannah, the governor accidentally fell between the steamboats *Dunleith* and *Minnehaha*. Darkness and a strong current thwarted the immediate strenuous rescue efforts. His body was recovered sixty-five miles downriver.[84]

Meanwhile, military operations continued, after a fashion. On April 8, Grant dispatched Sherman with his division to make at least a modest pursuit of the retreating Rebel army. Along the way, Sherman's men found ample evidence of the battered condition of that army—abandoned weapons, equipment, and personal possessions, as well as fresh graves and unburied dead. About five miles from camp, however, Rebel cavalry under Nathan Bedford Forrest attacked the lead regiment, the 77th Ohio. The hard-riding Forrest caught the regiment unprepared and inflicted a number of casualties. Sherman himself, who was riding with the advance, narrowly escaped being one of them. The 77th fell back on the rest of the division, and one of Sherman's men put a bullet into Forrest before the tough and wily cavalryman made off. Unfortunately, Forrest recovered. The brief fight came to be called "Fallen Timber," because of the large number of downed trees on the battlefield. Skirmish or not, Sherman had pursued about as far as seemed prudent, so he turned around and marched his division back to camp, arriving at about 11:00 that night.[85]

The enemy may have been retreating in front, but Halleck was bearing down on Grant and the Army of the Tennessee from the rear. Two days after the battle, Halleck wired Grant from St. Louis, "I leave here to join you with considerable reinforcements. Avoid another battle if you can 'till all arrive, we shall then be able to beat them without fail."[86] Of course, Halleck's plan all along had been to go to Pittsburg Landing in person, to concentrate there all the manpower of the Western department, and then to advance on Corinth. In Halleck's reckoning, beating the Rebels did not mean defeating them in pitched battle, which he believed was always to be avoided, but rather maneuvering skillfully enough to compel them to retreat from strategic points such as Corinth.[87]

Halleck and his staff arrived on April 11, and Old Brains at once got busy setting things to rights. First order of business was "the necessity of greater discipline and order" in the Army of the Tennessee.[88] "Your army is not now in condition to resist an attack," he lectured Grant in an April 14 dispatch. "It must be made so without delay."[89] To that end, he had his staff officer Capt. Nathaniel H. McLean write to Grant the same day: "The Major General Commanding desires that you will again call the attention of your officers to the necessity of forwarding official communication through the proper military channel. Letters should relate to one matter only, and be properly folded."[90] Halleck never understood Grant. How could this upstart from a Galena leather-goods store ever expect to win a war if he allowed his subordinates to fold letters improperly?

And so Halleck went on, spewing out orders over his own and his staff officers' signatures—drill, reorganize, patrol, picket, fix the roads, stockpile supplies—everything that Grant would have done if Halleck had been exploring for an all-water route to the Orient or otherwise rendering himself more useful to the nation—except perhaps for the proper folding of letters.[91]

Reorganization, of course, was inevitable. The hard-hit Second and Sixth divisions especially came in for heavy shuffling. The remaining fragments of the various regiments captured near the Hornets' Nest, men who had been sick or furloughed on the day of the battle, were conglomerated into a battalion-sized unit called the Union Brigade.[92] A new Iowa brigade was put together out of the 15th and 16th Iowa, both assigned to Prentiss's division on the day of the battle, and the 11th and 13th Iowa, formerly of what had been Oglesby's brigade. It was to become one of the most organizationally stable—and hardest-fighting—brigades in the Army of the Tennessee, its composition remaining unchanged for so long that it came to be called the "Old Iowa Brigade."[93]

Halleck, however, had a larger reorganization in mind. Maj. Gen. John Pope's Army of the Mississippi arrived later in April. This force had operated in cooperation with naval forces in taking Confederate strongpoints on the Mississippi River including Island Number Ten and New Madrid. With Pope's arrival, Halleck's force, encamped from Pittsburg Landing southward to Hamburg, five miles upstream, totaled more than 100,000 men. Halleck organized this host into a left, a center, a right, and a reserve. The left was Pope's Army of the Mississippi. The center was Buell's Army of the Ohio, less one division. The right was the Second, Fourth, Fifth, and Sixth divisions of the Army of the Tennessee, plus Maj. Gen. George H. Thomas's division of the Army of the Ohio. Thomas outranked Sherman, Hurlbut, and the new Second and Sixth division commanders, Thomas A. Davies and Thomas W. Sherman. Halleck's purpose in transferring George Thomas's division to the Army of the Tennessee was so that Thomas could then command the right wing. For that purpose he also placed the First and Third divisions in the reserve, since both divisions' commanders outranked Thomas. McClernand would command the reserve.[94]

Although the Army of the Tennessee continued to exist in theory, and although Grant remained nominally its commander, "in the present movements," as Halleck's orders specified, "he will act as second in command under the major-general commanding the department."[95] The only problem with that, as far as Grant was concerned, was that there was nothing whatsoever for the second-in-command to do. For all the good he was doing for the country and its cause, he may as well have been clerking in his father's leather-goods store back in Galena.

Thus reorganized, and presumably folding its letters correctly, Halleck's mighty juggernaut of three combined armies began its advance toward Corinth, some twenty miles away, on April 29.[96] Halleck could have marched straight to Corinth, arriving there about noon of the second day. Beauregard's Confederate army could have done no better than to get out of his way. With energy and skill, however, Halleck might have caught Beauregard and crushed his army, but rapid marches and the annihilation of enemy armies had no part in Halleck's plans. The objective was Corinth, not the Rebel army, and the chief concern was absolute security. The advance was therefore made at a snail's pace, alternating brief periods of slow, cautious marching with much longer periods spent building extensive field fortifications.

"The advance on Corinth was a new experience to every man in our command," wrote Capt. E. B. Soper of the Union Brigade. The enemy seemed to contest every mile of ground, but in fact the resistance came only from light skirmishing forces that Halleck's massive army could have brushed aside almost effortlessly. "Every advance was made in line of battle preceded by skirmishers," Soper added. "When the popping on the skirmish line became hot, lines were dressed up at favorable positions, every other man holding two rifles, and his file-mate industriously using the shovel or ax, relieving each other every minute or two. A strong line of rifle pits was in this way speedily constructed."[97] As Maj. William W. Belknap of the 15th Iowa pointed out, at least the Corinth campaign taught the men how to build breastworks.[98]

Many of the soldiers were growing less prepossessed with Halleck with each passing day and its average 1,200-yard advance in the face of an enemy who showed little inclination or capacity for serious resistance. Behind his back, they began to refer to him as "Grandmother Halleck."[99] "The strongest evidence that I see of Halleck's weakness is his delaying the battle so long," wrote Illinois soldier Charles Wills in his diary on May 11. He believed the hot weather was sapping the men's strength so that "the army [is] in better condition every day than it will be the next day." Yet Halleck did not attack the enemy. Four days later, Wills wrote, "What under the sun our Halleck is waiting for we can't guess."[100]

Grant, meanwhile, continued in his anomalous position, "apparently neither private nor general," as a junior officer put it.[101] For him it was one of the most difficult periods of the war. As second-in-command, he was simply superfluous. "I was little more than an observer," he later wrote. Halleck sent orders directly to the Army of the Tennessee units in the right and reserve wings and maneuvered them without Grant's knowledge. When Grant offered a possible means of trapping the enemy, Halleck dismissed his suggestion contemptuously. "My position was so embarrassing in fact," Grant wrote, "that I made several applications during the siege to be relieved."[102]

In fact, it almost went further than that. One day Sherman stopped by Halleck's headquarters. Sherman and Halleck were Old Army acquaintances, and as they chatted, Halleck mentioned that Grant "was going away the next morning." Sherman asked why, and Halleck said Grant had applied for thirty days' leave. Sherman sensed that if Grant left he would probably not be back—ever—and determined to have a talk with him. He found Grant at his headquarters tent, tidying up his desk, as it were. After a bit of small talk, Sherman asked if Grant was really leaving, and Grant affirmed that he was. Sherman asked why. "Sherman, you know. You know that I am in the way here. I have stood it as long as I can, and can endure it no longer." Where was he going? "St. Louis." Did he have anything to do there? "Not a bit." Sherman urged him not to leave. "Before the battle of Shiloh," Sherman later recounted his argument, "I had been cast down by a mere newspaper assertion of 'crazy'; but that single battle had given me new life, and now I was in high feather; and I argued with him that, if he went away, events would go right along, and he would be left out; whereas, if he remained, some happy accident might restore him to favor and his true place." Grant appreciated Sherman's concern and promised to delay his going indefinitely and not to leave without seeing Sherman again.[103] Sherman went on to do much toward winning the war, but this may have been his greatest service.

The constant low-grade skirmishing with the enemy came to mean little to the soldiers as they grew more and more hardened to combat. It was the smallest enemies who were the biggest nuisances to the soldiers during the creep to Corinth. "The gnats and wood ticks almost eat us up," wrote the 30th Illinois's David Poak to his sister.[104] Luther Cowan of the 45th Illinois added mosquitoes to his list of pests who were giving the men "particular and marked attention (for they really leave their mark)."[105] The weather, which earlier that spring had been cold and rainy, became first hot and rainy and then hot and dry, as the region started into a major summer-long drought.[106]

By May 29, one month into the twenty-mile advance, the army was at last on the outskirts of Corinth. That night the pickets heard "unusual noises" and "a series of explosions" coming from the town.[107] Early the next morning, Sherman ordered a brigade to probe forward. The troops advanced in skirmish formation and went all the way into the main Confederate fortifications without making contact with the Rebels.[108]

The enemy had evacuated. The noises during the night had been caused by their withdrawal, and the explosions were the detonation of the ammunition magazines that the Rebels had not been able to take with them. The rest of Halleck's mighty host either moved into Corinth that day and the next or encamped around the town.[109] Halleck ordered a brief pursuit by part of his forces, including the Second Division of the Army of the Tennessee. As Marion Morrison of the 9th Illinois pointed out, the halfhearted nature of the pursuit could be noted in the fact that they marched five miles after the enemy the first day, three the second, and then camped for five days before returning to Corinth.[110]

Soldiers in the army and civilians back home generally regarded the capture of Corinth as a hollow victory. True, as Allen Geer pointed out, Corinth was a "great strategical point," but because the Rebel army had escaped to fight again another day, "it is generally thought Halleck had been out generalled by Beauregard."[111] The public back in the Midwest was not pleased either. "They were prepared to hear of many slain in the effort to take Corinth," wrote an Illinoisan, "but not to hear that the enemy had fled and was out of reach."[112]

CHAPTER TWELVE

Iuka

AFTER CAPTURING the empty town of Corinth, Halleck's next move was to build around it a massive system of fortifications large enough for his entire 100,000-man army and requiring that many men to occupy it. Convinced in his own mind that his possession of that strategic point threatened checkmate of the Confederacy, he assumed that the South would hurl its armies at those fortifications in the desperate effort to retake Corinth. When this did not occur, he began to parcel out his forces to guard his supply lines and control the territory he had gained in West Tennessee and northern Mississippi. Units of the Army of the Tennessee were soon making the acquaintance of Purdy, Bolivar, Jackson, Lafayette, La Grange, Bethel, and other small towns in the region as well as the major city of Memphis. They skirmished occasionally with raiding Rebel cavalry but fought no major engagements.[1]

Hard marching was frequent, as Halleck shifted units from one place to another in response to perceived Confederate threats. Summer heat made such marches especially difficult.[2] "Marched through clouds of dust and excessive heat for twelve miles," noted a diarist in the 55th Illinois of a June 16 jaunt in northern Mississippi, adding, "Water scarce and much suffering therefore." The wearisome excursions did sometimes have their compensations. "Occasionally a regiment or two suddenly goes quick-step out into the country in pursuit of evanescent guerillas, and returns with each haversack bulging with peaches and sweet potatoes," wrote the Illinois soldier.[3]

Fruit was abundant in the region during the summer months, and the soldiers made the most of it. "Where I was with a large Guard detail the last three weeks," wrote Luther Cowan on August 12, "we could get just as many apples and peaches as we wanted for nothing and there was a blackberry patch close to our camp where I believe our boys picked twenty bushels of berries."[4] The proverbially plentiful blackberries were great favorites with the soldiers, mentioned in diaries and letters more often than any other fruit. The soldiers considered them a sovereign remedy for all intestinal complaints.[5] Other favorites included sweet potatoes, watermel-ons, milk (from surreptitiously milked cows), honey, and plums.[6]

Marches and garrison duty in Tennessee and Mississippi brought the Army of the Tennessee into contact not only with the fruits of the land but also with the inhabitants. Often the soldiers reacted with curiosity or sur-prise to the strange ways of the Southerners they encountered. One of the greatest shocks for the Northern boys was the Southern girls' use of tobacco. "You have no idea to what an extent the habit of dipping is carried here," wrote Illinois soldier Charles Wills. "I have, while talking to women who really had in every way the appearance of being ladies, seen them spit tobacco juice, and chew their dipping sticks, perfectly at ease."[7]

Other differences ran deeper and had larger consequences. The reac-tions of white Southerners to the presence of the army was all but univer-sally hostile. When Union troops marched into a Tennessee or Mississippi town, they were met with sullen stares and occasional expressions of hope for their future defeat.[8] The more time the troops spent in the South, the more they realized that many professed Unionists were in fact lying about their allegiance. The great majority of the white population was implacably hostile, and no amount of restraint or gentle treatment would win them over. "Those in Illinois, or elsewhere, who assert that there is a strong union sentiment prevailing among the citizens, are entirely mistaken," wrote James Dugan of the 14th Illinois. "*They are all Secessionists!* They hate the North, and wish to be divorced from it in every way, politically, socially, religiously, and commercially."[9]

Many white Southerners would simply reward the army's restraint by committing any hostile acts they could, when they thought they could get away with them. "They resort to all kinds of means to injure our cause," wrote Ohio soldier Thomas Cartwright from Memphis that summer. "They invent lies of reverses to our arms and circulate them through the city, tear down flags in the dead hour of night, when they get a chance, and have been detected conveying information to the enemy." Cartwright's conclusion was: "There is no doubt that there has been too much leniency shown towards these rebels all through this war."[10]

Through the first fifteen months or so of the war, almost all Union com-manders, in keeping with Lincoln's policy, strove to restrain their soldiers from taking the property of Southerners. Grant and Sherman had done so, as did Halleck, though the results of all such efforts were at best limited. Some degree of foraging had occurred from the first time Union troops moved into secessionist territory. Times were changing, however, in the summer of 1862. Union attitudes were shifting, beginning among the common soldiers and working upward toward the commander-in-chief. Even more than the staunch Confederate fighting at Shiloh or at the eastern battles that summer, what led Union men to reevaluate their treatment of white Southerners was the persistent bitter refusal of Southern white civilians to be conciliated by any means whatsoever. If they would not be conciliated, then they must be conquered, and every just means should be used to accomplish that goal as speedily as possible.

For Congress the new attitude led to the series of confiscation acts. For Lincoln it eventually led to the Emancipation Proclamation. Those with the most abundant and direct opportunities to observe the behavior of Southern whites were the common soldiers of the Army of the Tennessee, and for them the response was a renewed and redoubled determination to take Southern property, both to punish the disloyal owners and to boost the Union war effort.[11]

Generals like Halleck were among the last Northerners to recognize the realities of the situation and realize what action was necessary. Through the late spring of 1862, he continued to enforce the outmoded orders against foraging, much to the disgust of the soldiers. As Lucien Crooker of the 55th Illinois observed, such restraint "never had any particular effect upon the fealty of the people, because they were hopelessly hostile, and all favors to them seemed to generate contempt rather than gratitude."[12] The soldiers evaded such orders as best they could, until they were finally repealed. As always, the men would respect the persons of civilians; but now more than ever, they would take what property they could.

This also applied to the species of "property"—as claimed by white Southerners—over which the war was being fought. Many Midwesterners, including those in uniform in the Army of the Tennessee, continued to harbor racist attitudes, and among such soldiers the idea of enlisting black troops or even freeing the slaves was abhorrent.[13] For a growing number of soldiers, however, the role of slavery as the single essential cause of the war became increasingly clear. Using every just means to win the war clearly meant taking a new approach to slavery and the slaves. As Lucien Crooker put it, his regiment, "like most of the army, solved for itself the true relation of slavery to the rebellion, while statesmen and generals were groping in the mazes of impracticable speculation."[14] One of the first ways in which soldiers acted on their new attitude toward slavery was in showing an increased willingness to receive and harbor slaves in camp and to thwart slaveholders' efforts to retrieve them. Many regiments from the upper Midwest had always shown such willingness, but now it became more widespread.

Even as attitudes were changing, the Army of the Tennessee was coming into contact with tens of thousands of slaves, who saw the blue-clad soldiers as their deliverers from bondage. Large numbers of blacks flocked to the Union camps and columns wherever they could reach them. Swarms of escaping slaves followed the army's units as they marched between the various garrison towns of West Tennessee and northern Mississippi. When a brigade marched into a town, the whites glared sullenly at the troops while the black population received them joyously.[15] Sometimes escaping slaves brought valuable information to the Union army.[16]

In the army's camps, blacks came to perform much of the fatigue duty—digging trenches, repairing roads, and the like—and at times it seemed that almost every soldier had a black personal servant. Sometimes soldiers' attitudes toward the former slaves, or "contrabands," as they were called, were altruistic; sometimes they were not so at all. Yet even the dullest soldier could see that depriving the South of the slaves' labor and using that labor for the Union might well hasten the day of victory when they could all go home.[17]

The same spring and summer developments that showed that a more resolute and forceful prosecution of the war was necessary also showed that the United States needed more soldiers. During the fall and winter of 1861–62, a great surge of patriotic enlistment had fulfilled the demands of Lincoln's summer 1861 call for troops. In the early spring of 1862, with the fall of Forts Henry and Donelson as well as Union victories on the periphery of the war, the end of the conflict seemed to be in sight. Secretary of War Edwin M. Stanton even suspended additional recruitment. The perspective changed in late spring and early summer. Shiloh showed Confederate will to fight. The continued animosity of Southern civilians showed how far they were from being conciliated, and the successful Confederate defense of Richmond, Virginia, proved that the war was far from over. One of Lincoln's responses to the summer setbacks was to issue a call for 300,000 more volunteers, and Congress obligingly provided that if the requisite number of volunteers should not be forthcoming in any particular state or district, the draft would make up the difference.

Relatively few men were actually drafted that year, as a final great surge of patriotic enlistment during the late summer of 1862 fulfilled the quotas set by Lincoln's call. James Sloan Gibbons expressed the spirit of this movement, in somewhat idealized form, in his poem "We Are Coming, Father Abra'am, Three Hundred Thousand More." The recruiting went on all across the North, but many of those Midwesterners who responded to the call were destined to become the final major element in the composition of the Army of the Tennessee.

"We leave our plows and workshops,/Our wives and children dear," Gibbons had his patriotic volunteers sing. It sounds melodramatic, but it was often the simple truth. By this time, it was clear that army pay was little enough—and often months in arrears—and that soldiers' families would essentially be without their breadwinners. Nor were early efforts to subsidize soldiers' families proving adequate. Such concerns made the decision to enlist extremely difficult for married men.

In Newton, Iowa, forty-year-old Taylor Peirce and his wife, Katharine, "had a long talk" about whether Taylor should enlist. His going would leave her without help in maintaining their home and caring for their three children. On the other hand, it appeared that "the rebellion could not be put down without the government got more help." Other men were enlisting and leaving families in situations as difficult as theirs, and Katharine "would not have it said that her selfishness kept her husband from his post." She gave her consent. Taylor finished up some sawing he had to do, and two days later he was on the rolls of the newly organizing 22nd Iowa Regiment.[18]

In like manner, thirty-one-year-old William Winters talked with his wife, Hattie, before leaving her, their three children, and his harness-making shop in Hope, Indiana, and joining another new regiment, the 67th Indiana.[19] Another thirty-one-year-old, Daniel Winegar, left his wife, Elvira, and their two small children when he left Belvidere, Illinois, in the ranks of the 95th Illinois Regiment. "I would not have enlisted," he later wrote, "only I thought it was my duty to defend our Country."[20] And so, in like manner, men all over the Midwest left wife, children, and livelihood to enter the army.[21]

George Willison of Massillon, Ohio, was over forty years of age, had a wife and five children, and just enough money to get by. He seriously considered enlisting but decided the hardship on his family would be too great. Reluctantly he gave in to his eldest son's urgent pleas and signed the papers for the young man to enlist instead. Young Charles Willison was just four months beyond his sixteenth birthday when he mustered in. Unlike most of the new recruits, Charles joined an established regiment, the 76th Ohio, rather than a new one.[22]

Other young men also gained the reluctant consent of their parents. William Eddington's mother, a widow, had turned him down the year before. Now "Mother told me if I still wanted to go in the army I might do so." He enlisted in the 97th Illinois.[23] The parting was hard on the mothers. Before the brand-new 32nd Iowa left the little town of Nevada, the community held a banquet for the new recruits, "but there was so much sorrow and weeping at the thought of parting that our appetites were small," recalled recruit John Ritland. "Mother could not swallow a morsel. I gave her an apple to take home."[24]

On a farm near Cedarville, Illinois, nineteen-year-old Jefferson Moses had something special on his mind when the call came for "three hundred thousand more." That May the body of Capt. Silas W. Field of the 11th Illinois had lain in state in one of the churches in nearby Freeport, and Moses had gone "to see him laying in his coffin." That experience affected him deeply. "I got home and told pa and ma I wanted to go to war," Moses later wrote. "I never felt so in my life. I just felt a great duty that I never before thought of." That summer there was a recruiting rally at the high school in Cedarville. "I was there," Moses later explained, "and got the fever." All of his friends enlisted, but he held off to get his parents' consent. When he asked them, his father said, "You have our consent to go and may God's blessing go with you." His mother said nothing but "stood beside me with her hands to her face crying to most break my heart."[25]

Perhaps the recruit who best articulated his reasons for enlisting in the summer of 1862 was Sam Jones of Iowa City, Iowa, who that summer enlisted in the 22nd Iowa Regiment. "Up to this time," Jones later wrote, "I had not thought it necessary that I should go. I had had a feeling that those who were enlisting were doing it because they delighted in the public martial display of the soldier life; but a feeling came over me at this time that I was needed in the defense of my country." For Jones the whole issue of what he should do came down to two fundamental questions: "Could the government subdue the slave power, the power that was in rebellion?" And "For the government to do it—am I needed?" The answer he gave himself was "We, the people, are the government." With that thought in mind, he explained, "I made up my mind to be a soldier and fight for my country, as many thousands like me were doing."[26]

Not all enlistments were patriotic. Some men enlisted for fear that if they did not they might suffer the unspeakable disgrace of being drafted. Others signed up for the enlistment bounties offered by counties and states in order to fill their quotas and avoid the implementation of conscription. Still, receipt of a bounty was no proof of mercenary motive. When Cedar Falls, Iowa, raised a company for what was to become the 31st Iowa, the unmarried men of the company all donated their county bounties to be distributed among the married men and help support their families in their absence.[27]

Meanwhile, military operations continued. In mid-June, Halleck dispatched Buell and his Army of the Ohio to proceed eastward along the Memphis & Charleston Railroad, across northern Alabama, to take the town of Chattanooga, but Buell's army became bogged down in Alabama, vainly trying to maintain the Memphis & Charleston as a supply line while Rebel raiders destroyed its bridges and trestles faster than his repair crews could mend them. Buell was not a fast mover at the best of times, and his plodding progress across Alabama effectively took his army out of the war for several weeks and handed the initiative back to the Confederates.

By that time, Halleck was not in the Western theater to experience the results. On July 11, Lincoln promoted him to overall command of all Union armies and summoned him urgently to Washington. There the president hoped Halleck would apply to the vexing problems of the Virginia theater the same incisive leadership he had displayed in the West. He did, and Lincoln soon came to recognize him for the "first-rate clerk" he was. Halleck remained in Washington the rest of the war, handling bureaucratic matters but not attempting to interfere very much with field operations beyond giving rather tentative advice.

With Halleck gone, Grant was left as a department commander, reporting directly to Washington. George Thomas and his division had gone with Buell, so Grant was again direct commander of the Army of the Tennessee. As senior officer in the department, he also directed the Army of the Mississippi, now commanded by William S. Rosecrans in place of John Pope. Several divisions of the Army of the Mississippi would eventually be incorporated into the Army of the Tennessee.

Grant did not, however, immediately take the offensive. Halleck had committed the forces in West Tennessee and northern Mississippi to holding so many different points that it was impossible for Grant to assemble an army of respectable size for offensive operations. To have abandoned a large proportion of those posts would have entailed serious problems, not least of all with Grant's superior in Washington, the same Henry W. Halleck. Perhaps most important to Grant, over the past six months his superiors had demonstrated that an aggressive general who took risks and energetically advanced the cause of the Union was not what they wanted in a subordinate. Twice, Grant had been all but relieved of command in the wake of winning a major victory. He would have been a man of remarkable self-confidence indeed if all of that had not rendered him somewhat confused and a trifle hesitant to undertake another aggressive campaign. Before he felt ready to do that, he needed reassurance that his superiors desired an advance and would support him rather than stab him in the back.[28]

So, for a different set of reasons, Grant's army, like Buell's, remained essentially passive during the summer of 1862. Their Confederate counterparts did not. After evacuating Corinth, Beauregard withdrew his army to

Tupelo, Mississippi, and then took sick leave to go to a health spa. An unhappy Confederate president Jefferson Davis relieved Beauregard of his command and turned the job over to Braxton Bragg. At first Bragg was as stymied as Grant and Buell by problems of supply, insufficient forces, and the scarcity of water during the summer drought. Then, in response to Confederate concerns about Buell's very slowly developing threat to Chattanooga, he came up with a brilliant plan. He would move most of his army by rail to Chattanooga via Mobile, get there ahead of Buell, and then head north out of Chattanooga, turning Buell and threatening Middle Tennessee and perhaps eventually even the Kentucky Bluegrass region.

In Mississippi, Bragg left two Rebel forces, 16,000 in the northern part of the state under Maj. Gen. Sterling Price, and another 16,000, under Maj. Gen. Earl Van Dorn, to guard Vicksburg. Union naval forces advancing northward from the Gulf of Mexico had captured New Orleans in May. The river gunboat fleet had taken Memphis in early June. That left Vicksburg, for the present, as the only remaining Confederate bastion on the entire course of the Mississippi River, and it was briefly threatened in early summer by the combined seagoing and riverine Union naval squadrons. In the end, they could not take Vicksburg because they lacked a land force sufficient to drive off Van Dorn. Now Bragg wanted Van Dorn and Price to hold Mississippi during his absence, keep Grant from reinforcing Buell, and possibly strike northeastward into Middle Tennessee themselves in support of Bragg's campaign.

By early September, Bragg was in Kentucky, where Union authorities believed he posed a grave threat to Louisville and Cincinnati. Bragg's move had forced Buell to give up his slow advance to Chattanooga and pursue instead across Tennessee and into Kentucky as well. With the campaign approaching a climax in the Bluegrass, Bragg sent word to his subordinates in Mississippi to get busy and fulfill their part of the program. Price and Van Dorn dithered and declined to cooperate with each other. Finally, Price felt compelled to aid Bragg by striking toward the Union outpost at Iuka, Mississippi, twenty-two miles east of Corinth and not far from where the Memphis & Charleston crossed the Tennessee River at the eastern border of Mississippi.[29]

Grant had distributed his forces for best defense of the key railroads and towns. At and around his headquarters at Corinth, he had Thomas Davies's and Thomas McKean's divisions of the Army of the Tennessee along with two divisions of the Army of the Mississippi, which henceforth may as well be considered as part of the Army of the Tennessee. This four-division wing of his army Grant entrusted to Rosecrans. He had another concentration of force at Jackson, Tennessee, fifty-five miles north of Corinth, where Brig. Gen. E. O. C. Ord's division had its headquarters. Sherman's and Hurlbut's divisions had their base at Memphis.[30]

Grant had already dispatched two divisions of reinforcements—former Army of the Mississippi units—to Buell. On September 7 he got wind that Price and possibly Van Dorn were moving northward either to threaten his force or to attempt to pass him and join Bragg in Kentucky. At once Grant ordered Rosecrans to pull in all of his outposts on the railroad east of Corinth. Price seemed to be heading that way. Recalling the outposts would prevent the Confederates from gobbling them up, and it would also strengthen the defenses of Corinth itself, in case the Confederates should make a direct attack. By September 13, all of the outposts were in except for the one at Iuka, where a detachment was guarding a stockpile of supplies that still needed to be brought to safety in Corinth.[31]

Iuka was the easternmost point on the Memphis & Charleston Railroad held by Grant's forces. Guarding the supply depot there was part of a brigade under the command of Col. Robert C. Murphy of the 8th Wisconsin. Along with his own regiment, he had the 5th Minnesota and the 2nd Illinois Cavalry.[32] Up until the summer's de facto reorganization, Murphy and his infantry regiments had been part of the Army of the Mississippi.

About 10:00 a.m. on September 13, Confederate cavalry attacked Murphy's pickets outside Iuka, taking prisoners. Murphy's men counterattacked, capturing two prisoners of their own.[33] These informed Murphy that Price's main body was about a day's march behind them and coming this way. The Confederates had cut the telegraph wires, so Murphy sent word of the situation to Rosecrans by courier.[34] Meanwhile, the Confederate cavalry continued to hover around the town, skirmishing occasionally with Union pickets. Since the Rebels had also destroyed the railroad leading to Corinth, there was no way that Murphy could get the carloads of supplies to safety.[35]

Before dawn the next morning, Murphy had his men set fire to the supplies and then marched his command out of Iuka, headed in the direction of Corinth. Accompanying the retiring Union force was a large number of fleeing slaves, estimated by one soldier at 2,000. The Rebels detected the withdrawal of the Union troops and dashed into the town as soon as Murphy's column departed, putting out the fires and saving an immense bonanza of supplies as a welcoming feast for Price and his men, who marched into Iuka that day. Grant and Rosecrans were displeased with Murphy for allowing the supplies to fall into Confederate hands, and Rosecrans relieved the hapless colonel of command and brought him up on court-martial charges.[36] Rosecrans gave command of Murphy's brigade to Col. Joseph A. Mower of the 11th Missouri.

When Grant ordered Rosecrans to send a brigade to probe the enemy force at Iuka, Rosecrans selected Mower's. So on the morning of September 15, the brigade, soon to be called "the Eagle Brigade," in honor of the 8th Wisconsin's mascot, Abe, turned around and marched back over the road it had tramped the day before. About two miles from the town, it came up against Confederate infantry, probed aggressively, found the Rebels in heavy force, and withdrew a short distance.

As night fell, Mower had his men build campfires—"huge fires," a member of the 8th Wisconsin wrote in his diary—and get their suppers. Sometime after dark, a Confederate deserter entered the lines with the report that Price was in Iuka with 12,000 men. In fact, he had at least that many.[37] Mower had gained the information Grant wanted; now it was time to leave. He had his men build even more campfires, so as to create the impression that a larger force had arrived and was planning to stay the night. Then at about 10:00 p.m., they marched away. The story went the rounds in the brigade that the Rebels had surrounded their empty campsite during the night, not knowing they were gone, and the men were delighted with the savvy of their new commander, whom they soon nicknamed "the Wolf."[38]

On receiving Mower's confirmation that Price was at Iuka, Grant determined to attack him at once. For a change, he could now be confident that Halleck would not object to aggressive action. The new general-in-chief, frantic about affairs in Kentucky, urged Grant to let nothing delay the reinforcements he had sent and, as for whatever Rebels he might be facing in Mississippi, "there can be no very large force to attack you," Halleck had wired on September 11. "Attack the enemy if you can reach him with advantage."[39]

Grant needed no second invitation. An added reason for haste was the presence of Van Dorn's force at least four days' march to the southwest. If Grant moved quickly, he had the chance to snap up Price before Van Dorn could either join him or threaten Corinth. Rosecrans's command could spare 9,000 men while still holding Corinth and environs. Thanks to Grant's careful placement of his available forces, he was able to bring together another 8,000 from other parts of his department. Grant's plan was to combine these two forces and march them to Iuka.[40]

Rosecrans, however, thought he had a better idea. He would lead his 9,000 men via Jacinto to approach Iuka from the southwest, while Grant's other column, under the command of Ord, moved via Burnsville and approached Iuka from the northwest. Since Rosecrans had previously made his headquarters in Iuka and had a highly touted map of the area, Grant deferred to him and adopted the more complicated plan.[41]

The troops moved out on September 18, near the end of a twenty-four-hour rain.[42] The dirt roads turned to quagmires, and Rosecrans fell far behind schedule. He communicated with Grant by courier, and Grant postponed Ord's attack to coincide with Rosecrans's new projected time of arrival at Iuka, the morning of September 19. However, shortly after midnight on the morning of the nineteenth, Grant received word from Rosecrans that he was still twenty miles from Iuka. One of his divisions had taken a wrong turn and had to backtrack. Rosecrans promised, however, that he would start for the town at 4:30 the next morning and be there, he thought, by 2:00 p.m. Grant cautioned Ord not to launch his attack until he heard the sound of Rosecrans's guns from the south side of Iuka.[43]

Early on the morning of September 19, Ord advanced his skirmishers as ordered by Grant to within six miles of Iuka, making and holding contact with the Confederate skirmishers. The Rebels were still presenting "a bold front" toward Ord's column, a sure sign that Rosecrans had not yet attacked. So Ord's column halted and waited for the sound of Rosecrans's guns. Noon came and went. Grant and Ord discussed the situation and agreed that Rosecrans would not be able to get his troops into position for an attack that day. Nevertheless, Grant directed Ord to crowd the Rebels a bit and push to within four miles of Iuka but not to bring on a full-scale engagement until he heard Rosecrans's guns. From the south came only silence.[44]

While Grant and Ord waited, Rosecrans's column pressed on toward Iuka. Although the original plan had called for his two divisions to cover the final miles to Iuka on two different roads approaching from the south, Rosecrans decided at the last minute that he did not have enough troops to do that, and instead put the entire column on the same road, leaving the other road open.[45]

Leading the column was Col. John B. Sanborn's brigade of Charles Hamilton's division, screened by several squadrons of cavalry. Around 1:00 p.m. on September 19 the cavalrymen began to encounter enemy skirmishers, whom they drove for a mile or two. Then resistance stiffened. The cavalry commander reported to Sanborn that he could not push the Confederates any farther. "They were protected in houses, barns and outhouses on the plantations," Sanborn later explained, "and could not be dislodged."[46] Hamilton ordered Sanborn to use his infantry and push the stubborn Confederates out of the way. The colonel sent out four companies in skirmish formation, and the advance went on.[47]

It was perhaps 4:30 p.m. when the skirmishers, struggling through thickets and scrub timber on either side of the road, emerged in front of a full-strength Confederate line of battle that blasted them with a volley. "Our skirmishers got into a hornet's nest," recalled a soldier of the 5th Iowa. Sanborn sent word to Rosecrans, and back came an order from the commander. Clearly, Rosecrans, who was some distance back in the column, did not believe they were up against anything solid. Get the skirmishers back out in front, he directed, and get the column moving again. The officer commanding Sanborn's skirmishers flatly refused to obey the order. Momentarily at a loss about what to do in the face of his subordinate's defiance to his superior, Sanborn sent for Hamilton to come and deal with the situation.[48]

Hamilton rode forward far enough to see the Confederate line of battle and at once realized the truth. "He immediately became very much agitated," Sanborn dryly recounted, "and said that we must go into line of battle immediately, and as rapidly as possible." Sanborn hurried his regiments forward and into line on the double. With Hamilton's advice, he put his artillery, the 11th Ohio Battery, straddling the road, just where it topped a rise. One regiment he placed to the right of the battery and two on the left, with two more regiments in reserve, sheltered in a hollow behind the line.[49]

Sanborn was just making some final adjustments to the position of one of his regiments when Rosecrans rode up with his staff. The general was unhappy because Sanborn was, as he saw it, wasting time forming line of battle when he ought to be getting up the road as rapidly as possible. As Sanborn delicately put it, Rosecrans was "in a fault-finding mood." In fact, Rosecrans's raging tirades and torrents of profane verbal abuse were to become well known in the army. Only a minute or two passed, and Rosecrans probably did not have time to work up to full cry before being interrupted by the colonel of one of Sanborn's regiments, who shouted that "the whole rebel army was advancing." Brush and scrub timber was thick out in front, and Rosecrans and those with him still could see nothing.[50]

Sanborn, who was having a very trying afternoon, offered to ride forward and see for himself. He did and almost immediately repeated the experience of the skirmishers, coming face-to-face with the Rebel line. "The entire rebel line opened fire with both artillery and musketry," Sanborn recalled. Somehow they missed him, and he went galloping back to his brigade. Passing between the battery and the neighboring infantry regiment, he shouted for both to open fire, "and the battle opened as fiercely as it is possible to conceive. Leaves, twigs, men, horses—everything—was falling."[51]

This was the first fight for Sanborn's men, and they were eager to prove themselves. A member of the 5th Iowa thought his comrades were "loading and firing amid a storm of lead, as if they were drilling."[52] "The cries of the wounded and the roar of the cannon and musketry was like the rush and thundering of a mighty waterfall," recalled another Iowan.[53] Casualties mounted rapidly as the Rebels focused their assault toward capturing the 11th Ohio Battery. Battery commander Lt. Cyrus Sears ordered his gunners, "Use canister, aim low, and give them h———!"[54] From the 4th Minnesota's position on the left of Sanborn's line, Q. O. Russell saw scores of gray-clad soldiers fall before the repeated blasts of double canister from the battery.[55] Nevertheless, the Rebels pushed forward aggressively, even crossing bayonets in hand-to-hand combat with the 5th Iowa, just to the right of the guns.[56]

On the left of the battery the situation was even worse. There the 48th Indiana's field of fire was a scant twenty-five or thirty yards due to a sharp downward slope that distance in front of its line. Dense brush also concealed the Rebels, who were pouring a heavy short-range fire into the regiment's ranks. As the enemy charged forward, the Hoosiers broke for the rear, plunging into and through the tangled woods behind them. In rear of the 48th's line, less than 100 yards distant, was the 16th Iowa, veterans of Shiloh, which Sanborn had placed in reserve. As the tide of battle surged toward them, the Iowans rose from the ground and leveled their rifles. In front of them chaos was approaching—soldiers dodging between tree trunks, bushes, and vines, officers trying to get their men to rally, and the enemy only a few steps behind, sometimes actually among the fleeing Hoosiers.[57]

Sanborn saw what was about to happen and shouted again and again at the top of his voice for the 16th to hold its fire until the 48th had cleared their front. The veteran Iowans were cool, and Sanborn saw them look toward him and thought they had understood. Then, however, they looked back over their sights and, with half of the 48th still in the line of fire, cut loose a devastating volley. The Confederate attackers had simply been too close. The volley stopped them, but a soldier of a neighboring regiment estimated that it had also killed or wounded more than 100 of the 48th. Sanborn called it "the most cruel and destructive sight that I witnessed in the war," but admitted that under the circumstances the 16th could not have been expected to hold its fire any longer. For the time being, the 16th Iowa held the enemy advance in check.[58]

Meanwhile, pressure continued to build around the 11th Ohio Battery. The cannoneers stood by their guns doggedly, but the Confederates shot them down and swarmed over the battery.[59] Forty-six of fifty-four gunners became casualties, and three of the battery's four officers.[60] Almost immediately the Federals counterattacked and took the guns back. Fighting raged intensely around them as the battery changed hands repeatedly. Drummer boy T. G. Orr of the 5th Iowa later vividly remembered Capt. E. B. Bascom of his regiment pulling with all his might on the wheel of one of the cannon, trying desperately to draw it back away from the attacking Confederates, while with the other hand he wielded his saber, parrying the blows of Rebel rifle butts aimed at his head.[61]

Additional Union troops moved up and joined the fight, which continued unabated until nightfall. Through the blackness of an unusually dark night, both sides pulled back a short distance and the firing stopped.[62] Those who experienced the battle said that this hour-and-a-half-long struggle on a hillside choked with hazel and blackjack thickets was, for its duration and extent, one of the most intense encounters of the war. Two Confederate brigades numbering just over 3,100 had fought it out with two Union brigades of about 2,800. Casualties totaled 525 Confederates, 790 among the less experienced Union troops. The Rebels briefly had possession of the six guns of the 11th Ohio Battery, although they were unable to draw them off, since almost all the battery's horses were dead.[63]

Through it all, neither Grant, nor Ord, nor any member of their column heard any sound of battle drifting up from the south. The wind blew from the north all day, and the air was humid and heavy. Somehow these factors, perhaps along with other atmospheric conditions, combined to prevent the sounds of battle from reaching the northern column, only a few miles away. Ord's men maintained pressure on the Confederate skirmishers throughout the evening but never attacked. Not until late that night did Grant receive Rosecrans's dispatch—carried over a roundabout route by a courier—notifying him that a battle had taken place. He responded by directing Ord to attack at daybreak.[64]

But when the army advanced in the morning, the Confederates were gone. Likewise on Rosecrans's front, the previous evening's battlefield stood silent, deserted by living, unwounded Confederates. "The dead lay on top of each other" in some places along the line, and in the sector where the Rebels had charged toward the 11th Ohio Battery, Iowa soldier W. G. McElrea wrote, "the scene was terrible beyond description. Arms and legs, heads and shattered trunks were lying in every direction. It seems unreasonable to relate, but in many instances the legs, arms, and heads were entirely blown away from the mangled trunks and in other instances bodies were cut entirely in two by grape and canister."[65]

"The guns of the 11th Ohio were standing the next morning between the two lines of battle in the road with 10-penny board nails in their vents, the enemy being unable to take them from the field," recalled A. L. Brown of the 4th Minnesota.[66] He was correct in that observation, save that there was no Confederate line of battle by that time, only the trampled brush where it had been. Encountering only very light skirmishing from rapidly retiring cavalrymen, Ord's forces marched through Iuka, discovering that Price's army had escaped southward.[67] As Colonel Sanborn later pointed out, the key point had been Rosecrans's decision not to block both of the roads leading south out of Iuka. "When General Grant understood that," Sanborn explained after the war, "he was not disposed to forgive it in General Rosecrans, and General Rosecrans was never disposed to forgive Grant for not forgiving it."[68]

On the morning of September 20, Grant ordered Rosecrans's entire force after Price immediately and rode with Rosecrans for the first several miles. Not long after Grant left the column, however, Rosecrans called off the pursuit, much to Grant's displeasure.[69]

Two days later and half a continent away, Lincoln issued his preliminary Emancipation Proclamation, declaring that all slaves in areas still in rebellion against the United States as of January 1, 1863, would henceforth be free. Word of the proclamation had reached the troops in Mississippi and West Tennessee within a few days. John Campbell of the 5th Iowa was enthusiastic. "The 1st of January 1863 is to be the day of our nation's second birth," the Iuka veteran wrote. "God bless and help Abraham Lincoln—help him to 'break every yoke and let the oppressed go free.' The President has placed the Union pry under the corner stone of the Confederacy and the structure *will* fall."[70]

CHAPTER THIRTEEN

Corinth

AFTER THE BATTLE OF IUKA, the demand for reinforcements for Buell continued to draw troops out of Grant's department. This forced Grant more and more onto the defensive, and compelled him to pull back the garrisons from some of his smaller outposts. Corinth was more than ever the centerpiece and linchpin of the Union position in northern Mississippi and West Tennessee. Grant made his headquarters at Jackson, Tennessee, whence he could best communicate with Corinth, Memphis, and other possibly threatened outposts of his command.[1]

After successfully escaping from Iuka, Price had joined forces with Van Dorn, and their field army now totaled 22,000 men. During the closing days of September, Van Dorn, commanding the combined force, marched northward into Tennessee about twenty-five miles west of Corinth. That put the Confederates in a position from which they could threaten several of Grant's posts, including Corinth and Hurlbut's command at Bolivar, Tennessee, forty-five miles northwest of Corinth. By October 1, it was clear to Grant that Van Dorn's target was Corinth. The crafty Rebel turned toward the key railroad junction and approached it from the northwest, cutting Corinth off from the most direct sources of reinforcement in the rest of Grant's department.[2]

Grant acted energetically to counter the Confederate threat. In the general vicinity of Corinth were Rosecrans's four divisions—Davies's, McKean's, Hamilton's, and Stanley's—about 18,000 men. To strengthen Rosecrans, Grant started McPherson, now a brigadier general, marching an ad hoc brigade of about 1,500 men from Jackson to Corinth. He also directed Hurlbut to take four brigades, 5,400 men, and advance southward from Bolivar on the west bank of the Hatchie River, threatening the rear of the Confederates moving against Corinth and positioning themselves to cut off the rebels when they retreated. For Grant the eventual defeat and retreat of the Confederates was a given. His efforts were aimed at assuring that when that happened Van Dorn's army would be trapped and destroyed.[3]

Rosecrans was not as quick to recognize Van Dorn's purpose. Fearful lest the Confederate general merely feint against Corinth and then slide by to the north into Middle Tennessee, Rosecrans delayed concentrating his troops in the defenses of Corinth. Belatedly, on October 2, he began ordering his units to march for Corinth, but by that evening the only troops he had there were two brigades of Brig. Gen. Thomas McKean's division. With Van Dorn's army at Chewalla that night, just across the state line in Tennessee and only eleven miles northwest of Corinth, Rosecrans's position was becoming precarious.[4]

His troops certainly knew less than he did of the maneuverings of the army and the specific sorts of action that might result, but they were very clear about the fact that some sort of major battle was brewing. "There is a something in and about the camps which indicates trouble ahead," wrote Charles Hubert of the 50th Illinois. "The troops are quiet, the duties of the camp are silently performed." On the evening of October 2, the regular nightly prayer meeting in the camp of the 50th was unusually well attended. "As taps were sounding," Hubert wrote, "the meeting broke up. The men shook hands solemnly all around, and then someone spoke up: 'We will not all meet again on earth; let us do our duty and pray that we may meet in Heaven.' "[5]

Rosecrans's plan for October 3 was to deploy his forces in an arc covering Corinth from the northwest to the northeast—McKean's division on the left, Davies's in the center, and Hamilton's on the right. These three divisions would take positions about two and a half miles outside Corinth along the line of the old Confederate breastworks built under Beauregard's supervision back in May. If it became clear that the Rebels were making a serious advance against Corinth, the troops on this perimeter would make a fighting withdrawal to an inner line of works, known as the College Hill line, only a few hundred yards outside Corinth, for the decisive stand.[6]

Hamilton and Davies were still two and a half hours from their intended positions when at 7:30 a.m. the enemy began pressing against a detached brigade of McKean's division seven miles up the Chewalla Road. That brigade was commanded by Col. John M. Oliver. As part of the Sixth Division, Oliver's regiments had been under Prentiss's command at Shiloh. Now once again they were among the first to meet the enemy's approach. Oliver fell back toward Corinth, skirmishing actively with the Confederate advance, until he reached the line of the old breastworks. McKean reinforced him with the brigade of John McArthur, who had transferred from the Second to the Sixth Division since Shiloh. Most of the regiments of his brigade had been Everett Peabody's at the April battle.[7]

About ten o'clock, Davies's Second Division moved up to take position in the old breastworks on Oliver's right, though not in contact with him—there was simply too much front to cover. Davies had been confused this morning by a series of vague and contradictory verbal orders from Rosecrans and his staff officers. The planned action to develop the enemy attack along the old breastworks gave way first to an order to halt well short of that line and then an order to occupy the works after all and to make a serious stand there. To Davies, Rosecrans sent orders "not to let the enemy penetrate beyond the Rebel breastworks." The Second Division had seen heavy action in the past eight months—C. F. Smith's charge at Fort Donelson, the Sunken Road at Shiloh—and heavy losses too, which had reduced its numbers so that it was now carrying somewhat less than 3,000 infantrymen into this battle, half the strength of McKean's division. These 3,000 were not nearly enough to stretch the length of the sector Rosecrans had assigned to Davies. The men stood three or four feet apart in line, and large gaps intervened between several of the regiments and brigades.[8]

In the thin ranks of the 81st Ohio, Cpl. Charles Wright could not understand why Rosecrans wanted the division all the way out at the old Confederate breastworks. The position back on the College Hill line, closer to town, "would be a splendid place to make the fight," he thought. The Confederate breastwork was "a slight affair," in Wright's judgment, "and would only serve as protection against musketry." Halleck had at least made the troops connoisseurs of entrenchments, and they knew a flimsy one when they saw it.[9]

When the Confederates launched their assault, the end result was a foregone conclusion. Davies's and McKean's divisions nevertheless put up a game fight, inflicting heavy casualties on the attackers and making a series of defensive stands that prolonged the battle throughout the day. "We poured volley after volley into the advancing lines with seemingly little effect," wrote Capt. E. B. Soper of the 12th Iowa, and "they continued to advance."[10]

When Union regiments were flanked and overwhelmed and had to retreat during this day's fighting, their withdrawal was not the panic-driven flight that some had made at Shiloh, nor did their regiments lose cohesion. They might retire as fast as their legs would carry them to get out of range of an impossible position, and an observer would have discerned no formation during the sprint. However, the regiments reconstituted themselves in line of battle almost spontaneously as soon as they came to a place where they could make a stand. "The men were not panic stricken nor demoralized," wrote a member of the 50th Illinois, "but were easily re-formed and gave a good account of themselves."[11]

Hamilton's division, on the right of the Union line, remained largely unengaged. Rosecrans tried to order it to swing to the left and flank the Rebels attacking Davies's division. As often happened during battles, however, Rosecrans became rattled and sent a garbled message. Hamilton could make no sense of it and so remained idle for hours. When Rosecrans sent a clarification, Hamilton's division moved slowly, and the day was over before it could get into action.[12]

The only help McKean and Davies got that day was from a single brigade of Stanley's division—Mower's Eagle Brigade—sent forward in the afternoon as reinforcement. Mower was, as one of his men remarked, "a perfect war horse when in hearing of a battle," and double-quicked his men toward the scene of the fighting. The day was unseasonably warm, well over 90 degrees, and all of the soldiers on both sides suffered intensely from heat and thirst. The Eagle Brigade initially deployed behind some of Davies's troops, then moved forward to relieve them and was immediately hotly engaged. "The shot and shell fell fast and furious for a few moments," a soldier of the 47th Illinois later wrote, "and we returned the shots as fast as we could load and fire." It seemed only a few minutes that the regiment was in action, though Mower estimated it at two hours. As the soldier observed, "Once under fire and at work the soldier has little conception of time." The 47th made a brief and locally successful bayonet charge, in which its commander, Lt. Col. William Thrush, was killed.[13]

Elsewhere along the line of Mower's brigade, the eagle himself screamed and flapped his wings as he sat on his perch beside the colors. As the fighting around him became more intense, Abe grew so excited that he flew up suddenly and broke his tether. Back and forth the eagle soared over the contending battle lines, screaming all the while. Finally, perhaps spotting the familiar colors of the 8th Wisconsin, he swooped back down and voluntarily resumed his perch.[14]

That evening the Union troops withdrew to the College Hill line.[15] Many members of Rosecrans's command were discouraged about their prospects that evening. Hamilton told John Sanborn "that we had probably lost the field, and that our army would retreat during the night." Sanborn also overheard statements among his soldiers such as "We are outnumbered two to one"; "The rebels had got every advantage of us"; and "We cannot win this field."[16]

Rosecrans himself was confused and uncertain. Not until midafternoon had it dawned on him that Corinth was the Confederates' main objective. In a midday dispatch to Grant, he accused Oliver's brigade of acting "feebly," and slandered the sterling performance of the Second and Sixth divisions. "Our men did not act or fight well," he complained.[17]

In fact, it was Rosecrans who had not done well. He had failed to anticipate the enemy's action, put little more than half his troops into the battle, and called on his men to fight on ground they could not possibly hold. He had sent a series of confusing and unrealistic orders to his division commanders and had done nothing to coordinate their activities, while he personally remained safely back in Corinth. The movements of the army that day had had nothing to do with any plan of his to develop the enemy or make a fighting withdrawal. The troops and their officers had simply held on as best they could. At least by evening his surviving troops were back on the College Hill line, the strongest position for defending Corinth and the only real hope of holding the town.[18]

Davies met with Rosecrans in Corinth at about eight o'clock that evening and informed him that all three of his division's brigade commanders were down. Oglesby, Brig. Gen. Pleasant Hackleman, and Col. Silas D. Baldwin were even then in the nearby Tishomingo Hotel, which Union surgeons had transformed into a hospital. Hackleman died at about midnight. Oglesby was not expected to recover. Davies's division had taken significant casualties in its rank and file as well, and its temporary losses to heat exhaustion were even greater than those caused by enemy action. At Davies's request, Rosecrans agreed to hold the Second Division in reserve the next day. Several hours later, however, he changed his mind and ordered Davies's exhausted troops to march back into the front lines. The shuffling of units went on until almost 4:00 a.m.[19]

The line had a number of glaring weaknesses. Batteries Robinett and Powell formed projecting salients of the line and would be vulnerable because they could be hit by converging fire and attacked from several directions at once. Worse, a 500-yard gap existed in the center of the line. The situation of Davies's division was an additional weakness. Its remaining 2,200 men were simply stretched over a much wider front than they had any hope of holding, even if they had not been exhausted by the previous day's intense combat under a blazing sun.[20]

The last troops had been in their assigned positions for only a short time when well before dawn the second day's fighting opened with a heavy barrage of artillery. The Confederates had brought up several batteries, and Van Dorn hoped that these fourteen guns would prepare the way for an assault. The predawn bombardment was spectacular, "a real display of fireworks," one of the Federals called it. Col. John W. Fuller recalled, "Nothing we had ever seen looked like the flashes of those guns. No rockets ever scattered fire like the bursting of those shells!" Many projectiles sailed over Union lines to crash into the town of Corinth itself, killing civilians and one wounded Union soldier who was in the Tishomingo Hotel. Medical personnel hastily evacuated the many wounded to a safer location.[21]

The Union cannoneers held their fire for more than an hour, until the light had grown sufficient to allow for accurate shooting. Then, as usual, the Federal artillery proved superior, and this superiority was enhanced by the presence of heavy guns in several prepared positions such as Batteries Robinett and Powell. Within thirty minutes, the Union guns had silenced the Rebel artillery and forced it to withdraw. In front of Davies's division, Birge's Sharpshooters also lent a hand, picking off so many horses and gunners that when one of the Rebel batteries retired, it had to leave behind two 12-pounder brass Napoleon guns, whereupon the "Squirrel Tails," as Birge's men were known, dashed forward and dragged them in as trophies of war. Elsewhere the battered Confederate artillerymen left behind another gun, a British-made brass James rifle, which the skirmishers of the 63rd Ohio brought in as a prize.[22]

For the next several hours, the only action was between the skirmishers. The most notable incident of that stage of the battle came when Joseph Mower, always aggressive, was visiting the skirmish line and got into the midst of a sharp exchange with the Rebels. His horse went down, and Mower himself received a minor flesh wound in the neck and was captured.[23]

During these hours, Rosecrans ordered large numbers of skirmishers to advance well beyond his lines, but this arrangement did not serve him well when at about 10:00 a.m. the Rebels launched their mass assault. The first Confederate attack was aimed directly at Davies's weakened division on the Union right-center. Although the advancing Rebels could be seen at a considerable distance, the Union artillery had to wait until their own fleeing skirmishers cleared their front, and by that time it was too late for the big guns to break up the attack. Birge's Sharpshooters had not completely cleared the front when the artillery finally did open up, and a number of the Squirrel Tails fell to friendly fire.[24]

Along Davies's line, the infantry lay prone, awaiting the Confederate onslaught. Company officers walked along the line, repeating quietly, "Steady, boys; be firm, aim low, do not fire until you hear the word." Finally, Pvt. Hanson Alexander of the 50th Illinois could stand it no longer. He drew a bead on a Confederate battle flag waving prominently in the front line of the advancing host. Excitedly he bawled out a request for permission to fire and at almost the same moment triggered his shot. Within seconds the whole of Davies's line was blazing away.[25]

The Confederates, Brig. Gen. Martin E. Green's division, mostly Missourians and Mississippians, with contingents from several other Rebel states, came on across a field of weeds and tree stumps, lowering their heads as if advancing into a driving rainstorm. Many of them fell, but they were too many and too close, the defenders spread too thin. Disaster struck in the center of Davies's line, in the sector of the Union Brigade.[26] Actually a battalion-sized unit, the Union Brigade was composed of fragments of the 8th, 12th, and 14th Iowa and the 58th Illinois that had escaped capture at Shiloh. Mostly these were men who had been on the sick list or on furlough at the time of the battle. Morale had always been low in the Union Brigade, as its soldiers pined for their original regiments and griped that they should have received indefinite furloughs to live at home until their regimental comrades were exchanged.[27]

Now the Union Brigade proved a weak link in Davies's line. As Confederate pressure increased, it broke and scattered to the rear, with the Rebels in hot pursuit. "It was every man for himself and the rebels for the hindmost," recalled Jonathan Labrant of the Union Brigade.[28] The triumphant Confederates rolled up the right of Davies's hard-pressed line, overrunning Battery Powell and the left brigade of Hamilton's division in the process. Davies's left brigade held on somewhat longer, but the Rebels turned the captured cannon from Battery Powell on them, and the Second Division, the shock troops of Grant's 1862 victories, fell back in retreat.[29]

The division had no reserves and no place to rally short of Corinth, in some places only a few dozen yards to the rear of its battle line. Into the town went Davies's bluecoats, and the Rebels rushed after them. Some of Davies's regiments retained their order until they reached the town, but among the houses, the last vestiges of regimental organization disintegrated. In contrast, however, to units that had lost their organization at Shiloh, Davies's men did not turn tail and flee but continued fighting for the town street by street and house by house.[30]

"I was falling back with my company," recalled Pvt. Silas Bagley of the 50th Illinois, "when reaching some houses some forty yards in rear, we stopped and commenced firing on the advancing lines of the enemy." A few moments later a bullet broke Bagley's ankle. Nearby, Pvt. Charles Hubert, from another company of the 50th, had been loading and firing rapidly. Seeing Bagley fall, Hubert rushed over to try to help him escape the advancing Confederates. Unfortunately, Hubert was a diminutive 125 pounds, and Bagley twice his weight. Struggling gamely, the little soldier exclaimed, "What shall I do—you're too big and I'm too little." There was only one thing to do. Hubert hurried off to catch up with the regiment's retreat, recommending that Bagley crawl under a nearby house and hide. Bagley started to do so, but then it occurred to him that "I might get in there and my wound might disable me so I could not crawl out if the enemy should set fire to the building." So he stayed where he was and held up his hands in a gesture of surrender when the Confederates approached. To his dismay, a Rebel captain lay down behind him, using his bulky form as a barricade. The next few minutes were intensely unpleasant for Bagley, until a shell exploded only a few feet away. A fragment tore a gash in Bagley's leg, but the explosion blew off one leg of the Confederate captain's pants. The Rebel officer fled.[31]

The Rebels were almost among the army's baggage wagons. The wagons of Col. John DuBois's (formerly Baldwin's) brigade, along with the brigade's wounded, were under the charge of the 50th Illinois's Chaplain Matthew Bigger. As Bigger was sizing up the suddenly dangerous situation and deciding what to do with his charges, a highly agitated Union officer galloped up to him shouting that the army was whipped and demanding that he immediately set fire to all of the baggage wagons. The chaplain would have none of it. "We are not whipped, sir," he replied and led his wagons to a safer position in the rear, circled them, and began organizing stragglers and convalescents to defend them if necessary. The next day, the officer who had ordered Bigger to burn the wagons was pointed out to him as none other than Rosecrans himself.[32]

In fact, while the troops of the Second Division were retaining a remarkable degree of composure in their desperate struggle for the town, Rosecrans had entirely lost his own. He rode furiously this way and that, screaming curses and profanity. It was hard to say whether his efforts did any good or not. Aside from cursing his men as cowards, his recorded statements seem to have been mostly announcements that the battle was lost and orders for setting fire to various stockpiles of supplies. His soldiers ignored him.[33]

The battle was far from lost. The attacking Rebels were near the end of their endurance. They had suffered devastating casualties during the charge and were now as disorganized by the houses of Corinth as were the Union defenders. Federal artillery on either side of the breakthrough hammered the Confederate supporting troops with a deadly cross fire. Units of Hamilton's and Stanley's divisions pressured the Confederate attackers from both sides, and DuBois's brigade of Davies's division rallied and counterattacked them head-on through the streets of Corinth. DuBois's men, soon joined by the other regiments of Davies's division, drove the Rebels until they had to give up the pursuit because they themselves were beginning to suffer from the heavy cross fire of Union artillery. The Confederates continued their flight. It was about 1:00 p.m., and the crisis on the Union right had passed.[34]

Meanwhile, the dramatic climax of the battle was building on the Union left-center. Brig. Gen. Dabney Maury's division of Van Dorn's army, mostly Arkansans with a fair proportion of Texans and a few others, marched out of the woods in front of Battery Robinett. The defenders, members of Stanley's division, waited tensely as the Rebels formed their ranks in plain view but beyond effective range. "All the firing ceased and everything was silent as the grave," wrote twenty-two-year-old Capt. Oscar Jackson of the 63rd Ohio, directly in the path of the Rebel assault. "I thought they would never stop coming out of the timber." Finally the Confederate formations were ready. "They started at us with a firm, slow, steady step."[35]

Jackson thought he had "never seen anything so hard to stand as that slow, steady tramp. Not a sound was heard but they looked as if they intended to walk over us." He glanced down the line of his company and could tell that his men were impressed by the sight. Here and there, a man checked the load in his rifle or repositioned his cartridge box or cap pouch or simply shifted his weight nervously, but except for an occasional glance down at his rifle, every man's eyes remained fixed on the enemy. Jackson thought the sight was unnerving them, so to get their minds off it he made a little speech: "Boys, I guess we are going to have a fight. I have two things I want you to remember today. One is, we own all the ground behind us. The enemy may go over us but all the rebels yonder can't drive Company H back. The other is, if the butternuts come close enough, remember you have good bayonets on your rifles and use them."[36]

As the attackers came closer, they struggled through a thick abatis under heavy fire from the Union artillery, including Lt. Henry Robinett's three 20-pounder Parrott guns in the small earthwork that bore his name. As the Confederates progressed beyond the abatis, about 100 yards in front of Robinett, the line of Union infantry on either side of the battery rose and poured a volley into them. The slaughter in the first line of attackers was terrific. "As the smoke cleared away," wrote Oscar Jackson of the scene in front of his own company, "there was apparently ten yards square of a mass of struggling bodies and butternut clothes. Their column appeared to reel like a rope shaken at the end." The Rebel line broke and the survivors fell back, but a second wave of Confederates moved past them and advanced to the attack in their turn.[37]

The struggle for the battery became a stand-up fight at murderous range. The Union infantry on either side of Robinett, members of Fuller's Ohio Brigade, had no breastworks at all, and both sides suffered appalling casualties. The company of the 63rd Ohio closest to the right of Battery Robinett was all but annihilated. "Captain Jackson," roared Col. John Sprague, "move your company up to those guns and hold them." The captain saluted and led his men into the gap. As they reached their new position, Jackson saw a body of Confederates headed straight toward him. As he watched, the Confederate officer commanding the force turned to his men and said, "Boys, when you charge, give a good yell." Jackson heard it and then with a shudder heard the Rebels raise their yell and saw them rush toward his men at a dead run.

Jackson's company, now scarcely more than two dozen men, fired a volley. There was no time to reload. "Let them have the bayonet!" yelled Jackson, then, with the enemy only a few yards away, "Charge!" The Ohioans rushed forward to meet their attackers, and for a few minutes all was thrust and parry.[38] Other Rebels were surging around Jackson's little band, pushing the rest of Fuller's men back step by step and swarming up and over the ramparts of Battery Robinett. Lieutenant Robinett fell, and his men pulled back.

Waiting in reserve behind the battery was the 11th Missouri, of Mower's Eagle Brigade. Now Stanley ordered them to charge and give the Rebels the bayonet. Someone even spotted the general, dismounted, serving as a sort of extra file closer for the 11th. He was running right behind the regiment's line, arms spread wide, as if pushing the men forward. Missourians and Ohioans joined in driving back over Battery Robinett, sending the Rebels—those who were still on their feet—fleeing back toward their own lines. Fifty-four Confederates lay dead in the ditch of Battery Robinett, including the much-respected Col. William P. Rogers of the 2nd Texas, who had been hit thirteen times.[39]

Oscar Jackson and eleven of his men were still standing. "Never have I felt so proud of anything as I was of my men," Jackson wrote. "I thought that no such company was in that army." They had fought the enemy hand-to-hand, and the Rebels were in full retreat. As Jackson stood looking after the fleeing enemy, he saw one of them quickly turn and fire. Then something struck him heavily in the face. "It felt as if I had been hit with a piece of timber." He fell, rose, staggered a few steps to the rear, and fell again. Remarkably, he survived.[40]

As the Confederate survivors streamed back from their repulse at Battery Robinett, the Battle of Corinth was over. In all, Confederate casualties during the two days totaled nearly 4,000. Maury's division, which had assaulted Battery Robinett, lost nearly two-thirds of its strength. Union casualties were slightly over 2,500.[41]

Grant had high hopes of trapping Van Dorn after the battle at Corinth. The price Van Dorn paid for attacking Corinth from the rear was that his own line of retreat was highly precarious. He had to march his army back to the northwest, retracing the route by which it had approached, in order to reach the bridge over the Hatchie River. Only when west of the Hatchie would the Rebel army be able to turn south and escape Union pursuers. Grant already had Hurlbut's column moving down the west side of the Hatchie, well positioned to block Van Dorn's crossing. All that was needed now was for Rosecrans to pursue the Rebels as soon as they began their retreat. Even before the battle, Grant had sent him orders to do so, and now he repeated them. Yet Rosecrans's army stayed put.[42]

Van Dorn and his army marched away from the battlefield, beginning their retreat late on the afternoon of October 4. Instead of following, Rosecrans rode his lines, congratulating his men on their victory and admonishing them to fill their cartridge boxes, haversacks, and stomachs, go to bed early, and be ready to start after the Rebels first thing in the morning. McPherson's brigade arrived before the fighting was over, having marched ten miles that day, listening to the sound of cannon at Corinth all the way. Rosecrans gave McPherson the same orders he had given the rest of his troops. Van Dorn was stealing a march on him, and Rosecrans knew it. There was no denying that most of his men were tired and hungry, but Van Dorn's men were more so. McPherson's brigade was fresh, and McKean's division relatively so. Those units could have led a vigorous pursuit, but the afternoon passed, and Rosecrans did nothing.[43]

The only action of this first phase of the Confederate retreat was entirely extemporized by eager Union soldiers acting without orders. William McCord of Birge's Sharpshooters noted that "squads of soldiers from our lines" rushed forward "and made prisoners of large numbers of the enemy, in some instances one man capturing from five to twenty and in another instance twenty men capturing three hundred." Most of the Rebels picked up in this way were too exhausted or too demoralized to offer any resistance.[44] Another Federal who took advantage of Confederate exhaustion and disarray was the irrepressible Joseph Mower, who somehow saw his chance to snatch a horse and gallop back to Union lines.

By contrast to Rosecrans's restful afternoon, Hurlbut drove his men hard all that day. They were up at 3:00 a.m., and some units covered as much as twenty-three miles before nightfall. By evening their advance guard was skirmishing with Rebel cavalry. They bivouacked that night just beyond Middleton, Tennessee, and less than seven miles from the key Davis's Bridge over the Hatchie River between Metamora, Mississippi, and Pocahontas, Tennessee.[45]

Then next morning the column moved out early once again, with Brig. Gen. James C. Veatch's brigade in the lead. They advanced several miles against increasingly frantic but ineffectual resistance by Confederate cavalry. The terrain was rough, broken, and heavily wooded. Finally they emerged at the top of the forty-foot bluffs overlooking the Hatchie bottoms and, about 600 yards away, Davis's Bridge. At this time, about 8:00 a.m., General Ord joined Hurlbut and as senior officer took command of the expedition.[46]

Van Dorn was striving desperately to keep his escape route open. That morning he had rushed forward a brigade of infantry and a battery of artillery to bolster his cavalry and hold the bridge until his army and wagon trains could reach and cross it. John C. Moore's infantry brigade, however, was badly depleted and, like all of Van Dorn's troops, weak with hunger and fatigue. These were the troops who were spread out in the river bottom as Veatch approached, blocking his path to the bridge.

The Confederate artillery opened up on Veatch, and his guns replied. For an hour a spectacular artillery duel raged across the broad panorama of the river bottom. "Here were thousands of men on each side, bent on the destruction of human life," wrote a soldier of the 14th Illinois, "and using all the means to effect that purpose that human ingenuity, since the beginning of time, has been able to devise. . . . The air was filled with their awful thunderbolts, hurled at each other, and the shock was grand and awful beyond the power of pen to describe."[47]

About 10:00 a.m., Veatch ordered his brigade forward in line of battle. His batteries limbered up and followed. In the 14th Illinois, Lute Barber thought the brigade crossing the Hatchie bottoms made a "thrilling military sight such as one seldom sees." Moore's Confederate brigade offered only feeble resistance, then turned and fled—too late for many of them. "We poured in our fire at short range," wrote Barber, "and with a fierce yell rushed forward to the charge." Some of the Confederates surrendered, and Veatch's men rounded up several hundred prisoners. Other Rebels, cut off from the bridge, leapt into the river and struck out swimming for the eastern shore. Some made it, others drowned. Meanwhile, all four guns of the hapless Confederate battery fell into Veatch's hands.[48]

The rest of Hurlbut's division joined Veatch in the advance, along with two regiments that had been added to his command for this expedition, the 12th Michigan and the 68th Ohio. As the 68th advanced, the captain commanding the two left-flank companies, which happened to be the extreme left of the Union line, misunderstood his orders and advanced a couple of hundred yards ahead of the rest of the regiment. The 68th's colonel, R. K. Scott, dispatched adjutant Lt. George E. Welles to get the errant captain and his command back in line. No sooner had Welles conveyed the colonel's orders, however, than General Ord himself came galloping along the line in a towering rage. What did Welles mean ordering troops to retreat? "There were no orders given to retreat, but to advance on the enemy," roared Ord, and without giving the lieutenant a chance to explain, Ord smacked him with the flat of his sword. Welles was a very popular officer in the 68th, and immediately a number of nearby soldiers leveled their rifles at Ord and yelled for him to get away. This got Ord's attention enough to make him listen to Welles's hurried explanation, and then he rode off, unscathed, at least for the moment.[49]

Presently the Rebels on the other side of the river would do a valuable favor for the men of the 68th, as well as the rest of the Union troops present, by shooting General Ord and saving his own men the trouble of doing it. First, however, Ord managed to get his command into quite a mess.

He decided that his force should cross the river in the very teeth of Van Dorn's advance. This was an exceptionally bold move since his column of less than 6,000 men was outnumbered three to one by what was left of Van Dorn's army. Ord may have assumed that Rosecrans was pressing Van Dorn hard in the rear as Grant had ordered, but there was no sound of artillery from the southeast to indicate that this was the case. At any rate, Ord's specific orders for crossing the river were inappropriate because, unlike Hurlbut and his men, who had previously encamped at this location, Ord was not at all familiar with the terrain. He directed the troops to cross and then deploy on either side of the road. However, a sharp bend in the river left no room for those regiments assigned to deploy on the right-hand side of the road. The result was crowding and confusion that threw the troops into a jumble and made them an excellent target for the several batteries of Rebel artillery that had, in the meantime, taken position on a hill a few hundred yards east of the river and opened fire.[50]

Ord seemed oblivious to the problem and galloped about ordering more troops across the river. In telling Col. William Graves to take his 12th Michigan over the bridge, he stated that some other regiments had refused to go, though that seems doubtful. Perhaps the general was still confused about the left companies of the 68th Ohio. Like the other regiments of Veatch's brigade, as well as the 68th Ohio, the 12th crossed the bridge on the run, cheering, and joined the crush on the other side.[51] The crowded troops took heavy casualties from Confederate fire, and some regiments became disorganized. While trying to form his brigade on the east bank, Veatch went down with a painful wound but refused to be carried off the field. Ordering his men to lay him on the ground, he insisted, "If I can not lead my men on to victory, I will at least stay where I can see them win it." A few minutes later, Ord rode toward the bridge to try to sort out the mess he had made and took a bullet in the leg.[52]

Fortunately at this time, about 11:00 a.m., Hurlbut arrived at this particular part of the battlefield and resumed the active command of his division. He hurried to straighten out the confused regiments on the east bank and began moving them into positions where they could deploy properly and have a fighting chance against the enemy. That took time, and while the left of the division was being untangled, the right had to wait in position under fire. They were veteran troops, however, and took the situation with a considerable degree of nonchalance. The men of the 15th Illinois lay behind a rail fence as calmly as if they were enjoying a rest during a noonday halt on a march. Their colonel, George C. Rogers, sat placidly on the top rail of the fence while bullets were, in the words of one onlooker, "tattooing on the rails around him like gravel in a gourd."[53]

Next in line, most of the men of the 14th Illinois took shelter behind large pieces of driftwood that were piled and scattered around the river bottom. Some of their comrades, however, found a thicket covered with muscadine grapevines. One man shook down the fruit while the others sat below and feasted on what had that autumn become one of the soldiers' favorite delicacies.[54]

At last the line was ready. Staff officers passed Hurlbut's orders, and regimental officers shouted them to the men. The soldiers left their fences, driftwood, and muscadine vines, formed up and fixed bayonets, and the advance began. Once again, Confederate resistance proved feeble and collapsed as soon as Hurlbut's troops launched a concerted attack. They took the Rebel-held hill within about thirty minutes of his resuming command. Thereafter, the battle settled down to a stalemate. Hurlbut brought up his artillery, and from the hilltop the Union guns once again dueled successfully with their Confederate counterparts. The Rebels tried a couple of abortive infantry assaults, easily brushed back by the Union line, and then at about 3:30 p.m., the Confederate army retreated southward, giving up hope of crossing the Hatchie by Davis's Bridge.[55]

Outnumbered as Hurlbut was, it would have been foolhardy for him to pursue the Rebels. He had learned from some of the first prisoners taken that morning of the defeat of the Confederates at Corinth, and all day long he had expected to hear the sound of Rosecrans's artillery as the victor of Corinth closed in on the rear of Van Dorn's fleeing army, but no sound of battle came from the southeast. Without some indication that Rosecrans was engaging simultaneously, Hurlbut could not risk advancing.[56]

This time the problem was not an acoustic shadow. There were no sounds of battle from the southeast because Rosecrans was not in contact with the enemy. He had rested his troops throughout the afternoon and evening of October 4, while Van Dorn's army desperately marched away. Then on the morning of October 5, Rosecrans started after the Rebels, but the march, according to a soldier of the 50th Illinois, "was oppressively slow." Encumbered with artillery and supply wagons, the army crept forward, while "a spirit of impatience ruled the men; they were anxious to strike the hot trail of the enemy and reach them before they could cross the river." Despite a dispatch from Grant that day urging him to "push the enemy to the wall," Rosecrans advanced only eight miles and camped near the hamlet of Chewalla, Tennessee, still thirteen miles short of Davis's Bridge and the Hatchie River. All his column accomplished was to sweep up and make prisoners of several hundred Rebel stragglers.[57] McPherson's brigade, leading Rosecrans's pursuit, got a little farther and skirmished with Van Dorn's rear guard shortly before nightfall but stopped well short of the Hatchie.[58] Hurlbut's men finally heard the sound of McPherson's fighting about an hour after their own battle had ended.[59]

If Rosecrans had been pressing Van Dorn as Grant had ordered, the Confederates' situation at the Hatchie would have been desperate. Very possibly, Van Dorn and his army might have been trapped against the Hatchie and forced to surrender. As it was, however, free of pressure from the east, Van Dorn was able to turn his army southward, march six miles up the east bank of the Hatchie, and cross the river at Crum's Mill. His battered army escaped with only the damage it had sustained on the battlefields of Corinth and the Hatchie, much to Grant's dismay.[60] "The delay in pursuing the enemy by General Rosecrans was unaccountable," wrote an officer in the army at Corinth.[61] Augustus Chetlain believed that "Grant never fully forgave Rosecrans for this virtual disobedience of orders."[62]

Once Van Dorn was across the Hatchie, little chance remained of catching him before he could get his army safely behind prepared defensive works at Holly Springs, Mississippi. Attacking him there would require a major campaign, with extensive preparations. More important, it would offer no opportunity of trapping Van Dorn, only of driving him farther into the interior. The opportunity to capitalize on the hard-won victory at Corinth was gone. Grant realized it and on October 7 ordered Rosecrans to break off the now pointless pursuit and return to Corinth. Perversely, Rosecrans, who never understood the concept of momentum in war or gained the knack of trapping and capturing an enemy army, now announced that he wanted to continue the pursuit and complained that Grant was robbing him of a great opportunity. Grant knew better, however, and the campaign was over.[63]

PART TWO

Vicksburg

CHAPTER FOURTEEN

The Mississippi Central Campaign

A WEEK AFTER the Battle of Corinth, the weather, and the season, changed. A cold, rainy spell ended the siege of unseasonable heat, and then gave way to two weeks of pleasant Indian summer with mellow days and chilly nights during the latter half of the month. At the end of October, a freak storm brought a hard freeze and an inch of snow. It melted in a few days, and thereafter the weather continued for some weeks mostly clear and crisp.[1]

For the soldiers in Grant's army, October was a time of guard duty, drill, and building more entrenchments at the various posts that Halleck had assigned the army to hold several months before. When not engaged in the monotonous duties of military life, they were "cracking jokes, singing, playing eucre, whist, checkers, reading newspapers, love letters, novels." Many of them rejoiced at the coming of the first hard freeze—it would relieve them "from the annoyance of flies, mosquitoes, ticks, ants, worms, spiders, lizards, and snakes," and, above all, the ever-present lice, or "graybacks."[2]

October 1862 was also a time of laying the hard hand of war a little more heavily on the rebellious citizens of Union-held West Tennessee and northern Mississippi. The evolution of Union policy from conciliation to more stringent measures was proceeding apace. With Lincoln's announcement of his preliminary Emancipation Proclamation, in late September, had vanished any last hopes of assuaging white Southerners' hostility. They must now be subdued. With each passing week more of the implications of this policy worked their way into the day-to-day practice of the Union armies in the South, and no other army, save small detachments in coastal enclaves, occupied ground as far south as did the Army of the Tennessee. To its men would fall the task of making war real to rebellious Southerners.

In the daily practice of the soldiers, the new severe policy appeared first and most prevalently in the mundane pursuit of food and firewood, otherwise known as foraging. Letters and diaries from this period contain many of the by now common references to "feasting on hog and sweet potatoes." Allen Geer wrote that he and his comrades in the 20th Illinois "lived high, better than ever before in the service."[3]

More significantly, Edward Stanfield of the 48th Indiana wrote that the inhabitants of a road along which his regiment marched "were astonished at our conduct." When the Federals had passed that way before, Stanfield explained in a letter to his father, "every thing was guarded by our men." Now, however, it was different. "We lived high . . . taking from the inhabitants every thing in the eating line we wanted."[4] "We don't exactly steal," John Given explained in a letter to his parents back in Putnam County, Illinois, "but go in broad day light and don't care who sees us at it." This was justified, he continued, because the population of the county they were in was overwhelmingly secessionist.[5]

That same month, some of the highest-ranking officers were also coming to see such matters in a different light. Sherman was foremost in grasping the new realities of the war. He still disliked his men's tendency to "rob and steal occasionally," which, he told a fellow officer, was a "mortification" to him, but he realized that in order for the good cause to triumph, good men were going to have to be prepared to be as hard as evil men forced them to be.[6]

Sherman grasped this first because he had a bright, restless mind and because his assignment that fall was maintaining Union authority in and around Memphis and along the Mississippi above and below. Here he began to encounter the problem of Confederate guerrilla warfare, particularly in the form of gunfire ambushes of riverboats. The Mississippi had been the major highway of commerce for the midsection of the continent. Restoring it to that function was an important Union war aim and a key motivating factor for many Midwestern soldiers. Conversely, the Confederacy's interest was to interdict such commerce. When conventional Rebel forces in established positions could no longer do so—as was the case everywhere on the river north of Vicksburg—Rebel guerrillas strove to make riverborne transport and commerce impractical through hit-and-run tactics. Sherman saw this not only as a threatening tactic but also, when the guerrillas fired on unarmed vessels, an illegitimate form of warfare.

After Rebels a few miles below Memphis fired on the steamboats *Catahoula, Gladiator,* and *Continental* on October 17 and 18, Sherman dispatched a regiment with orders "to destroy all the houses, farms, and corn fields" near the scene of the crime. His purpose was "to let the guerrillas who attacked the Catahoula feel that certain destruction awaits the country for firing on steamboats engaged in carrying supplies needed by the planters between Memphis and Helena [in Arkansas]."[7]

Nor was Sherman finished. After guerrillas had fired on another steamboat back in September, Sherman had issued an order and had it circulated widely and published in the Memphis newspapers. As Sherman stated it, this policy mandated that "upon every case of firing on unarmed Boats engaged in peaceful traffic the families of ten men known to be in arms against us must quit Memphis." The expelled were allowed to take all of their household goods and movable property and were required to "remove to a distance of 25 miles from Memphis." In the wake of the *Catahoula* incident, Sherman made good his threat.[8]

"I know from their actions that it is not agreeable," Sherman explained in a letter to Rawlins, "but it is not to be expected that we should feed and clothe the families of men who are engaged in firing upon boats engaged in peaceful commerce."[9] If guerrilla attacks "were done by the direct or implied concert of the Confederate authorities," he wrote in his reply to an appeal from a civilian, "we are not going to chase through the canebrakes and swamps the individuals who did the deeds, but will visit punishment upon the adherents of that cause which employs such agents."[10] A week later, staff officer William S. Hillyer wrote to Sherman that Grant "heartily approves your course in expelling secession families as a punishment and preventive example for Guerillas firing into boats."[11]

Yet Sherman was no monster, and, in a war remarkable for its stark contrasts, the voluble, red-bearded Ohioan provided his share. Late in October, he issued a circular to the troops under his command noting that "there are many poor families in and about Memphis, who, unless aided, will suffer for wood, clothing, and provisions." He urged the soldiers to save any excess "bread, flour, meat, rice, coffee, sugar" in their rations and bring or send them to "the Central Relief Committee, in Jefferson Block, Second street," Memphis, for distribution to "poor and sick families."[12] Grant suggested that it would be better to support the poor by levies on wealthy local secessionists, and that eventually became Union army practice.[13] There was neither contradiction nor inconsistency in Sherman's policies. He was committed to using as much force as was necessary to end an unjustifiable rebellion, but he was eager to extend as much kindness as possible to those who were no longer aiding the Rebel cause.

The month of October was also a time of organizational changes. The District of West Tennessee became formally the Department of the Tennessee, and the troops in it, officially, the Army of the Tennessee. Grant commanded both.[14] The new department contained 48,500 troops—4,800 guarding rear areas in Kentucky and Illinois, 7,000 in Memphis under Sherman, 17,500 in Corinth, and another 19,200 in various garrisons and outposts in West Tennessee and northern Mississippi.[15] The force was too small to allow Grant to advance while still holding the many posts that Halleck had set up and which Grant did not feel authorized to abandon without his permission.

Personnel changes also followed the end of the Corinth campaign. Brig. Gen. Grenville Dodge replaced Davies as commander of the battered old Second Division. Dodge was a good choice, a man who could bring the worn-out division back to its previous hard-hitting fighting trim, but it would take time. Like several other successful officers in the Army of the Tennessee, Dodge was a graduate of Norwich Military Academy. After graduation in 1851, he had become a railroad engineer, eventually settling in Council Bluffs, Iowa. As colonel of the 4th Iowa, he had served at the March 1862 Battle of Pea Ridge, in Arkansas, before transferring to the east side of the Mississippi. One of his first duties there was using his railroad expertise to restore the Mobile & Ohio from Columbus, Kentucky, to Corinth.

Summoned to Grant's headquarters at Jackson, Tennessee, this October, Dodge hurried to meet the department commander but worried that his work uniform might make a bad impression. He need not have been concerned; Grant habitually dressed in the plainest of uniforms. For the next eighteen months, Dodge and the battle-weary Second Division would patrol rear areas, restoring the railroads and keeping them running, fighting off guerrillas and pushing supplies forward to the troops at the front.[16]

The most significant change of personnel involved Rosecrans. Although he was basking in the glow of the victory at Corinth, he had in fact mismanaged the battle and campaign about as thoroughly as he had the miserable affair at Iuka. He would, over the course of the war, prove himself to be an excellent general as long as his enemy gave him plenty of time to prepare and did nothing unexpected. As the Corinth campaign demonstrated, however, Rosecrans was rendered all but helpless by an aggressive enemy, even one as inept as Earl Van Dorn. At Corinth he had handled his troops poorly, and in the crisis he had given way to almost complete panic and consequent ineffectiveness.

Compounding Rosecrans's unfitness was his practice of denouncing others for miscues that were often his own. On the battlefield of Corinth, after the Confederate retreat, Rosecrans had loudly condemned the Second Division. They were "a set of cowards" and they "never should have any military standing in [his] army till they had won it on the field of battle; that they had disgraced themselves." Davies heard the slander and was furious. He wrote to Rosecrans a few days later, demanding an apology. Rosecrans, who could have been expected to be magnanimous in the wake of his nationally acclaimed victory, instead gave a sort of left-handed retraction, allowing that some units of the division may have fought well at some times during the battle but still mentioning the alleged "cowardly stampeding."[17] The men of Second Division had also heard of Rosecrans's slander and were as furious with him as was their commander.[18]

Nor were the soldiers of the Second Division the only ones who had problems with Rosecrans. Grant himself was finding his subordinate difficult to deal with. Members of Rosecrans's staff, very possibly with their commander's knowledge, leaked information to the press designed to make Rosecrans look good at Grant's expense. When Grant admonished Rosecrans to keep a better rein on his staff, the victor of Corinth took umbrage, denouncing the well-substantiated reports as false, and concluding with a virtual ultimatum: "If you do not meet me frankly with a declaration that you are satisfied I shall consider my power to be useful in this Department ended." Rosecrans also insisted on implying in subtle ways that his command was separate and independent from Grant's. Worse, he had a distinct tendency to ignore Grant's orders.[19]

By October 23, Grant had made up his mind to relieve Rosecrans of his command. That would have been a difficult step, since Rosecrans was widely viewed as being responsible for the victory at Corinth. A message that very day from Halleck in Washington, however, spared Grant the necessity of giving such a controversial order. Halleck directed Rosecrans to report at once to Cincinnati, where he was to take over the Army and Department of the Ohio from the lackluster Buell. Rosecrans was glad to have the promotion and glad to be out from under Grant's authority. Grant was very glad to see him go. It was a happy arrangement for all concerned— except Buell.[20]

A very different sort of organizational issue concerned the thousands of slaves who had fled their plantations and flocked to the Union army in hopes of freedom. Like the question of what to do with Southern white civilians, this was an issue that was peculiarly the Army of the Tennessee's own, because it was the only Union army that had penetrated the heartland of the Deep South. The old policy of returning runaways to their Rebel masters had long since been abandoned, and the Emancipation Proclamation assured that these Mississippi slaves would soon be officially free— unless the state returned to its Federal allegiance before the end of the year.

However, no policy governed the practical day-to-day issues of what they should do and how they should be fed. "Humanity forbade allowing them to starve," Grant later wrote, but he had no authority for feeding them except for those the army employed as teamsters and the like. The army could not use nearly as many as there were and most were unsuitable for the work anyway. "Negroes coming in by wagon loads," he telegraphed Halleck from La Grange, Tennessee, that November. "What will I do with them?"[21]

For want of any other solution, Grant put the contrabands to work picking cotton that had been left standing in the fields of the many abandoned plantations in the area. Halleck promptly approved the solution. It worked well, so Grant appointed Chaplain John Eaton of the 27th Ohio to supervise the soon-to-be-former slaves in picking, ginning, and baling the local cotton crop on a more extensive basis. The quartermaster's department shipped the cotton north for the U.S. government, which paid a set wage for the labor of picking. That money was administered by Eaton to provide food, clothing, and shelter for the thousands of blacks who had flocked to the army. Later the freedmen also chopped wood to supply the boilers of the many steamboats the army used on the rivers. Planters whose slaves had run off and had cotton to pick could apply to Eaton to hire the contrabands under his supervision to harvest their crops.[22]

The idea was a grand success. Under the auspices of this program, the former slaves were enabled, with the supervision of Eaton and his assistants, both to support themselves and to help support the war effort. Grant believed this scheme probably gave birth to the idea of the Freedmen's Bureau, a postwar government agency aimed at helping the former slaves.[23]

Grant's mind was also on the prospect of future operations. He wrote to Halleck proposing an advance into the interior of Mississippi but received no reply.[24] Old Brains had never been particularly helpful about planning operations, but this time he had an especially good reason for being unwilling to explain to Grant what military operations were to be undertaken in the Mississippi Valley. Curious schemes were afoot at the highest levels of power, and no one seemed to have a very clear view of exactly what the Union forces were going to undertake, although John McClernand thought he did.

McClernand had missed the Army of the Tennessee's fall battles, but he had been a busy man nonetheless, waging a different sort of campaign. He had long chafed under Grant's command and pined for greater military glory. In June he wrote to Lincoln, requesting an independent command where all the glory would be his and none shared with a superior. He suggested that the trans-Mississippi would be the most promising field.[25] Lincoln, however, made no response. The following month, McClernand sent his fellow Illinois politicians Elihu Washburne and Orville Browning a bizarre request that they use their influence to have McClernand transferred to the Army of the Potomac along with two divisions of Illinois troops. He would not have been independent there, but he would have been elevated to corps command and serving in the seemingly prestigious Eastern theater of the war. Browning presented the request to Secretary of War Edwin Stanton, who referred the matter to Halleck. Nothing came of it.[26]

So the next month, McClernand tried writing to Lincoln again, this time requesting a leave of absence. The purpose of this was probably to allow him to visit his political power base in Illinois and also to visit the national capital to press the flesh a bit there. Lincoln referred the request to Stanton, who passed it to Halleck, who sent McClernand a sharp rebuke for this repeated instance of violating army regulations by ignoring proper channels and the chain of command.[27]

However, another political gambit, started at the same time, paid off much better for McClernand. The same day that he wrote to Lincoln requesting leave, he also wrote to Illinois governor Richard Yates: "I think I could offer some information and assistance in regard to the refilling of our old regiments. Ask the Secretary of War to order me to visit you at Springfield for that purpose." Yates was happy to oblige the powerful Illinois politician and did as McClernand asked. War governors were vital to the Union war effort, and Illinois was an important state currently struggling to meet its quota under the call for "three hundred thousand more." Stanton granted Yates's request and McClernand soon got orders for Springfield.[28] After making a farewell address to his troops in which one soldier remembered that "he expressed great regret that he was called away," McClernand set out for Illinois.[29]

Back in the Prairie State, McClernand worked hard at organizing the new regiments the state was raising and in his spare time gave speeches denouncing West Point generals and the use of strategy in war. In late September, Yates prepared to attend a meeting of governors in Altoona, Pennsylvania, and, probably at McClernand's own behest, asked the general to go with him. The governors adopted a resolution of support for the Lincoln administration and the vigorous prosecution of the war, and on September 26 brought it to Washington to present to the president. That same day, McClernand was busily campaigning among them as well as among the members of Lincoln's cabinet in favor of a new scheme. He successfully obtained a letter, addressed to the president and signed by eight of the governors, recommending that he be given "a wider field of discretion and action" in the form of "an independent command, either of a Department or army, in some active field of operations, particularly in the Mississippi Valley."[30]

Two days later, he laid out his plan in a lengthy letter to Lincoln. He pointed out the obvious fact that the Mississippi River was important militarily and commercially and then stated that it was being kept closed by a "comparatively insignificant rebel garrison at Vicksburg." McClernand's plan was to take 60,000 men, load them on transports, and carry them to the Yazoo River, just north of Vicksburg. There they would land, successfully assault the Rebel-held bluffs on the south side of the Yazoo, and capture Vicksburg. From that idea McClernand proceeded with a number of possible elaborations, like plans for the conquest of Opelika, Alabama, and other key points, all of which might have sounded much like an attempt at strategy, had McClernand been a West Point graduate. If 60,000 men could not be had at the moment, McClernand proposed to take a smaller force, capture Vicksburg, and open the Mississippi River at once, leaving Opelika and other strategic points for a "more favorable period."[31]

Lincoln was initially ambivalent. He told Stanton that McClernand was "brave and capable" but "too desirous to be independent of everybody else." On September 30, McClernand met with the president again, and Lincoln invited him to come along on a visit to the Army of the Potomac, resting near Sharpsburg, Maryland, after a hard-fought battle there on September 17. The trip gave McClernand more time to bend the president's ear, as well as the opportunity to look good in comparison to that epitome of all that seemed wrong with West Point and "scientific war," George McClellan. Lincoln's party remained several days at Sharpsburg, and thus while the Army of the Tennessee fought at Corinth, McClernand accompanied the president, inspecting the camps of the Army of the Potomac and attending reviews. After the party's return to Washington, McClernand continued his campaign with Lincoln and Stanton, eventually scaling down his request for troops to 24,000.[32]

Success finally came on October 21 with an order signed by the secretary of war. It directed McClernand to finish organizing the remaining troops being raised in Indiana, Illinois, and Iowa, and, in Stanton's words,

> forward them with all dispatch to Memphis, Cairo, or such other points as may hereafter be designated by the general-in-chief, to the end that, when a sufficient force not required by the operations of General Grant's command shall be raised, an expedition may be organized under General McClernand's

command against Vicksburg and to clear the Mississippi River and open navigation to New Orleans.

The forces so organized will remain subject to the designation of the general-in-chief, and be employed according to such exigencies as the service in his judgment may require.[33]

Lincoln added a brief postscript to the order stating, "This order, though marked confidential, may be shown by Gen. McClernand, to Governors, and even others, when, in his discretion, he believes so doing to be indispensable to the progress of the expedition. I add that I feel deep interest in the success of the expedition. And desire it to be pushed forward with all possible despatch, consistently with the other parts of the military service."[34]

Convinced that he now had special authority, direct from the commander-in-chief, to lead an expedition against Vicksburg without regard for Grant or anyone else, McClernand returned to Springfield to finish raising his army. As quickly as he could get each regiment organized and equipped, he shipped it off to Cairo, whence it usually departed for Memphis. He anticipated following as soon as his army was complete and then setting out for Vicksburg, glory, and an unlimited political future.

Thus it was that when on October 26 Grant wrote Halleck asking for guidance about the offensive movement he wished to undertake, the general-in-chief was reluctant to give any clear reply. Halleck had been opposed to McClernand's plan from the beginning. It represented everything he abhorred in this unscientific war, and by comparison, Grant looked very good to him indeed. It had been at Halleck's urging that Lincoln and Stanton had included in McClernand's instructions the clause stating that McClernand's force would "remain subject to the designation of the general-in-chief, and be employed according to such exigencies as the service in his judgment may require."[35] For Halleck to have said exactly what he thought of the whole affair, and what he hoped would come of it, would have been little short of mutiny. Consequently, he was evasive, biding his time and awaiting an opportunity to employ his penchant for intrigue. In the long run, that was good for Grant. At the moment, it was only perplexing. For now, Grant would have to rely for his information of the matter on rumors and newspapers reports.[36]

Those, at least, were plentiful. Several newspapers were soon speculating about the expedition. By October 29, Grant's aide Col. William S. Hillyer wrote to Sherman, "From the Newspapers and other reports it is probable that McClernand will go to Helena and lead whatever expedition may move from there, and report to Curtis."[37] Helena, Arkansas, was on the west side of the Mississippi, where Maj. Gen. Samuel Curtis was department commander. Having had no official notification of McClernand's mission, Grant might very naturally have assumed that it must be outside his own department. Early in November, Lt. James H. Wilson reported for duty on Grant's staff. Wilson was a West Pointer but was from McClernand's hometown of Shawneetown, Illinois. The general had met him in Washington and told him at least something of the planned expedition, and Wilson passed the word on to Grant.[38]

On November 9, the post commander at Cairo telegraphed Grant that various new regiments were passing through Cairo, headed south, "with a kind of loose order to report to Gen McClernand."[39] Others had heard of such things too, and Charles Hamilton mentioned it in a dispatch to Grant that day. In reply, Grant said he was "not advised" about any orders for troops to report to McClernand. "I imagine if any such order has been issued it is to report to him as general forwarding officer," Grant surmised, "and he is instructed to send them here."[40]

Grant had started his advance on November 2. His first objective was the railroad nexus at Grand Junction, Tennessee, near the Tennessee-Mississippi line about halfway between Corinth and Memphis. There the tracks of the Mississippi Central Railroad crossed those of the Memphis & Charleston. The Rebels retreated, and Grant's troops occupied Grand Junction and the nearby town of La Grange, Tennessee, on November 4, without serious fighting. There, Grant halted to bring up supplies before continuing his advance. His next objective was Holly Springs, twenty-seven miles to the south-southwest on the Mississippi Central Railroad, where the Rebels were said to have 30,000 troops. Grant planned to have Sherman make a feint with his force from Memphis, while Grant advanced against Holly Springs with about 31,000 troops.[41]

Grant's soldiers hailed the opening of the new campaign. "They have been soldiers too long to be anxious to fight for fun," explained Capt. Luther Cowan of his men in the veteran 45th Illinois. However, he noted that his men "had become perfectly used up with camp and guard duties and drilling, and are in fact in a fighting mood." They were tired of seeing the war "managed just to suit the Secesh, not to interrupt them in their camping, marching or plan of battles, and let them have all the advantages all the time."[42] Grant would have said the same.

In the midst of this campaign, however, mixed signals from Washington, combined with the strange rumors of McClernand, proved confusing to Grant. On November 6, he received a dispatch from Halleck promising heavy reinforcements in the form of the new regiments then forming in the Midwest.[43] Unbeknownst to Grant, Halleck was using Grant's need for reinforcements—and the clause in McClernand's instructions about "such exigencies as the service in his judgment may require"—to see to it that the regiments McClernand was forwarding from the Midwest did not sit still in Cairo waiting for him but instead immediately went south and became part of Grant's army.[44] Grant could only be pleased at the prospect of more troops, and in response, he decided to await their arrival, extending his pause at La Grange and exulting that he would soon have a sufficient force to handle the Rebels at Holly Springs "without gloves."[45]

By November 10, however, he was disturbed. Halleck had informed him that a combined military and naval expedition would be moving against Vicksburg from Memphis. That was in Grant's department after all, not Curtis's. "This taken in connection with the misterious rumors of McClernands command," Grant explained to Sherman several days later, "left me in doubt as to what I should do."[46] He telegraphed Halleck seeking clarification. "Am I to understand that I lie still here while an expedition is fitted out from Memphis, or do you want me to push as far south as possible?" Grant asked. "Am I to have Sherman move subject to my order, or is he and his forces reserved for some special service? Will not more forces be sent here?" Halleck's reply came the next day and was both reassuring and cryptic: "You have command of all troops sent to your department, and have permission to fight the enemy where you please."[47]

With that settled, Grant determined to get on with his campaign. "I am exceedingly anxious to do something before the roads get bad and before the enemy can entrenc[h] and reinforce," he wrote to Sherman. Grant now instructed Sherman to move down from Memphis as a full-fledged part of the campaign. With new regiments from Illinois, Indiana, and Wisconsin that had recently reported to him, Sherman would have a force of three divisions and would form the right wing of Grant's army. Hamilton's three divisions would compose the left, McPherson's two divisions the center. Grant proposed to start his columns from La Grange as soon as Sherman was ready to march from Memphis, and he urged Sherman to make that as soon as possible. Halleck approved the movement, but warned Grant not to go too far.[48]

The opposing Confederate army, now commanded by newly appointed department commander Lt. Gen. John C. Pemberton, had by this time retreated from Holly Springs to a position behind the Tallahatchie River, about fifteen miles farther south and some forty miles from Grant's jumping-off point at La Grange.[49]

For this campaign, Grant planned to rely on the countryside for forage—fodder for the army's animals and, to some extent, food for its men. These were the bulkiest and most significant items in the supply train of a Civil War army, so whatever could be raised locally would greatly ease the supply situation. A deliberate plan to draw maximum supplies from the countryside was a new thing in this war and another indication of the less restrained Union policy. Grant was not, however, planning to do without a supply line altogether. A conventional supply train would still be hauling all of the army's ammunition needs as well as supplementing the supply of locally acquired food and fodder.[50]

New regiments continued to arrive at Grant's camps around La Grange at an average rate of one per day during the first seventeen days of November.[51] Grant brigaded these new regiments with his old ones. David Poak of the 30th Illinois wrote that in his brigade "the two new regiments are placed in between the old ones." Poak and his fellow veterans found amusement in the new recruits, who were as green as they themselves had been a year before. "It would make you laugh to hear the questions the new soldiers have to ask our boys about what a battle is like and how men feel when under fire," he wrote to his sister back in Illinois.[52]

Sometimes the veterans found other ways to amuse themselves at the expense of the green troops, and there was nothing friendly in the humor. The men who had joined the army in 1861 liked to believe themselves more patriotic than those who enlisted the following year, though often the difference was simply a question of family responsibilities. The veterans especially resented the fact that some of the 1862 recruits had received a $40 enlistment bounty. When the brand-new 93rd Illinois joined the 5th and 10th Iowa and 26th Missouri, veterans of the vortex of the fighting at Iuka, the first greeting the new men heard on marching into camp was, "How are you, forty dollar rats?"

The veterans then proceeded to add injury to insult. That night they stole "almost every frying-pan, coffee-pot, tin plate, cup, knife and fork" belonging to the 93rd. The next morning, the new soldiers noticed that their neighbors of the 5th Iowa had just "drawn" a like number of similar, shiny-new utensils. The Illinoisans went to their colonel, former Freeport banker Holden Putnam. "Well, boys," Putnam replied, "I don't think you will gain much by complaint." That was an astute observation, since their brigade commander at this time, Brig. Gen. Charles Matthies, was the former colonel of the 5th Iowa and shared his men's contempt of the newcomers. Putnam, however, had a solution. "You are different men than I took you to be," the former banker told his men, "if you can not get your own back with interest." That night the Illinoisans recovered most of their stolen property, along with much of the 5th Iowa's personal equipment, even including articles of clothing. When a furious Matthies came around to berate Putnam for his regiment's thievery, the colonel made the situation clear and offered a truce and general return of all stolen items. On this basis, peace returned to the brigade, and the veteran regiments showed a grudging respect for their new comrades.[53]

While the troops waited for the campaign to resume, religious interest was strong in the camps. Chaplains in Grant's army preached both in the camps and in church buildings in La Grange each evening. John Campbell of the 5th Iowa attended an interesting "conversation meeting"—a format in which individual soldiers stood and shared how Jesus Christ had changed their lives. "The church was crowded to overflowing," Campbell noted. The next evening, he found the building so packed that he could not even get in.[54] Not all soldiers took an interest in such matters, of course. Joseph Stockton noted that in his company of the brand-new 72nd Illinois, there were two professed atheists.[55]

Meanwhile, constant drilling and frequent reviews reminded the soldiers that action might be coming soon. "One thing certain is that we are generally reviewed before we start out on an active campaign," wrote David Poak, "but we do not always march after we are reviewed."[56]

Sherman's column moved out on schedule on Thursday, November 26, in pleasant fall weather.[57] The bands were playing "We Are Coming, Father Abra'am, Three Hundred Thousand More," as well as "I Will Never Be a Coward, I Will Never Be a Slave," and that perennial favorite of the Union soldiers, "John Brown's Body." The 83rd Indiana was making its very first march, and the new Hoosier soldiers wanted to look good as they paraded out of the city. Beneath the jaunty music of the bands, bystanders could have heard several hundred men nervously repeating, "Left, left, left," as they tried to keep in step.[58]

Part of the education of the new regiments was in what to carry on a march. As their comrades of the veteran regiments had done the year before, the men of the new regiments learned on their first serious march that the ideal load was much lighter than they had imagined and that they had brought with them many items they did not truly need. "All soon got rid of some of our things," wrote a new recruit from Illinois, "overcoats, blankets, pants, shirts, sox was discarded. Some places the side of the road was strewn with clothes."[59]

Baggage had been reduced for this campaign, and as part of that reduction, the troops had been forced to bid a regretful farewell to the Sibley tents. Henceforth such large and cumbersome equipment would be reserved for company and regimental headquarters. In their place, the individual soldiers received the despised shelter tent. Each man carried a rectangle of canvas that could be buttoned together with a comrade's rectangle so as to form a tent just large enough for the two men to lie in—if they were not unusually large men. Because they had to enter these tents on all fours, the soldiers derisively named them "dog tents" or "pup tents." Most of the regiments erected their dog tents for the first time on this march.[60]

By December 2, Sherman's column had covered fifty miles and reached the Tallahatchie River near Wyatt, Mississippi. Grant's column, having departed La Grange on November 28, had taken Holly Springs without opposition. The men were impressed with Holly Springs. "A very beautiful town," recalled Jefferson Moses of the 93rd Illinois. "I don't think I seen a neater and cleaner town in the south."[61] Many of the inhabitants had fled at the approach of the Union army, however, and those that remained greeted the soldiers "with long faces and sour countenances"—as well as taunts that the Rebel army would soon arrive and defeat them.[62]

The army's behavior on the march demonstrated that opinions still varied intensely as to the practical aspects of exactly how to treat Southern civilians. Grant, Sherman, and other high-ranking officers favored a pragmatic policy. They wanted the army to supply itself as far as possible from the property of guilty secessionists, but they wanted this done in an orderly, disciplined manner, and they wanted care taken to discriminate between the property of secessionists and Unionists and between the destitute and those who were members of the wealthy—especially slaveholding—class that had pushed the South into secession and Civil War.[63]

The troops of the veteran regiments, and probably most of the new ones as well, agreed with this in part. They too were prepared to live off of the secessionists, but they wanted to do their jayhawking on an informal basis, without the nuisance of commissaries and official procedures. "As soon as arms were stacked at the new camping place," wrote a soldier of the 55th Illinois, "the veterans scattered over the country in pursuit of plunder. This was against orders, as it was desired to do the foraging systematically by detail."[64] Compared to the high-ranking officers, the veteran soldiers also tended to be far more apt to believe citizens were secessionists and far more skeptical of professed Unionism on the part of civilians owning foodstuffs. "They all pretend to be Union men here, every man," wrote a Wisconsin soldier, "but I know better."[65]

Isaac Jackson of the 83rd Ohio was incensed when his brigade commander, Col. Stephen G. Burbridge, insisted on paying restitution to what

Jackson and his comrades were convinced was a thoroughly secessionist farmer.[66] Jefferson Moses found his commander more reasonable. When the 93rd Illinois camped along the road between Holly Springs and Lumpkins Mill, Col. Holden Putnam addressed the regiment. "Boys, you know the orders against foraging," Moses recalled him saying. "But over across the creek are a lot of hogs. But don't let an officer catch you."[67] Many officers, however, took very seriously Grant's orders against unauthorized foraging and made stringent, if not very successful, efforts to suppress it.[68]

Besides these two views, however, a third seemed to exist. Old John Brown's body might be moldering in the grave, but his spirit of harsh retribution was marching with some of the soldiers of Grant's army. "Along our march this time there has been more property destroyed than I ever saw before," wrote David Poak to his family back in Mercer County, Illinois. "Along the road between this and Bolivar the fences on nearly every plantation were fired and the grass and stubbles in the fields were also set on fire which caused the destruction of quite a number of buildings."[69] It was not an isolated phenomenon. John Campbell noted, "All along the line of our march, fences and houses have been ruthlessly burned by straggling soldiers."[70]

This differed from the common practice of using fence rails for firewood. Instead, the fences were simply being burned where they stood in an act of wanton vandalism. That the acts were committed by stragglers, as Campbell noted, was obvious. Soldiers in the ranks would have attracted the immediate attention of their officers had they committed such acts, and almost no officer would have tolerated that kind of behavior. Gen. David Stuart "threatened to have the first man shot who should be caught burning property." Stuart was especially incensed with the incendiaries because he had lost two hours on the march when he found that his road passed through a small village that was in flames, and he dared not take his artillery and ammunition wagons through it for fear of explosion.[71]

The question was, who were these stragglers and why were they doing this? Theories abounded. John Roberts of the 83rd Indiana believed that the arsonists in Sherman's column were members of the 6th and 8th Missouri regiments "that had been burned out by the 'Rebs' before they left home." Out of a desire for revenge, Roberts believed, these men burned "every cotton gin" they saw, despite the strenuous efforts of officers like Stuart.[72]

Pvt. Elisha Stockwell of the 14th Wisconsin marched in Grant's column from La Grange to the Tallahatchie. Recalling the events many years later, he wrote that men taken prisoner at Corinth had been marched over this same road by their Confederate captors "and had been ill treated by the cit-izens." Stockwell had heard that "in one case a woman had spit in one boy's face while stopped to rest and being exhibited by their captors to the citizens along the road." Now the former prisoners, since then exchanged and returned to the ranks, were determined to take their revenge. "There was lots of foraging on this march and houses burned," Stockwell recalled. "The fences on both sides of the road, which were what was called worm fences, built of oak rails, were on fire in places. The smoke was stifling. This was said to have been done by men that had been prisoners." Stock-well noted further that the civilians now pretended to be good Unionists and the officers tried hard to prevent foraging, straggling, and destruction, but to little avail.[73]

Brig. Gen. James W. Denver, who commanded a division in Sherman's column, believed the vandals were to be found among the new troops. "Some of the new regiments," he wrote, "seem to be possessed with the idea that in order to carry on war men must throw aside civilization and become savages. . . . We have very little trouble with the old regiments with the exception that they will upon occasion take chickens and pigs. But the new ones want to sweep the country as with the besom of destruction, leav-ing nothing on the road for any troops that may come after us."[74]

Denver told how Sherman himself came upon a group of soldiers who had taken a "splendid carriage and four horses" from a planter and were riding down the road in style, "cutting a grand splash in the very middle of a regiment." Sherman ordered the men to get off the carriage, and when one of them refused, the furious general snatched a rifle from one of the other soldiers and would have shot the man if the weapon had been loaded. He then made the carriage riders unhitch the horses, put the harness on themselves, and pull the carriage more than two miles back to its owner's house.[75]

Denver may well have been right about the destructiveness of the new troops. Charles Wills was a veteran of the 8th Illinois serving with the newly recruited 103rd. He noted that his new regiment did not light any of the fires and that the smoke and heat caused by the burning fences were unpleasant. "Yet I think the 103d generally approved of the proceedings," he noted. For himself, however, Wills was happy that his regiment had not taken part.[76]

John G. Given of the newly recruited 124th Illinois freely admitted that he and his comrades were among the vandals. "We marched 18 miles yes-terday," he wrote on November 5, "came through Grand Junction, burned almost everything on the road, stole lots of niggers, killed a cow and five calves for supper, then camped within the enclosure of Lagrange College, burned all the fence around it for firewood and had one of the most jovial nights I ever experienced."[77] Given's testimony would tend to bear out Denver's theory that the new troops were the most destructive. It also demonstrates that he was perfectly comfortable with his actions.

By the time Sherman's column reached the Tallahatchie at Wyatt, Grant and his troops were a few miles upstream on the Tallahatchie, already preparing to cross. Union cavalry screening Grant's advance had skirmished smartly with their Rebel counterparts, but otherwise the advance was unopposed. The immediate prospect, however, seemed to be a stiffly contested crossing of the Tallahatchie, "a bold, deep stream, with a newly-constructed fort behind," as Sherman later wrote.[78] Swollen by recent heavy rains, the Tallahatchie was a major obstacle, and the army expected to fight there. "We look for a battle tomorrow or next day. A severe one," wrote Lt. Otis Whitney of the green 27th Iowa in a letter to his wife. "We have had pale cheeks in camp already."[79] The Confederates had destroyed the railroad bridge and strongly fortified the south bank. As Grant later wrote in his memoirs, "A crossing would have been impossible in the presence of an enemy."[80]

Once again, however, Pemberton retreated without giving battle. Grant's army began crossing early on the morning of December 1, and Grant wired Halleck, "Our troops will be in Abbyville tomorrow or a battle will be fought." Abbeville, a town two or three miles beyond the river, fell without a fight. The Confederates abandoned their extensive fortifications and destroyed what supplies they could not take with them. Grant's forces pursued beyond Oxford, skirmishing occasionally with the Rebel rear guard.[81]

Meanwhile, the rainy weather that had raised the Tallahatchie above fording stage also made the roads all but impassable. Before linking up with Grant's forces near the Yocona River, seven miles south of Oxford, Sherman's column had to pause for several days to rebuild the bridge over the Tallahatchie at the village of Wyatt.[82] The Confederates had burned the span in their retreat. The only materials for rebuilding it were to be found in the boards and timbers of the houses of Wyatt, and these Sherman's pioneer detachment used without hesitation. Sherman's headquarters during this time was a large timber house. In the evenings, sitting around the fireplace smoking their pipes, members of Sherman's staff would amuse themselves by commenting on "the value of the ceiling and roof timbers for use in the new bridge." This never failed to get a rise out of the owner. "General," he remonstrated with Sherman, "you certainly would not take down your own

quarters and sleep out on the lawn in the rain—you will all die of colds."
Sherman's response was characteristic: "That bridge must be built if it takes
the last house in the town." Once the bridge was finished and Sherman's
column was marching away, a number of Wyatt's citizens came to Sherman
demanding vouchers against the U.S. government for the value of their dismantled houses. "Call upon the Southern Confederacy," Sherman replied.
"You let them burn the old bridge, and I was forced to build another. To do
this I was forced to use your houses, in exchange for which I give to you the
bridge. Take good care of it; do not force me to build another."[83]

By the time Sherman joined him, Grant had now advanced sixty-three
miles down the Mississippi Central Railroad in the space of little more than
a week. Only the heavy rains had prevented the operation from progressing
even more rapidly and fully meeting Grant's original schedule.[84]

While his army halted to bring up supplies and rebuild the Tallahatchie
bridge, the question Grant pondered was what to do next. Pemberton's
army had escaped serious damage and was sure to entrench again somewhere farther south. Grenada was still sixty miles beyond Grant's advance
guard, and Jackson another hundred miles beyond that. Grant did not have
sufficient force to guard such long supply lines and still meet Pemberton in
battle. So he devised another plan. He would send Sherman with one division back to Memphis, have them board transports, ride down the Mississippi, and threaten Vicksburg by direct attack. Pemberton would be unable
to counter both the threat of Sherman's assault on Vicksburg and the threat
of Grant's overland advance toward Jackson, which, if successful, would
doom Vicksburg.

Halleck approved the plan but stipulated that the river column should
number at least 25,000 men. He promised to provide a contingent from the
west bank of the Mississippi to bring it up to that strength. Significantly, in
view of what Halleck by this time knew of McClernand's grand scheme, he
suggested that Grant get his expedition under way before December 20.[85]
Grant, for his part, recorded in his memoirs more than two decades later that
he had "learned that an expedition down the Mississippi now was inevitable"
and that he desired to "have a competent commander in charge" of it.[86]

Meanwhile, with the force under his immediate command, Grant proposed to press slowly on Pemberton, keeping him occupied in the center of
the state and unable to confront Sherman. If Pemberton should make
another of his lightning retreats, Grant would follow and be on his heels
when he reached the vicinity of Vicksburg.[87]

On December 9, Sherman, accompanied by the division of Morgan L.
Smith, crossed back over the Tallahatchie and set out for Memphis.[88]

CHAPTER FIFTEEN

Chickasaw Bayou

AFTER RECEIVING Grant's December 8 order to return to Memphis, Sherman selected Morgan L. Smith's division to go with him—judging it his "best fighting division"—and held a farewell review of his other two divisions. "The men cheered till my little mare Dolly nearly jumped out of her skin," Sherman wrote proudly to his wife. The review, as well as the march back to Memphis, were under clear skies in pleasant weather.[1] Leaving the camps below the Tallahatchie at noon on December 10, Smith's division, by two days of hard marching, was back in Memphis by midday on December 13.[2]

Sherman made his preparations rapidly and was ready to depart Memphis less than five days after his arrival. The expedition would number about 32,000. Getting enough steamboats took time, however, especially because the Mississippi River was unusually low and travel above Memphis was difficult. Not until December 20 and 21 did Sherman's troops go aboard the steamboats at the Memphis docks. The first division departed around midnight on December 20, and over the next thirty-six hours the other two divisions, each conveyed in twelve to fifteen steamboats, cast off and steamed down the river.[3]

The last days in Memphis were a noisy, busy time for Sherman's soldiers. "The continued ringing of bells and blowing of whistles kept us awake a good share of the night," wrote Illinois soldier Wilson Chapel on the morning of December 21. "All is bustle and excitement," wrote Iowa soldier Judson Withrow at 1:20 a.m., "boats loading, Drums beating, officers hallowing, mules braying, darkies swearing, and in fact, every noise it is possible to conceive of, to make confusion worse confounded."[4] The next night, Wilson Chapel and many of his comrades of the 13th Illinois had to work all night to get coal aboard the steamboat that would carry them south.[5] In case coal ran short, Sherman saw to it that all of the boats had ample supplies of axes for gathering firewood along the way.[6]

When boats departed during daylight hours, it was often "with flags flying, bands playing and the men cheering."[7] Once again the massed fleet of transports and gunboats made an imposing sight, and many of the soldiers, especially those going to war for the first time, commented on the grandeur of the scene and the feeling of strength it imparted.[8] "One of the grandest spectacles to be seen," Indiana soldier William Winters described it—"fifteen boats all with colors flying & covered with men all dressed in uniforms & cheering each other as they pass, a fitting sight for an artist's pencil."[9] The men were optimistic about the expedition. Soldiers of the recently organized 69th Indiana referred to it as the "Castor Oil Expedition" because they expected it would quickly go through the Confederacy.[10]

About twelve miles below Helena, some of the boats came under rifle fire from a small settlement called Friar's Point on the Mississippi side of the river. The gunboats convoying that part of the transport fleet immediately shelled the town. Then troops went ashore and burned several buildings, presumably those closest to the suspected source of the shots.[11] In the long, strung-out column of transports, many of the troops were not even in sight of the action at Friar's Point. Far upstream, John Roberts of the 83rd Indiana recognized the distant sounds as the cannon of the gunboats and thought how it reminded him "of Ripley county coon dogs that had treed a coon or possum on Plum Creek or a half mile off in a hollow log."[12]

It was nearly evening by this time, and the lead boats tied up at Friar's Point, which Sherman had previously designated a general rendezvous for the fleet. Throughout the night, the rest of the convoy continued arriving. As at any time when the boats tied up to shore, commanders established picket lines several hundred yards inland.[13] When daylight rose on the morning of December 22, many of the soldiers who had remained on board asleep when their boats arrived during the night before made their first discovery of their whereabouts. Hoosier soldier William Winters awoke and climbed to the upper deck of his transport to find not only that he was at Friar's Point but also that the town was on fire again.[14]

Whenever the boats tied up, the soldiers were eager to go ashore to escape the cramped quarters on board and see what was to be seen. Early that morning, many had gone into Friar's Point. As the troops that had arrived during the night wandered around what was left of the village and talked with one another about the excitement of the previous evening, somehow the story made the rounds that, as William Wiley of the 77th Illinois put it, "rebel citizens had caught some of our men a short time before and had nailed them up in sugar hogsheads and rolled them into the river."[15] That was all the provocation the soldiers needed to send them on a rampage of looting, at the conclusion of which they torched the town.

The rapidly spreading fire attracted the attention of officers, who sent the provost guard on the double to arrest the perpetrators. When the provost guards marched their prisoners—a considerable collection of soldiers from a number of regiments—back to the river, the guilty parties made quite a spectacle. Many of them had pulled on various plundered garments over their uniforms. Calico dresses seemed to be much in demand. The guards made them shuck their purloined finery and pile it near the river, then marched them back to their regiments, where in at least some cases they faced no disciplinary action at all.[16] Winters noted that some of his comrades in the 67th Indiana had picked up "ribbons, books, paper, ink stands, & some checkers," and by the time the story got out to him on board the steamer *J. S. Pringle* the reason for the pillaging had evolved further into retaliation for shots fired at a steamboat "some ten days ago."[17]

Meanwhile, other Union troops were struggling to save the rest of the town of Friar's Point from going up in flames. Ultimately seven or eight buildings burned, and two others were destroyed when soldiers pulled them down in order to form a firebreak and prevent the rest of the town from burning as well.[18] More transports continued to pass by on the river, the soldiers gaping at what a new recruit of the 114th Ohio called their first "realistic picture of war." It was a dramatic picture, at any rate, as the rising sun shone through the rising flames and smoke of the burning buildings.[19]

In several other places along the river that day, Confederate guerrillas took potshots at the passing steamers. In some of these locations, Sherman's soldiers burned small settlements to the ground, leaving only chimneys to mark the spot.[20]

The landscape along the Mississippi was drab, flat, and uninteresting. "On a cast of the eye over any five miles of its country," wrote Asa Munn of the 13th Illinois, "there can be nothing worse in the way of scenery, unless it is the next five miles."[21] The very importance of Vicksburg lay in the fact that it was the first piece of high ground adjacent to the river anywhere south of Memphis. Behind the passing riverbanks on either side lay the low, often swampy lands of the Mississippi Delta, where watercourse, swamp, and dry land intertwined with bewildering complexity.

From time to time, each boat had to stop alongshore somewhere while large details of soldiers disembarked to chop out tree stumps or gather fence rails to feed the boat's boilers. Officers allowed the rest of the troops to go ashore in order to rest and cook rations, but the soldiers often made use of the opportunity for unauthorized foraging. "Stopped for wood," Michael Sweetman of the 114th Ohio noted in his diary on Christmas Eve. "Here some of us went foraging and I got some molasses and sweet potatoes."[22]

While Sherman was preparing to leave Memphis and then proceeding down the river, events were transpiring elsewhere that would significantly affect his campaign. On December 18, Grant received a telegram from Halleck. "The troops in your department, including those from Curtis' command which join down-river expedition," Halleck instructed, "will be divided into four army corps. It is the wish of the President that General McClernand's corps shall constitute a part of the river expedition, and that he shall have the immediate command, under your direction."[23]

With that, the suspense, at least, was over, and Grant could contemplate the measure of how much authority McClernand had been able to wrangle in Washington. He promptly forwarded the telegram to Sherman, but it did not reach him before he had gone down the river. Grant also drafted an order to McClernand, who was still in Illinois, officially notifying him of his assignment as senior corps commander on the Mississippi expedition, and spelling out which divisions would constitute his corps and which Sherman's. The four corps, initially numbered one through four, would eventually receive new numbers to reflect the existence of twelve corps in Virginia, and another, the Fourteenth, under Rosecrans. McClernand's would be the Thirteenth Corps, Sherman's the Fifteenth. The Sixteenth Corps went to Hurlbut, and the Seventeenth to McPherson.[24]

Halleck's missive, finally notifying Grant officially of McClernand's unwelcome insertion of himself and his political ambitions into the high command in the Mississippi Valley, was at least expected. Two days later, an event occurred that Grant had not expected. Confederate general Earl Van Dorn, defeated at Corinth in October and thereafter demoted to cavalry commander under Pemberton, now scored his greatest success of the war. On December 20, the day Sherman began loading his steamers in Memphis, Van Dorn led a raiding force of cavalry in striking Grant's advanced supply depot at Holly Springs. Commanding the post at Holly Springs was Col. Robert C. Murphy, who had narrowly escaped court-martial for his abandonment of supplies at Iuka in September. He was now detached from his 8th Wisconsin Regiment and commanded a mix of units guarding this even larger mountain of supplies. Despite warnings to be on the alert for Van Dorn, Murphy took so little precaution and then surrendered with so little effort at resistance that many came to believe him guilty of treachery.[25] Grant was furious with Murphy, rightly believing that the town could have been defended as other small outposts had successfully held off Van Dorn's attacks.[26] He lost no time in having Murphy dismissed from the service. This time the colonel was finished.[27]

So, however, was Grant's overland campaign. During his brief occupation of Holly Springs, Van Dorn burned the vast stocks of supplies and ammunition there. With that, and the breaking of the rail line by Van Dorn, Grant's supply situation, already very difficult, became impossible. He had no choice but to retreat. That same December 20, Grant issued orders to McPherson to begin the retreat, destroying railroads, bridges, and mills behind him as he went.[28]

Foraging had been an important part of Grant's plans for supply on the advance, and now it was doubly important—and more difficult. Advancing into the enemy's country, the army had encountered abundant foodstuffs, but as Illinois soldier David Poak noted, he and his comrades found foraging on the return trip to be "dry work, as the country had been scoured by the troops as they went southward."[29] On December 21, the first day of the retreat, Grant's whole army went on half rations, and the food situation deteriorated from there. The next day, the men of the 47th Illinois found their allotment only a single square of hardtack per day, while the 12th Wisconsin, recalled Hosea Rood, "marched two days with scarcely anything to eat."[30] Other troops reported being on third or even quarter rations for extended periods during the retreat, and virtually every soldier who left a record of that time wrote of hunger.[31]

By December 22, Grant's column was marching back through Holly Springs. The once-attractive town was now in a poor state of repair. When Van Dorn's men had set fire to the supplies, the flames had spread and burned up entire blocks of the town. Worse, they had reached the stocks of ammunition, which had exploded, breaking nearly every window in town, and laying several "fine, large public and business buildings" in ruins.[32] "We saw in the city many, many ruins and dreadful evidence of the great destruction of property by the Rebs in their late Raid," wrote Wisconsin soldier George Carter.[33]

The last Union regiment marched out of Holly Springs on the evening of January 10, and it was back across the Tennessee line within twenty-four hours. Grant's army once again had functioning supply lines, but it was back in the same area of West Tennessee whence Grant's fall offensive had started two months before.[34]

Blissfully ignorant of most of these events, Sherman had pressed ahead with his river campaign against Vicksburg. He did not receive Grant's notice of McClernand's official status in the expedition, nor did he learn of the Holly Springs debacle before departing on his expedition. The first day out, he did receive an unconfirmed report stating that a handful of Union soldiers had arrived in Memphis claiming that Holly Springs had fallen to the Confederates and they alone had escaped to tell the tale. "I hardly know what faith to put in such a report," Sherman wrote to Grant on December 21, "but suppose whatever may be the case you will attend to it."[35] Sherman did not know of Grant's retreat.

The army arrived at the settlement of Milliken's Bend, on the Louisiana shore north of Vicksburg, on Christmas Day amid fine weather. Consistent with the pattern of the campaign thus far, Confederate guerrillas fired on some of the boats, and the troops retaliated by burning Milliken's Bend.[36] Sherman landed Brig. Gen. Stephen G. Burbridge's brigade of Brig. Gen. A. J. Smith's division to march southwest and break the Vicksburg & Shreveport Railroad. Burbridge's troops set off into the hinterland at ten o'clock on Christmas morning and returned thirty-six hours later, footsore but successful, having marched seventy-five miles, cut telegraph wires, destroyed a number of railroad bridges and trestles, captured 196 head of beef cattle, 100 mules, and numerous horses, and destroyed various stockpiles of Confederate government property.[37]

Sherman did not wait for Burbridge to return before advancing to the second phase of the operation. Leaving A. J. Smith's division moored in its transports, Sherman led the rest of the fleet away from Milliken's Bend while the houses were still burning. The fleet proceeded down the river to Young's Point, below the mouth of the Yazoo and just around a sharp bend of the river from the Vicksburg waterfront.[38]

After conferring with Rear Admiral David D. Porter on Christmas afternoon, Sherman issued orders for the army to move at eight o'clock the next morning. At that hour, he took the three divisions that were with him at Young's Point and headed for the Yazoo. The gunboat squadron had previously secured the Yazoo and cleared it of Confederate mines, and thus the army's transports were free to proceed twelve miles upstream and land the troops, while the naval vessels provided gunfire support. The next day, Burbridge having returned, A. J. Smith's division arrived and joined the rest of the army on the south bank of the Yazoo.[39]

As the boats turned into the Yazoo, many of the Midwesterners on board got their first introduction to the strange world of the Mississippi Delta. "The banks are covered with a very thick growth of timber and underbrush of all kinds—swamp and cane break," wrote Jake Ritner of the brand-new 25th Iowa, "and the trees are covered with a kind of moss which grows all over the trees and hangs down almost to the ground. It is of a kind of gray color, and looks very curious and makes it impossible to see any distance although there are no leaves on the trees."[40] Spanish moss was only one of the elements that made this country different from what most of the men or their officers had ever encountered before.

The terrain of the Delta was a nightmare landscape in which to conduct military operations. Watercourses writhed like twisting serpents across the flat alluvial ground, and every few years one or another of them seemed to tire of its tortuous bed and forsake it for another, equally serpentine. The abandoned riverbeds became sloughs, bayous, backwaters, and, when silt deposits severed them from the main stream, oxbow lakes. Sherman's task now was to advance his army through, over, and around these obstacles in order to reach the foot of the Walnut Hills, the high ground on which Vicksburg stood. Only then could he launch his assault against the Confederate breastworks atop those hills.

The army camped that evening in the woods between the swamps and bayous and endured a night of cold rain without tents.[41] They rolled up in their oilcloths and leaned against tree trunks or exposed roots.[42] The men of the new regiments were especially eager to get at the enemy. "So you see we are getting to war in earnest," wrote Ritner to his wife back in Iowa after describing the army's preparations that day. That, he maintained, "is just what we want. The men are all in good spirits and keen to start at any time."[43] Even the old soldiers of the 55th Illinois, veterans of Shiloh, marched forward the next morning singing "The Battle Cry of Freedom."[44]

Throughout December 27 and 28, Sherman's divisions worked their way forward. Aided by the natural obstructions, Rebel skirmishers took every opportunity to hinder the advance of Sherman's four divisional columns, either passively by felled trees across roads and levies, or actively by small defensive stands that led to flare-ups of fighting and hours of sniping. One new soldier thought the noise of the firing sounded like "several thousand men at a wood chopping with the crack, crack of their axes."[45] Where the terrain was not covered by dense thickets and canebrakes, the soldiers found old cotton fields, still dotted with dead trees, and, as Cpl. Michael Sweetman of the 114th Ohio recalled, "covered with a dense growth of cockle-burs, four or five feet high, well ripened."[46] By evening the leading elements of the four divisions had advanced roughly a mile and a half from the Yazoo and stopped along the line of Chickasaw Bayou, chief obstruction in their path. Fordable at only a few places and staunchly defended by Confederates on the other side, it presented a serious obstacle to Sherman and his men.[47]

Where the 55th Illinois halted for the night, on the right-center of Sherman's line, the men had immediately in front of them a fifty-yard-wide abatis of felled timber. Just beyond the abatis was Chickasaw Bayou. Behind the bayou and less than 100 yards from where the Illinoisans lay was the Confederate skirmish line, well dug in on the levee. Beyond that stretched another three-quarters of a mile of swampy bottomland and then the Walnut Hills.[48] As Sherman explained in a note to Admiral Porter, "This piece of land is all cut up with Bayous. We get across one only to find ourselves on the bank of another."[49]

The Confederate line was anchored on the east by the heavy fortifications and big guns on Snyder's and Drumgould's bluffs, seven miles above Sherman's landing point, which barred steamboat access any farther up the Yazoo. On the west end of the line was Vicksburg itself, also heavily fortified. The line in between stretched fourteen miles—too long to be held everywhere in heavy numbers. Its strength came from its position on commanding bluffs—the Walnut Hills—as well as its multiple lines of entrenchments, and the maze of bayous and oxbow lakes in front. With considerable effort, the army discovered two possible crossing points on Chickasaw Bayou, and the divisions slowly and laboriously snaked their way through the difficult terrain to mass themselves along those two routes.

One of the two crossing points was a corduroy bridge on the army's left-center. It lay at a moderately safe distance from the Confederate defenses, and two Union brigades—one from Brig. Gen. Frederick Steele's division and the other from Brig. Gen. George W. Morgan's—were soon across and sparring with the Confederate skirmishers on the far side. The other was a ford formed by a sand spit on the right-center of the army, just where the 55th Illinois and the rest of David Stuart's brigade had halted on the evening of December 27. Heavily dug-in Rebels on the opposite bank held the crossing in force. Sherman assigned Morgan L. Smith's division to prepare to force its way across the bayou there.[50]

Sunday, December 28, saw dense fog, eventually replaced by powder smoke. Otherwise the weather was pleasant.[51] "The ball opened very early this morning just where it ceased at nightfall on yesterday," the 32nd Missouri's Maj. A. J. Seay recorded in his diary.[52] Early that day, Smith received Sherman's order for the crossing and rode forward to view the ground for himself. When he passed through the line of the 55th Illinois, the men warned him that Confederate sharpshooters were active. They liked Smith. Under his gruff exterior, the soldiers of his division maintained, "was a kind heart and a deep interest in the welfare of his men." He would crack jokes with the men in a free and easy way that was immensely popular.[53]

Smith continued almost to the bayou, observed the enemy lines for a few moments through his field glass, and then turned and rode back. As the general passed, Chaplain Milton Haney of the 55th noticed that he looked pale and saw blood on his stirrup. Still Smith did not falter. Turning to the men he shouted, "Boys, give them h——ll!" Then he rode off.[54]

In fact, Smith had taken a rifle bullet in the hip while observing Confederate lines. "He took this terrible shot so impassively that not a shudder seemed to affect him," wrote an eyewitness, "but coolly put up the glass and turned his horse around and rode back to the rear." Only later did most of the soldiers who had witnessed the scene learn that Smith had been wounded. After he rode to the rear, however, and was examined by a surgeon, it became apparent just how serious the wound was. The bullet had lodged near his spine, and surgeons and fellow officers doubted that he would survive. He was soon carried to one of the steamboats.[55]

David Stuart took over command of the division, and preparations for crossing the bayou continued. Batteries A and B, Chicago Light Artillery, came up and opened fire on the Rebels with their 20-pounder Parrott guns. So too did a strong line of Union skirmishers, sheltering in the brush along the creek. Early in the afternoon, Stuart ordered the 54th Ohio to clear a path through the abatis. To cover them, Col. T. Kilby Smith, who had succeeded to brigade command when Stuart took over the division, strengthened his line of sharpshooters even more. In the 55th Illinois, the men became "exceedingly expert in seeking cover among the logs and trees, and draped themselves with the moss hanging everywhere from the limbs for further disguise." The slightest careless exposure was sure to draw a shot from the watchful Confederates across the bayou.[56]

Also manning the skirmish line along the north bank of Chickasaw Bayou was the 83rd Indiana. When the regiment had moved out that morning, Col. Benjamin J. Spooner had reminded his men, "Boys, Jeff Davis said in the Mexican War that Indiana soldiers were cowards. Remember your state. Forward!" Once they were in position along the bank of the bayou, Spooner gave the order: "Fire, and continue to fire as long as you can see a man's head above the breastworks." The Rebels were well protected by their entrenchments, but occasionally one of the Hoosiers scored a hit. "I saw one poor Rebel jump up like a buck rabbit and fall back in the pit," wrote John Roberts. "I suppose he had been shot in the head and never knew what had hurt him." Spooner exhorted his men: "Pour it into them, boys, keep them down so our batteries can shell them."[57]

Roberts believed he and his comrades were doing a good job of making the Rebels keep their heads down. Confederate fire from the breastworks slacked off, but a party of sharpshooters worked their way down a gully that opened onto the bayou in a dense brushy thicket. From there they began methodically picking off the members of Roberts's company. As a member of the color guard, Roberts had not yet fired. He pointed out the sharpshooters' lair to his captain, who borrowed Roberts's rifle and took a shot himself. In reply the Rebels fired a volley of shots that came uncomfortably close to the colors. Roberts told the captain that "that was an insult to our little squad and asked permission to return the fire."

The captain responded by ordering Roberts to take half the color guard, six men, and cross fifty yards of open ground to a large log that would provide cover and give him a favorable angle for shooting the Rebels in the gully. As he ran, Roberts saw a Confederate rise up from behind the breastworks and fire at him. A bullet sang past his head. Before the Rebel could reload, the six-man squad dove behind the log and lay for a moment panting. The captain had judged correctly, and they had an excellent vantage point from which to fire on the Rebels in the thicket at the mouth of the gully. At the Hoosiers' first volley, the Confederates broke cover and scrambled back up the ravine like "frightened turkeys."

Roberts still had a problem, however. The man who had fired at him on the way to the log knew where he was and had undoubtedly reloaded by this time. Roberts carefully reloaded and peered over his log. The man across the bayou was watching, and they fired simultaneously. He heard the bullet pass over his head and saw that he had missed the Rebel as well. They reloaded and traded shots again. This time the Rebel's ball came close enough to "tingle" his right ear.

Roberts decided that his only chance was to get his rifle loaded first. He did, and took his aim at the Confederate parapet. When the Rebel's head rose, the Hoosier squeezed the trigger. Around the puff of white smoke from his own rifle's muzzle, he saw the other man's gun fall backward into the Confederate trench. "It had to be one of us," Roberts recalled years later, "and it was the other one."

His difficulties were not yet over, however. His comrades had used the cover of his duel with the Rebel sharpshooter to make their own escapes back to the rest of the regiment. Roberts's success attracted the notice of a Confederate battery, which sprayed the bank with canister, while Roberts hugged the ground behind his log. The Confederate artillery fire drew the reply of a Union battery, which cut its fuses so short that Roberts decided they were more of a threat than the enemy's fire and climbed over to the Confederate side of the log. After what seemed an interminable barrage, the artillery fell silent, and Roberts was able to hustle to the rear, just as his regiment was being relieved by the 8th Missouri.[58]

Despite all the efforts of Roberts and his comrades in the 83rd Indiana, as well as the other Union regiments on the skirmish line, the 54th Ohio suffered severe casualties in clearing the abatis. "The first man who struck an ax into a tree was shot dead," reported Stuart. Moments later a short round from one of the Union batteries exploded among the road-clearing party, killing three and wounding others. More short rounds followed. Somehow the work party kept at its task until it had cleared a path through the abatis.[59]

Confederate sharpshooters were active all day everywhere along the front—"the skulking rebels," Major Seay called them, as the Confederate skirmishers took maximum advantage of the abundant cover in the tangled river bottom.[60] Shortly after noon, as Brig. Gen. Frank Blair's brigade sparred with them on the Union left-center, a sharpshooter's bullet struck Col. John B. Wyman of the 13th Illinois, a very popular officer. Stretcher-bearers carried the colonel to the rear, where a surgeon examined him and realized at once that his case, a bullet wound through the chest cavity, was beyond the medicine of the day. The surgeon immediately sent word to the front for Cpl. Osgood Wyman, the colonel's son, to come to the field hospital at once. The younger Wyman arrived in time to exchange farewells with his father.[61]

The 13th lost two other men killed and eight wounded that day. Oddly enough, although the 13th was one of the 1861 regiments, these were its first losses in battle. They were no worse than average, however, for the regiments skirmishing along the line that day. From his position in reserve, Charles Willison of the 76th Ohio noted, "Ambulances loaded with wounded men from the front, and wounded men able to walk, were streaming past us to the rear."[62]

Late on December 28, Morgan, whose division's place in line was between Smith's and Blair's, near the center of the Union position, noticed that few or no Rebel defenders were in position directly opposite his division. The Confederates had reckoned that this stretch of Chickasaw Bayou, eighty feet wide and too deep to ford, would be defense enough in this sector and so had massed their forces opposite the natural crossings. Morgan got permission from Sherman to use the army's pontoon train to force a crossing that night and try to capitalize on the gap in the defenders' line.[63]

That evening Sherman's men bedded down once again on the cold, muddy ground, without campfires, which would have given away their position to watching Rebel eyes, and thus without warm food or the soldiers' beloved coffee. Across the way, they could hear the Confederate bands on the bluffs playing "Dixie."[64] Under cover of darkness, Capt. William F. Patterson's Kentucky Company of Engineers and Mechanics brought forward eight pontoons and got to work on the bridging operation.

Shortly before daybreak, Morgan discovered that Patterson and his men were bridging the wrong stream, a minor bayou that the army had no need of crossing. These bayous all started to look the same after a while, especially in the dark. So Patterson and his engineers, along with fatigue parties from other units of Morgan's division, got to work taking up the bridge, loading the pontoons back on the wagons, and heading for the real Chickasaw Bayou. Daylight revealed that the Confederates still had not occupied the line opposite Morgan's intended crossing point, and the bridge builders fell to work once more, promising Morgan that they would have the bayou spanned in two hours. The Rebels noticed the activity, however, and Confederate artillery took the bridge builders under fire. Union guns replied to cover them. The alerted Confederate commander, Brig. Gen. Stephen D. Lee, shifted troops to cover the sector, and work on the bridge proceeded much more slowly as the engineers took casualties and sometimes had to take cover.[65]

Sherman's plan was for Morgan to cross two brigades of his division at this formerly unguarded central point in the Confederate line. Then Morgan's artillery would fire a massed volley as the signal for the general advance. Two brigades of Steele's division and one of Morgan's would advance on the left from a position just beyond the corduroy bridge, followed up if necessary by Steele's third brigade. At the same time, Col. Giles Smith's brigade would storm across Chickasaw Bayou at the ford on the right and from there join the attack on the bluffs of the Walnut Hills. Meanwhile, the whole Union line of battle would move forward in the most threatening manner it could manage, in order to distract the defenders from the true focus of the assault in the center. Morgan was to have overall command of the main assault, which would be launched from the corduroy bridge on the left and the pontoon bridge, still not complete, in the center. A. J. Smith, commanding his own and Stuart's division, would have overall responsibility for operations on the right, including Giles Smith's cross-bayou assault.[66]

Throughout the morning, an artillery duel raged back and forth across the bottomland between dozens of Union and Confederate guns. Units moved into position for the assault in various places around the battlefield, but in the center Morgan's crucial bridging operation was making little progress in the face of Confederate opposition. Still, he continued to allow two brigades of his division to wait behind the bridge site, without any means of joining the attack.

Sometime after eleven o'clock that morning, Sherman made the decision to launch the attack. The circumstances surrounding it became a matter of dispute in later years. In his report, written five days after the battle, Sherman stated that he had given the order to advance "when Morgan was ready," shortly before noon.[67] In his own report, written three days after the battle, Morgan stated simply that he launched the advance when "informed of the desire of General Sherman that the assault should be promptly made."[68]

In his memoirs, written in 1875, Sherman recalled Morgan telling him, "General, in ten minutes after you give the signal I'll be on those hills."[69] But Morgan told the story somewhat differently. In his own version, he had himself recognizing that an advance on the left would be impossible and sending word to Sherman. Sherman then came to the front and joined Morgan in observing the terrain. Pointing to the bluffs, Sherman announced, "That is the route to take!" Then he rode back to his headquarters. The order to advance, according to Morgan, was conveyed by an officer of Sherman's staff: "Tell Morgan to give the signal for the assault; that we will lose 5,000 men before we take Vicksburg, and may as well lose them here as anywhere else." To this, Morgan had himself replying that he "would order the assault; that we might lose 5,000 men, but that his entire army could not carry the enemy's position." The larger the attacking force, Morgan added, "the greater would be the number slaughtered."[70]

What is clear in all of this is that Sherman had been acutely conscious of the need for rapid movement ever since he had departed from Grant back on the Tallahatchie. He believed that his expedition's chance of success depended on catching the Rebels unprepared, still focused on Grant's threat along the Mississippi Central. He believed, correctly, that Confederate reinforcements were arriving steadily in Vicksburg and would continue to do so. Therefore, Sherman believed he needed to launch his attack as soon as possible.[71]

On the other hand, it is just as clear that Morgan had been expressing great confidence before the December 29 assault. Enamored with the idea of his pontoon bridge that would soon span the "impassable" segment of Chickasaw Bayou, he had been making exactly the kind of statements Sherman recorded in his memoirs. On meeting Frederick Steele that morning, Morgan mentioned the bridge, said it would be finished in two hours, and boasted that "within thirty minutes thereafter he would have possession of the heights, to a moral certainty."[72] Twice the specified two hours had passed, however, before Sherman gave the order for the assault to begin, yet the bridge was still not ready.

Ten minutes before noon Morgan's artillery fired its massed volley. On the right of the line, A. J. Smith's skirmishers moved up to the edge of

Chickasaw Bayou and opened a brisk fire on the Confederates. At the ford where Stuart's brigade had fought the day before, Giles Smith's brigade advanced to storm the crossing, the 6th Missouri in the lead. Thanks to the work of the 54th Ohio the evening before, the abatis no longer barred their path. The first obstacle in their way would come only after they crossed the bayou. The south bank of Chickasaw Bayou here was in fact a levee, partially undercut so as to form a twenty-to-twenty-five-foot almost vertical dirt embankment. A narrow path angled up the slope, but it was wide enough for only two men to advance abreast, and Confederate cannon were positioned to rake it from end to end.[73]

Anticipating this problem, Giles Smith had ordered that the first troops across be a working party, tasked with widening the path. The men reached the foot of the bank, where they were fairly safe from Confederate fire, but they found that the only practical way of widening the access to the top would be by undermining the bank so that it would slump and provide a slope gradual enough for climbing. While the rest of the column waited, the men dug furiously at the embankment.

Thinking he spied another possible path to the top of the embankment a few yards up the bayou, Smith sent the rest of the 6th Missouri, a company at a time, splashing through the ford to join the knot of men at the foot of the embankment. In the middle of the bayou was a sandbar with a row of willows on it. Each company of Missourians would dash across the near channel and fling themselves down behind the willows. Then after catching their breath, they would make the final lunge to the south bank. Most of them got across safely.[74]

The new path Smith had spied proved as impractical as the first had been, so the Missourians had nothing to do but wait and take turns with the shovels, digging away at the embankment. Rebels held their rifles outside the parapet vertically in order to fire down on the Missourians, who used their hands to claw out hollows in the side of the bank in which to shelter.[75]

As if that was not bad enough, sometimes the covering fire from the 13th U.S. Infantry on the north bank of the bayou was aimed too low and would further endanger the Missourians crouching under the embankment, prompting shouts of "Shoot higher, for God's sake—shoot higher!"[76]

In the center of the Union line, Morgan had entrusted Col. Daniel W. Lindsey, commander of his Second Brigade, with the task of completing the pontoon bridge and leading the attack across it. By the time the artillery volley signaled the beginning of the general assault, Captain Patterson and his engineers, along with a fatigue party of the 114th Ohio, had been driven completely away from the bridge site by incessant and accurate Confederate fire. At the signal to advance, Lindsey moved his brigade up to the bank of the bayou and opened up with every rifle and cannon in his command. Under cover of this fusillade, Patterson, the engineers, and the detachment of Ohioans dashed back to the bank and hurriedly began wrestling the bulky, heavy pontoons into the water, then lashing them together and nailing the balks and chesses on top. They got six of the eight boats in place and were only twenty yards from the south bank before close-range Confederate fire drove them back again. Without the bridge, Lindsey's men were powerless to join the attack. The bayou was clearly too deep to wade, and they could see no Confederates among the brush and cane that covered the opposite hillside—only the numerous puffs of white smoke that told of the discharge of their rifles. The bluecoats stood on their side of the bayou and blazed away obstinately.[77]

On the Union left, Brig. Gen. Frank Blair's and Col. John F. De Courcy's brigades advanced side by side. At least in theory, these troops had no more serious obstacles between them and the bluffs than a few minor side channels of the bayou. De Courcy's brigade was on the right, two regiments up on the front line, two back in reserve. They had no sooner stepped off their line of departure than the leading regiments came under heavy fire. Then De Courcy's right-flank regiments ran into what he considered a "nearly impassable" abatis. After struggling through the tangle of interlocking tree branches, they emerged from the abatis only to find themselves on the bank of a deep bayou. With more effort and delay, they worked their way to the left, where the other regiments of the brigade had found a crossing. One of the right-flank regiments never got into the fight at all.[78]

Meanwhile, the regiments on De Courcy's left came under heavy fire as they advanced. Casualties were high and included the commanding officers of both the 16th Ohio and the 22nd Kentucky. In front of their advance, the Confederates abandoned some of their outlying defensive works, and when De Courcy's men reached those positions, they took shelter there and would advance no farther. The 22nd Kentucky had lost 81 men killed and wounded; the 16th Ohio, 117; and the large, new 54th Indiana, 129.[79]

Blair's brigade advanced on De Courcy's left. He ordered his four regiments, two from Missouri and one each from Ohio and Illinois, to fix bayonets. Then his order was "Guide right, double-quick," and troops moved out, yelling wildly. Blair, whose father had been an advisor to Andrew Jackson and whose brother was postmaster general of the United States, rode with them. The brigade advanced through heavy timber, then emerged at the top of a ten-foot bank that led down to the level of a branch of the bayou. At the bottom of the bank had stood a dense thicket of cottonwood saplings, but the Rebels had cut them all off at about three or four feet from the ground and left the fallen trunks lying every which way. Laboriously the men clambered over this obstruction and moved on.[80]

The branch bayou here was only about five yards wide and two feet deep but with a floor of seemingly bottomless mud that some said was quicksand. Pvt. Henry Kuck of the 31st Missouri called it an "old creek" where he and his comrades "got water and mud in our shoes and boots."[81] As color-bearer Jesse Betts was struggling across this narrow stream carrying the national colors of the 13th Illinois, Ensign Jesse Pierce, commander of the color guard, turned back from the far bank and reach down to take the flag from the floundering Betts. Betts gave him the flag and Pierce hurried forward with the regiment.[82]

Up another ten-foot bank, through another abatis, and they finally came face-to-face with the first line of Confederate entrenchments. An exploding shell felled Ensign Pierce. The color guard, like the rest of the regiment and, indeed, the whole brigade, had become badly mixed and scattered in working through the obstructions. Now with the flag of the 13th hidden among the tall cockleburs, no rallying point remained on which to form the regiment, and the color guard could not find the colors. Nevertheless, the regiment kept on advancing. The Rebels hastily withdrew from their first trench, but multiple lines of breastworks still lay ahead.[83]

Col. Peter Dister's horse mired down so badly that he abandoned it and preceded on foot. As Dister dressed the ranks of his 58th Ohio Regiment just beyond the first Confederate trench, Cincinnati German Johann Stuber was startled to see how thin those ranks had already become. The line moved forward again, and Stuber noticed the brigade's two newly recruited Missouri regiments going to ground, unwilling to advance any farther. The 58th, veterans of the second day at Shiloh, swept past them and, along with the 13th Illinois, pushed on and took a second set of works.[84] Jumping down into the second trench, Charles Wilson of the 13th sprained his ankle but scrambled out the other side and hobbled on with his regiment.[85]

Blair looked back and saw De Courcy's men swarming into the first line of trenches. What little order and formation remained in the two brigades was rapidly being lost. Wilson Chapel of the 13th Illinois, which was supposed to be Blair's right-front regiment, wrote of his regiment being further fragmented by passing through the ranks of the 16th Ohio, by this time De Courcy's left-front regiment, where the men of the latter regiment were taking shelter at the first line of Confederate trenches. The attacking force had become little more than an irregular swarm of men struggling over the soft, muddy ground of a wide-open field of cockleburs. "The only way we could do," Chapel recalled, "was to press forward, every man for himself."[86]

The 13th Illinois and 58th Ohio struggled forward, disorganized and scattered but still advancing. As they had been aligned at the start of the attack, the 13th was still generally in front of the 58th. Both regiments were taking a terrific pounding. "That was a terrible slaughter," recalled Johann Stuber, "too gruesome to be described, much less understood." Three decades later, he still vividly remembered seeing his wounded comrades writhing in the mud, their screams drowning out the commands of the remaining officers.[87]

They did not get far beyond the second line of breastworks. Indeed, the 58th Ohio never crossed the second breastwork at all. Dister had paused there a minute or two in order to let the slower men catch up and allow the regiment to re-form its ranks somewhat. Then he stepped atop the breastwork, swung his sword, and called, "Forward, 58th Ohio!" At that moment, a bullet struck him in the head, and he toppled backward to land dead at the feet of his soldiers.[88]

Beyond the breastwork, the 13th Illinois pressed on. They were running now, and men were falling at every step. "It rained a perfect shower of shot and shell around us," wrote Chapel, who remembered General Blair in the midst of it, waving his sword over his head and cheering the men on. A bullet shattered Chapel's canteen, and a shell fragment hit him in the leg and knocked him down, though it only bruised his leg.[89] Ahead was a third line of Rebel works, no outlying entrenchment now but the main line of resistance. Here the Rebels were not falling back but making a determined stand, and the lonely and depleted 13th Illinois was not going to drive them from this position. Blair saw that the situation was hopeless and gave the order to retreat. The surviving Illinoisans turned and started back, as Chapel described it, "in the same manner we advanced, every man for himself."[90]

Immediately to the rear, at the second breastwork, Dister's body had just rolled to a stop at the foot of the parapet, and several members of the 58th Ohio were stooping to pick up his corpse and carry it to the rear. Shouts of "retreat" swept along the line as the men saw Blair and the 13th Illinois turning back in front of them. Blair's losses in the assault approached one-third of his entire force.[91]

Meanwhile, even before Blair's and De Courcy's attacks had failed, Brig. Gen. John M. Thayer's brigade moved forward to join the assault. Thayer's orders were to go in on the right of De Courcy. His brigade consisted of five Iowa regiments, the veteran and relatively small 4th Iowa and four large, new regiments. Thayer formed them in column of fours, the 4th in front, and he ordered each of his colonels to follow the regiment in front of him. At Morgan's direction, he dismounted and sent his horse to the rear so as not to present too good a target for sharpshooters. Then he took his place at the head of the column and led the brigade forward.

Advancing behind De Courcy, the Iowans had relatively little difficulty at first. They crossed the first line of trenches, still in column, via a road that the Confederates had left unobstructed, and Thayer noticed Union troops sheltering in the trenches, unwilling to go forward. Well beyond the first trench, Thayer decided the time had come to have his brigade file right, deploy, and assault the hill.

As the 4th Iowa swung to the right, however, Thayer looked back along his column and found that all four of the other regiments were gone. Thayer told Col. James A. Williamson to hold his 4th Iowa in place as long as he could while Thayer went back to try to find and bring up the other regiments. They were nowhere to be seen, so Thayer, hurrying along on foot, decided to try to rally the troops sheltering in the first line of Confederate trenches and bring them forward to support the 4th. When he arrived, he found Blair was already there, "in a very earnest and excited conversation" with De Courcy, urging him "to get his men forward." Thayer joined in, but even the two of them could not convince De Courcy to renew the advance, nor could Thayer convince the men themselves to leave the safety of the trench. Both De Courcy and his soldiers had had enough.

When Thayer headed back to the front, he met Colonel Williamson bringing out the 4th Iowa. Blair's brigade had already started for the rear, and the 4th had taken 30 percent casualties in less than thirty minutes. In those circumstances, Williamson had decided, not unreasonably, that he was getting his men killed for no good purpose and so ordered the regiment to retreat.[92]

As Stuber and his comrades of the 58th Ohio turned back from the second breastwork after Blair had given the order to retreat, Stuber noticed an attacking column just moving forward to the right of his brigade. Those troops were probably Thayer's 4th Iowa. Stuber was not concerned with them. He had worries enough of his own. "I kept trying to stay with my regiment," he wrote, "but I could not catch any glimpse of a flag; I saw no officers; and there was no regimental line left. All was confusion." Stuber ran until he reached the first entrenchment. A shell fragment ripped through his hat, and another stuck in his rolled-up blanket.[93]

Back in Union lines, an angry Thayer went looking for his missing regiments and the reason they had gone astray. He discovered that Morgan had ordered the second regiment in his column to turn aside before crossing the bayou. The other regiments in the column, obeying Thayer's order to follow the regiment in front of them, had marched after it, and all four regiments, totaling some 3,000 men, had marched into the sector where Union troops were bottled up by the uncrossable stretch of the bayou. In later years, Thayer regretted not bringing court-martial charges against Morgan, and even Steele, for not preventing Morgan's blunder.[94]

Hundreds of live, unwounded Union soldiers still remained in the area between the bayou and the bluffs. After the assault foundered, Confederate troops made a major foray into no-man's-land and bagged large numbers of Federals who had been sheltering there, unable or unwilling to go either forward or back. The regiment that had the largest number taken prisoner was the 16th Ohio, with 194; the 54th Indiana was second with 135. These two regiments comprised the left wing of De Courcy's brigade, and their high number of prisoners suggests that they were indeed the troops who were sheltering in the first Confederate trench. Similarly, in Blair's brigade the two Missouri regiments that had gone to ground early and remained there, as it were, frozen by fear, also had the highest number captured, 121 in all. By contrast, the 13th Illinois and 58th Ohio, while suffering much higher numbers of men killed and wounded, lost well under half as many taken prisoner. In the veteran 58th, only 11 men were captured.[95]

Even the Confederate sortie did not sweep up all of the men sheltering in no-man's-land. John Dykeman and Charles Wilson of the 13th Illinois hid among the cockleburs until dusk and then made their escape, carrying with them a badly wounded member of the 4th Iowa, even though Wilson was still hobbling on the ankle he had sprained jumping into the second Confederate trench.[96]

After the failure of the noon assault, Sherman canceled a planned advance by Hovey's brigade over the same ground on which Blair, De Courcy, and Thayer had come to grief. At the ford on the Union right, Giles Smith ordered the 6th Missouri to withdraw from its awkward position on the south bank of the bayou, though the regiment remained pinned down on the south bank the rest of the day and could only withdraw after nightfall.[97] By midafternoon the grand assault was over. As Sgt. J. E. Leasure of the 16th Ohio noted, "We had bitten off a bigger chunk than we could chaw."[98] It had been as spectacular and complete a failure as any major operation of the war. Sherman's total casualties from the time his army landed on the banks of the Yazoo came to 1,776 men. Confederate casualties were light.[99]

The Chickasaw bottoms were a confusing and difficult place to fight, but the operation had not been very impressive for all that. In the one sector that offered any reasonable hope of success, no attack was ever launched because a pontoon bridge could not be built in time in the right place. The attack that did take place, on the Union left, should have been made by three brigades totaling thirteen regiments. Only eight of those regiments advanced even to the first line of Confederate entrenchments, and of those only three pressed home their attack with determination beyond that point. One of those three, the 4th Iowa, arrived so late as to be no help at all to the other two. The 13th Illinois and 58th Ohio were already starting to retreat by the time the 4th Iowa was approaching.

There were several reasons for the dismal outcome of the operations. The inexperience of regiments like the 54th Indiana and the 29th and 31st Missouri had been a factor. The 16th Ohio had less excuse. On the whole, however, the troops had done about as well as could have been expected under the circumstances, given their level of experience. The 4th Iowa, 58th Ohio, and especially the 13th Illinois had performed prodigies of valor.

The generals had not done as well. Morgan's performance had been nothing short of abysmal. He failed to ensure that the bridge was built in the right place the first time, failed to take the necessary measures to cover the bridge-building party during the morning, failed to be certain that De Courcy's brigade was aligned properly to cross the bayou, and gave an ill-considered order that resulted in diverting four of Thayer's five regiments with six-sevenths of his manpower.

Sherman ultimately bears the responsibility for the failure. Although his command consisted of only four divisions, he was remarkably quick to delegate authority to subordinates A. J. Smith, for operations on the right, and Morgan, for those on the left. It was Sherman's business to see to it that Morgan did his job correctly. Sherman gave the final order to attack with apparent disregard for the circumstances or the fact that preparations in the crucial center sector were far from complete. Whatever exoneration can be found for Sherman in the weak performance of Morgan, the fact remains that Sherman was simply not a very good offensive commander.

In a war in which nearly all generals struggled to find successful offensive tactics to cope with the new weapons of the mid-nineteenth century, Sherman stands out for exceptional ineptitude on the tactical offensive. A splendid defensive tactician, a tower of strength in the midst of intense fighting, a profound thinker about the nature of the war, and a brilliant strategist and logistician, Sherman simply did not have the knack for planning and executing successful assaults. A sense of his own weakness in this area may have prompted him to turn over direction of the Chickasaw Bayou operation to Smith and Morgan. Sherman's success as a general was going to depend on how well he could work around this one glaring gap in his abilities.

That evening a cold, hard rain began to fall and continued all night. The army's campsites were on low ground, and the soldiers huddled miserably or tried to sleep while sitting leaning against trees, without a single dry spot of earth to lie down on. Some who had reclined on the ground to sleep woke up after an hour or two of exhausted slumber to find themselves lying in several inches of chilly water. Others who had started work on entrenchments spent the night sitting in trenches with six inches of water. Cpl. Michael Sweetman and two comrades tried to shelter under a single piece of oilcloth while muttering imprecations at Confederate artillerists who kept up a sporadic harassing fire throughout the night.[100]

Some soldiers crept back into no-man's-land that night in search of dead or wounded comrades. Pvt. Jack Kenyon of the 13th Illinois went on a long crawl through the mud in search of his company's two lieutenants, George A. Napier and Jordan J. Cole, neither of whom had returned from the day's assault. To his surprise, he saw lying on the ground in the moonlight a flag with the numerals 1 and 3 on it. The 13th had lost both its regimental and national colors that day, and Kenyon assumed this was one of them. Removing the flag from the staff, he wrapped it around his waist and continued his search for the missing officers. With daylight approaching, he finally had to give up, never having found Napier or Cole, and sadly returned to camp. Chagrin was added to his sadness there, however, when he discovered that the flag he had rescued was not his own regiment's standard but rather the regimental colors of the 31st Missouri.

Meanwhile, Pvt. George W. Sutherland, also of the 13th, had made his way to the scene of the fighting with the specific purpose of recovering one of his regiment's flags. During the retreat the previous day, Sutherland had spied a banner lying beneath the body of a dead color-bearer. He had had no time to stop and get it then, but he had noted that the part of the flag protruding from under its fallen bearer featured the figure 3. He remembered roughly where this had been, but a midnight search while crawling through a muddy field of cockleburs was still tedious. The imminent possibility of a fusillade from the Confederate lines did not help matters. Finally he found the flag and brought it back to camp, staff and all. To his dismay, he discovered it was the national colors of the 31st Missouri.[101]

Sherman was unwilling to accept defeat. He considered renewing the assault across the Chickasaw bottoms but wisely decided against it. Instead he conferred with Porter about the possibility of conveying one or more divisions up the Yazoo in steamboats to make a direct assault on Haynes's

Bluff. Taking the bluff would, theoretically, open the way for communication with Grant, still assumed to be moving down from the interior of Mississippi, as well as for operations against Vicksburg from the only direction the town could practically be approached by a hostile army, the east and northeast.[102]

Sherman gave orders for Steele's division and one brigade of Stuart's to embark on the night of December 30, proceed to Haynes's Bluff, and launch an assault at daybreak on the last day of 1862. Meanwhile, he had his army entrench along the north bank of Chickasaw Bayou and be ready to renew the cross-bayou assault as soon as Steele's operation began upriver. The Confederates would not be able to meet both threats, Sherman hoped, and their lines would be bound to break somewhere.[103]

Late on the night of December 30, the troops boarded the steamboats as ordered. Steele's men lit large campfires in the evening and left them burning as they departed their camps in complete silence, hoping to conceal their absence from the Confederates. Morale was not high among the troops waiting to go upriver in the boats. Charles Willison of the 76th Ohio noticed officers bracing themselves up with whiskey. There was not enough whiskey to go around, so the privates were expected to provide their own courage.[104] The officers of the 76th may have had reason to feel uneasy. One member of the 25th Iowa noted that the orders were for each brigade to make the assault in column of companies, and the 76th Ohio was to occupy the front of the center column with the 25th Iowa right behind it. "The men were to throw away blankets and overcoats and charge with no loads in their guns," he added.[105]

As the expedition was about to get under way, however, a dense fog settled on the river, making travel by steamboat impossible, and Sherman abandoned the Haynes's Bluff operation.[106] Capt. Strew Emmons of the 76th Ohio was immensely relieved. "We was to take them with cold steele or die," he wrote to his wife. "It would have been the latter." The plan for the attack on Haynes Bluff was, in Emmons's opinion, "a most reckless fool hardy undertaking & could not possibly have succeeded." Emmons had had a presentiment that had he gone into that charge, he would not have come out alive. "I never before or since felt so in going into battle," he later wrote.[107]

With no further hope of immediate offensive operations, Sherman asked for a truce to retrieve the dead and wounded from the battlefield. Many of the dead were found to have been robbed and stripped by the Rebels, and some of Sherman's men believed from the nature of wounds they found on the corpses that they had been shot in the head at close range while lying wounded on the ground. Nevertheless, many soldiers took advantage of the truce to walk out and enter into conversation with their enemies.[108]

New Year's Day, 1863, passed quietly. That evening the Rebels held a celebration behind their fortifications on the Chickasaw bluffs. From their lines in the bottoms, the Federals could occasionally hear shouts and laughter and could see the flickering reflection of firelight above the Rebel parapets. Later a Confederate brass band played "Dixie," "The Bonnie Blue Flag," and a popular piece of that day entitled "Get Out of the Wilderness." Sherman's men figured that that one was intended for their ears.[109]

That night the Union army was stirring again. In the 114th Ohio, non-commissioned officers silently awakened the men at about 11:00 p.m. and in low tones directed them to pack and sling their knapsacks and fall in line with full accoutrements. More whispered orders directed them to take their weapons silently from the stacks and then to file by companies to the rear. "We marched out of the woods as silent as a funeral," wrote Sgt. Elias Moore in his diary. During the next three-quarters of a mile of marching, much speculation in the ranks focused on what this new movement might mean. "A night attack upon the enemy's works was the general impression," recalled Cpl. Michael Sweetman.[110]

Then they marched past a section of artillery, gunners standing by, ammunition ready, and the muzzles of the cannon pointing back in the direction from which the 114th had come. Only then did it begin to dawn on the men that they were retreating. Confirmation came when officers dispatched a detail with axes to fell trees across the road behind them and destroy a small bridge the army had built over one of the many side channels of the bayou. "Here for the first time we realized that we were beaten," wrote Sweetman.[111]

Other regiments' experiences were similar. The 55th Illinois was on a fatigue detail that night, working on gun emplacements for Battery A, 1st Illinois Light Artillery, when they received their own whispered orders to march. They too wondered what it all meant and realized that a retreat was in progress only when they arrived at the Yazoo and saw the steamboats waiting to take them aboard.[112] After waiting in skirmish line some time to cover the withdrawal of other troops, the 114th Ohio went aboard a steamboat at around 4:00 a.m. The next morning, while the transport fleet still lay moored in the river, Rebel skirmishers began nosing about the Chickasaw bottoms, but the firepower of the gunboats easily held them at bay. On board the steamer *Pembina*, a weary Sergeant Moore curled up in his blanket and went to sleep.[113] Sherman had decided on New Year's Day that nothing could be accomplished along Chickasaw Bayou and had ordered the stealthy departure that night.[114]

The soldiers were discouraged at their setback along Chickasaw Bayou. "No engagement in which I was afterward involved impressed me with the nightmarish sensations of this one," wrote Charles Willison of the 76th Ohio many years later.[115] Some of their anger and frustration was directed toward Sherman. "What makes this so deplorable is that it was a useless sacrifice of life," Henry Ankeny of the 4th Iowa wrote to his wife on the last day of 1862. "Our Generals do not understand their business and do not appear to care for the loss of life no more than were we so many brutes; that we are I suppose."[116] Ankeny was not alone in thinking that Sherman had blundered. "I think that this has been one of the foolishest moves that was ever made by any General that had common sense," wrote James Northup of the 23rd Wisconsin.[117]

The discouragement went much deeper than distrust for a specific general, however. "A general depression prevailed in the whole command," wrote Charles Miller of the 76th Ohio.[118] The news from other theaters of the war was also discouraging. Rumor told of a great Union defeat in Virginia during December. "It seems strange to me that we are so unfortunate," wrote Ankeny. "Our men are brave and loyal, but there is a fatality hanging over us that I cannot account for."[119] At the heart of the discouragement was the suspicion that the cause might be lost and all their sacrifices in vain. "At no time previous during the war had a doubt ever entered my mind on the ultimate success of our armies in suppressing this wicked rebellion," wrote Miller. Now, however, "the future seemed a dark blank."[120]

CHAPTER SIXTEEN

Winter on the Mississippi

O N THE MORNING of January 2, Sherman and his army, once again
afloat in steamboats, prepared to depart the scene of their defeat at
Chickasaw Bayou. Before they could leave, however, Porter brought Sherman news that McClernand had arrived at the mouth of the Yazoo on board
Tigress. Sherman knew that McClernand had come to take over command
of the expedition, and so he left the rest of the fleet moored where it was
and hastened down the Yazoo on a tugboat to meet with McClernand and
see what his orders would be. On board *Tigress*, Sherman briefed McClernand on the battle that had just taken place. The Rebels in Vicksburg were
receiving reinforcements, he told McClernand, and that would mean that
Grant must not be far away, close on the heels of Pemberton's fleeing army.
To Sherman's surprise, McClernand informed him that Grant had retreated
after the Holly Springs debacle and some elements of his army had already
reached Memphis before McClernand left.[1]

The question for Sherman and McClernand was what to do next. Sherman had a suggestion. A few days before, Confederates operating from a
post on the Arkansas River had captured the steamboat *Red Wing*, with a
load of the army's mail, on the banks of the Mississippi near the mouth of
the Arkansas. The Rebel garrison on the tributary was not large, but it was
a constant nuisance to Union communications on the great river, and Sherman now proposed to eliminate it.

McClernand was in a foul mood and behaved obnoxiously to both Sherman and Porter, but he recognized the value of Sherman's suggestion and
immediately gave orders for his force, which he styled "the Army of the
Mississippi," to head upriver toward the mouth of the Arkansas. Some distance up that river they came to the Confederate fort at a place called
Arkansas Post and captured it after a short, sharp fight on January 11.
McClernand was enraptured with his success. "Glorious! Glorious! My star
is ever in the ascendant!" he raved, and spun plans to take his army far up
the Arkansas, away from Grant's supervision.[2]

Grant, who by this time had reached Memphis, was less impressed and ordered McClernand to bring the expedition back to the Mississippi River for operations against the main objective, Vicksburg. It reached the mouth of the Arkansas River on January 17, and there met Grant, who that day had taken a steamer down from Memphis. While the boats were moored there, Grant visited with various officers, including Sherman and Porter. They convinced him that the capture of Arkansas Post had been a good idea and would indeed help clear the way for the capture of Vicksburg. However, they also made plain to him that they considered McClernand incompetent to lead the expedition. Both Porter and Sherman urged Grant to take command of it himself. Since Grant was the only officer in the department who outranked McClernand, only his presence could spare the army what Sherman and Porter both believed would be a debacle when they reached stoutly defended Vicksburg.[3]

Grant agreed. He ordered the expedition to proceed to Milliken's Bend, where he would join it in a few days. In the meantime, he hurried back to Memphis to make necessary preparations and have additional troops sent down the river. He gave orders for McPherson's Seventeenth Corps to ship out for Vicksburg as soon as possible, while Hurlbut's Sixteenth Corps would remain to garrison the various Union posts in West Tennessee.[4]

Next, Grant turned his attention to the question of how to take Vicksburg. It was a problem that seemed to have no solution at all. A direct landing at the foot of the bluff on which the city sat was a prospect too horrible to contemplate. An advance down the east bank of the Mississippi led straight into the Chickasaw Bayou bottoms and against the impregnable bluffs of the Walnut Hills. The only direction from which to approach Vicksburg with any reasonable chance of success was along the ridge between the Yazoo and the Big Black rivers. That broad belt of high, dry ground angled toward Vicksburg from the northeast. It could in turn be reached from the north in two ways—either via central Mississippi, where Grant's late-fall offensive had come to grief, or by crossing the Mississippi Delta, a belt of swamps that lay just behind the natural levees along the east side of the Mississippi from the Walnut Hills almost all the way north to Memphis. Crossing the delta would have been a questionable undertaking at the best of times, and the heavy rains of early January gave ample notice that this winter was going to be anything but the best of times in the delta swamps.[5]

One other way existed, at least in theory, to gain the high ground east of Vicksburg. That would be to march down the west bank of the river—also a maze of swamps, bayous, and natural levees—cross over to the east bank below Vicksburg, and then proceed northeastward by relatively firm, dry roads to the ridge between the Yazoo and the Big Black. What made this option difficult was that the army could not possibly cross the Mississippi without steamboats, which dared not attempt to pass the heavy guns of Vicksburg.

The problem facing Grant, therefore, was to put his army on the high ground east of Vicksburg, either by finding a way to get it across the delta north of Vicksburg or by discovering a method to get his steamboats into the river south of the city. His first solution to this problem was to have his men dig a canal across the peninsula, De Soto Point, opposite Vicksburg. The city sat at the outside end of a hairpin bend of the river. If the Federals could dig their way across the base of that bend, and get the river's power-ful current to scour their ditch into a viable channel, then the boats could bypass the batteries and reach the river south of Vicksburg.[6]

The idea was not new. The previous summer, a U.S. naval squadron had run up the Mississippi River from New Orleans. Only a modest land force had accompanied the warships, and they had been unable to capture Vicksburg. Brig. Gen. Thomas Williams's brigade had spent several weeks attempting to dig a canal across De Soto Point, but the falling level of the river during the summer drought had endangered the deep-draft men-of-war and forced the withdrawal of the expedition. Since that time, the Con-federates had fortified Port Hudson, Louisiana, 150 miles downriver, ruling out any prospect of help from that direction. Grant believed, however, that the canal could be altered and completed so as to fulfill its intended purpose. Back in Washington, Lincoln read of the plan with interest. Having once taken a flatboat down the Mississippi, the president knew the river's propen-sity to cut off its bends and believed the plan would work. He had Halleck send a note to Grant expressing his enthusiasm for the scheme.[7]

In order to push it to completion, Grant directed Sherman and McCler-nand to take their corps to Young's Point, just above De Soto Point, where they could provide security and manpower for another attempt at digging a canal.[8] The steamboats arrived there on January 22. As successive divisions reached the point, what struck the soldiers first was the sight of Vicksburg, about four miles away and plainly visible on a hill that rose steeply from the river.[9] When the 76th Ohio arrived on January 23, Frank Wise wrote in his diary, "The soldiers nearly all got on the hurricane decks with eyes widely opened while looking at the city and its fortifications of Vixburgh."[10]

The soldiers' next reaction was one of relief at finally being permitted to get off the transports. "We are disembarking from the boat, having made it our home (or prison) for 38 days," wrote Maj. A. J. Seay in his diary.[11] The troops worked hard, disembarking from the transports, unloading the army's impedimenta, and setting up their camps. Exposure, fatigue, poor diet, and extreme crowding had combined to make the transports into veritable pestholes of disease. A member of the 48th Ohio believed that nearly half the men on his transport, *City of Alton,* were disabled by sickness by the time they reached Young's Point. Significantly, he noted that while his own regiment suffered relatively little sickness, the big, new 108th Illinois, which shared the same crowded boat, had nearly three-fourths of its men unfit for duty from sickness. The new regiments were suffering the high rate of sickness common to Civil War soldiers in their first winter in uniform, but they were doing it in the cold, wet misery of the crowded transports or the muddy camps at Young's Point. Many were too sick to leave the transports, while others were ailing as they marched down the gangplanks and into the new camps.[12]

Sherman, to whose Fifteenth Corps was assigned the job of completing the canal across De Soto Point, went immediately to view the task at hand. He and his staff rode from the steamboat landing to the line of the unfinished canal. Reining in his horse at the edge of the canal, Sherman exclaimed, "It is no bigger than a plantation ditch." In fact, the segments of the canal that were the most complete at this time were barely ten feet wide and six feet deep. If that had been the only problem with the canal, it could have been remedied by large numbers of men with shovels. However, the Confederates had positioned heavy guns on the bluffs across the river so as to lob shells onto the whole length of the canal. As a further discouragement, both ends of the canal met the river in areas of slack water, where the forces of the river were unlikely to provide the necessary scouring to enlarge the channel. Sherman's quick reconnaissance had raised serious questions about the canal's prospects of success.[13]

Meanwhile, others had been pursuing their own sources of information about the canal. Sherman and his staff were discussing its possibilities when a courier rode up with an order from McClernand to Sherman. It read, "You will proceed immediately to blow up the bottom of the canal. It is important that this be done tonight, as tomorrow it may be too late." Sherman read the order and handed it to his chief engineer officer, William L. B. Jenney, directing that he carry it out. Jenney read it and looked up, puzzled, but Sherman understood the order no better than he. This left Jenney the unenviable necessity of going to McClernand for clarification and risking that general's well-known temper. Finding McClernand, Jenney diplomatically asked for more specific instructions as to exactly what the general wanted. True to form, McClernand flew into a rage. "You can dig a hole, can't you?" he roared. "You can put powder into it, can't you? You can touch it off, can't you? Well, then, won't it blow up?" Since the bottom of the ditch contained a small amount of water and any hole would have filled with water before it could have been filled with powder, these orders were impossible to carry out.

Later, Jenney and Sherman learned that while they had been reconnoitering the canal, McClernand had been talking to the captain of one of the steamboats, who had told him that the bottom of the canal was a thin layer of hard clay overlaying sand. If a hole were blown in the clay, the rapidly rising river, once it began to flow through the canal, would wash out the clay and the underlying sand. Unfortunately, as far as anyone in the Army of the Tennessee was ever able to ascertain, the clay in the bottom of the canal might have extended all the way to China.[14]

Although McClernand's order was not feasible, no reason existed why the army could not at least attempt to carry out Grant's order to dig the canal deeper and wider and to move its entrance and exit in hopes of making it effective. Sherman and his staff got busy supervising the operation in the days that followed. They assigned each regiment a segment 160 feet long—about the length of a veteran regiment's line as it stood in two ranks. Orders were to dig the canal sixty feet wide and nine feet deep. Provided the canal could be made to flow bank-full, those dimensions would be just large enough to allow passage of the navy's city-class ironclads, backbone of the river fleet.[15]

The Confederates did their best to interfere, lobbing shells at the canal whenever they suspected work was in progress. One particular gun on the Mississippi bluffs won from Sherman's men the derisive nickname "Whistling Dick" for the sound its shells made. The soldiers found it a noisy but not particularly dangerous accompaniment to their twelve-hour shifts on the canal. "Sometimes it would knock over staging, wheelbarrows and planks all over the place," recalled Illinois soldier W. R. Eddington. "We would sit down under the bank until they got in better humor and then we would get up and go to work again."[16]

Being sons of the Old Northwest, many of the soldiers knew the Mississippi and its ways. Around campfires at night, they discussed the canal, the eddy at its proposed entrance, and the stiff clay into which they were digging. The consensus was that it was not going to work. Each day they returned for another twelve-hour shift, but, as one of them later explained, there was "not much heart put into the work." As far as the men were concerned, they were simply "marking time" along this muddy ditch, and they wondered what the next plan would be for getting at the seemingly impregnable fortress of Vicksburg.[17]

By March 6, some regiments had finished their assigned segments but others still had digging to do and stumps to remove when the rising waters of the Mississippi that night broke through the levee at the upper end of the canal. Water not only rushed through the canal but also spread over the Young's Point peninsula, forcing thousands of Union troops to seek new and drier campsites, generally along the levee itself.[18] Yet the influx of water did not have the hoped-for effect on the canal itself. The stiff clay resisted even the turbid rush of the mighty river and the canal refused to scour out to a depth that would have permitted the passage of steamboats. Rather than accepting the soldiers' laborious offer of a new bed, the river, with its customary perversity, seemed bent on channeling its awesome power toward flooding the army completely out of its valley. Soon more than half the available manpower was committed to shoring up levees and repairing the several roaring crevasses that had opened in them.

Efforts on the canal continued, including the use of two steam dredges sent down from the North. In the end, however, the project proved as unavailing as the soldiers had suspected it would be.[19]

BY JANUARY 29, Grant had concluded his business in Memphis and joined the expedition at Young's Point. In his quiet way, he inspected the camps and the work on the canal. It was the first time Ohio soldier Charles Willison had seen his commanding general, and he was impressed with Grant's modesty and lack of pretense. "He came without any ostentation," Willison wrote, "almost alone, to inspect the work being done on the canal, and stood a while watching our company. I remember the attitude so characteristic of him, as he stood smoking the inevitable cigar, and with one hand in his pants pocket."[20] An Ohio officer wrote in a letter to his wife that day, "It gives the troops hope to see him in Command."[21]

At least one member of the expedition was not at all pleased to see Grant. McClernand seethed at his superior's presence. Grant, for his part, was eager to assuage him as much as possible. Although Halleck's January 11 telegram had explicitly authorized him to take direct command of the expedition, Grant was eager to give Lincoln all the political leeway he could.[22] So on first arriving at Young's Point, Grant mentioned to McClernand that he did not foresee changing McClernand's "relation to the forces here." That is, McClernand would continue as expedition commander, and Grant would give orders through him.[23]

It took less than twenty-four hours to demonstrate what a bad idea that was. The day following Grant's arrival, McClernand complained bitterly in a dispatch to Grant that one of his subordinates had gone over his head to Grant regarding some trivial matter of the assignment of campsites. Although that was exactly the sort of thing McClernand himself had done on a vastly larger scale by going over Grant's head to Lincoln, he found it infuriating when he was on the receiving end of such behavior. It would subvert his authority, he complained, and the one who did it ought to be arrested for insubordination. This might have seemed insubordinate in itself, but McClernand was just getting warmed up.

"I understand that orders are being issued from your Head Quarters directly to Army Corps Commanders, and not through me," he lectured Grant in his dispatch. "As I am invested, by order of the Secretary of War, endorsed by the President—and by order of the President communicated to you by the General-in-Chief, with the command of all the forces operating on the Mississippi river, I claim that all orders affecting the condition or operations of those forces should pass through these Head Quarters." If Grant disagreed, McClernand continued, "the question should be immediately referred to Washington, and one or other, or both of us relieved." Then in a statement with which Grant undoubtedly agreed, he concluded, "One thing is certain: two Generals cannot command this army, issuing independent and direct orders to subordinate officers, and the public service be promoted."[24]

This was a remarkable communication, not only because it was, as Grant later pointed out, "more in the nature of a reprimand than a protest," but also because McClernand had known for six weeks that the authorities in Washington had assigned him to command of the Thirteenth Corps. Clearly, however, in inventing "the Army of the Mississippi" and in insisting that Sherman refer to the Thirteenth Corps as Morgan's corps, McClernand was doing his best to overturn the intent of the president as expressed in Halleck's December 18 telegram to Grant.[25]

In order to make the command situation completely clear and unequivocal, Grant immediately issued General Orders No. 13, officially assuming "immediate command of the expedition against Vicksburg" and directing that "Army corps commanders will resume the immediate command of their respective corps, and will report to and receive orders direct from these headquarters."[26] That, of course, meant McClernand.

The politician was not slow to respond. "General orders No. 13 is this moment received," he wrote on that same busy January 30. "I hasten to inquire whether its purpose is to relieve me from the command of all or any portion of the forces composing the Mississippi River expedition, or, in other words, whether its purpose is to limit my command to the Thirteenth Army Corps."[27] That, of course, was exactly what it was meant to do. Whether Lincoln had tricked McClernand, or Halleck had tricked Lincoln, or the exigencies of war had betrayed the expectations of them all, the fact remained that McClernand's orders did not, as he repeatedly and obnoxiously claimed, endow him with the inalienable right to win military glory for himself at the head of an independent force. Lincoln, Stanton, and Halleck had framed the orders in such a way as to give McClernand command of the river expedition by seniority and only if Grant were occupied in central Mississippi or elsewhere in his department, as had been the case at the time the orders were issued.

Grant wrote a calm reply the following day. "The intention of General Orders, No. 13, is that I will take direct command of the Mississippi River expedition, which necessarily limits your command to the Thirteenth Army Corps," Grant explained. "I regard the President as Commander-in-Chief of the Army, and will obey every order of his, but as yet I have seen no order to prevent my taking immediate command in the field, and since the dispatch referred to in your note, I have received another from the General-in-Chief of the Army, authorizing me directly to take command of this army." He went on to explain that he had not at first anticipated issuing such an order, "but soon saw it would be much more convenient" to do so.[28]

Still not content, McClernand fired back again. He would acquiesce for the present, but he demanded that Grant forward the entire correspondence to Washington. "I claim the right to command the expedition," he defiantly asserted. Grant did forward the papers, but Washington did not intervene.[29] Meanwhile, on February 1, the same day that he launched the parting shot in that exchange with Grant, McClernand sent him another dispatch requesting permission to take his corps on an odyssey of more than 250 miles through Pine Bluff and Little Rock, Arkansas, and all the way to Arkadelphia, in the western part of the state—anything to get out from under Grant's control and have an independent command. Grant declined the request.[30]

While the high command struggled over such matters, the soldiers had struggles of their own. "The weather is pretty ugly, very muddy, rained part of the time," wrote the 76th Ohio's Frank Wise in his diary on January 26. Two days later, he wrote, "The mud froze hard, Ice ¼ of an inch thick."[31] Brig. Gen. John B. Sanborn later wrote of "the gloomy winter of 1862–63. The winter was cold, stormy, and disagreeable in the last degree. Snow fell at Memphis, on more than one occasion, to the depth of a foot or more."[32] In the camps at Young's Point, the soldiers of the Army of the Tennessee were in a position to suffer as much of the winter's misery as anyone could at their latitude.

The army had to camp on low ground. The 77th Illinois found its designated campsite to be a low-lying cornfield in which water stood in all of the furrows. Nearby, a levee rose some fifteen to twenty feet above the field in which the regiment's tents were pitched. When the regiment arrived and set up camp, the soldiers, warily eyeing their tents and the level of the river from the vantage point of the top of the levee, estimated that the surface of the river was ten or twelve feet higher than the ground on which they slept each night. During the course of the next month, the river rose steadily higher until it had nearly reached the top of the levee.[33]

In order to make the camp minimally habitable, the men had to find a way to drain off the standing water that kept collecting there. "We had to dig a deep ditch on each side of our rows of tents and between each tent to drain the water from the tents," wrote William Wiley. They threw the dirt from the ditches into their tents "to raise us above the water line." Then they gathered "corn stalks, weeds, brush, and whatever we could find to lay on to keep us out of the mud."[34]

The black, sticky mud was ubiquitous and usually impossible to stay out of. It sucked men's shoes right off their feet as they tried to walk or else clung to their footwear in amazing quantities. During the day, they worked "midleg deep in mud and water," and at night they lay down to sleep in shallower mud.[35] "If you want to see mud come to Louisiana and camp in a swamp," wrote Jake Ritner. "The driest place I could find to sleep last night the mud was four inches deep."[36] "We would about as soon see a few rebs as so much rain and mud," wrote William Wade in his diary.[37]

Every rain would cover the surrounding ground with a sheet of water several inches deep—much more in some places—so that it looked as if the troops were camping on clusters of low mud bars in the midst of a vast lake, and, as an Ohio soldier pointed out, "It rained nearly every day for weeks." Some patches of low ground never seemed to drain, so that troops coming and going from picket duty always had to wade waist-deep in icy water.[38]

In many of the camps, the only firewood available was cypress, green and unseasoned, which the soldiers complained would hardly burn even when dry, which it rarely was. They could barely coax enough fire out of it to make their coffee, the closest thing to a luxury the soldiers had. Even the inferior firewood had to be hauled with enormous effort from swamps sometimes as much as a mile away.[39]

So soft and muddy was the ground that wagons with even light loads would often mire down all the way to their hubs.[40] W. R. Eddington saw six mules attempting to pull a wagon loaded with only a single barrel of pork. Both mules and wagon finally mired down so badly that the soldiers had to unhitch the mules and then get several hundred men pulling on long ropes to drag them out of the mud hole, subsequently retrieving the wagon in the same manner.[41] "There are hundreds of teams all around here sticking fast," wrote Ritner. "The only way to transport anything is on the backs of men and mules—wagoning is played out."[42]

Despite being surrounded by water and almost never able to get dry, the soldiers found it impossible to secure pure drinking water. "Drinking water was reached by digging only a couple of feet, and was stagnant," recalled Charles Willison.[43] The impure water became a transmitter of disease germs.

Disease ran rampant through the camps that winter. Here and there, surgeons appropriated a cabin or two as a field hospital, and several of the steamboats became floating hospitals. Many of the patients succumbed. John Wiley wrote of seeing three or four new corpses laid out in front of the 77th Illinois's regimental hospital each day.[44] Similarly, on board the hospital steamer *Fanny Bullitt,* nurse William Winters kept a diary that recorded three or four deaths each day and some days as many as eight.[45] An Iowa officer reported an incredible seventeen bodies removed from one hospital boat in a single day.[46] At some periods during the encampment, Wiley wrote, "there was hardly an hour in the day but what we could hear the drums beating the dead march as some pour comrade was carried to his last resting place." Wiley, who was badly ill himself, could not help wondering how long it would be until the drums beat for him.[47] As always, it was the new soldiers who stood the highest chances of dying of disease. "They seemed to succumb so easily and quickly when sickness seized them," wrote Willison.[48]

It was impossible to bury the dead in the low-lying ground around the camps. Any hole in the ground large enough to receive a body would immediately fill with water. So the army had to bury its dead along the levees, until, in the words of Charles Miller of the 76th Ohio, "they became a vast cemetery stretching for miles along the river," with small boards in place of headstones. Walking on the levee one day, Miller was startled to read, scratched into one of the headboards, the name of a boyhood friend he had not seen for years, then another, and another. He had strayed unwittingly into the section of the levee where the 96th Ohio was interring its dead. The 96th, recruited largely from Miller's boyhood home of Mt. Vernon, Ohio, had, unbeknownst to Miller, contained many whom he had known in the past but was not destined to see again in this life.[49]

The soldiers might have born their hardships with their accustomed fortitude, but the worst of this winter encampment along the Mississippi was the discouragement, almost despair, that seemed to settle down on the camps like the dark, heavy rain clouds that came day after day. "These were the dark days of the war," wrote the 69th Indiana's Oran Perry.[50] At the heart of the discouragement was a gnawing doubt that the war could ever be won. "The war will never be over by fighting," wrote a dispirited officer to his wife in January. "Nothing but a compromise will save us, I fear—such work is horrible."[51]

"The news from the North was dispiriting in the extreme," wrote John B. Sanborn of that winter. Maj. Gen. Ambrose Burnside had led the ponderous Army of the Potomac to spectacular defeat at the December 1862 Battle of Fredericksburg. Rosecrans had won a costly and equivocal victory in Middle Tennessee at the turn of the year, and some accounts depicted great dissatisfaction and war-weariness in the Northern civilian population.[52] "Our cause never looked darker than at the present time," a Hoosier in the Army of the Tennessee wrote to his father that January. "Completely whipped everywhere, outgeneralled and outwitted in the east and in the west we are all completely disgusted and dispair of ultimate success."[53]

"The times look gloomy and the darkness that surrounds the Republic can almost be felt," wrote Iowa soldier Cyrus Boyd in his diary in January. "Shall I ever forget how dark and intensely hopeless every feature of our struggle looks now. The eastern army is totally routed and the enemy is strong and defiant everywhere." He wondered if perhaps this might be the "dark hour just before dawn. I know it cannot get much darker."[54] An ominous indicator of the army's low morale could be seen in its rising rate of desertion. "A tremendous number have deserted of late and the evil is growing," wrote Charles Wills in a letter home. Thousands more would desert, Wills believed, if stationed closer to home.[55]

Many officers and enlisted men believed that the most significant reason for the low morale and desertion lay in disloyal words and actions of some of those back home in the North.[56] "I am afraid our country is in a bad fix now between the Secesh and the Democrats," wrote the 45th Illinois's Luther Cowan.[57] Charles Wills believed "disloyal talk" by civilians was "the cause of all the desertions." Noting the high numbers of desertions, he added, "Nine-tenths of the discontent and demoralization spring from the same source."[58]

Letters from acquaintances or even family members back home sometimes contained denunciations of the war or predictions that it was bound to end in failure. "Many of the boys got letters from their Butternut friends telling them to desert and come home and they would be protected," recalled John Roberts of the 83rd Indiana.[59] Butternuts were pro-Confederate residents of southern Illinois, Indiana, and Ohio. The problem was widespread. Isaac Jackson of the 83rd Ohio wrote of persons "writing discouraging letters and sending traitorous scraps of printed matter to their sons and friends in the army."[60] The Cincinnati newspapers, avidly read by many soldiers, were sometimes little more than antiwar propaganda. "It was all very discouraging," wrote Roberts.[61]

On occasion, disloyal Northern civilians actually visited the army's camps for the purpose of encouraging the soldiers to give up the war and desert. Oran Perry recalled one such "reptile" from his home state who made a visit of several days with the 69th Indiana. The regiment, which had previously had no desertions, suddenly lost three or four in two days. Col. Tom Bennett of the 69th rose from his sickbed, had the regiment assembled, and delivered a roaring denunciation of Copperheads and cowards. Perry believed Bennett "made such a magnificent appeal to the patriotism of the men that the current was completely turned," both in the 69th and in the other regiments of the brigade. The visiting Copperhead fled the camp and headed back up the river.[62]

The disloyalty in the North cast a gloomy pall over current operations and led the soldiers of the Army of the Tennessee to suspect that they might be experiencing yet another failure as they labored and wallowed and sickened and sometimes died in this unnatural land where mud could be both sticky and slippery at the same time—and in every imaginable place—and nights were loud with "the piping and creaking and croaking of all sorts of creatures in the woods and swamps."[63] As Charles Willison summed it up, "The men could and were perfectly willing to march and fight even until death. But this helpless waiting and digging ditches, and disease and ignoble way of dying were very hard to endure with patience."[64] Some, a small minority, ran out of patience. "The old soldiers are very, very tired of the war," wrote an Illinois soldier. "Any number of them would recognize three or four confederacies to get home, and their influence over the new men is boundless."[65]

Helping to keep the soldiers going through these hard times were the tangible evidence of support from the home front. The most common such tokens were encouraging letters from friends and family. Equally welcome were boxes of good things from home—desirable food items not readily available at the front, especially vegetables, which could help ward off scurvy. Shipments also included clothing, and one soldier described a particularly welcome box as containing "socks, mittens, needle books." The town of Cedar Falls, Iowa, alone shipped 1,517 pounds of vegetables to its men at the front, and other communities made similar efforts to support their troops. Such shipments, in the opinion of one Illinois soldier, "went a long ways in reviving our spirits and failing health."[66]

CHAPTER SEVENTEEN

Into the Bayous

G RANT'S FIRST inspection of the canal convinced him that the project was very unlikely to be successful. About the only thing it would do would be to force the Confederates to spread their defenses along a somewhat greater length of bluffs, as they would want to place cannon to cover the exit of the canal.[1] That in itself might not have been a sufficient reason to have kept men at work on the canal, but Grant would try to humor the president, whether it be in tolerating McClernand or in continuing work on the canal about which Lincoln was so enthusiastic.

Meanwhile, Grant turned his attention to what he hoped would be a more practical means of accomplishing his goal of putting his army on dry land in rear of Vicksburg. For this purpose, he gave orders for the simultaneous exploration of two possible routes to the high ground behind Vicksburg, Yazoo Pass and Lake Providence. Once a bend of the river, Lake Providence had at some past date been spurned by the current of the Mississippi, cut off, and silted up at both ends to become an oxbow lake. It was now a six-mile-long crescent of amazingly clear water only a short distance from the west bank of the Mississippi some seventy-five river miles above Vicksburg.[2]

The lake was the scenic location of several picturesque plantations as well as a small village of the same name, but what made it interesting to Grant was that with a bit of engineering and some hard work with pick, shovel, ax, and saw, it might be made to connect both with the Mississippi and with a 200-mile-long network of bayous that would lead into the Red River, which in turn emptied into the Mississippi 130 miles below Vicksburg, in the stretch of hitherto Confederate-controlled river between Vicksburg and Port Hudson. If Grant could get the transports and gunboats into that stretch of river, he would be able to cross his army to the east bank of the Mississippi and approach Vicksburg from the rear by dry land.[3]

Grant assigned the task of opening the Lake Providence route to the Seventeenth Corps. Most of the corps was still in Memphis, awaiting sufficient steamboat transportation for the trip down to Young's Point. The Thirteenth and Fifteenth corps bivouacs already took up most of the available camping sites on the peninsula, however; so diverting the Seventeenth Corps to Lake Providence offered the additional benefit of providing ample space for it to camp. Finally, the commander of the Seventeenth Corps, James B. McPherson, was one of the most capable engineers in the army, well qualified to direct an operation of this sort.

The Seventeenth Corps began unloading at Lake Providence during the first week of February, and immediately went to work digging a canal from the river to the lake. To help in the work, the men confiscated plows and scrapers from the nearby plantations and from the same source also recruited large numbers of blacks. The former slaves flocked eagerly to the Union enclave. "The negroes are coming in droves every day," wrote Illinois soldier Daniel Winegar. "There must be over 1,000 here now. I don't know what we are going to do with them."[4] The fleeing slaves brought with them so many mules that the army had surplus and turned the extras loose to fend for themselves. As it had done in northern Mississippi, the army put the blacks to work not only on the canal but also picking cotton in nearby fields and paid them wages for their work.[5]

Despite the normal round of work details, the men had time to play "town ball" in their off-duty hours, and also to forage.[6] "It is the first time our soldiers have made a stop here," wrote an Illinois soldier, "so there is lots of stuff here to jayhawk. We have a stove in our tent, a parlor stove, with two holes on the top, so we can do our cooking. We have furniture enough too, so we get along first rate. In the line of provisions, we lack nothing except butter. We have had chicken, beef, and pork."[7] Headquarters for the encampment was Bellagio, the opulent plantation of Confederate senator Edward Sparrow. The senator seemed to have business elsewhere, but his guests made themselves at home in his absence.[8] In the town of Providence, the soldiers took possession of an abandoned church building and held services there on Sundays. The building filled to capacity, and there were even two ladies present. "It made me think of home," wrote Daniel Winegar.[9]

The soldiers were not slow to notice the beauty of Lake Providence. "As pretty a lake as ever was made," wrote Newton in a letter to his parents.[10] The banks of the lake were uniform and about fifteen feet high, lined with live oaks, magnolias, and cypress, draped with long, trailing Spanish moss. Here and there a stately plantation interrupted the foliage.[11] Spring was on the way. The peach blossoms were out and flower gardens already coming into bloom in February.[12]

Rainstorms were as frequent and violent at Lake Providence as they were farther down the river. "You never saw it rain as it does here," wrote Luther Cowan to his daughter back in Illinois. "It just pours. More water will fall in five minutes when it rains hard here than I ever saw fall in Jo Davies county in a half hour and the lightning and thunder is most beautiful."[13]

The campsites around the lake, as well as the opportunities to acquire palatable food and comfortable quarters, were far superior to anything at Young's Point. When troops at Lake Providence found themselves compelled to camp in a muddy cotton field, they were able to jayhawk enough boards from nearby structures to provide not only floors for their tents but porches in front of each one. "It was an ideal camp," wrote Col. Manning F. Force of the 20th Ohio.[14]

McPherson himself was still in Memphis trying to round up steamboats enough to transport the rest of his corps. Early reports from Col. George W. Deitzler and Lt. Col. W. L. Duff were encouraging. They noted that because the Mississippi was eight feet higher than Lake Providence, the cutting of the levee would result in the inundation of the by now largely abandoned town of Providence, but they were confident of opening a waterway that would allow shallow-draft boats access to the Red River and thus to the Mississippi below Vicksburg.[15]

By the end of February, McPherson, along with two of the three divisions of the Seventeenth Corps, had arrived at Lake Providence.[16] One of his first actions was to order his men to move a small steam tugboat, christened *J. A. Rawlins* in honor of Grant's chief of staff, from the Mississippi to the lake. Using block and tackle, they pulled *Rawlins* over the levee and then dragged her inch by inch down the main street of Providence. Pvt. Jonathan Thatcher, who was among those detailed for the job, estimated the total dry-land journey of the tug to have been a mile and a half, covered in the space of ten days. The purpose for putting *Rawlins* in the lake was to facilitate the exploration and clearing of possible routes through Bayou Baxter and the cypress swamp by which it connected to Bayou Macon. Thatcher, however, with typical enlisted man's cynicism, believed that the real purpose was to provide pleasure excursions for the generals and their staffs.[17]

If the staffs made any pleasure excursions in *Rawlins,* they were certainly not alone on the water. Numerous soldiers built or acquired small craft. "We spend much of our time especially in the evening boating on the lake," wrote one soldier.[18] Fishing was another favorite pastime for the men.[19] Occasionally the tug would carry one of the regimental bands out on the lake for a waterborne serenade, which was pleasant to many of the soldiers but presumably not very helpful to those who were fishing at the time.[20]

Between pleasure boating, fishing, ball games, and band concerts on the lake, work continued on the waterway that was to connect Lake Providence with the Red River. The chief obstacles were the many cypress trees that grew in the swamp between Bayou Baxter and Bayou Macon. If these could be cleared, it would be easy enough to raise the water level or dredge a channel that would allow boats from Lake Providence to proceed through Bayou Baxter and the cypress swamp to Bayou Macon, down Bayou Macon to the Tensas River, and down the Tensas to the Red. Removing the trees from the flooded swamp, and doing so below the waterline, was a difficult task. "Boys stand on rafts in the water to chop and saw," wrote Illinois soldier Allen Geer. When the big trees fell, the men snaked them out of the swamp with long cables.[21]

McPherson, however, became concerned that they might not be able to cut the trees low enough to permit boats to pass over them, even after they raised the water level by breaking the levee. Early in March, he investigated another possible route. With the river at its current extremely high stage, cutting the levee a few miles north of Lake Providence, near the Arkansas line, should inundate the open lands west of the river to such an extent that boats would be able to steam directly into Bayou Macon across several miles of flooded cotton fields. The strange ways of the river, however, could baffle even as brilliant an engineer as McPherson. When he had the levee cut, the water flooded the cotton fields but not deep enough for the steamboats.[22]

The upstream crevasse in the Mississippi levee raised the water level in Bayou Macon to the point that the bayou flowed backward through the cypress swamp and Bayou Baxter into Lake Providence, forcing the soldiers to suspend their tree-clearing operations. The men at Lake Providence were ignorant of their general's other scheme and assumed the sudden inconvenient rise in the bayou was the result of Rebel guerrillas either damming an outlet somewhere downstream or cutting a levee above.[23]

Grant made several trips up the river by steamboat to visit Lake Providence and observe the progress of the work there.[24] On one trip in early March, he and McPherson, accompanied by their staffs, boarded *Rawlins* and explored the lake, traveling down Bayou Baxter as far as it was cleared. The prospect was not encouraging. Grant was convinced that even if his men succeeded in clearing bayous Baxter and Macon, the Rebels would be able to hinder their progress on the Tensas and Red rivers to such a degree

as to make the project impractical. He did not order the work stopped, however. It gave the men something to do and the Seventeenth Corps someplace to camp. It also might attract Confederate attention away from
potentially more promising endeavors.[25]

By March 10, McPherson was convinced that a little more depth of
water in the back country would be all that was needed to enable boat traffic into Bayou Macon. He was confident that the extra depth could be
achieved by cutting the levee at Lake Providence and letting the Mississippi
directly into the lake. As soon as his men had completed the necessary evacuation of campsites, McPherson gave the order.[26]

The process of breaking the levee began at five o'clock on the evening
of March 16. The troops were excited, and many volunteered for duty with
the fatigue party that would make the cut. The workers dug two trenches
through the levee, each four feet wide. The two ditches were from thirty to
fifty feet apart—eyewitness accounts varied. The work crew deliberately
left the earth in between the trenches to be washed away by the in-rushing
water dropping twelve feet from the surface of the river to that of Lake
Providence. Soon two narrow streams of water were rushing briskly
through the levee and into the lake.[27]

The next morning, a cataract 200 feet wide, variously estimated to be
from 8 to 20 feet deep, was thundering through the levee with a roar said to
have been heard five miles away. Jonathan Thatcher thought it "looked as if
one-half of the Mississippi was coming through it."[28] It reminded Chaplain
Thomas M. Stevenson of the Muskingum River at high-water stage, rushing over one of the dams near his home in southeastern Ohio.[29] Col.
William Belknap thought the force and sound of the cataract were such as
"to make one remember the falls of Niagara."[30]

Many members of the Seventeenth Corps watched and listened to the
spectacle from the decks of the transports, moored at a safe distance on
the Mississippi. McPherson had sent them aboard both to get them out of
the way of the floodwaters and also to have them ready for other duty to
which Grant had already assigned them. Those of the soldiers who were
still ashore became almost wild with excitement. Even as the floodwaters
were creeping into the town of Providence, some of the men set fire to a
house. Maj. Luther Cowan of the 45th Illinois glanced up from a letter he
was writing to his wife. From his vantage point on the steamboat *Iatan,*
about 100 yards from the town, he had a ringside seat for all of the action
without being able to do anything about it except give his wife a moment-
by-moment account. "It is an old frame building," he penned, "and makes a
splendid fire."[31]

Next, the rowdy soldiers got into the church building and began ringing the bell wildly, "while thousands are shouting and hurrahing, but nobody trying to put out the fire." Next the rowdies in the church building began "breaking out the windows and tearing up things generally." This looked bad, Cowan admitted, but added, "I believe if the plan was adopted by our army of destroying everything we come to, that the war would come to an end much sooner." While Cowan sat philosophizing about how to hasten the end of the war, the blue-clad mob on shore progressed to the point of setting fire to the church. When the flames appeared, steam whistles sounded on several of the boats, calling the remaining troops to go aboard, probably in hopes of curbing their excesses on shore. Meanwhile, other soldiers hurried to extinguish the blaze in the church, and Lieutenant Colonel Cowan thought it was a good thing. "It looks too bad to see so nice a little house burned down." Still, he doubted that a church building would be of much use to the impious Rebels to whom they would be leaving it.[32]

The few remaining local inhabitants told soldiers that the break in the levee would flood seven counties.[33] Cowan guessed that it would "destroy millions of dollars worth of property" in the rich plantations in the area.[34] It would not, however, succeed in opening a practical waterway for Union forces to bypass Vicksburg via the Red River. Grant had already turned his attention and his hopes elsewhere.

During February and March, while most of the Seventeenth Corps was at work at Lake Providence, other elements of the Army of the Tennessee were endeavoring to achieve the same ultimate goal via a very different route. While Lake Providence seemed to offer the possibility of a west-bank bypass that would make possible a circuit three-quarters of the way around Vicksburg to reach the high ground behind it, Yazoo Pass held out the prospect of a departure from the east bank on a route that would lead across the Mississippi Delta to reach the Yazoo River, and the high ground beyond it, many miles north of the Confederate fortifications around Vicksburg.

The Yazoo is a curious sort of river that flows entirely through the low-lying Mississippi Delta, roughly paralleling the great river for more than 100 miles before finally joining it just above Vicksburg. About 6 miles below Helena, Arkansas, and on the opposite side of the river, some 200 miles north of Vicksburg, was an inlet on the Mississippi called Yazoo Pass. It had once led into another of the river's many abandoned bends, this one named Moon Lake. Moon Lake, in turn, connected to the Coldwater River, which flowed into the Tallahatchie River, which joined the Yallabusha River at Greenwood, Mississippi, to form the Yazoo. In years gone by, steamboats had used this route to reach the many rich plantations of the Mississippi Delta country, but in 1856 the State of Mississippi had built a strong levee across Yazoo Pass as a flood-control measure. Henceforth access to the Yazoo and its tributaries was to be only via the mouth of the Yazoo, near Vicksburg. With that route now barred by the Confederate fortifications at Haynes's and Snyder's bluffs, Grant proposed to restore the old means of access to the Delta.[35]

He had suggested the possibility of a movement through Yazoo Pass to McClernand a week before joining the army at Young's Point. On his first evening at Young's Point, January 29, Grant ordered Lt. Col. James H. Wilson, a topographical engineer on his staff, to take a gunboat and a detachment of troops from Helena and begin the active exploration of the route via Yazoo Pass.[36] Wilson found the situation promising, obtained a 500-man fatigue party from the garrison at Helena, and cut the levee. Picks, shovels, and gunpowder proved effective, and the water was soon rushing through the gap with a satisfying roar. Next, Wilson put his men to work clearing the deadfalls and overhanging trees that almost choked the narrow waterway. They also had to clear large numbers of trees that the Confederates had deliberately felled across the pass in an effort to obstruct it. Frequent reinforcements and rotations from Helena kept the working party going as it hacked its way through the tangle of logs.[37]

By February 15, the work on Yazoo Pass had progressed to the point that Grant ordered Brig. Gen. Leonard Ross's division of the Thirteenth Corps, 4,500 men, accompanied by some of Porter's ironclads, to proceed out of the Mississippi, through the pass, and into the Coldwater River.[38] Even after all of the hard work done by the advance party, negotiating the narrow waters of Yazoo Pass proved difficult for the steamboats. "The passage almost dismantled the boats," wrote soldier Enoch Weiss. "The overhanging branches of the forest trees in many places raked off the guards [i.e., railings] and the ornamental work on the decks and even mashed some of the wheel houses." Heavy tree limbs crashed through the cabin bulkheads, and if the pilot could not halt the boat quickly enough, ripped out whole sections, leaving a much more airy cabin deck. Soldiers lay flat and clung to the deck for dear life to avoid being swept off. Smokestacks had to be lowered to pass under some of the overhanging trees, then raised again to provide sufficient draft for the boiler fires, and the men had to repeat the process again and again.[39] Sometimes pilots miscalculated and simply knocked the stacks over by running under stout tree limbs.[40]

The winding pass frequently bent so sharply that the boat crews had to fasten cables to trees on shore and work the boat's capstan in order to bring the vessel's head around to the new course of the waterway. Details stood on deck with long poles ready to fend off against trees or the bank if necessary. "Peering through the woods we see a vessel abreast of us steaming in the opposite direction," recalled Weiss, "and yet it is one of our own Division following the same course." He heard that in one stretch they had steamed thirty-five miles in order to cover a crow's-flight distance of only five.[41]

Not until the morning of March 2 did the last of the steamboats clear Yazoo Pass and enter the Coldwater River, and it was the evening of the fifth before they reached the Tallahatchie.[42] Steaming was much easier there. The expedition soon passed a Rebel steamboat, aground and in flames. She was loaded with cotton and the Rebels had set her alight to prevent that valuable commodity from falling into Union hands. Shortly thereafter, the fleet tied up for the night. "All night a constant stream of burning cotton floated past the fleet," recalled an Indiana soldier, "keeping all hands busy saving the boats from conflagration."[43]

Some of the men took advantage of opportunities to forage on shore at the prosperous plantations along the Tallahatchie. Some officers were still determined to halt this sort of helter-skelter individual foraging. When Brig. Gen. Clinton Fisk's boat caught up with the steamer *Ida May*, he found that the latter's uniformed passengers were on shore ransacking a plantation, "shooting cattle, and many of them rushing pell-mell through and around the house on the plantation, catching chickens, turkeys, geese, pigs, &c. The women at the house were greatly frightened, and fearful that they were to be slaughtered." Outraged, Fisk threatened to shoot every officer and enlisted man he should subsequently find engaged in individual foraging. "I fully believe in taking from the enemy whatever he may have that we, as an army, need," he explained in a note to Ross, "or if what is left with him would strengthen the rebels," but he was determined to put a stop to disorderly, do-it-yourself resupply operations.[44]

Much of the destruction to the plantations along the Tallahatchie was the work not of Ross's men but of the Rebels themselves. Anxious to prevent valuable cotton from falling into the hands of the Federals, Confederates continued to set fire to their stockpiles of the white fiber. "At every farm cotton was burning or had been burnt lately," wrote an Indiana soldier.[45]

The white civilian population had mostly fled, leaving the large black population in de facto possession of the many plantations. The former slaves "greeted us with every demonstration they could think of," wrote Capt. Elihu Enos of the 28th Wisconsin, "waving of hats and handkerchiefs, jumping up and down, clapping of hands, shouting, &c. In some instances there were the whole black population of a plantation standing upon the bank, with their bundles, a mule or two, [and] a bale of cotton which they had succeeded in saving from the rebels."[46]

Meanwhile, back on the Mississippi, Grant could get very little news of the expedition's progress. Ross and Wilson were sending reports daily, sometimes several times a day, but a shortage of dispatch boats kept the messages a long time in transit.[47] Hearing reports that the Confederates at Vicksburg were sending troops north to counter the Union force coming through Yazoo Pass, Grant on March 7 directed that Brig. Gen. Isaac F. Quinby's and then Logan's divisions of the Seventeenth Corps should follow Ross. Grant had high hopes for the Yazoo Pass expedition and wanted to be sure it would not fail for want of sufficient troops.[48]

Ross's division approached Greenwood, Mississippi, and the forks of the Yazoo, on the morning of March 11. The ironclad gunboat *Chillicothe*, probing forward ahead of the fleet, encountered dug-in Rebel artillery and exchanged a few shots at long range. The fleet halted, and the troops began to disembark. Ross sent two companies of the 46th Indiana forward as skirmishers, but about 500 yards in front of the Rebel fort they came to an uncrossable "slough" and began to exchange fire with the Rebel pickets on the other side of it, part of a force of some 7,000 Confederates under Maj. Gen. W. W. Loring. After a brief firefight, the Hoosiers fell back to the vicinity of the boats.[49] The rest of Ross's division took up positions ashore. "We marched into the woods toward the fort with our drum corps playing a lively tune and the Rebel shell screaming over our heads," recalled Sgt. Lauren Barker of the 28th Wisconsin.[50]

That afternoon *Chillicothe* once again advanced against the Confederate heavy guns. This time the gunboat took the fight to the Rebels, in a serious attempt to drive them from their earthworks. The result was disappointing. A shell entered *Chillicothe* through a gun port and touched off a shell that was about to be loaded, killing four and wounding nine of her crew. The Rebels, protected by breastworks of earth-covered cotton bales, suffered no perceptible damage.[51]

Undeterred, Ross and Wilson that night had their men build a cotton-bale emplacement of their own about 500 yards from the Rebel battery, and over the next two days they put in it two 30-pounder Parrott guns. From this vantage point, better protected than any gunboat could be, they hoped to pound the Confederate batteries into silence. On the morning of March 13, the new battery opened fire, joined by *Chillicothe* and her sister gunboat *Baron De Kalb*, as well as a mortar boat. The Union guns might just as well have been firing blank cartridges, however, for any discernible effect they produced on the Confederate fortifications.[52]

The Rebels had only two heavy guns in their newly constructed position, named Fort Pemberton in honor of the Confederate department commander. The terrain, however, was all in their favor. The navigable waterway was so constricted that the gunboats could not gain a good angle to engage the fort. On the other hand, dry land—limited as it was to the curving strips of natural levee—was so scarce that Ross's division could not deploy and use its strength against the much weaker Confederate garrison.[53]

Wilson was disgusted with the senior naval officer of the expedition, Lt. Cdr. Watson Smith, whom, as he wryly observed in a letter to Rawlins, "I don't regard as the equal of Lord Nelson." He believed Smith should run his boats up to a range of 200 yards and "make a spoon or spoil a horn." Still, he had to admit that the light construction of these shallow-water gunboats was fearfully vulnerable to the fire of heavy guns, even at fairly long range. He also recognized that if the gunboats should be destroyed, the Rebels stood a good chance of bagging Ross's entire division.[54]

On March 16 the combined army and navy forces made another effort to take Fort Pemberton. During the night before, work parties added one 8-inch naval gun to the shore battery. Ross's infantry worked their way forward along narrow strips of dry land to within 450 yards of the fort, where they were to keep up a long-range harassing fire through the Confederate embrasures. Ross picked his three best regiments and placed them aboard shallow-draft boats. If the combined fire of the gunboats and shore battery silenced the Confederate heavy guns, the boats would advance, clear the obstructions the Rebels had placed in the channel in front of the fort, and then land the infantry to carry the place by storm.[55]

The plan went awry almost from the outset. The shore battery opened fire first, but the Confederate cotton-and-earth breastwork was so stout that the guns could make almost no impression. When the gunboats joined the fight, the lightly built *Chillicothe* took a pounding. By the time she had fired seven shots she had taken six hits, the last of which jammed both of her forward gun ports shut. Both gunboats beat a hasty retreat, and the attempt to take the fort came to an abrupt end.[56] As far as Sergeant Barker was concerned, his 28th Wisconsin, detailed as one of the regiments for the amphibious assault on the fort, had thus been "saved from slaughter."[57]

Ross kept his division in front of Fort Pemberton for four more days, scouting for some means of getting at it. The small fort at the forks of the

Yazoo seemed to have the same quality that Vicksburg possessed on a larger scale: it simply could not be approached in any manner that held out the least prospect of military success. The Union camps were close enough to hear the drums in Fort Pemberton, but impassable swamps separated them. On March 20, Ross loaded up his men and started back up the Tallahatchie. The next day, he met Quinby and his division coming down. Quinby, who was senior, was unwilling to turn back without having a go at Fort Pemberton himself, so the combined expedition turned around and went back to its position in front of the Rebel battery.[58] "This goes rather against the grain with most of us," wrote Cpl. Charles Wildish of Ross's division.[59]

For the next week, the troops settled down to a quasi-siege of Fort Pemberton with little prospect of success. A supply boat brought newspapers from up the river, and the men read that their expedition had reached Yazoo City, a good seventy miles farther down the Yazoo, beyond the Rebel fort that none of them had been able to pass. "So much for the papers," quipped a soldier. The desultory campaign against Fort Pemberton continued until April 4, when Quinby received an order from Grant to return to the Mississippi. That night the soldiers labored to load the steamboats, and the next morning the vessels cast off and steamed up the Tallahatchie. The troops were disappointed at the failure of the expedition, but generally recognized the impossible situation they had faced.[60]

Grant had held high hopes for the Yazoo Pass expedition. "I will have Vicksburg this month, or fail in the attempt," he had written to Halleck on March 6.[61] Ten days later, with the De Soto Point canal an obvious failure, the Lake Providence route useless, and the issue of the Yazoo Pass expedition in doubt, Grant was eager to lend all the support he could to a scheme of Porter's for introducing heavy gunboats into the Yazoo River between Haynes's Bluff and Fort Pemberton. This involved an even more convoluted series of connecting waterways than either the Lake Providence or Yazoo Pass routes. Gunboats and small transports could pass from the Mississippi into Steele's Bayou. Steele's Bayou led into Black Bayou, which connected to Deer Creek, which could be ascended to Rolling Fork, which gave access to the Big Sunflower River, which fed into just the stretch of the Yazoo that Grant wanted to reach, about twenty miles below Yazoo City and thirty or so from the mouth of the Yazoo, near Vicksburg.[62]

Porter had explored the first stretch of the route on March 14 and taken Grant with him on another probe the following day. Grant was so impressed he ordered Sherman to take a division of his troops into Steele's Bayou and support Porter. The bayou, like all of the streams by which it connected to the Big Sunflower River, was surprisingly deep. In other respects, however, it was very much like Yazoo Pass—narrow, winding, and choked with large trees, some growing in the stream, some beside it, some fallen across it either naturally or by the work of the enemy. As compared to the transports, the heavy gunboats were far better able to negotiate these hazards, in some cases simply bulling over trees as thick as twelve inches through the trunk. Lying lower in the water, the gunboats presented less top-hamper to be caught and ripped apart by overhanging limbs.[63]

Messages from Wilson and Ross had already suggested that one of the chief reasons for the difficulties that were even then developing for the Yazoo Pass expedition was that the naval commander did not thrust forward quickly enough to deny the Confederates the opportunity of preparing fortifications. Porter was not one to dally in any case, and so he forged ahead with his fleet of gunboats, leaving the slow-moving transports behind.[64]

Throughout the day of March 19, Sherman and his men, working on clearing Steele's Bayou, could hear the booming of the big naval guns farther inland. That night at 3:00 a.m., a black man reached Sherman's camp bearing a message from Porter, written on tissue paper and concealed in tobacco.[65] The admiral was in trouble. He had gotten up Deer Creek almost all the way to Rolling Fork when he had encountered a strong force of enemy sharpshooters. The Rebels shot down sailors who came on deck to fend off against the bank with poles. Without those measures, the clumsy gunboats were all but helpless in such constricted waters, completely unable to steer since they could not get up sufficient speed to make the vessels answer their rudders. The Confederates had far more infantry present than Porter had sailors on his boats, and they were vigorously felling trees ahead of the squadron.[66]

When the message reached him, Sherman was at Hill's Plantation, where Black Bayou joined Deer Creek, with a force of only 800 men from Giles Smith's brigade. Sherman dispatched Smith's force immediately, with orders to march along the natural levee of Deer Creek until they reached the gunboats and there tell Porter that Sherman would follow with all the troops he could get. The remainder of Sherman's troops were back in Black and Steele's bayous, so the general got into a canoe and paddled down Black Bayou a distance of four miles before meeting the transport *Silver Wave,* which was bringing another load of troops up the bayou. Sherman took command, roused a number of the fatigue parties that were encamped along the bayou, loaded the extra troops into an empty coal barge towed by a navy tug, and set out back up the bayou.[67]

It was a wild midnight ride at speeds the steamboats scarcely dared by day in such constricted waters, and, as Sherman recalled, "the night was absolutely black." *Silver Wave* was "crashing through the trees, carrying away pilot-house, smoke-stacks, and everything above-deck." After two and a half miles of such running, the boat came up against obstructions it simply could not pass. Hill's Plantation was still another mile and a half away. So Sherman and his men disembarked and pushed on through the canebrakes, carrying lighted candles to find their way. They had no horses, so everyone, including the general, walked. They reached the plantation shortly before daylight and there paused for rest.[68]

At first light they were on the march once more. They could hear the sound of Porter's guns again, much closer now, and they double-quicked most of the time, Sherman jogging along like everyone else. With him at the head of the column was his old regiment, the 13th U.S. Infantry. Sometimes they had to cross swamps, wading through hip-deep water with cartridge boxes slung around their necks to keep them dry.[69]

By noon they had covered twenty-one miles. Four miles more brought them into contact with some of Giles Smith's troops, who were guarding the vicinity of the naval squadron as well as their numbers would allow. As Sherman's force approached the gunboats, its leading troops had a brief brush with a party of Confederates who were trying to work their way around behind the squadron so as to fell trees across the creek there and seal off the gunboats' escape. Sherman's men easily drove off this Rebel party. Then Sherman deployed his troops in line of battle across the natural levee, from the road on the creek bank all the way into the swamp, and ordered them forward.[70] They swept through the woods and out into a large cotton field, across which they could see the gunboats, still firing their heavy guns into the swamp where the Rebels were lurking. One of Smith's officers had found a horse the night before and now offered it to Sherman. The general jumped on bareback and galloped along the levee to meet Porter, while the cheering sailors swarmed out onto the decks of their ironclads.[71]

It had been nip and tuck for Porter, who had about made up his mind that he would have to blow up his gunboats and lead his men on foot through the swamp to try to make their way back to Union lines. With the cover of Sherman's troops, though, it was a relatively simple matter to work the boats back out of Deer Creek, but it still took them three days to cover the distance that Sherman and his men had marched in one morning. It was not a pleasant journey for Sherman's men either, as an all-day rain turned their road into knee-deep mire. "This was one of the worst day's march I ever experienced," recalled Hoosier soldier John Roberts.[72] As the army withdrew, large numbers of blacks went with them, fleeing slavery.

By March 27, the gunboats were back in the Mississippi and Sherman's troops back in their camps at Young's Point. Even before the final cancellation of the Yazoo Pass expedition, the Steele's Bayou route had proven a failure.[73]

In early March, the adjutant general of the U.S. Army, Lorenzo Thomas, arrived at the camps of the Army of the Tennessee, sent from Washington on a mission to rally the troops in support of Lincoln's policy of enlisting black troops to fight for the cause of Union and liberty. Rigorous inspections preceded his arrival, as officers strove to make a good impression.[74] At the various divisional camps, commanders drew their men up in formation, and then Thomas would stride into the encampment, accompanied by the corps commander, his staff, and various other high-ranking officers, while cannons boomed a salute.[75] Thomas and the other generals then mounted the speakers' stand—usually an army wagon. At the camps near Lake Providence, McPherson usually introduced the adjutant general, and after Thomas had finished his speech, several of the other generals followed up with speeches of their own.[76]

Among those who spoke was John A. Logan, the former proslavery congressman now commanding a division of the Seventeenth Corps and one of the most popular generals in the army. As soon as Thomas finished his speech to Logan's division, the men began to clamor for their division commander. As always, Logan's speech was memorable. Allen Geer thought he had never heard such a speech before—"so lofty, eloquent, & patriotic it electrified, convinced."[77] Wimer Bedford remembered Logan proclaiming during his speech, "I once loved the man who loved slavery, and now I hate the man who loves rebellion."[78] At the camp of McArthur's division, Thomas apparently felt confident enough to put the matter of raising black troops to a "vote" of the men present. The response from the troops was "one thunderous 'aye.' "[79] A number of men in all of the divisions eagerly volunteered for service as officers in the newly organizing black regiments.[80]

The positive response to Thomas's mission showed not only a shift in the army's attitudes about blacks but also its drastically improved morale. The transformation was visible elsewhere. It could be seen in the way the soldiers went through their drills. "A much greater *interest* is now taken in the drill," wrote an Iowa soldier. Colonels began requiring more drill and requiring that all commissioned officers turn out to drill their troops, rather than leaving the task to the sergeants.[81]

A number of regiments held meetings and passed resolutions affirming their support for the war, the administration and all its measures, and their contempt for all Copperheads, whom they threatened with "terrible retribution" when the war was over. Most such resolutions were mailed to the newspapers back home for publication.[82] "Now a great change has taken place," wrote Isaac Jackson of the 83rd Ohio. "The health of the army is very good, the troops have been paid off, the people at home have been aroused to a sense of their duty, and now all things are cheerful. The dark cloud has passed away and the bright sky appears once more. The men are in excellent spirits."[83] Jackson had touched on the major reasons for rising morale.

One of these was the army's improving health. Perhaps it was in part the warmer spring weather, which in itself was a source of improved spirits. Perhaps the men had simply weathered the illnesses of the winter. Those who had survived were men of robust constitution and strong immune systems. Whatever the reason, the number of sick declined markedly. "The health of the army is 'A No. 1,' " wrote Henry Ankeny to his wife back in Iowa. "I don't think it could be better. Very few on the sick list."[84] Just as clearly, the decline in illnesses and deaths helped produce higher morale.

Another cause of rising morale was the appearance of the paymaster in many of the camps. Generally the army was many months in arrears. Without pay, the men could not send money home to help support their families, nor could they buy items from the sutlers to vary their monotonous and not very healthy diet of salt pork and hardtack. The distribution of pay changed all that and raised spirits wonderfully. "I feel more than well, as we have actually been paid off," wrote William Winters on April 4. "The boys are all like me in the best of spirits, all haveing had the blues, but the sight of green backs makes them all jubilent."[85] Such concerns were especially important to Winters, who had a wife and three children to support back in Hope, Indiana.

A third reason for rising morale in the Army of the Tennessee was a perceived change in the tone of letters and newspapers coming from the home country. Whether morale on the Northern home front had really changed that month, or whether the soldiers' perceptions had merely shifted, the men believed they once again had the support of the communities from which they had marched off to fight many months before. "Noticed a better sentiment pervading the northern press and society," wrote Allen Geer in his diary in early April.[86]

An additional reason for the rising morale may have been found in the soldiers' growing awareness of themselves as part of a superb army. Whereas at the turn of the year the army had seemed to be the essence of failure—checkmated on the Mississippi Central and bloodied along Chickasaw Bayou—now the men felt a deep confidence in their ultimate success. The schemes of the winter—the canal, Lake Providence, Yazoo Pass, and Steele's Bayou—had all ended in failure. Yet it had been primarily the forces of nature, and not their human enemies, who had foiled their efforts. Even at Fort Pemberton and the Confederate ambush of Porter's ironclads on Deer Creek, the Rebels had added only a slight impediment to the already almost insurmountable natural difficulties. The winter's struggle had been with the great river itself, as its power emanated through its delta full of tangled backwaters, and the Midwestern boys of the Army of the Tennessee were familiar with their region's long, often disappointing, but ultimately inevitable struggle with the mighty Mississippi. Seen in those terms, taking Vicksburg was just another job to be accomplished by persistent effort.

As for the Rebels, the soldiers now realized that they were not the invincibles they might have seemed in the dark days of winter. The Rebels had spent four months hiding behind the forces of nature, and whatever the wisdom of that course, it did not speak well of their courage. All of the Union efforts had been aimed at gaining a stand-up fight in the open. All of the Confederate efforts strove to avoid that. Such a course, continued month after month, could not fail to produce a subtle effect in minds on both sides of the Mississippi. Like Alexander the Great at the River Granicus, the men of the Army of the Tennessee saw their enemies' eagerness to stay behind a river and interpreted it to mean that their enemies knew them to be their masters. Subtly at first, but with growing certainty throughout the rest of the war, the soldiers of the Army of the Tennessee came to believe in their hearts that they would defeat their enemies every time they met. They would henceforth suffer no defeats but only temporary setbacks, because that is what they believed such events to be. The end result was certain, and they believed their enemies knew it too.

If anything in the Civil War could compare to the Continental Army's winter encampment at Valley Forge, it was the Army of the Tennessee's winter along the Mississippi River—discouraged by recent setbacks, betrayed by antiwar agitation on the home front, miserable in their cold, wet encampments, and dying, as a Wisconsin soldier put it, "like sheep with the rot."[87] Yet this hard experience toughened them and forged them together into a unified and confident fighting force.

They would never be professional warriors. Though they would be second to none in their fighting prowess, their goal remained the same as it had been since they had seen their first battles and learned the reality of war. John Barney of the 29th Wisconsin might have been expressing the views of the whole army when he wrote to his family that spring: "I used to have some ambition for something, I hardly know what. Now the only ambition I have, the only goal I want to reach is *home*." If only he could get home, he would be content, but he did not want to go before Union victory ended the war. "And more than that," he added, "we are going to make it end . . . *just as we want it to*."[88]

CHAPTER EIGHTEEN

Down the West Bank

B Y THE END OF MARCH, the De Soto Point Canal, as well as the Lake Providence and Steele's Bayou expeditions, had proven to be failures. The Yazoo Pass expedition, for which Grant had entertained the highest hopes, was then winding down to a similar conclusion in front of the ridiculously weak yet somehow invincible Fort Pemberton.

So on March 29, Grant took a fateful step and decided to implement a plan he had long been contemplating. On that day, he sent a message to Porter requesting a movement of the gunboats that would be irreversible. Unlike the Yazoo Pass and Steele's Bayou schemes, the new plan would not allow the gunboats to be committed and then withdrawn to their original position in the Mississippi. If this operation should fail, the navy would be unable to support any subsequent effort.

Grant's plan called for Porter to run his gunboats past the Vicksburg batteries and seize control of the stretch of river below the city. Having gotten a fleet below Vicksburg, it would then remain for Grant to get an army there and supply it. He planned to accomplish those goals by a movement down the west bank of the river. It sounded simple, but in its own way it was as difficult, and as susceptible to failure, as any of the other expeditions through the waterlogged valley of the Mississippi.

In dry seasons—usually late summer and fall—those lowlands were composed of a maze of winding bayous, the natural levees that followed their tortuous courses, and a great expanse of dark and trackless swamps. Spring was high-water season and this spring unusually so. With the man-made levees perforated with dozens of crevasses, the entire valley was a vast lake of varying depth, its surface broken by a few housetops, here and there, and a larger number of treetops over most of its extent. The only dry land was on the natural levees, often cut off from one another—narrow, curving islands a foot or two above the surface of the waters and looking on the map like several dozen horseshoes that someone had carelessly tossed on the ground, sometimes touching one another at odd angles, sometimes separated.

All of the plantations, and what passed for roads in that region, were on those levees. There, at least in theory, the army would march, picking its way through the watery wasteland, bridging or ferrying across intervening channels. There too the army's supplies would have to follow.

Another element of the plan involved running a fleet of transports—ordinary wooden riverboats—past the Vicksburg batteries several days after the gunboats had done so. That operation would not take nearly as long as the semiaquatic march down the west bank, but it would be at least as risky. The chances were that some of the fragile vessels would be destroyed by Confederate fire. Nevertheless, the transports were essential if the army was to cross the river below Vicksburg and do so rapidly enough to have a chance of success. The risk to the transports would simply have to be accepted.

Grant's first step, taken on March 29, was to notify Porter of his plan and request the admiral's cooperation. Porter was willing, but he reminded Grant what a momentous step this would be. Grant had suggested running one or two vessels past Vicksburg in order to control the downstream stretch of water and to suppress outlying Confederate batteries at Warrenton and Grand Gulf, south of Vicksburg, but Porter pointed out that fulfilling those tasks would require most of his vessels. "You must recollect," Porter wrote, "that when these gun-boats once go below we give up all hopes of ever getting them up again." The boats would be safe enough and could, if necessary, join Adm. David Farragut's squadron at the mouth of the Red River or proceed all the way downriver to Union-held Baton Rouge. What they could not do was run back upstream past the Vicksburg batteries. Six-knot armored gunboats in a four-knot current should be relatively secure going downstream, but breasting the current upstream under the guns of Vicksburg, they would be sitting ducks. If the boats ran the batteries, it would be the last operation against Vicksburg for which Grant could hope for significant naval support.[1]

While alerting Porter of the need to run the batteries, Grant had given orders for his infantry to begin moving south. The route down the west bank was typical of the Mississippi Delta, following the banks of Walnut Bayou to aptly named Roundaway Bayou and finally Bayou Vidal. Its starting point was near Milliken's Bend, where the Thirteenth Corps had been encamped ever since high water had driven it off Young's Point a few weeks before. The task of leading the march would therefore fall to McClernand.

The politician had been busy of late, though not with the same sorts of pursuits that had occupied Grant, Sherman, and McPherson. In February he had written to Lincoln that the failure of his vaunted Mississippi River plan, as executed by Sherman, had been attributable to Grant's retreat on the Mississippi Central Railroad.[2] Not that the plan he had hawked in Altoona and Washington had ever included an overland expedition like Grant's, but it made a convenient way to excuse his own obvious miscalculation and, he hoped, undermine Grant with Lincoln at the same time.

Sensing that his anti-Grant efforts were not gaining traction with the president, McClernand next tried a different tack. In a campaign as roundabout as any bayou in the Mississippi Delta and a good deal more twisted, McClernand set out to convince Lincoln and the country that Grant was a drunken sot. The first phase was a whispering campaign to the press. Soon reporters attached to the Thirteenth Corps were filing stories about Grant's alleged drunkenness. Next, McClernand contacted Capt. William J. Kountz. A year earlier, just before the army left Cairo, the corrupt Kountz had been in charge of arranging steamboat transportation. Grant had had to arrest him, and Kountz had retaliated by charging Grant with drunkenness. McClernand had tried to make use of Kountz back then, and now he hoped to do so again and much more effectively. He provided Kountz a letter of introduction to Lincoln describing the habitual shyster as "an honest and reliable gentleman." Kountz hurried off for Washington eager to recite a story that Grant had been intoxicated one day in March 1863.[3]

McClernand's winter campaign did not succeed in securing Grant's removal and his own elevation to the coveted command. However, along with various other murmurings sparked by jealousy as well as by disappointment that Grant had not yet taken Vicksburg, it did help to prompt the Lincoln administration to dispatch Assistant Secretary of War Charles A. Dana to Grant's headquarters on an extended fact-finding mission. Everyone knew that the primary fact Dana was supposed to find out was whether or not Grant was keeping sober. Grant's staff officers were disposed to resent the intruder at headquarters, but Grant treated Dana courteously and insisted that his staff do so as well. Dana arrived at Grant's headquarters boat, by then moored at Milliken's Bend, on April 7, just as the new campaign was getting under way.[4]

On March 30, Grant interrupted McClernand's personal winter campaign with orders to move immediately down the west bank to the settlement of New Carthage, Louisiana. McClernand assigned the task of leading the advance to Maj. Gen. Peter Osterhaus's division, and Osterhaus, in turn, detailed Col. Thomas W. Bennett and his 69th Indiana to probe southward in advance of the rest of the division. With Bennett and his regiment

would go two companies of the 2nd Illinois Cavalry, two mountain howitzers manned by a detachment of the 6th Missouri Cavalry, and an engineer company, bringing "a long train of pontoons" as well as a number of
light yawls, or skiffs, borrowed from the steamboats. They were about
1,000 men in all and would soon be calling themselves the "Argonauts."
They were in high spirits as they stayed up most of the night preparing to
depart on their adventure.[5]

At eight o'clock on the morning of March 31, Bennett's Argonauts
became the first troops to take to the road in what would become the Army
of the Tennessee's greatest campaign. "It was an exceedingly beautiful
day," recalled Lt. Col. Oran Perry of the 69th. "The sun shone as we had not
seen it for months." The pleasant weather and new spring verdure height-
ened the soldiers' excitement almost as much as the prospect of abundant
foraging in a region of rich plantations previously little touched by war.[6]

By two o'clock that afternoon, they had covered twelve miles of muddy
road and were approaching the village of Richmond, Louisiana, where
Walnut Bayou joined Roundaway Bayou. In order to get into Richmond,
the Argonauts had to cross Roundaway, and a light force of Confederate
cavalry waited to dispute their passage. While Bennett's artillery and most
of the infantry put down covering fire, a detachment under Perry piled into
the skiffs, crossed the bayou, and easily drove off the Rebel cavalry.[7]

The engineers went to work to build a bridge over Roundaway, and the
next morning McClernand and Osterhaus came out to view the position.
They decided to garrison Richmond with several more regiments and
ordered them down from Milliken's Bend at once. While awaiting completion of the bridge, they sent cavalry forward to probe as far down the road
toward New Carthage as they could. The horsemen returned that evening
having encountered Confederate resistance about ten miles beyond Richmond, near Holmes' Plantation.[8]

Engineers finished the Roundaway Bayou bridge at 7:00 p.m. on April 3.
It was an impressive structure, 200 feet long, made of logs taken from
nearby houses, and it enabled Osterhaus to continue his southward movement in force. At five o'clock the next morning, he marched out of Richmond with two regiments of infantry, a battalion of cavalry, and four
mountain howitzers. By 9:00 a.m. they had reached Holmes' Plantation.
The Rebel cavalry offered no serious resistance but fell back skirmishing in
front of the column. By evening they had marched another seven miles to
Smith's Plantation, also known as Pointe Clear, where Roundaway Bayou
joined Bayou Vidal. Here the outlook suddenly became much less encouraging. The road to New Carthage, some two miles farther south, abruptly

disappeared beneath a wide sheet of water. "To the south, as far as the eye could reach, the country was like a sea," recalled Perry. Only the narrow top of the man-made levee rose above the surface of the water, and it was broken at several points.[9]

To the west, however, a strip of land ran upstream along the right bank of Bayou Vidal. The Rebel cavalry retreated onto this strip of land and kept up its harassing fire. Osterhaus decided to try to find out where the Confederate horsemen had their base, so he ordered his own cavalry to follow them. The Rebels continued to fall back in front of the Union cavalry for several more miles to Dunbar's Plantation. There the dry ground ended and the Rebels took to boats. Local inhabitants informed the Federals that the Confederates were based at Perkins Plantation, several miles away and much of it under water. Osterhaus posted a small cavalry garrison at Dunbar's and encamped his main force at Pointe Clear for the night.[10]

On April 5, McClernand and Osterhaus, along with several members of their staffs, got into skiffs and set out to reconnoiter. They followed the man-made levee and found that the first two crevasses were too wide and carried too swift a current to permit bridging. At the third crevasse, about half a mile from New Carthage, they came under fire from the ubiquitous Confederate cavalry videttes and had to turn back. Their voyage confirmed that New Carthage was entirely under water, save for the rooftops, and that the badly broken artificial levee would not be a practical way to get there.[11]

Back in camp at Pointe Clear that afternoon, Osterhaus started making preparations to move his command, or at least a portion of it, by boat. Five black men who came into camp that day informed him that the Rebels had made an effort to sweep the area clear of boats but that a flatboat could be found eight miles up Bayou Vidal, and they could lead a Union patrol to it. A cavalry platoon Osterhaus sent with them brought back the boat, despite a brush with a superior force of Rebel horsemen. The flatboat was large but not well adapted for combat. To remedy that, Osterhaus had his engineers go to work on the vessel. Appropriating a supply of three-inch-thick boards from nearby buildings, they planked up the sides of the boat to the height of a man's head, made portholes for oars and rifles, and a gun port forward to accommodate one of the mountain howitzers. "Altogether," observed Perry, "she was something wonderful to behold." They christened their new man-of-war *Opossum*.[12]

The next day, Monday, April 6, was the anniversary of Shiloh, though neither regiment accompanying Osterhaus, the 49th and 69th Indiana, had been with the Army of the Tennessee on that desperate day. Under much different auspices, the Hoosiers rose early on this fine spring day and prepared to advance. Most of the command marched along the man-made levee and used skiffs to boat around the crevasses. Meanwhile, Osterhaus set out with two companies aboard *Opossum* and another collection of skiffs. "It was a quaint voyage," Perry later wrote. "Spread out like a line of skirmishers, we rowed down the bayous, across the fields and through the woods; at one time locking with the thick, heavy limbs of the trees, and then again anchoring in the stubborn undergrowth with which the woods were covered." Fickle currents played odd tricks on them, pushing them this way and that. They passed the mostly submerged village of New Carthage and shortly beyond it came to a twenty-acre ridge of dry ground, on which perched an impressive plantation house with its outbuildings.

Confederate cavalry made a stand in the plantation's gin house, which commanded the whole island. In the brief fight that followed, *Opossum* proved her worth and helped Osterhaus's men rout the Rebels. Taking possession of the establishment, the Federals found that its name was Ione and its proprietor a haughty but polite Southern gentleman named Joshua James, who announced with pride that he had been a member of Louisiana's secession convention and that he had four sons currently serving in the Rebel army. From James the Federals learned that the force they had been opposing was composed of a battalion of Louisiana cavalry and that it was supported by at least one regiment of Confederate Missouri infantry located several miles downstream at Perkins Plantation. They also discovered that the strip of dry land they were on actually continued southward to Perkins and beyond, winding along the back side of two oxbow lakes all the way to the town of St. Joseph.[13]

The grounds of Ione were bordered on the east by the Mississippi and on the west by flooded swamps that stretched to Bayou Vidal. Just across the Mississippi from Ione was Davis Bend, site of the plantations of Jefferson Davis and his brother. Osterhaus called the prospect across the river "a very tempting view."[14] He posted the 69th Indiana at Ione and parceled out the rest of his available forces to hold key points along the route between there and Milliken's Bend. Over the course of the next week, Osterhaus's advance party fought several small skirmishes with the elusive enemy cavalry.[15] Then, on April 15, the Confederates launched what was meant to be a more serious attack.

The Rebels had built fortifications at Grand Gulf, Mississippi, on the river thirty miles below Vicksburg. The commander there, Maj. Gen. John S. Bowen, noticed Grant's nascent downriver movement and reported it to Pemberton. The Confederate department commander was not inclined to see the movement as a serious threat, in part because Grant had planned it that way. To distract Pemberton's attention, he had ordered Sherman to send a division up the river to Greenville, Mississippi, and do a bit of foraging in the surrounding rich plantation district. Since two previous operations aimed at Vicksburg had come through that general region of the Mississippi Delta, Pemberton naturally paid close attention.[16]

He interpreted Bowen's report of Yankees on the west bank as a minor diversion and ordered the Grand Gulf command to send two or three regiments of the crack Missouri brigade across the river to put a stop to whatever it was Grant was trying to do there. This was a technical violation of Confederate military policy, since the Mississippi was the dividing line between Pemberton's department and that of Gen. Edmund Kirby Smith on the west. However, Smith's forces were all but isolated from the action along the Mississippi by the extensive flooded back swamps on the west side of the river. Besides, Smith had other operations on his mind and was not particularly interested in the Vicksburg campaign.[17]

So the Missouri Rebels crossed over, and, on April 15, one of their regiments attacked the Union cavalry outpost at Dunbar's Plantation. The 2nd Illinois Cavalry fought stoutly, Union infantry soon moved up in support, and the Missourians had to retreat to the main Confederate camp at the Perkins Plantation.[18]

While McClernand's lead elements skirmished with the Confederates among the bayous, the rest of his corps slowly worked its way southward over the muddy road on the narrow strip of land. After making the slog from Milliken's Bend to Richmond, a soldier of the 23rd Wisconsin wrote that he and some of his comrades had been marching through "some of the worst Mud Louisiana can afford."[19] Those words meant something, coming from a man who had camped along the Mississippi that winter.

As the Thirteenth Corps vacated the available campsites at Milliken's Bend, Grant ordered the Seventeenth Corps, many of whose units were just then withdrawing from the failed Yazoo Pass expedition, to move down from Lake Providence and encamp at Milliken's Bend, where it would be ready to follow immediately in the southward movement.[20] McClernand's advance was slowed, however, by the need to ferry troops laboriously by small boat around various crevasses in the levees. It was also endangered by the fact that the Confederates had two light gunboats somewhere along the river. Though unarmored, they could be deadly to any of McClernand's troops they should happen to catch exposed on the low, flat, narrow levees. At Ione the men of the 69th Indiana had a scare on the afternoon of April 16, when one of the Rebel boats, *Queen of the West,* steamed by their position but did not open fire.[21]

Both the problem of transportation and that of security from Rebel craft would be solved if Porter's U.S. Navy gunboats and some of the army-chartered transports could manage to run the Vicksburg batteries. For several days, Porter made careful preparations for the attempt. By April 16, all was in readiness and Porter gave orders for seven ironclads, one armed ram, three army transports, and a tug to stand down the Mississippi toward the guns of Vicksburg. Each boat had barges lashed to either side, loaded with coal or supplies and baggage for the army, both to carry more of such cargoes as would otherwise have to be hauled by wagons over muddy roads and also to stop some of the incoming shells. The big ironclads *Benton* and *Lafayette* had the ram and the tugboat lashed to their sheltered sides, in place of barges, in order to protect those vulnerable vessels. For further protection, the wooden vessels had cotton bales stacked along their sides and around their engines. Grant's command boat, *Henry von Phul,* followed them down the river to just outside the range of the Confederate guns, then stood off in the middle of the river, so that Grant could observe what happened. Shortly after 11:00 p.m. the fleet rounded De Soto Point and came under fire.[22]

The roar of Vicksburg's guns and the replies of the gunboats reverberated up and down the river from Lake Providence, thirty-eight crow's-flight miles north of Vicksburg, to New Carthage, twenty miles south. Almost the entire Army of the Tennessee could hear it. At Milliken's Bend, fifteen miles from the Vicksburg waterfront, men felt the earth tremble. Many of the soldiers guessed what was happening and felt uneasy about the result. Sherman's troops on Young's Point were close enough to see the flashes of the guns and the light of bonfires that Confederates lit on the shore of De Soto Point to illuminate the river.[23]

Twenty miles downriver at Ione Plantation, the officers of the 49th and 69th Indiana, at the sharp end of the spearhead of the Army of the Tennessee's advance, were enjoying a pleasant evening sitting on the second-floor gallery of the manor house. "We had an unusual number of good singers among us," recalled Lieutnant Colonel Perry, and one of them had obtained a copy of a relatively new song by George F. Root. Root had published it in Chicago the year before, and some of the army's bands had already added it to their repertoires, but none of these officers had heard it before. It had a catchy, rousing tune and stirring patriotic words, and the group on the veranda "sang it over and over again" until they had learned it thoroughly and "were almost in a camp-meeting frenzy."[24]

Yes, we'll rally round the flag, boys,
Rally once again,
Shouting the Battle Cry of Freedom.
We will rally from the hillside;
We'll gather from the plains,
Shouting the Battle Cry of Freedom![25]

Even old Mr. James himself, who sat up with his unwelcome guests, enjoyed the music, though he could not agree with the sentiments expressed in the lyrics that went on through multiple verses, exalting freedom and condemning slavery and rebellion. He complacently told the officers that they showed remarkable pluck and high spirits for men who were certain to be defeated and captured.[26]

"About 11 o'clock," wrote Perry, "when the excitement was at the highest, there came from up the river a heavy boom, then another, and another in quick succession, until the air was filled with the deep bellowing of the guns." As they gazed intently in the direction of the sounds, they saw "a great light" go up. It lit the sky above the northern horizon for more than an hour. "Speculation was rife as to the cause," Perry wrote. The officers listened as the firing progressed southward along the series of Confederate batteries ranged over more than a dozen miles of the east bank. Silence fell at last at around 3:00 a.m., and everyone turned in for a few hours' sleep, "strong in the hope of success."[27]

At first light next morning, the river at Ione was still empty. Then, shortly before 8:00 a.m., smoke appeared above the treetops of the next point of land up the river. All waited anxiously for the steamer to round the bend. Presently it did and proved to be the smoldering, almost burnt-out hulk of what had once been a steamboat, or part of one, drifting helplessly on the current. Also floating down the river were large numbers of burning cotton bales. Some minutes later, several barges appeared, also drifting aimlessly down the river from the direction of Vicksburg. The troops hurriedly launched skiffs and brought the errant craft to the shoreline of the plantation. Obviously the barges had broken loose from other vessels at some point upstream, though where those vessels might be now no one knew and few cared to speculate. On the barges, they found camp baggage, including a large, new silk United States flag. With what Perry admitted was "bravado," they hoisted the flag from the balcony of the mansion, "where it could be seen alike by friend and foe," but as the morning hours passed with painful slowness, the lieutenant colonel had to admit, "we were in a very troubled state of mind."[28]

The sun was nearly overhead when the many eyes still scanning the upper bend of the river spied another smudge of smoke above the trees. As they waited tensely for the source of the smoke to come into view, Perry thought the old Rebel, Mr. James, had the look on his face "of the gambler about to cast his last dice," and he had to admit that he and his comrades felt about the same way, though with just the opposite hopes and fears. Finally, around the bend, plowing a broad bow wave, steamed the flagship and pride of the fleet, *Benton*, the Stars and Stripes snapping jauntily from her flagstaff. Behind her, one after another, five more gunboats, one fast ram, one transport, and a tug rounded the bend, foam splashing from their bows and black coal smoke pouring from their stacks.

To the officers on the gallery of Ione, nothing ever looked better than that line of vessels as they churned down the river toward the wildly cheering bluecoats lining the shore. Mr. James "gazed at the fleet a few moments in a dazed sort of way," then sank to his knees and bowed his head over the balcony railing, "sobbing as if his heart would break." The officers on the balcony decided to take their celebration elsewhere, leaving the old planter to weep while the shadow of the big, billowing silk flag flitted over him.[29]

The celebration that followed when the fleet tied up at Ione "was something to be remembered the rest of our lives," Perry wrote years later.[30] The running of the batteries had been a stunning success, despite the losses. Porter's fleet had tied up along the shore just below the batteries that morning before proceeding down the river. During the passage of the batteries, the transport *Henry Clay* had taken repeated hits and had burst into flames. Its crew had abandoned ship, and its burned-out hulk was the derelict that had been the first element of the fleet to reach Ione. The transport *Forest Queen* had been disabled with a shot through the steam drum and had remained tied up while the crew made repairs. Most of the boats had taken hits and had one or more men wounded—the total was a dozen wounded in the entire fleet. Otherwise, the vessels had suffered remarkably little damage from the enormous quantities of powder and shot the Rebels had expended at them.[31]

When Sherman learned of the planned attempt to run the batteries, he personally led a detail carrying four yawls from Young's Point across to a point on the west bank of the river just below Vicksburg. There they put out into the river and took up positions in the channel, ready to pick up swimmers if necessary. From that position, Sherman and his men had a ringside seat for the fiery spectacle of the fleet's run past the batteries. After the fleet had cleared the batteries, Sherman boarded *Benton* and conferred briefly with Porter before setting out to return to shore. One of his boats fulfilled its lifeguard duty by picking up the pilot of *Henry Clay,* who was clinging to a floating board.[32]

Grant saw the flashes of the guns but could not be sure of the outcome of the operation. Anxious to find out, he went ashore, mounted a horse, and set out for the New Carthage area, where he arrived the next morning.[33] He was in time to get in on the celebration at Ione and to be serenaded by the newly formed officers' glee club of the 49th and 69th Indiana.[34]

Besides learning of the success of Porter's run past the batteries, Grant also made use of his ride along the levees to gain a much clearer understanding of the route and its difficulties. "The process of getting troops through in the way we were doing was so tedious that a better method must be devised," Grant later wrote. The Duckport Canal was not the answer. Water in the bayous connecting to the canal had never reached the depth engineers had hoped and steamboats needed. Now as the Mississippi began to recede from its previous extreme high level, thus drawing down the level of its interconnecting network of backwaters and bayous, it was clear that the requisite depth would never be achieved.[35]

The only alternative was to improve the land route. This involved corduroying many miles of muddy road and, most important, it required finding some alternative to the badly crevassed man-made levee between Pointe Clear and Ione. Probes along the various natural levees in that vicinity during the past week had revealed an alternate route that wound around the backside of another oxbow lake and came out on the riverside again at Perkins Plantation, about six miles downstream from Ione. The Rebels who had been encamped at Perkins had beaten a hasty retreat to the east bank of the river as soon as they learned that Porter had run the batteries, threatening to cut off their withdrawal at any time.[36] That left Perkins the logical place for Grant to begin concentrating the advance elements of his army, and he immediately set engineers and fatigue parties to work on bringing the new route into usable condition. That required building four bridges, two of which were each more than 600 feet in length. The total length of the four bridges came to more than 2,000 feet. Although the crow's-flight distance from Milliken's Bend to Perkins was only twenty-five miles, a wagon following the roundabout road along the bayous would travel forty between those two points.[37]

The advance of the army to Perkins did not need to wait on the completion of the new road. With the aid of the newly arrived transports and barges, McClernand moved two of his divisions to the same section of natural levee on which Ione lay.[38] However, supplying the army below Young's Point would be difficult even after the road was finished and impossible until then. To solve the immediate problem of supply and ease the long-term outlook, Grant decided to have several more transports run the Vicksburg batteries with massive loads of supplies.[39] If successful in their passage, these extra transports would also give Grant the practical ability to throw a significant number of troops across the river before the Confederates could respond.

This second running of the batteries would be an all-army operation and a very dangerous one. The boats would have neither armor nor cannon with which to fire back and make the Confederates keep their heads down—and their fire slow and inaccurate. The defenders of Vicksburg could be expected to be alert and ready for the new attempt. The civilian crews of the transports, all of which were chartered, wanted no part of this undertaking. At the first running of the batteries, only one captain and crew had agreed to take their boat through. The other chartered vessels had been taken down the river by scratch crews of soldier volunteers. Now, only a single man, a pilot, could be persuaded to risk life and limb in front of Vicksburg.

So the army turned once again to its own personnel for volunteers to crew the transports on their perilous journey. Logan's division was selected, and throughout its camps on April 21, colonels assembled their men into line, described the operation, and called for volunteers. The colonel of the 45th Illinois "told the soldiers of the dangerous undertaking," as one of them remembered, and "that in all probability the steamers would be riddled with shot and shell and many might perish." Then he called for those willing to go to take three paces to the front. The response was gratifying. Half of the 45th Illinois stepped forward. The story was the same in the 8th Illinois, where Logan himself made the appeal. Allen Geer remembered his own regiment, the 20th Illinois, as having volunteered to a man. At any rate, enough men volunteered throughout the division to have manned the fleet a dozen times over.[40]

In preparation for the trip, the men stacked cotton bales around the engines and boilers of the steamboats and along the sides. They laid sacks of oats, corn, and bran in layers two or three deep on the upper deck and cabin floors in order to prevent enemy shot from going right through the decks and hull or, worse, into the boilers. To guard against the kind of conflagration that had destroyed *Henry Clay,* the men placed buckets ready to hand and had hoses attached to the boats' pumps, ready for firefighting use.[41]

Another preparation for the attempt involved the positive use of fire. During the first running of the batteries, the Confederates had illuminated the river, and thus their targets in it, by torching several houses in the aban-

doned settlement of De Soto, just across the river from Vicksburg. To prevent them from using this means of illumination again, Grant sent a detachment to burn the remainder of the houses there during daylight hours. The
30th Iowa made the attempt on April 20, but Confederate skirmishers, with
artillery support from the Vicksburg batteries, drove them off. The Federals tried again that night, but again the determined Confederate defense
denied them the opportunity to burn the houses. The buildings would thus
remain until the Confederates were good and ready to burn them.[42]

On the evening of April 21, the six boats assigned to make the dangerous
voyage formed up in the river near the mouth of the Yazoo and turned
downstream. At the head of the line steamed *Tigress*, Grant's old command
boat, which had carried him from Savannah to Pittsburg Landing just over
a year before. Leading the operation from *Tigress*'s hurricane deck was Col.
Clark B. Lagow of Grant's staff. Commanding *Tigress* herself was Lt. Col.
William S. Oliver of the 7th Missouri, and his crew consisted of one civilian pilot—the only civilian in the whole operation—and thirty-nine officers and enlisted men of the 7th Missouri. Oliver was taking no chances
with his civilian pilot. He detailed Sgt. Robert Managh, an experienced
river man, as second pilot, and instructed the sergeant "to keep a sharp eye
on the citizen pilot, and to kill him and take the wheel if he attempted to
leave the boat or refused to steer as ordered."[43]

The five other boats were similarly manned, although without any civilians. The steamer *Anglo-Saxon* had a crew from the 45th Illinois, from the
lead mines of the northwestern part of the state, while *Horizon* was manned
by volunteers of the 20th Illinois, from the farms of central and northeast-
ern Illinois.[44]

The plan was patterned after Porter's successful operation of the week
before. The boats would proceed with utmost quietness, with maximum
pressure in the boilers but minimum steam to the engines—almost drifting—
in order to delay detection for as long as possible. Crews carefully extinguished or covered all lights and even stacked cotton bales or spread
tarpaulins to conceal the telltale light of boiler fires. Once detected, they
would immediately put on speed and race down the eastern edge of the
river, immediately in front of the Vicksburg batteries. It was a known fact
that many of the Confederate gun emplacements did not allow their pieces
to be depressed sufficiently to hit the near side of the river. The boats would
therefore boldly attempt to dash by under the very muzzles of the Rebel
cannon.[45]

As the flotilla approached De Soto Point, Confederate picket boats fired
warning shots and signal rockets went up. So much for the element of sur-

prise. *Tigress* went to full speed and raced around the point, the other vessels keeping pace behind her. As they rounded the bend and looked down the long, straight reach of river along the Vicksburg waterfront, the remaining houses of De Soto were already engulfed in flames, and men on the Vicksburg side of the river were lighting bonfires and barrels of tar. Down the river raced *Tigress* and her consorts, hugging the Vicksburg shore. Dozens of cannon hammered at them, while the transports could make no response. Miles away in the Union camps, the ground shook again from the heavy concussions of the guns.[46] "It was the most magnificent display of fireworks ever witnessed by man," recalled Oliver. "We were so wrapped up in the awful grandeur and sublimity of the scene, that we were in reality unconscious of danger and gave no thought to our own safety."[47]

The danger was in fact considerable. Oliver and Lagow could see many cannonballs striking the water short of them and skipping all the way over the vessel, but other Confederate gunners were more fortunate in their aim. A shot carried away the auxiliary tiller wheel. Another carried off the railing on which Oliver was resting his foot. Moments later yet another cut the guy rope of a spar on which he had placed his hand to steady himself. Then an eight-inch shell crashed into *Tigress*'s cabin and exploded, hurling broken pieces of boards in all directions. One of the splinters hit Oliver and knocked him down. Staggering to his feet, the lieutenant colonel continued to command his battered vessel. "As we heard their shots come crashing through our timbers," Oliver wrote in his report, "we wondered how she could live a moment under the raining fire of shot and shell."[48]

In the strong and treacherous currents in front of Vicksburg, the barges lashed to the sides of the transports sometimes rendered them almost unmanageable. The barge on the port side of *Tigress* somehow caught in an eddy and almost pulled the boat right into the shore. So suicidal did this maneuver appear that the Confederate gunners and riflemen on shore momentarily ceased firing at her, thinking the steamer's crew meant to surrender. They soon corrected their mistake and poured in their fire more heavily than ever, while Lt. D. W. McBride and Cpl. Patrick Flannigan raced to the port side with axes and chopped through the lashings that held *Tigress* pinioned to the balky barge. Miraculously, both men performed the task unscathed, and *Tigress* was freed to resume her dash down the river.[49]

On board the steamer *Anglo-Saxon*, Capt. Leander B. Fisk, of Mount Caroll, Illinois, commanded a volunteer crew from the 45th Illinois. Dozens of officers of the 45th had volunteered for the duty, but since only one was needed, they had "decided by lot who should go." Fisk had been the lucky man.[50] Now, however, he was having just the opposite sort of steering problem from that being experienced by the crew of *Tigress*. A Confederate shot parted the bow cable of his starboard barge. The heavily laden craft pivoted on the stern cable until it was almost perpendicular to *Anglo-Saxon*'s keel. The best efforts of helmsman Charlie Evans of Galena could not prevent *Anglo-Saxon,* under a full head of steam, from steering hard astarboard and jamming her bow into the soft mud of the Louisiana shore. Fisk's crew hurriedly cut the barge loose and got their boat under way again and steaming down the river.[51]

Meanwhile, *J. W. Cheesman* had struck a sandbar that had turned her all the way around, bow pointing back up the river. With some difficulty, her volunteer captain and crew got her off the bar and turned her back down the river.[52]

As they passed the Warren County Courthouse in the heart of Vicksburg, the scene was surreal. The river and the Vicksburg waterfront were lit up as bright as day, and it occurred to Oliver that a man could easily have read a newspaper on the hurricane deck of *Tigress*. Instead, however, he and Lagow could see the Rebel gunners clearly and could even see large crowds of Vicksburg civilians, including ladies, who had come out to see the spectacle. Noticing that the clock on the courthouse read 12:20, the officers pulled out their watches and checked to see if it was correct.[53]

The hapless *Anglo-Saxon* was coming in for more punishment. No sooner had Fisk and his men gotten her off the Louisiana shore than she took a hit in her starboard engine, rendering it useless. At almost the same moment a shell slammed into the pilothouse, demolishing it and hurling Evans out onto the hurricane deck, where he lay unconscious. Pvt. Joshua Kendall of Henderson, Illinois, jumped in and took the wheel but found that *Anglo-Saxon* would no longer answer her helm. Nothing remained now for Fisk and his crew but to drift helplessly past Vicksburg while the guns hammered their vessel relentlessly. Fisk counted thirty hits, not including canister and rifle bullets.[54]

Horizon made it past Vicksburg with relative ease. Capt. George W. Kennard of Champaign, Illinois, counted only fifteen or sixteen hits. The steamer and its volunteer crew from the 20th Illinois reached safe water with steering and engines intact and a dry hold.[55]

As they began to leave the Vicksburg waterfront behind them, men naturally felt relief. *Tigress,* however, was in serious trouble. She had been hit thirty-five times, and fourteen of those shots had entered her hull below the waterline. In the hold, a team of men from the 7th Missouri were desperately using cotton, cotton bags, and planks to plug the holes, but they now reported to the chief engineer that they were losing the struggle and would not be able to keep her afloat much longer. Then when they were almost two miles beyond Vicksburg, a parting shot from a long-range rifled gun ripped into *Tigress*, tearing a hole four feet square in her stern and letting the river in with a rush. Oliver ordered the pilot to run her aground on the Louisiana shore, while in the hold, with water knee deep, chief engineer Capt. Philip D. Toomer of the 7th Missouri ordered his men to get out but stayed behind himself to keep the engine running and give *Tigress* power for her desperate lunge for the bank.

On deck Lieutenant McBride and three of his men stood ready with the hawser. With the boat still twice her length from shore and Toomer standing in waist-deep water in the hold, *Tigress* finally lost steerage way. With permission from Oliver, McBride and his party jumped overboard in the attempt to swim to shore carrying the heavy hawser. It was no good, however, as the boat began drifting back into the channel, and McBride and his men had to drop the hawser and climb back on board. Toomer struggled out of the hold through neck-deep water, and presently *Tigress*'s bow struck a submerged obstruction and the steamer's keel snapped. Only her hog chains held her together as she slowly settled to the bottom, leaving most of her cabin and hurricane deck protruding above the surface.[56]

Perched atop the wreck, Lagow, Oliver, and their men hailed the passing *J. W. Cheesman* to take them off, but *Cheesman*'s engines were so badly damaged by hits that she could not reach them. Seeing their best chance of rescue beginning to float away downstream, *Tigress*'s crew abandoned ship on cotton bales and pieces of wreckage and paddled after the *Cheesman*. Reaching her and climbing aboard, the dripping but dauntless Toomer repaired the damage to her power plant and put her under way again. That was fortunate, for just then they spied *Empire City*, disabled and floating helplessly toward the Vicksburg side of the river, where a Confederate field battery was pounding her mercilessly. *Cheesman* took her in tow and headed down the river. When they reached the batteries at Warrenton, however, Oliver, who had taken over command, found that *Cheesman* could not be steered with *Empire City* in tow, so the latter had to be cut loose to float past the guns as best she could. Although dawn had broken by now, both vessels made it past the Warrenton batteries with only minor additional damage.[57]

Anglo-Saxon had a similar experience. Once clear of the Vicksburg batteries, Captain Fisk attempted to drop anchor and make repairs but found that her damage prevented him from anchoring. Seeing *Anglo-Saxon* floating by helplessly, Captain Kennard gave chase in *Horizon*. Before he could catch her, however, they had both come within range of the guns of Warrenton. Rather than place the two vessels adjacent to each other and present the gunners with a target they could not miss, Kennard let *Anglo-Saxon* drift past the batteries on the current and then took her in tow below Warrenton.[58]

The second running of the batteries was a mixed success. Clearly, running unarmored steamers past the batteries without aid of naval gunfire support was a desperate undertaking. All of the steamers took serious damage. *Tigress* sank, and of the five that reached McClernand's position below New Carthage, only *Horizon* and *Cheesman* were able to make steam. Mechanics and engineers got to work on the battered vessels, but it would be a week before they were fit for service. Then, however, Grant would have at his disposal seven transports and would have the capability to set his army on the east bank of the Mississippi almost whenever and wherever he might choose, outside the range of the Confederate batteries at Vicksburg, Warrenton, and Grand Gulf. Also, the supplies carried by the boats and barges that did make it through were of immense value.[59]

Sherman and his lifeboat patrol were on duty again below the batteries and fished Clark Lagow out of the river, among others. The staff officer, Sherman thought, "was satisfied never to attempt such a thing again."[60]

CHAPTER NINETEEN

Across the Mississippi

THE TASK FOR GRANT now was to cross the river, and he proposed to do so at Grand Gulf, where the Confederates had established a subsidiary stronghold. The immediate difficulties, besides the prospect of Rebel opposition, were the shortage of transports and the fact that the amount of dry land at Perkins Plantation was not sufficient to hold more than two divisions. Grant believed he needed to throw three divisions across the river in quick succession in order to be prepared to fight off the inevitable Confederate counterattack. Crossing the troops rapidly might be difficult if they were not already arrayed in the staging area when the operation started. To remedy this problem, Grant decided to shift the army's staging area farther downstream to Hard Times Landing, where Porter assured him there was plenty of room for his army. As an added benefit, Hard Times was closer to Grand Gulf, and therefore the transports would have shorter hauls and could make more frequent shuttles, speeding up the process of putting the army across the river.[1]

Grant was eager to proceed with the planned assault on Grand Gulf before the Rebels could further strengthen their defenses there, which observation indicated they were doing each day. He therefore set in motion several simultaneous processes aimed at getting the army to Hard Times Landing and getting its lead elements across the river as soon as possible. To Osterhaus he gave the task of scouting and securing a road leading to Hard Times via the west bank of a big oxbow lake called Lake St. Joseph, and Osterhaus once again called on Col. James Keigwin and his Argonaut detachment. Keigwin received his orders on April 24, and by April 29 his detachment had made it through to Hard Times via the Lake St. Joseph route, having bridged four bayous and driven off a band of pesky Confederate horsemen.[2]

Grant had no need to await the completion of Keigwin's operation before launching his assault on Grand Gulf, which could be carried out with the support of the gunboats and transports. He was disappointed, however, with the performance of his lead corps commander. He had given orders that officers were not to bring along their horses and baggage on the transports. McClernand had not only ignored the order, but had further delayed the transports by having them haul his wife, along with her servants and baggage. As a result, McClernand's corps was slower than it should have been in reaching Perkins Plantation and Hard Times. This in turn slowed McPherson's corps, which was following behind.[3]

When Grant arrived at Perkins Plantation on April 26, he was dismayed to find, in the words of Dana, who was with him, "the steamboats and barges were scattered about in the river and in the bayou as if there were no idea of the imperative necessity of the promptest possible movements." Grant meant to have prompt movements anyway, and ordered McClernand to embark his two divisions then encamped at Perkins—Osterhaus's and Brig. Gen. Eugene A. Carr's—and have them ready to make a landing at Grand Gulf as soon as the navy could suppress the Confederate batteries there.[4]

McClernand was loath to do so. He wanted to wait until all four of his divisions were on hand. That was nonsense, however, since more troops would not have fit on the dry ground at Perkins and McClernand already had more troops present than could be placed on the available transports. Grant went to visit other parts of his far-flung army, fully expecting McClernand to obey his orders. Nonetheless, in the twenty-four hours that followed, the politician in shoulder straps made not the least effort to comply. Instead, on April 27 he staged a grand review at Perkins in honor of Governor Yates, who was visiting again and addressed the troops in a fine political speech. Naturally, McClernand had to respond with a few appropriate remarks of his own. Then the general had his artillery fire a salute to Yates, which was another violation of orders, since Grant had directed that the scant supply of powder in the advanced camps be reserved for use on the enemy.[5]

That morning Grant wrote McClernand a very severe letter, but on finding that his subordinate had finally gotten his transports and barges sorted out and looked as if he might be about to accomplish something after all, he decided not to send it. Instead, he worked throughout a day of continuous rain, directing the embarkation of Carr's and Osterhaus's divisions. By the morning of April 28, the troops were on board and ready for transportation to the east bank.[6]

Doing at least some of McClernand's work for him added to Grant's already extensive duties. His energy amazed his subordinates. John Sanborn wrote that during these days "Grant seemed to make superhuman efforts and to be endowed with superhuman power." He hardly recognized in the new Grant the same placid general he had known the previous year. Then he had held his horse habitually to a walk. Now, "whenever he was seen, his horse was upon a fast trot or gallop; he seemed wrought up to the last pitch of determination and energy, and the whole army partook of this spirit."[7]

While working hard to get McClernand's men on the steamboats, Grant took time out on April 27 to write a note to Sherman suggesting he use the Fifteenth Corps to make a feint against the Confederate fortifications along the Walnut Hills, overlooking the lower Yazoo River. This was the same stretch of country in which Sherman's offensive had come to grief the preceding December, and Grant was sensitive to the castigation his friend had received in the newspapers after that operation. He therefore couched his message to Sherman in terms of a suggestion rather than an order, for fear that the troops might not understand and "our people at home would characterize it as a repulse." Still, it would be very helpful to have the Confederates looking anxiously to their defenses at Snyder's, Haynes's, and Drumgould's bluffs rather than rushing reinforcements in the opposite direction to bolster the defenses of Grand Gulf, which, Grant said in conclusion, he would probably attack the next day, April 28.[8]

Sherman had profound contempt for the newspapers and was not about to start letting fear of them dictate operational decisions. "The troops will all understand the purpose and will not be hurt by the repulse," he wrote back to Grant upon receiving the dispatch. "The People of the Country must find out the Truth as they best can. It is none of their business. You are engaged in a hazardous enterprise and for good reason wish to divert attention. That is sufficient to me and it shall be done."[9] Obtaining the cooperation of the naval officer commanding above Vicksburg, Sherman the next day took ten transports and eight gunboats up the Yazoo and landed ten regiments of infantry. The troops advanced until they drew the fire of the Confederate guns, then withdrew. The gunboats continued to bombard the defenses intermittently for the next several days.[10]

Sherman's feint was only one of several operations Grant had devised in order to confuse Pemberton. The most important of these was a raid by a brigade of cavalry under the command of Col. Benjamin Grierson that had left Hurlbut's lines in northern Mississippi ten days before and was even now scarcely forty miles east of Grand Gulf, heading for a linkup with the Union troops of Maj. Gen. Nathaniel P. Banks near Port Hudson, Louisiana, and tearing up railroad tracks and telegraph lines along the way. The cumulative effect of Grant's several diversions was powerful. Pemberton, never the most agile-minded of generals, was in an almost dizzy state of confusion.[11]

Delays prevented the attack from taking place on April 28 as Grant had originally hoped, but at 7:00 a.m. on April 29, Porter's gunboats advanced against the batteries at Grand Gulf. Grant had 10,000 of McClernand's men waiting in transports and barges to land on the Mississippi shore as soon as the navy had silenced the Confederate guns. That, however, proved to be no easy matter. The Rebel position was a strong one, atop commanding bluffs. The battle was a spectacular show for the troops of the Thirteenth Corps who had ringside seats from their transports. "It was something I had longed to see," wrote Ohio soldier Isaac Jackson, "and now my curiosity was satisfied." Union shells blasted dirt geysers forty or fifty feet high from the Rebel parapets. The gunboats "would come creeping up slow, one after another, and let broadside after broadside into the batteries," while Confederate shots skipped across the water, kicking up towering columns of spray. Dense clouds of white smoke hid the scene from time to time until a stiff breeze cleared them away again.[12]

Many of the Confederate shots found their targets. After five and a half hours of furious bombardment, the navy had suffered seventy-five casualties—including Admiral Porter, slightly wounded—as well as damage to three of its vessels. The gunboats had silenced most but not all of the Confederate guns, and it was obvious that trying to bring unarmored transports packed with troops under the muzzles of those remaining cannon would result in ghastly failure. The navy pulled back, and Grant had to come up with a new plan for crossing the river.[13]

In broad terms, the decision of what to do next was not difficult. Grant could accept defeat and take the army back to Milliken's Bend, or he could go farther down the river. The latter prospect was unappealing because it entailed further lengthening of his already tenuous supply line, stretched over sixty miles of muddy roads and makeshift bridges. The former prospect, however, was unthinkable. Therefore, down the river Grant would go. He boarded the flagship, *Benton*, to ask Porter to take the gunboats and the transports below the batteries that night. The scene of carnage on *Benton*'s gun deck was appalling, but Porter, who was in pain from a wound inflicted when a shell fragment struck the back of his head, nevertheless agreed to do so. The troops went ashore so that the transports could run the batteries empty. The army would march around on another looping natural levee and meet the fleet downstream. That night the boats ran the Grand Gulf batteries. Under cover of the gunboats' fire, the transports and barges made the passage substantially unscathed.[14]

To reconnoiter landing places farther down the east side, Grant had Osterhaus dispatch a small scouting party to the east bank. Osterhaus selected Capt. Richard H. Ballinger of Company A, 3rd Illinois Cavalry, to take eight men across the river. Ballinger had already volunteered for service with one of the newly raised black regiments and was slated to be colonel of the 3rd Mississippi, African Descent. For now, however, he had a smaller command of great responsibility.

Where *Benton* was lying tied up along the riverbank, numerous soldiers were standing around gawking at the damage from the day's fight. Ballinger, who had orders to use *Benton*'s yawl in crossing the river, showed up and asked for soldier volunteers to serve as oarsmen. Volunteers were plentiful, and after nightfall the party set out in the yawl, departing via a gunport on *Benton*'s outboard side. The Rebels were patrolling the east bank, but the party succeeded in landing without being detected. Ballinger's object seems to have been finding a black man who could serve as a source of information and possibly a guide. His search eventually turned up such a man, and all was going well until the informant learned that he was to be taken across to the west side of the river. At that point, he and his family began to kick up a ruckus. "After some delay," one of the volunteer oarsmen dryly noted, "he was landed in the boat." The proceeding had served to alert the Confederates, however, and the boat's return trip across the Mississippi was made under a brisk fire of musketry. Bullets lashed the water around the boat, but the night was too dark for accurate shooting.

Having escaped the Confederate pickets, the party next became the target of their Union comrades. The Federal pickets had become alarmed by the sound of firing from the other side of the river and sent a volley of their own in the direction of the splashing oars before Ballinger hailed the pickets. They required him to come ashore and explain the boat's presence in their front. The "explanation was in forceful language, but seemed to be satisfactory." Continuing up the river, Ballinger and his party reached Grant's headquarters and delivered their unwilling informant. The black man reported that he had lived in the neighborhood all his life and knew the roads well. The best place to land and find a dry road leading inland, he advised, would be Bruinsburg, eight miles farther down the river. Grant had thought he would have to go all the way to Rodney, Mississippi, another nine miles downstream, but took the recently freed slave's advice and set Bruinsburg as the army's target instead.[15]

The Thirteenth Corps hiked across the point of land opposite Grand Gulf and reached the river below and out of range of the Confederate batteries before nightfall on April 29. They camped that night at Disharoon's

Plantation and felt the ground tremble again as the fleet ran past Grand Gulf. McPherson's Seventeenth Corps was backed up along the roads behind them, with no room to advance until McClernand's men moved on. Most of Sherman's Fifteenth Corps was still at Young's Point that night, but preparing to march southward behind the rest of the army.[16]

At daylight on April 30, the men of the Thirteenth Corps filed back on board the steamboats. Grant meant to use every available vessel for this operation so that he could ferry as many troops as possible across the river as rapidly as possible. The transports each had a barge lashed on either side, and Porter agreed to use the gunboats too. The rule was standing room only and priority for combat strength. The only horses on the boats were for the artillery—no baggage wagons, no ambulances, no officers' horses, not even Grant's own. "They drove us on the boat just like we were a flock of sheep," wrote Illinois soldier W. R. Eddington, "until there was not standing room for another man."[17]

Grant joined Porter on board *Benton*. Even the flagship was not exempt from carrying the maximum number of soldiers, and the general and admiral were joined by two regiments of Brig. Gen. George F. McGinnis's brigade of the Thirteenth Corps. The 24th Indiana piled onto the open upper deck while most of the 46th Indiana crowded among the massive cannon on the gun deck below. Three companies of the 46th stood tightly packed together on the open bow of the gunboat. The other gunboats carried similar loads. As far as possible in these crowded conditions, the boats were cleared for action, and the gun crews stood by their guns amid the crowds of soldiers. The infantry anxiously eyed the east-bank bluffs and wondered what resistance they would meet there. Standing high atop *Benton*'s wheelhouse, Grant and Porter also surveyed the high ground to the east.[18]

Somehow a band had squeezed on board *Benton* and now struck up "The Red, White, and Blue." The patriotic music carried across the water. Standing crowded on board *Benton* or one of the other boats, or waiting on shore for transport in the next wave, thousands of soldiers responded with cheers.[19] The winter of suffering and futility was now a thing of the past, and the Army of the Tennessee was at last taking the fight to the enemy with what all of the soldiers sensed were at least even odds of success.

As *Benton* nosed into the muddy east bank of the river, the troops of the 24th and 46th Indiana swarmed ashore, scrambled into skirmish formation, and began moving inland to form a perimeter and secure the landing area. They found only one person in the vicinity, a Mississippi farmer whom they promptly took into custody to prevent him from spreading news of their arrival. The other boats grounded in rapid succession and disgorged their human cargoes, then began shuttling back and forth across the river with more loads of troops until by about noon that day the entire 17,000-man Thirteenth Corps was ashore in the state of Mississippi and the boats were ready to begin ferrying the Seventeenth Corps, which had moved up to the west bank in preparation for crossing.[20]

Despite the rapid buildup of Union forces on the east bank, Grant's entire offensive could still be stopped dead in its tracks if the Confederates took possession of the route up out of the bottomland and onto the plateau that formed the interior of Mississippi. If any substantial number of Rebel defenders held the road that climbed up the bluffs about two miles from where Grant's troops had landed, they could bid defiance to his whole army as easily as they had done Sherman's at Chickasaw Bayou four months before. It was therefore all the more vexatious to Grant to discover some-time after reaching the east bank that McClernand had neglected the obvi-ous preparatory step of issuing rations to his men the night before. Having the soldiers draw three days' rations was the all-but-automatic precursor of every significant troop movement, but here the men of the Thirteenth Corps had empty haversacks as they were about to set out on a rapid advance that would at least temporarily leave their supply wagons behind. Nothing could be done now but wait while the rations were brought over the river, a process that delayed the advance by four hours.[21]

Finally at about four in the afternoon, the column moved out, marching toward the bluffs, with Carr's division in the lead. The officers of the divi-sion, sharing Grant's urgency to get moving, had decided to forgo for the moment the issuing of rations to individual soldiers. Instead, they detailed men to carry the big boxes of hardtack, two men to a box. The pair stood one behind the other with one rifle spanning their left shoulders and the other their right. The box was then laid across the two rifles between them and off they marched. When the column stopped for supper, the supply ser-geants broke open the boxes and distributed the contents. When meat rations were too generous for the capacity of haversacks, the men fixed bayonets and impaled their portions. Then with rifles at right shoulder shift, the column marched down the road under myriad swaying chunks of pork.[22] Carr himself presented a curious spectacle, astride a commandeered mount, "a great big ugly poor mule," looking anything but the dashing cav-alry officer he had been in the prewar army. Grant himself fared somewhat better and succeeded in appropriating a horse to ride.[23]

Despite the delay for rations, Grant was in high spirits. He knew there were many challenges still to face before Vicksburg would be his, but he felt tremendous relief at having gotten nearly half his army across the river. All four divisions of the Thirteenth Corps were already on the east bank, and Logan's division of the Seventeenth was even then in the process of crossing. "I was now in the enemy's country," Grant wrote years later, "with a vast river and the stronghold of Vicksburg between me and my base of supplies. But I was on dry ground on the same side of the river with the enemy. All the campaigns, labors, hardships and exposures from the month of December previous to this time that had been made and endured, were for the accomplishment of this one object."[24]

When the column reached the bluffs, about an hour before sunset, they found the heights unoccupied. The road led up the bluffs through a deep cut with high banks on either side and came out onto the plateau beyond. The lead elements of the Thirteenth Corps halted for supper some distance beyond the bluffs, and there McClernand ordered his corps to "push on by a forced march that night as far as practicable." At the head of the column was Col. C. L. Harris's brigade, composed of the 11th Wisconsin and the 21st, 22nd, and 23rd Iowa. After the supper break, Harris assigned the 21st Iowa to relieve the 11th Wisconsin as the advance guard of the army. Col. Samuel Merrill of the 21st assigned Lt. Col. James Dunlap to take four companies, two deployed as skirmishers and two in reserve, along with a single gun of the attached 1st Ohio Battery, and proceed a short distance out in front, while the rest of the regiment followed in support.[25]

They resumed the march at about 5:30 p.m., advancing through the loess hills, a plateau cut by innumerable deep, steep, and winding ravines. The bottoms of the ravines were choked with vines, brambles, and cane. The land between the ravines stood in meandering steep-sided ridges with flat but often fairly narrow tops, upon which the roads ran and all of the local inhabitants' crops grew. As Grant put it, "The country in this part of Mississippi stands on edge, as it were, the roads running along the ridges except when they occasionally pass from one ridge to another." The military significance of this terrain Grant realized at once: "This makes it easy for an inferior force to delay, if not defeat, a far superior one."[26]

As darkness fell, Dunlap drew in his two-company skirmish force. Rather than have his men beat their way through the rough terrain in the dark, he sent a sixteen-man patrol with orders to push on ahead of the column along the road until they drew enemy fire.[27] A full moon rose, casting a surreal light on the already surreal landscape. "In many places the road seems to end abruptly, but [when] we come to the place we find it turning at right angles, passing through narrow valleys, sometimes through hills," recalled Sgt. Charles Hobbs of the 99th Illinois. At each halt, the soldiers in the long march column dropped to the ground and were asleep at once, and the officers and sergeants had hard work to rouse them again ten minutes later. About 10:00 p.m., Colonel Harris became incapacitated with severe stomach cramps and had to go to the rear. Command of his brigade passed to Col. William M. Stone of the 22nd Iowa. Stone moved forward to travel with Dunlap's advance force, and the march continued.[28]

They had come about twelve miles from the river when around midnight the lead patrol of Iowans drew a scattering of shots from the darkness out in front. One man was hit. Stone quickly brought the supporting companies into skirmish line, ordered the rest of the 21st Iowa to come up on the double, and had his skirmishers advance slowly through the ravines and thickets. The enemy had made off into the night, however, and was nowhere to be found. Stone brought his weary soldiers back into the road, where they formed column and trudged on. They had gone about three-quarters of a mile and were approaching a building called Magnolia Church when they were startled by a sudden volley of rifle fire just ahead. Back in the marching column, Lt. William Charleton heard the volley, looked at his watch, and noted that the time was 12:50 a.m.[29]

This time the Confederates obviously meant to offer serious resistance. Stone immediately ordered up the rest of his brigade and had his artillery piece go into battery in the road. Before the Iowa gunners could get off a shot, however, the Confederates had a whole battery in action. The Federals rushed forward the rest of the 1st Iowa Battery as well as the 1st Indiana, and a spectacular nighttime artillery battle ensued. The flash and boom of the guns and the scream of shells made a stunning contrast to the nighttime stillness, and Stone thought it one of the most memorable scenes of the whole campaign. Nearby infantry were impressed by the courage of Capt. Henry H. Griffiths, commanding the 1st Iowa Battery. "All night long we could hear him giving his commands with a clear loud voice," wrote Taylor Peirce of the 22nd Iowa, "and urging his men to give it to them while he sat or moved round amongst the guns on his horse amid a perfect shower of grape, canister, and shell." By 2:00 a.m. or perhaps a little later, the Union gunners had gotten the upper hand and silenced the Confederate artillerists. A lull settled over the battlefield. "For an hour before daylight there was perfect silence," noted Sgt. George Remley of the 22nd Iowa. At least it was quiet enough for Remley to snatch a few minutes of sleep.[30]

During the remaining hours of darkness, the other brigade of Carr's division, Brig. Gen. William P. Benton's, moved up behind Stone's, but Carr decided to wait until morning before deploying them. The moon had set, and the terrain was obviously too complicated for anyone to figure it out in the dark. The first light of dawn proved Carr had been right. The tangle of ridges and ravines between the army and the town of Port Gibson, on Bayou Pierre, was almost too complex to be understood in any light. The ridgetops were mostly clear, with excellent visibility, and the roads followed their roundabout routes. The ravines were abysses of jungle. The Union position was a few yards west of Magnolia Church. Just behind the Union position was a crossroads. From that crossroads the main road to Port Gibson, known as the Rodney Road, ran southeast past Magnolia Church and continued on a mostly northeasterly course to reach the town. The other fork, however, was a farm road that ran northwest to join the Bruinsburg Road, which almost paralleled the Rodney Road, running more or less due east, about a mile or so north of the Rodney Road, until the two gradually converged just outside Port Gibson. Between them lay the tangle of ravines that was the basin of Center Creek.

The sun rose through a hazy mist into a clear sky. Maj. Luther Cowan thought the morning had more the feel of midsummer back home in Warren, Illinois, than it did of May Day. McClernand arrived on the battlefield at daybreak, and he and his officers surveyed the terrain ahead. He determined to have Carr's division attack the Rebels with which it had collided that night around Magnolia Church and then continue to drive east along the Rodney Road. As he prepared to do so, however, he spotted Confederate troops on the ridge to the north of him, which carried the Bruinsburg Road. If those Confederates should advance down the farm road to the fork, they would be headed straight for the rear of Carr's men around Magnolia Church. McClernand decided that the Confederates to the north needed to be neutralized, and so as Osterhaus's division came marching up the road behind Carr's, he ordered the German general to take his men north, up the farm road to the Bruinsburg Road ridge and clear it of Rebels.[31]

The two Rebel forces both belonged to the Confederate division of Maj. Gen. John S. Bowen, who had been assigned to hold Grand Gulf and the southern approaches of Vicksburg. Bowen had been befuddled by Grant's recent maneuvering and so had kept his best brigade, Brig. Gen. Francis Cockrell's Missourians, back at Grand Gulf. Similarly, Pemberton, who was confused both by Grierson's cavalry raid through the center of the state and by Sherman's threatening demonstrations along the lower Yazoo, had declined to send any reinforcements to Bowen. Thus to meet the Army of the Tennessee outside Port Gibson, Bowen had Brig. Gen. Martin Green's brigade of Arkansans and Mississippians, holding the Rodney Road near Magnolia Church, and Brig. Gen. Edward Tracy's brigade of

Alabamians, posted on the Bruinsburg Road. Bowen's inferiority in numbers might have been instantly fatal on another battlefield, but here the odd mix of ridges and ravines conferred enormous advantages on an outnumbered defender, since the attacker had either to advance along the narrow ridges or else try to flail his way through the ravines, where his organization was almost sure to disintegrate.[32]

While his artillery banged away at the Rebels to the north, Osterhaus deployed his division as best he could and advanced with difficulty through the rough terrain. Once he got his troops up to the Confederate position, he easily drove the Rebels back. Yet the graycoats simply retreated to the next ridge or the one after that, and Osterhaus's Federals had their work to do all over again, struggling forward through underbrush and following ravines that curved this way and that, subtly pulling units off their proper alignments. Hours passed as the division slowly crept forward toward the Bruinsburg Road. Osterhaus was cautious and declined to press the attack even when he could have done so. Instead he insisted that he must have reinforcements, and only when joined by a brigade of John A. Logan's division, the lead unit of the Seventeenth Corps, did he renew his advance.[33]

Meanwhile, back on the Rodney Road, the rest of the Thirteenth Corps was fighting a separate battle. Firing had resumed shortly after daybreak, and to Taylor Peirce, waiting to take part in his first battle, the passing bullets sounded like so many angry bees flying by. At McClernand's order, Carr prepared to advance. He deployed his brigades on either side of the road, Stone's on the north, Benton's on the south. Then he had Benton press forward to drive the Rebel skirmishers off the ridge on which Magnolia Church stood. This proved successful, and Carr hoped next to use Benton to turn the southern flank of the main Confederate line, but difficulties arose. As on Osterhaus's front, the terrain made it almost impossible to maintain formation or alignment during a movement in line of battle. As Benton's brigade had been moving up into position that morning, the soldiers pulling themselves up the side of a ravine by clinging to the vines and cane, some of the men said they saw a black bear making off through the thick brush. The claim was entirely plausible, for the terrain was certainly more suited to beasts than to soldiers in line of battle.[34]

Now as Benton's brigade scrambled forward against the foe, its advance had carried it a little too far to the right, opening a gap in Carr's center, between Stone and Benton. A small Confederate counterattack exploited this problem, gaining a temporary advantage. Fierce fighting raged on either side of the Rodney Road. The 18th Indiana lost two color-bearers, and Col. H. D. Washburn took the flag himself and waved it while shouting encouragement to his men. Carr asked McClernand for reinforcements. The two brigades of Alvin Hovey's division were waiting just behind the zone of fighting, eating breakfast, drinking coffee, and, in some cases, thinking about snatching a nap. McClernand's order got them up and moving quickly to advance and plug the gap in the Union line.[35]

McClernand then took over direction of the attack and imposed his own tactical scheme. No West Point strategy for him—this attack was going to be a matter of brute force right up the middle, and he had the manpower to do it. He brought up the remaining division of the Thirteenth Corps, A. J. Smith's, and packed his troops into the constricted space on either side of the Rodney Road, in some places three or four regiments deep. While Hovey's men struggled to get into position, Benton, whose troops were now waiting in the shelter of a ravine, put them through the manual of arms in the time-honored tradition of steadying the men in preparation for a desperate charge. At last McClernand had his corps ready, and despite the limitations of the terrain, his line extended beyond the flanks of the Confederate defenders.[36]

When the Thirteenth Corps advanced, most of the soldiers agreed that they had not received any regular orders. They saw other troops around them beginning to move and simply joined in. The charge overwhelmed the Confederate defenders. Men of half a dozen regiments swarmed over the Botetourt Virginia Artillery before the Confederate gunners could even get off their final rounds of canister. Soldiers of the 11th Indiana swung the guns around and loosed the loads into the backs of the fleeing Rebels. So deep was McClernand's formation that some of the soldiers barely got to participate in this segment of the fight at all. Israel Ritter and his comrades of the 24th Iowa were in their first battle, but they were in the fourth line, with three other regiments in front of them. "It is impossible to describe the sound," noted Ritter in his diary. "It appeared that all the forest was crashing to pieces." The 24th got the order to advance, and "went over a field double quick, but the enemy had run and we did not get to fire."[37]

Grant had just arrived on the battlefield, and now he and McClernand rode along the lines of their victorious soldiers, accompanied by Governor Yates of Illinois. The troops cheered wildly and swung their hats. "A great day for the northwest," exulted McClernand, and both he and the governor could not resist the temptation to make short speeches to some of the nearby troops. Grant, impassive as ever, suggested that the advance should be resumed.[38]

It took time to get the troops sorted out and realigned. Long lines of prisoners were marched to the rear, while the wounded were carried to

Magnolia Church, which became a temporary field hospital. Then came a slow advance as the troops in line of battle scrambled down into ravines and clawed their way up the other sides, discovering that the cane growing in the ravines had sharp edges when broken. The day had already become fiercely hot—participants guessed more than 90 degrees—and some men collapsed of heat exhaustion. About half a mile farther up the road, they once again encountered the Confederates in a defensive position. Bowen's other brigade, Cockrell's Missourians, had finally reached the battlefield, along with reinforcements that Pemberton had belatedly released. Bowen posted the Missourians alongside Brig. Gen. William E. Baldwin's brigade of Mississippians and Louisianans, in a strong position that once again blocked the Army of the Tennessee's route to Port Gibson.[39]

Initial efforts to push the Confederates aside proved unsuccessful, so McClernand began preparing for a repetition of the tactics he had used before, massing his three divisions in front of the Confederate center, poised for another crushing assault. Bowen, however, preempted him by making an attack of his own. The Confederate commander had scant reserves, but he ordered Cockrell's brigade, the best Rebel unit in Mississippi, to assault the Union right. Hovey, whose division held that sector, saw Cockrell's men forming up for the attack and made preparations to receive them, gathering four batteries of artillery with a total of twenty-four guns. When the Rebel Missourians advanced, Hovey's massed artillery blasted them, but Cockrell's men came on undaunted and plowed into the Union infantry.

The battle raged for some time on the right. A veteran Union officer spoke of the mixture of sounds that made up "the voices of the battlefield" and that he remembered especially vividly in connection with these minutes: "the crash of musketry, the crack of the rifle, the roar of the guns, the shriek of shells, the rebel whoop, the Federal cheer, and that indescribable undertone of grinding, rumbling, splintering sound." Gradually the Federals gained the upper hand and began to drive the Confederates back, while Hovey's artillery continued to hammer them. In the counterattack, Ritter and his comrades of the inexperienced 24th Iowa finally got to use their rifles. Advancing in the thick of the fight along with other regiments, the 24th fired several volleys before Cockrell's brigade broke and fell back in disorder. Ritter noted that at the firing of his regiment's first volley a bullet had grazed his ear, and he suspected it came from the rifle of one of his inexpert comrades.[40]

Cockrell's attack had cost the Confederates heavy casualties among their best troops, but it had thrown McClernand's plans into disarray. Getting formations straightened out again and resupplied with ammunition would take time, and as always the terrain multiplied the difficulty and delay involved in every task. On top of that, McClernand seemed to be out of ideas and did not act aggressively to prepare his troops to resume the offensive. Instead, he indulged in a pastime popular among Civil War generals uncertain about what orders to give, that of personally sighting the guns of a nearby battery. Bowen, who possessed aggressiveness enough for any two generals, had no intention of waiting for McClernand to come up with something. About four o'clock that afternoon, while McClernand still delayed, Bowen launched Baldwin's Mississippi and Louisiana brigade in yet another spoiling attack. Baldwin's men met even rougher treatment than Cockrell's, as the Federals hurled them back almost as soon as they began their advance.[41]

As the afternoon waned toward evening, the Thirteenth Corps, now reinforced by a brigade of Logan's division, began to put heavy pressure on Bowen's line, gradually forcing the Confederates back. There was no charge this time, but a steady buildup along the skirmish line until the Confederates had to yield ground. Capt. Samuel De Golyer of the 8th Michigan Battery, attached to Logan's division, was especially bold in displaying the potential of artillery as a skirmish weapon. He had his men load their six cannon in a ravine and then manhandle them up the slope toward the ridge held by the Confederates. De Golyer's sweating artillerists managed to poke the muzzles of their cannon over the lip of the ravine and almost into the faces of the defenders before loosing devastating blasts of canister. Elsewhere, Union infantry pressed steadily forward by more conventional means.

About this time, Osterhaus's division, reinforced by a brigade of Logan's, finally resumed its advance along the Bruinsburg Road. Osterhaus himself dismounted and led the 114th Ohio in a charge on foot, capturing two brass cannon. Along this front, as on the Rodney Road, Confederate resistance was beginning to crumble. At about 6:00 p.m., Bowen ordered what was left of his battered division to retreat. Once again rough terrain and tangled foliage came to the aid of the outnumbered Confederates, and they were able to make their escape unmolested by the victorious Federals, disappearing both from Osterhaus's front on the Bruinsburg Road and from McClernand's on the Rodney Road.[42]

By the time the Federal commanders realized that the enemy had broken contact, daylight was fading, and McClernand ordered his men to halt for the night. The Battle of Port Gibson was over. Neither McClernand's nor Osterhaus's performances had been especially impressive, but they were

good enough to get the job done with the heavy local superiority in numbers that Grant's operational skill had provided them. The troops of the
Army of the Tennessee, both veterans and the as-yet-unbloodied regiments
of the "three hundred thousand more," had performed admirably.

Just after the fighting closed, Grant rode along Osterhaus's lines, accompanied by McPherson, Logan, Osterhaus, and Yates. The troops cheered
their commander enthusiastically. "Boys," Grant told them, "you have
done well today, but you'll have more of the same thing tomorrow!" When
the men shouted for Osterhaus, the German-American general added his
own exhortation (spelled out phonetically by one of the soldiers who heard
it): "Vell, boys, I dells you vat it is: you do as vell tomorrow as you does to
day and we whip dem repels undil they can't eat sauerkraut."[43]

The cheering was not confined to the Bruinsburg Road. All across the
darkening battlefield, Union troops gave voice to their jubilation. "When
the victory was complete," wrote Taylor Peirce to his wife back in Iowa,
"you ought to have heard the shout that rung out on the evening air. It was
enough to pay us for all our fatigue and dangers."[44]

CHAPTER TWENTY

Jackson

G RANT'S FIRST STRATEGIC objective after the success on May 1 was to get across Little Bayou Pierre and secure Grand Gulf as a base for operations farther into the interior. Unsure whether the Confederates had completely vacated the Port Gibson area, Grant advanced his army at first light on the morning of May 2, skirmishers out in front. "We moved on slowly in advance," wrote Isaac Jackson of the 83rd Ohio, "expecting to have the battery open every moment."[1] They discovered, however, that the Rebels had abandoned Port Gibson. Gone too were the Little Bayou Pierre bridges, now reduced to smoking ruins. A soldier of the 48th Ohio remembered that his regiment "stacked arms on the side-walk, under the shade trees," and waited to see what Grant would order next.[2]

Grant assigned his staff topographical engineer, Lt. Col. James H. Wilson, to build some sort of makeshift bridge over Little Bayou Pierre at Port Gibson and ordered McPherson to have Logan's division scout potential crossings both up- and downstream from the town. They found bridges burned and, in some cases, crossings covered by significant numbers of Confederate defenders.[3]

While Logan's men sparred with Confederates on the opposite bank elsewhere along the bayou, Wilson and his detachment of pioneers went to work to build a bridge in Port Gibson. He decided to build a raft-type bridge and put his fatigue parties to work tearing down nearby buildings to get the necessary lumber. When the span was finished, he sent a single cannon across to test it. Halfway across the bridge, the platform tipped and dumped the gun into Little Bayou Pierre. Wilson and his crew made some improvements and had a usable bridge open for traffic by 4:00 p.m.[4]

First across were the men of Marcellus Crocker's division of the Seventeenth Corps, which had come up too late to see action the previous day. Logan's division fell in behind. Their route followed the course of the Old Natchez Trace of Mississippi's frontier days, as they marched from Port Gibson northeastward to the crossing of Big Bayou Pierre at Grindstone

Ford, where a suspension bridge, quite modern for the time, ran 300 feet across and 40 feet above the surface of the bayou. It was 7:30 when Crocker's vanguard approached Grindstone Ford, and the bridge was in flames. The troops extinguished the fire before the span was completely destroyed. By nightfall they had possession of a ford that was usable for infantry only and a bridge that would not be usable by anyone until substantial repairs were completed. Wilson rounded up another fatigue party and went to work again. His second bridge project in twenty-four hours was open for business by 5:30 a.m., May 3.[5]

Again, Grant was wasting no time. As soon as the bridge at Grindstone Ford was finished, he sent the two available divisions of the Seventeenth Corps marching across it. This was a daring move, with the Thirteenth Corps still resting back at Port Gibson. In theory, Bowen's Confederates, heavily reinforced since the battle two days before, could have counterattacked and put McPherson's divisions in a desperate situation.[6]

By this time, however, Grant was gaining an ascendancy over the Confederate generals he faced—even the best of them, like the sturdy and astute Bowen. Grant was far ahead of his opponents in perceiving and assessing the operational situation and determining what to do next—often doing it while his foes were still trying to sort out the results of his previous move, or the one before that. Grant's edge was also one of confidence and aggressiveness. Every movement of his army expressed its commander's assurance that he would whip any force that stood in his path. His foes, cut from much flimsier cloth, could not help starting to believe it. Grant and the Army of the Tennessee would be coming for them, of that they could be sure, and increasingly their reaction to that certainty was an impulse to get out of the way. Confederate major general W. W. Loring had superseded Bowen by seniority. His response to word that a Union column was penetrating north of Big Bayou Pierre was to order his command, the southern wing of Pemberton's forces, to withdraw north of the Big Black River, abandoning Grand Gulf.[7]

Grant rode with McPherson's advance. The column encountered Confederate skirmishers almost immediately but drove them easily. Off and on for the rest of the day, McPherson's troops met varying degrees of resistance, sometimes in almost division strength. It was soon apparent, however, that the Confederates constituted a rearguard covering a retreat. While Logan's and Crocker's divisions continued to drive the Rebels northward, Grant turned aside to the west and rode into Grand Gulf with a small escort. Arriving at the river bastion, he found that the navy had taken possession in the wake of the Confederate evacuation. Grant paused with the fleet for a bath and a change of underclothes, then studied the dispatches from Washington and from Nathaniel P. Banks, commanding the Union forces operating against Port Hudson, Louisiana.

News from Banks forced Grant to make a decision. Not surprisingly, the unusually inept commander of the Department of the Gulf was not at all prepared to cooperate with Grant's operations. Up to this point, Grant had been open to the possibility of detaching McClernand's command and sending it to help Banks. In theory, Banks would use the reinforcements to capture Port Hudson quickly and would then bring his force north to help Grant take Vicksburg. The authorities in Washington had been encouraging Grant to consider such a course, though how serious he was about such a plan is difficult to say. It would in all probability have been an unmitigated disaster. Banks outranked Grant and would have commanded when their forces were united. If any general could yet have snatched defeat out of the jaws of Union victory in Mississippi, Banks was the man. In this case, his ineptitude saved the day by keeping him out of the Vicksburg campaign. Grant would be on his own and would have to get on about the business of taking Vicksburg without the dubious assistance of Banks.[8]

Either Grant had been thinking about this possibility for a long time or else he did a great deal of very fast thinking during several hours on the night of May 3, after several days spent mostly in the saddle and with very little sleep. Either way it was an impressive performance. His army would strike inland, he decided, and of necessity it would operate with an extremely tenuous supply line. The army would endeavor to supply its men with salt, coffee, perhaps some hardtack—and none too much of those commodities. Other than that, they would have to make their scant rations last as long as possible by eking them out with aggressive foraging. Grant wrote the necessary orders to get the movement started and the maximum, if still inadequate, amount of supplies flowing along behind his advance. He also directed Hurlbut at Memphis to send down a division to secure the west-bank positions so that Sherman's entire corps could join him for the march into Mississippi. Then he penned a dispatch to Halleck, notifying him of the movement, which he knew Old Brains would not like. By midnight, Grant was back in the saddle and riding to catch up with the advance of his army.[9]

By dawn of May 4, Grant had overtaken McPherson's two divisions at Hankinson's Ferry on the Big Black River. Logan's division had arrived there the previous afternoon and had advanced so rapidly that the Rebels had been unable to destroy the bridge. Logan's men took it intact and pushed across to the north bank of the Big Black, the last river barrier between Grant's army and Vicksburg, which lay about twenty-five miles due north of Hankinson's Ferry. Rising from the north side of the Big Black bottoms was that broad range of high ground that Grant had been trying to reach for the past six months. Now, however, he was not so sure he should move onto it—at least, not yet.[10]

An advance directly toward Vicksburg from Hankinson's Ferry would cross the same sort of ravine-slashed landscape on which Grant's army had fought the Battle of Port Gibson. Pemberton could concentrate his force around Vicksburg and might well succeed in holding Grant at bay, all the while receiving a steady flow of supplies from the east via the railroad that ran from Jackson to Vicksburg. Rejecting this option, Grant chose instead to withdraw the bridgehead at Hankinson's and march northeastward toward Jackson. There he could operate on the rolling terrain of central Mississippi, cut Pemberton's supply line through Jackson, and then approach Vicksburg directly from the east. It would mean crossing the Big Black at a later date, for that river flowed between Jackson and Vicksburg, but overall it seemed the better plan.[11]

Before first light on May 7, the Army of the Tennessee's three-day pause came to an end as the vanguard once again took up the advance. During the preceding night, McPherson's troops had pulled back to the south side of the Big Black and early that morning strode out on the road leading toward Jackson. That same day, two divisions of Sherman's Fifteenth Corps crossed the Mississippi and took up their march toward Hankinson's Ferry. During the next several days, the army spread out to march on parallel roads, so as to maximize the extent of country it could forage. McPherson's Seventeenth Corps took the right, McClernand's Thirteenth the left, and Sherman's Fifteenth, after dismantling the bridge at Hankinson's Ferry, followed in the middle and behind the other two corps.[12]

As the army marched northeast, it skirmished frequently with Confederate cavalry in front and on the right flank, along the Big Black. By seizing and holding the various crossings of the river as they advanced, Grant's men could keep the Rebels off the flank of the column and away from the trains of 200 to 300 wagons that overtook the army each day, shuttling supplies forward from Grand Gulf.

The first few days of the campaign, the weather had been hot and the roads dusty.[13] Some relief had come when a front moved through in the predawn hours of May 5, bringing a heavy rainstorm and subsequently four days of mostly cool, cloudy weather with strong north winds.[14] By May 9, however, the heat had returned with a vengeance and the roads were as dusty as ever.[15] "Extremely hot," wrote Maj. Luther Cowan of the 45th Illinois in

his diary, "water scarce and bad." The roads were "all dust . . . almost suffo-
cating the men."[16]

Food was a constant concern. Regular rations reached the troops only
sporadically and in scant supply. Most of the soldiers' sustenance had to
come from the country through which they passed. On May 6, William
Carroll noted in his diary that the forage detail of his 24th Indiana had
brought in "plenty of meat & sugar but no bread." Carroll and his buddies
eked out a meal with their few remaining hardtack crackers and some local
corn they had ground into meal.[17]

Sometimes the same troops could experience feast and famine within a
few days of each other. On May 6, Aurelius Voorhis noted that his haversack was nearly empty, and by the eighth he and several of his comrades in
the 46th Indiana were hungry enough to use a cotton gin to grind some
recently liberated corn into meal for baking, but that evening "we drew
rations which brought everybody back to an uncommon good humor,"
Voorhis wrote in his diary. "Corn bread is below par now as we have plenty
of crackers."[18]

Soldiers in one unit might have surfeit while others had to tighten their
belts. On May 10, Joseph Williamson and his comrades in the 33rd Illinois
found themselves carrying five days' rations, "wich was quite a lode."[19] At
the opposite extreme, Illinois soldier W. R. Eddington wrote in his diary,
"Our rations are running low and we are stripping the bark from slippery
elm trees and eating it as we march along and picking the buds and leaves
off the trees and eating them." Eddington managed to steal an ear of corn
from the supply set aside for the artillery horses and noted that it "helps
some to prolong existence." He hoped something better might turn up the
next day.[20]

If the soldiers occasionally fared poorly, they made sure that Mississippi's secessionists, as far as they could be identified, felt their pain. "The
citizens would like very much to have us leave as soon as convenient,"
wrote Luther Cowan. "The boys have great times taking bacon, sugar,
molasses, and whatever they can get from the old secesh, while they stand
around begging like culprits to be left alone."[21]

In a situation in which soldiers, often individually and without officers
present, searched civilian residences for food, it was unavoidable that some
bluecoats would avail themselves of the opportunity for plunder. When the
24th Indiana passed through Rocky Springs, Israel Ritter noticed that "a
crowd was gathering up the articles" at several stores. He helped himself to
"a couple of books and some secesh envelops."[22] McPherson had an order
read in all of his regiments, "forbidding pilfering robing or the destroying

of citizens property under heavy penalties in case of detection."[23] McClernand tried to suppress plundering by holding regimental officers responsible for their men's actions. On May 5, he arrested Cowan, of McPherson's
corps, "for not arresting a man for pillaging a house a few days ago." The
major was released the next day.[24] The generals' efforts probably helped a
little but could never be completely effective.

Although all of the soldiers relied on foraging for a substantial part of
their diet, by no means all of them were inclined to pillaging. Some had
very different ideas on how to use Mississippians' property. When soldiers
of the Thirteenth Corps in Cayuga, Mississippi, found a church building
unused on Sunday, May 10, they went in and held services. Isaac Jackson of
the 83rd Ohio was passing on his way back from drawing water when he
was surprised to hear singing coming from the building. Entering, he found
the hall packed with men in uniform. A chaplain preached, taking his text
from the book of Hebrews, twelfth chapter and second verse—"Looking
unto Jesus, the Author and Finisher of our faith . . ."[25]

Throughout the mundane daily concerns of getting enough to eat and
water to drink—cool if possible—and hoping, usually in vain, that the next
day's march would not be too hot or too dusty, the soldiers remained
intensely aware that they were making history. By May 5, Grant's army had
"performed the hardest march, and the best one that has been done in the
war," wrote Cowan proudly to his daughter back in Warren, Illinois. "We
have marched about ninety miles in eight days, through rain, mud, dust, the
hottest kind of weather, without tents to lie in and on short rations, foraging and subsisting the men in a great measure on the country. But the men
have stood it remarkable well."[26]

An example of one of the men standing the hard campaigning was John
Barney, whose 29th Wisconsin had squared off at point-blank range against
Cockrell's Missourians at Port Gibson. "We *thrashed* them *good* and are still
after them to give them another one," he wrote to "all at Home" back in
Hartford, Wisconsin, several days after the battle. "I hope we shall be kept
on the move until this war ends be it one year or three."[27] Like his comrades
throughout the Army of the Tennessee, Barney's drive to be moving on
and to "thrash" the Rebels stemmed not from a thirst for military glory but
from an intense longing to finish an unpleasant job that needed to be done
and then to return to his home. Just before the campaign started, John,
whose brother William was a member of the same regiment, had also written to "all at Home," urging them not to worry. Some of the soldiers were
bound to survive the war and get back home again, "and perhaps Wm and I
are among that number, at any rate it is no worse for us to die than anyone

else." On a more hopeful note he added, "I expect to go back to Hartford with Wm yet and hold plow."[28]

By May 12, McClernand's corps was encountering solid Confederate resistance along Fourteenmile Creek, about five miles south of Edwards Station, a small town on the railroad between Jackson and Vicksburg.[29] McPherson, marching on a roughly parallel road a half dozen miles to the southeast, set out that day to cover the eleven miles from the Roach farm, where water was available in Tallahala Creek, to the village of Raymond, at which point water could be found in numerous wells. To avoid the heat of the day, the march began at 4:30 a.m.[30]

Like persistent mosquitoes, Confederate skirmishers swarmed in front of the column but were brushed aside by the screening cavalry battalion. At the sound of the first shots, a soldier of the 20th Ohio, marching at the front of McPherson's infantry column, quipped, "Hello, somebody is shooting squirrels." A cascade of further shots prompted one of his comrades to remark dryly, "The squirrels are shooting back."[31]

By midmorning the heat and dust had already grown oppressive. The troops marched "through dust that came to the shoe top," wrote Maj. Samuel Byers of the 5th Iowa. "The atmosphere was yellow with it."[32] The separate brigades and divisions of the column deliberately lengthened the intervals between themselves in order to minimize the amount of one another's dust they had to eat.[33]

Out in front of the column, the Rebel skirmishers' resistance stiffened to the point that the cavalry could no longer drive them. Logan responded by ordering Brig. Gen. Elias S. Dennis, commanding his lead brigade, to shake out a line of infantry skirmishers and move those loitering Rebels along. Dennis called on the 20th Ohio and 30th Illinois. Col. Manning F. Force deployed his Ohioans in open order on the right of the road, while on the left of the road Lt. Col. William C. Rhodes directed a similar movement of his 30th Illinois, veterans of Belmont and many fights since.[34]

Forming the skirmish line was no easy task. "The road lay through the very thickest kind of woods," recalled a member of the regiment. Visibility was less than five yards, and deploying the regiment in skirmish line took half an hour. When that task was complete, the line stretched three-quarters of a mile, and none of the men could see more than three of his comrades. "It was enough to make a parson swear," wrote Ohioan Henry Dwight, "when the bugles sounded forward, and that huge line had to try to keep some sort of an alignment." Sometimes the Rebels in front seemed to be the least of their worries. Through tangles of thorny vines and over massive fallen tree trunks, the skirmish line struggled forward, occasionally fragmenting as rough terrain and poor visibility misdirected one or another of its segments. "Then," Lieutenant Dwight recalled, "there would be a great expense of time, breath and strong language, in trying to get the ends of the broken line together."[35]

Dwight thought they must have clawed their way through the woods for two hours, though it was probably not that long, and he and his comrades were feeling impatient with the cavalrymen for prompting the deployment, something he thought was like sending a "town meeting into a raspberry patch to catch a chipmunk." Some astute officer—Dwight thought it was Logan, his division commander—realized that the long skirmish line was impractical and had it reduced to a few companies while the rest of the regiments filed along on the road behind.[36]

It seemed like noon to the men of the skirmish companies when they finally emerged into an open field. Those who had not been crawling through the briars thought it was more like ten o'clock. The skirmishers crossed the field, followed by the rest of Dennis's brigade, climbed a fence, and entered the woods beyond. Capt. Samuel De Golyer's 8th Michigan Battery, which was attached to Dennis's brigade, halted in the road nearby. McPherson sent orders for the captain to place one of his three two-gun sections in battery, aimed up the road. Still, the threat did not seem severe, and De Golyer availed himself of this prime opportunity to water his horses in Fourteenmile Creek, which lay a few yards inside the woods. Logan seemed less concerned than his superior and quite comfortable with his division's relaxed state of readiness, since Dwight saw him dismounted quite close by, "over in the road," and, as Dwight thought, "getting ready for lunch."[37]

Back on the ridge in the open field to the rear, McPherson weighed the reports his scouts had brought him and peered through field glasses toward the far ridgeline. He decided that Confederates in division strength were apparently planning to contest his advance at the next ridge beyond the valley of Fourteenmile Creek, perhaps a mile and a half this side of Raymond. To fulfill his orders from Grant to occupy Raymond that day, McPherson figured he would have to push these Rebels aside and for that task he would need all of Logan's division with Crocker's in close support. He gave orders to move the wagon trains out of the road and pass the infantry to the front on the double.[38]

Since Dennis's brigade was already in position for the anticipated advance toward Raymond, his men had nothing to do but wait for the rest of the division and corps to come up. The woods in which the men of the 20th Ohio now found themselves were free of underbrush and far more open and pleasant than those they had recently traversed. The ground on the south, or near, bank of the creek was covered with grass and clover instead of briars, though moderate underbrush grew on the far side. Fourteenmile Creek itself was about a dozen yards wide but scarcely that many inches deep in most places. It flowed through a winding bed with steep banks four or five feet high in most places, higher in some. The town of Raymond lay about two miles farther up the road.[39]

Dennis's infantrymen remained skeptical about the presence of any significant Confederate force in front of them. They stacked arms and sprawled out on the shady grass, as Dwight recalled, "grumbling, chaffing, munching hard tack, or making fires to boil coffee in their tin cups." Some removed their shoes and socks and washed their hot feet in the waters of Fourteenmile Creek, while here and there a squad gathered for a game of euchre. Company cooks got busy fixing lunch. A few even strolled off to the skirmish line or over to the road, to see if they could find out what had spooked their cavalry and occasioned their unpleasant morning of clawing through the thickets. "The whole country was still with the stillness which you only see at nooning after a hard day's work in the fields." Dwight remembered listening to a mockingbird and watching a squirrel climbing along the trunk of a dead tree.[40]

The bird, the squirrel, Dwight, and several hundred of his blue-clad comrades suddenly jumped at the sound of a cannon shot several hundred yards away, followed in quick succession by several more. A Confederate battery began lobbing shells over the woods and into the field beyond. De Golyer's guns answered immediately. As the first salvo crashed out, the heavy white clouds of powder smoke from the discharge of the guns billowed out and hung near the ground, held down by a meteorological phenomenon known (today) as an inversion layer. Guns and gunners were soon invisible in their own sulfurous atmosphere. At the same time, the muzzle blast of the guns kicked up roiling clouds of yellow dust, thickening the murk around the battery. Conditions were definitely not favorable for accurate artillery fire.[41]

Dennis's infantrymen were still clutching their coffee cups or grabbing for footwear when "a crashing roar of musketry" erupted from the woods on the other side of the creek, felling dozens of Federals—twenty or thirty in the 20th Ohio alone. On its heels rose the demoniac wail of the Rebel yell from a charging line of battle coming straight toward them.[42]

"Attention battalion," came the voice of Colonel Force above the din. "Take arms, forward march." Men dropped their tin cups, playing cards, or shoes, snatched their rifles from the stacks, and scrambled into line of battle, some of them barefoot. Moments earlier, Dennis, or perhaps Logan, had sensed the need for a stronger skirmish line, farther out, and had directed Force to move the 20th forward, but the Confederate onslaught had started before he could give the order. Now the Ohioans splashed through the creek and up the bank on the other side.[43]

On the left of the 20th, the 78th Ohio also snatched up its rifles but, not receiving an order to advance, remained on the south bank. On the 20th's right, John E. Smith's brigade, which had been in the field behind and started forward when the shelling began, hurried up to take position on the right of Dennis's brigade.[44]

Force's Buckeyes did not advance far. As they scrambled to the top of the bank on the far side of the stream, the Rebel battle line came crashing through the underbrush less than fifty yards away. The Ohioans quickly jumped back down behind the steep bank and, using the creek bed as a natural trench, opened fire on the charging Rebels. Loading and firing as fast as they could, they succeeded in stopping the onslaught.

The attackers, members of the renowned 7th Texas Regiment, remained in front of them in the underbrush, firing back and working their way gradually forward until they were only fifteen or twenty yards from the 20th's line. In some parts of the line, the fighting became hand-to-hand. Many of the dead and wounded had powder burns, indicating that they were hit at point-blank range. "They kept trying to pass through our fire, jumping up, pushing forward a step, and then falling back into the same place," recalled Dwight, "just as you may see a lot of dead leaves in a gale of wind, eddying to and fro under a bank, often rising up to fly away, but never able to advance a peg."[45]

To the left of the 20th Ohio's position in the creek bed, the 68th and 78th Ohio, the 30th Illinois, and De Golyer's battery fell back to the edge of the woods but successfully fought off Confederate efforts to take the guns.[46]

On the right, however, the situation remained murky. The regiments of Smith's brigade had reached the edge of the woods on the right-hand side of the road just after the cannonade opened. They halted and sent forward skirmishers to try to determine the Confederate position and how the brigade should be inserted. But the woods in this sector formed another tangled thicket, and before the skirmishers could get far at all, the Rebel yell sounded and, as one of Smith's soldiers recalled, "the timber was swarming with them."[47]

Smith's regiments plunged forward in an attempt to extend the line of Dennis's brigade and prevent it from being flanked. The underbrush was too thick, however, and the 45th and 124th Illinois lost their way and had to return to their starting point.[48] The 20th Illinois, on the far right of the line, penetrated only a few yards into the woods when it ran head-on into a Confederate battle line coming the other way and began a desperate struggle.[49]

"The battle was now fierce," wrote Sgt. Ira Blanchard, "almost hand to hand, so close were they, that some of our boys fixed their bayonets ready to stab them." Blanchard could see, only a few yards in front of the Union line, a continuous line of muzzle flashes through the brush, which marked the position of the Confederate line. Here it was the Rebels who had possession of the creek bed, much to their advantage. The Illinoisans crouched as low as they could and fired back.[50]

Commanding the 20th that day was Lt. Col. Evan Richards of Mt. Pleasant, Illinois. Richards ordered his men to drop back about fifteen yards and get behind the rail fence at the edge of the woods, hoping the rails might provide at least some scant protection. As they clambered over the fence, however, a number of the Illinoisans were shot, including Richards himself, who was killed instantly. Command of the regiment passed to Maj. Daniel Bradley of Champaign. From its new position, the 20th Illinois went on fighting. To Blanchard the determination of both sides suggested "a couple of bull dogs engaged in a death struggle."[51]

Allen Geer and at least one other member of the regiment did not hear Richards's order to move back to the fence. Seeing that his comrades had fallen back on either side, Geer turned to join them. He dashed back to a tree several yards to the rear and there paused to squeeze off a shot. As he did so, a bullet struck him in the neck. Bleeding profusely and noticing that the Rebels were closing in on the other side of his tree, Geer "prayed for mercy, life & victory," and staggered back toward the rest of the regiment. There, he "found our men behind the fence fighting like tigers." He gave his gun to a comrade, stuffed a handkerchief in his wound, and set off for the field hospital.[52]

On the left of Smith's brigade and near the center of the Union line, the 23rd Indiana was supposed to link up with Dennis's right but could find neither Dennis's brigade nor their own. The regiment struggled through the thick brush and finally reached Fourteenmile Creek, only to find that this stretch flowed through a bed some fifteen feet deep with near-vertical sides. As Lt. Col. William P. Davis dryly noted in his report, the regiment crossed this obstacle "with much difficulty." A few yards beyond the creek, Davis realized that his regiment was all alone and ordered a halt while he sent men to find out where the rest of the brigade was.[53]

Davis was still wondering about that when a Confederate line of battle appeared over the ridgeline fifty yards in front and came charging toward the lonely Hoosiers of the 23rd. The Confederates were launching their attacking units in succession from their right to their left. Thus the Rebel attackers here, the 3rd Tennessee, struck a few minutes after the 7th Texas had hit Dennis's line. The Tennesseeans fired a volley into the 23rd Indiana and then charged. The Hoosiers fired back, but in moments the attackers were on top of them. They had not even had time to fix bayonets. Desperately they clubbed their muskets and literally attempted to beat back the Rebels.[54]

It was no use. Smith believed they were outnumbered, and he was probably right. Both their flanks were in the air, and no sign of the rest of the brigade was to be seen. He gave the order to fall back. Retreating in good order would have been difficult under that much pressure. Once they reached the creek, with its high, steep banks, it was impossible, and the withdrawal became a stampede. Smith finally managed to re-form his regiment on the right of the 20th Illinois, well to the rear of his brush with the Confederates and at the opposite end of the brigade's line.[55]

Logan was at his fiery best, riding his lines, energetically bolstering his troops' fighting spirit. At the beginning of the battle, he drew an unmarked cloak over his uniform in order to conceal his rank from Rebel marksmen. As he rode along the line, Ira Blanchard heard him shouting to some wavering troops, "For God's sake men, don't disgrace your country." Then pointing to other troops who were standing firm, he added, "See how they're holding them!"[56] Several members of the 20th Ohio spotted him riding to rally the 23rd Indiana on their right, and one described him as giving "the shriek of an eagle."[57]

The 20th Ohio was able to hang on alone in its advanced position near the center of the line due partially to the inspiration of Logan, partially to the tenacity of its soldiers, and a great deal to the fact that this section of creek bed was an ideal trench. Its meanders prevented Confederate troops who gained the regiment's flank from enfilading it and at the same time allowed Ohio soldiers on the curves to face toward their tormentors on the flank.[58]

Also, as Sgt. Osborn Oldroyd pointed out, it helped to know that they had no choice. "We had behind us a bank seven feet high—made slippery by the wading and climbing back of the wounded." If they retreated, they would have to scramble up that muddy bank with the enemy only a few feet away, firing directly into them. If the Ohioans could not hold the forward bank of the streambed, a great many of them were going to die.[59]

Pressure from the 7th Texas was still intense. The Buckeyes clung desperately to the creek bank, "digging our toes into the ground for fear that the mass of men in front would push us back over the bank after all," Dwight recalled.[60] Colonel Force noticed bits and pieces of leaves, cut by passing bullets, falling almost like green snow.[61]

Dwight saw a Texas officer ten yards away calmly loading his meerschaum pipe while his revolver hung by a strap from his wrist. Once he had the pipe drawing well, the Rebel clamped it in his mouth, gripped his revolver, "and went on popping away at us as leisurely as if he had been shooting rats." Dwight later explained how this could happen without the Texan's being shot. "The fact is when you start to draw a bead on any chap in such a fight you have got to make up your mind mighty quick who you'll shoot. There are so many on the other side that look as if they were just getting a bead on you that it takes a lot of nerve to stick to the one you first wanted to attend to. You generally feel like trying to kind of distribute your bullet so as to take in all who ought to be hit."[62] On the other hand, Osborn Oldroyd spotted a Texan wearing a red shirt and heard one of his comrades say as he raised his rifle, "See me bring that red shirt down." One of the other Ohioans yelled, "Hold on, that is my man." Both fired simultaneously, and the red-shirted Texan fell.[63]

The danger was real enough on both sides. About one in four members of the 20th Ohio was hit by the Texans' fire, and they gave about as good as they got. Command of Company C, 20th Ohio, devolved finally on a private.[64] Fourteenmile Creek ran red.[65]

While he rode along the line rallying his men, Logan sent his staff officers galloping back along the column to bring up the rest of the division as rapidly as possible.[66] McPherson did the same, and one of his staff officers found the 8th Illinois, which had that day been detailed to guard the division's ammunition train. The staff officer told them to see that the wagons were parked off the road and then come on at the double-quick. "We was needed Bad," wrote James Jessee in his diary.[67]

As the 8th approached the scene of the fighting, Logan himself met them, and "told us to hurry up for God sake," wrote Jessee; he "was some excited." Logan directed the 8th to the far right of his line, where increasing Confederate pressure threatened to overwhelm the 20th Illinois. The 8th passed through the line of the 20th and charged into the brush. The Rebel line broke in front of them, and the Illinoisans drove the Confederates for more than 200 yards. There the 8th stopped to regroup while the Rebels continued their flight. Jessee and his comrades in the 8th believed their regiment's "charge turned the fortune of the day in our favor."[68]

The 8th had done well, but a number of regiments entered the fight during this phase of the battle, and it was the cumulative effect of their arrival, along with the stout fighting of Dennis's and Smith's brigades, that finally turned back the Confederate attack. McPherson positioned several regiments of Brig. Gen. John D. Stevenson's brigade facing east, ready to repel a Rebel flanking column that scouts warned him was on the way. So effective was this deployment that when the Confederate skirmishers reached the edge of the open field and saw Stevenson's front facing toward them, the commander of the flanking column gave up the attack and withdrew as rapidly as possible.[69]

With the threat to his flank removed, McPherson was free to use Stevenson's regiments to reinforce his line along Fourteenmile Creek. Shortly thereafter, Col. John B. Sanborn's brigade, lead unit of Crocker's division, also came up and joined the fray. Like the 8th Illinois, Sanborn's men had double-quicked to the battlefield, assured by their officers that the troops at the front "never had more need of us." Edward Stanfield of the 48th Indiana concluded that the brigade's deployment had convinced the Rebels to retreat.[70] Like Jessee, he was partially right. The Confederate line along the creek, already strained to the utmost, finally began to give way under the increased weight of Union numbers.[71]

The hard-pressed 20th Ohio, still fighting for the creek bed, heard the cheers of the new Union troops going into battle on either side of them. "Pretty soon we found the Rebs in front of us were edging off a bit," recalled Dwight. "Somehow we were not pressed so hard. The firing kept up, but the smoke did not puff into our mouths so much." As the distance between the opposing lines increased, the Ohioans found that for the first time during the battle they could hear the sounds of passing bullets. Finally the firing stopped altogether, and the dazed and powder-grimed Buckeyes could stand and stretch for the first time since the fight started. They could also try to rinse the taste of gunpowder out of their mouths. "The smoke had blackened our faces, our lips and our throats so far down that it took a week to get the last of it out," wrote Dwight. "The most dandified officer in the regiment looked like a coalheaver."[72]

Union forces followed the fleeing Rebels. The 20th Ohio advanced along with the rest, giving a cheer as they climbed out of the creek bed. Then they stepped carefully "over the ghastly pile of Texans" who had fallen in the fight. As they advanced out of the woods and into an open cornfield, Dwight spied lying on the ground the very meerschaum he had seen the Texas officer smoking with such sangfroid during the fight. He picked it up and began to smoke it himself.[73]

The advance continued through the town of Raymond and out the other side, where they deployed skirmishers and camped for the night.[74] Passing through the town itself, the troops found a sumptuous picnic laid out on tables beneath stately shade trees. The ladies of Raymond had prepared the repast as a victory meal for the Confederates of Brig. Gen. John Gregg's brigade. As events had developed during the course of the day, victory had eluded Gregg's men, and pressing circumstances had made it inconvenient for them to stop and enjoy the ladies' hospitality while passing rapidly through town in the late afternoon. The men of Logan's division, arriving a few minutes later, made sure none of the food went to waste.[75]

The Battle of Raymond was as confused a fight as the Army of the Tennessee would ever experience. The Confederate commander, Gregg, had only a large brigade, but he had believed, on the basis of a previous false assessment by Pemberton, that the Union column approaching Raymond was a small flank guard to the main column, with not more than a brigade of infantry. Gregg's brigade constituted at that time the primary part of the garrison of Jackson, Mississippi, and Pemberton had ordered him to launch out to the southwest and strike the presumed Union flank guard. Gregg's plan was to hit the Federals in front with the 7th Texas and 3rd Tennessee, and send the rest of his brigade to flank the Union right. The 7th and 3rd were large regiments, about half again the size of the typical Union regiment, and they had fought with determination. What had given them their initial success was the rugged and confusing nature of the terrain, along with the element of surprise.

The 20th Ohio had absorbed almost the full weight of the Texans' attack, while the other regiments of Dennis's brigade fell back and escaped relatively unscathed. The 20th Ohio sustained 80 percent of the casualties suffered by Dennis's brigade, but its heroic stand in the bed of Fourteenmile Creek blunted one wing of the Confederate attack. The other half of the attack, the 3rd Tennessee, fell first on the 23rd Indiana and then on the 20th Illinois. Here the reason was the dense underbrush that prevented three of Smith's five regiments from entering the first phase of the fight and led to the situation in which two regiments fought alone and isolated from other units. Between them, the 20th and 23rd suffered almost 90 percent of the casualties inflicted on Smith's brigade. Total Union casualties came to 442. Confederate losses totaled 515.[76]

As long as the battle had been a contest between two large Confederate regiments and three smaller, and isolated, Union ones, numbers had been about equal and the struggle was a fierce and bloody deadlock. Once additional Union regiments marched up from the Seventeenth Corps's long column, or found their way through the underbrush to join the fight, it quickly became an unequal contest, and the Confederates had to take their leave.

Gregg's planned flanking attack was canceled in the face of the unexpected Union numerical superiority.

Raymond was not a masterpiece of tactics on any general's part—more of a confused collision in smoky thickets. The stubborn fighting of the soldiers in the lead regiments was the decisive factor, preventing the Confederate attack from knocking over Union regiments in succession along the column, like a row of falling dominoes. The stand of about 1,000 Buckeyes, Hoosiers, and Illinoisans provided the time for the rest of the corps to come forward to support them and eventually achieve victory.

Grant rode with Sherman that day and camped that evening at the Dillon Plantation, seven miles west of Raymond. There he received McPherson's message notifying him of the fight. It was obvious that the Confederate attackers had come from Jackson, and this fact emphasized the danger of allowing the Rebels to maintain a base of operations there, only fifty miles from Vicksburg. Besides being a potential sally port for strikes like the one at Raymond, Jackson was also a key railroad nexus and conduit for most of the supplies that reached Vicksburg from the rest of the Confederacy.

Furthermore, Grant had intelligence that Confederate reinforcements were on the way to Jackson, along with the Confederacy's Western theater commander (Pemberton's superior), Gen. Joseph E. Johnston. Johnston with a sizable army in Jackson would threaten Grant's flank and rear as he attacked Pemberton at Edwards Station and then, if successful, turned to the west against Vicksburg. Pemberton, in theory, would pose the same sort of flank threat should Grant move against Jackson, but Grant was already taking the measure of Pemberton and believed he had little to fear from the Confederate commander at Vicksburg. On the other hand, Grant, like many others who had known Johnston in the Old Army, respected his reputation as a general. Taking these factors into consideration, he made the supremely audacious decision to turn away from Pemberton and toward Jackson, further stretching his already tenuous supply line and pushing even deeper into enemy territory.[77]

That same evening, Grant sent orders to all three of his corps commanders, directing a feint toward Pemberton's force at Edwards Station and then a turn toward Jackson. Sherman was to bring his Fifteenth Corps up from its reserve position to join McPherson in leading the advance, while McClernand, whose corps was closest to the Rebels at Edwards Station, would handle the feint and then bring up the rear in the march on Jackson.[78]

As the various elements of the army marched the next morning, the men noticed with surprise that their columns took roads that led not northward, as their general direction had been the day before, but rather west. A march of eight miles brought McPherson's corps to the town of Clinton, Mississippi. Crocker's division led the way, spelling Logan's after its fight of the previous day. One of Crocker's soldiers wrote that they were "expecting a fight every mile," but the Confederates made no serious challenge to the advance—nothing the cavalry could not brush aside with ease. The day was hot, sunny, and dusty, like the previous five days. Isaac Vanderwarker of the 4th Minnesota noted that the countryside was full of prosperous-looking farms and plantations but the people were "not very cordial" except for the blacks, who always received the Union soldiers joyfully.[79]

Clinton lay on the line of the Southern Railroad of Mississippi, about ten miles west and a bit north of Jackson and eighteen miles east of Edwards Station. Vicksburg lay another twenty-two miles to the west of Edwards along the same tracks. "As we passed through town," recalled John Campbell of the 5th Iowa, "the inhabitants—men, women, and children—turned out to see the first yankee troops that had ever visited their quiet burgh."[80] McPherson had no sooner arrived in Clinton than he put his men to work tearing up the tracks, breaking for the first time the railroad connection between Vicksburg and the rest of the Confederacy. By that evening, Sherman was at Mississippi Springs, about ten miles southwest of Jackson and seven from Clinton. On Grant's orders the two prepared to advance toward Jackson the next day, keeping in communication by couriers who would crisscross the open country between their converging roads.[81]

The night of May 13 brought heavy rains to the parched Mississippi countryside, saturating it with amazing speed and transforming the roads from ankle-deep dust to even deeper mud. The rains continued the following morning as the Fifteenth and Seventeenth corps set out for Jackson along their separate roads before 6:00 a.m. Along Sherman's line of march, the road was in places covered with a foot or more of water, but the soldiers splashed on cheerfully. Morale was high that morning among the troops approaching Jackson, "that long talked of city towards which we had been going since the evacuation of Corinth," Edward Stanfield explained in a letter to his father back in Indiana. "And now that we were but 10 miles from it you may believe we were in high spirits."[82]

The men of the 8th Illinois noticed ladies standing in the doors and at the windows of the houses they marched by in the downpour. Some of the Southern ladies shouted taunts about the whipping the Yankees were going to get at Jackson, but "the Boys took it fine," one of the Illinoisans recorded in his diary, and marched along singing patriotic songs for the ladies' benefit.[83]

Rain was still falling heavily, accompanied by thunder and lightning, when at 9:30 a.m. the 5th Minnesota, skirmishing in front of McPherson's column, made contact with the enemy about two miles outside of Jackson. While the Minnesotans traded shots with the Rebels, men joked along the sodden column that they had finally "found the confederacy." They stood for about five minutes waiting for orders in the pouring rain and then received directions to deploy into line of battle in the plowed fields on either side of the road. Confederate artillery opened on them, and despite the veil of rapidly falling rain, "the solid shot and shell dropped around rather lively," Stanfield wrote. The officers had their men lie down in the muddy fields while the skirmishers pressed forward to probe the enemy positions. The thunderstorm raged over them with such violence that men had difficulty telling the discharges of nearby cannon from the peals of thunder, which seemed to come constantly.[84]

Some units in both Crocker's and Logan's divisions had to deal with a special problem, more vexing in its own way than the rain, mud, thunder, lightning, or even the Rebel artillery. Angry bees bedeviled both Smith's brigade of Logan's division and Sanborn's brigade of Crocker's. The story in the 48th Indiana was that some sweet-toothed Hoosier had raided a bee-hive and then run back to the ranks with the whole colony of bees in pursuit. In the 45th Illinois, however, Wilbur Crummer heard that stray bullets had struck the hives, disturbing the insects. "Men can stand up and be shot at all day with the deadly musket," Crummer explained, "but when a swarm of bees pounces upon a company of men in concert, it's beyond human nature to stand it." After some delay and much vexation, the affected regiments succeeded in forming their ranks—with the lines displaced so as to give a wide berth to the angry bees.[85]

Two miles to the south, Sherman's men heard the thump of artillery coming from McPherson's front. Almost simultaneously they encountered Confederate artillery fire on their own front. As McClernand's men were doing on the Clinton Road, Sherman's troops prepared to give battle. Brig. Gen. James M. Tuttle's division deployed in front of the Confederate works, with Brig. Gen. Joseph "the Wolf" Mower's Eagle Brigade on the left and Brig. Gen. Charles L. Matthies's brigade of Iowans on the right. Brig. Gen. Ralph P. Buckland's brigade followed in reserve. Tuttle's artillery, two batteries totaling twelve guns, wheeled into battery and opened fire.[86]

After a pause for the heaviest of the rain to spend itself, McPherson's and Sherman's troops pushed forward as planned, aligned with each other, as they closed in on Jackson by converging roads.[87] McPherson's advance came to a dramatic climax. "We advanced from one hollow to another until within half a mile of the rebs," wrote Stanfield. "Then we were ordered to charge double quick which we did with a Hoosier yell."[88] Linus Parrish of the 17th Iowa recalled how he and his comrades charged forward with fixed bayonets and "a yell like Indians."[89] The advancing line of blue-clad soldiers was an inspiring spectacle. Out on the far left flank, a soldier of the 93rd Illinois thought it "a sight beyond description."[90]

McPherson's flanks overlapped the short Confederate line it faced. His troops surged around both ends of the defenders' line and routed them after a short, sharp fight. Despite the brevity of the fight, there were losses. As the 17th Iowa charged along the Vicksburg-Jackson Road, Rebel gunners loosed a blast of double canister that toppled eighteen or twenty of the Iowans.[91] With the battery captured and the Rebels in headlong flight toward Jackson, the survivors of the 17th gathered around the regimental colors and sang "Rally Round the Flag." "I never heard it sung before nor since when it sounded so well nor so appropriate," recalled Parrish years later. He hoped the fleeing Rebels had heard the singing. The 17th had lost eighty men killed or wounded in the fight, 27 percent of the Union total.[92]

On Sherman's front, where Grant again rode with his favorite subordinate, Union artillery pounded the Rebels. Grant personally helped direct the 95th Ohio into a flanking position to which Sherman had dispatched it.[93] Tactical niceties were hardly necessary, however, in view of the weakness of the Rebel line. Mower rode forward a short distance and then trotted back, telling his men and those of neighboring regiments, "Boys, we can take those works and not half try." Minutes later his and Matthies's brigades swept forward, "and the yell that those wet Northern boys gave was enough to scare even the ghosts of the Southern Confederacy," wrote an Iowa soldier. Another Iowan reported that the defenders ran before the attacking line actually came within rifle range.[94] "The rebels licked," an Illinois soldier wrote in his diary that night, "running as usual or captured."[95]

Johnston had arrived at Jackson the day before. Reinforcements had brought total numbers there to 6,000 men, and Johnston had hope of that many more within the next twenty-four hours or so. Well before dawn on May 14, and well before any of Grant's troops made contact with his outlying scouts, Johnston had decided that Jackson must be evacuated. The fight later that morning was simply a rearguard action to cover the Confederate retreat.[96]

None of that mattered much to Grant and his men. For the second time in three days, they had met the Rebels and the graycoats had fled, leaving guns, flags, and, in this case, the capital city of Mississippi as the spoils of the victors. Johnston's army was dispersed and displaced and would be a long time recovering enough to think of taking the initiative. Grant was free to neutralize the Confederacy's supply and transportation hub in Mississippi and then turn toward Vicksburg at last. For a third time in the campaign, his forces had enjoyed an overwhelming numerical superiority in a battle, even though the Confederate troops in Mississippi still outnumbered his army. Once again, Grant's generalship had proven dazzlingly superior. "It was a grand victory," wrote James Jessee in his diary that night, before adding an astute assessment of the campaign: "Our movements have been made so rapid and with such determination that the rebels have been perfectly confounded. They could not anticipate where we was going to strike nor when & consequently could not reinforce any place. I think Gen. Grant will wake them up in a good many places."[97]

Grant's men marched triumphantly into Jackson and raised "an enormous cheer as they took possession of the capitol."[98] Soon the United States flag of the 59th Indiana was waving over the statehouse.[99] Sherman assigned the Eagle Brigade as provost guard for the brief expected duration of the army's stay in Jackson, with responsibility for destroying the large amount of Confederate quartermaster stores and cotton, as well as factories and railroads. Not all the soldiers' duties were destructive. The Rebels in their retreat set fire to large amounts of food, which Mower's men and other Union soldiers worked hard and for the most part successfully to save.[100] The troops enjoyed an abundance of peanuts, cornmeal, tobacco, and whiskey that the Confederates had left behind in Jackson, though Edward Stanfield complained that the whiskey was of very poor quality.[101]

In the work of destruction, the Eagle Brigade had the assistance of numerous other Union troops also assigned to the task. The men tore up railroads, heated and bent the rails, burned bridges, and "destroyed almost all the public buildings," as an officer of the 76th Ohio recalled.[102] Among the structures consigned to the flames were an iron foundry, an arsenal, railroad depots, and various factories that produced war supplies. Grant and Sherman visited a textile mill where the workers were keeping their looms running apace, manufacturing tent cloth out of cotton, apparently unmindful that the city had changed hands. Manager and operatives, most of whom were young women, paid no attention to the two generals who stood quietly watching the proceedings. On each bolt of tent cloth were the letters "C.S.A." After watching for a time, Grant commented to Sherman that he "thought they had done work enough." He had the employees sent home after allowing them to take as much cloth as they could carry, and then he had his men torch the factory.[103]

An incongruous addition to the list of destroyed buildings was a large hotel near the railroad depot. The owner begged Sherman to protect his hotel because he was a good Union man. Sherman observed dryly that he could tell that from the name of the hotel: Confederate House. The former name "United States House" had been painted over but could still be seen faintly under the word "Confederate." Still, Sherman assured the hotelier he had no particular intention of burning the place. Burn it did, however, to Sherman's surprise and apparently as an act of retaliation. More than a year earlier, as Union prisoners of war were being transported south after the Battle of Shiloh, the proprietor had refused to sell a meal to prisoners for U.S. currency and had also insulted the prisoners. Some of those prisoners had since been exchanged and were now back in the ranks of the army and determined to pay back the hotel owner in coin he would have to accept.[104] On the other hand, although some of the soldiers and perhaps local civilians looted stores, even the citizens of Jackson had to admit that private houses were neither plundered nor burned.[105]

One public building that was not destroyed was the statehouse itself. In the hall where Jefferson Davis had addressed Mississippi legislators five months before, a large assembly of soldiers elected themselves as a mock legislature for the state and carried on various preposterous proceedings. The most memorable of their acts was one providing for the ample payment of all Union soldiers with the abundant stocks of Confederate money found in the town. "If it had been worth anything we would have been rich," wrote Linus Parrish. Instead, some of the men used $500 or $1,000 bills to light their pipes or cigars.[106]

Grant, Sherman, and McPherson met for serious discussions that afternoon. The night before, Johnston had sent an order to Pemberton directing him to advance eastward and attack Grant, whom Johnston then believed to be at Clinton. Johnston would attempt to join him there so that the two could combine their forces. To make sure his subordinate received the message, Johnston had sent three different couriers, each carrying a copy. One of those couriers, unbeknownst to Johnston, was a Union spy and delivered the message to Grant instead of Pemberton. Armed with this information, Grant gave his corps commanders their orders for the next day. The key now was to prevent Johnston and the 12,000 men of the Jackson force from linking up with Pemberton. Therefore, while Sherman was to stay at Jackson until he had completed its destruction as a Confederate base and manufacturing center, McPherson would march west first thing in the morning to join McClernand in confronting Pemberton somewhere along the Southern Railroad of Mississippi. With arrangements complete, Grant then sought out quarters for the night and slept, as he was informed, in the same room Joe Johnston had occupied the night before.[107]

The soldiers made camp that evening—some of them in the capitol square—built fires, got supper, and tried to dry out. Many of the troops appropriated cotton bales, tore them open, and slept on soft beds of the valuable fiber. Their uniforms, however, most of them still damp when they turned in, carried a good bit of cotton with them when they rose next morning.[108]

Not everyone slept well. Sitting by the campfire at 2:00 a.m., surrounded by thousands of sleeping soldiers, Maj. Luther Cowan reflected on himself and the war. He now had temporary command of the 45th Illinois, the old Lead Mine Regiment, while its colonel and lieutenant colonel were absent sick. "I am so full of conflicting thoughts, emotions, and cares," he penned in his diary by the firelight. "Anxious for the future, grateful for the past, thankful that so many of us are able to stand the hardships of our hard marches and so favored as to escape wounds or death on the battlefield. So I sit here alone trying to think, hardly knowing whether I do or not. Hardly know whether it is Lute Cowan 'as went to war' or if it is some new being in some other world." He thought on that for a time and then decided that his continued "fidgety anxiety and multitude of cares" proved he was, after all, still "the same old Lute." His diary does not state whether he got any sleep that night, but at 5:00 a.m. he rode westward toward Vicksburg at the head of the Lead Mine Regiment.[109]

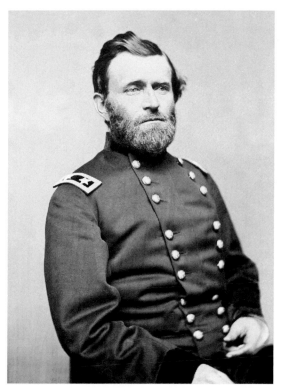

Ulysses S. Grant *(Library of Congress)*

Lew Wallace *(Library of Congress)*

John A. Rawlins *(National Archives)*

John A. McClernand *(Library of Congress)*

John A. Logan *(Library of Congress)*

John C. Frémont *(Library of Congress)*

Charles F. Smith *(Library of Congress)*

Henry W. Halleck *(Library of Congress)*

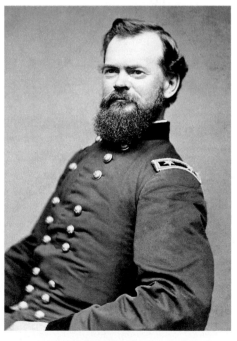

James B. McPherson *(Library of Congress)*

River gunboat *St. Louis*, later renamed *Baron de Kalb* (*National Archives*)

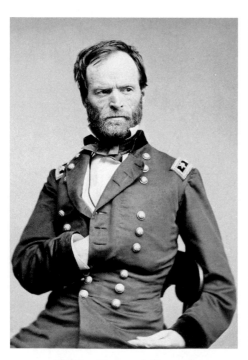

William Tecumseh Sherman
(*Library of Congress*)

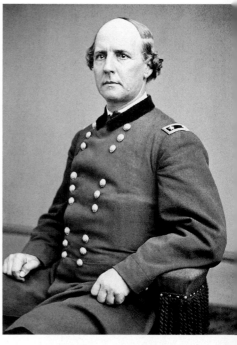

Stephen A. Hurlbut
(*Library of Congress*)

Andrew H. Foote *(National Archives)*

Benjamin M. Prentiss *(Library of Congress)*

Ralph P. Buckland *(Library of Congress)*

John McArthur *(Library of Congress)*

James M. Tuttle *(Library of Congress)*

Grenville M. Dodge *(Library of Congress)*

Alvin P. Hovey *(Library of Congress)*   Joseph A. Mower *(Library of Congress)*

David D. Porter *(Library of Congress)*

Giles A. Smith *(Library of Congress)*

A. J. Smith *(Library of Congress)*

CHAPTER TWENTY-ONE

Champion's Hill

McPHERSON AND McCLERNAND marched early on the morning of May 15. Skies were cloudy but no rain fell. The roads were drying—in most places—and the troops moved along at a lively pace.¹ The advance of the army camped that night near Bolton, Mississippi, on the railroad eighteen miles west of Jackson. Other columns were nearby on parallel roads.

Grant's forces were now in a position to block Pemberton from reaching Johnston's designated rendezvous point at Clinton. Still, Grant expected that Pemberton, whom he had known in the Old Army as a stickler about obeying orders, would try. Somewhere along this road they could expect to meet him. Grant rode over to McClernand's headquarters that evening to caution him to be on the lookout for Pemberton's approach during the next day's march and not to plunge into a battle unless he knew he could handle the Confederates in his front. He well knew McClernand's impetuosity and tendency to glory-hunting and did not want the politician-general to hurl the Thirteenth Corps into a fight with the whole of Pemberton's army just to ensure himself an inside track in a future presidential election.²

About five o'clock on the morning of May 16, Grant received intelligence that Pemberton was near Edwards Station with an army of about 25,000 men and marching toward him. Grant sent orders to Sherman to hurry his departure from Jackson so as to move up and support the other two corps. He ordered McPherson and McClernand to press forward toward Edwards Station and, presumably, the enemy.³

The Army of the Tennessee advanced westward along three parallel roads. The left, or southernmost, of these was the Raymond Road. On it marched A. J. Smith's division of the Thirteenth Corps followed by Frank Blair's division of the Fifteenth. (Blair's division was temporarily attached to the Thirteenth Corps.) In the center, on the appropriately named Middle Road, moved the divisions of Osterhaus and Carr, both of the Thirteenth Corps. McClernand also rode with this column.

On the right, or north, Alvin Hovey's division led the way out of Bolton that morning along the main Jackson Road. Though part of the Thirteenth Corps, Hovey was functioning this day as part of the Seventeenth. McPherson's two divisions followed close behind Hovey's, first that of John Logan and then that of Marcellus Crocker.[4] Grant and McPherson rode with the column on the Jackson Road. The Raymond and Jackson roads converged at Edwards Station. The Middle Road joined the Jackson Road about five miles east of Edwards. Hovey's division moved out on the Jackson Road at six o'clock, his troops in high spirits. As they marched, they apprehended a number of Rebel stragglers.[5]

A. J. Smith's skirmishers on the Raymond Road were the first to encounter Confederate pickets, about six miles east of Edwards Station. Minutes later, Osterhaus's men on the Middle Road also ran into Confederate resistance at roughly the same distance from Edwards. On the Jackson Road, where Hovey's division marched in the lead, the sound of firing to the south was followed quickly by the rattle of rifle and carbine fire from a patrol of the 1st Indiana Cavalry, riding just ahead of their own column. Sgt. Charles Longley of the 24th Iowa vividly remembered years later how the men around him looked at one another and blurted, "Did you hear that?"[6] The same sounds reached the camp of the 30th Illinois, part of Logan's division, two miles farther east. "They are pulling down a barn to build a bridge," one of the men guessed. "Yes," Capt. Lindsay Steele replied grimly, "that is a h———— of a barn."[7]

As Hovey's column continued forward on the Jackson Road, an elderly slave woman told the men of the 11th Indiana, Lew Wallace's old Zouave regiment, "Yes, sah—yes, sah, dars just thousands of them, thousands of 'em just on ahead dar." Hearing this, the Hoosiers let out a yell that was taken up well back in the column.[8] Within minutes, Hovey's skirmishers were hotly engaged. Clearly the Army of the Tennessee had located the main Confederate army in Mississippi.[9]

Grant was back in Clinton, and McPherson sent him word of the encounter with a suggestion that he come to the front. Grant was in the saddle by 7:30 and galloped west on the Jackson Road, ordering all wagon trains off the road as he went, so that the right-of-way would be clear for infantry and artillery moving to the front. "Today we shall fight the battle for Vicksburg," he shouted to Col. John Sanborn as he rode past his brigade of the Seventeenth Corps.[10] By midmorning, when he arrived at the battlefield, the skirmishing on Hovey's front had grown intense.[11] Hovey's division was already deployed, and McPherson was deploying Logan's on

Hovey's right as rapidly as possible. Crocker's division hastened up the road to join them at the best speed it could make.

Confederate counsels were far more confused than Grant could well have imagined. After sending his unrealistic order to Pemberton, Johnston encamped a dozen miles north of Jackson and did nothing. Pemberton vacillated from his own ideas, to plans urged on him by his fractious subordinates, to occasional impulses to try to obey Johnston's orders, and in the process moved his army haltingly first one way and then another. Pemberton was no fool, but Grant had by this time gained a complete mental advantage over him, winning the battle of minds before the clash of armies had reached its climax. Like a grand master of chess playing an outclassed opponent, Grant left Pemberton dazed and confused, wondering which move had been his great blunder when, in fact, in the face of the master's brilliant play, each of the loser's moves had been a worse blunder than the one before.

At the moment the Army of the Tennessee encountered him six miles east of Edwards Station, Pemberton was in the midst of yet another change of plan, abandoning the idea of marching east and striking the Army of the Tennessee from behind while it engaged the Confederates at Jackson. Pemberton now adopted a program of swinging north of Jackson to try to join forces with Johnston. The road grid being what it was, this new undertaking entailed about-facing and marching back to Edwards Station, whence a road angled northeast toward Johnston's supposed position. While Pemberton's teamsters were at work getting his 400-wagon supply train turned around and started back westward, Grant's skirmishers began to press against the Confederate outposts on the Jackson, Middle, and Raymond roads. Reluctantly, Pemberton realized he was not going to have the luxury of making and changing any more plans but was going to have to fight it out with Grant and the Army of the Tennessee right here and now.[12]

From Pemberton's perspective, the situation could have been worse. Only on the Jackson Road did the Federals show any disposition at all to take the fight to him. The Union columns on the Middle and Raymond roads were studies in passivity. Grant had in fact sent orders for McClernand to attack, but the courier, a member of McClernand's own staff, took the long way around instead of riding cross-country and thus did not deliver the message until midafternoon. In the meantime, McClernand, perversely misconstruing Grant's instructions not to start a battle, stubbornly refused to attack without further express orders from Grant. The divisions of his command—over half the force Grant had available—sat idly by while McPherson's three divisions fought the battle. The key to the battle, then, would be how fast Pemberton would realize that he had nothing to fear on his right and center and how quickly and completely he would succeed in shifting his forces to concentrate against Grant's column on his left.[13]

Grant and McPherson naturally knew none of this as they hurried to get Hovey's and Logan's divisions deployed and launched against the Confederates in their front. The lay of the local roads and ridges dictated the form of the battlefield in front of them. Some 1,500 yards before it reached the Confederate position, the Jackson Road curved from west to south. About 800 yards beyond the Confederate lines that Grant and McPherson could see in front of them, the Jackson Road met the Middle Road and at that point bent abruptly ninety degrees to the right, changing course from south back to west. Thus on a map, it could appear almost as if the Jackson Road were joining the Middle Road, rather than the other way around. At the same crossroads, the Ratliff Road came up from the south and joined the Jackson Road, connecting it to the Raymond Road. A man standing at the crossroads would see a four-way intersection, with the Jackson Road to the north and to the west, the Middle Road to the east, and the Ratliff Road to the south.

This network lay atop a formation of ridges that might, for purposes of the battle, be thought of as resembling a backward uppercase letter F. The long vertical stroke of the F was Ratliff Ridge, which ran north and south (not a precise compass bearing, but close enough). South of the crossroads, the Ratliff Road occupied the top of this ridge. North of the crossroads, the Jackson Road ran along the crest. The middle stroke of the F (running to the left rather than the right, since this F is to be backward) was Austin Ridge. The crossroads lay where Austin Ridge joined the long north-south spine of Ratliff Ridge. From that point, the Jackson Road proceeded westward along the crest of Austin Ridge. Finally, the upper stroke of this backward F is another ridge running west from the north end of the Ratliff Ridge. After the battle, some came to call this last ridge Lee's Ridge, after Confederate Brig. Gen. Stephen D. Lee, whose brigade fought there.

All the battlefield ridges were generally higher at their north and east ends and sloped downward along their crests toward their south and west ends. Where the north end of Ratliff Ridge met the east end of Lee's Ridge lay the high point of both, an eminence known as Champion's Hill (named for the local landowner), which rose about 140 feet above most of the surrounding terrain. Farmer Champion's house stood beside the Jackson Road about three-quarters of a mile north of the hill.

West of the battlefield lay Baker's Creek. Surging bank-full after the recent heavy rains, the creek could not be forded. Because high water had washed out the bridge on the Raymond Road, the only remaining crossing was the bridge on the Jackson Road, 3,300 yards west of the crossroads. The presence of Baker's Creek, well above fording stage, raised the stakes in the coming battle. Pemberton would be fighting with that raging torrent at his back.[14]

Pemberton's line initially ran along Ratliff Ridge from a point south of the Raymond Road all the way north to Champion's Hill, where Lee's Alabama brigade anchored the Rebel flank. The whole line faced east, the direction from which Pemberton expected Grant to advance. When Lee's outpost on the Jackson Road alerted him of the enemy's approach directly against his and the army's left flank, Lee shifted his brigade to Lee's Ridge, facing north now, toward Grant and the deploying divisions of Hovey and Logan. Lee's skirmishers began to exchange fire with those of Hovey.

Once Hovey's division was in position on the north slope of Champion's Hill, there was nothing for them to do but lie there in line of battle, waiting for Logan's division to complete its deployment. The lower slopes of the hill were cleared, but the upper slopes were heavily wooded. Just to the left of the Jackson Road, Lt. T. J. Williams of the 56th Ohio, part of Col. James R. Slack's brigade, listened to the bullets pattering against the ground around him and gazed uphill, into the woods, without being able to spot the enemy. During this "time of watchful foreboding," Williams saw Capt. John Cook, commander of another company of the 56th, walking up the line. Cook had been too sick to march lately and had been riding in an ambulance. The captain of Williams's company tried to talk Cook into going back to the rear, but he stubbornly replied, "I am going in with the boys if it is the last thing I ever do."[15]

Nearby, the 24th Iowa likewise sweated out the tense minutes before going into battle. "There were jokes and laughter," recalled Sergeant Longley, "—no one is going to blanch and advertise it—but the jokes were not able bodied nor the laughter natural." Other men gave each other messages to be conveyed to their loved ones if they should fall, or penned such messages themselves.[16]

Logan's men were sweating out the morning in a different way. Loaded with their equipment, they double-quicked up the road to reach the battlefield. The weather, as a soldier of the 31st Illinois described it, was "dense and hot," but the men were experienced enough by now to know that more sweat and fatigue now might well translate into saved lives later, if they could thereby gain an advantage on the Rebels. Thanks to Grant's order,

Hovey's wagon train was not an impediment. Teamsters and wagon guards had already jammed the vehicles against the trees that lined the way, and Logan's men had open road in front of them. By this time the skirmish fight between Hovey and the Rebels was getting noisy, and the sound of heavy firing as well as the "wild Confederate yell" spurred Logan's troops to greater speed as they loped toward their assigned places in line.[17]

Meanwhile, Grant deployed four batteries of artillery and pounded the Rebels along Lee's Ridge. Presently more Confederates joined Lee's brigade atop the ridge. Maj. Gen. Carter L. Stevenson sent two more brigades of his division to the aid of the sorely threatened Alabamians. The new brigades, both composed of Georgia troops, moved up—Brig. Gen. Alfred Cumming's on Lee's right, atop Champion's Hill, and Brig. Gen. Seth Barton's on Lee's left, occupying the lower end of Lee's Ridge.[18]

By this time, some of Logan's skirmishers had reached the crest of the ridge west of Lee's line. Barton's Georgians easily pushed them back, but overestimating the extent of their success, Barton's men charged down the north face of the ridge in pursuit. The four Union batteries and the rifles of Logan's division pounded them. James Jessee of the 8th Illinois noted that they got within forty yards of one of the more advanced batteries but were "mowed down like grain" by the combined effect of canister and rifle fire. The survivors retreated to the crest of Lee's Ridge, where they regrouped and assumed their intended position extending the left of Lee's line.[19]

McPherson ordered Brig. Gen. John D. Stevenson's brigade of Logan's division to advance at the double-quick and take up a position in a patch of woods on the right of Logan's line. From that ground, Stevenson's men could pour an enfilading fire into any Confederates who tried to repeat Barton's attack and, at the same time, were poised to launch an attack of their own with good prospects of flanking the Georgians on Lee's Ridge.[20]

As unlikely as it might have seemed, minutes later a Confederate force did advance. Lee thought he saw a gap in the Union line and an opportunity to snatch one of the batteries that had been pounding his men, and he dispatched the 23rd Alabama to do so. Seeing a Rebel column beginning to march down from the crest of the ridge, Maj. C. J. Stolbrand, Logan's German-born chief of artillery, galloped up to John E. Smith. "Sheneral Schmidt, dey are sharging you mitt doubled column," Stolbrand cried. "They vant mine guns."

"Let 'em come," roared Smith, "we're ready to receive them." Then, "Fix bayonets." His brigade obeyed and stood waiting expectantly. McPherson and Logan came riding down the line just then. The corps commander, at least, was on his way out to Stevenson's brigade, on the right flank. "Give them Jesse, boys," shouted the suave McPherson. "Give them Jesse."

Logan rose in the stirrups. "We are about to fight the battle for Vicksburg," he roared. "We must whip them here or all go under the sod together." As McPherson rode away, Smith paused, then shouted, "Forward—double quick—march," and the brigade surged forward to meet the advancing Rebels of the 23rd Alabama. Beset by flanking fire from some of Hovey's men on their right, hammered by the massed Union artillery, and suddenly faced with a massive charge, they turned and ran.[21]

Whether Smith gave that order on his own authority, or on Logan's, McPherson's, or Grant's, is unclear. McPherson was probably not its author, for he had by this time passed on to Stevenson's brigade, where he seemed bent on following quite a different program. One of Stevenson's soldiers noted in his diary that Smith's people started forward before Stevenson's brigade.[22]

Logan is the prime suspect for having launched the attack. He was with McPherson when the two of them visited Smith's brigade, but when McPherson rode on to the right to join Stevenson's brigade, Logan seems to have turned back toward the left brigade of his division.[23] A soldier of that brigade noted, "General Logan must have found some whiskey somewhere for he was quite silly for him." When a staff officer rode up and asked where he could be found during the battle, Logan replied, "Where the bullets fly the thickest, by G——d."

Then he rode along the brigade's line of battle thundering his exhortation to the men. "Boys, we have got work in front of us. The rascals are all there waiting for us. Now all we want to do is to get at them to make them 'git.' We always make them 'git' when we get at them. You won't have to go alone, I'm going down with you," he shouted, gesturing to the ravine that lay between them and Champion's Hill. "Now forward; double quick!" The men responded with a wild yell, brandishing their bayoneted rifles above their heads, and then started forward on a dead run.[24]

Meanwhile, McPherson reached Stevenson's brigade in the patch of woods out on the right flank and angling in front of the rest of the line. He wanted the men there to wait and let the Confederate regiment advance until it was directly opposite them and their flanking fire could rake down the length of it. With the enemy "in easy range and full view," however, the temptation was too great for some of Stevenson's men, and they fired without orders. All along the brigade's line other men were shouting, "Let us fire. Let us advance."[25]

According to Jessee, Smith's brigade began to advance just at this moment, and that was what finally forced McPherson to abandon his scheme of waiting to deliver a surprise flanking volley. He ordered Stevenson to join the advance. "The boys was on their feet in an instant," wrote Jessee, and the brigade was soon marching forward eagerly.[26]

Wherever the order originated, the advance quickly became general. Hovey's skirmishers were already hotly engaged along the upper slopes of Champion's Hill. Seeing Logan's division begin its charge, Hovey lost no time in getting his main line of battle started toward the crest. His men were much closer to the enemy than Logan's and did not have a large ravine to cross, so their attack struck first.[27]

On either side of the Jackson Road, officers shouted, "Attention," and the soldiers scrambled to their feet and dressed ranks. "Forward," came the next command, and the division strode uphill, colors flying.[28] Sergeant Longley remembered the adrenaline rush as they advanced and recalled with satisfaction that, although the slope was cut by small ravines, his own 24th Iowa was able to maintain "touch of elbows."[29] Over in McGinnis's brigade, however, the shape of the ground forced the line to constrict, pushing the 46th Indiana out of the front line and back into a reserve position.[30]

As the line advanced into the trees, casualties began to fall. "I remember the lurch, the stagger and collapse with which Corporal Neely left Company C," Longley wrote of his regiment's first loss. In the 56th Ohio, two brothers were shot dead within moments of each other. Another early casualty was Captain Cook, who had been sick and come back to be with his men in the battle.[31]

Pushing upward through the underbrush, the Federals at last came in sight of the Confederate battle line, a row of stabbing flames and a long cloud of white powder smoke. A Confederate battery spewed canister at them.[32] Directly in front of the guns, Lt. Thomas Durham of the 11th Indiana saw three of the four guns discharge a moment too early, hurling their loads of canister just over the heads of Company E. The fourth gun crew delayed firing because they had spotted Durham's own Company G and were hastily swinging their gun to point directly at Durham and his comrades. In their haste, however, the gunners failed to notice that the muzzle of their piece was also pointed directly at the bole of a huge hickory tree, only a few feet away. The whole load of canister slammed into the trunk and nearly cut the tree in two. "It would have torn my company to pieces had it not been for this tree," Durham recalled.[33]

The 24th Iowa halted and returned the fire. Longley spied a Confederate up the slope, sheltering behind a tree while loading a rifle. As the man leaned back to draw out the ramrod, Longley took aim and fired. The Rebel toppled backward and Longley let out a scream of triumph. For the moment, his only thought and feeling was "kill, *kill*, KILL."[34]

The 11th Indiana reached the Rebel battery before the gunners could reload, and a fierce hand-to-hand fight broke out. The Confederate infantry, Cumming's Georgians, rushed in to support the battery. "We were stabbing with bayonets, clubbing with guns, officers shooting with revolvers and slashing and thrusting with swords," recalled Durham. One big, raw-boned, muscular Hoosier grasped the barrel of his rifle and wielded it like a club, crushing the skull of one Rebel after another. Finally one of the Georgians ran a bayonet clear through him and he fell dead atop the bodies of those he had killed.[35]

McGinnis brought the 46th back up from its reserve position and threw it into the fight as well. The contest raged intensely around a log cabin near the Rebel battery. Back and forth, the tide of battle shifted repeatedly as the lines surged past the cabin several times.[36] Finally the Rebel line broke, and the Confederates fled down the back side of the hill. The shape of the ground funneled some of the fugitives into a ravine. Hovey's advancing troops gained both sides of the ravine and poured their fire down on the fleeing Rebels, cutting down many. "They were really piled on top of each other," wrote Durham, and the small stream at the bottom of the ravine, an upper branch of Austin Creek, ran red with blood.[37]

Just to the right of Hovey's fight, Mortimer Leggett's brigade of Logan's division struggled through a deep ravine full of tangled thickets. The going was rough, but the troops covered as much of the ground as possible at a dead run, with their bayoneted rifles thrust in front of them. The color-bearer of the 20th Illinois ran so fast that the men "had hard work to keep up with him," Ira Blanchard recalled. At the bottom of the ravine, they gathered up a number of prisoners, probably part of Cumming's skirmish line and possibly some of the fugitives of the hapless 23rd Alabama.[38]

They wasted as little time as possible with the prisoners and rushed on, working their way up the slope of Champion's Hill and Lee's Ridge. "Here we met some opposition," Blanchard later explained, but it did not delay them much. After a brief exchange of fire, they carried the Rebel line at the point of the bayonet and were in time to stake a claim, along with nearly every regiment in Hovey's division, to part of the credit for the capture of the guns at the top of Champion's Hill.[39]

In the center of Logan's line, in front of Smith's brigade, a handful of fugitives from the 23rd Alabama still fled through the brush back toward the top of the ridge, with Smith's soldiers in hot pursuit. Like Leggett's brigade on their left, Smith's men charged up the hill yelling and tore through the Confederate line with relatively little delay. Some of Smith's men did not perceive any specific Confederate line of resistance but considered the entire operation as a continuation of the chase after the fleeing 23rd Alabama.[40]

On Logan's right, Stevenson's men charged up the ridge and flanked the defending line, even as it was collapsing under the assault of Hovey's and the rest of Logan's division. Then, however, Stevenson's Illinoisans and Ohioans came under fire from artillery posted on the next ridge. Pemberton had long remained uncertain that Hovey's and Logan's divisions constituted the main threat to his position, so rather than shift infantry from his other two divisions to support Carter Stevenson's line along Lee's Ridge, the Confederate commander sent two batteries of artillery out the Jackson Road to the west to take up a position on Austin Ridge, the middle stroke of the backward **F**. This put them beyond, and about 500 yards behind, the Confederate left flank on Lee's Ridge, where Pemberton hoped their fire would secure that flank of his line. Coming under fire from those guns, John Stevenson's Federals turned directly toward them, struggled through a ravine choked with briars, across Austin Creek, and up the slope of Austin Ridge.[41]

The artillery had little infantry support. Indeed, the only infantry in the area seemed to be more of the fleeing remnants of Carter Stevenson's routed division. John Stevenson's Union troops gave a yell as they emerged from the brushy ravine and rushed toward the guns. The Rebels gave them blasts of double canister, but the Federals closed in relentlessly. The Confederate artillerists proved as brave and determined as those on Champion's Hill. They fired their last shot after the Midwesterners already had their hands on some of the guns. One of the battery commanders remained in the midst of the guns, urging his men on, until an attacking bluecoat shot him from his horse at a range of only a few feet. John Stevenson's Illinoisans and Ohioans now found themselves in possession not only of seven cannon but also of the Jackson Road, squarely between Pemberton's army and the bridge over Baker's Creek.[42]

While Stevenson's men attacked the Rebel batteries at the west end of Austin Ridge, the rest of Logan's division and all of Hovey's continued to advance. Leggett and Smith moved over the top of Lee's Ridge and into the ravine of Austin Creek. Hovey drove forward toward the crossroads, where the Jackson, Middle, and Ratliff roads met, 700 yards south of Champion's Hill. Two regiments of Cumming's Georgia brigade were posted at the crossroads, facing east. On Hovey's approach, Cumming's regiments, together with a four-gun battery of artillery, pivoted to face north and took position behind a stout rail fence with the Middle Road at their backs and a cornfield in front of them in hopes of fending off the Federal onslaught and saving the Confederate army's escape route via the crossroads.[43]

As Slack's brigade advanced straight toward the crossroads, the Rebels' initial volley staggered the Federals, but they kept on coming. A few yards farther into the cornfield, the Midwesterners halted to fire a volley of their own.

John H. Williams of the 56th Ohio was just bringing his rifle up to his shoulder when a Rebel bullet struck him in the heart, killing him instantly. As he fell, his rifle pitched forward, its bayonet stuck into the ground, and it remained thus standing. His captain snatched it up and fired it at the enemy. Only two places away in the front rank, Williams's brother, Lt. T. J. Williams, saw him fall and stooped over him, but the stricken man never moved. As Lieutenant Williams turned back toward the line, an artillery round took off the arm of the man on the other side of him. Others were falling all around, but the Iowans and Ohioans charged forward relentlessly across the cornfield, routing the Georgians and taking all four cannon. "The Rebs ran like sheep," wrote Israel Ritter of the 24th Iowa.[44]

By this time, it was 1:30 p.m. Hovey's and Logan's divisions, five brigades in all, about 10,000 strong, had fought their way up one side of Champion's Hill and Lee's Ridge and down the other. Along the way, they had completely thrashed three large Confederate brigades numbering probably 7,500 men and holding strong terrain. Of those three brigades, only Lee's Alabamians continued as an organized fighting force at this point in the battle, and it was much the worse for wear as Lee tried desperately to hold on to a stretch of the Jackson Road between John Stevenson's Union brigade on the west and Hovey's division on the east, while Leggett and Smith pressed against his line in front.

Hovey's and Logan's divisions had performed an impressive feat of arms, and they now held the key Jackson Road at two different places between the bulk of Pemberton's army and the vital Baker's Creek bridge. They had the Rebel army by the throat, but their formations were partially disorganized as a result of all of the hard fighting and rough terrain they had passed through. The men were hot, tired, and thirsty in the torrid midday heat, and their cartridge boxes were getting disturbingly light.

More disturbing to Grant was the fact that he still had heard nothing at all from McClernand's four divisions, which were supposed to be advancing on the Middle and Raymond roads. No sounds of battle came from either location. Indeed, now that Hovey's men held the piece of the Middle

Road at its junction with the Jackson Road, they should have been able to make contact with Osterhaus's division advancing from the east, but there was no sign of him. McClernand continued to interpret his previous orders from Grant not to initiate a battle as meaning that he should not join in a battle that was obviously raging less than a mile from where his troops sat idle. Unable to account for McClernand's nonappearance, Grant dispatched message after message urging him to attack at once.[45]

Meanwhile, Pemberton was having his own difficulties with disloyal subordinates. As Logan's and Hovey's assault began to buckle the Confederate line on Champion's Hill and Lee's Ridge, Pemberton realized that Grant's true threat lay there and not on the Middle and Raymond roads. Accordingly he called on his two divisions fronting those roads to send reinforcements immediately to aid in the desperate struggle at the north end of the battlefield. Both division commanders, John S. Bowen and W. W. Loring, despised Pemberton and flatly refused his order for reinforcements. He thus had nothing available to stay the disaster to Stevenson's division on his left. Only after the catastrophe on Champion's Hill and at the crossroads did Bowen relent and bring his division north up the Ratliff Road. They arrived minutes after Hovey's troops, winded and disordered, had taken possession of the crossroads.

Bowen's division at this time consisted of only two brigades, but they were among the best in the Western Confederate armies. One of them, the Missouri brigade, may well have been the best in any Confederate army. Together, Bowen's two brigades probably numbered about 5,000, significantly more than the approximately 4,200 that Hovey had taken into the attack a few hours before.[46] Reduced by the losses of the fight for Champion's Hill and the crossroads and the inevitable separation of soldiers from their units due to the disorganizing effects of hard fighting in rough terrain, Hovey's division was now badly outnumbered and in no shape to take on Bowen.

Confusion reigned in Slack's brigade, recalled Sgt. Charles Longley. Some eager soldiers had pursued their foes into a large field beyond the crossroads. Others were scattered among the newly captured guns. Key officers had fallen during the attack, and no one took the initiative to get the companies and regiments of the brigade back into their formations.[47] During the few minutes after the fighting had stopped around the crossroads, Lt. T. J. Williams got permission from his captain to go back to where the body of his brother lay. "I spread his rubber blanket over him," Williams later wrote. It was all he could do.[48]

As Bowen's division approached the crossroads, confusion continued among the Union troops. By the time Lieutenant Williams returned from visiting his brother's corpse, he and his comrades could see the Confederates forming up to begin the attack. As soon as the Rebels advanced within range, Williams's own company opened fire. "Most of the regiment at this time, so far as I could see, were lying down behind the fence," Williams recalled, "and they called to us from along the line to stop firing; that we were shooting our own men." Williams and his men knew better, so they kept up their fire. Finally their captain said nervously, "You had better stop, boys; they may be our men."

"Captain, take a look at them," replied Cpl. David Evans.

The captain did and needed no more convincing. "Up boys and give them h——," he shouted.[49]

The Rebels "were coming on fast," Williams wrote. They plowed into the 24th Iowa and drove it back in ferocious hand-to-hand fighting. Israel Ritter and another Iowan tried to drag a wounded comrade to the rear with them "but were compelled to leave him to escape." Another wounded comrade called to Ritter as he fled, "but it was folly to remain," he later wrote.[50]

The 56th Ohio found itself caught in a withering cross fire from the front and both flanks. The Ohioans had to give up their hold on the rail fence and fall back across the cornfield. When they did, the Rebels came after them with a rush. Men fell by the dozen but at least a portion of the regiment retreated slowly, loading and firing as they went, halting when they could to fire a few rounds, then falling back again.[51]

Williams was sheltering behind a large tree stump along with Pvt. Richard Davis. Davis admonished Williams that he must be more careful or the Rebels would get him. Moments later Davis collapsed across Williams's feet with a bullet in the chest. A shell cut down Corporal Evans, who had captured the flag of the 23rd Alabama at Port Gibson just fifteen days before. The Confederates made a rush for the colors of the 56th, but a captain led a wild countercharge in which much of the regiment participated and saved the flag. Ammunition began to be a critical concern, with staff officers bringing and distributing what few rounds could be obtained from the division's wagons far to the rear. Men rummaged the cartridge boxes of the dead and wounded. By this time in the fight, some of Hovey's men had fired as many as eighty rounds, twice an infantryman's normal ammunition load.[52]

Throughout Hovey's division, the story was much the same. Like the 56th Ohio, almost every regiment along the line seemed at one time or another to experience the sensation of being attacked in front and on both flanks at once, as the gaps and irregularities in Hovey's line, caused by the rapid advance over rough ground, became weaknesses that the enemy exploited.[53] As disorganization increased, resisting the Rebel onslaught became even more difficult. Aurelius Voorhis admitted in his diary that night that the 46th Indiana had fallen back "slowly at first, but we got so mixed up that it was impossible to reform in the face of the enemy."[54] The pace of the retreat quickened.

Hovey and his brigade commanders had sent several messages to the rear calling for reinforcements, but until Crocker's division arrived on the field, Grant had none to send them. The first of Crocker's brigades to appear, Sanborn's, McPherson parceled out by regiment to several sectors that seemed to need help. By the time the next brigade, that of Col. George B. Boomer, came up, having marched twelve miles already that day, it was clear that Hovey's need was the most acute, and Grant dispatched Boomer's four regiments to his aid.[55]

The brigade attempted to move into position on the far left, so as to extend Hovey's flank. The terrain in that direction, however, proved to be impassable; so Boomer pulled his men back to an open field along the Jackson Road where they waited in reserve. Some minutes later, General McGinnis came riding back over the hill to see if he could get some help for his men. Galloping up to Boomer, he shouted, "For God's sake, put this brigade into this fight." Boomer complied at once, marching his men at the double-quick up the slope, deploying them into line of battle shortly before reaching the crest, and then, still on the double, over the hilltop and down the other side.[56]

By the time Boomer's men topped Champion's Hill, they discovered Hovey's disorganized division retreating up the other side. Boomer gave the order to fix bayonets, but the noise of battle in front of them was so intense that most of his men could not hear him but did see him wave them forward. "We charged with a yell (but without bayonets)," wrote John Campbell of the 5th Iowa.[57] Boomer's numbers were too few to hold Bowen for long, but he slowed the Confederate advance, giving Hovey's men more time to fall back to someplace where they would have a fair chance to re-form their ranks. Step by step, the Rebels drove Boomer's Iowans, Illinoisans, and Missourians back over the crest of Champion's Hill and down the north side. The fighting was intense, and Boomer's brigade was well on its way to losing one-third of its numbers killed and wounded.[58]

Grant's situation was beginning to look critical. McClernand's four divisions, more than half the force Grant had available for this battle, might as well have been back in Louisiana. Wherever they were, they were not fighting, and Grant could get no news of them. Aside from the troops he had already committed to battle, Grant's only remaining reserve was Crocker's last brigade, that of Col. Samuel A. Holmes, which was even then double-quicking up the Jackson Road, approaching the Champion House. Holmes's one regiment of Missourians and one of Iowans, along with Boomer's desperately fighting brigade and Hovey's fleeing remnants, were all that stood between the seemingly unstoppable Rebels and the Union artillery and supply wagons. If Bowen got that far, Grant's army would be split in two and on the brink of destruction.

Grant's only other available resource was Logan's division. When he received word of the growing crisis on Champion's Hill, Grant was visiting Logan on the far right flank. He had spent the battle up to this time behind Hovey's division but had ridden to the right to see how things were going there. He found Logan near Stevenson's position on Austin Ridge and the Jackson Road where it led down to Baker's Creek. Neither Grant nor Logan realized that that road constituted Pemberton's only viable line of retreat at the moment. Learning of the impending disaster north of Champion's Hill, Grant ordered Logan to pull Stevenson's brigade back, abandoning Austin Ridge and the Jackson Road, and send it marching around to the left to reinforce the seriously threatened sector in front of the Champion House.[59]

In the center of Grant's front, Leggett's and Smith's brigades were still fighting. They had been working their way up Austin Ridge, engaging Lee's Alabamians and what remained of Barton's Georgians when Bowen's counterattack had struck Hovey. On Logan's extreme left, soldiers of the 30th Illinois, noticing the Rebel column charging up the Jackson Road, "remarked that there would soon be a lively racket to our left." The "lively racket," of course, was the sound of Bowen's two brigades attacking on a narrow front on either side of the Jackson Road, driving Hovey and sweeping past the left flank of Logan's line without paying it much attention.[60]

The extreme right-flank regiment of McGinnis's brigade, which joined onto the left of Leggett's, was the 34th Indiana. Hit hard by the fire of Cockrell's Missourians and nearly out of ammunition themselves, the 34th began to fall back in what looked to their neighbors of the 30th Illinois like a good deal of confusion. One of the Hoosiers had to admit that "as this was our first fall back, many of the boys forgot the numbers and were falling back at will—some, in fact, were on the double-quick for the rear." Meanwhile, the 30th Illinois was soon taking heavy fire from the flank and had to pull back a short distance too.[61]

Logan had just finished his conference with Grant several hundred yards to the right when he caught sight of these events transpiring on his division's left flank. He headed in that direction with his horse at a dead run, straight into the fleeing mass of Hoosiers. "What regiment is this?" roared Logan.

"The 34th Indiana," came the reply.

"Men, for God's sake, don't disgrace your state," thundered Logan.

"Of course, we stopped," recalled one of the Hoosiers, but old "Black Jack" Logan was just getting warmed up: "Not a mother of one of you, but what would rather see her son brought home dead, than to disgrace yourself." Just then the adjutant of the 34th came riding up. Logan recognized his rank and called out, "Adjutant, get your men together."

"General, the Rebels are awful thick up there," replied the adjutant.

"D—— it, that's the place to kill them—where they are thick," roared Logan. "While they are shooting you, you can be shooting them. You do not belong to my command, but you must fight." The general launched into quite a harangue, according to Sgt. R. M. Dihel of the 30th Illinois. "His language was forcible, inspiring, and savored a little of brimstone. Every word weighed a pound, and went straight to the mark." As always when Logan sought to inspire the troops, it worked. The 34th rallied and fought the rest of the battle alongside Leggett's brigade.[62]

Briefly isolated in the ravine of Austin Creek, Leggett and Smith nevertheless had serious fighting to do and an important role to play in the battle. First they repulsed a feeble frontal assault by Lee's Alabamians. In this they had the aid of very effective artillery fire from the 8th Michigan Battery. Somehow the redoubtable De Golyer had gotten his guns forward to this inaccessible position and now did good service helping to break up the Alabamians' attack. Next, Leggett turned his brigade to the left and launched an advance up the ravine of Austin Creek toward the Jackson Road and the left and rear of Bowen's division, by then fighting on the other side of Champion's Hill. Opposing Leggett were various fragments of Cumming's Georgia brigade, and he steadily drove them back, threatening to cut off Bowen's troops.[63]

Back on the north side of Champion's Hill, the question was, who would or could stop Bowen's Confederates? Unease about the lack of an answer to that question had prompted Grant to call in Stevenson's brigade from its position on the right flank, but before Stevenson could arrive, several elements of the Army of the Tennessee combined to provide a solution. As Bowen's advancing Rebels emerged from the woods near the top of Champion's Hill onto the open lower slopes, the massed Union artillery opened up on them with deadly effect, driving parts of the division back into the shelter of the wooded ravines near the top of the hill.

Eugene A. Carr *(Library of Congress)*

Frederick Steele *(Library of Congress)*

Peter J. Osterhaus *(Library of Congress)*

John M. Corse *(Library of Congress)*

James R. Slack *(Library of Congress)*

Manning F. Force *(Library of Congress)*

Vicksburg waterfront *(National Archives)*

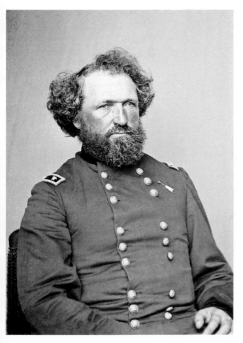

Mortimer D. Leggett *(Library of Congress)*   Charles C. Walcutt *(Library of Congress)*

Frank Blair with the staff of the Seventeenth Corps *(Library of Congress)*

Kennesaw Mountain *(National Archives)*

Oliver O. Howard (Harper's Weekly)

Confederate fortifications at Atlanta *(Library of Congress)*

William W. Belknap *(Library of Congress)*

William B. Hazen *(Library of Congress)*

Artist William Waud's sketch of Lt. Col. Justin C. Kennedy, 13th Iowa, raising
the U.S. flag over the South Carolina statehouse *(Library of Congress)*

Ruins of Columbia seen from the unfinished capitol *(Library of Congress)*

Frank Blair and staff lead the Seventeenth Corps through
the streets of Washington, D.C. *(Library of Congress)*

The Grand Review

While the Rebels were stalled by the artillery and by Boomer's sturdy brigade, Holmes's men came panting up the road and deployed into line. As they charged forward to take a position on Boomer's left, their yell was the first news Boomer's hard-pressed men received that help was on the way. "It was a most glorious shout," recalled a soldier of Boomer's brigade.[64] Simultaneously, Hovey's brigades, albeit somewhat depleted, had formed their ranks again and were drawing a fresh supply of ammunition in preparation for rejoining the battle.[65]

Imperceptibly at first, then all at once, the momentum in the battle swung to the Union side. Holmes's two regiments drove deeply into the Rebel position, which began to crumble. Now it was the turn of Bowen's men to run low on ammunition and begin scavenging the cartridge boxes of their fallen comrades in search of the last few rounds. The Midwesterners left them no time for that. Boomer's men joined the counterattack, then Slack's, McGinnis's, and Sanborn's.

Up the slope the attackers surged, then over the crest of Champion's Hill once again, while Leggett's flank attack threatened to trap every grayback north of the crossroads. Bowen's line faltered and began to lose its grip, then buckled completely. The Rebels were running. Charging after them, the Federals saw nothing but the backs and heels of Cockrell's Missourians in what was now no longer a fight but a footrace.[66]

Seeing that Stevenson's brigade was no longer needed on Champion's Hill, Grant sent it hurrying back to its position on Logan's right. It arrived in time to join the big push, retaking its former position astride Austin Ridge and the Jackson Road. As Smith's and Leggett's brigades advanced alongside, Lee's Alabama brigade folded up for the last time and headed south. Barton's and Cumming's men had already taken leg bail. Grant's troops took possession of the whole length of the Jackson Road from the crossroads, along Austin Ridge, all the way to the Baker's Creek bridge.

From the top of the ridge, the Federals halted to catch their breath, reform their lines, and herd hundreds of prisoners to the rear. Across the fields in front of them, they could see two-thirds of Pemberton's army in disorderly flight, while the remaining third, Loring's division, fell back slowly in line of battle, covering their comrades' retreat. Neither Logan, Hovey, nor Crocker saw fit to press the pursuit farther with their exhausted troops. The time was about 4:30 p.m.

Had the battle ended in this manner several hours earlier, Pemberton's only remaining course would have been to abandon his wagons and artillery and take his infantry cross-country southward on the east bank of Baker's Creek, and such a movement would almost certainly have been the prelude to the disintegration of his army. Now, however, the situation had changed. Throughout the day, Confederate engineers had worked at rebuilding the washed-out bridge over Baker's Creek on the Raymond Road and had at last succeeded. The elements also rewarded Pemberton for his army's daylong fight. The water level in Baker's Creek had been dropping steadily until now it had once again reached fording stage in the vicinity of the Raymond Road crossing. Pemberton could thus move his defeated army rapidly across the creek by simultaneous use of bridge and ford.[67]

At this point, the Union column on the Raymond Road, which had first made contact with the Rebels early that morning and had done nothing ever since, now suddenly came back to life. A. J. Smith's division pushed westward somewhat tentatively and took possession of the intersection of Raymond and Ratliff roads. A single Confederate brigade under Brig. Gen. Lloyd Tilghman—the man who had surrendered Fort Henry to the navy fifteen months before—fought a delaying action along the Raymond Road that succeeded, though it cost Tilghman his life. Pemberton's army was able to use a back road to reach the Raymond Road bridge over Baker's Creek without passing near the intersection with the Ratliff Road or encountering Smith's ineffectual attempt to hinder his escape. Loring, whose division, including Tilghman's brigade, was covering the withdrawal, became cut off from the crossings of Baker's Creek. Instead of crossing to the west bank, he traveled south for some miles, then swung to the east, abandoning Pemberton's army and eventually uniting with Johnston's force north of Jackson.

Around 2:30 in the afternoon, McClernand finally received the first of Grant's unequivocal orders to engage the enemy. Others followed in quick succession. In response, he had Osterhaus's division advance and drive off a small Confederate detachment that was manning a roadblock on the Middle Road in his front. A few yards farther on, he halted his advance and sat out the rest of the battle only 600 yards east of the crossroads. He sent instructions for A. J. Smith to put his column in motion, but made no effort to see that his orders were carried out energetically. They were not.[68]

McClernand's soldiers could not understand why they did not advance. "For four hours we stood there listening, waiting and wondering why we were not put into the fight," wrote a soldier in Carr's division on the Middle Road. "Fifteen minutes would have put us into the battle any time that day. It was a matter of speculation in the regiment at the time, and long afterward, why we were not moved forward."[69] Down on the Raymond Road, a soldier of the 55th Illinois recalled that by 11:00 a.m., he and his comrades could hear "the continuous roar of battle" from the direction of Champion's Hill. "We were momentarily expecting orders to advance upon the foe supposed to be in our front, or to move by the right flank to the aid of those there hotly engaged," he wrote. "No orders came, and for hours we lay idly on our arms, unmolested and unmolesting."[70]

If McClernand sincerely thought that Grant's orders not to initiate a battle prohibited him from joining one already in progress less than half a mile away, he would have been unfit to command a regiment, much less a corps. The politician from Shawneetown certainly possessed a distinctly spotty record, but no other incident of his career suggested he was as witless as that. Even when he did receive Grant's order to advance, McClernand did so in such a way as to give the minimum possible assistance to the Union forces engaged. It seems more likely that he resented Grant's admonition against overaggressiveness and wanted to pay him back for it. That, coupled with his long-standing jealousy and resentment of Grant, leads to the conclusion that McClernand would not particularly have minded seeing Grant defeated at Champion's Hill. If Grant suspected this, he kept it to himself.

Grant had fought the battle with about 15,500 men, and Pemberton had committed almost exactly that many of his own troops to battle, plus the additional 7,800 of Loring's division who entered the battle only to cover the retreat. McClernand idled the day away with just over 17,500 troops. If he had seen fit instead to join the battle, the Confederate front almost certainly would have collapsed before noon on the Jackson, Middle, and Raymond roads, and it is difficult to imagine how more than a corporal's guard of Pemberton's army could have escaped.[71] Several weeks and several thousand lives might have been saved. Brig. Gen. Stephen G. Burbridge, commanding the lead brigade on the Raymond Road, wrote that if his column had made a forceful advance, "we could have captured the whole rebel force opposed to us, and reached Edwards Station before sunset."[72]

Even with less than half his army, Grant had won an impressive victory. He had captured twenty-seven Rebel cannon and a number of battle flags. For total losses of 2,441 Union soldiers killed, wounded, and missing, Grant's army had inflicted more than 4,700 Confederate casualties including more than 2,400 missing—mostly captured.[73] In addition, he had separated Pemberton from Loring's division, one-third of his field army. The two forces had little prospect of rejoining, since Grant's victorious army soon lay squarely between them. What was left of the army with Pemberton in the field was battered, weary, and demoralized, fleeing toward Vicksburg.

Grant dispatched McClernand's fresh troops in pursuit. Carr's and

Osterhaus's divisions marched all the way to Edwards Station late that night. There they found a number of flaming railroad cars loaded with supplies and ammunition, torched by the Confederates in their retreat. The bluecoats joined with the citizens of Edwards Station in putting out the fires.[74] Most of the rest of the army camped between there and the battlefield.[75]

Grant left Hovey's division, which had taken 30 percent casualties, on the battlefield to care for the wounded, bury the dead, and recover salvageable equipment.[76] The men were exhausted. Lt. Thomas Durham found he had shouted so much during the battle that he had lost his voice. "I could make a noise no louder than a wheeze," he recalled, "and could not speak above a whisper for several days after."[77]

Salvageable equipment meant particularly weapons, and sometimes this was done informally. Before they marched away from the battlefield the next day, six companies of the 46th Indiana exchanged their hated Austrian rifles for good Springfields left on the field of battle, much to the long-term confusion of the army ordnance bureau, which for years kept demanding that the colonel explain what had happened to the missing Austrians.[78]

The task of caring for the wounded could not be completed before nightfall, and continued in the dark. That night, as the 46th Indiana's Col. Thomas H. Bringhurst observed, "the division divided the ground with the dead and wounded. All night the ambulance corps, with their torches of splinters, came among the sleeping soldiers, hunting and carrying out those to whom surgical attention would be a benefit."[79] Among those out on the battlefield that night was T. J. Williams. He and another of the 56th Ohio's lieutenants took a squad of soldiers on a torchlight expedition in search of members of the regiment who had fallen during the battle. The flickering light revealed a succession of grisly scenes. "One always remembered," Williams wrote, "was a very large rebel, sitting with his back against a large stump, with more than a deathly pallor, having bled to death." They proceeded on and found and buried their dead comrades.[80]

The field hospitals were harrowing scenes, in some ways worse than the battlefields. George Remley of the 22nd Iowa volunteered to help in one of them and worked there all night and until noon the next day. "I hope that I may never again be called upon to witness such scenes of suffering and horror as I looked upon that night," Remley wrote in a letter to a friend a few days later. "Were I to live a thousand years their impression could never be effaced from my memory." Here and there, a man would complain that his leg was cold and beg to have it covered with a blanket, but Remley could do nothing to help him because the limb that "felt cold" had been amputated.

Dying men would gasp for water or plead to be allowed to get up and leave the hospital so that they would not have to suffer. "These things and far more than these greeted my senses," Remley wrote, "as with a candle in one hand and a pail of water and a cup in the other, I picked my way among the wounded and over the amputated limbs that were scattered around the Hospital grounds."

It was a night for unwounded men to contemplate what they had passed through and why they had remained unscathed while so many around them had fallen. In the camp of the 5th Iowa, midway between the battlefield and Edwards Station, John Campbell sat scratching in his diary. Completing his account of the day's action, he added a concluding line: "To *Him* who hath preserved me through so many dangers, I return thanks that I have again passed safely through the perils of the bloody field."[81]

CHAPTER TWENTY-TWO

To the Gates of Vicksburg

G RANT'S ORDERS for the morning of May 17 called for McClernand's corps, less Hovey's division, to lead the march westward from Edwards Station along the Jackson Road, which roughly paralleled the Southern Railroad of Mississippi in linking Vicksburg with the state capital. McPherson would follow in McClernand's wake. Sherman had pulled out of Jackson the day before and marched his two divisions hard to catch up with the rest of the army. Today he would continue to the west, but on roads north of the Jackson Road. His objective would be Bridgeport, Mississippi, and there Blair's division would join him, reuniting the Fifteenth Corps.

The purpose of the day's operations was to obtain a bridgehead on the west bank of the Big Black River. That stream, with its mouth at Grand Gulf, on the Mississippi, had been on the army's left flank, usually just over the horizon, during its march from Bruinsburg to Jackson. Vicksburg lay on the other side, so with Jackson neutralized and Pemberton defeated, crossing the Big Black was next on Grant's agenda. The Southern Railroad of Mississippi crossed the Big Black on a trestle, Big Black Bridge, about six miles west of Edwards Station. The Jackson Road had to rely on a ferry a few hundred yards south of the railroad bridge. As McClernand pushed westward that morning, his troops would reach Big Black Bridge, where the Rebels were reported to have prepared breastworks. Sherman's march would also take him to the banks of the Big Black but at Bridgeport, eleven miles north of Big Black Bridge. There he would set up a pontoon bridge. Once he put his corps across, the Confederates would have to abandon the line of the Big Black and fall back toward Vicksburg.[1]

McClernand's men were up well before dawn. The armies had been in such close proximity the past several days that the men had had little opportunity to forage. Rations were scarce, and breakfast that morning for many of the soldiers consisted of a little cornmeal mush cooked in a tin cup.[2] The lead division, Carr's, marched at half past three o'clock that morning but advanced slowly. Along the way, they found the road strewn with discarded canteens, knapsacks, and cartridge boxes, sure signs of the Rebels' precipitate retreat the evening before. Even more significantly, the 33rd Illinois, advancing as skirmishers ahead of Carr's column, found a large number of Confederate stragglers sleeping here and there in the woods and behind fence corners. The Illinoisans awakened the slumbering Rebels and sent them to the rear as prisoners.[3]

Shortly after daybreak, the 33rd Illinois made contact with Confederate skirmishers, drove them back, and discovered a heavily manned line of breastworks covering Big Black Bridge. The Illinoisans took cover and waited for the rest of the command to come up. When they did, McClernand deployed Carr's division on the right of the road, Osterhaus's on the left, then Burbridge's brigade of A. J. Smith's division still farther to the left, extending the line almost to Gin Lake.[4]

Big Black Bridge lay on a westward-looping bend of the river. The east side of the river was a wide, level plain of bottomland. The west bank rose in a sixty-foot bluff. The Confederate position constituted a fortified bridgehead on the east side of the river. The breastworks were made of cotton bales with dirt thrown over them and ran across the open east side of the bend, from the river above the bend to what used to be the river below—but now was an oxbow lake called Gin Lake. For much of their length, the breastworks ran along the western bank of a small bayou—actually another abandoned bed of the river—in which only a foot or two of water stood at this time of year. The Confederate engineer who had designed the works hoped to make use of the bayou as a sort of moat for his defenses.

Pemberton's forces were holding the breastworks at Big Black Bridge only because their commander still hoped that Loring's division would arrive to join him. He had heard nothing from Loring since the beginning of the retreat from the battlefield of Champion's Hill the day before and could only guess at his subordinate's whereabouts. What Pemberton did not realize was that Loring had no intention of even trying to rejoin his army and was already on his way to Johnston. So Pemberton kept three brigades on the dangerous east bank of the Big Black, vainly extending a hand to comrades who were not coming. The immediate commander of the bridgehead was Maj. Gen. John Bowen, and for its defense he had the two brigades of his own division—rather roughly used at Champion's Hill the day before—and an extra brigade of East Tennesseeans under Brig. Gen. John C. Vaughn. Vaughn's men had not been present at Champion's Hill, but, as draftees from a region opposed to secession, their morale was low.[5]

As McClernand's artillery rumbled up the Jackson Road behind him, terrain features made him deploy it asymmetrically. South of the road, the bottomland was nothing but wide-open cotton fields. North of the road, a broad belt of woods covered much of the plain and extended to within about 400 yards of the Rebel breastworks. So dense were the woods that artillery generally could not pass through. McClernand therefore deployed almost all of his artillery south of the road, where firing positions were accessible and fields of fire ample. These guns were soon involved in a lively duel with the Confederate artillery.

Osterhaus, on learning from scouts that an opportunity beckoned on the far right flank, led a two-gun section of 20-pounder Parrotts from Capt. Jacob Foster's 1st Wisconsin Battery to deploy north of the road. "I shows you a place where you gets a good chance at 'em," Osterhaus told the section commander, and directed him to an old farm track leading through the forest to an acceptable firing position on the forward edge of the woods, well out on the right flank. A range of 400 yards was almost point-blank for the big 20-pounder Parrotts, and they were soon knocking apart the cotton-bale parapets.[6]

While Osterhaus was directing the deployment of Foster's other four 20-pounders near the railroad in about the center of the Union line, a Confederate shell touched off one of the ammunition chests. The blast killed one gunner and wounded three, as well as Foster and Osterhaus, who soon had to be carried to the rear with a relatively minor but nevertheless incapacitating wound in the thigh. Before leaving he turned over command of the Ninth Division to Brig. Gen. Albert L. Lee.[7]

Meanwhile, the Union skirmishers continued to edge their way closer to the Confederate breastworks, slithering forward through plowed fields that were wet from a heavy dew. They were soon "as soaking wet as if they had been swimming in a river," and coated with multiple layers of mud. "It was serious business," wrote Capt. Isaac Elliott of the 33rd Illinois, "but at the same time the fun of it was indescribable." Elliott later thought that if he had ordered his men to charge then, the Rebels might not have known how to react to the sight of such mud-covered monstrosities running toward them. Prudently, however, he kept his men slithering forward.[8]

Commanding Carr's right-flank brigade, and thus the right flank of McClernand's line, was Brig. Gen. Michael K. Lawler. Well over six feet tall and said to weigh more than 300 pounds, Lawler "could mount his horse only with great difficulty," a soldier observed, "and when he was mounted it was pretty hard on the horse." Coarse and ill mannered, Lawler nonetheless had a reputation as an excellent officer, "brave as a lion."[9] Lawler's brigade was composed of the 21st, 22nd, and 23rd Iowa, and the

11th Wisconsin, and these regiments now formed their line along the edge of the woods about 400 yards from the Confederate defenses.

Lawler's scouts informed him of an interesting terrain feature in front of his position. The bottomland here looked flat, and most of it was. However, the Big Black meandered across its floodplain and changed its course often. Here and there across the level plain, long, twisting indentations marked old abandoned beds of the river. One such natural ditch lay in front of Lawler's position and only a few score yards from the Confederate breast-works. Lawler believed that his brigade could use this depression as a launching point for a successful attack. After obtaining permission from Carr, Lawler shortly before 9:00 a.m. led his men in a headlong rush across the open field toward the sheltering meander scar. They arrived relatively unscathed, and then he took his time forming his column of attack in com-plete safety from Rebel fire while the single nearby section of 20-pounder Parrotts hammered away at the Confederate parapet.[10]

Then, when his men had thoroughly caught their breath, were in perfect formation, and understood fully what was expected of them, Lawler led them up out of the swale and straight for the Rebels. His men charged after him with a terrific shout. In the 23rd Iowa, Col. William H. Kinsman shouted, "Captains, lead your companies, and I will lead you." Struck by a bullet, he kept going, yelling, "They have not killed me yet." Hit a second time, he collapsed but still encouraged his men, "Go on, go on, I cannot go with you farther."[11] A young soldier in the ranks, also wounded, likewise urged his comrades on. "Go in, boys, give 'em h———," he called, "they have fixed me." Lawler's men splashed through the shallow bayou that fronted the Confederate works and then charged up the slope to the Rebel parapet.[12]

The Iowans and Wisconsin men came over the parapet in a massive rush. The effect was like the Mississippi in full flood stage breaking through a levee. Vaughn's East Tennessee brigade instantly collapsed into a con-fused mass of men either running away or surrendering.

Seeing Lawler's brigade charge, the other Federal units advanced with a shout, so that a wave of sound rolled along the army's line from right to left, and the attack became a mass assault on the whole length of the Con-federate breastworks.[13] A soldier in Carr's division later wrote that if his brigade had received orders to charge, he "did not hear them nor never knew that we had orders, but we charged just the same, every fellow for himself and as many 'Rebs' as possible."[14]

Few of the Rebels stayed in the works to receive them. They might as well have tried to stand in the way of a cataract roaring through a crevasse in a levee, trying to stem its tide. "When we were within a few rods of the rebel rifle pit," recalled R. M. Aiken of the 33rd Illinois, "the 'rebs' broke and most of them went pell mell to the rear." Brig. Gen. Martin E. Green's Arkansas brigade made a brief effort to resist. Then it too gave way almost as spectacularly as had Vaughn's. By that time, every member of Cockrell's Missouri brigade appeared to be in a contest to see who could reach the bridge first. For the Army of the Tennessee, another battle had turned into a footrace and without all the preliminary slaughter that had marred the previous day's cross-country event.[15]

The victorious Federals exulted over the many cannon they captured. Jimmy Adkins, one of the mud-slathered soldiers of the 33rd Illinois, was the first Union soldier to reach one of the Confederate guns. In his excitement at capturing a cannon, Adkins leapt atop the gun, flapped his elbows, and crowed like a rooster. He noticed the gun's lanyard in position at the breech. Not being an artillerist, Adkins did not realize that attaching the primer and lanyard was the last step of loading a cannon. Bending down, he grabbed the lanyard and yanked on it. The gun went off with a roar, sending a shell sailing off over the heads of the other advancing Union troops and a badly frightened Adkins somersaulting to the ground. "It created quite a sensation," Captain Elliott observed, but the elevation of the gun prevented Union casualties. "It was the first time," added the captain, "that Jimmy was known to be frightened."[16]

Most of the Confederates got across the river, though some of them had to swim in order to do so, and a few drowned in the attempt. Large numbers of surrendering Rebels all along the breastworks distracted, and got in the way of, rapid pursuit. Those who did make the run for the bridge often did so unhindered by equipment. "They left everything behind that would keep them from hurrying to Vicksburg," wrote Ohio soldier Isaac Jackson.[17]

Some of the Federals turned captured Confederate cannon and opened fire on the Rebels as they crossed the bridge. Many of the Confederates could not, or did not care to, run the gauntlet to reach the bridge. The 60th Tennessee Regiment attempted to move southward within the bridgehead to escape the debacle where Lawler struck. As the Tennesseans marched, however, Burbridge's brigade cut off their retreat, and virtually the entire regiment surrendered. The 61st and 62nd Tennessee fared little better.[18]

In all the confusion, quick-moving Confederate engineers torched the bridge, as well as a nearby steamboat that had served as a makeshift bridge. By the time the Federals approached, both structures were in flames. Two fresh Confederate brigades held positions on the sixty-foot bluff on the west bank, and their fire forced McClernand's men to keep a respectful distance while the bridge burned. The Army of the Tennessee was not going to be crossing at Big Black Bridge within the next few hours at any rate.[19]

Grant was on hand to watch the entire action. Shortly before the battle reached its climax, Brig. Gen. William Dwight rode up and introduced himself to Grant. He was not a member of the Army of the Tennessee but rather was attached to the staff of Maj. Gen. Nathaniel P. Banks. He handed Grant a copy of a telegram from Henry Halleck to Banks, dated May 11. In it, Halleck stated, "It is hoped you will unite with General Grant so as to attack Vicksburg and Port Hudson separately. If within your power to operate between the two places, and with your combined strength to attack a divided enemy, your success will be almost certain."[20] Grant had received a telegram from Halleck the night before with a similar message. It was a familiar theme in Halleck's writing, something he had suggested from time to time for weeks.[21]

Such a concept cropping up again at a time like this was a forceful reminder that even with the Rebel army soundly thrashed and fleeing disconsolately to Vicksburg, the Union high command could still find ways of losing the campaign. Diverting all or part of Grant's army in order to bring it under the command of the inveterate bungler Banks in his less significant campaign against Port Hudson would have been one of the most effective ways of turning success into failure. Grant had decided against such a course back at Grand Gulf when he opted to strike inland rather than go downriver and try to join Banks. Now he wisely reaffirmed that decision. To Dwight he explained that the situation had changed drastically since Halleck had written his dispatch and that if the general-in-chief were aware of the new circumstances he would not suggest such a course.[22]

Getting control of all or part of Grant's army was naturally a very enticing idea for Banks and his strap-hangers like Dwight. The latter misrepresented Halleck's missive as an order to Grant and demanded that he obey it. He continued belaboring Grant with wearisome and irrelevant reasons why he ought to do so until a terrific shout went up from the right of the Union line, indicating that Lawler had launched his assault. With relief Grant galloped off to be closer to the scene of the action, leaving Dwight behind. Twenty-two years later, Grant wrote that he could not remember ever having seen Dwight again.[23] The authorities in Washington would be inclined to forgive Grant for ignoring Halleck's advice if the result should be the capture of Vicksburg.

Although sporadic firing continued until nightfall, the Battle of Big Black Bridge was over by midmorning.[24] It had been a dramatic and one-sided Union victory. Grant's troops captured another eighteen Confederate cannon, five battle flags, and 1,751 prisoners, all for a cost of less than 300 Union soldiers killed or wounded.[25] For the fifth time since crossing the Mississippi, the Army of the Tennessee had met and defeated its foes. The superiority of Grant's generalship was visible in the fact that although the Confederates had more men in Mississippi participating in the campaign than he did, every time the forces had clashed during the month of May, the Army of the Tennessee had enjoyed overwhelming numerical superiority on the battlefield.

Once again, some units made use of the detritus of the battlefield to upgrade their equipment. Several companies of the 33rd Illinois equipped themselves with Enfield rifles, leaving their hated Dresden rifles lying on the field instead.[26] Members of the 22nd Iowa were more interested in other items left on the battlefield. They rifled the haversacks of dead Confederates for corn pones, which they ate with an appetite born of very short rations.[27]

With Big Black Bridge in flames, Grant gave orders for the building of new spans. He directed McClernand to build one in the vicinity of the one that had just been destroyed. Confederate skirmishers on the west bank bedeviled the efforts there, however, until the Rebels pulled out and retreated in the middle of the night. Then the work could go on apace. By the morning of May 18, McClernand had a makeshift bridge in place and his troops were crossing.[28]

McPherson's corps was marching for Amsterdam, Mississippi, about eight miles upstream from Big Black Bridge, and Grant directed him to build another bridge there. McPherson had his men build two spans, one a mile or so above Amsterdam and the other a like distance below. At the former location, McPherson's chief engineer, Andrew Hickenlooper, came up with an ingenious solution. He noticed a nearby warehouse full of cotton bales. Using the bales as floats and the beams and boards of the warehouse as the structural members, he built a floating cotton-bale bridge that probably had no equal in the world. It lasted about thirty-six hours, but that was long enough. As water gradually saturated the cotton, the bridge sank lower and lower until its deck was covered by water. Troops continued to splash across until the bridge was no longer needed, and could be cut loose, having served its purpose.[29] By early morning of May 18, the troops of the Seventeenth Corps were tramping across both Hickenlooper's bridge and a more conventional model a couple of miles downstream.[30]

The Fifteenth Corps had arrived at Bridgeport before midday, May 17. Sherman had a pontoon bridge and orders to get his men across the river.

The leading elements of the Fifteenth Corps captured a few Confederate pickets near the river, and then a small party of the 55th Illinois rowed over in a pontoon boat to become the first members of the Army of the Tennessee to cross the Big Black. With both banks secured, the engineers got to work on the pontoon bridge and had it complete before nightfall on the seventeenth. Most of the night, Sherman's troops were marching across the swaying span by the light of torches and bonfires on shore.[31] Grant rode up to Bridgeport to visit with Sherman that night, and they sat on a log, talking and watching the columns of troops crossing the bridge.[32]

The next morning, May 18, Sherman's Fifteenth Corps continued its westward march, with McPherson's Seventeenth falling in behind as it moved west from the bridges at Amsterdam. They were now astride the ridge of high ground between the Big Black and the Yazoo, immediately in rear of Vicksburg, the position that had been the goal of Grant's and Sherman's operations since the preceding November. Sherman dispatched a regiment of cavalry to take the Confederate fortifications at Haynes's Bluff from the rear as the army's main columns continued on their way to Vicksburg. When the horsemen got there, they found the fortifications abandoned. Pemberton had pulled all of his outlying garrisons into the fortified lines of Vicksburg proper. The cavalrymen made contact with a Union gunboat on the Yazoo.[33]

Sherman's main column proceeded cautiously toward Vicksburg, expecting to encounter the Rebels at any moment. The day was hot and the roads very dusty. About two miles, as the crow flies, from the Vicksburg waterfront, they came to a fork in the road. The main Jackson Road veered to the left and ran south along a ridge before turning west, on the back of another ridge, and going into the town of Vicksburg. The right fork, known locally as the Graveyard Road, ran north along a ridge for a short distance before curving around to the west and entering Vicksburg from the northeast. They were back in the zone of deep, steep-sided ravines and narrow, winding ridges, so roads could not be expected to follow direct routes.[34]

Grant, who was still riding with Sherman, directed him to follow the Graveyard Road and thus form the Army of the Tennessee's right flank as it approached Vicksburg. McPherson would take the left fork and follow the Jackson Road on the direct route to Vicksburg, forming the center of the Union line, and McClernand would swing over to the Baldwin's Ferry Road and approach the town from the southeast. He would form the Union left.[35]

Late that afternoon, Sherman's skirmishers came under fire. They pushed back the Rebel skirmishers and sighted, on the next chain of ridges, the earthworks of the Vicksburg defenses. General Blair, commanding Sherman's lead division, brought up a battery of artillery and had it start shelling the Rebels. As the rest of the Fifteenth Corps came up, Sherman had Steele's division file to the right, wrapping around the north end of the Confederate defenses and making contact with the Yazoo River.[36]

When McPherson's and McClernand's corps came up later that evening, they took positions fronting the Confederate works on the center and left, as assigned by Grant. As McPherson's column reached the forks of the Jackson and Graveyard roads and filed left, the men of the Seventeenth Corps got their first look at the fortifications of Vicksburg, frowning from the high ridges across the way, backlit by the setting sun, studded with artillery and battle flags. McPherson sat his horse beside the road, surveying the defenses with the practiced eye of a military engineer, as well as the fading light would allow. As his men tramped by him in the road on their way to their assigned positions, they cheered and threw their hats in the air. The regimental bands, one after another, struck up "The Girl I Left Behind Me," and the soldiers, most of whom had had nothing at all to eat in the past twelve hours and did not know when they might get more, continued to cheer vociferously as they marched by. An officer nearby noted that tears came to McPherson's eyes.[37]

While the troops were moving into their positions, Grant and Sherman rode to the top of the bluffs overlooking the Yazoo River and Chickasaw Bayou, the dreaded Walnut Hills from which the Confederates had slaughtered Sherman's men when he had advanced on Vicksburg the preceding December. Sherman turned to Grant and stated that up to that moment he had not felt certain of success. Now he was. The campaign that had just concluded was one of the greatest in history, Sherman thought. They had not taken Vicksburg yet, but even if they never did, the series of movements that had ejected the enemy from this seemingly impregnable position and placed the Army of the Tennessee in exactly the only place from which Vicksburg could be attacked with any hope of success constituted "a complete and successful campaign."[38]

By the morning of May 19, Union engineers had completed a bridge across the Yazoo River, near the scene of the previous December's debacle, and had a supply line officially open for business by which supplies could move from steamboats on the Mississippi above Vicksburg directly to the camps of Grant's army. For the first time since entering the state of Mississippi, Grant's troops had a full-service supply line, and wagon trains began moving across it immediately.[39]

As far as the soldiers were concerned, it was high time. "Not more than five days' rations had been issued to the army since May 1st," wrote a soldier in the 31st Illinois, "and everything along the line of march from water mill to farm house had been eaten. Everything that grunted, squawked, gobbled, or cackled had found its way into the mess pan, or had been stewed in the camp kettle, or roasted on a ramrod." As far as the soldiers knew, the country had been completely emptied of foodstuffs from Port Gibson to Jackson and thence to Vicksburg, and it had been none too much to eke out their scant army-issued rations.[40] Just the day before, Col. Manning Force of the 20th Ohio, seeing one of his soldiers with a small piece of cornbread, had offered to buy it for five dollars—more than one-third of a month's income for a private soldier. The man refused.[41] With most of the army suffering from hunger, a soldier of the 55th Illinois noted that "there was general and noisy rejoicing when the reopening of the 'cracker-line' was announced."[42]

Besides its new supply line, the Army of the Tennessee that morning also had Vicksburg closely invested along about two-thirds of its fortified lines, the northern and central sectors. On the south, no Federals at all faced about a third of the total length of the Confederate defenses, partially because Grant did not believe he had troops enough to stretch that far and partly because that sector offered Pemberton no viable escape route. Moving the Confederate army that way would only put it into a cul-de-sac formed by the confluence of the Mississippi and the Big Black—just as trapped as it was in Vicksburg but without the supplies and fortifications Vicksburg offered. Grant could hope, but hardly expect, that his opponent would be fool enough to walk into that trap.[43]

Grant believed, with good reason, that the Confederates his men had soundly thrashed at Champion's Hill and Big Black Bridge were badly demoralized. The detritus left in the wake of the Confederate retreat to Vicksburg, including large numbers of stragglers, had all the hallmarks of a rout. Grant hoped that if he hit them again immediately, he might be able to break their lines and rout them again as he had at Big Black Bridge. On the evening of May 18, he advised his corps commanders that he intended to attack the Rebel defenses the next day. At 9:00 a.m. on the nineteenth he issued the order for the assault, scheduled to begin at 2:00 p.m. The signal would be three massed salvos by Sherman's artillery.[44]

Throughout the morning, all three corps of the Army of the Tennessee continued to work their way into position. It was a deceptively difficult task. The terrain was like that at Port Gibson—narrow flat-topped ridges with cleared land and good visibility, interlaced with deep, dark ravines, steep-sided, bramble-choked, and likely as not to be swampy. Laboriously the troops moved forward over terrain that broke up their formations, confused their sense of direction, and left them exhausted and drenched in sweat. A soldier of the 31st Illinois wrote of "zig-zag hills and deep gulches that were of such irregular formation that they seemed to mock at the points of the compass."[45]

At the time Grant had appointed for the attack, 2:00 p.m., McClernand's line still faced a long scramble across an appalling tangle of ridges and ravines. The advance was necessarily slow, with many pauses while officers figured out how best to negotiate the next terrain obstacle. As A. J. Smith's division of McClernand's corps crept forward, William R. Eddington of the 97th Illinois made use of the breaks to jot occasional notes in his pocket diary. "They are pouring shot and shell into us. The next man to me on my left has just been killed. He is shot through the breast with a grape shot. We are moving forward slowly," Eddington wrote. "My Second Lieutenant is right next in front of me has just been killed, being shot through the head with a musket ball. We are still moving on slowly. The man next to me is knocked down by the wind of a cannon ball. He is not seriously hurt."[46]

And so it went for McClernand's men throughout the rest of that difficult day. The terrain made the advance so slow and its impact so diffuse that the Confederate defenders perceived no assault at all in this sector but merely a steady process of blue-clad soldiers moving in closer to the defensive works.

A. J. Smith tried to make a full-scale assault with his division. He had his regimental commanders announce to their men at about ten o'clock that morning that they were going ahead at 2:00 p.m. The men waited nervously, and their suspense "was somewhat like that of the culprit awaiting the hour of his execution," as one of them recalled. A member of the 48th Ohio wrote that at the time appointed, his colonel gave the order, "Forward, 48th!" and they advanced gamely up one ridge and down into the next ravine, taking heavy fire while crossing the crest. After hours of struggling "through brush and over fallen trees," they halted to allow the troops on their left to close up with them. "By the time they made the connection," the Ohioan wrote, "the sun was setting in the west."[47]

The story was much the same in the rest of McClernand's sector as well as McPherson's. In some cases, it became apparent that the officers' previous concept about the location of the main Rebel line was mistaken and that the troops needed to advance as much as 500 yards farther before actually approaching it. Here and there, a regiment managed to get into position, find a way through the abatis, and charge the Rebel works. Some even got close, but there was never any chance of a breakthrough. About sundown the troops pulled back slightly into protected hollows to sleep for the night.[48]

Meanwhile, Sherman's corps made the only serious impact on the Rebel lines that day. His troops on either side of the Graveyard Road had approached the closest to the defenses on the evening before. They now were the only ones really in position to launch an attack. Yet the task facing them was a grim one. At the salient where the Graveyard Road entered the Vicksburg defenses, the Confederates had built a special strongpoint known as the Stockade Redan because it was near a stockade of logs that blocked the Graveyard Road. The redan itself was an ordinary—but very strong—earthwork. Since the Stockade Redan stood at a projecting angle to the Confederate works, the Federals could attack it from two directions at once, both from the east and from the north. That was at least some consolation, but not much. Other nearby strongpoints could lay down a deadly cross fire on the approaches to the Stockade Redan, especially on the only relatively easy direct access to it, the Graveyard Road Ridge.[49]

The task of attacking the Stockade Redan fell to Frank Blair's division. As soon as he got Sherman's order to prepare for an attack, at about 9:30 that morning, Blair got his artillery into action. Sixteen guns went to work trying to batter down the side of the Confederate earthwork so that it would collapse into the ditch and allow attacking infantry to cross. Several hours of bombardment, however, proved only that Blair would need more guns and much heavier metal if he was going to accomplish anything of that sort. This was bad news, since his men had neither scaling ladders nor fascines for crossing the ditch or climbing the scarp of the Confederate earthworks.

Nervously, Blair's infantry waited for the order to advance. In the 83rd Indiana, Col. Benjamin Spooner gave his men a pep talk. "This is the day of all days you are expected to show your valor," Spooner said, "and to show Jeff Davis that Indiana soldiers are not cowards"—another reference to the old Mexican War Battle of Buena Vista and the Confederate president's alleged contempt for Hoosier courage. Spooner added that orders from higher headquarters forbade the men from stopping to aid any of their wounded comrades. "We were not even to turn him over or give him a drink of water until the battle was over," recalled John Roberts.[50]

Shortly before 2:00 p.m., the artillery ceased firing. Then at the stroke of 2:00, the guns fired three massed salvos, one after another, the signal for the infantry to attack. "Boys, remember your state," shouted Spooner to his Hoosiers. "Forward!" Col. Thomas Kilby Smith's brigade, including the 83rd Indiana, rushed westward on either side of the Graveyard Road, toward the east face of Stockade Redan, cheering wildly, while Col. Giles A. Smith's brigade charged from north to south, aiming for the north side of the work. All met sharp rifle fire as soon as they began their advance, but they looked and felt like "a human wave that seemed irresistible" when they set out.[51]

Kilby Smith had given command of his brigade's right wing, the 127th Illinois and the 83rd Indiana, to Spooner, while he accompanied the left wing himself. Spooner's two regiments advanced on the north side of the Graveyard Road and Kilby Smith's other three regiments on the south. The two wings could not see each other because the crest of the Graveyard Road Ridge was between them. The regiments struggled forward over the almost impossible terrain, pausing several times to dress their ranks. After advancing about 400 yards, Kilby Smith found that his wing of the brigade was exhausted and had scant chance of storming the final steep slope to reach the Stockade Redan. He halted them in a place about 65 to 75 yards short of the Confederate ditch where the steep hillside provided cover from Rebel fire as long as the men lay prostrate.[52]

Scrambling to the top of the Graveyard Road Ridge, Kilby Smith was surprised to see the colors of the 83rd Indiana and 127th Illinois waving immediately in front of the parapet of the Stockade Redan, actually in the ditch that fronted the earthworks. On this face of the fortress, Spooner's men could cooperate with Giles Smith's brigade, whose charge was converging on their right. Giles Smith had deployed the 8th Missouri as sharpshooters in order to force the Rebels to keep their heads down. Alongside Spooner's two regiments, the 13th U.S. Infantry, Sherman's own, and the 116th Illinois also made it into the ditch.[53]

It had not been easy getting there. The 83rd's color guard was down to color-bearer Sgt. John Cassens and Sgt. John Roberts when they paused just below the crest. Spooner ordered them over the top and into the ditch, to plant the flag at the foot of the Confederate works. As they did so, Roberts saw a rifle protruding from a firing port in the logs of the breastwork a few yards away. He brought up his own rifle to aim at the firing port, but before he could shoot he felt "something like a mule had kicked me in the breast" and fell backward. The Confederate bullet passed through the rolled-up blanket he was wearing across his body, then through the belt of his cartridge box, struck his breastbone, and entered his body. Cassens had already gotten to shelter at the base of the Confederate fort, so Roberts dragged himself a few yards to the rear and took shelter as best he could in a ravine. Finding that he was bleeding profusely, he remembered an article he had read in the *Cincinnati Commercial* that had claimed that gunpowder would stop bleeding. He tore open a cartridge and poured the gunpowder on his wound and was relieved when he thought the bleeding was diminishing.[54]

Meanwhile, the rest of his regiment, along with the 127th Illinois, 13th U.S., and 116th Illinois, made it into the ditch but found themselves unable to scale the steep scarp that led up from the ditch to the parapet. Without scaling ladders, they could do little but hunker down in the ditch, shoot at every Rebel who raised his head, and throw back the hand grenades that the Rebels lobbed over the parapet at them. Kilby Smith sent back to division headquarters for further orders and received instructions from Sherman "to get my men as close to the parapet as possible, and be ready to jump in when they began to yield." Sherman assured Smith's staff officer that McPherson was also assaulting the Confederate works and that more progress was imminent.[55]

From his perspective well forward of Sherman, Kilby Smith was actually in a better position to see, as he looked along the front of the Confederate fortifications to the south of his position, that no significant action was taking place in McPherson's sector, only desultory skirmish firing and sharpshooting. Still, he obediently ordered his men to cease firing and fix bayonets, ready to charge up and over the parapet when the order came. As he waited, however, he took a closer look at the scarp of the parapet in front of him and discovered that, like the works on the other side of the Graveyard Road, it was "too steep and high to scale without proper appliances"— scaling ladders. He thought about having his men form a makeshift ladder by driving their bayonets into the slope, but the small trickle of men who could have reached the top of the parapet by that means would have been going to their deaths without the least prospect of doing any damage to the enemy. "Therefore," Smith reported, "I determined to maintain the position and await developments."[56]

There were no further developments, however. The attack had sputtered out at the foot of the Confederate scarp. Kilby Smith deployed selected sharpshooters forward to pick off what Rebels they could, and he tried to keep them well supplied with ammunition.[57] That proved no easy task, as most of the members of the brigade were soon blazing away at any head that appeared above the parapet. Ammunition-bearers had to run a gauntlet made difficult by terrain and Confederate fire. In the 55th Illinois, the situation became serious enough that Col. Oscar Malmborg detailed the sergeant major to bring up the regimental band and have the members make individual runs with what ammunition they could carry, thus not giving the Rebels a large target.

It came as a surprise to the combat troops, including Malmborg, when some minutes later diminutive fourteen-year-old drummer boy Orion P. Howe, son of the regimental bandmaster, came dashing across the ravine with his blouse bulging with cartridges. Howe was not supposed to be part of the resupply operation, but was tending the wounded in a sheltered ravine. Learning that ammunition was needed at the front, he had gleaned all he could from the cartridge boxes of the wounded and made the dash. He not only survived but made several more runs bearing ammunition. Finally receiving a flesh wound in the leg, Howe hobbled to the rear, met Sherman himself sitting his horse in the Graveyard Road, and called out, "General Sherman, send some cartridges to Colonel Malmborg; the men are all out." Sherman ordered him to the rear at once and promised to see to a supply of ammunition for the 55th.

As Sherman reported in a letter to the secretary of war a few weeks later, Howe's parting shout as he went to the rear was "Calibre 54!" If so, the young drummer had made a mistake, for the 55th's Enfields took .577 cartridges. That took nothing away from the courage Howe had displayed in carrying cartridges, and that courage made Howe a national celebrity of sorts, the subject of a poem in the *Atlantic Monthly* the following year that opened with the lines "While Sherman stood beneath the hottest fire / That from the lines of Vicksburg gleam'd," and concluded, "More cartridges, sir, calibre fifty-four!" Howe also became the youngest soldier to receive the Congressional Medal of Honor for service at Vicksburg.[58]

Yet despite the heroics of Howe and many others, nothing remained for the troops of Blair's division but to hang on in such cover as they had been able to find and wait until nightfall would enable them to withdraw. When darkness did come, the Rebels built fires on their parapet to illuminate the ground in front. That proved to be a mistake for which Kilby Smith's sharpshooters made a number of graycoats pay. It "proved more dangerous to them than to us," recalled a soldier of the 55th Illinois, and the Confederates, with belated good judgment, let the fires die out. By midnight the Federals clinging to the slopes in front of the Stockade Redan were able to make their withdrawal in safety.[59]

John Roberts lay all afternoon in the ravine to which he had crawled for shelter after being wounded, where he was gradually joined by dozens of his wounded comrades of the 83rd Indiana, especially officers, who were the special targets of the Confederate sharpshooters. He lay most of the time beside the dead body of his captain. Night was coming, and he knew that after dark his comrades would try to reach him and bring him back inside the lines. At some point, he lost consciousness. Hours later he heard a voice speak his name, and in his dreamlike state of semi-consciousness was uncertain of the nature of the call. He thought that if it was from this world, he would get to see his wife and children again, if from the next, he would see his mother, who had died years before. It turned out to be the former—two comrades from his company who had made their way back through the darkness in search of him. The Rebels heard noises and opened fire, but the three Hoosiers successfully made it to the rear, where his friends deposited Roberts at the field hospital.[60]

The May 19 attacks were never close to success. Vicksburg's defenders were not as demoralized as the Federals might have supposed. Inside the Confederate works were not only the three divisions that Grant's men had mauled and chased all the way from Champion's Hill in the last few days but also two other divisions that had been in Vicksburg the whole time, completely fresh and unbloodied. Even most of the fugitives of Champion's Hill and Big Black Bridge recovered an adequate will to fight when they found themselves inside the magnificent fortifications of Vicksburg and sheltered by the difficult surrounding terrain. It was the terrain that really stopped Grant's May 19 assault, or at least weakened it to the point of insignificance.

If a quick strike failed to trigger Confederate collapse, perhaps a concerted and coordinated mass attack, with the strength of the entire Army of the Tennessee, would be sufficient to crush the Vicksburg defenses. Grant decided he ought to try it. Johnston was still lurking in the middle of the state with an army of uncertain size but certain to be reinforced when the authorities in Richmond realized what was at stake. That made the idea of a protracted siege worrisome. Besides, Grant's army as well as the additional troops that would have to be sent to it in order to sustain a siege could be used elsewhere in the war if they were not tied up in front of Vicksburg for weeks on end. Finally, Grant believed that the rank and file of the Army of the Tennessee would not be reconciled to the tedious drudgery of a siege unless he gave them another chance to take the place by storm.[61]

On May 20, he called a consultation of his three corps commanders. They agreed that the natural strength of the position was what had stopped them the day before, and Grant gave orders for another assault, this time with full preparation, to be launched on May 22 at precisely 10:00 a.m.[62]

The army spent May 20 and 21 making preparations, improving its positions and its supply situation. Though the process of hauling matériel up from the river had begun on the nineteenth, it was taking time to get the new rations into the hands of the soldiers. Riding his line on May 21, Grant heard one of the soldiers say, quietly, but just loud enough for the general to hear him, "Hard tack." That was all it took, and within moments hundreds of men had taken up the chant of "Hard tack! Hard tack!" and it spread rapidly along the line in both directions. Grant assured the soldiers nearby that the food was on the way, and the shouts of "Hard tack!" changed to cheers. By that evening the army was able to issue full rations to all of its troops around Vicksburg.[63]

Preparations for assault took many forms. In some places, commanders continued to edge their lines closer to the fortifications. In most locations, the Union officers had their men dig in to protect themselves from artillery and from any possible breakout attempt by the cornered Rebels. Union guns kept up a steady pounding against the defenses, while the blue-clad skirmishers picked off Rebel artillerists so effectively that they often drove the gunners away from their pieces.[64]

Joining in softening Vicksburg up for the assault were the guns of the fleet. From above and below, the gunboats closed in and went to work methodically, lobbing shell after shell into the city and its defenses. From a safe distance upriver, the mortar boats heaved their thirteen-inch projectiles into the Rebel stronghold. "The scene at night is splendid," wrote George Remley of the 22nd Iowa. "First the flash, like that of distant lightning, coming up from the river, then the track of the shell, describing a parabola in the air, distinctly traced by the burning fuse, and last but not least the vivid glare of intense sulphuric flame, quickly followed by the loud report echoing and reechoing among the surrounding hills." By contrast, the Rebels used their artillery only very sparingly on these days.[65]

Casualties were not heavy on May 20 or 21, but the constant skirmishing exacted a small but steady and continuous price in blood. The slow trickle of casualties seemed to allow the men to dwell more painfully on each loss. One who fell on May 20 was Capt. Henry M. Kellogg of the 33rd Illinois, the highly educated "Normal Regiment," and his loss led a fellow officer to reflect about the cost of the war and its guilt. "It is sad to have such a man killed," wrote the 33rd's Col. Charles E. Lippincott. "It is a great price the country is paying to suppress this rebellion, and it makes the wickedness of all the history which has led to this rebellion, and so to the necessity of this war, seem very great."[66]

CHAPTER TWENTY-THREE

The Great Assault

MAY 20 AND 21 WERE HOT, dry, and dusty until an afternoon thunderstorm on the twenty-first laid the dust and cooled the air.[1] The soldiers had anticipated another assault, but not until the evening of May 21 did they actually receive orders for the next day's 10:00 a.m. attack. Morale was not high. In the camp of the veteran 8th Illinois that evening, James Jessee heard a number of his fellow soldiers making statements to the effect that they would refuse to advance, though most said they would go if ordered.[2]

In a letter to his father, Edward Stanfield of the 48th Indiana wrote, "We always obey orders," but this time he and his comrades prepared to do so with the conviction that the attack would fail and they would not survive. "We expected to die as sure as there was such a thing as death," Stanfield later wrote.[3] In the camp of the 17th Illinois, the scene that evening was grim, as many of the men were exchanging final messages for loved ones. William Alexander turned to his tent mate George Smith and said, "George, if we go into the fight tomorrow I will be killed." This did nothing to help Smith's state of mind, for he had the same feeling about himself. Smith did some serious praying that night, promising God "that if spared I would serve Him the rest of my life."[4]

The Rebel cannon had been almost completely silent the past day or two.[5] Union artillery and sharpshooters had made it extremely hazardous and almost impossible for the Confederate artillerists to serve their guns.[6] The Union guns, by contrast, stepped up the tempo of their fire until, on the morning of May 22, there was a continuous thundering bombardment. No special salvos would be needed to signal the beginning of this day's attack. Grant had his senior officers synchronize their watches—an almost novel measure in those days—so that the assault could begin simultaneously all along the front. He also directed that, except for skirmishers and sharpshooters, the troops should advance with bayonets fixed and not fire their weapons until they were inside the enemy's works.[7]

All along the Union lines, men waited tensely for the order to advance. One soldier recalled "the exhausting suspense of that painful wait. How the past of our lives lived anew—our boyhood friends and frolics, our fathers, our mothers, the girls we left behind. Was this to be the end of all our joys and sorrows, or would we live years to come, maybe with mutilated bodies?" Union and Confederate artillery, the latter newly reawakened in anticipation of the attack, hammered back and forth across the lines, and the infantrymen could hear loads of canister passing over their heads sounding "like a flock of partridges."[8]

Promptly at 10:00 a.m. the infantry surged forward all along the front. On the far right of the Union line, Steele's division of the Fifteenth Corps charged forward over difficult ground. On Steele's right, Col. Charles R. Woods's brigade had to follow a narrow roadway for some distance under enemy fire before it could gain a position to launch an attack. Woods took fifty or sixty casualties before his brigade could deploy out of column and into line of battle. Henry Kircher of the 12th Missouri wrote that they had to go up a "little pathway" and took two hours getting to a place where they could deploy. Several stretches along their route were particularly exposed to Rebel fire, and the troops rushed through at the double-quick.[9]

Once the lead regiment, the 25th Iowa, was deployed, however, its fire provided cover for the regiments that followed. As soon as the brigade was in position, Woods ordered it forward. Col. Hugo Wangelin's 12th Missouri had the lead, with 200 uphill yards to go to reach the works. No formation and no amount of preparation seemed to offer an answer to this miserable terrain. The Missourians struggled forward, taking heavy losses and approaching within a few score yards of the breastworks.[10]

Attacking alongside the 12th Missouri was Capt. F. S. Washburn's 9th Iowa, the lead regiment of Brig. Gen. John M. Thayer's neighboring brigade of Steele's division. Thayer's other three Iowa regiments were not far behind. "Oh! what a fire they pored into us," wrote Pvt. Bruce Hoadley of the 26th Iowa. "We were swept down like grass before the scythe." Elements of the 26th got so close to the works that when the color-bearer went down, the flag fell across the parapet. Somehow the Iowans were able to snatch it back. They had to flatten themselves against the ground, however, for protection against the devastating fire. Hoadley found himself lying between a dead comrade and one who was dying.[11] The color guard of the 9th, fearing that they would all be shot and the flag captured, had the members of the regiment pass the banner downslope from man to man to get it farther away from the parapet.[12]

Thayer's brigade and the 12th Missouri were far too weak to break the line by themselves, and the rest of Steele's division could not get up in time to support them. Indeed, an irate Kircher thought the other regiments' chief contribution was putting an occasional stray bullet into the back of one of his fellow Missourians.[13]

From the right rear of the 12th Missouri, where his regiment guarded the right flank of the attack and the entire army, Capt. R. W. Burt of the 76th Ohio looked on in admiration. "It beat any thing I ever witnessed," he wrote, but he and his men were unable to do anything to help the Missourians and Iowans out there on the slope.[14]

Wangelin's and Thayer's men held on, exchanging fire with the Rebels from a range of ten or fifteen paces. Washburn fell mortally wounded. The 9th Iowa lost 78 men out of 300 it had carried into the fight, including all 4 of its color guard. The 12th Missouri suffered even more heavily, taking 108 casualties out of a similar number engaged. Finally nightfall gave the survivors cover to fall back. The terrain had defeated Steele's attack, with a slight assist from the Rebels.[15]

Sherman had not really expected Steele to break through, but he hoped the move on the far right would attract the Rebels' attention away from the centerpiece of the Fifteenth Corps's assault. This was to be an even more massive effort to succeed where the May 19 attack had failed in taking the Stockade Redan. Sherman had studied the ground in front of the redan carefully and come up with a plan he hoped would enable his troops to overcome the obstacles of the terrain. Rather than have his men attempt to advance in line of battle through the broken ravines, he would have them charge at top speed in a narrow column along the only clear, open corridor of approach in his sector, the Graveyard Road itself.[16]

Leading this desperate rush straight into the teeth of the defenses would be a party of about 150 volunteers—50 enlisted men and 2 officers from each brigade in Blair's division—carrying scaling ladders, bundles of cane, and planks—along with their rifles—so that they could bridge the ditch and provide those who followed them with the means of ascending the scarp. If the day's entire assault seemed like a desperate undertaking, the advance party was a veritable suicide squad. Sherman called them "a forlorn hope." Still, the commanders of Blair's brigades and regiments reported easily obtaining more than their quota of volunteers.[17] Following closely behind the party would be the brigade of Brig. Gen. Hugh Ewing, Sherman's brother-in-law and stepbrother. Ewing's headquarters flag would accompany the forlorn hope, which would be commanded by Capt. John H. Groce of Ewing's lead regiment, the 30th Ohio.[18]

As ten o'clock approached and the artillery hammered away, the forlorn hope formed up in the road where an intervening crest sheltered them from observation by the enemy. Sherman was there, along with Blair and Ewing. Some of the volunteers from John E. Smith's brigade remembered their brigade commander making a brief speech, shouted above the roar of the guns, in which he promised that if they captured the fort, every man in the party would have a sixty-day furlough. A very tense wait followed while the officers' watches ticked off the minutes and seconds until ten o'clock.

At 10:00 a.m., "to the minute," Sherman reported, he gave the order. Groce yelled to his men, and the forlorn hope dashed up the road at a run. For a few moments, the parapet remained deserted, the graycoats still sheltering behind it, riding out the Union bombardment. Then with the party only 100 feet away, the Confederates reared up and fired a ragged volley. Some of the attackers fell, but the others pressed on, past a lone oak where the road bent to the right and up the last few yards to the ditch and scarp of the earthwork. They dived into the ditch for cover and lay panting, ready to lead the rest of the column into the fort. Lt. William C. Porter of the 55th Illinois—a member of the forlorn hope—glanced at his watch and noted that it had taken them just three minutes to carry their load of ladders, planks, fascines, and rifles from the ravine where they had launched their attack.[19]

Young Pvt. Howell G. Trogden of the 8th Missouri, bearing the headquarters flag of Ewing's brigade, climbed partway up the slope of the earthwork and planted the colors. Many others in the party also advanced up the scarp and began digging shallow holes in its slope for cover. The defenders immediately above them could not shoot them now, but they continued to take incoming fire and occasional casualties from marksmen in the works on either side. The Rebels made a quick foray to try to snatch Trogden's flag, but the Federals fought them off. Beyond that, however, all the storming party could do was wait for support.[20]

That support was supposed to come from Ewing's brigade. The 30th Ohio double-quicked up the road, torn by Rebel rifle and artillery fire, but some made it all the way to the ditch to join Groce's forlorn hope. Others sheltered on the slope nearby. Behind them came the 37th Ohio, and now the assault ran into trouble. Like the forlorn hope and the 30th before it, the 37th had to run a deadly gauntlet of fire. Unlike their comrades in the first two units, however, the men of the 37th went to ground in the road, eagerly seeking any undulation in the surface that might afford some cover. The reason was apparently the accumulation of casualties in the roadway. Each company as it passed had left a number of its personnel lying where they fell dead or wounded. Subsequent units were naturally unwilling to step on their fallen comrades and became demoralized from stepping over or around them. By the time the 37th advanced, this reluctance had reached the point of a complete balk.[21]

Blair and Ewing, along with the 37th's commander, Lt. Col. Louis von Blessingh, and their staffs, were conspicuous, vigorously urging the men to move forward. The 37th's sergeant major, Louis Sebastian, walked the whole line of the regiment, where his comrades were lying in the road, calling on them to get up and move on, but to no avail. The men were not budging.[22]

The presence of a full regiment lying down in the road blocked it as an avenue of advance for other troops. So Blair ordered the rear two regiments of Ewing's brigade to leave the road and strike out across the rough ground to the left of it, the same ground over which the left of Kilby Smith's brigade had advanced three days earlier and failed to reach the Stockade Redan. In similar fashion, Ewing's remaining regiments and then Col. Giles A. Smith's brigade, which followed them, lost cohesion among the ravines and ran out of momentum about 150 yards short of the Confederate fortifications.[23]

As additional troops continued to press forward, Blair, with no good options left to him, sent them into the fight behind Giles Smith. When Kilby Smith's brigade topped the ridge and came in sight of the fighting, its commander was amazed to see not a compact column driving forward as briefed but, instead, scattered clumps of Union soldiers spread here and there over the same ground his brigade had vainly attempted to charge across three days before. Blair told him to move forward and to the left and see if he could not help Giles Smith's efforts there.[24]

Meanwhile, on the scarp, Porter, Trogden, and a few score hardy souls of the forlorn hope were still hanging on. A number of soldiers from the 30th Ohio had joined them now, but Porter could not find Groce or any other officer of the 30th and so continued to exercise command of his little section of the outer slope of the fortifications. Even with the new men from the 30th, his force was obviously too small to break the line, and Porter did not feel justified in sending his handful of soldiers "over the ramparts, to be either slaughtered or taken prisoners."[25]

From the Rebel side of the parapet came the shout, "Surrender, Yanks!"

"Come and get us" was the reply from the ditch. The Rebels tried, charging over the top of the parapet and down into the ditch, but Porter's men fought them off. Then the Confederates, safely back on their own side of the works, began throwing grenades over the parapet. This tactic proved ineffective, since the Rebels tended to overthrow their grenades, most of which carried over the ditch and landed harmlessly beyond it.

Noon passed. The Rebels improved their technique and began rolling the grenades down the outer slope. The Federals on the slope found some fence rails, and members of the party crawled almost to the top of the slope, pushing a fence rail ahead of them with their bayonets. In this manner, they caught many of the grenades at the very edge of the crest. The detonations there were relatively harmless to men flattened against the slope below, but catching grenades on a rail balanced on the end of two bayoneted rifles required considerable nerve. The party's only fatality to grenades that afternoon came when one somehow missed or bounded over the intercepting rails and reached the men below. Sgt. Richard Haney of Marietta, Illinois, threw himself on it, smothering the blast and saving the lives of several of his comrades, though at the loss of his own.[26] Before that day ended, the forlorn hope would include seventy-eight Medal of Honor winners.[27]

So the forlorn hope and their handful of reinforcements from the 30th Ohio hung on as best they could, exposed, as Porter dryly observed in his report, "to the fire from the flanks of the enemy, and a direct fire from the skirmishers of the First Brigade." By that he meant Giles Smith's men, who were trying to shoot over the heads of their comrades on the scarp but were apparently finding that tricky when aiming steeply uphill. When one of the Federals on the outer slope of the entrenchments was hit by a shot that his comrades judged to have come from the rear, Porter, Trogden, and the rest of the group by unanimous consent scrambled back down into the ditch itself, which would give them some cover from both enemy and friendly fire.[28]

While the assault of the Fifteenth Corps was bogging down in complete futility, McPherson's Seventeenth, next in line, launched its own. Immediately on the left of Giles Smith's brigade, Brig. Gen. T. E. G. Ransom's charged over similar ground, endeavoring to cooperate with Smith. The result, however, was similar futility. In the forefront of the assault was the old 11th Illinois, which Will Wallace had organized back in Springfield in the first month of the war, and which Ransom himself had led through the carnage of Fort Donelson. Today it was commanded by Col. Garrett Nevins, who had led the Rockford Zouaves into the 11th as Company D back at Camp Butler. During this charge at Vicksburg, he fell within a few feet of the breastworks, killed instantly by a bullet to the forehead.[29]

"The groans of the dying, the shrieks of the wounded, and the almost unearthly screaming of shells and cannonballs, mingled with the rattle of musketry, made up a scene that men see but a few times in a lifetime," wrote Sgt. Stephen A. Rollins of the 95th Illinois, adding, "and the fewer the better." Rollins was full of admiration for the officers of his brigade, who "were brave and daring to a fault." Ransom was "bolder than a lion," and Capt. Gabriel E. Cornwell, of Company K of the 95th, fell "while cheering on and trying to rally his men; but all was of no avail." Ransom's attack met no better success than those in Sherman's sector.[30]

McPherson directed his heaviest attack against the largest and strongest bastions on the defenses, the Great Redoubt and the 3rd Louisiana Redan, which was named after the regiment that garrisoned it. These two earthworks flanked and guarded the Jackson Road's entrance into the fortifications. They were mutually supporting, so that storming one would require taking both. The task of doing so fell to John A. Logan's division. Logan assigned John Stevenson's brigade to attack the Great Redoubt and John E. Smith's the 3rd Louisiana Redan.[31]

In preparation, Stevenson formed his brigade in a sheltered ravine 200 yards from the Great Redoubt. He strengthened his skirmish line by adding to it the entire 17th Illinois, hoping that the heavy fire from this swarm of skirmishers would make the Rebels keep their heads down. His remaining four regiments he divided into two columns of two regiments each, to advance by parallel routes. Columns would be much easier to move over rough terrain than would lines of battle. Stevenson's men had scaling ladders that work details had been building during the night, and they now had two for each company or about one for every ten or fifteen men.[32]

James Jessee of the 8th Illinois jotted in his diary that morning that he felt "fine as regards any physical condition but not so well as regards the prospect of the day's work that is before us."[33] The artillery continued to pound the Rebel works, as it had virtually all night long. Logan's infantry formed up in their sheltered ravine and waited for ten o'clock. Another member of the 8th Illinois, Gould Molineaux, sat writing in his diary. "We have drawn rations and are now preparing for the charge. The Lord Almighty protect me. I put my trust in Him alone now."[34]

At precisely ten o'clock, Logan's infantry marched "steadily up the slope with 'bayonets fixed' and orders not to fire guns." At first the parapets remained deserted. Then, when the attackers were relatively close, the "breastworks and forts swarmed with butternuts who poured volley after volley into our advancing columns." The artillery and supporting infantry tried to make the Rebels keep their heads down, but most of the supporting infantry was unable to fire for fear of hitting their own men.[35] Stevenson's two columns reached the edge of the ditch and deployed from column into line under heavy fire, taking casualties. The Rebels were "mowing us down like grass," wrote Jessee. "I never witnessed such a galling fire in my life."[36]

Reacting to heavy fire from the right, the right column veered left. At the head of the column, the hard-hit 7th Missouri faltered and fell back into the ranks of the 8th Illinois, which was bringing up the rear of the left column. Stevenson, along with Capt. Robert Buchanan, who commanded the 7th, rallied the regiment and deployed it in position to storm the works. Then Stevenson ordered his men to lie down just outside the ditch while the Union artillery shot over their heads into the Great Redoubt. After some time, fire from the redoubt almost ceased; so Stevenson ordered his men up and into the ditch, where they would deploy their scaling ladders against the scarp and take the fort by storm. Yelling wildly, the 7th Missouri and 81st Ohio surged forward. Somehow the left of the brigade never got the order and did not advance.[37]

The Confederates had been playing possum under the pounding of the Union guns, and as the right of Stevenson's brigade charged, a solid line of infantry reappeared on the parapet and poured a deadly, close-range fire into Stevenson's men. Confederate artillery swept them with devastating blasts of canister. The 7th Missouri, a regiment of Irishmen from St. Louis, planted its green Harp-of-Erin flag in the ditch of the redoubt. On the parapet above them flew another green flag with a similar device, belonging to a regiment of Confederate Irishmen also recruited in St. Louis. The Union Irishmen, along with other troops of Stevenson's brigade who got into the ditch, found that their scaling ladders were too short to reach the parapet, and their attack stalled. The 81st Ohio lost its colonel and so many other officers that it fell back in confusion. Most of the rest of Stevenson's brigade hung on grimly, some in the ditch, others farther down the slope, waiting for nightfall.[38]

"It is an almost if not entirely human impossibility to take this fort from this side," wrote Gould Molineaux in his diary as he sat with his back to a tree stump that sheltered him from the continued patter of enemy bullets landing nearby. Even if the ladders had been long enough, he reflected, "just think of one man to mount the ladder at a time." Casualties in his brigade had been high, he believed. "Oh, it is a miserable business. They never fired a shot as we were instructed not to until we gained the fort."[39]

Simultaneous with Stevenson's attack on the Great Redoubt, John E. Smith's brigade charged the 3rd Louisiana Redan. Like every other Union commander whose troops were to advance that day, Smith had given thought to how his men might be able to overcome the enormous odds in favor of the defenders. His first solution was to have the 23rd Indiana and 20th Illinois use some of the same sheltered ground that allowed Stevenson's men to advance within a few hundred yards of the Great Redoubt. From there, the regiments were to dash forward until the steep slope above them gave some cover from Confederate fire, then turn sharply to the right and advance against the 3rd Louisiana Redan along the front of the other fortifications. The concept looked feasible as Smith viewed the terrain from Union lines, but when the 23rd Indiana, at the head of the attacking column, began to move to the right along the Rebel front, the Hoosiers discovered their path blocked by a deep ravine that had been invisible from Smith's vantage point. The ravine was choked with abatis and swept by Rebel fire. Smith ordered the attackers to withdraw.

His first plan having failed almost before it got started, Smith came up with another, similar to Sherman's plan for the attack on the Stockade Redan. Like Sherman, Smith decided to give up the attempt to keep his column under cover and instead hope that rapid movement would protect it from extreme casualties. His regiments would move along the Jackson Road where it made a cut in a ridgetop and then deploy on the far side and charge the Rebel works. This time Smith assigned the 20th Illinois to lead the attack. The Illinoisans charged up the road four abreast. They took heavy casualties but succeeded in getting into the ditch of the 3rd Louisiana Redan. There, however, they discovered that the ditch was too deep and the scarp too steep to be scaled without ladders. Incredibly, Smith had provided them with none, so the attack stalled again. Smith sent word for the 20th to take cover as best they could.[40]

Farther south, in McClernand's sector, the major axis of advance was the line of the Southern Railroad of Mississippi as it passed through the Confederate works on its way into Vicksburg. Guarding the passage of the railroad were two powerful earthworks, the Railroad Redoubt and the 2nd Texas Lunette. McClernand assigned Carr's division to attack in this sector, supported by A. J. Smith's. Unfortunately, Carr, to whom McPherson gave command of the operation, arranged the two divisions one behind the other rather than having his own target one of the Rebel forts and Smith's the other. As it was, each earthwork would be the target of one brigade from each division, with resulting confusion.[41]

As in other sectors of the front, the infantrymen waited tensely for their turn. Taylor Peirce noted that in his own Company C, 22nd Iowa, a number of enlisted men complained of illness, but the captain was having none of it and ordered the sergeants to prod them with bayonets if they shirked during the advance.[42] Even the bravest of soldiers felt uneasy at what they were being asked to do. "I could not see any prospect of success in the assault," recalled Cornelius Dubois of the 33rd Illinois. When a comrade asked him to take charge of his personal effects and forward them to his family after his death in the charge—an event he regarded as a certainty—Dubois lamely tried to cheer him up by observing that his friend's chances of survival were as good as his own. It was not an especially encouraging thought to either of them. In Company E, Pvt. Daniel H. Graves looked at his watch and announced, "Boys, you have just fifteen minutes to live."[43]

Promptly at 10:00 a.m., McClernand's troops advanced. Benton's brigade led the assault against the 2nd Texas Lunette. The initial approach followed the usual pattern—advance by the flank through rough terrain or up a ravine, then break cover on the run and deploy into line of battle. Benton's men charged with determination all the way to the foot of the Confederate works, taking appalling casualties.

The colonels of Benton's regiments had drawn lots for the honor of leading the charge, and George W. K. Bailey of the 99th Illinois was the lucky winner. He had his men remove their coats before the charge and strode along at the head of their column in his shirtsleeves.[44] When color-bearer William Sitton of the 99th fell wounded, Tom Higgins snatched up the colors and carried them all the way to the Confederate trench line. Unfortunately he had become separated from the rest of the regiment and was captured along with the flag.[45]

From his position on the left of Company C, 33rd Illinois, Corporal Dubois knew his job was to keep a steady eye on the colors, at the opposite end of the company line, so he could maintain his unit's alignment. As they advanced, he saw the members of the color guard go down one after another until only his best friend and tent mate Sgt. Sam Shaw remained to take up the Stars and Stripes. Bullets riddled the flag, shot away Shaw's canteen and tin cup, and ripped open his haversack, but he kept going, miraculously unhurt.

Then Dubois saw the bearer of the regimental flag, beside Shaw, stagger and fall. He ran the length of the company and got to the color-bearer in time to hear him say to Lt. Edward J. Lewis, "Take the flag." Lewis did, but Dubois immediately took it from him, saying, "Lieutenant, I'll carry this flag." Proudly bearing the banner, he took his place on the left of his friend. "I'm with you, Sammie," he said, and the two of them strode forward with the flags.[46]

Generally the men obeyed the orders not to fire, though Dubois remembered a man in his company who defiantly took a shot at some of the Texans who were standing out in the open atop their parapet, aiming carefully at the Federals.[47] The advancing regiments tended to become scattered both because of the terrain they crossed and because of heavy losses among their officers. When Col. Charles Lippincott fell wounded, his regiment, the 33rd Illinois, began to lose cohesion. Seeing the disorder in the ranks of the neighboring regiment, Col. David Shunk of the 8th Indiana shouted, "Come on, my brave 33rd, I will lead you." Some did follow Shunk, but as one of its officers admitted, the 33rd, like the other regiments of Benton's brigade, became "more or less disorganized."[48]

Here and there, considerable numbers of men nevertheless made it all the way into the ditch. Lt. Lyman Pratt found himself the only unwounded man left in his company and alone in the ditch. Unlike color-bearer Higgins of the 99th, he managed to escape. Vinton Howell, also of the 33rd, got into the ditch along with a group of others and spent much of the afternoon throwing back over the breastworks the grenades the Rebels lobbed at them. As an officer of the 33rd pointed out, "It was a mere matter of chance on which side they would explode." Where the breastworks were low enough, Illinoisans crouched on the outside, held their rifles over their heads, and fired into the Rebels.[49]

Pvt. Charles Morris found himself in the ditch along with a composite group from several regiments commanded by Col. H. D. Washburn of the 18th Indiana. They planted several regimental colors along the outer slope of the works and then fought off Confederate attempts to snatch them. Their situation was a dangerous one. "We could keep them down in our front," Morris recalled, "but from both right and left they could murder us."[50]

As the day wore on and the men continued to be pinned down in front of the works in the blazing sun, thirst became a problem all along the lines. Some of the casualties fell to sunstroke or heat exhaustion rather than enemy shells or bullets. "I never suffered more from heat at any time," wrote John Campbell of the 5th Iowa.[51] When word that the soldiers needed water reached the camp of the 33rd Illinois back in a sheltered hollow in the rear, two members of the regimental drum corps volunteered to carry water to them. Filling all the canteens they could carry, they set out. Bullets shot off the heel of one man's shoe, cut canteen strings, and ripped holes in clothing, but somehow both men succeeded in the mission of mercy without receiving a scratch.[52]

Simultaneous with Benton's attack on the 2nd Texas Lunette came the charge of Lawler's brigade against the Railroad Redoubt. Lawler's men had broken the Confederate line at Big Black Bridge, but now they faced an immensely more difficult task. As in the attacks elsewhere along the Vicksburg lines this day, they crossed difficult ground and suffered a degree of disorganization. Here too the Rebels stood up on the top of their parapet to get better shots at the attackers, despite the efforts of the Union sharp-shooters to pick off as many as possible.[53]

Reaching the ditch of the Railroad Redoubt, Lawler's men plunged into it. Here, however, some of them found something much different than any of the other attacking brigades came upon that day. In the 22nd Iowa's sec-tor, Union artillery had succeeded in blasting a small breach in the parapet, allowing perhaps a dozen or more Iowans led by Sgt. Joseph E. Griffith and Sgt. Nicholas C. Messenger to scramble through into the interior of the Railroad Redoubt.

Large earth-and-log walls bisected the redoubt into several compart-ments, open to the Confederate rear but enclosed on the other three sides. Griffith, Messenger, and their men found themselves in one of these, along with a number of Rebels. Desperate hand-to-hand fighting ensued, and when it was over, Griffith and Messenger were in possession of fifteen pris-oners and one compartment of the redoubt. They found it difficult to remain there, however, as they were exposed to heavy fire from Confeder-ate troops behind the redoubt. The Iowans pulled back through the breach in the parapet, leaving this compartment of the fort a no-man's-land.[54]

Thereafter, the fight on the outer slope of the Railroad Redoubt became very much like the battles that were taking place at the same time at Stock-ade Redan, the Great Redoubt, the 3rd Louisiana Redan, and the 2nd Texas Lunette. The flags of several regiments of Lawler's brigade as well as Lan-dram's brigade of A. J. Smith's division waved in various proximity to the Rebel works, sometimes only a few feet from the crest of the parapet. Eighteen-year-old drummer Frank Dunn waved the colors of the 130th Illinois just below the parapet. When the staff was shot in two, Dunn picked up the flag itself and waved it without a staff.[55]

Occasional Confederate forays aimed at capturing a flag or clearing the Federals out of a section of trench met disaster in the face of fierce Union resistance, but neither could the bluecoats get possession of the Rebel side of the works, at least not on a basis that would allow them to stay there long. Out on the exposed slopes, Lawler's and Landrum's men sought what cover they could find or dug shallow fighting positions with their bayonets.[56]

As elsewhere, the Rebels tossed grenades and artillery shells over the parapet. Sometimes the Federals could throw them back, but the Rebels tried to cut the fuses short enough to prevent that. "When our men seen one was going to explode," wrote William Wiley of the 77th Illinois, "they would lay down flat with their faces on the ground and a good many saved

their lives in this way as the fragments of the shells would fly over them."
Wiley and his comrades no longer thought of taking the fort but of hanging
on until darkness gave them cover to pull back from their precarious
position.[57]

From his location several hundred yards to the rear, McClernand had a
somewhat different view of the situation. He believed his men had captured
one of the forts and were on the verge of a major breakthrough, and he
wanted support from the rest of Grant's army to make sure they achieved
it. The attack was little more than an hour old when at 11:15 a.m. McClernand sent a dispatch to Grant asserting that the Confederates were massing
against the Thirteenth Corps and urging that McPherson's Seventeenth
should "make a diversion" for him, though with Logan's division hurling
itself at the Great Redoubt and the 3rd Louisiana Redan, it is hard to imagine what other diversion McClernand thought he needed.[58]

Grant wrote back to say that if McClernand's advanced forces needed
help, he should reinforce them from his reserves. McClernand, however,
unlike the other two corps commanders, had not retained any reserves.
While he had launched Carr's and A. J. Smith's divisions at the strongholds
flanking the railroad, he had directed Osterhaus, reinforced by the only
available brigade of Hovey's division, to attack the fortifications farther to
the left, where they were of course making as little impression as any of the
other attacking columns.[59]

McClernand wrote again to say that his forces had "gained the enemy's
intrenchments at several points, but are brought to a stand," and then at
noon yet again, stating, "We have part possession of two forts, and the Stars
and Stripes are floating over them. A vigorous push ought to be made all
along the line."[60]

Grant received the message at his observation post on a high hill behind
McPherson's lines. He had selected that point because from it he could see
the entire line of the Rebel fortifications from the Stockade Redan all the
way to the Railroad Redoubt and beyond. Looking toward McClernand's
sector, about a mile and a half away, Grant could see nothing to indicate the
sort of success McClernand claimed. Indeed, reports and observation from
the whole line had already convinced him that it was time to call off the
attack. After reading McClernand's note, Grant rode over to Sherman's
headquarters. Handing the note to Sherman, he commented, "If only I
could believe it." Sherman remonstrated that since the note was official, it
had to be presumed true. "A corps commander would not write a misstate-
ment over his own signature at such a time," he urged.

"I do not know," Grant replied.[61]

One of the reasons for the Army of the Tennessee's unusual effectiveness was the great degree of mutual trust among its officers. This was nowhere more apparent than in the relationships among Grant, Sherman, and McPherson. No one seemed much inclined to trust the schemer McClernand. Yet, as Sherman pointed out, the army could not perform up to its potential on any other basis than trust between officers.

Grant still doubted McClernand's claims, but what if they should prove true? What if the Thirteenth Corps really was on the verge of a breakthrough but was allowed to fail through lack of support from the rest of the army? That possibility was too horrible to contemplate. Grant would just have to act on the basis that the message was accurate. He prepared to ride over to McClernand's sector and ordered Sherman to renew the assault at 3:00 p.m. if he had not by then received further orders from him to the contrary. He dispatched a similar order to McPherson and also directed him to send Quinby's division to reinforce McClernand directly.[62]

To renew the assault in his sector, Sherman ordered Giles Smith to press forward once again across the rugged ravines on the left of Sherman's sector. To try the Graveyard Road route again, Sherman chose Mower's Eagle Brigade, part of Tuttle's division. Mower had received his commission as brigadier general only two days before, and his men had presented him with a fine horse, saddle, and bridle on the occasion and then had given "cheer after cheer," as one of them recorded in his diary, "for the General is our idol."[63]

Summoning Mower, Sherman pointed to the Stockade Redan. "General Mower," he said, "can you carry those works?" Mower shook his head slowly and replied, "I can try."

"Then do it," Sherman ordered.[64]

The brigade formed up in the sheltered section of the road and prepared to charge forward in columns of four. Mower's own 11th Missouri was in the lead, the 47th Illinois next, then the 8th Wisconsin with Abe the eagle on his perch beside the colors, and finally the 5th Minnesota. From their position in the road, the men of the brigade could see Sherman, Tuttle, and Mower on a nearby hilltop, watching them, and felt inspired to do their best. Mower left the group and came over to take his position at the head of his brigade.[65]

Along the ridges on either side, Union infantry and artillery poured a heavier fire than ever into the Confederate works. Precisely at three o'clock, the brigade charged up the road. As the head of the column came within sight of the Rebel breastworks, a hurricane of fire tore into it. "It was terrible," recalled a participant. "The roar of cannon, and the crash of musketry was something which cannot be described."[66] The defenders had the range better than ever. Ninety-two men fell in the 11th Missouri and about forty in the 47th Illinois.[67]

Watching from his vantage point, Sherman turned to Tuttle and said, "This is murder; order those troops back." Tuttle dispatched a staff officer, who succeeded in halting the attack before the full fury of the Rebel fire could strike the last two regiments. The 11th Missouri, 47th Illinois, and at least one company of the 8th Wisconsin had already gone too far. They charged onward and joined the survivors of the forlorn hope and Ewing's brigade in the Rebel ditch. J. W. Greenman of the 8th Wisconsin wrote that the color-bearer of the 11th Missouri, "a tall brave young fellow, planted his flag on the rebel works, but he could not stay with his flag, but jumped back into the ditch, and only when darkness came on could he venture up to get his flag, which he successfully done."[68] Most of the 8th Wisconsin, including Abe, halted well short of that point, on Sherman's orders, but still suffered about twenty casualties, included a slightly wounded eagle.[69]

Giles Smith's brigade also made another brave attempt. The 8th Missouri and 55th Illinois, partners in several desperate endeavors in the past, were to lead the assault. Smith had been lying on the ground along with his men. Now he rose to his feet, waved his sword, and shouted, "Boys, they'll give us one volley; before they can reload, we'll be inside their works. Forward, double-quick, march! And hurrah like h———!" They did, and charged nearly to the parapet. Then, like the others that day, they could not manage the final few yards into the teeth of the Rebel fire and had to take shelter outside the works.[70]

In the Seventeenth Corps, McPherson ordered Logan to renew the assault on the Great Redoubt. The only viable approach was the Jackson Road, used by John E. Smith's brigade that morning. Logan now reinforced Smith with the 20th Ohio from Leggett's brigade and ordered him to attack again. This would once more be an affair in which only one regiment could advance at a time, and then only by the flank. Smith chose the Lead Mine Regiment, the 45th Illinois, to lead the way. The 45th had been Smith's own regiment, back when he was a colonel, and he knew "they would go wherever I ordered and where it was possible to go." They had not gotten their turn to attack in the morning, and so were fresh.[71]

Forming the 45th in a sheltered section of the roadway was the regiment's current commander, Maj. Luther Cowan, who had sat by the campfire a week before and wondered if he was still the same Lute Cowan who had left wife and children back in Warren, Illinois, two years before, or "some new being in some other world." His continued anxieties had convinced him then that he was still the same man. Now he had plenty to be anxious about, for his regiment faced incredible odds. Still, he had assured his wife two months before, "If we are there and happen to be the ones to charge, I intend to have it said afterwards that I finished my work there, or that I was one of the first to stand on the rebels works. I have no fear of the consequences, for I don't believe my time is yet up nor that it is my destiny to be hurt in a fight."[72]

Cowan made sure his men understood what they were about to do. They would march up the road to where it emerged from a cut out onto a slope in full view of the works about 200 yards away. Then the column would turn left and go to double-quick time until the head of the column had gone far enough to make room for the entire regiment in line of battle. At that point Cowan would give the order, "By the right flank, charge," and they would plunge up the hill and over the Rebel parapet. With explanations complete, they waited tensely for 3:00 p.m., as their comrades had waited five hours before.[73]

The time came. "Let every man stand to his post," shouted Cowan, "Forward, 45th!" The Lead Mine Regiment stepped off. As they emerged from the mouth of the cut, the Great Redoubt loomed ahead and above. The column swung to the left, and Cowan shouted, "Double-quick!" They had taken only a couple of steps when a volley rippled along the Rebel parapet and ripped into the head of the column. Dozens of blueclad bodies crumpled to the ground, but the others kept on running. At the head of the column, Sgt. Wilbur Crummer looked around and realized he had no officers with him. Luther Cowan had finished his life's work, as he had promised. His body lay where the first volley had caught the regiment, only a few yards from the mouth of the cut.[74]

Crummer had to make a quick decision. Technically the 45th was now under the command of the senior surviving captain, Leander Fisk, but that officer did not yet know it. As first sergeant of Company A, Crummer was now the ranking man at the head of the column. He kept going until he judged there was room for the whole regiment to clear the road. Then he dived for the ground, and everyone behind him did the same. Thanks to an undulation of the terrain, they could find some cover if they flattened themselves very close to the ground.[75]

Here they waited until Fisk, who had conned *Anglo-Saxon* past the Vicksburg batteries exactly one month ago, took command and ordered them to charge for the earthworks. Confederate fire "mowed the men down in bunches," but a few hardy members of the Lead Mine Regiment actually succeeded in reaching the top of the parapet before they too were shot down. The survivors sheltered against the scarp, as hundreds of other Union troops were doing by now all along the line of the fortifications. Seeing the disaster to the 45th, General Smith called off the attack and spared the 20th Ohio a similar bloodletting.[76]

In McClernand's sector, the renewal of the assault was carried out not by his own Thirteenth Corps, but by the reinforcements from McPherson, Quinby's division. Inexplicably, rather than massing this fresh division against the Railroad Redoubt, which seemed to offer the best chance of success, McClernand sent one of its three brigades to Osterhaus, whose attack was going nowhere. The other two brigades he dispatched to Carr. Carr then divided them, directing Col. John Sanborn's brigade against the 2nd Texas Lunette and Col. George B. Boomer's against the trenches, or in the parlance of the time, "rifle pits," between the lunette and the Railroad Redoubt. Lt. Henry G. Hicks, adjutant of the 93rd Illinois, noted that all of Quinby's officers understood both the desperation and the "utter folly" of this undertaking, but orders were orders.[77] "It was much like marching men to their graves in line of battle," wrote another soldier in the division.[78]

Only minutes before, the Confederates inside the Railroad Redoubt had counterattacked and succeeded in driving the Union troops away from the ditch, capturing the colors of the 77th Illinois and the 22nd Iowa. This extinguished whatever vestige of a reason there had ever been for committing Quinby's division. Nevertheless, Carr gave the orders, and Boomer and Sanborn grimly prepared to execute them.[79]

"Attention, Third Brigade!" shouted Boomer. "Shoulder arms! Right shoulder shift, arms! Forward, Common time, March!" The brigade had to cross a badly exposed ridge and then a brush-tangled ravine before reaching the final ridgeline in front of the Confederate works. By that time, Hicks estimated the brigade had lost a quarter of its numbers as casualties. On the last ridge, the brigade paused to catch its breath and re-form its ranks. Then as Boomer was about to give the order to charge, a bullet struck his head, killing him almost instantly. He lived just long enough to tell those bending over him, "Tell Col. Putnam not to go over that hill"— meaning the ridge the brigade was about to cross in its advance toward the Confederate works.[80] His own honor now beyond question, perhaps Boomer felt able to give directions that his men should be spared slaughter. "He was a man beloved by all who knew him," wrote Hicks, "and his loss was keenly felt. But his death unquestionably saved the brigade from practical annihilation."[81]

Col. Holden Putnam of the 93rd Illinois took over command of the brigade, and, either ignorant of or unconvinced by Boomer's dying advice, gave the order for the final charge. At this, however, the commanders of some of the regiments balked, refusing to obey the order and complaining that "it was murder to go further." Putnam told the men to lie down again and sent to the rear for instructions. When they came, they directed him to hold his ground until nightfall. "How any man escaped from that slaughter-pen that we got into that afternoon, has always been a mystery to me," reminisced W. A. Bartholomew of the 59th Indiana many years later.[82]

Sanborn's attack was, if anything, even more futile. His brigade suffered some 216 casualties, more than it had lost in all the rest of the campaign. To Sanborn, it seemed "all for no good." The advance never had any chance of accomplishing anything and was a complete waste of life. "I can but feel that there was official misrepresentation or misconduct that led to this matter which requires investigation," he wrote in his report three days later.[83]

At long last, the sun sank behind the Vicksburg fortifications and the shadows crept up from the ravines, finally ending a long, weary, bloody day for the Army of the Tennessee. The firing ceased as the battlefield darkened. Lying down in front of the Railroad Redoubt to shelter from the final Confederate shots, Adjutant Hicks noticed that it was a beautiful starry night. Lying on the ground beside him, Capt. Charles Taggart quoted Thomas Campbell's lines:

> Our bugles sang truce for night-cloud had lower'd,
> And the sentinel stars set their watch in the sky,
> And thousands had sunk on the ground overpower'd,
> The weary to sleep and the wounded to die.[84]

CHAPTER TWENTY-FOUR

Vicksburg Siege

T HE SIEGE OF VICKSBURG began before the last shots had been fired on May 22. Here and there in the positions they had seized during the day's attacks, or to which they had withdrawn after the attacks had failed, the Federals began to dig in, first with bayonets and later with spades and shovels. In some cases, these new lines were as little as 100 yards from the Confederate parapet. That night's work was the first of many nights of digging the army was destined to do in the coming weeks.

For some soldiers, the first order of business, after darkness fell, was to escape from the impossible positions into which the day's attack had carried them, often at the base of the enemy's earthworks. "As soon as it became dusk we darted from our secluded places and ran to the rear, each for himself," wrote Sam Jones of the 22nd Iowa. "We could only wait until each one would see his chance to get out."[1]

Sgt. William Eddington found himself in command of his company of the 97th Illinois that night, and after some uncertainty he realized that the company was all alone. The rest of the regiment—indeed, of the army, it seemed—had retreated. "I did not know what to do," Eddington wrote. "I knew that it was my duty to wait for orders. I waited for quite a while but no orders came, so I made up my mind that something was wrong." Quietly he led the company back to camp, where he found the rest of the regiment and learned that a runner had been sent to recall the company but somehow never arrived.[2] Eddington and his comrades were far from the only Union troops creeping out of no-man's-land in the middle of the night. It was well after midnight before all the members of the 93rd Illinois could make their way to the rear.[3]

Getting the wounded men back to camp was especially troublesome. Men crept through the darkness toward the places where they remembered seeing friends fall, constantly on the alert for shots or shells from the breastworks. Illinois soldiers Charles Morris and George Kendall took a stretcher forward almost to the Confederate works in order to retrieve their wounded comrade Billy Burlingame. Before they could find him, a Rebel on the other side of the works tossed a lighted 12-pounder shell over at them. Kendall reacted quickly, scooping up the hissing shell and throwing it over the top of the earthwork a fraction of a second before it exploded.[4]

Tales of courage that night were many, especially among the wounded. Parmenas Hills of the 33rd Illinois lost a leg to a Confederate shell that day, but once his comrades carried him off the field and had reached a safe distance from Confederate lines, he quipped, "Now I can go home and make stump speeches." Sadly, one of his comrades noted, "The splendid young fellow died a short time after."[5]

Sometimes the tales were simply of the wonder of being alive at the end of such a day. William Alexander, who had told his friend George Smith that he was bound to die that day, had fulfilled his prediction. Smith had thought himself equally certain of death before sundown but had promised to serve God if He spared his life, and day's end found him unscathed and still in the ranks of the 17th Illinois. Somewhat more remarkably, Smith could write fifty years later that he had faithfully kept the promise he had made to God as a very frightened young man on the morning of May 22, 1863.[6]

When all the living were finally back in their camps that night, the men had time for sorrow over those they had lost. The 22nd Iowa's regimental quartermaster met the returning soldiers and directed them to where a hot meal was waiting for them. They were ravenously hungry, wrote Jones, but "it was a very solemn banquet. The outlines of our faces were pale and rigid. Our hearts were sad, many friends had fallen since morn." Of those who actually went into the fight, the 22nd Iowa had lost 83 percent in the assault.[7]

The day's losses were much more than numbers to their comrades. "The saddest news that I have got to write is that we have lost our Major," wrote 45th Illinois soldier Kingsley Olds to his father three days later. "I am very sorry Major Cowan was killed, for he was as brave a man as ever lived and made a good officer."[8] Similarly, the 26th Missouri mourned the loss of "the gallant Col. Boomer."[9]

Jake Ritner of the 25th Iowa faced a particularly difficult loss. His friend Sgt. James Freeman had died within fifty yards of the breastworks that day. Shot through the lower abdomen, the popular sergeant "may have lived some time, but the place was exposed to such a raking fire of the enemy that we could not go to him till after dark, when he was found dead."[10]

Freeman was Ritner's best friend. "He was such a faithful soldier, always ready for duty," Ritner wrote. "He and I marched side by side at least 150 miles since the first of May, through dust, rain and mud, day and night; and wherever he was wanted he was sure to be found." He was also Ritner's wife's sister's husband. Ritner knew the loss would fall heavily on his sister-in-law, Caroline Freeman, back in Jefferson, Iowa. "I have been thinking all day that I must write to her," he explained in a letter to his wife, Emeline, the next day, "but I have concluded that I can't do it." Would Emeline be willing to break the sad news to her sister? She hurried to Caroline's house the same day she received word. Neighbors had already heard and were trying to comfort Mrs. Freeman. "She could hardly believe it till I got there," wrote her sister Emeline, "then she knew it was true and she commenced screaming. . . . I felt so bad for her."[11]

In the camps outside of Vicksburg, the evening of May 22 was a time for postmortems on the day's decisions. Grant would later write in his memoirs that the assault had been necessary because the men believed they could take Vicksburg by storm and wanted to try. This may have been a bit of self-justification after the fact, or Grant may honestly have believed as much. Most of his soldiers had not been of that mind at all, believing they were being sent to their deaths. The outcome of the assault confirmed their skepticism. "Thus ended the first assault made contrary to the dictates of common sence & the opinion of everyone," concluded Indiana soldier Edward Stanfield after the attack was over.[12] Two days later, Iowan Henry Ankeny wrote, "It was a useless expenditure of life and no one had any confidence in the successful end of the assault, but it has satisfied our generals that the enemy works cannot be taken by storm."[13]

Some soldiers were more willing to forgive Grant's decision. Although Edward Ingraham of the 33rd Illinois admitted that "the affair is now looked upon as a sad mistake," he added, "I do not blame Gen. Grant." Ingraham believed Grant had harbored legitimate concerns about the possible approach of a Confederate relieving army and therefore was justified, or at least excusable, for making "a bold strike."[14]

In hindsight, everyone, including Grant, knew that he had erred in ordering the attack. The results of the day's fighting had made clear that the Army of the Tennessee had had no realistic chance of breaking through the Vicksburg defenses from the positions it then occupied. Assaulting those lines on May 22 was the sort of blunder that a bad general might make but that every truly great Civil War general did make on more than one occasion. The evolution of weapons and tactics in the mid-nineteenth century made attacks in the Civil War difficult, costly, and prone to fail, yet still often necessary in order to achieve the purpose of a campaign. A general who was sufficiently aggressive to achieve great results in this war would have to be willing to launch major assaults without perfect knowledge of the terrain and the enemy's strength. Sometimes the result was Big Black Bridge and sometimes it was the May 22 assault on the Vicksburg fortifications.

Grant was among the most aggressive of Civil War generals and also the most successful. He had built the Army of the Tennessee in his own image and infused it with his own confidence and aggressiveness at every level, making it the perfect instrument of his successful style of war. May 22 at Vicksburg, however, was the price the Army of the Tennessee had to pay for being Grant's army.

The army had paid a price for having McClernand too, and many within the army knew it. "That night there were stirring times at Grant's headquarters," recalled staff engineer William Jenney. Most of the corps and division commanders gathered there, and "McClernand was spoken of in no complimentary terms." Rawlins was in a towering rage and announced that the records should "charge the loss of a thousand lives to that ———— McClernand."[15] John Sanborn, whose brigade had suffered in front of the 2nd Texas Lunette thanks to McClernand's message, was in some ways even more bitter. "Probably not less than two thousand men were killed and wounded," he wrote, "as a result of a despatch which seemed to have no foundation in fact."[16]

The army's casualties for the day totaled 3,199 men killed, wounded, and captured. Of those, probably a third fell in the renewed assaults Grant had ordered in response to McClernand's claims of success. In more personal terms, men like Col. George Boomer and Maj. Luther Cowan would have been alive that night had it not been for McClernand's mistake. And his insistence that his men had scored significant gains and could achieve a major breakthrough if reinforced and supported by attacks elsewhere along the line was a mistake, pure and simple.

His own soldiers knew as much. "This may have appeared true to him," wrote Charles D. Morris of the 33rd Illinois, "but he was not near enough to see for himself."[17] The verdict of Thirteenth and Seventeenth corps soldiers involved in the sector around the Railroad Redoubt was that if any chance of success had existed it was long gone by the time Quinby's division arrived. Some of Carr's division wondered why McClernand had not reinforced them with the one available brigade of Hovey's unengaged division rather than sending for reinforcements from McPherson that could not possibly arrive for several hours. Morris believed that with the help of Hovey's men "we would have broken their line."[18] As it was, the reinforcement was a complete waste.

On May 25, Pemberton requested a truce to allow for the removal of

Union dead from the slopes outside his forts, along with any wounded who might still be alive there. The stench of decomposing bodies had been a powerful motivation for the Confederate commander to take this course. Some of the Union wounded, no one can say just how many, had already been recovered by their comrades during the intervening nights. Some were still alive on the battlefield. Privates John W. Ross and James Scantlin of the 33rd Illinois, "one with a leg shot off, the other an arm," had survived by taking water from the canteens and food from the haversacks of their dead comrades. Surviving members of the 33rd retrieved them during the truce, but they died several days later.[19] The soldiers who kept diaries and letters expressed no expectation of such a truce and assigned no blame for its delay. Indeed, many of them thought it meant Pemberton was about to surrender. A number of Confederate soldiers took the opportunity of the truce to make their own individual surrenders, though some Union officers would not allow this under a flag of truce and told the would-be deserters to go back to their lines and desert in accordance with the laws of war.[20]

With the wasteful assault and the gruesome recovery of its victims finally over, those who had survived could thank God for their preservation and turn their attention to the business of getting into Vicksburg by the slower and surer means of siege. The most striking feature of siege warfare, either on the first or last day of such operations, was the constant roar of the artillery. The guns would now and then fall silent for a few minutes, but four weeks into the siege Ohio soldier Isaac Jackson could note in his diary, "There has not been an hour hardly but we can hear the report of a gun along the line somewhere."[21] Most soldiers simply described the cannonading as continuous.[22]

Most soldiers of the Army of the Tennessee were spectators to the work of the artillerists. For the infantrymen, hostile action during the siege consisted of sharpshooting. "During the siege I fired at least one thousand rounds," wrote young Charles Willison of the 76th Ohio. "Sharpshooting was kept up constantly and systematically." For days he kept watch on a certain point opposite his regiment's position where he had seen Rebels moving from time to time, and finally his patience paid off. "At this place I hit the only man I was sure of during the war," he wrote years later. "I could tell by the throwing up of his hands and a stretcher being immediately rushed to the spot."[23]

In an average morning during the siege, a man on sharpshooting duty might shoot anywhere from twenty to fifty rounds.[24] Nathan Dye wrote of expending forty rounds in four hours and noted that some men would take that many shots in an hour.[25] Thousands of men were doing the same throughout the daylight hours. "The fighting is incessant all day," wrote Edward Ingraham. "The rifle pits are full of men watching for rebel heads to appear above their breastworks."[26] The cumulative sound of all that sharpshooting was almost like the noise of a battle, though men found in their own homely experiences other sounds to which to liken the sharpshooters "constantly popping away." To Taylor Peirce, it sounded like "a chopping frolic where the axes are going continually."[27] It reminded Isaac Jackson of a number of men shingling a house, all hammering away at the shingles. "First one pops and then another."[28]

Aside from sharpshooting, and enduring as best they could the efforts of the enemy's sharpshooters and artillerymen, the task of the infantry during the siege was to push the entrenchments ever closer to the Rebel fortifications until the Union position became so advantageous that a final assault could succeed without unacceptable casualties. The process of doing this was as close to a science as any activity within the business of war. Day by day and night by night, the Army of the Tennessee pressed its siege lines closer and closer to the Confederate ramparts. In each sector all along the lines around Vicksburg, engineer officers planned new trenches and gun emplacements a little farther forward, and details of troops crept out into no-man's-land under cover of darkness to construct them.

Throughout the course of the siege, Confederate hopes for saving Vicksburg, or at least Pemberton's army, were pinned on another Confederate army under Joseph Johnston, which hovered northwest of Jackson, apparently waiting until Johnston thought the time was right to attack Grant and try to relieve Vicksburg. Grant detached part of his army under Sherman's immediate command to move some miles inland and prepare to block any effort by Johnston. The Confederate, however, did nothing.

While the siege works progressed methodically, relations between John A. McClernand and the rest of the army's officer corps reached a critical point. He had sat idly by while half the army fought for its life at Champion's Hill, and his exaggerated claims had cost the army in blood during the May 22 assault. Even such gaffes might perhaps have been forgiven if the man could ever have stopped his nefarious politicking. The fallout from one of McClernand's political maneuvers caught up with him during the middle of June and became the occasion of his downfall and final exit from the Army of the Tennessee.

Storm clouds had been brewing with renewed energy ever since the failed assault. McClernand had gotten wind of the hard things Grant's staffers were saying about him and became more embittered than ever against his commander. He was unguarded in expressing his feelings in conversation with his much younger townsman Col. James H. Wilson, a member of Grant's staff. To Wilson, McClernand raged profanely that he would obey no more orders from Grant. "I am tired of being dictated to— I won't stand it any longer, and you can go back and tell General Grant," McClernand announced before launching into a string of curses at Wilson. The staff officer took umbrage and demanded that McClernand apologize or fight him on the spot. "I was simply expressing my intense vehemence on the subject matter, sir," McClernand explained, "and I beg your pardon." Thereafter, whenever anyone was heard to utter an oath around army headquarters—something Rawlins was known to do from time to time— the waggish explanation was, "He's not swearing—he's just expressing his intense vehemence on the subject matter."[29]

By June 4, McClernand claimed to have heard that there were rumors making the rounds to the effect that he had been relieved, or arrested, or had not performed well in the May 22 assault. In a letter to Grant of that day, he reeled off a whole litany of rumors that he complained were "finding their way from the landings up the river." He could not resist including a barb by adding to the list the supposed rumor "that I am responsible for your failure" on May 22.[30]

Then on June 17, Grant learned that a piece had appeared in the June 10 edition of the *Missouri Democrat* and also in the June 13 edition of the *Memphis Evening Bulletin*, "purporting to be a congratulatory order from Maj. Gen. John A. McClernand to his command." That is exactly what it was, though in the best tradition of egocentric generals from Julius Caesar to Napoleon, McClernand had used the pretense of praising his troops as a vehicle to heap enormous praise on himself. The lengthy document rehearsed the whole course of recent operations, dwelling on the accomplishments of the Thirteenth Corps in such a way as to suggest that it had waged the entire campaign with no more than an occasional slight assist from the other two corps.[31]

McClernand's account was the most offensive at the two points of the campaign at which his actual performance had been worst. He implied that he had in fact fought the Battle of Champion's Hill and that on May 22 the Thirteenth Corps had truly had a lodgment in the Confederate works and that the other two corps had let it down, causing the failure of the assault. Still, the wording of the address was subtle enough that a reader sympathetic to McClernand could take it as nearly true. To feel the full sting of McClernand's insinuations, it was probably necessary to have a keen sense of his ways. The officers of the Army of the Tennessee knew him, and from brigade to corps commanders, those outside the Thirteenth Corps reacted with raw, throbbing fury when they read McClernand's address.

Frank Blair, a division commander in Sherman's Fifteenth Corps, was among the first to become aware of McClernand's self-congratulatory publication, seeing it in the Memphis paper. Seething with rage, Blair had gone to see Sherman on the evening of June 16. If Sherman and McPherson did not see fit to take up the matter with McClernand, Blair said he would declare political war on McClernand.[32] That was no idle threat. Blair's father had been a close advisor of Andrew Jackson and was still a respected senior statesman; his brother was Lincoln's postmaster general; and it had often been said of the family that when it came to political feuds, "They don't go in for a fight; they go in for a funeral."

Sherman needed little urging from Blair. The next morning, June 17, he penned a letter to Grant, roundly denouncing McClernand's latest offense—"such an effusion of vain-glory and hypocrisy." He rightly observed that the "order" was "manifestly addressed not to an army, but to a constituency in Illinois," and, Sherman might have added, across the rest of the country as well. Finally he pointed out that McClernand's order was not only unjust to his fellow officers, but, having been published in the newspapers, was also a blatant violation of army regulations. General Orders No. 151, of 1862, forbade the publication of reports, which is what McClernand's "Congratulatory Order" really was. Furthermore, this report had never even been submitted to McClernand's commanding officer, Grant.[33]

Grant knew he would have to take action now. The note he sent to McClernand was brief and to the point: "Inclosed I send you what purports to be your congratulatory address to the Thirteenth Army Corps," Grant wrote. "I would respectfully ask if it is a true copy. If it is not a correct copy, furnish me one by bearer, as required both by regulations and existing orders of the Department."[34]

McClernand was away from his headquarters when the note arrived, but he replied the next morning, stating that the newspaper clipping was indeed an accurate copy of his congratulatory order and adding, "I am prepared to maintain its statements." That Grant had not yet received a copy of it, McClernand blamed on his adjutant, Lt. Col. Walter B. Scates. McClernand said he thought Scates had forwarded the copy as he ought to have done.[35] Such excuses were entirely irrelevant to the major offense McClernand had committed by releasing the order to reporters without permission. He might—or might not—have believed that Grant had received a copy of the order, but he could not possibly have thought that Grant had given his approval to have it published.

By the time Grant received McClernand's reply, he also had a letter from McPherson. McPherson seems to have heard of the matter via a different route than Sherman, since in his letter he referred to the *Missouri Democrat* rather than the *Memphis Evening Appeal*. As always, McPherson was polite and well mannered. "The whole tenor of the order is so ungenerous, and the insinuations and criminations against the other corps of your army are so manifestly at variance with the facts," that McPherson had felt it his duty to call the matter to Grant's attention. Every one of his division and brigade commanders had expressed outrage at McClernand's order. In his most cutting remark, McPherson quipped, "Though born a warrior, as he himself stated," McClernand had forgotten that a soldier ought to be fair in his statements.[36] The "born warrior" allusion referred to a report in the army that McClernand, in a speech to some voters up in Illinois, had said, "Some men were born to one walk in life, and some to another. Thank God, I was born a warrior insensible to fear."[37] McClernand was the sort of man people believed would say such things.

Grant had no reason to hesitate. He had given McClernand responsibility because he thought that was what the president wanted. McClernand had endangered the army at Champion's Hill and cost it 1,000 casualties on May 22. Now he was threatening to poison completely the relationships within the Army of the Tennessee's officer corps, fomenting a spirit of self-serving jealousy and mistrust that, although Grant may well have been unaware of it, had by then palsied the upper echelons of Pemberton's army as well as the Confederate Army of Tennessee and, to a lesser extent, the Union Army of the Potomac. The substantial absence of such attitudes in the Army of the Tennessee had been an important ingredient in its success, and that ingredient existed by and large because Grant's personality demanded it.

By this time, it was clear to Grant that McClernand had to go, not later, after Vicksburg fell, but right now. Late on the evening of June 17, he had Rawlins compose the appropriate order: "Maj. Gen. John A. McClernand is hereby relieved from the command of the Thirteenth Army Corps. He will proceed to any point he may select in the State of Illinois, and report by letter to Headquarters of the Army for orders."[38] Grant intended the order to be delivered the next morning, but Rawlins and Wilson decided between them that it needed to be delivered at once. Rawlins was bitter at McClernand for his failures on May 16 and 22. Wilson had long disliked McClernand for what he believed to be the general's constant condescending treatment and belittling remarks. So at 2:00 a.m. on June 18, Wilson put on full dress uniform, took the army's provost marshal, a sergeant and four privates, and rode over to McClernand's headquarters. The general was in bed; so Wilson had him awakened. Some time later Wilson was shown into McClernand's headquarters tent, where the general waited, also in full uniform. Wilson handed him the order, and McClernand tossed it on the table, unopened. Wilson announced that his orders were to stay and see the order read. McClernand opened and read the order, then looked up and said, "Well sir! I am relieved! By God sir, we are both relieved." The last was perhaps McClernand's reference to the fact that Wilson would feel much better with him out of the army.[39]

As engineer officer William Jenney observed, "The departure of McClernand was a relief to the whole army."[40] Those who paid serious attention to such matters thought the departure a great improvement and long overdue.[41] Most of the common soldiers had very little to say on the matter. Command of the Thirteenth Corps went to Maj. Gen. Edward O. C. Ord, a move that Jenney believed "materially increased the efficiency of the Thirteenth Corps."[42]

McClernand was not about to go quietly up the river. He announced to Wilson at the time of his relief that he "very much doubted the authority of General Grant to relieve a general officer appointed by the President, but he would not make a point of it."[43] The next morning, he wrote to Grant, acknowledging receipt of the order and once again stating his exaggerated idea of his authority from Lincoln: "Having been appointed by the President to the command of that corps, under a definite act of Congress, I might justly challenge your authority in the premises, but forbear to do so at present."[44] He did not forbear very long, and before the end of the month he was bombarding Lincoln, Stanton, and Halleck with appeals for redress and denunciations of Grant. "I have been relieved for an omission of my adjutant. Hear me," he telegraphed the president from Cairo on June 23. He was soon back to hauling on political wires and enlisted Governor Yates in his cause.[45]

This time, however, it was not going to work. A popular politician in uniform might be all very well, but for Lincoln nothing was better than a general who would give him major victories. Grant was obviously in the process of doing that, so if forced to choose between Grant and McClernand, Lincoln would now stick with Grant. McClernand's complaints went unrewarded.

Meanwhile, the siege continued.

CHAPTER TWENTY-FIVE

Triumph at Vicksburg

T HE MOST IMPORTANT of the many approaches Grant's soldiers were steadily pushing closer to the Confederate works was in the sector of Logan's division of the Seventeenth Corps, along the axis of the Jackson Road, where the Great Redoubt and the 3rd Louisiana Redan barred advance. The 3rd Louisiana Redan was known to Union soldiers as Fort Hill, because of the towering bluff on which it stood. Both fortresses looked down menacingly on the terrain in front of them.

Hours after the failure of the May 22 assaults, McPherson assigned his chief engineer, Capt. Andrew Hickenlooper, to direct the siege operations in this sector. Hickenlooper realized that the 3rd Louisiana Redan was the key to this whole stretch of the Confederate line and that it could be approached from only one direction—along the ridge that carried the Jackson Road. This would lead the besiegers straight into the strength of the Confederate position, with the Great Redoubt standing just on the south side of the road and the 3rd Louisiana Redan on the north, but there was no other way. He surveyed the first section of terrain for the approach on the night of May 23, while Logan's pickets made a foray against their counterparts in order to provide cover. During the May 25 truce for burial of the dead, Hickenlooper observed more of the ground his men would be crossing.[1]

With his plans complete, he secured a 150-man work detail from Leggett's brigade of Logan's division. At daybreak on May 26, he had his men start digging at a point about 400 yards east of Fort Hill, near a two-story frame house belonging to James Shirley. To protect them from the fire of the Confederates in the redan, the soldiers used a sap roller, a wicker cylinder about five feet in diameter and ten feet long, tightly packed with cotton. This they gradually pushed out ahead of their work, affording them more or less immunity from the fire of Rebel sharpshooters. The soil was easy to work, fatigue details relieved one another at regular intervals, and with no Confederate countermeasures to worry about, they got on rapidly. The night shift would push the trench, or sap, forward as far as possible, and then the day shift would widen and deepen it until it was seven feet deep and eight feet wide. After two days of digging, Hickenlooper cut the size of the work details. They were getting closer, and the larger number of men could no longer work with safety.[2]

The Rebels would have liked to have made it more unsafe still. That day they opened fire with a three-inch rifled gun mounted in the 3rd Louisiana Redan, but the Union artillery smothered the lone gun in a thunderous, one-sided bombardment. Unfortunately, it was in this artillery duel that the gallant De Golyer fell, the victim of a sharpshooter. Though they could not stop the digging of the approach, the Rebels could at least bolster the strength of the defenses. Pemberton dispatched Cockrell's crack Missouri brigade to reinforce the defenders in the Jackson Road sector in preparation for the attack that was bound to come when the approach was complete.[3]

The digging went on apace, though the rate of advance slowed as the head of the sap drew closer to the redan. By May 29, the sap extended 180 yards and was just a furlong from the Rebel parapet. Five days later, the head of the sap reached a knoll 130 yards from Fort Hill, the highest point between the 3rd Louisiana Redan and the Shirley House. While viewing the ground on May 25, Hickenlooper had picked out this site for an advanced battery. He cut his fatigue details to 100 men and set them to work on a fortified emplacement for multiple guns. They revetted its face with gabions and fascines and built up eight-foot-thick earthen parapets behind them. They covered the gun embrasures with movable shutters of thick planks so that the artillerists would be protected while loading. By June 7, the new emplacement, dubbed Battery Hickenlooper, was ready to receive its armament of two 24-pounder howitzers and one 6-pounder gun. Meanwhile, Brigadier General Leggett was bossing the work in the sap, with a separate seventy-man detail, advancing its head to within seventy-five yards of the parapet by the time Battery Hickenlooper was finished.[4]

As the sappers continued to push the approach trench closer and closer to the fortress, someone got the idea of making a more effective sap roller. The men obtained a railroad flatcar and piled it high with some twenty bales of cotton. It provided more cover than an ordinary sap roller, and sharpshooters could use it for cover as well. The soldiers called it their "gunboat" or "Logan's car." They completed it on June 5 and put it into action for the first time that night. The Rebels were quick to react and made a skirmish foray that night aimed at destroying the gunboat, but the Federals drove them back. The next night, the Confederates tried again, and again the bluecoats beat them off.[5]

The inexorable land gunboat became almost an obsession to the Louisianans in the redan, and on the night of June 8 they contrived a new method of attacking it. An officer stuffed the hollow bases of several minié balls with cotton wads soaked in turpentine. He then fired these bullets from an ordinary Enfield rifle into the looming bulk of the gunboat. The cotton ignited when the rifle discharged, and the wads of burning fiber embedded themselves with the bullets in the cotton bales of the gunboat. Before the Federals realized what was happening, their gunboat was on fire. The Confederates maintained a heavy volume of rifle fire in order to hinder efforts to extinguish the blaze. The bluecoats tried throwing water and dirt at the fire, but their efforts were unavailing, and the higher the flames blazed up, the more they lit up the would-be firefighters and made them targets. Much to the frustration of Logan's men, their gunboat burned down to the axles while the Confederates jeered and hooted from the ramparts of the redan. Within days, however, the sap was advancing again, this time protected by more conventional sap rollers.[6]

On June 13, the Rebels tried a new type of weapon—new, at least, to the Vicksburg siege lines. They emplaced a mortar in the low ground to the rear of the 3rd Louisiana Redan, safely out of sight of the Yankees, and that evening opened fire, lobbing shells at the besiegers and into their camps. Every Union gun in that entire sector of the lines immediately returned the fire. Because they were all primarily direct-fire weapons, they could not quite reach the mortar, hidden as it was in its hollow behind the lines. They could, however, put so many shells into the general area that, as a Louisiana soldier noted, "it was almost certain death to remain in its vicinity." The Confederates made several other attempts to use their mortar over the next few days, but each time the ferocious return fire drove the crew away from their piece.[7]

Meanwhile, the battle of the sharpshooters grew more intense as the distance separating the two sides decreased. With their artillery all but silenced, daring to fire but rarely, the Confederates had to rely on rifle marksmanship as their only means of hindering the Union approach. Union sharpshooters, in turn, had the responsibility of protecting their comrades working in the saps and batteries. One of the most successful, Lt. Henry C. Foster of the 23rd Indiana in Leggett's brigade, was known as "Coonskin" because of his favorite nonregulation headgear. Foster would take rifle, ammunition, and several days' rations, and creep forward through no-man's-land during the night. Finding a position he liked, he would build a concealed underground burrow with an unobtrusive loophole bearing on the Confederate works. There he would remain for days at a time, picking off Rebels in their earthworks.[8]

During the first week of June, Foster arranged for a more convenient lair. With the aid of a large detail from his regiment, he removed railroad ties from the Southern Railroad of Mississippi and under cover of darkness used them to construct a tower just south of Battery Hickenlooper. "Coonskin's Tower," as the structure became known, was high enough to give a sharpshooter posted in it a view of part of the interior of the redan. The tower would have been vulnerable to artillery fire, but the Confederates dared not use their guns on it for fear of drawing a devastating counter-bombardment. The railroad ties were plenty thick enough to stop Confederate rifle bullets, so Foster and his associates could fire through the chinks between the ties with almost perfect impunity. The Rebels inside the redan simply had to be more careful.[9]

The sappers had to be more careful as well. David Poak of the 30th Illinois was part of the fatigue party on June 15 and wrote that the worst part of the job was moving the sap rollers. "The ground over which we had to move them was so rough and steep that some were obliged to expose themselves to keep the bales from rolling clear out of our reach, and whenever a man got high enough above the cotton bales to be seen by the Rebs, he was treated to some Minnie balls, some of which came too close to be agreeable."[10]

By June 16, they were within about twenty feet of the redan, and Hickenlooper canceled night shifts for fear that the Confederates might sortie and fall on the sappers only a few yards away. To compensate, Hickenlooper doubled the day shifts and, as further protection from Rebel sorties, had his men construct two rifle pits, or trenches, branching off to the south of the sap, one fifty yards from the redan and the other twenty-five. These provided positions from which Union infantry could protect the men working on the approach. Sharpshooters also found them useful, enhancing the Federal domination of the top of the parapet.[11]

On the night of June 17, the Louisianans in the redan succeeded in burning another sap roller with their turpentine-soaked cotton-loaded bullets. Two days later the Union sappers had another in service, and the work went on. On June 20, during a general Union bombardment, Federals boldly worked almost at the foot of the 3rd Louisiana Redan. The Union artillery and sharpshooters had gained such dominance of the Confederate parapet that the Federals at the head of the sap could occasionally venture out of their trench. Several of them apparently crept up the exterior slope of the redan and peeped over the top of the parapet. The Confederates shot and killed one man in the act of doing so, though stories vary widely as to just what he was trying to accomplish and why. Inside the fort, Louisianan Will Tunnard thought the man was trying to gain information about the interior. John Campbell of the 5th Iowa heard that the luckless soldier "was reaching over with a boarding pike to haul a butternut out." In the nearby 20th Illinois, Allen Geer's information was that the man was a member of the 45th Illinois who got drunk and "went over the rebel fort and shook his hat at them." Sgt. Will Crummer of the 45th Illinois later wrote that during the siege a soldier of the regiment, whom he referred to as "E," became inebriated and climbed to the top of the fort, where he was shot by the Rebels. The Illinois adjutant general's records indicate that Pvt. William H. Eddy of Crummer's own Company A was killed on June 21.[12]

By the evening of June 21, the head of the sap had almost reached the foot of the redan's exterior slope, and the Confederate defenders began employing a new tactic, lobbing hand grenades and 6- and 12-pounder shells into the sap. Each grenade weighed about a pound and consisted of an oval-shaped, hollow iron shell a little larger than a hen's egg. On one end was a feathered shaft; on the other, a percussion igniter. When thrown, the grenade usually landed on that igniter and exploded on contact. If that contact was with human flesh, the wounds created were hideous. Nevertheless, the sappers struggled on, digging when they could and trying to dodge or else catch and toss back the grenades that sailed over the parapet. Another day's work brought the sap right up against the exterior slope.[13]

While the mostly quiet war of the spade continued, Hickenlooper pursued noisier tactics as well. On June 18, he added two powerful 30-pounder Parrott rifles to the two 24-pounders in Battery Hickenlooper. The 30-pounders, borrowed from a battery farther to the rear, were among the most powerful guns on the Vicksburg siege lines, and at point-blank range their fire began to tear great gouges out of the parapet of the redan. By day's end they had battered a breach in the wall, but the Confederates built it back up during the night. The howitzers, on the other hand, could often drop their shells just over the parapet, producing a steady trickle of casualties among the increasingly hard-pressed defenders of the 3rd Louisiana Redan.[14]

While large fatigue details continued to work on the approach, improving the sap and the rifle pits, Hickenlooper prepared for the next stage of his campaign against the 3rd Louisiana Redan. He asked for volunteers who "had a practical knowledge of coal mining." Quite a number of men offered their services, and of them Hickenlooper selected thirty-six of the "strongest and most experienced," whom he organized into a mining detail under the command of Lt. Thomas Russell of the 7th Missouri and Sgt. William Morris of the 32nd Ohio, both from Stevenson's brigade of Logan's division. He divided the miners into day and night shifts, with three reliefs in each shift. Equipping them with drills, shovels, and short-handled picks, he set them to work on the night of June 22 digging a gallery, or tunnel, into the exterior face of the redan. Each relief worked for an hour, two men picking, two shoveling, and two hauling dirt out of the tunnel in grain sacks. The loess soil lent itself to such work, for it cut easily but stood stiffly so that little bracing was needed. They dug the tunnel four feet high and three feet wide and drove it forward some forty-five feet into the hillside. From the end of it, they dug three smaller galleries, each fifteen feet long, somewhat in the pattern of a bird's foot, one straight ahead and the others angling off at fifteen degrees to each side.[15]

Inside the redan, the Rebels could hear the sounds of digging below, and they in turn began digging a countermine in hopes of intercepting the Union tunnel and killing or driving off the miners. Working in the cramped, hot confines of the tunnel late on the evening of June 24, the Union miners heard the noise of the Confederates' digging so close it seemed their picks and shovels were about to come through the walls of the gallery. Indeed, the miners could hear not only the sound of the Confederates' digging but also their conversation and the orders spoken in the nearby tunnel. The Union miners panicked and scrambled out. In the morning, however, Hickenlooper persuaded them to go back to work, and by 9:00 a.m. on June 25 the tunnel and side galleries were finished.[16]

Immediately, Hickenlooper sent his miners hurrying back down the sap to bring up the black powder, 2,200 pounds of it that he had acquired from the navy, brought to the front in barrels, and stored safely behind the lines. Now the men of the mining detail carefully transferred the powder into grain sacks, 25 pounds in each sack, and carried it up the sap to the tunnel. It was particularly nerve-racking work because the Confederates were still tossing grenades and lighted shells over the parapet. Each man carrying a sack of powder had to wait and then time his rush over the final few yards between the explosion of Confederate grenades. Somehow, Hickenlooper's men managed to move all eighty-eight sacks of powder into the tunnel without mishap. They stuffed 800 pounds into the center gallery and 700 into each of the side galleries, fused them, and then blocked up the main gallery with more grain sacks filled with earth and shored up with timbers to prevent the energy of the blast from escaping back along the tunnel. At 1:00 p.m., Hickenlooper reported to McPherson that the mine was ready.[17]

Grant had been keeping track of the progress of Hickenlooper's approach and making plans for exploiting the detonation of the mine. He issued orders to all of his corps commanders to have their troops in readiness on the afternoon of June 25 and to initiate a mass artillery bombardment all along the line at the moment the mine went off. The major infantry assault would be confined to Logan's sector, with troops charging up the sap and surging through the gap that the mine was sure to create, but Grant wanted to keep Pemberton's attention diverted to other areas of his line so that the Confederate commander would not be able to send heavy reinforcements to the defenders of the 3rd Louisiana Redan. Grant further instructed his corps commanders that if they saw the enemy beginning to shift troops away from their fronts they were to fake infantry attacks of their own to hold the enemy in place. The hour for the explosion of the mine was set for 3:00 p.m., and all forward trenches were to be manned and ready by 2:00.[18]

To make the assault on the redan, McPherson designated Leggett's brigade, with two regiments of Col. Green B. Raum's brigade and one of Ransom's waiting in support in case reinforcements were needed. Leading Leggett's column was the veteran 45th Illinois, the Lead Mine Regiment. Foster and 100 picked sharpshooters would occupy the rifle trench branching south from the approach just twenty-five yards outside the Confederate works to assure absolute Union control of the parapet and to help exploit any breakthrough Leggett's men might achieve. As the hour for the blast approached, Hickenlooper, with Capt. Stewart Tresilian and ten pioneer troops, took up his own position a short distance down the approach from the mouth of the tunnel, near the base of Coonskin's Tower. Just behind him, the 45th Illinois waited with bayonets fixed. Grant himself, with his staff, was in Battery Hickenlooper, with a ringside seat for the coming struggle.[19]

"Many were the eyes turned upon that fort," wrote Illinois soldier Isaac Jackson, "for it can be seen a long ways." Indeed, all the way from the lines of the Fifteenth Corps on the north down to the Thirteenth Corps sector on the south, soldiers had their eyes fixed on the prominent fort on the hilltop near the Jackson Road. Nearly the entire Army of the Tennessee was up in the firing trenches, waiting with their rifles trained on the parapet. "What a picture," Jackson wrote, "thousands of men outside in the rifle pits awaiting the signal for to commence firing on the Army inside."[20]

Three o'clock came and went without a sound. Deadly quiet prevailed all along the siege lines as men watched and waited, gunners with the lanyards of loaded cannon in their hands—more than 200 guns and gunners. Men began to speculate whether something had gone wrong. Finally, at 3:30 p.m., the ground trembled, emitting a "dull, thundering sound," and the earthen rampart at the apex of the 3rd Louisiana Redan began to rise—slowly, it seemed, especially to distant observers, almost majestically—a huge piece of the landscape levitating skyward, then, in Hickenlooper's words, "gradually breaking into fragments and growing less bulky in appearance, until it looked like an immense fountain of the finely pulverized earth, mingled with flashes of fire and clouds of smoke, through which could occasionally be caught glimpses of dark objects—men, gun carriages, shelters, and so on." Hickenlooper, Foster, and the Lead Miners braced themselves as the earth heaved beneath their feet and dirt clods rained down on their heads. Then an even louder roar drowned the sound of the explosion, as every gun that would bear on the Vicksburg defenses burst into action, and the entire Army of the Tennessee sent up a tremendous shout.[21]

Through the thick clouds of dust, while dirt clods continued to rain down, the 45th Illinois charged up the sap. Hickenlooper and his pioneers quickly cleared the head of the sap of debris tossed out by the explosion, and the Lead Miners stormed through the breach. They found themselves in a bowl-shaped crater forty feet wide and twelve feet deep. To their dismay, they found that the Rebels, apparently anticipating something of this sort, had built another earthen rampart across the formerly open gorge, or back, of the 3rd Louisiana Redan. Now the 45th was streaming through a narrow gap into an open space commanded by another of the almost impregnable breastworks that had stopped the attacks of May 22. Worse, the Confederate commander had pulled his men out of the redan, sheltering them safely behind the new breastwork before the explosion. The only Rebels who had remained in the fort were six volunteers who had continued to work in the countermine in hopes of reaching and defusing the Union explosives. They were never heard from again. The rest of the Rebels, though shaken and dusted by the blast, were more than ready to defend their new parapet.[22]

Bad as the situation was, there was nothing for the Lead Miners to do now but try to break through the new Rebel line. Led by Lt. Col. Melancthon Smith, they surged across the crater and scrambled up the far side to the base of the breastwork. Smith was waving his sword and urging his men on when he fell mortally wounded just outside the parapet. The Confederate volley cut down others at the head of the Union column and stopped the assault just under the lip of the crater, only a few feet short of the new breastwork.

"Both sides fought with a desperation amounting almost to madness," wrote a soldier of the 45th Illinois. So close was the fighting in some places that a Rebel reached over the breastwork and grabbed the fabric of the 45th's flag. A brief tug-of-war followed between the color guard and the audacious Rebel. Then the flag tore and the Rebel was left with a swatch of red-and-white-striped cloth in his hands. At some point during the fight, a Confederate bullet shot away the brass head that was on top of the flagstaff.[23]

Col. Jasper Maltby of the 45th acted quickly to prevent the complete slaughter of his regiment. Realizing that no more than two companies could deploy and fight in the crater, Maltby ordered the rest of the 45th to halt outside the breach. Inside the crater, Maltby had one-third of his men climb up to the lip of the crater and fire as rapidly as they could at the Rebels behind the parapet while the other two-thirds loaded rifles for them from the relative security of the bottom of the crater. Often the men firing would keep their heads below the rim of the crater, hold their rifles above their heads with the muzzles protruding over the breastwork, and shoot down into the Confederates. Men fought with bayonets, or hurled bayoneted rifles like harpoons. Some men succeeded in snatching rifles out of the hands of enemy soldiers across the parapet. Every thirty minutes, Maltby relieved the two companies in the crater with two of those waiting in the approach trench. By the time they finished their thirty minutes in the crater, the men had expended nearly all of their ammunition, and their rifles were fouled with powder residue and nearly too hot to handle.[24]

Both sides hurled grenades in large numbers, producing hideous casualties in the crater. The ground underfoot became slippery with blood, and more than 130 yards away, back at Battery Hickenlooper, Grant and others there could hear above the roar of battle the screams of the wounded in the crater. The Confederates also lit shells and rolled them down the forward slope of their earthwork. Pvt. William Lazarus of the 1st U.S. Infantry, siege gun detachment, was specially detailed to take a large number of grenades into the crater and throw them into the Confederate works. He threw twenty before the Rebels shot him. Thereafter, Leggett detailed three more members of the 1st U.S. to the same duty. Some soldiers caught incoming grenades and threw them back at the Rebels. When the troops in the crater ran out of grenades, Captain Tresilian ran back to Battery Hickenlooper, fetched three 10-pounder Parrott shells, cut their fuses to five seconds, lit them, and threw them over the parapet.[25]

Meanwhile, Sergeants Will Crummer and Axel Esping gained a position in the northwest corner of the crater. From where they were, it was plain that Hickenlooper had calculated correctly when he judged that Fort Hill was the key to this entire sector of the defenses. They could look right down the length of the Confederate trenches running northwest from the crater, "and we had a splendid chance of doing good work," Crummer recalled, as they could hardly help hitting a Confederate defender with every shot. Then, however, Esping was shot through the head.[26]

Hickenlooper had tried to anticipate every eventuality, and so before the attack he had had his pioneers prepare ready-made head logs, complete with loopholes. These logs could be carried forward and mounted quickly atop any embankment to transform it into a finished breastwork comparable to what the defenders would have. With the attackers stalled in the crater in a furious exchange of fire with breastwork-protected defenders, Hickenlooper led his pioneers hustling forward with the head logs, deploying them on the forward lip of the crater. At first the logs seemed to perform as advertised, but then a nasty complication developed. Here, essentially inside the still-formidable remains of the great earthen ramparts of the 3rd Louisiana Redan, they were out of reach of the dominant long arm of the Union artillery. So the Confederates were once again free to use their own cannon, if they had any. They did, a single three-inch rifle that was soon getting hits on the prefabricated head logs. The effect was devastating, as splinters sprayed all over the crater, causing numerous casualties. One of the jagged pieces of timber hit Colonel Maltby, who had to be carried out of the crater, badly wounded. When Leggett heard what was happening, he ordered what was left of the head logs taken to the rear.[27]

The Confederates thought the time was ripe to launch an attack into the crater and eliminate the Union lodgment in their lines. Cockrell's Missourians were in reserve not far from the 3rd Louisiana Redan, and elements of the brigade were on their way there before the dust of the explosion had settled. As soon as the Confederate 6th Missouri Regiment arrived on the scene, its colonel led a counterattack against the Federals in the crater. The badly shot-up 45th Illinois proved more than a match for the Missourians, however. The Missouri colonel fell, and his men retreated. The deadlock in the redan continued.[28]

Watching what he could see of the action from Battery Hickenlooper and hearing much more, Grant judged that if his troops could just manage to hang on to the crater until morning, the Confederates would have to give up their line of rifle pits north of the redan, and the Federals might just be able to parlay that into a major breakthrough. He therefore ordered Leggett to keep fighting for the crater. Logan, to whose division Leggett belonged, was almost distraught about the casualties this was costing. At one point, upon seeing wounded soldiers being carried to the rear, he exclaimed, "My God! They are killing my bravest men in that hole." When a staff officer suggested evacuating the crater, Logan replied, "I can't; my commanding officer orders me to hold every inch of ground."[29]

So the fight went on. At 6:00 p.m., Leggett relieved the 45th Illinois with the 20th Illinois, and throughout the night and the next day six more regiments took their turns. In addition, the 31st Illinois took two turns, and the 45th took its second turn the following morning. The fighting remained as desperate as ever. Maj. C. J. Stolbrand, Logan's chief of artillery, stayed in the crater almost all night, catching Confederate grenades and lighted shells and throwing them back. The Rebels resorted to fusing boxes of rifle cartridges or light artillery shells, setting them atop their parapet, lighting them, and then sending them tumbling into the crater. In a number of cases, Stolbrand stamped out the fuses or pulled them out before the boxes could explode. His survival seemed little short of miraculous, as bullets cut his clothes and grazed his skin and grenades and shells exploded all around him. Yet he suffered nothing more serious than powder burns to his face, hands, and hair.[30]

Grant ordered Hickenlooper to build an emplacement for two guns right in the crater, so that they could batter the new breastwork at point-blank range. Hickenlooper and his men tried to construct such an emplacement, a sort of dugout protected by a casemate of heavy timbers, but the hail of shells and grenades, bouncing and rolling down the slope from the parapet, made it impractical to bring up artillery. By 5:00 p.m. on June 26, it was clear that no breakthrough was at hand and nothing more was to be gained by attempting to storm the breastworks of the 3rd Louisiana Redan. Grant ordered McPherson to pull his troops back to the middle of the crater, on a line with Hickenlooper's dugout and casemate, where they would be in less danger from grenades. There they built their own line of breastworks and settled down for the long haul. That corner of the 3rd Louisiana Redan would remain Union property for the rest of the siege. The cost for that gain had been 34 men killed and 209 wounded. Confederate losses for the operation were reported as 21 killed and 73 wounded in the regiments most directly affected.[31]

Nothing daunted, Hickenlooper started digging again the next day. With McPherson's authorization, he drifted a tunnel to the right of the crater, using the dugout in the middle of the crater as the starting point. By June 30, the Confederates were once again aware that their position was being undermined. This time they decided to try to attack the entrance of the mine with a petard, a very large explosive charge. They took an entire barrel of powder, fused it for fifteen seconds, and rolled it down the forward slope of their parapet, hoping that it would blow the pestilent structure into kindling wood. The petard did explode with an impressive roar but not close enough to the casemate to do it any damage. The digging went on.[32]

Next the Rebels attempted another countermine. This time they took steps to make sure that no more of their soldiers would be lost if the Union mine should go off. They sent eight slaves to do the digging under the supervision of a single white man. Once again, the opposing miners engaged in a tense underground battle of nerves. On July 1, Hickenlooper passed the word to McPherson that the sounds of digging as well as voices in the Confederate countermine were growing distinctly and disturbingly louder. McPherson asked Grant if he could go ahead and blow the mine rather than take the chance of having the Confederates break into it. Knowing that there was little practical chance of a major breakthrough, Grant authorized him to go ahead. McPherson planned no infantry assault. The purpose of this blast would be purely to harass the enemy and weaken his fortifications.[33]

This time the miners carried 1,800 pounds of powder into the mine, fused and shored it as before, and at 3:00 p.m. set it off. Despite the smaller charge, the damage to the redan was even greater this time, coming after the structure had already been weakened by the first blast six days earlier. Large sections of the original earthen ramparts collapsed, and the new gorge parapet was breached. The Confederates suffered a number of casualties as a result of the blast. The countermining party was wiped out save for a single slave who, miraculously, was blown all the way into Union lines, where he landed with minor injuries. Asked how high he had gone, he replied, "Dunno, massa, but t'ink bout t'ree mile."[34]

As the blast subsided, the Confederates, many of whom had been bruised and half-buried by the earth blown out of the new crater, rushed to their breastworks ready to repel the infantry attack they thought was sure to follow. Instead, the Union artillery opened up with a heavy bombardment, knocking the dirt out of the gorge parapet as fast as the Rebels could shovel it back from the inside. Finally, in desperation, the defenders made giant sandbags out of tent flies and wagon covers. Teams of sweating Confederates—Cockrell's elite Missourians—wrestled the unwieldy loads into place and thus were able to close up the breach and gain some protection from direct Union rifle and artillery fire.[35]

Meanwhile, Captain Tresilian had brought some new weapons into action. So far during the siege, the navy had used large coehorn mortars mounted on barges out in the river to lob shells into the town of Vicksburg. Because of the range from which they were fired and the limitations of their accuracy, it was not safe to aim the heavy mortars at the defensive perimeter for fear of hitting the encircling friendly forces. Tresilian had nevertheless worked out a way to hit the Confederate lines with indirect fire. Taking short sections of hardwood logs, he shrunk iron bands around them and then bored out their centers to take either 6- or 12-pound shells. He had completed construction of these makeshift trench mortars—one 6-pounder and two 12-pounders—that very morning.[36]

When the mine exploded and the bombardment opened, Tresilian and his men joined in with their mortars. For the Confederates, this high-angle fire proved to be the most vexatious and deadly element of the bombardment. Even after the conventional guns halted their bombardment at nightfall, Tresilian continued to lob his shells over the Confederate parapet. The effectiveness of the bombardment, including that of the conventional guns, is revealed in the fact that the 6th Missouri (Confederate) suffered more than twice as many casualties on July 1 simply manning the works as it had in the action of June 25 that included its unsuccessful counterattack. A Confederate staff officer calculated that Tresilian's mortars alone killed twenty-one and wounded seventy-two during the forty-eight hours immediately following the second mine explosion.[37]

All along the Vicksburg lines, similar though less dramatic contests of siege warfare took place during the month of June as the Federals worked their way steadily closer to the defenses. By early July, the opposing lines in many places were separated by only the thickness of a single parapet, Union on one side, Confederate on the other. Grant was planning an assault for July 6, and he had decided to delay the detonation of any further mines to occur in conjunction with the big push. Several others were currently in progress, and one in Sherman's sector was almost ready to receive its charge of powder. Grant ordered all approach trenches widened so as to allow troops to charge up them four abreast and for planks and other materials to be on hand for easy bridging of the Confederate ditches, where those still lay between the besieger and the besieged. The great assault, however, never took place.[38]

By midmorning on July 3, the sun had already grown hot, blazing out of a clear blue sky. The pickets of the 96th Ohio, part of Brig. Gen. Stephen G. Burbridge's brigade of A. J. Smith's division of the Thirteenth Corps, were in the advance trenches, sharpshooting, as they had done in shifts for the past six weeks. As usual, their task was to cover the division's sappers, who on this day were widening the approach trench only six feet from the ditch that fronted the 2nd Texas Lunette, a Confederate stronghold on the southeast side of the Vicksburg lines. Each man had his rifle cocked and ready and his eyes fixed on the Rebel parapet, ready to shoot any shape that rose above it. At about 10:00 a.m., however, an unusual shape arose—a white handkerchief on a stick. Behind it rose the forms of two Confederate officers. As two dozen rifles automatically swung to train on the two men, one of them barked out in an authoritative voice, "Cease firing."

"What is wanted?" shouted Capt. Joseph Leonard, commander of the skirmish detail. The two Confederates stated that they were authorized to negotiate terms of surrender and asked to be conducted to the Union commanding general. Leonard told the two officers to enter his skirmish line, where they identified themselves as Maj. Gen. John Bowen and Col. L. M. Montgomery of Pemberton's staff. Following standard procedures, Leonard had both Confederates blindfolded and assigned Sgt. George Lohr and a squad of soldiers to conduct them to division headquarters. As Lohr was leading the blindfolded Bowen across some of the Union trenches, the general made a misstep and fell. As the anxious sergeant helped him to his feet, Bowen quipped, "I never expected to cross Yankee breastworks without something happening, and I feel truly thankful that it was no worse."[39]

At division headquarters, A. J. Smith received the Confederate commissioners. Bowen handed Smith a letter he carried from Pemberton for delivery to Grant. In it Pemberton requested an armistice of several hours so that commissioners from both sides could meet to arrange terms for the capitulation of Vicksburg, concluding, "I make this proposition to save the further effusion of blood, which must otherwise be shed to a frightful extent, feeling myself fully able to maintain my position for a yet indefinite period." That statement was not going to fool anyone, least of all Grant. Bowen was eager to meet with Grant personally, and Smith forwarded the letter and Bowen's request to Grant by messenger. Grant denied the request. He and the Confederate general had been neighbors and friends when Grant had lived in Missouri, and apparently Grant did not want personal feelings interfering with the serious business at hand.[40]

Instead he sent back a reply that he would be willing to meet with Pemberton at three o'clock that afternoon in front of McPherson's lines, on the Jackson Road, within a few hundred yards of the Great Redoubt and the 3rd Louisiana Redan. Grant also sent a letter to Pemberton by the hand of Bowen, in which he stated,

The useless effusion of blood you propose stopping by this course can be ended at any time you may choose, by the unconditional surrender of the city and garrison. Men who have shown so much endurance and courage as those now in Vicksburg, will always challenge the respect of an adversary, and I can assure you will be treated with all the respect due to prisoners of war. I do not favor the proposition of appointing commissioners to arrange the terms of capitulation, because I have no terms other than those indicated above.[41]

FOR THE MEN in the trenches, peace had broken out very suddenly that morning. The troops of the Thirteenth Corps swarmed their breastworks within minutes of seeing the white flag. News that a flag-of-truce party had crossed into Union lines spread rapidly from the Thirteenth Corps sector through the other two corps and the detached division of the Sixteenth that had recently boosted the army's strength. Firing stopped, and the soldiers stood around on the parapets of their trenches, where it would have been worth a man's life to show the top of his head a few hours earlier.[42]

Around midday a Confederate took a shot at the colonel of the 32nd Ohio and wounded a nearby Union soldier. The colonel ordered his pickets to return the fire, and a Union artillery piece discharged a load of canister, leading to a widespread seeking of shelter and additional rifle and artillery fire in the Thirteenth and Seventeenth corps sectors. The firing died down early in the afternoon, and the unwonted quiet returned to the siege lines.[43]

By 3:00 p.m. the flare-up was over, and Grant, accompanied by McPherson, Ord, Logan, A. J. Smith, and several members of his staff, rode out to the place appointed for the meeting, a stunted oak tree that stood beside the Jackson Road between the lines. Grant and his party dismounted within 100 yards of the parapet of the 3rd Louisiana Redan, and their orderlies led the horses to the rear. Soldiers of both sides lined their entrenchments, eager to see the historic meeting. It was a sultry afternoon with not a puff of wind to stir the humid air or flap the white flags that hung limp all along both armies' trenches. To the southwest, however, towering dark thunderheads told of an approaching storm.[44]

Pemberton was late arriving, and Grant and his fellow officers waited in the hot sun while fifteen or twenty minutes passed. Grant's staff officers could tell he was annoyed, though he said nothing. Finally the Confederate commander emerged from the Vicksburg defenses, accompanied by Bowen and Montgomery, and rode out the Jackson Road to where the Union officers waited. Grant and Pemberton had served in the same division during the Mexican War and so were acquainted. Pemberton and his officers dismounted about thirty feet from Grant's group. Grant took several paces toward them and stopped, waiting for Pemberton to speak. As the general seeking terms of surrender, Pemberton should have spoken first, but he apparently wanted to force Grant to do so. The prolonged silence had become embarrassing to all present before at last Montgomery stepped forward and said, "General Grant, this is General Pemberton." At that the two generals advanced and shook hands. With no further amenities, Pemberton blurted, "What terms of capitulation do you propose to grant me?" Standing nearby, Union staff officer William E. Strong thought Pemberton's manner "insolent and overbearing."[45]

"Those terms stated in my letter of this morning," Grant replied.

At this Pemberton very nearly flew into a rage. "I have been present at the capitulation of two cities in my life," he stormed, "and commissioners were appointed to settle the terms, and I believe it is always customary to appoint them. If this is all you have to offer, the conference may as well terminate, and hostilities be at once resumed."

"Very well," said Grant in his accustomed matter-of-fact manner. "I am quite content to have it so." With that he turned away and called for his horse. The conference would have ended had not Bowen hastily intervened. He suggested that one or two subordinate officers from each side should confer on the matter while Grant and Pemberton went off a little ways by themselves. Grant, who apparently had no fear of forming an emotional attachment with Pemberton, readily agreed, so long as the decisions of his subordinates were not binding on him. He appointed McPherson and A. J. Smith to confer with Bowen and Montgomery while he and Pemberton retired a short distance toward Confederate lines and sat down on the slope in front of Fort Hill. Curious staff officers could not hear them but could watch their gestures. Pemberton was obviously still very excited, while Grant sat puffing his cigar impassively.

At the end of fifteen minutes, Grant had apparently heard enough from Pemberton, and the two strolled back to see if their subordinates had made any progress. The only proposal they had come up with was a Confederate suggestion that the Rebel army be permitted to go free, marching out of Vicksburg with colors flying and "all the honors of war," retaining all of its small arms and field artillery and free to resume hostilities as soon as it crossed the Big Black. This was a laughable proposal, and Grant, who considered the Confederate army in Vicksburg to be a more lucrative prize than the city itself, dismissed it out of hand. The meeting ended then, but

Grant told Pemberton that by ten o'clock that night he would send him his final offer of terms.[46]

That evening the quiet continued along the lines. Sent out on picket with "orders not to fire until further orders," James Jessee felt "quite lost."[47] At the north end of the siege lines, the most likely direction for a Confederate breakout attempt, Steele had his division's picket lines beefed up but ordered his men not to fire until they heard firing from the other sectors of the line. Anxious to know the outcome of the current negotiations, many soldiers spent a sleepless night.[48]

Grant was never much in favor of counsels of war. In his memoirs, he later admitted that the closest he ever came to holding one was on this afternoon. He sent for all of the corps and division commanders on the Vicksburg lines to come to his headquarters, where he presented the situation to them and asked their recommendations. McPherson suggested they take the Rebels prisoner but immediately parole them. Steele disagreed, arguing instead for unconditional surrender, but the majority, indeed everyone else, advocated McPherson's plan. The logistical demands of transporting so many prisoners back to Cairo would temporarily cripple Union operations in the Western theater. Under the terms of the prisoner-of-war cartel in effect at that time, each side would rapidly parole any excess prisoners it might take; so the Vicksburg Confederates would, at least in theory, soon be paroled even if Grant did ship them north. Grant's instincts were against it, but he reluctantly agreed. Perhaps the Rebel soldiers were so demoralized that they would refuse to serve the Confederacy any more and might even spread despair in their home districts.[49]

At 6:00 p.m., he dispatched a letter to Pemberton by the hands of Logan and Lt. Col. James H. Wilson offering to parole the Vicksburg garrison. Officers could keep their side arms and horses. Pemberton, after a bit of quibbling about trivial procedures, agreed to accept Grant's terms. The surrender was to take effect at 10:00 a.m. the next day, July 4.[50]

By the time Grant received Pemberton's final reply, it was past midnight. McPherson was still at Grant's headquarters at that time, and Grant notified him that Logan's division of the Seventeenth Corps would march into Vicksburg the next morning. Upon returning to his own headquarters, McPherson ordered two of his staff officers, George Coolbaugh and William Strong, to take the Seventeenth Corps headquarters flag and raise it from the Vicksburg courthouse as soon as the surrender occurred. Coolbaugh and Strong secured two orderlies, bundled the flag and tied it to one of their horses, and waited for morning.[51]

A few minutes before 10:00 a.m., Grant, McPherson, and their staffs rode through the lines and out to the tree on the Jackson Road where the previous afternoon's interview with Pemberton had taken place. At the hour appointed, white flags went up all along the Confederate lines, and a tremendous shout of victory went up from the Army of the Tennessee. The Rebels marched over their breastworks, halted, and stacked their arms in front, then turned and marched back.[52]

Grant and his entourage rode up the Jackson Road past the Great Redoubt and the 3rd Louisiana Redan. Behind them rode Logan, and just behind him, leading the division column, marched the 45th Illinois, with its flag still tattered from the hard fight in the crater. That morning McPherson had requested of Grant permission to give the 45th the lead, stating that the Lead Mine Regiment had "borne the brunt of the battle oftener than any other in my command, and always behaved nobly." A few days later, a soldier who marched in the ranks of the 45th that morning wrote, "This was the most glorious Fourth of July we ever spent, and the proudest day of our lives."[53]

Grant, McPherson, and their staffs stopped about half a mile beyond Confederate lines, where Pemberton and his staff had established themselves in a house. The Confederate officers behaved boorishly. All of them were sitting, and there was no chair for Grant. It was some time before a Confederate officer offered him a seat. A little later, when Grant asked for a drink of water, the Rebels told him he could find some inside the house. When he got back, his seat was taken again and not yielded back. Grant kept the discussion brief. As the party of Union officers was preparing to leave, McPherson signaled Coolbaugh and Strong to take the flag and head for the courthouse.[54]

Mounting up, the staff officers, their two orderlies, and two cavalrymen rode off and were soon ahead of Logan's division again, receiving hard looks and occasional "vile epithets" from civilians and recently surrendered soldiers they passed. They found a large crowd milling around in front of the courthouse. Forcing their way as far as they could through the throng on horseback, they finally dismounted, left their horses with their orderlies, and, accompanied by the two cavalrymen, made their way to the building and climbed the steps.[55]

"The scene that burst upon us as we gained the great bell in the cupola, the highest point attainable, was indescribably beautiful," wrote Strong. "For a moment we forgot our mission, and were fairly wrapped up in the grand panorama which lay spread out before us. At our feet lay the city of Vicksburg—a magnificent plateau extending for four or five miles north and south by two and a half or three east and west. . . . The outline of the Rebel intrenchments which encircled the city, and a perfect labyrinth of bold bluffs and sharp ridges this side and beyond, were in view, clearly cut against the sky." They could see the river with the fleet resting on it in two squadrons, one upstream and one down, while to the west and north lay the forested swamps of the delta.

After gazing for a few moments at the magnificent view, they returned to their mission. Lashing the flag securely to one of the pillars that supported the roof of the cupola, they let the stiff northeast breeze billow it out above the town. Strong took out his watch to check the time. It was just 11:15. He was startled by the sound of cannon fire and looked up to see the two gunboat squadrons steaming toward Vicksburg with every flag flying and their guns booming massed salutes. In a few minutes, the fleet was approaching the landing, with steam whistles blowing and cannon still firing a national salute. In the other direction, he could see the head of Logan's column approaching with colors flying and bands playing. When the 45th Illinois reached the courthouse, its battle-torn flag joined that of the Seventeenth Corps atop the cupola.[56]

Along the perimeter, Union and Confederate troops intermingled and fraternized freely, talking over the siege. Many of the Rebels, for their part, seemed happy about the surrender, or at least happy that the siege was over and they were still alive. "They hallooed about as much as our men," wrote Illinois soldier William Reid. Sgt. Stephen Rollins of the 95th Illinois agreed. "They were a starved, dirty, squalid set of rascals. They would come to our camps and beg rations from us, which we freely divided with them." The Federals were generous in sharing their food, and Col. Thomas Bringhurst estimated that his 46th Indiana alone fed more than 100 Confederates.[57]

Inside the city, the men of Logan's division also found their erstwhile enemies willing to talk civilly and receive handouts of food. "Groups of Union and Confederate soldiers could be seen wherever there was a shady place," wrote a soldier of the 45th Illinois, "the Union soldier pumping the rebel and giving him in return for the information hard tack and bacon, which the poor famished fellows accepted with a grateful look." William Jenney thought "the place seemed filled with a gigantic picnic." Here and there, a man would find a relative or acquaintance in the opposing army. A Confederate chaplain noted that the conduct of the Union troops was "respectful and considerate. No insolence of manner, and but little offensive taunting." A Louisiana soldier agreed. "No word of exultation was uttered to irritate the feelings of the prisoners. On the contrary, every sentinel who came upon post brought haversacks filled with provisions, which he would give to some famished Southerner, with the remark, 'Here, reb, I know you are starved nearly to death.' "[58]

Word of Vicksburg's fall, and with it the removal of the greatest obstacle to free navigation of the Mississippi, spread up the valley of the Father of Waters and its tributaries over the next few days. In the region whose economy had always been dependent on the river and whose sons and husbands now comprised the Army of the Tennessee, the news was cause for great rejoicing. In Mount Pleasant, Iowa, Emeline Ritner was washing the noon dishes between one and two o'clock on the afternoon of Tuesday, July 7. Her daughters were at school, and she may well have been thinking about her husband, Jake, with the 25th Iowa outside Vicksburg. She was startled to hear the church bell ringing. "I didn't know what it meant," she later recalled, "as there was no meeting." Even more strangely, the bell "rang by jerks as though they were pounding it with a stick." Soon every bell in town was ringing, men and boys were shouting, and people were going by waving flags and ringing cowbells. This was too much for Emeline. "I couldn't stand it," she explained, "I thought I must go up and see what was the matter." Before she was halfway to the square, she heard the news. *"Vicksburg had surrendered."* That afternoon, crowds of boys stood around shouting and ringing cowbells outside the houses of the town's three antiwar residents, and the local menfolk made the three Copperheads display the Stars and Stripes. "That night we had cannonading and the grandest fireworks I ever saw," wrote Emeline.[59]

In Warren, Illinois, the news arrived about an hour and a half later and the reaction was much the same. Men rang church bells, fired guns into the air, and set off small charges of gunpowder against anvils. Boys lit firecrackers, and everybody yelled. The engineers of the Mineral Point and Illinois Central railroads had heard the news too, and every locomotive that came through town did so with its whistle screaming. The country folk roundabout heard the commotion, piled into their wagons, and set out for town to see what was up. The celebration ran late into the evening, with a band, a parade, and a grand illumination. Warren was the hometown of Company B of the 45th Illinois.[60]

Cedar Falls, Iowa, was only 135 miles north of Mount Pleasant and west of Warren, but for some reason the news did not arrive there until July 9. The town had been worried about its boys in the 3rd and 31st regiments and about the outcome of the ongoing operations around Vicksburg—too worried to hold an Independence Day celebration that year. No one had felt like celebrating on the Fourth, but all that changed in a matter of minutes when the dispatch arrived announcing Vicksburg's surrender. Main Street was thronged with a boisterous, cheering crowd, flags appeared everywhere, and the members of the town's brass band ran to fetch their instruments. The rest of the day was given over to parades, bonfires, and hilarious jollification. Someone dragged an outhouse into the middle of Main Street and set it ablaze. An effigy of Jeff Davis was produced, hanged, then cast into the blazing outhouse.[61]

By the time the folks at home heard the news of Vicksburg, most of the Army of the Tennessee had turned its back on the conquered city and were marching eastward, toward Jackson and Joe Johnston's Rebel army. Grant was eager to get at the Confederate general who had long threatened to disrupt the siege of Vicksburg. Being able to do so quickly was one of the chief factors that motivated him to parole Pemberton's army. While the Union troops were still savoring their victory on the afternoon of July 4, Grant sent out orders for most of the army to prepare to march the next morning to reinforce Sherman for the pursuit of Johnston. It was a difficult campaign, coming on the heels of the fatiguing siege. The marches were long and the heat and dust were the worst the veterans had ever seen. Johnston's army skirmished briefly with them at Jackson before withdrawing into the piney woods of eastern Mississippi. Sherman decided not to pursue at this time, and marched his force back to rejoin the rest of the army encamped in various bivouacs between the Big Black and Vicksburg. The long campaign for the Gibraltar of the South was at last over. In Lincoln's words, "the Father of Waters flow[ed] again unvexed to the sea." And the men of the Army of the Tennessee could enjoy a well-earned rest.

PART THREE

Nothing but Victory

Chattanooga

I N THE LATE SUMMER of 1863, the men of the Army of the Tennessee
finally got the rest they had longed for during the hard marches, hard
fighting, and hard digging of the Vicksburg campaign. They would not
have had nearly so much rest if Grant could have had his way. He believed
momentum ought to be used, and he had plans for following up the conquest of the Mississippi Valley with a campaign against the important Confederate port of Mobile, Alabama. Halleck and Lincoln saw matters in a
different light. The general-in-chief had never understood the concept of
momentum in war, and the president was preoccupied with the French presence in Mexico. Over the next nine months, they diverted various elements
of the Army of the Tennessee to several ill-conceived schemes aimed at
securing territory west of the Mississippi and showing the United States
flag in Texas as a political statement to the French.

Shaping military operations to achieve political goals is the business of
wise statesmen, but political goals usually are not achieved through failure.
The French would not be impressed by military ineptitude or poor strategy.
They certainly were not impressed by the succession of Union blunders
that occupied good troops in the trans-Mississippi theater for the first nine
months after the fall of Vicksburg had made the trans-Mississippi strategically irrelevant to the outcome of the war. They might have been impressed
by major Union successes and a more rapid defeat of the Confederacy—
and Grant might well have contributed significantly to such successes if
given freedom of action and the full strength of the army he had molded
into the most effective fighting force of the war. But the authorities in
Washington thought otherwise, and dispersed the army, in Grant's words,
"where it would do the least good." The most significant immediate sub-
traction was that of the Thirteenth Corps, transferred to the command of
the dismal Nathaniel P. Banks west of the Mississippi, never to serve with
the Army of the Tennessee again.[1]

The Fifteenth, Sixteenth, and Seventeenth corps drilled, rested, and chased minor guerrillas during the late summer weeks while the strategic focus of the war shifted elsewhere. On August 16, William S. Rosecrans's Army of the Cumberland advanced from its bases around Winchester, Tennessee, and maneuvered skillfully across the Cumberland Plateau and the Tennessee River, turning Braxton Bragg's Confederate Army of Tennessee and forcing it to abandon the town of Chattanooga, located at a key transportation junction in the southern Appalachians. Rosecrans pursued aggressively with his army's three corps widely spread out to use three different mountain passes, but Bragg turned at bay in northwest Georgia. With reinforcements from Johnston as well as Robert E. Lee, Bragg soon had a numerical advantage over Rosecrans.

By the second week in September, it was clear that Rosecrans was in serious trouble, as Bragg with his newly enlarged army maneuvered to cut him off in the North Georgia mountains. A worried Halleck ordered Grant to send troops to Rosecrans's assistance. On the heels of this message came others, far more alarming, announcing that Rosecrans had fought a great battle, Chickamauga, and had been routed and driven into Chattanooga, where he was all but under siege by Bragg's victorious Rebels. Grant directed Sherman to take three of his own divisions and one of McPherson's—the units that happened to be handiest for quick shipment—transport them up the river to Memphis, and move east to join Rosecrans. Halleck's orders stressed Rosecrans's problems of supply, which were indeed severe, and therefore directed that Sherman repair the Memphis & Charleston Railroad as he went.[2]

Sherman arrived in Memphis on October 2 and set out eastward on the eleventh, saddened by the death of his son Willie to typhoid fever a few days before.[3] The railroad was intact as far as Corinth. Beyond it, Sherman pressed eastward as rapidly as he could while repairing the tracks and attempting to guard them against the seemingly ubiquitous Rebel raiders. During the advance, Sherman received official notice that he was now commander of the Army of the Tennessee. Grant had been promoted to command of the newly created Military Division of the Mississippi, encompassing the armies of the Ohio, the Cumberland, and the Tennessee, and was headed for Chattanooga to see about getting the Army of the Cumberland out of its predicament.[4]

By October 27, Sherman's forces had reached Tuscumbia, Alabama, when a Union scout, having come all the way down the Tennessee River from Chattanooga, arrived with a message from Grant: "Drop all work on Memphis & Charleston Railroad, cross the Tennessee, and hurry eastward with all possible dispatch toward Bridgeport, till you meet further orders from me."[5]

The new program was as much like Grant as the old one was vintage Halleck. Sherman lost no time in complying, ordering his divisions to abandon the railroad and march eastward as rapidly as possible. At the same time, however, he acted on another order from Grant and directed Grenville Dodge with the Second Division (part of Hurlbut's Sixteenth Corps) to continue the work on the railroad—not this time the hopeless Memphis & Charleston but rather the much more practical Nashville & Decatur. Giving Dodge the job of getting the railroad going was the ideal assignment, as he was both an excellent soldier and an excellent railroad man. His work in Tennessee and Alabama while Sherman and his four divisions fought farther east proved a big help in bringing up supplies not only for the Army of the Tennessee but also for the other Union troops in Chattanooga.[6]

During the first days of November, the four divisions of the Army of the Tennessee crossed their namesake river and tramped steadily eastward over good roads, through inviting countryside, under pleasant weather. They made good time, covering as much as twenty-five miles in a day's march. Weather and conditions changed on November 4, and the soldiers encountered roads "literally *bottomless*" with mud under steadily rainy skies. Conditions notwithstanding, they made long marches each day.[7]

On the day the weather changed, the head of the column found the bridge over the Elk River in ruins. The Elk was deep and wide here, near its mouth, and though a ferry was available for crossing, Sherman thought it would be far too slow for crossing his army. So he turned northeast instead, up the valley of the Elk. They crossed into Tennessee on November 6, under clearing skies. The roads were still muddy and difficult, and the terrain was gradually becoming more hilly and rugged. The troops frequently forded broad, shallow streams of clear, swift-flowing water.[8]

On November 8, the head of the column reached Fayetteville and crossed the Elk on a six-span limestone bridge. The following day, they reached the vicinity of Decherd, at the northwestern foot of the Cumberland Plateau and astride the Nashville & Chattanooga Railroad, which was the main supply artery for the Army of the Cumberland. There, for the first time since leaving Memphis, Sherman was in telegraphic communication with Grant.[9]

The column slowly snaked its way up the tortuous roads on the face of the rugged Cumberland Plateau. The road up the escarpment was fre-

quently interrupted by rock ledges two or three feet high, and the men had
to lift the wagons up onto the next ledge. The bare rock was often slippery,
and the mules fell down from time to time. "But after all we make better
head way than I expected," wrote a member of the 5th Iowa. He noted that
the hillsides were covered with a thick stand of timber. "How it grows is a
mystery to me," he wrote, "for not a particle of earth is to be seen, nothing
but solid rock." Roads on top of the plateau were sandy and relatively
good.[10]

By November 13, the head of the column had descended the southeast
side of the plateau and reached Bridgeport, Alabama, on the Tennessee
River about thirty-five miles below Chattanooga.[11] There, Sherman found
a dispatch from Grant directing him to proceed to Chattanooga in person
for conference, leaving his troops to follow as rapidly as possible. Several
small steamers were shuttling supplies on the river between Bridgeport and
Chattanooga, and Sherman took passage in one on the evening of November
14, found orderlies with one of Grant's own horses waiting for him at
the landing at Brown's Ferry, and rode into Chattanooga on the fifteenth.
Grant welcomed him warmly and the next morning took him for a tour of
the fortifications.[12]

From the Union earthworks, Sherman surveyed the setting. To the
southwest was the towering bulk of Lookout Mountain. To the southeast
was the long rampart of Missionary Ridge, rising 600 feet above the town
and lined with Confederate tents. The Rebels possessed the heights, and at
one time their outposts had stretched very nearly from the river above the
town to the river below it. Three weeks earlier, Grant had arrived, taken
command, and ejected the Rebels from Lookout Valley. That opened a supply line for the hitherto all but besieged Army of the Cumberland. Yet to
Sherman, viewing the situation on November 15, the situation looked bad
enough. "Why, General Grant," he exclaimed, "you are besieged."

"It is too true," Grant replied, though, he might have added, not nearly
as true as it had been three weeks before. He explained to Sherman that
Bragg had detached Lt. Gen. James Longstreet to capture or destroy Burnside's Army of the Ohio in East Tennessee, and dispatches from that quarter indicated that the situation there was grave. Here in Chattanooga, the
Army of the Cumberland's horses were all dead of starvation or nearly so.
Unable to move its guns or its supply wagons, that army was now rooted to
Chattanooga, unable to carry out operations more than a few miles from
the town. Grant was also uncertain about the Army of the Cumberland's
morale after its defeat at Chickamauga and subsequent starving time in
Chattanooga. It might not be eager to open a new offensive; certainly its

new commander, George H. Thomas, was in no hurry to attack anything or anybody. Grant had the Eleventh and Twelfth corps from the Army of the Potomac, recently arrived and waiting over in Looking Valley, but they had been accounted the hard-luck units of the hard-luck Army of the Potomac and did not seem likely candidates to spearhead an offensive. For that task, Grant wanted his invincibles of the Army of the Tennessee.

Grant went on to describe his plan for the coming battle. The Army of the Tennessee would march into the hills behind Chattanooga on the north bank of the Tennessee River. There, in a sheltered valley out of sight of Confederate eyes, it would wait until all was in readiness. Then it would cross the Tennessee upstream from Chattanooga and march to the north end of Missionary Ridge. Once the Army of the Tennessee started rolling up the Confederate line, Grant was confident the rest of his troops would fight well.[13]

Grant believed the north end of Missionary Ridge was not fortified and invited Sherman to accompany him to view the ground. They rode some four miles back into the hills north of the Tennessee. From one of the hill-tops, they gazed across the river and about two and a half miles of inter-vening terrain toward the long, slightly lumpy profile of Missionary Ridge. Near the northern end of the ridge, the Chattanooga & Cleveland Railroad passed through it via a tunnel. "From the hills we looked down on the amphitheater of Chattanooga as on a map," Sherman reported, "and noth-ing remained but for me to put my troops in the desired position." That seemed like a straightforward proposition, and Sherman was eager to get his army up and get to work.[14]

The party returned to Chattanooga, and there Sherman took his leave of Grant and hastened back to his army to try to expedite his march. To his dismay, when he reached the steamboat landing that evening, he found that the last boat had left for the night and he would have to wait until the next day. Unwilling to accept that delay, he got the commanding officer at the landing to loan him a rowboat and four soldiers, with which he set off down the river. They traveled all night, with Sherman occasionally taking a turn at the oars. At Shellmound, he swapped his crew for a fresh set of oarsmen and pressed on, reaching Bridgeport about daylight.[15]

Sherman immediately put his troops in motion, across the Tennessee, through Running Water Gap, and down into Lookout Valley. The weather had turned frosty cold several days before and now was raw, damp, and miserable under intermittent drizzle. The roads were muddy and difficult. Nevertheless, by November 20 the head of the Army of the Tennessee's column was marching past the camps of the Army of the Potomac detach-

ment at the lower end of Lookout Valley, though the tail of Sherman's column stretched all the way back to Bridgeport.[16]

It was the first meeting, at least on a large scale, between soldiers of the
Army of the Tennessee and of the Army of the Potomac, two very different organizations. Reactions were mixed. At the head of the Army of the
Tennessee's column that day was the 5th Iowa, and its members registered
generally favorable reactions. They noticed Maj. Gen. Joseph Hooker,
commanding the detachment of the Army of the Potomac, standing in
front of his tent in the steady rain to watch the new troops pass, and thought
him the finest-looking specimen of a general they had ever seen. The
Potomac troops seemed to react favorably. "The arrival of Sherman's army
is hailed by the troops here with a great deal of pleasure," noted Iowan John
Campbell. "What regiment is that?" shouted some of the Potomac men.

"The 5th Iowa," replied Sherman's men.

"Bully for Iowa."[17]

A New York soldier in the Twelfth Corps, observing Sherman's men
pass, thought they marched carelessly, not keeping their formations closed
up neatly the way the Eastern soldiers had been taught to do. The Army of
the Tennessee soldiers "all wore large hats instead of caps; were carelessly
dressed, both officers and men" and boasted that they "put on no style."
Still, "they were a large fine type of men, all westerners." The New York
soldier had the feeling that, if danger threatened, these slouching Westerners would "close up and be there." The soldiers from different sections did
"a good deal of friendly chaffing." "Oh look at their little caps," an Army
of the Tennessee man would cry out, and then, "Where are your paper
collars?"[18]

It was probably later that day that one of Sherman's men, a member of
the Fifteenth Corps, stopped to share a campfire and a bit of talk with several members of the Army of the Potomac's Twelfth Corps. He noticed
they all had a cloth patch in the shape of a star sewed to their caps and asked
its meaning. They explained that it was their corps badge. Each of the corps
in the Army of the Potomac had one. The Twelfth Corps men then asked
their visitor what his corps badge was. "Why," he replied slapping his cartridge box, "forty rounds in the cartridge-box and twenty in the pocket!"
Some months later when John A. Logan became commander of the Fifteenth Corps, he instituted a corps badge that depicted a cartridge box with
the words "Forty Rounds."[19]

Not all of the interaction between the two armies was cordial. Friction
between them seemed to grow with better acquaintance. "The feeling
between the western & eastern troops is very bitter," wrote Iowan W. G.

McElrea. "I am afraid that it will end badly yet. The eastern men have always been defeated while the western men have been victorious & yet these yankees pretend to look down on the western men & officers with contempt," McElrea explained. "This wont do," he added, "it will cause a rumpus yet & get some of these yankees an all fired thrashing."[20]

Despite the hardships of the march, morale among the Army of the Tennessee contingent was high. "Our army never was in better spirits or more enthusiastic in the cause than at present," wrote Capt. Jacob Ritner of the 25th Iowa. "We all expect a hot fight before long, but we expect nothing but victory." Ritner felt proud of the men of his company for the "fortitude and good will" with which they bore hardship and fatigue. "They don't talk now like they did in the 'dark days' at Young's Point last winter," he added, "but they all say they don't want to go home till the rebellion is put down."[21]

Throughout November 20 and 21, while rain poured down incessantly, the first two divisions of Sherman's troops tramped across the pontoon bridge at Brown's Ferry and then slogged over three miles of muddy road into the hills north of Chattanooga, pitching their camps in the concealed valley as planned. During the past month, they had marched more than 200 miles through three states, crossing numerous rivers, including the Tennessee twice, and had endured a considerable amount of cold, rainy weather and muddy roads. It was one of the epic marches of the war.[22]

The heavy rains of November 20 and 21 strained the pontoon bridge at Brown's Ferry to the point that it broke repeatedly and had to be repaired again and again during the next two days. By the twenty-third, it had stabilized to the point that Hugh Ewing's division was able to march across and join Morgan L. Smith's and John E. Smith's divisions in the concealed valley. Then, however, the bridge gave way again, leaving Osterhaus's division on the wrong side of the river and the wrong side of Lookout Mountain. It was hard to say just when the division might be able to make its crossing.[23]

Grant had been intensely impatient to begin the battle, especially since Washington had been pestering him with a continuous stream of messages reminding him of the grave threat to Burnside and wanting to know when Grant would be in a position to send help to the forces in East Tennessee. He decided that he could not wait for the river to subside or the bridge to be repaired and sent orders to Osterhaus to report to Hooker for service in Lookout Valley if he could not get across the river by eight o'clock the next morning. Sherman would begin the offensive with the three divisions on hand, bolstered for the occasion by a division borrowed from the Army of the Cumberland.[24]

The men in the concealed valley had been speculating about what lay in store for them. Clearly their superiors were taking considerable pains to keep them out of the Rebels' sight, and that was suggestive. "There is evidently some strategic move on hand," wrote Col. Jabez Banbury of the 5th Iowa, "but of what character we are unable to conjecture." They could take a guess or two on the basis of the fact that orders had come down for every man to prepare three days' rations and carry 100 rounds of ammunition, two and a half times the normal load. Like many of his soldiers, Banbury took the opportunity to climb the steep hill that screened them from the Tennessee and view the great natural amphitheater of Chattanooga. Confederate tents and campfires looked numerous along Missionary Ridge, and their defensive position seemed impregnable. Morale was high, but the men were still sober as they contemplated the coming battle.[25]

On November 23, Sherman sent Giles Smith's brigade of Morgan Smith's division marching northward five miles, still sheltered by the hills, to a position near North Chickamauga Creek. Engineer details had built 116 pontoon boats, enough for a bridge to span the Tennessee near the mouth of the creek. Sherman's orders were to load the men into the boats at midnight, then shove off and head downstream into the Tennessee River. Smith's brigade would seize the Rebel pickets before they could give the alarm and then establish a beachhead on the southeast bank of the Tennessee. The rest of the corps would follow. If all went as planned, the remainder of Sherman's troops would get to Smith's brigade before Bragg's army did.[26]

About 11:00 p.m. Smith's officers began making boat assignments. Four oarsmen to each craft, detailed from experienced boatmen throughout the Fifteenth Corps. This composite detail, along with the boats themselves, was under the command of Maj. Charles Hipp of the 37th Ohio. Smith's men were told off in twenty-five-man teams, one to a boat. Orders were strict: rifles were to be loaded but not capped, and on no pretense whatsoever was any man to fire his rifle without an order from an officer. Even the oars were muffled to minimize creaking. The brigade manned the boats in the darkness along the narrow creek. The 8th Missouri would lead the flotilla, then came the 55th Illinois, and behind it followed the other six regiments of the brigade.

At midnight they cast off and rowed rapidly down the creek, then into the broad, turbulent Tennessee, swollen by recent rains. The current was strong, even along the northwest shore, which the boats hugged in order to remain concealed for as long as possible. Heavy clouds covered the moon, and the darkness was so dense that men could scarcely make out the form of the boat next in front of them. They spoke in whispers when they had to speak at all. Ahead of them and to the left, they began to make out through the mist the Rebel pickets' campfires.

At the first picket post, the lead boat veered across the river as planned and, as soon as it grounded, its twenty-five men splashed ashore and captured the whole post without a shot being fired. They ferried the Rebel pickets to the northwest bank as prisoners and then set off again to rejoin the flotilla. The second boat repeated the process at the next campfire, and so it went at each post down the river. At the last outpost, a Confederate sentinel was so startled by the sudden approach of armed Yankees that his trigger finger twitched and fired his rifle harmlessly into the air. The rest of the Rebel army seemed to take no notice, and the last Confederate picket detachment was soon on its way to a Union prison.[27]

Still following the plan, the 8th Missouri and 116th Illinois landed near the mouth of South Chickamauga Creek while the other five regiments, led by the 55th Illinois, continued down the river some distance to a prearranged landing point, marked by signal fires on the opposite bank, and there landed and began to entrench. Major Hipp and his oarsmen took their boats across to the northwest shore to pick up more troops, who awaited ferrying there. At first the major had difficulty finding them in the darkness. In desperation, he shouted for the Second Division of the Fifteenth Corps. Out of the darkness came a suppressed but angry voice telling him to keep quiet or he would be arrested. Impatiently, Hipp shouted, "Where in the h———l is Gen. Sherman?"

"What do you want?" came the general's own voice from the darkness some fifty feet away.

"I want a brigade. The boats are waiting," answered Hipp.

"Did you make the landing?" asked Sherman.

"Yes," replied the major, "and captured the picket."

At that Sherman himself let out a yell of delight, and, as reported by those closer to him, took off his hat and waved it over his head. No need for silence remained as the only Rebels within earshot were now prisoners.[28]

Hipp found the troops and began ferrying them across the river. In a remarkably short time, Giles Smith's men had constructed a substantial earthwork from which to defend the planned bridgehead. By the time the sun rose on the morning of November 24, the rest of Morgan Smith's division had crossed along with all of John E. Smith's division, 8,000 men in all, well entrenched and ready for the Confederate reaction.[29]

November 24 dawned cloudy and misty, with the threat of rain. As soon as daylight came, the engineers diverted some of the boats from ferrying troops and began to incorporate them into a rapidly growing pontoon bridge. Some time later, the small steamboat *Dunbar* came up the river from Chattanooga and took over the ferrying duties. By noon Ewing's men were on the southeast bank, and the Army of the Cumberland division commanded by Brig. Gen. Jefferson C. Davis was ready to begin crossing. By that time, the pontoon bridge was complete. Sherman was highly impressed with the work of the engineers under the direction of Brig. Gen. William F. Smith of the Army of the Cumberland. "I have never beheld any work done so quietly, so well," wrote Sherman of the bridging operation, "and I doubt if the history of war can show a bridge of that extent (viz, 1,350 feet) laid down so noiselessly and well in so short a time."[30]

By 1:00 p.m., Sherman had all four of his divisions on the southeast bank of the Tennessee. The operation thus far had proceeded exactly as planned. The element of surprise had been achieved and the Confederate pickets silenced without giving the alarm. Bragg's army still had not reacted, and the ragged, low clouds hanging thickly around the tops of the mountains and hills gave promise that it might be some time yet before the Confederates discovered what was afoot on their right flank. Presently a drizzling rain began to fall, further veiling distant Missionary Ridge and Lookout Mountain into indistinct gray shapes.[31]

All that remained now was for Sherman to advance across the more or less level plain in front of him and seize the high ground at the north end of Missionary Ridge, near where the railroad tunnel passed through. Then he would be in a position both to roll up Bragg's line and to cut off his communications, dual threats so deadly the Confederates were bound to respond.

At 1:00 p.m., Sherman moved out toward Missionary Ridge with three divisions, leaving Davis's men to hold the bridgehead.[32] Other than a few Rebel skirmishers, the advancing Federals encountered no resistance at all. "We expected to have a desperate struggle," wrote an officer in the 47th Ohio. "Judge of our surprise when we found no enemy when we expected to experience our hardest fight."[33] About 3:30 that afternoon they approached the high ground that had been the goal of the operation. Here the terrain proved to be more complicated than it had appeared from the other side of the river. Missionary Ridge was not continuous and uniform. Its crest undulated, and in some places it had fairly significant saddles.

The 47th Ohio, of Brig. Gen. Joseph A. J. Lightburn's brigade, was skirmishing in front of Morgan L. Smith's division and was perhaps first to reach the high ground toward which the Army of the Tennessee had been marching. The Ohioans scrambled up the wooded slope and proceeded southward along its crest but found that they were not on a ridge at all but, rather, on a hill, separated from the high ground to the south by a deep saddle. Lightburn ordered his skirmishers to press on and take the "main hill" just south of them. The 47th Ohio advanced up that elevation and discovered that it too was separated from the rest of Missionary Ridge by a saddle about 150 feet deep. Rolling up Bragg's army by advancing southward along the crest of Missionary Ridge might not be quite as straightforward a task as it had once seemed.[34]

Over the second crest went the Ohioans and they started down the other side. Immediately they encountered a heavy Confederate skirmish line coming the other way. By this time the skirmishers of the other two Union divisions were closing in on the same point, as Sherman's force gradually converged on its target. Caught in the cross fire of three Union skirmish lines, the Rebels promptly fell back across the saddle and up the slope on the far side. That slope was the end of Missionary Ridge proper. The Union skirmishers pressed on across the saddle themselves and halted, on orders from Sherman, at the foot of the slope.[35]

The skies had been gloomy all day under a heavy overcast that hid the tops of the mountains. By the time Sherman's men secured the second summit and the saddle, a heavy fog had moved in, obscuring visibility and bringing a premature close to the short afternoon of a late autumn day. Lightburn's brigade consolidated its position on the second hilltop, the rest of Sherman's command on either side and behind it in reserve. The troops dug in and engaged in some minor sparring with Confederate outposts. Union troops of the Eleventh Corps moved up from Chattanooga and made contact with Sherman's right flank before nightfall. On Sherman's left flank, near South Chickamauga Creek, Confederate forces from the other side of the creek made a brief and ineffective foray against Giles Smith's brigade. The attackers were obviously not present in force, and Smith's men easily drove them off. Casualties were few, but one of them was Smith himself, severely wounded. Command of his brigade devolved on Col. Nathan Tupper of the 116th Illinois.[36]

The situation Sherman faced was confusing. The terrain of Missionary Ridge, which had looked so simple when viewed from the other side of the river, turned out to be very complicated indeed. The face of the ridge was scored by numerous large ravines separated by substantial spurs, and the crest was distinctly lumpy, with a succession of knolls and saddles, though none as big as that which now separated Sherman's command from the rest of the ridge. The next hump of the ridge to the south of Sherman's position was Tunnel Hill, under which the railroad tracks passed.

As darkness fell, Sherman sent a dispatch to Grant that his troops had got astride Missionary Ridge and were almost to Tunnel Hill. That was true, in a manner of speaking, although the situation was not quite what Grant and Sherman had envisioned when they made their plans. In many respects, those plans had worked to perfection. The Army of the Tennessee had indeed crossed the river and gotten onto the Rebel flank without the Confederates finding out about it. Only at the last moment, as Sherman's troops began to move over the northernmost detached humps of the ridge, did Confederate troops move to counter the Union advance. These were the troops the skirmishers had driven off of Lightburn's Hill and across the saddle onto Tunnel Hill, Texans of Brig. Gen. James Smith's brigade of Maj. Gen. Patrick R. Cleburne's division. Cleburne was easily the best division commander in the Confederate army, and his training and discipline had made his division into the best in the army as well. To Cleburne, Bragg now entrusted the task of holding the Confederate right flank on the north end of Missionary Ridge.

Grant, for his part, was delighted that Sherman had made such good progress that day. He was also delighted, and rather surprised, with the success of his opposite flank. On the Union right, Hooker had led Osterhaus's division along with one division from the Army of the Cumberland and one from the Army of the Potomac against the Confederate positions on the flanks and shoulders of Lookout Mountain. In an often fog-shrouded "battle above the clouds," Hooker's men drove the Rebels from the slopes, capturing many prisoners.

Late that night, Grant sat down to write his orders for the following day. Sherman would attack "at early dawn" and sweep down the crest and back slope of Missionary Ridge, rolling up Bragg's army and driving it away from its railroad supply line. Thomas would make his own attack simultaneously with Sherman's and in cooperation with it. "Your command," Grant instructed Thomas, "will either carry the rifle-pits and ridge directly in front of them or move to the left, as the presence of the enemy may require." Hooker would secure the summit of Lookout Mountain, where the enemy was still believed to lurk.[37]

During the first part of the night, rain fell heavily and then turned to sleet and freezing rain. Later the clouds and fog passed off and the night became crystal clear and bitterly cold under a bright full moon. Troops on Lightburn's Hill found that their vantage point gave them a panoramic view over Chattanooga to the surrounding heights. Many of the men were too cold to sleep. Where their position permitted them to do so with safety, they built fires to keep warm. Sitting around the crackling blazes sipping coffee or lying shivering on the ground, thousands of them watched an eclipse of the moon.[38]

November 25 dawned clear and bright. Before first light, Sherman was on horseback, riding his lines and trying to get a sense of how to proceed.[39] In theory, his task was simple. He was on the flank of the Confederate line, and all he had to do was roll it up. In reality, the problem before him was immensely intricate. The mountainous terrain around Chattanooga made a mockery of the standard tactical concepts of the war, devised as they were for rolling farmlands.

Sherman's line straddled the ridge, whose top was narrow, with room for scarcely a single regiment in line of battle. Since the defenders could mass as many men on that front as could the attackers, and since defenders behind breastworks had a three-to-one advantage, man for man, over attackers, the flanking assault that should have been easy was in fact almost impossible. Troops that advanced on either side of the ridge crest would be at a further disadvantage against the defenders, at least in theory, since they would be attacking up a steep slope. Perhaps the solution was a coordinated assault that hit the ridge on the end and both sides at once, but that would be maddeningly difficult to accomplish, since the attackers would be out of sight of one another, separated by the broad, rugged base of the ridge, while the defenders had a compact, open, yet sheltered position on their hilltop. Sherman's men could have used an assist in the form of an inept defense, but instead, defending that hilltop position, just above the tunnel, was the best brigade of one of the best divisions in the Confederate army, with the Confederacy's best division commander directing its defense.

Sherman decided to assign the primary attack to the division of his brother-in-law, Brig. Gen. Hugh Ewing. One of Ewing's brigades, Brig. Gen. John M. Corse's, would attack directly along the crest of the ridge. Another, that of Col. John M. Loomis, would advance on the low ground west of the ridge until it was even with Tunnel Hill, then turn and advance directly toward the Rebel strongpoint. Ewing's third brigade, Col. Joseph R. Cockerill's, would remain in reserve. Since Corse's brigade was small, only about 920 men, Sherman had Lightburn send 200 men of his brigade to cooperate with Corse. This would create an additional converging effect, since Lightburn's men would advance from Lightburn's Hill, while Corse's would start their advance from the other hill, which was held primarily by Col. Jessee I. Alexander's brigade of John E. Smith's division. Lightburn's contingent would form the left of the attack, Corse's the center, and Loomis's the right.[40]

Problems of coordination began at once. To make sure his orders were delivered correctly, Sherman rode over to Lightburn's Hill and personally gave the instructions for the advance of one of Lightburn's regiments. Lightburn chose the 30th Ohio, but, like many of the regiments in this campaign, it was so depleted that the general had to add two companies of the 4th West Virginia to bring the detachment up to Sherman's specified 200-man strength. Col. Theodore Jones of the 30th led the detachment forward through the early-morning light. They descended into the saddle between Lightburn's Hill and the rest of Missionary Ridge and there encountered the skirmishers of Smith's Texas brigade. "Without much trouble," one of Lightburn's officers recorded, Jones's Ohioans and West Virginians drove the Texans up the slope and followed them onto Missionary Ridge itself.[41]

As the Texas skirmishers continued to retreat southward along the crest of the ridge, the Ohioans and West Virginians found themselves in possession of a set of abandoned Confederate log-and-earth breastworks on a knoll at the north end of the ridge. To the south, the land atop the ridge sloped very gently downward into a shallow swale and then just as gently upward to a second knoll, higher than the first. That second knoll was Tunnel Hill. It was about 250 yards from the knoll that Jones's men had just taken. Crowned with more breastworks, still occupied by the Rebels, Tunnel Hill also boasted a battery of artillery.

Conspicuously absent from the ridgetop was any sign of Corse or his brigade, which had for some reason gotten a late start. Jones decided to try to take Tunnel Hill anyway. His men advanced along the ridgetop, passing through the swale and starting up the far slope before close-range rifle and artillery fire drove them back to the captured breastworks. With Corse still missing, Jones sent back to Lightburn for reinforcements, and Lightburn ordered up Lt. Col. Louis von Blessingh's 37th Ohio from his brigade.[42]

By the time the men of the 37th joined their fellow Buckeyes atop the ridge, Corse's attacking line was also approaching. It was still very early. One of Corse's officers reported that when the brigade advanced it was 7:00 a.m., which, if his watch was correct, would have been about half an hour before sunrise. Sherman noted that "the sun had hardly risen" when he heard Corse's bugler sounding the advance. Reckoning on the narrow ridgetop, Corse led with a skirmish line composed of the 40th Illinois, of which only five companies were present, along with three companies of the 103rd Illinois, all under the command of Maj. Hiram Hall. Behind them in close order—but at a considerable interval—came the 46th Ohio. Hall's skirmish line easily brushed aside the Rebel skirmishers in their front, just as Jones's men had done a few minutes before, and then appeared atop the first knoll on Jones's right at about the same time that von Blessingh's 37th Ohio arrived on his left.[43]

Jones, Hall, and von Blessingh, with fewer than 600 men, went for the Rebels immediately. The ridgetop was too narrow for von Blessingh's men in addition to Hall's; so he led his regiment along the slope to the left and tried to swing them around to take the Rebel works in flank. He quickly discovered, however, that another Confederate brigade was in line facing north on a spur of the ridge running east from the main crest, in perfect position to pour enfilade fire into Federals trying to move up the east slope of the ridge.[44]

To make matters worse, at the far end of that brigade, the Rebel line hinged northward and another Confederate brigade held a position along a spur ridge roughly paralleling the main crest of Missionary Ridge, about 400 yards to the east. They could contribute little besides long-range sniping at the Federals on Jones's Knoll, but their presence further complicated any possible Union effort to deal with the Confederate right flank. The strange vagaries of the terrain seemed to allow the Rebels, who knew the ground and had had the chance to select their positions the day before, to use all their available strength while preventing the Federals from getting at them with more than a few hundred men.

The Confederate cross fire lashed von Blessingh's Ohioans. Seventeen-year-old drummer boy John Kountz had left his drum and taken up a rifle. As he advanced alongside his comrades, he noticed how the Confederate fire "fairly plowed up the leaves and made the very ground seem alive." Seconds later he was hit in the thigh and went down. Then the line fell back, leaving him among the dead not far from the Rebel breastworks. When the 37th fetched up back near Jones's Knoll, someone told Capt. John Hamm of Company A that Kountz was still out there, wounded. "Who will go and get him out?" Hamm asked his men. Will Smith volunteered, and crawled forward as far as he could under cover of the curve of the slope. He then dashed the last few yards under heavy fire, got the wounded Kountz on his back, and scrambled back to the regiment without either of them being hit by the Rebel bullets that hummed all around them.[45]

While von Blessingh made his futile attempt on the right flank of Tunnel Hill, Jones's and Hall's men charged directly toward the Confederate breastworks. They pressed in close and fought with bayonets across the parapet. One member of the 40th Illinois leaped over the Confederate works but was killed inside. Presently they had to fall back. Seeing this, a number of the Rebels jumped over the breastworks in pursuit, but the Federals got behind the captured works on Jones's Knoll and turned the tables on the charging Texans. On this constricted ridgetop, defenders behind breastworks held the high cards, and the Ohioans and Illinoisans easily sent the Rebel attackers fleeing back to Tunnel Hill.[46]

About this time, General Corse arrived at the head of the 46th Ohio. The Federals were continuing to have a hard time coordinating their attacks this morning. Within the confines of the ridgetop, however, such factors scarcely mattered. Jones already had as many troops as could profitably advance along the narrow spine of the crest. Corse determined to lead the next assault himself and took the five companies of the 40th Illinois, five from the 103rd, and five more from the 46th Ohio. The rest of the brigade remained in reserve.[47]

The result of this third assault was similar to that of the first two. The fighting raged intensely around the breastworks for about an hour, punctuated by occasional Rebel counterattacks, which Corse's men beat back. Once again, a few Federals reached the breastworks but were killed. Corse himself fell wounded, and his men carried him off the field. Command of the brigade passed to Col. Charles C. Walcutt of the 46th Ohio. Eventually the brigade's line fell back to the starting point of the attack at the captured Rebel breastworks on Jones's Knoll, but swarms of skirmishers remained on the far side of the swale, picking off careless Rebels on Tunnel Hill. After several hours of intense combat along the ridge crest, the two sides had fought each other to a standstill, which served the Confederates' purpose precisely.[48]

Meanwhile, down on the low ground on Sherman's right, Col. John M. Loomis's brigade of Ewing's division had gradually worked its way forward and then turned to the left toward Tunnel Hill, with its right flank near the railroad that led to the tunnel. Once again the problem emerged of trying to attack the end of the ridge without a cooperating attack along the entire front of the ridge. When a force like Loomis's attempted to wrap around the end of the ridge, its flank immediately became vulnerable to Confederate fire from farther down the ridge. Loomis's troops came under fire both from artillery on westward-projecting spurs of Missionary Ridge as well as from Rebel skirmishers just south of the railroad.[49]

Another problem caused by the terrain was the wide circumference of the Union lines as they encircled the broad, rugged lower slopes. The different units of Sherman's force thus often could not see one another, and communication between them was slow. Loomis's watch read 10:30 a.m. when Ewing informed him that Corse "was about to assault Tunnel Hill." In fact, assuming Loomis had the correct time, Corse's men had already been fighting on Jones's Knoll and the slopes of Tunnel Hill for as much as two and a half hours. Together with Col. Adolphus Buschbeck's brigade of the Eleventh Corps, which was attached to his command, Loomis pressed in close enough to the slope for his skirmishers to become hotly engaged with their Confederate counterparts and to be able to perceive when Corse's attack failed and the fighting atop the ridge subsided to a steady crackle of skirmish fire.[50]

There matters rested while Sherman weighed the situation and tried to come up with some answer to the tactical riddle of northern Missionary Ridge. His answer was to press the battle more closely on his right flank— Loomis's sector. There his troops would be closer to the rest of Grant's forces and would not have to deal with the strange convoluted ridge spurs and Confederate lines on the east side of Missionary Ridge or with the cramping proximity of Chickamauga Creek. At 12:30, Loomis received Sherman's order, relayed through Ewing, to push up to the foot of Tunnel Hill. His and Buschbeck's brigades advanced, driving Rebel skirmishers who resisted stoutly. At the same time, the advancing Federals came under fire from Confederate artillery on the ridge. Loomis's left reached a road that ran along the foot of the steep slope, while his right took control of the railroad embankment within 300 yards of the tunnel and sparred with Confederate skirmishers who were sheltering in the whitewashed house and nearby log-cabin slave quarters of a prosperous farmer named Glass.[51]

Loomis was not happy with the position of his left flank, however, and asked Buschbeck to bring up two of his regiments to buttress the position. Buschbeck sent the 27th and 73rd Pennsylvania regiments, which went in aggressively and drove the Rebel skirmishers up the slope of Tunnel Hill. Then without Loomis's order, they pursued, driving upward to within a few yards of Cleburne's breastworks, but could go no farther. Crouching on the damp fallen leaves that covered the slope, sheltering as best they could behind stumps, logs, and tree trunks, the Pennsylvanians, like Walcutt's men a few yards to their left front, engaged in a fierce firefight with the Confederates behind the breastworks.[52]

Even while the Pennsylvanians were fighting higher up the slope, a small Confederate counterattack convinced Loomis that his left was still in danger. He asked Ewing for reinforcements. A couple of hours earlier, Ewing had called on John E. Smith to send him a brigade, and Smith had forwarded Brig. Gen. Charles L. Matthies's brigade. Now Ewing sent Matthies to support Loomis, and asked Smith for another. Smith forwarded Col. Green Berry Raum's brigade, his last, and then, having no more troops to command, hurried forward to see if he could help. Reaching Loomis's position, Smith was not completely satisfied with the way Ewing and Loomis had positioned his brigades. Passing over that, however, he noticed a formation of Union troops charging up the face of Missionary Ridge north of the tunnel. At first, Smith thought the troops were Loomis's but on closer investigation he learned that they were Matthies's, part of his own division. Hurriedly, Smith ordered Raum to advance in support of Matthies.[53]

What had happened was that Loomis had directed Matthies to take the Glass House. Matthies's troops had done so, though the retreating Confederates had torched the building on their way out. The Glass farmstead was a hot place anyway. Rebel cannon on the ridge swept the ground all around the house and the slave cabins. One shell passed so close to John Campbell's head that he "felt the heat of it very plainly."[54]

Matthies's brigade had not been in the vicinity of the Glass House for very long when Col. Holden Putnam, the sometime Freeport banker commanding the 93rd Illinois on Matthies's left, received a message from the colonel of the 27th Pennsylvania stating that his men could hold their position on the hillside if they were reinforced. Putnam forwarded the request to Matthies, who ordered the 93rd up the hill and shortly thereafter sent most of the rest of his brigade after it, leaving the 5th Iowa to hold the Glass farmstead. It was the advance of Matthies's three regiments that got Smith's attention and prompted him to order Raum up the hill to support him.[55]

Matthies caught up with his brigade and found his regiments in line on either side of the 27th Pennsylvania. He was just about to caution his men to "fire low and sure," when a bullet cut him down, badly wounded, and he had to turn over command of the brigade to Col. Benjamin Dean of the 26th Missouri. Putnam went up the hill on horseback, sword in one hand and the regiment's flag in the other. He continued cheering on his men after they reached the brow of the hill and were closely engaged with the enemy until he was shot through the head and killed instantly. His regiment, along with the rest of the Union troops on the upper slope of the hill, kept on fighting for some two hours after he fell. The lines were only twenty yards apart, and several Illinoisans were injured by rocks thrown by the Confederates, who were apparently running low on ammunition.[56]

As Union pressure from the brigades of Walcutt, Loomis, Buschbeck, Matthies, and Raum threatened to overwhelm the defenders of Tunnel Hill late in the afternoon, Cleburne determined on a counterattack and selected the ideal place for it, a fifty-yard gap in the Union line between the right of the 27th Pennsylvania and the left of the 5th Iowa, which was strung out in skirmish line covering the Glass farmstead and extending the Union line to the railroad. A fold in the slope concealed Cleburne's charging column from the view of most of the Union troops on Tunnel Hill, and the Confederates burst through the line almost before the Federals realized what was happening. Many of the Union troops struck by this unexpected onslaught continued to insist for years that the Rebels had gotten in rear of them by passing through the railroad tunnel. That would have been impractical as well as unnecessary; the tricky terrain of Missionary Ridge was sufficient for the purpose.[57]

The 5th Iowa, strung out in skirmish formation, never had a chance. The Confederates engulfed its left, capturing its colors, color guard, and about a third of its men. The rest, including Colonel Banbury, had to "cut our way through their lines [and] use our legs to carry us out of their midst." On the opposite side of the Confederate attack, the 27th Pennsylvania gave way in disorder, and the Rebels rolled up the Union line along the brow of Tunnel Hill, sending Matthies's and Raum's men dashing and tumbling down the slope "like chaff before a cyclone," one of them recalled. As soon as the Union infantry was out of the way, Sherman's batteries opened up on their pursuers. Cleburne's men scrambled back into their breastworks, and Matthies's and Raum's troops re-formed their lines as soon as they got clear of their impossible position on the slope.[58]

Watching the action from Lightburn's Hill, Sherman "chewed the stump of his cigar earnestly," a nearby officer noted. By now it was late afternoon, and it was plain that he was not going to be able to take Tunnel Hill in the hour or two of daylight that remained. The simultaneous attack by Thomas's Army of the Cumberland, which Grant had ordered the night before, had not occurred. Finally, however, at about the time Sherman's assault was sputtering out, Grant renewed his order to Thomas and, after a couple of repetitions, finally got the stolid commander in motion. The attack along the long, straight, western face of Missionary Ridge could be—and was—a coordinated mass assault. The Confederate commanders in those sectors were less skillful than Cleburne, and their troops were much less expertly sited. As a result, the deceptively complicated terrain of Missionary Ridge worked in favor of the attackers of the Army of the Cumberland, providing them cover much of the way up the slope. In the last light of the short autumn afternoon, Thomas's troops broke through the long, thin Rebel line and routed Bragg's army.[59]

Receiving word of the Union success in the center, which was out of his line of sight, Sherman ordered Morgan L. Smith's division to probe forward as far as the tunnel. They found that the enemy had pulled out. Cleburne's division was even then covering the Confederate retreat.[60] The Army of the Tennessee saw no action during the pursuit, except for Osterhaus's division, which, under Hooker's command, clashed with Cleburne's rear guard at Ringgold Gap on November 27.[61]

By that day, Grant could see that the Confederate army was in full retreat but that little was to be gained by further pursuit of it unless he was ready to undertake a new campaign. He was not, partially because the Army of the Cumberland could not stir far from its supply source and partially because the authorities in Washington were nagging him daily about the need to get help to Burnside, whose dispatches were dwelling darkly on the possibilities of starvation, surrender, or a desperate break-out attempt. So Grant canceled further pursuit of Bragg and sent orders to Thomas, who was still in Chattanooga, to start Maj. Gen. Gordon Granger's Fourth Corps on its way to Knoxville at once. Sherman was to "move slowly and leisurely back to Chattanooga," destroying the railroad as he went.[62] On November 29, Grant arrived in Chattanooga and was appalled to find that Granger had not even started. When Grant questioned him, Granger opined that marching on Knoxville to relieve Burnside was not a good idea. In his quiet way, Grant was furious. He got Granger in motion as ordered but determined to put the job in the hands of someone he could trust. He immediately sent orders for Sherman to bypass Chattanooga and march immediately for Knoxville, taking command of Granger on the way. By this time, Sherman's troops had been away from their camps for seven days, having taken with them two days' rations and one blanket or overcoat per man.[63]

It was a hard, cold, hungry march into East Tennessee. By the evening of December 5, however, as the head of the column reached Marysville, fifteen miles from Knoxville, Sherman received a message from Burnside notifying him that Longstreet, having learned of Sherman's approach, had lifted the siege and retreated northeastward, toward Virginia. Leaving his men to rest at Maryville, Sherman continued to Knoxville. He found that Burnside and his men—far from starving, as his dispatches had suggested—had in fact been eating considerably better than the Army of the Tennessee had lately been faring. Still, Burnside was appropriately grateful for Sherman's rapid march. Sherman determined to leave the Fourth Corps to reinforce Burnside, despite whining from Granger. Then with Howard's and Davis's commands, as well as the Army of the Tennessee, Sherman set out for Chattanooga, where he arrived on December 16. Grant ordered Howard's and Davis's commands to rejoin their original organizations and sent Sherman with the Fifteenth Corps and J. E. Smith's division of the Seventeenth into winter quarters in northern Alabama. The Army of the Tennessee's 1863 campaigning was finally at an end.[64]

CHAPTER TWENTY-SEVEN

Meridian

IN LATE DECEMBER 1863, Grant and Sherman met in Nashville to confer on future operations. Sherman suggested that he should return to Mississippi and clean out any remaining Confederate forces that might potentially threaten navigation of the river. Clearing out such backwaters of the war would help free troops for the major campaigns of the coming year.

Sherman's primary target would be the town of Meridian, near the eastern edge of the state, about 135 miles from Vicksburg. Meridian was the headquarters of Leonidas Polk, commanding Confederate forces in Mississippi. It was also an important transportation center and depot, the almost indispensable base for any major Confederate attempt to strike westward toward the river. Grant readily assented.[1]

Sherman arrived in Memphis on January 10 and began preparing for the expedition and conferring with Memphis garrison commander Stephen Hurlbut. By some accounts, Hurlbut had adapted well to the life of an occupation commander in Memphis, where there was plenty to drink, plenty to get, and not too much to do. Sherman now informed him that, at least for the time being, his comfortable duty was at an end: he would be taking the field for a winter campaign as a corps commander.

He had Hurlbut collect as large a field force as he could spare—two divisions—from his Sixteenth Corps, which had been occupying West Tennessee and northern Mississippi during the previous year. The troops thus amassed were sent down the river to Vicksburg. McPherson's Seventeenth Corps had been occupying Vicksburg and environs for the past six months. Sherman planned to take a similar force from the Seventeenth Corps in order to achieve a field army of some 20,000. He was very specific about one particular man in Hurlbut's department whom he wanted to accompany the expedition, and that was Maj. Gen. Andrew Jackson Smith. Smith was currently commanding a garrison in the distant backwater of Columbus, Kentucky, but he had previously led a division of the Thirteenth Corps throughout the Vicksburg campaign. Aggressive and highly competent, he had made a good impression on Sherman.[2]

While in Memphis, Sherman met with Brig. Gen. William Sooy Smith, whom Grant had sent from Middle Tennessee with 2,500 cavalry. Sherman directed Smith to move with his own cavalry and another division of horsemen provided by Hurlbut—7,000 troopers in all—on February 1 and head straight for Meridian, there to link up with Sherman. On his way, Smith was bound to encounter the cavalry force of Confederate raider Nathan Bedford Forrest, and Sherman warned him to be prepared to fight Forrest aggressively.[3]

By January 27, Sherman's Memphis preparations were complete and he took ship for Vicksburg. Arriving there on February 1, he conferred with Hurlbut and McPherson and received the report of a spy who informed him that Polk had two divisions of infantry—one under Maj. Gen. W. W. Loring at Canton, Mississippi, twenty-five miles northeast of Jackson, and the other under Maj. Gen. Samuel G. French at Brandon, fifteen miles due east of the Mississippi capital. Polk also had two divisions of cavalry—one operating under Forrest's command in northern Mississippi, and the other in the middle part of the state. Sherman noted with satisfaction, "General Polk seemed to have no suspicion of our intentions to disturb his serenity."[4]

Thanks to Sherman's strict secrecy, his own troops were themselves not quite clear about where they would be going and what they would be doing. Sgt. David Poak of the 30th Illinois wrote his sister on February 1, "What the exact object of the expedition is, is not known."[5] Late on the evening of February 2, as preparations were afoot for departure early the next morning, William McCarty scrawled in his diary that they were about to march, "Destination unknown."[6] Whatever the purpose of the march and wherever it might lead, the soldiers were eager to embark on it. "The boys get so tired staying in camp doing nothing," wrote Poak, "that they resort to almost every thing to keep in amusement." The march, he believed, would be a splendid form of amusement.[7]

Reveille sounded at 4:00 a.m. on the morning of February 3, and at six the columns took to the roads. Total strength was larger than planned, approximately 27,000 men. The expedition marched in two columns, the two divisions of the Sixteenth Corps under Hurlbut on the left and two divisions of the Seventeenth under McPherson on the right. Sherman was careful to keep his own headquarters near that of the slightly suspect Hurlbut throughout the operation. Scouting and screening ahead of them was a cavalry detachment under the command of Col. E. F. Winslow.[8]

The expedition's wagon train was sparse. This was to be a raid. In contrast to Grant during the May 1863 Vicksburg campaign, Sherman would make no attempt to maintain any sort of supply line whatsoever. His men would live on the rations in their haversacks and the three wagons per regiment that accompanied the march—along with what they could forage off the countryside.

They reached the Big Black River on the first afternoon of the march, crossed, and encamped four or five miles east of it.[9] As soon as they were east of the Big Black, they had to contend with the almost constant presence of Confederate cavalry, members of Brig. Gen. Wirt Adams's brigade. The Rebel horsemen skirmished in front of the column and marauded the flanks and rear. Some of the first significant skirmishing took place near the old Champion's Hill battlefield. Sherman's infantrymen had little difficulty brushing aside the pesky horsemen. The skirmishing "slightly hindered our progress," wrote Hosea Rood of the 12th Wisconsin. Later that day, however, three members of the 12th were killed when Confederate horse artillery lobbed a shell right into the center of Company I.[10] For the most part, the cavalry was merely a nuisance, and it did have the redeeming value of encouraging everyone to keep well closed up most of the time.[11]

Somewhat remarkably, however, it did not prevent foraging, which Sherman's veterans had refined to an art form. In vain did Mississippians attempt to conceal their bacon and hams in swamps and other out-of-the-way places. The troops had become expert at guessing hiding places, and when they were unable to turn up a suspected cache of foodstuffs, the local slaves were usually more than happy to provide the needed information. Lute Barber of the 15th Illinois saw on several occasions "load after load of the nicest hams" being brought up from hiding places back in the swamps and woods. Barber had to give the Mississippians credit for their excellent cured meat. "The Southern people surpassed the North in curing hams," he noted with a connoisseur's fine discrimination. "I never ate so sweet meat as in the South. They use a great deal of saltpeter and molasses in curing them and smoke them but little."[12] Live poultry, hogs, and cattle were also swept up by the column in large amounts without straying far from the main line of march.[13]

Sherman was in sympathy with his men on the subject of foraging. When a woman along the route of march applied to him to post a guard over her meat house during the passage of the army in order to prevent soldiers from raiding it, he replied that the soldiers needed the meat, and since the Southerners "had brought the war on themselves, they must bear the consequences." "Bully for Sherman," wrote an Illinois soldier in his diary.[14]

The presence of Confederate cavalry not only failed to prevent foraging but also did nothing to reduce the destruction of property along the army's line of march. Indeed, the constant skirmishing may have increased the devastation, as each side opted to burn buildings that were havens for enemy sharpshooters. A soldier of the 8th Illinois wrote of the February 4 march, "The fences, houses, and farms all on fire, quite a grand spectacle after night," but did not note the reason for the conflagrations.[15]

The pattern continued the following day, with constant skirmishing at the front of the column. That day McPherson's lead brigade covered nine miles in line of battle, spread out in the fields and woods on either side of the road, during the morning hours. Then another brigade took over the lead and continued beating the bushes throughout the afternoon. The constant firing produced a steady trickle of casualties. Rood saw seventeen dead and wounded men at the crossing of Baker's Creek alone. Confederate batteries continued to toss shells into the Union columns and camps, killing a man or two occasionally. The Union guns would unlimber and return the compliment. A similar process took place at the head of Hurlbut's column. When the expedition finally halted for the night, Sgt. James Jessee of the 8th Illinois noted in his diary that it had been "the hardest days march we have made for some time." That night the tired men "made fire, eat supper, gathered some leaves, made a Bed and lay down to rest & dream of Battles, and of home."[16]

Trailing its ever-lengthening column of black freedom-seekers and still driving Wirt Adams's cavalry in front of it, the expedition reached Jackson on February 6, and for the third time the capital city of Mississippi fell to troops under Sherman's command.[17] "We remained in Jackson long enough for the city to suffer on account of our presence," wrote Hosea Rood. "Just who set the fires none of us could tell. A building here and there would be seen with the flames just bursting through windows or roof, and that is all any of us knew about it." James Jessee wrote in his diary, "Boys perfectly crazy setting the houses a fire." Somewhat remarkably, both the statehouse and the courthouse were spared. By the time Sherman's troops marched out of the city the next day, Jackson "presented a sorry appearance," Rood noted, and the town was still on fire.[18]

Leaving Jackson, the expedition crossed the Pearl River on a pontoon bridge captured from the Rebels and continued eastward, reaching the town of Brandon. French's Confederate infantry division was nowhere to be seen. As destructive as the expedition may have been to civilian property in Mississippi, the persons of civilians were strictly exempt from harm. Confident in this, Confederate civilians, especially women, made no effort to get out of the path of the Union advance. In Brandon many of them were in evidence, frowning at the Union troops, who proceeded to burn the jail, a recruiting office, and several stores and public buildings.[19]

As they continued eastward, their route led through areas of towering pine forests interspersed with districts of rich plantations, where the soldiers "saw thousands of dollars worth of cotton in flames."[20] On February 9, the head of the column reached Morton, thirty-five miles from Jackson and sixty from Meridian. There, Sherman's cavalry began detecting the presence of Confederate infantry ahead of them. Yet the Rebel foot soldiers made no effort to block the march but continued to fall back.[21] The town of Morton was on fire when Sherman's troops reached it, having been torched by the retreating cavalry in order to deny the Federals the benefit of the commissary stores there. For a change, Sherman's men played the role of fire brigade and succeeded in extinguishing the flames in time to rescue considerable amounts of flour and meat.[22]

Near Morton, Confederate troops made one of their stands immediately behind a dwelling house in which, unknown to the Federals, the family was still present. Fire from the Confederate position behind the house drew a Union volley in return. Numerous bullets passed through the house, one of which killed a mother of five. The Union soldiers were saddened by this tragedy, but, as Hosea Rood noted, it had been "more chargeable to the Rebels than to our troops" because the Rebels "knew the family were in the house." Two Confederate soldiers were killed by the same volley, and the rest fled.[23]

On this march and others that came after, questions often arose as to what ought to be burned, what had actually been burned, and who had done it. Orders from Sherman clearly required the torching of railroad tracks, bridges, depots, factories, storehouses, and the like. Except in cases of specific retaliation, the burning of other structures was unofficial. The most likely targets were outbuildings such as barns and gin houses, with unoccupied private dwellings also being reduced to ashes on a fairly regular basis. The rarest target for burning was a private dwelling whose occupants had not fled the army's approach. There is no known case of a house being deliberately burned with the occupants still in it, but there were instances in which incendiaries unceremoniously chased the occupants out of a house before setting fire to it. Except in cases of specific retaliation, the latter activity was condemned by the great majority of soldiers. Lute Barber wrote that such deeds were the work of "gangs of ruffians, who always followed the wake of armies, to pillage and destroy," and he was probably right about most of the cases.[24]

At Tallahatta Creek, twenty miles from Meridian, they encountered felled trees across the road, an obvious attempt to slow the advance. Sherman surmised from this that Polk needed more time in order to salvage valuable assets from Meridian. He therefore decided to park his wagon trains, detach one regiment from each division to guard them, and, with the rest of his force unencumbered, press on toward Meridian at top speed. At Oktibbeha Creek, they found the bridge in flames, too far gone to save, but Sherman's men dismantled a large cotton gin nearby and used the materials to build a new bridge within about two hours. Finally, at 3:30 p.m. on Valentine's Day, Sherman's troops marched into Meridian, still having encountered no significant resistance from major formations of Confederate infantry. Once again the only resistance came from Rebel horsemen, and a single battalion of Winslow's cavalry sufficed to drive them off.[25]

Having reached the objective of his expedition, Sherman turned methodically to the task of eliminating the town's ability to serve as a base for Rebel operations. After giving his men a day to rest, on February 16 he put them to work. He had them destroy the Confederate arsenal and storehouses in town, and then sent large detachments in four directions in order to make a thorough job of destroying the tracks of the Mobile & Ohio Railroad north and south of Meridian and of the Jackson & Selma Railroad east and west of town. Hurlbut's Sixteenth Corps worked north and east of Meridian, and Hurlbut reported that they tore up sixty miles of track, burned the ties, and bent the rails. They also ignited eight bridges and destroyed one locomotive. McPherson's Seventeenth handled matters to the south and west of town. There McPherson reported eliminating fifty-five miles of track including fifty-three bridges and culverts and some 6,075 feet of trestlework across a swamp more than twenty miles south of Meridian. The Seventeenth could also boast the demolition of nineteen locomotives and three steam sawmills. When the work was finished, Sherman could state in his report, "Meridian, with its depots, store-houses, arsenal, hospitals, offices, hotels, and cantonments no longer exists."[26]

Another step toward Sherman's goal of neutralizing Meridian was removing excess foodstuffs. Union troops searched the town carefully for stocks of victuals, finding some ingeniously hidden. One women hid a sack of sugar in a cradle—to no avail. The search parties left each family what was deemed to be a reasonable amount of food for the family's own use, and then a guard was posted over the house to prevent off-duty soldiers from jayhawking what remained—or from setting fire to the house. Sometimes even a guard was not sufficient, and, as one of the soldiers wrote in his diary, "now and then a house would go up in flames."[27]

Several hours of rain on the morning of February 15 was the first since the expedition left Vicksburg. The entire outbound trip had been made in mild, sunny spring weather. Now temperatures turned bitter cold, and the morning of February 18 brought snow flurries.[28]

The one aspect of Sherman's program that had not yet developed was the rendezvous with Sooy Smith's cavalry command. Smith should have been in Meridian by now, and Sherman worried about what might have happened to him. In fact, Smith had gotten a late start, not riding out of Memphis until February 6. His subsequent progress had been dilatory, and while Sherman waited anxiously in Meridian, Smith was still far to the north. Unaware of this, Sherman waited for five days, using the time to complete the destruction. He needed to be back in Vicksburg by March 1, or shortly thereafter, in order to lend troops to Nathaniel Banks for operations west of the Mississippi—as ordered in Washington. Finally he decided he could wait no longer and turned back for Vicksburg.[29]

Many of the citizens of the by now very battered town "manifested some joy at our leaving," a soldier wrote. On the other hand, "quite a number of families" of white Unionists left Meridian with the army to travel to Vicksburg and a new life outside of Rebel lines. The column of blacks behind the army had grown steadily until by the time the expedition turned back toward Vicksburg, it was followed by what one soldier called "an innumerable host of contrabands."[30]

At first the return trip promised much scantier fare than the outbound journey because the army would be marching back over the same ground it had foraged so efficiently only a few days before. Foraging parties had to venture out farther away from the flanks of the column and collided more frequently with Rebel cavalry. Sometimes they were forced back empty-handed.[31] Then matters took a turn for the better, at least for the men of the Sixteenth Corps, when Sherman ordered it to take a more northerly road from Decatur through the towns of Marion and Union, in hopes of making contact with Sooy Smith, presumed to be somewhere to the north.[32]

In fact, Smith was much farther north than Sherman imagined. On February 21, he had a brush with Forrest, with about equal numbers, and decided to retreat to Memphis. The next day, at Okolona, Mississippi, Forrest attacked with his usual ferocity. By the time the fight was over, Smith had lost 388 men, six cannon, and his nerve. He lost no time in getting his expedition safely back to Memphis.

By February 27, Sherman's force reached Canton, which Lute Barber found to be a pleasant place, so thrifty and neat that it reminded him of Northern towns.[33] Reassured by a month's campaigning as to Hurlbut's competence and reliability and eager to get back in touch with the outside world, Sherman turned over command of the expedition to him as senior corps commander and, escorted by Winslow's cavalry, hastened back to Vicksburg.[34]

There he learned of Sooy Smith's failure. He also received the expected messages from Banks, calling for troops. Banks was planning an expedition up the Red River and wanted to borrow three of Sherman's divisions for that dubious purpose. He already had his own Nineteenth Corps, plus the Thirteenth Corps, which had been added to his command after Vicksburg, but the strategically ill-conceived Red River expedition was very dear to the hearts of Lincoln and Halleck. Sherman would have to send the troops as requested, but Grant, who was about to be promoted to commanding general of all U.S. armies, stipulated that they had to be back to Sherman in time for a spring campaign in Georgia. To Louisiana went the two-division field force of the Sixteenth Corps along with one division of the Seventeenth. Hurlbut would be returning to Memphis, however, and the Red River detachment would be commanded by A. J. Smith. Those three divisions would never again serve with the Army of the Tennessee but were destined to write their own chapters in the history of the last year of the war.[35]

The expedition arrived at Vicksburg on March 3. Following behind the troops, the column of nonmilitary persons had by now grown to enormous proportions. In addition to perhaps 150 white Unionist families, one soldier estimated there were 5,000 contrabands.[36] They were an amazing sight to the soldiers. Men, women, and children, the very young and the very old, the hale and healthy as well as the crippled and infirm, in every shade from light brown to jet black. Many were on foot and brought only what goods and possessions they could carry on their backs. Yet others were traveling in every type of wagon, buggy, sulky, and cart that central Mississippi had to offer, drawn by every imaginable combination of horses, donkeys, and oxen. A soldier counted more than thirty black children and two women in a single large plantation wagon. Other wagons carried a great deal of wealth and finery that the newly freed blacks had taken from the mansions of former masters.[37]

It had been at times, and in parts, a joyous procession, as the slaves reveled in the first concrete experiences of their new freedom. Seeing one young boy striding along carrying a bundle, a Union soldier asked, "Where are you going to, youngster?" To which the grinning boy replied, "I'm gui-in to glory, marster!"[38]

At the same time, this procession could also be one of sorrow and suffering. Freedom's circumstances could be harsh and unpleasant, as the newly freed slaves were quickly learning. Oddly, in view of the large amount of miscellaneous household goods they carried with them, few of the escapees carried much food. In a region where armed, aggressive, and experienced soldiers could scarcely find enough to eat, the former slaves were bound to go hungry, and many of them suffered terribly. Hunger and exposure, as well as crowding, made the contrabands vulnerable to infectious diseases, to which many succumbed before they could be forwarded to the contraband camps in the area.[39]

The soldiers themselves were a sight to behold as they marched into the camps they had left a month before, and they knew it. They had had no clothes on the march save those on their backs, and after thirty days of outdoor living in all weathers and tramping over roads that were sometimes very muddy, some of those clothes were wearing out. Soldiers marched along in tattered shreds of garments or even in their drawers, and a Wisconsin soldier estimated that "one man in every five or six came back barefooted," his shoes having fallen apart. They knew they were a comical sight and enjoyed the fact at least as much as any observers. "Our general appearance created much merriment among the boys who remained behind," recalled Hosea Rood.[40] When William McCarty got back to his tent in Vicksburg, he "put on clean clothes & burnt the old ones."[41]

They returned in high spirits nonetheless, believing that they had accomplished on this expedition everything that could possibly have been desired. The three brigades of Leggett's division covered twenty-seven miles on the last day of the march, making a race of it and double-quicking for the last eight miles. Back in camp, they were happy to find a large supply of the one thing every soldier wanted most, next to food—letters from home.[42]

Sherman wrote an enthusiastic report of the campaign, listing the various items of Confederate property destroyed, but such things, he said, were merely incidental to the real value of the Meridian expedition, which was convincing the men of the Army of the Tennessee—if they needed any such convincing—that they could march where they pleased through enemy country and live off the land as they went. "The great result attained," he wrote, "is the hardihood and confidence imparted to the command, which is now better fitted for war."[43] In fact, the expedition had been educational for all concerned. Sherman and his officers had learned much about the feasibility and effectiveness of raids deep into Confederate territory.

The destructiveness of the march showed no immediate signs of bringing the Rebels to their knees. In fact, James Jessee and his comrades in the 8th Illinois felt much less inclined to think that the Confederacy could be "starved out." Food was so abundant in the countryside that Jessee had to conclude the South could feed itself for another year even without the crop that was about to be put into the ground. Jessee and his friends concluded that the only thing that would speed the successful conclusion of the war would be the reelection of Abraham Lincoln in the fall of 1864. "It will strike terror into the leaders of the rebellion, convince them that the policy of the present administration is going to be carried out, and that the great mass of the people of the North give it their support and approbation." Jessee came to the conclusion that anyone who voted against Lincoln was voting "for the prolonging of the war."[44]

After the conclusion of the Meridian expedition, the next item on the agenda was the long-awaited reenlistment furlough. In late 1863, the Union high command had addressed a looming problem. The hundreds of thousands of veteran troops who had signed three-year enlistments in 1861 would be finishing their hitches in the midst of the 1864 summer campaigns. Their departure would devastate the Union armies in numbers and, much more important, in experience. As an inducement to reenlist, the army offered to allow the boys of '61 to reenlist early, during the winter of 1864. Regiments in which most of the men reenlisted could retain their identity and henceforth add the word "veteran" to their names. Best of all, every man who reenlisted was entitled to a thirty-day furlough. For many of them it would be the first chance to see parents, wives, or children since marching away to war two and a half years before.

Response was good in the Army of the Tennessee, as in the other Union armies in the West. Unlike the hard-luck soldiers in the Army of the Potomac, the Union fighting men in the West had experienced success and could see and feel the progress toward final victory. So they reenlisted in such numbers that the army soon owed a major segment of its soldiers thirty days in their home states.

Sherman felt distinctly ambivalent about the whole business. He admitted that it was "a judicious and wise measure" that kept good men in the army, but he lamented the need to furlough so many troops at one time. It was, he said, "like disbanding an army in the very midst of battle."[45] The soldiers suffered from no such mixed feelings. "Oh, my joy can never be told with our simple language," wrote 32nd Ohio soldier William Hubbell when the order came for his regiment to prepare for the trip back to Ohio.[46] Such orders came earlier, often near the beginning of February, for regiments in the Fifteenth Corps, which had not participated in the Meridian expedition. The regiments in the Sixteenth and Seventeenth corps got their orders at various times during March.

The furloughed soldiers returned to heroes' welcomes in their home-towns. "Never will I forget our reception at Massillon," wrote Charles Willison of the 76th Ohio regarding his regiment's return to its hometown. "The population turned out en masse to meet us at the depot, with bands and guard of home militia. The train had no more than stopped till we were almost carried bodily out of the car. When finally we were able to form in line, the procession, headed by the band and militia, marched to the principal hotel of the city, where a banquet was in waiting."[47]

In anticipation of the arrival of their contingent from the 3rd Iowa, the people of Cedar Falls decorated the railroad depot in cedar boughs, flags, and signs reading "Welcome" and "Honor to Whom All Honor Is Due; Iowa Boys, Bully for You!" Archways of cedar branches spanned the railroad platform and the bridge leading into town, with signs listing the regiment's skirmishes and battles. Hundreds thronged the station, and the Cedar Falls Brass Band was on hand when the soldiers' train pulled in. The troops filed off the train and formed in line to hear a welcoming speech. Then, escorted by the band and cheering crowd, they marched into Main Street, where a huge U.S. flag hung from a rope stretched between the upper floors of buildings and countless smaller versions of the Stars and Stripes floated from businesses and from the upstairs windows of the houses. At Horticultural Hall, the soldiers sat down to a feast prepared by the Cedar Falls Ladies' Soldiers' Aid Society.[48]

In this and similar welcomes at towns all across the Midwest, the tacit contract between the soldiers and their communities was renewed. The men would continue to face hardship and danger for the good of the community, and the citizens back home would honor the sacrifices their soldiers made. The practical demonstrations of support continued throughout the furlough. "It appeared as if the community spent its time and effort those thirty days seeing how nearly they could overwhelm us with glory," recalled Willison.[49]

The greatest joy of the furlough was being home with family, the goal toward which the soldiers of the Army of the Tennessee had been marching and fighting for two years—the opportunity to come home in honor and victory with the country and the Constitution saved. The furlough provided a foretaste of that ultimate satisfaction. William Hubbell wrote blissfully of how on his first morning back home the "sunlight streamed again through that same space between the curtains of my little bedroom window and rested on my face." At the breakfast table his father, as was his custom, read a chapter from the Bible. The young soldier recalled other mornings in years gone by when he had heard his father read that same chapter and had then "fretted and wondered why it was so long!" Now he could hardly imagine ever tiring of hearing his father read it.[50]

The thirty days of furlough passed quickly, and the day came when the regiments assembled at the railroad depots, once again amid bands and flags and cheering crowds. Yet as short as the furlough had seemed to the men, events in the war had been rushing ahead while they were gone. Congress passed and Lincoln signed an act reviving the rank of lieutenant general, last held by George Washington. As everyone expected, Lincoln nominated and the Senate confirmed Grant for the new rank, which Lincoln formally conferred on March 9. The following day, as expected, Grant received orders assigning him to command all the armies of the United States, replacing Halleck, who was reduced to the role of chief of staff. That vacated the post of commander of the Military Division of the Mississippi, which naturally went to Sherman. Just as naturally, James B. McPherson was tapped to move up and fill the vacancy thus created as commander of the Army of the Tennessee.

As general-in-chief, Grant planned a grand offensive for the spring of 1864, with five different armies (or groups of armies) advancing toward vital Confederate targets. Three of the planned thrusts were to be in Virginia. In the West, Nathaniel Banks was to finish his fool's errand up the Red River, return Sherman's borrowed divisions, and then direct his own Army of the Gulf in a campaign aimed at the vital Confederate port of Mobile. Sherman himself would lead the main Western effort. With the Army of the Tennessee, the Army of the Cumberland, and the Army of the Ohio—a combined force of about 100,000 men—he was to advance from Chattanooga southeastward toward Atlanta, Georgia, following the line of the Western & Atlantic Railroad. Opposing him would be one of the Confederacy's two remaining major armies, commanded now by the much-respected Joseph E. Johnston in place of the defeated Braxton Bragg. Grant confidently reckoned that the Confederacy would never be able to counter all of those threats.

The general-in-chief would make his headquarters with the Army of the Potomac, but Sherman thought that was a mistake. "Come out West," he urged his friend, "take to yourself the whole Mississippi Valley," by which Sherman meant the whole Western theater of the war. "The Atlantic slope and Pacific shores will follow its destiny as sure as the limbs of a tree live or die with the main trunk!" Virginia was simply too close to Washington. Political intrigues and complications would always hamstring any general who operated there. "Here lies the seat of the coming empire," Sherman exhorted, "and from the West, when our task is done, we will make short work of Charleston and Richmond, and the impoverished coast of the Atlantic."[51]

Grant in direct command of the 1864 Western campaign is one of the more interesting might-have-beens in a war filled with such tantalizing contingencies. To Grant, however, the situation in Virginia cried out for his presence. The very difficulty of the Virginia front—the skill of Robert E. Lee, the clumsiness of the Army of the Potomac, and the political snake pit of Washington—all pointed to the fact that only Grant's presence could mend Union fortunes there. Yet Sherman had been correct. The outcome of the war in the West would decide the future of the continent, regardless of what happened east of the Appalachians. To Sherman himself, however, would fall the duty of finishing the task in the West and then turning to "make short work" of the Atlantic coast. The job would begin in northwestern Georgia in May 1864.

CHAPTER TWENTY-EIGHT

Resaca

O N THE FIRST DAY OF MAY 1864, at various camps from Huntsville, Alabama, to Pulaski, Tennessee, the regiments that composed five divisions of the Army of the Tennessee packed up their camp equipment, slung their knapsacks or blanket rolls, took their last looks at the muddy scenes of their winter encampments, and marched out along roads leading toward Chattanooga. Heavy rain fell across much of the area on the night of April 30, rendering roads muddy and difficult the next day. The soldiers splashing through the mud on the various roads leading into Chattanooga were on their way to a campaign in which the Army of the Tennessee would operate in close concert with two other Union armies but would have a starring role as Sherman's maneuvering and striking force.[1]

Sherman's plan called for the Army of the Tennessee to flank Johnston's impregnable position on Rocky Face Ridge by passing through winding, three-mile-long Snake Creek Gap. From the eastern mouth of Snake Creek Gap, the Army of the Tennessee would be within a few miles of Johnston's supply line, the Western & Atlantic Railroad, near the town of Resaca, Georgia, where the rails crossed the Oostenaula River. As Sherman envisioned the operation, McPherson would debouch from the gap, break the railroad, then retire and take up a strong defensive position in the mouth of the gap. With his supply line cut, Johnston would presumably retreat, and when he did, the armies of the Cumberland and Ohio would fall on his rear while the Army of the Tennessee tore at his flank.[2]

Despite the muddy roads, the army covered as much as twenty-five miles per day during the march to Chattanooga, where units began arriving on May 4 and continued pouring through the town for the next several days. Some of the troops got to ride the rails for the last few dozen miles of their journey, embarking in trains at either Larkinsville or Woodville, Alabama, to Chattanooga. John McKee of the 2nd Iowa noted that from the railroad car on which he was riding, "We saw troops and wagons all along the road coming this way. Everything is going to the front." As the troops neared Chattanooga, they entered the region fought over in the previous autumn's campaigns. Surgeon William Allen of the 9th Illinois noted the sight and smell of thousands of rotting mule carcasses along the road.[3]

At Chattanooga on May 5, McPherson issued a message to "the soldiers of the Army of the Tennessee." "We are about to enter upon one of the most important campaigns of the war," he told the men. As they had "shown their valor and patriotism on many a hard-fought field" in the past, so he was counting on them to do so again. "Stand firmly by your posts," he admonished. "Let not the storm of battle nor the vigorous onsets of the enemy shake your faith in the righteousness of our cause, and the conviction of our ultimate success." They must remember that "the successful issue of the battle may depend on your individual bravery, and the stubbornness with which you hold your position." Then came the specific advice: conserve ammunition, make every shot count, aim low, and if the enemy charges with bayonets, meet him halfway with your own. Let the ambulance corps take care of the wounded, and "obey cheerfully and promptly the orders of your officers." Regimental adjutants read the order to the troops on dress parade the following day, and the soldiers, who idolized McPherson, found it encouraging.[4]

In Chattanooga the troops turned in most of their baggage and all of their garrison equipment, tents, and the like, and proceeded in light marching order with three days' cooked rations in their haversacks. After the wet first day of the march, back in Alabama, the weather had turned hot and dry, and now the roads were dusty as the army tramped southward through Rossville and past the old Chickamauga battlefield. On the evening of May 7, Col. J. W. Sprague's brigade of the Fourth Division of Dodge's Sixteenth Corps, leading the march, skirmished briefly with Confederate cavalry at Shipp's Gap in Taylor's Ridge. Sprague had no difficulty driving off the Rebel horsemen and holding the gap for the rest of the army to march through the next morning.

On May 8 the Army of the Tennessee entered the western end of Snake Creek Gap and encamped in the three-mile-long valley.[5] That night McPherson, who was accompanying the Sixteenth Corps, gave Dodge his orders for the next day. He was to advance at 6:00 a.m. toward Resaca, about eight miles east of the mouth of the gap. As Dodge understood his orders, his task was "to demonstrate on Resaca while other troops would cut the railroad north of that place."[6]

At daybreak, however, Dodge's skirmishers encountered Confederate cavalry. Reinforced by the 66th Illinois—Birge's Western Sharpshooters—the skirmish line was soon driving the Rebels.[7] The Western Sharpshooters had not only been selected for their marksmanship but were now using sixteen-shot Henry repeating rifles that they had purchased with their own funds. The Illinoisans advanced, "driving the enemy like sheep before them," as Brig. Gen. Thomas W. Sweeny reported. Behind the steadily advancing skirmish line of the 66th, the Sixteenth Corps took up its march at the head of the army's column, and the Western Sharpshooters drove the Confederate cavalry so steadily that the column never had to halt or slow down because of them. During the course of the seven-mile advance to the vicinity of Resaca, the 66th took seventy-six of the Rebel horsemen captive.[8]

Around noon McPherson ordered Dodge to keep going until he either encountered a Confederate line of battle or else reached a crossroads about a mile from Resaca. There he should wait for the Fifteenth Corps to come up. In a note he penned to Sherman a few minutes later, McPherson wrote that he did not know whether any significant number of Confederate infantry were in Resaca, but he would find out shortly.[9]

Just as Dodge reached the crossroads, he encountered Confederates drawn up in line of battle, both in their entrenchments immediately in front of Resaca and on a bald hill about three quarters of a mile from the town. He quickly deployed his lead division, that of Brig. Gen. James Veatch, at the crossroads, and brought up the other—the old Second Division, which had once been C. F. Smith's but now was commanded by Thomas W. Sweeny—on the right. Dodge ordered Sweeny to take the bald hill, and with little difficulty he did so, driving away the Rebels who had held it in brigade strength. The assault was spearheaded by the fast-shooting 66th Illinois with their Henry rifles, advancing in skirmish line in front of the division. The Western Sharpshooters alone broke the Confederate line and sent it fleeing toward Resaca before the rest of the Second Division got into the fight. With the bald hill secured, Dodge reported the situation to McPherson, who was at that time a mile or two back down the column.[10]

McPherson hastened forward. Looking over the ground in front of Resaca, he ordered Dodge to hold the hill and the crossroads and wait until the Fifteenth Corps came up.[11] About two o'clock, McPherson wrote a short note to Joe Hooker, commanding the Twentieth Corps, which was the closest part of the rest of Sherman's forces. McPherson indicated that he was still proceeding on Sherman's program: "If I succeed in breaking the railroad I intend to withdraw my command back and take a strong defensive position on the east entrance to the gap and await orders from Major-General Sherman."[12]

About 4:00 p.m., the Fifteenth Corps arrived and halted in rear of the

Sixteenth, ready to support it if necessary. McPherson ordered Dodge to advance his left division, Veatch's, from the crossroads to take the railroad north of Resaca. Dodge quickly got the division moving, personally accompanying the lead brigade, John W. Fuller's. The Confederates could see the movement from the breastworks and opened a heavy but largely ineffective fire. McPherson, however, became concerned that Sweeny's division on the bald hill was in danger, and also that the Rebels might exploit the gap that was growing between Sweeny and Veatch as the latter's division charged toward the railroad. He detached Veatch's trailing brigade, Sprague's, to shore up Sweeny's left. Sweeny seemed not to share McPherson's concerns about the safety of his position, reporting that he was "awaiting patiently for orders to assault the enemy's works."[13]

Those orders never came. Dodge, still advancing with Fuller's brigade, came within sight of the railroad and found it defended by what appeared to be a single regiment of infantry supported by a battery of artillery—easy prey for Fuller's brigade. As he was closing in and preparing to flank the Rebels on the north while attacking them from the front, Dodge received an order from McPherson directing him to withdraw Fuller's brigade to a position immediately on the left of Sprague, who was directly on the left of Sweeny's division on the bald hill. Dodge complied. By the time Fuller's brigade had taken up its new position, the sun was setting, and McPherson ordered everyone to pull back to the eastern outlet of Snake Creek Gap.[14]

The seven-mile tramp back to the gap in the darkness took several hours, and it was 1:00 a.m. before the last of the troops made their camps in more or less the same positions from which they had started out early that morning. They were tired, and, due to the fact that many of the supply wagons had not yet caught up with the column, many were hungry as well. The total casualties in the Sixteenth Corps for the day's fighting amounted to twenty-nine men killed, wounded, and missing.[15]

McPherson was in camp by 10:30 p.m., writing a dispatch to Sherman. He explained that he "could not succeed in cutting the railroad before dark, or getting to it," and so had "decided to withdraw the command" to the mouth of Snake Creek Gap. Good roads led down from Dalton, and he feared that a large portion of Johnston's army might descend on him at any moment. Besides, he needed to let the supply wagons catch up with the troops. He added that he would have to allow the men at least the following morning to rest and draw rations.[16]

In fact, the Rebels had had only 4,000 men near Resaca, and many of those were inexperienced. The Fifteenth and Sixteenth corps could have overwhelmed the defenders with ease, but McPherson could not have known that. He could perhaps have known that Dodge and Fuller were within minutes of taking a section of the railroad, but confusion is common in battles. McPherson was far from the first general to halt just short of success. Even after taking the railroad, more time would have been necessary to destroy it, and McPherson was convinced that he dared not linger around Resaca any longer. It was a reasonable decision, based on his lack of knowledge of the situation, but it is not the decision Grant would have made. Both men were highly intelligent and could calculate what the enemy's best move would be, but unlike Grant, McPherson had never learned to discount those calculations with a knowledge that the enemy might be mistaken, ignorant, or afraid. He tended to assume that the enemy would make the best possible move, and that rendered him cautious.

McPherson had his troops up and in line, ready to repel attack, before dawn on May 10, but no attack came. The Army of the Tennessee spent the day entrenching its position at the mouth of Snake Creek Gap, while minor skirmishing went on more or less continually along the front. Rain fell for about four hours in the middle of the day. McPherson noted that the Confederate skirmish line was "a very light one, easily driven back, and composed of cavalry," but did not draw from that observation the conclusion that he faced no significant Rebel opposition. Instead he continued to expect an attack from Johnston, though he felt confident of handling it in his strong position.[17]

He wrote to Sherman suggesting he bring the whole of his force through Snake Creek Gap as the best means of getting at Johnston. Long before McPherson's dispatch reached him, Sherman had come to the same conclusion. Nothing was to be gained by frontal assaults on Rocky Face Ridge; reaching Resaca via Snake Creek Gap was the best way to get Johnston into a fight in the open field, outside of his entrenchments, where Sherman might crush him. Accordingly, he issued orders to his various subordinates to send all of the Army of the Ohio and most of the Army of the Cumberland in that direction. Only Oliver O. Howard's Fourth Corps would remain behind, keeping up a lonely feint in front of Rocky Face. Sherman ordered McPherson to hold his position, which was exactly what the Army of the Tennessee's commander was inclined to do.[18]

The rain started again on the evening of May 10 and continued all night, a cold, pelting downpour accompanied by thunder and lightning. Late that night, a planned shift of some units to new positions in the line led to confusion and false reports of a Confederate attack. In response, officers routed the men out of their blanket rolls and marched them to the breastworks "in an awful hurry," as one of them noted. Few of them got much sleep that night. The next day was the same. Under a steady rain, the troops continued to work on their breastworks.[19] Local civilians reported that the Rebels were planning an attack, and from time to time McPherson shifted troops from one part of his front to another as the skirmish firing seemed to increase somewhat in a particular sector, but May 11 passed, and the anticipated attack still did not come.[20]

During these several days at the mouth of Snake Creek Gap, the Army of the Tennessee was a stationary point in the midst of a slow, stately hesitation waltz by the rest of the forces on both sides. Sherman delayed his movement to Snake Creek Gap in order to await the arrival of additional cavalry. Confused by McPherson's advance and retreat on May 9 and then by Sherman's slow movement to join McPherson, Johnston remained uncertain whether the Federals were feinting against Resaca in preparation for an attack on Rocky Face or the other way around. He started some of his units south, then stopped them and returned them to their former positions.[21]

Sketchy reports of the abortive Confederate movement reached Sherman and McPherson as indications that Johnston really was rushing to Resaca. McPherson ordered an attached cavalry division, sent down by Sherman, to scout the matter and see if the Rebels were indeed falling back. He also alerted his corps commanders to be ready "to move out promptly to attack the enemy in flank should he be really retreating." The reconnaissance revealed that the Rebels had not moved—yet—but the probe may have helped convince Johnston that it was time to pull his army back to Resaca. In any case, by the evening of May 11, Leonidas Polk's 15,000 troops from the Confederate Department of Mississippi and Alabama had reached Resaca and now held the fortifications there.[22]

Sherman arrived at McPherson's headquarters near the eastern end of Snake Creek Gap on the afternoon of a chilly, breezy May 12. He greeted McPherson warmly, but added, "Well, Mac, you have missed the opportunity of a lifetime," referring to the failure to break the railroad three days before.[23] Years later, in his memoirs, Sherman wrote generously that McPherson had been "perfectly justified by his orders" in falling back. That was true, as far as it went, but Sherman's orders had called for McPherson to cut the railroad before falling back. It was not in retreating that McPherson had failed but in not destroying the railroad first.[24] That evening signal officers from observation posts on strategically located hilltops sent Sherman definite information that Johnston's army was pulling out of Dalton and moving toward Resaca. The following morning, Howard probed forward and occupied the town of Dalton.[25]

Sherman meanwhile had given orders for his force in Snake Creek Gap to advance on Resaca at daybreak on May 13. The Army of the Tennessee would form the right; the Army of the Cumberland, the left. McPherson would proceed until he encountered the Resaca defenses, and then the Army of the Cumberland would pivot on him in a grand right wheel, swinging east and attempting to break the railroad north of Resaca. Sherman hoped that in so doing he would trap at least part of Johnston's army north of the town.[26]

May 13 dawned foggy. The troops formed up and advanced, with a division of cavalry skirmishing in front. After several miles of rough ground and through woods and thickets, the cavalry came up against Confederate resistance and fell back while the infantry passed to the front. Troops of Morgan L. Smith's and Osterhaus's divisions of the Fifteenth Corps and Veatch's division of the Sixteenth deployed into line of battle and at about 1:00 p.m. began fighting their way forward against stubborn Confederate skirmishers. By about 4:30 p.m., they had reached a line of hills—including the hill Dodge's men had taken on May 9—within sight of the Confederate entrenchments around Resaca.

Between McPherson's men and the Confederate lines was the valley of Camp Creek, a small tributary of the Oostenaula. The 1,200-yard-wide valley was mostly cleared of timber, and the Rebels had set fire to the brush piles to prevent their being used as cover by advancing Federals. To their left, the men of the Fifteenth Corps could see Confederate troops and wagon trains traveling southward along the railroad, toward Resaca. The last elements of Johnston's army were arriving from Dalton to join Polk's men at Resaca, bringing Rebel numbers within the entrenchments to between 60,000 and 65,000. It was now too late to trap Johnston or any part of his army north of Resaca.[27]

Sherman's new plan was to pin Johnston's army in place with small attacks along the lines around Resaca while part of his force established a bridgehead over the Oostenaula several miles upstream at Lay's Ferry. That would turn Johnston's position and force him into a hasty retreat to avoid being trapped. To take the bridgehead, Sherman assigned Sweeny's division of the Sixteenth Corps.

While Sweeny's men marched toward Lay's Ferry, the rest of the army distracted the Rebels. Sharp skirmishing and heavy artillery exchanges started all along the Resaca lines at dawn. Not long after that, the men of the Army of the Tennessee heard the roar of battle rising loudly on their left, as the Army of the Cumberland launched and then received medium-sized assaults at that end of the battlefield. The lines remained stable, although casualties were considerable. McPherson ordered Logan to make a diversionary attack, in order to prevent the Rebels from shifting troops to meet the Army of the Cumberland's attacks.[28]

Logan's target was a series of low hills between the main battle lines. Confederate skirmishers held the hills, well dug in, as was already becoming the pattern in this campaign. From the tops of the hills, if they could take them, Logan's men would be less than 700 yards from the main Confederate line and only about half a mile from the railroad bridge over the Oostenaula. With the bridge in easy artillery range, Logan's guns would be able to interdict Johnston's supplies and make his position north of the Oostenaula very difficult.[29]

The assignment went to Brig. Gen. Charles R. Woods's brigade of Osterhaus's division and Giles Smith's brigade of his brother Morgan's division. At 5:30 p.m., they made their way across Camp Creek as best they could. Some passed over a small bridge Osterhaus's men had taken that morning, while others crossed on fallen logs, and some were able to wade, holding their arms and ammunition over their heads. On the far bank they formed up, Woods's brigade on the left, Smith's on the right, both in two lines of battle. Between them and their goal lay about 500 yards of bottomland, marshy in places, cleared mostly, but obstructed here and there with tree trunks and thickets.[30]

The bugles sounded the advance at 5:50. The men cheered, and the two brigades moved forward at the double-quick under heavy fire from infantry and artillery. "The grass and bushes around us were riddled with bullets," wrote Capt. Charles Miller of the 76th Ohio, "and the dead trees were cut off by cannon balls and came crashing down about our heads." Logan's veterans continued despite losses, keeping low to the ground in order to minimize casualties and straightening their formations on the run as quickly as the rough terrain disrupted them. The attackers were visible along a large sector of the lines, and the whole Fifteenth Corps cheered wildly as they watched their comrades' advance.

The storming column was strong enough to dislodge even well-entrenched skirmishers, and within a few minutes they had taken the hilltops. Some of the Confederates in the position resisted stoutly, holding their ground until the Federals were almost on top of them. Soldiers of the 76th Ohio called on one of them to surrender, but the doughty Rebel shouted that "he would never surrender to a Yankee," fired at Miller, missed, and was shot dead by one of the Ohioans. Those Confederates who did not flee soon met a similar fate.[31]

Logan immediately sent pioneer troops and entrenching tools over to the two brigades in their advanced position to help them dig in as rapidly as possible and be prepared for a counterattack. Shortly before 8:00 p.m., the expected assault came—three brigades of Rebels from Tennessee, Arkansas, and Alabama. Woods's and Smith's brigades beat off the Rebels' first onset, but Logan could see that the attacking Confederate line was longer than that of his two brigades on the hills and was bound to flank them as the fight continued. To counter this threat, he ordered Lightburn's brigade of Morgan Smith's division to advance and join their comrades on the hills.[32]

Lightburn's men had been following the progress of the fight by the flashes of the guns through the gathering darkness and fretting at seeing their comrades engaged while they were unable to help. When the order came, they advanced eagerly, wading Camp Creek neck-deep and double-quicking across the rough ground beyond it. They soon joined on the right of Giles Smith's line and were in time to help fight off the next Rebel assault.[33]

Osterhaus dispatched three regiments to shore up Woods's left flank, and McPherson himself, watching the conflict, pulled two regiments out of the lines of Veatch's division of the Sixteenth Corps, on the far right, and hustled them around to reinforce Woods. Fighting continued until ten o'clock, when the Confederates apparently gave up on recovering the key terrain they had lost that evening. Logan's loss in the operation was a little more than 600 men killed, wounded, and missing.[34]

While the Fifteenth Corps sparred with the enemy along the Resaca fortifications, Sweeny's division of the Sixteenth approached the Oostenaula at Lay's Ferry, arriving shortly before noon and finding that the Confederates held the south bank of the river and were well dug in. Sweeny had Brig. Gen. Elliott W. Rice's brigade deploy and exchange fire with the Rebels in order to attract their attention. At the same time, he sent Col. Patrick E. Burke's brigade about half a mile farther upstream to the mouth of Snake Creek with orders to make the actual crossing there, using pontoon boats to get across the river.

The boats they were slated to use were actually the property of the Army of the Cumberland and were not yet on hand. While everyone waited, Rice's brigade continued skirmishing. Both sides plied each other with artillery fire as well. The Confederates moved their skirmishers down close to the south bank of the river in order to pick off the gunners of Capt. Frederick Welker's Battery H, 1st Missouri Light Artillery. To counter that move, Rice sent the 66th Indiana forward to his own bank of the river in order to suppress the Rebel sharpshooters.

As the Hoosiers traded fire with the enemy across the river, Pvt. Asahel

M. Pyburn, of the 66th Indiana, noticed that a Confederate color guard had taken its flag right up to the south edge of the river and planted the base of the staff in the mud of the bank. In one of the more astonishing feats of the war, Pyburn took off his clothes and swam the 100-yard-wide river, while his comrades fired as fast as they could to keep the Rebels' heads down. Reaching the south bank, he snatched the flag and swam back. Seeing their flag suddenly vanish into the river, the Rebels blazed away as fast as they could, and their bullets churned up the water all around Pyburn. Somehow he escaped unscathed, still carrying the captured flag, and was promoted to color sergeant.[35]

Shortly after four o'clock that afternoon, the pioneer detachment of the Army of the Cumberland reached Lay's Ferry, hauling the boats in wagons. The boats themselves were wood-and-canvas collapsibles, a clever new design made to order for the Army of the Cumberland, which seemed to have a wealth of ingenious gadgets and patent maps. The detachment assembled the vessels, each capable of carrying twenty men, and then the Army of the Tennessee took over. Sweeny detailed the 2nd and 7th Iowa regiments to carry the boats to Snake Creek, just above its mouth.[36]

From the sheltered ground where the pioneers had assembled the boats to the creek bank where the Hawkeyes would have to launch them was about three-quarters of a mile, across a large field with only a few scattered trees and scraggly brush to provide scant cover from the fire of Confederate artillery and sharpshooters on the opposite side of the Oostenaula. The Iowans were veterans of the Sunken Road at Shiloh, but one of them later wrote that carrying those boats across the field was "the most disagreeable job we were called upon to perform during our four years of service."[37]

Eight men stood on each side of a boat, and then the sixteen of them hoisted the craft to their shoulders. Even patent collapsible boats contained a considerable weight of wood and canvas, and Iowan J. W. Long wrote that it was a heavy load for sixteen men. Thus laden, the Hawkeyes set off at the fastest pace they could manage. Bullets buzzed past them, and without his rifle Long said he felt as naked as if he were "in a bathtub" with several thousand men shooting at him. During their dash, the fire grew so hot and close at times that Long and his comrades had to drop their boat and dive for cover. Each time, they scrambled back to continue the gauntlet. At last they got the clumsy craft into the waters of Snake Creek just short of the Oostenaula.

At about 5:00 p.m., the 81st Ohio and 66th Illinois made their assault. Following behind the Iowans who carried the boats, the two regiments made their way to the edge of Snake Creek and followed its course so as to avail themselves of what little shelter its banks offered against the heavy Confederate fire. Then about 400 yards from the river, the head of the column turned right, scrambled up the bank, and continued across the open field until the tail of the column had cleared the bank. The whole line faced left, raised the "Western Yell," and charged toward the river across an old cornfield. Cpl. Charles Wright of the 81st Ohio thought last year's dead cornstalks, still lying in the field, made an immensely satisfying crackling as the whole regiment tramped across them.[38]

Reaching the riverbank, the troops dropped to a knee behind a rail fence and began firing as rapidly as they could at the Confederate sharpshooters across the river. Two companies of the 81st and one of the 66th piled into the ungainly craft and paddled down the creek and out into the Oostenaula. Capt. Albert Arndt's Battery B, 1st Michigan Light Artillery, laid down covering fire, and the infantry continued to add the fire of their Springfields and sixteen-shooters to the barrage that was forcing the Confederates to keep their heads down.[39]

Sitting grimly in one of the canvas boats, Wright saw the oarsman next to him suddenly drop his oar and sit still. The boat immediately began to swing in the current. "Why don't you row?" asked Wright. "Don't you see we're going down stream?"

"I can't row," replied the oarsman with a grimace, "I'm shot."

Only then did Wright notice that a bullet had struck the man's back and passed clear through his body, exiting his chest. One of the Ohio soldiers who knew how to row put down his rifle, picked up the fallen oar, and got the boat moving across the river again.[40]

Several oarsmen were hit during the crossing, but as in Wright's boat, other soldiers took up the oars and kept the vessels moving across the river. One of the craft became briefly stuck on some obstruction in the middle of the river but got loose again after several intensely unpleasant moments. As they approached the south bank, Capt. W. H. Chamberlin, commanding the first landing party, thought that if he got out of this fight alive it would be straight into a Confederate prison. Nonetheless, the Ohioans and Western Sharpshooters formed up on the south bank as if they "had been drilled in that very movement fifty times before." Chamberlin found that his veteran soldiers anticipated his orders. With his troops in formation, he led them in rushing forward and capturing or chasing off the nearest Confederates. One group of three Ohioans captured eleven Rebels.[41] Under the cover of Chamberlin's detachment now firmly ensconced on the south bank, four more companies of the 81st and another of the 66th crossed and successfully took additional Confederate positions and prisoners, at a total cost of fifty-nine Union casualties.[42]

Burke was quickly making preparations to put the rest of his brigade across the river when Union cavalry brought Sweeny a report that the Confederates had built one or more bridges of their own and were now crossing the Oostenaula at Calhoun's Ferry, about halfway between Lay's Ferry and the rest of Sherman's army. If that were true, Sweeny's division—and especially Burke's troops on the south bank—could be in serious trouble. So Sweeny ordered them back to the north bank. It was just getting dark, and the men on the south bank withdrew quietly, apparently without attracting the notice of the nearest Confederates.[43]

To find out the truth about the Calhoun's Ferry report, Sweeny sent Col. Moses M. Bane's brigade to reconnoiter in that direction. Bane's men reached Calhoun's Ferry shortly after sundown, skirmished briefly with the Rebels on the opposite bank, but found no Confederates on the north side of the river. Two of Sweeny's staff officers made an extensive search, walking more than a mile along the riverbank, but found no bridges. Sweeny was reassured, but it was too late to prevent the withdrawal of Burke's troops from the south side at Lay's Ferry. The Federals were right back where they had started that morning, holding the north bank of the river and looking across at Rebels on the opposite shore, but now the Rebels had good reason to know exactly where Sherman's troops wished to make their crossing.[44]

The next morning, Sweeny ordered his men to cross the river again. This time the assignment fell to Rice's brigade. They marched down to the river shortly after eight o'clock and prepared to repeat the previous evening's harrowing operation. Rice decided to make use of the ferryboat, an old scow that was tied up at the landing. It was large enough to carry sixty men, and Rice decided to use it as his primary assault craft. Leading the way were two companies of the 66th Illinois, borrowed from Burke's brigade. The small detachment of Western Sharpshooters crossed the river in the flatboat, deployed in skirmish line, and put their sixteen-shooters to work. The 2nd Iowa crossed in pontoon boats just behind the Illinoisans, and the 66th Indiana charged down to the riverbank to deliver covering fire. From a hill a short distance to the rear, Welker's Missouri gunners added their thunder. The operation went off smoothly, and the Confederate skirmishers promptly fled.[45]

Using flatboat and pontoons, Rice shuttled the rest of his brigade to the south bank as rapidly as possible, giving up pontoons to the engineers as quickly as they were able to incorporate them into a rapidly growing bridge. Within an hour and a quarter from the time the two companies of the Western Sharpshooters had led the way across the river, Rice had his entire brigade on the south bank. The pontoon bridge was complete, and Burke's brigade began marching across. The time was scarcely 10:00 a.m.[46]

As soon as both brigades were over, they began entrenching a defensive position, Rice's brigade on the right in the woods and Burke's on the left in an open field. By midday they had completed the perimeter and two batteries of artillery had joined them.[47]

Up to that time, the Union force on the south bank had encountered resistance only from Confederate skirmishers, but Rice, who as senior officer in the bridgehead commanded both brigades, believed the Rebels were present in strength. About noon he probed forward with two regiments. The Rebels responded with a brigade-sized assault, which the Second Division easily beat off. Union casualties for the entire day totaled fewer than 200 men, while Rice's troops captured 23 of the enemy and one battle flag.[48]

The new entrenched bridgehead on the south bank of the Oostenaula put the Army of the Tennessee within striking distance of Johnston's vital supply line, the Western & Atlantic Railroad south of Resaca. Those who were aware of the situation expected Johnston to react to their presence, by either attacking or retreating. That night Sweeny ordered his brigade commanders to send out special listening parties that advanced gingerly through the darkness as far as the Rome Road. Through the nocturnal stillness, the scouts thought they could hear both railroad and wagon trains, sure signs that Johnston was evacuating Resaca.[49]

Meanwhile, on the other side of the Oostenaula, half a dozen miles away, the men of Logan's Fifteenth Corps were also listening. The day had seen desultory skirmishing in front and more sounds of heavy combat on the left, as Confederate and Union forces continued to struggle for the advantage on the north end of the battlefield. Logan's project that day had been to have a number of artillery pieces hauled out to the hills his men had captured the evening before, whence they would be able to bombard the bridges at Resaca beginning on the morning of May 16. Well before dawn, Logan's men heard more sounds of heavy firing coming from their left. No one knew just what to make of the racket, but Logan decided to take no chances. He ordered both Osterhaus and Morgan Smith to reinforce their skirmish lines.[50]

In fact, the sounds of battle on the left were caused by a division of the Army of the Cumberland renewing the previous day's dispute over possession of several pieces of artillery abandoned between the opposing lines of battle. What the Cumberlanders had clashed with was in fact the Confederate rearguard, for Johnston was indeed evacuating Resaca during the night. Shortly before dawn, Logan's skirmishers found the opposing lines deserted. As they cautiously advanced, loud noises and a lurid light in the sky in the direction of the railroad bridge confirmed their suspicions. They pressed forward rapidly into the town of Resaca itself, capturing numerous Confederate stragglers and exchanging shots with some of the last of the Rebel rearguard as the latter set fire to the road bridge. Logan's men succeeded in putting out the fire and saving the road bridge, but the railroad bridge was too far gone and burned completely.[51]

Johnston was gone, and the Battle of Resaca was over. Sherman's troops—specifically Sweeny's division of the Sixteenth Corps—had already breached the first of three major river barriers between their starting point and the city of Atlanta. The Oostenaula was behind them; the Etowah and Chattahoochee lay ahead. In the ten days since McPherson had announced to the Army of the Tennessee back in Chattanooga that they were "about to enter upon one of the most important campaigns of the war," they had covered more than one-third of the distance to Atlanta, which now lay scarcely seventy miles southeast of Sixteenth Corps lines. Along with the rest of Sherman's armies, they had forced Johnston back more than twenty miles from his previous base in Dalton.

Yet Johnston's army was still intact, and there had been times during the Snake Creek operation when, at least in hindsight, it seemed as if McPherson might have had the opportunity to trap the Rebels. In James B. McPherson, the Army of the Tennessee had its least aggressive commander, and at Snake Creek Gap, McPherson's caution may have lost an enormous opportunity. McPherson had not fulfilled his orders from Sherman to cut the railroad before pulling back into Snake Creek Gap. However, in order to achieve truly decisive results, McPherson would have had to take Resaca and hold it, something Sherman would probably have ordered and McPherson could easily have done if he had had the additional three divisions of the Seventeenth Corps and two of the Sixteenth and if Polk had been occupied, as he should have been, by a Union offensive toward Mobile. Whether McPherson could and should have taken and held Resaca anyway is one of the many unknowable might-have-beens that will always be part of warfare as long as generals are human and have to proceed on the basis of imperfect knowledge.

CHAPTER TWENTY-NINE

Kennesaw

ONCE SHERMAN LEARNED that Johnston was in retreat, he ordered a full-scale pursuit. To expedite the movement, he directed that his three armies cross the Oostenaula at three different points. The Army of the Tennessee's assigned crossing was Lay's Ferry, where two pontoon bridges now spanned the river.[1] The Sixteenth Corps's Second Division had the lead and early in the afternoon met and fought off a small attack by the Confederate rearguard. Among the fifty Union casualties was Colonel Burke, mortally wounded. Command of his brigade passed to Lt. Col. Robert N. Adams of the 81st Ohio.[2]

During the next three days, the Army of the Tennessee marched eight to ten miles each day, moving south on the heels of the Confederates parallel to the tracks of the Western & Atlantic. On the morning of May 19, the column began arriving near Kingston, Georgia, two miles north of the Etowah River and less than sixty from Atlanta. The Army of the Tennessee encamped on the west side of Kingston, while the Army of the Cumberland went into bivouac east of town. Maj. Gen. John M. Schofield and the Army of the Ohio were still moving up somewhat farther east.[3]

From Resaca to Kingston, the Western & Atlantic ran almost due south. At Kingston, however, two tracks took different directions. A spur line diverged west to Rome, Georgia, which a detachment of Sherman's troops had already occupied. The main line of the Western & Atlantic continued southeast out of Kingston, passing south of Cassville, six miles to the east of Kingston, then through Cartersville, gradually converging with the Etowah until it finally crossed the river about thirteen miles southeast of Kingston. The opposing forces had frequently been in contact with each other during the march down from Resaca, and at Adairsville on May 17 the Army of the Cumberland had bumped hard against the rear of the retreating column as Johnston paused to think about fighting a battle. The jolt from Thomas, along with the prospect of being flanked on either side by Schofield and McPherson, got him moving again.

Sherman had thought Johnston might turn at bay at Kingston, but his troops occupied the area without opposition. Somewhat to his surprise, however, he discovered that Johnston had taken up a position near Cassville and was threatening the Union left flank. Sherman ordered McPherson to swing the Army of the Tennessee forward and to the left so as to come in on Thomas's right flank, but such movements proved unnecessary, as the Confederate army was gone by the next morning. After moderate fighting, Johnston had once again retreated, this time across the Etowah. Unknown to Sherman and his troops, the Confederate commander had planned a major counterattack at Cassville but had called it off when some of Sherman's cavalry showed up in an unexpected quarter.[4]

With the Rebels having abandoned all of the country north of the Etowah, Sherman decided to rest his armies for a few days, repair the damaged railroad north of his position, and make sure of a steady flow of supplies before continuing the campaign. For the soldiers, this meant a welcome three days to rest and refit. "The trains came up," recalled Cpl. Charles Wright, "and we drew new clothing, fitted ourselves with good shoes, which are an important part of a soldier's outfit, and made ourselves ready generally for continuing the pursuit of the rebel army."[5]

The pause gave Sherman time to prepare for his next move. His forces now controlled all of Georgia north of the Etowah River, but difficult country lay ahead. About five miles south of the Etowah, the tracks of the Western & Atlantic ran through Allatoona Pass, a high and narrow defile. Familiar with the geography of North Georgia from his service there as a young officer in 1844, Sherman knew better than to attempt to force the pass in a head-on assault. Instead, he planned to diverge from the railroad, heading due south while the tracks ran off to the southeast. This would amount to a wide movement to his right, swinging far west of the railroad to turn the defenses of Allatoona Pass via the town of Dallas, Georgia. From Dallas, Sherman could turn back to the east, regaining the railroad and, he hoped, Johnston's rear at the town of Marietta, scarcely twenty miles from the heart of Atlanta.[6]

Sherman had his armies accumulate twenty days' reduced rations and make plans to bring them along in wagons and on the hoof. McPherson issued orders to the Army of the Tennessee directing that "regular foraging parties will be organized in each division and brigade," and that these would "invariably be in charge of reliable officers, who will be strictly responsible for any unauthorized seizures, pillaging, or plundering."[7]

Early on the morning of May 23, the armies marched again, with the Army of the Tennessee on the right. Sherman wanted McPherson on the west side of Dallas by May 25, when Thomas would be approaching the town from the north and Schofield would be covering the left flank and rear against any possible aggressive action by Johnston. The march began at 6:00 a.m. with the Fifteenth Corps in the lead. The column crossed the Etowah without incident, second of the three great river barriers that had barred their way to Atlanta when the campaign began. Only the Chattahoochee remained.[8]

The Army of the Tennessee marched eighteen miles on May 23 and camped in the valley of Euharlee Creek, just north of Van Wert. For some of the troops, the march continued late into the night before they made camp. Of the weary stumbling through the dark, Capt. Charles Miller of the 76th Ohio wrote, "It was one of the hardest marches and trials of human endurance that I ever experienced." The countryside they passed was mostly wooded. "As fine pine timber as I ever saw," commented Maj. A. J. Seay of the 32nd Missouri. The next day's march was much easier, only about eight miles for most units, as the column tramped through the town of Van Wert and continued to within ten miles of Dallas. For much of the day, the head of the column skirmished with Confederate cavalry.[9]

Right on schedule, the Army of the Tennessee approached Dallas from the west late on the morning of May 25, marching through a heavy rain that had begun the evening before. About three miles west of the town, the head of the column encountered somewhat stiffer Confederate resistance. Rebel skirmishers held positions behind Pumpkin Vine Creek, and Osterhaus's division, leading the march that day, deployed into line of battle in the midst of the streaming downpour. The rest of the Army of the Tennessee moved up during the course of the afternoon and evening to join the deployment along the creek. Logan's other two divisions moved into line on the right of Osterhaus. Dodge's Sixteenth Corps, which had been behind Logan's wagon train, arrived late that night, and McPherson ordered him to the left of Osterhaus. McPherson himself had an unpleasant adventure. In the darkness and rough terrain, he rode up to a Rebel picket post but made off safely under a hail of bullets.[10]

While the Army of the Tennessee approached Dallas from the west, the Army of the Cumberland, as Sherman had planned, moved in from the north. It too encountered Confederate resistance. The Rebels had burned the bridge on the main road to Dallas, so Thomas's column shifted a mile and a half to the northeast in order to cross Pumpkin Vine Creek. Once across, two of the Cumberland divisions had what Sherman called "a pretty hard fight" late in the afternoon. Clearly, Sherman's turning movement had not taken Johnston by surprise. The Confederates were in place, blocking Sherman's effort to get around Allatoona and reach Marietta without a fight.

That evening Sherman ordered McPherson to push through Dallas the next day and strike the left flank of the Rebels now confronting Thomas in a strong position near New Hope Church. Howard's Fourth Corps would hit the enemy right. "Use your artillery freely," Sherman added, hoping in that way to be able to gauge McPherson's position in this heavily wooded country. McPherson passed the word to his corps commanders, and they in turn to the divisions, that "the indications are that we will have a heavy battle tomorrow." Officers were to have rations issued and see that their men carried full cartridge boxes. Dodge's weary soldiers were to march at 3:00 a.m.[11]

To the men of the Sixteenth Corps, it seemed they had hardly made camp before reveille sounded and orders came to prepare to advance. More difficult marching over muddy roads was necessary in order to reach and cross Pumpkin Vine Creek, where the Sixteenth Corps would be ready to cooperate with the Fifteenth's advance. It was 10:30 a.m. before Dodge's corps was in position and the general advance began. The Rebels offered surprisingly little resistance. Shortly before two o'clock that afternoon, the Army of the Tennessee advanced through the town and three miles beyond before running up against a solid line of battle, well entrenched on a high ridge.[12]

McPherson's forces took up a corresponding line of battle along a ridge of their own several hundred yards to the west. Sharp skirmishing continued along the front, particularly in a sector near the center of the Army of the Tennessee's front, where one of Osterhaus's brigades became involved in a minor dispute with the Confederates over possession of a small hill between the lines. Eventually the brigade commander, Col. James A. Williamson, decided the hill was not worth the price and let the Rebels keep it. That night all along the line of the Army of the Tennessee, troops dug entrenchments—when they were not exchanging shots with the aggressive Confederate skirmishers.[13]

Early the next morning, the Confederates attacked the left flank of Osterhaus's division, which was not yet connected to Dodge's Sixteenth Corps line. After fierce fighting, Osterhaus's men repelled the assault, and shortly afterward tied in their line solidly on the right of the Sixteenth Corps, which moved up to support them.[14] Along the rest of the Army of the Tennessee's front that day, skirmishers advanced and drove their Confederate counterparts back into their fortified line, but that line was solid, well entrenched, and going nowhere. McPherson was not foolish enough to launch a frontal assault against it.[15]

That afternoon the Confederates made another local attack, this time against the right end of the Army of the Tennessee's line. It struck the center of Brig. Gen. William Harrow's division of the Fifteenth Corps. Harrow was a Hoosier recently transferred from the Army of the Potomac, where he had helped repulse Pickett's Charge at Gettysburg. Col. Charles C. Walcutt commanded Harrow's center brigade. Walcutt's right rested on the Villa Rica Road, where it was joined by the left of Col. Reuben Williams's brigade. As the extreme right of the army, Williams's brigade was refused, or bent back from the main line of battle, so that it joined Walcutt's command at the Villa Rica road at a right angle.[16]

About 500 yards in front of Walcutt's right was a Confederate battery on a commanding hill. The Rebel guns had been making Walcutt's life difficult for several hours when at 1:00 p.m. they and other Confederate artillery "commenced a terrific shelling." The men of Walcutt's brigade had not had time to complete their system of entrenchments, but as was often the case with long- or medium-range shelling, this barrage proved to be more noisy than dangerous. When the shelling stopped, the Rebel infantry charged. Walcutt's men held their fire until the attackers reached the foot of the rise on which they were stationed and then tore into them with deadly effect. The enemy kept coming, and the 6th Iowa, on Walcutt's right, met them with a bayonet charge. The Rebels retaliated by attacking the Iowans' exposed right flank, but Lt. Col. Alexander J. Miller deftly countered by refusing his right three companies. The attackers, Mississippians, retreated, leaving behind their dead, wounded, and a number of prisoners.[17]

Meanwhile, Sherman had changed his mind about the best way to deal with Johnston's position around New Hope Church. Gone was the idea of turning both of Johnston's flanks, replaced by a plan to lunge back toward the railroad and turn Johnston's right flank on a grand scale. "We don't want to turn the enemy's left flank," Sherman wrote on May 27, "but his right, so as to put our concentrated army between him and the railroad. Of which we want to make use." Sherman had come to the conclusion that the terrain in McPherson's front simply did not offer the possibility of decisive action. Instead, he now wanted McPherson to forget about "compassing the enemy's flank" and instead move left to close up on Thomas and keep pace with the rest of Sherman's forces as they too sidled to the left.[18]

This presented a problem for McPherson, since the wagon trains of the Army of the Tennessee were still parked back on the west bank of Pumpkin

Vine Creek. Any leftward movement would leave an open path for the enemy to capture the trains, and, as the Rebels' afternoon foray against the army's right indicated, they would not be slow about using it. The first step was to move the trains around to the left, where they would be covered by elements of the Army of the Cumberland. Then the Army of the Tennessee would be free to shift its position. McPherson gave orders for this movement on the evening of May 27.[19]

By midmorning of the next day, Sherman had once again become dissatisfied with his favorite subordinate's progress. "We are working round by the left," Sherman wrote to McPherson shortly after 10:00 a.m., "and, if you don't keep up, our line will become attenuated and liable to disaster." Sherman said he did not care whether the Army of the Tennessee moved by the left flank or pulled out of line to the rear and then shifted to the left, but he wanted it to move and soon. McPherson, however, was doing the best he could. He could not abandon his wagon train, and no one could make it move any faster. His plan was to pull the army out of line and shift it left that night.[20]

While the wagons trundled over the hilly roads toward their new assigned position in rear of the Army of the Cumberland, along the front lines May 28 began as a continuation of the preceding three days of constant, intense skirmishing. The situation was almost like that which the soldiers had experienced along the Vicksburg lines. "There is continuous firing kept up by pickets," wrote Surgeon John McKee of the 2nd Iowa. "A man durst not put up his head above the breastworks."[21] Matters were even worse out on the skirmish line. Charles Miller found that in posting his skirmishers in front of Osterhaus's division he had to make sure that every man had a rifle pit or a log for shelter, since "the sharpshooters of the enemy picked off all who were exposed." Miller himself found it a vexatious and highly dangerous task to move along his skirmish line, a duty that had to be accomplished by much crawling and dodging, with Rebel bullets humming close over his head.[22]

Late that afternoon, the Confederates launched an all-out assault on Harrow's division, charging along the ridge that carried the Villa Rica Road. The nature of the ground there was such that the attackers could approach to within 150 yards of the Union position without being seen. "A heavy column of Rebels rose from the brush with a yell the devil ought to copyright," wrote Charles Wills. The Confederates surged forward in column of battalions and almost immediately engulfed three 10-pounder Parrott guns of the 1st Iowa Battery. Harrow's chief of artillery, Capt. Henry H. Griffiths, had just moved the guns out to the skirmish line, about 150 yards in front of the main parapet, in order to get a better shot at the Confederate battery opposite. Each piece had fired two rounds before the attack started.[23]

The charging Rebel infantry swept around the Parrotts almost before the gunners had a chance to respond. For a time, neither side controlled the guns, and anyone who approached them was shot down. The battle raged "close and deadly," Logan reported. As usual, he was in the thick of it, inspiring and directing his troops, who cheered wherever he appeared. "When the musketry was playing the hottest," wrote Captain Wills, "Logan came dashing up along our line, waved his hat and told the boys to 'give them h——, boys.' You should have heard them cheer him." He came galloping up to the lines of the 100th Indiana and jumped his horse over the breastworks, shouting for the men to save the guns of the 1st Iowa Battery. The Hoosiers swarmed over the breastworks after him. Joined by the 6th Iowa, they charged forward and took the guns.[24]

Walcutt's brigade was at the vortex of the fighting, and its regimental commanders fell in quick succession. Col. Willard A. Dickerman of the 103rd Illinois and Maj. Henry H. Giesy of the 46th Ohio were shot dead. Lt. Col. Alexander J. Miller of the 6th Iowa went down severely wounded. Walcutt himself stood atop the parapet directing his men. As the attackers relentlessly closed in, it began to look as if no amount of gunfire would stop them, and Walcutt had his men fix bayonets.[25]

With heavy Confederate columns assailing the weakest part of his line, Logan ordered Osterhaus, whose division was on the left of the Fifteenth Corps, to send a brigade to reinforce the right of Harrow's division, where the enemy threatened to turn his flank. Osterhaus had Williamson's brigade in reserve at that time, and since his sector was still fairly quiet, he turned over command of his other two brigades to the senior brigadier and led the brigade in a rapid march that angled across the rear of the Fifteenth Corps's position, more or less following the hypotenuse of the right triangle formed by Harrow's refused right flank.

Williamson's brigade threaded its way between hills a distance of some two and a half miles to reach a position on Harrow's right. As they neared the scene of the fighting, they met members of the 1st Iowa Battery going to the rear, who told them of the loss of the three guns. Hurrying forward at an even faster pace, Williamson's men moved up on the right end of the line, securing the flank.[26]

A few minutes after the Rebels hit Harrow, other Confederate columns advanced to attack Morgan Smith and, shortly thereafter, Osterhaus's remaining two brigades, then the Sixteenth Corps, as the Confederates assaulted in succession along the line. Leaving Williamson in his new position on the flank, Osterhaus galloped back to join the rest of his division. He found the situation there well under control. The positions of the center and left of the Fifteenth Corps offered much better fields of fire than was available on the right, and Smith's and Osterhaus's men had a much easier time than did Harrow's. Only on the Union right did the Confederate attack seem to have a chance of success.[27]

Harrow's fight lasted about two hours. At length the stubborn Rebels fell back, leaving the ground covered with their dead and wounded. The Confederates attacking Smith and Osterhaus hung on a few minutes longer before they too retreated. On the Sixteenth Corps's front, the Rebels pressed their attacks to within twenty feet of the breastworks but could go no farther.[28] In the final minutes of the fighting, as the guns were already falling silent in some sectors, Logan came riding from his own lines along the line of the Sixteenth Corps, "with his hat in his hand, looking like the very god of war." Black Jack had an amazing ability to inspire his soldiers. J. W. Long of the 2nd Iowa wrote, "No one can describe how Logan looked in battle any more than he could describe the raging sea." Long thought "the biggest coward in the world would stand on his head on top of the breastworks if Logan was present and told him to do so."[29] Fifteenth Corps casualties in this fight, known as the Battle of Dallas, totaled 30 killed, 295 wounded, and 54 missing.[30]

The attacking Confederate force had been composed of Maj. Gen. William Bate's division augmented by a brigade of dismounted cavalry. Bate still walked with a cane as a result of a wound he received in front of Shiloh Church two years and fifty-two days before. During that period, he had won a reputation as one of the Confederacy's hardest-hitting commanders. His decision to attack that day had been based on the faulty premise that the Army of the Tennessee had already withdrawn from in front of Dallas, leaving only a skirmish line. It had been a costly mistake. Confederate casualties totaled between 1,000 and 1,500 men killed, wounded, and missing.[31]

That evening McPherson rode over to Sherman's headquarters to confer. The heavy attack on the Army of the Tennessee, especially its right flank, suggested that the enemy might have suspected his planned withdrawal. McPherson did not see how he could move the army that night, while his men were still involved in sending wounded and prisoners to the rear. Pulling the troops out of line on the heels of an enemy assault would tell the men that they had been defeated. Also, a Confederate officer captured in the attack told his captors that another assault would be made at midnight. Sherman agreed to allow the Army of the Tennessee to remain in its present position that night and another day and withdraw after nightfall on May 29, rather than twenty-four hours earlier as originally planned. That night the soldiers manned the trenches, but no attack came.[32]

On the evening of May 29, the Army of the Tennessee made elaborate preparations to conceal from the enemy their nocturnal withdrawal. Officers maintained normal skirmish lines and did not inform the skirmishers of the impending movement. They would be told only after the main battle line was already gone, and then they could slip away quietly. Troops lit campfires as usual in the rear, and officers detailed men to stay behind and keep them going while the rest of the troops marched away. During the course of the day, pioneer troops had been busy slashing timber in front of the works, to create the impression that the army intended to stay a while.[33]

Night fell, and the soldiers got their meager possessions together, ready to move out. Logan began withdrawing the right of the Fifteenth Corps from its works but had not gotten far when the skirmishers came rushing in with reports that the enemy was attacking. The troops in the main line of battle blazed away into the darkness. "Roll after roll of musketry opened on our right and left and soon the line in front of us opened a terrific fire," wrote Charles Miller, whose 76th Ohio was in a reserve position. The artillery opened up with a roar. Union guns on the hills behind the line hurled shot and shell over the breastworks, rending the forest and sending limbs crashing down around the infantrymen. Batteries along the firing line itself sent great blasts of canister into the darkened woods in front.[34]

"The noise and confusion were beyond description," wrote Miller. "Long sheets of flame blazed along our rifle pits and the air was full of smoke and sulphur."[35] The 66th Illinois had been skirmishing in front of Col. Robert N. Adams's brigade of the Sixteenth Corps. When they dashed back into the lines along with the rest of the Union skirmishers, they lay down behind the troops who manned the breastworks, and many of them let the men on the front line borrow their sixteen-shooters, with which they pumped out a tremendous volume of fire.[36] "It was the most terrifying battle of small arms I have ever heard," wrote Henry Ankeny of the 4th Iowa, "the booming and flashes of the artillery so sudden that at times we thought that our lines had given way."[37]

Ammunition expenditure was prodigious. The 12th Illinois completely exhausted its supply; so the 2nd Iowa moved up to replace it in line and keep up the fusillade. When one battery ran low on ammunition, General Dodge took a box of shells on his horse and carried it to the sweating gunners himself.[38]

As the roar of battle began to rise along the lines, Logan quickly hurried his troops back into the breastworks and postponed the withdrawal. The firing went on at intervals all night long. A. J. Seay called it "the most terrific firing I ever witnessed."[39] Going by the sound of the gunfire, some members of the Army of the Tennessee judged that there must have been five separate Rebel attacks, others seven, and some as many as eight. "The firing did not cease until nearly daylight," wrote Captain Miller, "hence none of us slept." For most of the men it was at least their second consecutive night without sleep.[40]

"Whether there was any real occasion for the great turmoil," Miller shrewdly observed, "was hard to find out. One thing was sure; the Rebels kept us in such an uproar that we could not march out of our position that night at least." In fact, the Rebels had done nothing in the night. An ordinary skirmish flare-up, common when hostile armies remained in close contact during the night, had triggered the massive nocturnal exhibition of the Army of the Tennessee's firepower. "Our line acted foolishly," wrote Seay.[41]

The next morning, Sherman rode to McPherson's front to view the situation for himself. He was standing with McPherson, Logan, and several other officers when a sharpshooter's bullet passed through Logan's sleeve, scratching the skin, and then struck and wounded one of the junior officers. After completing his inspection and discussions with McPherson, Sherman was again satisfied with his subordinate's performance and convinced that no hasty withdrawal was possible or necessary.[42]

Of the days the Army of the Tennessee faced the enemy along the lines east of Dallas, Charles Wright of the 81st Ohio wrote, "It was almost a continuous fight day and night."[43] The weather that had started spectacularly rainy when the army arrived near Dallas had now turned hot and dry. Rations had grown short, as the supply wagons could not follow the army closely in this rough and wooded country. Seay wrote of having "nothing to feed on except a little green wheat." "Rough times," he added in his diary.[44]

Throughout May 30 and 31, McPherson had his pioneer troops build another system of entrenchments just outside the town of Dallas, about a mile behind his current lines on the left and two and a half miles behind those on the right. Then early on the morning of June 1, before most of the men had time to get breakfast, McPherson began the withdrawal again. Following a plan suggested by Sherman, he withdrew first his reserves, then the frontline divisions from right to left, and last the skirmishers. The Confederate skirmishers followed as far as the new line of works, and there the army was able to break contact and begin its march to the left.[45]

While the Army of the Tennessee had been engaged near Dallas, the Armies of the Cumberland and the Ohio had been fighting around New Hope Church and Pickett's Mill, still farther east. When the Army of the Tennessee relieved elements of the Cumberlanders along the lines in front of New Hope Church, it allowed Thomas and finally Schofield to slide to the left and closer to the line of the Western & Atlantic Railroad where it passed through the town of Acworth, about eight miles away.[46]

Sherman had hoped to use the approaching Seventeenth Corps to reach even farther to the left, all the way to the pass at Allatoona itself. If the two divisions of the Seventeenth Corps, under the command of Maj. Gen. Frank Blair, could get through the pass and entrench at the southeast end of it while Johnston's Confederate army was occupied along the lines around Dallas and New Hope Church, it would accomplish the purpose that Sherman's foiled turning maneuver had been meant to achieve. He had to abandon that idea, however, when he learned that Blair's troops were too far away, still west of Rome. Instead, he gave the task of taking Allatoona to the cavalry. The main body of the army would continue to sidle to the east, hoping to edge Johnston out of the chain of natural defensive positions provided by the fifteen-mile-wide belt of mountains—an extension of the Blue Ridge—that angled across the line of the railroad between Allatoona and Marietta.[47]

On June 2, rain began to fall around noon, the beginning of a rainy spell that lasted for weeks. Since the soldiers did not have tents, the rain was particularly uncomfortable for them. On June 4, Sherman ordered McPherson once again to pull the army out of its position on the Union right but this time to march it around behind the Armies of the Cumberland and the Ohio to extend the Union left flank all the way to Acworth. The next morning as the Army of the Tennessee prepared to move, skirmishers discovered that Johnston's army was gone. The Confederate general, perceiving the movements Sherman had already made in the direction of Acworth, had begun to feel that his own right flank was threatened and had retreated to positions on the high ridges just south of Big Shanty, five miles southeast of Acworth.[48]

McPherson's troops marched that same day, and the next morning, June 6, with Osterhaus's division in the lead, the Army of the Tennessee passed through Acworth, took the road toward Marietta, and deployed two miles southeast of town. Over the course of the next three days, the Armies of the Cumberland and the Ohio moved up and took position to the right of McPherson's command. With that Sherman's force was back astride the

Western & Atlantic Railroad, and by June 10 his highly efficient railroad-repair details had the Etowah River bridge open for business and the trains running all the way to the front. Once again rations were plentiful.[49] On June 8, Blair arrived with the two divisions of the Seventeenth Corps. After deductions for various necessary garrisons, they totaled some 9,000 men, and their addition brought McPherson's total force to more than 29,000.[50]

Sherman's turning maneuver toward Dallas had accomplished his primary goal of forcing the Confederates to abandon Allatoona Pass but not his secondary goal of taking Marietta and forcing Johnston clear through the belt of mountains and across the Chattahoochee. Sherman's position in front of Acworth was not quite halfway through the belt of mountainous terrain between the Etowah and the Chattahoochee, seven miles southeast of Allatoona Pass and ten miles northwest of Marietta. Still, he had advanced some twenty-five miles since leaving the vicinity of Kingston, through some of the toughest and most defensible terrain in North Georgia. Chattanooga was ninety miles to the rear, and Atlanta now lay just thirty miles southeast of Logan's skirmish line.

Sherman had high hopes for the next phase of the campaign, in which he now planned to stick close to the tracks of the Western & Atlantic. Believing that Johnston had retired behind the Chattahoochee, Sherman still expected to advance rapidly.[51]

Among the troops, spirits and confidence were high, though this had been, as Henry Ankeny explained in a letter to his wife, "the hardest campaign that we have yet experienced." Like Sherman, some of the soldiers were beginning to feel frustration at their inability to bring the slippery Johnston to bay. "It is the wish of all," wrote Ankeny, "to settle the campaign at one grand stroke, rather than these continued flank movements that appear to put off the grande finale to the very last."[52]

On June 10, the armies marched again, their persons and equipment—if not their spirits—somewhat dampened by the eighth consecutive day of rain. Reconnaissance during the past few days had suggested the possible presence of the Confederates on the high mountain ridges south of Big Shanty, particularly Kennesaw Mountain, and Sherman directed his army commanders to be prepared. As before, Sherman kept the Army of the Cumberland in the center, but this time the Army of the Ohio was on the right and the Army of the Tennessee on the left. McPherson's troops advanced four miles that day, through the village of Big Shanty and a mile beyond, until they discovered first Rebel skirmishers and then a well-entrenched Confederate battle line on the slopes of Brush Mountain.

There the advance stopped. The other two armies made even less progress that day.[53]

Johnston held a position that stretched from Lost Mountain, southwest of the railroad, to Pine Mountain, and then on to Brush Mountain on the northeast side of the tracks. During the next several days, Sherman's armies gradually worked closer to the Confederate positions, probing for flanks or other weak points. Pine Mountain formed a salient in Johnston's line, and by June 14 it was clearly threatened with envelopment. Johnston ordered it evacuated that night. Two days later, Schofield's Army of the Ohio got around the weak southwestern flank of the Rebel line and forced it to fall back several miles to another ridge.

Meanwhile, the Army of the Tennessee continued to operate against the Confederate right. Each day brought heavy skirmishing and cannonading, and McPherson gradually worked the army forward and to the left in order to threaten the Confederate flank. On June 15, Sherman ordered McPherson to make a demonstration to distract attention away from an operation by the Army of the Cumberland. McPherson assigned Harrow's division to make a limited attack against a hilltop position on the Confederate flank. Harrow assigned Walcutt's brigade to spearhead the attack. They first had to cross a large open field with woods on the far side, and Walcutt sent word along the line that they would "have to get to that woods as quickly as possible." On his order, the brigade advanced with a loud cheer and surged forward in "regular storm fashion" under a heavy Confederate fire, wrote Charles Wills.[54]

They reached the woods and plunged in. A few yards farther on, they encountered the heavily entrenched Confederate picket line. The Rebel pickets were numerous but eager to surrender. "If you ever heard begging for life it was then," wrote Wills. Walcutt's men left the prisoners to find their own way to the rear and pushed on. Struggling through the dense underbrush, they emerged unexpectedly on the banks of Noonday Creek, which had been hidden in the thickets at the foot of the hill that was their objective. Fast and muddy, Noonday Creek was about ten to fifteen feet wide. No fords or bridges were in sight, and this was no place to halt. So, as Wills wrote, "We plunged in." The stream proved to be chest-deep and its banks "steep and slippery and muddy," but somehow they got across.

From the creek banks they began the ascent of the hill. All formation was gone, and it seemed to be "every man for himself" as they scrambled upward, expecting a hard fight at the top. Instead, the Rebels fled. Walcutt's winded soldiers halted at the top of the hill and contented themselves with taking a few potshots at the defenders as they ran away across an open field on the back side of the hill. In the day's action, the brigade took 542 prisoners at a cost of only 63 casualties.[55]

By June 18, the cumulative pressure on Johnston's position finally produced results. That night the Confederates pulled back again, this time to a new line centered about four miles southeast of Big Shanty, on Kennesaw Mountain itself. The Army of the Tennessee, alongside the rest of Sherman's forces, advanced to the foot of the mountain and, as always when troops halted for more than a few minutes during this campaign, began to entrench their position. Again, the contest became one of constant skirmishing and cannonading.[56]

Building entrenchments was hard, tedious work. Hosea Rood of the 12th Wisconsin noted that their lines were often so close to the enemy's that they could work on their entrenchments only at night. "We had to chop down large trees along the line of our proposed entrenchments, and then these had all to be moved and put in place by hand," wrote Rood. "An oak log forty feet long and two feet through at the big end is not easily lifted up and carried in the dark over stumps, and piles of brush for a distance of several yards. Yet such work had to be done in spite of stumbling, and grumbling, and sweating, and aching." The job was all the more unpleasant in the rain, which continued as the men dug into the mud.[57]

Sharpshooting and long-range artillery firing continued to provide motivation for the troops to entrench well. Gunner Albion Gross of the 1st Minnesota Battery rose from writing a letter to his wife moments before a bullet slammed into some of his gear in the place where he had been sitting. Such close calls were common and did not always have such happy endings. Gross had the privilege of returning the Rebels' compliments. "We are keeping watch on the rebs," he wrote to his wife, "and as they move their troops *bang* goes a shell at *them*." One evening Gross and his comrades spotted a campfire behind the Rebel lines, one mile away—"in plain sight of us and that was too bad we thought." Having obtained permission to fire, Gross, an expert gunlayer, took careful aim and fired a shell that burst directly over the target, scattering the fire and, presumably, the Rebels around it, drawing cheers from the Union infantrymen who had witnessed the shot.[58]

Yet the campaign was clearly stalled. "This is becoming tedious," wrote Charles Wills in his diary on June 20. "Johnston has no regard for one's feelings. We are all exceedingly anxious to see what is the other side of these mountains, but this abominable Johnston has no idea of letting us take a look until he is forced to."[59] Sherman felt the same.

On June 22, no rain fell. That day the Armies of the Cumberland and

the Ohio failed in an effort to turn the Confederate left but handily beat off
a counterattack. Skies continued clear and the roads dried during the several days that followed, while Sherman contemplated the failure of recent
efforts to get around Johnston's flanks. He was reluctant to venture far from
the railroad as he had in the Dallas operation, and Grant was counting on
him to keep the pressure on Johnston. Yet it seemed he had stretched his
forces as far as he could, while still holding the railroad, and always found
at the limit of his reach that Johnston was there to meet him. The opposing
lines had indeed grown very long. "Johnston must have full fifty miles of
connected trenches," Sherman wrote. Since Johnston's force was the
weaker, it must be very thin someplace, perhaps almost everyplace, perhaps
in the center—on Kennesaw Mountain.[60]

Kennesaw Mountain is in fact a ridge that slants from northeast to southwest, two miles long and with three distinct summits separated by saddles in
between. The highest peak is Big Kennesaw, at the northeast end of the
ridge, which rises 691 feet above the neighboring valley. In the middle, Little Kennesaw rises 400 feet from its base to its bald top, and on the southwestern end, Pigeon Hill tops out just 200 feet above the low ground at the
foot of its slopes. With the Confederates dug in near its crest, Kennesaw
Mountain presented the most formidable defensive position anywhere
along the Western & Atlantic between Chattanooga and Atlanta. In Sherman's words, it was "the key to the whole country."[61]

On June 24, Sherman issued an order for his armies to prepare for an
assault. McPherson and Schofield would each make demonstrations far out
on the flanks, but the main effort would be directed toward three separate
attacks, one by each of the three armies. Only the Army of the Tennessee
was slated to strike Kennesaw Mountain itself, and then only the Pigeon
Hill summit. The Army of the Cumberland would attack farther to the
right, against a smaller detached hill. The Army of the Ohio was originally
intended to attack still farther to the right, but when Sherman saw the
strength of the Confederate defenses in that sector, he called off that part of
his plan and had Schofield's troops concentrate on their demonstration on
the far right. He admonished his army commanders to maintain the strictest
secrecy about the planned attack, even from their own staff officers as much
as possible. The time appointed for the operation was 8:00 a.m., June 27.[62]

The same day that Sherman issued those orders, June 24, Logan made a
reconnaissance based on more or less the same supposition that lay behind
Sherman's order—of which Logan at that time was unaware. Nothing had
been heard recently from the Rebels on top of the mountain, and no one
could see them in the dense forest. Logan's three division commanders,

Osterhaus, Morgan Smith, and Harrow, all believed that the Confederates were holding Kennesaw with nothing but "a strong skirmish line." In that case, an even stronger skirmish line ought to be able to drive them off. With that purpose in mind, Logan sent a double line of skirmishers up the mountain. His men met Rebel skirmishers, all right—plenty of them, fighting fiercely all the way up the mountainside to within 200 yards of the crest. There they encountered solid resistance that would not be driven any farther. Having no orders to make a general attack on the mountain, Logan was reluctant to up the ante by heavily reinforcing his skirmish line. The only alternative was to withdraw them, which he did. "This advance," Logan dryly noted in his report, "proved the enemy to be still in possession of the mountain in force."[63]

To make the assault on the lower end of Kennesaw Mountain, McPherson selected Logan's Fifteenth Corps, the largest in the Army of the Tennessee. The army's assigned target for the assault, the Pigeon Hill end of Kennesaw, currently lay in the sector of the Army of the Cumberland, while the Fifteenth Corps held the center of the Army of the Tennessee. So during June 25 and 26, McPherson shifted the Fifteenth Corps around the Sixteenth to a position on the right of the Army of the Tennessee, replacing two divisions of the Army of the Cumberland, which pulled out of line and moved farther to the right. The Seventeenth Corps, on the left, and the Sixteenth, now in the center of the Army of the Tennessee, extended their lines to fill in the gap left by the Fifteenth's departure from its previous position. To avoid Rebel notice, the army made these maneuvers under cover of dense woods and completed the final stage of the movement during the night of June 26–27.[64]

In keeping with Sherman's orders for maximum secrecy, many in the Fifteenth Corps did not know what lay ahead. Even as they received orders to march silently to their new positions after nightfall on the twenty-sixth, the consensus opinion was that they were making a flanking movement to the right. Some of the brigade commanders waited until 7:00 a.m., one hour before starting time, to brief their officers.[65]

Col. Charles C. Walcutt waited until the morning of the attack to move his brigade into position, but he told his officers on the evening before. To Capt. Charles Wills, the announcement came as little surprise. He had noticed that Walcutt had been out with McPherson a good deal that day examining the terrain in front. Wills had already turned in when his regimental commander, Lt. Col. George W. Wright, woke him. "Have your men get their breakfasts by daylight," Wright ordered, "at 6 a.m. the fight will begin on the right, and at 8 a.m. our brigade will, with one from the 1st and 2nd divisions, charge a spur of the mountain." Wills directed his orderly sergeant to have him awakened in good time the next morning, and then lay down again. After thinking the matter over, he concluded, "Good-bye, vain world," and went to sleep.[66]

Early on the morning of June 27, the troops stacked knapsacks and other paraphernalia, to be left under guard, and then moved to their final jumping-off points, concealed by the forest from Rebel eyes atop Kennesaw. In the 55th Illinois, veterans of Shiloh and most of the army's fights since, soldiers ate their breakfasts with good appetite and sat around casually, smoking pipes, and talking as if nothing out of the ordinary was on schedule for the day.[67]

Yet comrades who knew one another well could note a greater seriousness. Some were open about their fears. A sergeant who had proved his courage in previous battles now approached his captain to confess that it had failed him this time. Could he remain with the baggage? The captain referred the matter to the regimental commander, Capt. Jacob M. Augustine, who granted the request. Though outwardly calm, Augustine had his own private misgivings. While his men munched their hardtack and sipped their coffee, he took out his pocket memorandum book. "We marched last night until eleven," he wrote, "got up at seven this morning—are to make an assault upon the breastworks at half-past seven. Our division takes the lead. Now may God protect the right. Am doubting our success."[68]

McPherson's orders called for the Sixteenth and Seventeenth corps to advance skirmishers up the slopes of Kennesaw in order to keep the enemy pinned down in those sectors. If the skirmishers found resistance light, they were to go ahead and take the summit, digging in and awaiting reinforcements. The Fifteenth was to make its assault on Pigeon Hill with four brigades, holding the rest in reserve. Logan designated Morgan Smith's division, in the center of his line, to make the attack, reinforced to a strength of four brigades by Walcutt's, on loan from Harrow. In the end, Smith used only three: Walcutt's, Lightburn's, and Giles Smith's. In all, the assault force numbered some 5,500 rifles.[69]

At 8:00 a.m., the troops marched forward, three brigades side by side, each in two lines. Immediately they came under heavy fire. Advancing on the left, Walcutt's 1,500-man brigade had orders from Smith to move toward the saddle between Pigeon Hill and Little Kennesaw. Since this route would give his men partial cover from Confederate artillery whose guns would be unable to depress enough to hit them, Smith ordered the brigade to lead off the advance, with the others ordered to step out when they heard the roar of firing from those guns that could hit Walcutt. There were plenty of them, and the other brigades had no trouble hearing them.[70]

Next to Walcutt, in the center of Smith's attacking force, Giles Smith's brigade advanced directly toward the peak of Pigeon Hill. Side by side with Walcutt's brigade, Smith's men overran the Confederate skirmishers, who were entrenched in rifle pits at the base and on the lower slopes of Kennesaw. The Federals hustled their prisoners to the rear and moved on. They scrambled down into a ravine, across its swampy bottom, and up the other side. There the brigadiers halted their men, dressed their lines, and gave the order to fix bayonets. Then they plunged upward through the tangled underbrush, clambering over boulders and pulling themselves up by the roots of trees.

So difficult was the terrain that Morgan Smith thought "trees had been felled and brush and rocks piled in such a manner as to make it impossible to advance with any regularity." Sometimes Giles Smith's men went on all fours to get under the tangled vines. Taking casualties all the way, the brigades approached the main Confederate defensive works, just below the mountain's crest. Their formation now was neither a line nor a column but, as a participant later wrote, "a swarm of desperate men clambering up between boulders and over tree trunks."[71]

While Walcutt's and Smith's brigades climbed toward the breastworks in their front, Lightburn's brigade, on the right, was aiming for a section of breastworks that ran through a small orchard about 400 yards to the right of Pigeon Hill. To reach that target, Lightburn's men had to cross a slough, choked with a dense thicket, where the men sank to their knees in the mud and water. Struggling forward, they splashed out of the swamp and burst free of the thicket so suddenly that they took the Confederate picket line by surprise, killing and wounding many of the Rebels and taking thirty-eight prisoners. That, however, was the end of Lightburn's success for the day. Out in the open, his men were exposed to a vicious enfilading cross fire that made advance all but suicidal. The brigade went to ground well short of the orchard.[72]

Walcutt's and Smith's brigades also had to stop short of their goal. In some places stark rock faces, twenty or twenty-five feet high, barred the way forward, leading officers to assert that they could not have gotten their troops to the top in two hours even if no defenders had been present. Walcutt particularly found that the saddle between Pigeon Hill and Little Kennesaw was an impassable gorge, and he diverted his advance more toward the hill itself.[73]

The underbrush was so thick that Captain Wills did not realize his company was moving parallel to a line of Confederate breastworks until one of his men pointed to the right and shouted, "Look there, Captain, may I shoot?" Just visible through the gaps in the foliage some sixty yards to the right across a narrow, deep ravine were the breastworks, blazing with rifle fire. Confederate skirmishers were still fleeing up the ravine, and the three companies on the right of the 103rd Illinois had already turned across it and charged the breastworks. Wills turned his own company toward the enemy, and they made it across the bottom of the ravine and about a third of the way up the far side before being pinned down by enemy fire. His men fired back as best they could, but they had little cover, and Wills thought Rebel marksmanship must have been very poor or his regiment would have been practically annihilated.[74] In fact the defenders were Cockrell's Missouri brigade. Looking uphill toward the Confederates in the breastworks, George Richardson of the 6th Iowa thought they looked more fiendish than anything he had ever seen before.[75]

Throughout the two desperate Union brigades, officers tried to inspire their men, and both officers and enlisted men performed prodigies of valor. Lt. Col. Rigdon S. Barnhill of the 40th Illinois fell dead near the top of the slope. As troops of the 6th Iowa rushed toward the breastworks, the Rebels manning the line in front of them broke for the rear, but the Confederate second line quickly moved up in overwhelming force and threw back the small band of Iowans who had made it that far.[76]

In Giles Smith's brigade, Col. Benjamin Spooner of the 83rd Indiana was shot through the leg, and Col. A. V. Rice of the 57th Ohio was shot in the right leg, the left foot, and the forehead. Miraculously, he survived, but he was out of the action. Most of the Union troops took cover as best they could behind logs, rocks, or folds of the ground about thirty feet from the Confederate breastworks.[77] Capt. William C. Porter, of the 55th Illinois, had gotten out of tight scrapes before. He had been one of the officers of the forlorn hope at Vicksburg, and had escaped injury or death through several difficult hours crouching on the scarp of the Stockade Redan. This time he did not escape, receiving a mortal wound near the top of the hill.[78]

Captain Augustine, commanding the 55th, seeing that his men had stopped advancing, stood up, stepped out in front of the regiment, and shouted, "Forward men!" For one moment, a survivor wrote, Augustine was "the grandest figure in that terrible scene." The next moment, he was shot through the chest. Some of his men did charge all the way to the breastworks and cross bayonets with the Rebels. None of those men returned from the charge, but some were said to have fallen inside the Rebel breastworks.

"Finding that so many gallant men were being uselessly slain," Logan ordered his troops back to the upper line of Confederate skirmishers' rifle pits and sent pioneer detachments forward to help transform the rifle pits into a full-scale system of entrenchments. High on the slope of Pigeon Hill, Captain Wills had just received word that Lieutenant Colonel Wright had fallen and that he was now in command of the 103rd Illinois. When the order came to withdraw, Wills worked his way along the regimental line, making sure that everyone got out. By the time he reached the bottom of the tangled slope, however, he had only about thirty men with him. The rest turned up over the next couple of hours, having become separated by the rough terrain and thick underbrush.[79]

Some of the Union troops were so close to the Confederate works that they could not withdraw until nightfall.[80] Even once they reached the ravine and creek at the base of the mountain, the soldiers were not necessarily safe. After helping to carry the dying Captain Augustine down from near the crest, Joseph Putnam ran to fetch a stretcher to transport the wounded officer to the rear. He had taken only a few steps when he received a severe wound in the upper thigh, one that veteran soldiers at once recognized as mortal. Putnam was one of the most popular soldiers in the regiment, known for his beautiful singing voice. He died singing "We're Going Home to Die No More."[81]

While Logan's men made their assault, Blair and Dodge sent skirmishers up the mountain as ordered. Dodge sent three regiments in skirmish line, including the Western Sharpshooters, but it was the 64th Illinois—the Yates Sharpshooters—also equipped with privately purchased Henry repeaters, that won special accolades that day, pressing up to within a few yards of the Rebel works. Blair's skirmishers also pushed forward vigorously, suffering some 200 casualties.[82]

Logan's casualties were significant and included seven regimental commanders. In all, his losses were 80 killed, 506 wounded, and 17 missing, a total of about 11 percent of the assault force.[83] Simultaneously the Army of the Cumberland's attack failed, with perhaps another 2,000 casualties. Kennesaw Mountain was a tragic experience for the regiments that participated in the attack. For the Army of the Tennessee it was a loss much less severe than it had suffered at Chickasaw Bayou. For Sherman's force as a whole, it was a setback. Yet neither in the size of the butcher's bill nor in casualty percentage was it comparable to the most disastrous repulses of the war. In the campaign Grant was simultaneously waging in Virginia, losses like those at Kennesaw were the small change of everyday operations. The June 27 attack stands out in the Atlanta campaign simply because Sherman, with the unintentional cooperation of the passive Johnston, was normally very sparing of the lives of his men.

He would be even more so in the future. The lesson of Kennesaw Mountain was plain to everyone in Sherman's armies, from the general himself on down. As Maj. A. J. Seay put it, "The rebel works and position are too strong to be carried by assault. We must flank 'em."[84]

Flanking the Rebels would be Sherman's next move. While the Armies of the Tennessee and the Cumberland were making their doomed charges against Kennesaw, the Army of the Ohio had been making a demonstration to the southwest, Sherman's far right. In one sense the demonstration was a failure—it did not draw Confederate troops away from the center. However, in another sense it was a surprising success. Confederate attention was so focused on the defense of Kennesaw Mountain that insufficient troops remained in front of Schofield to prevent him making a key lodgment on the far right, threatening to turn Johnston's position. Somewhat reluctantly, but with no other choice if he meant to keep advancing toward Atlanta, Sherman decided to cast loose of the railroad once again and turn Schofield's gain into something decisive.[85]

In order to do that, Sherman ordered the Army of the Tennessee to pull out of its position on the railroad in front of Big Shanty and swing behind the Armies of the Cumberland and the Ohio to come in on the far right, putting teeth into Schofield's implied threat. The day after the attack on Kennesaw Mountain, Sherman asked McPherson how long it would take his army to load up and be ready for a ten-day operation away from the railroad. McPherson replied that he could be ready to go as soon as the railroad brought up six days' rations for his men and five days' forage for his horses. The army spent the next few days in preparation, with McPherson checking to make sure that his pontoon bridge was long enough to span the Chattahoochee.[86]

On the morning of July 2, the Army of the Tennessee pulled out of line and marched toward the far right of Sherman's army group. During the night, however, Johnston reacted to Schofield's presence on his flank in exactly the way that Sherman and nearly everyone else had by now come to expect: he pulled his army out of the Kennesaw Mountain lines and retreated toward Atlanta. This time he halted at Smyrna. There his army had its back to the Chattahoochee and was less than ten miles from the center of Atlanta. Johnston had had large numbers of slaves at work for some time constructing a line of entrenchments that Sherman later called "one of the strongest pieces of field-fortification I ever saw."[87]

The Army of the Tennessee marched through Marietta and took up its assigned position on the far right of Sherman's armies. During the days that followed, while the Army of the Tennessee and the Army of the Cumberland skirmished vigorously with the entrenched Rebels, the Army of the Ohio, along with one of Sherman's cavalry divisions, succeeded in making a lodgment on the southeast bank of the Chattahoochee well upstream from Smyrna. Sherman reinforced the bridgehead by sending the Sixteenth Corps around to the left to join Schofield, and on the night of July 9–10, Johnston retreated yet again, pulling his army back to the south bank of the Chattahoochee. On July 12, the Fifteenth Corps marched to join Dodge's command on the left, and four days later the Seventeenth followed, arriving near the camps of the Fifteenth and Sixteenth in the vicinity of Roswell, Georgia, on July 17.[88]

With the exception of the march from the right to the left of Sherman's armies, July 10 to 17 was a time of rest for the Army of the Tennessee. They bathed in the river, washed their clothes, and stood inspection. "You could have seen your face in our belt plates & gun barrels," wrote Edward Allen to his parents back in Wisconsin. The soldiers foraged locally, and the most popular items were green apples—eaten as sauce—and the ubiquitous blackberries. "We found a great abundance of blackberries through the hills in this region," wrote Capt. Charles Miller. "It was a 'godsend' to the soldiers in a dietary point of view and scarcely a soldier in that vast army who did not eat his quart of blackberries, worth more than all the doctors' prescriptions." Scurvy had begun to make its appearance in the ranks, and the blackberries cured that as well as performing their usual function, still highly touted among the soldiers, of regulating the digestive tract.[89]

The weather was oppressively hot except during and immediately after thunderstorms. On the evening of July 14, an especially severe storm struck, with howling winds, tropical downpour, and the loudest peals of thunder and brightest flashes of lightning many of the Midwesterners had ever experienced. Lightning strikes killed a number of soldiers. The artillery park of the Sixteenth Corps, on an open hillside, seemed to be a particular target.[90]

On July 17, the Army of the Tennessee marched out on another operation. Sherman had been contemplating his next move toward Atlanta. His general concept was to cut the railroads leading into the city from both the east and the west, rendering its supply situation impossible and at least hindering the arrival of any possible reinforcements from Virginia. His first concrete attempt to implement the policy took the form of dispatching Maj.

Gen. George Stoneman's cavalry division to cut the Atlanta & West Point Railroad west of the city. The attempt was a dismal failure, as Stoneman never even reached the railroad. This confirmed Sherman's suspicions that his cavalry was not good for much of anything. It also confirmed his determination to carry out the next step of his plan: breaking the Georgia Railroad. This time, however, he would use a real fighting force to do the job, his "whiplash," as he called it, the Army of the Tennessee.

CHAPTER THIRTY

Across the Chattahoochee

WHILE THE MEN of the Army of the Tennessee swam, washed, dug entrenchments, and picked blackberries along the Chattahoochee, deliberations among generals and their superiors set the stage for their next operation. Grant sent Sherman word that as many as 25,000 Confederate troops might leave Virginia to reinforce Johnston. That made it all the more important for Sherman to cut the railroad east of Atlanta—and fast. To Thomas and McPherson, he wrote the same day he received Grant's warning, July 16, "It behooves us, therefore, to hurry." The several armies, Sherman directed, were to march the next morning. His plan was that while the Army of the Tennessee swung to the east, toward Decatur, in order to break the railroad and turn the Confederates yet again, the Armies of the Cumberland and the Ohio would advance more or less straight toward Atlanta.[1] The Army of the Tennessee marched early on July 17, each man carrying three days' rations and forty rounds. They covered eight miles and camped that night near Nancy's Creek.[2]

While they marched that day, more high-command deliberations brought another important change for the Army of the Tennessee's operations. This time, however, the enemy high command did the deliberating. As Johnston had retreated again and again, for more than 100 miles, and across the Oostenaula, Etowah, and Chattahoochee, dissatisfaction with him had grown in numerous quarters of the Confederacy, most significantly in its White House, where Jefferson Davis was none too well disposed toward Johnston in the first place. Lately, Johnston's orders to remove certain supplies from Atlanta and then to evacuate prisoners at Andersonville, 100 miles south of Atlanta, had startled Davis. When the general steadfastly refused to disclose to the president any plan for saving Atlanta—probably because he had none—Davis finally had enough. He sacked Johnston and replaced him with the best eligible general on hand, the aggressive John Bell Hood. After Johnston's last retreat, Hood had no room for another withdrawal without abandoning the city. The next time a Union turning maneuver presented the alternative of fight or retreat, Hood would have no choice.

On July 18, the Army of the Tennessee marched at 5:00 a.m., continuing its turning maneuver toward the Georgia Railroad east of Atlanta. Throughout the morning, they moved toward the great monolith of Stone Mountain, rising as a lone hump amid the otherwise rolling landscape. About 2:00 p.m., the army halted about seven miles east of Decatur, four miles west of Stone Mountain, and very near the Georgia Railroad.[3] McPherson assigned Lightburn's brigade, along with an attached cavalry division, to work on the railroad, and they tore up three full miles of track.[4]

Sherman's orders for July 19 were for more of the same. Thomas and Schofield, side by side, were to advance straight toward Atlanta from the north. Schofield's left flank was to reach Decatur and make contact with McPherson, who was to continue moving westward through and around Decatur toward Atlanta, tearing up the railroad as he came. Sherman, who still did not know that Hood had replaced Johnston, was pleased with McPherson's work in breaking the Georgia Railroad on the eighteenth, and wrote to him, "Now we must look after Joe Johnston."[5]

As ordered, the Fifteenth Corps was up early on the morning of July 19, and marched to the Georgia Railroad at Decatur—an "old-fashioned tree-embowered town," as an Illinois soldier described it, with about 800 inhabitants and a nice courthouse. Fires were already burning in some parts of the town when Logan's soldiers marched in, as the Confederates had torched supplies and wagons that they had not had time to take with them. That suited Illinois soldier Amariah Spencer just fine. "I say let them burn and destroy all they will," he wrote to his mother. "The more they burn the sooner they will play out."[6]

The Fifteenth Corps spent the day wrecking the rails, and camped that night on the north side of Decatur about six miles from Atlanta. As they had the day before, Confederate cavalry and horse artillery harassed the operation but could not slow Logan's advance. The Sixteenth moved up on Logan's right and made contact with Schofield's Army of the Ohio, farther to the right, while the Seventeenth continued to bring up the rear.[7]

Dodge, who had a special talent for intelligence gathering, had infiltrated several "scouts," or spies, inside the city of Atlanta. On the morning of July 19, one of them made his way through the lines to report the interesting news that Hood had superceded Johnston. Dodge immediately passed the information on to McPherson and Sherman.[8] At Sherman's headquarters, the commanding general discussed the change with one of Hood's old classmates, Schofield, and decided that it was a good thing.

According to Schofield, Hood was "bold even to rashness, and courageous in the extreme." Sherman's assessment was "that the change of commanders meant 'fight,' " and a fight in the open, outside of entrenchments, was just what he had been wanting and not able to get all the way down from Chattanooga. He sent notice to his army commanders to be on the alert for aggressive action by Hood.[9]

Sherman's orders for July 20 were for all three of his armies, now connected flank to flank, to advance directly toward Atlanta. "Each army commander will accept battle on anything like fair terms," if the enemy offered it outside of entrenchments. Otherwise they were to advance to within cannon shot of the entrenched lines of Atlanta, halt, dig in, and wait for orders.[10]

A sense of expectation prevailed in the camps of the Army of the Tennessee on the morning of July 20 as the troops prepared to advance on Atlanta. The band of Brig. Gen. R. K. Scott's brigade of the Seventeenth Corps played "The Star-Spangled Banner," as the brigade took up the march.[11] With or without musical accompaniment, the various units of the army advanced that morning with the Sixteenth Corps on the right, the Fifteenth in the center straddling the Georgia Railroad, and the Seventeenth moving up to take position on the left.

The enemy contested the advance with skirmishers and occasional artillery fire, but McPherson's troops had no difficulty pushing forward to what Logan estimated to be about two and a half miles from the city, where they approached the outer line of the Atlanta fortifications. There, Logan halted in order to let Dodge catch up to him on the right and Blair on the left. Before them in plain view lay Atlanta, the object of two and a half months of hard campaigning.[12]

As if to prove that he had fulfilled Sherman's orders to approach to within cannon shot of the city, Logan at about 1:00 p.m. brought up Capt. Francis De Gress's Battery H, 1st Illinois Light Artillery. With four 20-pounder Parrott rifles, De Gress's battery was the pride of the Fifteenth Corps. He had De Gress fire three rounds toward Atlanta, and a signal officer using a field glass observed the shot impacting inside the city, the first Union gunfire to strike Atlanta during the course of the war.[13]

On the left, the Seventeenth Corps got into heavier skirmishing. As Brig. Gen. Walter Q. Gresham's division advanced alongside the Fifteenth, they encountered more determined resistance near the outer line of fortifications, although their opponents continued to be dismounted cavalry supporting artillery. Blair rode up to Gresham and told him there was nothing but cavalry in front of him. According to one account, Blair told Gresham that Sherman had said they could go right into Atlanta and that he, Blair, wanted Gresham's division to "push ahead and get in there before any one else."[14]

Gresham pushed ahead a short distance, skirmishing heavily, and sent back word that he thought he was facing Confederate infantry. His troops were coming under sharp fire from skirmishers on a bald hill to their left front. If they advanced farther, the hill and its pestilent sharpshooters would be on their left flank. Gresham considered assaulting the hill, but the intervening ground was partly hidden in defilade. Suspecting that a deep ravine might lie in that hidden area between his division and the hill, Gresham feared that if he sent his men charging toward the Bald Hill, they could be trapped and slaughtered in the ravine—if one actually existed behind those woods. He sent two staff officers to view the ground, but the sharpshooters' fire was too hot, and the staffers came back without an answer. So Gresham decided to see for himself, creeping forward all the way to the skirmish line. He had just satisfied himself that there was no ravine when a sharpshooter's bullet slammed into his leg, and his men carried him off the field, badly wounded. Roughly an hour of daylight remained.[15]

When Gresham fell, he sent word to Blair, who hurried back to that sector to view the situation for himself. Surveying the ground, he sent orders for his reserve division, Brig. Gen. Mortimer D. Leggett's, to deploy on Gresham's left, directly in front of the Bald Hill. Leggett was not so sure about that. If his division formed up on line with Gresham's, that would put it in the middle of an open field in easy range of a Rebel battery positioned in front of Gresham's line. At the same time, there would still be a belt of thick timber between Leggett's men and the Bald Hill.[16]

Leggett sent an aide back to Blair for a clarification of his orders. Did Blair intend Leggett to assault the hill? The aide found Blair with McPherson. Approaching the generals, the aide saluted and said, "General Blair, General Leggett wishes to know if he shall attack the enemy in his front."

"Let's see," replied McPherson. Together with Blair, he rode over to Leggett's position. Looking over the ground, McPherson suggested that they push a strong skirmish line into the belt of timber as a possible prelude to assaulting the hill beyond it. Leggett dispatched Col. Gilbert D. Munson of his staff to direct the skirmish line and see that it got far enough forward to find the extreme southern flank of the opposing forces. A short time later, Munson was back reporting that the Confederate line extended only a short distance south of the Bald Hill.[17]

With daylight beginning to fade, "General McPherson decided that it was too late to assault the hill that night," Leggett later explained, "but directed that we should do so in the morning, unless we got orders to the contrary." Lt. Col. William E. Strong, inspector general on McPherson's staff, later thought that if Gresham had not been wounded that evening, the Seventeenth Corps might have gone all the way into Atlanta. Blair later reflected that if Leggett had attacked immediately, they could at least have taken the Bald Hill easily. Over in the Fifteenth, which had sat still throughout the evening waiting for the other corps to take position on its flanks, Capt. Tom Taylor watched the sun setting behind the opposite ridge, silhouetting a two-story red-brick house that stood near the railroad, and wrote bitterly in his diary, "How long, O Lord, will our leaders continue to let such opportunities slip through their fingers & afterwards sacrifice hundreds of lives in vain efforts to take the same position they let the enemy fortify & occupy under their very noses?" As always, it was easier to know what the commanding general should do when one was not the commanding general.[18]

In fact, only light forces had stood between the Army of the Tennessee and the city of Atlanta that day—about 2,500 Confederate cavalry and a single battery of artillery. The great bulk of Hood's army had attacked the Army of the Cumberland just south of Peachtree Creek late that afternoon. After several hours of fighting, Thomas's Federals beat back the attackers. Union casualties totaled about 1,600; Confederate, approximately 2,500. The sound of the heavy gunfire along Peachtree Creek was inaudible at the Army of the Tennessee's position on the east side of Atlanta.

Having decided not to attack that evening, McPherson directed Leggett to move his division forward and to the left, into the belt of woods and fronting the Bald Hill. The belt proved to be several hundred yards wide and composed largely of scrub oak. Leggett's right brigade, that of Brig. Gen. Manning F. Force, was directly in front of the hill. His skirmishers, as well as Brig. Gen. R. K. Scott's, in Leggett's center, advanced to the western edge of the belt of woods, looking out onto the open cornfield, about 400 yards wide and just ready to tassel. The field sloped upward to the Bald Hill.[19]

Leggett rode over to Force's position to inform him of the planned assault. "I want you to carry that hill, General," said Leggett. "Move as soon as it is light enough to see. I will support your left and rear with the rest of the division." He assured Force that the Seventeenth Corps's other division, until that evening Gresham's, would "make a demonstration as you go up to distract the attention of the enemy in their front."[20]

Force said he wished he had known about the planned attack sooner. If he had, he would not have placed the large but relatively inexperienced 12th Wisconsin in his front line. The 12th had been in the service for nearly three years but somehow had never been in the right place to get into a major battle. Leggett had to admit it was a fine-looking regiment. Its colonel, George E. Bryant, had assured him of its quality and begged, "Now, General, if you have any fighting to do, give us a chance." It now appeared that Bryant and his badgers would get their chance. Force would rather have depended on the small but tried and proven veteran regiments of his brigade, but he was uneasy about the message it would send the 12th if he yanked them out of line now. Bryant and the rest of his officers were confident their men could do the job, so Leggett and Force, with some misgivings, left the 12th in position to lead the next morning's assault.[21]

Another matter remained to be dealt with that night. After Gresham's wounding, the next senior officer in his division was a colonel; so Blair sent McPherson word that he needed a new division commander. McPherson sent one of the Fifteenth Corps's premier brigade commanders, Brig. Gen. Giles A. Smith. Smith arrived and took command of his new division at about 2:00 a.m., July 21.[22]

It was 1:00 a.m. when Sherman sat down to write a reply to McPherson's dispatch informing him of the evening's action. "I was in hopes you could have made a closer approach to Atlanta," Sherman wrote in mild rebuke, adding his suspicion that McPherson would face stronger breastworks manned by more troops in the morning. He also informed McPherson of the fight at Peachtree Creek and speculated that Hood might abandon Atlanta after the drubbing he had received on July 20.[23]

As Sherman, Blair, Taylor, and probably a number of others had feared, the Confederates in front of the Army of the Tennessee received substantial reinforcements during the night. Just before dawn, Cleburne's division, the Army of the Tennessee's old nemesis from Tunnel Hill at Chattanooga, arrived and took position opposite the Fifteenth Corps, straddling the Georgia Railroad and the Decatur Road. The dismounted Confederate cavalry therefore could hold the rest of the line in greater force than the day before.

In the predawn hours, Force made his plans to assault the Bald Hill at daybreak. He strengthened his skirmish line and had it press forward through the darkness as close as possible to the enemy lines without tipping off the Rebels that something was up. As soon as Force's main line of battle began to advance, the skirmishers were to "rush for the top of the hill, firing rapidly," as brigade picket officer Gilbert Munson recalled.[24]

Dawn broke, but the attack did not begin. Watching the hill from a vantage point near his headquarters, McPherson sent his chief of artillery, Capt. Andrew Hickenlooper, to ride over to the Seventeenth Corps and see that the attack was made promptly and with vigor. The problem involved Giles Smith's division, which was to launch a cooperating attack on the lines in its front. Possibly as a result of the late-night command change, Smith had not received the order for the morning's advance until quite late, and his division was not ready. Leggett's could not begin without it. On the slope of the Bald Hill, Force's skirmishers lay quiet and concealed while they watched the smoke of breakfast fires rise from the lines of the unsuspecting Confederate defenders and wondered what was delaying the assault.[25]

Back in the woods, the men of the 12th Wisconsin had plenty of time to contemplate what they were about to do. Hosea Rood, in Company E, wondered how many of them were going to be killed, mortally wounded, or maimed for life, and which ones they would be. Home, family, and sweetheart had never been so precious, and it seemed "very hard to give them all up." Still "conscience, manhood, and patriotism" steeled him for the task ahead, along with the thought that he was fighting so that his loved ones could "enjoy the blessings of liberty in a home made safe by the majesty of law." A few feet away, one of Rood's comrades sat leaning against a tree, humming quietly to himself. Rood recognized the tune. It was "Just Before the Battle, Mother."[26]

Finally, Giles Smith's division was ready. In Force's brigade, quiet orders passed along the front directed the men to pile their knapsacks and fall in outside their breastworks. Color-bearers unfurled the flags, and Rood thought the Stars and Stripes "looked brighter and more beautiful then they ever did before." General Force rode along just behind the line, speaking quietly to the men. "Boys, now be cool and firm," Force said. "Don't waver, don't falter; just make up your mind to drive the enemy from yonder hill, and you'll do it. Be cool and determined, boys, and it will be all right."[27]

Then at about 7:00 a.m., raising his voice to a booming shout, Force commanded, "Right shoulder shift arms! Forward, March!" In the stillness, the skirmishers well to the front heard the order and sprang forward even before the brigade's battle line emerged from the woods. The 12th and 16th Wisconsin formed the first line; 20th, 30th, and 31st Illinois, the second, all marching with bayonets fixed. Force and his staff were mounted, riding right behind the front line. For a minute or two, the skirmishers distracted the defenders' fire.

As the line of battle approached the brow of the hill, it caught up with the skirmishers, who fell in with their comrades in the ranks. At close range, the Rebels poured their fire into the attacking line. "Our men fell in bunches," wrote Munson, and file-closers could be heard above the din of gunfire shouting, "Close up! Close up!" The men filled the gaps, closing on their regimental colors. In the front line, the inexperienced 12th Wisconsin never flinched, despite losing 5 color-bearers and 134 out of fewer than 600 men it carried into the fight.[28]

Force's voice came booming again over the roar of battle, "Charge bayonets! Forward, double-quick, March!" Rifles came down from shoulders and bayonets were thrust forward as the line surged up the last few yards toward the enemy works, yelling wildly. In another minute or so, it was over. The Rebels broke for the rear. Force's men swarmed over the parapet and poured deadly volleys into the fleeing Confederates. The 12th and 16th Wisconsin pursued the fugitives down the back slope and into the woods, rounding up a number of prisoners and finally encountering another line of Confederate works. A staff officer reminded Force that their orders were only to take the Bald Hill, and the brigade commander, though muttering that they could take "the next hill too," sent an aide to recall the eager Wisconsin boys.[29]

The deed had been smartly done. When a staff officer brought word to Giles Smith that Force had already taken the Bald Hill, Smith could hardly believe it and thought at first the officer was joking. Force's brigade had met and routed Brig. Gen. Samuel W. Ferguson's Confederate cavalry, fighting dismounted as infantry. To the left of Force's brigade, the 20th and 78th Ohio regiments of Scott's brigade had also advanced but encountered no resistance at all, since they completely overlapped the southern end of the Confederate line. The Ohioans moved up to the same alignment as Force, extending his line farther south.[30]

On the other flank of Force's newly won hilltop position, Giles Smith's division advanced across an open field about 600 yards wide and sloping gently uphill to the Rebel works located in the edge of the woods. The troops pressed to within short range of the breastworks and exchanged fire with the Rebels. Two brigades of dismounted Confederate cavalry and the extreme right-flank regiment of Cleburne's division broke under the pressure of Smith's attack and fell back a short distance before rallying and returning to their works. Deeming that his attack had accomplished its purpose of distracting attention away from Leggett on the Bald Hill and also that his men were accomplishing little in exchanging fire with entrenched Confederates, Smith withdrew his division to its own breastworks.[31]

In fact, the enemy was by no means finished with Force or with the Bald

Hill. Cleburne's troops and the Rebel cavalry subsequently counterattacked, and the battle for the hill raged for several more hours. The tables were turned this time from what they had been at Tunnel Hill eight months before. Now it was a brigade of the Army of the Tennessee that possessed an important hilltop and Cleburne's division that strove to take it away from them. Force's Wisconsin and Illinois boys were stubborn, though, and when the smoke cleared, they were still holding the Bald Hill. Cleburne later referred to the struggle as "the bitterest of his life."[32]

Scattered thunderstorms moved through the area that afternoon, but most of the time the troops experienced intense heat, humidity, and sunshine. On the hilltop, with no hint of shade, some of Force's men suffered from sunstroke or heatstroke. Through the shimmering heat waves, Force noticed something off to the west and called Leggett's attention to it. In the distance, Confederate columns were marching southward, toward the Union left. Soon everyone on the Bald Hill could see it. Leggett reported the matter to Blair and McPherson, and McPherson, in turn, passed the information along to Sherman, who thought it meant that Hood had decided to abandon Atlanta and was withdrawing southward. In fact, these troops were additional reinforcements for the Confederates directly in front and just to the left of the Bald Hill, whose goal was to keep McPherson from breaking into Atlanta that afternoon.[33]

McPherson was apprehensive. That morning while he had been watching the progress of Leggett's fight for the Bald Hill, a scout had brought him an Atlanta newspaper from three days before, containing a copy of Johnston's farewell address to his army, turning over command to Hood. McPherson had already known of his former West Point classmate's recent promotion, but this was the first he had seen an official Confederate document confirming it. After reading Johnston's address, McPherson commented to several members of his staff who were nearby that "we must now look out for different tactics; that Hood though he might lack in judgment, would certainly fight his army at every opportunity that offered, and with desperation; and that we must take unusual precautions to guard against surprise."[34]

McPherson was inclined to suspect that the current movements in Hood's army had something to do with the Army of the Tennessee's dangling left flank. As the extreme left-flank unit of Sherman's forces, the army had no friendly units beyond its own left—only hilly, mostly forested country that might conceal approaching Rebels. That flank would ordinarily have been screened by Union cavalry, but Sherman had ordered Brig. Gen. Kenner Garrard's division, which was attached directly to his own headquarters, to leave its position on the left of the Army of the Tennessee and ride eastward to break the Georgia Railroad east of Stone Mountain at as many places as possible.[35]

Sherman was still worried that troops from Lee's army might arrive to reinforce Hood, and his concern for the complete destruction of the Georgia Railroad sprang from a desire to rule that out. It did not, however, help to allay McPherson's concerns. Garrard's errand to the east also required the detachment of one brigade of the Sixteenth Corps to Decatur to guard the large portion of the Army of the Tennessee's wagon train that was parked there that had previously been covered by Garrard's horsemen. McPherson sent Sprague's brigade of Fuller's (formerly Veatch's) division, leaving Fuller with only a single brigade.[36]

When the Confederates extended their line southward to counter Leggett's presence on the Bald Hill, McPherson responded in kind. He had Logan bring up Harrow's division from its position in reserve and place it on the left of Morgan Smith, replacing Giles Smith's division of the Seventeenth Corps and freeing it to move around to the left of Leggett's division. That extended the Army of the Tennessee's line several hundred yards to the south. Smith deployed his division on a line more or less continuing that held by Leggett, but whereas Leggett's line ran due north and south, Smith's new line slanted back somewhat to the east.[37]

The left of Smith's division—now the left of the Army of the Tennessee and of Sherman's forces—was held by Col. William Hall's "Old Iowa Brigade," organized during the spring 1862 advance on Corinth from four regiments that had had their baptism of fire at Shiloh the month before. Smith had Hall refuse his two left regiments so that the brigade's line curved from a facing of south-southwest to south-southeast. This would provide at least minimal protection against a flanking attack. He also deployed a picket line running a mile and a half to the east of his flank, to guard against any possible move into his and the army's rear. As added insurance, McPherson moved Fuller's lone brigade to a position in reserve behind the Seventeenth Corps.[38]

At nightfall on July 21, the Army of the Tennessee held a front the length of about five and a half divisions. On the far right of the army, adjoining the Army of the Ohio, was Sweeny's division of the Sixteenth Corps, one brigade in the front line, one behind it in reserve. Next came the three divisions of Logan's Fifteenth Corps, first Brig. Gen. Charles Woods's (formerly Osterhaus's), then Morgan Smith's straddling the Georgia Railroad and the Decatur Road in the center, and then Harrow's. To the left of Harrow's division was Leggett's division of the Seventeenth, still anchored on the Bald Hill it had taken that morning. Next came Giles Smith's division of the Seventeenth, with Fuller's brigade of the Sixteenth behind it in reserve.[39]

Many of the troops had passed much of July 21 digging trenches and erecting breastworks, and they were destined to spend the night in the same activity. "There was enough apprehension of danger among the men to make them work vigorously," Leggett later recalled.[40] The men were tired, but morale was high. "We have the best army I ever saw," wrote Amariah Spencer to his mother that evening. "The men are all in fine spirits and all seem to feel shure of success. I never saw an army so confident of success in my life. No one seems to feel any ways uneasy about the coming Battle."[41]

While most of the men dug, chopped, and manhandled logs into place that night, others had the duty of keeping track of the Rebels. As the new owner of the Bald Hill, Mortimer Leggett's division was the army's closest outpost to Atlanta. Leggett and Giles Smith were both concerned about the Confederate troop movements they had observed that day and discussed the matter late that evening. When Leggett expressed his concerns to Blair, the corps commander proved unreceptive. Blair was of the opinion that the Rebels were in the process of abandoning Atlanta. McPherson, however, continued to suspect that something more sinister was afoot. Shortly before midnight, he sent orders for his corps commanders to strengthen their breastworks and be prepared in case the Rebels should attack at dawn.[42]

A few minutes later, as Leggett was making the rounds of his lines, encouraging the men in their digging, he met with Lt. Col. George Welles of the 68th Ohio, who reported "considerable noise" somewhere off beyond the picket line. Leggett decided to see if he could find out more about what the Rebels were doing out there in the darkness. He and Wells asked for volunteers from the 68th for a scouting mission and from those who stepped forward selected two "shrewd, reliable men." Leggett instructed them to creep as far forward as they safely could and report back to him. They were gone for over an hour, and when they returned, they reported that they had found no Confederates for a long ways and had gotten close enough to the city to make out in the moonlight a column of Confederate troops marching southward out of Atlanta. Leggett forwarded the information to Blair and noted the time. It was just 1:30 a.m.[43]

CHAPTER THIRTY-ONE

Atlanta

Rumors on the night of July 21 had it that the Rebels would evacuate Atlanta. Around 3:00 a.m., July 22, the Army of the Tennessee's skirmishers, probing forward through the darkness, encountered only token resistance and in some cases none at all. Cpl. Charles Wright was among those who found no Confederate skirmishers to dispute his progress. "We would advance a few steps, then stop and listen, expecting every moment to be fired on," Wright recalled. "Finally we came to the works and hesitatingly mounted them and looked down into the trenches—not a Confederate to be seen, all gone!" Skirmishers exchanged nods, as if they had expected something of the sort. "Now we are going into Atlanta," said some of them.[1] In Blair's front, the Confederates had left behind an almost completed set of earthworks about 1,000 yards west of those that Blair's men had dug that night. In Logan's front, the abandoned breastworks were a continuation of the same line Leggett had stormed the day before in attacking the Bald Hill.

About 4:00 a.m., Col. Willard Warner of Sherman's staff arrived at McPherson's headquarters with a verbal order from Sherman, who believed the Rebels' absence from their breastworks was confirmation that Hood was indeed abandoning Atlanta. If so, he should be pursued, and Sherman dispatched orders to each of his army commanders for that purpose. Warner brought instructions for the Army of the Tennessee to move at once, "passing to the south and east of Atlanta, without entering the town," and try to cut off as many of the enemy as possible. Meanwhile, the Army of the Cumberland would move around the west side of Atlanta, and the Army of the Ohio straight through the city.[2]

At 6:00 a.m., McPherson issued to his corps commanders written orders for a pursuit. "The enemy having evacuated their works in front of our lines," he wrote in preface to the order, "the supposition of Major-General Sherman is that they have given up Atlanta and are retreating." McPherson and Blair rode out to Leggett's position at around sunrise. The two generals and their staffs continued "well out in front without drawing the enemy's fire," Leggett recalled, noting that "both seemed to believe that the enemy had evacuated." Since neither Leggett nor his officers shared that view, McPherson's and Blair's actions made them intensely nervous. Finally, Leggett and his staff "succeeded in detaining" the generals until the skirmish line advanced and drew enough fire to indicate a significant continued Rebel presence between them and Atlanta.[3]

If necessary, the generals could soon satisfy themselves of this by the evidence of their own eyes. From the high vantage point of the Bald Hill, they had a clear view of Atlanta, about three-quarters of a mile away. The light of the newly risen sun revealed Confederates in significant numbers behind the inner ring of fortifications around Atlanta. Clearly, Hood had not abandoned Atlanta after all, and McPherson countermanded his pursuit orders to the corps commanders, who had not had time to act on them anyway. To the commander of the Army of the Tennessee this was the confirmation that his old West Point roommate meant to fight for Atlanta. To his staff, he said several times that morning that "we were likely to have during that day the severest battle of the campaign."[4]

In the new state of affairs, McPherson directed Blair and Logan to send out pioneer detachments with spades and shovels to "reverse" the works, changing the shape of their cross section so as to make them useful for defending against attacks from the direction of Atlanta. As soon as the new works were ready, the Seventeenth Corps should move forward and occupy them. Logan wasted no time with preliminaries or advance parties of pioneers. He had the Fifteenth advance immediately into the abandoned Rebel works, bringing his corps back into line with the Seventeenth, which since Leggett's successful assault of the previous morning had been about 400 yards to the west of Logan's line. Logan had his men immediately begin reversing the Rebel breastworks.[5]

Capt. Jacob Ritner, like officers throughout the Fifteenth Corps, had to supervise his men in transforming the earthworks. The new task kept him from getting back to a letter to his wife, Emeline, that he had been writing before the order to advance had interrupted him. "I don't think there will be much fighting here anymore," he had written, "and we will have the town in a day or two." This new uncontested advance seemed to bear that out, even if it did mean more work.[6]

If Seventeenth Corps officers like Leggett and Giles Smith tended to expect a Confederate attack, a number of officers in the Fifteenth were of a contrary opinion and seemed unconcerned about defensive arrangements. Among those were Morgan Smith. The point where the Georgia Railroad passed through the Union line on its way from Atlanta to Decatur fell in the sector of Lightburn's brigade of Smith's division. Because the Union position was on a ridge, the railroad there was in a cut about fifteen feet deep, with thick brush growing along it and in a ravine to the left of it, about twenty yards from the breastworks. Nearby was a white frame house and several outbuildings. Col. Wells S. Jones of the 53rd Ohio requested permission to burn the buildings, since they obstructed his men's field of fire. He also suggested that they ought to barricade the railroad cut, to prevent Rebel attackers from using it as a covered approach. To both these requests, Lightburn responded with a peremptory refusal, in which he was supported by Smith, who had climbed a tree that morning to observe the dust cloud kicked up by large columns of Confederate troops moving off to the south.

Maj. Charles Hipp commanded the 37th Ohio, which was about 200 yards north of the railroad and directly in front of an unfinished two-and-a-half-story brick house, belonging to a man named Troup Hurt, where Morgan Smith had his headquarters. Hipp made the same suggestion directly to the division commander, but Smith refused, explaining that it would be a waste of time because they "would take dinner in Atlanta" that day. Maj. Thomas Taylor of the 47th Ohio, also part of Lightburn's brigade, was divisional picket officer that morning. He requested shovels so that the skirmishers could dig in. These too were refused, apparently by order of division headquarters. Taylor believed that the reason was that all the higher officers still expected the Rebels to evacuate Atlanta.[7]

About eight o'clock, McPherson rode over to Dodge's headquarters and directed him to send Sweeny's division of the Sixteenth Corps from its position on the right of the Fifteenth southward to a new position on the left of the Seventeenth.[8] McPherson notified Sherman of this but shortly thereafter received a note from him: "Instead of sending Dodge to your left, I wish you would put his whole corps at work destroying absolutely the railroad back to and including Decatur. I want that road absolutely and completely destroyed; every tie burned and every rail twisted." Sherman went on to explain that as soon as Garrard's cavalry got back from their raid to the east, he planned to send the Army of the Tennessee around to the extreme right to try to get at Hood's communications in that direction.[9]

To McPherson this seemed all wrong. He kept telling his staff that he believed the enemy was going to attack him that day, probably on his left front—the Seventeenth Corps—and he wanted the Sixteenth covering the Seventeenth's southern flank. The matter was serious enough that McPherson decided to ride over to Sherman's headquarters with several of his staff for a conference with the commander of the Military Division of the Mississippi. He reached Sherman's headquarters, which were behind Schofield's command, at around eleven o'clock. He and Sherman were convivial as always and then got down to business. McPherson explained that he thought it unwise to remove Dodge from the army's left until later in the day. Sherman readily acquiesced and said that the time for the execution of the order would be up to McPherson's discretion. He could wait and detach Dodge's command whenever he thought it was safe. McPherson in turn allowed that if the enemy was going to attack that day, it would probably be before 1:00 p.m. If no attack came by that hour, McPherson would go ahead and send the Sixteenth Corps to its railroad wrecking duties.[10]

After his meeting with Sherman, McPherson and his staff rode along the line of the Army of the Tennessee. Riding due south, they passed Woods's division of the Fifteenth Corps, then Morgan Smith's with De Gress's fearsome 20-pounder Parrotts, and continued on to Harrow's division. The pioneers and regular fatigue details were still working hard under the sweltering sun, turning the Rebels' works to face Atlanta. McPherson rode fast, but he stopped frequently to converse with division and brigade commanders as well as to greet common soldiers. He had a pleasant smile for the men of the 20th Ohio as they sat laughing and joking and eating their stewed green apples with hardtack just behind their lines on the south slope of the Bald Hill. Just south of the hill, where the left flank of Leggett's division joined the right of Giles Smith's, the line angled to the southeast. At that point, it also left the open fields and continued through the woods. At the far southern end of the Seventeenth Corps's lines, McPherson reached Col. William Hall's Old Iowa Brigade, which held a curving position that faced mostly south. He complimented Lt. Col. Addison Sanders of the 16th Iowa on his regiment's excellent performance in support of the previous morning's assault on the Bald Hill, in which the 16th had lost sixty-five men. "The old Sixteenth shall be remembered," McPherson promised before he rode off. From the Iowa Brigade, McPherson followed a woodland track that led half or three-quarters of a mile east to the camp of Fuller's one-brigade division of the Sixteenth Corps.[11]

Satisfied with the state of his army, McPherson turned back to the north and met Logan, Blair, and several of the division commanders and their staffs a few minutes before noon, just south of the railroad. The lines were quiet, and the generals and their staffs sat down in the shade of a grove of oaks about three-quarters of a mile behind the line of Morgan Smith's division for a leisurely noon meal. After lunch, the officers sat chatting in the dappled shade of the oaks, several of them puffing on cigars. Along the lines of the Army of the Tennessee, all continued as peaceful and still as a noon break from work in the grain fields back up in Illinois or Ohio. The prolonged silence was quite a luxury in this campaign of almost constant skirmishing.

Others too were enjoying a peaceful noontide. Near the southern end of the army's line, Lt. Richard Tuthill of Battery H, 1st Michigan Light Artillery, finished his meal of bean soup, hardtack, and coffee, then opened his valise, took out paper, ink, and pen, and started writing a letter.[12] A short distance to the north, Capt. E. E. Nutt of the 20th Ohio sat down on a log to read a book.[13]

Back in the oak grove near the railroad, McPherson decided to begin implementation of his promise to Sherman to send Dodge's men to work on the railroad. It was not one o'clock yet, but this was already shaping up to be the sort of drowsy afternoon in which nothing ever happened. Securing a pencil and some paper, McPherson scribbled an order to Grenville Dodge, dating it twelve noon. Since Sweeney's division had just arrived at the south end of the line, McPherson directed Dodge to let it stay there for the rest of the day. Fuller's division, however—the single brigade that was present at the front—was to start at once, and march to the line of the railroad west of Decatur. Finishing the note, McPherson handed it to a staff officer, who rode off southward toward the position of the Sixteenth Corps on the far left flank.[14]

About a mile or so to the south of the grove of oaks, Dodge was at the headquarters of Fuller's division, where he had arrived with Sweeny's division a few minutes before noon. Fuller's troops were in their camps behind the Seventeenth Corps. Sweeny's were resting alongside the road on which they had just been marching. Dodge informed Fuller of McPherson's order for the Sixteenth to move up and form the extreme left of the army as soon as Blair's pioneer details finished turning the Confederate works and the Seventeenth moved forward to occupy them. Since that would not take place before nightfall, the troops should encamp, entrench, and prepare to stay where they were until that time. While Dodge and Fuller were talking, Lt. Seth Laird reported his 14th Ohio Battery present, having just arrived from the other end of the army. Fuller told him he could park his guns on a small rise near the camp. Laird wanted to know if he would have time to unhitch and water his horses in a nearby brook.[15]

"Oh, yes," replied Fuller airily. "We may stay here half the afternoon."

Fuller's mess attendant announced dinner, and Dodge sat down with Fuller and his staff to a noon repast. As they were eating, several rifle shots sounded somewhere to the east of them, the opposite direction from the enemy's supposed location in the Atlanta fortifications. The officers dropped their knives and forks and listened. More shots came in quick succession, louder, closer, and more numerous. The skirmishers on the left rear were apparently having a very hot time of it. "There must be some Rebel cavalry raiding in our rear," Dodge observed. "You had better post one of your regiments so as to cover our trains."

A large segment of the Army of the Tennessee's wagon train was parked in rear of McPherson's headquarters on the south side of the railroad. If Rebel cavalry were in the army's rear, those wagons were vulnerable, and the Sixteenth Corps represented the closest Union force. Fuller quickly dispatched a staff officer hurrying into the woods, where Col. John Morrill's brigade of his division was camped, with orders to bring up a regiment. Dodge hastily mounted up and rode back toward where Sweeny's division was halted. The sound of the firing swelled dramatically and was soon mixed with the boom of artillery. That was enough for Fuller; he sent another staff officer with orders to turn out the whole brigade.[16]

Along the lines of the Seventeenth Corps, Captain Nutt closed his book and jumped up from the log. Lieutenant Tuthill laid down his pen. Orders were to return any artillery firing from the Confederate batteries on the Atlanta lines, and suddenly it seemed the Confederates had opened up with every gun they had. Leaving his letter, Tuthill rushed off to get his section of the battery into action. Along the lines nearby, infantry officers were shouting, "Fall in! Fall in!" as the soldiers scrambled for the breastworks.[17]

Back in the oak grove near the railroad, McPherson and the other lounging officers sprang to their feet at the first sound of gunfire from the southeast, every officer shouting for his orderly to bring his horse at once. Before the orderlies could obey, incoming shells were tearing through the treetops. Logan and Blair rode off to see to their lines, and McPherson set out for the Sixteenth Corps and the sound of what one staff officer described as "rattling volleys of small arms."[18]

The skirmishers whose rifle fire had first startled the generals were Sweeny's men as well as a single regiment of Leggett's division of the Seventeenth Corps, far from its parent unit. Sweeney had sent out skirmishers after scouts had informed him of the possible presence of Rebels in the woods to the south and east. Blair had received a report that Rebels, apparently cavalry raiders, were menacing his field hospital, in the army's rear, and had Leggett detach the 68th Ohio to provide security. The Buckeye regiment reached its assigned position and discovered not Confederate cavalry but rather a long, solid, advancing line of gray-clad infantry. The Ohioans fired a volley and slowly fell back, keeping up a steady fire. The swelling volume of gunfire coming from the 68th Ohio and the scattering shots from Sweeny's skirmishers was all the proof Dodge, Sweeny, and Fuller needed that what was out there was not a small band of cavalry raiders but rather a major formation of Confederate infantry—and it was moving toward them. The steadily approaching clatter of gunfire in the woods indicated plainly that the Rebels were driving in Sweeny's skirmishers. With only moments left to prepare, Dodge ordered Sweeny's division into line of battle right where it was along the road.[19]

Corporal Wright and his comrades in Sweeney's division had been resting on their knapsacks, munching hardtack or dozing in the hot sun. So inured to the sound of gunfire had they become that many of them gave little heed to the skirmish fire. It was the higher-ranking officers, for the most part, who knew that no firing should have been occurring in that direction. Wright and the men near him were aroused from their torpor by Capt. William C. Henry. "Men, get up and prepare for immediate action!" shouted Henry. Startled, the soldiers jumped up and looked around, as their comrades in the other regiments were doing. They had half-expected to see a Confederate line of battle bearing down on them at a range of fifty yards with bayonets fixed, but no Rebels were in sight. "Who the deuce are we going to fight?" quipped one of Sweeny's soldiers.[20] Another heard the firing and made the same surmise Dodge had done: "That's Wheeler after our hardtack."[21]

The officers were too busy to answer questions as they barked orders to get their troops into position to receive the coming attack. Col. August Mersy's brigade was at the head of Sweeny's column. Dodge directed it to turn right, westward, into the open field and continue for the length of the brigade, about 300 yards, before halting and facing left in line of battle, looking south. Then he had the brigade advance across the field until it reached the knoll where Laird had parked the guns of the 14th Ohio Battery.

Col. Elliott Rice's brigade, which had been behind Mersy's, continued marching by the right flank with the head of its column near Mersy's left flank. When the latter halted, Rice faced his brigade left into line of battle, looking eastward. Mersy's and Rice's brigades thus made a right angle at the knoll where the guns of the 14th Ohio were posted. Fuller's order to park the guns there was providential. It proved an ideal position, giving Laird's six three-inch ordnance rifles an excellent field of fire across the front of either Mersy's or Rice's brigades. With the battery's horses back at the brook for watering, Laird could never have moved the guns in time to meet the Confederate onslaught.[22]

While Sweeny's division took up its position, Fuller hurried Morrill's brigade into place on its right, continuing Mersy's line in that direction, facing south. The Sixteenth Corps thus formed a large L, with two brigades facing south and one facing east. No time remained for digging entrenchments or making breastworks, but Wright took a moment to look at his surroundings. To his right, he could see Morrill's brigade hurrying into line beyond the flank of his own. Beyond them, he thought he could glimpse through the woods the extreme right end of the breastworks of the Seventeenth Corps, variously estimated to be from a quarter-mile to a little more than a mile away. The works were there, manned by the Old Iowa Brigade, but Wright was probably mistaken in thinking that this was what he had seen through the underbrush. Across the open ground to his right rear, the army's supply wagons were beginning to move north, toward the railroad and away from the threatened left flank. Looking to either side, he observed his comrades standing at order-arms, gazing calmly at the woods about 300 yards away, one of them munching a hardtack cracker. Some of the men reflected on the bitter irony that after having dug dozens of trenches during the campaign, they were now apparently about to fight their biggest battle in the open with no time for digging.[23]

Moments later the Union skirmishers fell back out of the woods and quickly moved by the flank to clear the front and allow their comrades to open fire. Behind them Rebel banners and then battle lines appeared along the edge of the woods both to the south and east and then marched out into the open field, while Confederate artillery on high ground fired over the heads of the attackers into the lines of the Sixteenth Corps. To Dodge it seemed that the Rebels were assaulting in three separate columns, one from the east on Rice's brigade, another from the south on Mersy and Morrill, and a third surging into the woods to the west of the Sixteenth Corps, between it and Blair's Seventeenth.[24]

Laird opened up as soon as his gunners could see their targets, sending shells into the Rebel ranks with deadly effectiveness. About 100 yards north of Laird's position, Lt. A. T. Blodgett's Battery H, 1st Missouri Light Artillery, hammered away. Battery H would fire some 600 rounds during the course of the afternoon, and Laird's Ohioans were matching it blast for blast. A Union staff officer watching the scene recalled how the two batteries "mowed great swaths in the advancing columns." Still the Confederates kept coming.[25]

Dodge's infantry waited and held their fire. "Captain, they're close enough now," said a soldier in the 81st Ohio.

"Don't fire yet, boys," came the reply.

"Captain, they're close enough; I can hit 'em every time."

Finally the order came, and Dodge's men poured a volley into the faces of the advancing Confederates. The attacking line faltered as scores of graycoats went down, but their surviving comrades rallied and came on, officers conspicuously urging their men forward. "It was a square face-to-face grapple in open field, neither line advancing or retreating," wrote Col. Robert Adams of the 81st Ohio. "The rattle of musketry and the booming of cannon on both sides were indescribable; the air was full of flying missiles and the dense smoke furnished the only protection."[26] Years later, Maj. W. H. Chamberlin wrote, "I remember yet how the sight of our banners advancing amid the smoke thrilled me as it gave them a new beauty."[27]

A Rebel color-bearer found cover in a shallow ravine and advanced to within a few dozen yards of Laird's battery. Emerging from the ravine, he dived to the ground, holding the flagstaff erect in front of him with the flag waving as a rallying point for his comrades. So close was he to the guns that every time they fired, the muzzle blast caused his banner to billow out. Elsewhere along the lines, Iowan John McKee could see another Rebel flag emerging from the drifting clouds of powder smoke. "Their colors fell repeatedly," McKee recorded in his diary, "and finally I saw one stand fall and no one picked them up and then the whole line faltered and fell back in confusion." Parts of the Confederate attacking force broke and fell back to the woods, only to rally and advance again.[28]

As the battle continued in front of his lines, Dodge noticed that the formation attacking Morrill's brigade had veered too far west and exposed its flank to counterattack by Mersy. Dodge ordered Mersy's right and center regiments, the 12th Illinois and the 81st Ohio, to charge, and the two old regiments of Shiloh veterans rolled up the attacking formation and swept it away, taking 466 prisoners as well as two Rebel flags. Morrill's brigade also charged, and the advance continued all the way to the edge of the woods.[29]

There they took heavy fire in flank and rear from Confederates in the woods to the west. Fuller pivoted the brigade on its left flank, swinging back the right end of the line to face its tormentors in the woods. It was a complicated maneuver carried out under the most trying of circumstances. The 27th Ohio, on the right of Morrill's line, had to make the movement at almost a dead run in order to keep the line straight. Doing so, the regiment fell into confusion and appeared ready to fall back.

Fuller knew he could not make himself heard over the din of battle, so he led the 27th's color-bearer forward to the position he wanted the regiment to take and then gestured vigorously with his sword to show them the line he wanted to form. Relieved to know what they should do, the men of the 27th raised a great shout and swarmed into position along the line Fuller was indicating. He then had the brigade's first line, the 27th and 39th Ohio, fix bayonets and charge westward toward the enemy in the woods, now scarcely 100 yards away.

The Rebels broke and ran, but again Fuller found more of the enemy on his right flank. He had Morrill's second line, the 64th Illinois and the 18th Missouri, wheel to the right and attack them. The 64th Illinois—the Yates Sharpshooters—were another of the army's growing number of Henry-equipped regiments, its members having purchased the sixteen-shot Henry repeating rifles at their own expense—$41 per rifle on a monthly wage of $13—during the preceding several months. The extra firepower proved to be worth every cent they had paid. The Confederates tried to make a stand along a rail fence, but the Illinoisans and Missourians crushed them so completely that, after the fight, burial parties found as many as thirteen dead Rebels in a single fence corner.[30]

With Fuller's successful action in the woods that lay between the Sixteenth and Seventeenth corps, the first phase of the Battle of Atlanta came to an end. It had lasted about an hour.[31] Thanks in part to McPherson's foresight, the Sixteenth had been in exactly the right place at the right time to ward off the opening blow of Hood's ambitious offensive. Dodge's three brigades had just repulsed the six brigades of Maj. Gen. William H. T. Walker's and Maj. Gen. William B. Bate's divisions. Walker himself was among the slain, and the two divisions would be good for little more than skirmishing the rest of the day. Frank Blair had been on hand to watch a good bit of the fight. He was not a devout man, but he commented, "The Lord put Dodge in the right place today."[32]

That was not at all the way Hood had planned his attack to open. After nightfall on July 21, he had pulled Lt. Gen. William J. Hardee's corps, including the divisions of Bate and Walker, out of the lines facing the Army of the Tennessee and had sent them on a long roundabout march to attack the rear of that army. Had the Sixteenth Corps been busy tearing up the railroad as Sherman had intended, Bate and Walker would have gobbled up the portion of the wagon train present with the army and then taken the Seventeenth squarely in rear, while, as per Hood's plan, the troops of Maj. Gen. Benjamin F. Cheatham's corps attacked it and the Fifteenth head-on. If all went according to plan, the Army of the Tennessee, assailed front, flank, and rear, would collapse, with vast numbers of its personnel killed and wounded, many times more captured, and the rest scattered in headlong flight not likely to stop this side of the Chattahoochee. With the bold stand of the Sixteenth, Hood's plan was not off to a good start.

McPherson had arrived on Dodge's front within minutes of the first shots, having ordered the movement of the wagon train that Wright had observed just before the Rebel charge. From a knoll behind Morrill's brigade, McPherson had watched with satisfaction as the Sixteenth Corps hammered the Rebels back into the woods. It was the ultimate validation of his concerns during the last two days and of his appeal to Sherman to allow the Sixteenth to remain on his left flank. It was also proof positive that McPherson was not mistaken about the personality and likely actions of his old West Point roommate. That was still the same old "Sam" Hood across the way there in Atlanta, as daring and aggressive as ever.[33]

As soon as Fuller had finished off the last of the attackers and cleared the Rebels out of the woods toward the Seventeenth Corps, McPherson dispatched staff officer William E. Strong to ride over to the Seventeenth and check on the condition of affairs there. He instructed Strong to tell Giles Smith to hold his position and McPherson would order up troops to fill the gap between the Sixteenth and the Seventeenth. The staffer found Blair and Smith together near the extreme left flank of the Seventeenth, where Hall's Old Iowa Brigade held its curved, mostly southward-facing position. The generals informed him that Confederate columns had been spotted moving out of Atlanta and in a general direction that might well bring them onto the left flank of the Seventeenth or the sensitive half-mile gap between its flank and the Sixteenth.

With this information, Strong galloped back to rejoin McPherson on the knoll near the right of Dodge's lines. McPherson at once determined to ride across the gap and view the situation for himself. Accompanied by Strong and an orderly, he set out riding west along the woodland track he had traveled coming the other direction in his ride around the lines shortly before noon, and which Strong had just now crossed both coming and going. It ran more or less along a continuation of the line Mersy's and Morrill's brigades were holding and emerged near Hall's brigade of the Seventeenth Corps.[34]

Just as they were starting out, Lt. William Sherfy of the Signal Corps rode up to McPherson and warned him that the extended skirmish line of the Seventeenth Corps, covering the gap, was beginning to engage Confederate skirmishers in the woods to the south. Rebels might begin to infest the woods along the forest track at any time. Undeterred, and more eager than ever to find a solution for the problem, McPherson hurried on. Sherfy followed, as did several other signal officers of the Army of the Tennessee staff, though they apparently started later and were strung out for quite a distance behind McPherson, Strong, and the orderly.[35]

Also galloping along the woodland track in McPherson's wake was Col. R. K. Scott, who commanded a brigade in Leggett's division. One of his regiments, the 68th Ohio, was on detached duty guarding the Seventeenth Corps hospital in the rear. Scott heard a report that they were engaged and had ridden back to check on them. Hearing the sound of firing along the front of the army, Scott decided he had better get back to his brigade. The route he chose led along the same road that McPherson, Strong, and the orderly were riding some distance ahead.[36]

As they rode, the general explained to Strong that Logan had a brigade in reserve, Col. Hugo Wangelin's of Woods's division, and McPherson planned to use it to plug this gap. About halfway across the gap, McPherson pulled up and looked around. He guided his horse off the road and through the woods and underbrush on the south side of it to a ridge that paralleled the road a few yards to the south. After riding along the ridge for some distance, carefully surveying the ground, he turned his horse back to the road. This rise would be just the place to post Wangelin's brigade, he explained to Strong. Then he told the staff officer to ride to Logan immediately with orders to send Wangelin at once. Strong was then to stay with the brigade, guide it right to this spot, and direct its deployment. After that, Strong could join him at Giles Smith's position. The staffer turned back to the east while McPherson, accompanied by his orderly, put his horse to the gallop in the other direction, toward the lines of the Seventeenth Corps.[37]

McPherson and his orderly, cavalry trooper A. J. Thompson, rode perhaps 100 or 150 yards. Strong, now going rapidly away from them, was out of sight to the rear, and Sherfy had just gained sight of McPherson and Thompson from behind and was riding hard to catch up with them. Following behind Sherfy were Scott and several other officers. Suddenly a Confederate line of battle appeared out of the thick brush on the south, or left, side of the trail a few yards ahead of McPherson. Several of the Rebels shouted, "Halt! Stop there! Halt!"

McPherson was already wheeling his horse to the right as he tipped his hat to the Rebels "as politely as if he was saluting a lady," one of them recalled, then horse and general plunged into the woods on the north side of the road. Thompson was right behind him, clinging low to the neck of his horse to dodge the bullets that were sure to follow them. The Rebel volley crashed out a second or two later. Thompson felt several bullets pass close along the back of his neck, and then he saw McPherson topple from the saddle in front of him. Just as McPherson fell, his horse passed through a narrow gap between two small trees, and when Thompson's horse followed, the orderly, hanging almost on the side of the beast, was knocked out cold against one of the trees.[38]

Sherfy, a few yards farther back down the trail, saw the whole scene and was trying to make his own escape into the woods when he slammed into a tree and fell unconscious. The impact with the tree also smashed his watch, which stopped at 2:02 p.m. Almost simultaneously a bullet felled Scott's horse, and the colonel took a nasty spill that left him shaken and slightly injured. Capt. Ocran Howard, the Army of the Tennessee's chief signal officer, along with several others, was far enough back on the trail to see the smoke of the volley but not its result. They turned and fled back up the trail and so escaped.[39]

Sherfy recovered his wits in time to make off into the underbrush on the north side of the road. Thompson came to and crawled to where McPherson was lying. "General, are you hurt?" gasped Thompson.

"Oh, orderly, I am," McPherson replied. The general was lying on his right side with his right hand clasped to his chest and blood spurting between his fingers. There was little Thompson could do, and at that moment the Rebels swarmed over them, jerking the orderly to his feet and sending him to the rear, a prisoner. Nearby, Scott sat with tears in his eyes. A Confederate captain pointed to McPherson and asked Scott, "Who is this man lying here?"

"Sir, it is General McPherson," Scott replied. "You have killed the best man in our army."[40]

McPherson asked the Rebels for water, which they gave him. He asked for his hat, which one of the Rebel officers decided to keep. Then relieving the general of his sword belt, pocketbook, watch, field glasses, and some papers, they went their way. A few minutes later, George Reynolds, a wounded member of Hall's Iowa Brigade making his way to a field hospital, found McPherson lying alone in the woods. The general was still breathing but could not speak. Reynolds, whose left elbow was smashed, uncorked his canteen, gave the general a drink, carefully placed his own blanket under McPherson's head, and stayed with him until he expired.[41]

News of McPherson's death spread rapidly through the Army of the Tennessee. It struck deep sadness into the hearts of his soldiers. "We men in the ranks had learned to love and admire the smiling and courteous general," recalled Charles Wright.[42] The news of their loss also fired the men with a fierce desire to avenge his death, and that was just as well, for they had much more fighting to do. On this day, they would have need to bear in mind their late commander's order to the army at the commencement of the campaign: "Stand firmly by your posts," McPherson had told them back in May. "Let not the storm of battle nor the vigorous onsets of the enemy shake your faith in the righteousness of our cause, and the conviction of our ultimate success. Remember that notwithstanding the contest may be severe, strong arms and brave hearts are nearby to support you, and that the successful issue of the battle may depend on your individual bravery, and the stubbornness with which you hold your position."[43]

As a further boost to the army's morale in the wake of the loss of its beloved leader, word arrived simultaneously that command of the army had devolved on John A. "Black Jack" Logan. In a tight spot like this one, there was no other general soldiers would rather have followed than Logan. Several times during the battle, he rode the lines of the Fifteenth and Seventeenth corps on his impressive black warhorse, Slasher, hat and reins in his left hand, sword in his right, shouting, "Boys, avenge your fallen chief!" and "McPherson and revenge!" The men met him with frenzied cheers, and, as one of them recalled, "This seemed to inspire the army with renewed energy and courage." After the battle, an officer wrote that "the sight of him upon the battlefield was as good as a full brigade of fresh troops." Observers were often at a loss to explain the electric effect Logan's presence produced on soldiers in battle. Lt. Richard Tuthill tried: "He was one of those rare men who are natural leaders," Tuthill wrote, "under whom soldiers love to fight, having confidence in their valor and their ability to accomplish the thing undertaken." If an artist were ever to try to paint a picture of "the spirit of victorious war," Tuthill thought, he could do no better than render a portrait of Logan that day as he galloped along the lines of the Army of the Tennessee.[44]

His men were going to need all the inspiration they could get, for the key phases of the climactic battle for Atlanta still lay ahead of them. The Confederates who killed McPherson belonged to Cleburne's division. After its tough fight with the Seventeenth Corps on July 21, the division was among the Confederate forces that had pulled out of line and made the long roundabout march to hit the Army of the Tennessee in the flank and rear. Advancing alongside it and just to the west was Brig. Gen. George Maney's division, which formed the left of Hardee's corps. By the time Cleburne and Maney struck the Union defenders, Walker and Bate had already suffered defeat, but Cleburne's and Maney's troops were headed directly toward the flank of the Seventeenth Corps, Maney toward its flank and front and Cleburne toward its flank and rear.

Guarding that flank was Hall's Old Iowa Brigade.[45] The Iowans got their first warning of the Confederate approach several minutes before the first shots sounded to their left and rear. Two members of the 11th Iowa who had been foraging came rushing into camp to report that while they were up in an apple tree about a quarter mile south of the brigade's position, they had heard Confederate officers giving orders. Hall got his men into the trenches and posted extra skirmishers 200 yards to the front before action started in his sector. They did their job well, giving ample warning of the enemy's approach through the dense underbrush.

The pickets scrambled out of the bushes and jumped into the trenches. Not far behind came the Confederates. Simultaneously, Rebel artillery, firing over the heads of the attackers, pounded the lines of the Seventeenth Corps. Giles Smith had received McPherson's message through Lieutenant Colonel Strong to hold his position and expect support on his left rear. He passed the word to Hall and ordered him to stand fast. The Confederates struck hard, overlapping both of the brigade's flanks but pouring especially heavy fire into the left flank.[46]

The Iowans stood their ground. Lt. Col. Addison Sanders of the 16th had his men hold their fire until the attacking line entered the fifty-yard-deep cleared space in front of the regiment's trenches. Then on Sanders's order the regiment blasted a deadly volley into the faces of the attackers, stopping the advance in its tracks for the moment. Minutes later the Rebels rallied and came on again. The Iowans loaded and fired their rifles as rapidly as experienced soldiers could do in a desperate situation, until the barrels became so hot they were difficult to handle and the powder sometimes flashed when poured into the muzzle. Officers stood behind the firing line, tearing off the tops of the paper cartridges and handing the open cartridges to the men to speed the loading process.

Nearby, the two 12-pounder Napoleon guns of Lt. W. H. Powell's section of Battery F, 2nd Illinois Light Artillery, blasted canister into the charging Rebels. A large number of the enemy, mostly Arkansans with a few Texans, found themselves pinned down in front of the Iowans' breastworks, unable to advance or retreat. Some of these began to wave white handkerchiefs in token of surrender. Sanders ordered his men to cease firing long enough for the surrendering Rebels to come in, and the regiment soon found itself with double its own number of prisoners.[47]

Realizing that the assault would be more than Hall's Iowans could handle alone, Smith ordered Col. Benjamin F. Potts, commanding the division's other brigade, to send two regiments to bolster the Iowans' left flank, where it appeared that a powerful Confederate formation was already reaching the rear of the Seventeenth Corps. Smith did not realize that of Potts's two reserve regiments, most of one was serving on the corps's extended left-flank picket line. That left just the 3rd Iowa to try to stem the tide that was flowing around the left of Hall's brigade, and the Hawkeyes quickly discovered that it was already too late, as they collided against a large body of Confederate troops that had passed around Hall's left. The

3rd charged boldly into the Rebels, taking thirty prisoners at their first onset. After standing their ground for a few minutes more, however, they found the enemy sweeping around their left and had to fall back to rejoin the rest of their brigade at the breastworks.[48]

As the threat to the rear of his division became more serious, Smith ordered Hall to march his brigade by the right flank in order to escape what was rapidly becoming a complete envelopment and then move around the front (west) side of the division's breastworks to join the rest of the division farther north. Many soldiers of the 11th Iowa still had had no sight of the enemy through the thick underbrush in front of them but had been firing on orders to the left oblique in support of the 16th. It was a shock to them when the regimental adjutant came along the line passing the word, "March out by the right flank; the enemy are in the rear." For the 16th Iowa and several companies of the 13th, as well as Powell's section of Battery F, 2nd Illinois Light Artillery, the order came too late.

In fact, they never received the order. Realization that they were surrounded came in different ways. Sanders knew something was up when the men he detailed to take prisoners to the rear informed him that the trenches of the 13th, immediately behind their own, were occupied by the enemy. A sergeant of the 13th was with a part of that regiment assigned to the front line alongside the 16th. When his men ran low on ammunition, he dashed back to get a fresh supply. Jumping into his regiment's trenches in rear of the position where his men were fighting, he found himself in the midst of a crowd of Rebels, who promptly made him a prisoner. In all, some 230 men surrendered, along with two cannon. The rest of the Iowa Brigade escaped in fairly good order.[49]

At the same time that Smith told the Iowa Brigade to get out if it could, he also ordered Potts's and the rest of Hall's brigades to climb over the works to the west side, turn their backs to Atlanta, and face back over the parapet of their own breastworks. Here it came in handy that the works had been constructed without a deep ditch in front. Instead, as a simple log-and-earth breastwork, it was about as useful from one side as from the other.[50]

That feature of the breastworks was already proving a valuable asset to the men of Leggett's division, just north of Giles Smith's sector. While the Iowa Brigade was extricating itself and falling back to join Potts's brigade on the west side of the works, the Texans who had flanked them on the east swept past Smith's division and aimed straight for the Bald Hill, approaching Leggett's lines from the rear. On the summit of the hill, Colonel Bryant of the 12th Wisconsin was shouting for his men to get into the breastworks. "Which side, Colonel, which side?" called one of his soldiers.

"I don't care which side," roared Bryant, "but get into the works! And do it quick!"[51]

As the troops on the hill began to take fire from the rear, someone suggested that maybe the Union troops back there thought the hill had fallen to the Confederates and were now firing on it. General Force decided to rule out that possibility and barked out an order to bring him "a flag." A frightened young subaltern, thinking the presence of the enemy in their rear was cause to surrender, began running around, looking for a handkerchief or some other piece of white cloth. When Force noticed him, he let out an oath. "I don't want a flag of truce," he thundered, "I want the American flag!" Shortly he got one and planted it prominently on the works at the peak of the hill. With that settled, his men and the rest of the division quickly took to the west side of the works, "their faces to the east and their backs toward Atlanta," as Leggett reported, and there prepared to receive the attackers.[52]

On came the Texans "with demoniac yells" amid thick clouds of powder smoke that made a dense fog even under the July sun. The "unearthly yell," noted Tuthill, "could be heard above the sound of the muskets and cannon." Leggett's men stood on the west side of their breastworks and delivered "a cool, deliberate, and well-aimed fire" that halted the first onrush. The Texans rallied and made a second attempt, but again Leggett's men drove them back, leaving the ground covered with Confederate dead and wounded.

"For vindictive desperation," Leggett later wrote, "this encounter was probably never exceeded." There was special irony in the fact that the Confederates were charging over the same ground on which Leggett's men had attacked the day before when they successfully took the hill. One of the first to fall in the lines of Leggett's division was Force, struck by a bullet that entered below his left eye and exited near his right ear. Amazingly, he survived and returned to duty four months later. For now, his absence was a severe loss to his brigade, for he was a capable officer and his men had confidence in him. Bryant of the 12th Wisconsin had to step in and lead the brigade in its fight to hang on to the Bald Hill.[53]

Some of Cleburne's attackers went as far north as the left flank of the Fifteenth Corps, just beyond Leggett's division. The two brigades on the left of the Fifteenth, those of Colonels Charles C. Walcutt and John M. Oliver, pivoted to face toward the left rear, directly at the oncoming Rebels. Walcutt brought up two 24-pounder howitzers to add their firepower to that of his infantrymen. The result was devastating for the attackers. Walcutt reported that the cross fire from his brigade and Leggett's division "slaughtered the rebels by the hundreds." Both Walcutt's and Oliver's brigades then charged and captured a large number of Rebels. Among the prisoners was almost the entire strength of the 5th Confederate Infantry Regiment. On the persons of some of the prisoners, Walcutt's troops found McPherson's hat, field glasses, and some memoranda and dispatches.[54]

Just as Leggett's men were doing farther north, so in Giles Smith's sector Potts's brigade took to the Atlanta side of its breastworks and faced east. From that position Potts beat off a Confederate advance from that direction. A brief lull followed, and Smith deployed skirmishers who sent back word that the enemy was still not far off, but showed no disposition to renew the attack right away.[55]

That was a good break for Smith's men, because another Confederate formation presently appeared approaching from the south, straight toward the right flank of the new line. The 13th and 15th Iowa swung their line back to face the new attackers, but they were hopelessly outnumbered, flanked on the right, and driven back, as Hall had to admit, "in some confusion." However, because the divisional skirmish line was providing at least some security against the Confederates to the east, Hall's Iowans were able to jump back over to the original side of their works and shoot west again, firing into the Confederates who had just driven them from their south-facing position.[56]

By this time, Potts's brigade had also swung to face south and were lying down in the cornfield, ready to meet the Confederate onslaught head-on. As they waited among the corn rows, unable to see the enemy's approach and uncertain whether it would be from the south, east, or west, Chaplain Russell B. Bennett of the 32nd Ohio crept forward to a tree stump in the field forty or fifty yards south of the line. Bennett had been a private in the ranks at the beginning of the war and later succeeded to the office of chaplain. From his tree stump, he spotted the Confederates advancing from the south and shouted the news to his regiment, warning the men to stay low until the enemy was close. Then, still standing erect on the tree stump, he took a borrowed rifle and started taking long-range shots at the advancing Confederates while a comrade crouched below him, loading and handing up rifles. Ironically, the chaplain remained unscathed, while his more sheltered loader was killed. When the Confederate line came close, Potts's brigade rose up and poured fire into them, and Hall's Iowans fired into the attackers' flank. After a tough fight, the Rebels gave way and retreated in the direction from which they had come. It was now about four o'clock.[57]

Scarcely five minutes after the repulse of this attack from the south, the skirmishers reported that the Confederates on the east side were advancing again. During each lull in the attacks, a number of Union soldiers had run forward and picked up all of the rifles left lying on the ground by the fallen Rebels. Now many of the Federals had piles of extra weapons on hand. "We had plenty of guns," recalled the 15th Iowa's Col. William W. Belknap, "and we kept them loaded." Warned of the impending return of Cleburne's Confederates, Hall's men took their stocks of extra rifles and scrambled back over to the west side of the breastworks. Potts's brigade swung back into line facing east alongside them.[58]

The combat in this renewed assault from the east was more intense than anything that had gone before. As the Rebels approached, Belknap ordered his men "not to fire until each had marked his man," and they loosed a deadly close-range volley that staggered the attackers. The Confederates came on again and again. The Federals poured fire into them from their stockpiles of loaded rifles. Then some men loaded and passed rifles to others who stood along the breastworks and kept up a steady fire. In many parts of the line, however, dense underbrush on the east side of the breastworks allowed the Confederates to approach within a few yards before being seen. First in such places and then along most of the line, the fighting became hand-to-hand. Rebels held the east side of the works while the Federals clung to the west, in a contest of sheer stubbornness to see who would possess them in the end. Men bayoneted one another across the breastworks, and officers fought with their swords alongside their men.[59]

That morning Belknap had disciplined one of his soldiers for skulking in the previous day's fight. The soldier had promised to do better in the regiment's next battle, which came much sooner than either of them expected. Throughout the battle thus far, he had stood a few yards away from the colonel, "doing his work like a soldier." Now with the lines face-to-face in desperate combat, Belknap saw a Confederate on the other side of the works preparing to fire. "Shoot that man, John!" he shouted to the soldier who had funked the previous day's fight. John fired, and the Rebel fell.[60]

Sgt. Maj. John G. Safley of the 11th Iowa led a scratch party of thirty or forty men in a sally across the breastworks that netted two Confederate colors and ninety-three prisoners. Then the colonel of the 45th Alabama led his regiment charging toward the section of breastworks held by the 15th Iowa. Reaching the works, the Alabama colonel turned and looked back to discover that he was alone. So startled was he that he began cursing his men for cowards. At that point, Belknap reached across the works, grabbed his counterpart, and dragged him over the parapet as a prisoner, saying at the same time, "Look at your men! They are all dead! What are you cursing them for?" In fact, they were not quite all dead, and several of them fired at

Belknap while he was grappling with their colonel. One of the bullets passed through Belknap's beard, but he remained unharmed. The 15th Iowa also proudly counted the lieutenant colonel of the 38th Tennessee among its bag of prisoners.[61]

Sixty-five-year-old Lt. Col. William Jones of the 53rd Indiana was wounded through both thighs. Unable to remain on his feet and direct the regiment, he had his men prop him up behind the lines, where he drew his revolver and helped guard prisoners until a shell fragment struck his head and killed him.[62]

While Giles Smith's men fought their battle with the Tennesseeans and Alabamians, Leggett's division once again clambered over its breastworks, took the east side, faced west, and successfully repelled another assault from Atlanta. By now it was approximately 6:00 p.m. So far, with the exception of the loss of McPherson and the pounding taken by the Iowa Brigade, the battle had been going amazingly well for the Army of the Tennessee, despite the fact that Rebels in superior numbers had attacked it front, flank, and rear. Except for slight tactical adjustments of the lines, the Sixteenth Corps had scarcely taken a backward step since the battle opened. The Seventeenth had lost only about 300 yards at the southern end of its line, mostly the ground from which the Rebels had driven the Iowa Brigade and the left flank of Potts's brigade. Strong had successfully led a party into the woods to recover McPherson's body, which they sent to the rear in an ambulance.[63]

The Army of the Tennessee had fought magnificently and gotten a slight assist from the fact that the Rebels' tactics were not working exactly as planned. The front, flank, and rear attack could be devastating if all three blows fell exactly at the same time, but it was almost beyond human skill to make that happen. Hitherto, the assaults had fallen just a few minutes apart, close enough to have routed most Civil War troops, but not close enough to overcome the superb tactical virtuosity of the Army of the Tennessee's veterans.

Indeed, it was partially the defenders' skill that had made the attacks fall separately. Leggett, expecting an assault from the direction of Atlanta once those on the flank and rear were under way, sent Colonel Munson, his staff specialist on skirmishing, to take command of the division's skirmish line and use it to delay the advance from the west for as long as possible. Leggett had great confidence in Munson's abilities, later writing, "A skirmish line under his control was equal to a line of battle in the hands of some others." To Munson, Leggett gave some of the credit for the ability of his men to take to the west side of the works with impunity.[64]

Then, shortly after 6:00 p.m., the Confederate tactics suddenly fell together into a perfectly coordinated attack. Cleburne's division renewed its advance, and Maj. Gen. Carter L. Stevenson's division did the same. It was not so much a matter of the Confederate generals' skill as it was the dogged tenacity of their troops, who rallied again and again, until, more or less by chance, Giles Smith's Federals found Confederate formations advancing toward them simultaneously from east, south, and west, supported by artillery at close range firing canister. "They would jump first on one side of the works and then on the other," wrote a Confederate of the 12th Tennessee, "but we being on both sides and pouring upon them such a galling fire, they continued steadily to give way, firing back at us as they went."[65] On the receiving end of the assault, Captain Nutt of the 20th Ohio recalled, "They struck our left flank broadside—yelling, firing, bayonets flashing, smoke blinding, on they came literally walking over our left companies, pushing them back along our line."[66]

In short order, all of Smith's division and part of Leggett's had to fall back northward, crowding in on the rest of Leggett's division until the two organizations were completely intermingled. Despite the confusion, the soldiers continued to fight tenaciously at every place where they could make a stand, including the various traverses in Leggett's breastworks. The men in the ranks were experienced enough by now not to have to rely on familiar organizations and officers around them in order to fight well but rather recognized almost instinctively what needed to be done and did it, often without being ordered, and even if the troops on either side of them belonged to another brigade or division. Indeed, Lieutenant Tuthill was of the opinion that it was the individual soldiers who recognized when they had reached a point where they could and should turn and make a determined stand. "They had been in so many fights," he wrote, "that they did not need a general to tell them where and when to stop running and begin shooting."[67]

Nevertheless, Giles Smith and Mortimer Leggett labored mightily to establish a new line running almost straight east from the Bald Hill and facing south. This required the left brigade of Leggett's division to swing backward and face south as well, maintaining the link between Smith's right flank and the all-important hilltop. That was no easy task, and for a moment it looked as if Leggett's troops would not be able to make the connection, leaving a gap in the line that was sure to be fatal and entail the loss of the Bald Hill, key to the entire position.

Then the 68th Ohio came marching up to rejoin its brigade after the detached odyssey that had enabled it to fire some of the first shots of the battle. Of 68th commander Col. George E. Welles, Leggett wrote that his "instincts always seemed to guide him exactly to the place where most needed." He and his Buckeyes were certainly needed here and now. Leggett, Munson, and Welles arranged the regiment as the anchor of the new line, with its right resting against the breastworks on the Bald Hill.[68]

To help cover the new line while it was forming, Leggett had his right brigade, under Col. Adam G. Malloy, pivot forward on his left flank so that it came into alignment with the new line, facing south and extending toward Atlanta. The fire of Malloy's infantrymen administered a check to the pursuing Confederates, taking some of the pressure off the line Leggett and Smith were trying to cobble together. Once the new line was partially established, Leggett had Malloy swing his brigade back into place behind its breastworks. This made the summit of the Bald Hill the apex of the Union line. From the hilltop, the line ran at right angles to the north and to the east.[69]

On the far east end of that line, Wangelin's brigade of the Fifteenth corps, after having sought for several hours to find the appropriate position to carry out McPherson's last orders and link the Sixteenth and Seventeenth corps, now moved into position to extend the line farther east. It was still not long enough to make contact with the Sixteenth, but it helped. Dodge extended his line somewhat more in the direction of Blair's flank, and although the lines never quite came together, the gap became small enough to discourage further enemy penetration.[70]

The new line was hardly complete before the Confederates closed in. Pvt. Joseph Brown of the 78th Ohio fired once at the approaching attackers, and by the time he was nearly finished reloading, the smoke was so thick he could not tell friend from foe at five paces, but he could hear the Rebels all around him yelling, "Surrender, you ———!" Brown fired, then snatched up a loaded rifle just dropped by a fallen comrade and fired again.[71]

All around him, soldiers were using bayonets, clubbed rifles, fists, or grappling with the attackers who were threatening to overrun their line. The Confederates seized the flag of the 78th, but the Ohioans fought back savagely and Pvt. Russ Bethel came up with the colors. A big Rebel grabbed the fabric of the flag and for a moment was dragging it and the struggling Bethel toward the Rebel side of the lines. Holding the flagstaff with his left hand, Bethel slammed his right fist into the hulking Rebel's jaw, staggering the Confederate an instant before Pvt. Charles McBurney bayoneted the attacker. While McBurney was extracting his bayonet from the fallen Rebel, another Confederate seized the flag just as Bethel took a bullet in the right shoulder. With his right arm hanging useless, Bethel clung to the flagstaff like grim death with his left. The Rebel dragged both flag and bearer until Capt. John Orr of the 78th lunged forward, slashing savagely with his sword and nearly beheading the Confederate with a single stroke.[72]

Hand-to-hand fighting raged all along the lines of the Seventeenth Corps. Lt. Col. Daniel Bradley of the 20th Illinois fought with his revolver, sword, and even fists to help his hard-pressed regiment hold the line. When the 48th Illinois seemed to falter, twenty-two-year-old Col. Lucien Greathouse seized the colors, strode a few paces to the front of his regiment, and waved them defiantly at the Rebels. He was still waving the flag when a bullet struck him in the chest, killing him almost instantly, but the 48th stood its ground.[73]

Leggett thought this evening onslaught was "not exceeded in fierceness by any assault during the day." The Seventeenth Corps fended off attack after attack in the waning daylight, until in some parts of the line Rebel bodies were piled one atop the other outside the breastworks. Between onslaughts, the men along the new sections of the line dug, scraped, and scooped out the beginnings of entrenchments or piled up fence rails for cover. The fiercest assaults were aimed at the apex of the lines at the top of the Bald Hill. There the four big 24-pounder howitzers of Battery D, 1st Illinois, hurled heavy loads of canister into the faces of the attackers. Fierce fighting continued on the slopes until long after dark.[74]

Meanwhile, the Fifteenth Corps was fighting its own battle. About the time the coordinated attack struck the Seventeenth, other Confederates had advanced directly from Atlanta against the lines held by the Fifteenth on the right of the Army of the Tennessee. That sector had hitherto seen only moderate skirmishing and shelling. Wangelin's brigade of Woods's division, as well as three regiments of Col. James S. Martin's brigade of Morgan Smith's division, had been transferred from this quiet sector to try to plug the gap between the Sixteenth and Seventeenth.[75]

Throughout the afternoon, the men of the Fifteenth had followed the sounds of battle to the south and recognized a pattern. First would come the rising chorus of shrill Rebel yells as an attack started, then the crash of artillery and musketry that might continue for some time, and then the deep, baritone roar of Union cheers that told them their comrades had successfully beaten off another attack. The pattern was repeated again and again as the afternoon progressed.[76]

Then at about 6:00 p.m., heavy formations of Confederate troops advanced from the Atlanta fortifications directly across the shallow intervening valley toward the lines of the Fifteenth. There was nothing subtle about this attack. Union signal officers on the cupola of the Troup Hurt House observed Confederate preparations and sent down word to Morgan Smith. Smith replied that he was ready. Minutes later skirmishers observed the Rebels forming in line of battle in front of their works—a dead give-away of impending attack—and reported this.[77]

"Look yonder; they are coming for us!" blurted a skirmisher of the 111th Illinois as the Rebel line began to advance. "It looked like the whole rebel army was coming at once," one of his comrades recalled. The attackers were in fact Brig. Gen. John C. Brown's and Maj. Gen. Henry D. Clayton's divisions of Cheatham's corps. "On came Hood's brigades with the usual ear-piercing yell," recalled a soldier in the ranks of the 55th Illinois. Rapid and accurate fire from the veteran Fifteenth Corps tore into the Rebel lines at a range of 150 yards and drove them back. The Confederates rallied and came on again, and again the Fifteenth's lines held steady.[78]

Then the danger that Colonel Jones and Majors Taylor and Hipp had warned of that morning became a reality. Rebels used the houses and out-buildings in front of the lines as cover. From there they swarmed up the railroad, hidden by the underbrush along it and in the nearby ravine and then by the fifteen-foot walls of the cut. Simultaneously others charged on either side of the cut, including along the Decatur wagon road, about twenty yards north of the railroad cut.

Like the railroad, the wagon road was not obstructed by any sort of bar-ricade. South of the railroad cut was one section of Battery A, 1st Illinois. Another section was just north of the wagon road. In the whole eighty yards from the southernmost to the northernmost guns of the battery, the only infantry was Company K, 47th Ohio, stationed behind a short, low log breastwork between the cut and the wagon road. So short was the breast-work that only a single sixteen-man platoon could engage the enemy while the other platoon lay prone some yards to the rear. This arrangement might have worked if the troops on either flank could have laid down an effective cross fire. In this case, however, the other troops were directing their fire against the attackers in their own front; the buildings, brush, and railroad cut provided cover for the attackers; and the powder smoke had produced a dense fog, providing further cover.

The defenders did their best. Battery A, 1st Illinois, had been consoli-dated out of batteries A and B of the old Chicago Light Artillery, which had done sterling service at Belmont, Donelson, Shiloh, and many other fields. Once again the Chicago artillerists served their guns with skill and vigor.

The detonations rolled out from the muzzles of their 12-pounder Napoleons so rapidly that many of the hapless soldiers of Company K, between the two sections, were bleeding from the ears and nose as a result of the concussions. With little warning, the Rebels charged out of the billowing smoke a few yards away. The crouching Ohioans gave them a volley and then rose up to receive them on their bayonets. For a few minutes, it was all slashing bayonets and thudding rifle butts along the low log breastwork. Then the isolated platoon was overwhelmed, borne down by sheer weight of numbers, twelve of its sixteen men killed or wounded and the survivors forced to flee. The second platoon had no opportunity to resist, for by that time Rebels were already surging out of the eastern end of the railroad cut, seventy-five yards behind the Union position.[79]

For the remaining Federals in the sector, the operative question was now one of sprinting speed, as they strove to escape encirclement and avoid capture. Rebels swept over the Chicago Light Artillery, bayoneting some of the gunners and capturing many more, along with all four guns. The disaster spread rapidly, as the Confederates who had penetrated the railroad cut swarmed out in both directions, rolling up regiment after regiment as the Union troops fought the attackers in front and were astonished to find Rebels sweeping down on their flank and rear. Some could not get away without a fight. An intense struggle erupted over possession of the colors of the 47th Ohio. Pvt. Joseph Bedoll broke his rifle over the head of one of the Rebels, then waded into the attackers with his fists and succeeded in knocking down four of them and making his escape. Somehow the color guard managed to save both flags.[80]

In the Troup Hurt House, just a few yards behind the lines and about 200 yards north of the railroad, a squad of Union sharpshooters from the 37th Ohio found themselves cut off in the second story as Confederates poured into the ground floor. Several of the Ohioans made their bid for escape by jumping from the second-floor windows. Henry Puck landed atop the piled knapsacks of the 37th, which broke his fall but sent him tumbling. He was on his feet in an instant and ever afterward felt that the running he did over the next several hundred yards was the fastest of his life.[81]

The officers of Lightburn's brigade strove to rally their men and form a new line, though Lightburn himself "went off on a run," according to one of his officers. The lieutenant colonel of the 47th Ohio was captured while trying to form a new line, as was one of his captains. Major Taylor had halted a few men in the woods just behind the lines when he heard someone shouting in the road a few yards away. Thinking it was a fellow officer trying to get the men into line, Taylor burst out of the underbrush to find himself "within five feet of a rebel officer on a white horse with a flag in one hand and a revolver in the other."

"Halt!" shouted the Confederate officer. "We'll treat you like men."

"H———, stranger," blurted Taylor, "this is no place for me to halt!" and he dived into the bushes. The Confederate officer fired his revolver at him but missed, and Taylor told one of his men to try to shoot the Rebel.[82]

Col. Wells Jones of the 53rd Ohio now commanded Lightburn's brigade in place of Lightburn, who commanded the division in place of Smith, who now commanded the Fifteenth Corps in place of Logan. Jones was an excellent young officer and did his best to rally the brigade, but the situation was hopeless. Like the rest of Lightburn's division, his men had to retreat. So too did their neighboring troops on the left in the northern half of Harrow's division. On the far right of Lightburn's division, not far from the Troup Hurt House and near an 800-yard gap that separated Lightburn's from Woods's division farther to the north, the Confederates overran De Gress's battery before they could limber to the rear. The captain had no choice but to spike his prized 20-pounder Parrotts and flee.[83]

Lightburn's troops rallied on the ridge where the Fifteenth Corps's line had been located before the morning's advance. There Lightburn ordered Jones to retake the works they had just lost. Apparently, Lightburn thought the situation was still fluid enough that a quick counterattack, even by a weak force, could restore the line. This was nonsense. Jones led his brigade forward with bayonets fixed, but when they approached the works, "a hail storm of fire and bullets" swept their line. Bullets snapped off both flagstaffs of the 47th Ohio, cut down the color-bearers, and felled dozens of others. The Rebels had turned the captured guns of the Chicago Light Artillery and were firing them at the Federals. With the enemy closing in on both flanks, Jones ordered a retreat.[84]

It seemed incredible—the Fifteenth Corps staring into the ugly face of defeat. The Army of the Tennessee had survived an afternoon of hammering at its flanks and rear, only to have a hole the size of a two-division front ripped in its right-center by a head-on assault. In theory, if they could exploit their success, Hood's Confederates now had the opportunity to slice through the Army of the Tennessee, envelop it (except for Woods's division on the northern flank), and destroy it—unless Logan and his troops could do something to stop it.

At the time of the breakthrough, Logan was with Dodge on the Sixteenth Corps's front. Learning of the debacle to his old Fifteenth Corps, Logan quickly ordered Colonel Martin to take his three regiments back to join the rest of his brigade in Lightburn's division. He directed Dodge to send Col. August Mersy's brigade of Sweeny's division as additional rein-forcement, and then, as had been his habit on battlefields from Belmont to Champion's Hill, he set out for the threatened point at a gallop.[85]

On the opposite side of the break in the line, Sherman watched the bat-tle unfold from his headquarters at the Howard House, about half a mile north of the Troup Hurt House, and had seen with dismay the collapse of Lightburn's division. De Gress himself fled north, into the lines of Woods's division, not far from Sherman's headquarters. "My battery is gone," he lamented to an officer of the 76th Ohio, and on reaching Sherman's head-quarters he was almost in tears. Some minutes later, Woods's troops were alarmed to see the Rebels turning the big 20-pounder Parrotts toward them, but De Gress, who by that time was back on the front line, shouted: "Stand your ground, boys. They are only fooling you. Those guns are all spiked. I know it, for I did it myself."[86]

About that time, Sherman sent orders for Woods to turn his division southward, attack into the gap, flank the Confederates there, and restore the line. Woods moved out promptly, bearing down on the Rebels around the Troup Hurt House and De Gress's abandoned guns across a shallow, clear valley with all the pomp and circumstance of war. "Never did troops keep better alignment in marching in the face of an enemy," wrote Capt. Charles Miller of the 76th Ohio. "To the right and to the left we could see the straight blue lines with their banners gaily waving in the breeze."[87]

Back at the railroad, Harrow's troops were already pressing back toward their old position, and Lightburn's division was sorting itself out for yet another charge toward its former lines. Just as Lightburn's men were beginning to move forward again, someone spotted a familiar form on a big black horse galloping toward them from the left rear. Every man in the Army of the Tennessee knew Black Jack Logan with the rage of battle on him.

An Illinois soldier who saw him remembered vividly how he looked: "coal-black charger streaked with foam, hatless, his long black hair flying, his eyes flashing with wrath—a human hurricane on horseback." Close behind Logan came Martin's three regiments and Mersy's brigade at a dead run. The ground across which Logan was riding was visible for half a mile in almost any direction, and all through Harrow's and Lightburn's divisions the roar of cheers rose above the crash of gunfire and, with the cheers, shouts of "Black Jack!" until thousands of soldiers were shouting, "Black Jack! Black Jack! Black Jack!"[88]

The whole mass of Union troops surged forward—Harrow, Lightburn, Mersy, and Woods. Confederate generals Brown and Clayton ordered their troops to retreat, but few Rebels got the word in time to leave. Instead they stood their ground and fired a volley into the charging Federals. Then as Logan's men kept coming, most of the Confederates turned and ran.[89]

As Woods's division swept past the Troup Hurt House, the 76th Ohio charged through the right section of De Gress's battery and engaged in hand-to-hand fighting with the Rebels among the cannon. De Gress, who had accompanied the charge, "put his arms around the guns and cried for joy."[90]

Then he hurried on to the left section of his battery, a few dozen yards farther south, which had been retaken by the quick-firing Western Sharpshooters of Mersy's brigade. The battery commander effusively thanked Col. Robert Adams, who had succeeded to command of the brigade when Mersy was wounded a few minutes before. De Gress somehow managed to unspike his guns (a theoretical impossibility) and was eager to get them in action again. With his artillerists either dead or fled, he gathered a detail of equally eager volunteers from Mersy's brigade and began sending shots after the Rebels.

Pvt. Joe Schum of the 81st Ohio had seen artillerymen using double charges of canister but did not quite understand the concept. Someone had loaded a 20-pound percussion shell into one of the big guns, and Schum shoved another in after it, shouting, "Feed 'em—give 'em double rations." Someone pulled the lanyard, and the cannon exploded with a roar, sending chunks of its shattered breech in all directions. One fragment, about two feet by six inches, went spinning up into the air as high as the treetops. Miraculously none of the dozens of Union troops nearby was seriously hurt. Staring wide-eyed at his handiwork, Schum quipped, "Send her to the hospital!" and hurried to get back into the ranks of his regiment, once again very much an ordinary infantryman. De Gress reported that that particular gun had been damaged a month before and was probably unsound.[91]

Farther south, Lightburn's troops charged back into the sector around the railroad. The 47th Ohio retook two of the guns of Battery A, 1st Illinois, turned them back around to face the enemy, and fired several rounds at the retreating Rebels.[92] The firing would continue on the Bald Hill for several hours yet, sometimes with great intensity, but for practical purposes the Battle of Atlanta was over.

The July 22, 1864, Battle of Atlanta was the campaign's climatic fight but not its conclusion. It had been Hood's last chance to reverse the course of the previous eleven weeks, to crush Sherman's armies and drive them back to Chattanooga, but Hood was not prepared to admit that, much less to give up Atlanta.

In some ways, the July 22 battle was also the climax of the Army of the Tennessee's wartime career. About 27,000 troops had successfully defeated the attacks of nearly 40,000 Confederates who had the advantages of surprise and position. Union casualties for the Battle of Atlanta totaled 3,722, while Confederate losses have been variously estimated at anywhere from 5,500 to 10,000.[93]

The victory would have been impossible without the experience, skill, and toughness the soldiers had gained along the way in the campaigns that had taken them from Cairo to the outskirts of Atlanta by way of Shiloh and Vicksburg. Above all, they had gained along that difficult path a high degree of confidence in their commanders, their fellow soldiers, and themselves— confidence that they would find a way to win somehow. This confidence enabled the Army of the Tennessee's soldiers to continue fighting in circumstances in which they could reasonably have been expected to surrender or flee. Confidence between commanders allowed them to respond without hesitation to requests for help from their fellow corps, division, and brigade commanders. The spirit of mutual loyalty, cooperation, and teamwork that Grant had begun cultivating in the army's earliest days back in Cairo had by now become a settled feature of its personality.

The Army of the Tennessee had become, for its size, the most effective fighting force on the continent, but the goal of its soldiers was still the same as it had been since they had first "seen the elephant" and quenched their youthful desire for adventure. They wanted to go home. But for them, the road back to Cedar Falls, Iowa; Mineral Point, Wisconsin; Warren, Illinois; and hundreds of other Midwestern hometowns would have to lead through Atlanta and as many other centers of Confederate power as might need to feel what Sherman would call "the hard hand of war" before the power of the slaveholders' rebellion was broken, and the Great Republic and its Constitution were finally saved.

CHAPTER THIRTY-TWO

Ezra Church and Jonesboro

O N   T H E   M O R N I N G   O F   J U L Y   2 3 , the Confederates were gone from
the previous day's battlefield, having withdrawn into the Atlanta fortifications during the night. The Army of the Tennessee remained in position
for another four days burying the dead, digging more trenches, and wreak-
ing still more destruction on the Georgia Railroad. The day after the battle,
Sherman rode along the army's lines, pausing to speak to the soldiers. They
greeted him with "wild cheers." In regiment after regiment, men tossed
their hats in the air and shouted themselves hoarse. Sherman "thanked us
for the way we had conducted ourselves the day before, and lamented the
death of McPherson," wrote Elisha Stockwell of the 14th Wisconsin. "We
thought more of him for those few words."[1] Sherman also had words of
practical advice here and there along the line. He gave "some useful hints"
to Maj. Tom Taylor of the 47th Ohio, and quipped humorously to the headquarters staff of the Seventeenth Corps that "the only unmilitary move that
they made was not to surrender."[2]

Yet gloom hung over the Army of the Tennessee on July 23. "This was
a sad, sad day," wrote Hosea Rood, "for in some respects the horrors of the
battlefield are much greater after the strife is over then during the combat.
There is no excitement to keep up the nerves; dead friends are found here
and there; the dead are bloated to twice their natural size; faces are so blackened by decomposition that one can scarcely recognize his own tent-mate;
the stench is terribly offensive—but I must not say more of it."[3]

Many faces were missing from the ranks. "McPherson was beloved by
every soldier in his command," wrote Wisconsin soldier William Covill,
"and there is not one but mourns the loss of so valuable a leader." In addition, each unit had its own particular losses to mourn. The 48th Illinois
missed its colonel, twenty-two-year-old Lucien Greathouse. "He was as
brave and patriotic a man as ever drew life breath," wrote Chief Musician
William Odell a few days later. "I loved him as a brother for he always
treated me as such."[4]

One of the first issues with which Sherman had to deal after the battle was the question of permanent command of the Army of the Tennessee. Logan had succeeded to the post on a temporary basis by reason of seniority, and he had done a good job. Indeed, in a battle in which the army had to fight for its life, he was almost the ideal commander. The question was whether he had the steadiness, administrative ability, and technical skill to command the army on a permanent basis. Sherman was inclined to be doubtful.[5]

Instead, Sherman gave the command to Oliver Howard, until this point the commander of the Fourth Corps in the Army of the Cumberland.[6] Born in Maine in 1830, Howard had graduated from Bowdoin College in 1850 before entering West Point, where he finished fourth in the class of 1854. He served in the Eastern theater of the war until late summer of 1863, losing his right arm at Fair Oaks and rising to corps command. In his first two battles as corps commander, Chancellorsville and Gettysburg, his superiors' misjudgments and the tides of battle had handed him impossible situations, leading to disasters that Howard could do little to prevent. Still, he had received a congressional vote of thanks for his selection of the winning position at Gettysburg, and his continued promotion to responsible positions, without any powerful political patrons, indicated that the War Department, at least, recognized him as an officer of merit. Howard was brave, conscientious, aggressive, and solidly competent.

Logan, of course, was profoundly disappointed, and for the rest of his life remained bitter toward West Point and the officers who came out of it, whom he saw as a clique that arrogated all high positions to themselves. He refrained, however, from any open display of his displeasure in the midst of the campaign and quietly reverted to command of the Fifteenth Corps.[7] Sherman penned him a kindly note on July 27. "No one could have a higher appreciation of the responsibility that devolved on you so unexpectedly and the noble manner in which you met it," he wrote. "I fear you will be disappointed at not succeeding permanently to the command of the Army & Dept. I assure you in giving preference to Gen. Howard, I will not fail to give you every credit for having done so well. You have command of a good corps, a command that I would prefer to the more complicated one of a Dept., and if you will be patient it will come to you soon enough. Be assured of my entire confidence." Sherman signed the note, "Your friend."[8]

Howard was the first outsider and the first Easterner to command the Army of the Tennessee, but he was accepted almost immediately by the men, who appreciated his courage, earnestness, and competence. In any case, they seemed to possess little regional chauvinism. Despite replacing the immensely popular Logan, Howard was well liked within the Army of the Tennessee almost from his first day in command. That was a good thing, because the day he took it over the Army of the Tennessee was on the march on another turning maneuver around Atlanta, as Sherman once again wielded his "whiplash" toward Hood's railroad supply lines.

On Sherman's orders, the Army of the Tennessee pulled out of line by moonlight in the predawn hours of July 27 and began a march behind the Armies of the Ohio and the Cumberland, headed for the far right, where Sherman had been planning to send them before the battle. "The cannon wheels are all muffled and we are ordered to leave as quietly as possible," wrote an Iowa soldier in his diary.[9]

Howard assumed command while the army was on the move at about daylight that morning. It was a long, hard day of marching, much of it through rain and mud. "The tiresomely slow tramp, tramp, hour after hour, seemed as though it never would end," wrote an Illinois soldier. As the march continued late into the night, the men would make use of even brief halts to drop down beside the road and fall so soundly asleep that their comrades had difficulty waking them when the order was given to resume five minutes later.[10] They maintained their good humor as best they could, laughing as they heard the sound of Confederate artillery bombarding the empty entrenchments they had just left.[11]

Arriving west of Atlanta, Dodge's Sixteenth Corps moved into position on the right of the Army of the Cumberland, facing Atlanta. Blair's Seventeenth passed it and moved into line on the right of Dodge, somewhat refused. The Fifteenth was headed for a position on the right of Blair, even more sharply refused so as to deal with any repetition of Hood's audacious flanking tactics. Last in the column, Logan's men still had not reached their assigned position when, at seven or eight o'clock that evening, the officers called a halt and told the men that they would have time enough to cook supper. They had just gotten their fires going well—their coffee had not yet come to a boil—when Confederate gunners inside the Atlanta defenses detected their position and opened a bombardment that forced Logan's men to march on at once, without any supper. They halted at about midnight, still short of their intended destination, on an east-west ridge that lay just south of the position of the Seventeenth Corps.[12]

Well before dawn on July 28, after the soldiers had slept only a few hours, the Fifteenth, resumed its march. Riding behind it were Howard and Sherman. Around midday, skirmishing intensified sharply in front of the

Fifteenth, and artillery joined the fight. Confederate shells broke tree limbs over the generals' heads, and Howard remarked, "General, Hood will attack me here."

"I guess not," Sherman replied, "he will hardly try it again."

Howard was another of the younger generals who had prior knowledge of Hood, having been one year behind him at West Point. He replied that he knew the Confederate to be a man who would not be deterred by setbacks.[13]

Sherman and Howard inspected the position of the Fifteenth Corps. Woods's division faced generally east, prolonging the line of the Seventeenth. His right flank was posted on a low ridge near a meetinghouse known as Ezra Church. At that point, the line angled about ninety degrees to the right, with Harrow's and Morgan Smith's divisions aligned along a connected east-west ridge. Their position overlooked open fields to the south. As battle was obviously imminent, the men were hastily piling up logs and rails as a makeshift breastwork. At best it offered only partial protection for a man kneeling or even lying down. One soldier recalled that the barricade along his regiment's front was "about knee high." No time remained for proper entrenching. Sherman turned and rode toward the Army of the Cumberland so as to be ready to order up reinforcements if Howard should need them.[14]

On the far right of Logan's line was Lightburn's brigade of Morgan Smith's division. Lightburn had become a problem. His troops were excellent, but he had been quite open in blaming them for the debacle on July 22, which had really been caused by his and Morgan Smith's refusal to place their line in a condition of defense. This was not Lightburn's first act of gross unfairness, and his troops were becoming bitter toward him.

Now Lightburn got an idea. He noticed a knoll on the next ridge in front of his lines, occupied by Confederate skirmishers, and decided that his should occupy it instead. So he sent Col. Wells Jones with the 47th and 53rd Ohio to take it. A sharp little fight ensued. The Confederates brought in artillery; Morgan Smith did the same. Jones asked for reinforcements. Lightburn dispatched the 54th Ohio, and the struggle for the hill began to take on the appearance of a small battle in itself when it was abruptly swallowed up by a much larger one.[15] The familiar sound of "the cornbread yelp" rose from the woods, and the Confederates emerged from the forest and strode across the valley all along the front of the Fifteenth Corps's southward-facing two divisions.[16]

Jones and his two regiments fell back quickly to the main line, narrowly escaping being cut off. As they began to withdraw, Lt. Henry Bremfoerder, adjutant of the 47th Ohio, announced to his comrades that he was not going to retreat until he had given the Rebels every one of the bullets in his revolver. Major Taylor was having none of that nonsense. He grabbed Bremfoerder and carried him off bodily. With Jones's detachment back on the main line, the battle was joined in earnest. The time was approximately 11:30 a.m.[17]

As heavy firing began to break out all along the main line of the Fifteenth Corps, a soldier of the 55th Illinois saw Logan pass along the line with "an almost exultant expression lighting up his dark face." "Hold them!" exhorted Logan. "Steady, boys, we've got them now." Some regiments opened fire at a range of several hundred yards, utilizing sharpshooting skills honed the previous summer at Vicksburg. Others reserved their fire for an initial volley at much closer range. Both tactics proved successful. Along most of the line of the Fifteenth, the Rebels broke and fell back.[18]

The Confederate line overlapped Logan's right, however, and a sizable body of Rebels swept past his flank, forcing several of Lightburn's regiments to fall back from the ridge and threatening more of the dire circumstances the army had experienced six days before. Ironically, the attackers in this charge belonged to the same division that had broken through Lightburn's brigade via the railroad cut on the twenty-second. This time, however, Lightburn's men rallied on the back slope of the ridge, and Jones and Taylor led them back uphill, yelling wildly. In his report, Taylor claimed that they drove the Rebels off the ridge "more by noise than by numbers."[19]

Even after Lightburn's troops had regained the ridge, the Confederates attempted to hang on to what they had won, and a fierce conflict ensued. Lightburn's own whereabouts during the fight are unclear. With Jones directing them, the four regiments on the right were able to extend their line far enough to counter the Confederate flanking attempt. They were spread thin, but Jones placed them skillfully, and they fought off the next four assaults.[20]

To strengthen his hard-pressed right, Logan requested help from his fellow corps commanders. Dodge detached four regiments, and Blair sent two more. Logan used the reinforcements mostly to spell his hot, tired men. By this time, Lightburn's soldiers were running low on ammunition, and their rifles were becoming fouled with powder residue. Their replacements performed equally well in holding the extended line against several more assaults. Once again, the 64th and 66th Illinois were formidable with their Henry repeaters. To further buttress the right, Howard ordered Hickenlooper, in his capacity as chief of artillery, to bring up and carefully site several batteries of guns—twenty-six in all—to sweep the ground beyond the flank. By that time, however, the crisis on the right was well under control. Most of the firing continued to come from the infantrymen's rifles.[21]

The Confederates renewed their assaults again and again, hammering at Logan's front with stubborn persistence. Some members of the Fifteenth Corps counted nine separate attacks, others seven, five, or as few as four. "From twelve o'clock till near night the firing was incessant, swelling out, as the rebels charged, into a fierce and steady roar, and again dying away as they receded, to a fitful rattling," wrote a member of the 31st Missouri.[22]

During lulls, the soldiers scrambled to get more logs, rocks, and rails for their breastworks but quickly had to return to fighting—according to Logan such breaks in the action lasted only three to five minutes. Pvt. Albert Crummell of the 30th Ohio made much different use of those precious minutes. As soon as the Rebels turned their backs in retreat, he hopped over the scant breastworks and dashed forward to ransack the knapsacks of the fallen Confederates in search of tobacco, one of the few items of which the Rebels had plenty and the Federals were in short supply. He did not have to go far; some of the fallen lay within twenty feet of the Union line.[23]

The intensity of the fighting varied from one sector to another. A soldier of the 55th Illinois, on the right of the Fifteenth Corps, thought the second assault "lacked the verve and tenacity of the first." In front of Oliver's brigade, on the left near the angle of the line at Ezra Church, Rebels closed to within a few feet of the breastworks, and Oliver's men caught some of them and hauled them over as prisoners. The fourth assault was even worse in this sector. Lt. Col. Robert A. Gillmore of the 26th Illinois counted five Confederate flags along his regimental front within ten paces of the barricades. Some were much closer than that. One Rebel color-bearer used the spearhead on the top of his flagstaff to impale a member of the 26th. Members of the regiment captured one flag. A few yards down the line, in Walcutt's brigade, Pvt. Harry Davis of the 46th Ohio took the flag of the 30th Louisiana, prying the staff from the hands of the dead lieutenant colonel of the regiment. After the battle, Walcutt recognized the fallen officer as Thomas Shields, a former schoolmate of his in Columbus, Ohio.[24]

On his fourth and final tobacco-hunting foray in no-man's-land, Private Crummell encountered a wounded Rebel who pled desperately to be taken into Union lines. Loath to abandon the plugs of "the precious weed" with which both his hands were by then full, Crummell finally agreed to get down on hands and knees and let the Confederate crawl on his back and put his arms around his neck. Thus encumbered, Crummell got back to the Union lines just ahead of the next attacking wave.[25]

By late afternoon, many of the soldiers' rifles were growing almost too hot to use. Powder flashed as men poured it down the barrels. Many suffered second-degree burns on their hands from such premature ignitions, and a soldier of the 47th Ohio had his hand punctured by his own ramrod when the charge in his rifle exploded while he was ramming it. Taylor ordered the rest of the 47th to cease firing, fix bayonets, and prepare to meet the next advance with cold steel. Soldiers of the 116th Illinois resorted to pouring water from their canteens down the barrels of their rifles.[26]

Howard and Logan ranged up and down the embattled lines, encouraging the men and making adjustments where necessary. It was just after the repulse of the second attack that Howard passed by the 55th Illinois. "We heard cheering on our left," recalled an Illinoisan, "which regiment after regiment in succession took up." Shortly, Howard, who had been the occasion of the cheering, came into sight, "a neatly dressed officer of kindly face and martial bearing," with the empty right sleeve of his uniform pinned up. The 55th hurrahed liked the other regiments. "Well, boys," said Howard, "I thought I had seen fighting before, but I never saw anything like this." As the army's new commander continued along the line, he paused now and then to make complimentary remarks to the soldiers. The men liked him at once.[27]

The tactical situation offered very little for any general to do besides encourage his men, as this proved to be in many ways the simplest battle the Army of the Tennessee ever fought. The soldiers stayed where they were and shot every Rebel who attempted to approach their line. The Rebels shot back, of course, and although the battle may have been simple, it required hard fighting and considerable courage for Logan's men to stand up to repeated attacks from a foe that greatly outnumbered them. Nor were the Confederates the only ones suffering casualties. Captain J. F. Summers of the 70th Ohio was encouraging his men—"There they come!" he cried, "Pour it into them!"—when he was shot through the chest and fell mortally wounded. During the course of the battle, a number of Union soldiers collapsed—and some died—from sunstroke or heatstroke.[28]

Toward evening the attacks ceased and the Rebels withdrew from the battlefield. The Battle of Ezra Church, as it was called, was a lopsided Union victory. Federal casualties totaled 562; Confederate losses, about 3,000. "The rails saved us," wrote Illinois soldier Charles Wills, referring to the hastily erected log-and-rail breastworks that had helped make the casualty figures so wildly disproportionate.[29] On the Confederate side, the battle had not been conducted according to Hood's plan. Desiring to check Sherman's latest flanking maneuver, Hood had dispatched two corps, those of Stephen D. Lee and Alexander P. Stewart, with orders to take up a position near Ezra Church and the Lick Skillet Road. On approaching the position, Lee, who had been in corps command for only a few days but outranked Stewart, found that Logan already occupied it. The only thing to do, therefore, as Lee saw it, was attack, and at his orders both corps hurled themselves ineffectually at Logan's lines, giving the Army of the Tennessee what was in some ways an easy victory though a hard fight.

The victory served to smooth relations in the army's high command after the changes of the past week. Howard was delighted with the army's performance and had high praise for all of his generals, especially Logan, whom he called "spirited and energetic," and praised for his direction of the battle as well as his "decision and resolution."[30] As for Howard, a junior officer noted that at Ezra Church he "won the respect and esteem of the officers and men of the Army of the Tennessee," feelings that continued to increase the longer they served under him.[31] Howard had allowed Logan to direct his corps without interference, but he had been present to encourage the men and to intervene if necessary. Sherman believed this had done much to reconcile Logan to his subordinate position. It was a relief to Sherman to know that his favorite army was still running as smoothly as ever.[32]

Ezra Church had displayed once again the spirit of warm cooperation and mutual trust among the generals, as Dodge and Blair had responded to Logan's request for reinforcements without awaiting formal orders. Throughout its ranks, from commanding general to private soldier, the army was becoming more than ever an organization in which men recognized quickly what needed to be done, and did it without standing on formalities. Morale among the rank and file remained as high as ever. No one liked all this fighting, but they were confident that, as one soldier wrote home, "the rebels are getting the worst of it" and "the army feels confident of victory."[33]

That night the army rested in the positions it had held during the day. "It was everything else but pleasant to hear the groans and cries of the wounded and dying on the field," wrote an Ohio soldier. Many spent the night strengthening their breastworks and digging trenches in anticipation of a Confederate assault, but the only Rebels in the immediate front the next morning were the dead and wounded, who lay scattered across the field in appalling numbers.[34] "Acre upon acre of the open field lay before us at daylight strewn with dead men, guns, accoutrements and clothing," wrote a member of the 55th Illinois. Along a fence where the Confederate formations had paused in their advance, "the rebels lay in a windrow, in some places two or three piled across each other." Another thick belt of corpses lay along a tiny stream that trickled through the bottom of the shallow valley, where wounded Confederates had crawled to drink or bathe their wounds and then had expired. In between such windrows of the dead, a soldier of the 68th Ohio noted, "so thickly was the ground covered with slain that one could have stepped from body to body over the ground without touching it!" It was, wrote Jake Ritner of the 25th Iowa, "a horribly sickening sight."[35] The army spent July 29 burying the dead. The continued hot weather was cause for haste. Already, noted Capt. Charles Miller, "the smell of the dead rapidly decomposing in the sun," was producing "a sickening sensation that I shall never forget."[36]

During August, Sherman continued his efforts to reach Hood's last railroad supply line. He gradually stretched the lines of his infantry farther and farther around the west side of Atlanta, while waiting to learn the results of the cavalry raid he had dispatched against the railroad. That raid, however, proved to be a failure and led Sherman to the conclusion that "cavalry could not, or would not, make a sufficient lodgment on the railroad below Atlanta and that nothing would suffice but for us to reach it with the main army." At first he attempted to accomplish this by further stretching his lines, both thinning them behind increasingly elaborate entrenchments and pressing them closer to the Atlanta defenses so as to reduce the circumference they had to cover.[37] The Army of the Tennessee spent the month in activities similar to those they had experienced during the Vicksburg siege, digging trenches and battery emplacements, sharpshooting, and shelling Atlanta. Over the course of the month, the movement of the lines was such that the Ezra Church ridge, which had been the position of the Army of the Tennessee's right flank on the day of the battle, was, by the end of the month, the position of its left.[38]

Several changes of personnel took place in late July and August. Brig. Gen. Thomas W. Sweeny, the fiery one-armed Irishman, had helped Will Wallace hold the line at Shiloh but was a difficult character. On July 24, Sweeny had gotten into an argument with his fellow Sixteenth Corps division commander, English-born Brig. Gen. John W. Fuller, and kicked Fuller out of his tent—literally. Grenville Dodge considered the kicking of a fellow general to be conduct unbecoming an officer and a gentleman and had Sweeny arrested and sent back to Nashville to await court-martial.

Sherman assigned Brig. Gen. John M. Corse, who had been serving on his staff, to take command of the old Second Division.[39]

Dodge himself left the army during the following month, under different circumstances. While observing the enemy's positions on August 19, he was struck by a sharpshooter's bullet, which plowed a furrow through his scalp just above his forehead, leaving him unconscious. He eventually recovered, but was out of action for several months. His men were sorry to see him go. Brig. Gen. Thomas E. G. Ransom, a highly capable officer who had started the war as Will Wallace's lieutenant colonel in the 11th Illinois and was currently just recovering from a severe wound received in Banks's wretched Red River fiasco, took command of the Sixteenth Corps.[40]

In the Fifteenth, Morgan L. Smith's old Chickasaw Bayou wound flared up, forcing him to take sick leave. That left Lightburn in command of Smith's division, once Sherman's own, much to the dismay of its troops, who were absolutely convinced of his "incompetence—or worse."[41] Sherman imported Brig. Gen. William B. Hazen, one of the most capable and hard-driving young brigade commanders in the Army of the Cumberland, to take over the division, and Lightburn returned to his brigade. A few days later, he received a wound very much like that which had put Dodge out of action. In contrast to the case of Dodge, everyone was glad to see Lightburn go.[42]

Hazen found the command atmosphere of the Army of the Tennessee a refreshing change from what he had known in the Army of the Cumberland. The first thing that struck him was how relatively young and junior-ranking its officers were. Hazen had been one of the junior brigade commanders in the Army of the Cumberland but now found himself the second-ranking officer in the Fifteenth Corps. Promotion had been rapid for men of ability. To this Hazen attributed the "perfect harmony and good will" that prevailed throughout the army's officer corps, in contrast to the "jealousies, dislikes, and dissensions" he had known in the Army of the Cumberland. He was probably at least partially right about that, although the mutual trust and confidence among the Army of the Tennessee's officers probably owed a good deal to the personality that Grant had imparted to the army from the beginning. Hazen quickly went to work to remedy the administrative slackness of Lightburn and get Sherman's old division back into fighting trim.[43]

By late August, Sherman was convinced that he would once again have to cut most of his army loose from its supply line in order to separate Hood from his. He had the Twentieth Corps, now in the capable hands of Maj. Gen. Henry W. Slocum, entrench north of Atlanta in order to cover the

Chattahoochee River railroad bridge and major stockpiles of supplies. With the rest of his command and twenty days' rations, Sherman prepared to march south, keeping to the west of Atlanta, with the goal of seizing the Atlanta & West Point and the Macon & Western Railroad at points south and west of Atlanta.

The two railroads ran on the same track from Atlanta seven miles southwest to East Point. There the Atlanta & West Point continued southwest while the Macon & Western turned southeast for a half-dozen miles and then curved to a generally southerly course. Confederate fortifications stretched from Atlanta to East Point and a mile or so beyond. Since frontal assaults on those works were out of the question, the cutting of the railroads would have to be done beyond East Point, and both would have to be broken. Once again the Army of the Tennessee was to be the whiplash, on the outer edge of the broad wheeling movement Sherman's three armies were undertaking. Its ultimate target was the town of Jonesboro, on the Macon & Western seventeen miles south of Atlanta.[44]

During the night of August 26, the army withdrew from its positions near Ezra Church. Although the lines had been in some places as little as twenty-five yards apart, the Federals moved out so quietly that the Confederates remained unaware of it until the Union column was more than a mile away. The Rebel artillerists tossed a few shells after them but with little effect. The army marched in two columns on parallel roads, the Fifteenth Corps on the left, the Seventeenth followed by the Sixteenth on the right. They continued until 11:00 a.m. on the twenty-seventh, covering about sixteen miles before making camp. Around 7:00 a.m. on the morning of August 28, the army took up the march again and at noon reached the tracks of the Atlanta & West Point Railroad at the town of Fairburn, twenty miles southwest of Atlanta.[45]

The Army of the Tennessee quickly entrenched so as to be ready for any surprises Hood might have in store and then went to work on the railroad, tearing up the tracks, burning the ties, heating, bending, and twisting the rails, and filling up the cuts with "earth, rocks, trunks of trees, and other rubbish," as Howard reported. The activity occupied most of the army through the rest of that day and the next. Early on the morning of August 30, the command moved out again, this time with the Sixteenth Corps leading on the right, the Fifteenth on the left, and the Seventeenth in reserve. The lead infantry brigades occasionally had to deploy to drive off Confederate horsemen too powerful to be moved by the Federal cavalry screen. Wells Jones's brigade of Hazen's division covered a good bit of the distance in skirmish formation, often through thick underbrush. "Whenever they would halt and make a stand," wrote Maj. Tom Taylor of the 47th Ohio, "the regiment raised a shout and cheer and the rebels executed the 'Southern quickstep' to a charm." Still, with the process being repeated every half mile or so, Howard noted, "everybody became weary and impatient." By late afternoon, the head of the Fifteenth Corps had reached Renfro Place, the objective Sherman had designated for the Army of the Tennessee for that day.[46]

Since there was no water to be had at Renfro Place and since Sherman's orders gave him the option of pressing farther if opportunity offered, Howard did so. He kept his men marching another six miles to the Flint River, with a detachment of cavalry still driving the Confederates in front of them. The Rebel horsemen set fire to the Flint River bridge as they fled, but the Union cavalry, closely followed by troops of the Fifteenth Corps, put out the flames and rushed across. By dusk, Logan's entire corps was on the east bank of the Flint and had reached a wooded ridge a half mile short of the Macon & Western Railroad and the town of Jonesboro, where the Confederates had breastworks. During the night, Logan's men entrenched their position and built additional bridges across the Flint. The Sixteenth and Seventeenth corps, delayed by rough terrain and lack of good roads, spent most of the night marching to catch up with their comrades of the Fifteenth.[47]

By midmorning on August 31, the Army of the Tennessee occupied a position in which the Fifteenth, in the center, faced east; the Seventeenth, on the left, was refused to face northeast; and the Sixteenth, on the right, was even more sharply refused so as to face south. Most of the Seventeenth and Sixteenth were still on the west bank of the Flint, but enough additional pontoon bridges were in position to ensure quick movement of troops between the various corps if that became necessary. Artillery along Logan's lines was only 800 yards from the railroad, comfortable range for even smoothbore cannon. No Confederate supply trains would be traveling those rails while Union guns held such a position. In effect, the Army of the Tennessee had already accomplished the purpose of the operation, and by doing it in this way, Howard had arranged the situation so that the enemy, and not his own troops, would have to bear the burden of mounting an attack against entrenchments.[48]

As Howard was well aware, Hood had to respond to his presence near Jonesboro in some way, either by withdrawing from Atlanta or by attacking and driving the Federals off his line of communication. True to form, he chose the latter. To expel the Federals from their position at Jonesboro, Hood dispatched Hardee with two of the three Confederate corps during the night of August 30, but Hardee was not ready to launch his attack until 3:00 p.m. the next day.

As had been the case at Ezra Church the month before, this assault fell mostly on the Fifteenth Corps, though this time it struck part of the Sixteenth as well. Along many parts of Logan's line, the attackers approached to within fifty yards of the breastworks. The Rebels "advanced boldly through the open field up in the direction of our works, with their colors flying, and yelling like so many wild Indians," recalled Illinois soldier Ephraim Wilson. In many regiments, the officers had their men wait until the attackers reached close range before opening fire. The 10th Illinois let them approach to within eighty yards. Then Wilson and his comrades "poured volley after volley into the faces of the gallant foe."[49] Eyewitnesses on the Union side counted from two to four separate assaults or renewals of the attack after initial repulses.[50] At the height of the battle, Logan and his staff rode the lines of the Fifteenth Corps. One soldier wrote in his diary that night of Logan "waving his hat & cheering the boys. This sight alone was worth a year's service. His looks alone told the boys that things were going to suit him & did a world of good to assure the men. A person could almost tell the position of the troops by the cheers that followed him round the lines."[51]

After about an hour and a half, the attack subsided. It had never even come close to success, and the slaughter among the attackers was terrific. Protected by their entrenchments, the Army of the Tennessee lost only 172 men killed, wounded, and missing. Confederate casualties totaled approximately 2,200.[52]

As determined and bloody as the Rebel assault was, the Confederates did not display the fire and zeal they had exhibited in July. The summer's hard fighting was beginning to tell on Hood's army, and it did not press home the attacks at Jonesboro with quite the same abandon it had at Ezra Church. "The assault altogether was the least determined of any I ever saw them make," wrote Taylor. Even when the Confederates advanced bravely, it had been with a resignation to be killed if necessary but without hope of victory. "The enemy came up on a dog trot," wrote a Wisconsin soldier, "with their heads down & firing but little." Captain Wills noted that it seemed "more like a butchery than a battle." In one sense, however, the Confederate attack at Jonesboro resembled that at Ezra Church, and that lay in the fact that it was poorly planned and coordinated.[53]

While the Army of the Tennessee faced Hardee's two corps outside Jonesboro, the rest of Sherman's forces—less the Twentieth Corps—took up positions astride the Macon & Western between Jonesboro and Atlanta.

Each of Sherman's three armies now occupied a position that, by itself, would have been fatal to Hood's continued efforts to hold Atlanta. On September 1, Thomas's forces moved south and drove in Hardee's northern flank around Jonesboro, further emphasizing the hopelessness of the Confederate situation. The Army of the Tennessee's role in that day's action was to maintain its position and make occasional feints to keep the Rebels from concentrating their attention on Thomas. After two days of defeat at Jonesboro, all that was left for Hood was to evacuate Atlanta as rapidly as possible, since any delay was fraught with peril of losing his army as well.[54]

At around midnight on the night of September 1–2, Howard's soldiers heard the sounds of a battle in the direction of Atlanta. Many surmised that Hood's remaining force in the city must have lashed out to try to restore the severed Confederate supply lines and had collided with Schofield's Twenty-third Corps just south of the city. The sounds of gunfire and explosions waxed and waned in intensity several times and then ceased altogether not long before sunrise.[55]

The next morning Hardee was gone. Sherman put his forces in pursuit, heading down the Macon & Western Railroad about seven miles to Lovejoy's Station, where dug-in Confederate infantry blocked further advance.[56] While Sherman's forces were moving into position, news arrived that the Rebels had evacuated Atlanta and Slocum's Twentieth Corps had marched in. The sounds during the night had been Hood's men blowing up stocks of surplus ammunition in Atlanta preparatory to fleeing the city. Regimental commanders read the official announcement to their troops, and, despite an all-day rain, the lines resounded with cheers and the sounds of brass bands. "Atlanta is ours!!" wrote Iowan John McKee in his diary, "Glory to God. Bully for Sherman."[57]

Sherman decided not to pursue Hood any farther for the time being but rather to pull back slowly to Atlanta and vicinity and there spend the next few weeks resting, refitting, and considering the next move. On September 5, he issued orders for the Army of the Cumberland to garrison Atlanta proper, the Army of the Ohio to bivouac at Decatur, and the Army of the Tennessee to encamp at East Point.[58]

As the soldiers of the Army of the Tennessee contemplated the campaign that had just concluded, they felt more confident than ever in their commanders. "What a sharp game Genl Sherman played on Hood to get him out of Atlanta & his breastworks," wrote Ohioan Charles Weiser. "Indeed, there never has been a more successful campaign on record. There never was a bolder strike than Sherman made when we started from before Atlanta." Others agreed. "Uncle Billy Sherman is too smart for old Hood," wrote Illinois soldier Isaiah Dillon. "I never saw troops have so much confidence in a man in my life."[59]

The capture of Atlanta was one of the great epochs of the war, on a level with the seizure of Vicksburg. While Sherman's armies had been fighting their way through North Georgia during the summer of 1864, the North had been engaged in a presidential election campaign. The Democratic Party had adopted a platform calling the war a failure and demanding immediate negotiations that could end only in Confederate independence. It had nominated as its candidate failed Army of the Potomac commander George B. McClellan. McClellan claimed that he would continue the war to a victory that would mean the restoration of the Union and the preservation of slavery, yet all over the continent, both North and South, most Americans understood that a vote for McClellan was a vote to give up the war. Lincoln believed that if he were defeated in the election, he would have to win the war while a lame duck, for McClellan surely would not win it after taking office. We can never know for sure what would have happened had the majority of Northern voters accepted the Democratic argument that the war was a failure and should be abandoned, but with casualty lists growing to appalling lengths during the summer months and no spectacular military successes of the sort that newspapers could understand and communicate to their readers, Lincoln and many others believed that the North was about to suffer just such a loss of will to fight. The fall of Atlanta removed that possibility. It guaranteed that the Northern will to carry on the war would remain solid for as long as it might take to achieve victory, and in so doing it nailed the coffin shut on any realistic hopes for the independence of the Southern slaveholders' republic. Now all that remained was to convince Southerners of this fact.

CHAPTER THIRTY-THREE

Marching Through Georgia

WITH THE ATLANTA CAMPAIGN at last over, the Army of the Tennessee on September 7 marched from Lovejoy's Station to East Point, and there encamped. Regimental adjutants read congratulatory orders to the troops from Lincoln and Grant, "and we cheered ourselves hoarse over them," wrote an Illinois soldier. In the days that followed, they built a system of modest southward-facing earthworks as insurance against attack, but none came. "All firing has stopped," wrote William Wade of the 11th Iowa. "It is so still that it seems strange."[1]

During the next several weeks, the army took up the routine of camp life it had not known for four months. "Our promised rest is pretty well taken up between Co[mpany] & Reg[iment]al drill 4 hours each day, cleaning camp, guns & accouterments, Inspections, parades, &c., &c.," groused Wisconsin soldier Edward Allen in a letter home. The men turned in their worn-out uniforms, shoes, knapsacks, haversacks, canteens, and other equipment in exchange for new issues.[2]

Changes occurred in the organization of the army as well as in the personnel of its high command. Logan and Blair took leaves of absence to attend to political matters of importance to the Lincoln administration, and Peter Osterhaus, who had several weeks earlier returned from his own leave, took over temporary command of the Fifteenth Corps. Temporary command of the Seventeenth went to Thomas E. G. Ransom. The Sixteenth was badly understrength because of various detachments, so Sherman disbanded it, assigning one of its divisions to the Fifteenth and the other to the Seventeenth. For the remainder of the war, the Army of the Tennessee would consist of those two corps.[3]

When the men had nothing else to do, they sat around camp and discussed politics, chiefly the current presidential race. The soldiers overwhelmingly supported Lincoln, since he represented the cause of the Union for which they were fighting. Even the few die-hard Democrats among them could hardly stomach the current well-nigh treasonous Democratic plat-form. Allen Geer, a lonely McClellan supporter in the 20th Ohio, decided that it would be wise not to speak of his preference openly.[4]

During these weeks, a number of escaped Union prisoners of war made their way into the army's lines after having spent time in the notorious Andersonville prison. Some were members of the Army of the Tennessee who had been captured only two months before at the Battle of Atlanta. Yet even that short span under the inhuman conditions at Andersonville had broken their health to such an extent that almost none of them was able to return to duty with his regiment. One sergeant who had weighed nearly 200 pounds when captured two months before was down to 136 when he made it to Union lines around Atlanta. The appearance of these walking skeletons and the obvious mistreatment they had suffered made an impression on their comrades.[5]

On October 3, the camp routine came to an end with the arrival of orders from Sherman to prepare to march, and at five o'clock the next morning the army took to the roads again.[6] The reason was that John Bell Hood had started his next campaign. Passing well to the west of Atlanta, Hood had moved into North Georgia to threaten Sherman's vulnerable supply line, the rails of the Western & Atlantic. Sherman responded to early signs of Hood's movement by dispatching two divisions to guard key points along the railroad, and when it became apparent that Hood was moving north with his whole army, Sherman followed with most of his, leaving Slocum with the Twentieth Corps to garrison Atlanta.[7]

On October 5, major elements of Hood's army struck a Union garrison of slightly fewer than 2,000 men under the command of John Corse at Allatoona Pass. Corse's little band of Army of the Tennessee troops—including such veteran regiments as the 7th and 93rd Illinois—succeeded in beating off a daylong series of assaults by several times their numbers of Confederates, inflicting ruinous casualties on the attackers. The approach of Sherman's main force finally compelled the Rebels to break off their efforts and withdraw.

For the better part of the next month, Sherman chased Hood around the hills of North Georgia, and as part of his force in that campaign, the Army of the Tennessee footed it for more than 300 miles.[8] "We've done some hard marching day and night running old Hood," wrote Isaiah Dillon of the 111th Illinois, "and can't get fight out of him."[9] The Confederate general had learned his lesson, at least for now, and refused to engage Sherman in battle. The situation was as frustrating to Sherman as it was to his men.

Much of the time, rations could not catch up with them or were interrupted when Hood's men made temporary breaks in the railroad, but Sherman's men were too resourceful to go hungry in an inhabited country. "For most of the time we have been on ⅔ rations but have foraged so much off the country (which we find very rich since we left the R[ail]R[oad]) that we have lived better than at any time since we came south. We get sweet potatoes, chickens, fresh pork, beef, flour, meal, mutton & molasses," wrote one of the soldiers. In some places, the farmers had not yet processed their sorghum into molasses, so the soldiers did it for them—and ate the molasses.[10]

Both Sherman and Hood eventually tired of the game. Hood conceived a scheme for invading Middle Tennessee via North Alabama and marched his army off to the west. Sherman had already assigned George Thomas to cover Union communications in Tennessee. In response to Hood's movement, Sherman sent Thomas the Fourth and Twenty-third corps, which, along with other forces already in Tennessee or on the way, comprised a force far more than sufficient to deal with Hood.

For the rest of his forces, the Fourteenth and Twentieth corps as well as both corps of the Army of the Tennessee, Sherman had a different operation in mind. For several weeks, he had been corresponding with Grant and the War Department about the futility of trying to defend his long railroad supply line against constant attack by both guerrillas and Hood's army. "It will be a physical impossibility to protect the [rail]roads, now that Hood, Forrest, Wheeler, and the whole batch of devils, are turned loose without home or habitation," Sherman warned, adding farther down the page, "By attempting to hold the roads, we will lose a thousand men each month, and will gain no result." Instead, Sherman proposed a giant raid, in which he would lead a force of 60,000 in cutting completely loose from all supply lines and march it clear across the state of Georgia. "I propose that we break up the railroad from Chattanooga forward, and that we strike out with our wagons for Milledgeville, Millen, and Savannah," he wrote. It was useless, he claimed, to attempt to occupy Georgia, but by destroying its railroads, bridges, factories, warehouses, and the like, he could destroy its ability to contribute to the Confederate war effort. At the same time, he might help the Southern people to see that the war was over and they had lost. "I can make this march," he wrote, "and make Georgia howl."[11]

Grant and Halleck had their reservations about this audacious plan that seemed to flirt with the possibility of having a 60,000-man army trapped deep in the interior of the enemy's country. Sherman's arguments eventually won them over, however, and in mid-October he received from Halleck, on behalf of Grant, official authorization to undertake the operation. The navy would be on hand to meet him at Ossabaw Sound, near Savannah.[12]

Sherman spent the rest of October and early November carefully preparing for his expedition, and for Thomas's defense of Tennessee. Supplies stockpiled in Atlanta and between there and Chattanooga were hauled north. "All the surplus ordnance stores, camp utensils, officers' property— everything that could not well be borne upon the soldier's person or slung to the regimental mules—had been sent back to Chattanooga," wrote an Illinois soldier.[13] Garrisons pulled out of the various strongpoints from which they had protected the railroad. Sick and wounded men were shipped back to Chattanooga, as were all of the weak mules and horses.[14] The army's wagons were carefully overhauled and loaded.

During the first few days of November, commissioners from the various states came around to take the votes of the men for the presidential election. The soldiers voted overwhelmingly for Lincoln. In the 20th Illinois, where Allen Geer had decided it would be best to keep quiet about his support for McClellan, the tally was ninety-seven to one.[15]

New faces appeared in the camps as well as some that had not been seen for a time, and others disappeared. Soldiers who had thoroughly recovered from wounds or sickness returned to their regiments. Frank Blair returned from furlough and resumed command of the Seventeenth Corps. Also just in time to take part in the expedition, Joseph A. Mower arrived, a transfer from the detachment of the Sixteenth Corps that was still serving in the Mississippi Valley. Sherman, who rightly considered him one of the most skillful and aggressive young generals in the army, was delighted to have Mower back and assigned him to command a division in the Seventeenth.[16] Sadly, however, Thomas E. G. Ransom, another bright young general and one of the rising stars of the army, fell ill and died at Rome, Georgia, on October 29, one month short of his thirtieth birthday. His constitution had been fatally weakened by the several wounds he had received during the course of the war.

The rank and file of the army knew that something was up but could only guess what it was. Isaiah Dillon wrote his wife that they had been ordered to prepare for "a raid somewhere," with lots of hard marching— "some say to Savannah, some to Mobile and other places. I can't tell where."[17] Allen Geer heard that the destination might be Memphis, Tennessee.[18] "Don't even know whether we are starting on a campaign or not," wrote Charles Wills. "Hood is reported across the Tennessee. We understand that Thomas has men enough to attend to him, and that Sherman intends to use us to Christianize this country. Many think we are now on the way to Montgomery or Selma."[19] Wherever they might be bound, confidence was high. "We are in fine shape and I think could go anywhere Uncle Billy would lead," wrote Theodore Upson of the 100th Indiana.[20]

Finally, on November 10, Sherman issued orders for the units that were to take part in the march to begin making their way from their various positions in North Georgia down to Atlanta in preparation for immediate departure. He directed John Corse and his division of the Army of the Tennessee that had been garrisoning Rome, Georgia, to pull out and head for Atlanta, after burning "all the mills, factories, etc., etc.," of that northwestern Georgia town. Marietta received the same treatment.[21] That evening in the various camps of the Army of the Tennessee, the soldiers scribbled the last letters home that they would be able to mail until the expedition was completed. The last trains of convalescent soldiers and surplus supplies rolled north, and then on November 12, Sherman had the railroad and telegraph broken, severing the final links of supply or communication with the North. Among the last information to come over the wires before the break was news that Lincoln had won reelection, at which the soldiers rejoiced boisterously.[22] "The Rubicon is passed, the die is cast, and all that sort of thing," wrote Wills that day. "At 11 a.m. ours and the 17th Corps were let loose on the railroad. The men worked with a will and before dark the 12 miles of track between here and Marietta were destroyed."[23] The troops completed their trek to Atlanta, tearing up the railroad as they went.[24]

The Army of the Tennessee crossed the Chattahoochee on the evening of November 13 and went into camp on the southwest side of Atlanta. Already columns of smoke were rising from the city. "Destruction of public works in Atlanta progressing rapidly," noted Tom Taylor in his diary. Factories, warehouses, machine shops, foundries, arsenals, the railroad depot, and other public buildings were in flames. "Coming through Atlanta the smoke almost blinded us," wrote Wills.[25]

As it lay encamped southwest of Atlanta on November 13 and 14, the Army of the Tennessee was larger than it had been at any time since the Vicksburg campaign. With the return of those who had recovered from wounds and sickness, the arrival of new recruits, and the addition of John E. Smith's division of the Fifteenth Corps, which had guarded supply lines throughout the Atlanta campaign, the army's field strength was approximately 33,000. It was a lean, experienced, highly confident fighting force.[26] "Such an army as we have I doubt if ever was got together before," wrote Theodore Upson. "All are in the finest condition. We have weeded out all the sick, feeble ones and all the faint hearted ones, and all the boys are ready for a meal or a fight and don't seem to care which it is."[27]

On the morning of November 15, the armies turned their backs to the still-smoking city of Atlanta and marched south, "relying on our strength and the Providence of God," wrote Maj. A. J. Seay.[28] Sherman rode with Slocum's wing of the advance, soon to be known as the Army of Georgia, consisting of the Fourteenth and Twentieth corps. They would take the left, while the Army of the Tennessee formed the right. Howard's troops marched south-southeast, the Fifteenth and Seventeenth corps, as was to be standard practice during the campaign, moving on parallel roads.[29]

The army was traveling light. Orders allowed one pack mule per company, and that meant the soldiers generally had to carry their own mess equipment. Six men constituted a mess and shared the duty of carrying coffeepot, camp kettle, and frying pan, along with their individual tin cups and mess knives. In his knapsack, a man usually had a change of underclothes, an overcoat, a blanket, and a shelter half.[30] Some reduced their load even more. Upson noted that many of his comrades carried only "a blanket made into a roll with the rubber 'poncho' which is doubled around and tied at the ends and hung over the left shoulder. Of course, we have our haversacks and canteens and our guns and cartridge boxes with 40 rounds of ammunition. Some of the boys carry 20 more in their pockets."[31] In order to keep the column as short as possible, the wagons had priority in the road, with most of the troops marching in two files on either side of the wagons.[32]

Although the commissaries had loaded the wagons with as much food as they could carry, that would not be enough for the trip. "The army will forage liberally on the country during the march," Sherman's orders stated. Individual soldiers could take what they found during halts within sight of the column, but ranging farther afield—which was a necessity if the army was not to starve—was reserved for specially detailed and organized foraging parties under the command of officers. They were not to enter houses or use "abusive or threatening language," and they were to "endeavor to leave with each family a reasonable portion for their maintenance." They could take whatever the army needed of food, horses, or mules, but they were to discriminate "between the rich, who are usually hostile, and the poor and industrious, usually neutral or friendly."[33]

Each brigade had a foraging detail of from twenty-five to fifty, detailed from its various regiments. A divisional foraging officer would assign each party a different direction, so that they did not get in one another's way or attempt to forage the same country.[34] The foragers ranged ahead and to the flanks of the advancing column and brought food to points along the road over which the army would be passing later that day. Sometimes they commandeered teams and farm wagons and brought them into their brigade's camp that evening, heavily loaded with food.[35]

Duty in the foraging parties was highly sought after but also demanding and sometimes dangerous. The members would be up well before reveille, preparing to march, while their commanding officer would visit division headquarters for briefing on his assigned sector and where he could expect to find the command that evening. Once they were out in the countryside, the brigade foraging parties would break up into their separate regimental detachments in order to cover more of the countryside. Rebel horsemen often lurked just out of sight of the main columns, and encounters were frequent. "Scarcely a day passed," wrote an Illinois soldier regarding his regiment's foragers, "but they were required to engage in more or less skirmishing, and often hard fighting was necessary to drive away the Confederate cavalry."[36] The foragers were usually victorious in such clashes, but occasionally an entire party would be taken prisoner. On other rare occasions, subsequent patrols would find the foragers' bodies scattered around a farmstead or thicket, along with ample evidence that they had sold their lives dearly. In their encounters with cavalry, the foragers were performing a valuable secondary service to the army, scouting the country ahead and screening the marching columns from enemy horsemen.[37]

In addition to the regular foraging parties were the "bummers." During the march through Georgia, the term "bummer" referred to any soldier who in violation of orders would sneak away from the column to forage on his own. According to one soldier, the bummers may have been as numerous as the authorized foragers, though still probably not more than 5 or 10 percent of the army's total numbers. Most were simply seeking variety and adventure, as well as the assurance of tasty and plentiful meals for themselves and their comrades. Though operating individually, the bummers would quickly band together if they encountered Confederate cavalry, each man hurrying to the sound of shots. Although no officers were present on such occasions and the men came from different regiments and brigades, they almost instinctively came together into tactical formations for combat. Bummers also reinforced regularly authorized foraging parties in combat.[38]

Some of the bummers were guilty of abuses of one sort or another. To the extent that thefts or other crimes took place during the march, they were almost exclusively the work of bummers. Soldiers who remained in the ranks had minimal opportunities for plunder—limited largely to houses in the immediate vicinity of their regiments' camp each night. "Houses occupied by families were seldom seriously disturbed," wrote Charles Willison. "Orders were strict that such were not to be entered or their occupants ill treated." Smokehouses and barns were another matter, of course, and, Willison added, "houses were often found deserted, and in such we felt more at liberty to ransack and take away what evidently had been left for us."[39]

In such cases, some of the soldiers might help themselves to jewelry, watches, silverware, or the like. Large amounts of such items would have been very difficult to carry while taking part in a march such as this, or to conceal from the officers, who did their best to prevent such abuses. Howard especially, as a devout Christian, was adamant that no theft should take place and gave orders that any man found stealing should be tried by drumhead court-martial and, if convicted, summarily shot. Most officers were not willing to go that far, and so when courts-martial were held, they declined to convict soldiers of theft, which would have meant death, and instead found them guilty of some lesser charge, entailing perhaps the forfeiture of six months' pay. Such events were rare, however, since the great majority of the soldiers were prevented both by circumstances and by their consciences from plundering. It remained for embittered white Southerners of later generations to exaggerate such isolated thefts into a legend of wholesale plunder.[40]

Indeed, the mythmaking about the March to the Sea started almost before the march itself and grew apace while Sherman's men made their first few days of advance southeastward from Atlanta. Stories circulated that Sherman's men were burning all the houses and abusing all the women in their path. Union soldiers encountered such stories again and again during their progress across the state, told to them by frightened locals who were incredulous at the degree of restraint they displayed. Mrs. Elizabeth C. Pye, who lived near Hillsboro, had heard that the Yankees burned all private houses and so had all of her furniture, including a big feather bed, moved into the woods and hidden. Foragers of the 103rd Illinois found the items and carried them back into her house for her. Capt. Charles Wills noted in his diary, "I think there is less pillaging this trip than I ever saw before."[41]

Although a small number of crimes against property did occur, crimes against persons were all but unheard of. General Hazen was not aware of a single case of rape during the entire march.[42] Despite their rhetoric both before and after the march, most Georgians seemed to expect such restraint. Male civilians who judged their farms to be in the path of Sherman's armies frequently took their livestock and fled, leaving their womenfolk behind to greet the approaching soldiers, since it was a well-known fact that an occupied house was far less likely to be robbed than an empty one. Their confidence that Sherman's men would respect their women proved well founded.[43]

Of course, no matter how gentlemanly the behavior of Sherman's soldiers or how many times they thoughtfully retrieved someone's furniture from the woods, they were not going to win the hearts and minds of the majority of Southerners. They seethed with hatred toward Sherman's men, not only because of the loss of food, livestock, and sometimes outbuildings, but also because the very presence of those victorious Union soldiers in the heartland of the Deep South was conclusive proof that the slaveholders' Confederacy had failed and the cause of Union and freedom had triumphed.

For a sizable minority, however, those very facts called forth exactly the opposite reaction. The black population hailed the Union soldiers as deliverers. "It is most ludicrous to see the action of the negro women as we pass," wrote Wills. "They seem to be half crazy with joy, and when a band strikes up they go stark mad."[44] Not content merely to cheer the passing of the Union armies, thousands of slaves flocked from miles around to follow it. "The Darkies came to us from every direction," wrote Indiana soldier Theodore Upson. "They are all looking for freedom but really don't seem to know just what freedom means."[45]

Thousands of them seemed to believe that freedom meant chiefly the ability to leave the plantations, which they did, flocking after the army. In vain did Sherman and his officers tell the slaves that the army was not able to accommodate or feed them now, that they should remain patiently at home and await liberation at the end of the war. Some wanted to go and try to find family members in Macon, Savannah, or other distant places, from whom they had been separated by sale. Despite orders to turn back, innumerable multitudes followed behind the army. Many of them carried "bundles and bags of clothing, bedding and cooking utensils on their heads." Those who could took wheeled transportation and various draft animals from their plantations. Now they presented a curious spectacle with their "assortment of animals and vehicles, limping horses, gaunt mules, oxen and cows, hitched to old wobbly buggies, coaches, carriages and carts," wrote Illinois soldier Enoch Weiss.[46]

The presence of the blacks affected Sherman's soldiers in different ways. Some found infinite humor in the situation and enjoyed playing jokes on the former slaves. Some of the soldiers were cruel, but most were not extremely so. Soldiers might tell blacks that a particular junior officer or even an ordinary bummer was Sherman himself and then enjoy the slaves' extravagant reactions to what they took to be their liberator. Others found the situation sobering. The former slaves were leaving places where they had food and shelter in their "abiding faith that the Yankees would lead them to a land of liberty and to a land filled with plenty for them," but the more reflective knew that the army was in no position to help the slaves at the moment. Such soldiers were sobered by the knowledge that they were the objects of blind faith that they knew they could not help but disappoint. They tried to do what they could. General Hazen frequently provided wagon transportation to a frail old woman who said she was going "out to freedom," but she survived the march by only a few days.[47]

The former slaves enthusiastically approved of the soldiers' policies regarding foraging and the destruction of property. Again and again, it was the slaves of each plantation who either slyly or boldly tipped off Union foragers as to the hiding places of their master's food, livestock, and even valuables before leaving the plantation and following behind Sherman's troops. Thomas Stevenson of the 78th Ohio remembered that whenever the Union troops burned a factory the blacks went wild with joy.[48] At the J. B. Jones Plantation near Herndon, staff officer Henry Hitchcock talked with a black mammy who seemed very affectionate toward the white children in her charge. He mentioned to the slave that, after the army had departed, the white inhabitants would probably denounce the Union soldiers just as much as if they had actually burned the plantation house.

"It *ought* to be burned," said the black woman bitterly.

"Why?" asked the shocked staff officer.

" 'Cause there has been so much devilment here," replied the woman, "whipping niggers most to death to make 'em work to pay for it."[49]

During the first week of the march, the army traveled through the plantation region. This area had always produced a significant amount of foodstuffs for local consumption alongside its predominant staple crop, cotton. In recent years, both the exhortations of the Confederate government and the difficulty of marketing cotton had prompted many planters and farmers to forgo the white fiber in favor of food crops such as corn and sweet potatoes. Hostile armies had never before passed over this country, and as a result, the foraging was the most bountiful the soldiers had encountered. "It was surprising to us to see, through Georgia, so great a cultivation of corn," wrote Enoch Weiss. "There was field after field of ungathered corn." More sought after by the soldiers, however, were the hogs and sweet potatoes. Some of the sweet potatoes were reported to be as much as eighteen inches long and to weigh from eight to fifteen pounds. They were a delicacy to the soldiers in whatever size they came.[50] Other favorites included chickens, honey, molasses, peanuts, and persimmons—"the best I ever ate," wrote Ohioan Cornelius Platter.[51]

The Georgians did their best to hide their food, resorting to varied stratagems from concealing the items in the woods to actually burying them. How often such tricks worked will probably never be known, but they failed often enough to keep the army eating the fat of the land and to provide stories the soldiers would tell for years. Some planters also buried their silver and jewelry outdoors, which was by far the most likely means of losing them, since the Federals were adept at finding newly buried items and were more likely to keep something they dug up than to go into a house and steal it.

Throughout the march, the army commandeered horses and mules. Many of these were taken by foragers both to enhance their mobility and to carry their haul back to camp at the end of the day. Artillery units, wagoneers, and mounted officers often traded their weak or worn-out beasts for fresh new ones, so that by the end of the march the army was superbly supplied with the best horseflesh it had ever enjoyed. Beyond that, horses and mules became fairly common in the army. Most of the foraging parties went mounted all the time. Soldiers whose shoes had worn out were also allowed to ride, and many others were soon on horseback with perfectly good footwear. Sometimes surplus horses were simply shot in order to deny their use to the enemy. This was especially the case at river crossings, which division or corps commanders would use as checkpoints to cull surplus or unauthorized beasts out of their column. At the crossing of the Ocmulgee, so many horses and mules were shot that soldiers and civilians at a distance thought a skirmish was in progress.[52]

Most of the troops remained ignorant of the intended destination of the march. "It is still a mystery where we are going," wrote Cornelius Platter. He speculated that it might be Milledgeville or Macon, and others wondered about Mobile, Alabama, or Beaufort, South Carolina.[53] The uncertainty was very deliberate on Sherman's part but directed at the enemy. In order to prevent the Confederate authorities from being able to concentrate their forces to oppose him, Sherman selected his route of march in such a way as to appear to threaten more than one target. While the Army of the Tennessee appeared to be headed toward Macon, the Army of Georgia—Slocum's wing—threatened Augusta. Instead of visiting either city, Sherman directed both wings of his force in between them, encountering only scattered cavalry. Although Sherman possessed great combat power, he could not afford to meet the enemy in comparable strength, since his army's daily food supply depended on a steady, rapid advance. Sherman's excellent strategy and skillful management made the march look easy, almost as if his army might have wandered effortlessly to any point in the Confederacy. That was not quite the case.

During the first three days of the march, the army enjoyed good roads and dry weather. Some of the soldiers actually found it uncomfortably warm. On November 18, rain began to fall though temperatures remained balmy. Roads became muddy and the march much more of a struggle. After having averaged more than fifteen miles per day since leaving East Point, the Army of the Tennessee made scarcely more than half a dozen on that day, delayed not only by the rain but also by the need to lay pontoon bridges and begin crossing the Ocmulgee River north of Macon.

As the weather system that had first brought rain progressed across central Georgia, the rain persisted and temperatures fell precipitately. Cold rain fell on November 20 and 21, and on the latter night temperatures dropped well below freezing. On November 22 the soldiers saw snow falling while they marched midway between Macon and Milledgeville, and ice on puddles froze an inch thick. When not washboards of frozen ruts, the roads were deep quagmires. The army struggled forward through the next several days, usually covering eight or ten miles per day. "As the mules drop down from exhaustion they are rolled out to one side and left more dead than alive," wrote a soldier of the 50th Illinois. The heavy pontoon trains proved especially troublesome to haul over the bottomless roads, but they were absolutely essential to the army's survival.[54]

On the frosty, snowy morning of November 22, the Fifteenth Corps reached the tracks of the Macon & Savannah Railroad near Gordon, about twenty miles east of Macon. Wrecking railroads was one of the chief objects of the March to the Sea, and by this time Sherman's armies had developed the process to an art form. They now not only burned the ties and heated the rails but also used a special tool on the end of a handspike to reshape the hot iron. One soldier would grasp the end of a hot rail while another held the other end, each using the special tool. Then they would turn the ends of the rail in opposite directions, twisting the heated center into a corkscrew. Nothing short of a rolling mill would ever make that rail usable again. With such methods, a regiment could wreck a mile of track in about six hours, and Osterhaus put a good many regiments to work east of Macon, the men keeping warm amid the snow by the heat of bonfires of railroad ties.[55]

From the west came the sound of intermittent gunfire. The day before, Judson Kilpatrick's cavalry, which was handling most of the skirmishing, had sparred with Confederate forces on the eastern edge of Macon, and by the sounds coming from that direction, they were at it again. Howard directed Osterhaus to send Brig. Gen. Charles Woods's division a few miles to the west to support Kilpatrick, if needed, and provide security for the rest of the Fifteenth Corps as it directed its attention to the routine task of tearing up the railroad. Howard was also concerned about the wagon trains, which were toiling over the muddy roads and vulnerable to attack. Woods deployed as ordered and sent one brigade, Walcutt's, two miles farther west to the vicinity of the whistle-stop station of Griswoldville, about ten miles east of Macon.[56]

Walcutt's skirmishers tangled briskly with the Confederate cavalry, easily driving them beyond Griswoldville. Then Walcutt pulled back to a position just east of the town, on the edge of a large field—forest behind him and 600 yards of open ground in front. His men built a perfunctory barricade of rails, as usual, though no one really expected the Rebels to approach them in such a position. Then with the obligatory breastwork in place, Walcutt's men turned their attention to cooking some dinner.[57]

Their culinary pursuits were interrupted by the rattle of shots from the picket line. A minute or two later, the pickets themselves came dashing in, warning of the approach of a heavy enemy force. Moments later a solid Confederate line of battle emerged on the far edge of the field and advanced toward the Union position as if it were on review. Instantly the Federals forgot about dinner and got serious about their breastwork. In the three or four minutes it took the stately Confederate formation to advance halfway across the broad field, Walcutt's men scrambled around, calmly but intensely piling more rails and even logs on their barricade. By the time the approaching line had reached the midway point of the field, the breastwork was stout enough to stop a rifle bullet. Meanwhile, two Rebel batteries had come out into the field and opened fire. Walcutt's two-gun section replied gamely but was almost immediately silenced by the six-fold Confederate advantage in weight of metal. By that time, Walcutt himself was out of action, having taken a wound in the leg while reconnoitering in front of the lines. Command of the brigade passed to Col. R. F. Catterson of the 97th Indiana.[58]

Gazing across their newly completed breastwork, the Federals sized up the situation with the experienced eyes of veterans and wondered which Rebel general had blundered this time. "We all felt that we had a sure thing," recalled Charles Wills. This should be easy, especially for the men of the 46th Ohio, who carried seven-shot Spencer repeating rifles. Then a second wave of Confederate infantry emerged from the far tree line about

150 yards behind the first and another behind that a minute or two later. "It really looked as though we had a big job ahead us," recalled Maj. Asias Willison of the 103rd Illinois.[59]

Walcutt's men liked to let their attackers approach within prime killing range before opening fire, but against this human avalanche, such tactics might end up getting them overrun. Some of them were already casting anxious glances at Colonel Catterson when at 250 yards he gave the order to open fire. The Rebels kept on advancing into the hail of Union bullets until they were within 45 yards of the line and tried to exchange fire with the defenders behind the breastwork. At one point, the 103rd Illinois ran out of ammunition and grimly fixed bayonets to await the Confederate onslaught. Before it came to that, the details sent to the rear for more cartridges returned with a fresh supply, and the 103rd opened fire again. Finally the survivors of the first wave had had enough and broke for the rear. The second wave came forward and met the same fate, as did the third. "One after another their lines crumbled to pieces," wrote Wills, "and they took the run to save themselves."[60]

With that, the Battle of Griswoldville was over. Walcutt's 1,500 men had faced a full division of Georgia militia, 4,400 strong, but though the numbers had favored the Rebels, experience was all on the side of Walcutt's veterans. Wills estimated that five out of every six bullets the militiamen fired had passed at least twenty feet above the heads of his men. Total casualties in Walcutt's brigade came to 14 killed and 62 wounded. Confederate casualties totaled 473. Walking the battlefield, the Federals realized the full horror of the situation. The dead and wounded were "old grey-haired and weakly-looking men" as well as boys who looked to be no more than fifteen years of age. The Union soldiers did their best to help the wounded, carrying those who could be moved to the brigade's field hospital. "I hope we will never have to shoot at such men again," wrote Wills. "They knew nothing at all about fighting."[61]

The march went on, and the troops continued wrecking the Macon & Savannah Railroad for the next several days. Indeed, for most of the rest of the march, some element of the army was usually demolishing a railroad on any given day. Iowa soldier Abijah Gore also noted that before they left Gordon, "most of the Town was destroyed." A Union scout attached to Howard's headquarters had been killed in Gordon a day or two before, but it remains unclear whether greater destruction was visited on the town as a retaliation.[62]

For many members of the Army of the Tennessee, the devastation of property fell into a different category than theft. As a general rule, they considered it much more acceptable and honorable, even when not sanctioned by orders, which called for the destruction only of factories, foundries, arsenals, warehouses, railroads, depots, public buildings, and the like, except in cases of specific retaliation. Many, though by no means all, of the soldiers believed that the South, or perhaps only slaveholders and secessionists, deserved punishment for their wrongdoing, ranging from their mistreatment of slaves, Southern Unionists, and Federal prisoners of war to the very fact that by secession they had plunged the country into civil war.

It is very difficult to say whether those who felt that way comprised a majority of Sherman's soldiers, but they were certainly numerous enough to make their presence felt. Their favorite targets were barns and cotton gins. Cotton was an important element of the Confederate economy, and so it and the gins that processed it were fair game.[63] It was less common for soldiers to burn houses.[64] On November 20, the day his regiment marched through Hillsboro, Tom Taylor saw three houses burn in a single day, and the fact was notable enough to be recorded in his diary. Taylor did not record the burning of any other dwellings during the march.[65] The next day, November 21, Cornelius Platter marched through Hillsboro and noted that much of it was in ashes.[66] It may just be possible that the cold weather of the fourth week of November put the Union soldiers into an incendiary temper, but Abijah Gore noted that the reason for the large amount of destruction in Hillsboro was that "it was a manufacturing town."[67] "All the principal buildings" of Irwinton were consigned to the flames, but then it was a county seat, and Sherman's troops routinely burned county courthouses.[68]

When private residences burned, it was often an indication of peculiar animosity on the part of the soldiers, who perceived the owner of the burning house to be especially hostile or guilty. An example was the case of a Mr. Stubbs, who lived not far from Savannah. Stubbs was well known for his pack of bloodhounds, which he used to hunt down escaped slaves and Union prisoners of war. Some of the Union soldiers he caught were subsequently exchanged or escaped and were now back in the ranks. Henry Hitchcock, of Sherman's staff, knew of a colonel who had escaped and been caught by dogs and now had "sworn that no dog (hound) shall be left alive on the road he marches on."[69]

The rank and file agreed and had been killing dogs all along the route. As the army approached the neighborhood where Stubbs was reputed to live, the troops began making inquiries for his whereabouts. After two days of searching, they found the place. When Thomas Stevenson went by the plantation with his comrades of the 78th Ohio, "the house, cotton gin, press, corn ricks, stable, everything that could burn, was in flames." Stevenson also noticed that the bodies of the dead bloodhounds lay in the dooryard. "Wherever our army has passed," Stevenson wrote, "everything in the shape of a dog has been killed. The soldiers and officers are determined that no flying fugitives, white men or Negroes, shall be followed by trackhounds that come within reach of their powder and ball."[70] Another way a man could get his house burned was by placing obstructions in the road over which the army would be marching. In at least one case, officers succeeded in ascertaining the identity of one who had headed up a party of men felling trees across the road and had his house burned in retaliation.[71]

Some members of the army strongly disapproved of wanton destruction such as the burning of barns and cotton gins, to say nothing of houses. Tom Taylor spoke for many when he referred to the fires as "a shameful spectacle," believing that such acts did nothing to hasten the coming of peace.[72] By contrast, others within the army believed that everything that increased the sum total of the burden of the war on Confederate states served to bring peace and victory that much closer.

Yet even when there was clear provocation and presumptive guilt, a Georgia resident might very well receive the benefit of the doubt, especially if higher-ranking officers were cognizant of the situation. Not far from Savannah, Sherman and his staff, riding now with Blair at the head of the Seventeenth Corps, spent the night at the house of a Rev. Mr. Heidt of the Methodist Episcopal Church, South. Sherman's aide Capt. L. M. Dayton found a large quantity of cartridges hidden in the minister's chicken coop. Heidt "was badly scared," another staff officer recalled, and "protested he knew nothing about it."

"Must have been done by your soldiers," Heidt claimed.

"We don't draw ours from the Macon Arsenal," replied Dayton, displaying the label on the packages of rifle cartridges. Heidt hurried off to look into the matter and came back with what Maj. Henry Hitchcock characterized as "a cock and bull story" about his son having put the ammunition there without his knowledge. As the Union officers rode away from the house, officers of Blair's staff mentioned that Heidt's slaves had stated that their master had been behind the torching of a bridge over a creek not far away. The staff officers were eager to burn his house, but Blair was not sure of Heidt's guilt and not only forbade the burning of his house but also stationed a detail to guard it and see that it was left alone until the army moved away.[73]

Its progress marked by the pillars of smoke and fire from burning railroad ties as well as barns and cotton gins, the Army of the Tennessee toiled southeastward along muddy roads. Gradually the weather improved, and by November 28, a soldier reported that it was "quite warm," and the army was once again making about fifteen miles a day or better. As the weather improved, the countryside deteriorated, at least in terms of prosperity and availability of foodstuffs. They were in Georgia's piney woods now. As they continued past Irwinton, they noticed dense pine forests, miles and miles of them, along with sandy, relatively infertile soil, and a sparser, less prosperous population. Some of the inhabitants were so poor and backward that General Hazen came across one family that did not even know there was a war on. The ground in this region was often low and swampy, and the roadbed seemed to be made of quicksand. Pioneer detachments corduroyed miles of the route.[74]

Food was becoming much scarcer than it had been in the bountiful lands farther north, requiring foraging details as well as bummers to become more and more daring and enterprising. Using their ingenuity and experience, and ranging farther and farther from the column to find isolated cornfields in clearings, the foragers usually kept their regiments eating well.[75]

The pine woods could be pleasant. Except for occasional thick stands of young pines, the forest was open, without undergrowth, its floor carpeted with a thick covering of pine straw and here and there a stand of wire grass. The weather was delightful, almost too warm again, but after the bitter cold of the previous week, no one was inclined to complain. "March about 15 miles through swamp country covered with beautiful pine timber," recorded the 2nd Iowa's John McKee in his diary on November 29. "Weather hot but was very pleasant laying in the shade of the pine when we wanted to stop and rest."[76]

On November 25, the Army of the Tennessee reached the Oconee River. Confederate cavalry on the far bank were inclined to dispute the passage, but Howard pushed a brigade across in canvas boats upstream from where the Rebels were resisting, prompting the horsemen to mount up and ride. With the defenders gone, the army began crossing the Oconee on pontoon bridges. The country beyond was lower, flatter, and less rolling. The streams were muddier, and so were the roads. "We find the country growing more swampy," noted a soldier of the 50th Illinois in his diary. Providentially, the weather remained mostly dry while the army crossed the low-lying coastal plain. By December 4 the advance was approaching Statesboro. Farms were numerous and more prosperous, forage easier to get.[77]

They were now in the coastal section of Georgia, a region whose recorded history stretched back all the way to the Revolutionary War and the colonial period. For most of the Midwestern soldiers, this was the first time they had actually trod the ground on which the events in their schoolbooks had been played out. On December 5, a soldier of the 93rd Illinois was struck by the antiquity of the country through which he was marching. "A plantation was passed today that was cultivated during the Revolutionary War by the grandfather of the present proprietor," he wrote in his diary, adding, "There was a Negro on the place who was over a hundred years old."[78]

On November 30, the Seventeenth Corps reached the Ogeechee River, and again Rebel cavalry disputed the crossing. Corse, whose division led the march, used artillery to suppress enemy fire while a regiment made the crossing in canvas boats and soon put the Confederates to flight. That day and the next, the corps crossed the river, and on December 2 it marched into Millen, where the Confederates had kept a prison pen in which thousands of Union prisoners had lived and often died in appalling conditions. Soldiers found the open stockade where their comrades had been cooped up without shelter for months, and they discovered some 750 graves, but the living prisoners were gone. Several days before, Howard had dispatched a party of scouts under Capt. William Duncan of the 10th Illinois Cavalry to ride far ahead of the army and find out if there was any chance of rescuing the prisoners at Millen, but the Confederates had removed their suffering prisoners well before the scouting party arrived.[79]

The day after the first columns entered Millen, the 20th Illinois marched through. Sgt. Maj. Allen Geer described the place as "a flourishing station" at the junction of the Macon & Savannah Railroad with the Millen & Augusta Railroad, and added matter-of-factly, "Our troops destroy the whole place." Finished with Millen, the Seventeenth Corps moved down the east bank of the Ogeechee, tearing up the railroad as it went.[80]

The Fifteenth Corps continued down the west bank of the Ogeechee to Statesboro, which the soldiers described as a frame courthouse surrounded by a few cabins. There, on December 4, several of the mounted foraging detachments had a stiff fight with Confederate horsemen. The Fifteenth crossed the river at Wright's Bridge on December 6 and 7, after driving off the usual cavalry. The Confederates had burned the bridge there, as they had other spans across the Ogeechee, but Osterhaus's men tore down a number of nearby houses in order to get lumber to repair it.[81]

Beyond the Ogeechee, the army encountered more and bigger swamps, some of which were said to contain alligators and all of which definitely had snakes as well as more and larger specimens of the strange plants the men had been noticing in recent days—Spanish moss, as well as the cypress tree, the live oak, and the palmetto. The swamps were not usually deep, but sometimes the men had to wade in water to their knees or waist for a quarter mile at a time. "An awful country to get through," wrote Charles Wills five miles from Savannah, "all lakes and swamps." Confederate resistance also became more intense but still was limited to frequent skirmishing.

They were very close to Savannah now. Soldiers climbed trees from time to time to see if they could view the ocean yet. The pace of the march slowed as Sherman began to maneuver his forces carefully in order to invest the fortified Confederate city. The slow movement and constant harassment by cavalry made the task of the foragers harder and more dangerous than ever. To make matters worse, the surrounding countryside was not as rich as that which the army had traversed farther north. Even in the pine barrens the foragers had been able to find a sufficient supply of food, but ironically now that they had reached the land of rice plantations, food was scarcer.[82]

The troops encountered new dangers as well. The Confederates had planted land mines—what Civil War soldiers called "torpedoes"—in some of the roadways. On December 9, one of the mines exploded under the 1st Alabama (Union) Cavalry Regiment, killing a horse and wounding several troopers. The 1st Alabama was attached to Blair's Seventeenth Corps. Minutes later Lt. Col. Andrew Hickenlooper, inspector general on Blair's staff, found that there were other unexploded mines nearby. He began very carefully scraping the dirt away from one of them. Lt. Francis Tupper, adjutant of the 1st Alabama Cavalry, came back and joined him in stooping over the mine, also scraping dirt for a time. Then Tupper rose and stepped backward—directly onto another mine. The mine exploded, blowing off Tupper's foot. Hickenlooper escaped unscathed.

The use of land mines was still quite new, and it was considered to be outside the bounds of civilized warfare unless they were planted directly in front of a fort, within the range of its guns. Then they were allowable as part of the fort's defenses. But, as Henry Hitchcock of Sherman's staff wrote, to "leave hidden in an open public road, without warning or chance of defense, these murderous instruments of assassination" was "contrary to every rule of civilized warfare." Blair dealt with the matter by having Rebel prisoners brought up and ordered to clear the road of mines. Just as they were being assigned their task, Sherman and his staff rode up. Some of the prisoners "begged" Sherman "very hard to be left off, but" as Hitchcock noted, "of course to no purpose." Sherman told the prisoners that "their people had put these things there to assassinate our men instead of fighting them fair, and they must remove them; and if *they* got blown up he didn't care." The prisoners went to work "very carefully" and successfully cleared the minefield without further incident. Hitchcock and the rest of Sherman's troops heartily approved of the policy.[83]

By December 10, Sherman's army had invested the city of Savannah, closing off what seemed to be most of the practical routes of escape for its garrison. The overall situation was good, but with the army on short rations composed entirely of rice, which the men now had to spend nearly all their time threshing, it was important to open a supply line to the sea as soon as possible. Howard entrusted his scout, Duncan, with the assignment of going down the Ogeechee River in a dugout canoe, past various Confederate posts including Fort McAllister, in order to reach U.S. Navy vessels in Ossabaw Sound and alert them of the army's approach. Accompanied by Sgt. Myron J. Amick and Pvt. George W. Quimby and aided by numerous slaves along the way, Duncan succeeded in his task.[84]

With the investment of Savannah, the March to the Sea was over. The men of the Army of the Tennessee had experienced some difficult times—the rain, mud, snow, and bitter chill of the cold snap in central Georgia and the sparse rations of rice during the final days outside Savannah. Overall, however, they would remember the March to the Sea as the most enjoyable chapter of their army careers. "It beats everything I ever saw soldiering," wrote Charles Wills. "The march was little more than a grand picnic," recalled Hazen. "The country was full of what were luxuries to us." No army, he believed, had ever been in better health and vigor.[85] That was the most common way for participants to describe the march: "a picnic every day," or "a great picnic."[86]

The weather remained uncomfortably hot until heavy rains on the evening of December 10 heralded the arrival of another cold front. By the next night, Wills was recording in his diary, "Tonight promises to be the coldest night of the winter."[87] On December 13, Sherman ordered Howard to assign Hazen's division to storm Fort McAllister, which guarded the mouth of the Ogeechee River at Ossabaw Sound. Hazen's was the old Fifth Division, which had been Sherman's at Shiloh and for several months afterward. It was always a favorite of his, though by this time, thanks to several reorganizations, only five of the division's seventeen regiments had served in Sherman's division at Shiloh, and two of those, the 54th Ohio and 55th Illinois, had been part of David Stuart's detached brigade. The other three, the 53rd, 57th, and 70th Ohio, had been with Sherman for the heroic defense of the ridge near Shiloh Church and had proved themselves on many a battlefield since, as had the division's other regiments, several of which had joined the organization while Sherman was still its commander.[88]

Fort McAllister was immediately in rear of the Army of the Tennessee's lines facing Savannah, and more important, it blocked the landing of supplies from the fleet. Hazen had to wait for a pioneer and engineer detachment to rebuild the bridge over the mouth of the Cannoochee River, but he had his division in position for the attack by 1:00 p.m. that day. The garrison was not large, only about 200 men, but it defended a very well-built, powerful fort with twenty-three heavy guns, protected by an extensive abatis and a minefield covering all its approaches. In theory, the Rebels ought to have been able to fight off as large a force as would have room to attack.[89]

Hazen spent the afternoon carefully positioning his division. He placed one flank on the Ogeechee above McAllister and the other on the river below, and he carefully worked his skirmishers forward until they were in the abatis itself, sheltering behind the trunks of the felled trees that comprised the obstruction.[90]

Sherman, Howard, and their staffs watched anxiously from the opposite side of the Ogeechee, some three and a half miles away across salt marsh and open water. Army of the Tennessee signal officers had built a platform astride the ridgepole of a rice mill, and Sherman and the other officers climbed to the top of a shed adjoining the rice mill, where they had a good view and could easily communicate with the signalmen. Nearby they had a section of De Gress's 20-pounder Parrotts banging away at the fort, partially to divert the attention of the Confederates and partially to attract the attention of any U.S. naval vessels that might be within earshot. Local slaves had given Union officers information that led them to believe the fleet was looking for them. Each night, they said, the warships offshore fired rockets, and each day a smaller steamer ventured into Ossabaw Sound as far as it dared before being warned off by the guns of Fort McAllister.[91]

As the afternoon wore on, Sherman had his signalmen wigwag a message to Hazen's division reminding its commander that he wanted the fort taken today. Hazen sent back to say he would get the job done, but the sun was getting lower and Sherman was impatient.[92] About that time, someone noticed a smudge of smoke on the horizon far out in Ossabaw Sound. As the source of the smoke moved and drew closer, there could be no doubt that it was a steamer. Thereafter Sherman and his officers divided their observations between Hazen's methodical preparations and the slow approach of the vessel in the sound. As it came nearer, the officers could see through their field glasses that it flew the United States flag. Shortly before 5:00 p.m., the ship was close enough to exchange semaphore messages with

Sherman's signalmen atop the mill and to draw a few ineffective long-range shots from the fort's artillery. "Who are you?" signaled the vessel.

"General Sherman," the army flagman replied.

"Is Fort McAllister taken?" the navy wanted to know.

"Not yet," Sherman had his signalman send, "but it will be in a minute!"[93]

Almost at that moment, Hazen launched his assault, using nine regiments aimed at three specific objectives around the fort's perimeter. It was over in thirteen minutes. Hazen's men swarmed through the abatis, across the minefield—taking more casualties from the mines than from enemy fire—and over the parapet before the defenders could do them much damage. With the fort overrun, the Confederates had little choice but surrender. Hazen's casualties were about ninety killed and wounded. The Confederates lost forty or fifty killed and wounded, and the rest captured, along with all their guns.[94]

Through the haze of white powder smoke, Sherman, Howard, and the others could see the Stars and Stripes waving over the parapets and the blue-clad troops exuberantly celebrating, firing their rifles into the air. It even seemed as if the soldiers' shouts carried all the way across the expanse of river and salt marsh and were audible to the party at the rice mill. Sherman immediately ordered up a small boat to carry him across the river, accompanied by Howard. After congratulating Hazen and inspecting the fort, Sherman found another small boat to carry him out to the naval vessel, which he found to be the tug *Dandelion*. Later that night he returned to the fort.[95]

With a steady flow of supplies now assured, Sherman was able to turn his attention to taking Savannah and its defenders, who were commanded by Lt. Gen. William J. Hardee. Over the next few days, Sherman conferred with Adm. John A. Dahlgren on how best to cooperate on the capture of Savannah. As it turned out, however, Hardee proved slippery enough to extract his garrison across the swamps and islands around the mouth of the Savannah River and reach safety in South Carolina on December 20, the fourth anniversary of that state's declaration that it was no longer part of the nation. The following day, Union troops marched into the city. Sherman would have liked to have bagged Hardee's troops but was happy enough to take Savannah. In a dispatch to Lincoln, Sherman wrote, "I beg to present you, as a Christmas gift, the city of Savannah, with 150 heavy guns and plenty of ammunition, and also about 25,000 bales of cotton."[96]

For the next six weeks, the army encamped outside Savannah, and the men enjoyed a rest and a taste of a climate very different from what they had grown up with. One strange feature of life near Savannah was the availability of all the oysters the men cared to eat, a delicacy few of them had previously enjoyed in anything like such amounts.[97] When not gathering oysters, many took the opportunity to visit the city and do a little sightseeing, and their letters almost read like travelogues. "The streets are wide, unpaved and sandy, but laid out with great regularity, and well shaded with trees." Monuments to Revolutionary War heroes Nathanael Greene and Casimir Pulaski were special points of interest. Another was the waterfront, where many could see oceangoing ships for the first time.[98]

Howard made his headquarters in the house of Sir James Mullineaux, a British citizen. In one room, numerous citizens of Savannah had stored their fine liquors, hoping that they would not be confiscated if they were "under the protection of the British flag." In another room, they had stockpiled various other sorts of valuables, including books, with similar hopes of protection. Howard entrusted the keys to these rooms to Capt. Wimer Bedford of his staff. As Bedford recalled years later, all of the items in both rooms somehow made their way into the army. "We did not care much for the British flag," he wrote. The men of the Army of the Tennessee had seen far too much British military equipment in the hands of the Rebel army. "We had no respect therefore for the English Government and hence none for its flag."[99]

The moral effect of the March to the Sea could be noticed in the demeanor of the citizens of Savannah. "Here, for the first time," wrote Maj. James S. Reeves, "the people are submissive, and acknowledge our power. In other places they were defiant and insolent, but we see now the evidence that the conviction is deep, that our army can go over the Confederacy at will, and they have no army to stand before it."[100]

CHAPTER THIRTY-FOUR

Columbia

DURING THE WEEKS the army remained around Savannah, Sherman and Grant exchanged telegrams and contemplated the next campaign. Grant was inclined to favor transporting Sherman's army by sea to Virginia. Then Grant and Sherman and their combined armies would defeat Lee. There was no question that when Sherman arrived in Virginia, Lee's days would be numbered, and with Sherman having just finished overrunning the Confederate West, Lee's defeat would all but assure the end of the war. The difficulty, as usual, lay in logistics. It would take time to assemble enough shipping to transport Sherman's army, and Sherman believed he could get to Virginia just as fast, or faster, by marching, duplicating his journey across Georgia. While his army would be moving toward Virginia and a denouement whose issue could not be in doubt, it would also be further eviscerating both the Confederacy's economy and its will to resist. Grant agreed.

Sherman's soldiers were eager for such a march. For the first time in the war, it would take them into South Carolina, birthplace of secession. Frank Putney remembered how as early as the winter of 1862–63 his fellow soldiers around their campfires would "denounce South Carolina with bitter reproaches as the cause of the war and declare that when they got there they would give her a 'warming.' "[1] Even other Southerners desired to see the scourge of war laid on the back of South Carolina. As the army had marched through Georgia, citizens had frequently asked, "Why don't you go over to South Carolina, and serve them this way? They started it."[2]

During mid- and late January, the few available transport vessels slowly and laboriously ferried the Army of the Tennessee some forty miles up the coast to Beaufort, South Carolina, which had been held by Union forces as a coastal enclave for the past two years. For most of the men, it was their first ocean voyage, and many were seasick.[3] On January 15, the leading elements of the Army of the Tennessee advanced from Beaufort, skirmishing occasionally with small Confederate forces, and occupied Pocotaligo, about twenty-five miles inland. This was to be their jumping-off point for the coming offensive into the heart of the state. During the last two weeks of January, the rest of the army joined the vanguard around Pocotaligo. Once again the Army of the Tennessee would comprise the right wing of Sherman's combined force, while the Army of Georgia, under Slocum, advanced on the left from its starting point of Hardeeville, South Carolina, on the northeast bank of the Savannah River.[4]

During the advance from Beaufort to Pocotaligo, the soldiers got started on what they had come to South Carolina to do. "We were not out of sight of Port Royal Ferry," wrote General Hazen, "when the black columns of smoke began to ascend." Hazen was one of the few men of any rank in the Army of the Tennessee who did not desire to see South Carolina burn, but he found that his orders to spare this or that plantation house carried weight only in his immediate presence. As soon as he rode away, the structure went up in flames. "There was scarcely a building far or near on the line of that march that was not burned," wrote Hazen.[5] Charles Willison saw matters differently. He recorded that the soldiers spared occupied houses but burned abandoned ones.[6] The full story probably lay in between Hazen's and Willison's recollections. The soldiers spared some houses, but some families had to flee from their burning homes. Hazen, for his part, seems to have been most concerned with the wealthy planters, persons of cultivation and refinement, whose residences he especially wished to spare. However, those were precisely the places his soldiers especially wished to burn.

On January 29, the army received orders to march early the next morning. In a letter written a few days later, young soldier Edward Allen recalled the orders that were read to his regiment, the 16th Wisconsin, at dress parade that evening. They reminded "us that S[outh] C[arolina] was the state where the seeds of rebellion were first sown & ripened into fruit & giving us to understand that we were not to be so closely restricted as through G[eorgi]a., i.e., allowed more privileges, though pillaging, house entering, burning unless ordered by the generals, would be severely punished."[7] The orders might have been equivocal, but most of the soldiers were very clear in their minds about what they wanted to do to the state of South Carolina.

Early on the morning of January 30, the Army of the Tennessee advanced on its last campaign, moving northwestward from Pocotaligo to McPhersonville. The countryside was level, the soil sandy, and the trees were pine and live oak. The weather was cool but pleasant, and the roads were good.[8] Foraging began again in the same pattern on which it had operated so successfully during the March to the Sea. The army also used the

ame march configuration, each corps on a different road, wagons in the
oad, soldiers walking beside them on either side. As they had during the
ast phase of the March to the Sea, Sherman and his staff rode with the Seventeenth Corps.[9]

After that first relatively easy day's march, however, the army began to
get a taste of what the trek through the Carolinas was going to be like. As
the army turned from northwest to due north, it found in front of it the
wide, flooded swamps in the valley of the Salkehatchie River, the first of
numerous broad swamps and many-channeled rivers it would have to cross
as it moved through the Carolina Low Country. The Rebels had destroyed
all the bridges and felled trees across the roads. Their cavalry, which
harassed the edges of the columns constantly, now defended the far bank of
the Salkehatchie.

After pausing on January 31 to allow Slocum's wing to overcome difficulties it was experiencing in crossing the Savannah River, the Army of the
Tennessee plunged ahead on the first day of February. Pioneer detachments
made short work of the felled-tree obstructions, joking that they could
remove them faster than the Confederates could put them in place. Mower's
division had the lead and that day crossed Whippy Swamp, a tributary of
the Salkehatchie.[10] Forming line of battle, they "wadded a swamp ½ to three
quarters of a mile in width and from knee deep to hip deep," wrote Missouri
soldier F. J. Smith in his diary that night.[11] The men would shout out fanciful soundings to one another as they had heard the sailors do a few days
before, and when a man would stumble and duck under the water, someone
was sure to call out, "No bottom!"[12]

Swamp crossings, some of them more than a mile wide, became routine
during the march. The ever-precise Hazen counted thirty-six by his division in South Carolina, along with six large and eight small rivers and
thirty-six creeks. "It rained most of the time, day and night," recalled Manning Force. For six straight weeks the soldiers were rarely dry.[13]

Moving the army, its artillery, ambulances, and supply wagons through
the swampy Low Country, laced with flooded streams, involved an immense
amount of work. Hazen's division built an incredible 17.6 miles of corduroy
road during the course of the campaign. Force's division built 15.8 miles,
and the others were probably just as active. Pioneer details worked all day,
every day, constructing the roads and bridges, often reinforced by entire
regiments or even brigades, all wielding axes or shovels and helping to drag
logs into place. Other massive details had the task of helping—sometimes
dragging, almost carrying—the wagons through muddy sections of the
road that had not been corduroyed. Often the wagon wheels met no ade-

quate resistance from the soft mud, and the wagons rested on their beds. "Parties were detailed every day to lift wagons up out of the mud, when the teams could not pull them through," recalled Force. "The amount of work of which a large body of troops is capable is almost incredible," wrote Hazen. "When the will is right, the question is one merely of organization."[14]

On February 2, Mower's division, still leading the advance of the Seventeenth Corps, which was closer to the Salkehatchie, reached the river, but the bridge was destroyed. Pressing five miles farther upstream, Mower found another bridge intact but heavily defended by entrenched Rebels who laid down a deadly fire on the causeway that approached the bridge. The next day, while Mower continued to confront the Rebels with one brigade, he sent his other two on a flanking movement to the left. By sundown they had waded the Salkehatchie and its swamps, bridged seventeen unfordable streams, and flanked the Rebels out of their position. Simultaneously, Giles Smith's division waded the river downstream, fording thirty-four or thirty-five (depending on who was counting) separate channels. "The water averaged waist deep generally and at many points still deeper," recalled Brig. Gen. William Belknap, "in a dense cypress timber, full of the usual 'cypress knees,' which were mostly covered with water, and running through a thick underbrush and luxuriant creeping vines of all kinds, enough to satisfy the taste of any amateur botanist."[15]

By February 6, the army had crossed the Salkehatchie after capturing several more intact bridges. The rapid and relatively bloodless crossing was a surprise to everyone from Howard down to the lowest private. Rumor had had it that the Rebel general Hardee held the far bank with 30,000 men and was planning to make a determined stand.[16]

Howard's rapid crossing apparently surprised the Rebels too, for on the east bank the army's foraging parties found better hunting. Accepting the verdict of their military leaders that the swamps themselves were impassable, Confederate civilians had neglected to ship their supplies elsewhere.[17] On the day the army crossed the river, Lt. Cyrus Roberts, commanding a forage detail, wrote in his diary, "Pleasant day. Foraged 1 cart & 1 wagon & filled them with bacon, flour, meal, potatoes (sweet), tobacco, molasses, honey, turkeys, chickens &c., also several horses & mules." (Presumably the horses and mules had to walk.) The next day, the regiment was so abundantly supplied with food that Roberts had his foraging party concentrate on acquiring more horses and mules instead.[18]

Within days, however, the South Carolinians, like their neighbors in Georgia, were applying all their ingenuity to hiding both foodstuffs and valuables. The soldiers in turn became increasingly adept at finding such items.[19] "The smallest recent change in the appearance of the surface of the earth anywhere was cause for explorations," wrote Lt. Frank Putney. "A newly made flower bed, a newly planted tree, a newly graveled walk, even a newly ploughed field was such a suspicious circumstance as to require investigation by prodding with a ramrod, and if anything solid was struck, by digging with a spade." Burial proved to be an unwise policy for protecting valuable items. "Whatever was unearthed," Putney continued, "whether food or family jewels, was confiscated, for all buried treasure whatever its nature, was regarded as fair spoil of war."[20]

Manning Force told of a sergeant of a foraging detachment who approached the master and mistress of a plantation and asked, "Has any one died here lately?"

"No, nobody," the planter replied.

"I thought somebody had died here," suggested the sergeant again.

"No, sir," said the planter, but his wife butted in, "Oh, yes, don't you remember, my dear, don't you remember that colored boy that was buried yesterday?"

"Ah, yes," said the planter, "there was a colored boy buried yesterday."

"I only wanted to let you know," the sergeant said very solemnly, "that I have opened that grave and taken out the corpse." The "corpse," it turned out, was the plantation's supply of ham.[21]

Foraging was more difficult in this campaign than it had been during the march through Georgia. Confederate cavalry were more numerous than they had been in Georgia and were making a concerted effort to drive in the Union foragers. Contact with the enemy was more frequent and more serious, encouraging foragers to keep together in sizable groups. The same swamps and flooded creeks that impeded the movement of the army itself also hindered the roving of the foragers. Yet they regularly ranged up to fifteen miles to either side and in front of the column. Finding adequate supplies was more difficult in this campaign because of the army's slower pace, only about six miles per day between Pocotaligo and Columbia as compared to roughly ten miles per day between East Point and Savannah. Hence the foragers had to range two-thirds again as far from the column in order to cover the same amount of territory.[22]

In their difficult tasks, the foragers found steady allies in the plantation blacks, who regularly helped them locate hidden food and served as guides on the back roads and as teamsters for the commandeered wagons, buggies, and other conveyances that brought the forage back to the column. The foragers' own resourcefulness was their main reliance, whether in escaping the Rebel cavalry or, as frequently occurred, taking over a gristmill and running it themselves for as much as three days at a time in order to provide flour and cornmeal for the army. In all of this, the regular foraging parties maintained good discipline and generally followed the orders pertaining to foraging. Maj. Samuel Mahon, who commanded a party of Corse's division, wrote, "I never knew of an instance where people were left destitute of food, no matter how pressing were the needs of the army; enough was left to keep the people from hunger." Indeed, no evidence has ever come to light suggesting that anyone starved in any of the areas Sherman's army marched over.[23]

Foraging, wading, building corduroy roads, the march continued day by day, across the Little Salkehatchie, South Edisto, and North Edisto rivers. Each river had several channels and was lined with swamps, and at each crossing the lead divisions used skill and extreme aggressiveness to seize the objective, often taking control of multiple bridges before the enemy could burn them. Typically one division would threaten a crossing directly while another would wade the swamps or ferry itself across a channel using makeshift rafts in order to flank the defenders. Sometimes the aggressive, wide-ranging foragers themselves took and held important objectives. On February 7, as the army prepared to advance toward the line of the Charleston & Augusta Railroad in the vicinity of Midway, South Carolina, word reached headquarters that the foragers already had it and were building defensive works to hold it until the rest of the army arrived. It did later that day, and the next day the men plied their by now well-honed skills as railroad wreckers.[24]

The army crossed the North Edisto and its swamps on February 12, and Sherman waded right along with the soldiers of the Seventeenth Corps through ice-cold water, knee-deep or deeper. At one point, the men heard Sherman give a shout and found that he had "got into a place over 3 feet deep." With much laughter among all involved, the men of the 17th Wisconsin seized "Uncle Billy" and carried him the rest of the way across.[25]

That day the army took Orangeburg, South Carolina.[26] Many of its citizens fled before the arrival of the troops, and some set fire to the stockpiles of cotton they left behind. It was a strange irony of the march that Rebels would consistently burn their cotton to prevent it from falling into the hands of Sherman's troops, who were burning all the cotton they could find. In Orangeburg, the flames spread from the cotton to the surrounding buildings, and the town was on fire when the Union troops arrived. Howard noted that "the wind was high and the fire spread rapidly." The first Union regiment to enter the town, the 68th Ohio, went right to work fighting the fires. Years later, Cpl. Joshua Dicus of the 68th would wryly tell his grand-daughter that Sherman's men had not burned anything while marching through the South—they just went around putting out the fires the Rebels had set. Dicus and his comrades finally succeeded in containing the blaze, though not before it had destroyed a large part of the town. They did, how-ever, manage to save the Orphan Asylum of South Carolina, home of some 300 children. Thereafter, they found 200 bales of cotton that the retreating Confederates had neglected to torch. So, after carefully transporting the bales outside the town to open fields, the Federals burned the cotton, taking care not to allow the fire to spread to what was left of Orangeburg.[27]

In selecting the route of the campaign, Sherman was using the same method that had proved successful during the march through Georgia, keeping the Confederates uncertain as to his true destination so that they could not mass their forces in his path. In this case, Sherman shaped his route in such a way that Howard's Army of the Tennessee appeared to threaten Charleston while Slocum's Army of Georgia appeared to threaten Augusta. In fact, both armies passed by those targets, traveling about forty to fifty miles apart on a course toward the center of the state and the capital at Columbia. At Orangeburg, the Army of the Tennessee was about eighty-five miles from Beaufort and only forty from Columbia.

The march so far had been as destructive as the soldiers had anticipated, with most of the houses along the route going up in flames. "I never saw so much destruction of property before," Charles Wills wrote in his diary. "Orders are as strict as ever, but our men understand they are in South Car-olina and are making good their old threats. Very few houses escape burn-ing, as almost everybody has run away from before us, you may imagine there is not much left in our track. Where a family remains at home they save their house, but lose their stock, and eatables."[28]

"We are marching on through this wicked state," wrote Illinois soldier Isaiah Dillon to his wife. "Oh, the destruction of property, burning clean as we go, houses and all."[29] When John Corse's division of the Fifteenth Corps passed through Robertsville, the soldiers set fires that consumed almost every structure in the village except the church.[30] A soldier of the 55th Illinois, marching with the main column of the Fifteenth Corps, recorded that only abandoned houses were burned, as well as any that the soldiers thought belonged to slaveholders. He also noted that the officers of the Fifteenth made vigorous efforts to prevent the wholesale burning, but to no avail. "Through the state the progress of each corps was signaled far and wide by the columns of flame and smoke that day by day rose from burning buildings, as the army moved northward by parallel routes."[31] And rightly so, thought Sherman's men. "Thus the instigators and abettors of Rebellion get their reward," wrote Lt. Ensign King of the 15th Iowa.[32]

Near Midway one evening, Lt. Frank Putney and another staff officer were riding ahead of their brigade with orders to scout their assigned campground by daylight and be able to guide the several regiments to their places when they arrived after dark. As they approached a plantation house, a middle-aged gentleman asked that Putney post a guard to prevent the burning or looting of his property. Putney replied that he had no guard detail available, but the planter was insistent and asked where he could find the general in command of the troops then approaching. The general, he suggested, would surely be willing to protect his library from destruction, motioning toward a detached, one-story building near the house. Such a library was unusual on a plantation and prompted Putney to ask the man his name.

"William Gilmore Simms, Sir," said the man with a bow. Putney started. Simms was the foremost novelist of the South and, among American novelists of his day, second only to James Fenimore Cooper. His popularity and that of his "Border Stories" like *Richard Hurdis* and *Border Beagles* had spread well beyond his region, and his books had been the beloved boyhood reading of young Frank Putney in far-off Wisconsin. Putney immediately sought out his brigade commander, Brig. Gen. Charles Ewing, to urge the case for posting a guard over Simms's plantation, known as Woodlands. Ewing readily agreed, but he warned Simms that his writ ran only as far as his own brigade. The novelist would have to seek a like accommodation from the commander of each subsequent brigade that passed through the area. With the guard posted, Putney went off to attend to his delayed mission, wondering if Simms's library would ultimately be spared. It was not.[33]

Despite the destruction, however, very little theft of valuables took place, and personal violence toward civilians was unheard of. The soldiers were particular about keeping their loads as light as possible, and they would even trim off a few inches of their blankets, if they did not need the length, so as not to have to carry the extra weight. They were reluctant to take on the burden of carrying pilfered valuables. Manning Force related how one evening the provost marshals of the Seventeenth Corps made a surprise raid on the camps, searching the soldiers and their knapsacks for booty. All they found was a little tobacco and a few pieces of pilfered clothing. South Carolina civilians told Force that his troops and the Confederate cavalry were alike in taking their food and livestock. The difference was that the Federals would then burn their house whereas the Confederates 'abused and insulted them." Force never heard of a single case of "personal abuse" of a South Carolina civilian by a Union soldier.[34]

As Putney was riding ahead of the army one day, he was startled to hear "ear-piercing feminine screams" coming from a plantation house. Spurring his horse, Putney rode into the plantation yard, which was swarming with foragers methodically removing food from the premises. Putney excitedly demanded of one of the soldiers "why he did not go to the aid of the woman."

"Oh, she's all right," replied the soldier nonchalantly.

The puzzled lieutenant rode around the house to the source of the screaming. There he found a woman standing in a barrel of molasses, not only screaming but intermittently shrieking out curses at the soldiers. Putney had never heard a woman use such language before. He asked the soldiers what had happened, and they explained that some minutes earlier several men had entered the kitchen to get a dipper. The woman had snatched up the dipper and used it to fling boiling water in their faces, whereupon the rest of the soldiers had seized her, carried her outside, and dropped her in the barrel of molasses, suggesting that she stay there as "it might sweeten her temper." Reflecting on the situation, Putney decided that, given the woman's frame of mind and lack of self-control, she was probably safer in the barrel than out of it. So he quietly rode off, leaving her screaming imprecations from her treacle bath.[35]

As the army approached Columbia, it passed through countryside that was more thickly settled—and had more houses to burn. "The whole country seemed on fire at times," wrote an Illinois soldier, who surmised that the inhabitants of Columbia "could plainly see the columns of smoke rapidly coming nearer day by day, and anticipate the retribution about to overwhelm them."[36]

Sometimes the countryside really was on fire. A thick belt of pine woods extended across the army's path south of Columbia, containing many turpentine-making establishments. Some of the first troops through these woods, perhaps the foragers or bummers, had set them afire, apparently as a lark. Those who came behind had to make their way through or around the burning woods as best they could. "At one place, a short distance from the road had been stored several hundred barrels of rosin," recalled Charles Willison. "This caught and the roar of its burning could be heard long before we reached the scene, creating such a dense smoke as to obscure the sun." The infantry scattered through the woods looking for nonburning routes to the other side, and Willison thought it was nothing short of miraculous that the ammunition wagons had not blown up. The tarry smoke left the men looking like coal-heavers.[37]

Confederate cavalry, supported by artillery, continued to skirmish briskly with the lead elements of the army, disputing every bridge, causeway, or swamp crossing. On the night of February 15, Confederate artillery on the north bank of the Congaree River bombarded the camp of the army's lead divisions. Only a few men were killed and wounded, but "the annoyance was great," Hazen recalled. "We were all driven to dig holes in the ground to lie in, and the shrieking of shot in the darkness just over us was unpleasant beyond expression." Daylight on February 16 found the Rebels gone. The Army of the Tennessee followed, reached the banks of the Congaree, and gazed across at the city of Columbia on the far shore.

The Congaree was wide here and looked difficult to cross. Indeed, the engineer officers gave the opinion that the army's pontoon train was not adequate to span it. The river was formed by the confluence of the Saluda and Broad rivers just above the city, so Sherman ordered Howard to cross the Saluda about a mile above Columbia. Howard brought up artillery to silence the Confederate guns that were firing at the army from the edge of Columbia itself. The Union gunners succeeded in that task, as well as in scattering some cavalry and suppressing looters who were emptying a depot of food supplies that Sherman very much wanted for his own troops.

As Rebel sharpshooters continued to fire from the buildings of the town, the Union artillerists kept up their bombardment. "I was amused to see the gunners knock the chimneys off of buildings," wrote Sgt. John Bannan of the nearby 4th Iowa. On orders from Sherman, De Gress's gunners put a couple of 20-pounder Parrott solid shots into the statehouse. Then someone suggested that they "throw a few shots at the arsenal," which was more than a mile away. De Gress lent his field glass to one of his gun captains and pointed out the arsenal. The sergeant scrutinized the building and remarked, "I can knock the chimney off." There were several chimneys on the building, so an officer designated a specific one as the target. The sergeant carefully laid his piece, fired, and several seconds later the chimney toppled.[38]

Howard then had Hazen send a brigade several miles above the town, where a bridge spanned the Saluda, to secure a crossing there. To no one's surprise, the Rebels had burned the bridge. Hazen's men found some small boats and a larger one that could take horses, and with these a regiment of infantry and a few horsemen, including Hazen himself, got over the river, drove off the Confederate pickets, and made a dash for the covered bridge over the Broad River. The Rebels, however, had prepared the bridge with tinder and turpentine and lit it at the first sign that the Federals were across the Saluda. It was a roaring blaze by the time Hazen's party arrived.[39]

For the moment, that stopped the Union advance. The engineers soon had a pontoon bridge over the Saluda, and the rest of Hazen's division as well as Woods's marched across it during February 16, into the peninsula formed by the convergence of the Saluda and the Broad. That evening Woods alerted Col. George Stone, commanding his Third Brigade, to have his troops ready to cross the river at or before first light. Stone's men, five regiments of Iowans, spent a chilly and unpleasant night on the southwest bank of the Broad River with orders not to light any fires.[40]

Stone hoped to enter Columbia by daybreak on February 17, but the engineers had difficulty getting his brigade to the northeast bank. They had three pontoon boats available and hoped to ferry the brigade across. First, however, they had to get a rope across the fast-flowing river to guide the ferrying operation, and this they did not succeed in doing until 3:00 a.m., when two daring officers carried the rope across in a skiff, guided only by the light of the campfire of a Confederate picket post on the far shore. At 3:50 the first boatloads of troops—the 31st Iowa—crossed to the far bank and set up a perimeter. Colonel Stone was among the first across and found that his troops were on a crescent-shaped island about 25 yards wide and 200 yards long. Separating it from the northeast shore were only a few shallow, fordable channels, defended by Confederate cavalry. Stone deployed his brigade on the island and mounted a successful assault. His men charged through the side channels of the river, holding their rifles and cartridge boxes above their heads, and drove off the Rebel horsemen.[41]

Stone halted to allow the next brigade, Col. William B. Woods's, to begin crossing. As soon as it did, Stone took up the march again toward Columbia. About a mile from the city, he met a delegation in a carriage bearing a flag of truce, approaching from the other direction, composed of the mayor and two aldermen, who had come out to seek terms for the surrender of the city. Stone's reply was reminiscent of Grant's at Fort Donelson, two years and one day before: "I refused anything but an unconditional surrender." Since the Confederate cavalry was helpless to prevent the fall of Columbia, the officials had little choice but to accept. As the mayor, aldermen, Stone, a few staff officers, and a forty-man escort approached the city, they found about fifteen of Stone's advanced skirmishers being driven back by a battalion of Rebel cavalry, who either did not know or did not care that the city had been surrendered. Stone threatened to shoot the officials, but his escorts, together with the handful of advanced skirmishers, drove off the cavalry.[42]

Stone's brigade resumed its march into Columbia. Stone and Capt. William B. Pratt of the Fifteenth Corps staff hurried ahead and raised the U.S. flag of the 31st Iowa Regiment over the statehouse. As soon as the engineers had finished constructing a pontoon bridge over the Broad River, the rest of Woods's division marched into Columbia in column of fours.[43]

Whether they were the first U.S. troops to enter the city and whether the flag of the 31st Iowa was indeed the first to wave over the South Carolina statehouse was a matter of much dispute after the war. Very early that morning, while Stone's brigade was still working on its river crossing, Brig. Gen. William W. Belknap, who commanded the Old Iowa Brigade in the Seventeenth Corps, dispatched a party of eighteen men of the 13th Iowa under Lt. Col. Justin C. Kennedy, accompanied by two staff officers, in a small flatboat that he and his men had spent most of the night modifying. They crossed the Congaree much closer to Columbia, in more danger from the rapid and treacherous current than from the Rebels. "We put our over-coats on the edge of the boat to keep the water from coming in," recalled Iowan Thomas Oldham.

Ashore on the other side, they drove off some Confederate skirmishers, then pushed inland until they encountered a horse and buggy, which they immediately commandeered. The three officers, two color-bearers, and a couple of other soldiers piled in, and off they went toward the statehouse. A couple of blocks from their goal, they exchanged shots with some horse-men, who promptly fled. Then Kennedy and his men hoisted the national colors over the old statehouse, and their blue regimental flag over the new one. Kennedy's men and their flags were visible to much of the Seventeenth Corps across the river, and the men cheered heartily.[44]

Unaware of Kennedy's extracurricular adventure, Stone's troops marched into the city, proudly believing themselves the first Union soldiers to set foot in the capital of the first state to secede. They halted along the main street, stacked arms, and stood looking around at the wealthy and tasteful seat of government of South Carolina and also at the long piles of cotton bales in the middle of the street, still smoldering from fires lit by South Carolina general Wade Hampton's cavalrymen as they evacuated the city. Once again the Confederates were burning cotton to prevent it from falling into the hands of Sherman's Yankees—who could do nothing with it but burn it. At some point after the horsemen rode off, the local fire company turned out with a rather dilapidated fire engine to try to extin-guish the long ridge of blazing fiber in the middle of the city's principal thoroughfare—as well as numerous other streets—which was not only a waste of valuable cotton but also a serious fire hazard to the rest of Columbia. They were still trying when the soldiers arrived, with the fire far from completely extinguished.[45]

Aside from the long, burning heaps of cotton in many of its streets, Columbia was not looking quite itself that morning. Confederate stragglers and civilians had, between the departure of Hampton's cavalry and the arrival of the Union infantry, done a good deal of looting. Fires had destroyed or damaged several buildings. Stores and shops were broken open, and papers, rags, and various litter lay scattered on the floors, in the open doorways, and on the street and sidewalk outside. A stiff wind scattered the loose papers down the streets and festooned fences, trees, and bushes with loose cotton. To Howard, it looked like a grove in his native Maine after a snowstorm.[46]

To Stone's brigade fell the duty of taking possession of the public buildings and providing provost guards to keep order. The rest of the Fifteenth Corps marched through Columbia with Sherman and Howard in front of them, colors flying and bands playing, being careful to march on the windward side of the long ridges of burning cotton, which were still emitting thick, choking smoke. Blacks and some whites along the streets cheered Sherman as he passed. The Fifteenth encamped a mile or two beyond Columbia. The Seventeenth had to wait its turn at the bridges behind the Fifteenth. Its lead division marched through the city about at nightfall and camped near the Fifteenth, but the other two divisions halted before passing through the city and camped on the outskirts.[47]

Among those wandering the streets that afternoon were several dozen recent Union prisoners of war, escapees from a camp for captured officers just outside Columbia who had been hiding in the city since their escape. Instantly recognizable by their tattered clothes, usually bare heads and feet, and gaunt, almost skeletal appearance, the former prisoners had an agenda.[48] One of them approached several members of the 31st Iowa and told them, "If you do not burn the city we will."[49]

Among those who were happy to see the arrival of Union soldiers in Columbia were the slaves. As always, they received the Federals joyfully, eager to see them appropriate or destroy the property of their erstwhile masters. This day the interest of many of the soldiers seemed to be in getting drunk, and the slaves obligingly guided ever-growing numbers of stragglers to the cellars and warehouses where large stocks of alcohol were to be found.[50]

The slaves were also among those handing out liquor to the men. As the soldiers of Stone's brigade lounged in the street, civilians—black and white—approached, offering them liquor. When Hazen marched in at the head of his division somewhat later, liquors of various sorts were being "passed along the line in buckets and tin pans, and in one instance in a large tin boiler such as is used on kitchen stoves. Many men in the ranks," noted the strict disciplinarian Hazen, "were already drunk."[51]

As Sherman rode into the city with his staff, Howard noticed that not only were the newly freed slaves cheering lustily, but the Union soldiers lining the streets were cheering with unusual enthusiasm. A soldier wearing a plug hat and a long, ornate dressing gown over his uniform stepped gravely down off the sidewalk and approached the general, lifting his nonregulation headgear. "I have the honor (hic), General, to present (hic) you with (hic) the freedom of the (hic) City." Members of Sherman's escort lost no time in arresting the man. Sherman grinned and rode on.[52]

Subtly, almost imperceptibly at first, military control of the streets was growing perilously weak. Stone was away from his brigade for about an hour on his excursion to raise the flag over the statehouse. By the time he got back, many of his men were drunk. They were tired, he wrote, and many had not had time to eat and thus were drinking on empty stomachs. It was the only way he could account for the amount of intoxication in his command in such a short time. He might have had another explanation if he had been present to see the prodigious amounts of liquor some of his men had been consuming.[53] "Officers were flying around trying to stop it," recalled Lt. Samuel Snow of the 25th Iowa. Snow and a detail he led destroyed some twenty barrels of liquor.[54] Other officers were also having barrels of whiskey rolled out into the street and the heads of the barrels knocked in, allowing the liquor to pour out onto the street. "Some of the boys were trying to save some of it by dipping it out of the gutter," recalled Capt. William Duncan.[55]

The streets quieted down later in the afternoon, and nothing looked seriously amiss in the hours before sunset. Howard gave orders to post provost guards, and inspected many of the sentinels, questioning them about their orders and checking their sobriety. He noticed a number of drunken soldiers and gave orders to Logan, who was back at the helm of the Fifteenth Corps, to have the culprits arrested at once. Then, as fatigued as anyone else from the hard campaigning and constant skirmishing of recent days, Howard went to his headquarters, a commandeered house in the city, and tried to get some sleep.[56]

Several fires had already occurred in various buildings around the city, but Stone's troops, those who were sober at least, quickly put them out. Gradually, however, the pace began to accelerate. Around sundown, which came at 6:09 p.m., Hazen noticed several fires in "a clump of isolated wooden buildings a little to the north of the principal hotel." The buildings themselves looked to be beyond saving, but Hazen thought the fire could easily be stopped from spreading farther. Over the next two hours, additional fires broke out. Meanwhile, the day's stiff breeze from the south and southwest was gradually picking up into a howling windstorm devoid of rain.[57]

By eight o'clock, Stone's brigade was overwhelmed. Many of his men had continued doing their duty faithfully throughout the day, but some significant portion of the brigade was hopelessly drunk. This left the command critically shorthanded in the face of a challenge that might well have been too much for it even at full strength. Untold numbers of stragglers were pouring into the city from the camps of the Fifteenth Corps, northeast of the city, and the Seventeenth southwest of it. Stone even thought some of these nocturnal bummers came from Kilpatrick's cavalry division. All manner of civilians were roaming the streets, including large numbers of newly freed slaves. Nobody knew where the former prisoners of war were at this hour, and to make matters worse, someone had opened the city jail, and all of the inmates were now at large in the city. The fires had never really died inside the heaps of cotton in the streets, and under the stiff breeze they were now blazing merrily. Fire spread rapidly to nearby buildings.[58]

Twice during the early evening hours, Stone sent his division commander, Charles Woods, requests for another regiment or two as reinforcements. By 8:00 p.m., fires began to spread out of control. At about 9:00 p.m., Howard, whose rest had been very short-lived, decided that Stone's brigade had become inefficient and ordered Woods to relieve it with the brigade of his brother, Col. William Woods. For Stone's Iowans, at least those sober enough to know about it, the order was a humiliating reversal from the glorious flag-raising a few hours before. Stone ordered his regiments to march out to the divisional camps north of town, but he himself remained in the city throughout the night trying to fight the fires.[59]

It might have been scant consolation to Stone to know that Woods was faring little better. Hazen met him shortly after he took over the city and suggested that he turn out his men and pull down some buildings to create a fire break. With evident frustration, Woods replied that "he could not get men enough together to do any good."[60] That statement raises the suspicion that Woods's brigade was in no better shape than Stone's. They may not all have been drunk, but most seemed to have their own agenda that night, and saving the capital of South Carolina from burning was definitely not on it. A soldier of Woods's brigade, William Baugh of the 76th Ohio, wrote that he and his comrades attempted to use one of the town's fire engines to fight the fires, but someone cut the hose. "The soldiers were bound to burn the secession place," he wrote, "and they done it."[61]

At about the same time, or possibly a little later, Charles Woods dispatched his third brigade, Col. Robert F. Catterson's, into the city. Theodore Upson of the 100th Indiana was part of Catterson's brigade. "A good many of our men were drunk," he later recalled. "Our first business was to gather them up and get them out of the way." Thereafter, Upson and his comrades spent the rest of the night helping citizens of Columbia escape from the flames with as much of their property as possible. "All we could do was to hustle them out and if they had any little valuables help them get them to a safe place," Upson wrote. "Where we could get blankets we gave them without asking to whom they belonged. Some of the women we had to carry as best we could, and the little children too."[62]

All across the city, where soldiers had been detailed to act as guards at private residences, most of the sentinels remained faithful to their duty throughout the night, alternately fighting fires and fending off their drunken, off-duty comrades. An Iowa soldier found himself without a post when the house he was guarding burned down. He attached himself to another house where several ladies were staying who had been frightened by drunken soldiers on looting expeditions. The Iowan spent the rest of the night fending off would-be intruders, breaking his rifle over the head of one of them, and left the house and its inhabitants intact in the morning. Mrs. Campbell Bryce credited the faithfulness and energy of her two guards with saving her house from the flames, and she saw to it that they were well fed in the morning.

The drunken, rioting stragglers were bent on plunder but were neither vicious nor especially violent. A few male South Carolinians who attempted to interfere got knocked down for their troubles, but beyond that the residents suffered no personal violence. Harriet Ravenel wrote that a "stream of drunkards poured through the house, plundering and raging" but admitted that they were "curiously civil, and abstaining from personal insult. . . . They generally spoke to us as 'Lady,' and although they swore horribly, they seldom swore at us." Another Columbia woman noted, "The Yankees were just as gentlemanly as rough men could well be."[63]

Howard spent the night, along with Logan, Woods, and other generals, in trying to contain the fire and save the affected civilians. It was, he later wrote, "one of the most terrific scenes that I have ever witnessed." Burning buildings on all sides illuminated the soldiery, the riffraff, and the frightened civilians running in all directions. In several places, Howard noticed knots of soldiers protecting civilians from the released banditti and possibly from their own straggling and inebriated fellow soldiers.[64] Several hundred soldiers of Brig. Gen. William T. Clark's brigade of John E. Smith's division of the Fifteenth Corps obtained permission to go back into the city to help fight the fires.[65]

Around 3:00 a.m., Logan ordered Hazen to send another brigade into the city. Hazen dispatched Brig. Gen. John M. Oliver's brigade. By this time, Woods's troops in the city were already beginning to get control of the situation. The 40th Illinois formed ranks, fixed bayonets, and started sweeping the streets. Still, Oliver and his men found work to do when they got to town. "Called out to suppress riot," Oliver tersely reported, "did so, killing 2 men, wounding 30, and arresting 370."[66] The wind also died down at about that time, allowing the troops finally to halt the spread of the fire. About one-third of the city had burned, primarily the business district.[67]

After it was over, men began to discuss the causes of the Columbia fire, and the argument went on for as long as the participants lived. Pvt. Edwin Kimberly believed the smoldering cotton, fanned into a blaze and carried over the city by the high wind, was the source of the conflagration.[68] Logan and Hazen felt it was the work of drunk and disorderly Union soldiers.[69] Sgt. Maj. John G. Brown of the 55th Illinois, one of the regiments in Hazen's division, thought it was the recent prisoners of war, seeking revenge for their mistreatment and the deaths of many of their comrades in captivity.[70] Charles Woods, commander of the division to which Stone's brigade belonged, believed the fire stemmed from the burning cotton, perhaps aided by the common criminals who had been improperly released from the town jail the previous afternoon—as well as drunken slaves and soldiers.[71] His brother, Col. William B. Woods, who commanded the brigade that relieved Stone's, heard from "respectable citizens of the town" that the fire was "first set" by the local black population, and given the former slaves' frequently expressed desire for revenge against their onetime masters and their glee at the burning of large structures, he readily believed it.[72]

Eyewitness testimony is sufficient to establish that the smoldering cotton on the streets did flare up under the high winds and set fire to a number of surrounding buildings. The location of the destruction suggests that this was the primary source of the fire. Eyewitnesses among local civilians claimed to have seen both soldiers and recent jail inmates deliberately setting fires. No doubt members of the Army of the Tennessee were among the incendiaries. However, it is also clear that the majority of the soldiers either remained in their camps or struggled throughout the night to fight the fires or corral the riffraff.[73]

Some members of the Army of the Tennessee were sorry that Columbia had burned. "I do pity the women and poor little children that so many are made homeless and without anything," wrote Pvt. Jefferson Moses of the 93rd Illinois. "O, what a pity for them."[74] Others were pleased, but none were going to lose any sleep over it, then or later. "Little comment need be made respecting the manner of, and responsibility for, the burning of Columbia," wrote Sergeant Major Brown of the 55th Illinois some years after the war. "It only paid the just penalty for its treason. It was among the first to cry out for the war, and at length reaped its reward." Lt. Ensign H. King of the 15th Iowa agreed. "South Carolina, the nation state of John C. Calhoun, the hot-bed of treason, the first state to Rebel, the most defiant aider and abettor of the Rebellion, pays this small price for her crimes," he mused in his diary the day after the fire. "To our mind, the punishment is but commensurate with the crime." Reflecting on the night's long and ultimately futile firefighting efforts, Brown wrote, "The seal of destruction had been set upon the city, and it was doomed."[75] It was almost as if Columbia had burned by divine decree that night. "God only knows how much of this is in accordance with his will," concluded King.

CHAPTER THIRTY-FIVE

Washington and Home

ON FEBRUARY 20, the army took up the march again, followed by a large and constantly growing column of blacks fleeing slavery and even a number of white Unionists who feared for their safety among their secessionist fellow citizens. The refugees, both white and black, flocked to the army day after day as it marched northward. Foraging went on as usual. Provost guards tried to prevent looting. Raids on the wagons during the last week of February turned up a large number of items, which the soldiers, and perhaps especially the teamsters, had felt free to take from the ruins of Columbia. No one was allowed to keep such booty if discovered. The provosts either gave it to local civilians or destroyed it. In a pouring all-day rain on February 22, the army crossed the Wateree River near Camden, South Carolina.[1]

Shortly after crossing the river, Sherman had to deal with the problem of Confederate murder of Union prisoners. Such killings had begun against the men of Slocum's column as early as February 5, only a few days after the army had moved into South Carolina. Three of Slocum's men had been captured by Confederate cavalry, and a farmer named Trowell identified them to their captors as the men who had foraged at his farm. So the Confederates shot them and threw their bodies in the bushes not far from Trowell's house. Neither the house nor any of the outbuildings had been burned, but when Slocum learned the circumstances of the murders from slaves, he had the place torched and Trowell himself arrested and taken along with the army to be tried as an accessory to murder.[2]

Yet the problem continued. During the last week of February, Kilpatrick's cavalry found the mutilated bodies of an infantry lieutenant and seven enlisted men, lying close together, with papers pinned to their chests stating "Death to Foragers." That same day, Union cavalrymen discovered the remains of one of their own foraging parties, nine corpses, of which "two had their throats cut from ear to ear." Two soldiers of the Army of the Tennessee were found dead, "with their brains beaten out," and in circum-

stances in which it was clear that they had been captured first and then murdered.[3] On February 23, Sherman responded by ordering all of his subordinate commanders to carry out strict retaliation: "If any of your foragers are
murdered, take life for life, leaving a record of each case."[4]

They soon had opportunity. On February 24, Kilpatrick notified Sherman that his scouts had found in a ravine the bodies of twenty-one Union
infantrymen, apparently an entire foraging party, naked and with their
throats slit. One of Kilpatrick's troopers was hanged from a tree by the
roadside.[5] Sherman responded this time by sending a letter to Wade Hampton, informing him of these recent atrocities, pointing out that foraging was
entirely within the laws of war, and warning that if the murders continued
he would be forced to retaliate on a one-for-one basis. Hampton's reply
came back several days later, seething with hatred. It was the right of every
white Southern man, Hampton asserted, to "shoot down, as he would a
wild beast," any Union forager, and if Sherman retaliated, he would murder two more Union prisoners for every man Sherman executed.[6]

On February 25, a party of Rebel cavalry wearing captured Union uniforms struck a foraging party of Brig. Gen. William Clark's brigade within
a mile and a half of the brigade's camp. Clark's skirmishers pushed forward
and drove off the Rebels, but not before they had witnessed, at a distance, a
shocking scene. Two members of the foraging party, Pvt. William Barber
and Musician William Crackles, both of Company B, 63rd Illinois, surrendered. Then to the horror of their comrades several hundred yards away,
the Rebels shot them. Clark's men captured several of the Rebels in Union
uniforms, and his division commander, John E. Smith, ordered two of them
shot on the spot. His men grimly carried out the order.[7]

Nothing remained but to continue carrying out strict retaliation. On
March 1, Confederate cavalrymen captured and then beat to death Pvt.
Robert M. Woodruff of Company H, 30th Illinois. "His head had been
pounded to pieces with a pine club," wrote Allen Geer. Blair, to whose
corps the 30th belonged, ordered his provost marshal to "select from the
prisoners in his charge one man . . . to be shot to death in retaliation for the
murder."[8]

The men detailed to do the job prepared tickets, one of them marked for
death. Each prisoner had to draw one. The man who drew the fatal slip was
about forty-five years of age, a conscript, and the father of nine children.
The officer in charge gave him an hour to prepare, and he spent the time in
prayer. When the hour was up, the executioners blindfolded him and stood
him against a large tree. The firing squad consisted of twelve men from the
30th Illinois. Others had prepared the rifles in advance, six with ball car-

ridges and six with blanks. No member of the squad would know, except perhaps by the force of recoil, whether he had fired a bullet or not. The commander of the execution detail gave the order and the squad fired. The prisoner fell dead, struck by all six bullets. "Such are the necessities of War," wrote Lt. Cyrus Roberts of the 78th Ohio.[9] Despite Hampton's threats, the Confederates for a time refrained from murdering any more captured foragers.[10]

The army proceeded on. After a delay at the crossing of flooded Lynch's Creek, they reached Cheraw, on March 3. As at Columbia and Orangeburg, the troops found fires already burning when they arrived. In this case, it was a depot and several storehouses that the Rebels had torched in anticipation of the Union troops' arrival. Once on the scene, Howard's men gave Cheraw the standard treatment. "Everything in Cheraw of any value to the enemy, including cotton and business houses, is going up in smoke," wrote Capt. Charles Wills.[11] Leaving Cheraw, the army continued marching to the northeast, approaching the North Carolina line, which was only about twenty miles away by the route the army was taking. On March 7, Wills recorded in his diary, "We are about on the State line now, and will leave S[outh] C[arolina] tomorrow. I think she has her 'rights' now."[12]

In North Carolina, the nature of the march changed dramatically. Foraging continued, since the army still had to eat, but, as General Force noted, "destruction ceased. Not a house was burned."[13] The shift in behavior was universal throughout the army. "There was nothing more remarkable in this campaign than the entire change in the treatment of private property after we entered North Carolina," wrote Hazen. "The men all knew where the State line was."[14]

In one way, North Carolina was just like its neighbor to the south. Swamps and streams were abundant and the men seemed always to be crossing them. The weather was much the same too, mostly rainy, and the heavy rains seemed to turn the roads themselves into swamps. Force noted in his diary that "the roads were running" with water, and the corduroy that the men had laid was beginning to float away. Some of the soldiers remembered their first twenty-four hours in North Carolina as "the worst day and night the command ever saw in the service." Officers and men struggled side by side to get the cumbersome supply and pontoon wagons through the swamps, shouting in unison, "Hee, O hee!" Logan was much in evidence, one of the soldiers recalled, working "nearly all night, tugging at the ropes like a Trojan, covered with mud from head to feet."[15]

Shortly after crossing into North Carolina, Sherman asked Howard to slow his march in order to allow Slocum and the Army of Georgia to be first to take Fayetteville. Either Sherman thought it was Slocum's turn after the Army of the Tennessee had captured the last major city or else he was not quite sure about the behavior of his old command and wanted to be certain that Fayetteville did not get the Columbia treatment.[16]

As it turned out, the Army of the Tennessee's foragers were not party to the agreement and early on the morning of March 11 went into Fayetteville well ahead of Slocum's men. After the foragers had taken the town, a brigade of Confederate cavalry charged and drove them out, killing several and capturing several others, whom they subsequently murdered. The sound of firing brought dozens of additional foraging parties swarming in from the countryside, and one of the most amazing aspects of the entire incident is that this ad hoc collection of small groups immediately and spontaneously formed itself into an effective line of battle that maneuvered and fought with superb efficiency without the direction of any officers above the handful of lieutenants and captains with the individual parties. The soldiers of the Army of the Tennessee had so much experience fighting together that they at once recognized what needed to be done and what their own individual part in it should be. The second wave of foragers took Fayetteville and held it until Brig. Gen. Benjamin F. Potts's brigade of Giles Smith's division of the Seventeenth Corps came up to reinforce them. Later in the day, Slocum's Fourteenth Corps arrived to take over official control of the city.[17]

At Fayetteville the army made contact with Union vessels steaming up the Cape Fear River and received small amounts of supplies, though not nearly the number of shoes needed to replace those that the men had worn out in their hundreds of miles of marching. The army also used the contact to send its vast following column of refugees down the Cape Fear to Wilmington, for shipment by sea.[18]

March 12 was a Sunday, and many of the soldiers attended worship in one or another of the many churches in Fayetteville. Hoosier soldier Theodore Upson noted in his diary that he had heard "a pretty good sermon." It had been about "loving one's enemies," and Upton had to admit that the Southerners were going to have a hard time doing that. "But they would not have had any enemies if they had not tried to break up the Union," he added. "If they will give up that crazy notion and stop fighting us, we will be their best friends."[19]

By March 13, the destruction of military and industrial targets in Fayetteville was complete, and the army crossed the Cape Fear below the city and continued its progress northeastward, to Goldsboro, where Sherman planned to meet a force of some 20,000 men under the command of John M.

Schofield, moving inland from the coast, where Union forces had captured Fort Fisher, near Wilmington, two months before.[20] More caution was needed now, because for the first time since departing Atlanta they faced a significant Confederate field army. Hardee's force, now out of Savannah, Joseph Wheeler's and Wade Hampton's cavalry commands, various odds and ends of troops the Confederacy had been keeping in North Carolina, and, most significantly, a number of the component parts of the battered army that had once been Hood's had vainly attempted to hold Atlanta. After Hood's dismal campaign in Tennessee, the Confederate authorities ordered what was left of his army to move to North Carolina in hopes of halting Sherman's advance. The whole force was under the command of Joseph Johnston. It numbered scarcely more than half the size of Sherman's, but it was large enough to require attention.

On a rainy March 16, Johnston challenged the advance of Slocum's column at Averasborough, but Slocum's troops easily brushed him aside. Three days later, Johnston made a more serious attack at Bentonville. The wings had been keeping closer together of late, but on March 19 the shape of the road net had forced them about six miles apart. Beginning in the afternoon, Howard's soldiers could hear "very heavy artillery and musketry" coming from the west and knew that Slocum must be fighting. Howard sent a staff officer back down the column to have Hazen's division, the last in the Fifteenth Corps column, turn back onto Slocum's road so as to come up behind the Army of Georgia if needed. Initial reports, however, indicated that the fighting on the left was only a cavalry skirmish, so Howard halted Hazen. As the afternoon wore on, the sounds of battle from the west continued and seemed to increase, and finally one of Slocum's staff officers rode in on a lathered horse to report that the Army of Georgia was having a hard battle. At that point, both Howard and Sherman sent orders for Hazen to resume his movement.[21]

During the night, Howard and Sherman decided to send Blair as well, and the Seventeenth Corps moved out at midnight. Logan too, after tightening up his Fifteenth Corps column, turned toward the scene of the previous day's fighting.[22] Hazen's division marched all night and came into line on the right of the hard-pressed Fourteenth Corps at 6:00 a.m., March 20. During the course of the day, the division was slightly engaged, as the Rebels seemed much less aggressive than they had been the day before.[23]

Throughout March 20, the rest of the Army of the Tennessee continued toward Bentonville, driving Confederate skirmishers before them. Finally, at about three o'clock in the afternoon, the army came into position on the right of the Army of Georgia. The rest of the Fifteenth Corps, linking up

with Hazen's division, was on Slocum's immediate right, and the Seventeenth was to the right of the Fifteenth, on the far right.[24] Casualties from
the day's fighting were relatively light, but the experience was not a pleasant one. Robert Hoadley of the 26th Iowa wrote of digging entrenchments
in a pouring rain under heavy Confederate fire. His company lost only two
men badly wounded, "but when you come to see how few men we have, it is
like taking a Brother out of a family." His company was down to one sergeant, one corporal, and nine privates.[25]

On March 21, it was the Federals who took the offensive, despite heavy
rain that began late in the morning and continued throughout the day.
Action opened in earnest shortly after midday on the far right. In one sense,
the attack was a mistake, but it was just the sort of inspired "mistake" that
Joseph Mower could be expected to make, the kind of mistake generals
might hope their subordinates would make. The Wolf was still as aggressive as ever. Several days earlier, one of his soldiers had overheard a staff
officer ask him how long it would take to reach a certain point. "We will get
there in four days if the Johnnies don't bother us," Mower had replied. "If
they do, we'll go it in two."[26]

His was the extreme right-flank division in the Union line. Blair ordered
him to move up into position on the right of Force's division and to make
contact with the Confederate line in front of him. As Mower advanced into
the position ordered, he discovered a road leading from the right of his line
to Mill Creek, where it crossed by a ford. He decided that using the road
and the ford would be the best way to close in on the enemy's flank and so
led his division across. Struggling through woods and swamps, Mower's
men advanced until they made contact with the extreme left-rear of the
Confederate army and met rifle and artillery fire. Mower charged toward
the guns. The Rebel artillerists limbered up and headed for the rear, but not
before Mower's men were able to capture one of their caissons. More
important, the charge had ripped through the Confederate flank and penetrated deep behind Johnston's lines and was a serious threat to cut off his
retreat.

Only at this point did Mower learn from the commander of his left-flank
brigade that they had lost contact with Force's division some time ago.
Mower surmised that his own division must have drifted to the right while it
was working its way through the swamp. That was apparently the mistake
that had allowed him to turn the Confederate flank, rout its defenders, and
seize the important position he now held. Mower gave the order to move by
the left flank until the connection was restored, hoping to link up with the
rest of the army while continuing to hold the high ground beyond the

swamp. The movement had hardly started when the Rebels struck the division in front and on both flanks at the same time. By dint of Mower's skillful maneuvering and his men's hard fighting, the division successfully beat off the attacks while shifting left far enough to establish contact with Force. By that time, however, he was more or less back in the position from which he had started his foray across Mill Creek.[27]

While Mower waged his battle on the right, Howard reacted aggressively to the plight of his isolated division. He ordered Logan to put pressure on the Confederate lines in his front and Blair to support Mower with the entire Seventeenth Corps if necessary. Mower was distributing ammunition in preparation for renewing the attack when he received an order to hold his present position and entrench.[28]

Howard realized that they had the opportunity to do the enemy serious damage and was eager to begin. He was shocked therefore to see the Seventeenth Corps halting its advance and beginning to dig in. Riding rapidly to Blair, Howard demanded to know why he had stopped advancing.

"The withdrawal is by Sherman's order!" Blair replied. Howard was stunned and very dissatisfied, but there was nothing he could do. The Battle of Bentonville was over.[29]

In hindsight it is easy to see that Sherman's order to halt the attack was a mistake. Sherman himself said so in his memoirs. He did not know the size of Johnston's army and wanted to make contact with Schofield before fighting a general engagement. Clearly, if Sherman fully understood the situation on the battlefield on March 21, he would have realized that he had an opportunity for a much more decisive victory. True to form, Sherman at Bentonville demonstrated himself to be less effective at offensive tactics than he was at strategy and logistics, two areas in which his genius had made him one of the foremost architects of Union victory.[30]

Still, no one can know what would have happened had Mower been turned loose, any more than Sherman could have known how long the war would continue after an indecisive victory at Bentonville. In hindsight, trapping Johnston looked so easy that later-day historians would sneer that Sherman was overrated. Yet as easy as it might have appeared, trapping a Civil War army was, as the historical record proves, almost impossibly difficult. Only one general ever succeeded in doing so. That was Grant, and he did it on three separate occasions. With the knowledge we have today of Bentonville and what came after, it does seem that Sherman should have continued Mower's assault, but the historical odds are that Johnston would somehow have escaped anyway.

Johnston's troops pulled out at around 2:00 a.m. on March 22. Elements of the Army of the Tennessee pursued for several hours and skirmished with the Rebel rearguard until Sherman once again called them off.[31] "It was hardly a battle for us, though we have received orders to put it on our flags," wrote Theodore Upson in his diary. "I should think those fool Johnnys would quit. They might as well try to stop a tornado as Uncle Billy and his boys. Had our whole Army been there [at the beginning of the Battle of Bentonville] we would have eat them up."[32]

With Johnston gone from their immediate front, Sherman's army proceeded on, marching northeastward toward Goldsboro, now less than twenty-five miles away. The roads continued to be very difficult when the weather was rainy, as it often was. "I never saw such a country," wrote Captain Wills in his diary. "There seems to be a thick crust over a vast bed of quicksand." A wagon would roll along, its wheels making only shallow ruts in the firm surface strata. Then that layer would crack and drop the wagon into quicksand, where it would sink immediately to the hubs or even to the wagon bed. "I was riding tonight on apparently high ground in the woods," Wills wrote, "and three times the ground gave way just like rotten ice, and let my horse in belly deep." Day by day, the army laid down mile upon mile of corduroy road.[33]

The foragers were the first of Sherman's troops to make contact with Schofield's army, advancing northwest from the coast at Wilmington into the interior for a junction with Sherman at Goldsboro. Some of the foragers decided to take advantage of their travel-worn appearance to pose as Rebels and "capture" several small detachments of Schofield's troops. Schofield's men were veterans, but they were far from possessing the degree of nerve, toughness, and confidence—even cockiness—that had by now become standard in the Army of the Tennessee. They readily surrendered, and Sherman's men swapped their rusty and battered rifles for the newcomers' shiny ones before informing them of their true identity.[34]

On March 24, the Army of the Tennessee reached Goldsboro and linked up with Schofield, bringing Sherman's total numbers to about 80,000. For the Army of the Tennessee, the best thing about reaching Goldsboro was the unaccustomed luxury of full communications with the North and, above all, the arrival of long-awaited mail. "Today has been a glorious day in camp," wrote Edward Allen on March 26, "for after our long campaign we have opened communications & mail is coming in by the car load. The boys are nearly wild over their letters & valentines."[35]

The army remained at Goldsboro for two and a half weeks, resting, refitting, and drawing new clothes, shoes, and equipment. There it received news that Grant had taken Richmond on April 2. Sherman's men were ecstatic. "Victory! Victory! Glorious news from Gen. Grant," wrote an exuberant Cornelius Platter in his diary. "Everything is in a uprore," noted Musician John Bates. "Hollering all along the line is the order of the day."[36] Clearly, the end was near, but as Indiana soldier William Fifer wrote in a letter from Goldsboro, "I look to have some more fiting to do before they will give up."[37] From Goldsboro, Edward Allen wrote in a letter, "Since arriving here I have thought more of going home than at any time yet. There has been so much talk of 'peace, peace.' " Surely the army's next advance would end the war. "It must," Allen reasoned, "can't be otherwise."[38]

Throughout the past two months, Sherman's command had been drawing steadily closer to Lee's army and Richmond, gradually shrinking the size of the last significant enclave of Confederate power. As Bentonville made plain, Johnston could not hope to halt or even significantly slow Sherman's progress. The only possible Confederate countermove was for Lee to abandon Richmond, somehow escape Grant's clutches, and make his way south to combine with Johnston against Sherman. Even that was a slim chance and, after the junction with Schofield's command, no chance at all. Sherman would undoubtedly have given the combined forces of Lee and Johnston a severe drubbing. Had Lee remained in position around Richmond and Petersburg, it would only remain for Sherman to march into Virginia and combine with Grant to crush Lee and end the war, unless Grant managed it first without Sherman's help.

The fall of Richmond changed the strategic situation. With what was left of his army, Lee was fleeing westward with Grant in hot pursuit. In Goldsboro, Sherman received word of these developments on April 6 and a further update from Grant, dated the fifth, two days later. In response, Sherman promised to have his force, now consisting of the Army of the Tennessee under Howard, the Army of Georgia under Slocum, and the Army of the Ohio under Schofield, under way by April 10 to cooperate with Grant in the effort to run to earth the last two major Confederate armies.[39]

On a rainy April 10, Sherman's armies marched out of Goldsboro, as promised, heading northwest, toward Raleigh and Johnston's army. According to the exacting, seldom-satisfied Hazen, the Army of the Tennessee was at that time "as nearly perfect, in instruction, equipment, and general efficiency, as volunteer troops can be made while in the field."[40] For their part, the troops believed they were following one of the greatest generals who had ever lived. As Sgt. Young J. Powell of the 2nd Iowa put it, the troops "think that there never was such a man as Sherman or, as they call him, Crazy Bill, and he has got his men to believe that they can't be whipped."[41]

Confederate cavalry skirmished in front of the column without slowing its progress. "This Rebel cavalry ahead don't amount to a cent," wrote Charles Wills in his diary. "They keep shooting all the time, but are afraid to wait until we get within range of them. They have not hindered our march a minute."[42] The Rebel horsemen and irregulars were far more lethal against Union foragers whom they found in small numbers at a distance from the column. The Confederate practice of murdering captured foragers had revived in full force even before the army reached Goldsboro. "They get a great many of our boys while foraging," wrote Isaiah Dillon of the 111th Illinois from Goldsboro. "They kill them generally, I guess. We find them in the woods with their throats cut and some hanging to trees."[43] During the first few days that the army was encamped at Goldsboro, before the regular supply line was fully functional via the coast, foragers continued to venture into the countryside and Rebels continued to murder those they caught. On March 28, a forage detail consisting of a lieutenant and ten enlisted men was captured and subsequently shot. One of the men, badly wounded and left for dead, managed to crawl back to Union lines.[44]

No sooner did the army take to the road again than the Rebels resumed the practice of atrocities against captives. On April 12, a party of foragers was captured and then murdered "while trying to make their escape."[45] Several days later, Rebel guerrillas attacked a foraging party of the 68th Ohio, capturing Cpl. Joshua Dicus and two others. The Rebels disarmed them and ordered them to start running, then shot them in the back as they ran. A bullet struck Dicus in the back and exited his chest. His two comrades were killed, and the Rebels left him for dead. He subsequently revived and managed to crawl far enough to get help. Not all captured foragers were shot. As the army approached Raleigh, it was greeted by the sight of two hanged by the neck from a signpost.[46] This time there is no record of further retaliation by Union commanders. Perhaps no one had the heart to match the Rebels in brutality, but failing to respond allowed the killing to go on unchecked.

On the morning of April 12, news arrived that Lee had surrendered to Grant. "The troops became crazy with enthusiasm," recalled Sergeant Major Brown of the 55th Illinois. "The long column from van to rear guard was soon in an uproarious, uncontrollable state of excitement that did not subside during the day."[47] Charles Wills could not believe it at first, but then Logan himself rode down the column and personally assured him that "it is rue as gospel."[48] Augustus Van Dyke of the headquarters staff noted that many of the soldiers soon fell into discussions of what they would do when hey got home.[49]

The next day, the army marched into Raleigh. Sherman stood at the south gate of the state capitol grounds while the men passed in review.[50] Some of the citizens of Raleigh were on the sidewalks to see the army march by and seemed happy at least that the war was coming to a close. "The ladies particularly were lavish with smiles and greetings of welcome, which the soldiers acknowledged by cheers as they passed," recalled Sergeant Major Brown.[51]

With Lee and his army gone, Johnston had no stomach for further fighting. On April 14, he sent Sherman a flag of truce with a request to enter into negotiations—cause for another round of cheering and hat-tossing throughout the army. Sherman agreed to halt active operations while the negotiations were in progress, and the army remained encamped near Raleigh. Sherman and Johnston met in nearby Durham Station on April 17. As he was leaving to meet with Johnston, Sherman received a telegraph dispatch from the War Department notifying him of the April 14 assassination of Abraham Lincoln. In his meeting with Johnston, Sherman unwisely allowed the wily Confederate to draw him into negotiations reaching far beyond the surrender of the Rebel army in North Carolina and embracing a complete settlement of the entire sectional conflict, a breathtaking leap beyond Sherman's authority.

Worse still, Sherman agreed to terms that would have been absurdly generous even before Lincoln's assassination. Confederate regiments were to march to their various state capitals, store their weapons in state arsenals, and go home, promising not to wage war on the United States anymore. The president of the United States, now Andrew Johnson, was to recognize the existing—rebellious—state governments as soon as their members took an oath to be loyal to the United States from now on. It was as if the past four years had never happened. Scarcely able to believe his good fortune, Johnston departed from the meeting to gain the approval of his civil government, which, in the persons of Jefferson Davis and his cabinet, on the run after the fall of Richmond, was not far away.

Sherman returned to his headquarters and issued to his armies an order announcing Lincoln's assassination. The soldiers were stunned. Almost all of them tended to feel a close personal bond with the president whom most of them had never met. This was especially true of the Midwesterners, who comprised the majority of Sherman's armies and almost the entire manpower of the Army of the Tennessee. The initial reaction in the camps was one of shocked quietness. "Scarcely a word was spoken," wrote an Ohio soldier. "The camps were hushed to the utmost stillness." Over the course of several hours, this feeling gradually gave way to another. "The silent murmur of revenge was whispered from right to left of the whole army," recalled the same soldier.[52] The murmur rose steadily in volume until that evening Allen Geer of the 20th Illinois wrote in his diary, "The troops are in a blaze of excitement and bitterness of sad feeling."[53] Theodore Upson noted, "The men are fearfully angry, and I don't know what they may do."[54] Sherman and Howard, however, had anticipated their reaction and had already issued stringent orders that everyone was to be confined to camp that night with heavy guards posted to keep them from sneaking out.

During the night, a mob estimated at 2,000 or more started out for Raleigh with the avowed purpose of destroying it. General Logan learned of it and, true to form, rode to the point of conflict, placing himself in the path of the marauders. He ordered them back to their camps, but for once, Army of the Tennessee soldiers disregarded an order from Logan and kept marching. Only when he pointed out a battery of artillery that he had ordered up and warned them that he would have them blasted with canister if they persisted did they finally relent. Everyone knew that Black Jack would keep his promise. Upson wrote in his diary that the city of Raleigh owed Logan "a debt it never can pay."[55]

This time military discipline held, and Raleigh escaped the fate of Columbia. Numerous members of the army agreed that only the strict orders, heavy guards, and energetic efforts of commanding officers had prevented the city's "sudden transition to ashes."[56] The soldiers, however, were not assuaged. "More than one vow of vengeance was registered," wrote Augustus Van Dyke, "and if it should become necessary for this army to pursue the Rebels further, the lesson of war that the South has already learned will be as nothing to that which we would teach them."[57] Charles Willison of the 76th Ohio agreed. "Had hostilities been continued under this impression, there is no telling what the result might have been."[58]

On April 18, Sherman met Johnston a second time and signed the unduly generous surrender agreement they had negotiated the previous day, subject to ratification in Washington. When word of Sherman's deal reached the capital, Secretary of War Edwin Stanton, who for the moment was more or less running the government, flew into a rage. It was a given that Sherman's terms would be rejected, but Stanton, who was always very excitable, not to say unstable, decided that Sherman himself must be a traitor and was ready to have him arrested. Grant stepped in and offered to go to North Carolina himself. Though his orders were to remove Sherman ind take over affairs there himself, Grant instead gently informed Sherman of Washington's disapproval and then remained in the background while Sherman negotiated another agreement with Johnston. The final terms were still more generous than those Grant had given Lee at Appomattox— Sherman never could seem to hold his own with Johnston in negotiation— but they were at least acceptable.

For the soldiers, the on-and-off negotiations were confusing. On April 24, when news came of the nonratification, they received orders announcing that Johnston "hadn't surrendered yet" and that they were going to march the next morning "and clean him out," recalled James Williams of the 23rd Indiana, adding, "You had better believe that we felt like cleaning him out about that time." Williams and his comrades had marched only three miles the next morning when the renewal of negotiations halted them again. Then on April 26 came news that Johnston had surrendered a second time, sparking renewed intense jubilation among the troops.[59]

The army spent several days in camp near Raleigh in inspections and reviews. Foraging came to an absolute halt, as the army adopted peacetime manners. "Home is the principal gossip through the entire camp," wrote William Nugen of the 25th Iowa. The men had been longing for home for almost four years now, and were eager to go as soon as they could with honor and victory. Now at last that was possible, and it became very nearly the only idea on the soldiers' minds.[60]

The final road home for the Army of the Tennessee was to lead through Washington, D.C., for one last parade as an army, part of a Grand Review that was scheduled in the national capital for May 23 and 24. The columns formed up and marched out of their camps around Raleigh early on the morning of April 29. The pace was fast—no roads to corduroy, no swamps to wade, no burned bridges to rebuild, and absolutely no foraging. Charles Wills noted that there was "no foraging, no burning rails, or houses, and nothing naughty whatever." When they camped each night, there was "not a hand laid on a rail . . . with intent to burn, not a motion toward a chicken or smoke-house."[61]

On the evening of May 6, they arrived in Petersburg, Virginia, scene of the last Eastern campaign. Some of the men cast a professional eye over the battlefield and found it surprisingly flat and the fortifications not up to the standard that had been used around Atlanta.[62] Shortly thereafter, Howard was summoned to Washington to take over the new Freedmen's Bureau, which would endeavor to care for the recently freed slaves. Command of the Army of the Tennessee finally passed to John A. Logan.[63] North of

Petersburg, the march carried the Army of the Tennessee through Richmond, the storied capital of Virginia and the Confederacy, and then pas some of the battlefields of the Army of the Potomac's years of futility. Ye to many a soldier such scenes excited little interest. "It puzzles me that my memory has not retained more of the incidents and route of our final journey from Raleigh to Washington," wrote Charles Willison, "but with the elements of suffering and danger removed, I seem to have stopped charging my mind with the scenes and what happened on our peaceful route."[64]

On May 21, the Army of the Tennessee arrived at Alexandria, Virginia, on the Potomac River opposite Washington. The view across the river was impressive. From the hill on which the 20th Illinois was camped, Allen Geer ticked off the sights in the impressive panorama: "We are bivouacked on an eminence commanding a view of the Washington Monument, the Capitol, the White House, residence of General Lee, Arlington Heights, lunatic asylum, Potomac, and shifting ruins of the Smithsonian Institute & a star-bright evening affords a magnificent scene."[65] The Army of the Potomac was to march through Washington on May 23, and Sherman's armies were to parade the next day.

In preparation for the review, the troops spent May 23 cleaning and polishing equipment and brushing up their uniforms, somewhat concerned that they would make a poor appearance after the spit-and-polish Army of the Potomac. "We now have got to put on style," wrote artillerist Albion Gross to his wife. Some went into town to see the Easterners parade, however, and on returning to camp reassured their comrades that the Army of the Potomac soldiers "are no great shakes any way in marching."[66] Hazen also attended the May 23 festivities and appraised the Army of the Potomac with his perfectionist's eye. He noted that "frequent reviews, and the presence of distinguished personages, had bred some evil habits" in the Eastern troops. When they passed the reviewing stand, most of the Eastern regiments cheered, "many men swinging their hats, and so losing their cadence and military bearing." Hazen thought his men could do better.[67]

Early on May 24, the Western armies moved up, massed in column of companies, until the head of the column was on Pennsylvania Avenue at the foot of Capitol Hill. The Army of the Tennessee was in the lead. In front sat Sherman on horseback, along with Howard and their staffs. Behind them Logan and his staff sat their horses, and next came Gen. Charles Wood and his. Behind this small cavalcade of mounted officers stood the first of the infantry, the 100th Indiana, and behind it stretched the long column of the Army of the Tennessee, twenty men abreast. At 9:00 a.m., the signal gun boomed and the column stepped off. "Our boys fell into the long swinging step, every man in perfect time, our guns at a right shoulder shift," Theodore Upson proudly recalled, "and it seemed to me that the men never had marched so well before." At the head of each regiment strode the color-bearers, proudly carrying the flags with the name of their regiment and the battles it had fought.[68]

Soon they were moving between sidewalks packed with cheering men, women, and children. Watchers crowded the upper-story windows on either side of the street, and every tree seemed to have several boys in it. "How they cheered!" recalled Upson. "It was a constant roar." Countless flags of all sizes hung over the street or waved from the hands of eager citizens along the sidewalks. There were banners too, some stretched from one side of the street to the other over the marchers' heads, with inscriptions like "Welcome to Our Western Boys," and "Hail to Sherman's Army." A banner on the side of the Treasury Building read, "The Only Debt the NATION Can Never Pay Is That of Gratitude to Its Defenders." Young J. Powell of the 2nd Iowa wrote a few days later, "The streets through which we passed was strewn with flowers, and the ladies along the sidewalk throwed boquet after boquet to the boys as they passed along." Here and there along the sidewalk, a choir of children or young ladies sang "When Johnny Comes Marching Home," or other patriotic songs.[69]

Riding at the head of the column, Sherman hoped his Western boys were marching well but did not wish to be seen turning in the saddle to look at them. At the Treasury Building, he cast a glance over his shoulder. "The sight was simply magnificent," he recalled. "The column was compact, and the glittering muskets looked like a solid mass of steel, moving with the regularity of a pendulum." Ahead of them stood the reviewing stand near the White House, where sat President Johnson, General Grant, members of the cabinet, foreign ambassadors, and various other dignitaries.[70]

As they rode past the reviewing stand, Sherman and the other officers brought their swords to the salute. Behind them, on the command of Col. Ruel M. Johnson, the 100th Indiana brought their rifles crisply from right shoulder shift to carry arms, the marching salute. The great men on the reviewing stand rose to their feet and lifted their hats, returning the salute, and the crowds roared. Theodore Upson stole a quick glance along the line of his platoon. "Every man had his eyes front," he later wrote, "every step was perfect; and on the faces of the men was what one might call a *glory look*." After passing the reviewing stand, they recovered their arms to right shoulder shift, once again in crisp unison, and the crowds cheered again. "My, but I was proud of our boys," wrote Upson.[71]

Behind them regiment after regiment followed in perfect step, giving the same salute as they passed the reviewing stand. Tom Taylor rode by with the 47th Ohio, proud of his men—"I don't think I ever beheld them when they looked more immovable and formidable"—and especially proud that De Gress's battery was rolling along with his division, its three surviving 20-pounder Parrotts glistening in the bright sunlight.[72] A soldier of the 50th Illinois thought, "As we passed the stand no prouder set of men ever lived than those who marched by under the shadow of the Fiftieth flag." Here and there along the column, a band boomed out patriotic music, and often the crowd joined in singing along, especially if the tune was "The Battle Hymn of the Republic." The musicians seemed to be particular targets of women with wreaths and garlands, until the bands came to look like "moving flower gardens."[73] For Jefferson Moses, marching in the ranks of the 93rd Illinois, it was a banner day. He turned twenty-two years old that very May 24, and he had never had a birthday like this before.[74]

As prearranged, Sherman turned out of the column after passing the reviewing stand and joined the president and other dignitaries there. Each corps and division commander came to the stand to be introduced to Johnson while his unit marched by. For more than three hours, the Army of the Tennessee strode past the reviewing stand, and Slocum's Army of Georgia followed behind them. They were different from the men of the Eastern armies. Physically larger and more muscular, they marched with more precision and had a longer stride. Beyond that, there was a certain indefinable swagger. "They march like lords of the world!" one of the onlookers was heard to exclaim. It was a quietly radiated air of supreme confidence from men who had marched from Cairo through the Carolinas and everything the Rebels could throw in their way.[75]

The army camped two miles north of Washington that night. It had been a hard march, and as Upson put it, they "were a tired but happy lot of boys."[76] All that remained was to wait for the army's bureaucracy to get around to discharging them. During the next few days, many took the opportunity of going into Washington as sightseers.[77] Favorite destinations included the Capitol, the Patent Office, and the Smithsonian Institution, and the men wrote home of seeing things like "the camp chest of Washington, his plates, knives and forks, quilts, saddle and bridle." To facilitate their visits to the city, the men took over the Fourteenth Street Railroad and ran it for their own convenience, facetiously reporting to Sherman that they had "captured" it. The captain of the Capitol police might have been expected to do something about that, but perhaps he had difficulty getting out to the camps, since the men had appropriated his horse and buggy. Such

ɔranks shortly brought orders for Sherman to move the Army of the Tennessee away from Washington as quickly as possible.[78]

The various units of the army left between May 31 and June 6, bound for
Louisville, Kentucky. They traveled by rail as far as Parkersburg, West Virginia, and thence by steamboat on the Ohio. The citizenry greeted them
warmly along the way. They "thronged every depot," recalled a veteran,
"loaded with baskets of pies and cakes." The men of the 93rd Illinois had
especially fond memories of the people of Grafton, West Virginia, who met
their train at eleven o'clock at night. "They filled our canteens with coffee
and our haversacks with meats, and sent us on our way rejoicing."[79]

The men groused about how long it took the army to discharge them,
but gradually over the course of June, July, and August each regiment
shipped out for the Midwestern town where it had mustered in three or four
years before. Sometimes cheering crowds met their return. Sometimes no
advance notice had been received; a regiment piled out onto a darkened
railroad platform long after midnight, and young men for whom twenty-
mile night marches were all in a day's work now walked by moonlight on
familiar roads the last few miles to the farmsteads they had left as boys
when the war began. There would be adjustments in the coming days for
both the soldiers and the Midwest that had sent them off and now welcomed
them back, but throughout the rest of his life each veteran could look with
pride and satisfaction to the years when he had marched with the Army of
the Tennessee.

ACKNOWLEDGMENTS

It is a pleasure to acknowledge the kind assistance of many persons who helped to make this book possible. My friend and colleague Brooks D. Simpson suggested to me the idea for this book one day in the spring of 1996 while we were walking the Shiloh battlefield together. Walking battlefields with Brooks has been very profitable to me. It was on the battlefield of Perryville in November 1994 that he and Mark Grimsley suggested to me the topic for my book *While God Is Marching On: The Religious World of Civil War Soldiers.* I continue to appreciate his friendship and advice.

Stewart Bennett, Gary Ecelbarger, David Slay, and John Lundberg kindly shared research materials with me. Stewart sent me a whole box of materials he had collected on the 76th Ohio for his then-forthcoming book, *The Struggle for the Life of the Republic.* He also took time out on a West Coast trip he was making to take my shopping list to the Huntington Library and get some materials for me there. David called my attention to excellent resources in the Mississippi Department of Archives and History that I never would have found without his help, and he allowed me the use of his manuscript guide to Civil War sources in Georgia, an invaluable tool that I hope will soon be available to all Civil War researchers in published form. Gary sent me much first-class material and shared his profound insights on John A. Logan, on whom he is currently writing a biography. John Lundberg made available materials that definitely made my task much easier.

Jim Ogden, chief park historian for Chickamauga and Chattanooga National Military Park, took me on a guided tour of sites related to the Army of the Tennessee's participation in the Battle of Chattanooga. His expert commentary was immensely useful to me in sorting out the complicated operations there. I'm convinced that no one knows that battle or the ground on which it was fought the way Jim does. I have also benefited, in company with many others, from tramping the Shiloh battlefield with expert guides Brig. Gen. Parker Hills and Shiloh park historian Stacey Allen and from following the incomparable Ed Bearss over the field of Champion's Hill.

Larry Daniel, Tim Smith, Buck Foster, Kraig McNutt, David Slay, and Michael Ballard took time out from their own important work to read parts of the manuscript and give me the benefit of their excellent feedback. Ashbel Green, vice president and senior editor of Alfred A. Knopf, also provided a very useful critique of the manuscript. Of course, the final product is my own, and none of them is to blame for its shortcomings.

Archivists and librarians have been kind and helpful at all of the institutions mentioned in my list of sources, and I regret that I did not get the names of all of them so that I could acknowledge them here. Richard Sommers, David Keogh, Pam Cheney, and Richard Baughman of the U.S. Army Military History Institute archives were especially helpful in making my time there as useful as possible. So too was Nan Card of the Rutherford B. Hayes Presidential Center in Fremont, Ohio.

As always, my wife, Leah, has provided invaluable support and encouragement. I cannot imagine how I could do this without her.

Steven E. Woodworth
Benbrook, Texas
November 11, 2004

NOTES

ABBREVIATIONS USED

ACL   Augustana College Library
AHC   Atlanta History Center
HLUGA   Hargrett Library, University of Georgia–Athens
IHS   Indiana Historical Society
ISHL   Illinois State Historical Library
LC   Library of Congress
MDAH   Mississippi Department of Archives and History
MOLLUS   *Papers of the Military Order of the Loyal Legion of the United States*
OR   *Official Records* (U.S. War Department, *The War of the Rebellion: Official Records of the Union and Confederate Armies,* 128 vols. [Washington, D.C.: Government Printing Office, 1881–1901]. Except as otherwise noted, all references are to Series I).
PLDU   Perkins Library, Duke University
SHC   Southern Historical Collection
USAMHI   U.S. Army Military History Institute
WHMC   Western Historical Manuscript Collection
WHS   Wisconsin Historical Society
WRHS   Western Reserve Historical Society

INTRODUCTION

1. Ritner, *Love and Valor,* 238–39.

CHAPTER ONE: RAISING AN ARMY

1. Clark and Bowen, *University Recruits,* 6.
2. Lyftogt, *From Blue Mills to Columbia,* 18–24.
3. Bryner, *Bugle Echoes,* 15.
4. John L. Maxwell to Charles Sumner, January 27, 1865, Papers of Charles Sumner, Houghton Library, Harvard, reel 32, quoted in Mark E. Neely, Jr., *Retaliation: The Problem of Atrocity in the American Civil War,* 18.
5. George O. Smith Reminiscences, George O. Smith Papers, ISHL.
6. Bryner, *Bugle Echoes,* 15–17.
7. Ambrose, *History of the Seventh Regiment,* 5.

8. Wardner, "Reminiscences of a Surgeon," in *MOLLUS*, 12:172–77.

9. Chetlain, *Recollections of Seventy Years*, 69–80.

10. Gebhardt, "The Eleventh Illinois Infantry Regiment in the Civil War," 1–6.

11. Wallace, *Smoke, Sound & Fury*, 15–16, 18–19.

12. Tuttle, "Personal Recollections of 1861," in *MOLLUS*, 55:18–19.

13. Bryner, *Bugle Echoes*, 15–17.

14. A. G. Dinsmore Reminiscences, Autobiographical Notes, WHS; Hicken, *Illinois in the Civil War*, 3.

15. Gaff, *On Many a Bloody Field*, 3.

16. Wimer Bedford Reminiscences, Wimer Bedford Papers, LC.

17. Dietrich C. Smith to Carrie Pieper, April 21, 1861, Dietrich C. Smith Papers, ISHL.

18. Manuscript in Noah Beecher Sharp Papers, IHS.

19. Clark and Bowen, *University Recruits*, 10–11.

20. Elliott, *History of the Thirty-third Regiment*, 7–8.

21. Clark and Bowen, *University Recruits*, 14.

22. Rood, *Story of the Service of Company E*, 47–51.

23. Crooker, Nourse, and Brown, *The 55th Illinois*, 21–23.

24. Stevenson, *History of the 78th Regiment*, 97, 99.

25. Stuber, *Mein Tagebuch*, 4–5.

26. Barrett, *The Soldier Bird*, 7–11, 16–17, 20; Eunice Merriman manuscript, "Old Abe," FF80–84, John Erastus Perkins Papers, mircrofilm, WHS.

27. Connelly, *History of the Seventieth Ohio Regiment*, 8–9.

28. Bryner, *Bugle Echoes*, 15–17.

29. Campbell, *The Union Must Stand*, 3.

30. Lyftogt, *From Blue Mills to Columbia*, 18–24.

31. Adams, "My First Company," in *MOLLUS*, 31:288.

32. Rood, *Story of the Service of Company E*, 43.

33. Gebhardt, "The Eleventh Illinois Infantry Regiment in the Civil War," 6–7.

34. Campbell, *The Union Must Stand*, 2–3.

35. Dietrich C. Smith to Carrie Pieper, April 1861, Dietrich C. Smith Papers, ISHL.

36. Lyftogt, *From Blue Mills to Columbia*, 18–24.

37. Rood, *Story of the Service of Company E*, 64–67.

38. Adams, "My First Company," in *MOLLUS*, 31:289.

39. Dugan, *History of Hurlbut's Fighting Fourth Division*, 31.

40. Cyrus E. Dickey to Ann Wallace, April 24, Wallace-Dickey Family Papers, ISHL.

41. Paddock, "The Beginnings of an Illinois Volunteer Regiment in 1861," in *MOLLUS*, 11:258.

42. Hicken, *Illinois in the Civil War*, 5–6.

43. Daniel Buck to "Dear Mother," September 26, 1861, Daniel Buck Papers, WHS; Barrett, *The Soldier Bird*, 22–25.

44. Munn, Miller, and Newton, *Military History and Reminiscences of the Thirteenth*, 4.

45. E-mail to author from Bart Johnson of 11th Indiana reenactor group; Wallace, *Smoke, Sound & Fury*, 21.

46. Wallace, *Smoke, Sound & Fury*, 21–23; Dugan, *History of Hurlbut's Fighting Fourth Division*, 29–30.

47. Crooker, Nourse, and Brown, *The 55th Illinois*, 21, 25.

48. Day, "The Fifteenth Iowa at Shiloh," in *MOLLUS*, 56:174–75.

49. Regimental Order No. 2; William H. L. Wallace to Ann Wallace, May 12, 1861, Wallace-Dickey Family Papers, ISHL.

50. Cyrus E. Dickey to Ann Wallace, April 24, Wallace-Dickey Family Papers, ISHL.

51. *Warren (Illinois) Independent*, November 19, 1861.

52. Crooker, Nourse, and Brown, *The 55th Illinois,* 41–43.
53. "Civil War Reminiscences of Dr. John T. Hunt, Macedonia, Illinois, Company A., 40th Illinois Voluntary Infantry," in "The Yesterdays of Hamilton County," http://www.carolyar.com/Illinois/Hunt-Part1.htm.
54. Bryner, *Bugle Echoes,* 30.
55. Flemming, "The Battle of Shiloh as a Private Saw It," in *MOLLUS,* 6:132–33.
56. William H. L. Wallace to Ann Wallace, April 24 and 26, Wallace-Dickey Family Papers, ISHL.

CHAPTER TWO: CAIRO

1. Dugan, *History of Hurlbut's Fighting Fourth Division,* 21.
2. Wallace, *Smoke, Sound & Fury,* 21–22; "Lew Wallace," http://ehistory.com.
3. Luther H. Cowan Diary, January 1862, Luther H. Cowan Papers, WHS.
4. Logan, "Cairo in 1861," *National Tribune,* February 9, 1888, p. 1
5. J. W. Greenman Diary, January 22, 1862, MDAH.
6. Howard, *Illinois,* 122–23, 269, 299.
7. Dietrich C. Smith to Carrie Pieper [April 1861], Dietrich C. Smith Papers, ISHL.
8. Morrison, *A History of the Ninth Regiment,* 7–9.
9. Ibid., 7–9; *Report of the Adjutant General of the State of Illinois,* vol. 1, in "Illinois in the Civil War," http://www.illinoiscivilwar.org.
10. Howard, *Illinois,* 163.
11. "Civil War Reminiscences of Dr. John T. Hunt, Macedonia, Illinois, Company A., 40th Illinois Voluntary Infantry," in "The Yesterdays of Hamilton County," http://www.carolyar.com/Illinois/Hunt-Part1.htm.
12. Ibid.
13. Hicken, *Illinois in the Civil War,* 12; Kiper, *McClernand,* 22.
14. Jones, *Black Jack,* 83–84.
15. Ibid., 44.
16. Kiper, *McClernand,* 22; Jones, *Black Jack,* 88; Grant, *Personal Memoirs,* 1:244–46.
17. Jones, *Black Jack,* 94–106.
18. Kiper, *McClernand,* 20–23.
19. Hicken, *Illinois in the Civil War,* 12–13.
20. Douglas Hapeman Diary, May 5, 1861, ISHL; William H. L. Wallace to Ann Wallace, May 12, 1861, Wallace-Dickey Family Papers, ISHL.
21. Douglas Hapeman Diary, May 6, 1861, ISHL; William H. L. Wallace to Ann Wallace, May 12, 1861, and S. H. Freeland to William H. L. Wallace, May 7, 1861, Wallace-Dickey Family Papers, ISHL.
22. Douglas Hapeman Diary, May 6, 1861, ISHL; William H. L. Wallace to Ann Wallace, May 12, 1861; O. Ott to William H. L. Wallace, May 8, 1861, Wallace-Dickey Family Papers, ISHL.
23. William H. L. Wallace to Ann Wallace, May 12, 1861, and William H. L. Wallace to Maj. John B. Wyman, May 8, 1861, Wallace-Dickey Family Papers, ISHL.
24. Crooker, Nourse, and Brown, *The 55th Illinois,* 26.
25. Regimental Order No. 9, May 11, 1861, Wallace-Dickey Family Papers, ISHL.
26. N. R. Casey to William H. L. Wallace, May 9, 1861; Regimental Order No. 7, May 10, 1861; Regimental Order No. 9, May 11, 1861, all in Wallace-Dickey Family Papers, ISHL. William H. Austin to John S. Sargent, June 11, 1861, William H. Austin Papers, ISHL.
27. Geer, *The Civil War Diary,* 3–5.

28. David W. Poak to "Dear Sister," September 21, 1861, David W. Poak Papers, ISHL.
29. William H. L. Wallace to Ann Wallace, May 14, 1861, Wallace-Dickey Family Papers, ISHL.
30. Morrison, *A History of the Ninth Regiment*, 10.
31. Paddock, "The Beginnings of an Illinois Volunteer Regiment in 1861," in *MOLLUS* 11:263; Ambrose, *History of the Seventh Regiment*, 7; Douglas Hapeman Diary, May 30, 1861 ISHL.
32. The 13th through the 21st Illinois had originally been taken into state service and subsequently had to reenlist into Federal service. Most of their soldiers, like those whom Logan addressed in Grant's 21st Illinois, did so.
33. Benjamin M. Prentiss to William H. L. Wallace, May 7, 1861 (two letters), Wallace-Dickey Family Papers, ISHL.
34. Gebhardt, "The Eleventh Illinois Infantry Regiment in the Civil War," *Report of the Adjutant General of the State of Illinois*, 1:42–43; www.illinoiscivilwar.org.
35. Gebhardt, "The Eleventh Illinois Infantry Regiment in the Civil War," 42–44.
36. *Report of the Adjutant General of the State of Illinois*, 22nd Illinois Regiment, http://www.rootsweb.com/~ilcivilw/history/022.htm; Gebhardt, "The Eleventh Illinois Infantry Regiment in the Civil War," 53.
37. Wardner, "Reminiscences of a Surgeon," in *MOLLUS*, 12:177.

CHAPTER THREE: PADUCAH

1. Grant, *Personal Memoirs*, 1:264.
2. Simpson, *Ulysses S. Grant*, 87–92.
3. *OR*, vol. 3, p. 142.
4. Ibid., pp. 141, 144, 152.
5. Feis, *Grant's Secret Service*, 21–23.
6. Simon, ed., *Papers of Ulysses S. Grant*, 2:189.
7. Williams, *Grant Rises in the West: The First Year*, 55–56; Grant, *Personal Memoirs*, 265; Simon, ed., *Papers of Ulysses S. Grant*, 2:190–93.
8. Grant, *Personal Memoirs*, 265; *OR*, vol. 4, p. 196.
9. Grant, *Personal Memoirs*, 265.
10. Feis, *Grant's Secret Service*, 23–24.
11. *OR*, vol. 4, p. 197; Simon, ed., *Papers of Ulysses S. Grant*, 2:194.
12. On the initial Union conciliatory policy, see Grimsley, *The Hard Hand of War*, 1–66.
13. *OR*, vol. 4, p. 198.
14. Smith, *Grant*, 120.
15. Warner, *Generals in Blue*, 460; *OR*, vol. 4, p. 198; Wallace, *Smoke, Sound & Fury*, 54; Simon, ed., *Papers of Ulysses S. Grant*, 2:201–4.
16. Simon, ed., *Papers of Ulysses S. Grant*, 2:198.
17. Chetlain, "Recollections of General U.S. Grant, 1861–1863," in *MOLLUS*, 10:22.
18. Wallace, *Smoke, Sound & Fury*, 52.
19. Simon, ed., *Papers of Ulysses S. Grant*, 2:205; Chetlain, *Recollections of Seventy Years*, 80–83; Morrison, *History of the Ninth Regiment*, 15.
20. Brinton, *Personal Memoirs*, 37.
21. Catton, *Grant Moves South*, 63.
22. Simon, ed., *Papers of Ulysses S. Grant*, 2:248–50.
23. Ibid., 2:238.
24. Simpson, *Ulysses S. Grant*, 89–90; Catton, *Grant Moves South*, 67–69.

25. Simon, ed., *Papers of Ulysses S. Grant*, 2:225, 242; Hughes, *The Battle of Belmont*, 56–57.
26. Simon, ed., *Papers of Ulysses S. Grant*, 3:64.
27. *OR*, vol. 3, p. 169; Simon, ed., *Papers of Ulysses S. Grant*, 2:273; Jessee, *Civil War Diaries*, chap. 1, pp. 1–2.
28. Morrison, *History of the Ninth Regiment*, 15–16.
29. Kiper, *McClernand*, 26–28.
30. The deal did not work out; see the equipment of the 27th, 30th, and 31st Illinois in Baumann, *Arming the Suckers*, 99–106.
31. Morris, Hartwell, and Kuykendall, *History 31st Regiment*, 20.
32. *OR*, vol. 3, p. 558; Simon, ed., *Papers of Ulysses S. Grant*, 2:273.
33. *OR*, vol. 3, p. 267.
34. Ibid., p. 268.
35. Simon, ed., *Papers of Ulysses S. Grant*, 3:111; *OR*, vol. 3, p. 268.
36. Simon, ed., *Papers of Ulysses S. Grant*, 3:123–25; *OR*, vol. 3, p. 269.
37. Simon, ed., *Papers of Ulysses S. Grant*, 3:114.
38. Hughes, *The Battle of Belmont*, 46.
39. Simon, ed., *Papers of Ulysses S. Grant*, 3:113–15.
40. William H. Jones Diary, November 6, 1861, Civil War Miscellaneous Collection, USAMHI.
41. Morris, Hartwell, and Kuykendall, *History 31st Regiment*, 22.
42. Hughes, *The Battle of Belmont*, 49–50.

CHAPTER FOUR: BELMONT

1. Hughes, *The Battle of Belmont*, 50.
2. *OR*, vol. 3, pp. 269–70.
3. W. H. L. Wallace to Anne Wallace, November 6 and 14, 1861, Wallace-Dickey Family Papers, ISHL.
4. Feis, "Grant and the Belmont Campaign," 37–38; Hughes, *The Battle of Belmont*, 52–53; Simon, ed., *Papers of Ulysses S. Grant*, 3:150–51.
5. *OR*, vol. 3, p. 270.
6. Walter Scates to "Dear Father," November 13, 1861, Pearce Civil War Collection.
7. Ibid.
8. *OR*, vol. 3, pp. 275–76; Simon, ed., *The Papers of Ulysses S. Grant*, 3:137; Hughes, *The Battle of Belmont*, 57–62; Brinton, *Personal Memoirs*, 71–73.
9. Hughes, *The Battle of Belmont*, 78–80.
10. Morris, Hartwell, and Kuykendall, *History 31st Regiment*, 22; Simon, ed., *The Papers of Ulysses S. Grant*, 3:137; *OR*, vol. 3, pp. 291–92; Hughes, *The Battle of Belmont*, 84–87; Catton, *Grant Moves South*, 75.
11. Walter Scates to "Dear Father," November 13, 1861, Pearce Civil War Collection.
12. Hughes, *The Battle of Belmont*, 88–91; Walter Scates to "Dear Father," November 13, 1861, Pearce Civil War Collection; H. J. Walter, "Battle of Belmont," *National Tribune*, August 5, 1886, p. 3; *OR*, vol. 3, p. 296.
13. *OR*, vol. 3, p. 278; Hughes, *The Battle of Belmont*, 91–92.
14. Hughes, *The Battle of Belmont*, 93–106; Walter Scates to "Dear Father," November 13, 1861, Pearce Civil War Collection.
15. Hughes, *The Battle of Belmont*, 107–8, 115–16, 118–19, 121–22, 124–25; *OR*, vol. 3, pp. 279–84, 288, 292–93.
16. *OR*, vol. 3, p. 280; Hughes, *The Battle of Belmont*, 121–22.

17. Hughes, *The Battle of Belmont*, 115.
18. *OR*, vol. 3, p. 293; Kiper, *McClernand*, 45; Simon, ed., *The Papers of Ulysses S. Grant*, 3:194; Hughes, *The Battle of Belmont*, 127.
19. Hughes, *The Battle of Belmont*, 127.
20. Morris, Hartwell, and Kuykendall, *History 31st Regiment*, 24; Grant, *Personal Memoirs*, 1:274.
21. Brinton, *Personal Memoirs*, 77; Grant, *Personal Memoirs*, 1:276.
22. Hughes, *The Battle of Belmont*, 134–49; Brinton, *Personal Memoirs*, 77.
23. Walter, "Battle of Belmont," 3; Grant, *Personal Memoirs*, 1:276; Brinton, *Personal Memoirs*, 78.
24. Hughes, *The Battle of Belmont*, 151–52.
25. *OR*, vol. 3, pp. 280, 289.
26. Hughes, *The Battle of Belmont*, 152–53.
27. Walter, "Battle of Belmont," 3.
28. *OR*, vol. 3, p. 293; Simon, ed., *The Papers of Ulysses S. Grant*, 3:195.
29. Hughes, *The Battle of Belmont*, 154–56, 184.
30. Note in the front of William H. Jones Diary, William H. Jones Papers, Civil War Miscellaneous Collection, USAMHI.
31. Walter, "Battle of Belmont," 3.
32. Walter Scates to "Dear Father," November 13, 1861, Pearce Civil War Collection.
33. Ibid.
34. Ibid.
35. *OR*, vol. 3, pp. 287, 289.
36. Walter Scates to "Dear Father," November 13, 1861, Pearce Civil War Collection.
37. Grant, *Personal Memoirs*, 1:278–79.
38. Walter Scates to "Dear Father," November 13, 1861, Pearce Civil War Collection; *OR*, vol. 3, p. 281; Grant, *Personal Memoirs*, 1:280; Hughes, *The Battle of Belmont*, 166–74.
39. Jones, *Black Jack*, 114; Hughes, *The Battle of Belmont*, 166–74.
40. Grant, *Personal Memoirs*, 1:279.
41. Smith, *Grant*, 130–31.
42. W. H. L. Wallace to Ann Wallace, November 14, 1861, Wallace-Dickey Family Papers, ISHL.
43. Grant, *Personal Memoirs*, 1:280.
44. Hughes, *The Battle of Belmont*, 175.
45. Ibid., 184–85.
46. *OR*, vol. 3, p. 281; Kiper, *McClernand*, 46–47.
47. Simon, ed., *The Papers of Ulysses S. Grant*, 3:129.
48. Cooling, "Grant and Charles Ferguson Smith," in Woodworth, ed., *Grant's Lieutenants*, 46.
49. Catton, *Grant Moves South*, 80.
50. Hunt, "Civil War Reminiscences," http://www.carolyar.com/Illinois/Hunt-Part1.htm; Morrison, *History of the Ninth Regiment*, 16.
51. *OR*, vol. 3, pp. 299–300.
52. Hughes, *The Battle of Belmont*, 194.
53. Wills, *Army Life*, 42.
54. Simon, ed., *The Papers of Ulysses S. Grant*, 3:131–32, 134; Hughes, *The Battle of Belmont*, 178–79, 186–87.
55. Hughes, *The Battle of Belmont*, 178–79.
56. Smith, *Grant*, 131; Hughes, *The Battle of Belmont*, 196.
57. Simon, ed., *The Papers of Ulysses S. Grant*, 3:138.
58. Kiper, *McClernand*, 48.
59. *OR*, vol. 3, pp. 277–83; Winschel, "John A. McClernand," in Woodworth, ed., *Grant's Lieutenants*, 131–32.

60. Abraham Lincoln to John A. McClernand, November 10, 1861, Abraham Lincoln Papers, LC.

61. W. H. L. Wallace to Ann Wallace, November 14, 1861, Wallace-Dickey Family Papers, ISHL.

62. Simon, ed., *The Papers of Ulysses S. Grant*, 3:130, 137.

63. Brinton, *Personal Memoirs*, 79.

64. Catton, *Grant Moves South*, 84.

65. Grant, *Personal Memoirs*, 1:284.

66. Warner, *Generals in Blue*, 195–97; Catton, *Grant Moves South*, 85–87.

67. Grant, *Personal Memoirs*, 1:285.

68. Catton, *Grant Moves South*, 88–89.

69. Simon, ed., *The Papers of Ulysses S. Grant*, 3:204–5; McClernand to Lincoln, November 22, 1861, Abraham Lincoln Papers, LC.

70. Simon, ed., *The Papers of Ulysses S. Grant*, 3:214.

71. Ibid., 3:208–9.

72. Ibid., 3:205.

73. W. H. L. Wallace to Ann Wallace, November 26, 1861, Wallace-Dickey Family Papers, ISHL.

74. Jessee, *Civil War Diaries*, chap. 1, pp. 2–3; George W. Reese to "Dear Cousin," November 25, 1861, George W. Reese Papers, ISHL; W. H. L. Wallace to Ann Wallace, November 15 and 27, 1861, Wallace-Dickey Family Papers, ISHL; David W. Poak to "Dear Sister," November 30, David W. Poak Papers, ISHL.

75. Austin S. Andrew to "Dear Sisters," November 20, 1861, Austin S. Andrew Papers, ISHL.

76. W. H. L. Wallace to Ann Wallace, November 25, 1861, Wallace-Dickey Family Papers, ISHL.

77. Ibid., November 20, 1861.

78. Ibid., January 25, 1861.

79. David W. Poak to "Dear Sister," November 30, David W. Poak Papers, ISHL.

80. Morris, Hartwell, and Kuykendall, *History 31st Regiment*, 26.

CHAPTER FIVE: FORT HENRY

1. W. H. L. Wallace to Ann Wallace, January 8, Wallace-Dickey Family Papers, ISHL.

2. Catton, *Grant Moves South*, 118.

3. Ibid., 118–19.

4. David W. Poak to "Dear Sister," January 9, 1862, David W. Poak Papers, ISHL; W. H. L. Wallace to Ann Wallace, January 9, 1862, ISHL; U. S. Grant to Capt. R. B. Hatch, January 8, 1862, U. S. Grant Papers, Civil War Miscellaneous Collection, USAMHI.

5. W. H. L. Wallace to Ann Wallace, January 8, 1862, Wallace-Dickey Family Papers, ISHL.

6. David W. Poak to Sarah J. Poak, January 9, 1862, David W. Poak Papers, ISHL.

7. *OR*, vol. 7, pp. 541–43.

8. W. H. L. Wallace to Ann Wallace, January 9, 1862, Wallace-Dickey Family Papers, ISHL; Jessee, *Civil War Diaries*, chap. 1, p. 4.

9. Catton, *Grant Moves South*, 120; *OR*, vol. 7, pp. 68–72; Grant, *Personal Memoirs*, 1:286.

10. *OR*, vol. 7, pp. 72–74; William L. Sanderson to "Dear wife," January 26, 1862, "Letters from Col. William L. Sanderson, 23rd Indiana Infantry," in "Indiana in the Civil War," http://www.indianainthecivilwar.com/; John D. Kerr to "Dear wife," February 3, 1862, John D. Kerr Papers, ISHL; Morrison, *History of the Ninth Regiment*, 16–17.

11. W. H. L. Wallace to Ann Wallace, January 16 and 20, 1862, Wallace-Dickey Family Papers, ISHL.

12. Feis, *Grant's Secret Service*, 60–62.

13. Catton, *Grant Moves South*, 120.

14. Grant, *Personal Memoirs*, 1:286–87; Feis, *Grant's Secret Service*, 62–63.
15. Grant, *Personal Memoirs*, 1:287.
16. Williams, *Grant Rises in the West*, 123; *OR*, vol. 7, p. 440.
17. Feis, *Grant's Secret Service*, 66.
18. Grant, *Personal Memoirs*, 1:287–88.
19. Simon, ed., *The Papers of Ulysses S. Grant*, 4:103–4.
20. *OR*, vol. 5, p. 41.
21. Ibid., vol. 7, p. 571.
22. Ibid., p. 121.
23. Ibid., pp. 121–22; Grant, *Personal Memoirs*, 1:288.
24. *OR*, vol. 7, p. 122; Simpson, *Ulysses S. Grant*, 111.
25. Warner, *Generals in Blue*, 306–7.
26. Luther H. Cowan to "Dear Molly," January 18, 1862, Luther H. Cowan Papers, WHS.
27. Crooker, Nourse, and Brown, *The 55th Illinois*, 48.
28. Geer, *Civil War Diary*, 15; Douglas Hapeman Diary, January 28, 1862, ISHL; W. H. L. Wallace to Ann Wallace, January 29, 1862, Wallace-Dickey Family Papers, ISHL; Crooker, Nourse, and Brown, *The 55th Illinois*, 48; Clark and Bowen, *University Recruits*, 42.
29. W. H. L. Wallace to Ann Wallace, January 29, 1862, Wallace-Dickey Family Papers, ISHL.
30. Wallace, *Smoke, Sound & Fury*, 60.
31. Luther H. Cowan to Harriet Cowan, February 1, 1862, Luther H. Cowan Papers, WHS.
32. W. H. L. Wallace to Ann Wallace, February 1, 1862, Wallace-Dickey Family Papers, ISHL.
33. Geer, *Civil War Diary*, 15–16; W. H. L. Wallace to Ann Wallace, February 3, 1862, Wallace-Dickey Family Papers, ISHL; John D. Kerr to "Dear wife," February 3, 1862, John D. Kerr Papers, ISHL.
34. Grant, *Personal Memoirs*, 1:288.
35. *OR*, vol. 7, pp. 577, 583–85; Smith, *Grant*, 141.
36. *OR*, vol. 7, pp. 577, 579.
37. Douglas Hapeman Diary, February 1, 1862, ISHL; Luther H. Cowan to Harriet Cowan, February 1, 1862, Luther H. Cowan Papers, WHS.
38. Douglas Hapeman Diary, February 2 and 3, 1862, ISHL; Jessee, *Civil War Diaries*, chap. 1, p. 5.
39. Ambrose, *History of the Seventh Regiment*, 25.
40. Morris, Hartwell, and Kuykendall, *History 31st Regiment*, 30; W. H. L. Wallace to Ann Wallace, February 3, 1862, Wallace-Dickey Family Papers, ISHL.
41. Grant, *Personal Memoirs*, 1:288.
42. Smith, *Grant*, 141; Simpson, *Ulysses S. Grant*, 111.
43. *OR*, vol. 7, p. 126; Grant, *Personal Memoirs*, 1:288.
44. Grant, *Personal Memoirs*, 1:290; *OR*, vol. 7, pp. 126, 581; Tucker, *Unconditional Surrender*, 54; Morris, Hartwell, and Kuykendall, *History 31st Regiment*, 30; W. H. L. Wallace to Ann Wallace, February 4, 1862, Wallace-Dickey Family Papers, ISHL.
45. *OR*, vol. 7, p. 126.
46. Ibid., p. 579.
47. Clark and Bowen, *University Recruits*, 44.
48. W. H. L. Wallace to Ann Wallace, February 4, 1862, Wallace-Dickey Family Papers, ISHL; Lew Wallace, *Smoke, Sound & Fury*, 60; Crummer, *With Grant*, 13.
49. W. H. L. Wallace to Ann Wallace, February 4, 1862, Wallace-Dickey Family Papers, ISHL; Jessee, *Civil War Diaries*, chap. 1, p. 5; Ambrose, *History of the Seventh Regiment*, 25.
50. Geer, *Civil War Diary*, 16; Ambrose, *History of the Seventh Regiment*, 25–26; Cooling, *Forts Henry and Donelson*, 97.
51. *OR*, vol. 7, pp. 585–86; Grant, *Personal Memoirs*, 1:291.

52. Lew Wallace, *Smoke, Sound & Fury,* 61.
53. Geer, *Civil War Diary,* 16; Jessee, *Civil War Diaries,* chap. 1, p. 5; Douglas Hapeman Diary, February 5, 1862, ISHL.
54. Crummer, *With Grant,* 16.
55. Douglas Hapeman Diary, February 6, 1862, ISHL; Wallace, *Smoke, Sound & Fury,* 61.
56. Ira Merchant to Henry Yates, February 26, 1862, ISHL.
57. Hubert, *History of the Fiftieth Regiment,* 60; Crummer, *With Grant,* 19.
58. Crummer, *With Grant,* 19; Morris, Hartwell, and Kuykendall, *History 31st Regiment,* 31–32; Ira Merchant to Henry Yates, February 26, 1862, ISHL.
59. Douglas Hapeman Diary, February 6, 1862, ISHL; Luther H. Cowan Diary, February 6, 1862, Luther H. Cowan Papers, WHS.
60. Tucker, *Unconditional Surrender,* 56–59; Cooling, *Forts Henry and Donelson,* 101–8.
61. W. H. L. Wallace to Ann Wallace, February 7, 1862, Wallace-Dickey Family Papers, ISHL.
62. Wallace, *Smoke, Sound & Fury,* 62.
63. David W. Poak to Sarah J. Poak, February 8, 1862, David W. Poak Papers, ISHL; Clark and Bowen, *University Recruits,* 48; Luther H. Cowan Diary, February 6, 1862, Luther H. Cowan Papers, WHS; Jessee, *Civil War Diaries,* chap. 1, p. 5.
64. Morris, Hartwell, and Kuykendall, *History 31st Regiment,* 32.
65. Wallace, *Smoke, Sound & Fury,* 62.
66. Ira Merchant to Henry Yates, February 26, 1862, ISHL; David W. Poak to Sarah J. Poak, February 8, 1862, David W. Poak Papers, ISHL; Luther H. Cowan Diary, February 6, 1862, Luther H. Cowan Papers, WHS.
67. Crummer, *With Grant,* 21.
68. Smith, *Grant,* 147; Clark and Bowen, *University Recruits,* 48; Ira Merchant to Henry Yates, February 26, 1862, Ira Merchant Papers, ISHL; Horace Wardner, "Reminiscences of a Surgeon," in *MOLLUS,* 12:179.
69. Dietrich C. Smith to "My Dearest Carrie," February 20, 1862, Dietrich C. Smith Papers, ISHL.
70. Lew Wallace, *Smoke, Sound & Fury,* 63.

CHAPTER SIX: FROM HENRY TO DONELSON

1. David W. Poak to Sarah J. Poak, February 8, 1862, David W. Poak Papers, ISHL.
2. Hubert, *History of the Fiftieth Regiment,* 61.
3. Kiner, *One Year's Soldiering,* 9–11; Adolph Engelmann to Mina Engelmann, February 5 and 9, 1862, Engelmann-Kircher Family Papers, ISHL; Abram J. Vanauken Diary, February 9, 1862, ISHL.
4. Cooling, *Forts Henry and Donelson,* 117.
5. Adolph Engelmann to Mina Engelmann, February 10, 1862, Engelmann-Kircher Family Papers, ISHL.
6. Engle, *Struggle for the Heartland,* 59; Kiper, *McClernand,* 72.
7. Hicken, *Illinois in the Civil War,* 30; Kiper, *McClernand,* 72.
8. *OR,* vol. 7, p. 124.
9. Simpson, *Ulysses S. Grant,* 112–13.
10. Clark and Bowen, *University Recruits,* 50.
11. Simon, ed., *The Papers of Ulysses S. Grant,* 4:165–66.
12. Smith, *Grant,* 148.
13. Hicken, *Illinois in the Civil War,* 30.
14. *OR,* vol. 7, p. 594; Simon, ed., *The Papers of Ulysses S. Grant,* 4:196.

15. Smith, *Grant*, 151–52.

16. Simon, ed., *The Papers of Ulysses S. Grant*, 4:175.

17. W. H. L. Wallace to Ann Wallace, February 8, 1862, Wallace-Dickey Family Papers, ISHL.

18. Simon, ed., *The Papers of Ulysses S. Grant*, 4:179.

19. Jessee, *Civil War Diaries*, chap. 1, pp. 5–6; Adolph Engelmann to Mina Engelmann, February 10, 1862, Engelmann-Kircher Family Papers, ISHL.

20. Simon, ed., *The Papers of Ulysses S. Grant*, 4:176–79; Grant, *Personal Memoirs*, 1:294.

21. Grant, *Personal Memoirs*, 1:295–96.

22. Simon, ed., *The Papers of Ulysses S. Grant*, 4:184.

23. Ibid., 4:183; Kiper, *McClernand*, 73.

24. Wallace, *Smoke, Sound & Fury*, 65–66; Kiper, *McClernand*, 73; Hicken, *Illinois in the Civil War*, 31.

25. Ballard, *U. S. Grant*.

26. Geer, *Civil War Diary*, 17; Kiner, *One Year's Soldiering*, 11; Simon, ed., *The Papers of Ulysses S. Grant*, 4:191–93.

27. *OR*, vol. 7, p. 595; Simon, ed., *The Papers of Ulysses S. Grant*, 4:193–94.

28. Simon, ed., *The Papers of Ulysses S. Grant*, 4:195.

29. Ibid., 4:196.

30. Ambrose, *History of the Seventh Regiment*, 30–31; Morris, Hartwell, and Kuykendall, *History 31st Regiment*, 33–34.

31. Wallace, *Smoke, Sound & Fury*, 67.

32. Hicks, "Fort Donelson," in *MOLLUS*, 29:440.

33. Kiner, *One Year's Soldiering*, 11.

34. Douglas Hapeman Diary, February 12, 1862, ISHL; Crummer, *With Grant*, 25.

35. Hicks, "Fort Donelson," in *MOLLUS*, 29:440.

36. *OR*, vol. 7, pp. 170–71, 183–84, 188; Jessee, *Civil War Diaries*, chap. 1, p. 6; *Report of the Adjutant General of the State of Illinois*, 8th Infantry Regiment, http://www.rootsweb.com/~ilcivilw/history/008.htm; David Poak to "Dear Aunt," February 17, 1862, David W. Poak Papers, ISHL; Gould D. Molineaux Diary, February 12, 1862, Special Collections, ACL; Morris, Hartwell, and Kuykendall, *History 31st Regiment*, 33–34; Hicks, "Fort Donelson," in *MOLLUS*, 29:440–41; Geer, *Civil War Diary*, 17–18.

37. *OR*, vol. 7, p. 184; Jessee, *Civil War Diaries*, chap. 1, p. 6; Hicks, "Fort Donelson," in *MOLLUS*, 29:442.

38. *OR*, vol. 7, p. 162.

39. Ibid., pp. 162, 605.

40. Simon, ed., *Papers of Ulysses S. Grant*, 4:191.

41. William H. Brown to "Dear Parents," February 18, 1862, William H. Brown Letters, ISHL.

42. Morris, Hartwell, and Kuykendall, *History 31st Regiment*, 34.

43. J. F. Warner, "Smith's Division at Donelson," *National Tribune*, January 3, 1884, p. 3.

44. Barber, *Holding the Line*, 17–18.

45. Clark and Bowen, *University Recruits*, 56.

46. Douglas Hapeman Diary, February 13, 1862, ISHL.

47. Cooling, *Forts Henry and Donelson*, 140–45.

48. *OR*, vol. 7, pp. 227–28; 232.

49. Ibid., pp. 172–73, 193, 215; Barber, *Holding the Line*, 18; Crummer, *With Grant*, 28–29; Hicks, "Fort Donelson," in *MOLLUS*, 29:446.

50. *OR*, vol. 7, pp. 212–13; Cooling, *Forts Henry and Donelson*, 145.

51. Crummer, *With Grant*, 28–29; Hicks, "Fort Donelson," in *MOLLUS*, 29:446.

52. George O. Smith Reminiscences, George O. Smith Papers, ISHL; Barber, *Holding the Line*, 19.

53. *OR*, vol. 7, pp. 172–73.

54. Ibid., p. 163.

55. Barber, *Holding the Line*, 20; *OR*, vol. 7, p. 174.

56. Kiner, *One Year's Soldiering*, 13–14.

57. Gebhardt, "The Eleventh Illinois Infantry Regiment in the Civil War," 74–75.

58. Morrison, *History of the Ninth Regiment*, 22.

59. Gould D. Molineaux Diary, February 13, 1862, Special Collections, ACL.

60. Clark and Bowen, *University Recruits*, 57.

61. Ambrose, *History of the Seventh Regiment*, 32.

62. *Report of the Adjutant General of the State of Illinois*, 8th Infantry Regiment, http://www.rootsweb.com/~ilcivilw/history/008.htm; Crummer, *With Grant*, 30.

63. Clark and Bowen, *University Recruits*, 57.

64. Ibid., 57–58.

65. Kiner, *One Year's Soldiering*, 14; Clark and Bowen, *University Recruits*, 57; Gould D. Molineaux Diary, February 13, 1862, Special Collections, ACL.

66. *OR*, vol. 7, p. 174; Ambrose, *History of the Seventh Regiment*, 32; Barber, *Holding the Line*, 20; Kiner, *One Year's Soldiering*, 14–15.

67. Barber, *Holding the Line*, 20–21.

68. Clark and Bowen, *University Recruits*, 60–61.

69. Geer, *Civil War Diary*, 18.

70. *OR*, vol. 7, p. 166.

71. Gould D. Molineaux Diary, February 14, 1862, Special Collections, ACL.

72. *OR*, vol. 7, p. 166; Tucker, *Unconditional Surrender*, 83–86; Hicks, "Fort Donelson," in *MOLLUS*, 29:447; Wallace, *Smoke, Sound & Fury*, 75.

73. Grant, *Personal Memoirs*, 1:303–4.

74. Ibid., 1:305.

75. Simon, ed., *The Papers of Ulysses S. Grant*, 4:205; Grant, *Personal Memoirs*, 1:301–2.

76. Wallace, *Smoke, Sound & Fury*, 71–74.

77. *OR*, vol. 7, p. 174; Morrison, *History of the Ninth Regiment*, 22.

78. *OR*, vol. 7, p. 216.

79. Morris, Hartwell, and Kuykendall, *History 31st Regiment*, 35; Clark and Bowen, *University Recruits*, 61; Kiner, *One Year's Soldiering*, 14–15; Geer, *Civil War Diary*, 18.

80. Burt, "Experiences of the 76th Ohio in the Siege," *National Tribune*, September 13, 1906.

CHAPTER SEVEN: VICTORY AT FORT DONELSON

1. Grant, *Personal Memoirs*, 1:304.

2. Ibid.

3. Hicks, "Fort Donelson," in *MOLLUS*, 29:448; *OR*, vol. 7, p. 185.

4. *OR*, vol. 7, pp. 218–19.

5. Ibid., p. 217.

6. *Report of the Adjutant General of the State of Illinois*, 9th Infantry Regiment, http://www.rootsweb.com/~ilcivilw/history/009.htm; Morrison, *History of the Ninth Regiment*, 22–23.

7. Morrison, *History of the 9th Regiment*, 26.

8. Ibid., 22–23.

9. *OR*, vol. 7, pp. 168, 176.

10. Brinton, *Personal Memoirs*, 126–27.

11. *OR*, vol. 7, pp. 186, 190.

12. Gould D. Molineaux Diary, February 15, 1862, Special Collections, ACL; David W. Poak to "Dear Aunt," February 17, 1862, David W. Poak Papers, ISHL; Morris, Hartwell, and Kuykendall, *History 31st Regiment*, 35–36; *OR*, vol. 7, p. 186.

13. Jessee, *Civil War Diaries*, chap. 1, p. 6; Gould D. Molineaux Diary, February 15, 1862, Special Collections, ACL.

14. *OR*, vol. 7, p. 195.

15. Huffstodt, *Hard Dying Men*, 65–66; Churchill, "Wounded at Fort Donelson," in *MOLLUS*, 14:149.

16. *OR*, vol. 7, p. 210; Blanchard, *I Marched with Sherman*, 46.

17. Huffstodt, *Hard Dying Men*, 66–67; Luther H. Cowan to Harriet Cowan, February 19, 1862, Luther H. Cowan Papers, WHS; Churchill, "Wounded at Fort Donelson," in *MOLLUS*, 14:148.

18. Brinton, *Personal Memoirs*, 125–26; Brinsfield et al., *Faith in the Fight*, 130.

19. *OR*, vol. 7, p. 186.

20. Wallace, *Smoke, Sound & Fury*, 79–80.

21. *OR*, vol. 7, p. 175.

22. Wallace, *Smoke, Sound & Fury*, 80.

23. Jesse B. Connelly Diary, February 15, 1862, IHS.

24. *OR*, vol. 7, p. 244; Jessee, *Civil War Diaries*, chap. 1, p. 6; Gould D. Molineaux Diary, February 15, 1862, Special Collections, ACL.

25. Gould D. Molineaux Diary, February 15, 1862, Special Collections, ACL; *OR*, vol. 7, p. 244; Jesse B. Connelly Diary, February 15, 1862, IHS.

26. *OR*, vol. 7, p. 187.

27. Churchill, "Wounded at Fort Donelson," in *MOLLUS*, 14:148.

28. Morris, Hartwell, and Kuykendall, *History 31st Regiment*, 35–36; Churchill, "Wounded at Fort Donelson," in *MOLLUS*, 14:148.

29. Huffstodt, *Hard Dying Men*, 67–68; Churchill, "Wounded at Fort Donelson," in *MOLLUS*, 14:148–50.

30. Douglas Hapeman Diary, February 15, 1862, ISHL; Huffstodt, *Hard Dying Men*, 67–68.

31. *OR*, vol. 7, pp. 195–96; Churchill, "Wounded at Fort Donelson," in *MOLLUS*, 14:149.

32. Churchill, "Wounded at Fort Donelson," in *MOLLUS*, 14:150.

33. Ibid.

34. Huffstodt, *Hard Dying Men*, 72.

35. Ibid.

36. Ibid., 71–72.

37. *OR*, vol. 7, p. 200.

38. *Report of the Adjutant General of the State of Illinois*, 11th Infantry Regiment, http://www.rootsweb.com/~ilcivilw/history/011.htm; Gebhardt, "The Eleventh Illinois Infantry Regiment in the Civil War," 81–83.

39. Wallace, *Smoke, Sound & Fury*, 79–82.

40. Ibid., 83–84; *OR*, vol. 7, pp. 237–38.

41. *OR*, vol. 7, p. 210.

42. Stuber, *Mein Tagebuch*, 16–17.

43. Burt, "Experiences of the 76th Ohio in the Siege," *National Tribune*, September 13, 1906, p. 3.

44. Ibid.

45. Wallace, *Smoke, Sound & Fury*, 84–85.

46. Grant, *Personal Memoirs*, 1:305–06; Simpson, *Ulysses S. Grant*, 115.

47. Arnold, *The Armies of U.S. Grant*, 44–45.

48. Grant, *Personal Memoirs*, 1:307.

49. Ibid., 4:308.
50. Simpson, *Ulysses S. Grant*, 115; Wallace, *Smoke, Sound & Fury*, 86.
51. Cooling, *Forts Henry and Donelson*, 185; Simpson, *Ulysses S. Grant*, 115.
52. Simon, ed., *The Papers of Ulysses S. Grant*, 4:214; Williams, *Grant Rises in the West*, 244.
53. Grant, *Personal Memoirs*, 1:308.
54. *OR*, vol. 7, pp. 223, 229; Williams, *Grant Rises in the West*, 245.
55. Kiner, *One Year's Soldiering*, 13.
56. Cooling, *Forts Henry and Donelson*, 185.
57. *OR*, vol. 7, p. 230; Arnold, *The Armies of U.S. Grant*, 46.
58. *OR*, vol. 7, p. 230; Clark and Bowen, *University Recruits*, 57.
59. Clark and Bowen, *University Recruits*, 57.
60. Cooling, *Forts Henry and Donelson*, 185; Arnold, *The Armies of U.S. Grant*, 45–46.
61. Brinton, *Personal Memoirs*, 121.
62. *OR*, vol. 7, p. 230; Cooling, *Forts Henry and Donelson*, 185; Arnold, *The Armies of U.S. Grant*, 46.
63. McGillicuddy, "The 50th Illinois at Fort Donelson," *National Tribune*, May 1, 1884; Kiner, *One Year's Soldiering*, 15.
64. Clark and Bowen, *University Recruits*, 63.
65. Tucker, *Unconditional Surrender*, 94.
66. William H. Brown to "Dear Parents," February 18, 1862, William H. Brown Letters, ISHL.
67. Wallace, *Smoke, Sound & Fury*, 87–88.
68. Ibid., 88–89.
69. Ibid.; Cooling, *Forts Henry and Donelson*, 191.
70. William H. Brown to "Dear Parents," February 18, 1862, William H. Brown Letters, ISHL.
71. Rerick, *The Forty-fourth Indiana Volunteer Infantry*, 39; William H. Brown to "Dear Parents," February 18, 1862, William H. Brown Letters, ISHL; Wallace, *Smoke, Sound & Fury*, 90–91.
72. William H. Brown to "Dear Parents," February 18, 1862, William H. Brown Letters, ISHL.
73. Churchill, "Wounded at Fort Donelson," in *MOLLUS*, 14:146–64.
74. Rerick, *The Forty-fourth Indiana Volunteer Infantry*, 39–40.
75. Luther H. Cowan Diary, December 10, 1862, Luther H. Cowan Papers, WHS.
76. Catton, *Grant Moves South*, 173.
77. Brinton, *Personal Memoirs*, 129.
78. Simon, ed., *The Papers of Ulysses S. Grant*, 4:218.
79. Brinton, *Personal Memoirs*, 129–30; Simon, ed., *The Papers of Ulysses S. Grant*, 4:218.
80. Brinton, *Personal Memoirs*, 133.
81. S. M. Emmons, J. H. H. Hunter, and F. Morrison to the editor of the *East Liverpool Mercury*, May 15, 1862.
82. Clark and Bowen, *University Recruits*, 66.
83. Burt, "Experiences of the 76th Ohio in the Siege," 3; Hubert, *History of the Fiftieth Regiment*, 68; Stuber, *Mein Tagebuch*, 17–18; George O. Smith Diary, February 16, 1862, ISHL.
84. Crummer, *With Grant*, 43–44.
85. Hubert, *History of the Fiftieth Regiment*, 70–71; Crummer, *With Grant*, 43; Abram J. Vanauken Diary, February 16, 1862, Abram J. Vanauken Papers, ISHL.
86. Jonathan L. Labrant Reminiscences, Jonathan L. Labrant Diary, Civil War Miscellaneous Collection, USAMHI.
87. Victor H. Stevens to "Dear Uncle," February 28, 1862, Howard and Victor H. Stevens Papers, Civil War Miscellaneous Collection, USAMHI.
88. Barber, *Holding the Line*, 34.
89. Crummer, *With Grant*, 44.

90. Daniel, *Shiloh*, 30.
91. Grant, *Personal Memoirs*, 1:306.

CHAPTER EIGHT: UP THE TENNESSEE RIVER

1. Crummer, *With Grant*, 47.
2. William H. Tebbets to "My Dear Sister," March 2, 1862, William H. Tebbets Papers, ISHL.
3. Jessee, *Civil War Diaries*, chap. 1, p. 6; Gould D. Molineaux Diary, February 21, 1862, Special Collections, ACL; Clark and Bowen, *University Recruits*, 67; Geer, *Civil War Diary*, 20.
4. William W. McCarty to "My dear Daughter," February 20, 1862, William W. McCarty Papers, Civil War Miscellaneous Collection, USAMHI.
5. Geer, *Civil War Diary*, 23.
6. Jessee, *Civil War Diaries*, chap. 1, p. 6; Kiner, *One Year's Soldiering*, 19.
7. David W. Poak to Sarah J. Poak, February 28, 1862, David W. Poak Papers, ISHL; Luther H. Cowan to Harriet Cowan, March 1, 1862, Luther H. Cowan Papers, WHS; William W. McCarty to "My dear Daughter," March 2, 1862, William W. McCarty Papers, Civil War Miscellaneous Collection, USAMHI; Stevenson, *History of the 78th Regiment*, 142; Rerick, *The Forty-fourth Indiana Volunteer Infantry*, 43–44; Puterbaugh, *March and Countermarch*, 115.
8. Geer, *Civil War Diary*, 19–20; Charles H. Lutz to "Dear Brother," February 25, 1862, Charles H. Lutz Papers, Civil War Miscellaneous Collection, USAMHI.
9. Gould D. Molineaux Diary, February 21, 1862, Special Collections, ACL.
10. Luther H. Cowan to Harriet Cowan, February 19, 1862, Luther H. Cowan Papers, WHS.
11. Francis Marion Bateman to "My dear Parents," February 23, 1862, Francis Marion Bateman Papers, LC.
12. Ira Merchant to Henry Yates, February 26, 1862, Ira Merchant Papers, ISHL.
13. John A. McClernand, Field Order No. 145, February 17, 1862, Abraham Lincoln Papers, LC.
14. Ibid.
15. John A. McClernand to Abraham Lincoln, February 18, 1862, Abraham Lincoln Papers, LC.
16. Williams, *Grant Rises in the West*, 260–61.
17. *OR*, vol. 7, p. 641.
18. Ibid., p. 637.
19. Ibid., p. 645.
20. Simpson, *Ulysses S. Grant*, 119.
21. Simon, ed., *The Papers of Ulysses S. Grant*, 4:245, 284.
22. W. H. L. Wallace to Ann Wallace, February 20, 1862, Wallace-Dickey Family Papers, ISHL.
23. *OR*, vol. 7, p. 649.
24. Ibid., p. 649.
25. Lash, *A Politician Turned General*, 1–66.
26. Ibid., 67–92; Hurlbut obituary, *National Tribune*, April 29, 1882, p. 1; Dugan, *History of Hurlbut's Fighting Fourth Division*, 106.
27. Grant, *Personal Memoirs*, 1:317–18.
28. Simon, ed., *The Papers of Ulysses S. Grant*, 4:279, 282; Brinton, *Personal Memoirs*, 143.
29. Simon, ed., *The Papers of Ulysses S. Grant*, 4:299.
30. Grant, *Personal Memoirs*, 1:319–20; W. H. L. Wallace to Ann Wallace, February 28, 1862, Wallace-Dickey Family Papers, ISHL.
31. Grant, *Personal Memoirs*, 1:320–21.
32. Ibid., 1:321; W. H. L. Wallace to Ann Wallace, February 28, 1862, Wallace-Dickey Family Papers, ISHL.

33. Simon, ed., *The Papers of Ulysses S. Grant*, 4:293–94.

34. Brinton, *Personal Memoirs*, 143.

35. Grant, *Personal Memoirs*, 1:321.

36. Simon, ed., *The Papers of Ulysses S. Grant*, 4:310–12.

37. *OR*, vol. 7, pp. 679–80.

38. Ibid., p. 680.

39. Simon, ed., *The Papers of Ulysses S. Grant*, 4:319.

40. Grant, *Personal Memoirs*, 1:326.

41. Simon, ed., *The Papers of Ulysses S. Grant*, 4:319.

42. Ibid., 4:320n.

43. *OR*, vol. 10, pt. 2, pp. 13, 15.

44. Ibid., vol. 7, p. 682.

45. Smith, *Grant*, 173.

46. Simon, ed., *The Papers of Ulysses S. Grant*, 4:306.

47. Smith, *Grant*, 174–75.

48. Brinton, *Personal Memoirs*, 145, 148.

49. Barber, *Army Memoirs*, 46.

50. Dugan, *History of Hurlbut's Fighting Fourth Division*, 96–97; Douglas Hapeman Diary, March 4 and 5, 1862, ISHL; Geer, *Civil War Diary*, 20; Kiner, *One Year's Soldiering*, 20; William W. McCarty Reminiscences, William W. McCarty Papers, Civil War Miscellaneous Collection, USAMHI; Adolph Engelmann to Mina Engelmann, March 7, 1862, Engelmann-Kircher Family Papers, ISHL; Jessee, *Civil War Diaries*, chap. 1, p. 7.

51. Clark and Bowen, *University Recruits*, 81.

52. Barker, *With the Western Sharpshooters*, 9.

53. Kiner, *One Year's Soldiering*, 20; Abram J. Vanauken Diary, March 6, 1862, Abram J. Vanauken Papers, ISHL.

54. Daniel, *Shiloh*, 75.

55. Crummer, *With Grant*, 49.

56. Luther H. Cowan to Harriet Cowan, March 7, 1862, Luther H. Cowan Papers, WHS; Adoph Engelmann to Mina Engelmann, March 12, 1862, Engelmann-Kircher Family Papers, ISHL; Levi Losier to "Dear Lydia," March 16, 1862, Levi Losier Papers, Civil War Miscellaneous Collection, USAMHI; Puterbaugh, *March and Countermarch*, 111.

57. Brinton, *Personal Memoirs*, 148–49.

58. Grant, *Personal Memoirs*, 1:328.

59. Brinton, *Personal Memoirs*, 150.

60. Flemming, "The Battle of Shiloh as a Private Saw It," in *MOLLUS*, 6:132.

61. Shanks, "Recollections of Sherman," *Harper's New Monthly Magazine* 30, no. 175 (December 1864): 641.

62. Sherman, *Memoirs*, 232–36; Marszalek, *Sherman*, 162–170.

63. *OR*, vol. 7, p. 2; Simpson and Berlin, eds., *Sherman's Civil War*, 191.

64. Grant, *Personal Memoirs*, 1:315.

65. Simpson and Berlin, eds., *Sherman's Civil War*, 192–93; Dawes, "My First Day Under Fire at Shiloh," in *MOLLUS*, 3:2.

66. *OR*, vol. 10, pt. 2, pp. 12, 20; Simpson and Berlin, eds., *Sherman's Civil War*, 195; Sherman, *Memoirs*, 245–47; Crooker, Nourse, and Brown, *The 55th Illinois*, 63; *OR*, vol. 10, pt. 1, p. 28.

67. Douglas Hapeman Diary, March 10, 1862, ISHL.

68. Crooker, Nourse, and Brown, *The 55th Illinois*, 58–63; Douglas Hapeman Diary, February 11, 1862, ISHL; Hickenlooper, "The Battle of Shiloh," in *MOLLUS*, 5:410; Mason, "Shiloh," in *MOLLUS*, 10:93; Morrison, *A History of the Ninth Regiment*, 29; Puterbaugh, *March and Countermarch*, 112; Clark and Bowen, *University Recruits*, 82.

69. Mason, "Shiloh," in *MOLLUS*, 10:93.

70. Crooker, Nourse, and Brown, *The 55th Illinois*, 63.

71. Dugan, *History of Hurlbut's Fighting Fourth Division*, 98.

72. Clark and Bowen, *University Recruits*, 82.

73. *OR*, vol. 10, pt. 2, p. 16.

74. Kiner, *One Year's Soldiering*, 21.

75. Ibid.; Crooker, Nourse, and Brown, *The 55th Illinois*, 57; Bering and Montgomery, *History of the Forty-eighth Ohio*.

76. Wright, *A Corporal's Story*, 27–28; Douglas Hapeman Diary, March 11, 1862, ISHL; Adolph Engelmann to Mina Engelmann, March 12, 1862, Engelmann-Kircher Family Papers, ISHL.

77. Bering and Montgomery, *History of the Forty-eighth Ohio*.

78. Puterbaugh, *March and Countermarch*, 112.

79. Adolph Engelmann to Mina Engelmann, March 12, 1862, Engelmann-Kircher Family Papers, ISHL; Daniel, *Shiloh*, 75–76.

80. Dugan, *History of Hurlbut's Fighting Fourth Division*, 98.

81. Douglas Hapeman Diary, March 12, 1862, ISHL; Clark and Bowen, *University Recruits*, 83; Geer, *Civil War Diary*, 22.

82. W. H. L. Wallace to Ann Wallace, March 14, 1862, Wallace-Dickey Family Papers, ISHL.

83. Wallace, *Smoke, Sound & Fury*, 103–4.

84. Ibid.; *OR*, vol. 10, pt. 1, pp. 8–10.

85. *OR*, vol. 10, pt. 1, pp. 8, 22.

86. Ibid., p. 22; Crooker, Nourse, and Brown, *The 55th Illinois*, 64; Sherman, *Memoirs*, 247; Simpson and Berlin, eds., *Sherman's Civil War*, 197.

87. *OR*, vol. 10, pt. 1, p. 22; Crooker, Nourse, and Brown, *The 55th Illinois*, 64; Flemming, "The Battle of Shiloh as a Private Saw It," in *MOLLUS*, 6:132–33.

88. *OR*, vol. 10, pt. 1, pp. 22–23; Christian Zook to "Dear friends," March 23, 1862, Christian Zook Papers, Civil War Miscellaneous Collection, USAMHI.

89. *OR*, vol. 10, pt. 1, p. 23; Crooker, Nourse, and Brown, *The 55th Illinois*, 64; Flemming, "The Battle of Shiloh as a Private Saw It," in *MOLLUS*, 6:132–33.

90. *OR*, vol. 10, pt. 1, p. 23; Sherman, *Memoirs*, 247–48; Rerick, *The Forty-fourth Indiana Volunteer Infantry*, 43.

91. Barber, *Army Memoirs*, 46.

92. Mason, "Shiloh," in *MOLLUS*, 10:94; Kiner, *One Year's Soldiering*, 21.

93. Mason, "Shiloh," in *MOLLUS*, 10:94; Bering and Montgomery, *History of the Forty-eighth Ohio;* Crooker, Nourse, and Brown, *The 55th Illinois*, 66–67; Clark and Bowen, *University Recruits*, 84.

94. Sumbardo, "Some Facts About the Battle of Shiloh," in *MOLLUS*, 28:29; *OR*, vol. 10, pt. 2, p. 50.

CHAPTER NINE: "WE ARE ATTACKED!"

1. Puterbaugh, *March and Countermarch*, 114.

2. Crooker, Nourse, and Brown, *The 55th Illinois*, 68–69.

3. Puterbaugh, *March and Countermarch*, 114; Wright, *A Corporal's Story;* Sumbardo, "Some Facts About the Battle of Shiloh," in *MOLLUS*, 28:29; Barber, *Army Memoirs*, 48.

4. Puterbaugh, *March and Countermarch*, 117.

5. Adolph Engelmann to Mina Engelmann, March 30, 1862, Engelmann-Kircher Family Papers, ISHL; Stuber, *Mein Tagebuch*, 21; William L. Dillon to "Dear Brother & Sister," March 25, 1862, Isaiah T. and William L. Dillon Papers, ISHL.

6. Crooker, Nourse, and Brown, *The 55th Illinois*, 68.

7. W. H. L. Wallace to Ann Wallace, March 29, 1862, Wallace-Dickey Family Papers, ISHL.

8. William L. Wade Diary, March 26, 1862, Civil War Miscellaneous Collection, USAMHI.

9. Jonathan L. Labrant Diary, March 27, 1862, Civil War Miscellaneous Collection, USAMHI.

10. Luther H. Cowan to "My Dear Ones," March 30, 1862, Luther H. Cowan Papers, WHS.

11. William W. McCarty Papers, Civil War Miscellaneous Collection, USAMHI; Stuber, *Mein Tagebuch*, 20; William L. Wade Diary, March 27–28, 1862, Civil War Miscellaneous Collection, USAMHI; Barber, *Army Memoirs*, 48; Crooker, Nourse, and Brown, *The 55th Illinois*, 70–71.

12. Wright, *A Corporal's Story*, 29–30.

13. "An Iowa Soldier's Story of Shiloh," anonymous, *National Tribune*, May 3, 1883, p. 3.

14. William L. Wade Diary, April 1, 1862, Civil War Miscellaneous Collection, USAMHI.

15. Douglas Hapeman Diary, March 26, 1862, ISHL.

16. Clark and Bowen, *University Recruits*, 84.

17. Jonathan L. Labrant Diary, April 3, 1862, Civil War Miscellaneous Collection, USAMHI.

18. Barber, *Army Memoirs*, 48.

19. Smith, *Grant*, 176–79.

20. Ibid.; Simpson, *Ulysses S. Grant*, 123–27.

21. *OR*, vol. 10, pt. 2, pp. 15, 21, 32; Smith, *Grant*, 176–79; Simpson, *Ulysses S. Grant*, 123–27.

22. Crooker, Nourse, and Brown, *The 55th Illinois*, 63; Hancock, *The Fourteenth Wisconsin*, 2.

23. *OR*, vol. 10, pt. 2, p. 46.

24. Simon, ed., *Papers of Ulysses S. Grant*, 4:392.

25. Ibid., 4:398–99.

26. Ibid., 4:400.

27. *OR*, vol. 10, pt. 2, pp. 50–51.

28. Simon, ed., *Papers of Ulysses S. Grant*, 4:400.

29. *OR*, vol. 10, pt. 2, pp. 50, 55.

30. Puterbaugh, *March and Countermarch*, 117–18.

31. Levi P. Coman to "Dear Mattie," March 23, 1862, private collection.

32. Abram J. Vanauken Diary, March 22, 1862, ISHL.

33. Richardson, *"For My Country,"* 38; William L. Dillon to "Dear Brother & Sister," March 25, 1862, Isaiah T. and William L. Dillon Papers, ISHL.

34. John A. McClernand to Abraham Lincoln, February 27, 1862, Abraham Lincoln Papers, LC.

35. *OR*, vol. 7, pp. 170, 179.

36. John A. McClernand to Abraham Lincoln, March 31, 1862, Abraham Lincoln Papers, LC.

37. *OR*, vol. 10, pt. 2, p. 52.

38. Ibid., p. 67.

39. Jones, "The Battle of Shiloh: Reminiscences," in *MOLLUS*, 49:52, 54; Henry Miller Culbertson to "Dear Mother, Brother, and Sister," March 21–22, 1862, Henry Miller Culbertson Papers, WHS.

40. Sumbardo, "Some Facts About the Battle of Shiloh," in *MOLLUS*, 28:30–31.

41. *OR*, vol. 10, pt. 2, p. 70.

42. W. H. L. Wallace to Ann Wallace, April 3, 1862, and Special Orders No. 13, April 3, 1862, Wallace-Dickey Family Papers, ISHL.

43. W. H. L. Wallace to Ann Wallace, March 22, 1862, Wallace-Dickey Family Papers, ISHL.

44. Simpson, *Ulysses S. Grant*, 130.

45. William L. Wade Diary, March 28, 1862, Civil War Miscellaneous Collection, USAMHI.

46. Jonathan L. Labrant Diary, March 26, 1862, Civil War Miscellaneous Collection, USAMHI; Puterbaugh, *March and Countermarch*, 117–18.

47. Clark and Bowen, *University Recruits*, 85; William L. Wade Diary, April 3, 1862, Civil War

Miscellaneous Collection, USAMHI; Douglas Hapeman Diary, April 3, 1862, ISHL; Jessee, *Civil War Diaries,* chap. 1, p. 9.

48. Oates, "The Ninth Illinois at Shiloh," *National Tribune,* May 10, 1883, p. 1.
49. Sumbardo, "Some Facts About the Battle of Shiloh," in *MOLLUS,* 28:32.
50. Bering and Montgomery, *History of the Forty-eighth Ohio;* Connelly, *History of the Seventieth Ohio,* 19–20.
51. Baird, "Shiloh: The Services of the 21st Mo. on the Field," *National Tribune,* February 25, 1886, p. 3; *OR,* vol. 10, pt. 2, p. 90.
52. *Warren (Illinois) Independent,* April 22, 1862.
53. Flemming, "The Battle of Shiloh as a Private Saw It," in *MOLLUS,* 6:136–38.
54. French, "One Regiment That Was Not Surprised," *National Tribune,* April 12, 1883, p. 3; Daniel, *Shiloh,* 141.
55. *Warren (Illinois) Independent,* April 22, 1862.
56. Douglas Hapeman Diary, April 4, 1862, ISHL; Lyftogt, *From Blue Mills to Columbia,* 51; Connelly, *History of the Seventieth Ohio Regiment,* 20; "An Iowa Soldier's Story of Shiloh," *National Tribune,* May 3, 1883, p. 3; Abram J. Vanauken Diary, April 4, 1862, ISHL; Dawes, "My First Day Under Fire at Shiloh," in *MOLLUS,* 3:3; Crooker, Nourse, and Brown, *The 55th Illinois,* 73; Squier, *This Wilderness of War,* 10; Bering and Montgomery, *History of the Forty-eighth Ohio;* Geer, *Civil War Diary,* 24; Andrew Hickenlooper, "The Battle of Shiloh," in *MOLLUS,* 5:409–10; Jessee, *Civil War Diaries,* chap. 1, p. 9.
57. Daniel, *Shiloh,* 139; Grant, *Personal Memoirs,* 1:334–35.
58. Hickenlooper, "The Battle of Shiloh," in *MOLLUS,* 5:410.
59. William W. McCarty Reminiscences, William W. McCarty Papers, Civil War Miscellaneous Collection, USAMHI.
60. Dawes, "My First Day Under Fire at Shiloh," in *MOLLUS,* 3:3.
61. Gordon, "A Graphic Picture of the Battle of Shiloh," *National Tribune,* April 26, 1883, p. 1.
62. Sumbardo, "Some Facts About the Battle of Shiloh," in *MOLLUS,* 28:32.
63. Barber, *Army Memoirs,* 48–49.
64. W. H. L. Wallace to Ann Wallace, April 5, 1862, Wallace-Dickey Family Papers, ISHL.
65. Hickenlooper, "The Battle of Shiloh," in *MOLLUS,* 5:412.
66. Downing, *Civil War Diary,* 40.
67. Christian Zook to "Dear friends at home," April 5, 1862, Christian Zook Papers, Civil War Miscellaneous Collection, USAMHI.
68. Gordon, "A Graphic Picture of the Battle of Shiloh," *National Tribune,* April 26, 1883, p. 1.
69. *OR,* vol. 10, pt. 2, pp. 93–94.
70. Ibid., pt. 1, p. 89.
71. Hancock, *The Fourteenth Wisconsin,* 3.
72. Daniel, *Shiloh,* 139–40.
73. *OR,* vol. 10, pt. 2, p. 93.
74. Hubert, *History of the Fiftieth Regiment,* 85.
75. W. H. L. Wallace to Ann Wallace, April 5, 1862, Wallace-Dickey Family Papers, ISHL.
76. *OR,* vol. 10, pt. 2, p. 91.
77. Lewis Wallace to W. H. L. Wallace, April 5, 1862, Wallace-Dickey Family Papers, ISHL.
78. Cockerill, "A Boy at Shiloh," in *MOLLUS,* 6:17.
79. Connelly, *History of the Seventieth Ohio,* 20.
80. Dawes, "My First Day Under Fire at Shiloh," in *MOLLUS,* 3:3–5.
81. Ibid.
82. Sumbardo, "Some Facts About the Battle of Shiloh," in *MOLLUS,* 28:32.
83. Gordon, "A Graphic Picture of the Battle of Shiloh," *National Tribune,* May 3, 1883, p. 3.
84. Crooker, Nourse, and Brown, *The 55th Illinois,* 443.

85. Hubert, *History of the Fiftieth Regiment*, 89.

86. *OR*, vol. 10, pt. 1, p. 279; Baker, "How the Battle Began," *National Tribune*, April 12, 1883, p. 3; French, "One Regiment That Was Not Surprised," *National Tribune*, April 12, 1883, p. 3; Daniel, *Shiloh*, 141.

87. Jones, "The Battle of Shiloh: Reminiscences," in *MOLLUS*, 49:54.

88. Daniel, *Shiloh*, 142; Baker, "How the Battle Began," *National Tribune*, April 12, 1883, p. 3.

89. Gordon, "A Graphic Picture of the Battle of Shiloh," *National Tribune*, May 3, 1883, p. 3.

90. Ibid.

91. Baker, "How the Battle Began," *National Tribune*, April 12, 1883, p. 3; Daniel, *Shiloh*, 143–44.

92. Gordon, "A Graphic Picture of the Battle of Shiloh," *National Tribune*, May 3, 1883, p. 3.

93. *OR*, vol. 10, pt. 1, pp. 282–83; Daniel, *Shiloh*, 147; William B. Allmon, "The Much-Traveled 21st Missouri Fought for the Union in Tennessee and Texas, and at Points in Between," *America's Civil War*, September 1996; Baker, "How the Battle Began," *National Tribune*, April 12, 1883, p. 3; Abbott, "The 12th Mich.," *National Tribune*, October 15, 1885, p. 3; French, "One Regiment That Was Not Surprised," *National Tribune*, April 12, 1883, p. 3.

94. Mason, "Shiloh," in *MOLLUS*, 10:96.

95. Belknap, *History of the Fifteenth Regiment*, 190–91.

96. Day, "The Fifteenth Iowa at Shiloh," in *MOLLUS*, 65:187–79.

97. Sword, *Shiloh*, 290.

98. Dawes, "My First Day Under Fire at Shiloh," in *MOLLUS*, 3:5–7; Flemming, "The Battle of Shiloh as a Private Saw It," in *MOLLUS*, 6:138–39.

99. Bering and Montgomery, *History of the Forty-eighth Ohio*.

100. Flemming, "The Battle of Shiloh as a Private Saw It," in *MOLLUS*, 6:138–39. In this and subsequent discussions of the action on April 6, I will refer to Sherman's division as the three brigades that functioned together under him as a division, McDowell's, Buckland's, and Hildebrand's. Sherman's detached brigade under Col. David Stuart I will address separately.

101. Gordon, "A Graphic Picture of the Battle of Shiloh," *National Tribune*, May 3, 1883, p. 3.

102. Dawes, "My First Day Under Fire at Shiloh," in *MOLLUS*, 3:7–8.

103. *OR*, vol. 10, pt. 1, p. 278; Jones, "The Battle of Shiloh: Reminiscences," in *MOLLUS*, 49:54–59.

104. Edgar Embley to "Dear Brother & Sister," April 28, 1862, Edgar Embley Papers, Harrisburg Civil War Round Table Collection, USAMHI.

105. Henry Miller Culbertson to "Dear Mother, Brother and Sister," April 10, 1862, Henry Miller Culbertson Papers, WHS.

106. Hickenlooper, "The Battle of Shiloh," in *MOLLUS*, 5:414.

107. Easlick, "A Regiment Without Fodder for Its Guns," *National Tribune*, April 12, 1883, p. 3.

108. Dawes, "My First Day Under Fire at Shiloh," in *MOLLUS*, 3:8–9; Cockerill, "A Boy at Shiloh," in *MOLLUS*, 6:17.

109. Cockerill, "A Boy at Shiloh," in *MOLLUS*, 6:17.

110. Dawes, "My First Day Under Fire at Shiloh," in *MOLLUS*, 3:9.

111. Ibid.

112. Gordon, "A Graphic Picture of the Battle of Shiloh," *National Tribune*, May 3, 1883, p. 3.

113. Dawes, "My First Day Under Fire at Shiloh," in *MOLLUS*, 3:9; *OR*, vol. 10, pt. 1, p. 568.

114. *OR*, vol. 10, pt. 1, p. 278.

115. Hickenlooper, "The Battle of Shiloh," in *MOLLUS*, 5:415–17.

116. Baird, "Shiloh: The Services of the 21st Mo. on the Field," *National Tribune*, February 25, 1886, p. 3.

117. Hickenlooper, "The Battle of Shiloh," in *MOLLUS*, 5:417; *OR*, vol. 10, pt. 1, p. 280; Jones, "The Battle of Shiloh: Reminiscences," in *MOLLUS*, 49:57.

118. *OR*, vol. 10, pt. 1, p. 278.

119. Ibid., pp. 266–67, 270; Bering and Montgomery, *History of the Forty-eighth Ohio*.

120. Cockerill, "A Boy at Shiloh," in *MOLLUS*, 6:17.

121. Gordon, "A Graphic Picture of the Battle of Shiloh," *National Tribune*, April 26, 1883, p. 1.

122. Flemming, "The Battle of Shiloh as a Private Saw It," in *MOLLUS*, 6:142.

123. Dawes, "My First Day Under Fire at Shiloh," in *MOLLUS*, 3:2.

124. *OR*, vol. 20, pt. 1, p. 263.

125. Ibid., pp. 249–50.

126. Connelly, *History of the Seventeenth Ohio Regiment*, 22.

CHAPTER TEN: "THE DEVIL'S OWN DAY"

1. Grant, *Personal Memoirs*, 1:335–36; Catton, *Grant Moves South*, 222–23.

2. Catton, *Grant Moves South*, 223; Simon, ed., *The Papers of Ulysses S. Grant*, 5:17–18.

3. Wallace, *Smoke, Sound & Fury*, 111–12.

4. Ibid., 112; Putnam, "Reminiscences of the Battle of Shiloh," in *MOLLUS*, 2:198–207.

5. *OR*, vol. 10, pt. 1, p. 178.

6. Putnam, "Reminiscences of the Battle of Shiloh," in *MOLLUS*, 2:198–207; *OR*, vol. 10, pt. 1, pp. 180, 185; Smith, *Grant*, 191.

7. Lee, "Shiloh: Comrade Lee Criticizes Gen. Buell's Article on the Famous Battle," *National Tribune*, May 6, 1886, p. 3.

8. *OR*, vol. 10, pt. 1, p. 139.

9. Adolph Engelmann to Mina Engelmann, April 17, 1862, Engelmann-Kircher Family Papers, ISHL; *OR*, vol. 10, pt. 1, pp. 143–44.

10. Blanchard, *I Marched with Sherman*, 53–54.

11. Cockerill, "A Boy at Shiloh," in *MOLLUS*, 6:19.

12. Oates, "The Ninth Illinois at Shiloh," *National Tribune*, May 10, 1883, p. 1.

13. *OR*, vol. 10, pt. 1, p. 143.

14. Kiper, *McClernand*, 106; *OR*, vol. 10, pt. 1, p. 115.

15. Putnam, "Reminiscences of the Battle of Shiloh," in *MOLLUS*, 2:198–207; Connelly, *History of the Seventeenth Ohio Regiment*, 23.

16. Sherman, *Memoirs*, 266.

17. Grant, *Personal Memoirs*, 1:343; Smith, *Grant*, 192.

18. *OR*, vol. 10, pt. 1, p. 278.

19. Ibid.

20. Sumbardo, "Some Facts About the Battle of Shiloh," in *MOLLUS*, 28:34.

21. Squier, *This Wilderness of War*, 10–12.

22. *OR*, vol. 10, pt. 1, p. 235; Jesse B. Connelly Diary, April 9, 1862, IHS.

23. Squier, *This Wilderness of War*, 10–12.

24. Lyftogt, *From Blue Mills to Columbia*, 56.

25. Hickenlooper, "The Battle of Shiloh," in *MOLLUS*, 5:420.

26. *OR*, vol. 10, pt. 1, pp. 278, 281.

27. Kiner, *One Year's Soldiering*, 24–27.

28. *OR*, vol. 10, pt. 1, p. 153.

29. Squier, *This Wilderness of War*, 10–12.

30. *OR*, vol. 10, pt. 1, p. 181; Putnam, "Reminiscences of the Battle of Shiloh," in *MOLLUS*, 2:198–207.

31. *OR*, vol. 10, pt. 1, pp. 278–79.

32. Ibid., pp. 233, 235, 238.

33. Ibid., pp. 214–15.
34. Blanchard, *I Marched with Sherman*, 54.
35. Crummer, *With Grant*, 57–58.
36. Huffstodt, *Hard Dying Men*, 92.
37. Crummer, *With Grant*, 57–58.
38. Blanchard, *I Marched with Sherman*, 54.
39. Huffstodt, *Hard Dying Men*, 91.
40. Crummer, *With Grant*, 58–59; Blanchard, *I Marched with Sherman*, 54.
41. Crummer, *With Grant*, 59.
42. Nesbitt Baugher to "Dear Father," April 9, 1862, Luther H. Cowan Papers, WHS.
43. *OR*, vol. 1, pt. 1, p. 133.
44. Blanchard, *I Marched with Sherman*, 54.
45. George O. Smith Reminiscences, George O. Smith Papers, ISHL.
46. *OR*, vol. 1, pt. 1, p. 133.
47. Barber, *Army Memoirs*, 52–53.
48. Ibid., 53.
49. Puterbaugh, *March and Countermarch*, 124.
50. *OR*, vol. 1, pt. 1, pp. 220, 226; Barber, *Army Memoirs*, 54.
51. *OR*, vol. 1, pt. 1, p. 220.
52. Blanchard, *I Marched with Sherman*, 54.
53. *OR*, vol. 1, pt. 1, pp. 116–17, 220.
54. Downing, *Civil War Diary*, 41.
55. Gebhardt, "The Eleventh Illinois Infantry Regiment in the Civil War," 96; Downing, *Civil War Diary*, 41.
56. Downing, *Civil War Diary*, 41.
57. Sherman, *Memoirs*, 258; Daniel, *Shiloh*, 182–85.
58. Putnam, "Reminiscences of the Battle of Shiloh," in *MOLLUS*, 2:198–207.
59. *OR*, vol. 10, pt. 1, p. 179.
60. Stacy Allen, " 'If He Had Less Rank': Lewis Wallace," Woodworth, ed., *Grant's Lieutenants*, 74; *OR*, vol. 10, pt. 1, pp. 178–80.
61. Crooker, Nourse, and Brown, *The 55th Illinois*, 96, 102–8.
62. Ibid., 96–98; *OR*, vol. 10, pt. 1, p. 258; Fink, "Shiloh," *National Tribune*, May 3, 1883, p. 3.
63. Crooker, Nourse, and Brown, *The 55th Illinois*, 113–15, 445–47.
64. Ibid., 121.
65. Hickenlooper, "The Battle of Shiloh," in *MOLLUS*, 5:418.
66. Rerick, *The Forty-fourth Indiana Volunteer Infantry*, 53.
67. Sumbardo, "Some Facts About the Battle of Shiloh," in *MOLLUS*, 28:34–35.
68. Clark and Bowen, *University Recruits*, 96.
69. Sword, *Shiloh*, 444–45.
70. Hickenlooper, "The Battle of Shiloh," in *MOLLUS*, 5:421.
71. Kimbell, *History of Battery A*, 42.
72. *OR*, vol. 10, pt. 1, pp. 215, 218.
73. Crooker, Nourse, and Brown, *The 55th Illinois*, 100–2; *OR*, vol. 10, pt. 1, p. 259; Wheeler, "Shiloh," *National Tribune*, May 3, 1883, p. 3.
74. Crooker, Nourse, and Brown, *The 55th Illinois*, 109–10.
75. Ibid., 123.
76. Hubert, *History of the Fiftieth Regiment*, 90–93.
77. Cockerill, "A Boy at Shiloh," in *MOLLUS*, 6:22–23.
78. Morrison, *A History of the Ninth Regiment*, 29–30, 33–34.
79. Squier, *This Wilderness of War*, 10–12.

80. Mason, "Shiloh," in *MOLLUS*, 10:98; *OR*, vol. 10, pt. 1, p. 204.
81. Lyftogt, *From Blue Mills to Columbia*, 57.
82. Kimbell, *History of Battery A*, 42–43.
83. D. J. Benner to "Dear Uncle," April 9, 1862, Luther H. Cowan Papers, WHS.
84. *OR*, vol. 10, pt. 1, p. 279.
85. Crummer, *With Grant*, 64–65.
86. Cyrus Dickey to "My dear brother," April 10, 1862, Wallace-Dickey Family Papers, ISHL.
87. Sumbardo, "Some Facts About the Battle of Shiloh," in *MOLLUS*, 28:35–37.
88. Sword, *Shiloh*, 295–99; Daniel, *Shiloh*, 230–37.
89. Hickenlooper, "The Battle of Shiloh," in *MOLLUS*, 5:435.
90. Grant, *Personal Memoirs*, 1:344; *OR*, vol. 10, pt. 1, p. 186.
91. *OR*, vol. 10, pt. 1, p. 186.
92. Grant, *Personal Memoirs*, 1:344–45.
93. Flemming, "The Battle of Shiloh as a Private Saw It," in *MOLLUS*, 6:143; Bryant, "The Story of Shiloh," *National Tribune*, May 10, 1883, p. 1.
94. Grant, *Personal Memoirs*, 1:344–45.
95. Flemming, "The Battle of Shiloh as a Private Saw It," in *MOLLUS*, 6:143; Blanchard, *I Marched with Sherman*, 56–57; Belknap, *History of the Fifteenth Regiment*, 192–93; Putnam, "Reminiscences of the Battle of Shiloh," in *MOLLUS*, 2:198–207; Cockerill, "A Boy at Shiloh," in *MOLLUS*, 6:26.
96. Daniel, *Shiloh*, 244.
97. Sword, *Shiloh*, 361; Daniel, *Shiloh*, 246.
98. Kimbell, *History of Battery A*, 44; Bauman, *Arming the Suckers*, 11.
99. *OR*, vol. 10, pt. 1, p. 147.
100. D. J. Benner to "Dear Uncle," April 9, 1862, Luther H. Cowan Papers, WHS; *OR*, vol. 10, pt. 1, p. 204.
101. Morrison, *A History of the Ninth Regiment*, 30, 34.
102. Day, "The Fifteenth Iowa at Shiloh," in *MOLLUS*, 56:178–86; Belknap, "The Obedience and Courage of the Private Soldier," in *MOLLUS*, 55:161; Francis M. Harmon to "My Dear brother," April 11, 1862, Francis M. Harmon Papers, IHS.
103. Sherman, *Memoirs*, 266.
104. Hubert, *History of the Fiftieth Regiment*, 100.
105. Daniel, *Shiloh*, 245–46.
106. *OR*, vol. 10, pt. 1, p. 187.
107. Hubert, *History of the Fiftieth Regiment*, 93.
108. *OR*, vol. 10, pt. 1, p. 147.
109. Wright, *A Corporal's Story*, 36.
110. Simpson, *Ulysses S. Grant*, 133.
111. Hubert, *History of the Fiftieth Regiment*, 93.
112. D. J. Benner to "Dear Uncle," April 9, 1862, Luther H. Cowan Papers, WHS.
113. Wright, *A Corporal's Story*, 38; Dugan, *History of Hurlbut's Fighting Fourth Division*, 104.
114. Blanchard, *I Marched with Sherman*, 56–57; Cockerill, "A Boy at Shiloh," in *MOLLUS*, 6:25; Crooker, Nourse, and Brown, *The 55th Illinois*, 116.
115. Simpson, *Ulysses S. Grant*, 134.

CHAPTER ELEVEN: FROM PITTSBURG LANDING TO CORINTH

1. Hovey, "Pittsburg Landing," *National Tribune*, February 1, 1883, p. 1; Wallace, *Smoke, Sound & Fury*, 119; McGinnis, "Shiloh," in *MOLLUS*, 24:16.

2. Cockerill, "A Boy at Shiloh," in *MOLLUS*, 6:28.

3. Jones, "The Battle of Shiloh: Reminiscences," in *MOLLUS*, 49:59.

4. Cockerill, "A Boy at Shiloh," in *MOLLUS*, 6:28.

5. John T. Hunt, "Civil War Reminiscences of Dr. John T. Hunt, Macedonia, Illinois, Company A, 40th Illinois Volunteer Infantry," in "The Yesterdays of Hamilton County," http://www.carolyar.com/Illinois/Hunt-Part1.htm.

6. William L. Wade Diary, April 7, 1862, Civil War Miscellaneous Collection, USAMHI.

7. John T. Hunt, "Civil War Reminiscences of Dr. John T. Hunt, Macedonia, Illinois, Company A, 40th Illinois Volunteer Infantry," in "The Yesterdays of Hamilton County," http://www.carolyar.com/Illinois/Hunt-Part1.htm.

8. Oscar Eugene Stewart Memoir, Vicksburg National Military Park.

9. John T. Hunt, "Civil War Reminiscences of Dr. John T. Hunt, Macedonia, Illinois, Company A, 40th Illinois Volunteer Infantry," in "The Yesterdays of Hamilton County," http://www.carolyar.com/Illinois/Hunt-Part1.htm.

10. Jones, "The Battle of Shiloh: Reminiscences," in *MOLLUS*, 49:59; William L. Wade Diary, April 7, 1862, Civil War Miscellaneous Collection, USAMHI.

11. Mason, "Shiloh," in *MOLLUS*, 10:102.

12. Connelly, *History of the Seventieth Ohio Regiment*, 24.

13. Day, "The Fifteenth Iowa at Shiloh," in *MOLLUS*, 56:186.

14. Jones, "The Battle of Shiloh: Reminiscences," in *MOLLUS*, 49:59.

15. Cockerill, "A Boy at Shiloh," in *MOLLUS*, 6:28.

16. Hubert, *History of the Fiftieth Regiment*, 94.

17. Day, "The Fifteenth Iowa at Shiloh," in *MOLLUS*, 56:186.

18. Cockerill, "A Boy at Shiloh," in *MOLLUS*, 6:28.

19. George O. Smith Reminiscences, George O. Smith Papers, ISHL.

20. Ibid.

21. Post, ed., *Soldiers' Letters*, 179.

22. Wardner, "Reminiscences of a Surgeon," in *MOLLUS*, 12:186.

23. Crooker, Nourse, and Brown, *The 55th Illinois*, 124–25.

24. Cockerill, "A Boy at Shiloh," in *MOLLUS*, 6:28; Oscar Eugene Stewart Memoir, Vicksburg National Military Park.

25. Putnam, "Reminiscences of the Battle of Shiloh," in *MOLLUS*, 2:198–207.

26. Sherman, *Memoirs*, 266.

27. Carl von Clausewitz. *On War*. Anatol Rapoport, ed. (Baltimore: Penguin Books, 1968), 164.

28. Putnam, "Reminiscences of the Battle of Shiloh," in *MOLLUS*, 2:198–207.

29. McGinnis, "Shiloh," in *MOLLUS*, 24:16; Wallace, *Smoke, Sound & Fury*, 119.

30. William L. Sanderson to "My dear wife," May 22, 1862, "Letters from Col. William L. Sanderson, 23rd Indiana Infantry," in "Indiana in the Civil War," http://www.indianainthecivilwar.com.

31. Crooker, Nourse, and Brown, *The 55th Illinois*, 448.

32. John T. Hunt, "Civil War Reminiscences of Dr. John T. Hunt, Macedonia, Illinois, Company A, 40th Illinois Volunteer Infantry," in "The Yesterdays of Hamilton County," http://www.carolyar.com/Illinois/Hunt-Part1.htm.

33. *OR*, vol. 10, pt. 1, p. 170; McGinnis, "Shiloh," in *MOLLUS*, 24:17.

34. William L. Sanderson to "My dear wife," May 22, 1862, "Letters from Col. William L. Sanderson, 23rd Indiana Infantry," in "Indiana in the Civil War," http://www.indianainthecivilwar.com.

35. Ibid.

36. *OR*, vol. 10, pt. 1, p. 196.

37. Veatch, "The Battle of Shiloh," *National Tribune*, March 15, 1883, p. 1.

38. *OR,* vol. 10, pt. 1, pp. 190–91.

39. Ibid., pp. 251–52.

40. Wright, *A Corporal's Story,* 43–44, appendix pp. vi–viii.

41. Ibid., 43.

42. Grant, *Personal Memoirs,* 1:350–51; Lee, "Shiloh: Comrade Lee Criticizes Gen. Buell's Article on the Famous Battle," *National Tribune,* May 6, 1886, p. 3; Veatch, "The Battle of Shiloh," *National Tribune,* March 15, 1883, p. 1; Dugan, *History of Hurlbut's Fighting Fourth Division,* 105; *OR,* vol. 10, pt. 1, pp. 221, 224–25, 232.

43. D. J. Benner to "Dear Uncle," April 9, 1862, Luther H. Cowan Papers, WHS.

44. William L. Sanderson to "My dear wife," May 22, 1862, "Letters from Col. William L. Sanderson, 23rd Indiana Infantry," in "Indiana in the Civil War," http://www.indianainthecivilwar.com.

45. Simon, ed., *Papers of Ulysses S. Grant,* 5:50.

46. Henry Miller Culbertson to "Dear Mother, Brother and Sister," April 10, 1862, Henry Miller Culbertson Papers, WHS.

47. Dugan, *History of Hurlbut's Fighting Fourth Division,* 106.

48. Simon, ed., *Papers of Ulysses S. Grant,* 5:34.

49. Chetlain, *Recollections of Seventy Years,* 89.

50. Andreas, "The 'Ifs and Buts' of Shiloh," in *MOLLUS,* 10:116.

51. Simpson, *Ulysses S. Grant,* 137.

52. Morrison, *A History of the Ninth Regiment,* 34.

53. Wills, *Army Life,* 83–84.

54. Jessee B. Connelly Diary, April 9, 1862, IHS.

55. Belknap, *History of the Fifteenth Regiment,* 190–92.

56. Grant, *Personal Memoirs,* 1:368–69.

57. Abram J. Vanauken Diary, April 4, 1862, ISHL; Cockerill, "A Boy at Shiloh," in *MOLLUS,* 6:33–34; D. B. Baker, "How the Battle Began," *National Tribune,* April 12, 1883, p. 3.

58. *OR,* vol. 10, pt. 1, pp. 113–14.

59. Crummer, *With Grant,* 74; Douglas Hapeman Diary, April 7, 1862, ISHL.

60. Connelly, *History of the Seventieth Ohio Regiment,* 25.

61. William L. Wade Diary, April 7, 1862, Civil War Miscellaneous Collection, USAMHI.

62. George O. Smith Diary, April 7, 1862, ISHL.

63. Geer, *Civil War Diary,* 25.

64. Abram J. Vanauken Diary, April 9, 1862, ISHL.

65. Oscar Eugene Stewart Memoir, Vicksburg National Military Park.

66. Cyrus Dickey to "My dear brother," April 10, 1862, Wallace-Dickey Family Papers, ISHL; Douglas Hapeman Diary, April 9 and 10, 1862, ISHL.

67. Stuber, *Mein Tagebuch,* 23–24; Connelly, *History of the Seventieth Ohio Regiment,* 25.

68. William L. Wade Diary, April 8, 1862, Civil War Miscellaneous Collection, USAMHI; Abram J. Vanauken Diary, April 8, 1862, ISHL; Crooker, Nourse, and Brown, *The 55th Illinois,* 136.

69. Henry Miller Culbertson to "Dear Mother, Brother and Sister," April 10, 1862, Henry Miller Culbertson Letters, WHS.

70. Crummer, *With Grant,* 74.

71. William L. Wade Diary, April 8, 1862, Civil War Miscellaneous Collection, USAMHI; Barber, *Army Memoirs,* 60–61.

72. Grant, *Personal Memoirs,* 1:367.

73. Newton, *A Wisconsin Boy in Dixie,* 16.

74. John T. Hunt, "Civil War Reminiscences of Dr. John T. Hunt, Macedonia, Illinois, Company A, 40th Illinois Volunteer Infantry," in "The Yesterdays of Hamilton County," http://www.carolyar.com/Illinois/Hunt-Part1.htm.

75. Morrison, *History of the Ninth Regiment,* 35.

76. Puterbaugh, *March and Countermarch,* 124.

77. John Jay Dickey to "My dear dear Sister & friends," April 11, 1862, Wallace-Dickey Family Papers, ISHL.

78. Clark and Bowen, *University Recruits,* 136.

79. William L. Wade Diary, April 16, 1862, Civil War Miscellaneous Collection, USAMHI.

80. Dugan, *History of Hurlbut's Fighting Fourth Division,* 111.

81. Crooker, Nourse, and Brown, *The 55th Illinois,* 448.

82. Emilie Quiner Diary, April 9, 1862, WHS.

83. Rood, *Story of the Service of Company E,* 169.

84. Love, *Wisconsin in the War of the Rebellion,* 434.

85. Bering and Montgomery, *History of the Forty-eighth Ohio.*

86. Simon, ed., *Papers of Ulysses S. Grant,* 5:20.

87. Smith, *Grant,* 207–8.

88. Simon, ed., *Papers of Ulysses S. Grant,* 5:48.

89. *OR,* vol. 10, pt. 2, pp. 105–6.

90. Simon, ed., *Papers of Ulysses S. Grant,* 5:49.

91. Ibid., 5:48–52.

92. Soper, "A Chapter from the History of Company D, Twelfth Iowa Infantry Volunteers," in *MOLLUS,* 56:130–32.

93. Oscar Eugene Stewart Memoir, Vicksburg National Military Park; Belknap, *History of the Fifteenth Regiment,* 196.

94. *OR,* vol. 10, pt. 2, p. 144.

95. Ibid.

96. Crooker, Nourse, and Brown, *The 55th Illinois,* 138; Morrison, *History of the Ninth Regiment,* 35; Bering and Montgomery, *History of the Forty-eighth Ohio.*

97. Soper, "A Chapter from the History of Company D, Twelfth Iowa Infantry Volunteers," in *MOLLUS,* 56:133.

98. Belknap, "The Obedience and Courage of the Private Soldier," in *MOLLUS,* 55:159.

99. Crooker, Nourse, and Brown, *The 55th Illinois,* 142.

100. Wills, *Army Life,* 88–89.

101. Belknap, "The Obedience and Courage of the Private Soldier," in *MOLLUS,* 55:161.

102. Grant, *Personal Memoirs,* 1:379.

103. Sherman, *Memoirs,* 276.

104. David W. Poak to "Dear Sister," May 23, 1862, David W. Poak Papers, ISHL.

105. Luther H. Cowan to "Dear Wife," May 27, 1862, Luther H. Cowan Papers, WHS.

106. Douglas Hapeman Diary, May 13–23, 26, and 27, ISHL.

107. Francis M. Johnson Diary, May 29, 1862, Civil War Miscellaneous Collection, USAMHI; Soper, "A Chapter from the History of Company D, Twelfth Iowa Infantry Volunteers," in *MOLLUS,* 56:134.

108. Crooker, Nourse, and Brown, *The 55th Illinois,* 147.

109. Douglas Hapeman Diary, May 30 and 31, 1862, ISHL.

110. Morrison, *History of the Ninth Regiment,* 36.

111. Geer, *Civil War Diary,* 34–35.

112. Morrison, *History of the Ninth Regiment,* 35.

CHAPTER TWELVE: IUKA

1. Grant, *Personal Memoirs,* 1:385–400.

2. Crooker, Nourse, and Brown, *The 55th Illinois,* 148.

3. Ibid.

4. Luther H. Cowan to "Dear Molly," August 12, 1862, Luther H. Cowan Papers, WHS.

5. Barber, *Army Memoirs*, 67; Jessee, *Civil War Diaries*, chap. 1, pp. 16–17, 19; Francis M. Johnson Diary, June 22, July 6, 1862, Civil War Miscellaneous Collection, USAMHI; David W. Poak to "Dear Sister," June 26, 1862, David W. Poak Papers, ISHL; Geer, *Civil War Diary*, 39.

6. Barber, *Army Memoirs*, 69; George O. Smith Reminiscences, George O. Smith Papers, ISHL; Jessee, *Civil War Diaries*, chap. 1, p. 19.

7. Wills, *Army Life*, 123.

8. Douglas Hapeman Diary, June 8, 1862, ISHL; William W. McCarty Diary, June 7, 1862, Civil War Miscellaneous Collection, USAMHI; Fuller, "The 78th Ohio at Jackson, Tenn.," *National Tribune*, June 18, 1883, p. 3.

9. Dugan, *History of Hurlbut's Fighting Fourth Division*, 136. Emphasis in the original. See also Geer, *Civil War Diary*, 37.

10. Thomas Cartwright Letter, *East Liverpool Mercury* 2, no. 8 (July 1862): 2; Barber, *Army Memoirs*, 68.

11. Wills, *Army Life*, 121.

12. Crooker, Nourse, and Brown, *The 55th Illinois*, 158.

13. Wills, *Army Life*, 125; Thomas Cartwright letter, *East Liverpool Mercury*, vol. 2, no. 8 (July 1862): 2.

14. Crooker, Nourse, and Brown, *The 55th Illinois*, 152–53.

15. Connelly, *History of the Seventieth Ohio Regiment*, 36–37.

16. Francis M. Johnson, "Diary of a Soldier in Grant's Rear Guard (1862–1863)," in Granville W. Hough, ed., *Journal of Mississippi History*, in Francis M. Johnson Papers, Civil War Miscellaneous Collection, USAMHI.

17. Crooker, Nourse, and Brown, *The 55th Illinois*, 155; David W. Poak to "Sister Sadie," August 28, 1862, David W. Poak Papers, ISHL; Luther H. Cowan to Josephine J. Cowan, August 3, 1862, Luther H. Cowan Papers, WHS; George W. Reese to "Dear Cousin," July 17, 1862, George W. Reese Papers, ISHL; Geer, *Civil War Diary*, 43; Bering and Montgomery, *History of the Forty-eighth Ohio;* Connelly, *History of the Seventieth Ohio Regiment*, 36–37.

18. Peirce and Peirce, *Dear Catharine, Dear Taylor*, 189–90.

19. Winters, *Musick of the Mocking Birds*, 30–31.

20. Daniel G. Winegar to "Dear Wife," May 8, 1863, Daniel G. Winegar Papers, ISHL.

21. For other examples, see John Roberts, "A Pioneer's Story," IHS; "The History and Letters of Robert Bowlin, Co. G. 114th O.V.I.," http://www.fortunecity.com/westwood/makeover/347/id240.htm.

22. Willison, *Reminiscences of a Boy's Service*, 17–18.

23. William R. Eddington Reminiscences, William R. Eddington Papers, ISHL.

24. "The Civil War History of John Ritland," Iowa in the Civil War, http://members.cox.net/jritland/.

25. "The Memoirs, Diary, and Life of Private Jefferson Moses, Company G, 93rd Illinois Volunteers," http://www.ioweb.com/civilwar.

26. Jones, *Reminiscences of the Twenty-Second Iowa*, 5–6.

27. Lyftogt, *From Blue Mills to Columbia*, 68–71.

28. For these insights on Grant, I am indebted to Michael B. Ballard, who has developed these ideas for a forthcoming book on Grant and kindly shared them with me.

29. Hess, *Banners to the Breeze*, 121–29.

30. Grant, *Personal Memoirs*, 1:404–5; Hess, *Banners to the Breeze*, 123.

31. Grant, *Personal Memoirs*, 1:406.

32. Williams, *The Eagle Regiment*, 11.

33. J. W. Greenman Diary, September 13, 1862, MDAH; Smith, "A Few Days with the Eighth Regiment, Wisconsin Volunteers at Iuka and Corinth," in *MOLLUS*, 49:61.

34. *OR*, vol. 17, pt. 1, p. 60.

35. Ibid., p. 65; J. W. Greenman Diary, September 13, 1862, MDAH.

36. Smith, "A Few Days with the Eighth Regiment, Wisconsin Volunteers at Iuka and Corinth," in *MOLLUS*, 49:61–62; Williams, *The Eagle Regiment*, 11; Cozzens, *The Darkest Days of the War*, 61.

37. Williams, *The Eagle Regiment*, 11–12; Smith, "A Few Days with the Eighth Regiment, Wisconsin Volunteers at Iuka and Corinth," in *MOLLUS*, 49:62.

38. *OR*, vol. 17, pt. 1, p. 61; J. W. Greenman Diary, September 15, 17, 1862, MDAH; Cozzens, *The Darkest Days of the War*, 62.

39. *OR*, vol. 17, pt. 2, p. 214.

40. Ibid., pt. 1, p. 65.

41. Grant, *Personal Memoirs*, 1:407–8; *OR*, vol. 17, pt. 1, pp. 117–18.

42. Campbell, *The Union Must Stand*, 57; William W. McCarty Reminiscences, William W. McCarty Papers, Civil War Miscellaneous Collection, USAMHI.

43. Sanborn, "Battles and Campaigns of September, 1862," in *MOLLUS*, 30:214; *OR*, vol. 17, pt. 1, pp. 66–67; Grant, *Personal Memoirs*, 1:411; Hess, *Banners to the Breeze*, 132–33.

44. *OR*, vol. 17, pt. 1, pp. 67, 118–19.

45. Cozzens, *The Darkest Days of the War*, 72.

46. Sanborn, "Battles and Campaigns of September, 1862," in *MOLLUS*, 30:215; *OR*, vol. 17, pt. 1, p. 91.

47. *OR*, vol. 17, pt. 1, pp. 95, 102; Sanborn, "Battles and Campaigns of September, 1862," in *MOLLUS*, 30:215.

48. W. G. McElrea Diary, September 19, 1862, Civil War Miscellaneous Collection, USAMHI; Campbell, *The Union Must Stand*, 58; *OR*, vol. 17, pt. 1, pp. 95, 102; Sanborn, "Battles and Campaigns of September, 1862," in *MOLLUS*, 30:215.

49. Sanborn, "Battles and Campaigns of September, 1862," in *MOLLUS*, 30:215–16.

50. Ibid., 30:216.

51. Ibid.

52. Campbell, *The Union Must Stand*, 59.

53. W. G. McElrea Diary, September 19, 1862, Civil War Miscellaneous Collection, USAMHI.

54. Sears, "The 11th Ohio Battery at Iuka," *National Tribune*, November 6, 1884, p. 3.

55. Russell, "The Position of the Troops," *National Tribune*, October 2, 1884, p. 3.

56. Campbell, *The Union Must Stand*, 59.

57. *OR*, vol. 17, pt. 1, pp. 97, 101.

58. Brown, *History of the Fourth Regiment*, 88–89.

59. *OR*, vol. 17, pt. 1, p. 92; John B. Sanborn, "Battles and Campaigns of September, 1862," in *MOLLUS*, 30:219–20; Brown, *History of the Fourth Regiment*, 100–1.

60. Sears, "The 11th Ohio Battery at Iuka," *National Tribune*, November 6, 1884.

61. Orr, "The Battle of Iuka," *National Tribune*, September 11, 1884, p. 3.

62. Campbell, *The Union Must Stand*, 59; Sanborn, "Battles and Campaigns of September, 1862," in *MOLLUS*, 30:220–21; Brown, *History of the Fourth Regiment*, 92; *OR*, vol. 17, pt. 1, p. 85.

63. Hess, *Banners to the Breeze*, 136–37.

64. Grant, *Personal Memoirs*, 1:412.

65. W. G. McElrea Diary, September 20, 1862, Civil War Miscellaneous Collection, USAMHI.

66. Brown, "The 48th Ind.'s Conduct, and the 11th Ohio Battery's Losses," *National Tribune*, October 2, 1884, p. 3.

67. Grant, *Personal Memoirs*, 1:413.

68. Sanborn, "Battles and Campaigns of September, 1862," in *MOLLUS*, 30:229–30.

69. Grant, *Personal Memoirs*, 1:413.

70. Campbell, *The Union Must Stand*, 61.

CHAPTER THIRTEEN: CORINTH

1. Grant, *Personal Memoirs*, 1:414–15; Simon, ed., *The Papers of Ulysses S. Grant*, 6:85–95; Simpson, *Ulysses S. Grant*, 153–54.

2. Simon, ed., *Papers of Ulysses S. Grant*, 6:96–97; Grant, *Personal Memoirs*, 1:415–16.

3. Simon, ed., *Papers of Ulysses S. Grant*, 6:104–6; *OR*, vol. 17, pt. 1, pp. 154–55.

4. Cozzens, *The Darkest Days of the War*, 151–55.

5. Hubert, *History of the Fiftieth Regiment*, 124–25.

6. *OR*, vol. 17, pt. 1, pp. 205, 251, 336.

7. Ibid., pp. 205, 251, 336–37; Jonathan Labrant Diary, October 3, 1862, Civil War Miscellaneous Collection, USAMHI.

8. Cozzens, *The Darkest Days of the War*, 162–64; *OR*, vol. 17, pt. 1, p. 252.

9. Wright, *A Corporal's Story*, 56.

10. Soper, "A Chapter from the History of Company D, Twelfth Iowa Infantry Volunteers," in *MOLLUS*, 56:136–38.

11. Hubert, *History of the Fiftieth Regiment*, 132.

12. *OR*, vol. 17, pt. 1, pp. 160, 168, 205; Campbell, *The Union Must Stand*, 61–62.

13. A soldier of the 47th Illinois, "Attack on Corinth: How Price and Van Dorn Were Routed There," *National Tribune*, January 3, 1884, p. 3; *OR*, vol. 17, pt. 1, pp. 197–98; Bryner, *Bugle Echoes*, 58–59.

14. Bryner, *Bugle Echoes*, 59–60.

15. A soldier of the 47th Illinois, "Attack on Corinth: How Price and Van Dorn Were Routed There," *National Tribune*, January 3, 1884, p. 3; *OR*, vol. 17, pt. 1, pp. 197–98; Smith, "A Few Days with the Eighth Regiment, Wisconsin Volunteers at Iuka and Corinth," in *MOLLUS*, 49:62–64.

16. Sanborn, "Battles and Campaigns of September, 1862," in *MOLLUS*, 30:222.

17. *OR*, vol. 17, pt. 1, p. 160.

18. Cozzens, *The Darkest Days of the War*, 194–200.

19. Ibid., 224–28.

20. Hess, *Banners to the Breeze*, 157; Hubert, *History of the Fiftieth Regiment*, 138.

21. Morrison, *History of the Ninth Regiment*, 39; Wardner, "Reminiscences of a Surgeon," in *MOLLUS*, 12:189; Hess, *Banners to the Breeze*, 154; Cozzens, *The Darkest Days of the War*, 232–34.

22. Belknap, *History of the Fifteenth Regiment*, 212–13; Jackson, *The Colonel's Diary*, 69; Hess, *Banners to the Breeze*, 154; Cozzens, *The Darkest Days of the War*, 234; McCord, "Battle of Corinth: The Campaigns Preceding and Leading Up to This Battle and Its Results," in *MOLLUS*, 29:578; anonymous member of the 63rd Ohio, "Corinth," *National Tribune*, August 14, 1884, p. 3.

23. Bryner, *Bugle Echoes*, 61–62.

24. McCord, "Battle of Corinth: The Campaigns Preceding and Leading Up to This Battle and Its Results," in *MOLLUS*, 29:578.

25. Hubert, *History of the Fiftieth Regiment*, 142.

26. Cozzens, *The Darkest Days of the War*, 242; McCord, "Battle of Corinth: The Campaigns Preceding and Leading Up to This Battle and Its Results," in *MOLLUS*, 29:579.

27. Soper, "A Chapter from the History of Company D, Twelfth Iowa Infantry Volunteers," in *MOLLUS*, 56:130–32.

28. Jonathan L. Labrant Diary, October 3, 1862, Civil War Miscellaneous Collection, USAMHI.

29. Hubert, *History of the Fiftieth Regiment*, 142; *OR*, vol. 17, pt. 1, p. 293.

30. Hubert, *History of the Fiftieth Regiment*, 140–41; Belknap, *History of the Fifteenth Regiment*, 212–13; *OR*, vol. 17, pt. 1, p. 295.

31. Hubert, *History of the Fiftieth Regiment*, 145–46.

32. Ibid., 147.

33. Cozzens, *The Darkest Days of the War*, 251–52, 267–68.

34. Campbell, *The Union Must Stand*, 62–63; William B. McCord, "Battle of Corinth: The Campaigns Preceding and Leading Up to This Battle and Its Results," in *MOLLUS*, 29:580; Cozzens, *The Darkest Days of the War*, 266–70; Hess, *Banners to the Breeze*, 159–60.

35. Jackson, *The Colonel's Diary*, 71.

36. Ibid., 71–72.

37. Ibid., 72–73.

38. Ibid., 73–74.

39. William L. Wade Diary, October 4, 1862, Civil War Miscellaneous Collection, USAMHI; Wardner, "Reminiscences of a Surgeon," in *MOLLUS*, 12:190; Cozzens, *The Darkest Days of the War*, 261–67.

40. Jackson, *The Colonel's Diary*, 74–75.

41. Cozzens, *The Darkest Days of the War*, 305–6.

42. Grant, *Personal Memoirs*, 1:417.

43. Morris, Hartwell, and Kuykendall, *History 31st Regiment*, 49; Chetlain, *Recollections of Seventy Years*, 95–96; McCord, "Battle of Corinth: The Campaigns Preceding and Leading Up to This Battle and Its Results," in *MOLLUS*, 29:581–82; Smith, "A Few Days with the Eighth Regiment, Wisconsin Volunteers at Iuka and Corinth," in *MOLLUS*, 49:66; *OR*, vol. 17, pt. 1, p. 170.

44. McCord, "Battle of Corinth: The Campaigns Preceding and Leading Up to This Battle and Its Results," in *MOLLUS*, 29:582.

45. Cone, "On the Hatchie: The 12th Mich. the First to Cross the Bridge," *National Tribune*, April 22, 1886, p. 3; Meeker, "Hurlbut's Division at the Hatchie," *National Tribune*, June 10, 1886, p. 3; Hess, *Banners to the Breeze*, 168.

46. Meeker, "Hurlbut's Division at the Hatchie," *National Tribune*, June 10, 1886, p. 3; Hess, *Banners to the Breeze*, 168; Jackson, "On the Hatchie," *National Tribune*, January 14, 1886, p. 3.

47. Dugan, *History of Hurlbut's Fighting Fourth Division*, 175; *OR*, vol. 17, pt. 1, pp. 305, 332–33.

48. Francis M. Johnson Diary, October 5, 1862, Civil War Miscellaneous Collection, USAMHI; Barber, *Army Memoirs*, 81–85; Grant, *Personal Memoirs*, 1:418; Hess, *Banners to the Breeze*, 168–69; Jackson, "On the Hatchie," *National Tribune*, January 14, 1886, p. 3; Dugan, *History of Hurlbut's Fighting Fourth Division*, 176; *OR*, vol. 17, pt. 1, pp. 305–6.

49. Richardson, "On the Hatchie: How Gen. Ord Struck the Adjutant," *National Tribune*, March 25, 1886, p. 3.

50. Barber, *Army Memoirs*, 81–85; Jackson, "On the Hatchie," *National Tribune*, January 14, 1886, p. 3; *OR*, vol. 17, pt. 1, p. 306.

51. Cone, "On the Hatchie: The 12th Mich. the First to Cross the Bridge," *National Tribune*, April 22, 1886, p. 3.

52. Dugan, *History of Hurlbut's Fighting Fourth Division*, 176–77, 187–88; Jackson, "On the Hatchie," *National Tribune*, January 14, 1886, p. 3; *OR*, vol. 17, pt. 1, p. 306.

53. Jackson, "On the Hatchie," *National Tribune*, January 14, 1886, p. 3; *OR*, vol. 17, pt. 1, p. 306.

54. Dugan, *History of Hurlbut's Fighting Fourth Division*, 187.

55. Jackson, "On the Hatchie," *National Tribune*, January 14, 1886, p. 3; *OR*, vol. 17, pt. 1, p. 306.

56. *OR*, vol. 17, pt. 1, p. 306.
57. Hubert, *History of the Fiftieth Regiment*, 162; Simon, ed., *Papers of Ulysses S. Grant*, 6:123.
58. *OR*, vol. 17, pt. 1, p. 368.
59. Dugan, *History of Hurlbut's Fighting Fourth Division*, 181.
60. Hess, *Banners to the Breeze*, 170–71.
61. McCord, "Battle of Corinth: The Campaigns Preceding and Leading Up to This Battle and Its Results," in *MOLLUS*, 29:582.
62. Chetlain, *Recollections of Seventy Years*, 95–96.
63. Hess, *Banners to the Breeze*, 171; Simon, ed., *Papers of Ulysses S. Grant*, 6:131, 133.

CHAPTER FOURTEEN: THE MISSISSIPPI CENTRAL CAMPAIGN

1. Geer, *Civil War Diary*, 58–60, 65–66; Adolph Engelmann to "Dear Mina," October 10, 25, and 29, 1862, Engelmann-Kircher Family Papers, ISHL; Campbell, *The Union Must Stand*, 64; Hubert, *History of the Fiftieth Regiment*, 164; John G. Given to "Dear Father and Mother," October 23, 1862, John G. Given Papers, ISHL; Belknap, *History of the Fifteenth Regiment*, 230; Francis M. Johnson Diary, October 26–29, 1862, Civil War Miscellaneous Collection, USAMHI; David W. Poak to "Dear Sisters," October 30, 1862, David W. Poak Papers, ISHL.
2. Luther H. Cowan to "My Dear Children," October 26, 1862, Luther H. Cowan Papers, WHS; Campbell, *The Union Must Stand*, 65; David W. Poak to "Dear Sisters," October 30, 1862, David W. Poak Papers, ISHL; William W. McCarty Diary, October 9, 1862, Civil War Miscellaneous Collection, USAMHI; Belknap, *History of the Fifteenth Regiment*, 230.
3. Hubert, *History of the Fiftieth Regiment*, 164; Geer, *Civil War Diary*, 66.
4. Edward P. Stanfield to "Dear Father," October 12, 1862, Edward P. Stanfield Papers, IHS.
5. John G. Given to "Dear Father and Mother," October 23, 1862, John G. Given Papers, ISHL.
6. *OR*, vol. 17, pt. 2, p. 856.
7. Ibid., vol. 13, p. 749; vol. 17, pt. 2, pp. 280–81, 285.
8. Simpson and Berlin, eds., *Sherman's Civil War*, 346–47.
9. *OR*, vol. 13, p. 748; vol. 17, pt. 2, p. 285.
10. Ibid., vol. 17, pt. 2, pp. 287–88.
11. Simon, ed., *The Papers of Ulysses S. Grant*, 6:180.
12. *OR*, vol. 17, pt. 2, pp. 856–57.
13. Simon, ed., *Papers of Ulysses S. Grant*, 6:180.
14. *OR*, vol. 17, pt. 2, p. 278.
15. Simon, ed., *Papers of Ulysses S. Grant*, 6:155.
16. Feis, "The War of Spies and Supplies: Grant and Grenville M. Dodge in the West, 1862–1864," in Woodworth, ed., *Grant's Lieutenants*, 183–98.
17. *OR*, vol. 17, pt. 1, p. 267.
18. Hubert, *History of the Fiftieth Regiment*, 167–68.
19. Simon, ed., *Papers of Ulysses S. Grant*, 6:163–67.
20. Grant, *Personal Memoirs*, 1:420; *OR*, vol. 17, pt. 2, p. 290; Simon, ed., *Papers of Ulysses S. Grant*, 6:180.
21. Simon, ed., *Papers of Ulysses S. Grant*, 6:315; Grant, *Personal Memoirs*, 2:424–25; *OR*, vol. 17, pt. 1, p. 470.
22. *OR*, vol. 17, pt. 1, pp. 470–71; Simon, ed., *Papers of Ulysses S. Grant*, 6:315–16, 318; Grant, *Personal Memoirs*, 2:424–25.
23. Grant, *Personal Memoirs*, 2:424–25.

24. Simon, ed., *Papers of Ulysses S. Grant,* 6:199–200; Grant, *Personal Memoirs,* 2:422.

25. John A. McClernand to Abraham Lincoln, June 20, 1862, Abraham Lincoln Papers, LC.

26. Kiper, *McClernand,* 125, 128.

27. Ibid., 128.

28. Ibid., 131–32.

29. David W. Poak to "Dear Sister," September 10, 1862, David W. Poak Papers, ISHL.

30. Kiper, *McClernand,* 133–35; *OR,* series III, vol. 2, pp. 582–84; Richard Yates et al. to Abraham Lincoln, September 26, 1862, Abraham Lincoln Papers, LC.

31. John A. McClernand to Abraham Lincoln, September 28, 1862, Abraham Lincoln Papers, LC.

32. Kiper, *McClernand,* 137.

33. *OR,* vol. 17, pt. 2, p. 282.

34. Kiper, *McClernand,* 140.

35. Bearss, *Vicksburg Is the Key,* 27.

36. Kiper, *McClernand,* 140.

37. Simon, ed., *Papers of Ulysses S. Grant,* 6:180.

38. Kiper, *McClernand,* 142.

39. Simon, ed., *Papers of Ulysses S. Grant,* 6:279.

40. Ibid., 6:285.

41. Ibid., 6:243, 256, 262; *OR,* vol. 17, pt. 1, pp. 466–67.

42. Luther H. Cowan to "Dear Harriet," November 2, 1862, Luther H. Cowan Papers, WHS.

43. *OR,* vol. 17, pt. 1, p. 467.

44. Bearss, *Vicksburg Is the Key,* 31.

45. Simon, ed., *Papers of Ulysses S. Grant,* 6:262.

46. *OR,* vol. 17, pt. 1, pp. 468–69; Simon, ed., *Papers of Ulysses S. Grant,* 6:310.

47. *OR,* vol. 17, pt. 1, p. 469.

48. Simon, ed., *Papers of Ulysses S. Grant,* 6:293, 310–12; *OR,* vol. 17, pt. 1, p. 471.

49. *OR,* vol. 17, pt. 1, p. 470; Simon, ed., *Papers of Ulysses S. Grant,* 6:304–5, 310–12.

50. Simon, ed., *Papers of Ulysses S. Grant,* 6:300, 311, 398.

51. Ibid., 6:327.

52. David W. Poak to "Dear Sister," November 24, 1862, David W. Poak Papers, ISHL.

53. Hicks, "The Campaign and Capture of Vicksburg," in *MOLLUS,* 31:90–92.

54. Campbell, *The Union Must Stand,* 67.

55. Joseph Stockton Diary, September 30, 1862, Civil War Miscellaneous Collection, USAMHI.

56. David W. Poak to "Dear Sister," November 24, 1862, David W. Poak Papers, ISHL.

57. Crooker, Nourse, and Brown, *The 55th Illinois,* 181.

58. John M. Roberts Reminiscences, IHS.

59. Jefferson Moses, "The Memoirs, Diary, and Life of Private Jefferson Moses, Company G, 93rd Illinois Volunteers," http://www.ioweb.com/civilwar.

60. Crooker, Nourse, and Brown, *The 55th Illinois,* 179, 181; Dunbar, *History of the Ninety-third Regiment,* chap. 2.

61. Jefferson Moses, "The Memoirs, Diary, and Life of Private Jefferson Moses, Company G, 93rd Illinois Volunteers," http://www.ioweb.com/civilwar.

62. Campbell, *The Union Must Stand,* 212–14.

63. Grimsley, *The Hard Hand of War,* throughout.

64. Crooker, Nourse, and Brown, *The 55th Illinois,* 183.

65. John J. Barney to "All at Home," November 14, 1862, John J. Barney Papers, WHS.

66. Jackson, *Some of the Boys,* 27–28.

67. Jefferson Moses, "The Memoirs, Diary, and Life of Private Jefferson Moses, Company G, 93rd Illinois Volunteers," http://www.ioweb.com/civilwar.

68. Campbell, *The Union Must Stand*, 66; John G. Given to "Dear Home," November 13, 1862, John G. Given Papers, ISHL.

69. David W. Poak to "Dear Aunts," November 7, 1862, David W. Poak Papers, ISHL.

70. Campbell, *The Union Must Stand*, 65–66.

71. John M. Roberts Reminiscences, IHS.

72. Ibid.

73. Stockwell, *Private Elisha Stockwell*, 52–53.

74. James W. Denver to "My Dear Wife," November 29, 1862, James W. Denver Papers, Harrisburg Civil War Round Table Collection, USAMHI.

75. Ibid.

76. Wills, *Army Life*, 129–30.

77. John G. Given to "Dear Home," November 2, 1862, John G. Given Papers, ISHL.

78. David W. Poak to "Dear Aunt," November 30, 1862, David W. Poak Papers, ISHL; Sherman, *Memoirs*, 303; Simon, ed., *Papers of Ulysses S. Grant*, 6:360; OR, vol. 17, pt. 1, p. 471.

79. Otis Whitney to "My Dear Wife" (Hattie Whitney), November 29, 1862, private collection, Arlington, Texas.

80. Belknap, *History of the Fifteenth Regiment*, 234; Grant, *Personal Memoirs*, 1:428.

81. Simpson and Berlin, eds., *Sherman's Civil War*, 338–39; Sherman, *Memoirs*, 303; Simon, ed., *Papers of Ulysses S. Grant*, 6:367–72; OR, vol. 17, pt. 1, pp. 471–72.

82. Simpson and Berlin, eds., *Sherman's Civil War*, 338–39; Sherman, *Memoirs*, 303; Simon, ed., *Papers of Ulysses S. Grant*, 6:367–72; OR, vol. 17, pt. 1, pp. 471–72.

83. Jenney, "Personal Recollections of Vicksburg," in *MOLLUS*, 12:248–49.

84. Sherman, *Memoirs*, 303; Simon, ed., *Papers of Ulysses S. Grant*, 6:372; Grant, *Personal Memoirs*, 1:428.

85. Simon, ed., *Papers of Ulysses S. Grant*, 6:372; OR, vol. 17, pt. 1, p. 473.

86. Grant, *Personal Memoirs*, 1:428–29; Sherman, *Memoirs*, 304–6; OR, vol. 17., pt. 1, p. 474; Simon, ed., *Papers of Ulysses S. Grant*, 6:403.

87. Sherman, *Memoirs*, 304–5, 310–11; Grant, *Personal Memoirs*, 1:431–32.

88. Sherman, *Memoirs*, 311.

CHAPTER FIFTEEN: CHICKASAW BAYOU

1. Simpson and Berlin, eds., *Sherman's Civil War*, 342–43.

2. Crooker, Nourse, and Brown, *The 55th Illinois*, 184; Sherman, *Memoirs*, 308.

3. OR, vol. 17, pt. 2, pp. 426, 434, 441; Simpson and Berlin, eds., *Sherman's Civil War*, 348; Crooker, Nourse, and Brown, *The 55th Illinois*, 186; Wiley, *Civil War Diary*, 26; John M. Roberts Reminiscences, IHS; Ankeny, *Kiss Josey for Me*, 111; Bering and Montgomery, *History of the Forty-eighth Ohio;* Sweetman, "Chickasaw Bluffs," *National Tribune*, April 20, 1893, p. 1.

4. Adoniram Judson Withrow to "Dear Lib," December 21, 1862, Adoniram Judson Withrow Papers, SHC.

5. Munn, Miller, and Newton, *Military History and Reminiscences*, 234.

6. Sherman, *Memoirs*, 312.

7. Wiley, *Civil War Diary*, 26.

8. Crooker, Nourse, and Brown, *The 55th Illinois*, 186; Sweetman, "Chickasaw Bluffs," *National Tribune*, April 20, 1893, p. 1; Harper to "Dear Father and Mother," December 22, 1862, John and Alexander Harper Papers, ISHL; Munn, Miller, and Newton, *Military History and Reminiscences*, 235; Ritner, *Love and Valor*, 83–85.

9. Winters, *The Musick of the Mocking Birds*, 13.

10. Perry, "The Entering Wedge," in *MOLLUS*, 24:359.

11. "The Civil War Diary of Michael Sweetman," http://www.fortunecity.com/westwood/makeover/347/id229.htm; Sweetman, "Chickasaw Bluffs," *National Tribune,* April 20, 1893, p. 1; Northup, *Drifting to an Unknown Future,* 54; Alexander Harper to "Dear Father and Mother," December 22, 1862, John and Alexander Harper Papers, ISHL.

12. John M. Roberts Reminiscences, IHS.

13. Munn, Miller, and Newton, *Military History and Reminiscences,* 236.

14. *OR,* vol. 17, pt. 2, p. 434; Sherman, *Memoirs,* 308; Sweetman, "Chickasaw Bluffs," *National Tribune,* April 20, 1893, p. 1; Winters, *Musick of the Mocking Birds,* 13.

15. Wiley, *Civil War Diary,* 26–27.

16. Ibid.

17. Winters, *Musick of the Mocking Birds,* 13.

18. Ibid.

19. Sweetman, "Chickasaw Bluffs," *National Tribune,* April 20, 1893, p. 1.

20. Winters, *Musick of the Mocking Birds,* 13–14; John M. Roberts Reminiscences, IHS; Northup, *Drifting to an Unknown Future,* 54; Sweetman, "Chickasaw Bluffs," *National Tribune,* April 20, 1893, p. 1; Franklin A. Wise Diary, December 23, 1862, WRHS; "The Civil War Diary of Michael Sweetman," http://www.fortunecity.com/westwood/makeover/347/id229.htm.

21. Munn, Miller, and Newton, *Military History and Reminiscences,* 237.

22. "The Civil War Diary of Michael Sweetman," http://www.fortunecity.com/westwood/makeover/347/id229.htm; Crooker, Nourse, and Brown, *The 55th Illinois,* 187.

23. *OR,* vol. 17, pt. 2, p. 425.

24. Ibid., pp. 425, 432.

25. Joseph Stockton Diary, December 21, 1862, Civil War Miscellaneous Collection, USAMHI; David W. Poak to "Dear Sister," January 8, 1862 [*sic;* actually 1863], David W. Poak Papers, ISHL.

26. *OR,* vol. 17, pt. 2, p. 482; *Report of the Adjutant General of the State of Illinois,* 90th Illinois Infantry Regiment, http://www.illinoiscivilwar.org/cw90-agr.html; Bissell, "The Western Organization of Colored People for Furnishing Information to United States Troops in the South," in *MOLLUS,* 27:319.

27. *OR,* vol. 17, pt. 2, pp. 439–40; Williams, *The Eagle Regiment,* 14–15.

28. *OR,* vol. 17, pt. 2, pp. 442–43.

29. David W. Poak to "Dear Sister," January 8, 1862, David W. Poak Papers, ISHL.

30. Francis M. Johnson Diary, December 21, 1862, Civil War Miscellaneous Collection, USAMHI; Bryner, *Bugle Echoes,* 69; Rood, *Story of the Service of Company E,* 158.

31. Andrus, *Civil War Letters,* 43; Richardson, *For My Country,* 76–77; Geer, *Civil War Diary,* 74; Luther H. Cowan Diary, December 25, 1862, Luther H. Cowan Papers, WHS.

32. Belknap, *History of the Fifteenth Regiment,* 235–36; Stevenson,, *History of the 78th,* 203.

33. George B. Carter to "Dear Brother Bill," January 7, 1863, George B. Carter Papers, WHS.

34. *Report of the Adjutant General of the State of Illinois,* 76th Illinois Infantry Regiment, http://www.illinoiscivilwar.org/cw76-hist.html.

35. *OR,* vol. 17, pt. 1, p. 604.

36. Adoniram Judson Withrow to "Dear Lib," December 25, 1862, Adoniram Judson Withrow Papers, SHC; Franklin A. Wise Diary, December 25, 1862, WRHS.

37. Sherman, *Memoirs,* 312; *OR,* vol. 17, pt. 1, pp. 629–30; Jackson, *Some of the Boys,* 55; Chapel, *Civil War Journals,* 101.

38. Bearss, *Vicksburg Is the Key,* 157–58; *OR,* vol. 17, pt. 1, pp. 605, 620.

39. Sherman, *Memoirs,* 312; Munn, Miller, and Newton, *Military History and Reminiscences,* 235; *OR,* vol. 17, pt. 1, p. 605; Bearss, *Vicksburg Is the Key,* 157–59; Scheel, *Rain, Mud & Swamps,* 35.

40. Ritner, *Love and Valor*, 85.
41. Scheel, *Rain, Mud & Swamps*, 35; Franklin A. Wise Diary, December 27, 1862, WRHS Puck, ed., *Sacrifice at Vicksburg*, 43–44.
42. John M. Roberts Reminiscences, IHS.
43. Ritner, *Love and Valor*, 85.
44. Crooker, Nourse, and Brown, *The 55th Illinois*, 188–90.
45. John M. Roberts Reminiscences, IHS.
46. Crooker, Nourse, and Brown, *The 55th Illinois*, 188–90; Sweetman, "Chickasaw Bluffs," *National Tribune*, April 20, 1893, p. 1.
47. *OR*, vol. 17, pt. 1, pp. 626, 637.
48. Crooker, Nourse, and Brown, *The 55th Illinois*, 188–90.
49. Sherman to Porter, December 28, 1862, Sherman Papers, Huntington Library.
50. *OR*, vol. 17, pt. 1, pp. 606–7; Lucien B. Crooker, "Chickasaw Bayou," *National Tribune*, September 11, 1884, p. 3.
51. Scheel, *Rain, Mud & Swamps*, 38; Franklin A. Wise Diary, December 28, 1862, WRHS.
52. Quoted in Scheel, *Rain, Mud & Swamps*, 38.
53. Crooker, Nourse, and Brown, *The 55th Illinois*, 138–39.
54. *OR*, vol. 17, pt. 1, p. 635; Munn, Miller, and Newton, *Military History and Reminiscences*, 239; Crooker, Nourse, and Brown, *The 55th Illinois*, 452.
55. Crooker, "Chickasaw Bayou," *National Tribune*, September 11, 1884, p. 3.
56. *OR*, vol. 17, pt. 1, pp. 635–36; Crooker, Nourse, and Brown, *The 55th Illinois*, 193–95.
57. John M. Roberts Reminiscences, IHS.
58. Ibid.
59. Crooker, Nourse, and Brown, *The 55th Illinois*, 193–95; *OR*, vol. 17, pt. 1, p. 636.
60. Quoted in Scheel, *Rain, Mud & Swamps*, 38.
61. Munn, Miller, and Newton, *Military History and Reminiscences*, 239–40.
62. Ibid., 240; Stuber, *Mein Tagebuch*, 59; Willison, *Reminiscences of a Boy's Service*, 37–38.
63. Bearss, *Vicksburg Is the Key*, 194–95; *OR*, vol. 17, pt. 1, p. 637.
64. Leasure, "Chickasaw Bluffs," *National Tribune*, December 25, 1884, p. 3.
65. Bearss, *Vicksburg Is the Key*, 194–95; *OR*, vol. 17, pt. 1, p. 637.
66. Bearss, *Vicksburg Is the Key*, 195–207; *OR*, vol. 17, pt. 1, pp. 607–8.
67. *OR*, vol. 17, pt. 1, p. 608.
68. Ibid., p. 638.
69. Sherman, *Memoirs*, 314.
70. George W. Morgan, "The Assault on Chickasaw Bluffs," in Johnson and Buel, *Battles and Leaders*, 3:466–67.
71. *OR*, vol. 17, pt. 1, p. 607.
72. Ibid., pp. 651–52.
73. Ibid., pp. 633–34, 649.
74. Ibid., pp. 633–34; Jackson, *Some of the Boys*, 54.
75. *OR*, vol. 17, pt. 1, pp. 633–34; Sherman, *Memoirs*, 315.
76. Jackson, *Some of the Boys*, 54–55.
77. *OR*, vol. 17, pt. 1, p. 647; Sweetman, "Chickasaw Bluffs," *National Tribune*, April 20, 1893, p. 3.
78. *OR*, vol. 17, pt. 1, p. 650; Leasure, "Chickasaw Bluffs," *National Tribune*, December 25, 1884, p. 3.
79. *OR*, vol. 17, pt. 1, pp. 625, 650.
80. Stuber, *Mein Tagebuch*, 60–62; Munn, Miller, and Newton, *Military History and Reminiscences*, 245–48; *OR*, vol. 17, pt. 1, p. 655.
81. Kuck letter quoted in Scheel, *Rain, Mud & Swamps*, 55-56.

82. *OR*, vol. 17, pt. 1, p. 655; Munn, Miller, and Newton, *Military History and Reminiscences,* 247; Chapel, *Civil War Journals,* 104–6.

83. Munn, Miller, and Newton, *Military History and Reminiscences,* 247–48; *OR*, vol. 17, pt. 1, pp. 655–56.

84. Stuber, *Mein Tagebuch,* 60–62; Munn, Miller, and Newton, *Military History and Reminiscences,* 247–48; *OR*, vol. 17, pt. 1, pp. 655–56.

85. Charles C. Wilson notation in the margin of his copy of Munn, Miller, and Newton, *Military History and Reminiscences,* Charles C. Wilson Papers, Civil War Miscellaneous Papers, USAMHI.

86. *OR*, vol. 17, pt. 1, p. 656; Stuber, *Mein Tagebuch,* 60–62; Chapel, *Civil War Journals,* 104–6.

87. Stuber, *Mein Tagebuch,* 60–62.

88. Ibid.

89. *OR*, vol. 17, pt. 1, p. 656; Chapel, *Civil War Journals,* 104–6.

90. *OR*, vol. 17, pt. 1, p. 656; Chapel, *Civil War Journals,* 104–6.

91. Stuber, *Mein Tagebuch,* 60–62; *OR*, vol. 17, pt. 1, pp. 625, 656.

92. *OR*, vol. 17, pt. 1, pp. 658–59; John M. Thayer to "My Dear Sir and Comrade," September 18, 1891, quoted in Munn, Miller, and Newton, *Military History and Reminiscences,* 264–66.

93. Stuber, *Mein Tagebuch,* 60–62.

94. John M. Thayer to "My Dear Sir and Comrade," September 18, 1891, quoted in Munn, Miller, and Newton, *Military History and Reminiscences,* 264–66.

95. *OR*, vol. 17, pt. 1, p. 625.

96. Charles C. Wilson notation in the margin of his copy of Munn, Miller, and Newton, *Military History and Reminiscences,* Charles C. Wilson Papers, Civil War Miscellaneous Papers, USAMHI.

97. Sherman, *Memoirs,* 315.

98. Leasure, "Chickasaw Bluffs," *National Tribune,* December 25, 1884, p. 3.

99. *OR*, vol. 17, pt. 1, p. 625.

100. Wiley, *Civil War Diary,* 29–30; Crooker, Nourse, and Brown, *The 55th Illinois,* 195; Franklin A. Wise Diary, December 30, 1862, WRHS; Scheel, *Rain, Mud & Swamps,* 44; Sweetman, "Chickasaw Bluffs," *National Tribune,* April 20, 1893, p. 3.

101. Scheel, *Rain, Mud & Swamps,* 49–50; Munn, Miller, and Newton, *Military History and Reminiscences,* 282–83.

102. Sherman, *Memoirs,* 315.

103. Ibid., 316; Sherman to Porter, December 29, 1862, Sherman Papers, Huntington Library.

104. Sherman, *Memoirs,* 316; Chapel, *Civil War Journals,* 107; Ritner, *Love and Valor,* 90–91; Willison, *Reminiscences of a Boy's Service,* 38–39.

105. Ritner, *Love and Valor,* 91.

106. Sherman, *Memoirs,* 316; Chapel, *Civil War Journals,* 107; Ritner, *Love and Valor,* 90–91; Willison, *Reminiscences of a Boy's Service,* 38–39.

107. Emmons letter quoted in Willison, *Reminiscences of a Boy's Service,* 131.

108. "The Civil War Diary of Michael Sweetman," http://www.fortunecity.com/westwood/makeover/347/id229.htm; Scheel, *Rain, Mud & Swamps,* 51; Lyftogt, *From Blue Mills to Columbia,* 82–83; Winters, *Musick of the Mocking Birds,* 16–17; A. J. Sweetman, "Chickasaw Bluffs," *National Tribune,* April 20, 1893, p. 3.

109. Sweetman, "Chickasaw Bluffs," *National Tribune,* April 20, 1893, p. 3; "Diary of Elias D. Moore," January 1, 1863, http://www.fortunecity.com/westwood/makeover/347/diary_of_a_union_soldier_elias_d_moore_114th_ohio_volunteer_infantry113.htm.

110. Sweetman, "Chickasaw Bluffs," *National Tribune,* April 20, 1893, p. 3; "Diary of Elias D. Moore," January 1, 1863.

111. Sweetman, "Chickasaw Bluffs," *National Tribune,* April 20, 1893, p. 3; "Diary of Elias D. Moore," January 1, 1863.

112. Crooker, Nourse, and Brown, *The 55th Illinois*, 196.

113. Sweetman, "Chickasaw Bluffs," *National Tribune*, April 20, 1893, p. 3; "Diary of Elias D⬛ Moore," January 1 and 2, 1863.

114. Sherman, *Memoirs*, 316.

115. Willison, *Reminiscences of a Boy's Service*, 35.

116. Ankeny, *Kiss Josey for Me*, 115–16.

117. Northup, *Drifting to an Unknown Future*, 55.

118. Miller, *The Struggle for the Life of the Republic*, 72.

119. Ankeny, *Kiss Josey for Me*, 115–16.

120. Miller, *The Struggle for the Life of the Republic*, 72.

CHAPTER SIXTEEN: WINTER ON THE MISSISSIPPI

1. Sherman, *Memoirs*, 316–17.

2. Ibid., 324.

3. *OR*, vol. 17, pt. 2, pp. 570–71; Grant, *Personal Memoirs*, 1:440–41; Jenney, "With Sherman and Grant from Memphis to Chattanooga—A Reminiscence," in *MOLLUS*, 13:200.

4. Grant, *Personal Memoirs*, 1:441.

5. *OR*, vol. 24, pt. 1, p. 8.

6. Ibid.

7. Ibid., pp. 8, 10.

8. Ibid., p. 8.

9. Adoniram Judson Withrow to "Dear Lib," January 23, 1863, Adoniram Judson Withrow Papers, SHC; Crooker, Nourse, and Brown, *The 55th Illinois*, 210–11.

10. Franklin A. Wise Diary, January 23, 1863, WRHS.

11. Quoted in Scheel, *Rain, Mud & Swamps*, 76.

12. Bering and Montgomery, *History of the Forty-eighth Ohio;* Scheel, *Rain, Mud & Swamps*, 76;

13. Jenney, "Personal Recollections of Vicksburg," in *MOLLUS*, 12:252; Crooker, Nourse, and Brown, *The 55th Illinois*, 211.

14. Jenney, "Personal Recollections of Vicksburg," in *MOLLUS*, 12:252–53.

15. Bering and Montgomery, *History of the Forty-eighth Ohio;* Willison, *Reminiscences of a Boy's Service*, 45–46.

16. Crooker, Nourse, and Brown, *The 55th Illinois*, 212; W. R. Eddington Reminiscences, Civil War Miscellaneous Collection, USAMHI; John M. Roberts Reminiscences, IHS; Ankeny, *Kiss Josey for Me*, 121–22.

17. Crooker, Nourse, and Brown, *The 55th Illinois*, 211; Ankeny, *Kiss Josey for Me*, 121–22.

18. Bering and Montgomery, *History of the Forty-eighth Ohio; OR*, vol. 24, pt. 1, p. 19; Crooker, Nourse, and Brown, *The 55th Illinois*, 220.

19. Jenney, "With Sherman and Grant from Memphis to Chattanooga: A Reminiscence," in *MOLLUS*, 13:198–99.

20. Willison, *Reminiscences of a Boy's Service*, 45–46.

21. Strew M. Emmons to his wife, January 30, 1863, in Willison, *Reminiscences of a Boy's Service*, 133.

22. Grant, *Personal Memoirs*, 1:442–42.

23. Simon, ed., *The Papers of Ulysses S. Grant*, 7:264–65; *OR*, vol. 24, pt. 1, p. 12.

24. Simon, ed., *The Papers of Ulysses S. Grant*, 7:266–67.

25. Grant, *Personal Memoirs*, 1:441; Simon, ed., *The Papers of Ulysses S. Grant*, 7:62; *OR*, vol. 17, pt. 2, p. 425.

26. *OR*, vol. 24, pt. 1, p. 11.

27. Simon, ed., *The Papers of Ulysses S. Grant*, 7:265; *OR*, vol. 24, pt. 1, p. 12.
28. Simon, ed., *The Papers of Ulysses S. Grant*, 7:264; *OR*, vol. 24, pt. 1, p. 13.
29. Simon, ed., *The Papers of Ulysses S. Grant*, 7:264–68; *OR*, vol. 24, pt. 1, pp. 11–14.
30. Simon, ed., *The Papers of Ulysses S. Grant*, 7:267–681; *OR*, vol. 24, pt. 3, p. 56.
31. Franklin A. Wise Diary, January 26 and 28, 1863, WRHS.
32. Sanborn, "The Campaign Against Vicksburg," in *MOLLUS*, 27:116.
33. Wiley, *Civil War Diary*, 36–40.
34. Ibid., 37–40.
35. Crooker, Nourse, and Brown, *The 55th Illinois*, 212.
36. Ritner, *Love and Valor*, 108.
37. William L. Wade Diary, January 27, 1863, Civil War Miscellaneous Collection, USAMHI.
38. Wiley, *Civil War Diary*, 37–40; Miller, *The Struggle for the Life of the Republic*, 86.
39. Wiley, *Civil War Diary*, 37–40.
40. Ibid.
41. W. R. Eddington Reminiscences, Civil War Miscellaneous Collection, USAMHI.
42. Ritner, *Love and Valor*, 108.
43. Henry Clemons to "Dear Wife," January 18, 1863, Henry Clemons Letters, WHS; Willison, *Reminiscences of a Boy's Service*, 44.
44. Wiley, *Civil War Diary*, 37–40.
45. Winters, *The Musick of the Mocking Birds*, 26–28.
46. Lyftogt, *From Blue Mills to Columbia*, 85–86.
47. Wiley, *Civil War Diary*, 37–40.
48. Willison, *Reminiscences of a Boy's Service*, 44.
49. Miller, *The Struggle for the Life of the Republic*, 87.
50. Perry, "The Entering Wedge," in *MOLLUS*, 24:359–61.
51. Capt. Strew M. Emmons to his wife, January 20, 1863, in Willison, *Reminiscences of a Boy's Service*, 134.
52. Sanborn, "The Campaign Against Vicksburg," in *MOLLUS*, 27:116.
53. Edward P. Stanfield to "Dear Father," January 4, 1863, Edward P. Stanfield Papers, IHS.
54. Boyd, *Civil War Diary*, 110–11.
55. Wills, *Army Life*, 150.
56. Crooker, Nourse, and Brown, *The 55th Illinois*, 197, 205; Wills, *Army Life*, 152.
57. Luther H. Cowan to "Dear Mollie," January 14, 1863, Luther H. Cowan Papers, WHS.
58. Wills, *Army Life*, 150.
59. John M. Roberts Reminiscences, IHS.
60. Jackson, *Some of the Boys*, 78.
61. John M. Roberts Reminiscences, IHS.
62. Perry, "The Entering Wedge," in *MOLLUS*, 24:359–61.
63. Willison, *Reminiscences of a Boy's Service*, 44.
64. Ibid., 45–46.
65. Wills, *Army Life*, 150.
66. Lyftogt, *From Blue Mills to Columbia*, 86–87; Wiley, *Civil War Diary*, 37–40.

CHAPTER SEVENTEEN: INTO THE BAYOUS

1. *OR*, vol. 24, pt. 1, p. 14; Simon, ed., *The Papers of Ulysses S. Grant*, 7:253–54.
2. Grant, *Personal Memoirs*, 1:448; Newton, *A Wisconsin Boy in Dixie*, 55; Force, "Personal Recollections of the Vicksburg Campaign," in *MOLLUS*, 1:293.
3. Bearss, *Vicksburg Is the Key*, 467.

4. Robert Ridge Diary, February 2 and 3, 1863, ISHL; Daniel G. Winegar Diary, February 8 1863, ISHL.

5. Daniel G. Winegar Diary, February 17, 1863, ISHL; Robert Ridge Diary, February 18, 1863 ISHL; William L. Wade Diary, February 20, 1863, Civil War Miscellaneous Collection USAMHI.

6. Abram J. Vanauken Diary, February, 3, 7, 12, and 13, 1863, ISHL; Robert Ridge Diary, February 2, 1863, ISHL.

7. Daniel G. Winegar Diary, February 6, 1863, ISHL.

8. Wimer Bedford Reminiscences, LC; Luther H. Cowan Diary, February 23, 1863, Luther H. Cowan Papers, WHS.

9. Robert Ridge Diary, February 8, 1863, ISHL; Daniel G. Winegar Diary, February 8 and 17, 1863, ISHL.

10. Newton, *A Wisconsin Boy in Dixie*, 55.

11. Force, "Personal Recollections of the Vicksburg Campaign," in *MOLLUS*, 1:293; Luther H. Cowan Diary, February 23, 1863, Luther H. Cowan Papers, WHS.

12. Daniel G. Winegar Diary, February 9, 1863, ISHL; Stevenson, *History of the 78th Regiment*, 223–24.

13. Luther H. Cowan to "Dear Mollie," February 25, 1863, Luther H. Cowan Papers, WHS.

14. Force, "Personal Recollections of the Vicksburg Campaign," in *MOLLUS*, 1:293.

15. *OR*, vol. 24, pt. 1, pp. 15–16.

16. Stevenson, *History of the 78th Regiment*, 223–24; Force, "Personal Recollections of the Vicksburg Campaign," in *MOLLUS*, 1:293; Geer, *Civil War*, 80.

17. Daniel G. Winegar Diary, March 5, 1863, ISHL; Robert Ridge Diary March 4, 1863, ISHL; Jessee, *Civil War Diaries*, chap. 3, p. 11; Belknap, *History of the Fifteenth Regiment*, 245–46.

18. William L. Wade Diary, February 23, 1863, Civil War Miscellaneous Collection, USAMHI.

19. Geer, *Civil War Diaries*, 80.

20. Ibid., 81.

21. Ibid.

22. *OR*, vol. 24, pt. 3, p. 76.

23. Stevenson, *History of the 78th Regiment*, 224; Geer, *Civil War Diaries*, 81.

24. Robert Ridge Diary, February 24, 1863, ISHL.

25. Grant, *Personal Memoirs*, 1:448–49. Grant gives February 4 as the date of this visit, and other witnesses corroborate that he did visit Lake Providence on that date. However, he must have confused that visit with a later one, because the steam tug was not in the lake prior to March 4.

26. *OR*, vol. 24, pt. 3, pp. 98, 110.

27. Luther H. Cowan Diary, March 16, 1863, Luther H. Cowan Papers, WHS; Daniel G. Winegar Diary, March 19, 1863, ISHL; Geer, *Civil War Diaries*, 82; Stevenson, *History of the 78th Regiment*, 226–27; Luther H. Cowan to "Dear Harriet," March 17, 1863, Luther H. Cowan Papers, WHS.

28. Daniel G. Winegar Diary, March 19, 1863, ISHL; William L. Wade Diary, March 17, 1863; Belknap, *History of the Fifteenth Regiment*, 245–46.

29. Stevenson, *History of the 78th Regiment*, 227.

30. Belknap, *History of the Fifteenth Regiment*, 243.

31. Luther H. Cowan to "Dear Harriet," March 17, 1863, Luther H. Cowan Papers, WHS.

32. Ibid.

33. Daniel G. Winegar Diary, March 19, 1863, ISHL.

34. Luther H. Cowan to "Dear Harriet," March 17, 1863, Luther H. Cowan Papers, WHS.

35. Grant, *Personal Memoirs*, 1:450; Bearss, *Vicksburg Is the Key*, 481–83.

36. Simon, ed., *The Papers of Ulysses S. Grant*, 7:253–54.

37. Bearss, *Vicksburg Is the Key*, 486–92; *OR*, vol. 24, pt. 1, pp. 378, 388.

38. *OR*, vol. 24, pt. 3, p. 56; Grant, *Personal Memoirs*, 1:450.

39. Enoch Weiss Reminiscences, Civil War Miscellaneous Collection, USAMHI; Joseph Stockton Diary, March 15, 1863, Civil War Miscellaneous Collection, USAMHI; Dunbar, *History of the Ninety-third Regiment*.

40. Bringhurst and Swigart, *History of the Forty-sixth Regiment*, 47–48.

41. Linus Parrish Manuscript A, http://www.iowa-counties.com/civilwar/17th_inf/17th _Parrish_A.htm (site now discontinued); Enoch Weiss Reminiscences, Civil War Miscellaneous Collection, USAMHI.

42. Bearss, *Vicksburg Is the Key*, 509–14.

43. Bringhurst and Swigart, *History of the Forty-sixth Regiment*, 48; Aurelius Lyman Voorhis Diary, March 10, 1863, IHS.

44. *OR*, vol. 24, pt. 3, p. 87.

45. Aurelius Lyman Voorhis Diary, March 7, 1863, IHS.

46. Quoted in "The Yazoo Pass Expedition" in "Twenty-eighth Wisconsin Volunteer Infantry," http://people.msoe.edu/~peterson/28thwisconsin.

47. *OR*, vol. 24, pt. 1, p. 394.

48. Ibid., pt. 3, p. 90.

49. Ibid., pt. 1, pp. 378–81, 395; Aurelius Lyman Voorhis Diary, March 11, 1863, IHS.

50. Quoted in "The Yazoo Pass Expedition" in "Twenty-eighth Wisconsin Volunteer Infantry," http://people.msoe.edu/~peterson/28thwisconsin.

51. *OR*, vol. 24, pt. 1, pp. 378–81; Aurelius Lyman Voorhis Diary, March 11, 1863, IHS.

52. *OR*, vol. 24, pt. 1, pp. 379–81.

53. Ibid., 379–82.

54. Ibid.

55. Ibid., 382–84, 396–97.

56. Ibid., 382–84, 396.

57. Quoted in "The Yazoo Pass Expedition" in "Twenty-eighth Wisconsin Volunteer Infantry," http://people.msoe.edu/~peterson/28thwisconsin.

58. *OR*, vol. 24, pt. 1, pp. 297–98, 385, 407; Aurelius Lyman Voorhis Diary, March 18 and 21, 1863, IHS; Bringhurst and Swigart, *History of the Forty-sixth Regiment*, 49.

59. Quoted in "The Yazoo Pass Expedition" in "Twenty-eighth Wisconsin Volunteer Infantry," http://people.msoe.edu/~peterson/28thwisconsin.

60. Ibid.; Aurelius Lyman Voorhis Diary, March 22 and April 5, 1863, IHS; Isaac Vanderwarker Diary, April 5, 1863, Civil War Miscellaneous Collection, USAMHI; Joseph Stockton Diary, April 5, 1863, Civil War Miscellaneous Collection, USAMHI; Bringhurst and Swigart, *History of the Forty-sixth Regiment*, 50; Bearss, *Vicksburg Is the Key*, 546.

61. *OR*, vol. 24, pt. 1, p. 16.

62. Ibid., pp. 20–21.

63. Grant, *Personal Memoirs*, 1:452–53; Sherman, *Memoirs*, 330–31.

64. Grant, *Personal Memoirs*, 1:452–53; Sherman, *Memoirs*, 330–31.

65. *OR*, vol. 24, pt. 1, p. 439; Sherman, *Memoirs*, 332; Jenney, "Personal Recollections of Vicksburg," in *MOLLUS*, 12:252.

66. Sherman, *Memoirs*, 332, 334.

67. Ibid., 332.

68. Ibid.

69. Ibid., 333.

70. *OR*, vol. 24, pt. 1, pp. 440–41; Sherman, *Memoirs*, 333.

71. *OR*, vol. 24, pt. 1, p. 443; Sherman, *Memoirs*, 333–34.

72. *OR*, vol. 24, pt. 1, p. 444; John M. Roberts Reminiscences, IHS.

73. Willison, *Reminiscences of a Boy's Service*, 51; Sherman, *Memoirs*, 334–35.

74. William L. Wade Diary, March 1, 2, 4, 5, and 8, 1863, Civil War Miscellaneous Collection, USAMHI; Belknap, *History of the Fifteenth Regiment*, 242–43.

75. Jessee, *Civil War Diaries*, chap. 3, pp. 14–15.

76. Geer, *Civil War Diary*, 88–89; Belknap, *History of the Fifteenth Regiment*, 251–53.

77. Geer, *Civil War Diary*, 88–89.

78. David W. Poak to "Sister Sallie," April 14, 1863, David W. Poak Papers, ISHL; Wimer Bedford Papers, LC.

79. Charles H. Lutz to "Dear Brother," April 11, 1863, Charles H. Lutz Papers, Civil War Miscellaneous Collection, USAMHI; William L. Wade Diary, March 6, 1863, Civil War Miscellaneous Collection, USAMHI.

80. George O. Smith Reminiscences, George O. Smith Papers, ISHL; Jessee, *Civil War Diaries*, chap. 3, p. 15; Geer, *Civil War Diary*, 89.

81. Lycurgus Remley to "Dear Pa," April 11, 1863, George and Lycurgus Remley Papers, Pearce Civil War Collection.

82. Scheel, *Rain, Mud & Swamps*, 92–93.

83. Jackson, *Some of the Boys*, 79.

84. Ankeny, *Kiss Josey for Me*, 139.

85. Winters, *The Musick of the Mocking Birds*, 47.

86. Geer, *Civil War Diary*, 88.

87. Samuel C. Kirkpatrick to "Dear Father and Mother Brothers and Sisters," April 3, 1863, Samuel C. Kirkpatrick Papers, WHS.

88. John J. Barney to "all at Home," March 2, 1863, John J. Barney Papers, WHS.

CHAPTER EIGHTEEN: DOWN THE WEST BANK

1. Simon, ed., *The Papers of Ulysses S. Grant*, 7:486–87; Grabau, *Ninety-eight Days*, 61.

2. John A. McClernand to Abraham Lincoln, February 14, 1863, Abraham Lincoln Papers, LC.

3. Simpson, *Ulysses S. Grant*, 176.

4. Ibid., 179–80; Catton, *Grant Moves South*, 389.

5. *OR*, vol. 24, pt. 1, pp. 139, 491; Perry, "The Entering Wedge," in *MOLLUS*, 24:362–64; Grabau, *Ninety-eight Days*, 62.

6. Perry, "The Entering Wedge," in *MOLLUS*, 24:364.

7. Ibid., 364–65; *OR*, vol. 24, pt. 1, pp. 139, 491.

8. *OR*, vol. 24, pt. 1, p. 491.

9. Ibid., pp. 139, 491; Perry, "The Entering Wedge," in *MOLLUS*, 24:365.

10. *OR*, vol. 24, pt. 1, pp. 139, 491–92; Perry, "The Entering Wedge," in *MOLLUS*, 24:365.

11. *OR*, vol. 24, pt. 1, pp. 139–40, 492; Perry, "The Entering Wedge," in *MOLLUS*, 24:365.

12. *OR*, vol. 24, pt. 1, pp. 140, 490, 492; Perry, "The Entering Wedge," in *MOLLUS*, 24:365–66.

13. *OR*, vol. 24, pt. 1, pp. 140, 489–90, 492–93; Perry, "The Entering Wedge," in *MOLLUS*, 24:365–69.

14. *OR*, vol. 24, pt. 1, p. 140.

15. Ibid.; Perry, "The Entering Wedge," in *MOLLUS*, 24:369–70.

16. Grabau, *Ninety-eight Days*, 63, 67–69.

17. Ibid., 67–73.

18. *OR*, vol. 24, pt. 1, p. 490; Perry, "The Entering Wedge," in *MOLLUS*, 24:365–69.

19. Puck, ed., *Sacrifice at Vicksburg*, 59.

20. Sanborn, "The Campaign Against Vicksburg," in *MOLLUS*, 27:120–21.

21. *OR*, vol. 24, pt. 1, p. 141; Grabau, *Ninety-eight Days*, 65–66; Perry, "The Entering Wedge," in *MOLLUS*, 24:372.

22. Grant, *Personal Memoirs*, 1:462; Grabau, *Ninety-eight Days*, 75–77; Bearss, *Grant Strikes a Fatal Blow*, 57; Simpson, *Ulysses S. Grant*, 187–88.

23. Edward P. Stanfield to "Dear Father," April 18, 1863, Edward P. Stanfield Papers, IHS; Geer, *Civil War Diary*, 91; Bringhurst and Swigart, *History of the Forty-sixth Regiment*, 54; Elliott, *History of the Thirty-third Regiment*, 37; Jessee, *Civil War Diaries*, chap. 3, p. 15; Crooker, Nourse, and Brown, *The 55th Illinois*, 225–26; Isaac Vanderwarker Diary, April 16, 1863, Civil War Miscellaneous Collection, USAMHI.

24. Perry, "The Entering Wedge," in *MOLLUS*, 24:373.

25. Crawford, ed., *The Civil War Songbook*, 2–3.

26. Perry, "The Entering Wedge," in *MOLLUS*, 24:373.

27. Ibid., 374.

28. Grant, *Personal Memoirs*, 1:463; Grabau, *Ninety-eight Days*, 77; Bearss, *Grant Strikes a Fatal Blow*, 73; Perry, "The Entering Wedge," in *MOLLUS*, 24:374–75.

29. Perry, "The Entering Wedge," in *MOLLUS*, 24:375.

30. Grabau, *Ninety-eight Days*, 75–76; Perry, "The Entering Wedge," in *MOLLUS*, 24:375.

31. *OR*, vol. 24, pt. 1, p. 517; Grabau, *Ninety-eight Days*, 76–77; Bearss, *Grant Strikes a Fatal Blow*, 67–73.

32. Sherman, *Memoirs*, 343–44.

33. Simpson, *Ulysses S. Grant*, 188; Grant, *Personal Memoirs*, 1:466.

34. Perry, "The Entering Wedge," in *MOLLUS*, 24:375.

35. Grant, *Personal Memoirs*, 1:466.

36. Perry, "The Entering Wedge," in *MOLLUS*, 24:375.

37. Grant, *Personal Memoirs*, 1:466.

38. *OR*, vol. 24, pt. 1, p. 141.

39. Grant, *Personal Memoirs*, 1:471.

40. Crummer, *With Grant*, 93–94; Luther H. Cowan Diary, April 21, 1863, WHS; Luther H. Cowan to "Dear Harriet," April 22, 1863, Luther H. Cowan Papers, WHS; Jessee, *Civil War Diaries*, chap. 3, p. 16; Geer, *Civil War Diary*, 92.

41. Strong, "The Campaign Against Vicksburg," in *MOLLUS*, 11:321–22.

42. *OR*, vol. 24, pt. 3, pp. 215–16.

43. Ibid., pt. 1, pp. 565–67; Strong, "The Campaign Against Vicksburg," in *MOLLUS*, 11:323.

44. *OR*, vol. 24, pt. 1, pp. 565–69.

45. Strong, "The Campaign Against Vicksburg," in *MOLLUS*, 11:322.

46. Aurelius Lyman Voorhis Diary, April 23, 1863, IHS.

47. Strong, "The Campaign Against Vicksburg," in *MOLLUS*, 11:324.

48. *OR*, vol. 24, pt. 1, pp. 565–66; Strong, "The Campaign Against Vicksburg," in *MOLLUS*, 11:324–25.

49. *OR*, vol. 24, pt. 1, p. 566; Strong, "The Campaign Against Vicksburg," in *MOLLUS*, 11:324.

50. Luther H. Cowan Diary, April 21, 1863, WHS.

51. *OR*, vol. 24, pt. 1, p. 567; Crummer, *With Grant*, 94.

52. Strong, "The Campaign Against Vicksburg," in *MOLLUS*, 11:324.

53. Ibid.

54. *OR*, vol. 24, pt. 1, pp. 567–68.

55. Ibid., p. 568.

56. Ibid., p. 566; Strong, "The Campaign Against Vicksburg," in *MOLLUS*, 11:324–26.

57. *OR*, vol. 24, pt. 1, p. 566; Strong, "The Campaign Against Vicksburg," in *MOLLUS*, 11:326.

58. *OR*, vol. 24, pt. 1, pp. 568–69.

59. Sherman, *Memoirs*, 344.
60. Ibid.

CHAPTER NINETEEN: ACROSS THE MISSISSIPPI

1. Bearss, *Grant Strikes a Fatal Blow*, 277–301; Grabau, *Ninety-eight Days*, 81–90.
2. *OR*, vol. 24, pt. 1, pp. 571–73.
3. Ibid., 80–81.
4. Grant, *Personal Memoirs*, 1:474–75; *OR*, vol. 24, pt. 1, pp. 80–81.
5. *OR*, vol. 24, pt. 1, pp. 80–81; Elliott, *History of the Thirty-third Regiment*, 37.
6. *OR*, vol. 24, pt. 1, p. 81.
7. Sanborn, "The Campaign Against Vicksburg," in *MOLLUS*, 27:124–25.
8. Simon, ed., *The Papers of Ulysses S. Grant*, 8:130.
9. Ibid., 131.
10. *OR*, vol. 24, pt. 1, pp. 576–77.
11. Grabau, *Ninety-eight Days*, 112–122.
12. Jackson, *Some of the Boys*, 86–87; Israel M. Ritter Diary, April 29, 1863, Civil War Miscellaneous Collection, USAMHI; John H. Ferree to "Dear Brother," May 9, 1863, John H. Ferree Papers, IHS; Elliott, *History of the Thirty-third Regiment*, 37–38.
13. Bearss, *Grant Strikes a Fatal Blow*, 305–15; Grabau, *Ninety-eight Days*, 135–38.
14. Grant, *Personal Memoirs*, 1:476; Bearss, *Grant Strikes a Fatal Blow*, 312–13.
15. Elliott, *History of the Thirty-third Regiment*, 236–37; Grant, *Personal Memoirs*, 1:477–78.
16. Bearss, *Grant Strikes a Fatal Blow*, 317–18; Grabau, *Ninety-eight Days*, 138; Peirce and Peirce, *Dear Catharine, Dear Taylor*, 105; Jackson, *Some of the Boys*, 87; John H. Ferree to "Dear Brother," May 9, 1863, John H. Ferree Papers, IHS; Bringhurst and Swigart, *History of the Forty-sixth Regiment*, 55–56.
17. W. R. Eddington Reminiscences, Civil War Miscellaneous Collection, USAMHI.
18. Bringhurst and Swigart, *History of the Forty-sixth Regiment*, 56; Frank Swigart, "The First to Land at Bruinsburg," *National Tribune*, October 16, 1884, p. 3; Aurelius Lyman Voorhis Diary, April 30, 1863, IHS.
19. Bringhurst and Swigart, *History of the Forty-sixth Regiment*, 56; Aurelius Lyman Voorhis Diary, April 30, 1863, IHS.
20. Bringhurst and Swigart, *History of the Forty-sixth Regiment*, 56–57; Swigart, "The First to Land at Bruinsburg," *National Tribune*, October 16, 1884, p. 3; Israel M. Ritter Diary, May 1, 1863, Civil War Miscellaneous Collection, USAMHI.
21. Bearss, *Grant Strikes a Fatal Blow*, 318–19; *OR*, vol. 24, pt. 1, p. 143.
22. Jones, *Reminiscences of the Twenty-Second Iowa*, 29; Swigart, "The First to Land at Bruinsburg," *National Tribune*, October 16, 1884, p. 3.
23. *OR*, vol. 24, pt. 1, p. 143.
24. Grant, *Personal Memoirs*, 1:480–81.
25. *OR*, vol. 24, pt. 1, p. 631; Grant, *Personal Memoirs*, 1:483; Force, "Personal Recollections of the Vicksburg Campaign," in *MOLLUS*, 1:296.
26. Grant, *Personal Memoirs*, 1:483.
27. Bearss, *Grant Strikes a Fatal Blow*, 320.
28. Ibid., 345; *OR*, vol. 24, pt. 1, p. 628; Elliott, *History of the Thirty-third Regiment*, 38.
29. *OR*, vol. 24, pt. 1, pp. 628–29; Peirce and Peirce, *Dear Catharine, Dear Taylor*, 107; Holcomb, ed., *Southern Sons, Northern Soldiers*, 62; Charleton, "Port Gibson: Who Commenced the Fight," *National Tribune*, December 4, 1884, p. 3.

30. *OR*, vol. 24, pt. 1, pp. 628–29; Peirce and Peirce, *Dear Catharine, Dear Taylor*, 107; Holcomb, ed., *Southern Sons, Northern Soldiers*, 62.

31. *OR*, vol. 24, pt. 1, p. 143; Holcomb, ed., *Southern Sons, Northern Soldiers*, 62; Luther H. Cowan to "My dear Mollie," May 5, 1863, Luther H. Cowan Papers, WHS.

32. Bearrs, *Grant Strikes a Fatal Blow*, 359.

33. *OR*, vol. 24, pt. 1, pp. 143, 585–86, 588, 590–92, 625, 679.

34. Denny, "Who Captured the Guns at Magnolia Hills?" *National Tribune*, December 11, 1884, p. 3; Peirce and Peirce, *Dear Catharine, Dear Taylor*, 192; Bearss, *Grant Strikes a Fatal Blow*, 373–78.

35. *OR*, vol. 24, pt. 1, pp. 615–16, 620–21, 625–26, 664, 672–73; Martin, "Port Gibson," *National Tribune*, October 16, 1884, p. 3; Bearss, *Grant Strikes a Fatal Blow*, 373–78; Aurelius Lyman Voorhis Diary, May 1, 1863, IHS.

36. W. P. Pease, "Port Gibson Again," *National Tribune*, November 6, 1884; Bearss, *Grant Strikes a Fatal Blow*, 379–81.

37. Denny, "Who Captured the Guns at Magnolia Hills?" *National Tribune*, December 11, 1884, p. 3; Swigert, "Bruinsburg," *National Tribune*, December 11, 1884, p. 3; Morris, "Bruinsburg," *National Tribune*, October 2, 1884, p. 3; *OR*, vol. 24, pt. 1, pp. 602–3, 607, 609–10, 613–14, 622, 626; Martin, "Port Gibson," *National Tribune*, October 16, 1884, p. 3; Hobbs, "The Illinoisan's Story," *National Tribune*, October 16, 1884, p. 3; Bringhurst and Swigart, *History of the Forty-sixth Regiment*, 57; Holbrook, "Port Gibson: Still Another—the 11th Ind.," *National Tribune*, December 4, 1884, p. 3.

38. Bearss, *Grant Strikes a Fatal Blow*, 385–86; Holcomb, ed., *Southern Sons, Northern Soldiers*, 63.

39. Bearss, *Grant Strikes a Fatal Blow*, 386–88; Holcomb, ed., *Southern Sons, Northern Soldiers*, 63; Morris, Hartwell, and Kuykendall, *History 31st Regiment*, 57; Martin, "Port Gibson," *National Tribune*, October 16, 1884, p. 3; Peirce and Peirce, *Dear Catharine, Dear Taylor*, 108; Luther H. Cowan Diary, May 2, 1863, Luther H. Cowan Papers, WHS.

40. Bearss, *Grant Strikes a Fatal Blow*, 388–93; Luther H. Cowan Diary, May 5, 1863, Luther H. Cowan Papers, WHS; *OR*, vol. 24, pt. 1, pp. 603–4, 607, 611, 613, 664, 668–69; Israel M. Ritter Diary, May 1, 1863, Civil War Miscellaneous Collection, USAMHI.

41. Bearss, *Grant Strikes a Fatal Blow*, 393–94; Peirce and Peirce, *Dear Catharine, Dear Taylor*, 108.

42. Bearss, *Grant Strikes a Fatal Blow*, 394–99.

43. Hawk, "Port Gibson: From Another Participant," *National Tribune*, December 4, 1884, p. 3.

44. Grant, *Personal Memoirs*, 1:484; Peirce and Peirce, *Dear Catharine, Dear Taylor*, 108.

CHAPTER TWENTY: JACKSON

1. Jackson, *Some of the Boys*, 88–89.

2. Bering and Montgomery, *History of the Forty-eighth Ohio*.

3. Grant, *Personal Memoirs*, 1:485–86; Hickenlooper, "Our Volunteer Engineers," in *MOLLUS*, 2:308–9.

4. Grant, *Personal Memoirs*, 1:485; Elliott, *History of the Thirty-third Regiment*, 38; John H. Ferree to "Dear Brother," May 9, 1863, IHS; Bearss, *Grant Strikes a Fatal Blow*, 409–11; Grabau, *Ninety-eight Days*, 168–72.

5. Hickenlooper, "Our Volunteer Engineers," in *MOLLUS*, 2:308–9; Bearss, *Grant Strikes a Fatal Blow*, 411–16.

6. Bearss, *Grant Strikes a Fatal Blow*, 423–24.

7. Ibid., 421–23.

8. Luther H. Cowan Diary, May 3, 1863, Luther H. Cowan Papers, WHS; Force, "Personal Recollections of the Vicksburg Campaign," in *MOLLUS*, 1:297–98; Grant, *Personal Memoirs*, 1:491–92.

9. Grant, *Personal Memoirs*, 1:490–91.

10. Force, "Personal Recollections of the Vicksburg Campaign," in *MOLLUS*, 1:297–98; David W. Poak to "Sadie," May 4, 1863, David W. Poak Papers, ISHL; John H. Ferree to "Dear Brother," May 9, 1863, IHS; Geer, *Civil War Diary*, 96–97; Grabau, *Ninety-eight Days*, 174; Grant, *Personal Memoirs*, 1:492–94.

11. Grant, *Personal Memoirs*, 1:494.

12. Ibid.; Grabau, *Ninety-eight Days*, 209–13; Sherman, *Memoirs*, 346–47; Ankeny, *Kiss Josey for Me*, 149.

13. Gould D. Molineaux Diary, May 2, 1863, Special Collections, ACL; Isaac Vanderwarker Diary, May 3 and 4, 1863, Civil War Miscellaneous Collection, USAMHI; Israel M. Ritter Diary, May 3, 1863, Civil War Miscellaneous Collection, USAMHI; Campbell, *The Union Must Stand*, 92.

14. Isaac Vanderwarker Diary, May 6–8, 1863, Civil War Miscellaneous Collection, USAMHI; Thomas N. McCleur Diary, May 4, 1863, Jackson County Historical Society, Murphysboro, Illinois; Luther H. Cowan Diary, May 5, 1863, Luther H. Cowan Papers, WHS; Israel M. Ritter Diary, May 5 and 7, 1863, Civil War Miscellaneous Collection, USAMHI; Robert Ridge Diary, May 5 and 7, 1863, ISHL; Joseph B. Williamson Diary, May 6, 1863, ISHL; Campbell, *The Union Must Stand*, 92–93; Franklin A. Wise Diary, May 6, 1863, WRHS; Henry G. Ankeny, *Kiss Josey for Me*, 149.

15. Post, ed., *Soldiers' Letters*, 263–72; Isaac Vanderwarker Diary, May 9, 1863, Civil War Miscellaneous Collection, USAMHI; Luther H. Cowan Diary, May 9, 1863, Luther H. Cowan Papers, WHS; Franklin A. Wise Diary, May 9, 1863, WRHS.

16. Luther H. Cowan Diary, May 3, 1863, Luther H. Cowan Papers, WHS.

17. "Diary of William H. Carroll," May 6, 1863, http://www.indianainthecivilwar.com/letters/24th/May63.htm.

18. Aurelius Lyman Voorhis Diary, May 6 and 8, 1863, IHS.

19. Joseph B. Williamson Diary, May 10, 1863, ISHL.

20. W. R. Eddington Diary, May 11, 1863, Civil War Miscellaneous Collection, USAMHI.

21. Luther H. Cowan to "My dear Mollie," May 5, 1863, Luther H. Cowan Papers, WHS.

22. Israel M. Ritter Diary, May 6, 1863, Civil War Miscellaneous Collection, USAMHI.

23. Jessee, *Civil War Diaries*, chap. 3, p. 18.

24. Luther H. Cowan to "Dear Harriet," May 6, 1863, Luther H. Cowan Papers, WHS.

25. Jackson, *Some of the Boys*, 92.

26. Luther H. Cowan to "My dear Mollie," May 5, 1863, Luther H. Cowan Papers, WHS.

27. John J. Barney to "all at Home," May 5, 1863, John J. Barney Papers, WHS.

28. William K. Barney to "all at Home," April 26, 1863, William K. Barney Papers, WHS.

29. Aurelius Lyman Voorhis Diary, May 12, 1863, IHS; "Diary of William H. Carroll," May 12, 1863, http://www.indianainthecivilwar.com/letters/24th/May63.htm; Bringhurst and Swigart, *History of the Forty-sixth Regiment*, 59.

30. Grabau, *Ninety-eight Days*, 222; Luther H. Cowan Diary, May 12, 1863, Luther H. Cowan Papers, WHS.

31. *OR*, vol. 24, pt. 1, p. 735; Henry O. Dwight, "A Soldier's Story: The Affair on the Raymond Road," *New York Daily Tribune*, November 21, 1886.

32. Quoted in Drake, *In Their Own Words*, 18.

33. Grabau, *Ninety-eight Days*, 223–24.

34. *OR*, vol. 24, pt. 1, pp. 637, 714; Force, "Personal Recollections of the Vicksburg Campaign,"

in *MOLLUS*, 1:298–300; Dwight, "A Soldier's Story," *New York Daily Tribune*, November 21, 1886.

35. *OR*, vol. 24, pt. 1, p. 637; Dwight, "A Soldier's Story," *New York Daily Tribune*, November 21, 1886.

36. *OR*, vol. 24, pt. 1, p. 714; Dwight, "A Soldier's Story," *New York Daily Tribune*, November 21, 1886.

37. Dwight, "A Soldier's Story," *New York Daily Tribune*, November 21, 1886.

38. *OR*, vol. 24, pt. 1, p. 637.

39. Dwight, "A Soldier's Story," *New York Daily Tribune*, November 21, 1886; Force, "Personal Recollections of the Vicksburg Campaign," in *MOLLUS*, 1:298–300; Grabau, *Ninety-eight Days*, 223–24.

40. *OR*, vol. 24, pt. 1, p. 714; Dwight, "A Soldier's Story," *New York Daily Tribune*, November 21, 1886; Drake, *In Their Own Words*, 42.

41. *OR*, vol. 24, pt. 1, pp. 709, 714; Dwight, "A Soldier's Story," *New York Daily Tribune*, November 21, 1886; Force, "Personal Recollections of the Vicksburg Campaign," in *MOLLUS*, 1:298–300; Grabau, *Ninety-eight Days*, 222–24, 229.

42. *OR*, vol. 24, pt. 1, p. 714; Dwight, "A Soldier's Story," *New York Daily Tribune*, November 21, 1886.

43. *OR*, vol. 24, pt. 1, p. 714; Dwight, "A Soldier's Story," *New York Daily Tribune*, November 21, 1886; Force, "Personal Recollections of the Vicksburg Campaign," in *MOLLUS*, 1:298–300.

44. *OR*, vol. 24, pt. 1, p. 714; Dwight, "A Soldier's Story," *New York Daily Tribune*, November 21, 1886; Force, "Personal Recollections of the Vicksburg Campaign," in *MOLLUS*, 1:298–300.

45. Dwight, "A Soldier's Story," *New York Daily Tribune*, November 21, 1886; Force, "Personal Recollections of the Vicksburg Campaign," in *MOLLUS*, 1:298–300.

46. Dwight, "A Soldier's Story," *New York Daily Tribune*, November 21, 1886.

47. Blanchard, *I Marched with Sherman*, 87–88; Luther H. Cowan Diary, May 12, 1863, Luther H. Cowan Papers, WHS.

48. Bearss, *Grant Strikes a Fatal Blow*, 493.

49. *OR*, vol. 24, pt. 1, pp. 707–8; Blanchard, *I Marched with Sherman*, 88.

50. Blanchard, *I Marched with Sherman*, 88; Geer, *Civil War Diary*, 99.

51. Blanchard, *I Marched with Sherman*, 88.

52. Geer, *Civil War Diary*, 99–100.

53. *OR*, vol. 24, pt. 1, p. 711.

54. Ibid., p. 712.

55. Ibid., pp. 708, 711; Dwight, "A Soldier's Story," *New York Daily Tribune*, November 21, 1886.

56. Blanchard, *I Marched with Sherman*, 88.

57. Dwight, "A Soldier's Story," *New York Daily Tribune*, November 21, 1886; Drake, *In Their Own Words*, 47.

58. Bearss, *Grant Strikes a Fatal Blow*, 495–96.

59. Quoted in Drake, *In Their Own Words*, 46.

60. Dwight, "A Soldier's Story," *New York Daily Tribune*, November 21, 1886.

61. Force, "Personal Recollections of the Vicksburg Campaign," in *MOLLUS*, 1:298–300.

62. Dwight, "A Soldier's Story," *New York Daily Tribune*, November 21, 1886.

63. Drake, *In Their Own Words*, 47.

64. Dwight, "A Soldier's Story," *New York Daily Tribune*, November 21, 1886.

65. Drake, *In Their Own Words*, 50.

66. Dwight, "A Soldier's Story," *New York Daily Tribune*, November 21, 1886.

67. Jessee, *Civil War Diaries*, chap. 3, p. 19.

68. Ibid.

69. Grabau, *Ninety-eight Days*, 231–32; Bearss, *Grant Strikes a Fatal Blow*, 497–500.

70. Edward P. Stanfield to "Dear Father," May 26, 1863, Edward P. Stanfield Papers, IHS.

71. Grabau, *Ninety-eight Days*, 232–34; Bearss, *Grant Strikes a Fatal Blow*, 500–510.

72. Dwight, "A Soldier's Story," *New York Daily Tribune*, November 21, 1886.

73. Ibid.

74. Luther H. Cowan Diary, May 12, 1863, Luther H. Cowan Papers, WHS.

75. Dwight, "A Soldier's Story," *New York Daily Tribune*, November 21, 1886; Bearss, *Grant Strikes a Fatal Blow*, 510.

76. Bearss, *Grant Strikes a Fatal Blow*, 511.

77. Grant, *Personal Memoirs*, 1:499–500; Simon, ed., *The Papers of Ulysses S. Grant*, 8:204–8; Bearss, *Grant Strikes a Fatal Blow*, 512–14.

78. Grant, *Personal Memoirs*, 1:499–500; Simon, ed., *The Papers of Ulysses S. Grant*, 8:204–8; Israel M. Ritter Diary, May 13, 1863, Civil War Miscellaneous Collection, USAMHI.

79. Thomas N. McCleur Diary, May 13, 1863, Jackson County Historical Society, Murphysboro, Illinois; Joseph B. Williamson Diary, May 13, 1863, ISHL; Edward P. Stanfield to "Dear Father," May 26, 1863, Edward P. Stanfield Papers, IHS; Luther H. Cowan Diary, May 13, 1863, Luther H. Cowan Papers, WHS; Isaac Vanderwarker Diary, May 13, 1863, Civil War Miscellaneous Collection, USAMHI; Campbell, *The Union Must Stand*, 93–94.

80. Campbell, *The Union Must Stand*, 93–94.

81. Grant, *Personal Memoirs*, 1:501; Edward P. Stanfield to "Dear Father," May 26, 1863, Edward P. Stanfield Papers, IHS; Simon, ed., *The Papers of Ulysses S. Grant*, 8:212; Morris, Hartwell, and Kuykendall, *History 31st Regiment*, 61–62; Campbell, *The Union Must Stand*, 93–94.

82. Grant, *Personal Memoirs*, 1:503–4; Simon, ed., *The Papers of Ulysses S. Grant*, 8:212; Luther H. Cowan Diary, May 13, 1863, Luther H. Cowan Papers, WHS; Isaac Vanderwarker Diary, May 13, 1863, Civil War Miscellaneous Collection, USAMHI; Edward P. Stanfield to "Dear Father," May 26, 1863, Edward P. Stanfield Papers, IHS.

83. Jessee, *Civil War Diaries*, chap. 3, pp. 19–20.

84. Edward P. Stanfield to "Dear Father," May 26, 1863, Edward P. Stanfield Papers, IHS; Sanborn, "The Campaign Against Vicksburg," in *MOLLUS*, 27:130–31; Huston, "Who Planted the Flag at Jackson, Miss.?" *National Tribune*, February 19, 1885, p. 3.

85. Enoch Weiss Diary, May 14, 1863, Civil War Miscellaneous Collection, USAMHI; Crummer, *With Grant*, 100–1.

86. Bryner, *Bugle Echoes*, 79–80.

87. Blanchard, *I Marched with Sherman*, 89–90.

88. Edward P. Stanfield to "Dear Father," May 26, 1863, Edward P. Stanfield Papers, IHS.

89. Linus Parrish, "A Condensed History of My Army Life," http://www.iowa-counties.com/civilwar/17th_inf/17th_Parrish_B.htm (site now discontinued).

90. Dunbar, *History of the Ninety-third Regiment*.

91. Huston, "Who Planted the Flag at Jackson, Miss.?" *National Tribune*, February 19, 1885, p. 3.

92. Parrish, "At Jackson," *National Tribune*, August 11, 1887, p. 3.

93. Burke, "The 95th Ohio at Jackson, Miss.," *National Tribune*, May 1, 1884, p. 3; Grant, *Personal Memoirs*, 1:505.

94. Clark and Bowen, *University Recruits*, 176; Bryner, *Bugle Echoes*, 79–80.

95. Luther H. Cowan Diary, May 14, 1863, Luther H. Cowan Papers, WHS.

96. Grabau, *Ninety-eight Days*, 245–47.

97. Jessee, *Civil War Diaries*, chap. 3, pp. 19–20.

98. Franklin A. Wise Diary, May 15, 1863, WRHS.

99. Enoch Weiss Diary, May 14, 1863, Civil War Miscellaneous Collection, USAMHI; Dunbar, *History of the Ninety-third Regiment*, http://www.illinoiscivilwar.org/cw93-hist-ch4a.html.

00. Williams, *The Eagle Regiment*, 16–17; anonymous manuscript by a member of the 47th Illinois entitled "A Condensed History of the 47th Regiment of Illinois Volunteer Infantry," John Nelson Cromwell Papers, ISHL; Grant, *Personal Memoirs*, 1:506.

01. Edward P. Stanfield to "Dear Father," May 26, 1863, Edward P. Stanfield Papers, IHS.

02. R. W. Burt to "Dear Wife," May 23, 1863, R. W. Burt Papers, WHMC, 23 Ellis Library, University of Missouri–Columbia.

03. Grant, *Personal Memoirs*, 1:507.

04. Sherman, *Memoirs*, 347–48; Miller, *The Struggle for the Life of the Republic*, 94–95; Clark and Bowen, *University Recruits*, 178.

105. Scheel, *Rain, Mud & Swamps*, 117–18.

106. L. F. Parrish, "At Jackson," *National Tribune*, August 11, 1887, p. 3.

107. Grant, *Personal Memoirs*, 1:506–9; Sherman, *Memoirs*, 347.

108. Clark and Bowen, *University Recruits*, 176.

109. Luther H. Cowan Diary, May 15, 1863, Luther H. Cowan Papers, WHS.

CHAPTER TWENTY-ONE: CHAMPION'S HILL

1. Aurelius Lyman Voorhis Diary, May 15, 1863, IHS; Longley, "Champion's Hill," in *MOLLUS*, 55:209–10; Isaac Vanderwarker Diary, May 15, 1863, Civil War Miscellaneous Collection, USAMHI; Israel M. Ritter Diary, May 15, 1863, Civil War Miscellaneous Collection, USAMHI; Campbell, *The Union Must Stand*, 95; Bringhurst and Swigart, *History of the Forty-sixth Regiment*, 60; Joseph B. Williamson Diary, May 15, 1863, ISHL; Jessee, *Civil War Diaries*, chap. 3, p. 20.

2. Grant, *Personal Memoirs*, 1:510.

3. Ibid., 511–12.

4. *OR*, vol. 24, pt. 2, pp. 59–60.

5. Williams, "The Battle of Champion's Hill," in *MOLLUS*, 5:204; Bringhurst and Swigart, *History of the Forty-sixth Regiment*, 60.

6. Longley, "Champion's Hill," May 16, 1863, in *MOLLUS*, 55:211–14; Bringhurst and Swigart, *History of the Forty-sixth Regiment*, 60.

7. Steele, "Champion's Hill," *National Tribune*, November 29, 1888, p. 4.

8. Durham, *Three Years with Wallace's Zouaves*, 128–29.

9. Grant, *Personal Memoirs*, 1:512–13.

10. Sanborn, "The Campaign Against Vicksburg," in *MOLLUS*, 27:131.

11. Grant, *Personal Memoirs*, 1:513.

12. Grabau, *Ninety-eight Days*, 273–77.

13. Grant, *Personal Memoirs*, 1:513; Grabau, *Ninety-eight Days*, 279–80.

14. The discussion of the geography of the battlefield is based on Grabau, *Ninety-eight Days*, 269–70.

15. Williams, "The Battle of Champion's Hill," in *MOLLUS*, 5:205.

16. Longley, "Champion's Hill," May 16, 1863, in *MOLLUS*, 55:211–14.

17. Morris, Hartwell, and Kuykendall, *History 31st Regiment*, 63; Gould D. Molineaux Diary, May 16, 1863, Special Collections, ACL; Manning F. Force, "Personal Recollections of the Vicksburg Campaign," in *MOLLUS*, 1:301–3.

18. Bearss, *Grant Strikes a Fatal Blow*, 596–99.

19. Jessee, *Civil War Diaries*, chap. 3, pp. 20–21; *OR*, vol. 24, pt. 1, p. 640; Grabau, *Ninety-eight Days*, 287.

20. Jessee, *Civil War Diaries*, chap. 3, pp. 20–21; *OR*, vol. 24, pt. 1, p. 640.

21. Morris, Hartwell, and Kuykendall, *History 31st Regiment*, 64–65; *OR*, vol. 24, pt. 2, p. 53.

22. Jessee, *Civil War Diaries*, chap. 3, pp. 20–21.

23. *OR*, vol. 24, pt. 1, p. 647; Force, "Personal Recollections of the Vicksburg Campaign," i *MOLLUS*, 1:301–3.

24. Blanchard, *I Marched with Sherman*, 92.

25. Jessee, *Civil War Diaries*, chap. 3, pp. 20–21; Grabau, *Ninety-eight Days*, 288.

26. Jessee, *Civil War Diaries*, chap. 3, pp. 20–21.

27. *OR*, vol. 24, pt. 2, p. 42.

28. Williams, "The Battle of Champion's Hill," in *MOLLUS*, 5:205.

29. Longley, "Champion's Hill," May 16, 1863, in *MOLLUS*, 55:211–14.

30. Bringhurst and Swigart, *History of the Forty-sixth Regiment*, 60; *OR*, vol. 24, pt. 2, p. 49.

31. Longley, "Champion's Hill," May 16, 1863, in *MOLLUS*, 55:211–14; Williams, "The Battle of Champion's Hill," in *MOLLUS*, 5:205.

32. Longley, "Champion's Hill," May 16, 1863, in *MOLLUS*, 55:211–14; *OR*, vol. 24, pt. 2, p. 49.

33. Durham, *Three Years with Wallace's Zouaves*, 130.

34. Longley, "Champion's Hill," May 16, 1863, in *MOLLUS*, 55:211–14.

35. Durham, *Three Years with Wallace's Zouaves*, 131; *OR*, vol. 24, pt. 2, p. 49.

36. Bringhurst and Swigart, *History of the Forty-sixth Regiment*, 61; *OR*, vol. 24, pt. 2, p. 49.

37. Durham, *Three Years with Wallace's Zouaves*, 131.

38. Blanchard, *I Marched with Sherman*, 92.

39. Ibid; *OR*, vol. 24, pt. 2, pp. 42, 49, 55.

40. Morris, Hartwell, and Kuykendall, *History 31st Regiment*, 65.

41. Jessee, *Civil War Diaries*, chap. 3, p. 21.

42. Florey, "Champion Hills," *National Tribune*, August 4, 1887, p. 3; Jessee, *Civil War Diaries*, chap. 3, p. 21; Gould D. Molineaux Diary, May 16, 1863, Special Collections, ACL; *OR*, vol. 24, pt. 1, p. 640.

43. Arnold, *Grant Wins the War*, 162–63; Bearss, *Grant Strikes a Fatal Blow*, 601; Williams, "The Battle of Champion's Hill," in *MOLLUS*, 5:206.

44. Williams, "The Battle of Champion's Hill," in *MOLLUS* 5:206; Israel M. Ritter Diary, May 16, 1863, Civil War Miscellaneous Collection, USAMHI.

45. Grant, *Personal Memoirs*, 1:513.

46. *OR*, vol. 24, pt. 3, pp. 249, 907; Bearss, *Grant Strikes a Fatal Blow*, 403–5, 516, 611, 647; Williams, "The Battle of Champion's Hill," in *MOLLUS*, 5:211.

47. Longley, "Champion's Hill," in *MOLLUS*, 55:214.

48. Williams, "The Battle of Champion's Hill," in *MOLLUS*, 5:207.

49. Ibid., 208.

50. Israel M. Ritter Diary, May 16, 1863, Civil War Miscellaneous Collection, USAMHI.

51. Williams, "The Battle of Champion's Hill," in *MOLLUS*, 5:208–9.

52. *OR*, vol. 24, pt. 2, p. 50; Williams, "The Battle of Champion's Hill," in *MOLLUS*, 5:209–10.

53. *OR*, vol. 24, pt. 2, pp. 53, 59.

54. Aurelius Lyman Voorhis Diary, May 16, 1863, IHS.

55. *OR*, vol. 24, pt. 2, p. 63.

56. Ibid., p. 50; Dunbar, *History of the Ninety-third Regiment;* Campbell, *The Union Must Stand*, 95–98.

57. Campbell, *The Union Must Stand*, 95–98.

58. *OR*, vol. 24, pt. 2, p. 50; Dunbar, *History of the Ninety-third Regiment*.

59. Grant, *Personal Memoirs*, 1:517.

60. Dihel, "Champion's Hill: A Graphic Picture of a Most Exciting Time—Logan's Division at Champion's Hill," *National Tribune*, September 11, 1884, p. 3.

61. Grinnell, "The 34th Ind.," *National Tribune*, August 11, 1887, p. 3; Dihel, "Champion's

Hill," *National Tribune,* September 11, 1884, p. 3; Harris, "An Incident of Champion Hills—Gen. Logan's Advice," *National Tribune,* July 31, 1884, p. 3.

62. Harris, "An Incident of Champion Hills," *National Tribune,* July 31, 1884, p. 3; Dihel, "Champion's Hill," *National Tribune,* September 11, 1884, p. 3.

63. Grabau, *Ninety-eight Days,* 296.

64. Dunbar, *History of the Ninety-third Regiment.*

65. Bringhurst and Swigart, *History of the Forty-sixth Regiment,* 60.

66. Williams, "The Battle of Champion's Hill," in *MOLLUS,* 5:210; Edward P. Stanfield to "Dear Father," May 26, 1863, Edward P. Stanfield Letters, IHS; Campbell, *The Union Must Stand,* 95–98; Henry G. Hicks, "The Campaign and Capture of Vicksburg," in *MOLLUS,* 31:99; Dunbar, *History of the Ninety-third Regiment;* Morris, Hartwell, and Kuykendall, *History 31st Regiment,* 65.

67. Bearss, *Grant Strikes a Fatal Blow,* 625.

68. OR, vol. 24, pt. 2, p. 15; Bearss, *Grant Strikes a Fatal Blow,* 617–18, 625.

69. Elliott, *History of the Thirty-third Regiment,* 40.

70. Crooker, Nourse, and Brown, *The 55th Illinois,* 232–33.

71. Grant, *Personal Memoirs,* 1:520; Bearss, *Grant Strikes a Fatal Blow,* 640.

72. OR, vol. 24, pt. 2, p. 32.

73. Bearss, *Grant Strikes a Fatal Blow,* 642; Grabau, *Ninety-eight Days,* 312.

74. OR, vol. 24, pt. 2, pp. 16, 22, 24; Edward P. Stanfield to "Dear Father," May 26, 1863, Edward P. Stanfield Papers, IHS; Bearss, *Grant Strikes a Fatal Blow,* 632.

75. Grant, *Personal Memoirs,* 1:520.

76. Ibid.

77. Durham, *Three Years with Wallace's Zouaves,* 134.

78. Bringhurst and Swigart, *History of the Forty-sixth Regiment,* 66.

79. Ibid., 62.

80. Williams, "The Battle of Champion's Hill," in *MOLLUS,* 5:210–11.

81. Campbell, *The Union Must Stand,* 98.

CHAPTER TWENTY-TWO: TO THE GATES OF VICKSBURG

1. Grabau, *Ninety-eight Days,* 319–23; Grant, *Personal Memoirs,* 1:522–23.

2. Bering and Montgomery, *History of the Forty-eighth Ohio;* Elliott, *History of the Thirty-third Regiment,* 233; Wiley, *Civil War Diary,* 48–49.

3. OR, vol. 24, pt. 1, p. 151; Elliott, *History of the Thirty-third Regiment,* 233.

4. Elliott, *History of the Thirty-third Regiment,* 233; Joseph B. Williamson Diary, May 17, 1863, ISHL; Grant, *Personal Memoirs,* 1:523; Grabau, *Ninety-eight Days,* 328–29; Jackson, *Some of the Boys,* 96.

5. Grabau, *Ninety-eight Days,* 323–26.

6. Ibid., 329; Bearss, *Grant Strikes a Fatal Blow,* 666.

7. Bearrs, *Grant Strikes a Fatal Blow,* 666; Hess, "Peter J. Osterhaus: Grant's Ethnic General," 209.

8. Elliott, *History of the Thirty-third Regiment,* 41.

9. Ibid., 35.

10. Grabau, *Ninety-eight Days,* 329–30.

11. Wright, "Generals Curtis and Crocker," in *MOLLUS,* 55:219.

12. OR, vol. 24, pt. 2, p. 137; Jones, *Reminiscences of the Twenty-second Iowa,* 35.

13. Joseph B. Williamson Diary, May 17, 1863, ISHL; Jackson, *Some of the Boys,* 96.

14. Elliott, *History of the Thirty-third Regiment,* 233.

15. Ibid., Grabau, *Ninety-eight Days,* 330.

16. Elliott, *History of the Thirty-third Regiment,* 41.

17. Joseph B. Williamson Diary, May 17, 1863, ISHL; Jackson, *Some of the Boys,* 96.

18. Elliott, *History of the Thirty-third Regiment,* 233; Jackson, *Some of the Boys,* 96; W. R Eddington Reminiscences, Civil War Miscellaneous Collection, USAMHI.

19. Joseph B. Williamson Diary, May 17, 1863, ISHL; Grabau, *Ninety-eight Days,* 330–31.

20. Simon, ed., *The Papers of Ulysses S. Grant,* 8:221.

21. Ibid.; Simpson, *Ulysses S. Grant,* 201.

22. Grant, *Personal Memoirs,* 1:524.

23. Ibid., 524–26.

24. Joseph B. Williamson Diary, May 17, 1863, ISHL.

25. *OR,* vol. 24, pt. 1, p. 617; pt. 2, pp. 130–31.

26. Elliott, *History of the Thirty-third Regiment,* 233.

27. Jones, *Reminiscences of the Twenty-second Iowa,* 35–36.

28. Grant, *Personal Memoirs,* 1:526–27; Grabau, *Ninety-eight Days,* 342–43; *OR,* vol. 24, pt. 1, p. 153.

29. Enoch Weiss Reminiscences, Civil War Miscellaneous Collection, USAMHI.

30. Grabau, *Ninety-eight Days,* 341; Hickenlooper, "Our Volunteer Engineers," in *MOLLUS,* 2:309–10; Sanborn, "The Campaign Against Vicksburg," in *MOLLUS,* 27:132–33.

31. R. W. Burt to "Dear Wife," May 23, 1863, R. W. Burt Papers, WHMC; Crooker, Nourse, and Brown, *The 55th Illinois,* 233–34; Sherman, *Memoirs,* 349.

32. Bryner, *Bugle Echoes,* 83; Sherman, *Memoirs,* 349.

33. Sherman, *Memoirs,* 349–50.

34. Robert Ridge Diary, May 18, 1863, ISHL; Grabau, *Ninety-eight Days,* 348.

35. Grabau, *Ninety-eight Days,* 348; Sherman, *Memoirs,* 350; Grant, *Personal Memoirs,* 1:527.

36. Grabau, *Ninety-eight Days,* 348; Sherman, *Memoirs,* 350.

37. Strong, "The Campaign Against Vicksburg," in *MOLLUS,* 11:329–30.

38. Grant, *Personal Memoirs,* 1:528.

39. Jenney, "Personal Recollections of Vicksburg," in *MOLLUS,* 12:260–61.

40. Morris, Hartwell, and Kuykendall, *History 31st Regiment,* 68.

41. Force, "Personal Recollections of the Vicksburg Campaign," in *MOLLUS,* 1:304.

42. Crooker, Nourse, and Brown, *The 55th Illinois,* 235.

43. Grabau, *Ninety-eight Days,* 351–52; Grant, *Personal Memoirs,* 1:529.

44. Joseph B. Williamson Diary, May 18, 1863, ISHL; Bering and Montgomery, *History of the Forty-eighth Ohio;* Grant, *Personal Memoirs,* 1:529; Sherman, *Memoirs,* 351; Grabau, *Ninety-eight Days,* 356.

45. Morris, Hartwell, and Kuykendall, *History 31st Regiment,* 67–68; Grabau, *Ninety-eight Days,* 356.

46. W. R. Eddington Diary, May 19, 1863; Civil War Miscellaneous Collection, USAMHI.

47. Bering and Montgomery, *History of the Forty-eighth Ohio.*

48. Post, ed., *Soldiers' Letters,* 204–6; Tunnard, *A Southern Record,* 206; W. R. Eddington Diary, May 19, 1863, Civil War Miscellaneous Collection, USAMHI; Wiley, *Civil War Diary,* 49.

49. Grabau, *Ninety-eight Days,* 358; Shea and Winschel, *Vicksburg Is the Key,* 146.

50. John M. Roberts Reminiscences, IHS.

51. *OR,* vol. 24, pt. 2, p. 257; John M. Roberts Reminiscences, IHS; Crooker, Nourse, and Brown, *The 55th Illinois,* 235–36.

52. *OR,* vol. 24, pt. 2, pp. 257, 268; Crooker, Nourse, and Brown, *The 55th Illinois,* 235–36.

53. *OR,* vol. 24, pt. 2, pp. 257, 264, 268; John M. Roberts Reminiscences, IHS.

54. John M. Roberts Reminiscences, IHS.

55. *OR*, vol. 24, pt. 2, p. 268.

56. Ibid.

57. Ibid.

58. Crooker, Nourse, and Brown, *The 55th Illinois*, 237–39; Shea and Winschel, *Vicksburg Is the Key*, 147.

59. *OR*, vol. 24, pt. 2, p. 268; Crooker, Nourse, and Brown, *The 55th Illinois*, 235–36.

60. John M. Roberts Reminiscences, IHS.

61. Grant, *Personal Memoirs*, 1:530–31.

62. Sherman, *Memoirs*, 351.

63. Grant, *Personal Memoirs*, 1:530.

64. Dunbar, *History of the Ninety-third Regiment; OR*, vol. 24, pt. 2, p. 251; Abram J. Vanauken Diary, May 20, 1863, ISHL; Jessee, *Civil War Diaries*, chap. 3, pp. 20–21; Elliott, *History of the Thirty-third Regiment*, 42; Scheel, *Rain, Mud & Swamps*, 123–24; Campbell, *The Union Must Stand*, 99.

65. Tunnard, *A Southern Record*, 207; Bryner, *Bugle Echoes*, 84; Scheel, *Rain, Mud & Swamps*, 123–24; Campbell, *The Union Must Stand*, 99; Holcomb, ed., *Southern Sons, Northern Soldiers*, 69.

66. C. E. Lippincott to Newton Bateman, June 15, 1863, Newton Bateman Papers, ISHL.

CHAPTER TWENTY-THREE: THE GREAT ASSAULT

1. Jessee, *Civil War Diaries*, chap. 3, p. 22; Isaac Vanderwarker Diary, May 21, 1863, Civil War Miscellaneous Collection, USAMHI.

2. Jessee, *Civil War Diaries*, chap. 3, p. 22.

3. Edward P. Stanfield to "Dear Father," May 26, 1863, Edward P. Stanfield Papers, IHS.

4. George O. Smith Reminiscences, George O. Smith Papers, ISHL.

5. Isaac Vanderwarker Diary, May 21, 1863, Civil War Miscellaneous Collection, USAMHI.

6. Tunnard, *A Southern Record*, 207–8; Scheel, *Rain, Mud & Swamps*, 125.

7. Grant, *Personal Memoirs*, 1:531; Simon, ed., *The Papers of Ulysses S. Grant*, 8:246.

8. Enoch Weiss Reminiscences, p. 23, Civil War Miscellaneous Collection, USAMHI; Edward P. Stanfield to "Dear Father," May 26, 1863, Edward P. Stanfield Papers, IHS.

9. *OR*, vol. 24, pt. 2, pp. 251–52; Kircher, *A German in the Yankee Fatherland*, 99–100.

10. *OR*, vol. 24, pt. 2, pp. 251–52; Kircher, *A German in the Yankee Fatherland*, 99–100.

11. Robert Bruce Hoadley to "Dear Cousin," May 29, 1863, Robert Bruce Hoadley Papers, PLDU.

12. Kircher, *A German in the Yankee Fatherland*, 109.

13. *OR*, vol. 24, pt. 2, pp. 251–52; Kircher, *A German in the Yankee Fatherland*, 99–100.

14. R. W. Burt to "Dear Wife," May 23, 1863, R. W. Burt Letters, WHMC.

15. *OR*, vol. 24, pt. 2, pp. 251–52, 254; Kircher, *A German in the Yankee Fatherland*, 99–100; Bearss, *Unvexed to the Sea*, 864.

16. Sherman, *Memoirs*, 351.

17. Shea and Winschel, *Vicksburg Is the Key*, 149; Sherman, *Memoirs*, 351; *OR*, vol. 24, pt. 2, pp. 275, 280.

18. *OR*, vol. 24, pt. 2, p. 282; Crooker, Nourse, and Brown, *The 55th Illinois*, 244.

19. Crooker, Nourse, and Brown, *The 55th Illinois*, 244–46; *OR*, vol. 24, pt. 2, p. 273.

20. Crooker, Nourse, and Brown, *The 55th Illinois*, 244–46; *OR*, vol. 24, pt. 2, pp. 257, 273.

21. *OR*, vol. 24, pt. 2, p. 282; Kountz et al., *History of the 37th Regiment*, 21.

22. *OR*, vol. 24, pt. 2, p. 257; Kountz et al., *History of the 37th Regiment*, 21–22.

23. *OR*, vol. 24, pt. 2, p. 258.

24. Ibid., p. 269.

25. Ibid., p. 273.

26. Crooker, Nourse, and Brown, *The 55th Illinois*, 244–46.

27. Shea and Winschel, *Vicksburg Is the Key*, 149.

28. *OR*, vol. 24, pt. 2, p. 273; Crooker, Nourse, and Brown, *The 55th Illinois*, 244–46.

29. Carl Dean Gebhardt, "The Eleventh Illinois Infantry Regiment in the Civil War," M.A. thesis, Western Illinois University, 1968, 116.

30. Post, ed., *Soldiers' Letters*, 213–14.

31. *OR*, vol. 24, pt. 1, pp. 710, 719.

32. Ibid., p. 719; Jessee, *Civil War Diaries*, chap. 3, p. 22; Gould D. Molineaux Diary, May 22, 1863, Special Collections, ACL.

33. Jessee, *Civil War Diaries*, chap. 3, p. 22.

34. Gould D. Molineaux Diary, May 22, 1863, Special Collections, ACL.

35. Campbell, *The Union Must Stand*, 99–100.

36. *OR*, vol. 24, pt. 1, p. 719; Jessee, *Civil War Diaries*, chap. 3, p. 22.

37. *OR*, vol. 24, pt. 1, p. 719; Jessee, *Civil War Diaries*, chap. 3, p. 22; Gould D. Molineaux Diary, May 22, 1863, Special Collections, ACL.

38. *OR*, vol. 24, pt. 1, p. 719; Shea and Winschel, *Vicksburg Is the Key*, 149–50; Jessee, *Civil War Diaries*, chap. 3, p. 22; Campbell, *The Union Must Stand*, 99–100.

39. Gould D. Molineaux Diary, May 22, 1863, Special Collections, ACL.

40. *OR*, vol. 24, pt. 1, p. 710; Wimer Bedford Diary, May 22, 1863, LC.

41. Grabau, *Ninety-eight Days*, 376.

42. Peirce and Peirce, *Dear Catharine, Dear Taylor*, 118.

43. Elliott, *History of the Thirty-third Regiment*, 42, 242.

44. Ibid., 42.

45. George S. Marks Reminiscences, Civil War Miscellaneous Collection, USAMHI.

46. Elliott, *History of the Thirty-third Regiment*, 42, 243.

47. Ibid., 243.

48. Ibid., 44; Bearss, *Unvexed to the Sea*, 828–29.

49. Elliott, *History of the Thirty-third Regiment*, 42, 243.

50. Morris, "The Charge at Vicksburg," *National Tribune*, April 16, 1885, p. 3.

51. Campbell, *The Union Must Stand*, 99–100.

52. Elliott, *History of the Thirty-third Regiment*, 218.

53. *OR*, vol. 24, pt. 1, pp. 154–55; pt. 2, p. 140; Jones, *Reminiscences of the Twenty-second Iowa*, 38; Bearrs, *Unvexed to the Sea*, 825–27.

54. *OR*, vol. 24, pt. 1, pp. 154–55; pt. 2, p. 140; Jones, *Reminiscences of the Twenty-second Iowa*, 38; Frederick, "That Iowa Sergeant," *National Tribune*, August 14, 1884, p. 3; Bearrs, *Unvexed to the Sea*, 825–27.

55. Wilkin, "Vicksburg," in *MOLLUS*, 13:231–32.

56. Jones, *Reminiscences of the Twenty-second Iowa*, 38–39.

57. Wiley, *Civil War Diary*, 50–51.

58. *OR*, vol. 24, pt. 1, p. 172.

59. Ibid.; pt. 2, pp. 232, 240.

60. Ibid., pt. 1, p. 172.

61. Ibid., pp. 55–56; Jenney, "Personal Recollections of Vicksburg," in *MOLLUS*, 12:261; Sherman, *Memoirs*, 352.

62. Grant, *Personal Memoirs*, 1:531; Sherman, *Memoirs*, 352; *OR*, vol. 24, pt. 1, pp. 55–56.

63. J. W. Greenman Diary, May 20, 1862, MDAH.

64. Bryner, *Bugle Echoes*, 85.

65. Ibid., 85–86; Burdette, *The Drums of the 47th*, 80.

66. J. W. Greenman Diary, May 23, 1862, MDAH.

67. Bryner, *Bugle Echoes,* 85–86.

68. Ibid., 86; Burdette, *The Drums of the 47th,* 68–69; J. W. Greenman Diary, May 23, 1862, MDAH.

69. Bryner, *Bugle Echoes,* 86; Burdette, *The Drums of the 47th,* 68–69.

70. Crooker, Nourse, and Brown, *The 55th Illinois,* 244.

71. *OR,* vol. 24, pt. 1, p. 711.

72. Luther H. Cowan to "Dear Harriet," March 18, 1863, Luther H. Cowan Papers, WHS.

73. Crummer, *With Grant,* 111–12.

74. Post, ed., *Soldiers' Letters,* 263–72; Crummer, *With Grant,* 112.

75. Crummer, *With Grant,* 112–13.

76. Ibid.; Kingsley Olds to "Dear Father," May 25, 1863, Luther H. Cowan Papers, WHS; *OR,* vol. 24, pt. 1, p. 711.

77. Bearss, *Unvexed to the Sea,* 847; Dunbar, *History of the Ninety-third Regiment;* Henry G. Hicks, "The Campaign and Capture of Vicksburg," in *MOLLUS,* 31:103.

78. Dunbar, *History of the Ninety-third Regiment,* http://www.illinoiscivilwar.org/cw93-hist-ch4c.html.

79. Campbell, *The Union Must Stand,* 99–100.

80. Ibid.

81. Bearss, *Unvexed to the Sea,* 851–52; Dunbar, *History of the Ninety-third Regiment,* http://www.illinoiscivilwar.org/cw93-hist-ch4c.html; Hicks, "The Campaign and Capture of Vicksburg," in *MOLLUS,* 31:103; Campbell, *The Union Must Stand,* 99–100.

82. Bearss, *Unvexed to the Sea,* 851–52; Dunbar, *History of the Ninety-third Regiment,* http://www.illinoiscivilwar.org/cw93-hist-ch4c.html; Hicks, "The Campaign and Capture of Vicksburg," in *MOLLUS,* 31:103; Bartholomew, "The Charge at Vicksburg," *National Tribune,* November 27, 1884, p. 3.

83. *OR,* vol. 24, pt. 1, p. 733.

84. Hicks, "The Campaign and Capture of Vicksburg," in *MOLLUS,* 31:104.

CHAPTER TWENTY-FOUR: VICKSBURG SIEGE

1. Jones, *Reminiscences of the Twenty-Second Iowa,* 38.

2. W. R. Eddington Reminiscences, Civil War Miscellaneous Collection, USAMHI.

3. Hicks, "The Campaign and Capture of Vicksburg," in *MOLLUS,* 31:103–4.

4. Elliott, *History of the Thirty-third Regiment,* 42.

5. Ibid.

6. George O. Smith Reminiscences, George O. Smith Papers, ISHL.

7. Jones, *Reminiscences of the Twenty-second Iowa,* 39–40.

8. Kingsley Olds to "Dear Father," May 25, 1863, Luther H. Cowan Papers, WHS.

9. Bartholomew, "The Charge at Vicksburg," *National Tribune,* November 27, 1884, p. 3.

10. Ritner, *Love and Valor,* 168–70.

11. Ibid., 171–72; 181–82.

12. Edward P. Stanfield to "Dear Father," May 26, 1863, Edward P. Stanfield Papers, IHS.

13. Ankeny, *Kiss Josey for Me,* 154–55.

14. Edward H. Ingraham to "Dear Aunt," May 29, 1863, E. H. and D. G. Ingraham Papers, ISHL.

15. Jenney, "Personal Recollections of Vicksburg," in *MOLLUS,* 12:261.

16. Sanborn, "The Campaign Against Vicksburg," in *MOLLUS,* 27:134.

17. Morris, "The Charge at Vicksburg," *National Tribune,* April 16, 1885, p. 3.

18. Ibid.; Campbell, *The Union Must Stand*, 99–100.

19. Elliott, *History of the Thirty-third Regiment*, 45.

20. Aurelius Lyman Voorhis Diary, May 25, IHS; Jackson, *Some of the Boys*, 97–98; Miller, *The Struggle for the Life of the Republic*, 97; Gould D. Molineaux Diary, May 25, 1863, Special Collections, ACL; Wiley, *Civil War Diary*, 53.

21. Jackson, *Some of the Boys*, 97–98.

22. David S. Morgan to "Dear Father and Mother Decker," June 11, 1863, http://www.kiva.net/~bjohnson/DSMintro.htm.

23. Willison, *Reminiscences of a Boy's Service*, 61–62.

24. Israel M. Ritter Diary, May 25, 1863, Civil War Miscellaneous Collection, USAMHI; Joseph B. Williamson Diary, May 26, 1863, ISHL; Campbell, *The Union Must Stand*, 105.

25. David W. Poak to "Dear Sister," June 28, 1863, David W. Poak Papers, ISHL.

26. Edward H. Ingraham to "Dear Aunt," May 29, 1863, E. H. and D. G. Ingraham Papers, ISHL.

27. Peirce and Peirce, *Dear Catharine, Dear Taylor*, 115–16.

28. Jackson, *Some of the Boys*, 97–98.

29. Simpson, *Ulysses S. Grant*, 210; Kiper, *McClernand*, 168.

30. *OR*, vol. 24, pt. 1, pp. 165–66.

31. Ibid., pp. 161–63.

32. Jenney, "Personal Recollections of Vicksburg," in *MOLLUS*, 12:262.

33. *OR*, vol. 24, pt. 1, pp. 162–63.

34. Ibid., p. 159.

35. Ibid., p. 162.

36. Ibid., p. 164.

37. Jenney, "Personal Recollections of Vicksburg," in *MOLLUS*, 12:263–64.

38. *OR*, vol. 24, pt. 1, pp. 164–65.

39. Bearss, *Unvexed to the Sea*, 879–80; Jenney, in *MOLLUS*, 12:262–63.

40. Jenney, in *MOLLUS*, 12:263.

41. Kiper, *McClernand*, 272; Edward P. Stanfield to "Dear Father," June 22, 1863, Edward Stanfield Letters, IHS.

42. *OR*, vol. 24, pt. 1, p. 165; Jenney, in *MOLLUS*, 12:263.

43. Jenney, in *MOLLUS*, 12:262–63.

44. *OR*, vol. 24, pt. 1, p. 166.

45. Ibid., pp. 159–86.

CHAPTER TWENTY-FIVE: TRIUMPH AT VICKSBURG

1. Hickenlooper, "The Vicksburg Mine," in *MOLLUS*, 3:539–41; Bearss, *Unvexed to the Sea*, 908–9.

2. Hickenlooper, "The Vicksburg Mine," in *MOLLUS*, 3:539–41; Strong, "The Campaign Against Vicksburg," in *MOLLUS*, 11:338; Bearss, *Unvexed to the Sea*, 909.

3. Bearss, *Unvexed to the Sea*, 909.

4. Force, "Personal Recollections of the Vicksburg Campaign," in *MOLLUS*, 1:307; Hickenlooper, "The Vicksburg Mine," in *MOLLUS*, 3:539–41; Bearss, *Unvexed to the Sea*, 909–10.

5. Jessee, *Civil War Diaries*, chap. 3, p. 24; Campbell, *The Union Must Stand*, 105; Geer, *Civil War Diary*, 105; Tunnard, *A Southern Record*, 216.

6. Tunnard, *A Southern Record*, 217; Geer, *Civil War Diary*, 105; Campbell, *The Union Must Stand*, 105; Jessee, *Civil War Diaries*, chap. 3, p. 24; David W. Poak to "Sister Sadie," June 12, 1863, David W. Poak Papers, ISHL; Hickenlooper, "The Vicksburg Mine," in *MOLLUS*, 3:539–41; Bearss, *Unvexed to the Sea*, 911.

7. Tunnard, *A Southern Record*, 219–20; Campbell, *The Union Must Stand*, 106.

8. Bearss, *Unvexed to the Sea*, 911.

9. Ibid.

10. David W. Poak to "Dear Sister," June 28, 1863, David W. Poak Papers, ISHL.

11. Edward P. Stanfield to "Dear Father," June 22, 1863, Edward P. Stanfield Papers, IHS; David W. Poak to "Dear Sister," June 28, 1863, David W. Poak Papers, ISHL; Campbell, *The Union Must Stand*, 106; Bearss, *Unvexed to the Sea*, 912.

12. Jessee, *Civil War Diaries*, chap. 3, p. 26; Tunnard, *A Southern Record*, 224; Campbell, *The Union Must Stand*, 107; Geer, *Civil War Diary*, 108; Crummer, *With Grant*, 155–56; Roster of Company A, 45th Illinois, Illinois Civil War Project, http://www.rootsweb.com/~ilcivilw/r050/045-a-in.htm.

13. Edward P. Stanfield to "Dear Father," June 22, 1863, Edward P. Stanfield Papers, IHS; Force, "Personal Recollections of the Vicksburg Campaign," in *MOLLUS*, 1:307; Tunnard, *A Southern Record*, 227; Bearss, *Unvexed to the Sea*, 912–13.

14. Tunnard, *A Southern Record*, 218–19; Bearss, *Unvexed to the Sea*, 913.

15. Jessee, *Civil War Diaries*, chap. 3, p. 26; Hickenlooper, "The Vicksburg Mine," in *MOLLUS*, 3:541; Bearss, *Unvexed to the Sea*, 913.

16. Hickenlooper, "The Vicksburg Mine," in *MOLLUS*, 3:541–42; Bearss, *Unvexed to the Sea*, 913–14.

17. Hickenlooper, "The Vicksburg Mine," in *MOLLUS*, 3:542; Bearss, *Unvexed to the Sea*, 914–15.

18. Grant, *Personal Memoirs*, 1:551; Bearss, *Unvexed to the Sea*, 915.

19. Hickenlooper, "The Vicksburg Mine," in *MOLLUS*, 3:542; Strong, "The Campaign Against Vicksburg," in *MOLLUS*, 11:340; Bearss, *Unvexed to the Sea*, 915–18.

20. Jackson, *Some of the Boys*, 107–8; Strong, "The Campaign Against Vicksburg," in *MOLLUS*, 11:339; Crooker, Nourse, and Brown, *The 55th Illinois*, 252; Wiley, *Civil War Diary*, 58.

21. Hickenlooper, "The Vicksburg Mine," in *MOLLUS*, 3:542; Strong, "The Campaign Against Vicksburg," in *MOLLUS*, 11:340; Post, ed., *Soldiers' Letters*, 263–64; Crummer, *With Grant*, 136–38; Crooker, Nourse, and Brown, *The 55th Illinois*, 252; Wiley, *Civil War Diary;* Jackson, *Some of the Boys*, 107–8; William M. Reid Diary, June 25, 1863, ISHL; Aurelius Lyman Voorhis Diary, June 25, 1863, IHS; Nathan G. Dye to "Dear friends," June 26, 1863, Nathan G. Dye Papers, PLDU; Bearss, *Unvexed to the Sea*, 918.

22. Crummer, *With Grant*, 138; Bearss, *Unvexed to the Sea*, 918–19.

23. Post, ed., *Soldiers' Letters*, 263–67; Bearss, *Unvexed to the Sea*, 919–21; M. M. Yeakel to the editor of the *Warren (Illinois) Independent*, August 31, 1863, Luther H. Cowan Papers, WHS.

24. Hickenlooper, "The Vicksburg Mine," in *MOLLUS*, Morris, Hartwell, and Kuykendall, *History 31st Regiment*, 73–74; Bearss, *Unvexed to the Sea*, 919–21.

25. *OR*, vol. 24, pt. 2, p. 249; Strong, "The Campaign Against Vicksburg," in *MOLLUS*, 11:341–42; Grant, *Personal Memoirs*, 1:552; Morris, Hartwell, and Kuykendall, *History 31st Regiment*, 73–74; Crummer, *With Grant*, 139; Bearss, *Unvexed to the Sea*, 921.

26. Crummer, *With Grant*, 167–68.

27. Bearss, *Unvexed to the Sea*, 919.

28. Tunnard, *A Southern Record*, 227; Bearss, *Unvexed to the Sea*, 920–21.

29. Crummer, *With Grant*, 142; *OR*, vol. 24, pt. 2, p. 294.

30. Strong, "The Campaign Against Vicksburg," in *MOLLUS*, 11:342.

31. *OR*, vol. 24, pt. 2, p. 294.

32. Bearss, *Unvexed to the Sea*, 925.

33. Tunnard, *A Southern Record*, 232; Bearss, *Unvexed to the Sea*, 927–28.

34. Robert Ridge Diary, July 1, 1863, ISHL; Jessee, *Civil War Diaries*, chap. 3, p. 27; Grant, *Personal Memoirs*, 1:552; Bearss, *Unvexed to the Sea*, 928.

35. Tunnard, *A Southern Record*, 234; Bearss, *Unvexed to the Sea*, 929.

36. Tunnard, *A Southern Record*, 234; Bearss, *Unvexed to the Sea*, 929.

37. Bearss, *Unvexed to the Sea*, 929.

38. Grant, *Personal Memoirs*, 1:553, 555; Jenney, "Personal Recollections of Vicksburg," i MOLLUS, 12:264; Crooker, Nourse, and Brown, *The 55th Illinois*, 252; Hickenlooper, "Th Vicksburg Mine," in MOLLUS, 3:542.

39. Craven, "Vicksburg: The Offer to Surrender," *National Tribune*, October 30, 1884, p. Tressel, "The Surrender of Vicksburg," *National Tribune*, November 27, 1884, p. 3.

40. *OR*, vol. 24, pt. 1, p. 114.

41. Ibid.; Grant, *Personal Memoirs*, 1:557–58.

42. Bringhurst and Swigart, *History of the Forty-sixth Regiment*, 66; Jessee, *Civil War Diaries* chap. 3, p. 27; Peirce and Peirce, *Dear Catharine, Dear Taylor*, 125; William M. Reid Diary July 3, 1863, ISHL.

43. Jessee, *Civil War Diaries*, chap. 3, p. 27; Aurelius Lyman Voorhis Diary, July 3, 1863, IHS; Peirce and Peirce, *Dear Catharine, Dear Taylor*, 125; Joseph B. Williamson Diary, July 3, 1863, ISHL.

44. Strong, "The Campaign Against Vicksburg," in MOLLUS, 11:344; Tunnard, *A Southern Record*, 236–37.

45. Strong, "The Campaign Against Vicksburg," in MOLLUS, 11:345; Morris, Hartwell, and Kuykendall, *History 31st Regiment*, 76.

46. Strong, "The Campaign Against Vicksburg," in MOLLUS, 11:345–46; *OR*, vol. 24, pt. 1, p. 114; Grant, *Personal Memoirs*, 1:559.

47. Jessee, *Civil War Diaries*, chap. 3, p. 27.

48. Bringhurst and Swigart, *History of the Forty-sixth Regiment*, 66; Miller, *The Struggle for the Life of the Republic*, 101.

49. *OR*, vol. 24, pt. 1, p. 115; Grant, *Personal Memoirs*, 1:559–64.

50. Grant, *Personal Memoirs*, 1:559–64; *OR*, vol. 24, pt. 1, p. 115.

51. Strong, "The Campaign Against Vicksburg," in MOLLUS, 11:349–50.

52. Ibid., 350; Bringhurst and Swigart, *History of the Forty-sixth Regiment*, 66; Peirce and Peirce, *Dear Catharine, Dear Taylor*, 124; Holcomb, ed., *Southern Sons, Northern Soldiers*, 81.

53. Strong, "The Campaign Against Vicksburg," in MOLLUS, 11:351; *OR*, vol. 24, pt. 3, p. 476; Post, ed., *Soldiers' Letters*, 263–72. Post incorrectly identifies the author of this letter as Stephen A. Rollins of the 95th Illinois, but it was almost certainly written by John A. (or H.) Rollins of the 45th.

54. Strong, "The Campaign Against Vicksburg," in MOLLUS, 11:351.

55. Ibid., 351–52.

56. Strong, "The Campaign Against Vicksburg," in MOLLUS, 11:352–54; Crooker, Nourse, and Brown, *The 55th Illinois*, 254; Swards, "My Campaigning with the Army of the Tennessee," in MOLLUS, 55:78–79; Jenney, "With Sherman and Grant from Memphis to Chattanooga—A Reminiscence," in MOLLUS, 13:206; Tunnard, *A Southern Record*, 239.

57. Crooker, Nourse, and Brown, *The 55th Illinois*, 254; Peirce and Peirce, *Dear Catharine, Dear Taylor*, 124; William M. Reid Diary, July 4, 1863, ISHL; Post, ed., *Soldiers' Letters*, 343–44; Tunnard, *A Southern Record*, 240; Bringhurst and Swigart, *History of the Forty-sixth Regiment*, 66.

58. Crummer, *With Grant*, 159; Jenney, "Personal Recollections of Vicksburg," in MOLLUS, 12:265; Bennett, *Narrative of the Great Revival*, 319–20; Tunnard, *A Southern Record*, 240.

59. Ritner, *Love and Valor*, 198–99.

60. "Glorious News," *Warren (Illinois) Independent*, July 9, 1863.

61. Lyftogt, *From Blue Mills to Columbia*, 101.

CHAPTER TWENTY-SIX: CHATTANOOGA

1. Grant, *Personal Memoirs,* 1:578–82.
2. Ibid., 582–83; Sherman, *Memoirs,* 372–73.
3. Sherman, *Memoirs,* 373–76; Upson, *With Sherman to the Sea,* 70–71.
4. Sherman, *Memoirs,* 378–83.
5. Scheel, *Rain, Mud & Swamps,* 179; Sherman, *Memoirs,* 383; Grant, *Personal Memoirs,* 2:45.
6. Sherman, *Memoirs,* 385; Grant, *Personal Memoirs,* 2:47.
7. Jabez Banbury Diary, November 4–6, 1863, Civil War Miscellaneous Collection, USAMHI; Scheel, *Rain, Mud & Swamps,* 182; Crooker, Nourse, and Brown, *The 55th Illinois,* 277; Campbell, *The Union Must Stand,* 129–30.
8. Enoch Weiss Reminiscences, Civil War Miscellaneous Collection, USAMHI; Jabez Banbury Diary, November 4–6, 1863, Civil War Miscellaneous Collection, USAMHI; Scheel, *Rain, Mud & Swamps,* 182; Crooker, Nourse, and Brown, *The 55th Illinois,* 277; Campbell, *The Union Must Stand,* 129–30.
9. Connelly, *History of the Seventieth Ohio Regiment,* 56; Jabez Banbury Diary, November 10, 1863, Civil War Miscellaneous Collection, USAMHI; Sherman, *Memoirs,* 386–87.
10. W. G. McElrea Diary, November 13, 1863, Civil War Miscellaneous Collection, USAMHI.
11. Campbell, *The Union Must Stand,* 130–31; Crooker, Nourse, and Brown, *The 55th Illinois,* 278; Sherman, *Memoirs,* 386–87.
12. *OR,* vol. 31, pt. 2, p. 571; Sherman, *Memoirs,* 387.
13. Sherman, *Memoirs,* 387.
14. Ibid., 388; Grant, *Personal Memoirs,* 2:58.
15. Sherman, *Memoirs,* 388–89.
16. Campbell, *The Union Must Stand,* 130–31; Scheel, *Rain, Mud & Swamps,* 183–84; Sherman, *Memoirs,* 389; Grant, *Personal Memoirs,* 2:59.
17. Campbell, *The Union Must Stand,* 221–27.
18. Bull, *Soldiering,* 98.
19. Sherman, *Memoirs,* 389.
20. W. G. McElrea Diary, November 16, 1863, Civil War Miscellaneous Collection, USAMHI.
21. Ritner, *Love and Valor,* 238–39.
22. Campbell, *The Union Must Stand,* 221–27; Crooker, Nourse, and Brown, *The 55th Illinois,* 278; Sherman, *Memoirs,* 281.
23. Sherman, *Memoirs,* 389; Grant, *Personal Memoirs,* 2:65–66.
24. Dunbar, *History of the Ninety-third Regiment.*
25. Jabez Banbury Diary, November 20–21, 1863, Civil War Miscellaneous Collection, USAMHI; Campbell, *The Union Must Stand,* 133–34, 233–37; Henry T. Card to "Dear Brother & Sister," November 22, 1863, Henry T. Card Papers, Civil War Miscellaneous Collection, USAMHI.
26. Crooker, Nourse, and Brown, *The 55th Illinois,* 281–82; *OR,* vol. 31, pt. 2, p. 572.
27. Crooker, Nourse, and Brown, *The 55th Illinois,* 282–84; Kountz et al., *History of the 37th Regiment,* 31; *OR,* vol. 31, pt. 2, p. 572.
28. Kountz et al., *History of the 37th Regiment,* 26.
29. Crooker, Nourse, and Brown, *The 55th Illinois,* 282–84; *OR,* vol. 31, pt. 2, p. 572; Jabez Banbury Diary, Civil War Miscellaneous Collection, USAMHI; Campbell, *The Union Must Stand,* 134–36.
30. *OR,* vol. 31, pt. 2, p. 573.
31. Ibid.; Crooker, Nourse, and Brown, *The 55th Illinois,* 282–84.
32. *OR,* vol. 31, pt. 2, p. 573; Campbell, *The Union Must Stand,* 34–36, 224–27; Connelly, *History of the Seventieth Ohio Regiment,* 60–61.

33. Taylor, *Tom Taylor's Civil War*, 85.
34. Crooker, Nourse, and Brown, *The 55th Illinois*, 282–84; *OR*, vol. 31, pt. 2, pp. 573, 629.
35. *OR*, vol. 31, pt. 2, p. 646; Campbell, *The Union Must Stand*, 224–27; Taylor, *Tom Taylor Civil War*, 84–87.
36. Taylor, *Tom Taylor's Civil War*, 84–87; Crooker, Nourse, and Brown, *The 55th Illinois*, 285
37. *OR*, vol. 31, pt. 2, pp. 43–44.
38. Connelly, *History of the Seventieth Ohio Regiment*, 63; Taylor, *Tom Taylor's Civil War*, 84–8; Crooker, Nourse, and Brown, *The 55th Illinois*, 285; Enoch Weiss Reminiscences, Civil Wa Miscellaneous Collection, USAMHI.
39. Crooker, Nourse, and Brown, *The 55th Illinois*, 287; *OR*, vol. 31, pt. 2, p. 574.
40. *OR*, vol. 31, pt. 2, p. 574.
41. Ibid., p. 629; Taylor, *Tom Taylor's Civil War*, 87–90.
42. *OR*, vol. 31, pt. 2, p. 629; Taylor, *Tom Taylor's Civil War*, 87–90.
43. *OR*, vol. 31, pt. 2, pp. 574, 629, 636; Taylor, *Tom Taylor's Civil War*, 87–90; John T. Hunt "Civil War Reminiscences of Dr. John T. Hunt, Macedonia, Illinois, Company A, 40th Illinois Volunteer Infantry," in "The Yesterdays of Hamilton County," http://www.carolyar. com/Illinois/Hunt-Part1.htm.
44. Taylor, *Tom Taylor's Civil War*, 87–90; "Civil War Reminiscences of Dr. John T. Hunt."
45. John S. Kountz et al., *History of the 37th Regiment*, 28.
46. Taylor, *Tom Taylor's Civil War*, 87–90; "Civil War Reminiscences of Dr. John T. Hunt."
47. *OR*, vol. 31, pt. 2, p. 636.
48. Ibid., pp. 575, 636.
49. Ibid., p. 633.
50. Ibid.
51. Ibid., p. 634.
52. Ibid.
53. Ibid., pp. 634, 643–44.
54. Ibid., p. 652; Jabez Banbury Diary, November 25, 1863, Civil War Miscellaneous Collection, USAMHI; Campbell, *The Union Must Stand*, 136–38.
55. *OR*, vol. 31, pt. 2, p. 652; Campbell, *The Union Must Stand*, 136–38; Jabez Banbury Diary, November 25, 1863, Civil War Miscellaneous Collection, USAMHI.
56. *OR*, vol. 31, pt. 2, p. 653; Dunbar, *History of the Ninety-third Regiment*, http://www. illinoiscivilwar.org/cw93-hist-ch5d.html.
57. *OR*, vol. 31, pt. 2, p. 655; Dunbar, *History of the Ninety-Third Regiment*, http://www. illinoiscivilwar.org/cw93-hist-ch5d.html.
58. *OR*, vol. 31, pt. 2, pp. 575, 653, 655; Jabez Banbury Diary, November 25, 1863, Civil War Miscellaneous Collection, USAMHI; Dunbar, *History of the Ninety-third Regiment*, http:// www.illinoiscivilwar.org/cw93-hist-ch5d.html.
59. Taylor, *Tom Taylor's Civil War*, 87–90.
60. *OR*, vol. 31, pt. 2, p. 576.
61. Cozzens, *The Shipwreck of Their Hopes*, 364.
62. Grant, *Personal Memoirs*, 2:90–92; *OR*, vol. 31, pt. 2, p. 577.
63. Grant, *Personal Memoirs*, 2:92–93; *OR*, vol. 31, pt. 2, p. 577.
64. *OR*, vol. 31, pt. 2, p. 577–81; Sherman, *Memoirs*, 393–94.

CHAPTER TWENTY-SEVEN: MERIDIAN

1. Grant, *Personal Memoirs*, 2:107; Sherman, *Memoirs*, 413.
2. Grant, *Personal Memoirs*, 2:107; Sherman, *Memoirs*, 413–17; *OR*, vol. 32, pt. 1, p. 174.

3. Sherman, *Memoirs*, 417–18; *OR*, vol. 32, pt. 1, p. 174.

4. Sherman, *Memoirs*, 418–19.

5. David W. Poak to "Dear Sister," February 1, 1864, David W. Poak Papers, ISHL.

6. William W. McCarty Diary, February 2, 1864, Civil War Miscellaneous Collection, USAMHI; Post, ed., *Soldiers' Letters*, 323.

7. David W. Poak to "Dear Sister," February 1, 1864, David W. Poak Papers, ISHL.

8. Sherman, *Memoirs*, 419; *OR*, vol. 32, pt. 1, pp. 172, 175; Foster, "Dress Rehearsal for Hard War," 37.

9. Jessee, *Civil War Diaries*, chap. 5, p. 6; Sherman, *Memoirs*, 419; Rood, *Story of the Service of Company E*, 242; *OR*, vol. 32, pt. 2, p. 67.

10. Rood, *Story of the Service of Company E*, 242; *OR*, vol. 32, pt. 1, p. 175.

11. Sherman, *Memoirs*, 419; Jessee, *Civil War Diaries*, chap. 5, p. 6.

12. Barber, *Army Memoirs*, 135.

13. Jessee, *Civil War Diaries*, chap. 5, p. 8.

14. Ibid.

15. Ibid., p. 6.

16. William W. McCarty Diary, February 5, 1864, Civil War Miscellaneous Collection, USAMHI; Rood, *Story of the Service of Company E*, 243–44; Jessee, *Civil War Diaries*, chap. 5, p. 6.

17. Sherman, *Memoirs*, 419.

18. Rood, *Story of the Service of Company E*, 244–45; Jessee, *Civil War Diaries*, chap. 5, p. 7; William W. McCarty Diary, February 6, 1864, Civil War Miscellaneous Collection, USAMHI.

19. Jessee, *Civil War Diaries*, chap. 5, p. 7; Stephen H. Smith Diary, February 8, 1864, Civil War Miscellaneous Collection, USAMHI.

20. Jessee, *Civil War Diaries*, chap. 5, p. 7.

21. Sherman, *Memoirs*, 419; Rood, *Story of the Service of Company E*, 244–45; Jessee, *Civil War Diaries*, chap. 5, p. 7.

22. Jessee, *Civil War Diaries*, chap. 5, p. 8.

23. Rood, *Story of the Service of Company E*, 245.

24. Barber, *Army Memoirs*, 138.

25. *OR*, vol. 32, pt. 1, p. 175.

26. Sherman, *Memoirs*, 420; *OR*, vol. 32, pt. 1, p. 175.

27. Jessee, *Civil War Diaries*, chap. 5, p. 10.

28. Ibid., pp. 5–11; William W. McCarty Diary, February 15, 1864, Civil War Miscellaneous Collection, USAMHI.

29. Sherman, *Memoirs*, 422–23; *OR*, vol. 32, pt. 1, p. 176.

30. Jessee, *Civil War Diaries*, chap. 5, p. 11.

31. Barber, *Army Memoirs*, 138.

32. Sherman, *Memoirs*, 423; Rood, *Story of the Service of Company E*; Barber, *Army Memoirs*, 138.

33. Barber, *Army Memoirs*, 138.

34. Sherman, *Memoirs*, 423.

35. Ibid., 423–24.

36. Jessee, *Civil War Diaries*, chap. 5, p. 12.

37. Post, ed., *Soldiers' Letters*, 435.

38. Rood, *Story of the Service of Company E*, 250; Post, ed., *Soldiers' Letters*, 435.

39. Post, ed., *Soldiers' Letters*, 435.

40. Barber, *Army Memoirs*, 140; Rood, *Story of the Service of Company E*, 248–49.

41. William W. McCarty Diary, March 3, 1864, Civil War Miscellaneous Collection, USAMHI.

42. Jessee, *Civil War Diaries*, chap. 5, p. 14.

43. *OR*, vol. 32, pt. 1, p. 177.
44. Jessee, *Civil War Diaries*, chap. 5, p. 11.
45. Sherman, *Memoirs*, 424.
46. Post, ed., *Soldiers' Letters*, 338.
47. Willison, *Reminiscences of a Boy's Service*, 87–88.
48. Lyftogt, *From Blue Mills to Columbia*, 115–17.
49. Willison, *Reminiscences of a Boy's Service*, 87–88.
50. Post, ed., *Soldiers' Letters*, 338–39.
51. Simpson and Berlin, eds., *Sherman's Civil War*, 605–6.

CHAPTER TWENTY-EIGHT: RESACA

1. Miller, *The Struggle for the Life of the Republic*, 150–55; J. W. Long Letter, *National Tribune,* September 13, 1888, p. 3; John J. McKee Diary, May 1, 1864, Civil War Miscellaneous Collection, USAMHI.
2. McMurry, *Atlanta 1864*, 50–58.
3. John J. McKee Diary, May 3 and 4, 1864, Civil War Miscellaneous Collection, USAMHI; *OR*, vol. 38, pt. 3, pp. 169, 375; Wright, *A Corporal's Story*, 93; William Allen to "Dear Millie," May 6, 1864, William Anderson Allen Papers, ISHL.
4. *OR*, vol. 38, pt. 4, pp. 41–42; John J. McKee Diary, May 6, 1864, Civil War Miscellaneous Collection, USAMHI.
5. *OR*, vol. 38, pt. 3, pp. 16, 169, 375; Miller, *The Struggle for the Life of the Republic*, 157; John J. McKee Diary, May 7 and 8, 1864, Civil War Miscellaneous Collection, USAMHI; Scheel, *Rain, Mud & Swamps*, 260.
6. *OR*, vol. 38, pt. 3, p. 375.
7. Ibid., pp. 16, 375–76, 397, 452, 457.
8. Barker, *With the Western Sharpshooters*, 9; Baumann, *Arming the Suckers*, 153; Haldeman, "Who Recaptured the De Gres Battery in the Battle Before Atlanta: Other Versions," *National Tribune*, June 28, 1883, p. 3; *OR*, vol. 38, pt. 3, pp. 16, 375–76, 397, 452, 457.
9. *OR*, vol. 38, pt. 3, pp. 16, 375.
10. Ibid., pp. 16, 375–76, 398; Barker, *With the Western Sharpshooters*, 9.
11. *OR*, vol. 38, pt. 3, pp. 16, 375–76.
12. Ibid., pt. 4, p. 105.
13. Ibid., pt. 3, pp. 376, 398.
14. Ibid., pp. 376, 483.
15. Ibid., pp. 377, 457; Miller, *The Struggle for the Life of the Republic*, 157; Wright, *A Corporal's Story*, 96.
16. *OR*, vol. 38, pt. 3, pp. 16–17.
17. Ibid., p. 17; pt. 4, p. 111; Miller, *The Struggle for the Life of the Republic*, 157; John J. McKee Diary, May 10, 1864, Civil War Miscellaneous Collection, USAMHI.
18. *OR*, vol. 38, pt. 4, pp. 125–27, 138–39.
19. Ibid., pt. 3, pp. 398, 421; Miller, *The Struggle for the Life of the Republic*, 157; John J. McKee Diary, May 10 and 11, 1864, Civil War Miscellaneous Collection, USAMHI; Scheel, *Rain, Mud & Swamps*, 262.
20. *OR*, vol. 38, pt. 4, pp. 126–28, 138–39.
21. Ibid., pp. 691–97; Sherman, *Memoirs*, 500.
22. *OR*, vol. 38, pt. 4, pp. 139–40, 152–53, 695–96.
23. Quoted in Castel, *Decision in the West*, 150.
24. Sherman, *Memoirs*, 500.

25. *OR*, vol. 38, pt. 4, pp. 147, 163.

26. Ibid., p. 170.

27. Miller, *The Struggle for the Life of the Republic*, 159–61; *OR*, vol. 38, pt. 3, pp. 124, 141–42, 176–77, 225, 377.

28. *OR*, vol. 38, pt. 3, p. 92.

29. Ibid.

30. Ibid., pp. 92–93, 177.

31. Ibid., pp. 93, 126–27, 177, 190–91; Miller, *The Struggle for the Life of the Republic*, 159; Aldrich, "Resaca: The Part the 26th Iowa Took in That Fight," *National Tribune*, November 13, 1884, p. 3.

32. *OR*, vol. 38, pt. 3, pp. 93–94, 177, 191, 220.

33. Ibid., pp. 93–94, 177, 220; Taylor, *Tom Taylor's Civil War*, 115.

34. *OR*, vol. 38, pt. 3, pp. 93–94, 127.

35. Ibid., pp. 420, 436; Long, "Lay's Ferry," *National Tribune*, September 13, 1888, p. 3.

36. *OR*, vol. 38, pt. 3, pp. 376, 399–400, 439, 447–48, 457, 461; Chamberlin, "The Skirmish Line in the Atlanta Campaign," in *MOLLUS*, 2:185.

37. Wright, *A Corporal's Story*, 99; Long, "Lay's Ferry," *National Tribune*, September 13, 1888, p. 3; John J. McKee Diary, May 14, 1864, Civil War Miscellaneous Collection, USAMHI.

38. Wright, *A Corporal's Story*, 99–100.

39. *OR*, vol. 38, pt. 3, pp. 376, 399–400, 439, 447–48, 457, 461; Wright, *A Corporal's Story*, 100.

40. Wright, *A Corporal's Story*, 101.

41. Chamberlin, "The Skirmish Line in the Atlanta Campaign," in *MOLLUS*, 2:185.

42. *OR*, vol. 38, pt. 3, pp. 376, 400, 447–48, 457, 461.

43. Ibid., pp. 376, 400, 457, 461.

44. Ibid., pp. 376, 400, 457, 461, 465.

45. Ibid., pp. 421, 457–58; pt. 4, p. 196; John J. McKee Diary, May 15, 1864, Civil War Miscellaneous Collection, USAMHI.

46. *OR*, vol. 38, pt. 3, pp. 377–78, 400, 421.

47. Ibid.

48. Ibid., pp. 377–78, 400–1, 422; John J. McKee Diary, May 15, 1864, Civil War Miscellaneous Collection, USAMHI.

49. *OR*, vol. 38, pt. 3, p. 401; pt. 4, pp. 200–1.

50. Ibid., pp. 94, 127, 177.

51. Ibid., pp. 94, 127, 177, 213.

CHAPTER TWENTY-NINE: KENNESAW

1. *OR*, vol. 38, pt., 3, p. 94; Miller, *The Struggle for the Life of the Republic*, 161–62.

2. *OR*, vol. 38, pt. 3, pp. 33, 94, 378–79, 457–58, 461–62, 465; Wright, *A Corporal's Story*, 102–5; John J. McKee Diary, May 16, 1864, Civil War Miscellaneous Collection, USAMHI; Miller, *The Struggle for the Life of the Republic*, 161.

3. *OR*, vol. 38, pt. 3, pp. 33, 186, 205–6; Sherman, *Memoirs*, 503.

4. Sherman, *Memoirs*, 505–6.

5. Ibid., 506, 511; *OR*, vol. 38, pt. 3, pp. 33, 186, 205–6; Wright, *A Corporal's Story*, 105.

6. Sherman, *Memoirs*, 511–12; *OR*, vol. 38, pt. 4, p. 260.

7. *OR*, vol. 38, pt. 4, pp. 260, 273–74; Isaiah T. Dillon to "My ever dear wife," May 20, 1864, Isaiah T. Dillon Papers, ISHL.

8. *OR*, vol. 38, pt. 4, pp. 288–89, 292–93.

9. Ibid., pt. 3, pp. 95, 153, 186–87, 192–93, 205, 220, 379; pt. 4, pp. 308–9; Miller, *The Struggle f* the Life of the Republic, 162; Scheel, *Rain, Mud & Swamps*, 282.

10. *OR*, vol. 38, pt. 3, pp. 95, 129, 153, 187, 379; pt. 4, pp. 312, 315; John J. McKee Diary, Civ War Miscellaneous Collection, USAMHI; Wills, *Army Life*, 248.

11. *OR*, vol. 38, pt. 4, pp. 312–13.

12. Ibid., pt. 3, pp. 95, 129, 153, 187, 193, 220, 379–80; pt. 4, p. 321.

13. Ibid., pt. 3, pp. 95, 129, 153–55, 187, 193, 220, 379–80; Isaiah T. Dillon to "My Dear Sarah," June 2, 1864, Isaiah T. Dillon Papers, ISHL.

14. *OR*, vol. 38, pt. 3, pp. 129–31, 380.

15. Ibid., p. 95; pt. 4, p. 327.

16. Ibid., pt. 3, pp. 95, 278, 315–16; pt. 4, p. 327.

17. Ibid., pt. 3, pp. 95, 278, 316, 332; pt. 4, p. 327.

18. Ibid., pt. 4, pp. 326–27.

19. Ibid., pp. 327–29.

20. Ibid., p. 339.

21. John J. McKee Diary, May 28, 1864, Civil War Miscellaneous Collection, USAMHI.

22. Miller, *The Struggle for the Life of the Republic*, 163.

23. *OR*, vol. 38, pt. 3, p. 279, 366; Upson, *With Sherman to the Sea*, 109; Wills, *Army Life*, 250–51.

24. John A. Logan to Mary Logan, May 30, 1864, John A. Logan Papers, LC; Upson, *With Sherman to the Sea*, 109; Wills, *Army Life*, 250–51.

25. *OR*, vol. 38, pt. 3, pp. 95–96, 179, 316–17, 325, 332, 336.

26. Ibid., pp. 130–31, 155.

27. Ibid., pp. 96, 130–31.

28. John J. McKee Diary, May 28, 1864, Civil War Miscellaneous Collection, USAMHI.

29. Long, *National Tribune*, September 13, 1888, p. 3.

30. John A. Logan to Mary Logan, May 30, 1864, John A. Logan Papers, LC; *OR*, vol. 38, pt. 3, pp. 96, 279.

31. Castel, *Decision in the West*, 243–47.

32. *OR*, vol. 38, pt. 4, pp. 333, 338–40.

33. Ibid., p. 350.

34. Miller, *The Struggle for the Life of the Republic*, 165.

35. Ibid.; Wright, *A Corporal's Story*, 108–9.

36. Wright, *A Corporal's Story*, 108–9.

37. Ankeny, *Kiss Josey for Me*, 220–21.

38. John J. McKee Diary, May 30, 1864, Civil War Miscellaneous Collection, USAMHI.

39. Scheel, *Rain, Mud & Swamps*, 289.

40. *OR*, vol. 38, pt. 3, p. 96; John J. McKee Diary, May 30, 1864, Civil War Miscellaneous Collection, USAMHI; Isaiah T. Dillon to "My Dear Wife," May 30, 1864, Isaiah T. Dillon Papers, ISHL; Miller, *The Struggle for the Life of the Republic*, 165.

41. *OR*, vol. 38, pt. 3, p. 96; Miller, *The Struggle for the Life of the Republic*, 165; Scheel, *Rain, Mud & Swamps*, 289.

42. *OR*, vol. 38, pt. 3, pp. 96, 130; pt. 4, pp. 352, 366, 371–72; Sherman, *Memoirs*, 514.

43. Wright, *A Corporal's Story*, 105.

44. Scheel, *Rain, Mud & Swamps*, 289.

45. *OR*, vol. 38, pt. 3, pp. 96, 130; pt. 4, pp. 352, 366, 371–72; Miller, *The Struggle for the Life of the Republic*, 165–66; Taylor, *Tom Taylor's Civil War*, 124–25.

46. *OR*, vol. 38, pt. 4, pp. 361–62, 371, 385.

47. Ibid., pp. 347, 366–67.

48. Ibid., pt. 3, p. 97; pt. 4, pp. 404, 407; John J. McKee Diary, June 2, 1864, Civil War Miscellaneous Collection, USAMHI; Miller, *The Struggle for the Life of the Republic*, 167–68.

49. *OR*, vol. 38, pt. 3, p. 97; pt. 4, pp. 416–17, 420.

50. Ibid., pt. 4, pp. 415, 441; Castel, *Decision in the West*, 264.

51. *OR*, vol. 38, pt. 4, pp. 424, 427.

52. Ankeny, *Kiss Josey for Me*, 218–19.

53. *OR*, vol. 38, pt. 3, pp. 97, 131; pt. 4, pp. 445–46.

54. Ibid., pp. 97–98, 279, 317, 337; pt. 4, pp. 488–89; Wills, *Army Life*, 261–62.

55. *OR*, vol. 38, pt. 3, pp. 97–98, 279, 317, 337; pt. 4, pp. 488–89.

56. Ibid., pt. 3, pp. 98, 221.

57. Rood, *Story of the Service of Company E*, 285–86; Isaiah T. Dillon to Sarah Dillon, June 3, 1864, Isaiah T. Dillon Papers, ISHL; Miller, *The Struggle for the Life of the Republic*, 167.

58. Albion Gross to "My Dear Wife," June 14 and 24, 1864, Albion Gross Papers, Civil War Miscellaneous Collection, USAMHI.

59. Wills, *Army Life*, 265.

60. *OR*, vol. 38, pt. 4, pp. 572–73.

61. Castel, *Decision in the West*, 285; *OR*, vol. 38, pt. 4, p. 573.

62. *OR*, vol. 38, pt. 4, pp. 588–89.

63. Ibid., pt. 3, p. 98; Taylor, *Tom Taylor's Civil War*, 131–32.

64. *OR*, vol. 38, pt. 3, pp. 98–99, 279–80; pt. 4, pp. 595, 601, 605–6.

65. Crooker, Nourse, and Brown, *The 55th Illinois*, 322–24.

66. Wills, *Army Life*, 268–70.

67. Crooker, Nourse, and Brown, *The 55th Illinois*, 322–24; Wills, *Army Life*, 268–70.

68. Crooker, Nourse, and Brown, *The 55th Illinois*, 322–24.

69. *OR*, vol. 38, pt. 3, pp. 99, 178; pt. 4, pp. 605–6.

70. Ibid., pp. 178, 318.

71. Ibid., pp. 99, 194; Crooker, Nourse, and Brown, *The 55th Illinois*, 325.

72. *OR*, vol. 38, pt. 3, pp. 99, 178.

73. Ibid., pp. 99, 318.

74. Wills, *Army Life*, 270–71.

75. Richardson, *For My Country*, 160.

76. *OR*, vol. 38, pt. 3, pp. 99, 178, 194, 201, 216, 318; Richardson, *For My Country*, 160.

77. *OR*, vol. 38, pt. 3, pp. 99, 178, 194, 201, 216, 318; Crooker, Nourse, and Brown, *The 55th Illinois*, 326.

78. Crooker, Nourse, and Brown, *The 55th Illinois*, 327.

79. *OR*, vol. 38, pt. 3, pp. 99; Wills, *Army Life*, 270–71.

80. *OR*, vol. 38, pt. 3, pp. 99, 216.

81. Crooker, Nourse, and Brown, *The 55th Illinois*, 327.

82. *OR*, vol. 38, pt. 3, p. 381.

83. Ibid., pp. 99–100.

84. Scheel, *Rain, Mud & Swamps*, 309.

85. McMurry, *Atlanta 1864*, 110–11.

86. *OR*, vol. 38, pt. 4, pp. 631, 646–47.

87. Ibid., pt. 3, p. 100; pt. 5, pp. 11, 28–29; Sherman, *Memoirs*, 532–36.

88. *OR*, vol. 38, pt. 3, pp. 100–1, 383, 553; Chamberlin, "The Skirmish Line in the Atlanta Campaign," in *MOLLUS*, 2:188–92; William W. McCarty Diary, July 4, 1864, Civil War Miscellaneous Collection, USAMHI; David W. Poak to "Sister Sadie," July 7, 1864, David W. Poak Papers, ISHL.

89. Edward W. Allen to "Dear Parents," July 14, 1864, Edward W. Allen Papers, SHC; William W. McCarty Diary, July 15, 1864, Civil War Miscellaneous Collection, USAMHI; Albion Gross Diary, July 16, 1864, Civil War Miscellaneous Collection, USAMHI; Miller, *The Struggle for the Life of the Republic*, 177–78; Wills, *Army Life*, 274.

90. Ankeny, *Kiss Josey for Me*, 230; Connelly, *History of the Seventieth Ohio*, 88; Scheel, *Rain Mud & Swamps*, 323; John W. Bates Diary, July 15, 1864, Civil War Miscellaneous Collection, USAMHI; Isaiah T. Dillon to "Loveing wife," July 16, 1864, Isaiah T. Dillon Papers, ISHL; Miller, *The Struggle for the Life of the Republic*, 178; Wills, *Army Life*, 280.

CHAPTER THIRTY: ACROSS THE CHATTAHOOCHEE

1. *OR*, vol. 38, pt. 5, pp. 149–51.
2. Miller, *The Struggle for the Life of the Republic*, 177–78; Crooker, Nourse, and Brown, *The 55th Illinois*, 334; *OR*, vol. 38, pt. 3, p. 101; pt. 5, pp. 156–58, 165; Scheel, *Rain, Mud & Swamps*, 325; John W. Bates Diary, July 17, 1864, Civil War Miscellaneous Collection, USAMHI.
3. *OR*, vol. 38, pt. 3, pp. 19–20, 101; pt. 5, pp. 168–69.
4. Ibid., pt. 3, pt. 3, pp. 19–20, 101; Crooker, Nourse, and Brown, *The 55th Illinois*, 334; Kountz et al., *History of the 37th Regiment*, 48; Isaiah T. Dillon to "My Dear and Loveing Wife," July 26, 1864, Isaiah T. Dillon Papers, ISHL.
5. *OR*, vol. 38, pt. 5, pp. 179–82, 192.
6. Ibid., pt. 3, pp. 101, 383, 553; Crooker, Nourse, and Brown, *The 55th Illinois*, 334; Amariah S. Spencer to "Dear Mother," July 21, 1864, Spencer Family Papers, Civil War Miscellaneous Collection, USAMHI.
7. *OR*, vol. 38, pt. 3, pp. 101, 383, 553.
8. p. 383.
9. Sherman, *Memoirs*, 543–44.
10. *OR*, vol. 38, pt. 5, p. 193.
11. William W. McCarty Diary, July 20, 1864, Civil War Miscellaneous Collection, USAMHI.
12. *OR*, vol. 38, pt. 3, pp. 101–2, 384, 543; Strong, "The Death of General James B. McPherson," in *MOLLUS*, 10:312; Taylor, *Tom Taylor's Civil War*, 140–41.
13. *OR*, vol. 38, pt. 3, pp. 102, 265.
14. Strong, "The Death of General James B. McPherson," in *MOLLUS*, 10:312–13.
15. *OR*, vol. 38, pt. 3, pp. 543, 580; Strong, "The Death of General James B. McPherson," in *MOLLUS*, 10:313.
16. *OR*, vol. 38, pt. 3, p. 580; Leggett, *The Battle of Atlanta*, 2–3.
17. Leggett, *The Battle of Atlanta*, 2–3; Gilbert D. Munson, "Battle of Atlanta," in *MOLLUS*, 2:213.
18. Leggett, *The Battle of Atlanta*, 2–3; Munson, "Battle of Atlanta," in *MOLLUS*, 2:213; Strong, "The Death of General James B. McPherson," in *MOLLUS*, 10:313–14; *OR*, vol. 38, pt. 3, pp. 543, 580; Taylor, *Tom Taylor's Civil War*, 140–41.
19. Leggett, *The Battle of Atlanta*, 3–5; Rood, *Story of the Service of Company E*, 305–6; Morris, Hartwell, and Kuykendall, *History 31st Regiment*, 103–4.
20. Munson, "Battle of Atlanta," in *MOLLUS*, 2:213–14.
21. Leggett, *The Battle of Atlanta*, 3–5; Leggett, "Battle of Atlanta," *National Tribune*, May 6, 1886, p. 1.
22. *OR*, vol. 38, pt. 3, pp. 543, 580; pt. 5, p. 210.
23. Ibid., pt. 5, pp. 218–19.
24. Ibid., pt. 3, p. 564; Munson, "Battle of Atlanta," in *MOLLUS*, 2:214–15.
25. Munson, "Battle of Atlanta," in *MOLLUS*, 2:215–16; Leggett, *Battle of Atlanta*, 4–5; Strong, "The Death of General James B. McPherson," in *MOLLUS*, 10:314.
26. Rood, *Story of the Service of Company E*, 307–8.
27. Ibid., 308.

28. *OR*, vol. 38, pt. 3, p. 571; Munson, "Battle of Atlanta," in *MOLLUS*, 2:215–17.

29. *OR*, vol. 38, pt. 3, pp. 543, 564; Rood, *Story of the Service of Company E*, 309–10; Munson, "Battle of Atlanta," in *MOLLUS*, 2:215–17; Strong, "The Death of General James B. McPherson," in *MOLLUS*, 10:314–15.

30. *OR*, vol. 38, pt. 3, p. 952; Munson, "Battle of Atlanta," in *MOLLUS*, 2:216–17.

31. *OR*, vol. 38, pt. 3, pp. 543–44, 580, 746, 952; Munson, "Battle of Atlanta," in *MOLLUS*, 2:215–17; Strong, "The Death of General James B. McPherson," in *MOLLUS*, 10:315.

32. *OR*, vol. 38, pt. 3, p. 20; Munson, "Battle of Atlanta," in *MOLLUS*, 2:215–19; Strong, "The Death of General James B. McPherson," in *MOLLUS*, 10:315; Leggett, *Battle of Atlanta*, 5–6, 10–11.

33. John J. McKee Diary, July 21, 1864, Civil War Miscellaneous Collection, USAMHI; Leggett, *Battle of Atlanta*, 6–7, 9.

34. *OR*, vol. 38, pt. 3, pp. 20, 564; Strong, "The Death of General James B. McPherson," in *MOLLUS*, 10:316–17.

35. *OR*, vol. 38, pt. 3, p. 20.

36. Ibid., p. 384; pt. 5, p. 220.

37. Strong, "The Death of General James B. McPherson," in *MOLLUS*, 10:318; Fuller, "A Terrible Day," *National Tribune*, April 16, 1885, p. 1.

38. *OR*, vol. 38, pt. 3, p. 581; pt. 5, p. 220; Compton, "The Second Division of the 16th Army Corps, in the Atlanta Campaign," in *MOLLUS*, 30:117; Leggett, *Battle of Atlanta*, 9.

39. *OR*, vol. 38, pt. 3, pp. 102, 369, 544.

40. Ibid., pp. 102, 544; Munson, "Battle of Atlanta," in *MOLLUS*, 2:218–19; Robert N. Adams, "The Battle and Capture of Atlanta," in *MOLLUS*, 29:147; Leggett, "Battle of Atlanta," *National Tribune*, May 6, 1886, p. 1.

41. Amariah S. Spencer to "Dear Mother," July 21, 1864, Spencer Family Papers, Civil War Miscellaneous Collection, USAMHI.

42. Leggett, "Battle of Atlanta," *National Tribune*, May 6, 1886, p. 1.

43. Leggett, *Battle of Atlanta*, 11; Leggett, "Battle of Atlanta," *National Tribune*, May 6, 1886, p. 1.

CHAPTER THIRTY-ONE: ATLANTA

1. *OR*, vol. 38, pt. 3, pp. 102, 139, 179, 417, 425, 544–45, 581; Fink, "De Grasse's Battery," *National Tribune*, July 9, 1885, p. 3; Wright, *A Corporal's Story*, 126.

2. *OR*, vol. 38, pt. 5, p. 231; Strong, "The Death of General James B. McPherson," in *MOLLUS*, 10:317.

3. Leggett, "Battle of Atlanta," *National Tribune*, May 6, 1886, p. 1.

4. *OR*, vol. 38, pt. 3, p. 102; pt. 5, p. 231; Strong, "The Death of General James B. McPherson," in *MOLLUS*, 10:317.

5. *OR*, vol. 38, pt. 3, pp. 102, 139, 179, 417, 425, 544–45, 581; Fink, "De Grasse's Battery," *National Tribune*, July 9, 1885, p. 3; Wright, *A Corporal's Story*, 126.

6. Ritner, *Love and Valor*, 312–13.

7. Taylor, *Tom Taylor's Civil War*, 143–50; Kountz et al., *History of the 37th Regiment*, 49; Jeff [last name not given, a soldier in 6th Missouri], "Atlanta," *National Tribune*, July 9, 1885, p. 3.

8. *OR*, vol. 38, pt. 3, pp. 369, 417, 545.

9. Strong, "The Death of General James B. McPherson," in *MOLLUS*, 10:319.

10. Ibid.

11. *OR*, vol. 38, pt. 3, p. 608; Wood, "The 20th Ohio at Atlanta," *National Tribune*, August 14, 1884, p. 3; Leggett, "Battle of Atlanta," *National Tribune*, May 6, 1886, p. 1.

12. Tuthill, "An Artilleryman's Recollections of the Battle of Atlanta," in *MOLLUS*, 10:298.

13. Nutt, "Fight at Atlanta: Work of the Seventy-eighth and Twentieth Ohio That Day, *National Tribune*, January 3, 1884, p. 3.

14. Strong, "The Death of General James B. McPherson," in *MOLLUS*, 10:320–22, 324.

15. Fuller, "A Terrible Day," *National Tribune*, April 16, 1885, p. 1; *OR*, vol. 38, pt. 3, pp. 369, 475.

16. Fuller, "A Terrible Day," *National Tribune*, April 16, 1885, p. 1; *OR*, vol. 38, pt. 3, p. 475.

17. Nutt, "Fight at Atlanta: Work of the Seventy-eighth and Twentieth Ohio That Day," *National Tribune*, January 3, 1884, p. 3; Tuthill, "An Artilleryman's Recollections of the Battle of Atlanta," in *MOLLUS*, 10:298–99; Gilbert D. Munson, "Battle of Atlanta," in *MOLLUS*, 2:219–20; Rood, *Story of the Service of Company E*, 316.

18. Strong, "The Death of General James B. McPherson," in *MOLLUS*, 10:322.

19. *OR*, vol. 38, pt. 3, pp. 369, 418, 545; Leggett, *Battle of Atlanta*, 12–13; Leggett, "Battle of Atlanta," *National Tribune*, May 6, 1886, p. 1; Loop, "Sounding the Alarm: The 68th Ohio's Trying Time at the Battle of Atlanta," *National Tribune*, December 1, 1898, p. 3.

20. Wright, *A Corporal's Story*, 127.

21. Adams, "The Battle and Capture of Atlanta," in *MOLLUS*, 29:149.

22. Wright, *A Corporal's Story*, 127; *OR*, vol. 38, pt. 3, pp. 369, 418.

23. *OR*, vol. 38, pt. 3, pp. 369–70, 418, 545; Adams, "The Battle and Capture of Atlanta," in *MOLLUS*, 29:150; Wright, *A Corporal's Story*, 127–28.

24. Wright, *A Corporal's Story*, 128; Strong, "The Death of General James B. McPherson," in *MOLLUS*, 10:323; *OR*, vol. 38, pt. 3, pp. 370, 418.

25. Veteran, Dayton, Ohio, "Who Recaptured the De Gres Battery in the Battle Before Atlanta," *National Tribune*, June 28, 1883, p. 3; Strong, "The Death of General James B. McPherson," in *MOLLUS*, 10:323.

26. Adams, "The Battle and Capture of Atlanta," in *MOLLUS*, 29:151.

27. Chamberlin, "Hood's Second Sortie at Atlanta," in Johnson and Buel, *Battles and Leaders*, 327.

28. Wright, *A Corporal's Story*, 128; *OR*, vol. 38, pt. 3, p. 418; Compton, "The Second Division of the 16th Army Corps, in the Atlanta Campaign," in *MOLLUS*, 30:119; John J. McKee Diary, July 22, 1864, Civil War Miscellaneous Collection, USAMHI.

29. *OR*, vol. 38, pt. 3, pp. 370, 450–51; Wright, *A Corporal's Story*, 128.

30. *OR*, vol. 38, pt. 3, pp. 370, 450–51, 476; Baumann, *Arming the Suckers*, 149–50.

31. *OR*, vol. 38, pt. 3, pp. 450, 476.

32. Adams, "The Battle and Capture of Atlanta," in *MOLLUS*, 29:150.

33. Strong, "The Death of General James B. McPherson," in *MOLLUS*, 10:323.

34. *OR*, vol. 38, pt. 3, p. 476; Strong, "The Death of General James B. McPherson," in *MOLLUS*, 10:323–25.

35. *OR*, vol. 38, pt. 3, p. 395.

36. Leggett, "Battle of Atlanta," 25; Strong, "The Death of General James B. McPherson," in *MOLLUS*, 10:334–35.

37. Strong, "The Death of General James B. McPherson," in *MOLLUS*, 10:325.

38. Strong, "The Death of General James B. McPherson," in *MOLLUS*, 10:329–31; Richard Beard to the *Nashville Union and American*, June 27, 1875, Richard Beard Papers, LC; Thompson, "McPherson's Death: The Sad Story of His Orderly, Who Saw Him Die," *National Tribune*, July 23, 1885, p. 3.

39. Strong, "The Death of General James B. McPherson," in *MOLLUS*, 10:329–31; *OR*, vol. 38, pt. 3, pp. 81, 395.

40. Strong, "The Death of General James B. McPherson," in *MOLLUS*, 10:329–38; Thompson, "McPherson's Death," *National Tribune*, July 23, 1885, p. 3.

41. Reynolds, "General McPherson's Death," *National Tribune*, October 1, 1881, p. 1; Strong,

"The Death of General James B. McPherson," in *MOLLUS*, 10:331–32; Holcombe, "Who Cared for the Body of Gen. McPherson," *National Tribune*, April 30, 1885, p. 3.

42. Wright, *A Corporal's Story*, 132.

43. *OR*, vol. 38, pt. 4, p. 41.

44. Gary Ecelbarger, "A Human Hurricane on Horseback: General John A. Logan and the Atlanta Campaign," *North and South*, forthcoming; W. Connelly, *History of the Seventieth Ohio Regiment*, 95; Richard S. Tuthill, "An Artilleryman's Recollections of the Battle of Atlanta," in *MOLLUS*, 10:299–300.

45. C. T. Hull, "Atlanta," *National Tribune*, August 27, 1891, p. 3; *OR*, vol. 38, pt. 3, pp. 608–9.

46. C. T. Hull, "Atlanta," *National Tribune*, August 27, 1891, p. 3; *OR*, vol. 38, pt. 3, pp. 581, 594, 599, 608.

47. *OR*, vol. 38, pt. 3, pp. 576, 608–9.

48. Ibid., pp. 581, 588–89.

49. Ibid., pp. 576, 581–82, 594, 609–10; Rood, "Sketches of the Thirteenth Iowa," in *MOLLUS*, 55:131; Hull, "Atlanta," *National Tribune*, August 27, 1891, p. 3; Munger, "The 16th Iowa at Atlanta," *National Tribune*, August 26, 1886, p. 3.

50. *OR*, vol. 38, pt. 3, p. 582.

51. Rood, *Story of the Service of Company E*, 317.

52. *OR*, vol. 38, pt. 3, p. 564; Tuthill, "An Artilleryman's Recollections of the Battle of Atlanta," in *MOLLUS*, 10:305–6.

53. *OR*, vol. 38, pt. 3, pp. 564–65; 572; Leggett, *Battle of Atlanta*, 16–17, 25; Tuthill, "An Artilleryman's Recollections of the Battle of Atlanta," in *MOLLUS*, 10:304–5.

54. *OR*, vol. 38, pt. 3, pp. 318, 341.

55. Ibid., pp. 582, 594, 602, 606.

56. Ibid.

57. Ibid., pp. 582, 589, 594, 602, 606; W. L. Curry, *War History of Union County*, http://www.ohiocivilwar.com/stori/preacher.html.

58. *OR*, vol. 38, pt. 3, pp. 582, 594, 602; Belknap, *History of the Fifteenth Regiment*, 371.

59. *OR*, vol. 38, pt. 3, pp. 582–83, 594.

60. Belknap, "The Obedience and Courage of the Private Soldier," in *MOLLUS*, 55:166.

61. *OR*, vol. 38, pt. 3, pp. 582–83, 594–95, 600, 606; Belknap, *History of the Fifteenth Regiment*, 371–72.

62. *OR*, vol. 38, pt. 3, p. 588.

63. Strong, "The Death of General James B. McPherson," in *MOLLUS*, 10:327–28.

64. Leggett, *Battle of Atlanta*, 17.

65. Fielder, *Civil War Diaries*, 189.

66. Nutt, "Fight at Atlanta: Work of the Seventy-eighth and Twentieth Ohio That Day," *National Tribune*, January 3, 1884, p. 3.

67. Leggett, *Battle of Atlanta*, 20, 26–27; Tuthill, "An Artilleryman's Recollection of the Battle of Atlanta," in *MOLLUS*, 10:302.

68. *OR*, vol. 38, pt. 3, pp. 565, 583; Munson, "Battle of Atlanta," in *MOLLUS*, 2:225–27.

69. Leggett, *Battle of Atlanta*, 21.

70. *OR*, vol. 38, pt. 3, pp. 370, 565, 583; Leggett, *Battle of Atlanta*, 21.

71. Brown, "The 50th Illinois at Fort Donelson," *National Tribune*, February 21, 1884, p. 3.

72. Leggett, *Battle of Atlanta*, 27; W. W. DeHaven letter, *National Tribune*, July 16, 1891, p. 3.

73. Charles B. Loop to "My Dear Wife," July 26, 1864, Charles B. Loop Papers, Civil War Miscellaneous Collection, USAMHI; Connelly, *History of the Seventieth Ohio Regiment*, 91; *OR*, vol. 38, pt. 3, pp. 117, 282.

74. Leggett, *Battle of Atlanta*, 21–22; *OR*, vol. 38, pt. 3, pp. 58, 572; Tuthill, "An Artilleryman's Recollections of the Battle of Atlanta," in *MOLLUS*, 10:302.

75. Crooker, Nourse, and Brown, *The 55th Illinois,* 337.

76. *OR,* vol. 38, pt. 3, p. 246; Taylor, *Tom Taylor's Civil War,* 145.

77. Fink, "De Grasse's Battery," *National Tribune,* July 9, 1885, p. 3.

78. Ralston, "De Grasse's Battery: The Part the 111th Ill. Took in Its Recapture," *National Tribune,* August 27, 1885, p. 3; Kountz et al., *History of the 37th Regiment,* 49–50; Crooker, Nourse, and Brown, *The 55th Illinois,* 338.

79. *OR,* vol. 38, pt. 3, pp. 223, 246; Taylor, *Tom Taylor's Civil War,* 147.

80. Saunier, *A History of the Forty-Seventh Regiment, Ohio Veteran Volunteer Infantry,* 287–88; Kimbell, *History of Battery A,* 87.

81. Kountz et al., *History of the 37th Regiment,* 50–51.

82. Taylor, *Tom Taylor's Civil War,* 147–48.

83. *OR,* vol. 38, pt. 3, pp. 223, 265.

84. Ibid., p. 223; Taylor, *Tom Taylor's Civil War,* 148; Wright, *A Corporal's Story,* 132.

85. *OR,* vol. 38, pt. 3, p. 370; James Compton, "The Second Division of the 16th Army Corps, in the Atlanta Campaign," in *MOLLUS,* 30:121.

86. Sherman, *Memoirs,* 554; Hull, "DeGress's Battery," *National Tribune.*

87. Sherman, *Memoirs,* 554; Mendenhall, "Battle of Atlanta," *National Tribune,* August 5, 1886, p. 3; Miller, "Saving his Battery," *National Tribune,* April 23, 1885, p. 3.

88. Crooker, Nourse, and Brown, *The 55th Illinois,* 341; Childress, "Atlanta," *National Tribune,* August 5, 1886, p. 3; Ralston, "De Grasse's Battery: The Part the 111th Ill. Took in Its Recapture," *National Tribune,* August 27, 1885, p. 3; Fink, "De Grasse's Battery," *National Tribune,* July 9, 1885, p. 3; Jeff (last name not given, soldier in 6th Missouri), "Atlanta," *National Tribune,* July 9, 1885, p. 3.

89. Miller, *The Struggle for the Life of the Republic,* 187–88; Miller, "Saving his Battery," *National Tribune,* April 23, 1885, p. 3.

90. Hull, "DeGress's Battery," *National Tribune;* Shearer, "De Grasse's Battery Once More," *National Tribune,* September 3, 1885, p. 3; Mendenhall, "Battle of Atlanta," *National Tribune,* August 5, 1886, p. 3; Miller, *The Struggle for the Life of the Republic,* 188.

91. Adams, "The Battle and Capture of Atlanta," in *MOLLUS,* 29:157; Hull, "DeGress's Battery," *National Tribune;* Wright, *A Corporal's Story,* 133; Childress, "Atlanta," *National Tribune,* August 5, 1886, p. 3; Crosby Johnson, "Battle of Atlanta," *National Tribune,* October 10, 1886, p. 3; *OR,* vol. 38, pt. 3, pp. 265, 451; Naylor, "Who Recaptured the De Gres Battery in the Battle Before Atlanta," *National Tribune,* June 28, 1883, p. 3; Private, Company I, 81st Ohio, "Capture of the De Gres Battery: The Question Settled," *National Tribune,* July 19, 1883, p. 3. Another version of the story had an unnamed soldier or soldiers loading the Parrott gun with double canister or with a double powder charge at maximum elevation in order, as they hoped, to reach Atlanta. Haldeman, "Who Recaptured the De Gres Battery in the Battle Before Atlanta," *National Tribune,* June 28, 1883, p. 3.

92. Taylor, *Tom Taylor's Civil War,* 149.

93. *OR,* vol. 38, pt. 3, p. 21; Castel, *Decision in the West,* 412.

CHAPTER THIRTY-TWO: EZRA CHURCH AND JONESBORO

1. Munson, "Battle of Atlanta," in *MOLLUS,* 2:229; Stockwell, Jr., *Private Elisha Stockwell,* 97–98.

2. Taylor, *Tom Taylor's Civil War,* 151; Charles B. Loop to "My Dear Wife," July 26, 1864, Charles B. Loop Papers, Civil War Miscellaneous Collection, USAMHI.

3. Rood, *Story of the Service of Company E,* 319.

4. William S. Covill to "Dear Sister," August 4, 1864; William H. Odell to Joseph O. Burton, August 3, 1864, Jonathan Blair Papers, ISHL.

5. Sherman, *Memoirs*, 558–59.

6. *OR*, vol. 38, pt. 3, p. 40; pt. 5, pp. 240–41, 260–61; Sherman, *Memoirs*, 559; Howard, "The Struggle for Atlanta," in Johnson and Buel, *Battles and Leaders of the Civil War*, 4:319.

7. Ecelbarger, "A Human Hurricane on Horseback," *North and South*, forthcoming; *OR*, vol. 38, pt. 5, p. 278.

8. W. T. Sherman to John A. Logan, July 27, 1864, John A. Logan Papers, LC.

9. *OR*, vol. 38, pt. 3, p. 40; pt. 5, pp. 255, 267–70; John J. McKee Diary, July 26, 1864, Civil War Miscellaneous Collection, USAMHI.

10. *OR*, vol. 38, pt. 3, p. 40; pt. 5, pp. 255, 267–70; Wright, *A Corporal's Story*, 136; Howard, "The Struggle for Atlanta," 319; Howard, *Autobiography*, 17–19; William H. Hugen to "Sister Mary," July 29, 1864, William H. Nugen Papers, PLDU; Crooker, Nourse, and Brown, *The 55th Illinois*, 344.

11. Scheel, *Rain, Mud & Swamps*, 362; Miller, *The Struggle for the Life of the Republic*, 190.

12. *OR*, vol. 38, pt. 3, p. 40; pt. 5, pp. 255, 267–70; Kountz et al., *History of the 37th Regiment*, 52; Howard, "The Struggle for Atlanta," 319.

13. Howard, "The Struggle for Atlanta," 319; Howard, *Autobiography*, 2:19–20.

14. *OR*, vol. 38, pt. 3, p. 140; pt. 5, p. 282; Connelly, *History of the Seventieth Ohio Regiment*, 97–98; Howard, "The Struggle for Atlanta," 319; Sherman, *Memoirs*, 562.

15. *OR*, vol. 38, pt. 3, pp. 41, 222–23.

16. Ibid., pp. 222–23; Howard, "The Struggle for Atlanta," 319; Connelly, *History of the Seventieth Ohio Regiment*, 98.

17. Saunier, *A History of the Forty-seventh Regiment*, 298.

18. Crooker, Nourse, and Brown, *The 55th Illinois*, 345–46; Connelly, *History of the Seventieth Ohio Regiment*, 98.

19. *OR*, vol. 38, pt. 3, pp. 247–48; Taylor, *Tom Taylor's Civil War*, 153–58; Saunier, *A History of the Forty-seventh Regiment*, 299.

20. Taylor, *Tom Taylor's Civil War*, 153–58.

21. *OR*, vol. 38, pt. 3, pp. 41, 222–23; Taylor, *Tom Taylor's Civil War*, 153–58; Belknap, *History of the Fifteenth Regiment*, 378–81; Howard, "The Struggle for Atlanta," 319; Howard, *Autobiography*, 2:23–24.

22. Scheel, *Rain, Mud & Swamps*, 365, 374–80; Miller, *The Struggle for the Life of the Republic*, 190–91; Crummell, "Ezra Chapel," *National Tribune*, April 26, 1888, p. 3; Crooker, Nourse, and Brown, *The 55th Illinois*, 345–47; Connelly, *History of the Seventieth Ohio Regiment*, 98–99.

23. *OR*, vol. 38, pt. 3, pp. 42, 104, 189; pt. 5, pp. 282–83; Ritner, *Love and Valor*, 321–22; Crummell, "Ezra Chapel," *National Tribune*, April 26, 1888, p. 3.

24. *OR*, vol. 38, pt. 3, pp. 42, 104, 189, 294; pt. 5, pp. 282–83; Crooker, Nourse, and Brown, *The 55th Illinois*, 345–47; Connelly, *History of the Seventieth Ohio Regiment*, 98–99; Howard, "The Struggle for Atlanta," 319–20; Scheel, *Rain, Mud & Swamps*, 374–80.

25. Crummell, "Ezra Chapel," *National Tribune*, April 26, 1888, p. 3.

26. Saunier, *A History of the Forty-seventh Regiment*, 300; Coombe, "The 28th of July Before Atlanta," *National Tribune*, February 7, 1884, p. 3.

27. Crooker, Nourse, and Brown, *The 55th Illinois*, 347.

28. Connelly, *History of the Seventieth Ohio Regiment*, 99–100; Castel, *Decision in the West*, 434; Miller, *The Struggle for the Life of the Republic*, 191; Rood, *Story of the Service of Company E*, 323; Ritner, *Love and Valor*, 321–22.

29. *OR*, vol. 38, pt. 3, pp. 42, 104, 189; pt. 5, pp. 282–83; Crooker, Nourse, and Brown, *The 55th Illinois*, 345–46; Howard, "The Struggle for Atlanta," 319–20; Wills, *Army Life*, 287.

30. *OR*, vol. 38, pt. 3, pp. 41–42; Howard, "The Struggle for Atlanta," 319–20.

31. Duncan, "The Army of the Tennessee Under Major-General O. O. Howard," in *MOLLUS*, 29:166.

32. Sherman, *Memoirs*, 564.

33. Michael Cunningham letter, July 28, 1864, Michael Cunningham Papers, WHS.

34. Connelly, *History of the Seventieth Ohio Regiment*, 100–1; Crooker, Nourse, and Brown, *The 55th Illinois*, 348.

35. Crooker, Nourse, and Brown, *The 55th Illinois*, 348; Post, ed., *Soldiers' Letters*, 458–60; Ritner, *Love and Valor*, 321–22.

36. Connelly, *History of the Seventieth Ohio Regiment*, 101; Miller, *The Struggle for the Life of the Republic*, 192.

37. Sherman, *Memoirs*, 570–77.

38. Howard, "The Struggle for Atlanta," 320–21; *OR*, vol. 38, pt. 3, p. 43.

39. James Compton, "The Second Division of the 16th Army Corps in the Atlanta Campaign," in *MOLLUS*, 30:122.

40. Chamberlin, "The Skirmish Line in the Atlanta Campaign," in *MOLLUS*, 2:193; Howard, "The Struggle for Atlanta," 321; John J. McKee Diary, August 19, 1864, Civil War Miscellaneous Collection, USAMHI.

41. Crooker, Nourse, and Brown, *The 55th Illinois*, 350–51.

42. Special Field Orders No. 101, Headquarters Dept. and Army of the Tennessee, August 17, 1864, William B. Hazen Papers, Civil War Miscellaneous Collection, USAMHI; Hazen, *Narrative of Military Service*, 281; Crooker, Nourse, and Brown, *The 55th Illinois*, 360.

43. Hazen, *Narrative of Military Service*, 280–85, 299–300; Crooker, Nourse, and Brown, *The 55th Illinois*, 360.

44. Howard, "The Struggle for Atlanta," 321.

45. *OR*, vol. 38, pt. 3, p. 43; Wills, *Army Life*, 292–93; Howard, *Autobiography*, 2:30–31; Crooker, Nourse, and Brown, *The 55th Illinois*, 365; Hazen, *Narrative of Military Service*, 285.

46. Hazen, *Narrative of Military Service*, 289–90; Taylor, *Tom Taylor's Civil War*, 177; Howard, *Autobiography*, 2:34.

47. *OR*, vol. 38, pt. 3, pp. 43–44; Howard, "The Struggle for Atlanta," 321–22; Howard, *Autobiography*, 2:34; Crooker, Nourse, and Brown, *The 55th Illinois*, 366.

48. *OR*, vol. 38, pt. 3, pp. 44–45; Howard, *Autobiography*, 2:37.

49. Wilson, *Memoirs*, 358–59.

50. Ibid.; Hazen, *Narrative of Military Service*, 290; Edward W. Allen Diary, August 31, 1864, SHC.

51. Edward W. Allen Diary, August 31, 1864, SHC.

52. *OR*, vol. 38, pt. 3, p. 45; Andrus, *Civil War Letters*, 102–3.

53. *OR*, vol. 38, pt. 3, pp. 44–45; Howard, *Autobiography*, 2:37; Taylor, *Tom Taylor's Civil War*, 178; Edward W. Allen Diary, August 31, 1864, SHC; Wills, *Army Life*, 297.

54. Hazen, *Narrative of Military Service*, 294; Taylor, *Tom Taylor's Civil War*, 180–81.

55. Geer, *Civil War Diary*, 160.

56. Wright, *A Corporal's Story*, 140; Hazen, *Narrative of Military Service*, 291.

57. Sherman, *Memoirs*, 583; Geer, *Civil War Diary*, 160–61; John J. McKee Diary, September 2, 1864, Civil War Miscellaneous Collection, USAMHI.

58. Sherman, *Memoirs*, 584.

59. Charles Weiser to "Friend Hattie," Charles Weiser Papers, Civil War Miscellaneous Papers, USAMHI; Isaiah T. Dillon to "My Dear Wife," September 4, 1864, Isaiah T. Dillon Papers, ISHL.

CHAPTER THIRTY-THREE: MARCHING THROUGH GEORGIA

1. Hazen, *Narrative of Military Service*, 302; Crooker, Nourse, and Brown, *The 55th Illinois*, 371; William L. Wade Diary, September 7, 1864, Civil War Miscellaneous Collection, USAMHI.

2. Edward W. Allen to "Dear Father," September 16, 1864, Edward W. Allen Papers, SHC.

3. Sherman, *Memoirs*, 620–21.

4. Geer, *Civil War Diary*, 163.

5. Crooker, Nourse, and Brown, *The 55th Illinois*, 374; Hazen, *Narrative of Military Service*, 287; Isaiah T. Dillon to "My Dear Wife Sarah," September 29, 1864, Isaiah T. Dillon Papers, ISHL.

6. William L. Wade Diary, October 3 and 4, 1864, Civil War Miscellaneous Collection, USAMHI; William B. Hazen Diary, October 3 and 4, 1864, Civil War Miscellaneous Collection, USAMHI; Ankeny, *Kiss Josey for Me*, 245.

7. Sherman, *Memoirs*, 618–20.

8. Howard, *Autobiography*, 2:68–69; Isaiah T. Dillon to "My Dear Wife," November 6, 1864, Isaiah T. Dillon Papers, ISHL.

9. Isaiah T. Dillon to "My Dear Wife," October 22, 1864, Isaiah T. Dillon Papers, ISHL.

10. Edward E. Allen to "Friend Mary," October 23, 1864, Edward W. Allen Papers, SHC.

11. Sherman, *Memoirs*, 627–30.

12. Ibid., 631.

13. Crooker, Nourse, and Brown, *The 55th Illinois*, 380.

14. Howard, *Autobiography*, 2:68–69.

15. Edward W. Allen to "Dear Parents," November 8, 1864, Edward W. Allen Papers, SHC; Geer, *Civil War Diary*, 174–75.

16. Sherman, *Memoirs*, 634–43.

17. Isaiah T. Dillon to "My Dear Wife," October 22, 1864, Isaiah T. Dillon Papers, ISHL.

18. Geer, *Civil War Diary*, 172.

19. Wills, *Army Life*, 316.

20. Upson, *With Sherman to the Sea*, 133.

21. Enoch Weiss Diary, November 12, 1864, Civil War Miscellaneous Collection, USAMHI.

22. Richard Robert Crowe to "My Dear Mother," November 10, 1864, Richard Robert Crowe Papers, WHS; Diary of Operations of the Army of the Tennessee, November 12, 1864, Joseph A. Sladen Papers, Civil War Miscellaneous Collection, USAMHI; Crooker, Nourse, and Brown, *The 55th Illinois*, 386.

23. Wills, *Army Life*, 318–19.

24. Sherman, *Memoirs*, 643–46.

25. Howard, *Autography*, 2:70; Diary of Operations of the Army of the Tennessee, November 13, 1864, Joseph A. Sladen Papers, Civil War Miscellaneous Collection, USAMHI; Wimer Bedford Diary, November 13, 1864, LC; Taylor, *Tom Taylor's Civil War*, 194; Wills, *Army Life*, 318–19; Crooker, Nourse, and Brown, *The 55th Illinois*, 386–87.

26. Howard, *Autobiography*, 2:70.

27. Upson, *With Sherman to the Sea*, 134.

28. Scheel, *Rain, Mud & Swamps*, 455.

29. Hazen, *Narrative of Military Service*, 314; William B. Hazen Diary, November 15, 1864, Civil War Miscellaneous Collection, USAMHI; Diary of Operations of the Army of the Tennessee, November 15, 1864, Joseph A. Sladen Papers, Civil War Miscellaneous Collection, USAMHI.

30. Morris, Hartwell, and Kuykendall, *History 31st Regiment*, 132.

31. Upson, *With Sherman to the Sea*, 134.
32. Hubert, *History of the Fiftieth Regiment*, 322–23; Belknap, *History of the Fifteenth Regiment*, 413.
33. Sherman, *Memoirs*, 652.
34. Mahon, "The Forager in Sherman's Last Campaigns," in *MOLLUS*, 56:190; Crooker, Nourse, and Brown, *The 55th Illinois*, 388–90; Hubert, *History of the Fiftieth Regiment*, 323.
35. Hazen, *Narrative of Military Service*, 414–15.
36. Crooker, Nourse, and Brown, *The 55th Illinois*, 388–90.
37. Hazen, *Narrative of Military Service*, 320, 416; William B. Hazen Diary, December 3, 1864, Civil War Miscellaneous Collection, USAMHI.
38. Crooker, Nourse, and Brown, *The 55th Illinois*, 421–24.
39. Willison, *Reminiscences of a Boy's Service*, 101–3.
40. Dunbar, *History of the Ninety-third Regiment*, http://www.illinoiscivilwar.org/cw93-hist-ch9c.html; Hazen, *Narrative of Military Service*, 415–16.
41. Wills, *Army Life*, 320–22.
42. Hazen, *Narrative of Military Service*, 416.
43. Cornelius C. Platter Diary, November 28, 1864, HLUGA.
44. Wills, *Army Life*, 320–22.
45. Upson, *With Sherman to the Sea*, 136.
46. Ibid.; Stevenson, *History of the 78th*, 313–14; Enoch Weiss Reminiscences, 39–40, Civil War Miscellaneous Collection, USAMHI.
47. Upson, *With Sherman to the Sea*, 136; Enoch Weiss Reminiscences, 39–40, Civil War Miscellaneous Collection, USAMHI; Hazen, *Narrative of Military Service*, 328.
48. Crooker, Nourse, and Brown, *The 55th Illinois*, 392–93; Stevenson, *History of the 78th Regiment*, 314–15.
49. Hitchcock, *Marching with Sherman*, 122.
50. William B. Hazen Diary, November 17, 1864, Civil War Miscellaneous Collection, USAMHI; John J. McKee Diary, November 18, 1864, Civil War Miscellaneous Collection, USAMHI; Geer, *Civil War Diary*, 176–77; Abijah F. Gore Diary, November 17, 1864, Civil War Miscellaneous Collection, USAMHI; Enoch Weiss Reminiscences, pp. 39–41, Civil War Miscellaneous Collection, USAMHI; Hubert, *History of the Fiftieth Regiment*, 322–23.
51. Abijah F. Gore Diary, November 18, 1864, Civil War Miscellaneous Collection, USAMHI; Ritner, *Love and Valor*, 390; Cornelius C. Platter Diary, November 17, 1864, HLUGA.
52. Scheel, *Rain, Mud & Swamps*, 459; Diary of Operations of the Army of the Tennessee, November 24, 1864, Joseph A. Sladen Papers, Civil War Miscellaneous Collection, USAMHI; Cornelius C. Platter Diary, November 20, 1864, HLUGA.
53. Cornelius C. Platter Diary, November 17 and 28, 1864, HLUGA.
54. Hubert, *History of the Fiftieth Regiment*, 324; Cornelius C. Platter Diary, November 22, 1864, HLUGA.
55. Hazen, *Narrative of Military Service*, 416–18; Dunbar, *History of the Ninety-third Regiment Illinois Volunteer Infantry*, http://www.illinoiscivilwar.org/cw93-hist-ch9a.html.
56. Howard, *Autobiography*, 2:71–72, 74; Diary of Operations of the Army of the Tennessee, November 22, 1864, Joseph A. Sladen Papers, Civil War Miscellaneous Collection, USAMHI.
57. Howard, *Autobiography*, 2:72; Wills, *Army Life*, 322–24.
58. Wills, *Army Life*, 322–24.
59. Orendorff et al., *Reminiscences of the Civil War*, 154.
60. Ibid., 155; Upson, *With Sherman to the Sea*, 136–37; Wills, *Army Life*, 322–24.
61. Howard, *Autobiography*, 2:73; Wills, *Army Life*, 322–24.
62. Hubert, *History of the Fiftieth Regiment*, 325; Diary of Operations of the Army of the Ten-

nessee, November 27 and December 2–3, 1864, Joseph A. Sladen Papers, Civil War Miscellaneous Collection, USAMHI; Scheel, *Rain, Mud & Swamps*, 468, 471; Geer, *Civil War Diary*, 177–80; John J. McKee Diary, December 2, 1864, Civil War Miscellaneous Collection, USAMHI; Abijah F. Gore Diary, November 24, 1864, Civil War Miscellaneous Collection, USAMHI; William Duncan, "The Army of the Tennessee Under Major-General O. O. Howard," in *MOLLUS*, 29:168.

63. Taylor, *Tom Taylor's Civil War*, 196; Abijah F. Gore Diary, November 25, 1864, Civil War Miscellaneous Collection, USAMHI.

64. Thomas M. Stevenson, *History of the 78th Regiment*, 317.

65. Taylor, *Tom Taylor's Civil War*, 197.

66. Cornelius C. Platter Diary, November 21, 1864, HLUGA.

67. Abijah F. Gore Diary, November 21, Civil War Miscellaneous Collection, USAMHI.

68. Cornelius C. Platter Diary, November 25, 1864, HLUGA; Hubert, *History of the Fiftieth Regiment*, 325.

69. Hitchcock, *Marching with Sherman*, 142–43.

70. Ibid.; Stevenson, *History of the 78th Regiment*, 317.

71. Hitchcock, *Marching with Sherman*, 156.

72. Taylor, *Tom Taylor's Civil War*, 196.

73. Hitchcock, *Marching with Sherman*, 157.

74. Crooker, Nourse, and Brown, *The 55th Illinois*, 394; Hazen, *Narrative of Military Service*, 328.

75. Crooker, Nourse, and Brown, *The 55th Illinois*, 394; Abijah F. Gore Diary, November 27 and December 2, 1864, Civil War Miscellaneous Collection, USAMHI; William B. Hazen Diary, November 24, 1864, Civil War Miscellaneous Collection, USAMHI; Hitchcock, *Marching with Sherman*, 115–16.

76. Hitchcock, *Marching with Sherman*, 110; John J. McKee Diary, November 29, 1864, Civil War Miscellaneous Collection, USAMHI.

77. Howard, *Autobiography*, 2:79–80; Diary of Operations of the Army of the Tennessee, November 25, 1864, Joseph A. Sladen Papers, Civil War Miscellaneous Collection, USAMHI; Belknap, *History of the Fifteenth Regiment*, 413; Cornelius C. Platter Diary, December 4, 1864, HLUGA; Dunbar, *History of the Ninety-third Regiment*, http://www.illinoiscivilwar.org/cw93-hist-ch9b.html; Hubert, *History of the Fiftieth Regiment*, 326–27.

78. Dunbar, *History of the Ninety-third Regiment*, http://www.illinoiscivilwar.org/cw93-hist-ch9b.html.

79. *OR*, vol. 44, p. 69; Howard, *Autobiography*, 2:82; Belknap, *History of the Fifteenth Regiment*, 414; Stevenson, *History of the 78th Regiment*, 316–17; William Duncan, "The Army of the Tennessee Under Major-General O. O. Howard," in *MOLLUS*, 29:168; Wimer Bedford Diary, November 30, 1864, LC.

80. Geer, *Civil War Diary*, 180; Diary of Operations of the Army of the Tennessee, December 5, 1864, Joseph A. Sladen Papers, Civil War Miscellaneous Collection, USAMHI.

81. Howard, *Autobiography*, 2:79–84; Taylor, *Tom Taylor's Civil War*, 200–1; William B. Hazen Diary, December 4, 1864, Civil War Miscellaneous Collection, USAMHI; Diary of Operations of the Army of the Tennessee, December 4, 1864, Joseph A. Sladen Papers, Civil War Miscellaneous Collection, USAMHI; Ritner, *Love and Valor*, 392; John J. McKee Diary, December 7, 1864, Civil War Miscellaneous Collection, USAMHI.

82. Wimer Bedford Reminiscences, Wimer Bedford Papers, LC; Howard, *Autobiography*, 2:84; Cornelius C. Platter Diary, December 2, 1864, HLUGA; Taylor, *Tom Taylor's Civil War*, 201–2; Wills, *Army Life*, 333–35; Crooker, Nourse, and Brown, *The 55th Illinois*, 396.

83. Hitchcock, *Marching with Sherman*, 161–62; John W. Bates Diary, December 9, 1864, Civil War Miscellaneous Collection, USAMHI.

84. Mahon, "The Forager in Sherman's Last Campaigns," in *MOLLUS*, 56:191; Morris, Hartwell, and Kuykendall, *History 31st Regiment*, 138; Upson, *With Sherman to the Sea*, 137; Duncan, "The Army of the Tennessee Under Major-General O. O. Howard," in *MOLLUS*, 29:170–74; Howard, *Autobiography*, 2:83–85.

85. Wills, *Army Life*, 320–22; Hazen, *Narrative of Military Service*, 313.

86. Duncan, "The Army of the Tennessee Under Major-General O. O. Howard," in *MOLLUS*, 29:167; Wimer Bedford Reminiscences, Wimer Bedford Papers, LC.

87. Wills, *Army Life*, 333–35.

88. *OR*, vol. 44, p. 10; Sherman, *Memoirs*, 672.

89. *OR*, vol. 44, p. 10.

90. Ibid.

91. Ibid., pp. 10–11, 72; Sherman, *Memoirs*, 672.

92. *OR*, vol. 44, p. 72; Sherman, *Memoirs*, 672–73.

93. *OR*, vol. 44, pp. 10–11, 72.

94. Ibid.; Owen Stuart to "My Dear Wife," December 17, 1864, Owen Stuart Papers, ISHL.

95. *OR*, vol. 44, pp. 11, 72; Sherman, *Memoirs*, 673.

96. *OR*, vol. 44, p. 11.

97. Cornelius C. Platter Diary, December 25, 1864, HLUGA.

98. Stevenson, *History of the 78th Regiment*, 323; Morris, Hartwell, and Kuykendall, *History 31st Regiment*, 140; Moses , "Memoirs," December 26, 1864.

99. Wimer Bedford Reminiscences, Wimer Bedford Papers, LC.

100. Stevenson, *History of the 78th Regiment*, 322.

CHAPTER THIRTY-FOUR: COLUMBIA

1. Putney, "Incidents of Sherman's March Through the Carolinas," in *MOLLUS*, 48:381–82.

2. Hazen, *Narrative of Military Service*, 336.

3. Sherman, *Memoirs*, 721.

4. Howard, *Autobiography*, 2:102–3; Sherman, *Memoirs*, 719–21; Hazen, *Narrative of Military Service*, 335.

5. Hazen, *Narrative of Military Service*, 337.

6. Willison, *Reminiscences of a Boy's Service*, 108–9.

7. Edward W. Allen to "Dear Parents," February 4, 1865, Edward W. Allen Papers, SHC.

8. Cyrus M. Roberts Diary, January 29 and 30, 1865, Civil War Miscellaneous Collection, USAMHI; Diary of Operations of the Army of the Tennessee, January 30, 1865, Joseph A. Sladen Papers, Civil War Miscellaneous Collection, USAMHI; Cornelius C. Platter Diary, January 30, 1865, HLUGA.

9. Force, "Marching Across Carolina," in *MOLLUS*, 1:2–3; Sherman, *Memoirs*, 753.

10. *OR*, vol. 47, pt. 1, p. 192; Howard, *Autobiography*, 2:105–6.

11. Scheel, *Rain, Mud & Swamps*, 499.

12. William Duncan, "Through the Carolinas with the Army of the Tennessee," in *MOLLUS*, 29:330.

13. Memorandum on Carolina campaign in William B. Hazen Papers, Civil War Miscellaneous Collection, USAMHI; Force, "Marching Across Carolina," in *MOLLUS*, 1:2–3; Duncan, "Through the Carolinas with the Army of the Tennessee," in *MOLLUS*, 29:330.

14. Force, "Marching Across Carolina," in *MOLLUS*, 1:9–13; Hazen, *Narrative of Military Service*, 338.

15. *OR*, vol. 47, pt. 1, pp. 193–95; Force, "Marching Across Carolina," in *MOLLUS*, 1:5; Diary of Operations of the Army of the Tennessee, February 3, 1865, Joseph A. Sladen

Papers, Civil War Miscellaneous Collection, USAMHI; Belknap, *History of the Fifteenth Regiment,* 2:108.

16. Howard, *Autobiography,* 2:108; Crooker, Nourse, and Brown, *The 55th Illinois,* 404–5.

17. *OR,* vol. 47, pt. 1, pp. 194–95; Belknap, *History of the Fifteenth Regiment,* 448.

18. Cyrus M. Roberts Diary, February 5 and 6, 1865, Civil War Miscellaneous Collection, USAMHI.

19. *OR,* vol. 47, pt. 1, pp. 194–95.

20. Putney, "Incidents of Sherman's March Through the Carolinas," in *MOLLUS,* 48:384.

21. Force, "Marching Across Carolina," in *MOLLUS,* 1:12–13.

22. Mahon, "The Forager in Sherman's Last Campaigns," in *MOLLUS,* 56:192–96.

23. Ibid., 195–99.

24. Crooker, Nourse, and Brown, *The 55th Illinois,* 405; *OR,* vol. 47, pt. 1, p. 195.

25. Cyrus M. Roberts Diary, February 12, 1865, Civil War Miscellaneous Collection, USAMHI.

26. *OR,* vol. 47, pt. 1, p. 196.

27. Cyrus M. Roberts Diary, February 12, 1865, Civil War Miscellaneous Collection, USAMHI; Geer, *Civil War Diary,* 196; Ensign H. King Diary, February 15, 1865, Civil War Miscellaneous Collection, USAMHI; *OR,* vol. 47, pt. 1, p. 196.

28. Wills, *Army Life,* 342–43.

29. Isaiah T. Dillon to "My Dear Wife," February 4, 1865, Isaiah T. Dillon Papers, ISHL.

30. Hubert, *History of the Fiftieth Regiment,* 346.

31. Crooker, Nourse, and Brown, *The 55th Illinois,* 404.

32. Ensign H. King Diary, February 15, 1865, Civil War Miscellaneous Collection, USAMHI.

33. Frank Putney, "Incidents of Sherman's March Through the Carolinas," in *MOLLUS,* 48:385.

34. Force, "Marching Across Carolina," in *MOLLUS,* 1:15.

35. Putney, "Incidents of Sherman's March Through the Carolinas," in *MOLLUS,* 48:386–87.

36. Crooker, Nourse, and Brown, *The 55th Illinois,* 406–8.

37. Willison, *Reminiscences of a Boy's Service,* 110–11; Cornelius C. Platter Diary, February 13, 1865, HLUGA; Wills, *Army Life,* 344–45.

38. *OR,* vol. 47, pt. 1, pp. 197–98, 226; Belknap, *History of the Fifteenth Regiment,* 450–52; Hazen, *Narrative of Military Service,* 347–48; Howard, *Autobiography,* 2:119–20; Isaiah T. Dillon to "My Dear and devoted wife," March 22, 1865, Isaiah T. Dillon Papers, ISHL; Bannan, "Columbia, S.C.: A Member of the 4th Iowa Consults His Diary," *National Tribune,* August 20, 1885, p. 3.

39. Hazen, *Narrative of Military Service,* 347–49; Crooker, Nourse, and Brown, *The 55th Illinois,* 408.

40. Hazen, *Narrative of Military Service,* 347–49; *OR,* vol. 47, pt. 1, p. 263; Brannan, "Columbia, S.C.," *National Tribune,* August 20, 1885, p. 3.

41. *OR,* vol. 47, pt. 1, pp. 263–65; Humbert, "Columbia, S.C., and the Part W. M. Prouty and Montgomery Hulburt Took in the Capture," *National Tribune,* October 8, 1885, p. 3; Marvin, "The First Flag at Columbia, S.C.," *National Tribune,* September 17, 1885, p. 3.

42. *OR,* vol. 47, pt. 1, pp. 264–65; Brannan, "Columbia, S.C.," *National Tribune,* August 20, 1885, p. 3.

43. *OR,* vol. 47, pt. 1, p. 265; Brannan, "Columbia, S.C.," *National Tribune,* August 20, 1885, p. 3.

44. *OR,* vol. 47, pt. 1, pp. 379, 412; Ensign H. King Diary, February 17, 1865, Civil War Miscellaneous Collection, USAMHI; Belknap, *History of the Fifteenth Regiment,* 452–59; Rood, "Sketches of the Thirteenth Iowa," in *MOLLUS,* 55:123–24; Lee, "The Columbia, S.C., Controversy," *National Tribune,* July 16, 1885, p. 3; Wilson, "The 13th Iowa at Columbia," *National Tribune,* July 16, 1885, p. 3; Krone, "The 41st Ill. at Columbia, S.C.," *National Tribune,* September 10, 1885, p. 3; Ragsdale, "The First to Enter Columbia," *National Tribune,* August 6, 1885, p. 3.

45. Hazen, *Narrative of Military Service*, 349; Lucas, *Sherman and the Burning of Columbia*, 75–7...

46. Hazen, *Narrative of Military Service*, 349–50; Lucas, *Sherman and the Burning of Columbia*, 68–71; 90–91.

47. *OR*, vol. 47, pt. 1, pp. 198, 227, 412; Howard, *Autobiography*, 2:120; Kimberley, "Burning of Columbia," *National Tribune*, September 3, 1885; John W. Bates Diary, February 17, 1865, Civil War Miscellaneous Collection, USAMHI; Geer, *Civil War Diary*, 197.

48. Hazen, *Narrative of Military Service*, 350.

49. Marvin, "Columbia, S.C.," *National Tribune*, October 14, 1886, p. 3.

50. *OR*, vol. 47, pt. 1, pp. 228, 265.

51. Hazen, *Narrative of Military Service*, 349.

52. Howard, *Autobiography*, 2:120; Upson, *With Sherman to the Sea*, 152–54.

53. *OR*, vol. 47, pt. 1, p. 265.

54. Samuel W. Snow to "My Dear Parents," March 28, 1865, Snow Family Papers, PLDU.

55. Duncan, "Through the Carolinas with the Army of the Tennessee," in *MOLLUS*, 29:331–32.

56. *OR*, vol. 47, pt. 1, p. 198; Samuel W. Snow to "My Dear Parents," March 28, 1865, Snow Family Papers, PLDU; Lucas, *Sherman and the Burning of Columbia*, 85–86.

57. Hazen, *Narrative of Military Service*, 350.

58. *OR*, vol. 47, pt. 1, pp. 198–99, 265; Upson, *With Sherman to the Sea*, 152–54.

59. *OR*, vol. 47, pt. 1, p. 265; Howard, *Autobiography*, 2:120–24.

60. Hazen, *Narrative of Military Service*, 350.

61. William G. Baugh to "Mother," March 14, 1865, and William G. Baugh to "Dear Parents," March 27, 1865, William G. Baugh Papers, Emory University, Atlanta, Georgia.

62. Upson, *With Sherman to the Sea*, 152–54.

63. Lucas, *Sherman and the Burning of Columbia*, 111–16.

64. *OR*, vol. 47, pt. 1, p. 199.

65. Kimberley, "Burning of Columbia," *National Tribune*, September 3, 1885, p. 3.

66. Hazen, *Narrative of Military Service*, 353; Wills, *Army Life*, 350–51; *OR*, vol. 47, pt. 1, p. 310.

67. Dunbar, *History of the Ninety-third Regiment*, http://www.illinoiscivilwar.org/cw93-hist-ch10b.html.

68. Kimberley, "Burning of Columbia," *National Tribune*, September 3, 1885, p. 3.

69. Hazen, *Narrative of Military Service*, 347–52; *OR*, vol. 47, pt. 1, p. 227.

70. Crooker, Nourse, and Brown, *The 55th Illinois*, 410.

71. Wood letter quoted in Force, "Marching Across Carolina," in *MOLLUS*, 1:17; *OR*, vol. 47, pt. 1, p. 243.

72. *OR*, vol. 47, pt. 1, p. 252.

73. Dunbar, *History of the Ninety-third Regiment*, http://www.illinoiscivilwar.org/cw93-hist-ch10b.html; Lucas, *Sherman and the Burning of Columbia*, 119–62.

74. Stevenson, *History of the 78th Regiment*, 331; Moses, "Memoirs," February 18, 1865.

75. Crooker, Nourse, and Brown, *The 55th Illinois*, 408–10; Ensign H. King Diary, February 18, 1865, Civil War Miscellaneous Collection, USAMHI.

CHAPTER THIRTY-FIVE: WASHINGTON AND HOME

1. *OR*, vol. 47, pt. 1, pp. 199, 318; Hazen, *Narrative of Military Service*, 366; Geer, *Civil War Diary*, 200–1; Crooker, Nourse, and Brown, *The 55th Illinois*, 411; Wills, *Army Life*, 355; Howard, *Autobiography*, 2:130.

2. *OR*, vol. 47, pt. 1, p. 683.

3. Ibid., pp. 566, 860; pt. 2, p. 533; Howard, *Autobiography*, 2:130–31.

4. *OR*, vol. 47, pt. 2, p. 537.

5. Ibid., pp. 554–55.

6. Ibid., pp. 596–97.

7. Ibid., pt. 1, pp. 318–19, 327–28; Diary of Operations of the Army of the Tennessee, February 25, 1865, Joseph A. Sladen Papers, Civil War Miscellaneous Collection, USAMHI.

8. *OR*, vol. 47, pt. 1, pp. 649–50; Geer, *Civil War Diary*, 200.

9. Cyrus M. Roberts Diary, March 2, 1865, Civil War Miscellaneous Collection, USAMHI; Geer, *Civil War Diary*, 200–201; Stevenson, *History of the 78th Regiment*, 332–22.

10. Howard, *Autobiography*, 2:130–31; Dunbar, *History of the Ninety-third Regiment*, http://www.illinoiscivilwar.org/cw93-hist-ch10b.html.

11. Howard, *Autobiography*, 2:134; Ensign H. King Diary, March 3, 1865, Civil War Miscellaneous Collection, USAMHI; Wills, *Army Life*, 356–57.

12. Wills, *Army Life*, 358–59.

13. William B. Hazen Diary, March 8, 1865, Civil War Miscellaneous Collection, USAMHI; Force, "Marching Across Carolina," in *MOLLUS*, 1:16.

14. Hazen, *Narrative of Military Service*, 376.

15. Force, "Marching Across Carolina," in *MOLLUS*, 1:16; Dunbar, *History of the Ninety-third Regiment*, http://www.illinoiscivilwar.org/cw93-hist-ch10c.html.

16. Howard, *Autobiography*, 2:136–37.

17. Geer, *Civil War Diary*, 203; Diary of Operations of the Army of the Tennessee, March 11, 1865, Joseph A. Sladen Papers, Civil War Miscellaneous Collection, USAMHI; Wills, *Army Life*, 360–61; Stevenson, *History of the 78th Regiment*, 333–34; Edward W. Allen Diary, March 11, 1865, SHC.

18. Hazen, *Narrative of Military Service*, 358; Geer, *Civil War Diary*, 203.

19. Upson, *With Sherman Through the South*, 156.

20. Cyrus M. Roberts Diary, March 13, 1865, Civil War Miscellaneous Collection, USAMHI.

21. Wills, *Army Life*, 364; Cornelius C. Platter Diary, March 19, 1865, HLUGA; Howard, *Autobiography*, 2:142–43; Diary of Operations of the Army of the Tennessee, March 19, 1865, Joseph A. Sladen Papers, Civil War Miscellaneous Collection, USAMHI.

22. Diary of Operations of the Army of the Tennessee, March 20, 1865, Joseph A. Sladen Papers, Civil War Miscellaneous Collection, USAMHI.

23. Crooker, Nourse, and Brown, *The 55th Illinois*, 413; Hazen, *Narrative of Military Service*, 358.

24. Wills, *Army Life*, 364; Howard, *Autobiography*, 2:144–45; *OR*, vol. 47, pt. 1, pp. 235, 246, 262.

25. Robert Bruce Hoadley to "Cousin Em," April 8, 1865, Robert Bruce Hoadley Papers, PLDU.

26. F. M. Gee, "Capture of Gun at Cheraw, S.C.," *National Tribune*, October 2, 1884, p. 3; Edward W. Allen Diary, March 21, 1865, SHC; Cornelius C. Platter Diary, March 21, 1865, HLUGA.

27. *OR*, vol. 47, pt. 1, pp. 383, 391; Howard, *Autobiography*, 2:149; Diary of Operations of the Army of the Tennessee, March 21, 1865, Joseph A. Sladen Papers, Civil War Miscellaneous Collection, USAMHI.

28. Howard, *Autobiography*, 2:150; *OR*, vol. 47, pt. 1, p. 391.

29. Howard, *Autobiography*, 2:150.

30. Sherman, *Memoirs*, 786.

31. Wills, *Army Life*, 366–67; Diary of Operations of the Army of the Tennessee, March 22, 1865, Joseph A. Sladen Papers, Civil War Miscellaneous Collection, USAMHI.

32. Upson, *With Sherman Through the South*, 160.

33. Wills, *Army Life*, 359.

34. Cyrus M. Roberts Diary, March 21, 1865, Civil War Miscellaneous Collection, USAMHI.

35. Edward W. Allen to "Dear Friend," March 26, 1865, Edward W. Allen Papers, SHC.

36. Moses, "Memoirs," April 7, 1865; Cornelius C. Platter Diary, April 6, 1865, HLUGA; John W. Bates Diary, April 6, 1865, Civil War Miscellaneous Collection, USAMHI.

37. William Fifer to "Dear Brother and Sisters and Mother," April 6, 1865, William Fifer Papers, IHS.

38. Edward W. Allen to "Dear Friend Mary," April 3, 1865, Edward W. Allen Papers, SHC.

39. Sherman, *Memoirs*, 830–31.

40. Hazen, *Narrative of Military Service*, 359.

41. Young J. Powell to Ellen Aumack, March 27, 1865, Ellen Aumack Papers, PLDU.

42. Wills, *Army Life*, 367.

43. Isaiah T. Dillon to "My Dear and most devoted Sarah," April 1, 1865, Isaiah T. Dillon Papers, ISHL.

44. Hubert, *History of the Fiftieth Regiment*, 362.

45. Geer, *Civil War Diary*, 213.

46. Pennsylvania Infantry–52nd, Civil War Miscellaneous Collection, USAMHI.

47. Crooker, Nourse, and Brown, *The 55th Illinois*, 429–30.

48. Wills, *Army Life*, 368.

49. Augustus M. Van Dyke to "Dear Father," April 18, 1865, Augustus M. Van Dyke Papers, IHS.

50. Wills, *Army Life*, 369–70.

51. Crooker, Nourse, and Brown, *The 55th Illinois*, 430.

52. Stevenson, *History of the 78th Regiment*, 336–37.

53. Geer, *Civil War Diary*, 214.

54. Upson, *With Sherman Through the South*, 166–67.

55. Ibid.

56. Charles Weiser to "Cousin Katy," April 1865, Charles Weiser Papers, Civil War Miscellaneous Collection, USAMHI; Geer, *Civil War Diary*, 214; Stevenson, *History of the 78th Regiment*, 336–37.

57. Augustus M. Van Dyke to "Dear Father," April 18, 1865, Augustus M. Van Dyke Papers, IHS.

58. Willison, *Reminiscences of a Boy's Service*, 121.

59. James Williams Letter, April 27, 1865, James Williams Papers, Civil War Miscellaneous Collection, USAMHI; Geer, *Civil War Diary*, 217; R. W. Burt to "Dear Wife & Children," April 28, 1865, R. W. Burt Papers, WHMC.

60. Geer, *Civil War Diary*, 215–16; William H. Nugen to "Sister Mary," April 22, 1865, William H. Nugen, PLDU; Owen Stuart Letter, April 21, 1865, Owen Stuart Papers, ISHL; Circular No. 20, Raleigh, April 22, 1865, William B. Hazen Papers, Civil War Miscellaneous Collection, USAMHI; Howard, *Autobiography*, 2:158–59; Aaron Overstreet to "Dear companion and children," April 27, 1865, Aaron Overstreet Papers, Civil War Miscellaneous Collection, USAMHI.

61. Diary of Operations of the Army of the Tennessee, April 29, 1865, Joseph A. Sladen Papers, Civil War Miscellaneous Collection, USAMHI; Geer, *Civil War Diary*, 217; Wills, *Army Life*, 372–73.

62. Geer, *Civil War Diary*, 219; Moses, "Memoirs," May 5–7, 1865; Diary of Operations of the Army of the Tennessee, May 6, 1865, Joseph A. Sladen Papers, Civil War Miscellaneous Collection, USAMHI; Edward W. Allen to "Dear Friend," May 7, 1865, Edward W. Allen Papers, SHC; Stevenson, *History of the 78th Regiment*, 338.

63. Sherman, *Memoirs*, 863.

64. Willison, *Reminiscences of a Boy's Service*, 122–23.

65. Moses, "Memoirs," May 21, 1865; William B. Hazen Diary, May 21, 1865, Civil War Miscel-

laneous Collection, USAMHI; Stevenson, *History of the 78th Regiment*, 338–39; Geer, *Civil War Diary*, 223–24.

66. Albion Gross to "My Dear Companion," May 23, 1865, Albion Gross Papers, Civil War Miscellaneous Collection, USAMHI; Hubert, *History of the Fiftieth Regiment*, 393–94.

67. Hazen, *Narrative of Military Service*, 378.

68. Young J. Powell to Ellen Aumack, May 28, 1865, Ellen Aumack Papers, PLDU; Hubert, *History of the Fiftieth Regiment*, 394–95; Edward Schweitzer Papers, Civil War Times Illustrated Collection, USAMHI; Upson, *With Sherman Through the South*, 177–78; Sherman, *Memoirs*, 865.

69. Upson, *With Sherman Through the South*, 177–78; Isaiah T. Dillon to "My Dear wife Sarah," May 29, 1865, Isaiah T. Dillon Papers, ISHL; Rood, *Story of the Service of Company E*, 447–48; Young J. Powell to Ellen Aumack, May 28, 1865, Ellen Aumack Papers, PLDU; Hubert, *History of the Fiftieth Regiment*, 394–95.

70. Sherman, *Memoirs*, 865–66.

71. Upson, *With Sherman Through the South*, 177–78.

72. Taylor, *Tom Taylor's Civil War*, 221–22.

73. Dunbar, *History of the Ninety-third Regiment*, http://www.illinoiscivilwar.org/cw93-hist-ch12.html.

74. Moses, "Memoirs," May 24, 1865.

75. Sherman, *Memoirs*, 866; Hazen, *Narrative of Military Service*, 378; Overmyer, *A Stupendous Effort*, 168.

76. Upson, *With Sherman Through the South*, 178.

77. Crooker, Nourse, and Brown, *The 55th Illinois*, 433.

78. John J. McKee Diary, May 25, 1865, Civil War Miscellaneous Collection, USAMHI; Albion Gross to "Dear Wife," June 4, 1865, Albion Gross Papers, Civil War Miscellaneous Collection, USAMHI; Hazen, *Narrative of Military Service*, 377–78.

79. Stevenson, *History of the 78th Regiment*, 339; Dunbar, *History of the Ninety-third Regiment*, http://www.illinoiscivilwar.org/cw93-hist-ch13.html.

SOURCES

UNPUBLISHED PRIMARY SOURCES

ATLANTA HISTORY CENTER

Dwight Allen Papers

John Barnett Papers

AUGUSTANA COLLEGE LIBRARY, SPECIAL COLLECTIONS, ROCK ISLAND, ILLINOIS

Gould D. Molineaux Diary

HARGRETT LIBRARY, UNIVERSITY OF GEORGIA—ATHENS

Cornelius C. Platter Diary

ILLINOIS STATE HISTORICAL LIBRARY

William Anderson Allen Papers
Austin S. Andrew Papers
William H. Austin Papers
Newton Bateman Papers
Thomas Benson Beggs Papers
Jonathan Blair Papers
William H. Brown Papers
David Cornwall Papers
John Nelson Cromwell Papers
Isaiah T. Dillon Papers
William L. Dillon Papers
William R. Eddington Papers
Engelmann-Kircher Family Papers
John G. Given Papers
Douglas Hapeman Diary
John and Alexander Harper Papers

E. H. and D. G. Ingraham Papers
John D. Kerr Papers
Ira Merchant Papers
David W. Poak Papers
George W. Reese Papers
William M. Reid Diary
Robert Ridge Diary
Dietrich C. Smith Papers
George O. Smith Papers
Owen Stuart Papers
William H. Tebbets Papers
Abram J. Vanauken Papers
Wallace-Dickey Family Papers
Joseph B. Williamson Diary
Daniel G. Winegar Papers

INDIANA HISTORICAL SOCIETY

Jesse B. Connelly Diary
John H. Ferree Papers
William Fifer Papers

James Watts Hamilton Papers
John J. Hardin Papers
Francis M. Harmon Papers

Daniel Hughes Diary
George S. Johnson Papers
Willard Mendell Papers
John M. Roberts Reminiscences
Noah Beecher Sharp Papers

Benjamin J. Spooner Papers
Edward P. Stanfield Papers
Henry R. Strong Papers
Augustus M. Van Dyke Papers
Aurelius Lyman Voorhis Diary

JACKSON COUNTY HISTORICAL SOCIETY, MURPHYSBORO, ILLINOIS

Thomas N. McCleur Diary

LIBRARY OF CONGRESS

Chauncey E. Barton Papers
Francis Marion Bateman Papers
Richard Beard Papers

Wimer Bedford Papers
Abraham Lincoln Papers
John A. Logan Papers

MISSISSIPPI DEPARTMENT OF ARCHIVES AND HISTORY

J. W. Greenman Diary

PEARCE CIVIL WAR COLLECTION, NAVARRO COLLEGE, CORSICANA, TEXAS

George and Lycurgus Remley Papers

Walter Scates Letter

PERKINS LIBRARY, DUKE UNIVERSITY

Ellen Aumack Papers
Nathan G. Dye Papers
Robert Bruce Hoadley Papers

William H. Nugen Papers
Snow Family Papers

SOUTHERN HISTORICAL COLLECTION, UNIVERSITY OF NORTH CAROLINA,
CHAPEL HILL

Edward W. Allen Papers

Adoniram Judson Withrow Papers

U.S. ARMY MILITARY HISTORY INSTITUTE, CARLISLE BARRACKS, PENNSYLVANIA
CIVIL WAR MISCELLANEOUS COLLECTION

Anderson-Caphart-McCowan Family Papers
Jabez Banbury Diary
John W. Bates Diary
William N. Bullard Papers
Henry O. Dwight Papers
W. R. Eddington Papers
Brigham Foster Papers
U. S. Grant Papers
Abijah F. Gore Diary
Albion Gross Papers
William B. Hazen Papers
Francis M. Johnson Diary

William H. Jones Papers
Ensign H. King Diary
Jonathan L. Labrant Papers
John W. Latimer Papers
Charles B. Loop Papers
Levi Losier Papers
Charles H. Lutz Papers
William W. McCarty Papers
W. G. McElrea Diary
John J. McKee Diary
David McKinney Diary
Aaron Overstreet Papers

Israel M. Ritter Diary
Cyrus M. Roberts Diary
Joseph A. Sladen Papers
Stephen H. Smith Diary
Spencer Family Papers
Howard and Victor H. Stevens Papers
Joseph Stockton Diary

Isaac Vanderwarker Diary
William L. Wade Diary
Charles Weiser Papers
Enoch Weiss Diary
James Williams Papers
Charles C. Wilson Papers
Christian Zook Papers

CIVIL WAR TIMES ILLUSTRATED COLLECTION

Edward Schweitzer Papers

HARRISBURG CIVIL WAR ROUND TABLE COLLECTION

James W. Denver Papers

Edgar Embley Papers

VICKSBURG NATIONAL MILITARY PARK

Oscar Eugene Stewart Memoir

WESTERN HISTORICAL MANUSCRIPT COLLECTION, ELLIS LIBRARY, UNIVERSITY OF MISSOURI—COLUMBIA

R. W. Burt Papers

WESTERN RESERVE HISTORICAL SOCIETY

Franklin A. Wise Diary

WISCONSIN HISTORICAL SOCIETY

John J. Barney Papers
William Barney Papers
Daniel Buck Papers
George B. Carter Papers
Henry Clemons Papers
George A. Cooley Diary
Wilson S. Covill Papers
Luther H. Cowan Papers
Richard Robert Crowe Papers

Henry Miller Culbertson Papers
Michael Cunningham Papers
A. G. Dinsmore Reminiscences,
    Autobiographical Notes
Harrison Family Papers
Samuel C. Kirkpatrick Papers
John Erastus Perkins Papers
Emilie Quiner Diary

PUBLISHED PRIMARY SOURCES

Abbott, A. L. "The 12th Mich." *National Tribune.* October 15, 1885, p. 3.

Adams, Robert N. "My First Company." In *Military Order of the Loyal Legion of the United States.*
    56 vols., various publishers & dates; reprint, Wilmington, NC: Broadfoot Publishing Co.,
    1994, vol. 31.

Aldrich, M. G. "Resaca: The Part the 26th Iowa Took in That Fight." *National Tribune,* November 13, 1884, p. 3.

Ambrose, Daniel Leib. *History of the Seventh Regiment Illinois Volunteer Infantry.* Springfield: Illinois Journal Co., 1868.

Andreas, Alfred T. "The 'Ifs and Buts' of Shiloh." In *Military Order of the Loyal Legion of the United States*. 56 vols., various publishers & dates; reprint, Wilmington, NC: Broadfoot Publishing Co., 1994, vol. 10.

Andrus, Onley. *The Civil War Letters of Sergeant Onley Andrus*. Fred Albert Shannon, ed. Urbana: University of Illinois Press, 1947.

Ankeny, Henry G. *Kiss Josey for Me*. Florence Marie Ankeny Cox, ed. Santa Ana, CA: Friis-Pioneer Press, 1974.

Ayers, W. S. "The 78th Ohio at Bald Hill." *National Tribune*, January 17, 1884, p. 3.

Baird, T. W. "Shiloh: The Services of the 21st Mo. on the Field." *National Tribune*, February 25, 1886, p. 3.

Baker, D. B. "How the Battle Began." *National Tribune*, April 12, 1883, p. 3.

Barber, Flavel C. *Holding the Line: The Third Tennessee Infantry, 1861–1864*. Robert H. Ferrell, ed. Kent, OH: Kent State University Press, 1994.

Barber, Lucius W. *Army Memoirs of Lucius W. Barber, Company "D," 15th Illinois Volunteer Infantry*. Chicago: J. M. W. Jones Stationery & Printing Co., 1894.

Barker, Lorenzo A. *With the Western Sharpshooters: Michigan Boys of Company D, 66th Illinois*. Huntington, WV: Blue Acorn, 1994; originally published 1905.

Barney, Mitchell S. "That Prize Flag." *National Tribune*, March 4, 1886, p. 3.

Bartholomew, W. A. "The Charge at Vicksburg." *National Tribune*, November 27, 1884, p. 3.

Barton, R. H. "McPherson's Death." *National Tribune*, September 10, 1885, p. 3.

Bassett, C. E. "The Excelsior Banner." *National Tribune*, December 31, 1885, p. 3.

Belknap, William W. *History of the Fifteenth Regiment, Iowa Veteran Volunteer Infantry*. Keokuk, IA: R. B. Ogden & Son, 1887.

———. "The Obedience and Courage of the Private Soldier." In *Papers of the Military Order of the Loyal Legion of the United States*. 56 vols., various publishers and dates; reprint, Wilmington, NC: Broadfoot Publishing Co., 1994, vol. 55.

Bennett, William W. *A Narrative of the Great Revival in the Southern Armies During the Late Civil War Between the States of the Federal Union*. Philadelphia: Claxton, Remson and Haffelfinger, 1877.

Bering, John A., and Thomas Montgomery. *History of the Forty-eighth Ohio Veteran Volunteer Infantry*. Hillsboro, OH: Highland News Office, 1880 (http://www.48ovvi.org/oh48hist.html).

Bissell, J. W. "The Western Organization of Colored People for Furnishing Information to United States Troops in the South." In *Papers of the Military Order of the Loyal Legion of the United States*. 56 vols., various publishers and dates; reprint, Wilmington, NC: Broadfoot Publishing Co., 1994, vol. 27.

Blanchard, Ira. *I Marched with Sherman: Civil War Memoirs of the 20th Illinois Volunteer Infantry*. San Francisco: J. D. Huff, 1992.

Boyd, Cyrus F. *The Civil War Diary of Cyrus F. Boyd, Fifteenth Iowa Infantry, 1861–1863*. Mildred Throne, ed. Millwood, NY: Kraus, 1977.

Bringhurst, Thomas H., and Frank Swigart. *History of the Forty-sixth Regiment, Indiana Volunteer Infantry, September, 1861–September, 1865*. Logansport, IN: Wilson, Humphreys, 1888.

Brinsfield, John W., William C. Davis, Benedict Maryniak, and James I. Robertson, Jr., eds., *Faith in the Fight: Civil War Chaplains*. Mechanicsburg, PA: Stackpole Books, 2003.

Brinton, John H. *Personal Memoirs of John H. Brinton: Civil War Surgeon, 1861–1865*. Carbondale: Southern Illinois University Press, 1996.

Brown, A. L. "The 48th Ind.'s Conduct, and the 11th Ohio Battery's Losses." *National Tribune*, October 2, 1884, p. 3.

Brown, Alonzo L. *History of the Fourth Regiment of Minnesota Infantry Volunteers During the Great Rebellion, 1861–1865*. St. Paul: Pioneer Press, 189.

Brown, J. L. "The 50th Illinois at Fort Donelson." *National Tribune*, February 21, 1884, p. 3.

Bryner, Byron Cloyd. *Bugle Echoes: The Story of Illinois 47th*. Springfield, IL: Phillips Bros., Printers, 1905.

Bull, Rice C. *Soldiering: The Civil War Diary of Rice C. Bull, 123rd New York Volunteer Infantry*. K. Jack Bauer, ed., San Rafael, CA: Presidio Press, 1977.

Burdette, Robert J. *The Drums of the 47th*. Indianapolis: Bobbs-Merrill, 1914.

Burt, R. W. "Experiences of the 76th Ohio in the Siege." *National Tribune*, September 13, 1906, p. 3.

Campbell, John Quincy Adams. *The Union Must Stand: The Civil War Diary of John Quincy Adams Campbell, Fifth Iowa Volunteer Infantry*. Mark Grimsley and Todd D. Miller, eds. Knoxville: University of Tennessee Press, 2000.

Chapel, Wilson E. *The Civil War Journals of Wilson E. Chapel, March 1861 to January 1863*. DeKalb, IL: DeKalb County Historical and Genealogical Society, 1998.

Chetlain, Augustus L. *Recollections of Seventy Years*. Galena, IL: Gazette Publishing Co., 1899.

Childress, George L. "Atlanta." *National Tribune*, August 5, 1886, p. 3.

Churchill, James O. "Wounded at Fort Donelson." In *Papers of the Military Order of the Loyal Legion of the United States*. 56 vols., various publishers and dates; reprint, Wilmington, NC: Broadfoot Publishing Co., 1994, vol. 14.

Clemson, J. W. "Surprised the Johnnies." *National Tribune*, September 30, 1897, p. 3.

Cockerill, John A. "A Boy at Shiloh." In *Papers of the Military Order of the Loyal Legion of the United States*. 56 vols., various publishers and dates; reprint, Wilmington, NC: Broadfoot Publishing Co., 1994, vol. 6.

Compton, James. "The Second Division of the Sixteenth Army Corps in the Atlanta Campaign." In Papers of the Military Order of the Loyal Legion of the United States. 56 vols., various publishers and dates; reprint. Wilmington, NC: Broadfoot Publishing Co., 1994, vol. 30.

Cone, Charles M. "On the Hatchie: The 12th Mich. the First to Cross the Bridge." *National Tribune*, April 22, 1886, p. 3.

Connelly, Thomas W. *History of the Seventieth Ohio Regiment*. Cincinnati: Peak Bros., n.d.

Coombe, E. "The 28th of July Before Atlanta." *National Tribune*, February 7, 1884, p. 3.

Coulter, S. L. "De Grasse's Battery." *National Tribune*, May 21, 1885, p. 3.

Crawford, Richard, ed. *The Civil War Songbook: Complete Original Sheet Music for 37 Songs*. New York: Dover, 1977.

Crooker, Lucien B. "Chickasaw Bayou." *National Tribune*, September 11, 1884, p. 3.

Crooker, Lucien B., Henry S. Nourse, and John G. Brown. *The 55th Illinois, 1861–1865*. Huntington, WV: Blue Acorn Press, 1993.

Crummell, Albert B. "De Grasse's Battery: What a Comrade Saw Around the Howard House." *National Tribune*, September 10, 1885, p. 3.

———. "Ezra Chapel." *National Tribune*, April 26, 1888, p. 3.

Crummer, Wilbur F. *With Grant at Fort Donelson, Shiloh, and Vicksburg*. Oak Park, IL: E. C. Crummer & Co., 1915.

Dawes, E. C. "My First Day Under Fire at Shiloh." In *Papers of the Military Order of the Loyal Legion of the United States*. 56 vols., various publishers and dates; reprint, Wilmington, NC: Broadfoot Publishing Co., 1994, vol. 3.

Day, James G. "The Fifteenth Iowa at Shiloh." In *Papers of the Military Order of the Loyal Legion of the United States*. 56 vols., various publishers and dates; reprint, Wilmington, NC: Broadfoot Publishing Co., 1994, vol. 56.

Dihel, R. M. "Champion's Hill: A Graphic Picture of a Most Exciting Time—Logan's Division at Champion's Hill." *National Tribune*, September 11, 1884, p. 3.

Downing, Alexander G. *Downing's Civil War Diary*. Olynthus B. Clark, ed. Des Moines: Iowa State Department of History and Archives, 1916.

Dugan, James. *History of Hurlbut's Fighting Fourth Division*. Cincinnati: Morgan & Co., 1863.

Dunbar, Aaron. *History of the Ninety-third Regiment Illinois Volunteer Infantry: From Organization To Muster Out.* Harvey M. Trimble, ed. http://www.illinoiscivilwar.org/cw93-hist-toc.html.

Duncan, William. "The Army of the Tennessee Under Major-General O. O. Howard." In *Papers of the Military Order of the Loyal Legion of the United States.* 56 vols., various publishers and dates; reprint, Wilmington, NC: Broadfoot Publishing Co., 1994, vol. 29.

Durham, Thomas Wise. *Three Years with Wallace's Zouaves: The Civil War Memoirs of Thomas Wise Durham.* Jeffrey L. Patrick, ed. Macon, GA: Mercer University Press, 2003.

Dwight, Henry O. "A Soldier's Story: The Affair on the Raymond Road." *New York Daily Tribune,* November 21, 1886.

Easlick, William. "A Regiment Without Fodder for Its Guns." *National Tribune,* April 12, 1883, p. 3.

Elliott, Isaac H. *History of the Thirty-third Regiment Illinois Veteran Volunteer Infantry in the Civil War.* Gibson City, IL: Regimental Association of the Thirty-third Illinois, 1902.

Fink, Jacob. "De Grasse's Battery." *National Tribune,* July 9, 1885, p. 3.

———. "Shiloh." *National Tribune,* May 3, 1883, p. 3.

Fish, C. H. "The Signal Corps, Part 3." *National Tribune,* April 29, 1883, p. 3.

Flemming, Robert H. "The Battle of Shiloh as a Private Saw It." In *Papers of the Military Order of the Loyal Legion of the United States.* 56 vols., various publishers and dates; reprint, Wilmington, NC: Broadfoot Publishing Co., 1994, vol. 6.

Flint, Mortimer R. "The Battle of Allatoona." In *Papers of the Military Order of the Loyal Legion of the United States.* 56 vols., various publishers and dates; reprint, Wilmington, NC: Broadfoot Publishing Co., 1994, vol. 30.

Florey, A. J. "Champion Hills." *National Tribune,* August 4, 1887, p. 3.

Force, Manning F. "Marching Across Carolina." In *Papers of the Military Order of the Loyal Legion of the United States.* 56 vols., various publishers and dates; reprint, Wilmington, NC: Broadfoot Publishing Co., 1994, vol. 1.

———. "Personal Recollections of the Vicksburg Campaign." In *Papers of the Military Order of the Loyal Legion of the United States.* 56 vols., various publishers and dates; reprint, Wilmington, NC: Broadfoot Publishing Co., 1994, vol. 1.

Frederick, Noah T. "That Iowa Sergeant." *National Tribune,* August 14, 1884, p. 3.

French, William. "One Regiment That Was Not Surprised." *National Tribune,* April 12, 1883, p. 3.

Fuller, C. M. "The 78th Ohio at Jackson, Tenn." *National Tribune,* June 18, 1883, p. 3.

Fuller, John W. "A Terrible Day: The Fighting Before Atlanta, July 22, 1864." *National Tribune,* April 16, 1885.

Geer, Allen Morgan. *The Civil War Diary of Allen Morgan Geer, Twentieth Regiment, Illinois Volunteers.* Mary Ann Anderson, ed. Denver: Robert C. Appleman, 1977.

Gordon, Edward A. "A Graphic Picture of the Battle of Shiloh." *National Tribune,* April 26, 1883, p. 1.

Grant, Ulysses S. *Personal Memoirs of U. S. Grant.* 2 vols. New York: Charles L. Webster & Co., 1885.

Grinnell, J. L. "The 34th Ind." *National Tribune,* August 11, 1887, p. 3.

Haldeman, J. B. "Who Recaptured the De Gres Battery in the Battle Before Atlanta?: Other Versions." *National Tribune,* June 28, 1883, p. 3.

Hancock, John. *The Fourteenth Wisconsin at Corinth and Shiloh.* Indianapolis: F. E. Engle & Son, 1895.

Harris, J. B. "An Incident of Champion Hills—Gen. Logan's Advice." *National Tribune,* July 31, 1884, p. 3.

Hazen, William B. *A Narrative of Military Service.* Boston: Ticknor & Co., 1885.

Hickenlooper, Andrew. "The Battle of Shiloh." In *Papers of the Military Order of the Loyal Legion of the United States.* 56 vols., various publishers and dates; reprint, Wilmington, NC: Broadfoot Publishing Co., 1994, vol. 5.

Hicks, Henry G. "The Campaign and Capture of Vicksburg." In *Papers of the Military Order of the Loyal Legion of the United States.* 56 vols., various publishers and dates; reprint, Wilmington, NC: Broadfoot Publishing Co., 1994, vol. 31.

———. "Fort Donelson." In *Papers of the Military Order of the Loyal Legion of the United States.* 56 vols., various publishers and dates; reprint, Wilmington, NC: Broadfoot Publishing Co., 1994, vol. 29.

Hitchcock, Henry. *Marching with Sherman.* Lincoln: University of Nebraska Press, 1995.

Holcomb, Julie, ed. *Southern Sons, Northern Soldiers: The Civil War Letters of the Remley Brothers, 22nd Iowa Infantry.* DeKalb: Northern Illinois University Press, 2004.

Holcombe, R. I. "Who Cared for the Body of Gen. McPherson?" *National Tribune,* April 30, 1885, p. 3.

Hovey, Alvin P. "Pittsburg Landing." *National Tribune,* February 1, 1883, p. 1.

Howard, Oliver O. *Autobiography of Oliver Otis Howard, Major General, United States Army.* 2 vols. Freeport, NY: Books for Libraries Press, 1971.

Hubert, Charles F. *History of the Fiftieth Regiment, Illinois Volunteer Infantry in the War of the Union.* Kansas City, MO: Western Veteran Publishing Co., 1894.

Humbert, S. B. "Columbia, S.C., and the Part W. M. Prouty and Montgomery Hulburt Took in the Capture." *National Tribune,* October 8, 1885, p. 3.

Hunt, John T. "Civil War Reminiscences of Dr. John T. Hunt, Macedonia, Illinois, Company A., 40th Illinois Voluntary Infantry." In "The Yesterdays of Hamilton County, Illinois," http://www.carolyar.com/Illinois/Hunt-Part1.htm.

Huston, Joseph J. "Who Planted the Flag at Jackson, Miss.?" *National Tribune,* February 19, 1885, p. 3.

"An Iowa Soldier's Story of Shiloh." *National Tribune,* May 3, 1883, p. 3.

Jackson, Isaac. *Some of the Boys: The Civil War Letters of Isaac Jackson, 1862–1865.* Carbondale: Southern Illinois University Press, 1960.

Jackson, Oscar Lawrence. *The Colonel's Diary: Journals Kept Before and During the Civil War by the Late Colonel Oscar L. Jackson, Sometime Commander of the 63rd Regiment O.V.I.* David P. Jackson, ed. Privately published, 1922.

Jackson, W. W. "On the Hatchie." *National Tribune,* January 14, 1886, p. 3.

Jeff [last name not given, a soldier in 6th Missouri]. "Atlanta." *National Tribune,* July 9, 1885, p. 3.

Jenney, William L. B. "Personal Recollections of Vicksburg." In *Papers of the Military Order of the Loyal Legion of the United States.* 56 vols., various publishers and dates; reprint, Wilmington, NC: Broadfoot Publishing Co., 1994, vol. 12.

———. "With Sherman and Grant from Memphis to Chattanooga: A Reminiscence." In *Papers of the Military Order of the Loyal Legion of the United States.* 56 vols., various publishers and dates; reprint, Wilmington, NC: Broadfoot Publishing Co., 1994, vol. 13.

Jessee, James W. *Civil War Diaries of James W. Jessee, 1861–1865, Company K, 8th Regiment of Illinois Volunteer Infantry.* William P. LaBounty, ed. Normal, IL: McLean County Genealogical Society, 1997.

Johnson, Crosby. "Battle of Atlanta." *National Tribune,* October 10, 1886, p. 3.

Johnson, Robert U., and Clarence C. Buel. *Battles and Leaders of the Civil War.* New York: The Century Company, 1887.

Jones, D. Lloyd. "The Battle of Shiloh: Reminiscences." In *Papers of the Military Order of the Loyal Legion of the United States.* 56 vols., various publishers and dates; reprint, Wilmington, NC: Broadfoot Publishing Co., 1994, vol. 49.

Jones, Samuel Calvin. *Reminiscences of the Twenty-second Iowa Volunteer Infantry.* Iowa City: Camp Pope Book Shop, 1907; reprint, 1993.

Kennedy, John F. "The Excelsior Prize Drill." *National Tribune*, May 6, 1886, p. 3.

Kimbell, Charles B. *History of Battery A, First Illinois Light Artillery Volunteers*. Chicago: Cushing Printing Co., 1899.

Kimberley, E. O. "Burning of Columbia." *National Tribune*, September 3, 1885, p. 3.

Kiner, F. F. *One Year's Soldiering: Embracing the Battles of Fort Donelson and Shiloh*. Lancaster PA: E. H. Thomas, 1863. Reprint, Prior Lake, MN: Morgan Avenue Press, 2000.

Kircher, Henry A. *A German in the Yankee Fatherland: The Civil War Letters of Henry A. Kircher*. Earl J. Hess, ed. Kent, OH: Kent State University Press, 1983.

Kountz, John S., et al. *History of the 37th Regiment O.V.V.I.* Toledo: Montgomery & Vroomar Printers, 1889.

Krone, D. C. "The 41st Ill. at Columbia, S.C." *National Tribune*, September 10, 1885, p. 3.

Leasure, J. E. "Chickasaw Bluffs." *National Tribune*, December 25, 1884, p. 3.

Lee, E. T. "The Columbia, S.C., Controversy." *National Tribune*, July 16, 1885, p. 3.

———. "Shiloh: Comrade Lee Criticizes Gen. Buell's Article on the Famous Battle." *National Tribune*, May 6, 1886, p. 3.

Leggett, Mortimer D. "Battle of Atlanta." *National Tribune*, May 6, 1886, p. 1.

———. *The Battle of Atlanta: A Paper Read by General M. D. Leggett Before the Society of the Army of the Tennessee, October 18, 1883, at Cleveland*. Cleveland: John A. Davies, 1883.

Logan, Mrs. John A. [Mary C.] "Cairo in 1861." *National Tribune*, February 9, 1888, p. 1.

Long, J. W. Letter. *National Tribune*, September 13, 1888, p. 3.

Longley, Charles L. "Champion's Hill." In *Papers of the Military Order of the Loyal Legion of the United States*. 56 vols., various publishers and dates; reprint, Wilmington, NC: Broadfoot Publishing Co., 1994, vol. 55.

Loop, M. B. "Sounding the Alarm: The 68th Ohio's Trying Time at the Battle of Atlanta." *National Tribune*, December 1, 1898, p. 3.

Love, William DeLoss. *Wisconsin in the War of the Rebellion: A History of All Regiments and Batteries That State Has Sent to the Field*. Chicago: Church & Goodman, Publishers, 1866.

Mahon, Samuel. "The Forager in Sherman's Last Campaigns." In *Papers of the Military Order of the Loyal Legion of the United States*. 56 vols., various publishers and dates; reprint, Wilmington, NC: Broadfoot Publishing Co., 1994, vol. 56.

Marvin, R. M. "Columbia, S.C." *National Tribune*, October 14, 1886, p. 3.

———. "The First Flag at Columbia, S.C." *National Tribune*, September 17, 1885, p. 3.

Mason, George. "Shiloh." In *Papers of the Military Order of the Loyal Legion of the United States*. 56 vols., various publishers and dates; reprint, Wilmington, NC: Broadfoot Publishing Co., 1994, vol. 10.

McCord, William B. "Battle of Corinth: The Campaigns Preceding and Leading Up to this Battle and its Results." In *Papers of the Military Order of the Loyal Legion of the United States*. 56 vols., various publishers and dates; reprint, Wilmington, NC: Broadfoot Publishing Co., 1994, vol. 29.

McGillicuddy, T. D. "The 50th Illinois at Fort Donelson." *National Tribune*, May 1, 1884, p. 3.

McGinnis, George F. "Shiloh." In *Papers of the Military Order of the Loyal Legion of the United States*. 56 vols., various publishers and dates; reprint, Wilmington, NC: Broadfoot Publishing Co., 1994, vol. 24.

Meeker, W. D. "Hurlbut's Division at the Hatchie." *National Tribune*, June 10, 1886, p. 3.

Mendenhall, S. C. "Battle of Atlanta." *National Tribune*, August 5, 1886, p. 3.

Miller, Charles D. "Saving His Battery." *National Tribune*, April 23, 1885, p. 3.

———. *The Struggle for the Life of the Republic: A Civil War Narrative by Brevet Major Charles Dana Miller, 76th Ohio Volunteer Infantry*. Stewart Bennett, ed. Kent, OH: Kent State University Press, 2004.

Moore, Elias D. "Diaries of Elias D. Moore, 114th O.V.I., Company A." http://www.

fortunecity.com / westwood / makeover / 347 / civil_war_diary_of_a_union_soldier_elias_
d_moore_114th_ohio_volunteer_infantry.htm.

Morris, C. D. "The Charge at Vicksburg." *National Tribune,* April 16, 1885, p. 3.

Morris, W. S., L. D. Hartwell, and J. B. Kuykendall. *History 31st Regiment Illinois Volunteers Organized by John A. Logan.* Carbondale: Southern Illinois University Press, 1998; originally published 1902.

Morrison, Marion. *A History of the Ninth Regiment Illinois Volunteer Infantry.* Monmouth, IL, 1864; reprint, Carbondale: Southern Illinois University Press, 1997.

Moses, Jefferson. "The Memoirs, Diary, and Life of Private Jefferson Moses, Company G, 93rd Illinois Volunteers." http://www.ioweb.com/civilwar.

Munger, J. C. "The 16th Iowa at Atlanta." *National Tribune,* August 26, 1886, p. 3.

Munn, Asa B., Amos H. Miller, and W. O. Newton. *Military History and Reminiscences of the Thirteenth Regiment of Illinois Volunteer Infantry in the Civil War in the United States, 1861–1865.* Chicago: Woman's Temperance Publishing Association, 1892.

Naylor, J. M. "Who Recaptured the De Gres Battery in the Battle Before Atlanta?: Other Versions." *National Tribune,* June 28, 1883.

Newton, James K. *A Wisconsin Boy in Dixie: The Selected Letters of James K. Newton.* Stephen E. Ambrose, ed. Madison: University of Wisconsin Press, 1961.

Northup, James E., and Samuel W. Northup. *"Drifting to an Unknown Future": The Civil War Letters of James E. Northup and Samuel W. Northup.* Robert C. Steensma, ed. Sioux Falls, SD: Center for Western Studies, 2000.

Nutt, E. E. "Fight at Atlanta: Work of the Seventy-eighth and Twentieth Ohio That Day." *National Tribune,* January 3, 1884, p. 3.

Oates, James. "The Ninth Illinois at Shiloh." *National Tribune,* May 10, 1883, p. 1.

Orendorff, H. H., et al. *Reminiscences of the Civil War from Diaries of Members of the 103rd Illinois Volunteer Infantry.* N.p., 1904.

Orr, T. G. "The Battle of Iuka." *National Tribune,* September 11, 1884, p. 3.

Paddock, George L. "The Beginnings of an Illinois Volunteer Regiment in 1861." In *Papers of the Military Order of the Loyal Legion of the United States.* 56 vols., various publishers and dates; reprint, Wilmington, NC: Broadfoot Publishing Co., 1994, vol. 11.

Parrish, L. F. "At Jackson." *National Tribune,* August 11, 1887, p. 3.

Peirce, Taylor, and Catharine Peirce. *Dear Catharine, Dear Taylor: The Civil War Letters of Catharine and Taylor Peirce.* Richard L. Kiper, ed. Lawrence: University Press of Kansas, 2002.

Perry, Oran. "The Entering Wedge." In *Papers of the Military Order of the Loyal Legion of the United States.* 56 vols., various publishers and dates; reprint, Wilmington, NC: Broadfoot Publishing Co., 1994, vol. 24.

Pierson, Enos. "The 54th Ind. at Chickasaw." *National Tribune,* April 16, 1885, p. 3.

Post, Lydia Minturn, ed. *Soldiers' Letters from Camp, Battle-field, and Prison.* New York: Bunce & Huntington, 1865.

Private, 81st Ohio. "Capture of the De Gres Batery: The Question Settled." *National Tribune,* July 19, 1883, p. 3.

Puck, Susan T., ed. *Sacrifice at Vicksburg: Letters from the Front.* Shippensburg, PA: Burd Street Press, 1997.

Puterbaugh, John. *March and Countermarch: Letters from a Union Soldier, May 14, 1861, to April 3, 1862.* Ruth H. Kilbourn, ed. Grants Pass, OR: published by the editor, 1995.

Putnam, Douglas, Jr. "Reminiscences of the Battle of Shiloh." In *Papers of the Military Order of the Loyal Legion of the United States.* 56 vols., various publishers and dates; reprint, Wilmington, NC: Broadfoot Publishing Co., 1994, vol. 2.

Ragsdale, J. W. "The First to Enter Columbia." *National Tribune,* August 6, 1885, p. 3.

Ralston, Alexander. "De Grasse's Battery: The Part the 11th Ill. Took in Its Recapture." *Nation*
Tribune, August 27, 1885, p. 3.

Raney, David A. "In the Lord's Army: The United States Christian Commission, Soldiers, an
the Union War Effort." In Paul A. Cimbala and Randall M. Miller, eds., *Union Soldiers an*
the Northern Home Front: Wartime Experiences, Postwar Adjustments. New York: Fordhar
University Press, 2002.

Report of the Adjutant General of the State of Illinois. vol. 1, containing reports for the year
1861–66. Revised by Brig. Gen. J. N. Reece, Adjutant General. Springfield, IL: Phillip
Bros., State Printers, 1900. In "Illinois in the Civil War," www.illinoiscivilwar.org.

Rerick, John H. *The Forty-fourth Indiana Volunteer Infantry: History of Its Services in the War of the*
Rebellion. Lagrange, IN: published by the author, 1880.

Reynolds, George. "General McPherson's Death." *National Tribune*, October 1, 1881, p. 1.

Richardson, George Sidenbender, and William A. Richardson. *"For My Country": The Richardson*
Letters, 1861–1865. Gordon C. Jones, ed. Wilmington, NC: Broadfoot Publishing Co., 1984.

Richardson, L. W. "On the Hatchie: How Gen. Ord Struck the Adjutant." *National Tribune*,
March 25, 1886, p. 3.

Ritner, Jacob, and Emeline Ritner. *Love and Valor: The Intimate Civil War Letters Between Captain*
Jacob and Emeline Ritner. Charles F. Larimer, ed. Western Springs, IL: Sigourney Press,
2000.

Rood, H. H. "Sketches of the Thirteenth Iowa." In *Papers of the Military Order of the Loyal Legion*
of the United States. 56 vols., various publishers and dates; reprint, Wilmington, NC: Broadfoot Publishing Co., 1994, vol. 55.

Rood, Hosea W. *Story of the Service of Company E, Twelfth Wisconsin Regiment Veteran Volunteer*
Infantry in the War of the Rebellion. Milwaukee: Swain & Tate, 1893.

Russell, Q. O. "The Position of the Troops." *National Tribune*, October 2, 1884, p. 3.

Sanborn, John B. "Battles and Campaigns of September, 1862." In *Papers of the Military Order of*
the Loyal Legion of the United States. 56 vols., various publishers and dates; reprint, Wilmington, NC: Broadfoot Publishing Co., 1994, vol. 30.

———. "The Campaign Against Vicksburg." In *Papers of the Military Order of the Loyal Legion*
of the United States. 56 vols., various publishers and dates; reprint, Wilmington, NC: Broadfoot Publishing Co., 1994, vol. 27.

Sanderson, William L. "Letters from Col. William L. Sanderson, 23rd Indiana Infantry." In
"Indiana in the Civil War," http://www.indianainthecivilwar.com.

Saunier, Joseph A. *A History of the Forty-seventh Regiment, Ohio Veteran Volunteer Infantry.* Hillsboro, OH: Press the Lyle Printing Company, 1903.

Sears, Cyrus. "The 11th Ohio Battery at Iuka." *National Tribune*, November 6, 1884, p. 3.

Shanks, William F. G. "Recollections of Sherman." *Harper's New Monthly Magazine* 30, no. 175
(December 1864).

Shearer, Wells H. "De Grasse's Battery Once More." *National Tribune*, September 3, 1885, p. 3.

Sherman, William T. *Memoirs of General W. T. Sherman.* New York: Library of America, 1990.

Simon, John Y., ed. *The Papers of Ulysses S. Grant.* 26 vols. Carbondale: Southern Illinois University Press, 1969–.

Simpson, Brooks D., and Jean V. Berlin, eds. *Sherman's Civil War: Selected Correspondence of*
William T. Sherman, 1860–1865. Chapel Hill: University of North Carolina Press, 1999.

Smith, Albert E. "A Few Days with the Eighth Regiment, Wisconsin Volunteers at Iuka and
Corinth." In *Papers of the Military Order of the Loyal Legion of the United States.* 56 vols.,
various publishers and dates; reprint, Wilmington, NC: Broadfoot Publishing Co., 1994,
vol. 49.

Soper, E. B. "A Chapter from the History of Company D, Twelfth Iowa Infantry Volunteers." In

Papers of the Military Order of the Loyal Legion of the United States. 56 vols., various publishers and dates; reprint, Wilmington, NC: Broadfoot Publishing Co., 1994, vol. 56.

Squier, George W. *This Wilderness of War: The Civil War Letters of George W. Squier, Hoosier Volunteer*. Julie A. Doyle, John David Smith, and Richard M. McMurry, eds. Knoxville: University of Tennessee Press, 1998.

Steele, Lindsay. "Champion's Hill." *National Tribune*, November 29, 1888, p. 4.

Stevenson, Thomas M. *History of the 78th Regiment O.V.V.I. from its "Muster-in" to Its "Muster-out."* Zanesville, OH: Hugh Dunne, 1865.

Stockwell, Elisha, Jr. *Private Elisha Stockwell, Jr., Sees the Civil War*. Byron R. Abernethy, ed. Norman: University of Oklahoma Press, 1958.

Strong, William E. "The Campaign Against Vicksburg." In *Papers of the Military Order of the Loyal Legion of the United States*. 56 vols., various publishers and dates; reprint, Wilmington, NC: Broadfoot Publishing Co., 1994, vol. 11.

———. "The Death of General James B. McPherson." In *Papers of the Military Order of the Loyal Legion of the United States*. 56 vols., various publishers and dates; reprint, Wilmington, NC: Broadfoot Publishing Co., 1994, vol. 10.

Stuber, Johann. *Mein Tagebuch über die Erlebnisse im Revolutions-Kriege*. Cincinnati: S. Rosenthal & Co., 1896.

Sumbardo, C. L. "Some Facts About the Battle of Shiloh." In *Papers of the Military Order of the Loyal Legion of the United States*. 56 vols., various publishers and dates; reprint, Wilmington, NC: Broadfoot Publishing Co., 1994, vol. 28.

Sweetman, Alexander A. J. "Chickasaw Bluffs." *National Tribune*, April 20, 1893, p. 1.

Taylor, Thomas. *Tom Taylor's Civil War*. Albert Castel, ed. Lawrence: University Press of Kansas, 2000.

Thompson, A. J. "McPherson's Death: The Sad Story of His Orderly, Who Saw Him Die." *National Tribune*, July 23, 1885, p. 3.

Tunnard, William H. *A Southern Record: The History of the Third Regiment, Louisiana Infantry*. Fayetteville: University of Arkansas Press, 1997.

Tuttle, John M. "Personal Recollections of 1861." In *Papers of the Military Order of the Loyal Legion of the United States*. 56 vols., various publishers and dates; reprint, Wilmington, NC: Broadfoot Publishing Co., 1994, vol. 55.

United States War Department. *The War of the Rebellion: Official Records of the Union and Confederate Armies*. 128 vols. Washington, DC: Government Printing Office, 1881–1901.

Upson, Theodore F. *With Sherman to the Sea: The Civil War Letters, Diaries, and Reminiscences of Theodore F. Upson*. Oscar Osburn Winther, ed. Bloomington: Indiana University Press, 1958.

Veatch, James C. "The Battle of Shiloh." *National Tribune*, March 15, 1883, p. 1.

Veteran, "Who Recaptured the De Gres Battery in the Battle Before Atlanta?: Other Versions." *National Tribune*, June 28, 1883, p. 3.

Wallace, Isabel. *Life and Letters of General W. H. L. Wallace*. Carbondale: Southern Illinois University Press, 2000; originally published by R. R. Donnelley & Sons, 1909.

Wallace, Lew. *Smoke, Sound & Fury: The Civil War Memoirs of Major-General Lew Wallace, U.S. Volunteers*. Jim Leeke, ed. Portland, OR: Strawberry Hill Press, 1998.

Walter, H. J. "Battle of Belmont." *National Tribune*, August 5, 1886, p. 3.

Wardner, Horace. "Reminiscences of a Surgeon." In *Papers of the Military Order of the Loyal Legion of the United States*. 56 vols., various publishers and dates; reprint, Wilmington, NC: Broadfoot Publishing Co., 1994, vol. 12.

Warner, J. F. "Smith's Division at Donelson." *National Tribune*, January 3, 1884, p. 3.

Wheeler, John P. "Shiloh." *National Tribune*, May 3, 1883, p. 3.

Wiley, William. *The Civil War Diary of a Common Soldier.* Terrence J. Winschel, ed. Baton Rouge: Louisiana State University Press, 2001.

Wilkin, Jacob W. "Vicksburg." In *Papers of the Military Order of the Loyal Legion of the United States.* 56 vols., various publishers and dates; reprint, Wilmington, NC: Broadfoot Publishing Co., 1994, vol. 13.

Williams, John Melvin. *The Eagle Regiment.* Belleville, WI: Recorder Printing, 1890.

Williams, T. J. "The Battle of Champion's Hill." In *Papers of the Military Order of the Loyal Legion of the United States.* 56 vols., various publishers and dates; reprint, Wilmington, NC: Broadfoot Publishing Co., 1994, vol. 5.

Willison, Charles A. *Reminiscences of a Boy's Service with the 76th Ohio.* Huntington, WV: Blue Acorn Press, 1995; originally published 1908.

Wills, Charles W. *Army Life of an Illinois Soldier.* Carbondale: Southern Illinois University Press, 1996.

Wilson, Ephraim A. *Memoirs of the War.* Cleveland: W. M. Bayne Printing Co., 1893.

Wilson, G. W. "The 13th Iowa at Columbia." *National Tribune,* July 16, 1885, p. 3.

Wilson, William. "66th Illinois at Dallas." *National Tribune,* October 16, 1884, p. 3.

Winters, William. *The Musick of the Mocking Birds, the Roar of the Cannon: The Diary and Letters of William Winters.* Steven E. Woodworth, ed. Lincoln: University of Nebraska Press, 1998.

Wood, D. W. "The 20th Ohio at Atlanta." *National Tribune,* August 14, 1884, p. 3.

Worthington, Thomas. *A Brief History of the Forty-sixth Ohio Volunteers.* N.p.: published by the author, 1878.

Wright, Charles. *A Corporal's Story: Experiences in the Ranks of Company C, 81st Ohio Vol. Infantry.* W. H. Chamberlin, ed. Philadelphia: James Beal, Printer, 1887.

Wright, George G. "Generals Curtis and Crocker." In *Papers of the Military Order of the Loyal Legion of the United States.* 56 vols., various publishers and dates; reprint, Wilmington, NC: Broadfoot Publishing Co., 1994, vol. 55.

SECONDARY SOURCES

Allmon, William B. "The Much-Traveled 21st Missouri Fought for the Union in Tennessee and Texas, and at Points in Between." *America's Civil War,* September 1996.

Arnold, James R. *The Armies of U.S. Grant.* London: Arms & Armour Press, 1995.

———. *Grant Wins the War: Decision at Vicksburg.* New York: John Wiley, 1997.

Ballard, Michael B. *U. S. Grant: The Making of a General, 1861–1863.* Wilmington, DE: Scholarly Resources, 2004.

Barrett, Joseph O. *The Soldier Bird "Old Abe": The Live War-Eagle of Wisconsin.* Madison, WI: Atwood & Culver, 1876.

Baumann, Ken. *Arming the Suckers, 1861–1865: A Compilation of Illinois Civil War Weapons.* Dayton: Morningside Press, 1989.

Bearss, Edwin Cole. *The Campaign for Vicksburg.* 3 vols. Vol. 1, *Vicksburg Is the Key;* Vol. 2, *Grant Strikes a Fatal Blow;* Vol. 3, *Unvexed to the Sea.* Dayton: Morningside Press, 1985.

Brewer, James D. *Tom Worthington's Civil War: Shiloh, Sherman, and the Search for Vindication.* Jefferson, NC: McFarland, 2001.

Campbell, Jacqueline Glass. *When Sherman Marched North from the Sea: Resistance on the Confederate Home Front.* Chapel Hill: University of North Carolina Press, 2003.

Castel, Albert E. *Decision in the West: The Atlanta Campaign of 1864.* Lawrence: University Press of Kansas, 1992.

Catton, Bruce. *Grant Moves South.* Boston: Little, Brown, 1960.

Clark, Charles B., and Roger B. Bowen, *University Recruits—Company C, 12th Iowa Infantry Regiment, U.S.A., 1861–1866.* Elverson, PA: Mennonite Family History, 1991.

ooling, Benjamin Franklin. *Forts Henry and Donelson: The Key to the Confederate Heartland.* Knoxville: University of Tennessee Press, 1987.

ozzens, Peter. *The Darkest Days of the War: The Battles of Iuka and Corinth.* Chapel Hill: University of North Carolina Press, 1997.

———. *The Shipwreck of Their Hopes: The Battles for Chattanooga.* Urbana: University of Illinois Press, 1994.

)aniel, Larry J. *Shiloh: The Battle That Changed the Civil War.* New York: Simon & Schuster, 1997.

)oby, Joseph E. *The Last Full Measure of Devotion.* Raleigh, NC: Pentland Press, 1996.

)rake, Rebecca Blackwell. *In Their Own Words: Soldiers Tell the Story of the Battle of Raymond.* Raymond, MS: Friends of Raymond, 2001.

ingle, Stephen D. *Struggle for the Heartland: The Campaigns from Fort Henry to Corinth.* Lincoln: University of Nebraska Press, 2001.

eis, William B. "Grant and the Belmont Campaign: A Study in Intelligence and Command." In *The Art of Command in the Civil War.* Steven E. Woodworth, ed. Lincoln: University of Nebraska Press, 1998.

———. *Grant's Secret Service: The Intelligence War from Belmont to Appomattox.* Lincoln: University of Nebraska Press, 2002.

Foster, Buckley Thomas. "Dress Rehearsal for Hard War: William T. Sherman and the Meridian Expedition." Ph.D. dissertation, Mississippi State University, 2003.

Gaff, Alan D. *On Many a Bloody Field: Four Years in the Iron Brigade.* Bloomington: Indiana University Press, 1996.

Gebhardt, Carl Dean. "The Eleventh Illinois Infantry Regiment in the Civil War." M.A. thesis, Western Illinois University, 1968.

Gott, Kendall. *Where the South Lost the War: An Analysis of the Fort Henry–Fort Donelson Campaign, February 1862.* Mechanicsburg, PA: Stackpole Books, 2003.

Grabau, Warren E. *Ninety-eight Days: A Geographer's View of the Vicksburg Campaign.* Knoxville: University of Tennessee Press, 2000.

Grimsley, Mark. *The Hard Hand of War: Union Military Policy Toward Southern Civilians, 1861–1865.* New York: Cambridge University Press, 1995.

Hess, Earl J. *Banners to the Breeze: The Kentucky Campaign, Corinth, and Stones River.* Lincoln: University of Nebraska Press, 2000.

Hicken, Victor. *Illinois in the Civil War.* Urbana: University of Illinois Press, 1991.

Howard, Robert P. *Illinois: A History of the Prairie State.* Grand Rapids, MI: William B. Eerdmans Publishing Co., 1972.

Huffstodt, Jim. *Hard Dying Men: The Story of General W. H. L. Wallace, General T. E. G. Ransom, and their "Old Eleventh" Illinois Infantry in the American Civil War.* Bowie, MD: Heritage Books, 1991.

Hughes, Nathaniel Cheairs, Jr. *The Battle of Belmont: Grant Strikes South.* Chapel Hill: University of North Carolina Press, 1991.

Jones, James Pickett. *"Black Jack": John A. Logan and Southern Illinois in the Civil War Era.* Carbondale: Southern Illinois University Press, 1995; originally published by University Press of Florida, 1967.

Kiper, Richard L. *Major General John Alexander McClernand: Politician in Uniform.* Kent, OH: Kent State University Press, 1999.

Lash, Jeffrey N. *A Politician Turned General: The Civil War Career of Stephen Augustus Hurlbut.* Kent, OH: Kent State University Press, 2003.

Lucas, Marion B. *Sherman and the Burning of Columbia.* Columbia: University of South Carolina Press, 2000; originally published by Texas A&M University Press, 1976.

Lyftogt, Kenneth L. *From Blue Mills to Columbia: Cedar Falls and the Civil War.* Ames: Iowa State University Press, 1993.

Marszalek, John F. *Commander of All Lincoln's Armies: A Life of General Henry W. Halleck.* Belknap Press of Harvard University Press, 2004.

McMurry, Richard M. *Atlanta 1864: Last Chance for the Confederacy.* Lincoln: University of Nebraska Press, 2000.

———. *Sherman: A Soldier's Passion for Order.* New York: Free Press, 1993.

Neely, Mark E., Jr. *Retaliation: The Problem of Atrocity in the American Civil War.* Gettysburg, PA: Gettysburg College, 2002.

Overmyer, Jack K. *A Stupendous Effort: The 87th Indiana in the War of the Rebellion.* Bloomington: Indiana University Press, 1997.

Perret, Geoffrey. *Ulysses S. Grant: Soldier and President.* New York: Random House, 1997.

Scheel, Gary L. *Rain, Mud & Swamps: 31st Missouri Volunteer Infantry Regiment Marching Through the South During the Civil War with General William T. Sherman.* Pacific, MO: published by the author, 1998.

Shea, William L., and Terrence J. Winschel. *Vicksburg Is the Key: The Struggle for the Mississippi River.* Lincoln: University of Nebraska Press, 2003.

Simpson, Brooks D. *Ulysses S. Grant: Triumph over Adversity, 1822–1865.* New York: Houghton Mifflin, 2000.

Smith, Jean Edward. *Grant.* New York: Simon & Schuster, 2001.

Smith, Timothy B. *Champion Hill: Decisive Battle for Vicksburg.* New York: Savas Beatie, 2004.

Sword, Wiley. *Shiloh: Bloody April.* Dayton: Morningside Press, 1974.

Tucker, Spencer C. *Unconditional Surrender: The Capture of Forts Henry and Donelson.* Abilene, TX: McWhiney Foundation Press, 2001.

Warner, Ezra J. *Generals in Blue: Lives of the Union Commanders.* Baton Rouge: Louisiana State University Press, 1964.

Williams, Kenneth P. *Grant Rises in the West: The First Year, 1861–1862.* Lincoln: University of Nebraska Press, 1997; originally published 1952.

Woodworth, Steven E., ed. *Grant's Lieutenants: From Cairo to Vicksburg.* Lawrence: University Press of Kansas, 2001.

INDEX

A NOTE ABOUT THE AUTHOR

Steven Woodworth is a professor of history at Texas Christian University and the author of numerous books on the Civil War.

A NOTE ON THE TYPE

Pierre Simon Fournier le jeune, who designed the type used in this book, was both an originator and a collector of types. His services to the art of printing were his design of letters, his creation of ornaments and initials, and his standardization of type sizes. His types are old style in character and sharply cut. In 1764 and 1766 he published his *Manuel typographique,* a treatise on the history of French types and printing, on typefounding in all its details, and on what many consider his most important contribution to typography—the measurement of type by the point system.

Composed by North Market Street Graphics, Lancaster, Pennsylvania
Printed and bound by Berryville Graphics, Berryville, Virginia
Designed by Robert C. Olsson